Judith R. Gordon
BOSTON COLLEGE

Human Resource Management

A Practical Approach

Allyn and Bacon, Inc.
BOSTON • LONDON • SYDNEY • TORONTO

To my husband, children, and family

Photo Credits

p. 1: Richard Wood/THE PICTURE CUBE
p. 73: Frank Siteman/THE PICTURE CUBE
p. 217: Steven Stone/THE PICTURE CUBE
p. 427: Martha Stewart/THE PICTURE CUBE
p. 591: Frank Siteman/THE PICTURE CUBE

7 Wells Avenue, Newton, Massachusetts 02159.

Library of Congress Cataloging-in-Publication Data

Gordon, Judith R.
Human resource management.

Includes index.
1. Personnel management. I. Title.
HF5549.G6547 1986 658.3 85–15776
ISBN 0–205–08604–7

Series editor: John Peters
Editorial production service: Helyn Pultz
Text designer/photo researcher: Janis Capone
Cover coordinator: Linda K. Dickinson
Cover designer: David Ford

Printed in the United States of America

10 9 8 7 6 5 4 3 2 1 90 89 88 87 86

Brief Contents

Complete Contents

Preface

The last decade has witnessed a significant change in the personnel and labor relations functions in organizations. Top management has increasingly viewed them as essential for the organization's well-being and effectiveness. The new name "human resources management" given to these functions reflects the change in their status.

Executives have simultaneously accorded human resources professionals new respect, turning to them for advice and assistance in improving organizational productivity, worker satisfaction, and the overall quality of worklife. Human resources professionals now serve as expert resources in staffing, training and development, compensation, and labor relations. They have become well versed in the laws that influence human resources management in the areas of equal opportunity employment, safety and health, and pensions and benefits.

The role of line managers in human resources management has also changed over the past ten years. Managers are now charged with significant responsibility for implementing sophisticated personnel and labor relations programs. They work in partnership with human resources professionals to ensure that human resources policies and practices meet both the goals of the organization and the needs of its members.

This book describes state-of-the-art human resources management. It discusses the characteristics of effective practice in organizations of various sizes, types, and industries. Readers examine the roles played by managers and human resources professionals in managing human resources today. They also consider the increasing responsibilities that managers must assume in effective human resources management, as well as the nature of their partnership with human resources professionals.

The book is written for students of human resources management at all levels, including practicing managers and professionals, using a multifaceted pedagogical approach. Readers are encouraged to consider the roles human resources professionals and managers play in a range of different situations, by applying the concepts presented in the text and readings to the case analyses and experiential activities. The pedagogical approach emphasizes active learning and participation.

The following individuals have contributed to the development of this book: Dan Dalton, Indiana University, Bloomington; Gary Latham, University of Washington; Nancy Napier, University of Washington; Tom Patton, Michigan State University; Ken Rowland, University of Illinois at Urbana; Craig Russell, University of Pittsburgh; Susan Taylor, University of Maryland; and Ann Wendt, University of Utah. I extend my sincere thanks to them for the time and thoughtful comments they have contributed. I also wish to thank my colleagues at Boston College School of Management for their enthusiasm and support; and offer my appreciation and thanks to Jack Peters, Helyn Pultz, Caroline Esmond, and the staff of Allyn and Bacon, Inc., for their technical and editorial assistance. I extend a special thank you to Diane Weiss, who helped with the administrative tasks associated with this book. Finally, I wish to thank my extended family, who followed the project with encouragement and good wishes; as always, my husband and children were my mainstay during its many phases, and I will always be grateful to them.

PART 1

The Components of Human Resources Management

CHAPTER 1

Setting the Stage for Effective Human Resources Management

CHAPTER OUTLINE

Introduction
What Is Human Resources Management?
Why Is Human Resources Management Important to Organizations?
The Evolving Roles in Human Resources Management
- Human Resources Professionals
- Top Management
- Line Managers
- Unions
- Other Employees
- The Interaction of Professionals and Managers

A Practical Approach
- Diagnosis
- Evaluation
- Design
- Implementation

Organization of This Book
- Organization
- Using This Book

SUMMARY

Endnotes
Further Readings

LEARNING CHECKPOINTS

After completing this chapter, students will be able to

- define human resources management;
- discuss the significance of effective human resources management to organizations;
- identify the components of human resources management;
- specify the participants involved in human resources management;
- trace the changing roles in human resources management;
- describe the interaction between human resources professionals and managers;
- outline the practical approach to human resources management.

INTRODUCTION

Calvin Murray reviewed the memo he had just received. It read:

> This is to remind all supervisors that recommendations for annual pay raises must be completed today. As you know, this is the capstone of our yearly human resources management program. Please complete the attached form for each employee and return it to the human resources management department by the end of this week. Thank you for your cooperation.

Cal pondered the memo for a while, thinking about the decisions he had recently made regarding his subordinates' salary increases. He felt confident that his proposals were on target. Yet he knew that three of his subordinates would not be happy with his decisions. Two had threatened to quit if they didn't receive a substantial increase. From others he heard rumors of unionization attempts.

He had tried to prepare his subordinates to assume more responsibility, but didn't feel he had succeeded. He remembered nominating two or three of his employees for a special training program, but they never went. He had planned to meet with them four or five times during the year to keep them informed about their progress, but his good intentions had disappeared in an avalanche of deadlines. The department's productivity resembled a roller coaster—up one month and down the next.

Cal felt that he needed a new perspective on the situation. He recalled that another manager had commented about "the great help and useful insights" a member of the human resources department staff had provided when that manager had encountered similar problems.

Cal Murray called Gerald Atkins, a human resources staff member, on Monday and arranged a meeting for Wednesday. At the meeting Atkins explained some recent changes in the company's human resources policies and practices to Cal. In particular, they discussed ways for Cal to improve his evaluations of employee performance and identify appropriate training opportunities for his staff. By Friday they had developed a plan of action for Cal.

Cal valued this interaction with a human resources management professional and hoped it would continue.

How can managers such as Cal Murray and professionals such as Gerald Atkins increase the effectiveness of human resources management in their organizations? Should Cal spend more time talking with his employees? Should he give them all large pay increases? Should he provide each employee with more training? Should he hold more frequent discussions with them about their performance? Should he have selected different employees in the first place? Should he be concerned that they might unionize? What role should Gerald Atkins play? Should he give Cal a list of available training programs each month? Should he schedule meetings between Cal and his subordinates to discuss their performance? Should Atkins send Cal regular memos about new human resources policies?

In this book we will answer these questions. We will examine the nature of human resources management and consider the role that managers and human resources professionals should play in all aspects of it. We will examine the qualities of *effective* human resources management—what human resources management *should be,* not necessarily what human resources management *is.* We set the stage in this chapter by addressing questions such as the following:

- What is human resources management?
- Why is human resources management important?
- Who participates in human resources management?
- What roles do human resources professionals, top and middle managers, supervisors, union leaders, and other organizational members play?
- How should human resources professionals and managers interact to ensure effective human resources management?

WHAT IS HUMAN RESOURCES MANAGEMENT?

Human resources management refers to the use, development, assessment, reward, and management of individual organizational members or worker groups. It includes the design and implementation of systems for planning, staffing, developing employees, managing careers, evaluating performance, compensating workers, and smoothing labor relations.

Human resources, along with financial, material, or time resources, contribute to the production of goods or services in an organization. Effective human resources management calls for managers and human resources professionals to find the best way of using people to accomplish organizational goals and to improve organizational performance. But effective human resources management also requires organizational members to accomplish their personal goals. Because demographics are changing, the work force is more diverse, individual goals are becoming more heterogeneous, and therefore organizational leaders face a significant challenge. Managers and human resources professionals must find ways to increase employee satisfaction, commitment, and involvement in organizational life; improve the quality of working life; and increase worker efficiency and productivity. Effective human resources management can increase organizational effectiveness.

WHY IS HUMAN RESOURCES MANAGEMENT IMPORTANT TO ORGANIZATIONS?

Good human resources practice can first result in the increased ability of an organization to attract and retain the best people. Planning alerts the organization to the types of people it will need in the short, medium, and long run. Quality recruitment and selection activities identify the best people for available jobs and make sure they are placed in appropriate positions. Performance evaluations and training develop individuals who require skills, knowledge, and attitudes different from those they currently have.

Good human resources practice can also motivate organizational members to do outstanding work. It can encourage worker commitment to and involvement in work and the organization. The ability to advance in the organization, to experience career growth and development, and to receive rewards commensurate with performance can encourage high performance and positive attitudes toward work. Managers' skill in working with unions also positively influences worker performance and attitudes.

Who has the responsibility for ensuring high productivity, performance, satisfaction, commitment, involvement, and quality of working life? In the next section we will identify the participants in human resources management.

THE EVOLVING ROLES IN HUMAN RESOURCES MANAGEMENT

Diverse groups throughout the organization participate in the design and implementation of human resources activities. Their roles have evolved during the twentieth century. The early part of the century saw a concern for improved efficiency through careful design of work. During the middle part of the century, emphasis shifted to the availability of managerial personnel and employee productivity.[1] Recent decades have focused on the demand for technical personnel, responses to new legislation and governmental regulations, increased concern for the quality of working life, and a renewed emphasis on productivity.

The roles of organizational participants in the management of human resources have similarly evolved over the twentieth century. In this section we examine the current and future roles of five groups: (1) human resources professionals, (2) top management, (3) line management, (4) other organizational members, and (5) unions.

Human Resources Professionals

Most organizations charge certain employees with the responsibility for overseeing both personnel functions and labor relations. In the 1980s many organizations renamed these personnel, industrial relations, or employee relations functions *human resources.* The responsibility of the human resources department can range from simply maintaining payroll records to designing and implementing complex staffing, development, compensation, and grievance systems.

Design of the Department. The human resources department may be organized in several ways. Figure 1–1 shows one structure, where the department is divided into functions. In this structure there are separate divisions or groups for the

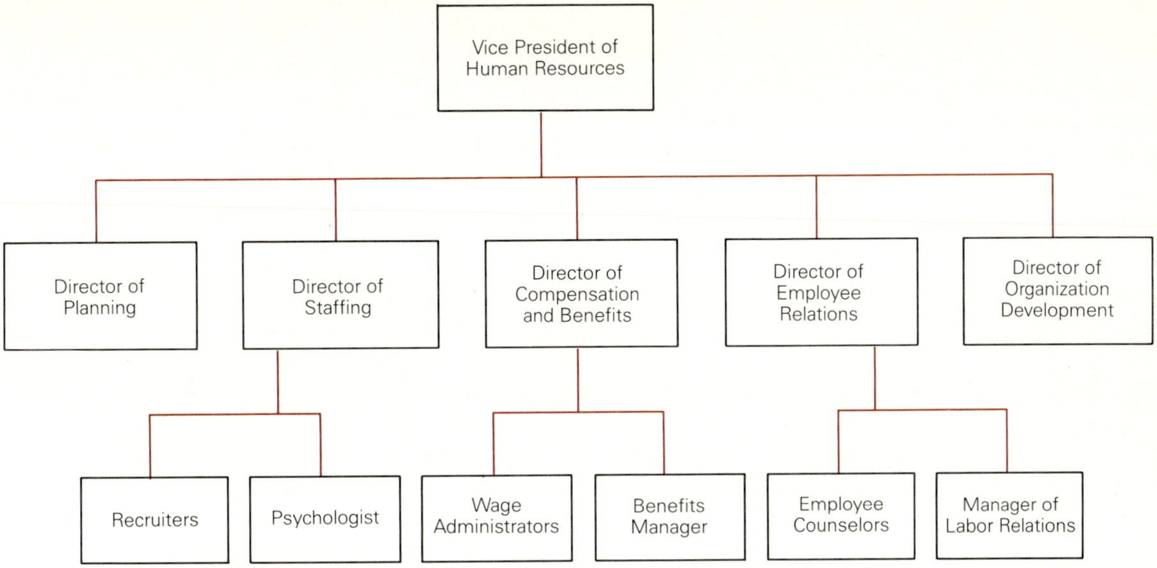

Figure 1–1 FUNCTIONAL STRUCTURE FOR A HUMAN RESOURCES MANAGEMENT DEPARTMENT

major human resources functions: planning, recruiting, training, compensation, employee relations, labor relations, and organizational development. Sometimes organizations combine diverse responsibilities into single positions, such as a wage-and-benefits administrator. Top management that views the human resources function as highly segmented and sees little need for integration between functions, such as staffing and development or planning and employee relations, often chooses this structure. Or management that values high specialization of knowledge among its employees, and wants a training expert or a collective bargaining expert may prefer this structure. Hospitals and large manufacturing organizations have traditionally used the functional structure.

Some organizations implement a structure that encourages human resources professionals to act as generalists. In this case, several personnel staff members may be assigned to support all human resources activities for an operating division, as illustrated in Figure 1–2. These human resources professionals know all human resources functions to some degree. They also learn about the activities of their operating group. In their jobs, human resources generalists emphasize the integration of human resources knowledge with their understanding of the specific concerns of their operating division. Often human resources specialists in a small, corporate-level human resources department act as resources and consultants to these personnel generalists and provide them the detailed, technical knowledge required to implement programs in the different divisions.

Top management chooses this structure when the operating groups have

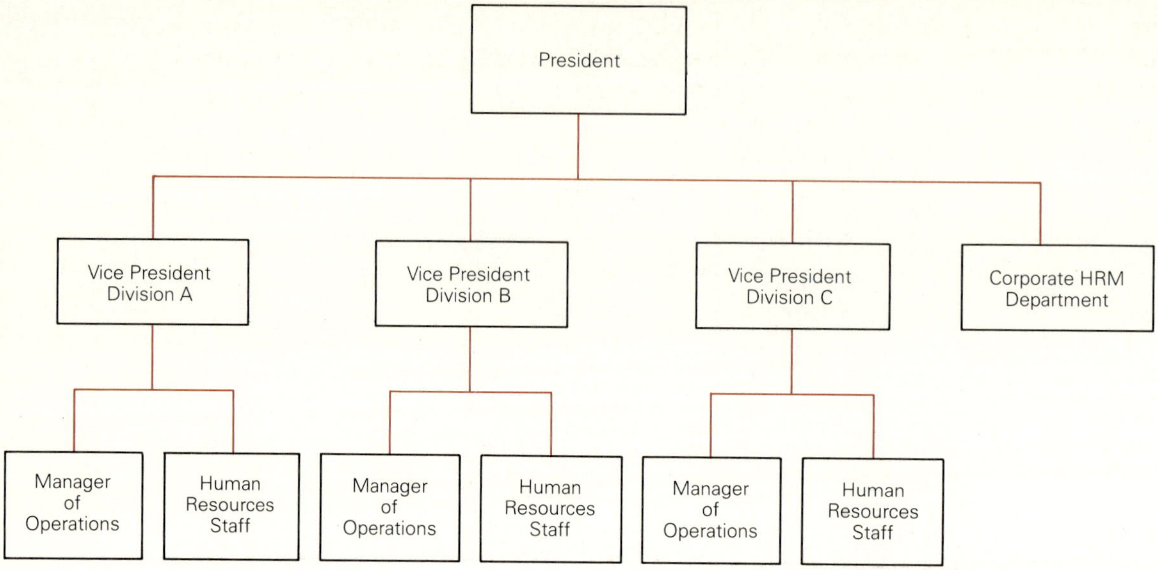

Figure 1–2 EXCERPT FROM ORGANIZATIONAL CHART INCLUDING PERSONNEL GENERALISTS

significantly different and pressing human resources needs, when these needs cross into diverse human resources functional areas, and when meeting these needs requires direct and frequent service by one or more human resources professionals. Many high technology companies have adopted this structure because in these organizations management believes it allows a faster response to a changing environment. Under this structure, for example, one operating group can request that its human resources professionals focus on developing a new hiring program, whereas another operating group might prefer to place greater emphasis on the training of current employees.

Activities of Human Resources Professionals. Contemporary human resources professionals perform diverse activities that fall into four categories: (1) setting policy, (2) giving advice, (3) providing information and activities in such areas as recruitment, selection, and training, and (4) offering control by monitoring performance and employee conformance to personnel policies.[2] Although a survey sent to a sample of executives, line managers, and personnel directors indicated that most view the personnel department as a service and advising unit, all groups indicated a desire for more involvement in all types of activities.[3] These preferences may reflect the desire of all groups to eliminate the arbitrary distinction in most organizations between line and staff positions, and to design positions that best meet the organization's and individuals' needs.

Additional roles for human resources professionals in the next decade are likely to focus on increasing the effectiveness of interaction with line managers and the transfer of some direct human resources management responsibilities to these line managers. Subsequently, the professional would act as (1) a *provider*, who offers expertise to assist line managers in human resources management; (2) a *delegator*, who assigns personnel roles to the manager; (3) an *auditor*, who evaluates the performance of line managers in implementing personnel policies; (4) an *innovator*, who upgrades the technical competence and access of managers to information, develops new programs and procedures, and communicates to top managers; and (5) a *policy formulator*, who develops consistent, cost-effective human resources policy.[4]

Each organization must determine the extent to which the development of human resources policy and the control of personnel-related activities should be centralized in the human resources management department or decentralized, along with implementation, to line managers. For example, human resources professionals may perform all recruiting activities, or they may relinquish all activities except organization-wide advertising or open houses to line managers. Regardless of the extent of centralization of personnel activities, the expanding role of human resources professionals as innovators and policy formulators calls for an upgrading of their technical competence and professional image.[5] It also calls for more power to make things happen in the organization.[6] As described in the next sections, line managers, too, must increase their knowledge of human resources functions and become more actively involved in human resources management.

In this book we assume that human resources professionals perform *active* roles of diagnostician, counselor, planner, and policy formulator in the management of human resources.[7] The precise performance of these roles may vary for different human resources functions, as described in subsequent chapters of this book. To be effective in each of these roles, however, human resources professionals must demonstrate the relevance of their knowledge to top management, look for places in the organization to have impact, develop a bottom-line orientation, and create programs that are likely to succeed.[8]

Top Management

Executives should sanction and legitimize all human resources functions. Although they most often delegate significant responsibility for the design and implementation of human resources policies, many top managers participate in the development of and oversee all human resources practices and procedures in the organization. In addition, top management should become directly involved in the human resources practices that influence their subordinates, such as interviewing candidates for executive positions or appraising other top managers.

In areas such as human resources planning and labor negotiations, top managers should also play a central role. Top managers can greatly influence whether an organization will unionize and, once unionized, what the quality of the relationship between union and management will be. Top managers can retain total control of the organization or divert some of their power to human resources professionals, line managers, or other subordinates. By clarifying personal and organizational goals, top managers can provide other organizational members with the framework in which human resources management functions.

They can also influence effective human resources management throughout the organization by clarifying the responsibilities of human resources professionals, as described above, and of line managers, as described in the next section.

What happens when executives do not value human resources management? This may occur when executives are overly concerned with bottom-line profit and view human resources management as an unnecessary cost. Or when they do not see the relationship between human resources management and organizational effectiveness. Such a situation places a heavy burden on human resources professionals to justify their existence. (See Chapter 15 for a discussion of cost-benefit analysis.) They—and managers committed to quality human resources management—should regularly seek ways to demonstrate its value to the organization. To do this, they might track the influence of management training on managerial performance or evaluate the introduction of greater worker participation (see Chapter 14) on the reduction of grievances. Executive training can also facilitate improved attitudes toward human resources management.

Line Managers

Line managers—middle managers and lower level supervisors—should have primary responsibility and accountability for the implementation of human resources policies developed by top management and human resources professionals.[9] They should systematically perform each human resources function, beginning most frequently with a situational audit and job analysis (described in Chapter 2), specification of criteria for effective human resources management, and implementation of human resources programs. For example, they must determine if training programs meet their subordinates' needs, if employees value specific organizational benefits, or if supervisors act collaboratively in dealing with union grievances. They should continually practice quality, state-of-the-art human resources management.

Line managers must develop sufficient knowledge of state-of-the-art human resources management so they can act as diagnosticians and assess the effectiveness of current human resources practices. This book is designed in part to provide such information.

Line managers are increasingly assuming a more active role in the design of human resources systems. In addition to providing feedback about current programs, they can clearly describe their own and subordinates' needs and limitations. In this way, human resources professionals or consultants who develop human resources systems receive first-hand information that they can use to improve human resources programs. Line managers can design additional activities that supplement the general human resources policies. For example, they can conduct more frequent performance evaluations than are conducted in the rest of the organization. Or they can design a special career path and career development program for the technical employees they supervise.

Finally, line managers should monitor the human resources practices of the managers they supervise. They should provide analysis and assistance where needed, or refer their subordinate managers to human resources professionals when special expertise is required. In the future, line managers are likely to shoulder primary responsibility for ensuring that human resources management is effective across the organization. But to encourage the active involvement of line managers in human resources management they must receive support and rewards for managing human resources effectively.

Unions

In some organizations members band together as part of a union. Representatives of this adjunct organization negotiate with management to specify rules under which members will work. Union leadership and membership can significantly influence the type of human resources management in an organization. Because the relationship between union and management has traditionally been adversarial, labor contracts have often specified the nature of human resources management practices such as selection, promotion, evaluation, and compensation in organizations. The constraints imposed by labor contracts can limit the ability of management to adapt to changing environmental or organizational conditions.

Recently, however, attempts to establish a more collaborative relationship have simultaneously encouraged the introduction of new human resources management practices in quality-of-working-life programs (see Chapters 11 and 14). Union leaders, human resources professionals, and managers should together continue to seek ways of effectively managing human resources in the organization.

Other Employees

The remaining employees, whether unionized or not, should lobby for high-quality human resources management. To do this requires that organizational members know the characteristics of effective human resources management. This book is intended to provide such information. Each employee should then be able to diagnose the quality of human resources practices in his or her organization, since workers often provide the most accurate identification of weaknesses and the most creative sources of improvements. In addition, workers should encourage managers to correct deficiencies that exist in human resources management. Informed employees contribute to an internal organizational environment (climate) that encourages growth and development as well as high quality performance and productivity in the organization.

The Interaction of Professionals and Managers

Today, more than ever before, human resources professionals and managers act *jointly* to manage human resources effectively. In the future, this partnership is likely to become stronger. For example, if human resources professionals design a performance evaluation system, managers will implement the system and provide feedback to the human resources professionals about its strengths and weaknesses. The human resources department should then revise the system to incorporate the managers' suggestions. Or, if a manager needs to fill a vacant staff position, he or she could use the human resources department as a source of recruits. The human resources department can advertise in local newspapers, organize an open house, or list employee referrals. In this way, human resources professionals can become expert resources to the managers who are charged with effective human resources management.

In this book we will consider the roles human resources professionals and managers should play in state-of-the-art human resources management. In addition, we will emphasize their interaction and its significance for effective human resources management. Although there are many approaches to increasing the effectiveness of human resources management, in this book we use the *practical approach,* which the next section describes in more detail.

A PRACTICAL APPROACH

Human resources professionals and managers can increase the effectiveness of human resources management by using a four-step approach in dealing with problems and issues: (1) diagnosis, (2) evaluation, (3) design, and (4) implementation.

First, human resources professionals and top management should *diagnose* the problems in managing human resources organization-wide. Managers should diagnose the problems in their own division, department, or area. All should analyze the needs of workers and managers and determine how well the organization meets them in each situation. Cal Murray, for example, should determine the needs and goals of employees he supervises and assess how well the human resources practices meet these needs and help accomplish these goals. A human resources professional can help managers with this diagnosis by acting as a sounding board or offering new perspectives on the situation. In addition, Cal, with the assistance of human resources professionals such as Gerald Atkins, should examine the nature of the environment, organization, and job. Together they should diagnose the context in which current human resources practices occur and, ultimately, fit the practices to the situation.

Second, managers and human resources professionals should *evaluate* the practices they or other organizational members currently use. They should assess the value of these practices and procedures to workers, their cost, and their effectiveness in accomplishing organizational goals.

Third, the human resources professionals must ensure that the approach to human resources management throughout the organization is a coherent one. They can assist managers in adapting and integrating organizational policies to the management of subordinates. Managers should specify procedures that fit with their own and subordinates' needs. Then human resources professionals can offer examples of practices in other organizations that might help improve the human resources management in their own. Together managers and human resources professionals should *design* human resources management systems. This means that at a strategic level, human resources professionals and top management should design general policies and practices to implement. At the operational level, they should identify, evaluate, and select specific alternatives. For example, at a strategic level, an organization can implement general guidelines for recruitment, including philosophy, resources, and responsibility. At a tactical level, decisions about recruitment would relate to the specific sources of recruitment to use.

Finally, the manager should then *implement* the resulting systems. Figure 1–3 summarizes these steps.

Diagnosis

Diagnosis requires a description of the existing organization, its jobs, employees, environment, and any other factors that influence the use of human resources in

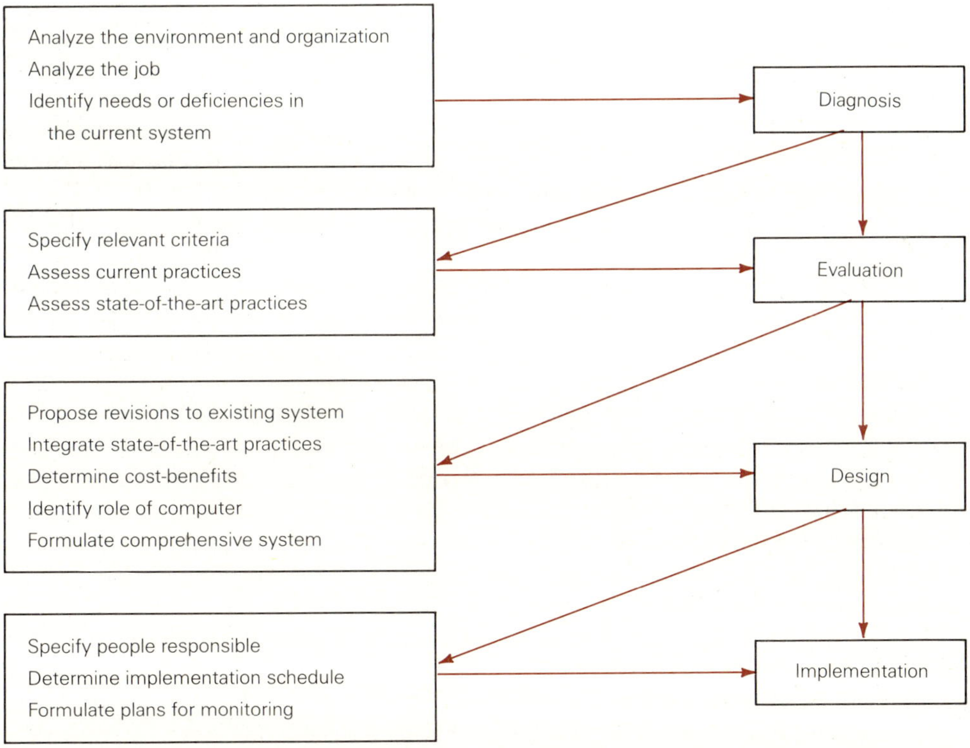

Figure 1–3 THE PRACTICAL APPROACH TO HUMAN RESOURCES MANAGEMENT

the organization. Human resources professionals, managers, or other employees can begin by analyzing the organizational and environmental context of human resources management. They should describe the organization's size, product, and location, as well as the nature of its social, legal, and economic environments. They should also analyze the jobs held by organizational members. Once the context has been identified, analysis of specific conditions should occur.

Diagnosis involves a determination of needs for certain human resources management practices in given situations. In the scenario that opens this chapter, for example, there seem to be deficiencies in the selection, training, and development of employees. Diagnosis calls for pinpointing the general areas of weakness, deficiency, or need in the management of human resources.

Evaluation

Evaluation involves an assessment of all current management practices to determine their effectiveness. Assessment of practices must consider the criteria discussed in each chapter of this book. For example, the selection of Cal Murray's subordinates should follow a well-defined selection process. Compensation should be based on a systematic job evaluation. A needs assessment should always precede employee training. Human resources professionals should review and evaluate practices used in other organizations for possible inclusion in their organization's program.

Design

The manager and human resources professional must design coherent systems for human resources management. How should they approach this challenge? They should correct deficiencies in existing systems and integrate state-of-the-art practices into them.

The costs of the proposed system should be detailed and, if possible, a cost-benefit analysis performed. Analyzing costs is important to ensure the cost-benefit of the proposed system and to strengthen management's commitment to its implementation.

Finally, where feasible, the use of a computer should be integrated into the newly designed system. Computerization has dramatically increased the amount of information that can be stored and retrieved for use with human resources management. Effective human resources management incorporates the use of computerized data bases and analyses. The low cost, high capability, and user-friendliness of computer hardware and software today facilitate their use by organizations of all sizes.

Gerald Atkins, then, should design a systematic, coherent approach to performance appraisal for the organization. Cal Murray should modify this approach to make it more effective for his particular subordinates. Cal might, for example, complete appraisal forms twice a year on his employees: one form to emphasize development and to be used primarily for counseling; the other to emphasize performance assessment and to be linked into compensation decisions. These formal evaluations could be accompanied by performance interviews three or four times a year. The resulting data could be maintained on a computerized data base with the result that managers or human resources professionals could access the data for identifying training and development needs.

Implementation

Design cannot be done in a vacuum. The last step is to consider who will implement the policies, how resources will be distributed, how the implementation will occur, and how to monitor human resources management.

First, the parties responsible for implementation must be identified. Will the line manager be solely responsible for the system? Will the human resources professionals share responsibility? What contribution must employees make to get the system to work? How much support must top management provide?

These parties can perform diverse roles. They can act as the actual change agents by implementing new procedures themselves. They can advise others and supervise the introduction of new programs. Or they can remain a resource to organizational members and dispense information as requested. Chapter 14 examines these roles in more detail.

Second, top management must allocate resources for the design and implementation of human resources programs. They must address questions such as the following: What resources (money, people, equipment) will the line manager have? What resources will human resources professionals control?

Next, the schedule for implementing the human resources procedures must be identified. Will performance interviews be held early in the day or on Friday afternoon? Will they be conducted in the manager's office or at a special off-site location?

Finally, plans for monitoring human resources practices in the organization must be delineated. Will a human resources auditor be appointed? Will human resources professionals have responsibility for control?

These four steps provide a generic approach to increasing the effectiveness of human resources management. Consider the case of a retail department store experiencing high turnover among its young professionals. Or consider the steel company forced to make layoffs in a declining economic situation. Or review the experience of the bank that must increase its work force by thirty employees within six months. In each of these situations (described in later chapters of this book) the practical approach can provide direction for assessing deficiencies and needs, evaluating current practices, and proposing new human resources management systems.

ORGANIZATION OF THIS BOOK

The remainder of this book incorporates the practical approach in its organization and pedagogy. Each chapter emphasizes the four stages of the approach; each encourages readers to diagnose the situation, evaluate current human resources management, design state-of-the-art human resources practices, and consider implementation issues. Readers can strengthen their knowledge of this approach through the textual material and readings, which they can then apply to cases and exercises.

Organization

This book includes five parts: (1) the components of human resources management, (2) personnel systems for staffing organizations, (3) personnel systems for evaluation and development, (4) labor relations systems, and (5) organizational effectiveness. Figure 1–4 illustrates this organization.

Part 1 describes the building blocks of human resources management. Specifically, Chapter 2 provides an approach for analyzing the context in which human resources management occurs. It also discusses job analysis and human resources planning.

Part 2 discusses personnel systems for staffing organizations. Chapter 3 discusses an approach for implementing systematic recruitment. Chapter 4 traces the steps in selecting employees. Chapter 5 concludes Part 2 with a specification of ways to reduce the number of employees in an organization.

In Part 3, personnel systems to evaluate and develop employees are introduced. Chapter 6 describes the components of an effective performance appraisal system. Chapter 7 discusses training and development. Chapter 8 presents an approach to career management that involves human resources professionals, managers, and individual workers. Chapter 9 describes compensation and reward systems, including wage and salary administration, benefits, and incentive plans.

Part 4 presents the labor relations systems. Chapter 10 describes the basic activities of introducing a union into an organization; it also examines the historical and legal context of unionization. Chapter 11 describes the collective bargaining process and offers strategies for increasing the effectiveness of negotiations. Chapter 12 presents a discussion of labor contract resolution and administration, emphasizing the issues involved in grievance resolution.

Part 5 concludes the book by investigating other issues related to organizational effectiveness. Chapter 13 summarizes the laws and legal issues that affect human resources management. Chapter 14 discusses issues surrounding the implementation of change in organizations. And Chapter 15 reviews the comprehensive, practical approach to effective human resources management.

Using This Book

Through the use of text, articles, case analyses, and experiential activities you are guided to understand, evaluate, design, and implement effective human resources management practices.

Text. The text emphasizes the practical approach to human resources management. It discusses the roles of and interaction between managers and professionals in each area of human resources management. Each chapter begins with a brief

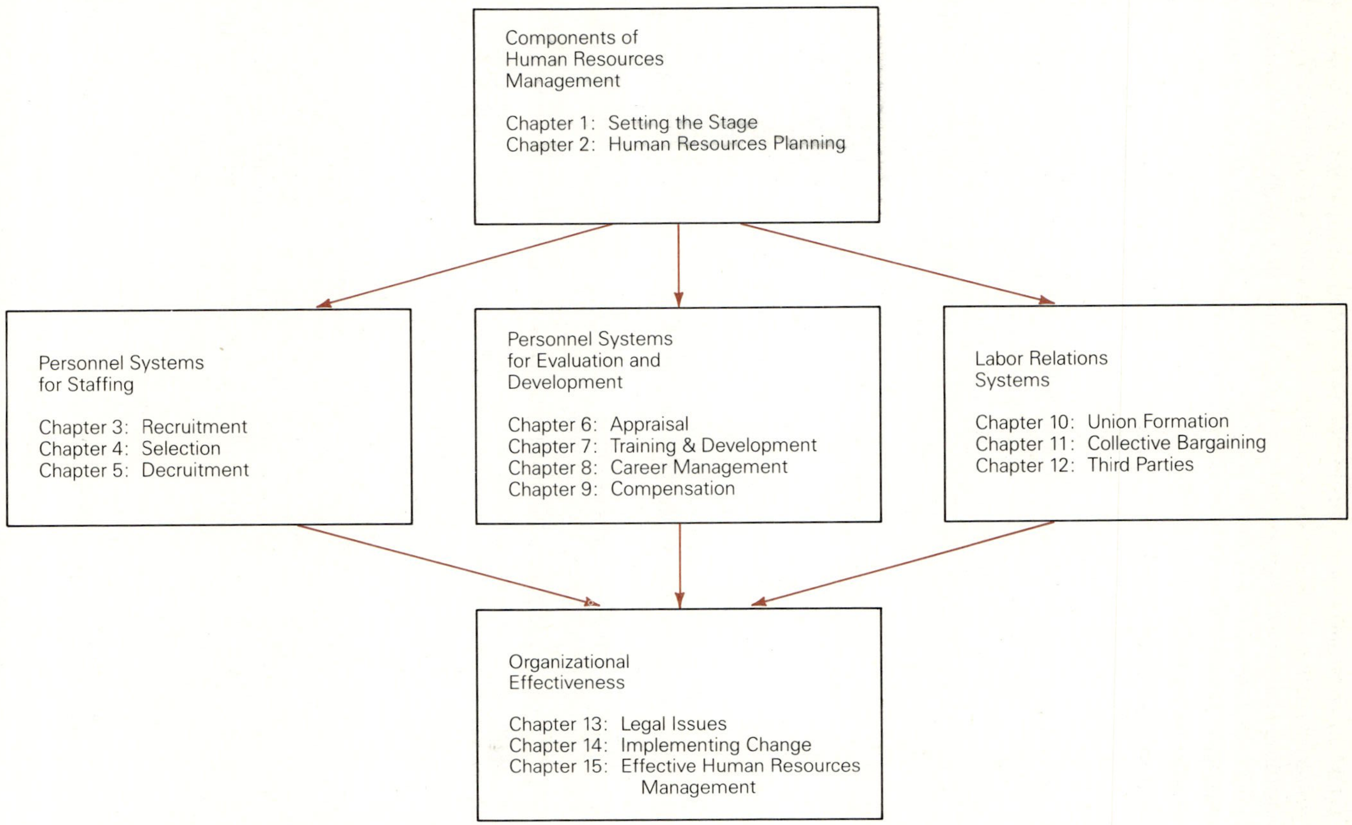

Figure 1–4 THE ORGANIZATION OF THIS BOOK

scenario that describes a problem. Then each chapter guides you to diagnose the situation. Next it presents a framework for evaluating the effectiveness of the human resources management system being discussed. Each chapter emphasizes characteristics of state-of-the-art programs in each area of human resources management, and offers suggestions, based on these models, for changing human resources practices and policies. Finally, the text concludes with implications for action by human resources professionals and managers.

Readings. Most chapters include two readings from professional literature in the field of human resources management. These readings have been selected to illustrate either state-of-the-art practices or frameworks for understanding, analyzing, and designing various human resources practices. You are encouraged through the accompanying discussion questions to integrate the information in the readings into the frameworks presented in the text.

Cases. The cases in this book provide examples of real-life situations. Typically, they describe organizational problems calling for changes in human resources practices. For example, one case might illustrate a situation where a manager has to deal with a problem worker. Another case might describe an organization where managers resisted using an existing appraisal system.

You should consider the interaction between managers and human resources professionals in diagnosing the problems in these cases, evaluating the current human resources management practices, designing more effective ways of managing human resources, and implementing these policies and procedures. The following highlights the practical approach to case analysis.[10]

First, list the facts of the situation. This requires you to separate the facts from assumptions you might make about them. Often in listing the facts you will note that important data are missing. You must attempt to secure these data or clearly specify the assumptions you are making about the data.

Consider the following facts:

> The negotiations between the Teamsters Union and the Johnson Can Company have broken down for the fourth time. This union and Johnson Can have a history of long, bitter negotiations and numerous strikes. The strike deadline (midnight) is only one hour away. Representatives of both sides have left the hotel where the negotiations were taking place. The union steward gave the following statement to the press: "Management is unwilling to negotiate. We have taken a strike vote and are prepared to strike if management does not accept our proposals in the next hour."

Second, identify the problems, deficiencies, and needs in the situation. In this example, both union and management must reach an acceptable agreement, yet there seem to be no mechanisms to prevent the union from striking. We can assume from the failure of past negotiations that union and management have taken win-lose, adversarial positions and have refused to collaborate or attempt joint problem-solving. We can test this assumption by gathering additional data through interviews or the review of written documents. The organization seems to lack ways of effectively managing the relationship between union and management.

Third, evaluate the effectiveness of the system. Here you should specify the criteria for effective labor negotiations. Such criteria might include reaching agreement before a strike occurs, or one that will result in gains for both parties. You should compare the current system to these criteria or to an ideal situation. You should analyze the assets and liabilities of the existing system. You should also look for and examine other practices or techniques that might increase the effectiveness of human resources management in this instance. In the case of the Johnson Can Company, you should examine all facets of labor-management relations now and in the past. Possible solutions might be to increase worker involvement in bargaining or provide more training in problem-solving to union and management.

Fourth, you redesign the system. In this step you should integrate the analyses and evaluations of steps 1 through 4. You must think creatively and propose ways to build more comprehensive and effective human resources management systems. In this case, you should propose ways of changing the labor negotiation system.

Fifth, you plan for the implementation of the redesigned system. Such a plan should specify the cost of the system, the constituencies involved in its introduction, and the extent to which computerization of the system can be used.

Exercises. Throughout the book you are presented with scenarios that allow you to role-play or simulate the experiences of a manager or human resources professional who faces tough personnel issues. For example, you may have the opportunity to select a manager for a vacant position, plan for recruiting accountants, or design a training program for newly hired welders. At the conclusion of each exercise you are encouraged to draw conclusions about ways of increasing the effectiveness of human resources management.

SUMMARY

Human resources management has become a major focus in the life of organizations of all sizes. Because it closely relates to worker productivity and satisfaction, human resources management has become a significant preoccupation of managers, human resources professionals, and other organizational members. Employees are becoming more sophisticated in their demands for high quality working environments, appropriate compensation, and adequate training and development. Managers must continually look for ways to improve their interactions with employees, other managers, and outside constituencies.

This book describes ways to improve human resources management. It emphasizes the interaction between managers and human resources professionals in the design and implementation of effective human resources practices and policies for organizations of all sizes.

ENDNOTES

[1]J.W. Walker, *Human Resource Planning* (New York: McGraw-Hill, 1980).

[2]G.W. Bohlander, H.C. White, and M.N. Wolfe, The three faces of personnel—or PAIR Department activities as seen by executives, line managers, and personnel directors, *Personnel* 60 (1983): 12–22.

[3]*Ibid.*

[4]J.W. English, The road ahead for the human resources function, *Personnel* 57 (March-April 1980).

[5]*Ibid.*

[6]H. Jain and V. Murray, Why the human resources management function fails, *California Management Review* 26 (Summer 1984): 95.

[7]T.F. Cawsey, Why line managers don't listen to their personnel departments, *Personnel* 57 (January-February 1980): 11–20.

[8]*Ibid.*

[9]*Ibid.*

[10]Other approaches to case analysis are presented in R. Ronstadt, *The Art of Case Analysis: A Student Guide* (Needham, Mass.: Lord Publishing, 1977) and J.R. Gordon, *A Diagnostic Approach to Organizational Behavior* (Boston: Allyn and Bacon, 1983).

FURTHER READINGS

BNA, Personnel Management Policy and Practice Series. Washington, D.C.: Bureau of National Affairs.

Daily Labor Report. Washington, D.C.: Bureau of National Affairs.

Personnel Management: Communications and Policies and Practices Series. Englewood Cliffs, N.J.: Prentice-Hall.

Ronstadt, R. *The Art of Case Analysis: A Student Guide.* Needham, Mass.: Lord Publishing, 1977.

CHAPTER 2

Conducting Human Resources Planning

CHAPTER OUTLINE

LEARNING CHECKPOINTS

After completing the text and activities in this chapter, students will be able to

- describe the components of human resources planning;
- show the relationship of human resources planning to strategic planning;
- analyze the nature of the changing environment and its impact on employment needs and availability;
- evaluate the organizational contingencies that influence human resources management;
- perform a situational analysis;
- describe the process of job analysis;
- construct a job description, job specification, and performance standard;
- compare and contrast various techniques for forecasting employment demand and supply;
- indicate the roles of managers and human resources professionals in planning.

INTRODUCTION

The Antron Computer Corporation, a subsidiary of Elliot, Inc., a diversified manufacturing operation, was recently sold to a group of investors. Antron Computer manufactures a state-of-the-art microcomputer with strong technical applications. Under its previous ownership Antron had focused on research and development of the new product and had just begun to sell computers at the time of its sale. Under its new ownership Antron continues to expand its sales effort. At the same time it continues to develop new computers.

Richard Irving has been hired as vice president of sales. After several weeks at Antron, Irving began receiving complaints. His salespeople complain that they are not getting good or quick responses to technical questions they ask. The customers are bypassing their sales representatives to get responses from the service department to problems they are encountering.

In addition, Antron is introducing a new computer at a major computer show next week. Irving expects that the current problems will not be solved but instead will be exacerbated with the introduction of the new computer. Irving thinks he needs to hire fifty sales and service employees. But he also knows that finding so many people and "getting them up to speed" will be difficult if not impossible. He wonders why the company has gotten into this trouble and how he could help in remedying the situation.

Janice Copeland recently joined Antron as its Director of Human Resources Planning. She was charged with the responsibility for developing forecasts and proposing plans for implementing them *jointly* with department managers. She knows that Antron has instituted few, if any, procedures related to planning. Some managers seem to do it intuitively; others do no human resources planning at all. She is now considering the best way to proceed from here.

What steps should Antron take now and in the future? What role should Irving perform? The other managers? Copeland? What types of planning practices should Antron institute? In this chapter we examine the process of human resources planning.

Human resources planning is "the process of analyzing an organization's human resource needs under changing conditions and developing the activities necessary to satisfy these needs."[1] Human resources planning involves (1) employment planning and (2) program planning. Employment planning refers to the identification of the human resources necessary to achieve future organizational objectives. To develop an employment plan, human resources professionals forecast the supply of and demand for human resources. The plan then specifies the difference between the supply and the demand; that is, whether there is an oversupply, undersupply, or an appropriate supply of human resources for a given employment category. The employment plan is closely linked to the strategic plan of the organization.

Program planning follows the development of an employment plan. It involves the selection of human resources tools that most effectively address an oversupply or undersupply of workers. Program planning includes the coordination of programs to meet employment plans in diverse personnel and labor relations areas. Planning requires both managers and human resources professionals to understand the context in which human resources management occurs. Such an analysis accompanies the formulation of organizational strategy, which forms the backbone of human resources planning.

In this chapter, we first examine the strategic backbone of planning. Second, we provide a way of auditing the context in which human resources management occurs. Next, we examine methods of job analysis and the significance of job analysis to human resources management. Fourth, we address issues related to employment planning, including the specification of supply and demand and the use of various forecasting techniques. Then we briefly consider issues related to program planning. We conclude the chapter with the implications of the planning process for managers and human resources professionals.

THE STRATEGIC BACKBONE

Management decisions on the strategic level specify the organization's plans for accomplishing their long-term objectives of profitability, service, market share, and performance. In its strategic planning, top management answers questions such as the following[2]:

- What kind of business should we be in?
- What market does this imply?
- What technological investment does this imply?
- What organizational changes does this imply?
- What effort and activity must be performed to achieve the market, technology, and organization desired?
- To what extent does the current situation have to be changed?
- What general changes in human resources are necessary to accomplish these changes?

Consider the case of Antron. What strategic decisions might Antron make? Clearly Antron's management and its parent, Elliot, Inc., have determined that Antron should be in the computer business; more specifically, that Antron should design, build, and sell high-end microcomputers and market its product to the scientific community. But Antron also has other issues to address. What resources should be devoted to research and development? How much emphasis should be placed on sales as opposed to service? How closely allied should engineering and manufacturing be?

The strategic plan sets the stage for human resources planning. Specifically, by identifying where the company is and in what direction it should be moving, strategic planning bears directly on questions such as the following:

- What skills, potential, and weaknesses currently exist in the organization?
- What work force will the company be likely to have if no change in current practices occurs?
- What work force should the company have?
- What employment policies and programs must be started or changed?
- What does the resulting employment plan look like?
- How will the employment plan be designed?
- How will the employment plan be monitored?
- What activities are necessary to support the employment plan?
- What types of activities will help acquire the employees required?
- How can the productivity of employees be ensured?

Consider Antron's decision to do its own technical support. What types of employees are required to implement this decision? Antron might need individuals with technical knowledge about certain types of computers; it also needs workers who can listen carefully to customers' complaints and diagnose the causes. Janice Copeland must determine how many individuals the company needs with the technical expertise, interpersonal expertise, and knowledge of the environment. She must also determine how many such employees currently work at Antron. Richard Irving can assist by providing data for making the necessary employment forecasts.

Management cannot answer these questions only by considering the organization's objectives as defined in the strategic plan. Managers and human resources professionals must assess external factors as well: the nature of the economy, all relevant legislation, and the political, social, and cultural climate in which the organization operates. They must also consider conditions created by past practices and existing structures. The next section describes the situational audit that managers and human resources professionals should perform to delineate these internal and external influences.

SITUATIONAL AUDIT

For a manager or human resources professional to develop an accurate human resources plan, he or she must analyze the situation in which human resources management occurs. Initially, a situational analysis can provide data for the development of a strategic plan. Later, performing a periodic situational analysis helps human resources professionals and managers develop and update employment and program plans.

The situational analysis is important to the practical approach to human resources management proposed in this book. Such a consideration of the environment and organization should increase the effectiveness of the design of human resources policies and programs. When organizational members resist performing a situational analysis, human resources professionals must emphasize its importance and lobby top management to provide resources to support it. In this section we detail the two components of a situational audit: (1) environmental analysis and (2) organizational assessment.

Environmental Analysis

What kind of environment does Antron face? During the past two decades organizational environments have become more dynamic, less predictable, and more complex than any time before. These changes have contributed to unique problems for organizations. Human resources professionals and managers who understand the reasons for these changes should be better prepared to design responsive human resources programs. They may also be able to predict future changes and plan for future program-environment fit.

Reasons for Environmental Change. What are the causes of these changes in the environment? The following seven major factors have contributed to them:

1. Technological advances—automation has allowed workers to triple and quadruple their productivity per day and computers have expedited the dissemination of information.
2. Geographical accessibility—nationalization and internationalization of organizations have become common.
3. Increased education level—the high percentage of individuals holding high school diplomas and college degrees has changed workers' expectations of organizational life, family dynamics, and leisure activities.[3]
4. Population redistribution—the population has shifted from the Northeast to the Sunbelt, the Southwest, and the West; and the relative age distributions have changed, resulting, for example, in larger numbers of workers now in their 30s and 40s who are demanding management positions in numbers disproportionate to the number of such positions available.[4]
5. Economic instability—inflation and increased competition have pressured organizations to reduce costs and enhance the effective use of human resources management.
6. Increased governmental regulation—the Occupational Safety and Health Act, the Equal Employment Opportunity Act, and other federal legislation have spurred organizations to reexamine their production procedures, physical facilities, and employment practices.
7. Productivity crises—industries such as automobile and steel manufacturing have experienced significant declines in efficiency, especially compared to international competitors.[5]

Because of these changes, ongoing diagnosis of the environment is the first step to effective human resources management that can respond to current external conditions.

The Nature of the Environment. An environmental audit delineates and evaluates the components of the environment relevant to human resources management. An environmental audit must (1) specify the major components of the environment faced by the organization; (2) note the significance of each component for organizational performance; and (3) assess the significance of each component for effective human resources management. Figure 2–1 lists questions managers or human resources professionals can use in evaluating various aspects of the environment.

The *economic* environment affecting an organization influences the availability of human resources as well as the effectiveness of specific human resources

Economic Environment

1. What is the current rate of inflation?
2. Is the current economic situation a fluctuation or an established trend?
3. How available is financing to organizations?
4. What pressures are consumers experiencing in the marketplace?
5. What economic expectations do employees hold?
6. What economic expectations are they likely to place on their organization?
7. How will economic conditions influence present human resources management activities?
8. Which activities should help organizations deal more effectively with the present environment?
9. What activities cannot be conducted because of economic conditions?

Social Environment

10. What social forces influence the behavior of organizational members?
11. What social groups exist in the workplace and outside the workplace?
12. What norms influence the behavior of organizational members?
13. What social expectations do workers have of the organization and their jobs?
14. What social attributes influence the organization and its functioning?

Political Environment

15. What political groups are in power?
16. What policies do the parties in power encourage?
17. What is the likelihood that the political situation will change in the short run? In the long run?
18. What resources will the government likely make available to organizations?

Legal Environment

19. What laws and regulations have an impact on human resources management?
20. What laws and regulations are pending?
21. How do the laws and regulations influence my organization?
22. How do the laws and regulations influence the human resources management practices that are necessary and appropriate?

Geographical Environment

23. Where is the organization located?
24. What are the implications of this location for employee attitudes?

Figure 2–1 QUESTIONS FOR ASSESSING THE ENVIRONMENT *Continued*

25. How proximate are various parts of the organization?
26. What are the implications of the physical location for human resources management practices?

Cultural Environment

27. How would you describe the culture in which the organization operates?
28. In what ways is the culture unique?
29. How does the culture influence human resources management practices?

Technological Environment

30. What recent technological innovations influence the organization?
31. With what frequency do such innovations occur?
32. In what ways do these innovations affect the organization?
33. What human resources management practices respond to the existing and new technology?
34. How can the organization cope with changes in technology?

Labor Environment

35. How common are unions among similar organizations?
36. Does the community support or oppose unionization?
37. What is the educational/professional level in the environment?
38. How have unions acted in the past? (Have they been strike-prone or strike-adverse, adversarial or collaborative?)

Figure 2–1 Continued

management practices. It directly affects an organization's financial status, which in turn determines the level of spending, extent of risk, and priorities in financing the organization will assume. A high rate of inflation, for example, may make an organization more cautious about spending; or it may reduce borrowing and eventually reduce funds for training, compensation, or safety improvements.

The *social* environment in which the organization operates can be described along a variety of dimensions: urban-rural, northeast-northwest, blue collar–white collar, professional-unskilled. The nature of the social environment contributes to the norms that influence the expectations of workers and management. Those in company towns may expect a greater integration of work and family life than those in noncompany towns. Norms, in turn, affect the human resources management policies that are expected and accepted. Expectations of upward mobility and career development may differ between blue-collar and white-collar workers for example.

The *political* environment includes governmental attitudes toward big business, union regulations, and social welfare. Changing governmental attitudes about the delivery of day care, health care, education, and retirement, for example, have encouraged some organizations to provide benefits in these areas. Increasing numbers of organizations offer day care centers on-site or day care vouchers to their employees.[6] And governmental enforcement of laws affecting the workplace varies; for example, under the Reagan administration enforcement of occupational safety and health regulations has decreased.[7]

The *legislative* environment at the federal, state, and local levels has inspired human resources practices encouraging equal employment opportunity, discouraging sexual harassment, and facilitating safety in the workplace.[8] Figure 2–2 summarizes the key pieces of legislation and their provisions, while Chapters 10 and 13 discuss these laws and their implications for human resources management in detail.

The *geographical* environment may influence employees' expectations regarding the relationship between work and leisure, the types of organizational benefits offered, or the extent of stress, alcoholism, or personal problems exhibited in the workplace. For example, compensation for oil pipeline workers in Alaska in the 1970s was disproportionately high for the jobs, in part because of Alaska's geographical isolation.[9] The geographical proximity of departments, divisions, or subsidiaries of an organization may affect the uniformity of human resources management practices within it. Divisions in different regions of the United States may find their human resources programs similar to that of competitors' rather than other divisions in the same organization.

The *cultural* environment includes factors relating to ethnicity, religion, social status, and other background experiences of the work force. Such factors influence the norms and expectations of organizational members. For example, many public

Norris LaGuardia Act of 1932 limits the use of injunctions in preventing union activity.

National Labor Relations Act of 1945 describes bargaining subjects and unfair management and labor practices.

Labor-Management Relations Act of 1947 states unfair union labor practices and prohibits the closed shop.

Landrum Griffin Act of 1959 regulates internal union affairs.

Equal Pay Act of 1963 prohibits discrimination on the basis of sex in compensation for jobs.

Title VII of the Civil Rights Act of 1964 prohibits discrimination in employment on the basis of race, color, religion, sex, and national origin.

Age Discrimination in Employment Act of 1967 (amended in 1978) prohibits discrimination for workers between the ages of forty and seventy.

Occupational Safety and Health Act of 1970 mandates specific safe and healthy working conditions.

Vocational Rehabilitation Act of 1973 prohibits discrimination against physically handicapped individuals.

Employment Retirement Income Security Act of 1974 protects against the misuse of pension monies.

Vietnam Era Veterans Readjustment Assistance Act of 1974 requires affirmative action in hiring and promoting Vietnam era veterans.

Figure 2–2 SUMMARY OF KEY LEGISLATION

schools in northern Maine close for vacation every September so that both students and teachers can participate in the potato harvest.

The *technological* environment influences the tools available and skills required to perform a job.[10] Most organizations have faced major human resources issues associated with the widespread computerization of business functions and automation of assembly processes. Some have instituted special training programs. Others have changed their selection criteria. Changing technology often requires special attention to recruitment, training, and career management.

The *labor* environment describes the general attitude of employees and residents toward unionization. In the Northeast and Midwest unions are more common and accepted than in the South, Southwest, and West.[11] The educational level of the population in a particular area also influences individuals' attitudes: traditionally, educational level correlates negatively with individuals' attitudes toward unions. Professionals, for example, who generally have a high educational level, react less favorably to unions than do blue-collar workers.[12] Union activity in the past—the nature and frequency of strikes, for example—also affects attitudes toward labor.

Understanding the nature of the environment and its direction of change helps managers and human resources professionals predict the type of work force that will be needed and available to meet the organization's objectives. Recognizing that legislative changes may call for more minority employees, or that technological developments may require more technically expert workers, for example, can help managers and human resources professionals focus their employment planning.

If Janice Copeland or Richard Irving performed an environmental audit by answering the questions listed in Figure 2–1, how might they characterize the economic, political, and technological environment faced by Antron? In the middle 1980s, companies similar to Antron faced a stabilizing but not totally predictable economic environment. With inflation under control, borrowing at the available, lower interest rates increased. Organizations faced a politically conservative government that generally supported business through favorable tax laws and other incentives. The technological environment changed so rapidly that some high technology companies found their products obsolete within six to twelve months.

But the environment is not the sole influence on employment and program planning. Characteristics of the organization, as described in the next section, also affect human resources management.

Organizational Assessment

Consider the ways in which human resources management would vary among IBM, United States Steel, and the Massachusetts General Hospital. Consider differences among a boutique, a major department store chain such as Lord and Taylor, and a large chain such as Sears Roebuck and Company. The situational audit must inventory the organization's characteristics before determining the most appropriate human resources programs. An organizational analysis will focus on four areas: (1) the organization's mission or goals, (2) its resources, (3) its climate, and (4) its structure. Human resources management practices must be congruent with these four elements.

An organization's *goals* are "the objects toward which organizations direct their energies and concerns."[13] Goals concern (1) creation and maintenance of societal values and public responsibility, (2) kinds and levels of output, (3) specific characteristics of products or services, (4) managerial activities and performance, including the use of power and motivation of employees, (5) levels of profitability, (6) use of resources, and (7) employee attitudes and performance, including satisfaction, turnover, absenteeism, and commitment.[14] Organizations develop strategic plans that help accomplish organizational goals. Since human resources planning should complement strategic planning, knowing an organization's mission or goals and their relationship to the strategic plan contributes to effective human resources planning. For example, if Antron's management perceives customer service as the key goal, then the number of service employees must increase; if sales are paramount, then the sales staff must expand.

The availability of financial *resources* can of course constrain human resources management. Consider the ways limited financial resources can influence such areas as compensation, labor negotiations, training, and recruitment. The amount of money allocated to compensation determines salary levels and the types of benefits offered. The recruiting budget influences the sources tapped for recruits; the selection budget may determine the extent to which standardized tests are used. Budgetary control by line managers instead of human resources managers or top managers can also affect the nature of their participation in staffing and training activities.

"The internal or psychological environment of an organization . . . known as *climate*"[15] influences the human resources management practices and policies acceptable to organizational members. Organizations that use selection criteria based on ability recruit a pool of candidates different from those that use selection criteria based on political connections. These two types of organizations probably differ in the instruments they use in the selection process, and the organizations' tracking of candidates for promotion would require collection of different data. The amount of job pressure tolerated by the organization may influence the extent to which stress management is incorporated into managerial training, the complexity of the job design in the organization, or the nature of individuals selected for the jobs. Those organizations with a climate that can be characterized as humane and participative accept and require human resources management practices different from those that can be described as autocratic.

The answers to questions such as those in Figure 2–3 provide information for determining effective human resources practices. For example, if the organizational climate encourages individuals to provide and receive feedback, managers may be more receptive to conducting frequent performance appraisals than if the climate does not support feedback. Or if promotion from within the organization is encouraged, managers should first tap internal rather than external sources.

1. To what extent are individual autonomy and responsibility encouraged?
2. To what extent are individuals involved in decision-making in the organization?
3. To what extent are individuals encouraged to provide and have an opportunity to receive feedback?
4. To what extent does top management exhibit a concern for organizational members' satisfaction and quality of work life as well as performance and productivity?
5. To what extent are organizational goals clear and accepted by organizational members?
6. To what extent is work clearly defined?
7. To what extent are managers and workers encouraged or expected to take risks?
8. To what extent does top management pay attention to the ideas of subordinates?
9. To what extent is promotion from inside versus outside the organization encouraged?
10. Is selection based on ability?
11. Is teamwork and intergroup cooperation encouraged?
12. Is sufficient time available to complete assigned work?

Based on dimensions identified in G.H. Litwin and R.A. Stringer, *Motivation and Organizational Climate* (Boston: Division of Research, Graduate School of Business Administration, Harvard University, 1968) and R.J. House and J.R. Rizzo, Organizational Practices Questionnaire (Toronto: University of Toronto, 1972; unpublished).

Figure 2–3 QUESTIONS FOR ASSESSING ORGANIZATIONAL CLIMATE

The nature of the organization's *structure*—its formal reporting relationships, the extent and type of the division of labor, and the means of coordinating the various parts—also influences the feasibility and appropriateness of alternative human resources management systems. Organizations differ in the extent to which they emphasize job specialization, use the hierarchy to resolve problems, rely on standardized policies and procedures, and implement a reward system encouraging obedience to superiors.[16] The structure also influences the nature and extent of individual motivation, which in turn can affect the impact of various human resources programs and practices.

The structure of an organization may also accommodate unions. Typically unions act as adjunct organizations to which some organizational members have an allegiance. The existence of unions and their legitimacy in organizational activities influence human resources practices, and may also exert influence over the design of jobs in the workplace.

JOB ANALYSIS

So far we have identified some environmental and organizational issues that contribute to the situation organizations may face. *Job analysis* complements the situational audit and forms the foundation for most human resources management practices. It acts as the cornerstone of the human resources functions of recruitment, selection, decruitment, performance appraisal, training and development, career management, compensation, and labor relations. Job analysis is "the process of obtaining information about jobs."[17] It refers to the delineation of the tasks performed, skills and experiences required, and performance expectations for each job. At Antron it might address questions such as these: How does Antron describe various jobs? What tasks and activities does each job include? How complex is each job? How challenging is each job? Does each job include a coherent set of activities?

Components of Job Analysis

A job analysis typically includes three components: (1) job description, (2) job specification, and (3) performance standards. The *job description* delineates the tasks performed by a job holder. It explains the duties, working conditions, and other aspects of a job. Figure 2–4 shows a job description for a Counselor I position in a large insurance company. The *job specification* describes what the job demands of employees. It includes the required skills, education, experience, and physical and mental demands for the job. Job specifications for the Counselor I position might include a master's degree in counseling psychology and one to three years of experience as a counselor. *Performance standards* identify the level of performance expected of the job holder and the criterion against which job success is measured. Performance standards for the Counselor I job might include provision of at least one session of psychological counseling to each referral or at least one-half day of training to managers each month.

Job Analysis Procedures

A job analysis system should be dynamic. As jobs change, managers or human resources professionals should automatically revise the job analysis. For example, if a secretary replaces his or her typewriter with a word processor, the job description should be rewritten and the change might entitle the worker to a higher salary. If a worker increases his or her supervisory responsibility but maintains the same job title, a new job analysis should be performed. The revised job specification might suggest areas of training needed by the job holder. All job analyses should be reviewed and, if necessary, revised regularly—yearly or biannually perhaps. In addition, managers and employees should be encouraged to request a new job analysis when they perceive that there have been significant changes in a job.

Job analysis procedures should ensure that the data collected are accurate, reliable, and complete. Diverse types of data can provide information about a job so the job analysis system should specify the nature of data to be collected and the individuals responsible for collecting it. Tradeoffs frequently occur between gathering high quality data and expending reasonable time, money, and staff resources on the analysis.

A job analysis involves four steps: (1) specifying the job to be analyzed; (2) assigning the job analyst; (3) collecting data about the job; and (4) writing the description, specification, or performance standards. Ideally job analyses should be performed jointly by human resources professionals, managers, and job holders. The professionals frequently provide guidelines for a manager to use

JOB DESCRIPTION NUMBER *711701–6R*

I. JOB TITLE: COUNSELOR I

Reports to: Director: EEO and Counseling

Department: Corp. Personnel Ops. Division: Counseling & Employee Services

Cost Center: 595

II. *JOB FUNCTION:*
Counsels employees on personal, psychological, and job-related problems; counsels management in dealing with problem employees; administers career and vocational testing; administers entire spectrum of Company-planned retirement activities; serves as a resource in the field for employees desiring psychology and social work referrals in the Boston area.

UNIT FUNCTION:
Provides psychological counseling and guidance to all levels of Home Office employees on personal problems (e.g., marital/family, stress, depression, anxiety disorders, and other psychological disorders) that affect workplace performance either directly or indirectly. Provides career counseling. Provides training programs for supervisory personnel. Investigates employee complaints as part of the Employee Complaint Review Procedure and refers cases to the Employee Relations Committee. Holds employee termination interviews. Furnishes retiree services to some 1,800 retired employees. Administers Service Award Program, Student and Personal Loan Programs.

III. A. *Briefly list principal duties and responsibilities in order of importance. Indicate frequency (daily, weekly, monthly, annually or irregularly) and percentage of overall time spent on each. Asterisk (*) items which involve use of confidential data.*

1. Provides psychological counseling to Home Office employees—self-referred, referred by management or by the Health Clinic—on job-related problems and problems of a personal nature (marital, family, and social problems, emotional disorders, alcohol and substance abuse) that affect employee performance either directly or indirectly. Independently analyzes and evaluates crisis situations, deciding on appropriate course of action (i.e., further counseling, psychiatric referrals, job transfers, legal aid, etc.). Guides employees to modify behavior to successfully meet job demands. (DAILY—20%)

2. Acting in a consulting capacity, counsels supervisors and managers in strategies for dealing with problem employees. Works with supervisory and/or management personnel to develop appropriate courses of action in order to minimize time-consuming involvement in problem resolution. Creates alternative strategies for management both through courses and individual consultation in order to handle current and emerging employee problems. Counsels managers to enhance their awareness of the effect that employees' psychobehavioral disorders, alcohol and substance abuse can have on workplace performance. Works with managers on strategies for early detection and prompt referral. (DAILY—15%)

3. Administers battery of Career Counseling tests. Evaluates test results, and discusses results with employees. (WEEKLY—5%)

4. Administers the entire range of activities and services offered by the company to retiring employees. Designs, coordinates, organizes, and follows through on the extensive number

Figure 2–4 SAMPLE JOB DESCRIPTION, JOB SPECIFICATION, AND PERFORMANCE STANDARDS *Continued* of planned retirement services. Aids prospective retirees in planning their retirement years. Administers retirement planning seminars. Organizes annual pre-retirement meeting, several series of preparation meetings and luncheons, and annual luncheon for Home Office retirees. Furnishes retirement preparation information privately to employees unable to attend meetings. Serves as Home Office contact for retirees, telephoning, corresponding, and meeting with retired employees to furnish information regarding Group or Pension coverage, Social Security benefits, etc. Conducts retirement termination interviews and reviews material covered in preparation meetings with all retiring employees. Prepares and/or updates Retiree Handbook. (MONTHLY—20%)

5. Designs and teaches, in coordination with Corporate Career Education, enrichment courses for management and employees on such general interest topics from the psychology field as Stress Management, Team Dynamics, Successful Weight Management, How to Handle Employee Problems, etc. (MONTHLY—5%)

6. Coordinates with psychologists and rehabilitation nurses in the Health Clinic regarding the placement of severely emotionally disturbed employees on disability leave and/or Group Disability coverage. (MONTHLY—5%)

7. Functions as a human resource information clearinghouse for the Company, acting as a liaison between employees and professional human service resources in the Greater Boston area. Maintains professional contact with other employee assistance counselors at companies of a comparable size, both in the Boston area and further afield. Attends local and regional conferences for employee assistance counselors. (AS NEEDED—5%)

8. Administers JH employee termination interview program. Conducts exit interviews of employees, writes up reports of interviews, and submits reports to area management with recommendations for action. (WEEKLY—20%)

9. Educates employees leaving for military service of company policy in effect, and of their rights and obligations under the law. Advises company management of obligations to employees entering the military or returning to employment following military service. Approves payment of military leave allowance where applicable. (MONTHLY—5%)

B. *Describe the skills and abilities needed to do this job. For example, list prior experience on certain jobs.*

A thorough knowledge of counseling theory and practice gained by a combination of education (a Masters degree in counseling or social work is required) and training in the field (a minimum 3 to 5 years required).

C. *Furnish any additional information which would help to describe or understand the duties of this job.*

An Employee Assistance Counselor should have the ability to perform the following as a matter of course. The ability to interpret the verbal and non-verbal messages conveyed by employees in times of emotional crisis, independently assessing the situation, deciding upon appropriate courses of action, and following through on resolution of the problem. The ability to create and maintain a relaxed, non-judgemental, and confidential atmosphere necessary for obtaining employee confidence, and working out employee personal, psychological, and work-related problems. The ability to maintain professional standards of confidentiality on emotionally highly-charged information. Seasoning and self-assurance are necessary to handle crisis situations as they arise, on-the-spot and without supervision.

Figure 2–4 **Continued**

in analyzing the jobs of subordinates. The manager may then use his or her own perceptions of the job coupled with reports from the job holders as basic data. Who would be the best person to analyze the jobs at Antron? Antron's president? Richard Irving? Janice Copeland? The salespeople? The most accurate and comprehensive job analysis would involve all of these people in collecting and analyzing data about the job.

Data collection includes a review of existing data about a job—for example, the job description, performance evaluations of job holders, or written goals of the job holder. Additional data should be gathered from observing the job and its functions by systematically observing a worker perform the job and documenting these observations. Job analysts could also administer standardized or specially constructed questionnaires to the job holder and supervisors. Figure 2–5 describes the Position Analysis Questionnaire and Management Position Description Questionnaire, both of which are frequently used in job analysis. Human resources professionals or other job analysts can also interview the job holder and supervisors to obtain their perceptions of the job's activities, specifications, and standards.

Often analysts supplement data collected through observations, interviews, or questionnaires by requesting that job holders maintain a log or diary of their work activities. In addition, supervisors can record critical incidents that occur in the job, providing a sample of key job activities. Videotaping a sample of job

Position Analysis Questionnaire[a]

Each of 194 job elements is rated according to extent of use, importance to the job, amount of time, possibility of occurrence, and applicability on a five-point scale from very minor to extreme, as well as does not apply. Job elements are divided into six divisions: (1) information input, such as use of written materials or near-visual discrimination; (2) mental processes, such as level of reasoning in problem-solving or coding/decoding; (3) work output, such as use of keyboard devices or assembling/disassembling; (4) relationships with other persons, such as instructing or contacts with public or customers; (5) job context, such as high temperature or interpersonal conflict situations; and (6) other job characteristics.

Management Position Description Questionnaire[b]

The MPDQ includes 208 items specifically designed for management positions. Respondents check those items that apply to their jobs. These items have been organized into thirteen job factors: (1) product, market, and financial planning; (2) coordination of other organizational units and personnel; (3) internal business control; (4) product sales and service responsibility; (5) public and customer relations; (6) advanced consulting; (7) autonomy of action; (8) approval of financial commitment; (9) staff service; (10) supervision; (11) complexity and stress; (12) advanced financial responsibility; and (13) broad personnel responsibility.

[a]Based on E.J. McCormick, *Job Analysis* (New York: AMACOM, 1979).
[b]Based on W.W. Tornow and P.R. Pinto, "The Development of Management Job Taxonomy: A System for Describing, Classifying and Evaluating Executive Positions," *Journal of Applied Psychology* 11 (1976): 410–418.

Figure 2–5 SAMPLE DIMENSIONS FROM POSITION ANALYSIS QUESTIONNAIRE AND MANAGEMENT POSITION DESCRIPTION QUESTIONNAIRE performance has also become popular as a way of completely and systematically representing the job's content.

Figure 2–6 lists a series of questions that the data should attempt to answer. Questions 1 through 8 provide data for the job description; questions 9 and 10 gather data for job specifications; questions 11 and 12 identify the performance standards. For example, for item 3 the counselor's daily diary might indicate that he or she spends an hour and a half each day counseling other employees and one hour each day acting as a resource to other supervisors. (Note that the job analysis for the Counselor I job in Figure 2–4 does not address answers to questions 11 and 12).

After collecting data, the analyst prepares a written document. A detailed description of the activities performed by the counselor, in this case, is translated into the written job description similar to sections IIIA1 and IIIA2 of the job description in Figure 2–4. The analyst lists all tasks involved, rates their complexity and frequency, groups similar tasks, then converts these data into short, concise, clearly written job descriptions, job specifications, and performance standards. The written job analysis should include action verbs to describe tasks, sufficient detail to accurately reflect acceptable performance, and grammatically correct language. A second analyst, known as a *job auditor,* reviews the document for accuracy. He or she may collect additional data and compare them to the original data to check the accuracy of the job analysis.

Uses of Job Analysis

What role does job analysis serve?[18] Job analysis assists in communicating the expectations of a job to a job holder, his or her supervisors, and peers. By reviewing existing job descriptions, specifications, and performance standards employees can more quickly learn the scope and boundaries of their responsibilities. A job analysis can focus employment forecasting and planning (as described in the next sections of this chapter). Human resources professionals and managers

1. What tasks comprise the job?
2. What does a typical work day look like?
3. What is the frequency and duration of each job activity?
4. How complex is each job activity?
5. What job activities are related, and how are they related?
6. How much supervisory responsibility does the job entail?
7. To whom does the job holder report?
8. What budgetary responsibility does the job involve?
9. What qualifications are required of job holders?
10. What mental and physical demands are placed on job holders?
11. What expectations do supervisors and coworkers have of the job holder?
12. What outcomes reflect acceptable job performance? Outstanding job performance?

Figure 2–6 SAMPLE QUESTIONS FOR DATA COLLECTION IN A JOB ANALYSIS can then forecast and compare supply and demand for specific jobs as well as inventory workers' skills and compare them to job requirements.

Job analysis also provides basic guidelines for ensuring the fit between potential employees and a job. Criteria for the recruitment and selection of employees (see Chapters 3 and 4) should be drawn from the job specifications. Job analysis can provide a focus for career development to ensure that current employees have the skills required to perform the activities of future jobs (see Chapter 8). Promotion, demotion, and transfer decisions (see Chapter 5) are also frequently made on the basis of the fit between individual and job.

Performance standards, which should delineate the performance requirements of any job holder, can be used as the basis of evaluation and the establishment of development goals (see Chapter 6). Job analysis should inform individuals of the evaluation criteria used. Job evaluations, on which pay scales are based (see Chapter 9), should also be closely linked to job analyses, which should list the key job activities which are ultimately rewarded. Job analysis also provides a framework for assessing training needs, selecting training programs, and evaluating the impact of training and development programs (see Chapter 7).

In addition, job analysis provides basic information for union-management negotiations. In a union setting, the data in a job analysis helps set performance standards, establish responsibility, authority, and accountability, conduct negotiations, handle grievances, and establish channels of communication between union and management (see Chapters 11 and 12).

Finally, a job analysis can serve as a focus of organizational change, including the alteration of job activities through programs such as job enrichment or work simplification (see Chapter 14).

An Effective Job Analysis Program

Human resources professionals must ensure that a job analysis program provides managers and job holders with accurate job descriptions, specifications, and performance standards on a timely basis. Because job analysis is the cornerstone of all human resources functions, requiring accuracy and currency for every position in the organization is essential. An inaccurate job analysis can cause managers or human resources professionals to identify incorrect criteria for recruitment or selection (see Chapters 3 and 4). Poor job analyses may result in inaccurate job evaluations and consequent inappropriate compensation decisions (see Chapter 9). Incomplete job analysis may result in incomplete or inaccurate performance evaluations (see Chapter 6). Managers and human resources professionals should establish a system for the review of existing job descriptions, collection of data to update the descriptions, and revision of the documents on a regular basis.

The success of job analysis programs depends on a variety of factors: (1) commitment of top management; (2) involvement of the union in unionized organizations; (3) involvement of employees; (4) effective communication of the purpose of the program; (5) assignment of a qualified and interested person to perform the job analysis; (6) use of human resources management experts as resources; (7) collection of data during regular work hours; (8) use of valid and reliable data collection methods and instruments; (9) use of a steering committee or other vehicle to oversee the analysis.[19] Errors result when there is inadequate sampling of behaviors, employees are not committed to providing accurate information about their jobs, or there are changes in the environment, organization, or job itself that are not monitored frequently enough.

EMPLOYMENT PLANNING

A key component of human resources planning is the determination of the types of employees that the organization will need in the short, medium, and long run. Employment planning includes forecasting future needs for employees of various job categories, forecasting the current and future supply of employees in various job categories, and comparing the demand to the supply. What types of people will Antron require to accomplish its goals in the next month? Year? Three years? Five years? Antron will require a certain number of salespeople and engineers. The company will also need production personnel, general managers, and human resources professionals, among others. How many and what kinds of engineers will Antron require? How many and what kinds of salespeople?

Forecasting the *demand* of employees means determining the number of employees in each job category *needed* to accomplish an organization's goals. Forecasting *supply* refers to a determination of the number of employees in specified job categories *available* for employment.

Both supply and demand can be determined at two levels. At a macroeconomic level supply and demand refer to the general availability and demand for certain types of workers in industry at large. Employment estimators evaluate labor force patterns, economic factors, or technological considerations to determine the external supply; they also note shifting industrial patterns to determine demand. In the early 1980s, for example, the supply of teachers in the labor force relative to demand was high in urban industrial areas, while the relative supply of engineers was low. The Department of Labor regularly issues reports that highlight the outlook for various professions.[20]

In this section we emphasize a more organizational view of supply and demand. (Planning at the individual level is addressed in Chapter 8, which describes career management.) To determine the supply of employees a manager or human resources professional could count those currently in sales jobs, those inside the company who could potentially hold a sales job, and the number of individuals available for sales positions outside the company. The techniques for forecasting demand and supply vary in sophistication, from judgmental techniques to statistical analyses. Many organizations rely on qualitative assessments, which are easy to perform and relatively inexpensive. The availability of low-cost computers and statistical data analysis packages, however, makes quantitative techniques more available and feasible.[21]

The next sections examine three types of forecasting techniques: (1) judgmental techniques, (2) matrix methods, and (3) quantitative approaches.[22] Table 2–1 shows the percentage of firms using each of the forecasting techniques described below.

Judgmental Forecasts

The simplest forecasting techniques involve estimating the number of employees needed or available in each category using an individual's *best judgment* in making the estimate. For example, a manager might make the following estimates: four extra sales people would double sales; the number of production workers can decrease by four if increased automation is introduced; worker turnover will be 10 percent; or the closing of a competitor's laboratory will make fifty engineers available for immediate employment. A production manager might estimate instead that, with improved technology and increased automation, the number of production workers can decrease by four during the next year. Or the foreman may estimate that turnover among her workers will be 10 percent, so that 90 percent of the present work force will be available during the next year. The engineering chief may learn that a competitor is closing its local laboratory, thus making available a significant supply of engineers. Managers, experts in the field, employees, and human resources professionals typically base their judgments on

	Percentage of Firms Reporting Forecasting Technique		
	Short Range *(less than 2 years)*	Intermediate Range *(2–5 years)*	Long Range *(more than 5 years)*
Supply Forecasts			
Markov or network flow models	12%	13%	10%
Personnel inventories	54	33	22
Computer simulation	10	15	5
Operations research	11	12	10
Succession planning or replacement charts	55	39	22
Others	6	6	2
Demand Forecasts			
Supervisor estimates	75	31	12
Rule-of-thumb	28	15	7
Replacement chart	36	34	18
Delphi	2	6	1
Time series regression analysis	13	19	13
Computer simulation	7	11	7
Other	8	6	0

Table 2–1 PERCENTAGE OF FIRMS USING VARIOUS FORECASTING TECHNIQUES

past experience, their general knowledge of an industry, or guesses about employment trends.

Judgmental techniques use two approaches: (1) a unit demand approach and (2) an organizational demand approach. The unit demand approach is a bottom-up approach. Supervisors estimate the number of employees they will need in a given time period and report this number to their superior. The supervisors then collect the predictions for each unit they supervise and estimate the demand for their unit. This collation of estimates continues until an estimate is obtained for the entire organization. The manager is actively involved in this type of forecasting by providing estimates of need, while the human resources professional provides guidance by focusing the estimates made or the issues considered in making them.

The organizational approach is a top-down approach. In this instance, top management makes the decisions about the number of employees needed in various job categories throughout the organization, based on their assessment of the work force required to fulfill the strategic plan. At Antron, for example, executives might determine that the sales force must add thirty employees, that the number of managers must double, and that the human resources department should add five professionals. Each of the judgmental techniques described below can be used from the unit demand or organizational perspective.

Estimates of supply focus on the internal and external labor markets. Supervisors or organizational experts can estimate the number of employees who will be available inside the company to hold particular jobs. For example, supervisors in high-technology industries expect as high as a 30 percent turnover rate in some jobs; for those positions they would estimate a lower supply of employees than the number that currently hold the job. They can also assess the number of individuals who could fill a position but are working for other organizations. A competitor, for example, might have 100 potential hires for Antron.

Formalized Judgments. Rule-of-thumb techniques provide general guidelines for the number of employees needed or available to do a particular job. For example, one salesperson might be needed for each $100,000 of sales, or one assembly worker might be needed for each 1000 cars produced. A rule-of-thumb for the availability of clerks, based on historical data, might be that nine will remain with the organization after six months, eight after eighteen months, and six after two years. The sophistication of rule-of-thumb techniques can vary significantly. At their simplest they resemble a supervisor or expert estimate that uses historical data. At their most sophisticated they approach the quantitative techniques described later in this chapter. The accuracy of rule-of-thumb techniques depends on the type of historical data available for determining the number of employees needed or available in various categories.

Skills Inventory. Skills inventories best help estimate the supply of workers within an organization. As shown in Figure 2–7, a skills inventory lists the skills possessed by each employee. Work experience, educational credentials, training

Name ______________________ Date ______________

Job Title ______________________ Years of Experience with Organization ______________

Education ____

Special Training ____

Job History ____

____

____

____

Skills: List below any skills you possess that are relevant to your job or any other job in this organization.

______________________ ______________________

______________________ ______________________

______________________ ______________________

______________________ ______________________

______________________ ______________________

Supervisory Responsibility:

Current number of employees supervised ______________

Previous supervisory responsibility: Job Title Number Supervised

______________________ ______________________

______________________ ______________________

______________________ ______________________

Other relevant information: ____

____

Figure 2–7 SAMPLE SKILLS INVENTORY

activities, skills, supervisory responsibility, and other job-related information are then coded.[23]

Human resources professionals should then compile the data from skills inventories for all organizational members. This summary reflects the skills available in the organization. Analyzing the summary, by computer whenever possible, should allow human resources professionals or managers to tabulate the supply of various skills organization-wide.

Replacement Chart. The replacement chart is an organizational chart that names and describes current job holders and potential replacements. Figure 2–8 shows a replacement chart for the human resources management department of a small manufacturing firm.

Note that each block in the organizational chart has the following information:

1. the position title;
2. the current job holder's name;
3. a rating of the job holder's current performance;
4. a rating of the job holder's promotability;

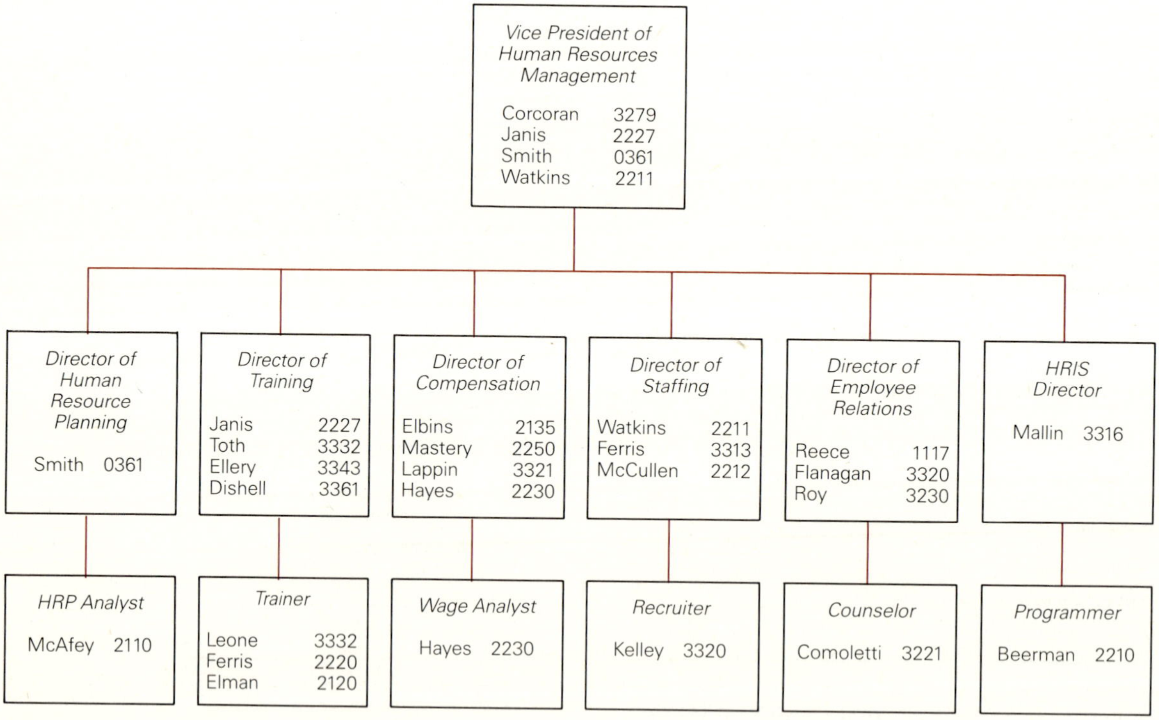

Key (ratings, given in order, after each name)
Performance: 1 (Poor), 2 (Satisfactory), 3 (Outstanding)
Promotability: 1 (not for 2 years), 2 (not for 1 year), 3 (promotable now)
Experience: Number of years
Supervisory: Number supervised

Figure 2–8 EXCERPTS FROM A REPLACEMENT CHART

5. the number of years the job holder has held the position;

6. other ratings of performance, such as participation in certain types of training programs, willingness to relocate geographically, or the extent and nature of supervisory experience;

7. the names of potential successors in the short and medium run;

8. a rating of the current performance of each potential successor;

9. a rating of the promotability of each potential successor;

10. other ratings of performance for each potential successor, such as the availability of successors, relative seniority, or supervisory or technical experience of the potential successor.

The replacement chart in Figure 2–8 would allow a manager or human resources professional to deduce supply as follows: (1) a successor to the Director of Human Resources Planning is not available; (2) individuals with employment counseling skills and experience are not available since the Employee Counselor lacks a ready replacement; and (3) there is a supply of individuals with expertise in training management since the Director of Training position has several highly promotable potential successors. Deducing demand is more difficult. If, for example, the Director of Human Resources Planning is a newly created position, then there would be a demand for individuals skilled enough to hold that position.

Replacement charts provide a manager with a clear representation of the current employment situation in a unit or organization. In addition to its ability to forecast demand or supply on a case-by-case basis, it also offers insight into the career development required for individuals or groups of employees. For example, a lack of individuals who can readily be promoted into supervisory positions may suggest the need for management development training. Or an overabundance of middle managers may suggest the need for more job rotation or lateral transfer programs.

Although constructing a chart takes time, it can provide useful, complete, and systematic information for employment decisions. The more a manager uses objective indices of performance and promotability in developing the chart, the more accurate the conclusions that can be drawn from it. Frequent updating of the data, however, is essential to its usefulness.

Supervisor Estimates. Many argue that no one knows the number of employees needed or available to do a job better than the person in charge of getting that job done. The supervisor uses intuition and experience to assess the number of employees needed or the number who will be available. Typically a component of bottom-up forecasting, supervisor assessments are simple and quick and can produce accurate results. At the same time, they are based heavily on opinion, can detract from the supervisor's other responsibilities, and may require knowledge about the organization or environment that a supervisor may not have.

In spite of these limitations, this type of forecasting remains a very popular one, particularly in small organizations or those lacking sophisticated technology or quantitative expertise. Richard Irving, using the organizational approach at Antron, for example, could estimate the needs of his department as well as predict the number of employees who will be available to fill these needs. Or Irving could ask all managers in the sales department to estimate their supply and demand, and amalgamate these data into a single estimate.

Expert Estimates. Instead of doing the estimate himself, Irving could hire an expert to evaluate supply and demand. Some industries have spawned individuals or firms that have become very knowledgeable about supply and demand for that industry. There are experts who can evaluate the impact of office automation on staffing requirements, for example. In some situations, such as the introduction of a new technology or changes in the legal regulations that affect staffing, a supervisor may lack sufficient knowledge to make good estimates of the people needed or available to do a job. Here experts can provide the best judgment about supply and demand to help meet the organization's goals.

Like supervisor estimates, expert estimates are relatively intuitive decisions. They have higher direct costs associated with them because experts are compensated for offering their expert opinion. Yet, because experts frequently do not provide quantitative or statistical support for their estimates, the relative cost remains low. Could an expert help Richard Irving forecast the needs of his department?

Delphi Estimates. Rather than relying solely on individual supervisor or expert judgments, the Delphi method is an iterative approach that obtains and uses opinions from a group to forecast demand or supply.

The procedure typically requires a facilitator, such as a human resources professional, who coordinates performance of the following steps:

1. Define a problem or question, such as the number of employees required for sales positions in two years;
2. Check that the problem is clear and answerable;
3. Identify, select, and orient a panel of experts, such as the sales managers, who offer estimates;
4. Issue a first-round questionnaire to request planning estimates from each sales manager;
5. Analyze and summarize responses;
6. Distribute a second questionnaire and summary of data to the expert panel members;
7. Analyze responses and determine degree of agreement among experts;
8. Initiate another round or convene a face-to-face meeting with the panel members to reconcile differences.[24]

This technique offers the advantage of eliciting multiple opinions while retaining the ability to poll individual members. The value of this approach depends on the knowledge of the panel members; therefore the facilitator must carefully select the Delphi group. The technique shares the advantages of low cost and ease of use with other judgmental techniques.

Matrix Methods

The matrix method bridges the gap between the judgmental techniques and the quantitative techniques. Rooted in the highly mathematical Markov analysis, the matrix method combines past experience and managerial judgment in formulating the probabilities for employee movement between jobs.[25]

As shown in Table 2–2, the transitional probability matrix helps identify the number of people likely to hold a job at a given time. It uses assumptions about the percentages of individuals moving from one labor pool into another in successive years. Such assumptions are based on historical data and managerial judgment. The procedures are as follows:

1. Historical records provide information for a five- to ten-year period about hirings, dates of job entry, promotions, transfers, and departures from jobs;

A. Human Resources Requirements

Initial Population		Human Resources Requirements	
		Year 1	Year 2
Job A	200	300	310
Job B	250	150	195

B. Matrix of Movement

From	To	
	Job A	Job B
Job A	.8	.1
Job B	.1	.7

C. Year 1 Inventory Projection

Year 0	Year 1	
	Job A	Job B
Job A	160	20
Job B	25	175
Total	185	195

D. Projected Need or Surplus

	Initial Population	Inventory at Year 1	Year 1 Requirements	Need (Surplus)
Job A	200	185	300	115
Job B	250	195	150	(45)

Table 2–2 SAMPLE MATRIX ANALYSIS

2. Historical data reflect the stability of patterns of movement in the past that can be expected to predict patterns of personnel in the future;
3. The data are analyzed to determine the probabilities of holding the same position, or receiving a transfer or promotion next year (What are the chances of a salesperson being a sales supervisor next year? Of remaining a salesperson? Of being transferred to production or merchandising?);
4. Using probabilities determined in number 3 and matrix algebra concepts, the distribution of personnel in subsequent years is predicted.

Table 2–2 shows the proportion of people moving from one job to another during successive years. Part A shows the initial number of job holders as well as the human resources requirements for the first and second subsequent years. Part B shows the matrix—the percentage of employees who historically move between Jobs A and B from one year to the next: 80 percent remain in Job A, 10 percent move from Job A to Job B, 10 percent move from Job B to Job A, 70 percent remain in Job B. Part C shows the inventory projection based on these expected transitions; for example, 80 percent of the 200 or 160 currently in Job A are projected to remain in Job A in Year 1. Part D shows the inventory expectations at Year 1 for both jobs and compares these to the requirements: in Year 1 115 people for Job A will be needed and 45 extra people will be in Job B.

The transitional matrix approach estimates the internal supply of individuals for particular jobs. Comparing the estimates of individuals required in various positions—the demand—to those expected to be available according to the matrix—the supply—yields the excess/deficiency to be entered into the employment plan.

The matrix approach systematically integrates historical knowledge into forecasts. Its cost, however, exceeds that of the judgmental techniques. In addition, the quality of the historical data determines the accuracy of the results. Should Janice Copeland use the matrix approach? What role would Richard Irving play?

Quantitative Techniques

Quantitative techniques incorporate the use of more sophisticated mathematical analysis. As such these approaches require human resources professionals and managers to make explicit the assumptions they use in making forecasts. They must specify the variables that predict the extent of human resources needed and available, as well as the interrelationships among the variables. This specification allows the forecasters to manipulate variables and run tests on them as a way of finding the best predictors and predictions of human resources supply and demand.

Statistics serve four functions in planning: (1) They provide summaries of data in understandable form. (2) They facilitate model building and forecasting by indicating patterns in personnel data. (3) They identify relationships between key human resources variables. (4) They identify sources of error and uncertainty in personnel data.[26] The next section describes four statistical approaches: (1) trend analyses, (2) multiple predictive techniques, (3) operations research techniques, and (4) simulations.

Trend Analysis. Trend analysis predicts future employment needs or availability in terms of the relationship of employees to such organizational variables as sales levels, production output, or loan revenues. Trend analysis can use judgments or the statistical technique of correlation, as shown in Table 2–3. Either past rates of change are extended into the future, or future employment is estimated by matching it with an index such as the Gross National Product, Consumer Price Index, or inflation rate.

Causal forecasting attempts to use historical data to determine the cause of various events or outcomes. Causal forecasting might show that increasing a sales staff increases sales dollars, for example. Time series forecasting does not attempt to attribute cause and effect to correlated variables. Over time, for example, such forecasting might track changes in staff levels as a function of the changing rate of inflation, but it does not imply that the inflation rate *causes* a certain staff level.

Trend analysis more explicitly and systematically considers the impact of diverse variables on the employment picture than do the judgmental and matrix approaches. The correct selection of such variables determines the accuracy of the predictions of supply and demand. The availability of computerized data bases and statistical packages increases the ability to use statistical techniques in trend analyses by reducing the time, cost, and expertise required to perform them.

Multiple Predictive Techniques. Highly accurate statistical models exist that can predict both demand for and supply of individuals in specific employment categories. Multiple predictive techniques include multiple regression and more complex trend analysis such as canonical correlations.[27] To predict the number of

Year	Sales	Production Workers
1977	$300K	8
1978	500K	10
1979	700K	14
1980	1000K	20
1981	1100K	20
1982	1200K	24
1983	1100K	25
1984	1500K	30
1985	1700K	27
1986	2000K	35

Number of production workers = (.016 × Sales) + (3.5)

Table 2–3 SAMPLE CORRELATION ANALYSIS

employees required or available, multiple regression first requires the manager or human resources professional to identify the factors that influence those employee levels and then to correlate the number of employees with those influences.

Multiple regression incorporates several predictors into a single model for determining level of employees. For example, if the number of production employees required relates to the rate of inflation, level of sales, degree of automation, and level of union wage demands, then multiple regression considers all these relationships simultaneously to predict the number of employees required.

The accuracy of multiple regression techniques depends on correctly identifying the relevant predictor variables and gathering complete data. There are new statistical packages that facilitate the use of these techniques and allow the manipulation of variables to test the effects of different predictors as well. Together, Richard Irving and Janice Copeland at Antron could use multiple regression techniques to predict staff needs and availability.

Operations Research Techniques. Linear programming can be used to specify the number of employees needed to meet organizational objectives within constraints such as total number of employees, total plant capacity, or total compensation level. Goal programming and dynamic programming are additional operations research techniques that have been used in forecasting.

These techniques require the user to be mathematically knowledgeable. Most schools of business offer courses in operations management that include practice in such techniques as they apply to inventory scheduling or transportation problems. However, translating the techniques for use in human resources management has been relatively uncommon.

Simulations. Computer simulations are representations of complex work situations that allow different aspects to be changed singly or in combination. The impact of these changes on employment level can then be studied. Although only organizations with large computer facilities have historically used such simulations, the increased availability of computer capacity now makes them more accessible to small organizations as well.

See Table 2–4 for a comparison of the various methods of forecasting supply and demand listed above.

Comparing Demand to Supply

Let us assume that Richard Irving and Janice Copeland gathered all possible data and have the analyses before them. What steps should Antron take next? Irving's estimates of demand indicate that Antron needs to add ten sales support people to the four currently in that position during each of the next two years. Analyses of skills inventories and supervisor estimates reveal that the organization currently employs only five people who could easily move into a sales support position. The organization faces a deficiency: demand exceeds supply.

Technique	Type	Focus	Computerized or Manual	Cost in Dollars	Cost in Time
Delphi estimate	judgmental	supply & demand	manual	low	high
Expert estimate	judgmental	supply & demand	manual	high	moderate
Formalized judgments	judgmental	supply & demand	manual	low	low
Multiple predictive techniques	quantitative	supply & demand	computerized	high	high
Operations research	quantitative	supply & demand	computerized	high	high
Replacement chart	judgmental	supply	manual or computerized	low to moderate	moderate
Simulations	quantitative	supply & demand	computerized	high	high
Skills inventory	judgmental	supply	manual or computerized	moderate	moderate to high
Supervisor estimate	judgmental	supply & demand	manual	low	low to moderate
Transitional matrix	matrix	supply & demand	manual or computerized	moderate to high	moderate to high
Trend analysis	quantitative	supply & demand	manual or computerized	moderate to high	moderate to high

Table 2–4 COMPARISON OF FORECASTING TECHNIQUES

Janice Copeland should then make comparisons of various ways Irving can secure the needed employees (see Table 2–5). She should try to take into account the major limitations in making these comparisons, however: the inaccuracy of forecasts, inadequate data bases, lack of acceptance of planning in the organization, and significant expense.[28]

Based on these forecasts, however, Copeland or Irving must determine the most reasonable actions to deal with the deficiency. The implementation of these actions comprises program planning—the second part of human resources planning.

PROGRAM PLANNING

Program planning follows employment planning. It focuses on the development and implementation of plans that help reach employment and organizational goals, and involves the selection of tools that most effectively address an oversupply or undersupply of human resources. A program plan must "help managers anticipate and meet changing needs relative to the acquisition, deployment, and utilization of people."[29]

But program planning involves *systems*—diverse personnel and labor relations activities, actions, and plans that must be compatible with one another. Management should agree to wage provisions in new labor contracts that do not contradict compensation policy for nonunion workers, for example. Management should also grant productivity incentives to individuals who receive positive performance appraisals. A comprehensive planning framework ensures the

		Supply of Managers: High	Supply of Managers: Low
Demand for Managers	High	Selection Placement Promotion	Internal: Training and development Compensation External: Recruitment
	Low	Change in company plans Outplacement Layoffs Demotions Early Retirement	Training and development if change in demand is expected in the future

Table 2–5 MANPOWER ACTIONS EMPHASIS BASED ON MANPOWER SUPPLY AND DEMAND WITHIN THE ENTERPRISE

congruence of human resources decisions in staffing, development, career management, compensation, collective bargaining, and organizational improvement. We examine each of these systems, as well as their interrelationships, in the rest of this book.

DEVELOPING AN APPROACH TO HUMAN RESOURCES PLANNING

Human resources planning should involve the *joint* effort of human resources professionals and managers. Human resources professionals should have primary responsibility for establishing and monitoring planning procedures. Managers in the organization should implement the procedures, emphasizing careful and complete collection and analysis of data.

When human resources planning is the sole responsibility of the personnel department and is not recognized as a legitimate part of business planning, "(1) plans are developed in a vacuum and bear little relationship to the business plans they are supposedly supporting; (2) plans are inadvertently tentative and emphasize short-term operational aspects of personnel management; (3) personnel management is placed in a reactive mode and must play catch-up to the rest of the organization; and (4) business objectives may suffer setbacks since to some degree all business plan objectives are people-dependent."[30] The following section offers a scenario for appropriately sharing planning responsibilities.

Implications for Human Resources Professionals

To ensure the effectiveness of planning, human resources professionals must monitor and evaluate existing planning practices. Effective practice includes the following:

1. Human resources professionals must diagnose the current situation, focusing specifically on the requirements for planning and the existence of planning practices. Diagnosis should also examine the results of the situational audit and job analyses.
2. Human resources professionals must ensure the existence of current job descriptions, specifications, and performance standards for all positions.
3. Human resources professionals should poll managers and other key organizational members about the planning practices they use to answer questions such as whether planning procedures exist, how elaborate the procedures are, how costly they are, how accurate the planning results are, whether there are forecasts for supply and demand for each position, and whether data bases for use in forecasting have been computerized.
4. Human resources professionals should review planning procedures used by other organizations.

5. Human resources professionals should provide managers with direction regarding the types of data to collect for employment planning. They should assist managers in using computers to store and evaluate these data.

6. Human resources professionals should coordinate and oversee planning of a comprehensive set of activities to achieve employment and organizational goals; and they should monitor the cost-effectiveness of these activities.

Implications for Managers

Managers have the primary responsibility for gathering data about supply and demand and implementing program plans. To do this effectively, they should follow these procedures:

1. Managers should periodically perform a situational audit involving both environmental and organizational analyses.
2. Managers should provide data for job analyses. They must also monitor current job descriptions, specifications, and performance standards since most human resources activities rely on comprehensive and accurate job analyses.
3. Managers should assist in forecasting demand and supply for each position they supervise; compare supply to demand for each position; and formulate strategies for dealing with deficiencies or surpluses.
4. Managers should carefully pilot-test and then implement the planning system. They should involve their subordinates in developing these implementation procedures and in training them to use the system.
5. Managers should employ computers in the human resources planning system. Essential to effective human resources planning is a comprehensive information system that "provides accurate and timely data about the status of the organization's people, job structure, and culture."[31]
6. Managers should periodically evaluate the relative costs and benefits of the entire system.

ACTIVITIES

Activity 2–1

PERFORMING A JOB ANALYSIS

Step 1: Select a partner.

Step 2: Select a job you currently hold. If you are not employed, select your job as a student.

Step 3: Interview your partner about his or her job. Ask questions such as the following:

1. How would you describe a typical day?
2. Who do you supervise?
3. Who supervises you?
4. What are your major responsibilities?
5. What activities do you perform during the week?
6. What percentage of time do you devote to each activity?
7. What mental and physical demands are made of you on the job?
8. What skills, knowledge, experience, or other credentials are required to hold your job?
9. What are the major outcomes or products of your job?
10. What constitutes good performance in your job?

Step 4: Reverse roles.

Step 5: Using the data collected, write the job description, specification, and performance standards for your partner's job.

Step 6: Now get a new partner. Check for accuracy—or audit—the job description completed on your partner's job. (This is likely to require the new partner to repeat steps 3 and 4 above.)

Step 7: Meet with the person who has analyzed and audited the same job in order to modify the written job description to fit with data collected by both of you.

Step 8: Discussion. In small groups or with the class as a whole, share your experiences in writing job descriptions, specifications, and performance standards. Then consider questions such as the following:

1. How accurate were the analyses that were performed?
2. How did the original analyses and those performed by the auditor compare?
3. What problems are there in doing a job analysis?
4. What procedures could have been specified to make the process easier? More reliable? More accurate?

Activity 2–2

BROWN, STEINBERG & COMPANY

Step 1: Read the case.

Step 2: Prepare the case for class discussion.

"This is the third job I have reviewed this quarter that has been run over budget," thought Blake. Late in October 1982, Jerome Blake, Senior Partner at the Boston Office of Brown, Steinberg & Company, was examining an audit for the fiscal year ended September 30, for Telecompter, Inc. The costs to complete the job were estimated at $40,000. Yet, due to excessive hours, the billing to Telecompter, Inc., had exceeded $50,000. Upon further investigation, Blake discovered that current year's billings to clients had increased at an average of 30%.

Case prepared by Steve Strand, MBA candidate, under the supervision of Assistant Professor Alberto Zanzi.

COMPANY'S BACKGROUND

Brown, Steinberg & Company is an international public accounting firm, with offices located throughout the United States and Europe. Through a series of mergers, acquisitions and successful services, Brown, Steinberg & Company has climbed to its current position of 12th largest in the United States. The Firm specializes in the hospitality industry (hotels, restaurants, clubs, etc.), but also services a wide range of other businesses as well. The Company's revenues have increased from $32 million in 1978 to a projected $50 million for 1982. The Boston Office is the Firm's second largest office, employing approximately sixty-five people and servicing approximately two hundred clients with an average sales volume of $20 million yearly. (See Figure 2–9 for organizational chart of Brown, Steinberg & Company.)

Public accounting firms basically "audit" businesses. A company's financial records are reviewed and verified by the auditors. The client's financial statements are then accompanied by an opinion from the accounting firm as to the reliability of the financial information presented.

Auditing a client requires a team composed of a senior accountant and from two to four staff accountants. The work is performed at the client's office and the job is then reviewed by the Supervisor, Manager and Partner-in-Charge.

The auditing fee to be charged is then calculated by multiplying the total hours incurred in performing and reviewing the job times the various wage ranges. A typical audit takes three to four weeks to complete at a cost ranging between $20,000 and $40,000 depending on the complexity of the job. (See Table 2–6.) The Firm also provides tax and management advisory services to their clients. Public accountants are required to hold a college degree, usually in Accounting.

Management's Opinions

The following day, Jerome Blake called Rosemary Janes into his office to express his concern. Rosemary Janes, 35, was the first female to achieve a Manager's position at Brown, Steinberg & Company. She has risen quickly through the ranks, and is viewed as being very aggressive.

> Blake: I have noticed lately that jobs have been running over budget and consequently our auditing fees have been rising steadily. Normally, I would expect fees to rise somewhat because of general cost increases each year. However, I think the 30% we have been averaging this year is excessive. I realize the current economic climate has presented certain problems in auditing our clients, but I think we are running into a problem of having to justify our fees. High fees have cost us the loss of one client already this year, and I am afraid we will have a difficult time explaining our bill to Telecompter, Inc. If we don't raise our fees to cover the increased costs, then we have to absorb the expenses and that is going to decrease our yearly profit. I intend on finding out what the problem is and I want you to do a little investigative work also.

> Janes: I noticed the same problem of overrunning our budgets. I detect a general lack of concentration by the staff in recent months. I made my way to Manager by working hard and putting in the hours when I had to. Invariably, I feel that public accounting is a terrific training ground and the staff can learn a lot by giving it their all. Most public accounting firms have a high turnover rate because staff are only putting in their required three years to become certified (CPA). I think the high turnover is inherent in public accounting and with 60% turnover we're no different than other firms. High turnover, plus the fact that the staff is just not performing properly, is causing an increase in our auditing costs. I think we should send out a memo on these overruns. That would shake up the staff!

Blake concluded the conversation by saying he was going to follow up on the problem and would talk to others within the Firm.

Charles Rubin, Partner-in-Charge

Charles Rubin, Partner-in-Charge of Personnel, also expresses his point of view to Blake:

> Rubin: I have worked for this Firm for over 25 years and I cannot believe the staff would have any complaints over their current pay. When we were on staff, we worked twice the hours for half the pay. However, we have had a bit

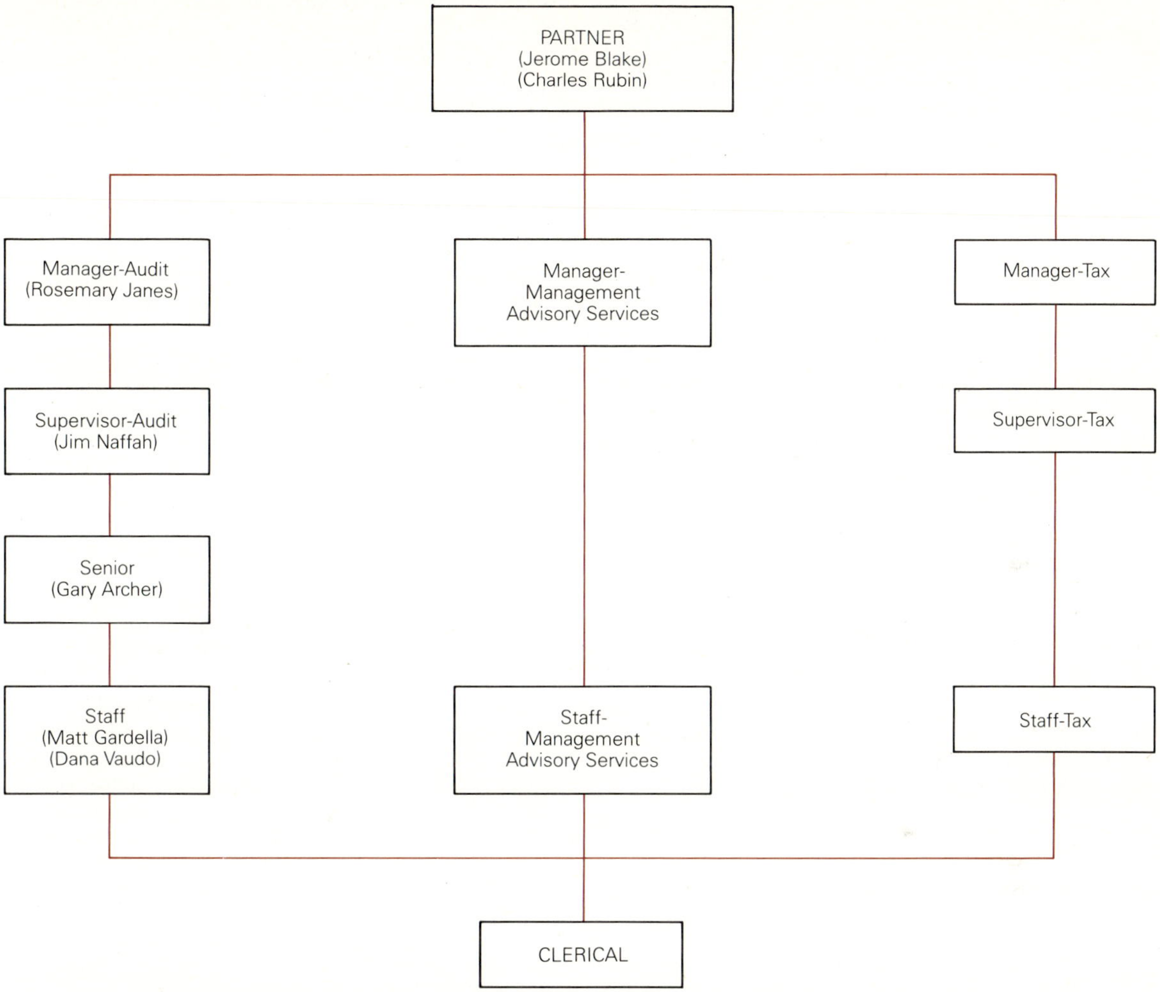

Figure 2–9 ORGANIZATIONAL CHART

of a turnover problem lately. While I don't think the turnover is outrageous, I think it's a little higher than we'd like. We have a large pool of college graduates anxious to work for this Firm and we enjoy the "healthy competition" that exists among the staff people. However, training new personnel is expensive and losing experienced people causes morale problems since a certain comradery exists among the staff. Also, experienced people generally cut down the time required to do the job each year since they are already familiar with the client's system. We have a good reputation as a stable employer within the accounting industry and I would hate to damage that reputation. But, if the present staff is not doing the job, then we will have to weed out the bad apples and replace them with more qualified accountants. You would think they would work hard just to justify their salary. The way the economy is, they should consider themselves lucky to be working at all.

Position	Chargeable Rate per Hour
Partner	$100
Manager	$75
Supervisor	$65–$55
Senior	$50–$40
Staff	$40–$30
Clerical	$10–$20

Table 2–6 **COMPENSATION BY RANK**

Rubin also stated that the Boston Office has recently been able to cut training costs. By establishing an in-house training program, Brown, Steinberg & Company does not have to send their employees to expensive seminars located out of the State.

The staff viewed these seminars as a social benefit, as well as being able to receive the needed technical updating. The seminars usually lasted one week and presented an opportunity for employees at the Company's various offices to meet and exchange ideas.

Rubin, however, felt that the traveling and course costs were getting excessive so he instituted a program whereby management personnel provided technical presentations at the Boston Office. Other offices were to follow Boston's precedent soon.

BID FOR NEW IMPORTANT JOBS

During the first week of November 1982, Brown, Steinberg & Company was preparing to bid for the audit of a new Boston hotel and for a large communications company looking to change accountants. The bids were to be submitted by November 30 of that year. These two new jobs, if obtained, would necessitate an increase in the size of the accounting staff and should generate some large additional revenues. Blake was concerned, however, about submitting a competitive bid since auditing costs have been rising too much.

Blake also realized that Brown, Steinberg & Company must have the experienced staff to properly service these new clients. Before final preparation of the bids, Blake asked Janes to speak to some staff members and to report their general attitudes to him.

SUPERVISOR AND SENIOR ATTITUDES

Jim Naffah had been recently promoted from staff level to Supervisor. He has been employed at Brown, Steinberg & Company a little over four years. He expresses his opinion to Janes as follows:

> Naffah: I know the staff has been kind of down lately and I guess you always hear grumblings from some people. I think, though, that some problems exist now that were not present when I was on staff.
>
> For one thing, the jobs seem to be scheduled tighter than they have been in the past. In attempting to work within the given time frame for the audits, we're forced to work longer and faster. With all the new regulations in accounting coming out lately, you have got to find your own time to stay up to date.
>
> The in-house training doesn't seem to give us the technical updating we need. The experienced people seem to be working more rather than being able to delegate some of the workload. I wish we had more people available for assignments.
>
> Some of the staff have also complained about there being no rotation of jobs. I know that going back to the same client year after year was easier, but you really don't learn as much that way. If these guys aren't interested in the assignment they are working on, then it seems to take them longer to complete the job and they are not nearly as efficient as they could be.
>
> Since being made Supervisor, I have had to actually do some detailed work that the senior or staff should be doing. If the work is not done correctly or within a reasonable amount of time, then people are going to get called on the carpet right down the line. This competitive atmosphere may be great to keep people on their toes, but I know some people I have started with that have yet to be promoted and feel as if they are being run over by new employees trying to climb the corporate ladder. It is tough to get the overlooked ones to give the job their best shot. We have got a pretty close-knit group on staff, but most of the people from my level have been leaving lately. I have mixed emotions about them leaving. I realize that turnover creates openings for me and everyone else for advancement. But, the

Partners and higher level Managers like yourself are very young. The Firm seems satisfied with its size, so I don't see any new Partners or Managers positions opening in the near future. How long will it be until a guy like me can move up? In spite of the opportunity thing, I miss the people that have been leaving lately. I don't think a lot of them necessarily wanted to go, they just felt they could do better elsewhere.

Gary Archer has been with Brown, Steinberg & Company for almost four years. He is senior staff member and is the most logical choice for the next Supervisor's position that arises.

Archer went straight to the point:

I have decided to accept a controller's position with Video-Market, Inc., in Boston. They are a good company and it is a nice job for me. I must admit I had some real apprehensions about leaving Brown, Steinberg & Company. I really enjoy most of the staff and I get along well with management. But, I'm getting tired of doing the same audits and being constantly under pressure to finish on time. I have always taken an interest in the work and I figure I am next in line for a promotion. No one mentions, though, about what plans they have for me, so who knows when any promotion would be?

I do not see the Firm expanding with any new clients; as a matter of fact, we seem to be losing a few lately. I'll tell you, too, I have had staffers working for me lately that make it obvious they are in public just to meet the time requirements for certification. They do the bare minimum of work and that is it. No one seems to read our evaluations. I know a couple of us seniors have written up some staff for lousy attitudes and bad work, but they remain on staff with the good workers.

You know that word gets around quickly, and I think some of the staff gets discouraged to see these jokers still around. I guess the Firm wants to maintain its reputation as a steady employer and does not want to lay people off.

The truth is, I'm not getting much of an increase with Video-Market, Inc., but the benefits will be much better. With the cost of my MBA classes, I cannot afford to keep paying for them myself. My wife is not too pleased about the hours I have had to put in lately either. I look at the Managers and see the overtime they have had to put in over the years to get where they are. It makes me wonder why I should strive for the top. I'll miss most of the people and the work, but I think it will be a good move for me and my family.

STAFF ACCOUNTANTS' VIEWPOINT

Matt Gardella has been a staff accountant with Brown, Steinberg & Company for approximately two years. Janes related to Blake an overheard conversation between Gardella and another staff member. She points out that Gardella's attitude is typical of other staff members.

Gardella: There sure seems to be a lot of tedious work at this Company. I discovered after a short time that public accounting is not for me. I am not thrilled about the jobs I have been assisting on and I do not appreciate the pressure we are constantly put under. But, until my three years are up, I will have to make the best of the situation here. I am looking forward to the day when I can get out of public accounting and enjoy my work.

Dana Vaudo was recently hired from college by Brown, Steinberg & Company. Vaudo has been an assistant for just over three months. Vaudo states his feelings to Janes in the following way:

Vaudo: I really like this company. The people seem friendly and I find the work challenging. I enjoy not having to go to the same office every day and I think the exposure to different businesses is good for me. I just wish people on staff would stop complaining. I almost feel guilty for being positive about this Firm. Maybe the complainers will leave soon and make it more pleasant for all of us.

BLAKE'S PROBLEM

At the end of November with the deadline for submitting new bids only two weeks away, Blake was considering what to do. He has weighed all the information received from Janes concerning staff attitudes and he is well aware of management's opinions. Blake thought that a bid to cover the average increase in expenses would not be competitive with other firms and Brown, Steinberg & Company would therefore lose out on the jobs. He is convinced that some steps can be taken to get control over rising audit costs. Before making a commitment on the new jobs, however, Blake felt that something must be done to change the present situation.

Step 3: Individually, in small groups, or with the entire class, as directed by your instructor, answer the following:

1. What environment has Brown, Steinberg & Company faced?
2. How is that environment changing?
3. What organizational issues influence the personnel activities in the firm?
4. What would a job analysis of the auditor's job look like?
5. What human resources changes will this firm be likely to experience in the next three years? Five years?
6. Offer an approach to employment planning for Brown, Steinberg & Company.

Step 4: Discussion. In small groups, with the entire class, or in written form, share your answers to the questions above.

Activity 2–3

TRANSITIONAL MATRIX AS A PLANNING TOOL

Step 1: Review the matrix reproduced in Table 2–7 below. Note that transitional probabilities are given for eight jobs between 1986 and 1987. Also note, in parentheses under each job, the number of job holders in each category in 1986.

Step 2: Determine the number of individuals who will be available for each job from within the organization in 1987, 1988, 1989, and 1990.

Step 3: Answer the following questions:

1. Assume your human resources forecast indicates that you will need forty sales supervisors in 1988. Should you plan to introduce a major external recruiting program for this position?
2. Assume your organization will require 400 sales support clerks in 1987. Should you plan to hire additional sales support clerks in 1987?
3. Which positions show an increase in the number of job holders over time?
4. Assume your organization will require 242 salespeople in 1989. Should you expect any difficulty in ensuring that the required number will be available?

Step 4: In small groups, or with the entire class, discuss the following questions:

1. Which job categories experience a decline in available job holders over time?
2. Which job categories experience an increase in available job holders over time?
3. What general trends can you observe in the movement of personnel over the next five years?
4. What problems will the organization experience in their supply of human resources during the next five years?

Activity 2–4

THE REPLACEMENT CHART

Step 1: Choose an organization, division, or department with which you are familiar.

Step 2: Draw the current organization chart for the organization, division, or department.

Step 3: For each person in the organization, assess

1. current performance;
2. current readiness for advancement;
3. number of years of experience;

	Job Held in 1986							
	Sales Manager *(100)*	Sales Support *(200)*	Sales Person *(300)*	Billing Clerk *(450)*	Inventory Clerk *(350)*	Market Analysts *(50)*	Stock Person *(200)*	Buyer *(100)*
Job Held in 1987								
Sales Manager	.8	.1	.1			.1		
Sales Support	.1	.4	.2			.1		.1
Sales Person		.2	.5				.1	.2
Billing Clerk				.3	.2		.2	
Inventory Clerk				.2	.3		.2	
Market Analyst		.1	.2			.4		.1
Stock Person					.2		.4	
Buyer		.1						.6
Leave organization	.1	.1		.5	.3	.4	.1	

Table 2–7 **TRANSITIONAL MATRIX**

4. extent of supervisory responsibility;
5. any other relevant criteria.

Indicate their ranking on each of the criteria on the chart.

Step 4: For each position on the chart, list, at most, five potential successors. If there is no potential successor for a position, leave those lines blank.

Step 5: Rate each potential successor on the criteria listed in step 3 above.

Step 6: Identify the following:

1. An individual who is ready to move and has a potential successor who can fill his or her current position;
2. An individual who is ready to move but has no ready successor;
3. An individual who is not ready to move but his or her immediate successor is;
4. An individual who is not ready to move and has no successors.

Step 7: With a partner, review your replacement charts and your answers to the questions in step 6. Make a list of all replacement problems in the organization, department, or division you have described. For each problem, offer a solution for alleviating it.

Step 8: Discussion. In small groups or with the entire class, list the potential replacement problems that organizations face. Then compile a list of possible solutions for each problem.

Activity 2–5

THE NEW WEST COMPANY

Step 1: Read the following description of the New West Company.

New West, Inc., located in a large southwestern city, is a medium-sized manufacturer of clothing and equipment relating to outdoor activities. The company was incorporated by the Singer family approximately 40 years ago; ten years ago the company offered shares to the public through the over-the-counter market. New West experienced significant growth approximately ten years ago. Recently they have been considering expanding their facilities and product lines again to take advantage of the rapidly growing outdoor activities industry.

While the company has grown slowly and has many loyal employees, the technical and marketing expertise of their current employees is questionable. New West has traditionally promoted from within. Occasionally they have recruited outside the organization. The production techniques, product lines, and potential customers have become very sophisticated and demanding in the last ten years. Top management recognizes that the company will have to be innovative and incorporate robotics and other sophisticated technologies if they are to be ready to face the next decade.

Currently New West employs 700 individuals in the following departments: 40 in accounting, 10 in data processing, 20 in finance, 20 in human resources management, 500 in manufacturing, 100 in marketing, and 10 in research and development.

New West is planning to begin increasing productive capacity within the next few months. Top management projects that they will increase the capacity by 30 percent within the next year, 30 percent within the following two years, and 40 percent in the following three years.

Sales within the last three years have increased consistently, from $10 million to $12 million to $15 million. The profit percentage has been decreasing slightly over the past five years, from 10 percent to 7 percent.

The accounting group consists of CPAs and bookkeepers. As a group they lack knowledge of recent computerization of accounting practices. In addition, several have failed to remain current about recent changes in corporate tax laws and other federal SEC regulations.

The finance department has traditionally managed the capital structure of the firm. Currently the firm has a relatively small debt. Increasingly, however, the organization has been experiencing cash flow problems.

The human resources department was titled the personnel department until recently. Its major function has been record keeping. The top position in the department is held by a former sales representative who was moved laterally into a staff position in the department and then inherited the top position when the former job holder retired. Recruitment, selection, and training of employees has been left to individual departments. The company has also been involved in affirmative action and union negotiations. Recently, threats of slowdowns have been heard from the manufacturing workers.

The manufacturing department is the largest in the company. It has lacked cohesion and has experienced significant inefficiencies due to out-of-date equipment and production techniques. The department has a rigid hierarchy; all managers have been promoted from within the department. Managers are salaried, and the rest of the department—all union workers—is paid on an hourly basis. During the past two years they have accrued significant amounts of overtime.

The marketing department has primarily included sales representatives and their managers. One manager has also had the responsibility for the advertising program in the company, which has been contracted to outside organizations.

The research and development group is small. Although increasing funds have been allocated to research and development, most managers in the company feel that it has had little impact. R & D has spent a lot of effort on developing new fabrics for outdoor clothing, but has done little product development or equipment innovation beyond that.

The data processing department includes primarily computer operators and a few programmers who are responsible for automating the accounting practices in the company. There is no management information system. The computer is primarily used for customer billings, payroll, and purchasing.

Step 2: Individually, in small groups, or with the entire class, develop a strategic plan for New West. To develop the plan, consider the following questions:

1. What kind of business should New West be in?
2. What market does this imply?
3. What technological investment does this imply?
4. What organizational changes does this imply?
5. What effort and activity must be performed to achieve the market, technology, and organization desired?
6. To what extent does the current situation have to be changed?

Step 3: Individually, in small groups, or with the entire class, forecast the human resources supply and demand for New West over the next five years. What changes in human resources are necessary to accomplish these strategic changes? In formulating your answer, consider the following questions:

1. What skills, potential, and weaknesses are there in the work force?
2. What work force should the company have?
3. What work force will the company be likely to have?
4. What employment policies and programs must be started or changed?

Step 4: Develop an employment plan for New West.

Step 5: Discussion. In small groups or with the entire class, share your employment plans. Then together formulate a final employment plan.

Activity 2–6

EASTERN STATE PSYCHIATRIC INSTITUTE

Step 1: Read the case.

Step 2: Prepare the case for class discussion.

Eastern State Psychiatric Institute (ESPI) is a facility of the Eastern State Department of Mental Hygiene located in the rural town of Birchville in Eastern

Reprinted by permission of Hak-Chong Lee, Professor of Management, Yonsei University, Seoul, Korea; and Thomas J. Rybaltowski, M.B.A., M.S. (State University of New York at Albany), who is presently serving as Treasurer of the North Colonie Central School District, Newtonville, New York. His previous experience includes management training with the Dominican Development Foundation and the U.S. Peace Corps. He has published numerous articles on management and educational administration.

State. Since its initial operation as a state mental hospital in 1920, ESPI has gradually evolved into a geographically organized in-patient facility with an increasing number of satellite programs established in individual communities of the "catchment area". This catchment area, or geographical region, served by the Institute includes all of York County, most of Warren County, and the eastern part of Duke County where ESPI is located. This area is diverse in nature, ranging from medium-sized cities to rural farming lands. It is currently incorporated under one of 5 regions in the state under the jurisdiction of the state's Department of Mental Hygiene (DMH).

MISSION AND ORGANIZATION

Eastern State's primary mission has been to offer intensive psychiatric service for those admitted to the hospital. Residential services include Adolescent, Mental Retardation, Geriatric, Medical/Surgical, and Alcoholic units. Patients in the hospital receive round the clock care. Specialized programs are provided for geriatric, alcoholic, and adolescent populations. Also included is a Campus School, a Halfway House and a Sheltered Workshop which utilizes vocational programs developed through the Institute's Community Store, Food Services and Department of Industrial Maintenance.

Educational training and employment opportunities are also offered to in-patients through the active involvement in patient education of the Duke County Office for Cooperative Educational Program (OCEP) and the Office of Vocational Training and Development (OVTD) in rehabilitative activities. Programs available at the Institute comprise an important part of the overall process which prepares a resident patient for return to community life. Aside from the medical units, there are also support services including offices in Personnel, Public Relations, Program Evaluation, and a Business Office (Figure 2–10).

As a self-contained hospital community, ESPI has been striving toward the treatment and care of mentally-ill persons with a continual desire to allow patients to effectively function outside the hospital environment.

DEVELOPMENTS IN MENTAL HEALTH

Over the last decade, the patient population of the nation's mental hospitals has declined from some 490,000 to just over 215,000. Largely responsible for this decline is the growing number of community-based out-patient mental health centers such as Community Clinics, Day Care Treatment Programs, Clinic Drop-in Centers, Coffee Houses, Adult Homes, Health-Related Facilities, Family Care Facilities, and Mobile Psychiatric Centers. Such centers, or clinics, account for about 70% of the decline of persons in state and county mental hospitals since 1950.[1]

The move toward community-based facilities, or "de-institutionalization" of mental health patients, has been initiated by changes in mental health treatment. Dr. Richard M. Restak, a Washington, D. C. neurologist with psychiatric training, says, "For too long, psychiatry has ignored the fact that emotional disturbances are largely biochemical in nature. Recent research has proved that many perhaps most emotional states are determined by changes in the chemistry of the brain."[2] In recent years, it has been discovered that heredity and various chemicals play a role in schizophrenia, depression, and manic diseases. A study has shown that the emphasis on psychiatric research, training, and treatment of mentally-ill patients has begun to shift from psychology and Freudianism to chemical and biological causes of mental illness.

Dr. Roy W. Menninger, president of the world-famous Menninger Foundation in Topeka, Kansas, says, "The overwhelming majority of psychological problems are being resolved favorably when the patient gets early, appropriate and sufficient treatment."[3] This treatment has been increasingly administered to patients on an out-patient basis through community-based mental health clinics. These community-based clinics have aided in the efficient and effective treatment of patients. It has been recognized by those in the caring professions that the mentally ill do not get better as often, or as quickly, in a hospital setting as they do in the normalizing atmosphere of the community at large.

Dr. Adams, Unit Chief of the Adolescent Unit at ESPI, also confirms the general trend in psychiatric care: "Anyone who lives long at an in-patient facility

[1] "New Ways to Heal Disturbed Minds: Where Will It All Lead?" *U. S. News and World Report,* February 16, 1976, p. 2.

[2] *Ibid.*

[3] *Ibid.*

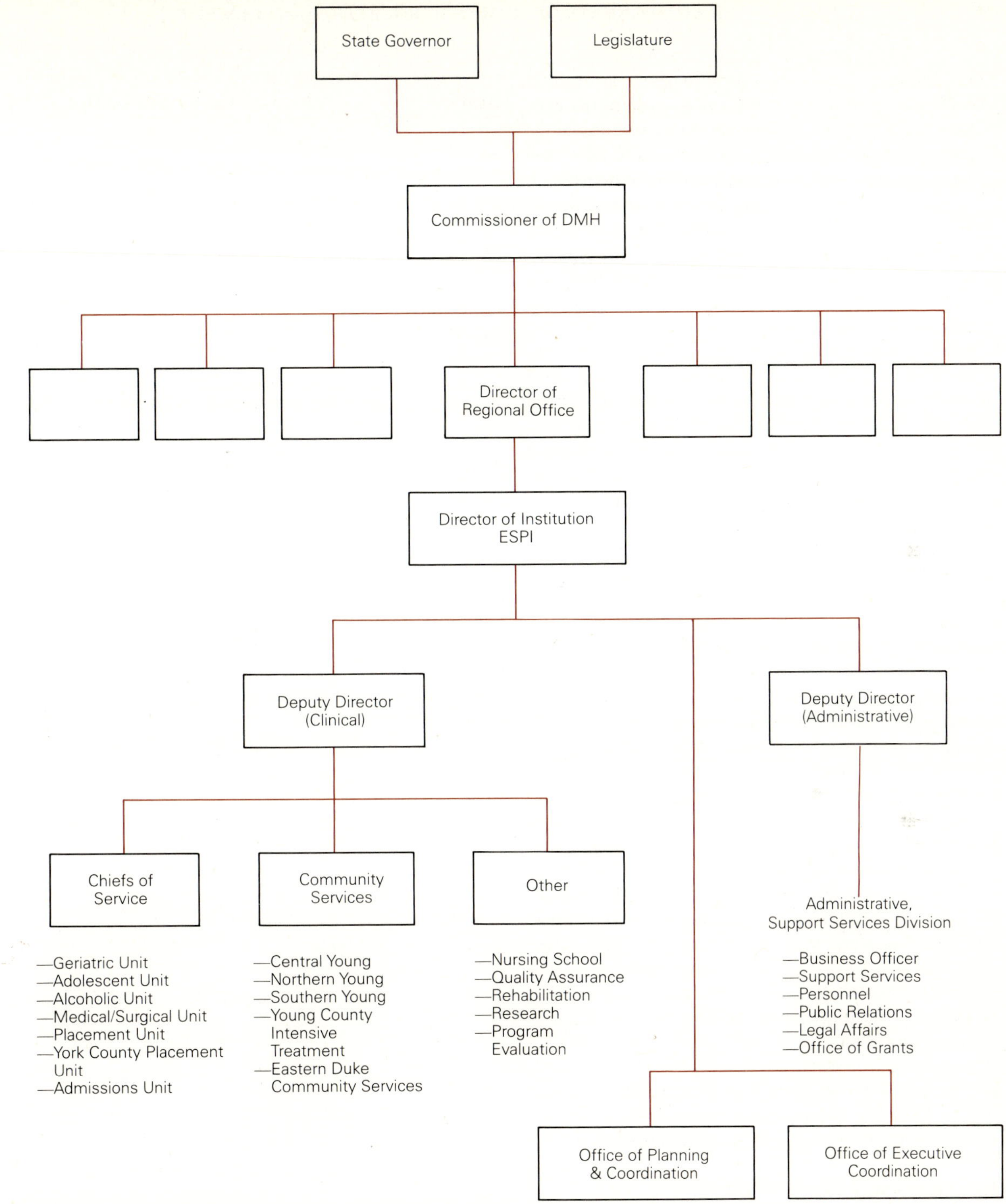

Figure 2–10 PARTIAL ORGANIZATION CHART

finds it much harder to return to the community. Priorities have shifted towards greater use of the out-patient facility, even though psychiatric knowledge is not advanced far enough to completely close the in-patient hospital. A total approach is needed which develops some optimal blend between the basic in-patient services now offered and flexible out-patient services. It has been my concern for the proper placement of patients into these out-patient facilities, for a reinstatement of patients back into the in-patient facility would be a crime."

Due to the apparent advantages of recent advances in mental hygiene care, a state-wide trend toward de-institutionalization has been initiated in Eastern State aimed at reducing the in-patient populations of all mental hospitals in the state. The move toward de-institutionalization has been accentuated in recent years by the increasing concern of the Eastern State Legislature to improve the organization and effectiveness of the state's Department of Mental Hygiene. The Mental Health Committees of the Eastern State Legislature have been developing a package of legislation to improve care of the state's mentally disabled, dilute the powers of the Department's commissioner, give localities more control over planning, and mandate certain mental care standards and administrative procedures to ensure increased efficiency in the delivery of mental care services.

For example, one major bill in the package seeks for a creation of a mental health planning unit, taking away some of the powers now vested in the Office of the DMH Commissioner. This unit would define the authority and responsibility for state and local participation in providing mental health service. Sponsors of these legislative moves argue that there has been no state-wide mental hygiene plan since 1965 and that such a plan is vitally needed at a time when the entire system is in transition from a primarily institution-based system to one that is community-based.

Due to the legislation of this kind, and as a psychiatric center responsive to current mental health needs, ESPI has been developing its services in the direction of community psychiatry and treatment and away from the centralized institution in recent years. The move away from the institutionalized hospital has been reflected at ESPI by the decline in their number of in-patients (Table 2–8 and Figure 2–11).

At the same time, the Institute has been constantly expanding the range of its programs and making them as readily available and accessible to rising community needs as possible. These services, which range from prevention through intensive treatment, are designed to permit clients to remain in their communities for treatment or assist them in returning to the community from the hospital. All treatment programs have sought to encourage growth and independence through rehabilitative activities; individual, group and family therapy; counseling and

Date	In-Patient Level
6/1/75	2,460
9/1/75	2,217
1/2/76	1,992
4/1/76	1,846
6/1/76	1,782
9/1/76	1,701
1/2/77	1,446
4/1/77	1,098
6/1/77	999
9/1/77	949
1/2/78	909

Table 2–8 IN-PATIENT POPULATION LEVELS

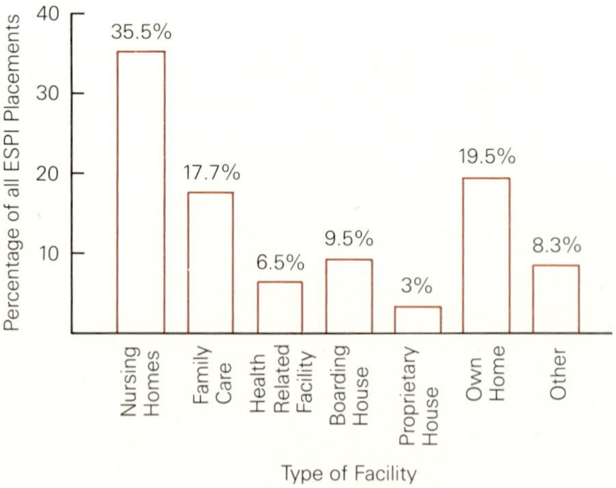

Figure 2–11 PLACEMENTS BY FACILITIES JULY-DECEMBER 1977

links with services of other agencies in the helping network.

Out-patient services provided by ESPI have also been increasingly based in the communities they serve, with permanent headquarters and staff in those communities. Although the central hospital in Birchville still serves an important function for those clients who need intensive care, the Institute's services are, for the most part, changing in accordance with current theories of mental health, or on a preventive, therapeutic out-patient basis.

PLACEMENT PROCESS

The effectiveness of de-institutionalization is mainly governed by the process of placing hospital patients into community-based facilities. This is a complicated process which requires close coordination among many professional, administrative and service people at the Institute as well as at the out-patient facilities (Figure 2–12).

Following is a partial list of typical activities involved in the placement process:

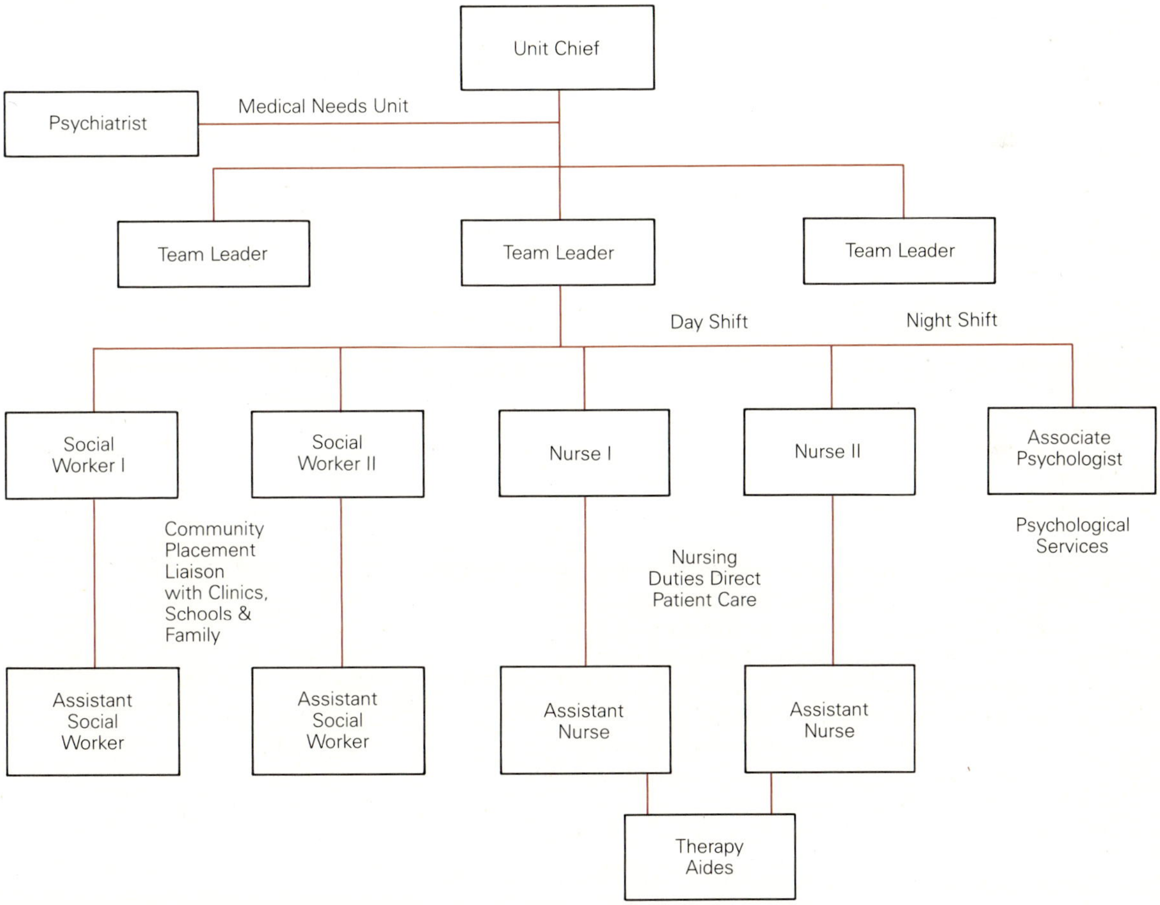

Figure 2–12 **PARTIAL ORGANIZATIONAL STRUCTURE OF A TYPICAL CLINICAL SERVICE UNIT**

- Meeting of placement team to assess the feasibility of releasing a patient.
- Laboratory and medical tests.
- Correction of medical difficulties.
- Letter to patient's family explaining movement of the patient out of the hospital.
- Contact county resource agent.
- Application for state/county funding.
- Complete forms for various state agencies including Department of Social Services, Department of Mental Hygiene, County approval forms, out-patient facility forms, and Hospital forms.
- Find out the availability of out-patient facilities and visit them.
- Confirmation of the availability.
- Wait for medical and funding approvals and doctor's signature.
- Contact out-patient medical teams concerning patient movement.
- Double-check financial funding, medical approvals, and facility confirmation.
- Actual placement.

The placement process is further complicated by the type of facility, the city or town of residence a patient is being placed in, and individual discretions of social workers and team leaders, as illustrated by the following:

- Boarding homes do not require as much money per patient as does an Adult Home. Therefore, funding is easier to come by. Moreover, the funding feasibility varies from one county to another.
- County medical approval for a patient is necessary in health-related facilities, but not in Adult Homes. No medical approval is necessary if a patient is returned to the care of his family, but clinical approval is needed.
- It is hoped that most patients can be placed in a facility in their home county. However, it was found that approximately 55% of geriatric patients were being placed into a neighboring state because of a lack of local facilities.
- Some counties have their own out-patient mobile team or liaison office which eases the transition from the hospital to the community facility. Thus, some facilities provide transportation in transferring the patient while others require the patient to be moved by the institution.
- The proprietor of a boarding house or a sponsor of a family care facility must give his approval before a patient can be transferred.
- Each placement team places a patient in their own individual manner. It is left to the discretion of social workers and team leaders as to what placement activities are to take priority.

Up to now, placement of in-patients has been accomplished through informal, "in-house" directives determined by top administrators at ESPI. A typical placement process took as long as 11 weeks, but ESPI was still able to achieve a steady increase in the number of patient placements until recently (Table 2–9).

However, under the increasing pressure toward rapid de-institutionalization, ESPI could no longer continue with the lengthy and informal placement practices, but had to develop a formal and efficient plan to deal with the drastic increases in patient placements which were being mandated by the Department of Mental Hygiene.

IMPACT OF ACCELERATED PLACEMENT OF PATIENTS

The increased rate of patient placement has brought a wide impact throughout the hospital. As Mrs. R.M. Link, R.N., a team leader in Geriatric Unit says, "There has been great pressure within this hospital to release patients. Just last week we got a request from the Director asking for a placement of 30 patients right away." Joe Pitman, Director of Planning at ESPI, also says, "High standards are being

Date	Placements
6/19/76	57
8/14/76	60
10/9/76	59
12/4/76	113
2/26/77	220
5/21/77	166
8/13/77	148
10/8/77	97
12/3/77	44

Table 2–9 PATIENT PLACEMENT RATE

set by the Director of this hospital; he has high expectations of what can be accomplished.''

However, the implementation of the high placement goal has drawn critical reactions. S.R. Simon, Chief of Admissions Unit, states:

> It's very hard now to place patients from ESPI. When we first started to reduce our in-patient population, the easily placeable ones had no problem in resettling. Now, we have come down to the hard-core, higher-risk patient who is extremely difficult to place. This is not only because he is the more chronic patient, but also because of a shortage of beds in community facilities. It is also very hard for someone like a social worker to coordinate all activities needed before a patient can be placed. Under such adverse conditions, we can't really expect strong commitment from placement teams.

C. Reynolds, Rehabilitation Department, Central Office, is concerned with current methods of planning for patients under increasing placement targets:

> What we need around here is some systematic procedure to transform us from our actual state to some desired one. Things are done too randomly around here. Our Director, Dr. King, has asked for an additional 500 patients to be placed in the next 6 months. How can we do that under the present system?

Although the relocation of patients is assisted by placement teams in the Placement Unit, the ward social worker is primarily responsible for the coordination of all the procedures and activities leading to the eventual discharge of a patient. Social workers interact with nurses, therapy aides, doctors, and the out-patient clinic in an effort to see that a patient is properly placed. Quite often, a strong bond develops between the patient and the social worker with great sympathy toward the patient. This at times causes the social worker to be reluctant to speed up the placement of the patient. The team leader usually oversees the activities of the social workers in the team and aids in coordinating of all placement activities. However, these activities are usually quite varied and detailed with seemingly endless forms to complete for numerous agencies.

Currently, over 41 different forms are required for placement purposes. Often, one to four or more copies of many forms are also required. The excessive amount of paperwork is admonished by V. Lawrence, Chairperson of DMH/DSS Liaison Coordinators Committee and Social Worker Supervisor:

> The process of resettling a patient in the community requires a great deal of paperwork, much of which is repetitive, filling out of numerous forms for referrals to community agencies for housing and financial assistance or other supportive services. Moreover, our own various community service units also require a good deal of referral information in order to accept the client for out-patient services. . . . The paperwork required is a hamper to the quality of care a patient receives. If our social workers spend all their time filling out forms, then obviously less time is left to be spent with patients who really need their services.

Mrs. R. Cusato, Team Leader of Geriatric Unit, also says:

> A lot of bottlenecks occur as all types of forms are being processed in various agencies. . . . Bureaucracy is really holding us back.

However, the paperwork is not the only activity required which slows down the release of a patient. Mrs. Link says:

> The doctor's cooperation is very important. Quite often, the patient is ready to be placed and we wait around for some doctor's signature. The forms may sit on his desk for a week. We waste more time than we need to. Doctors here don't really care if a patient is released or not. They prefer to treat patients slowly and at their leisure.

Organizational changes caused by the de-institutionalization program have also produced many problems. As the in-patient population decreased, the remaining patients were consolidated into fewer and fewer wards. As the number of wards declined, entire buildings were closed and whole wards moved into remaining facilities. At one time, 30 buildings were in operation. This has been reduced to 16. The School of Nursing has been on the list to be phased out as well as a Halfway House. This has resulted in the reassignments of all types of workers including clinical and staff workers (Table 2–10).

C. L. Daniels, Nurse Administrator in Medical/Surgical Unit, says:

> People are being laid off or moved around so much that morale is degenerating with all kinds of rumors. This is especially true among our older and less skilled employees. The younger and more educated workers can take a voluntary transfer to some other facility, but those who have worked here for years, when this hospital had three times the number of patients it has now, don't want to move. Job security is very important to these people.

Dr. D. J. Walker, Chief of Alcoholic Unit, says:

> With major organizational changes occurring constantly, the attitude of employees directly affects the quality of patient care. What we need to do is not to move so fast and reassess our ultimate goals.

Other problems are also expressed. V. Lawrence states:

> There are not enough community facilities to accept all patients and there may not be for a long time to come. Furthermore, I don't think that communities are ready to accept any more disturbed people in their neighborhood.

Pat Roberts, Team Leader in Placement Unit, points out another problem:

> Not only is available housing very important, but so is the need for adequate funding. Money is very tight these days and we are largely understaffed—in fact, we've been understaffed now for a few years. This places an added burden upon those presently working. The staff shortage is particularly serious with social workers. Maybe what we really need is more social workers and less psychologists. . . . Along with the manpower shortage, funding approvals and housing are the major bottlenecks in the placement process.

Date	Number of Employees
9/12/75	1,578
1/2 /76	1,564
4/24/76	1,578
8/14/76	1,573
10/8/76	1,553
2/26/77	1,512
8/13/77	1,524
10/8/77	1,426
11/5/77	1,362
12/3/77	1,285

Table 2–10 NUMBER OF EMPLOYEES AT ESPI

Dr. King, the Director of ESPI has been meeting regularly with key professional and administrative personnel each week for several hours to discuss various programs of the Institute. The problems associated with de-institutionalization have been brought up indirectly and briefly touched upon in past meetings. In May 1978, as the problems were becoming more serious, the Director sent out a memorandum stating that the next staff meeting would be entirely devoted to the discussion of ESPI's programs on de-institutionalization.

Step 3: Individually or in small groups answer the following:

1. What environmental changes is Eastern State Psychiatric Institute facing?
2. Describe the organizational situation at Eastern State Psychiatric Institute.
3. What changes in human resources are necessary?
4. Offer an employment plan for Eastern State Psychiatric Institute.

Step 4: Discussion. In small groups, with the entire class, or in written form, share your answers to the above questions.

SUMMARY

Equal employment opportunity legislation and other laws, the inability to get human resources to support organizational expansion and diversification, the changing composition of the labor market, the increasing costs of personnel benefits, the increase in personnel demands, and the need to increase worker productivity act as pressures for more employment planning.[32]

Still, many companies do very little. A survey of Fortune 200 firms indicated that only 37 percent did employment planning for the whole company, while less than one-fourth conducted planning for even parts of their organizations.[33] Table 2–11 summarizes attitudes toward employment planning from those human resources personnel polled.

Employment planning precedes the introduction of program planning for recruitment, selection, decruitment, performance evaluation, training and devel-

Statement	Strongly Agree or Agree	Undecided	Disagree or Strongly Disagree
Human resource planning suffers from lack of understanding of what human resource planning is	72.4%	5.7%	21.9%
Human resource planning suffers from lack of data in forecasting human resource demand and supply	62.8	9.3	27.9
Human resource planning suffers from lack of involvement by top management	60.9	1.1	37.9
Changes in government policy often frustrate planning efforts	50.6	14.1	35.3
Human resource planning suffers from lack of readily applicable planning techniques	50.6	4.6	44.8
Human resource planning suffers from non-existence of corporate plan	45.9	8.2	45.9
Human resource planning suffers from lack of personnel qualified for planning	42.6	8.0	49.4
Human resource planning is seen as an interference by line managers	23.3	17.4	59.3
Human resource planning is not for small and medium-sized companies	3.4	1.1	95.5
Technology is too static to justify human resource planning	1.2	2.3	96.5

Reprinted by permission of the publisher from *Human Resource Planning*, Vol. 3, No. 2, 1980. Copyright 1980 by the Human Resource Planning Society.

Table 2–11 AN ORDERED LIST OF ATTITUDES TOWARD HUMAN RESOURCE PLANNING

opment, career management, compensation, and labor relations. But a lack of comprehensive and integrated programs in these diverse functional areas most often characterizes human resources management.

In this chapter we discussed and applied general principles of employment planning. In the Brown, Steinberg & Company and Eastern State Psychiatric Institute activities we considered the impact of environmental changes on human resources needs and supply. We practiced the matrix method of forecasting and designed and analyzed a replacement chart. In the New West activity we developed an employment plan.

Deficiencies and surpluses of employees may call for different human resources program plans from managers or human resources professionals. We discuss the development of program plans in later chapters of this book.

Effective planning requires the involvement of all managers and employees to ensure that the data used in planning are complete and the resulting conclusions accurate. It includes the following features:

1. Unit plans linked to organizational plans;
2. Provisions for systematic and regular planning;
3. Long- and short-range components;
4. Provisions for review and modification of the plan;
5. Links between the plan and the budget;
6. Data-based planning;
7. Links between the plan and management activities; and
8. Opportunities for employee participation in development and execution.[34]

ENDNOTES

[1]J.W. Walker, *Human Resource Planning* (New York: McGraw-Hill, 1980).

[2]*Ibid.;* J.W. Walker, Linking human resources planning and strategic planning, *Human Resource Planning* 1 (1978): 1–18.

[3]*1980 United States Census* (Washington, D.C.: U.S. Government Printing Office, 1980).

[4]*Ibid.* T.L. Friedman, The baby boom comes of age: And finds executive suites as full as kindergartens and colleges were, *New York Times,* 10 January 1982, p. 18; A.R. Weber, In the 1980's: A dramatically different labor force, *Across the Board* (December 1979): 25–32.

[5]A. Fleming, Engineers blame top management for car makers' productivity lag, *Automotive News,* 15 February 1982, 1.

[6]R.W. Schram, Parents, kids, and companies: New rules for business, *Personnel Journal* (June 1981): 436.

[7]V. Cahan, The overhaul that could give OSHA lite under Reagan, *Business Week,* 19 January 1981; A lighter schedule of OSHA inspections, *Business Week,* 14 September 1981.

[8]Review of costs and benefits of job safety and health law, *Monthly Labor Review* 103 (August 1980): 24; Reform in OSHA—Vital need, *Journal of Commerce* 3550 (2 November, 1981): 312; *New York Times,* 16 January 1984.

[9]*New York Times,* 19 March 1975; *New York Times,* 13 October 1975; *Wall Street Journal,* 3 April 1975.

[10]See C. Perrow, A framework for the comparative analysis of organizations, *American Sociological Review* 32 (1967): 194–208; and J. Woodward, *Industrial Organizations: Theory and Practice* (London: Oxford University Press, 1965) for seminal discussions about the influence of technology.

[11]T.A. Kochan, How American workers view labor unions, *Monthly Labor Review* 102 (1979): 23–31.

[12]G. Strauss, Industrial relations: Time of change, *Industrial Relations* 23 (Winter 1984): 1–15.

[13]W.J. Gore, *Administrative Decision-Making* (New York: Wiley, 1964), pp. 184–185; F. Kast, Organizational and individual objectives. In *Contemporary Management: Issues and Viewpoints,* ed. J.W. McGuire (Englewood Cliffs, N.J.: Prentice-Hall, 1974).

[14]See C. Perrow, *Organizational Analysis: A Sociological View* (Belmont, Cal.: Wadsworth, 1970); P. Drucker, *The Practice of Management* (New York: Harper, 1954); and E. Gross, The definition of organizational goals, *British Journal of Sociology* 20 (1969): 277–294 for three typologies of organizational goals.

[15]W.R. LaFollette, How is the climate in your organization?, *Personnel Journal* 53 (1975).

[16]C.R. Gullett, Mechanistic vs. organic organizations: What does the future hold?, *The Personnel Administrator* 20 (1975): 17.

[17]E.J. McCormick, *Job Analysis* (New York: AMACOM, 1979), p. 20.

[18]See *Summary of National Job Analysis Methods Survey* (Long Beach, Cal.: California State College, Bureau of Business Research, 1968).

[19]F.M. Lopez et al., Empirical test of a trait oriented job analysis technique, *Personnel Psychology* 34 (1981): 479–502.

[20]See, for example, publications such as U.S. Department of Labor, *Perspectives on Working Women,* Bureau of Labor Statistics, June, 1980; U.S. Department of Labor, *Dictionary of Occupational Titles,* Employment and Training Administration, 1977; *Monthly Labor Review;* U.S. Department of Labor, *Specific Vocational Preparation Estimates for Occupations in the U.S. Department of Labor Dictionary of Occupational Titles,* Employment and Training Administration, February 1978.

[21]K.F. Misa and T. Stein, Strategic HRM and the bottom line, *Personnel Administrator* 28 (October 1983): 27–30.

[22]G.T. Milkovich and T.A. Mahoney, Human resource planning models: A perspective, *Human Resource Planning* 1 (1978): 19–30 offer another classification of forecasting techniques.

[23]A. Walker, *HRIS Development: A Project Team Guide to Building an Effective Personnel Information System* (New York: Van Nostrand Reinhold, 1982).

[24]E.H. Burack and N.J. Mathys, *Human Resource Planning: A Pragmatic Approach to Manpower Staffing and Development* (Lake Forest, Ill.: Brace-Park Press, 1980).

[25]See J.W. Walker, Trends in manpower management research, *Business Horizons* (August 1968): 37–46; Milkovich & Mahoney, *op. cit.;* V.H. Vroom and K.R. MacCrimmon, Toward a stochastic model of managerial careers, *Administrative Science Quarterly* 13 (1968): 26–46.

[26]D.J. Bartholomew, Statistics in human resource planning, *Human Resource Planning* 1 (1978): 67–77.

[27]See Milkovich & Mahoney, *op. cit.*

[28]C.R. Greer and D. Armstrong, Human resource forecasting and planning: A state-of-the-art investigation, *Human Resource Planning* 3 (1981).

[29]Walker, 1980, *op. cit.,* p. 10.

[30]G.M. Groe, Legitimizing human resource planning, *Human Resource Planning* 3 (1980): 11–26.

[31]Greer and Armstrong, *op. cit.*

[32]H. Kahalas et al., Human resource planning activities in U.S. firms, *Human Resource Planning* 1 (1981): 53–66.

[33]*Ibid.*

[34]L.J. Harvey, Effective planning for human resource development, *Personnel Administrator* 28 (October 1983): 45–52, 112.

FURTHER READINGS

Burack, E.H. and Mathys, N.J. *Human Resource Planning: A Pragmatic Approach to Manpower Staffing and Development.* Lake Forest, Ill.: Brace-Park Press, 1980.

DeSanto, J.F. Work force planning and corporate strategy. *Personnel Administrator* 28 (October 1983): 33–38.

Frohman, M., and Frohman, A.L. Organization adaptation: A personnel responsibility. *Personnel Administrator* 29 (January 1984): 45–47, 88.

Gael, D. *Job Analysis: A Guide to Assessing Work Activities.* San Francisco: Jossey-Bass, 1983.

McCormick, E.J. *Job Analysis.* New York: AMACOM, 1979.

Niehaus, R.J. *Computer-assisted Human Resources Planning.* New York: John Wiley, 1979.

Walker, J.W. *Human Resource Planning.* New York: McGraw-Hill, 1980.

PART 2

Personnel Systems for Staffing

CHAPTER 3

Performing Systematic Recruitment

CHAPTER OUTLINE

LEARNING CHECKPOINTS

After completing the reading and activities in this chapter, students will be able to

- state the steps in the recruiting process;
- perform a situational analysis for recruiting;
- show the use of job analyses in recruitment;
- state the advantages and disadvantages of internal and external sources of recruits;
- choose the most appropriate source of recruits for a specific situation;
- compare and contrast various recruiting methods;
- discuss the cost implications of various recruiting techniques;
- offer ways of using computerized data bases in recruitment;
- design an effective recruiting system.

INTRODUCTION

WXX Television and Radio is a medium-sized organization in the communications industry. It is a subsidiary of Major Communications which owns television and radio stations in fifty-six cities in the United States. The headquarters of Major Communications is in Miami, Florida. Although Major is a nationally known organization, WXX reaches viewers and listeners in Chicago and the tristate region of Indiana, Michigan, and Illinois.

Because television and radio have been glamour industries, attracting high-quality employees at low salaries has not been a problem. Yet turnover has been high at WXX. WXX's competitors have lured away management and on-air talent. Forecasts for the next five years show a lack of technically skilled workers in the labor force. Competitors who pay higher salaries continue to hire the best technicians—the type of technical workers top managers at WXX feel they need to compete in the technologically dynamic environment.

WXX Television and Radio has its own human resources department. In the past, this department has had the sole responsibility for hiring employees. Recently, however, the small staff of this department has been so overwhelmed with wage and salary administration that recruitment has suffered. The station manager and the corporate personnel director recently issued a joint memorandum that transferred some recruiting responsibility to department managers. Currently, WXX must recruit two camera technicians, an accountant, five clerks, and two reporters. Within the next three years, projections show a need for four additional technicians and a larger human resources staff.

How should the department managers proceed? What contribution should they make to the recruiting effort? What responsibilities should the human resources department retain? How can WXX ensure that it has an effective recruitment system?

This chapter proposes answers to these questions. It provides a framework for designing a recruitment system at WXX and other organizations. We begin by examining the steps in recruitment. Next, we investigate various sources of recruits and techniques for recruiting them. Then we look in depth at a major way of gathering data about recruits—the employment interview. We conclude the chapter with a summary of responsibilities that human resources professionals and managers should assume in recruitment.

STEPS IN RECRUITMENT

Recruitment is "the process of locating, identifying, and attracting applicants capable of and interested in filling job vacancies."[1] In addition to locating potential job holders, it serves "(1) to screen out inappropriate candidates and focus on those to be called back; (2) to 'sell' the organization as a potential employer by providing information about job and organizational characteristics; and (3) to build favorable public opinion toward the organization by influencing applicants' attitudes accordingly—whether they are hired or not."[2] In situations where the demand for employees exceeds the available supply, such as that at WXX, the organization often hires employees; recruitment gathers a *pool* of potential hires.

The fundamentals of a good recruiting program include the following factors: (1) it attracts a large number of well-qualified applicants; (2) it never compromises selection standards (see Chapter 4); (3) it takes place on a continuous basis; and (4) it is creative, imaginative, and innovative.[3] Recruitment can draw individuals from those currently employed by the organization, those employed by other organizations, or the unemployed.

Recruitment involves seven steps. Human resources professionals and managers must (1) analyze the situation calling for recruitment; (2) perform a job analysis for each job with openings; (3) list criteria for assessing potential recruits; (4) identify potential sources of recruits; (5) specify possible techniques for tapping these sources; (6) select the sources and techniques most appropriate for recruiting for each job; and (7) list individuals eligible for the job.

How should recruitment occur at WXX? It must start with a situational audit. Environmental and organizational assessment establishes the context in which recruitment occurs.

Job analysis should accompany the audit. As described in Chapter 2, managers and human resources professionals should take major responsibility for performing an accurate job analysis. For example, they must prepare job specifications for the technician's job.

Based on the job specifications the manager should list general criteria for potential job holders; these characteristics serve as recruitment guides. Such criteria reflect basic skills, experiences, or education a job holder should have. Recruitment criteria for WXX camera technicians might include technical education, experience in the television industry, and knowledge of computer technology. Criteria for accountants might include a C.P.A. and three years of experience in accounting. Recruitment criteria tend to be very general, particularly when compared to selection criteria.

Next, the managers should share the criteria with the human resources department. Together they can determine whether internal or external sources would be best. Then they can develop a comprehensive list of methods for tapping these sources, including advertisements, job posting, walk-in applications, employment agencies, and college visits.[4] Should WXX advertise in local or trade publications? Post notices of job openings? Use employment agencies? They might ask "headhunters" to locate reporters or other on-air talent, contact technical-school placement offices for qualified technicians, and rely on employment agencies or college recruiting for business staff.

Or they might use other methods to obtain a pool of recruits for these positions. The manager must assess the advantages and disadvantages associated with each method. For example, newspaper advertisements are expensive and attract a large number of responses. For the job of reporter this method would attract too many unqualified applicants; on the other hand, for clerical positions newspaper advertisements could attract a large pool of qualified applicants. To determine the best sources and methods, managers and human resources professionals should consider their *yield ratio*—the percentage of qualified applicants compared to the number of total applicants from a given source. For example, newspaper advertising probably has a lower yield ratio (e.g., 1 of 10 applicants qualified) than the use of executive recruiters (e.g., 1 of 3 applicants qualified).

Finally, the managers and human resources professionals must tap the appropriate sources of recruits by implementing the recruitment methods. They must place advertisements, contact professional associations, hold open houses, use employment agencies, or seek referrals. Through these methods they gather a pool of individuals eligible for the job.

THE SITUATIONAL AUDIT FOR RECRUITMENT

Auditing the situation calls for managers and human resources professionals to diagnose the environmental and organizational context in which recruitment occurs.

The Environment

An assessment of the environment allows human resources professionals and managers to predict the amount of effort required to recruit a certain number of potential employees. If a large external labor supply exists, for example, the organization can devote fewer resources to recruiting. Such analysis can identify specific problem areas where recruitment will be most and least difficult. For example, recruitment in the 1980s has focused more effort on attracting technical personnel than on managerial personnel because of the relative lack of technical workers in the labor force.[5]

The environmental audit should also identify the relevant labor market—the pool of individuals from which recruits can be drawn. For example, an organization might establish the relevant labor market as covering the entire country or being limited to a much smaller geographical area, such as New England or California. Or, the extent to which the labor pool consists of union members may determine an organization's abilities to recruit nonunion workers. The audit also would identify the legislative pressures on recruitment; since the early 1970s, for example, recruitment activities in most organizations have to reflect equal opportunity practices (see Chapter 13).

Consider the environment WXX-TV faces: changing technological environment, strong economic pressures, regional consumers, and unionized labor. This environment dictates the value of regularly identifying qualified technical employees, finding reporters who appeal to Midwestern audiences, and developing positive relationships with local unions. Strong competition for employees with other stations would suggest a need for *active* recruitment, supported by significant resources. Managers at WXX-TV must audit the environment and determine the implications of their conclusions for recruitment activities.

The Organization

The organization also influences recruitment. Managers must consider answers to questions such as the following:

- What will be the supply of recruits inside and outside the organization?
- Who has the responsibility for recruitment?
- What is the climate in the organization?
- How flexible is the assignment of responsibilities within the organization?
- How common is communication across departments or divisions?
- What attractions does the organization hold for potential recruits?

Organizational characteristics influence the design and implementation of a recruitment system. For example, organizations that emphasize decentralized decision-making more readily accept a manager's decision regarding recruitment activities and choice of the final pool. Organizations where lateral communication is common can rely more on internal movement of employees to fill vacant positions. Organizations that discourage advancement from within the ranks must rely more on advertising, use of employment agencies, and campus recruiting as ways of developing a pool of employees.

Organizational assessment should provide data that help top management assign responsibility for recruitment appropriately and identify the financial and staff resources available for recruitment activities. In addition, the employees at WXX-TV, for example, must deal with negotiated contract provisions for many jobs. Such regulations might limit recruiting to certain sources.

THE JOB ANALYSIS

Accurate job analyses act as the basic building block of effective recruiting. Managers should perform a job analysis for each available job. They can use the resulting job description and specifications to identify the recruitment criteria. Consider the following excerpt from the job description for a camera technician at WXX Television: (1) operates large studio camera; (2) moves camera on director's cue; (3) selects shots requested by the director; (4) calls for engineers when there are problems with equipment.

What *general* characteristics are required to fill this position? The job specifications would require the operator to have technical knowledge of camera equipment and experience in the television industry, preferably at a station with comparable job requirements. These general criteria provide guidelines for thinking about the sources of recruits and methods of tapping the appropriate sources.

SOURCES OF RECRUITS

Internal sources refer to current employees within the organization; *external sources* are individuals not currently employed by the organization. Both human resources professionals and managers can secure recruits from these sources.

Internal Sources

Current employees are a very effective source of recruits for all positions. Because current employees know the organization's expectations about performance, the skills and knowledge required for various jobs, and the required attitudes for organizational membership, they can identify individuals (including themselves) who would contribute effectively.

Many organizations have adopted the policy of using current employees to fill vacant positions if at all possible. The promotion-from-within policy acts as a strong performance incentive. Employees who want to advance within the organization tend to be more motivated when they know that good performance is rewarded with promotions. For organizations this policy encourages a steady stream of employees at a relatively low recruitment cost. Another advantage is that once an employee has learned the ropes, the organization does not need to invest further in orienting the employee to company expectations and standards.

In unionized organizations, promotion from within may be required by the labor contract. Although such policies may reduce the time and cost required to orient workers to the organization, advancement is frequently prescribed according to workers' seniority rather than the quality of their job performance. Unionized workers are not always placed in positions for which they are best suited.

If you are a manager or human resources professional with responsibility for recruitment, you should usually look inside the organization first for recruits. Only where inbreeding and lack of "new blood" could create problems, when current organizational members lack required skills or experience, or when the "best" rather than an "acceptable" applicant pool is desired, should you turn to external sources.

Should WXX-TV use internal sources of recruits? The possibility of promotion from within attracts young aspirants to low-paying clerical or other entry positions in the industry. In contrast, most recruitment for on-air positions seems to use external sources to bring "new blood" to the on-air presence. In addition, some technical positions at WXX-TV may require training that cannot be obtained on the job. These positions should be filled using external sources of recruits.

External Sources

External sources of recruits include individuals who currently are not members of the organization. Friends and acquaintances of current employees provide one source of recruits. These individuals tend to have some knowledge of the organization and its expectations of employees. The cost of identifying them and attracting them to the organization may be minimal.

Students provide a pool of recruits who are relatively current in an area of study, tend to be highly motivated, and want employment. Organizations have traditionally filled entry-level jobs with recent graduates of high schools or colleges. As the general population has become more educated, the focus of such recruitment has shifted primarily to colleges. Depending on the organization's size and the types of job vacancies, organizations may devote a significant part of their recruiting effort to college visits. One report indicated that 50% of college-educated talent hired each year came from college recruiting.[6] The Big Eight accounting firms, for example, attract most recruits for entry-level positions from undergraduate schools with competitive accounting departments. Because they regularly compete for the best of a limited pool of talented recruits, they consider campus recruiting essential.

Union rosters can act as an external, as well as internal, source of recruits. Particularly where skilled craftspeople are required, unions may provide the most complete listing of available individuals. By hiring from union lists the organization may improve its relationship with the union by supporting its members through employment. At the same time, this form of hiring may create inbreeding similar to that resulting from using internal sources.

Competitors' employees are another external source. These workers typically have the skills required to perform the job. However, the cost of attracting them away from their current employer may be high. In addition, the ill-will that may result from "robbing competitors" may be dysfunctional in the marketplace.

Table 3–1 compares the various sources of recruits. To determine the best source, a manager or human resources professional should answer the following questions:

1. Where are the most qualified individuals located?
2. Does the organization require "new blood"?
3. Does the organization encourage advancement from within?

Recruiting the most qualified applicants should be the highest priority. Beyond this, the likely impact of using internal or external sources on workers and on organizational performance must be evaluated.

METHODS OF RECRUITMENT

Human resources professionals and managers can use a variety of methods to secure a pool of recruits from either internal or external sources. We examine the following methods in this section: (1) job posting, (2) referrals, (3) college recruiting programs, (4) job fairs, (5) open houses, (6) newspaper and other media advertising, and (7) employment agencies.

Source	Advantages	Disadvantages
Current employees	know organization's expectations have required attitudes relatively low recruiting costs may require less training may motivate workers to perform so they can advance	may result in inbreeding may limit new ideas introduced
Friends of current employees	have some knowledge of organization and its expectations likely to be a good fit present workers are invested in their success relatively low cost	may result in favoritism may result in lack of diversity among employees
College students	typically have current knowledge generally motivated to perform well	may be costly to recruit useful only for entry jobs may require too much time to bring them on board
Union rosters	good source of specific types of workers (e.g., craftspeople) may encourage positive union-management relations may be relatively inexpensive	organization may feel pressured to hire may not result in best person-job fit
Competitors' employees	recruits may require little training fit with job is likely to be high encourages introduction of new ideas	tends to be costly does not foster good will with competitors may require resocializing to requirements of new employer

Table 3–1 ADVANTAGES AND DISADVANTAGES OF SOURCES OF RECRUITS

Job Posting

Recruitment of current employees can occur through *job posting*. A bona fide job posting system requires all openings to be posted or advertised to current employees. "Open" internal recruiting, such as job posting, encourages managers to *objectively* identify a pool of applicants for open positions; a manager cannot easily limit applications to friends or demonstrate favoritism in forming the pool. One study noted that 80% of organizations surveyed post blue-collar jobs and 50% post professional jobs.[7] Although job posting is commonly used for recruiting low- and middle-level jobs, comparatively few organizations use job posting to recruit middle- and top-management positions. Why? These organizations may rely on "closed" recruiting so they can give their own preferred candidates priority in applying for available jobs.

Some managers also reason that job posting may attract too many applicants who lack the needed qualifications for higher level positions. They note that employees who repeatedly apply for internal transfers or advancement but are not hired may experience dissatisfaction and other negative outcomes. Also, professionals may lose organizational status and privileges once others know they are looking for another position. However, to eliminate these problems, managers and human resources professionals should incorporate job posting into an employee development system and ensure the confidentiality of all applications. Reading 3–1, "Job Posting for Professional Staff," discusses one example of a job posting program.

Referrals

Employees who understand their organization's operations, standards, and goals can recognize other employees who will perform well in their organization. They may *refer* current employees for other jobs in the organization; or they can recommend friends or professional acquaintances for openings. Current employees intuitively assess the fit between the individual, the organization, and the job. Referrals can occur formally or informally. Using referrals reduces the danger of inbreeding that can result from internal sources, while still increasing the likelihood of a good fit between the person and the organization. However, negative fallout can occur when a referral does not make it in the organization.

Banks, for example, have instituted incentive programs to encourage employee referrals.[8] Particularly for jobs such as tellers, where recruitment may be difficult, costly, or continuous, banks give their employees bonuses for recruiting an employee who remains with the organization for a prespecified period of time, generally one to three months. If you are planning to introduce a referral incentive program, make sure it (1) offers merchandise as well as cash incentives, (2) offers prizes at each step of the hiring, not just once, (3) emphasizes management support to generate enthusiasm, (4) receives intensive promotion to enhance employee awareness, and (5) is administered efficiently.[9] One study of 6390 bank employees indicated that high school referrals and referrals by present employees were among the methods that provided the most stable employment.[10]

College Recruiting Programs

Managers and human resources professionals should use college recruiting if they want to hire employees with state-of-the-art knowledge who can quickly contribute to the organization, concentrate their recruiting efforts where they will obtain highest yield, and track the characteristics of the available labor supply. In this case, they must also have a relatively large recruiting budget since the costs of $1500 to $6000 per hire from college recruiting can be prohibitive.[11]

Human resources professionals or managers can conduct the campus recruiting program. To be effective they must have a clear knowledge of job requirements from the managers involved in hiring. They must then target the appropriate group of students. Campus recruiting offers fewer benefits for jobs with very general recruitment criteria where there is an extremely large potential pool of recruits.

Large and prestigious universities attract many recruiters, but the percentage of job offers varies. Often college visits serve a public relations, not a recruiting function, but are still considered worthwhile. Managers with limited resources, however, may not be able to expend them on this method.

To make college recruiting programs as effective as possible, top management must (1) train recruiters to emphasize the organization's strengths in areas important to applicants, (2) review recruitment literature to ensure that it addresses points students rate as important, (3) develop additional information sources such as faculty or campus newspapers to increase visibility, (4) keep time lags between campus interviews and on-site interviews to less than three weeks, (5) assign key human resources professionals and managers to determine the information students receive on-site, (6) provide opportunities for students to meet with supervisors and coworkers during their site visit, (7) use the site visit to provide information about important organizational characteristics, and (8) seek feedback on student reactions to their visit.[12]

Job Fairs

Organizations in related industries often join together at a central location to recruit individuals en masse. Although organizational representatives may recruit individuals at job fairs, in general they serve an information-dissemination rather than a recruiting function. Job fairs can attract many potential recruits at a relatively low cost. Managers and human resources professionals should participate in job fairs whenever possible to supplement other methods.

Open Houses

Some organizations have arranged times when potential recruits can tour the organization and meet representatives on-site. In this way individuals can learn first hand about the job and the organizational requirements. High technology organizations have used this approach quite successfully.[13] For organizations, open houses attract a large number of potential recruits at a relatively low expenditure of time and money. Although human resources professionals typically organize open houses, managers should play an active role as organizational representatives.

Newspaper and Other Media Advertising

In contrast to the methods described so far, this method involves no direct contact between organizational members and potential recruits. Advertising generally attracts a large, nonselective pool of applicants. Look at the advertisement in Figure 3–1. What types of employees do you think this advertisement would attract? Would the organization be likely to attract the precise people they would like for the job? Compare it to the advertisement in Figure 3–2. What differences are there in the effectiveness of these advertisements? A good advertisement clearly lists the criteria that the organization will use for a preliminary screening

Software Engineers—Operating Systems

Responsible for identifying hardware support features within operating system and control program software. Individual will work closely with the software development departments in developing, implementing and introducing these support features, especially those that pertain to Remote Assistance and Network products.

Position requires BS in EE, CS or CE with a minimum of 5 years' experience in software development, maintenance or support plus 3 years in hardware design or support. Strong communications background will be very helpful.

Reprinted by permission of *The Boston Globe.*

Figure 3–1 SAMPLE ADVERTISEMENT FOR A JOB OPENING

of applicants; it also provides a relatively complete description of the job opening given the space purchased.

Although relatively expensive to place, newspaper advertising effectively attracts large numbers of job applicants. To productively use advertisements, human resources professionals must answer the following questions:

- What type of advertisement will attract the desired recruits?
- Where should the advertisement be placed?
- How much should be spent for the advertisement?
- Is there a less expensive way of attracting the same pool of recruits?
- Is the advertisement likely to attract the type of recruit that will fit the position?
- What percentage of recruits will be misfits with the job?

SOFTWARE

$35K + HP/1000. Software development of real-time data collection, graphic display and links for mfg.

Reprinted by permission of *The Boston Globe.*

Figure 3–2 SAMPLE ADVERTISEMENT FOR A JOB OPENING

In writing advertisements, human resources professionals must attract the attention and generate the interest of potential job holders. The ad should generate qualified inquiries, create a favorable image of the organization, and have a positive effect on present employees (e.g., make them proud to be part of the organization).[14] The person writing a creative recruitment ad should make sure that it has impact on readers, suggests that the organization has an immediate need for applicants, provides believable and useful information about the job and organization, is addressed to individual readers and relates to their interests, shows the uniqueness of the organization, is visually attractive, and encourages applicants to act immediately.[15]

Table 3–2 lists other media that can be used for recruiting. You can use direct mail advertising, for example, to locate professional employees. Martin Marietta, Inc., used direct mail to find experienced professionals who were successful in their current position, not necessarily looking for a job change, not reading recruiting advertisements in traditional sources, and potentially motivated to explore new opportunities.[16] They sent a brochure and mini-resume reply card to 10,000 people whose names they secured from a firm that specializes in conducting these campaigns. The personnel representatives then followed up on the responses by asking for a formal resume or a completed resume questionnaire. Then applicants were treated with regular selection procedures. Recruitment cost approximately $700 per hire.

Employment Agencies

Managers or human resources professionals can ask employment agencies for a list of qualified applicants. These organizations match potential employees to job vacancies. Privately owned or government operated, they supply diverse types of employees, from low to highly skilled individuals for manual, clerical, technical, or managerial positions.

Because privately owned agencies receive compensation only when they succeed in placing workers, they try to identify individuals who best fit the needs of the recruiting organization. Managers and human resources professionals with significant time constraints but a relatively large budget should call on these agencies; such recruiting firms do much of the legwork for the hiring organization, but at a relatively high cost. Organizations often use employment agencies as a last resort, when internal sources of recruits or less costly external sources of recruits cannot be used.

Executive search firms resemble employment agencies, but fill only middle- to top-level technical and managerial positions. Called *headhunters* because of their reputation for stealing employees from other organizations, executive recruiters maintain a list of individuals with a variety of credentials. They are hired to search for and find individuals who qualify for a specific position. They prescreen those individuals to yield three to five recruits for the organization to evaluate. Fortune 500 companies use headhunters for jobs with salaries greater than $60,000.[17] The number of executive search firms is increasing; one of the largest

Type of Medium	Advantages	Disadvantages	When to Use
Newspapers	Short deadlines Ad size flexibility Circulation concentrated in specific geographic areas Classified sections well organized for easy access by active job seekers	Easy for prospects to ignore Considerable competitive clutter Circulation not specialized—you must pay for great amount of unwanted readers Poor printing quality	When you want to limit recruiting to a specific area When sufficient numbers of prospects are clustered in a specific area When enough prospects are reading help-wanted ads to fill hiring needs
Magazines	Specialized magazines reach pinpointed occupation categories Ad size flexibility High quality printing Prestigious editorial environment Long life—prospects keep magazines and reread them	Wide geographic circulation—usually cannot be used to limit recruiting to specific area Long lead time for ad placement	When job is specialized When time and geographic limitations are not of utmost importance When involved in ongoing recruiting programs
Directories	Specialized audiences Long life	Not timely Often have competitive clutter	Only appropriate for ongoing recruiting programs
Direct mail	Most personal form of advertising Unlimited number of formats and amount of space By selecting names by zip code, mailing can be pinpointed to precise geographic area	Difficult to find mailing list of prospects by occupation at home addresses Cost for reaching each prospect is high	If the right mailing list can be found, this is potentially the most effective medium—no other medium gives the prospect as much a feeling of being specially selected Particularly valuable in competitive situations
Radio and Television	Difficult to ignore. Can reach prospects who are not actively looking for a job better than newspapers and magazines Can be limited to specific geographic areas Creatively flexible. Can dramatize employment story more effectively than printed ads Little competitive recruitment clutter	Only brief, uncomplicated messages are possible Lack of permanence; prospect cannot refer back to it. (Repeated airings necessary to make impression.) Creation and production of commercials—particularly TV—can be time-consuming and costly Lack of special interest selectivity; paying for waste circulation	In competitive situations when not enough prospects are reading your printed ads When there are multiple job openings and there are enough prospects in specific geographic area When a large impact is needed quickly. A "blitz" campaign can saturate an area in two weeks or less Useful to call attention to printed ads

Table 3–2 ADVANTAGES AND DISADVANTAGES OF THE MAJOR TYPES OF MEDIA *Continued*

Type of Medium	Advantages	Disadvantages	When to Use
Outdoor (roadside billboards) and Transit (posters on buses & subways)	Difficult to ignore. Can reach prospects as they are literally traveling to their current jobs Precise geographic selectivity Reaches large numbers of people manv times at a low cost	Only very brief message is possible Requires long lead for preparation and must be in place for long period of time. (Usually one to three months.)	When there is a steady hiring need for large numbers of people that is expected to remain constant over a long period of time
"Point-of-Purchase" (Promotional materials at recruiting location)	Calls attention to employment story at time when prospects can take some type of immediate action Creative flexibility	Limited usefulness; prospects must visit a recruiting location before it can be effective	Posters, banners, brochures, audio-visual presentations at special events such as job fairs, open houses, conventions, as part of an employee referral program, at placement offices or whenever prospects visit at organization's location frequently.

"Planning for Recruitment Advertising: Part II," by Bernard S. Hodes, copyright June 1983. Reprinted with permission by *Personnel Journal,* Costa Mesa, California; all rights reserved.

Table 3–2 Continued

has 1250 clients, 400 consultants, 33 offices, and $40 million in recent annual billings.[18]

The cost of this service to the recruiting organization equals 25% to 33% of the first year's salary of the employee hired. Thus the choice of a recruiting firm should be based on its capability and reputation.[19]

Which methods of recruiting can WXX-TV use? An effective recruiting system should use diverse approaches, fitting the method to the recruiting need. For example, advertisements might draw a pool of clerical employees; college or graduate school recruiting might attract people to the accounting or marketing departments; executive search firms might obtain applicants for top management positions.

Comparison of Methods of Recruiting

Individual methods differ along the dimensions of cost, effectiveness, use, and expertise required, as shown in Table 3–3. To reap the benefits of the diverse approaches, organizations can use a multifaceted approach to recruitment. To reach a broader cross-section of potential recruits, one bank placed point-of-purchase displays with brochures in its branches, sent fliers with monthly customer statements, placed radio and transit advertisements, and advertised in shopping malls.[20] In the first month, the bank had 2000 responses, of which 800 were interviewed and 300 hired.

Source	Use	Advantages	Disadvantages
College recruiting	entry level positions	attract limited pool	moderate to high cost
Employee referrals	entry positions some managerial positions hard to fill or high turnover positions	low cost recruits that fit low cost	inbreeding
Employment agency	all positions	attract pool with good fit	high cost
Executive recruiters	top management	take total recruitment responsibility	high cost
Job fairs	all positions	attract large pool	too unselective
Job posting	non-entry or managerial positions	performance incentive low cost	inbreeding
Newspaper advertising	entry and middle-level positions	attract large pool	may attract wrong pool potentially high cost
Open houses	all positions	attract large pool present accurate picture of organization	too unselective

Table 3–3 SUMMARY OF ADVANTAGES AND DISADVANTAGES OF SOURCES OF RECRUITS

THE EMPLOYMENT INTERVIEW

As part of the recruitment system, human resources professionals and managers should conduct employment interviews; these serve as a major way of exchanging information about a job to be filled and the credentials of a potential recruit. College recruiting, employment agencies, and executive search firms also use interviews as data-gathering tools in recruiting. In this section we discuss the characteristics of an effective interview, as well as a special type of interview called the *realistic job preview.*

Characteristics of an Effective Interview

Managers use employment interviews to gain preliminary information about a job applicant and to present general information about the recruiting organization. They might use visual screening, critical or "knockout" questions (e.g., Can you travel 40% of the time?), review the application form with the applicant (see Chapter 4), or briefly describe the job to the applicant.[21] The manager or interviewer should demonstrate interest in the candidate and his or her potential contributions, show an understanding of the candidate's background and perspective, discuss the candidate's strengths and weaknesses, and answer the candidate's questions.[22] The manager should be certain to follow any legal constraints that influence recruitment interviewing (see Chapter 13). In the long run, the quality of the interview affects the job acceptance rate of candidates.[23]

An interviewer should recognize that there are major questions about the value of interviews as a data collection tool and carefully use the data obtained from them. For example, the tendency to pay more attention to information received first and to negative information may bias the interview.[24] Reading 3–2, "A Guide to Job-Related Employment Interviewing," by Robert Bloom and Erich Prien, offers an approach for increasing the accuracy and usefulness of employment interviews.

Realistic Job Preview

Traditional job recruitment portrays the job only in a favorable light to ensure the applicant's interest—negative aspects of the job are not mentioned. Rather than conducting a traditional employment interview, managers or human resources professionals should emphasize realistic recruitment through presenting a preview that gives applicants complete information about the activities, responsibilities, and other aspects of the job in the most accurate way possible.[25] A realistic job preview presents both positive and negative information. The interviewer presents the applicant with detailed and precise data about all aspects of the job and organization. For example, the interviewer might describe difficulties that previous job holders experienced and the reasons they left the organization. The applicant can then use this complete picture of the job to decide whether he or she fits with the organization.

This approach limits the turnover often resulting when an individual's expectations do not fit the job's reality. One study at Southern New England Telephone Company showed that traditional recruitment, which created highly inflated expectations, resulted in greater job dissatisfaction than realistic recruitment.[26] In addition to using the interview to present a realistic picture, other organizations (including a telephone company, a life insurance agency, the Marine Corps, and a college) used films, booklets, videotapes, and brochures, respectively, to realistically present the positive and negative features of jobs in their organizations.[27]

A manager who uses realistic job previews must (1) carefully choose the medium for conveying the message about the job; (2) try not to arouse the applicant's needs for achieving in an undesirable situation; (3) include the preview early in the recruitment process; (4) moderate the amount of realism presented so that the potential employee does not feel helpless; and (5) recognize that realistic recruitment cannot substitute for other organizational programs, such as strong selection or training practices.[28] When these principles are applied, realistic recruitment has effectively selected job holders for entry-level jobs in tight hiring situations.[29]

A COMPREHENSIVE RECRUITMENT SYSTEM

In a comprehensive system human resources professionals and managers must

1. diagnose as completely as possible (given constraints of time, financial resources, and staff availability) the environmental and organizational factors that affect the position to be filled and the recruitment activities;
2. construct detailed job descriptions, specifications, and performance standards;
3. specify the types of individuals most often employed by the organization in that type of position;
4. specify recruitment criteria;
5. evaluate various sources of recruits;
6. select the sources of recruits likely to yield the largest, most congruent pool of potential hires at the lowest cost;
7. identify methods for tapping these sources, including writing advertisements, scheduling college recruiting, designing incentive programs for internal referrals, and implementing a job posting system;
8. select the most cost-effective methods; and
9. develop a recruitment plan that includes a list of activities and a timetable for implementing them.

The quality of a recruitment system can be assessed by answering the following questions:

- Has a situational audit been performed?
- Are there recruitment criteria? Are they meaningful for the jobs to be filled?
- Has a range of potential sources been identified?
- Has each source been evaluated for usefulness, cost, and accessibility?
- Have alternative methods for tapping each relevant source been examined?
- Have recruitment methods been assessed for cost and benefit?
- Have responsibilities for recruitment been effectively allocated?
- Have contingency plans been developed in case sources do not yield as planned?

Managers and human resources professionals contribute in somewhat different ways to a comprehensive recruitment system. To the extent possible they should act in the ways discussed in the next sections.

Implications for Human Resources Professionals

To increase the effectiveness of recruitment in the organization, the human resources professional should coordinate and monitor the managerial recruitment activities described below.

1. They should combine the needs identified by individual managers into an organizational needs assessment. The professionals can identify sources and methods that would benefit more than one department, and thus reduce the relative cost to each group.
2. They should consider diverse sources of recruits and use diverse methods for tapping these sources. Establishing a network of contacts that lead to useful external sources should be a high priority and innovation in identifying new sources is essential.
3. Human resources professionals must coordinate in-house recruitment programs such as job posting, and introduce incentive programs for filling positions with high turnover.
4. They should be a source of information about the supply of various types of employees, internally and externally, in the short, medium, and long run. They should also know the types of recruitment activities that other organizations have used successfully.
5. Human resources professionals responsible for staffing should develop a data base of potential candidates. The availability of relatively inexpensive computerized data base managers should allow them to reduce their reliance on employment agencies and executive recruiters.
6. Professionals must frequently reassess the cost-effectiveness of various methods of recruiting for specific jobs. For example, the value of undergraduate college recruiting may decrease as positions require more on-the-job experience.
7. Human resources professionals must maintain a recruitment schedule, as well as monitor the implementation of recruitment activities organization-wide.

Implications for Managers

Managers, in contrast, must focus primarily on identifying their own recruitment needs and gathering a pool of candidates to meet those needs. Effective practice includes the following:

1. Managers must periodically update job analyses to ensure the correct identification of their employment needs. This means instituting a program for the regular revision of job descriptions, specifications, and performance standards.
2. They must carefully specify recruitment criteria based on current job analyses. Such criteria should predict job performance.
3. Although managers can rely on human resources professionals to identify and tap some sources of recruits, they should also actively propose and develop new sources of recruits. In particular, the development of a network of contacts inside the organization can facilitate internal recruitment.
4. Managers should practice their interviewing skills, and introduce realistic job previewing into employment interviews.
5. They should develop and implement a schedule of recruitment activities to ensure the availability of a pool of recruits when needed.

READINGS

Reading 3–1

JOB POSTING FOR PROFESSIONAL STAFF

J. Robert Garcia

The term "job announcement program" usually refers to the familiar concept of union job posting. In this process unions have a contractual agreement with management whereby the company posts all job vacancies for union-represented, graded manual and clerical jobs and notifies union members of successful applicants.

If this approach works reasonably well for union employees, why isn't it applied to professional staff—such as employees in a research and development (R&D) laboratory? Scientists and engineers (like everyone else) are concerned about how supervisors are selected, where the challenging jobs are, and how jobs are filled.

Management, too, should consider the federal regulations which require a clear statement of company guidelines governing internal opportunities and selection procedures and give job posting for professional staff a closer look.

APPREHENSIONS ABOUT A JOB ANNOUNCEMENT PROGRAM

Any job announcement program is certain to meet with mixed reactions from professional staff. Some of the common concerns voiced by staff in this situation are:

- If they seek a lateral transfer to another group, how will their current supervisors react?
- If they are not selected for the job they request, how will this affect their career?
- If a supervisory vacancy occurs, how do they seek an audience with the selecting manager and will their own supervisor recommend them?

"Job Posting for Professional Staff," by J. Robert Garcia, copyright March 1981. Reprinted with the permission of *Personnel Journal*, Costa Mesa, California; all rights reserved.

The very thought of a job announcement program in an R&D laboratory generates controversy among managers. Some think it's unprofessional to list staff jobs—a job announcement program may be appropriate for blue-collar workers, but not for professionals. Others say that to announce job vacancies could disrupt the work force because certain groups with more interesting work would benefit at the expense of groups with less interesting (but necessary) work.

Determining the effectiveness of job posting in selecting supervisors is also controversial. Through long experience, management feels it has developed reliable approaches for identifying supervisory talent by such methods as job rotations, understudies and special assignments. Other groups have used the management selection committee approach to list high-potential staff with the talent to fill future organizational needs.

Employees are seldom consulted in any of these approaches. Instead, they are often selected for reassignment by some all-knowing group that feels only it can identify the interests, ambitions and capabilities of staff and decide what is best for them.

Certainly it is important for management to maintain the stability of their organizations, especially during critical phases of an assignment or until completion of a sensitive project. At the same time, management recognizes that locking R&D staff into one organization or type of work risks dissatisfying professionals who may be tempted to look for opportunities outside the company. The possible loss of some of the laboratory's most talented professionals would mean not only the loss of their valuable expertise, but also the added expense of seeking qualified replacements.

SANDIA'S JOB ANNOUNCEMENT PROGRAM

Sandia National Laboratories has successfully implemented a job announcement program for approximately 7,700 employees, including professional and support staffs. Although Sandia Laboratories' principal mission is nuclear weapons systems engineering, in the past few years it has shifted some of its R&D talents toward improving the country's energy prospects. The energy programs were carefully selected to use existing capabilities and at the same time provide new and challenging work to the staff.

During the early stages of diversification, a few staff members were selected for assignment to the energy programs. However, most of the staff continued work in support of the laboratories' primary defense-related role. Some employees with years of experience, eager for the new challenges posed by energy R&D, were unhappy with management's staffing decisions.

In response, Sandia investigated the feasibility of a job announcement program. In July 1976, Sandia implemented a job announcement program designed to include the first two levels of supervision, the technical and administrative professional staff, and the technical and administrative support staff. This program provided two very different routes to nomination for a job: self-nomination and nomination by an employee's director.

JOB ANNOUNCEMENT PROCEDURE

If a decision has been made to not recruit from outside, the supervisor with a vacancy announces the open position and submits the vacancy announcement, along with a brief job description, to the personnel department by Tuesday.

Job announcements are then published in a weekly bulletin that is distributed to all employees on Thursday of the same week. Nominations for available jobs are open for one week from the date of the announcement.

Lateral nominations: employees may nominate themselves by calling a telephone number in the personnel department and giving their name, employee number and job of interest. Only nominations for lateral shifts into supervisory, professional and support positions are acceptable. Late nominations are permitted only for valid reasons, such as vacation or illness.

Promotional nominations to supervision: these nominations are made by upper management only. Management at the director level submit nominations by letter to the director with the vacancy. These letters describe the experience, education and performance of the director's candidate.

Thus, the director with a vacancy has two broad lists from which to choose: 1) candidates who want to be considered on a lateral basis, and 2) employees recommended for promotion by their directors.

In addition, copies of all promotional supervisory nominations are sent directly to the director of personnel; suspension or cancellation of job vacancies may occur under special circumstances; and final disposition of the vacancy is published in the weekly bulletin.

SPECIAL CONCERNS

A few of the following areas required special consideration:

- *Listing of vacancies at other geographical locations.* Sandia has main facilities in two different states and at several test sites and locations both inside and outside the continental United States. Identical systems of announcing vacancies were used at each location, with each issuing its own bulletin. However, the supervisor with the vacancy may ask for staff positions to be listed at other locations. Costs of relocation are reviewed before an announcement is made and before any employee is considered for a job elsewhere. Relocations are the exception rather than the rule.
- *Agreement on release date.* The supervisor releases the successful applicant from his or her current job within 30 days. Absence of a suitable replacement does not qualify as an exception to the 30-day rule. The need to complete a critical project phase may delay transfer up to 60 days with vice-presidential approval.
- *Reversal of decision.* During the first six months either the individual on a new assignment or the new supervisor can reverse the move and the employee returns to his or her former position.

EXCEPTIONS

Experience has resulted in few exceptions, which have been used thoughtfully and sparingly. A listing can be suspended totally or only for selected openings or projects, subject to approval by the company president. These exceptions include:

- Positions affected by functional transfers or reorganizations ("functional" means that the same job is moved in its entirety from one group to another)
- Placement of employees because of job evaluation considerations or physical disabilities that make it impossible for employees to continue in their present jobs
- Interchange of two or more employees for developmental purposes after mutual agreement of management and employee
- Moves of individuals consistent with the needs of the organization or to resolve a personnel problem

REACTIONS

Most of the staff are pleased that a job announcement program was established. Most participants who were selected are happy with their new assignments, and supervisors are satisfied with the responses of the staff and the quality of candidates. Very few decisions have resulted in employees returning to their former jobs. Both management and staff believe that communication has improved due to the public announcement of successful job candidates as well as to posting of vacancies. Employee morale appears to have improved. Employees say they now have a greater voice in where their talents can be put to best use and therefore the development of their own careers. They feel better just knowing about jobs that fit their capabilities, even though they may not nominate themselves for the vacancies.

Supervisors with vacancies have learned to state their needs and standards of performance more clearly, and have also improved their interviewing skills. Individual nominees have discovered that self-development and currency in their fields has paid off in better, more challenging assignments. Unsuccessful nominees have identified needed skills and gained a more realistic idea of additional training or experience required for particular career alternatives.

PROBLEMS

As with any new system, there were problems:

- Some supervisors went through the motions of announcing a vacancy, with the ultimate objective of canceling the announcement and employing a new hire.
- Occasionally employees alleged preselection—"Why bother to nominate yourself; they've already decided who they want to select."
- At least one interviewee grumbled that during his interview the supervisor made him feel undesirable by pointing out his faults and explaining why he would not be selected.
- Occasional long delays between posting and final disposition have caused some dissatisfaction. (During the past 3 years the frequency of delays and "pending" announcements has been reduced.)
- When no explanation was given when selections were not made, bidders were left to wonder whether no qualified applicant was found or the position was cancelled. (This was resolved by listing the deposition of all past openings in the weekly bulletin.)
- Many supervisors who made a selection failed to advise unsuccessful bidders (resolved the same way as in the above case).

PROGRAM REVIEW

Three months after its introduction the program was reviewed. One hundred fifty-four openings had been announced and 24 were canceled. The vacancies were well-distributed throughout technical and administrative groups and between supervisory and staff classifications. Most nominees were highly selective; the few overly frequent nominees were counseled to be more selective. Of the remaining 130 announcements, 717 nominations (or 5.5 per opening) were submitted. The nomination activity was higher in the support positions. Sixty nominations were received either laterally or as recommendations from directors for the 10 supervisory vacancies announced during the first quarter of the program.

One year later a detailed analysis of program experience was presented to upper management.

Management concluded that the program was not only good for the organization, but that it resulted in a better way to reassign staff to work of their own choosing. Management also felt that the program was a good means of improving communication among staff regarding internal job opportunities. Top management recommended expansion of the program to cover third-level managers.

As of June 1980, the program had been in operation for four years. Of the 2,331 announcements made, 61% were filled, 35% were canceled by the supervisor, and 4% are "pending." More announcements have been canceled in the professional, technical, administrative and technician categories than in supervisory and support categories. Why are so many of these jobs canceled? One reason is that supervisors with vacancies often post jobs and interview candidates, and when not satisfied with the quality of the candidates, disqualify all nominees and ask management for permission to recruit from outside.

At first the number of "pending" jobs posed a problem. We soon discovered that supervisors tended to delay selection for several weeks. This practice stopped after supervisors were informed that vacancies would be canceled if not filled within one month.

A look at the number of vacancies by job classification filled within and between organizations indicates that about 70% of the supervisory openings are filled from within the group with the position opening. This high percentage occurs because the selecting supervisor is more familiar with the work of candidates within the group. Likewise, in specialty or project groups with similar work, it is natural for an individual to move from staff into supervision under a manager who has firsthand knowledge about the quality of the candidate's work.

For the higher level management announcements (department level) begun after the first year of the program, nominations ranged from a low of 3 to a high of 10 per announcement. About half the jobs in this category were filled by candidates from outside the group having the vacancy.

CONCLUSION

Another benefit is that the program has aided college recruiting efforts. After features of the program are pointed out to college graduates, they see such a program as an opportunity to match their own career with the objectives of the organization. An organization that offers freedom of choice and encourages career growth has a definite advantage when recruiting.

Within the organization, the program has proved an orderly, effective way of announcing job opportunities. It also allows employees to express job interests and provides them with valuable feedback. Not only is the program well accepted by both the R&D staff and management, but it also complies with the intent of federal affirmative action rules and regulations.

DISCUSSION QUESTIONS

1. What is a job announcement program?
2. What problems are there in introducing such a program?
3. How can the effectiveness of a job announcement program be increased?
4. What role do human resources professionals and managers play in such a program?

Reading 3–2

A GUIDE TO JOB-RELATED EMPLOYMENT INTERVIEWING

Robert Bloom and Erich P. Prien

Business needs as well as legal concerns virtually mandate valid employee selection procedures. However, business practice and employee selection has lagged significantly behind research and development. In addition, a variety of myths that are obstacles to change have arisen, despite the strong potential of such changes for significantly improving personnel practices.

Reprinted from the October, 1983 issue of *Personnel Administrator*, copyright, 1983, The American Society for Personnel Administration, 606 North Washington Street, Alexandria, VA 22314, $30 per year.

A particularly troublesome myth is that the conduct of casual pre-employment selection interviews allows the employer to prevent or obstruct discriminatory employment practices litigation. The idea is that casual interviews avoid the creation of documentation that might be used as evidence in litigation.

The assumption that an absence of documentation has any effect upon litigation represents little more than ignorance of the litigation process. The fact is the courts have agreed that a *prima facie* case of discrimination can be established solely through the use of "bottom line" statistics, that is, a comparison of the makeup of an organization's workforce, or particular components of that work force, with data on the composition of some relevant population.

Initially, what is important to enforcement agencies and the courts are outcomes—the numbers of minority personnel hired. A lack of selection documentation will not protect an organization in discriminatory employment practice litigation cases when "bottom line" requirements are not met.

Otteman and Chapman (1977) have strongly advocated job-content-based personnel selection procedures. While some indication was provided for "how to do it," the link to any one specific practice was not clearly established.

However, in a more recent article, Macey, Prien and Goldstein (1982) elaborated on the technology for developing job content data for various personnel applications through systematic job analysis. Standing alone, the above two articles are little more than academic exercises with reference to the focus of this article.

The linking pin, though, is an article by Osburn, Timmreck and Bigby (1981), demonstrating that ratings based upon structured interviews differentiate among job candidates, whereas global interview ratings did not.

More specifically, when selection interviewers were asked to make judgments with reference to job-related and defined characteristics, those interviewers who rated candidates on specific and relevant dimensions were able to accurately discriminate between the more qualified and less qualified applicant. In sharp contrast, when the judgment task was not defined, interviewers rating on general job dimensions were not able to accurately discriminate between the more and less qualified applicant. In addition, there was greater agreement among interviewers who assessed the candidates on specific job dimensions than among interviewers who assessed on the general job dimensions.

Thus, Otteman and Chapman (1977) place the problem in an appropriate context; Macey, et al. (1982) spell out the techniques for developing job content data, and Osburn, et al. (1981) demonstrate the payoff in terms of the results obtained.

With a clearly established rationale and the general technology, what is now required for the personnel professional is a specific, well defined and step-by-step expansion of the job-content method applied to pre-employment interviewing.

ANALYSES

Macey, et al. (1982) have designed an approach that can be utilized for the development of specific information for pre-employment interviewing. These authors discuss two domains by which jobs can be characterized, identified and defined. The first domain reflects tasks or what individuals do in their jobs. Tasks are those activities or job operations engaged in by workers that produce an identifiable output. The determination of these tasks represent what McGehee and Thayer (1961) refer to as "task analysis."

Task analysis entails a process of observation or study of a job to obtain a description of the duties which comprise the target job(s). The product is a summary statement of the job(s) plus a listing of the important tasks comprising the job. However, in the context of selection, the task-oriented description is used mainly to define the boundaries or limits for a person-oriented job analysis. The reason for establishing a frame of reference in this way is that task-oriented job analyses deal primarily with observable data that require a minimum of judgment and inference. Such observations can be recorded and verified. A task-oriented job description can have substantial reliability. Thus, a task analysis becomes a strong foundation on which a person-oriented job analysis can be built.

The second domain focuses on those individual characteristics that are associated with variations in job performance. This domain is defined in terms of the knowledge, skills, abilities (KSAs) that individuals possess prior to job entry, or acquire through experience after job entry. This domain serves to explain why some individuals perform tasks in a manner contributing to the effectiveness of the organization, whereas others do not. The specification of this domain of personal characteristics corresponds to what McGehee and Thayer (1961) referred to as "person analysis."

Person analysis is performed in terms of knowledge, skills and abilities which are defined as follows:

Knowledge is the foundation upon which abilities and skills are built. It is defined as an organized body of information, usually of a factual, structured and/or procedural nature, which if applied, makes competent performance on the job possible. It should be noted that the mere possession of knowledge does not ensure its proper application.

Skill is defined as a proficient manual, verbal or mental manipulation of people, ideas or things. Usually a skill implies an observable psychomotor activity. Skills differ from abilities in that possession of a skill implies a performance standard that must be met.

Ability is defined as the present power to perform a job function—to carry through with an activity while applying or using the essential knowledge.

In the context of selection interviewing, KSAs distinguish qualified from unqualified candidates and assist in differentiating among qualified candidates for employment in the job. This is the purpose of the person-oriented job analysis and the isolation of all and only all of the essential KSAs related to the target job(s). A complete elaboration of the specific procedures used to collect information related to the task and person domains would be beyond the scope of this paper. However, the next several sections present an abbreviated version of the types of procedures utilized.

PHASE I

The collection of task and person information is greatly facilitated by an overall structure or framework describing the work done in the organization. A general framework is achieved through an examination of available job description records, direct observation of the work setting and process and/or work output records. Information acquired in this preparatory stage provides a general understanding of business operations, terminology and so on.

PHASE II

The second phase of the job analysis required interviews with individuals who are qualified as subject matter experts (SMEs). The purpose of these interviews is to collect detailed information about the tasks employees perform, and the KSAs required to perform those tasks. The result of these interviews is a set of descriptors in the task (task analysis) and in the KSA (person analysis) domains.

Examples of task descriptors or statements are presented in Figure 3–3. Task statements are written to represent duties of varying complexity and therefore will be of varying length and complexity. However, all task statements answer the questions "what," "to whom/what," "how" and "why." An optimum style in writing task statements results in specificity, clarity and accuracy. Task statements are reviewed by job analysts and SMEs to ensure that all and only all of the task domain is represented.

Examples of KSA statements are also presented in Figure 3–3. These statements specify the person attributes necessary to perform the duties specified in the development of the task analysis. As previously

Tasks	KSAs
Assist customers in opening or closing savings and checking accounts.	Ability to organize recorded information in a way which permits evaluation by others.
Take customer credit information and complete loan documentation form.	Knowledge of budget preparation procedures for department or specific area of responsibility.
Interview customers to complete loan application.	Knowledge of principles of finance.
Investigate and resolve customer problems with personal banking services.	Ability to express explanations of qualitative in narrative form.

Figure 3–3 EXAMPLES OF TASKS AND ELEMENTS

stated, person-oriented job analysis is usually accomplished by means of interview procedures.

The information sources are typically SMEs (i.e., job supervisors and/or experienced, successful incumbents). Of course, the burden of effort in deriving and defining KSAs is carried by the personnel specialist using the information obtained from the SMEs. In general, the preferred procedure in collecting KSA data is to obtain information from panels or groups of SMEs.

Information obtained from panels will tend to check and balance errors in individual judgment that can occur in any job analysis. An alternative and low-priority procedure is possible, however. The personnel specialist can perform the entire KSA analysis alone if they cross-check their results with SMEs.

There are several general rules for defining KSA statements. They are:

- Maintain a reasonable balance between generality and specificity. Exactly how generally or specifically a KSA statement should be stated will depend on its intended use. For pre-employment interviewing, the statement must be specific enough to characterize job skills that discriminate qualified from unqualified candidates and among qualified candidates.
- Avoid simply restating a task statement. Such an approach is redundant and usually provides very little new information about the job. It is necessary to ask what knowledge, skills or abilities are necessary to perform the task. For example, a task statement might be: "Researches legal questions by analyzing cases—." A redundant KSA statement would be "Ability to research legal questions by—." The correct phrasing which provides the interviewer with specific information to target questions and to determine the degree to which the applicant possesses the ability would be, "Ability to develop and organize an information search strategy and procedure using topic, key word or other parameters."
- Avoid the error of including trivial information when developing the KSAs. For example, in a supervisor's job, "knowledge of the procedure used to order personal office supplies" might be trivial. However, because the omission of key KSAs is a more serious error than including trivia, include KSAs if they are borderline.

The following two phases are optional and can be employed if the job analyst is developing task and/or KSA specifications for a large variety of different jobs and/or for a variety of different purposes (e.g., determination of minimum qualifications, training needs analysis, etc.). If the analyst is developing specifications for a single job or a small number of jobs, then the task is complete. All that remains is implementation.

PHASE III

In this phase, SMEs including job incumbents and supervisors provide further information about the two job content domains. In order to meet the requirement of identifying selection dimensions SMEs provide several judgments of the task and KSA statement developed in Phase II. Some of the kinds of judgments that could be obtained include the following:

For task statements:

- *Importance.* SMEs rate the criticality of the task for full job performance.
- *Frequency.* SMEs indicate the relative frequency with which tasks are performed on the job.
- *Difficulty in acquiring proficiency.* SMEs indicate how difficult it is to acquire proficiency at that task on the job.

For KSA statements:

- *Where acquired.* SMEs indicate whether the KSA must be acquired prior to job entry, can only be acquired after job entry or can be acquired at either point.
- *Difficulty in learning.* SMEs indicate how difficult it is to gain competence with reference to the KSAs necessary for full job performance.
- *Importance.* SMEs rate the criticality of KSAs for full job performance.
- *Opportunity to acquire.* Ratings are collected pertaining to the opportunity to acquire requisite KSAs on the job.

Obviously, for job-related interviewing the critical rating the analyst must have is the "where acquired" rating. This rating represents the SMEs' collective judgments as to those KSAs essential for successful job performance but which in the judgment of the SMEs must be acquired prior to job entry.

PHASE IV

Once SME ratings of task and KSA items are obtained, they are statistically analyzed by job. The analysis results in the identification of groups of task statements and groups of KSA statements. Each group of statements represents a logical set. They are variations upon a theme which are necessary to define more specifically the content of individual jobs.

Two different jobs having the same general requirement may be somewhat or quite different insofar as the specific character of that requirement is concerned. For example, an inside and outside sales job might both require a job dimension labeled, "sales ability," but because of the relatively different character of the work setting the specifics would be quite different. The outside sales job might require ability in face-to-face contact with customers while the inside sales job might require abilities dealing with telephone contact, correspondence, records, etc.

It is important to recognize that jobs that differ in terms of their main duties also differ in terms of the KSAs required for successful performance. The key results of a thorough and comprehensive job analysis will be the specification of those KSAs uniquely required for successful performance on the job. In the pre-employment selection interview, the key results of the job analysis will proscribe those KSAs which will be used in measuring or evaluating candidates for a position. That subset of job-related knowledge, skills and abilities related to a particular target position and only that subset should be used in job-related interviewing. Unless a job analysis has been conducted to establish and document the link between job tasks and KSAs, legal guidelines and professional standards relative to the development and use of selection procedures may be violated.

As an example of the outcome of a person-oriented job analysis, Figure 3–4 contains one of several subsets of KSAs. The subset was rationally derived with the process used for its production well documented. Figure 3–5 contains sample questions a selection interviewer might ask based upon the subset of KSA contained in Figure 3–4.

Knowledge of individual worker abilities and potential.

Ability to instruct employees in the correct methods/procedures for performing maintenance/service tasks by demonstrating, coaching and providing feedback on their performance.

Ability to estimate the maintenance work load in relation to equipment used, products, operations and production schedule.

Knowledge of the production schedule and needs of the plant for establishing maintenance priorities.

Ability to plan and schedule a preventative maintenance program to mesh with ongoing maintenance activity.

Figure 3–4 AN EXAMPLE OF ONE OF SEVERAL SUBSETS OF KSAS WHICH WERE DERIVED FROM A PERSON-ORIENTED JOB ANALYSIS

Figure 3–6 contains an example of one subset of several KSA statements arranged for a structured interview format. The interviewer scores each KSA statement based upon the response the candidate gives to the interviewer's job-related questions contained in Figure 3–5. The selection interviewer might use a five-, seven- or 10-point scale to rate the candidate's response to each KSA statement. A 10-point scale is illustrated.

The logic underlying the use of job-related KSAs for selection interviewing is that KSAs represent individual difference characteristics. The relative degree of possession or lack of possession of these characteristics will be associated with success or failure in performing the job tasks. To extend this principle one need only think of the major duty and associated KSAs in performing that duty. Individuals who do not possess the KSAs required will, of course, logically not be successful in performing the job.

Individuals who do possess the KSAs may be successful in performing the task. This brings out one of the dilemmas in personnel selection: the "can do versus will do" difference. If an individual possesses the necessary KSAs required for effective job performance, it is reasonably certain they can perform the job successfully, but there is no assurance that they will perform the job successfully if given the opportunity.

Knowledge of individual worker abilities and potential.
Q. How do you know when someone will be a good worker?
Q. How can you find out how to help someone improve their performance?

Ability to instruct employees in the correct methods/procedures for performing maintenance/service tasks by demonstrating, coaching and providing feedback on their performance.
Q. Tell me how you trained workers to do their job.
Q. What methods of training have you found useful with operators and/or mechanics?

Ability to estimate the maintenance work load in relation to equipment used, products, operations and production schedule.
Q. How can you tell how much work you and the maintenance crew will have to do during a day?
Q. What effect do such things as operations and plant products have on the maintenance staff work load?

Knowledge of the production schedule and needs of the plant for establishing maintenance priorities.
Q. What effect does the production schedule of the plant have on what a mechanic ought to repair first?
Q. How do you know what the needs of the plant are at any given time and what mechanics ought to be doing?

Ability to plan and schedule a preventative maintenance program to mesh with ongoing maintenance activity.
Q. How did/would you go about planning a preventative maintenance program in the plant?
Q. How would you mix the needed maintenance work load with the load created by the preventative maintenance program?

Figure 3–5 EXAMPLES OF SAMPLE QUESTIONS BASED UPON JOB-RELATED KSAS

Differentiating between those who can do and those who will do is difficult and beyond the scope of the present article. For the present, it is sufficient to think of each KSA and each subset of KSAs as individual differences which are singly and collectively related to job performance. In the pre-employment interview what the interviewer is essentially doing is collecting specific job-related information about the candidate to provide the basis for a selection decision.

References

Otteman, R. and Chapman, J. B., "A viable strategy for validation: content validity," *Personnel Administrator,* November 1977, pp. 17–22.

Macey, W.; Prien, E. P.; and Goldstein, I. W., "Multimethod job analysis: methodology and applications," 1982, unpublished manuscript, Memphis, TN.

Osburn, H. G.; Timmreck, C.; and Bigby, D., "Effect of dimensional relevance on accuracy of simulated hiring decisions by employment interviewers," *Journal of Applied Psychology,* 1981, Vol. 66, pp. 159–165.

McGehee, W. and Thayer, P. W., *Training in Business and Industry,* New York: Wiley, 1961.

DISCUSSION QUESTIONS

1. What problems do interviewers encounter in pre-employment interviewing in meeting legal constraints?
2. What is the job-content method?
3. How can a manager use the job-content method?
4. What advantages does it offer over other interviewing approaches?
5. What elements would a job-content interview conducted by a manager contain?

INTERVIEW RATINGS

APPLICANT NAME ______________________________	SCORE
Knowledge of individual worker abilities and potential.	( )
Ability to instruct employees in the correct methods/procedures for performing maintenance/ service tasks by demonstrating, coaching and providing feedback on their performance.	( )
Ability to estimate the maintenance work load in relation to equipment used, products, operations and production schedule.	( )
Knowledge of the production schedule and needs of the plant for establishing maintenance priorities.	( )
Ability to plan and schedule a preventative maintenance program to mesh with ongoing maintenance activity.	( )
Total =	________
[× 1/5] =	________

Job Requirement Rating Scale

0–2	2–4	4–6	6–8	8–10
There is clear and convincing evidence that the applicant does not possess the characteristic. The applicant is uniformly considered inferior with respect to other applicants on this requirement.	The evidence suggests that the applicant does not possess enough of the requirement to perform the job adequately.	The evidence is mixed. There are indications that the applicant possesses the characteristic; however, the evidence does not indicate superiority, merely presence.	The evidence clearly supports a judgment that the applicant possesses the characteristic to an adequate extent to meet the job demands. There is also evidence of factors which may limit the applicant.	There is clear and convincing evidence that the applicant possesses the characteristic and is uniformly judged superior in the absolute sense; equal to the hypothetical ideal employee for this job.

0 1 2 3 4 5 6 7 8 9 10

Figure 3–6 EXAMPLE OF A STRUCTURED, SCORABLE JOB-RELATED INTERVIEW FORMAT

ACTIVITIES

Activity 3–1

OVERSEAS HUMAN RESOURCES, INC.

Step 1: Read Overseas Human Resources, Inc.

Step 2: Prepare the case for class discussion.

In November of 1976, Takanobu Otani, an MBA student at the University of Michigan, approached a classmate about a business idea he wanted to pursue after graduation. He wanted to open an English school in Japan and he offered to pay all his friend's expenses if he'd come and be the school's first instructor. "Come for 6 months. We can travel and eat our way around Japan on weekends and set up the business during the week."

Business ideas which could involve both countries became *the* topic of conversation for months. After 2½ months, the two had considered approximately 30 separate businesses. The central premise for each was "it works in the U.S., will it work in Japan?" or vice versa. The businesses needed to be labor/service intensive since initial capital would be limited.

The two decided to open the English school and release a restaurant guidebook/couponbook in Osaka. They accepted 2 more partners (one who would supply only labor, one only capital) before graduation. When school ended, Tak returned to Japan, incorporated the business, set up an office and collected information on Osaka English schools. Steve Milgrom, his MBA partner, collected information on how guidebooks in the U.S. operated.

When Milgrom arrived, Otani and Matsumoto began to visit restaurants for Check and Check (the guidebook's name), while Milgrom began advertising and promotions for MLC, the English school. It took one month for the 3 of them to work out a successful sales pitch, but finally restaurants began to sign up at a rapid pace. They discovered that 2 other companies had tried to establish a guidebook/couponbook in the past, but couldn't get enough contracts from the restaurants.

PRODUCT

English schools are a business with significant economies of scale because of the high cost and importance of advertising. Still, it shared an office with Check and Check and offered unbelievable quality at low prices. Students sat on leather chairs and couches around a glass table. Classes, which ranged from 90 to 120 minutes, were broken up about midway with free coffee and donuts. Milgrom was a native speaker, had a master's degree, and had an owner's motivation. Revenues grew steadily for the school over the first 4 months with word of mouth bringing in many of the students.

But it was Check and Check which caused the real excitement. The product was better than they could've hoped to expect. They "chose" the better restaurants in the city—188 in the first issue. Over 90% of them had been written up in restaurant guidebooks without a coupon. The book was printed on quality paper and the format was "significantly better" than those found in the U.S. Coupons were valid from Nov. 10, 1977 to Dec. 31, 1978. Towards the end of the collecting period, they had hired another salesman, Doguchi, who had once been both Otani and Matsumoto's sales manager and trainer in the past. Good people were hard for a small company to get and he was looking for a new job.

DISTRIBUTION

The company had 2 primary ideas for distribution. First, they considered using the kiosks (small giftshop/bookstores in the train stations). One thousand kiosks were in the Osaka area. Generally, they sold mass-marketed products, however, and this was not matched well with the high quality image the restaurants would want to convey.

A second possibility involved Playguide, a group of about 40 shops around Osaka which had prime locations in the train stations. They sold tickets to musical and sporting events as well as newspapers, magazines and gift items. Their clientele was generally young, active and had considerable disposable income. A perfect fit.

The Playguides were franchised, however, and each store manager accepted or rejected items individually. The kiosks insisted on a proven track record, at least $100,000 in sales. Neither was feasible.

The company was forced to rely on the English school students for initial distribution. They believed the product was so excellent and inexpensive (2200 Y), though, that word of mouth would be sufficient.

COMPETITION

Two weeks before the actual release of the product, Albrighto JoHo, a company with over $100 million in sales, released a similar product of their own in Osaka. Lifting the idea from OHR, they put out a smallish pamphlet with 30 coupons valid for one month. The first 10,000 copies were given away free and because of their previous relationship with the kiosks, they were able to place the first issue there!

This event was not unexpected. Otani and Milgrom predicted this sort of competition to emerge. They had even predicted Albrighto JoHo as one of the two most likely entrants to the market. It was the speed of the emergence that caught them by surprise. The quality of the pamphlet was so poor, however, that neither restaurant owners nor consumers were satisfied. It also seemed highly probable that the basic concept of a one month coupon book was against FTC rules, and the product was withdrawn from the market.

INVESTMENT AND SALES

The company's fiscal year ran from April 1 to March 31, but neither this nor the calendar year made sense as a time period to measure company performance. The best period was November 10, when a book was issued until November 9 of the following year, before another book was issued.

During the start-up period from June 15, 1977 to November 10, 1977 when the first book was released, $25,000 in start-up costs were incurred. This figure was considered representative for other cities despite many detours and the low salaries which the owners survived on.

From November 10 to March 31, the company sold only 1625 books at $10 apiece. Doguchi, who was hired on a small salary plus commission threatened to quit unless his salary was raised. The company granted the raise, despite being near insolvency.

With their last remaining funds, a direct mailing was sent to the 1625 members. The members were offered gifts for signing up 5 or more new members and the cost of the book was dropped from 2200 Y to 1000 Y. The response was immediate. Over the next 3 months, 9000 new members were signed up.

On November 10, 1978, a second book was released. Besides the $25,000 in start-up costs, the company sustained a $5000 loss, and the other 3 workers lived on very minimal salaries. Another friend who had just graduated from the University of Michigan with an engineering degree was hired. Just before the release, a mailing was done to the 11,000 Check and Check members. Again, the company was totally out of funds and hadn't paid for the printing of the new book (× $25,000), but optimism was rampant. This would be the breakthrough year.

From Nov. 10, 1978 to Dec. 31, 1978, 5000 books were sold at $10 apiece. Sales for the year were estimated at 15,000 books, enough to wipe out the first year's loss, pay the workers well and cover at least $15,000 of the start-up costs. And the market potential was estimated at *over* 100,000 books/year in Osaka alone.

Otani and Milgrom never doubted this ultimate success, indeed expansion plans were drawn up in that first summer. They planned to introduce Check and Check in 10 cities in Japan, each having populations over 1,000,000. In March, they planned to expand to Kobe, letting Doguchi and Nori, the employees, handle sales there.

But while the owners were satisfied, the employees were not. Their salaries were just now in line with what they might expect to make in other jobs. They had no guarantee of lifetime employment and for them the future was uncertain. During holiday periods, when their families got together, they could not truly take pride in their positions. If they were "in on the ground floor" and were to grow with the company, they wanted the company to grow swiftly.

Indeed, the issues of controlled growth, employee satisfaction, and the source of future personnel were the major concerns of the owners. They wanted to grow quickly so as to be first into the 10 major Japanese cities, but they wanted to ensure OHR's survival too. Investors wouldn't recognize the potential of the company, so they believed that outside financing would be too expensive. Finally, since they needed salesmen at least 25 years old, they couldn't find men with strong management potential unless they hired students directly out of college and trained them for a few years.

The first meeting of the board of directors was scheduled for May. Each director began to consider solutions to these problems. Their dreams were dependent on them.

Step 3: Individually, in small groups, or with the entire class, as directed by your instructor, answer the questions below.

1. What features describe the environmental and organizational context faced by OHR?
2. What types of employees will OHR need in the next year? Three years? Five years?
3. What are the most appropriate sources of these employees?
4. What are the best methods to tap these sources?
5. What roles should human resources professionals play in meeting employment needs?
6. What roles should managers play in meeting employment needs?
7. What recommendations would you offer for the contents and implementation of a recruitment system?

Activity 3–2

LONGVILLE UNIVERSITY

Step 1: Read the following scenario.

Longville University has 20,000 full and part-time graduate students, 800 faculty, and 800 support staff. The university operates in a suburb of a large metropolitan city. It includes a business school, law school, medical school, college of arts and sciences, education school, and nursing school.

You recently received a degree in business and have been hired to assist the Dean of the School of Management. This school has experienced significant increases in student and faculty numbers in recent years in comparison to most other schools (with the exception of the law and medical schools) in the university. Previously all recruitment for faculty and staff positions in the School of Management had been done by the personnel office. However, because of the rapidly increasing size and some unique needs of the school, the dean has received permission to oversee the recruiting effort more directly.

As one of your first projects the dean has requested that you develop a recruitment plan for the School of Management that can be implemented immediately and that also can direct the recruitment effort for the next five to seven years. The following types of employees must be recruited: junior faculty for all departments, a few senior faculty members for key positions, secretarial staff for all departments and the deans' offices, and assistants for the computer lab which is located in the School of Management.

Step 2: Individually or in small groups as directed by your instructor, design a recruitment plan for the School of Management. The plan should include a diagnosis of the recruitment situation faced by the School of Management, options for tapping into various sources of recruits, provisions for maintaining an ongoing recruitment system, consideration of computerization of the system, and estimates of costs.

Step 3: In small groups or with the class as a whole share your designs. Formulate a master plan that integrates the elements of various recruitment plans.

Step 4: Discussion. With the class as a whole, address the following:

1. Diagnose the situation faced by the School of Management.
2. Design a recruitment plan.
3. Describe the issues involved in implementing the plan.

Activity 3–3

MEDIA CAMPAIGN

Step 1: Read the following scenario.

Kelso-McGrath, a large manufacturer of computer terminals, has grown approximately 30% in each of the last two years, and top management expects this rate of growth to continue. The company has experienced particularly high turnover among its engineers. These professionals fall into the following categories:

Software—develops prototypes and complex simulations for new hardware using C-language; interfaces artificial intelligence with advanced hardware technology
Design—performs the physical design and documentation of new products
Manufacturing—provides product support, including suggesting and implementing design and procedure modifications to improve the manufacturability and reliability of the product
Quality control—provides technical support for quality assessment of hardware; designs and implements quality assurance programs
Hardware—revises designs in response to comments from test sites; interacts with designers and users.

Step 2: Plan a media campaign for recruiting the approximately 400 engineers needed in the next two years. You expect that the demand for engineers will be equally divided in the five areas named above. Be sure to write any advertisements or other copy you plan to use. Include a schedule and budget for the campaign.

Step 3: In small groups or with the entire class, share your media campaigns.

For each campaign, answer the following questions:

1. What advantages and limitations does the plan have?
2. Will the campaign succeed in recruiting the needed candidates?
3. What will each recruit cost?
4. What changes should be made in the campaign to increase its effectiveness?
5. What roles should human resources professionals and managers play in the campaign?

Activity 3–4

THE EMPLOYMENT INTERVIEW

Step 1: Two members from the class are selected, one to play the role of Lee Elkins, the manager who conducts the employment interview, and the other the role of Mickey McCabe, the employee interviewed. All other members act as observers.

Step 2: All participants read the general instructions. The two participants should become familiar with their own roles. Both should play their parts without referring to their role sheets. All observers should read their roles and may read the roles of the two participants.

THE SITUATION

It is February 15th and Mickey McCabe has just applied for the new marketing research position in the marketing department of a computer software firm. The firm is three years old, but has tripled in size to approximately one hundred professionals and fifty support staff. Top management has previously directed the head of marketing to use an outside firm for all market research projects. Recently, however, the costs of this approach have escalated significantly and the responsiveness of the contractor has decreased. Management has decided to bring the market research function in-house. As one of the original employees of the marketing department, Lee Elkins has been asked to do some recruiting for the position. This recruiting has involved a significant number of interviews with potential candidates inside and outside the organization.

Step 3: The Role Play

1. When everyone is ready, Lee Elkins enters the office and sits at the desk. A moment later, Mickey McCabe enters the office and the scene begins.
2. The amount of time needed to complete the interview will vary, but twenty minutes is usually adequate. The interview is carried to the point of completion.

Step 4: Discussion. In small groups or with the entire class, answer the following:

1. Briefly summarize the main events of the meeting.
2. Describe the effectiveness of the interviewer.
3. Describe the effectiveness of the interviewee.
4. Were any biases evident in the meeting?

VARIATIONS

1. One or two new pairs of participants can role-play in order to permit comparison of different interview styles and their outcomes.
2. The two participants can exchange roles and role-play the case again.
3. The class is divided into small groups, each of which prepares one of the roles, and then representatives are chosen to role-play in front of the class.

INSTRUCTIONS FOR OBSERVERS

1. Observe the manner in which Elkins began the meeting.
   a. What kind of atmosphere was created?
   b. What types of verbal and nonverbal communication were used?
   c. Were the purpose and agenda stated clearly and concisely?
2. Observe how the interview was conducted.
   a. To what extent did the interviewer give a realistic job preview?
   b. Did the interviewer move from broad general questions to more specific ones or the reverse?
3. Evaluate the outcomes of the interview.
   a. Did the interviewer learn a sufficient amount about the interviewee?
   b. Did the interviewee learn a sufficient amount about the job?
   c. Did the interview accomplish the goals of the participants?
4. How could the interview have been conducted differently?

Activity 3–5

SUPREME STORES

Step 1: Read the following scenario.

Supreme Stores is a regional organization that has recently opened ten branch stores in Georgia and Florida. Although the organization has been growing, the public's view of it remains skeptical. It has been rumored to have major labor-management problems, although no hard evidence of these problems exists. It has also been rumored to have expanded too rapidly, and some people say that the company will bankrupt itself if it does not improve its controls and management talent. The recently hired president is known in the industry as being a tough, hard-line manager who is concerned more with the bottom line than with the people who work for Supreme Stores.

The company has recently decentralized its recruiting effort. You are the manager of one of the newest and largest stores in the chain. You must hire three bookkeepers who can interface with the organization's computerized information system, two buyers of special merchandise that only your store sells, three department heads, and twenty sales clerks.

Step 2: You must design a recruitment campaign for your store. In designing this campaign, you should consider incorporating the following activities:

1. Perform environmental, organizational, job, and individual analyses for each position.
2. Identify the recruitment criteria for each position.
3. Identify possible sources of recruits for each job.
4. Determine the costs of each source.
5. Finalize a set of recruitment activities, a timetable, and costs to present to top management.

Step 3: Discussion. Share your plans with the rest of the class. What similarities and differences are there in the plans? What are the advantages and disadvantages of each plan?

Activity 3–6

EUCLID AIRCRAFT PRODUCTS

Step 1: Read the Euclid Aircraft Products case.

Step 2: Prepare the case for class discussion.

The Apco Plant of the Euclid Aircraft Products Company manufactures a wide assortment of precision jet engine parts, used in both commercial and military aircraft. Apco is a high volume production facility operating on a three shift basis and employing 7000 people. Although five autonomous manufacturing divisions share the plant, certain housekeeping and operating support functions are centralized in a Plant General Group. One such function is the Tool Control Department, which orders, maintains inventories and dispenses several thousand machine tool parts, such as drill bits, cutting tools, dies and fixtures through its central tool room.

Precision tooling is a major cost item in the plant, and inventories are carefully controlled to balance between minimum stocking and effectively meeting the day-to-day requirements for tooling of the manufacturing divisions. For several years, the tool inventory control has been done manually by a section of seven clerks, five men and two women, located in a small office in the center of the factory area.

Reprinted with permission of the author, John W. Lewis III, Boston College School of Management.

Three of the men had previously held production jobs, while the rest had been hired into their present positions. Their ages were between 41 and 63 years old, and length of company service ranged from 12 to 23 years.

In 1958, a Business Systems Department had been organized within the Plant Comptroller's Office, and Max Wilder appointed as its manager. Its purpose was to analyze systems and procedures in use for operational planning and control, especially those information systems which could be more efficiently performed by the Company's computer. In addition to providing systems support to the plant accounting and financial staff departments, Business Systems analysts responded to requests for their services from executives in the operating divisions. Costs for such "consulting" services were charged to the requesting unit.

If a preliminary investigation of a request warranted, a feasibility study of an activity was undertaken to ascertain its adaptability to automation at a reasonable cost. Where favorable results were obtained and a joint decision between Business Systems and the operating units was made to proceed with the project, systems analysts aided by programmers developed the necessary computer "software," and also the procedures for effecting a changeover to the new system. Business systems then worked directly with the group where the system was being installed, and retained project responsibility until the changeover was completed and the computer system fully operational.

In the Fall of 1961, Ed Heartstone, the Director of Plant General became concerned over an alarming rise in tool inventory costs. The problem stemmed in part from a rapidly changing mix of products that required novel tooling with corresponding obsolescence of a large percentage of existing tooling inventories. The manual system of tool inventory control appeared unable to respond to the shifting demands placed on it, even though personnel in this section were regarded as both diligent and competent. Heartstone asked the Business Systems Department to study the operation for possible conversion to a computerized system, and alerted the supervisor of the inventory control section to provide necessary assistance.

A feasibility study produced positive results, and it was estimated by Business Systems that the changeover from the manual to computerized system would require approximately three months. Based on a promise of substantially improved inventory control efficiency and major long term cost savings, and with concurrence from top management, Heartstone made a decision to go ahead with the project. Wilder said he had the resources to begin the project immediately.

Tom Flasher, systems analyst, was assigned as the project leader to work with the supervisor and members of the inventory control section to install the new system. The analyst was young and while he had no prior experience in manufacturing operations, he had impressed upper management on a recent system design project in the accounting area. The tool inventory effort was the largest project Flasher had undertaken to date, and an important step for Business Systems in demonstrating its line support capability to operating divisions.

In his initial meeting with the inventory controllers, Flasher received a somewhat cool reception from most of them, but assumed this stemmed from a normal human resistance to change and mistrust of the computer. He was confident that as the project progressed and people began to see positive results, their attitudes would change. Since service to the plant could not be disrupted, the manual system was to be maintained throughout the changeover.

During the first full month of the project things went relatively smooth, with inventory controllers cooperating so that two major milestones in the changeover were achieved on schedule. Both the Plant General Director and the Business Systems manager were pleased with the progress and began preliminary discussions regarding an even larger systems analysis effort upon completion of this one. Wilder decided to promote Tom Flasher to a senior systems analyst and gave him a significant salary increase sixty days before it had been scheduled.

In the next month, however, the project moved more slowly as minor problems and "bugs" developed in the computer program, which forced delays in achieving a key milestone. To recover valuable lost time, and to get the inventory project back on schedule, a second systems analyst was taken off a financial planning program and transferred to the changeover effect.

During the third month, the project lagged still further, even with the additional specialist, and the use of substantial overtime, costs which had not been anticipated earlier. Wilder was forced to extend the completion date another sixty days, a fact which angered the Director of Plant General, who was beginning to receive strong complaints from manufacturing divisions because of poor service from the Tool Control department. One major production operation of a government contract had to be shut down for ten days due to a shortage of special tooling, which had been ordered late by inventory controllers.

The next two months saw the project bog down completely. Tempers flared on all sides. Though the problems encountered appeared to be minor ones, Flasher was heard to say at one point: "it seems that as fast as I solve one problem, two more bugs crop up to plague me." An important trial effort to run the inventory on the computer using the new system produced information outputs which the inventory control supervisor called "garbage." Due to mounting pressure from operating divisions, Heartstone ordered inventory control section to concentrate full-time with the manual system to restore effective service to the plant. He sent a memo to Wilder in which he asked him to "take your socalled system back to the drawing board until you can clearly demonstrate its workability."

In this period, relationships between Business Systems and the inventory control section deteriorated, and both the comptroller and the Plant Services Director were drawn into the dispute. Inventory control personnel were accused by Wilder and Flasher of sabotaging the new system, and they in turn countered with claims that the systems group was incompetent and vindictive.

Seven months after the project had been initiated, the tool inventory control changeover had not been completed, and no wrapup date was in sight. The vice president of the plant intervened when the director of Plant General refused to accept interdepartmental changes for programming and support services from the Business Systems department.

Step 3: Individually, in small groups, or in written form, answer the following questions:

1. What features describe the environmental and organizational context at Euclid Aircraft?
2. Comment about the staffing of the computerization program.
3. Should more systematic recruitment have occurred?
4. What are the best sources of new workers for the Tool Control department?
5. What are the best methods to tap these sources?
6. What recommendations would you offer for introducing a systematic recruitment system?

SUMMARY

Recruitment refers to the gathering of a pool of applicants who can fill a given position. Although recruitment is very common in organizations, the process frequently lacks systematic identification of recruitment criteria, comparison and evaluation of sources of recruits and methods of tapping them, or determination of the cost-effectiveness of them. In this chapter we have examined a systematic approach to recruitment. In the cases of Overseas Human Resources, Inc., and Euclid Aircraft Products you have proposed a recruitment plan. In the situations of Longville University, the Media Campaign, and Supreme Stores you have designed a variety of recruitment strategies.

Human resources professionals and managers increasingly support a marketing approach to recruitment.[30] They view the goal of recruitment as getting the best-qualified candidates, not filling vacancies quickly. They value creativity in recruitment: new sources and methods are developed. Recruitment has a long-term rather than a short-term orientation; human resources professionals and managers try to build a pool of recruits from which they can draw over a year or two and for numerous positions. A marketing approach also focuses recruitment on creating a company identity in advertising and recruiting, rather than merely listing openings. Finally, advertisements serve a sales function, like product advertising, rather than a listing of job requirements.

Managers and human resources professionals must act in partnership for effective recruitment. In addition to tapping sources of workers, recruitment activities include improving and elaborating an existing recruitment system by revising the recruiting plan; revising systems and policies; thinking of creative recruiting strategies; providing training for managers in recruiting and interviewing; developing recruiting standards; designing and gathering a candidate data base; making links with outside recruiters; conducting salary surveys; and improving public relations.[31]

ENDNOTES

[1]T.J. Bergmann and M.S. Taylor, College recruitment: What attracts students to organizations, *Personnel* 61 (May-June 1984): 34–46.

[2]*Ibid.*

[3]E.S. Stanton, *Successful Personnel Recruiting and Selection* (New York: AMACOM, 1977).

[4]H.Z. Levine, Consensus, *Personnel* 61 (January-February 1984): 4–10.

[5]T.L. Friedman, The baby boom comes of age: And finds executive suites as full as kindergartens and colleges were, *New York Times,* 19 January 1982, p. 18.

[6]Bergmann and Taylor, *op. cit.*

[7]L.S. Kleiman and K.J. Clark, An effective job posting system, *Personnel Journal* 63 (February 1984): 20–25; R.B. Crimmins, Miles' Laboratories, Inc. creates a job posting program, *Personnel Administrator* 28 (November 1983): 41–45.

[8]R. Stoops, Employee referral programs, *Personnel Journal* 62 (September 1983): 690–692.

[9]*Ibid.*

[10]M.J. Gannon, Sources of referral and employee turnover, *Journal of Applied Psychology* 55 (1971): 226–228.

[11]Bergmann and Taylor, *op. cit.*

[12]Bergmann and Taylor, *op. cit.*

[13]See *The Boston Sunday Globe,* 26 February 1984 for examples.

[14]*DS&E Recruitment Manual 1976–1977* (New York: Deutsch, Shea & Evans, Inc., 1976), cited in E.S. Stanton, *op. cit.*

[15]*Ibid.*

[16]R. Stoops, Direct mail: Luring the isolated professionals, *Personnel Journal* 63 (June 1984): 34–35.

[17]D. Bushness, "Headhunting" a competitive game, *Boston Globe,* 14 January 1985, p. 34.

[18]*Ibid.*

[19]T.C. Amory, Searching for a search firm, *Personnel Journal* 62 (February 1983): 114–116.

[20]R. Stoops, Recruitment in banking, *Personnel Journal* 62 (July 1983).

[21]Stanton, *op. cit.*

[22]N. Schmitt and B.W. Coyle, Applicant decisions in the employment interview, *Journal of Applied Psychology* 61 (1976): 184–192; Alderfer and McCord, Personal and situational factors in the recruitment interview, *Journal of Applied Psychology* 54 (1972): 377–385.

[23]C.P. Alderfer and C.G. McCord, *op. cit.*

[24]Schmitt, *op. cit.*; H.C. Osburn and S.W. Constantin, The selection interview: Some issues raised by research on decision making, unpublished manuscript cited in J.P. Wanous, *Organizational Entry: Recruitment, Selection, and Socialization of Newcomers* (Reading, Mass.: Addison-Wesley, 1980).

[25]*Ibid.*

[26]J.P. Wanous, Effects of a realistic job preview on job acceptance, job attitudes, and job survival, *Journal of Applied Psychology* 58 (1973): 327–332; J.P. Wanous, A job preview makes recruiting more effective, *Harvard Business Review* 53 (1975): 16; J.P. Wanous, Tell it like it is at realistic job previews, *Personnel* 52 (1975): 50–60.

[27]These programs are described in Wanous, *Harvard Business Review* (1975), *op cit.*; C.F. Youngberg, An experimental study of job satisfaction and turnover in relation to job expectations and self-expectations, Unpublished doctoral dissertation, New York University, 1963; Wanous, 1980, *op cit.*; T.J. Marchese, *Barat—A Prospectus, 1976–1977* (Lake Forest, Ill.: Barat College, 1976), respectively.

[28]Wanous, 1980, *op. cit.*

[29]Wanous, 1980, *op. cit.*

[30]R. Stoops, Reading survey supports market approaches to recruitment, *Personnel Journal* 63 (March 1984): 22–24.

[31]R. Roberts, What the recruiting department should do when it's not recruiting, *Personnel Journal* 62 (January 1983).

FURTHER READINGS

Arvey, R.D. *Fairness in Selecting Employees.* Reading, Mass.: Addison-Wesley, 1979.

Conarroe, R.R. *Executive Search: A Guide for Recruiting Outstanding Executives.* New York: Van Nostrand Reinhold, 1976.

Dreher, G.F., and Sackett, P.R. *Perspectives on Employee*

Staffing and Selection: Readings and Commentary. Homewood, Ill.: Irwin, 1983.

McCulloch, K.J. *Selecting Employees Safely Under the Law.* Englewood Cliffs, N.J.: Prentice-Hall, 1981.

Robertson, J. *How to Win in a Job Interview.* Englewood Cliffs, N.J.: Prentice-Hall, 1978.

Ryckman, W.G. *How to Pass the Employment Interview with Flying Colors.* Homewood, Ill.: Dow Jones–Irwin, 1982.

Schneider, B. *Staffing Organizations.* Glenview, Ill.: Scott, Foresman, 1976,

Wanous, J.P. *Organizational Entry: Recruitment, Selection, and Socialization of Newcomers.* Reading, Mass: Addison-Wesley, 1980.

CHAPTER 4

Specifying Selection Procedures

CHAPTER OUTLINE

LEARNING CHECKPOINTS

After completing the reading and activities in this chapter, students will be able to

- differentiate between selection and recruitment;
- list the steps in the selection process;
- show the significance of job analysis to selection;
- develop selection criteria for a given job;
- discuss the advantages and disadvantages of instruments and techniques used in selection;
- discuss the meaning and determination of reliability and validity for selection instruments and techniques;
- conduct an effective selection interview;
- evaluate the effectiveness of a selection system.

INTRODUCTION

The West Suburban Bank has been experiencing high turnover among its tellers since top management redefined the role. Now a teller processes transactions, performs all aspects of customer service, and sells the bank's services. West Suburban will have thirty openings for tellers during the next six months. Managers have the responsibility for hiring tellers for their own branches.

Jamie Boyce is the branch manager of West Suburban's oldest branch. Like the work force in other branches, hers has been relatively unstable. The location of the branch is very desirable; the pay and benefits are in line with those offered for comparable jobs; flexible hours are available; and Jamie and her two predecessors are considered effective and compassionate managers. The bank has spent large sums of money to train individuals for the new teller positions, but with little visible payback.

Jamie's branch has one of the highest turnover rates and poorest performance records in the bank. Jamie thinks she has not selected the best individuals for the new teller position.

Is ineffective selection causing the problems in Jamie's branch? Given the branch's efforts in training, compensation, and supervision, poor selection is a likely explanation.

This chapter offers a framework for evaluating and improving the selection of employees. We begin with an overview of the steps in selection. Then we consider the development of criteria for selecting employees. Next we focus on the effective choice and use of instruments and techniques in selection; we examine the use of application blanks, resumes, standardized and nonstandardized tests, assessment centers, and interviews. Then we discuss the procedure for the final selection of an employee. We conclude the chapter by looking at the interaction of human resources professionals and managers in the selection process.

STEPS IN EMPLOYEE SELECTION

How can organizations and managers systematically select employees to fill vacant positions? How should West Suburban Bank select employees for the new teller job?

Selection refers to the choice of an individual from a pool of candidates to fill an available position. It follows recruitment. Effective selection should include the following steps: (1) job analysis; (2) development of selection criteria; (3) choice of instruments or techniques to measure the selection criteria; (4) collection of data about candidates; and (5) analysis of data to identify the preferred candidate for the job.

The *first* step in selection requires the manager to complete a job analysis. Using the job description and job specifications, the human resources professional or manager can identify the characteristics the job holder should possess.

At West Suburban, the job description has recently changed. Thus the selection process must identify individuals who will perform well in the *new* teller job—they must be able to sell services as well as process transactions.

Second, based on the job analysis, the manager should specify the criteria for evaluating applicants for the vacant position. Selection criteria are characteristics derived from the job description and specifications. We would expect an applicant with these characteristics to perform well on the job and remain with the organization. For example, the criteria for the new teller position might include sales experience, knowledge of bank services, high motivation, and aggressiveness. Tracking high performers who remain with the organization and determining how they differ from low performers who leave the organization forms the basis for formulating the selection criteria.

Managers and human resources professionals might jointly specify the selection criteria. For example, the professionals could help the managers analyze the characteristics that distinguish high from low performers by systematically studying the correlates of performance and turnover. Human resources professionals could also act as a sounding board to ensure that managers pick complete, measurable, and appropriate criteria.

After specifying the selection criteria, the *third* step occurs: the choice of instruments or techniques for use in evaluating the criteria. Managers generally rely on interviews to assess the applicants' qualifications. Using a single source of data, however, limits the information on which managers base hiring decisions. They should consider using other instruments or techniques, including tests or assessment centers, to gather data about the selection criteria.

Both human resources professionals and managers should participate in the *fourth* step, data collection about job candidates using the instruments and techniques selected in step 3. The responsibility can be divided in a variety of ways. For example, a human resources professional could supervise the administration of instruments that require special expertise, such as certain standardized tests or assessment centers. The manager could collect data using less sophisticated methods, such as reviewing application blanks and resumes or conducting interviews. Alternatively, a human resources professional could do the initial screening of applicants using tests, application blanks, or resumes to reduce the pool. The manager could then gather data, primarily through interviews, from a greatly reduced pool. In either scenario, the manager should have the final responsibility for filling job vacancies; the human resources professional should oversee selection organization-wide to ensure that consistent procedures are used.

Fifth, the manager should analyze the data and rank the candidates. Typically the manager offers the job to the highest rated applicant.

Any selection process should include these five steps. In the next section we discuss each of them in greater detail.

DEVELOPING THE SELECTION CRITERIA

The ability to specify selection criteria derives from the thoroughness of the job analysis[1] as well as the precision and completeness of the listing of criteria.

The Job Analysis

Updating of the job description and specifications occurs as part of recruitment and precedes listing of the selection criteria. For the new teller position, for example, the job description might call for the job holder to (1) process all cash, checking, and savings transactions; (2) balance cash and transactions daily; (3) interact with customers in a positive and enthusiastic manner; (4) issue bank checks and money orders; (5) refer customers to appropriate departments for special problems and transactions; and (6) sell additional bank services, such as IRAs and money market accounts, directly to customers. What should selection criteria be for this position? What characteristics would correlate with high performance and low turnover? What conclusions would emerge from a systematic study of performance and turnover?

Listing the Selection Criteria

To help specify selection criteria a manager or human resources professional can identify the characteristics, experiences, or abilities that best predict high performance in the job. For the new teller's job, for example, basic competency in algebra might predict performance less well than the ability to cash a check correctly according to bank procedures; the ability to describe all services offered by the bank may predict performance better than the ability to repeat the bank's philosophy. Based on the job analysis, the following list includes some possible selection criteria for the new teller position:

- Ability to perform basic mathematical functions
- Facility with computerized operations
- Effective interpersonal skills
- Ability to deal with details
- Aggressiveness
- Knowledge of sales techniques
- Sales experience
- Skill in implementing sales techniques
- Knowledge of bank products and services

For each job to be filled, the manager should check that each criterion is job-related, observable, and measurable.[2] Figure 4–1 provides examples of such criteria for four different jobs.

Is the development of criteria always straightforward? Identifying the selection criteria for more complex jobs, such as middle-level or top executives, can be

Salesperson
2–4 years' experience in selling
knowledge of product market

Assembler of Circuit Boards
higher than average manual dexterity
punctuality and reliability

Finance Manager
knowledge of state-of-the-art financial management principles
higher than average intelligence
2–4 years' experience in a finance function

Custodian in Defense Installation
security clearance
previous experience in sensitive work areas

Figure 4–1 EXAMPLES OF JOB-RELATED, OBSERVABLE, AND MEASURABLE CRITERIA

difficult. Ideally a board of directors or the managers responsible for hiring these employees should develop a detailed and concrete set of criteria on which to base selection decisions, but in reality the criteria used may be more limited and general. Or those hiring executives may rely on only a few criteria, such as "track record" or experience, and base the final decision on their intuitive feel for the candidate's likely success. In part their failure to completely specify selection criteria may be a function of difficulty in defining success in these high-level positions. In spite of these difficulties all organizational members who make hiring decisions should specify the criteria as concretely as possible.

IDENTIFYING APPROPRIATE INSTRUMENTS AND MEASUREMENT TECHNIQUES

What types of instruments or techniques could be used to assess the criteria listed above for the position of teller? Answers might be a mathematics test, a personality test, other aptitude and ability tests, recommendations from a previous employer, or interviews. Such instruments and techniques represent the diverse ways of assessing selection criteria. In this section we first examine the factors that influence the choice of appropriate instruments or measuring techniques. Then we review (1) application blanks, (2) resumes, (3) standardized tests, (4) non-standardized tests, (5) assessment centers, and (6) interviews.

Criteria for Selecting Instruments or Measurement Techniques

How do you accurately measure a candidate's interpersonal skills? Knowledge of sales techniques? Loyalty and commitment? The choice of an instrument or technique should consider its (1) validity, (2) reliability, (3) cost, and (4) ease of administration.[3]

Validity. Validity refers, at one level, to the extent to which an instrument measures what it intends to measure.[4] For example, a resume or an application blank validly measures previous jobs held by a candidate. A typing test validly measures a typist's speed and error rate. But the validity of a technique is not always so clear. For example, does a resume validly measure management skills? Does a mechanical aptitude test validly measure a welder's skill? At a second level, validity refers to the correlation between an assessment procedure, such as a standardized test, and criterion data, such as performance or turnover.[5] In selecting an instrument for this type of validity the human resources professional or manager must try to pick one that accurately predicts scores on a given criterion.

One can assess three kinds of validity: (1) content validity, (2) criterion-related validity, and (3) construct validity.[6] Often intuitive guesses are used because of the expense of performing more sophisticated validity studies. The human resources professional should attempt to secure an accurate estimate of validity of an instrument or technique he or she plans to use or recommend for a manager's use.

Content validity refers to the extent to which the content of an instrument reflects the criterion it measures.[7] Also known as judgmental validity, content validity uses individual judgments to estimate the relevance of an assessment instrument or technique to specific criteria.[8] Content or judgmental validity, then, is the degree to which a test, other instrument, or technique adequately represents the job component being measured.[9]

The content of a typing test validly measures the range of skills and knowledge required to perform effectively in a typing position. An on-the-job test that requires a welder to merge two pieces of pipe validly, but only partially, measures a welder's performance as a pipe fitter. Such instruments have high content validity. In contrast, the tasks completed for an intelligence test differ from the activities of a managerial job; thus they do not reflect the key components of managerial performance. Likewise, the questions asked on a personality test differ from the activities associated with a salesperson's job, so such instruments most likely have a relatively low content validity for this job.

Criterion-related validity refers to the "extent to which scores on one variable, usually a predictor, may be used to infer performance on a different and operationally independent variable called a criterion. For convenience we often speak of criterion-related validities in terms of correlation coefficients, but the statistic has nothing to do with the definition."[10] For example, intelligence tests have been shown to correlate highly with measures of managerial performance.[11] Interviewers' ratings of candidates have been positively associated with the candidates' ultimate performance on the job.[12] Such instruments may or may not have high content validity, but they do have relatively high criterion-related validity. Instruments such as typing tests have both high content validity and high criterion-related validity.

We can assess two types of criterion-related validity: (1) concurrent validity and (2) predictive validity.[13] Concurrent validity is determined when the predictor (assessment instruments and techniques) and criterion data are collected at the same time on present employees. This establishes the validity of an instrument for present employees at the present time, but does not indicate validity for predicting future performance. Predictive validity is determined when the criterion data are obtained at a later time than the assessment data.

We can assess criterion-related validity by evaluating the degree to which individuals' scores on an instrument are positively associated with their performance in a job. Table 4–1 gives examples of the scores of job candidates on two sets of instruments as well as their performance ratings in their jobs. The order of their scores on instrument A parallels the order of their performance ratings more closely than does the order of their scores on instrument B. Thus instrument A has a higher criterion-related validity than does instrument B.

Human resources professionals or managers who attempt to assess criterion-related validity must carefully choose the measure of successful performance. For example, success for a manager might be reflected in the department's costs per year, revenues per year, or his or her supervisor's ratings of performance. Test scores or interviewer ratings may correlate differently with each of these measures and yield varying estimates of validity, confusing the issue of whether the instrument has validity for measuring performance. To determine the criterion-related validity of an instrument, a human resources professional or a manager must (1) identify the selection instruments or techniques and criterion of success and (2) correlate the scores on the instrument and on the success criterion for individuals holding similar jobs.[14]

Construct validity is concerned with the "psychological qualities a test measures"; it is evaluated by "demonstrating that certain explanatory constructs account to some degree for performance on the test."[15] This type of validity is "especially useful with reference to tasks measuring traits for which external criteria are not available."[16]

Although construct validity produces no single coefficient, its weight of evidence contributes to judgments that determine the extent of validity. Construct validity can be assessed by (1) determining if groups that should differ in theory—on certain personality constructs, for example—actually receive different test scores;

Candidate Number	Score on Test A	Score on Test B	Performance Rating
1	99	79	10
2	95	83	10
3	95	62	9
4	88	37	8
5	79	48	6
6	70	68	6
7	56	95	5
8	56	80	4
9	50	67	2
10	30	67	2

Table 4–1 EVALUATION OF PREDICTIVE VALIDITY

(2) seeing whether changes in the individual or environment result in predictable changes in test scores; (3) assessing the correlation between different tests that are assumed to measure the same variable; and (4) testing for a high correlation between single items, or different parts of the test, and the total test score.[17] A test is considered accurate to measure the trait of personability or aggressiveness if two groups considered to differ on these traits receive significantly different scores on the test. In practice, not only must such tests adequately measure construct validity, but the construct must be job-related for the test to be legally acceptable.

Reliability. A reliable instrument gives consistent results in measuring a behavior or attitude. If an aptitude test is administered to the same person twice within a twenty-four hour period, a highly reliable instrument would yield the same or very similar scores both times; a relatively unreliable instrument would yield very different scores. If two managers rate a subordinate's performance using an observation schedule, for example, a highly reliable scale would yield the same or similar ratings.

A manager or human resources professional should choose instruments that have the following types of reliability:

1. *Test-retest* reliability—the instrument or technique gives the same results when administered repeatedly to the same person. For example, if a person takes the same aptitude test twice during the week and receives the same score, the test-retest reliability is high.
2. *Inter-rater* reliability—the instrument or technique gives the same results when used by two or more different raters. For example, if two managers interview the same candidate and evaluate the candidate similarly, the interview has high inter-rater reliability.
3. *Intra-rater* reliability—the instrument or technique gives the same results when repeatedly used by the same rater to rate the same behaviors or attitudes at different times. For example, if a manager observes identical behavior on the job and assigns the same performance rating on a performance appraisal form, the form has intra-rater reliability.

Reliability coefficients differ from validity coefficients. A test may have high reliability (for example, repeated administrations yield the same results or scores), but have low validity (the test score does not correlate with performance ratings, or the test does not reflect job behaviors or job constructs). Alternatively, an instrument or technique may have high reliability and high validity, or low reliability and low validity.

Cost. Why would a manager not choose the most reliable or most valid instrument for measuring a behavior or attitude? A highly reliable and valid test may have a high purchase price. Or the time needed to create highly reliable and valid measures may be too great.

Too often human resources professionals or managers overlook the cost involved in administering certain instruments. For example, managers routinely use interviews for screening relatively large numbers of prospective employees. But interviews often have relatively low reliability and validity, and the time involved in interviewing a number of candidates can be very expensive.

Ease of Administration. This relates closely to the amount of time involved in administration, as well as the expertise required to administer an instrument. Many managers find standardized tests and rating scales easy to administer, but interviews more difficult. Other tests, such as the Thematic Apperception Test or the Rorschach Inkblot Test, require the administrator to have specialized knowledge which few human resources professionals and even fewer managers have.[18]

The instruments and techniques described in the next section vary significantly on these four characteristics—validity, reliability, cost, and ease of administration. Table 4–2 summarizes their strengths and weaknesses.

Instrument/Technique	Strengths	Weaknesses
Application blanks	yield reliable and valid data easy to administer relatively inexpensive	often ask questions that lack job-relatedness cannot assess complex behaviors
Assessment centers	generally yield reliable and valid data for selection, development, and identification of potential	very expensive time-consuming not easy to administer
Interviews	relatively inexpensive commonly used in organizations	time-consuming frequently lack reliability and validity
Resumes	yield reliable and valid data easy to administer relatively inexpensive	cannot assess complex behaviors
Specially designed tests	may have high validity often easy to administer	often lack reliability and validity data expensive to develop
Standardized tests	generally have high reliability and validity for a specific population often easy to administer	may not be appropriate for group of candidates expensive to purchase may require special skill to administer

Table 4–2 **STRENGTHS AND WEAKNESSES OF SELECTION INSTRUMENTS AND TECHNIQUES**

Evaluating Application Blanks

Applicants for entry-level jobs often complete application blanks as the first step in the selection process. This step is followed in turn by an employment interview (see Chapter 3), placement tests or exercises, a selection interview (as described later in this chapter), and an employment offer.[19]

Figure 4–2 shows a sample application blank. What types of criteria would such an instrument measure? Most would include

- Previous experience at the position
- Extent of supervisory responsibility
- Educational level
- Industry experience
- Leadership responsibilities

For entry-level jobs, the biographical data on application blanks have been known to have validity in predicting job performance (as reflected in supervisor ratings) second only to measures of ability.[20] Care must be taken, however, to ensure that the forms are used to collect data that have direct relevance to job performance. Application blanks often request information such as citizenship, salary history, or place of birth. What criteria do such data measure? How relevant are these criteria?

In evaluating application blanks, managers must consider the information given, the skills shown in the previous jobs held, and the type of thinking reflected by answers to application questions.[21] Managers should check the reasons for leaving previous jobs; educational background, signs of self-reliance, demonstrated intelligence, and attitudes.[22]

Applications frequently request that job candidates provide references. These are used to help assess an individual's past performance, personality, character, and good fit with the corporate culture. In checking references, an individual should (1) determine who should be contacted, (2) interview the references, and (3) sift the evidence gathered to assess the selection criteria.[23]

Although reference checking would seem to be the most valid way of obtaining information about past performance, there are questions about its reliability, validity, and cost-effectiveness.[24] Most personnel officers are reluctant to release all or even some information about former employees. In one study of sixty Fortune 500 companies, only nine firms would release all available information when a written release was provided by the employee; thirteen would confirm dates of employment and job title; the rest would provide only selected information.[25] To protect themselves, organizational representatives should make sure that the inquirer has a job-related need to know and that they themselves communicate information without malice.[26]

Recently managers have subjected application blanks to increased scrutiny. Many clearly violate legislation designed to eliminate discrimination in selection.[27] Table 4–3 lists the types of questions often found on application blanks that may violate federal law. (See Chapter 13 for the legal constraints on selection.)

APPLICATION FOR EMPLOYMENT

–an equal opportunity/affirmative action employer–

Name ____
First Middle Last

Address ____
No. Street

____
City State Zip

Tel. No. ____________________ Soc. Sec. No. ____________________

Position Applying For ____

Part-time ☐ Full-time ☐ Temporary ☐ Permanent ☐

Are you a citizen of the USA? Yes ☐ No ☐

Have you applied here before? ____________ Worked here before? ____________

Who referred you here? ____

If employed, who can be contacted during business hours in case of any emergency?

Name ____________________ Address ____
Street or Company City State

Relationship ____________________ Telephone Number ____________________

	Name, City, State of School	Major Course of Study	Day or Evening	Date Entered	Date Left	Graduated Yes	Graduated No
High School							
College							
College							
Graduate or other special training							

Special training or skills ____________________ Typing ________ wpm Shorthand ____________________ wpm

Figure 4–2 SAMPLE APPLICATION BLANK

Continued

Military Record (Include Reserves and National Guard)

Branch of Service ______________ From (date) ______ To (date) ______ Type of Discharge ______________

In the past 10 years have you been convicted for any reason other than a minor traffic violation? Yes No
If yes, explain:

Have you ever filed for or received industrial accident compensation? Yes No
If yes give date(s) and nature of accident(s):

Do you have any physical or mental limitations or disabilities? Yes No
If yes, please describe:

EMPLOYMENT HISTORY: (Begin with present or most recent employment. Include military experience.)

Organization			Supervisor	Title
Address		Tel. No.	May we contact for a reference? Yes No	
Your Title			Reason for Leaving	
Describe Duties:				
Starting Salary	Date Started	Last Salary	Date Left	Hours/Week

Organization			Supervisor	Title
Address		Tel. No.	May we contact for a reference? Yes No	
Your Title			Reason for Leaving	
Describe Duties:				
Starting Salary	Date Started	Last Salary	Date Left	Hours/Week

Organization			Supervisor	Title
Address		Tel. No.	May we contact for a reference? Yes No	
Your Title			Reason for Leaving	
Describe Duties:				
Starting Salary	Date Started	Last Salary	Date Left	Hours/Week

Organization			Supervisor	Title
Address		Tel. No.	May we contact for a reference? Yes No	
Your Title			Reason for Leaving	
Describe Duties:				
Starting Salary	Date Started	Last Salary	Date Left	Hours/Week

Organization			Supervisor	Title
Address		Tel. No.	May we contact for a reference? Yes No	
Your Title			Reason for Leaving	
Describe Duties:				
Starting Salary	Date Started	Last Salary	Date Left	Hours/Week

IMPORTANT—PLEASE READ BEFORE SIGNING

I certify that the information given in this application is true and acknowledge that misrepresentation and/or withholding information will result in the rejection of this application or will be considered just cause for discharge if discovered after employment begins.

Your Signature ______________________________ Date ______________

Reprinted with permission.

Figure 4–2 Continued

Subject	Fair pre-employment inquiries	Unfair pre-employment inquiries
a. Age	Inquiries as to birth date and proof of true age are permitted. . . .	Any inquiry which implies a preference for persons under 40 years of age.
b. Arrests (See also Convictions)	None. (Law enforcement agencies are exempt from this rule. . . .)	All inquiries relating to arrests.
c. Citizenship	Whether applicant is prevented from lawfully becoming employed in this country because of visa or immigration status. Whether applicant can provide proof of citizenship, visa, or alien registration number after being hired.	Whether applicant is citizen. Requirement before hiring that applicant present birth certificate, naturalization or baptismal record. Any inquiry into citizenship which would tend to divulge applicant's lineage, ancestry, national origin, descent, or birthplace.
d. Convictions (See also Arrests)	Inquiries concerning specified convictions which relate reasonably to fitness to perform the particular job(s) being applied for, *Provided* that such inquiries be limited to convictions for which the date of conviction or prison release, whichever is more recent, is within 7 years of the date of the job application. . . .	Any inquiry which does not meet the requirement for fair pre-employment inquiries.
e. Family	Whether applicant can meet specified work schedules or has activities, commitments or responsibilities that may prevent him or her from meeting work attendance requirements.	Specific inquiries concerning spouse, spouse's employment or salary, children, child care arrangements, or dependents.
f. Handicap	Whether applicant has certain specified sensory, mental or physical handicaps which relate reasonably to fitness to perform the particular job. Whether applicant has any handicaps or health problems which may affect work performance or which the employer should take into account in determining job placement.	Over-general inquiries (e.g. "Do you have any handicaps?") which would tend to divulge handicaps or health conditions which do not relate reasonably to fitness to perform the job.
g. Height and weight	Inquiries as to ability to perform actual job requirements. Being of a certain height or weight will not be considered to be a job requirement unless the employer can show that no employee with the ineligible height or weight could do the work.	Any inquiry which is not based on actual job requirements.
h. Marital status (See also Name and Family)	None.	( ) Mr. ( ) Miss ( ) Mrs. ( ) Ms. Whether the applicant is married, single, divorced, separated, engaged, widowed, etc.

Table 4–3 FAIR AND UNFAIR PRE-EMPLOYMENT INQUIRIES

Subject	Fair pre-employment inquiries	Unfair pre-employment inquiries
i. Military	Inquiries concerning education, training, or work experience in the armed forces of the United States.	Type or condition of military discharge. Applicant's experience in other than U.S. armed forces. Request for discharge papers.
j. Name	Whether applicant has worked for this company or a competitor under a different name and, if so, what name. Name under which applicant is known to references if different from present name.	Inquiry into original name where it has been changed by court order or marriage. Inquiries about a name which would divulge marital status, lineage, ancestry, national origin or descent.
k. National origin	Inquiries into applicant's ability to read, write and speak foreign languages, when such inquiries are based on job requirements.	Inquiries into applicant's lineage, ancestry, national origin, descent, birthplace, or mother tongue. National origin of applicant's parents or spouse.
l. Organizations	Inquiry into organization memberships, excluding any organization the name or character of which indicates the race, color, creed, sex, marital status, religion, or national origin or ancestry of its members.	Requirement that applicant list all organizations, clubs, societies, and lodges to which he or she belongs.
m. Photographs	May be requested *after* hiring for identification purposes.	Request that applicant submit a photograph, mandatorily or optionally, at any time before hiring.
n. Pregnancy (See also Handicap)	Inquiries as to a duration of stay on job or anticipated absences which are made to males and females alike.	All questions as to pregnancy, and medical history concerning pregnancy and related matters.
o. Race or color	None.	Any inquiry concerning race or color of skin, hair, eyes, etc.
p. Relatives	Names of applicant's relatives already employed by this company or by any competitor.	Names and addresses of any relative other than those listed as proper.
q. Religion or creed	None.	Inquiries concerning applicant's religious denomination, religious affiliations, church, parish, pastor, or religious holidays observed.
r. Residence	Inquiries about address to the extent needed to facilitate contacting the applicant.	Names or relationship of persons with whom applicant resides. Whether applicant owns or rents own home.
s. Sex	None.	Any inquiry.

SOURCE: *Pre-Employment Inquiries and Screening,* Washington State Human Rights Commission, July 1977, pp. 4–9.

Table 4–3 Continued

Reviewing Resumes

Resumes often substitute for the application blank in filling professional positions. They provide data to use in a preliminary screening of applicants such as experience, education, or job knowledge. Resumes also include information that can be used in initially forming a recruitment pool, as described in Chapter 3.

What types of data do resumes provide? They summarize an applicant's education, work history, special achievements, and hobbies, and often answer the following questions:

1. Has the individual held leadership positions?
2. Has the individual demonstrated academic achievement?
3. Has the individual been involved in extracurricular activities?
4. Does the individual have work experience?
5. Has the individual paid for part of his or her education?
6. What quantitative skills does the individual likely have?
7. What interpersonal skills does the individual likely have?
8. How well does the individual express himself or herself?

Look at the resume shown in Figure 4–3. What types of criteria might data from this resume assess? Resumes can measure criteria such as supervisory experience or experience with certain job-related tasks; in contrast, resumes cannot measure personality characteristics or leadership ability. How useful do you think these criteria are for selection? Generally managers and human resources professionals can use resumes to make a first reduction of the pool of applicants on educational and experiential criteria.

Most organizations lack a systematic way for evaluating resumes. Managers should formulate a series of resume evaluation questions that link to selection criteria. Further, a manager must ensure that the data presented in the resume are accurate. He or she should use other instruments or methods, such as interviews or reference checks, to check the accuracy of the resume.

Selecting Standardized Tests

Standardized tests are commercially developed, have been used with a variety of populations, and have fairly substantial reliability and validity data. To standardize a test, a test developer administers it to a large, heterogeneous group of individuals. Using various statistical techniques, the developer eliminates items that are ambiguous or that fail to discriminate between individuals who differ on the characteristic being measured. Repeated administrations of the test refine the items. Subsequently reliability and validity studies are performed using diverse samples of individuals. Additional revisions of the test occur until high validity is obtained for the relevant population and the test is shown to be reliable.

Among the best known of such tests are the Stanford Binet and Wechsler Intelligence Tests, the Minnesota Multiphasic Aptitude Test, the Rorschach Inkblot Test, among others developed by such organizations as the Educational Testing Service, Consulting Psychologists Press, and Psychological Testing Corporation.[28]

OBJECTIVE	To obtain an organizational planning and development position in Human Resources which utilizes my analytical, planning and strategic management skills.
EDUCATION	**BOSTON COLLEGE, SCHOOL OF MANAGEMENT** Bachelor of Science Degree, May 1984 **Double Major:** Human Resource Management and Marketing **Achievements:** Cum Laude, G.P.A. in concentrations 3.8/4.0 Dean's List 1980–1984 **Relevant Projects:** Human Resource emphasis: A Study on Resident Perceptions of the Resident Assistant Role at Boston College Critique and prescriptive analysis of the Human Resource Function at Western Electric Marketing emphasis: Strategic Analysis of the Executive Search Firm market in Boston Marketing campaign entitled "Travel to Mexico"
EXPERIENCE	**BANK OF BOSTON** 5/83–Present **Human Resource Systems Management Intern:** Project Manager for study of career pathing and internal job movement in Bank of Boston. Project involved questionnaire and interview design, analysis of existing job change data base, and presentation of results and recommendations to Human Resource Planning Management. Used descriptive statistics, Markovian analysis, and SAS graph tools. **OFFICE OF UNIVERSITY HOUSING, BOSTON COLLEGE** 8/82–Present **Resident Assistant:** Liaison between university and resident community in translating and administering university policy for upperclass apartment complex. Position involves peer counseling, developing and coordinating social, educational, and cultural activities, maintaining dorm security, and interviewing Resident Assistant candidates. **FREEDOM FEDERAL SAVINGS & LOAN ASSOCIATION** 2/80–8/82 **Customer Service Representative:** (Part-time and summers). Designed and managed customer notification and follow-up system for abandoned property. On-going responsibilities involved informing and advising customers on industry trends and interest rates, opening new accounts, interviewing student loan applicants and processing loan applications.
ACTIVITIES	Undergraduate Government of Boston College Senior Week Committee, Chairperson; Freshman Orientation Program, Leader; Personnel Management Academy; Marketing Academy; Admission Day Visits.
DISTINCTIONS	Daughters of the American Revolution Citizenship Award Recipient, 1980 Watertown's Massachusetts Girls' State Representative, 1979
TECHNICAL SUMMARY	BASIC Programming **Hardware:** IBM Mainframe, Wang VS 80, IBM PC, Apple II **Software:** SAS, SPSS, 1-2-3, TSO, SPF, Wangwriter, Visicalc
REFERENCES	Furnished Upon Request

Reprinted with permission.

Figure 4–3 SAMPLE RESUME

Research suggests that professionally developed cognitive ability tests are the most valid predictors of performance on the job.[29] Jamie Boyce, then, might administer standardized tests as part of the process of selecting tellers for her branch bank. Table 4–4 lists examples of such tests and their potential uses in organizational settings.

Test Name	Purpose	Sample Item
Adaptability Test	Measures mental adaptability or alertness. Distinguishes between persons who easily adapt to new situations and those who perform better on routine or repetitive jobs.	What is the seventh letter in the alphabet?
SRA Clerical Aptitudes	Measures three aptitudes that are basic for successful job performance in many office positions: vocabulary, office arithmetic, and detail checking.	*Big* means the SAME as *large*. An X has been marked in [S] on the Answer Pad. P-1. big — large p-2. left — right p-3. good — night p-4. forget — remember
Computer Operator Aptitude Battery	Three subtests measure aptitudes important to success in performing the computer operator job. Predicts ability to perform computer operator job and potential for learning computer programming.	In this test you will be given a series of letters, numbers, and punctuation marks called a format. This format can be changed to other alternate formats if certain rules are followed. Look at the sample below. On the left side the format is given along with a specific rule. On the right side are the alternate formats; some are correct and some are not. Your task is to determine if the alternate formats given have followed the general rules and the specific rule(s).
Flanagan Aptitude Classification Tests	Measures aptitudes for sixteen important on-the-job skills, including coding, coordination, ingenuity, precision, reasoning.	When you have decided which is the correct assembly, put an X in the box above that picture. 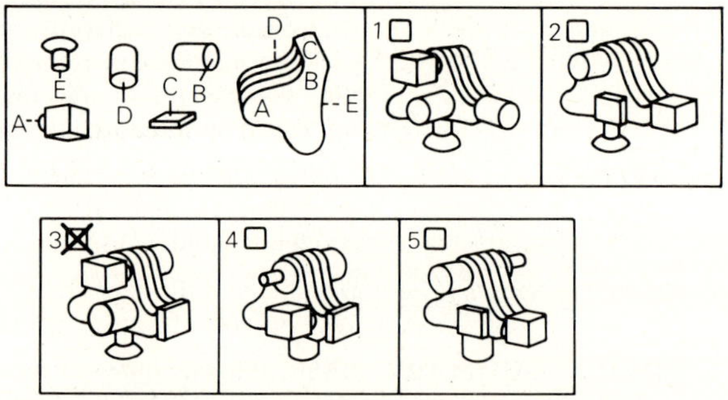
Flanagan Industrial Tests	Measures eighteen distinct aptitudes or functions important to supervisory, technical, office, skilled, and entry-level job demands.	In this booklet you are to draw a circle in the space between the inner and outer rings of each figure like the one in Sample 1 below. 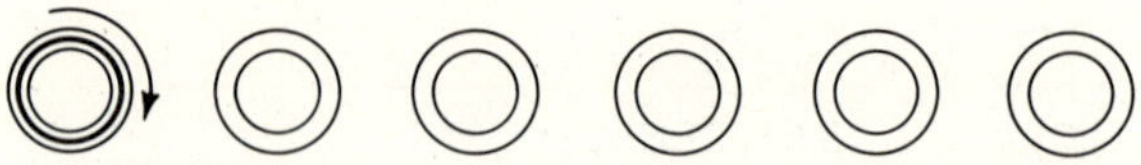
Leadership Opinion Questionnaire	Measures two important dimensions of supervisory leadership: consideration and structure.	For each item, choose the alternative which most nearly expresses your opinion on how frequently you *should* do what is described by that item. Always indicate what you, as a supervisor, or manager, sincerely believe to be the desirable way to act.

Table 4–4 **SAMPLE TESTS FOR EMPLOYEE ASSESSMENT** *Continued*

Test Name	Purpose	Sample Item
		Put the welfare of your unit above the welfare of any person in it. ☐ Always ☐ Often ☐ Occasionally ☐ Seldom ☐ Never
SRA Mechanical Aptitudes	Measures ability to learn mechanical skills in three major areas: mechanical knowledge, space relations, and shop arithmetic.	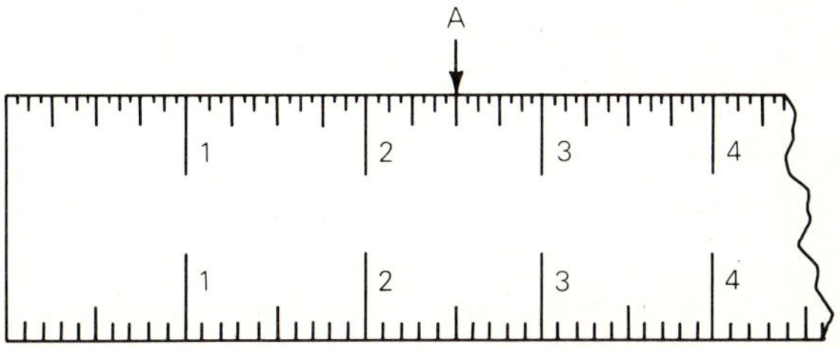 What is the reading at A? A. 2.80 inches B. 2.08 inches C. 1.50 inches D. 2.50 inches E. *none of these*
Office Skills Tests	Measures twelve aspects of most job tasks that are commonly performed in offices, such as spelling, typing, grammar.	Albert _?_ the letters that you dictated. ○ typing ○ have typed ○ is typed ○ typed ○ type
The Personal Audit	Measures personality traits objectively to assess personal adjustment essential to job satisfaction and success. For educational, clinical, and industrial use.	Indicate the degree of your liking for each of the following activities by drawing a circle around "M" if you would like it a *great deal,* around "S" if you would have *some* liking for it, around "L" if you would have a *little* liking for it, around "N" if you would have practically *no* liking for it. M S L N Acting as master of ceremonies at a night club. M S L N Introducing strangers at a party. M S L N Playing a part in a movie. M S L N Attending a masquerade party. M S L N Performing on the radio.
Sales Attitude Checklist	Reflects attitudes toward selling and habits in the selling situation.	This booklet contains statements that are commonly used by salespersons to describe their attitudes and behaviors. These statements are grouped into sets of four. Read over the four statements in a set and think of your performance as a salesperson. Select the one statement in the set that is most like you. Put an X in the box beside that statement in the column headed M (for most). Then consider the remaining three statements in the set. Decide which one of these three is least like you and put an X in the box beside that statement in

Table 4–4 Continued

Continued

Test Name	Purpose	Sample Item
		the column headed L (for least). Leave the boxes beside the other two statements in the set blank. Look at the completed example below. M L My selling is highly personal. ☐ ☐ I am a conservative dresser. ☐ ☐ I sometimes make price concessions to close a sale. ☐ ☒ I have a good feel for people's reactions. ☒ ☐

Table 4–4 Continued

What advantages do standardized tests offer? First, these tests often have high reliability and validity for certain groups or purposes. Second, many standardized tests, particularly the paper-and-pencil tests that measure skills, abilities, and attitudes, are relatively easy to administer and score. Third, the performance of candidates can easily be ranked. Finally, consistent measurement for positions in different parts of the organization is assured.

But these tests often command a relatively high purchase price because of the cost and time involved in their development. Some tests require that a manager or human resources professional have special training to administer the test and interpret the results. In these cases the manager may hire a testing specialist. Top executives often use outside psychologists to evaluate candidates for top managerial positions.

There are diverse types of standardized tests. *Aptitude tests* assess a person's ability to acquire knowledge or skills. There are tests that measure general intellectual ability, aptitude for specific occupations or a specific task, cognitive or motor aptitudes, or interpersonal competence.[30] Organizations may administer tests that assess individual aptitudes, or they may administer a multiaptitude battery. The usefulness of aptitude tests depends on the criterion to be predicted; for example, tests that measure specific aptitudes have been shown to accurately predict managerial effectiveness best.[31] As discussed in Chapter 13, test administrators must ensure that the test used measures job-related criteria.

Achievement tests assess the extent to which a person has acquired knowledge from learning situations. Paper-and-pencil tests are used to evaluate whether a person can judge the correctness of work that has been performed, can perform a task in a simulated setting, or can complete a work sample.[32] These tests tend to have high validity for evaluating certain key knowledge, but they often fail to assess individual performance or the process of performing various tasks since they focus on facts and principles.[33]

Some organizations use *personality tests* as selection instruments. These tests assess specific values and personality characteristics, such as aggressiveness, need for achievement, affiliation, or power. Other organizations complement these with *interest inventories* that determine the types of tasks, jobs, or occupations an individual would prefer to perform. In many cases the validity of both personality tests and interest inventories for predicting job performance is questionable.[34]

Some standardized tests are reliable and valid for groups other than those the manager wants to evaluate. In other cases there is no standardized test that will measure the required skills, abilities, or attitudes. In these situations a nonstandardized test may be more appropriate.

Developing Nonstandardized Tests

Managers and other organizational members often develop their own tests to measure various selection criteria. For example, a human resources professional might design a typing test for clerical applicants, or an observation checklist for telephone sales staff. Realistic work-sample tests have been shown to have the highest validity when job performance is the criterion.[35] Figure 4–4 illustrates a test used for the self-assessment of an applicant's qualifications for a job.

Name ______________ Address ______________ Phone ______________

Present Job ______________ Time on This Job ______________

1) Self-Rating of Present Competence: (1 = Some Familiarity, 2 = Generally Competent, 3 = Very Well Qualified)

______ Mechanical Engineering	______ Electrical Instrumentation	______ Elementary S.Q.C.
______ Advanced Statistical Techniques	______ Elementary Measuring Inspection	______ Advanced Measuring Inspection
______ Undestructive Testing	______ Live Testing	______ Plastic Physical Testing
______ Plastic ______________ Testing	______ A.S.M.E. Standards	______ Basic Physics
______ Basic Chemistry	______ Procedure Preparation	______ Report Writing
______ Injection Molding	______ High Volume Assembly	______ Job Shop Assembly
______ Tell Ideas Verbally	______ Tell Ideas in Writing	______ Operations Research
______ Desk Computer-Calculators	______ Full-sized Computers	______ Market Research
______ Consumer Surveying	______ Sampling ______________	______ Randomization
______ Job Enrichment	______ Cost Accounting	______ Information Storage & Retrieval
______ Basic Metallurgy	______ Production Methods	______ Data Analysis
______ Personnel Administration	______ Employee Supervision	______ Quality Managing
______ Systems Design	______ Specification Preparation	______ Vendor Rating Systems
______ Quality Cost Reporting	______ Theory & Practice	______ Tolerance

2) What are your three strongest areas of competence? ______________

Figure 4–4 SELF-ASSESSMENT QUESTIONNAIRE *Continued*

3) Self-Rating of Personal Traits: (Scale of 0, 1, 2, 3 with 3 being the highest rating)

______ Interest in Quality Engineering	______ Interest in Quality Management	______ Accept Direction
______ Give Direction	______ Work with Peers	______ Problem Solving
______ Group Problem Solving	______ Teaching Ability	______ Coaching Ability
______ Initiative	______ Industriousness	______ Learning Ability
______ Flexibility	______ Alertness	______ Intelligence
______ Business Sense	______ Ability to Field Human Factors	______ Ability to Select Personnel
______ Ability to Release Personnel	______ Ability to Develop Personnel	______ Long-Range Cognizance
______ Follow-through to Completion	______ Ability to Plan	______ Ability to Implement
______ Ability to Handle Multiple Problems	______ Self Starter	______ Self-Control
______ Ability to say "No"	______ Ability to Control Cost	______ Honesty

4) What is your strongest personal trait? ______________________________

How do you use it? ______________________________

5) What is your weakest personal trait? ______________ Why? ______________________________

6) Any comments or questions? ______________________________

Figure 4–4 Continued

Such tests can vary significantly in their sophistication, complexity, and length. Because they may also lack proven validity and reliability, human resources professionals and managers must determine their accuracy in measuring the selection criteria. Managers should be able to use human resources department members as a source for developing or validating such specially designed tests.

When an organization uses either standardized or nonstandardized tests to assess an individual, it has the responsibility to inform them that the test is a regular step in the hiring process. In addition, managers or human resources professionals must tell candidates what the test measures, why it is being used, and what passing or failing means to or about them.[36]

Evaluating Assessment Centers

First used in the 1940s by the Office of Strategic Services to select operatives, assessment centers were then introduced to the corporate world by American Telephone and Telegraph in the 1950s.[37] Assessment centers serve three purposes: (1) selection of individuals for specific, often managerial, jobs; (2) identification of individuals who have potential to advance in the organization, and (3) diagnosis of individual and organizational training and development needs.[38]

Assessment centers generally take place over three to five days and are conducted at off-site locations. Eight essential steps in the design of assessment centers include (1) setting objectives, (2) identifying the skills to be measured, (3) selecting and designing exercises to measure these skills, (4) training the assessors, (5) designing the schedule of activities, (6) defining the procedures for evaluating and observing participant performance, (7) developing the procedures for returning the results to participants and their managers, and (8) validating the results.[39]

Preparation for conducting assessment centers begins with top management selecting three to five lower level managers to act as administrators for a specific center. Top management shares with the administrators (managers) their goals for the center. Together they come to agreement on whether the center is to help select managers, identify managerial talent, or diagnose training needs.

The design of the assessment center differs depending on these objectives.[40] For personnel selection, the center may assess specific skills, conduct exercises that are fairly uniform in difficulty, and provide limited feedback to the participants. In contrast, for appraising managerial potential, the center may assess a range of skills that are generalizable to a family of management jobs, offer exercises that vary in difficulty so that individuals with different competence can be identified, and provide detailed feedback to participants.

Human resources professionals or outside consultants who are regularly involved with an organization's assessment center can provide managers with a set of activities to administer. The activities, such as role plays, generally emphasize peer interaction and feedback. They also use assessment methods that simulate the real-work environment, such as business simulations, in-baskets, or decision-making exercises.[41]

The human resources professionals or outside consultants train the administrators in how to conduct the activities. They may involve them in the design of supplementary activities as well. Together they sequence the activities and prepare the schedule for the center. At this time, the team of administrators also determines procedures for evaluating participants and feeding back the results to them and their superiors.

Next the managers conduct the assessment activities, usually for five to ten participants; and then evaluate participants' performance. To evaluate performance assessors must have expertise in six areas:

1. Knowledge of assessment techniques and the kinds of behaviors they are designed to elicit;
2. Knowledge of assessment dimensions and examples of behaviors related to them;
3. Skill in behavioral observation and recording;
4. Knowledge of evaluation and rating procedures;
5. Knowledge of organizational assessment policies and practices; and
6. Where appropriate, knowledge of feedback procedures.[42]

As part of the evaluation, administrators report the behavior they observe during assessment exercises, offer summaries of behavior, and rate the participants overall.

Such centers have been shown to yield reliable and valid results in meeting their objectives.[43] Still, human resources professionals or consultants should conduct regular analyses to show that the results effectively select managers, identify managerial talent, or diagnose needs. Some research suggests that they result, not in better selection decisions, but only in the identification of those likely to be promoted by current organizational standards.[44] But organizational members tend to accept them as useful and value participation in them.[45] And assessment centers have had a positive impact on minority groups and have yielded relatively useful results for them.[46]

When should managers use assessment centers? Because of the high cost of sending individuals to assessment centers, managers should be careful in determining whom to send. They should only send individuals about whom they require additional information to make placement or promotion decisions, individuals whose training needs are unclear, or individuals who could learn from the assessment center experience. Applicants for entry-level jobs, such as bank tellers, typically are not good candidates for assessment centers. Managers must recognize, however, that assessment centers can have negative effects on those not chosen, can impact careers, and can create stress for both participants and nonparticipants.[47]

The creation of an assessment center in organizations where one does not already exist involves determining the potential benefits in light of the relatively high costs. Where an in-house assessment center is not feasible, managers can use outside assessment centers. Reading 4–1, "Identifying Managerial Potential: An Alternative to Assessment Centers," by Donald Brush and Lyle Schoenfeldt, offers an examination of assessment centers and an alternative to them that links selection to appraisal of employees.

Conducting Interviews

A manager's use of an interview as a selection instrument generally occurs relatively late in the selection process. Sometimes a human resources professional may conduct screening interviews early in the process as well. Because interviewing requires a significant amount of a manager's time and few managers are willing to relinquish the interview as a selection instrument, it must be carefully designed to assure that selection criteria are as reliably and validly assessed as possible. Jamie Boyce, for example, might need to improve the quality of the interviews she conducts with teller applicants.

What should a manager consider in designing and conducting an interview? First, the manager should specify the criteria the interview is designed to measure. Second, the manager must design the interview questions to assess these criteria. Third, the manager must conduct the interview. Fourth, the manager must evaluate the data collected during the interview. (Also recall the advice offered about employment interviewing in Chapter 3.) Reading 4–2, "A Manager's Guide to Selection Interviewing," by Charles Tharp, complements the discussion below about the use of selection interviews.

Measurement of Selection Criteria. The first step in interviewing involves specifying the purpose of the interview and the information it is to collect. For example, the manager should determine whether the interview is to confirm information collected on the application blank, assess the applicant's ability to function in stressful situations, or test the applicant's knowledge of or ability to perform job-related tasks.

The manager should tie the interview's content to the selection criteria that have been derived from the job analysis. For example, an interview for the new teller position at West Suburban Bank might measure applicants' preferences for a sales position or their knowledge of sales techniques. Criteria for supervisory positions might include the candidate's interest in becoming a supervisor, attitude toward becoming a leader, willingness to take on responsibility, ability to recognize effective leadership, lack of sexual or racial bias, and ability to recognize his or her own shortcomings.[48]

In each case the manager should know the purpose of the interview and the criteria the interview assesses. As with other instruments, the manager should ensure that the interview is the instrument that most effectively measures specific criteria. The manager, together with human resources professionals, should assess the reliability, validity, ease of administration, and cost of the interview for assessing the selection criteria.

Types of Questions. The interviewer can ask open-ended questions or closed-ended questions. *Open-ended* questions, such as "Tell me about your experience in sales," or "What do you consider your strengths as an employee?" allow the interviewee to structure the response to the question and present information that he or she feels is important. *Closed-ended* questions, such as "Tell me the first thing you would say to a new customer," or "How many employees have you supervised during the past year?" allow the interviewer to focus a response more precisely. Some combination of the two approaches is most effective. The interview can move from open-ended questions to closed-ended questions, alternate the two types of questions, or begin with closed-ended questions and end with open-ended ones. Figure 4–5 offers one example of the structure of an interview.

The types of questions asked must also be geared to the nature of the position to be filled. For example, in interviewing supervisory candidates a manager might ask the following questions:

1. Why do you want to be a supervisor?
2. What are the functions and duties of a supervisor as you see them?
3. What personal characteristics and other qualifications do you have that would help you to become a good supervisor?

Opening

- Give a warm, friendly greeting—smile.
- Names are important—yours and the applicant's. Pronounce it correctly and use first and last names consistently. Tell the applicant what to call you and then ask the applicant for his or her preferred form of address.
- Talk briefly about yourself (your position in the company and then your personal background, hobbies, interests, etc.) to put the applicant at ease so that she or he might reciprocate with personal information.
- Ask the applicant about hobbies, activities, or some other topic that you believe will be of interest to "break the ice."

Structure the Interview

- State the purpose of interview: "The purpose of this interview is to discuss your qualifications and to see whether they match the skills needed to work as a selection interviewer. First, let's talk about your work experience and next your education and training. Then I will give you a preview of what the interviewer's job is really like. Finally, there will be a chance to ask about anything you want. How's that?"
- Since you plan to take notes, mention this to the applicant: "By the way, I will be taking some notes during the interview so that I don't miss any pertinent information that may come from our discussion. Okay?"

Work Experience: Most Relevant Job

- Use this comprehensive opening question: "Let's talk about your work experience. How about starting with the job that you feel gave you the best preparation for working as a selection interviewer. Tell me all about the job: how you got it, why you chose it, your actual job duties, what you learned on the job, the hours and your attendance record, the pay, why you left (or are leaving), and things like that."
- Probe and follow up to cover each of these items thoroughly: how the applicant got the job, reasons for choosing it, job duties, etc.
- Summarize the major facts and findings from the applicant's most relevant job. For example: "Let me summarize what we have covered to make sure that I've got it right. You worked as a _____ where most of your time was spent doing _________ and _________, and you used these skills, _________ and _________. You chose the job because of _________ and your reasons for leaving it are _________ and _________. Anything else to add?"

Other Work Experience

- If time is available, discuss other jobs the applicant has held that might be pertinent. Get a brief overview of each job the applicant has held. Emphasize jobs held in the last five years or less, since older experience is less likely to be relevant for your decision.
- Ask the work experience questions you specifically prepared for this applicant when you planned the interview.
- Summarize your major findings about all jobs. When the summary is satisfactory to the applicant, go on to discuss education and training.

After the Interview

- Take time to write summary notes immediately. Describe the applicant's behavior and the impressions he or she created. Cite facts and specific incidents from the interview or from the person's work or educational history.
- Wait a day and then complete the Evaluation Form.

Figure 4–5 INTERVIEW GUIDELINES

4. How do you feel about taking on the added responsibilities and demands that come with a supervisory job?
5. Do you think you could be a supervisor in any department other than your own? Where?
6. If you were a supervisor, could you motivate subordinates and take disciplinary action against employees, including former coworkers, if necessary? How would you handle, say, a worker with a high rate of absence?[49]

Questions that you might ask in interviewing a candidate for an executive position might include

1. What criteria would you (a) use in measuring your own performance over the next year and the following years, (b) like your performance measured by, and (c) use in measuring your superior's performance and your relation to him or her?
2. Assume we faced a significant cut in expenditures—for example, 10 to 20 percent within a year or two. How would you go about planning and implementing such a cut in the areas of your responsibility?[50]

In most interviews the interviewer tries to make the interviewee feel at ease by beginning with questions that are relatively easy to answer and then moving on to questions that the interviewee may find more difficult. Stress interviews, in contrast, take a different approach—asking very hard, even impossible-to-answer questions—as a way of testing the ability of an interviewee to function in stressful situations, such as medical school.

Think for a moment about interviews in which you have participated. Did the interviewer

- clearly state the purpose of the interview?
- ask only job-related questions?
- avoid stereotyping and other perceptual distortions?
- present realistic job previews?
- recognize the implications of nonverbal communication?
- speak with a vocabulary understood by the interviewee?
- avoid stress interviews?

Data Analysis. The information collected in an interview should be analyzed to determine the interviewee's status on each criterion measured. Effective analysis breaks down the interviewee's responses into categories. If a teller must communicate effectively, for example, then data analysis should tabulate responses about whether a candidate has the necessary communication skills. Where possible, the qualitative data collected during an interview should be converted to quantitative data.[51] This facilitates the ranking of candidates based on interview data.

The interviewer's background, attitudes, questions, variations in technique, or poor recording of results can detract from the quality of the interview.[52] Other factors that can reduce the reliability and validity of interviews include the use of untrained interviewers, variability in the content of the interviews, uneven interpretation of results, premature decisions about the interviewee's qualifications, and poor interviewing conditions, among others.[53]

INFLUENCES ON FINAL SELECTION

Human resources professionals and managers together must design a system that supports the administration of instruments and use of measurement techniques to reliably and validly assess selection criteria. As instruments are administered, organizations should develop a profile of each candidate on all criteria and store these data in computerized or manual data files. Such profiles should include all job-related information collected about the candidate. Human resources professionals can oversee the selection process organization-wide. Managers, however, should be responsible for selecting the job holder. A selection system that has a low *selection ratio,* that is, a system where a small number of individuals is selected from a large pool of applicants, is desirable.

Figure 4–6 shows two approaches to final selection. As shown in the top section, a manager can reduce a pool of candidates by *iteratively* applying one selection criterion at a time, in sequence, and eliminating at each step a candidate who does not meet the criterion. For example, if a high school-diploma measures an educational criterion required for performance in the new teller position, then the human resources professional can eliminate all candidates who lack such a credential. Next, a mathematics aptitude test to measure quantitative skills would be administered to the remaining recruits. After analysis of the results, the human resources professional or manager can eliminate all candidates who do not earn a prespecified score. Finally, the manager could interview the remainder of the pool. Afterward the manager would rank the candidates in order according to the prespecified job-related criteria and choose the best candidate.

Alternatively, the manager can use a *weighted* approach, as shown in the bottom section of Figure 4–6. With help from the human resources department he or she can first administer all instruments, then analyze all data simultaneously rather than sequentially. The manager weights the data, giving the most predictive the highest weight. The manager can assign a weight to each criterion according to its importance, score each person's performance on each criterion, multiply this score by the weight assigned to that criterion, and finally obtain a total score representing an individual's performance on the selection criteria. The manager can then rank-order individuals according to these scores and select either the highest scoring candidate or a group of finalists for further evaluation.

Use of rational selection approaches, as described previously, should result in identification of the best candidates. Organizational realities indicate, however, that many organizations do not use such rational approaches. Rather, a top manager might say, "Hire Smith." This approach may work, but it runs the risk

CANDIDATE INFORMATION

Candidate	Highest Degree	Experience	Score on Test A	Score on Interview	Performance Rating
1	H.S. diploma	Extensive	97	3	Outstanding
2	B.S.	Some	80	2	Satisfactory
3	B.S.	None	90	1	Satisfactory
4	M.S.	None	85	3	Unsatisfactory
5	Ph.D.	Some	88	1	Satisfactory

ITERATIVE PROCEDURE

1. Eliminate all candidates without experience (candidates 1, 2, 5 remain);
2. Eliminate all candidates with unsatisfactory performance rating (candidates 1, 2, 5 remain);
3. Eliminate all candidates who score below 2 on the interview (candidates 1, 2 remain);
4. Eliminate all candidates who score below 80 on test A (candidates 1, 2 remain);
5. Eliminate all candidates without a college degree (candidate 2 remains).
6. Offer the position to candidate 2.

WEIGHTED PROCEDURE

1. Assign a weight to each criterion (or to each test score that reflects the criterion).
2. Rate each person's performance on each criterion, based on the test, interview, and other data.

Candidate	Education *Weight: 1*	Experience *Weight: 5*	Test Score *Weight: 2*	Interview *Weight: 4*	Performance Rating *Weight: 4*
1	1	3	3	3	3
2	2	2	2	2	2
3	2	1	3	1	2
4	3	1	2	3	1
5	3	2	2	1	2

3. Multiply the ranking by weight assigned to the criteria for each person.

   Candidate 1: $(1 \times 1) + (3 \times 5) + (3 \times 2) + (3 \times 4) + (3 \times 4)$
   Candidate 2: $(2 \times 1) + (2 \times 5) + (2 \times 2) + (2 \times 4) + (2 \times 4)$
   Candidate 3: $(2 \times 1) + (1 \times 5) + (3 \times 2) + (1 \times 4) + (2 \times 4)$
   Candidate 4: $(3 \times 1) + (1 \times 5) + (2 \times 2) + (3 \times 4) + (1 \times 4)$
   Candidate 5: $(3 \times 1) + (2 \times 5) + (2 \times 2) + (1 \times 4) + (2 \times 4)$

4. Add the results.

   Candidate 1: 46
   Candidate 2: 32
   Candidate 3: 25
   Candidate 4: 28
   Candidate 5: 29

5. Choose the candidate with the highest score (candidate 1).

Figure 4–6 REDUCTION OF THE SELECTION POOL

of overlooking the most qualified candidate. At West Suburban Bank managers should use either the iterative or weighted approaches to rank-order candidates for the teller job.

Then the manager should make the job offer to the top-choice individual. The offer should be accompanied by a time limit within which the candidate must accept or reject the offer. If the applicant refuses the offer, then the manager offers the job to the next highly rated candidate.

AN INTEGRATED SELECTION SYSTEM

The selection system must go hand in hand with the recruitment system. The manager or human resources professional should answer the following questions to determine the effectiveness of the selection procedures:

1. Has a job analysis been performed?
2. Are there selection criteria? Are they appropriate for the jobs to be filled? Do they predict effective job performance?
3. Have instruments or techniques that measure the criteria been identified?
4. Are the chosen instruments reliable, valid, relatively inexpensive, and relatively easy to administer?
5. Are multiple instruments or techniques used to evaluate the candidates?
6. Is final selection of the candidate rational and systematic?

A data base that maintains records of available employees and their ratings on predetermined criteria can expedite selection. Continual updating of such information should allow the manager to administer relatively few instruments each time selection must take place. Regular updating of the job descriptions and associated criteria for each job should also facilitate the selection process.

Implications for Human Resources Professionals

Human resources professionals should act as resources and overseers in the selection process. Effective practice can be characterized as follows:

1. Human resources professionals must oversee managers' performance of job analyses; they must ensure that there is frequent updating of job analyses.
2. Human resources professionals should assist managers in selecting instruments to measure various criteria. They should maintain a comprehensive list of standardized instruments useful in selection; perform reliability and validity studies for particular groups; monitor the legality of questions asked in instruments such as application blanks or interviews; and track the cost of various instruments.
3. Human resources professionals can develop instruments for measuring unique criteria, study the reliability and validity of these instruments, and

administer them as necessary. They can design and implement assessment centers, for example.

4. Human resources professionals should maintain a data base of individual performance on various selection criteria and instruments.

5. Human resources professionals should oversee the selection procedures used by managers organization-wide. They can offer suggestions for increasing their consistency and effectiveness.

6. Human resources professionals can assist with a preliminary screening of applicants to reduce the time managers must devote to selection activities.

Implications for Managers

Managers should identify selection criteria, help specify and administer appropriate assessment instruments and techniques, and analyze the data obtained from them. Effective selection procedures include the following:

1. Managers must institute systems to ensure the frequent updating of job analyses.

2. Managers must identify measurable, observable, and job-related criteria that will accurately predict job performance, turnover, or other behaviors and attitudes.

3. Managers should select or develop instruments to measure selection criteria; and their choices should be the most reliable, valid, and cost-effective instruments possible. They can develop checklists and interview guidelines where they are appropriate.

4. Managers should systematically collect, record, and evaluate data. They should use all relevant data to systematically rank candidates. They should seek computer assistance in weighting performance on various criteria to increase the accuracy of the analysis.

5. Managers should practice interviewing and train their subordinates in interviewing skills.

6. Managers should retain the responsibility for making the final selection of employees. They should make job offers themselves, clearly specifying compensation, benefits, and a deadline for the candidate's response.

READINGS

Reading 4–1

IDENTIFYING MANAGERIAL POTENTIAL: AN ALTERNATIVE TO ASSESSMENT CENTERS

Donald H. Brush and Lyle F. Schoenfeldt

The identification of management talent has always been problematic and elusive. Despite the growing number of books, articles, and seminars devoted to the process of selecting and developing high-quality managers, little real progress in innovative appraisal techniques has actually been made. Many companies use their performance appraisal system to review their employees' past performance and to identify talented workers by having supervisors rate their subordinates' overall management potential. However, this can be a highly subjective and, too often, political exercise that leaves unanswered the question, "Potential for what?" In other words, the appraisers may be unfamiliar with the range and detail of a subordinate's performance and what is really required to perform satisfactorily at higher organizational levels.

One of the few innovative approaches to identifying and developing potential managers in existence is the assessment center method. First used to evaluate candidates for irregular warfare under the auspices of the Office of Strategic Services during World War II, assessment centers are now being used in hundreds of public and private organizations worldwide.

There are several important distinctions between the techniques used in assessment centers and the more traditional assessment methodology. These distinctions include, among other things, (1) the use of multiple contrived situations (for example, business simulations) to observe behavior, (2) the presence of several trained assessors who pool their evaluations along a variety of specified dimensions (for example, the assessee's leadership, risk taking, and administrative abilities), (3) the evaluation of several (usually six) employees at one time, and (4) extensive feedback, written or verbal, to either the employee or management, or both.

Although assessment centers have proved beneficial in identifying managerial talent, this approach still represents an "isolationist" view of the appraisal process. That is, appraisal actually takes the individual being appraised out of the context of the job by assessing skills and potential in simulated experiences divorced from the daily activities of the job. The purpose of this article is to analyze the strengths and weaknesses of assessment center methodology and then to outline an innovative system—the integral appraisal system—that uses some assessment center principles, but represents a shift toward systematically examining behavior as it occurs *on the job.*

ASSESSMENT CENTER STRENGTHS

First let's review some of the major strengths and weaknesses of assessment center methodology before describing the integrated appraisal process.

Assessor Training. A typical assessment center has a two-to-one ratio of assessees to assessors (exclusive of administrative staff), or three assessors to every six candidates. Although it is possible to have personnel staff trained as permanent assessors, many companies have taken this function out of the personnel department and made it the responsibility of line managers. This has done much more than enable managers to perform a direct service for the organization; it has helped them become more effective managers. As they are rotated through the role of assessor, they get the opportunity to acquire and develop such important skills as observing behavior, making decisions, and giving and receiving feedback. As a consequence of this training in observing, reporting, and evaluating dimensions critical to man-

Reprinted, by permission of the publisher, from PERSONNEL, May-June, 1980 agerial success, the managers frequently increase their own ability to handle personnel management functions (performance appraisals, for example) and administrative and planning responsibilities more effectively.

Reliability and Validity. The statistical results of assessment centers have been as good as, if not better than, most traditional assessment procedures. Interrater reliability has frequently been reported in the 70s and 80s range, and validity studies—in which assessment center ratings have been used to predict such criteria as management level, salary growth, frequency of promotions, and performance ratings—have also shown positive results, with validity coefficients often ranging from the 30s to the 60s.

Career Development. It goes almost without saying that feedback to the employee, in the form of effective career development counseling, is an important offshoot of the assessment center process. Candidates learn what their strong and weak points are and they are often advised as to how they can improve their skills in a particular area. This is an especially important aspect for growing companies that are looking for ways to identify and develop potential middle managers currently at lower-level positions.

It appears that both the business and scientific communities have accepted the idea that assessment centers constitute satisfactory evaluation procedures. However, a number of potential implementation problems have not been fully explained or solved to the satisfaction of at least some practitioners.

TECHNICAL ISSUES OF CONCERN

The question of what is really being measured by the assessment center process is one that most researchers have not closely examined. Recent studies suggest the possibility that assessment center staffs are appraising candidates not so much on an objective evaluation of observed performance as on their own familiarity with the preferences of management. Consequently, there may exist a rather subtle case of "criteria contamination" in which assessors are, at a very costly rate, duplicating decisions that will be made through already existing procedures.

Although most validity evidence that has been gathered supports the assessment center approach, only about 20 primary validity studies have so far been published. Of these, many were concerned with rated potential rather than actual performance. A close examination of the literature suggests that significantly higher correlations exist between assessment center predictions and job potential ratings (median $r = .63$) than between assessment center ratings and actual job performance (median $r = .33$).

The move to give content validity equal footing in the latest government guidelines on employee selection, including the recently adopted Uniform Guidelines on Employee Selection Procedures, has initiated a trend away from using criterion-oriented validity approaches to measure the effectiveness of assessment centers. A few people, such as Dr. William A. Gorham, formerly of the U.S. Civil Service Commission, have even said that content validity offers the only practical defense of assessment centers. However, as they now stand, assessment centers would probably have difficulty passing muster on a content-oriented basis. Several problems exist in this regard, the most serious being the lack of job relatedness among the exercises involved.

OPERATIONAL PROBLEMS

There are, of course, problems in implementing assessment centers, just as there are with any appraisal system. However, some of these problems are unique to assessment centers. They are:

Cost. Behavioral scientists, many of whom view cost as a matter for least concern in developing a technique, must become sensitive to the need for cost/benefit analysis. In an interesting note on the cost of assessment center evaluations as a selection method Joseph Steger, former dean of the School of Management at Rensselaer Polytechnic Institute in Troy, New York, estimated the difference in cost between traditional pencil-and-paper tests and assessment center evaluations. Taking an actual study, hypothetical but conservative cost estimates were applied for observer and assessee time spent off the job, lodging, travel, and overhead. Assessment center costs were found to far exceed those of the traditional test method. When comparing the cost relative to the validity of the two procedures, it was found that per correlational point, the testing cost was $68.82, whereas the assessment center cost was $540.25. It cost an additional $24,996 to go from a validity of 0.45 (tests) to 0.52 (assessment center). Clearly, then, cost plays an important role in setting up an assessment center and the benefits of the center should include more than just accurate selection.

Coaching. If employees who have participated in the assessment center evaluation procedure coach other employees on the techniques involved, future assessment center results for those who had been coached would obviously be distorted. This problem was highlighted when a divisional vice-president unfamiliar with his company's assessment center outlined in detail one of the exercises and the appropriate action to be taken to the assessment center director. In such a situation, uncontrollable bias is introduced into the performance of candidates and, indeed, the credibility of the entire process is jeopardized.

Heterogeneity of Assessees. One problem in implementing the centers arises when the assessees involved cut across hierarchical levels. Although most companies try to avoid this, those that run assessment centers sometimes find it necessary to add or substitute employees from different company levels. Although the employees might not know each other initially, when their differences in status become apparent, assessees at lower organizational levels defer to those at higher levels in the group exercises—thereby biasing assessment results.

Job Relatedness. Assessment center methodology utilizes contrived experimental exercises, such as leadership group discussions, role-playing interviews, and in-basket tests to elicit the behavior on which assessments are to be made. Although this procedure does have its advantages—for example, exercises are designed to target specific behaviors and are standardized for all participants—attention must be paid to the appropriateness of the exercises in satisfying the requirements mandated by government guidelines for job relatedness. If content validity with respect to assessment center methods is to be assumed, then exercises that elicit job-related behaviors—determined by a thorough job analysis—must be used. Potential problems can also arise from the use of "canned exercises"—exercises that, taken from other organizations, may be only tangentially related to the on-the-job activities involved at the company in question.

AN ALTERNATIVE STRATEGY

The alternative strategy we propose has some of the advantages of assessment center procedures yet minimizes the problems arising from excessive cost, difficulties, and the need for validity. It is the previously mentioned *integrated appraisal approach*.

A major benefit of the assessment center method—one that should be maintained in any alternative strategy—is the training of assessors. This results in increased understanding of the manager's role and his or her ability to observe and evaluate critical employee behavior. This "front end" training in assessor skills should be given not only to personnel staff specialists, but to all operating managers if an organization wants to build an effective management team.

The integrated appraisal strategy differs from the assessment center approach not so much in the training phase as in the evaluation phase. Why pull employees off the job for a week to put them through artificial experiences removed from what they normally do? We feel that the data already exist in most organizations that, if properly collected and interpreted, would allow for the processes of internal selection and promotion, identification of potential managers, and employee development. Furthermore, appropriately collected job-performance data would have the advantage of being (1) available without the use of costly and contrived experiences, (2) clearly job-related, (3) defensible on the basis of content-oriented validity, and (4) more meaningful for employee development.

Let's look at an example, drawn from the experience of three manufacturing companies, that illustrates how an "in-house" appraisal system is developed. The three firms wanted to improve their internal selection and promotion practices, with special attention paid to the identification of employee management potential in the R&D department of one firm, and in middle-level line management in several departments in the other two. Moreover, the firms wanted the assessment data obtained to be meaningfully integrated into ongoing organizational activities. In other words, the data were to be (1) based on performance in those current and anticipated job elements that indicate effective management behavior and potential, (2) collectible on a continuous basis, and (3) reflective of the dynamic nature of the job and career rather than based on a one-shot annual assessment event.

With these requirements in mind, the following steps were taken:

- *Job analysis.* A thorough job analysis was performed to establish the critical tasks and abilities required for each management position. Ten percent of the managers in the target groups were then interviewed, using a structured format; their responses formed the basis of a more extensive job analysis questionnaire that was then administered to 30 percent of the managers in the target groups. The structured interview and the subsequent questionnaire were based on a model of the manager's role that was developed at Rensselaer Polytechnic Institute and validated in a number of contexts.
- *Assessor training.* As previously noted, there are numerous advantages in training and involving line managers to evaluate effective management behavior. In these companies, the training program was based on job analysis results and included an understanding of the complexities of the manager's job with emphasis on the functions identified in job analysis, skills building in observing and evaluating behavior, and practice in giving employees feedback.
- *Procedures.* Systematic procedures for obtaining and evaluating performance data were developed, capitalizing on information obtained and utilized by the managers themselves on a regular basis. Table 4–5 illustrates some of the dimensions of the manager's job to be appraised and compares approaches used in the integrated appraisal method with the respective assessment center exercises that might be used.

Managerial Dimension to be Appraised	Integrated Appraisal Measure	Related Assessment Center Exercise
Motivation (work motivation and ability to motivate others)	Management presentations Unit productivity	Background interviews
Technical competence	Existing organizational measures such as patents, publications, awards	None available
Interpersonal skills (power mode, salesmanship, oral communication)	Management presentations Performance feedback Client relationships	Business games Leaderless group discussions
Administration	Timeliness of reports Coordinating work activities	In-basket exercises Business games
Ability to direct and make decisions	Performance in an environment with personal risk	In-basket exercises Leaderless group discussions Fault-finding exercises
Training and development	Quality of employee performance reviews Provision of informal development experiences for subordinates	Background interviews

Table 4–5 INTEGRATED APPRAISAL METHOD VERSUS ASSESSMENT CENTER METHOD

As the figure shows, there is a strong relationship between the kind of data that already exist in an organization and the data created by artificial work experiences. Other assessment center methods used by the integrated appraisal approach include multiple raters and a variety of evaluation methods.

- *Implementation.* As most managers already know, the implementation of any new program can be complex and difficult. Clearly, the success of developing and implementing an integrated appraisal system depends on the willingness of the personnel staff to educate corporate members in its benefits, to maintain it, and to pursue new areas of application.

In one organization using the system, managers meet annually with their subordinates, colleagues, and superiors to discuss their jobs and the dimensions on which they are to be evaluated. This approach can enhance communication and understanding of various jobs in the company. Simple forms were developed to assess managerial dimensions in a wide variety of company activities such as budget presentations, performance reviews, and written reports. Every fiscal quarter, each manager is required to obtain performance ratings from his or her superior and, in most cases, from selected colleagues, subordinates, and external groups. These ratings, when completed, are reviewed with the manager and then sent to the personnel department, where they are placed in a human resources data bank—thus providing a comprehensive historical performance record that includes information from a variety of sources and situations.

To illustrate how this method would work, let's examine the case of John Howard, a production manager in the steel division of his company. John had some new ideas that he felt would help increase finished-product yield, and he and his boss, Jeff Moore, presented his idea to the plant manager. Shortly after the decision was made to act further on John's idea, Moore evaluated his subordinate's technical competence in terms of the quality of the idea and John's salesmanship, tolerance for stress, and initiative in making the presentation. Moore then sent a brief summary of the evaluation to the personnel department, where the data were processed into the human resources data bank. In this way, John's assessments by his boss and others are processed throughout the year—making a comprehensive record of John's abilities and performance available for review at any time, including his annual performance appraisal.

Summary. The integrated appraisal method emphasizes profiling the requirements for all relevant managerial-level jobs and continuously assessing employee performance on job aspects that would allow determination of projected performance in logically related higher-level positions. Other highlights of the method include the following:

- Employee behavior is observed, recorded, and evaluated.
- Multiple lines of evidence are considered, and this evidence is collected over a longer period of time than the typical two- to three-day assessment center process.
- Multiple facets of the job are evaluated.
- Decisions are double-checked through converging lines of information.

Thus, this approach attempts to incorporate the strengths of assessment center evaluation procedures into the actual job itself.

SOME CRITICAL QUESTIONS

Following are several important aspects of the integrated appraisal approach of which organizations should be aware when considering implementing such a system.

Cost. Training managers in the integrated appraisal method can be expensive, but the cost should not exceed the cost of training managers in assessment center techniques or training them in the company's own performance appraisal methods. On the other hand, the substantial cost incurred when managers and subordinates are absent from the job for assessment procedures—travel, lodging, and so on—are avoided.

Validity. There is no guarantee that the integrated appraisal system will have any more empirical validity than that documented by assessment center procedures. The verdict on this issue cannot be presented until further research is completed. However, its content-oriented approach to validity, based as it is on thorough job analyses, should be consistent with government guidelines relative to measuring knowledge, skills, or abilities necessary for successful job performance.

Job Relatedness. The "exercises" used in the integrated appraisal method are not standardized for all participants, as they are in assessment center procedures. Although this can be criticized as a weakness, the exercises are more relevant because they are part of the job. The feedback from different assessors is extremely meaningful and directly applicable to what the assessee is doing. In addition, the dimensions upon which employees are appraised reflect the specific nature of the job they currently hold, as well as those to which they might ascend.

Commitment. The fact that the integrated appraisal system is conducted on the job and is therefore less artificial than the assessment center approach should tend to increase commitment to utilizing the information gathered. The evaluation and counseling of employees would occur at the time of the assessment and not six months later when it would have little impact on development. Of course, it goes without saying that any system must be clearly monitored and supported by top management if it is to succeed.

Would the integrated appraisal system fit in well with the organization's affirmative action goals? It should assist employers in complying with affirmative action because it casts the broadest net possible—that is, there is no need to select those to be evaluated, as would be the case with assessment center techniques.

Is Automation Necessary? Although the organizations involved in this research use automated management information systems, they are not a requirement for successful system implementation. Many firms, however, routinely keep performance data on computer files for various reasons. Electronic data processing (EDP) can assist in pulling together the various appraisals into a comprehensive, longitudinal picture of performance. If appropriate safeguards are introduced, such a system will not pose a "Big Brother" threat but rather will be treated as just another human resources file.

DISCUSSION QUESTIONS

1. For what purposes are assessment centers used?
2. What are the strengths of assessment centers?
3. What issues exist about the validity of assessment centers?
4. What are the operational problems in using assessment centers?
5. What alternatives are there to using assessment centers for selection? For development?
6. What roles do managers and human resources professionals play in the design and administration of assessment centers?

Reading 4–2

A MANAGER'S GUIDE TO SELECTION INTERVIEWING

Charles G. Tharp

In recent years, numerous factors have heightened the importance of more effective recruiting and screening potential employees. Some of the key factors affecting employee selection are:

- Equal employment/affirmative action regulations
- Scarcity of supply in several high tech labor markets
- Increasing geographic immobility of career couples
- Volume of staffing activities due to promotion and turnover trends
- Accelerating costs associated with poor selections: training, relocation, high salaries, morale, etc.

While not exhaustive, the above list illustrates that the selection process is becoming increasingly complex.

"A Manager's Guide to Selection Interviewing" by Charles G. Tharp, August 1983. Reprinted with the permission of *Personnel Journal*, Costa Mesa, California;

Given that the employee selection process is one of the more complex and is acknowledged to be the most critical function affecting managerial and employee success, a logical and structured approach is needed. This approach could increase the probability that the selection made will represent a productive fit between the individual's qualifications and career interests and the needs of the organization.

THE PREDICTIVE MODEL

The entire rationale for conducting selection interviews is that only through the interview process can a manager gather sufficient data to be able to predict whether a candidate will be successful in the position for which he or she is being considered. While it is equally true that the candidate uses the interview process as a means of assessing the job and the organization, this article focuses on the manager's side of the decision model.

The various factors cited in the research and literature on employee selection can be grouped under three major categories: past work experience, intelligence/education, and motivation and career expectations.

Past work experience is one of the primary factors that can be used to screen virtually all candidates for any open position. The major exception to this is in the case of new, inexperienced college or high school graduates. Some of the areas relevant to past work experience are:

- the degree to which previous work experiences are similar to the requirements of the position being interviewed for
- qualifications and skills gained in prior work that will be important to the successful performance of the position being interviewed for
- performance and accomplishments in similar positions
- situation and organizational context in which experience was gained and the similarity of this background to the organization and work climate of the position being interviewed for
- ability of the candidate to transfer, generalize, and capitalize on earlier work experiences as the individual progressed through his or her career

A clear understanding of previous work experiences will equip the assessing manager with a significant data base from which to predict the fit of the candidate's background and qualifications with those of the subject position.

SECOND MAJOR CATEGORY

The second major category of intelligence and education is important because probing this area will provide insights into the ability of the candidate to conceptually handle the new learning associated with the position. In the context of this analysis, intelligence is not the same as IQ but rather focuses on the exhibited behaviors of quickness of thought, verbal skills, and problem-solving ability. Education is relevant when the requirements of a position dictate that the individual has mastered a defined body of knowledge (for example, engineering or law) or is certified so that specific regularity or liability considerations are satisfied. Similarly, educational attainment can be used as an indicator of general intelligence level, motivation, and goal orientation.

The more the position being interviewed for requires problem solving, planning, and overall creativity, the more important the factors of intelligence and education become to successful performance. Some of the key areas relating to intelligence and education are:

- problems solved and data analyzed in previous positions
- planning and conceptualization exhibited in prior situations
- ability to clearly articulate ideas and experiences
- grade point average in school, especially in major
- performance on standardized tests and accreditation or licensing exams

Combining information about intelligence and educational background with past work experience will provide the assessor with a good feel for how quickly the candidate could master the new job, potential growth beyond the current job, and overall ability to perform the requirements of the position.

One of the obvious drawbacks of basing selection decisions on ability alone is that ability does not, in and of itself, guarantee performance. Ability, however, is a necessary but not sufficient condition for the realization of performance. Performance is the product of a multiplicative relationship between ability and motivation. Both factors must be present.

CAREER EXPECTATIONS

Career expectations of the candidate and the achievability of these within the organization are important to assess so that both the individual's career goals and the organization's need for continuity and valuable human resources can be satisfied. Failure to have a good match of career expectations and the organization's ability to develop and promote the individual will result in high levels of turnover and a loss of training investments.

Motivation and career expectations can be assessed by gathering information about the following areas:

- Candidate's need for managerial direction in previous assignments
- Extra areas worked in and ideas initiated by the candidate outside of the position description
- Nonwork-related activities that the candidate has pursued and what they achieved
- Independence and personal financial contribution to the candidate's educational costs
- Career plans and realism of the candidate's career timing and career objectives
- The candidate's satisfaction with career progress to date

The skilled interviewer will be able to conduct a selection interview in a smooth and orderly fashion that covers past work experience, intelligence, education, motivation, and career expectations. A good approach is to conduct the interview so as to get an overall picture of the candidate as a total person.

In addition to the specific areas outlined above, the interviewer will want to spend enough time with the candidate to establish "gut feelings" or interpersonal "chemistry" assessments. Questions regarding family background, social experiences, and outside interests will provide additional data on the personality fit between the manager and the candidate.

INTERVIEW FORMAT

Table 4–6 presents a suggested interview format that I have found helpful. To cover the areas outlined in Table 4–6 will require at least one to one and one-half hours. This length of time should also allow the manager to establish a "gut feeling" about the candidate.

Experience has shown that the use of a structured interview format, such as the one presented in Table 4–6, produces greater reliability and effectiveness in the selection process. Using a structured approach to gathering the necessary data about past work experience, intelligence, education, motivation, and career expectations should make the selection process much more enjoyable and more effective.

Some of the major benefits to be realized from an improved selection process are:

- reduced turnover
- higher levels of employee satisfaction relative to career
- increased performance because of better person/job matches
- less opportunity or chance for selection decisions based on illegal criteria (age, sex, race)
- improved management attention to job requirements and performance expectations

While it requires greater discipline, the suggested selection model should yield tremendous benefits that will be far greater than the time investment involved.

References

Arvey, Richard A. *Fairness in Selecting Employees* (Reading, MA: Addison-Wesley, 1979).

Dunnette, Marvin D. *Personnel Selection and Placement* (Wadsworth, 1966).

Fear, Richard A. *The Evaluation Interview* (New York: McGraw-Hill, 1973).

Mahler, Walter R. *How Effective Executives Interview* (Homewood, IL: Dow-Jones-Irwin, 1976).

Willing, Jules Z. "The Roundtable Interview—A Method of Selecting Trainees," *Personnel,* Vol. 39, No. 21 (March-April 1962), pp. 26–32.

Interview time: 1 to 1½ hours
Applicability: Exploratory as well as specific job interviewing

Step	Desired Result
Explain your role in the structure of the organization and how the position (if one exists) fits in with the rest of the organization. Discuss products, production facilities, geographic locations, employee population, and human resources philosophy. Also provide an overview of the organization's strategic plan. Discuss roles, positions, etc., of other interviewers who will be meeting the candidate.	Puts the candidate at ease and gives him or her a general feel for the organization and its philosophies.
Review resume information: education, work experience, hobbies, etc.	Makes sure data flows properly and is logical.
Probe early family experiences, educational achievements, part-time and summer jobs, extracurricular activities, etc.	Information is gained about the candidate's achievement orientation, balance of interests, general level of intelligence, social skills, and adjustment.
Probe specific post-degree job progression, especially the reasons for leaving a particular job and why the next job was selected.	Knowledge is gained about the candidate's career orientation, ability to make informed decisions, whether job changes were volitionary, ability to plan and execute plans, maturity, and personal learning curve.
Review job performance and responsibilities on last three jobs. Ask questions that require answers about the situation or environment within which performance was achieved; specific performance of the candidate; what the candidate personally did to bring about the performance; and what results were achieved by the individual (both qualitative and quantitative).	Knowledge is gained about the candidate's job performance under different conditions. The aim is to predict future performance within your organization in a specific job.
Present a hypothetical or actual problem from the subject position that needs to be solved.	Provides an assessment of the candidate's ability to conceptualize problems and his or her methods of searching for possible solutions.
Probe the candidate's career plans and aspirations and ask how he or she is with career progress to date. Specifically, evaluate the reference points and standards the candidate uses when assessing his or her own success and competency. Ask, "To what do you attribute your success or failure in your career progression?"	Illustrates the candidate's internal and external reference points, self-confidence and self-image, action orientation, and extent to which career successes or failure can be attributed to the candidate's actions.
Inquire about the candidate's feelings about his or her own strengths and developmental needs. Ask for work-related examples of where those strengths and weaknesses have been demonstrated.	Demonstrates the candidate's openness about developmental needs, self-confidence, assertiveness, and self-development activities.
Wrap up the interview. Ask, "What are two or three things I should know about you that I didn't ask about?" And, "Do you have any questions you want me to answer?"	Gives the candidate another chance to gather information about your organization and the position, and to discuss personal qualities not already discussed.

Table 4–6 SUGGESTED INTERVIEW FORMAT

DISCUSSION QUESTIONS

1. What value do selection interviews serve?
2. What pitfalls exist in using interviews to gather selection data?
3. Differentiate between exploratory and specific job interviewing.
4. What components comprise a selection interview?
5. Offer a sample agenda for a selection interview.

ACTIVITIES

Activity 4–1

GAMMA ENGINEERING CORPORATION

Step 1: You are the chief engineer at Gamma Engineering, a rapidly growing firm in a high-growth, high-technology industry. Similar to other companies in the industry, your division experiences a high turnover among group leaders. You currently have a vacancy in the group developing the operating system for a new computer that is due on the market in six months, but is running significantly behind schedule. You have reduced the pool to five individuals. You must choose among the applicants listed below.

John Witherspoon has been with Gamma Corporation for five years as an applications programmer in a different division. Before that he worked for two years in developing an operating system for one of Gamma's competitors.

William King is the group leader in the hardware engineering group at Gamma. He recently moved there from Aerodyne Appliances, where he managed the engineering support group.

Janine Kitay has been a member of the operating software group for three years. During that time she has earned a reputation as a bright, aggressive, hardworking individual.

Carol Martin is the group leader of a group working on a special component of the operating system. She joined Gamma six months ago after receiving a master's degree in computer science and seems to be struggling in her new role.

Paul Ordway worked for one of Gamma's competitors that recently went bankrupt. He had managed one of the engineering teams that worked on the operating system. Rumors suggest that Ordway's group may have contributed significantly to the company's inability to meet a rapidly changing environment.

INTELLIGENCE TEST SCORES

	Wechsler Adult Intelligence Test	Otis-Lennon Intelligence Test
Witherspoon	130	125
King	110	125
Kitay	135	140
Martin	120	115
Ordway	125	125

MANUAL DEXTERITY TEST RESULTS*

	Test scores	Most recent performance rating
Witherspoon	95	Satisfactory
King	55	Satisfactory
Kitay	90	Excellent
Martin	45	Unacceptable
Ordway	80	Satisfactory

*(Scores below 70 are considered unacceptable)

PERSONALITY TEST RESULTS

Witherspoon	works well under pressure, aggressive
King	introverted, dislikes challenges
Kitay	immature, likes pressure and challenges
Martin	sociable, responds poorly to pressure
Ordway	sociable, aggressive, unemotional responses

Step 2: Now, in groups of four to six, reach consensus about the person you would hire. Be prepared to justify your choice.

Step 3: Discussion. In small groups or with the entire class, address the following:

1. Explain your diagnosis of the situation faced by the chief engineer.
2. Describe the process you used in making the decision.
3. Evaluate the quality of this process.
4. Explain and justify your choice.
5. In what ways would you change the process or decision if given the opportunity to revise it?

Activity 4–2

A PROJECT MANAGEMENT CASE STUDY

Step 1: Read the case study.

Step 2: Prepare the case study for class discussion.

SELECTING A PROGRAM MANAGER

Following a weekly corporate staff meeting on finance and operations, Mr. J.R. Stewart, Executive Vice President of Eastern Electronics, Inc. (EEI), was discussing the selection of a Program Manager for the forthcoming Army BAT Program with Arnold Knepper, EEI Vice President and General Manager of EEI's Microwave Division.

Mr. Stewart had opened the discussion with, "Arnie, I saw M/Gen. Yager of AMC (Army Missile Command) at a symposium last week and he asked about our plans for the BAT Program. In particular, he was concerned about who would replace Jerry Carson as Program Manager now that he has accepted the OSD (Office of Secretary of Defense) appointment to work in DDR&E (Director Defense Research and Engineering)." (Carson was the prospective Program Manager for BAT. He led the proposal effort and accepted an OSD appointment three days before AMC announced that EEI had won the BAT award.)

"I've been working on that problem, Mr. Stewart, and I've narrowed the candidates down to two people: Jim Martin and Boyd Dowler. I'd like to discuss it with you because choosing between them is going to be difficult."

"Before we get down to details, Arnie, how did you select Martin and Dowler? What criteria did you use?"

"I didn't use any specific criteria. Since we're so shallow on candidates who would make good Program Managers, there weren't many options."

"Look, Arnie, Carson is gone and since Gen. Yager is keen on who manages his pet projects, I feel we'll have to be careful in our selection. This is particularly true since Gen. Yager championed the BAT Project and got OSD to approve it. Therefore, why don't you come back next week with a written list of selection

Reprinted with permission of the author, Larry Bennigson, and publisher, *Project Management Quarterly* 3 (June 1972): 14–16.

criteria and pertinent data on Martin and Dowler. Since we've got three weeks before we start negotiations on the BAT contract, I feel we can take another week on a decision this important. Also, let's talk a little about developing Program Managers so that our options won't be so thin in the future."

Background on EEI and the BAT Program

EEI is a leader in military electronics with products ranging from components to missile systems. Its primary strength is in radar technology with all three military services and NASA serving as customers for its radars. EEI has eight divisions scattered throughout the United States. The Microwave Division is the second largest with annual sales of 150 million. Three major programs account for 80 percent of the Microwave Division's sales.

Microwave uses Program Managers supported by staffs of various sizes to administer its programs. Traditionally, the Division's technical strength consists of several functional support groups and development laboratories, many of which were formed when the Division was first organized in 1943.

In late May, 1966, the Microwave Division won the BAT Program. The BAT Program will develop and test several prototypes of an advanced surface-to-air defense missile. The missile will use a new and relatively untried guidance technique. If prototype tests are successful, a production program with a potential of several hundred million dollars could follow. The Army has a "wait and see" attitude about production commitments. EEI feels that it won the award because of its technical approach on the BAT. If the BAT is successful, it could represent over half of Microwave's business from 1969 through 1973.

Meeting to Select the BAT Program Manager

Knepper opened the 13 June meeting by showing Mr. Stewart the criteria he had listed for Program Managers (shown as Figure 4–7).

Stewart commented, "I like your list, Arnie, but let me add my nickel's worth.

"To begin with, we want people who are experienced engineers. A good Program Manager has to be able to sort through the pieces himself if a technical problem begins to inhibit progress. Our Program Managers should be able to relate technical details of their programs to the customer or to top management at a moment's notice. Further, they should be able to provide an up-to-the-minute status report on the project.

"Also, we want managers. We want people who can work out the best balance between the technical objectives of the program and the estimated cost and schedule. Too many times in the past our technical oriented Program Managers have overemphasized technical performance at the expense of cost and schedule.

"In addition, they must have loyalty and dedication. Not only is loyalty to the project and upper management necessary, but loyalty to their people. They must sacrifice themselves when necessary to demonstrate that the confidence placed in them is repaid with their best efforts to accomplish the task.

"Moreover, Program Managers must be able to obtain customer acceptance and approval on technical and program issues. In many ways this is more of an art than a science and is very much a function of the type of program involved. Above all else, Program Managers must not dictate to the customer what the best approach or alternative is. The most effective Program Managers have a way of getting the customer to select or ratify the approach that we feel is in our best interest.

"And finally, the world loves a tiger! We need high rpm-type guys who will rattle a cage or two when it is necessary to get things done.

"Okay, Arnie, so much for my views, let's talk about your two candidates."

"Well, sir, both Martin and Dowler are currently managing other programs. Martin manages the USAF Ripper (air-to-air missile); Dowler, the Army CW

1. Must know the product.
2. Should know the customer and be acceptable to him.
3. Must be capable of managing a large program. (BAT Program will be the largest Microwave program, if successful; twice as large as any current program.)
4. Must have sales ability.
5. Must be capable of obtaining internal cooperation from support groups.

Figure 4–7 JOB REQUIREMENTS—BAT PROGRAM MANAGER

Tracker (surface-to-air tracking radar). The Ripper is established in production now after those painful development problems we had. The CW Tracker is finishing test and evaluation and is just starting production. Both programs are in shape for the assistant program managers to take over, if necessary.

"Martin is 44 years old and has been with us 22 years. He is stronger technically than Dowler, who is 38 and has been with us 9 years. Dowler is quick to grasp technical issues, but just does not profess to be the engineer that Martin is. I feel that Martin could do a better job getting the BAT guidance package developed.

"In addition, I had members of my staff discuss Martin and Dowler with their peers and observe their management techniques. Also, I personally interviewed each of them. Here's how their peers size them up."

People who have worked for both Martin and Dowler expressed no significant preference on which one they preferred to work for. They felt that Dowler did more to develop them personally than Martin.

Other Program Managers rated Dowler over Martin in responding to customer desires. On the other hand, they rated Martin higher than Dowler on getting along with the functional line managers at Microwave. Also, they felt that Martin was more sensitive to top management policy than Dowler.

The other Program Managers seem to feel that Dowler was somewhat inconsistent concerning his subordinates' problems. Sometimes he told them exactly what to do and the next time he would ignore them until they solved their own problems. However, his own subordinates thought he was reasonable in deciding when to help them and when to leave them alone. On the other hand, Martin made most all of the decisions and always let the people know what had to be done. He left little doubt as to who was boss and in control.

One point that seemed to irritate other Program Managers was Dowler's approach to organization. To satisfy the customer's request, he had projectized his program to the maximum extent possible. This was somewhat contrary to management's aim of centralizing control and using functional groups to serve all the program offices. By way of contrast, Martin didn't try as hard to sell us on projectizing his program when his customer suggested it.

The functional department managers liked working with Martin best and they had mixed emotions about Dowler. They felt Martin was willing to understand their problems while Dowler had a rather product-oriented, hard-headed attitude about their groups. They further stated that if Dowler didn't get the services he expected, he didn't care to discuss the reason, he would go to top division management and obtain approval to assume direct control of certain portions of their groups.

In addition, members of my staff were able to observe specific program management techniques of both Martin and Dowler. To make a side-by-side comparison of the performance on present programs is difficult due to the different nature of each program. It seems that Martin's program is characterized as a particularly difficult one technically. Tough technical problems caused panic and indecision with occasional complaints from the customer. On the other hand, Dowler's program, which was less of a technical challenge, seems to run smoother. Occasionally, I have to throttle his fore-handedness at turning things on and starting activities that our functional managers look on as being unnecessary or premature.

Attitudes on Selling

Martin has mixed views about how much of his effort should go into selling. He feels that running his program constitutes his prime job and selling belongs to marketing. Further, there is no better way to upset him than to borrow a man from his program to support a sales effort. Somewhat like Martin, Dowler feels that once he becomes involved in a program, he considers it his primary job. And, when the program is under control, he feels that it is appropriate to devote a portion of his time to selling advanced versions of the project and/or broadening the applications of the existing product. He considers his selling responsibilities to revolve around selling the Microwave Division through excellent performance on the existing program.

The two men differed significantly in their attitude toward contracting and contract negotiations. Dowler feels Contract Administration should get program office approval for all agreements. He likes to participate actively in initial negotiations and then fade into the background once the initial ground work has been laid. His active participation has created an abrasion or two with our Manager of Contracts. On the other hand, Martin feels company procedure clearly makes such negotiations the responsibility of the Contracts Department.

Control

While Dowler maintained personal contact with his subordinates, he strongly supported use of advanced techniques whether or not they were required by the contract. However, initially, he did not comply with the use of PERT on the CW Tracker Project nearly as closely or as readily as did Martin on the Ripper Program. In fact, Dowler took several months to get his PERT system underway. The customer complained that he was dragging his feet. Dowler's position was that it took him months to get PERT reliably successful and he wanted a workable system. Having completed his PERT system shakedown, he now relies heavily on it.

Martin stated that he doesn't delegate his program control to mechanical techniques like PERT or PERT/Cost. Although he used them on the Ripper Program, he preferred to rely on eyeball-to-eyeball observations and control things through personal "contact with the troops." He feels that in complex technical developments it's the informal communication system that gets the decisive activities to occur.

Employing Company Procedures

Dowler consistently ignores company procedures if he feels he has a reason to do so. He feels that time is worth too much money to use established procedures and have to wait for decisions and action to result from them. His reputation for taking charge often carries functional people along with his approach even though they may be reluctant. The functional managers often complain that his "take-over" attitude is fragmenting their groups.

Martin normally employed company procedures to the letter. It was rare indeed when he violated them or ever found occasion to challenge them.

Mr. Knepper's Interviews with Dowler and Martin

Dowler explained his organization in the following way. Other Program Managers and their staffs of 20 to 40 people are supplemented by "procuring" services from the functional groups. Dowler tried such an arrangement, he said, but gradually increased his staff to about 170 and projectized. The Army's request to projectize helped Dowler sell us (the Microwave Division management) on the change. Dowler explained that time and time again he was dissatisfied with performance of the services he had to "procure." He said he had to demand approval for direct control of certain functional personnel to end poor performance and late deliveries.

Dowler is the first to admit that his "take-overs" have created friction with functional managers. He feels the functional managers expected him to "break his pick" in attempting to direct individuals in their groups.

Dowler notes that now functional managers cooperate in giving him what he wants because they figure he'll get it one way or another.

His attitude about other organizations in the Microwave Division is somewhat condescending. In fact, he has commented freely that he would like to have his own estimating and pricing group since he has no confidence in estimating or pricing as it is now done. I'm not sure I agree. Estimating and pricing must be oriented to division-wide objectives and cannot yield to the Program Managers when there is a conflict in objectives and trades to be made.

He feels that many schedule slippages on Microwave programs would be prevented in the program offices through proper planning rather than blaming them on supporting organizations. He felt the key was to anticipate trouble spots and "pursue two or more courses of action" when the outcome of one could set the program back if it were unsuccessful.

Dowler summarized his interview by stating that people at Microwave feel his program's success was due to luck and rule breaking. He stated this was an unfortunate conclusion and added that people didn't realize how proper planning and Program Office control eliminates most of the usual problems. He said that on his program there was no great show of the Program Manager putting out fires, insisting on weekend work, and living in a general crisis status.

Martin's interview was somewhat less candid than Dowler's. Martin started by stating that the Program Manager's role was to stay on top of things through actually getting into the swim and seeing what was being done. He stated that he didn't exercise himself unnecessarily about unavoidable cost and schedule problems which were largely out of his control in Microwave's functional setup. It was impossible for him to directly control the functional groups that spent the money. He concentrated his energy on the items he could control, which he felt were major and primarily technical in nature. He said, "In the last analysis, technical performance would normally make up for a little overrun or a delivery slip. Customer satisfaction and product performance overshadows the rest." He freely admitted that the Ripper Program had more than its share of development problems. He stated that he was handcuffed by a poorly structured contract. Also, he complained about late reporting of actual expenditures from the Accounting Department. In addition, Martin stated that priority conflicts in manufacturing were largely to blame for the late deliveries of Ripper missiles. He said that despite his efforts, manufacturing never seemed to fully understand his position and the specific needs of the Ripper Program.

Finally, Martin said he felt projectizing was helpful in some companies but was unnecessary at Microwave. He said that when he was assigned to the Ripper Program, company procedures required him to use the existing functional organization to accomplish the task. He felt there was no opportunity foregone in not projectizing his program because in the long run projectizing would tend to fragment the functional groups wherein Microwave's technical strength lies. In his summary, Martin expressed his approach as one of following established division policy and keeping abreast of the program. "After all," he said, "administration is largely a matter of giving attention to the right details."

At this point, Mr. Stewart says, "Well, Arnie, it looks like you've researched the alternatives. I've got to go to a meeting, but when I get back let's discuss our corporate objectives on the BAT Program. We should give some thought to 'where the battle will be won or lost.' In particular, how can we ensure that we develop the guidance package successfully? Then, you can tell me which one you have chosen and why. We'll discuss your choice a few minutes and then I want to hear about your plans for developing future program managers."

Step 3: Individually, in small groups, or with the entire class, as directed by your instructor, answer the following questions:

1. Analyze the situation at Eastern Electronics.
2. Describe the job to be filled.
3. What selection criteria are appropriate?
4. What instruments have been used to evaluate each candidate?
5. Assess the validity, reliability, cost, and ease of administration of these instruments.
6. Who should Mr. Knepper select? Why?

Step 4: Discussion. In small groups, with the entire class, or in written form, share your answers to the questions above.

Activity 4–3

THE APPLICATION BLANK

Step 1: Secure job application blanks from three different organizations.

Step 2: Evaluate the effectiveness of the application blanks.

1. For what jobs is the application blank used?
2. What types of information does it gather?
3. Does the application blank provide job-related information?
4. Does the application blank ask any questions that are illegal?
5. Does the application blank provide reliable and valid data for selecting individuals for the various jobs it's used for?

Step 3: If appropriate, redesign the application blank.

Activity 4–4

MEASURING TEST RELIABILITY AND VALIDITY

Step 1: The following lists the scores of twenty applicants on the Action Dexterity Test at two testing times approximately three days apart and their performance ratings on the same test one year later.

Applicant	First Test Score	Second Test Score	Performance Rating
1	90	88	15
2	89	84	10
3	44	68	11
4	76	68	6
5	52	68	10
6	100	95	9
7	83	99	11
8	67	78	11
9	67	79	5
10	57	67	9
11	60	89	15
12	88	75	13
13	91	90	14
14	85	67	5
15	30	79	1
16	45	79	10
17	50	59	7
18	73	77	8
19	77	85	10
20	61	80	4

Step 2: Determine the reliability of the Action Dexterity Test.

Step 3: Determine the validity of the Action Dexterity Test.

Step 4: Discussion. With the entire class, compare your estimates of reliability and validity. What types of reliability and validity did you determine? What other types can be determined from these data? What types cannot be determined from these data?

Activity 4–5

SELECTION INTERVIEW

Step 1: Read the following scenario.

Sandy Burkhardt is the office manager of the business office of the local telephone company. Recent firings have left two service positions available. The service staff answers customers' phone calls and either files a work order or refers the customer to the person who can best handle the problem. The office has experienced significant turnover. Sandy feels that this is a result of poor selection procedures. Those who have been hired seem to lack strong interpersonal skills and common sense. In addition, they seem unwilling to learn enough about other parts of the business office operation to make appropriate referrals.

Step 2: Two members from the class are selected, one to role-play the manager who conducts the selection interview and the other to role-play the employee interviewed. All other members act as observers. The manager plays the role of Sandy Burkhardt, and the applicant plays the role of Shelley Einhorn.

Step 3: The role play. When everyone is ready, Shelley Einhorn enters Sandy Burkhardt's office, and the role play begins. The interview is carried to completion.

VARIATIONS

1. One or two new pairs of participants can role-play in order to permit comparison of different interview styles and their outcomes.
2. The class can be divided into small groups, with each preparing the role of either Burkhardt or Einhorn, and representatives are chosen to role-play in front of the class.
3. The class can be divided into groups of three, with one person in each group playing Burkhardt, Einhorn, and an observer. The interview can then be conducted simultaneously in the different groups.

Step 4: Discussion. Report what you saw happening in the interview and then answer the following questions:

1. Describe the parts of the interview. How did Burkhardt proceed from the beginning to the end?
2. What objectives did the interview accomplish?
3. How reliable were the data gathered during the interview?
4. What data did Burkhardt gather during the interview?
5. What additional data should Burkhardt have gathered?
6. How could the interview have been improved?

Activity 4–6

STATE TROOPER EXAMINATION

Step 1: Read the State Trooper Examination Case.

Step 2: Prepare the case for class discussion.

Sarah Spence of the State Personnel Department decided to ascertain the validity of questions used in the two recent written state trooper examinations, using the "criterion" method. By this method, an attempt would be made to determine the correlation between troopers' performance on examination questions and on the job. If most troopers who correctly answered an examination question had subsequently performed well on the job, that would suggest that the question was a valid predictor of job performance. In order to measure job performance, Spence prepared a new performance appraisal form, which asked supervisors to rate troopers on each of the "performance dimensions" found to be "important" (mean score of 3.0 or above) for beginning police officers as a result of the brainstorming session and follow-up questionnaires.

The existing forms used to evaluate troopers and those proposed by the 1972 management consultant's study were considered unacceptable for this purpose because neither rated precisely the correct dimensions.

The results of the special evaluations were disappointing. Though the Personnel Department wanted to get two evaluations of every trooper, in many cases there was only one sergeant who had supervised the trooper since graduation from the academy. Where there were two supervisory appraisals, the correlation between the two was extremely low. Finally, most evaluations showed a strong "halo effect." That is, supervisors tended to give uniform ratings to troopers on all of the criteria, suggesting that a strong impression formed in the application of one criterion had colored the evaluator's application of other criteria.

Lacking useful performance evaluations and short on time, Spence finally decided to construct the written examination by using two "power of observation" tableaus (a total of 30 questions), plus fifty questions from the old examinations the responses to which had proved to be most job relevant according to the recent job analysis and least discriminatory by race or ethnicity. The "power of observation" questions were based on questions used in a recent examination for state corrections officer. The passing rate for minorities on those questions had been approximately the same as for whites.

During the final preparation stages, the State Police conducted an extensive promotional effort aimed at attracting women, blacks, and Hispanics to take the examination. The examination was held on January 17, 1976. The recruiting effort proved to be so successful that, although the passing rate for blacks and Hispanics was very low, the total number of women and minorities among those passing the test was much higher than ever before:

Candidate Group	Number Examined	Number Passing	Percent Passing
All candidates	4028	2432	60.4
Women	350	250	71.4
Blacks	193	44	22.8
Hispanics	123	37	30.1

For the physical examination, Spence eventually developed a test consisting of an obstacle course and a mile run, and pretested it on a sample of state troopers, policewomen and State University coeds:

> The pretest was a disaster. The State Police monitor said that it was a mickey-mouse test and if anyone couldn't pass it, they should shoot themselves. There was a lot of resentment on the part of the State Police. The state troopers breezed through it. So did most of the women.

With time running out, Spence, using the advice of an ad hoc panel of physical training specialists, decided to drop a few events, consolidate others and tighten time limits. The final version included the following events:

1. a mile run (to measure stamina)
2. balance beam (to screen out gross acrophobia or lack of bodily control)
3. an obstacle course (to measure agility, speed and various types of strength), consisting of:
    - **a.** a window wall;
    - **b.** two hurdles;
    - **c.** a car window; and
    - **d.** a sand bag pull
4. a weight lift (to measure "static strength")

Candidates for the position of "state policewoman" were required only to run a mile in ten minutes.

The physical performance test was administered in late March and early April, 1976, to 1,827 candidates. The progress of the field of candidates through the physical performance testing process is shown on the following table:

Candidate Group	Scheduled For Test	Absent or Withdrew Before Test	Tested	Failed	Later With-drew	Eligible for Certification
All candidates	2432	606	1826	211	17	1598
Women[1]	15	0	15	8	0	7
Blacks	44	15	29	6	1	22
Hispanics	37	12	25	2	0	23

The final list of eligible candidates for the position of state trooper trainee, then, contained 1,598 names. The names were grouped by rank on the written test (the physical test having been scored pass-fail only) from a theoretical high raw score of 80 (80 correct answers out of 80 questions) to a low of 56 (70 percent correct). Since there were only 25 passing scores (56 through 80) and 56 vacancies to be filled, the Personnel Department certified the entire list to the State Police. This meant that the State Police could lawfully choose *any* 56 of the 1,598 people whose names appeared on the list.

Once the list had been prepared and certified to the State Police by the Personnel Department, responsibility for the selection process shifted to the State Police Department. It then fell to Captain Kenneth O'Brien, State Police Personnel Officer, to administer the process of distilling the 1,598 certified candidates down to 56 trainees. As the State Police Officer designated by the Commissioner to prepare the Department's annual affirmative action plan, O'Brien knew as well as anyone in the Department the constraints under which he must operate. Somehow he must attempt to satisfy the legal obligation imposed by state and federal antidiscrimination laws without impairing the quality or the discipline of the force.

Captain Kenneth O'Brien, Personnel Officer for the State Police, decided to maintain the essential ingredients of the traditional State Police screening process, but with modifications designed to maximize the number of female and minority candidates considered. Accordingly, he decided to limit the pool of candidates (from among the 1,598 certified) to the following: all women and minority candidates, excluding those whose score was precisely 70 percent, plus those white males scoring in the ten highest ranks. If necessary, the pool would be expanded to include white males in successively lower ranks. As in the past, this group was interviewed by the Selection Board, at which time candidates were asked a series of highly personal questions about their personal habits and affairs.

[1]This table shows only those women who chose to apply for certification for a "state trooper" position. Women passing the written test were required to specify whether they wished to be considered for the position of "state trooper" or "state policewoman" prior to the physical test. Most of the women chose "policewoman."

	On Eligibility List	Interviewed by State Police	Examined by Polygraph	Appointed to Training Class	Completed Training[1]
White Males	1546	394	133	46	43
Black Males	22	21	7	2	2
Hispanic Males	23	17	10	4	3
Females	7	7	5	4	4

[1]Four candidates dropped out before training was completed—three white males and one Hispanic male. All four dropped out for personal reasons. This was the lowest dropout rate for Academy Training of any Trooper Trainee class.

Table 4–7 EXAMINATION RESULTS

Candidates deemed acceptable as a result of the interviews and follow-up polygraph test were then given a medical examination and an extensive background check. The results are shown in Table 4–7.

Step 3: Individually, in small groups, or with the entire class, as directed by your instructor, answer the questions that follow.

1. Evaluate the selection process for the position of State Trooper and State Policewoman.
2. Assess the validity of the State Trooper Examination.
3. What changes would you recommend in the selection procedure?
4. How should the State Trooper Examination be changed?

Step 4: Discussion. In small groups, with the entire class, or in written form, share your answers to the questions above.

SUMMARY

How can a manager make more effective choices regarding the people he or she employs? How can Jamie Boyce at West Suburban Bank ensure that her selection of tellers is effective?

In this chapter we have examined a process that should increase the effectiveness of selection. The manager and human resources professionals must first perform a detailed job analysis. Next, the manager must determine the criteria a successful candidate should have. Third, with the assistance of human resources professionals, the manager must identify the best available instruments or techniques for assessing these criteria; instruments that demonstrate high reliability and validity, ease of administration, and reasonable cost. The more instruments or techniques used, the more accurate will be the prediction of performance.[54] Next, the manager or human resources professional must collect data about candidates, using these instruments or techniques. Finally, they must analyze the data and rank-order the candidates.

You analyzed how well the selection systems used in the Eastern Electronics Company and the State Personnel Department follow these steps for effective selection. In both situations you identified deficiencies in the selection system. You had the chance to practice effective selection in choosing an engineer for the Gamma Engineering Corporation. You also examined job application blanks, practiced conducting selection interviews, and assessed the usefulness of these instruments in measuring job-related criteria. Finally, you determined the reliability and validity of two tests.

Effective selection means identifying and securing the appropriate person for a particular job. Identification of the best person must be accompanied by organizational procedures that facilitate that person's acceptance of the job. This means strong communication between the organization and the candidate, after the choice is made, to convince the candidate to accept the offer.

ENDNOTES

[1]H. Jain and V. Murray, Why the human resources management function fails, *California Management Review* 26 (1984): 95.

[2]See *Albemarle Paper Company v. Moody*, 422 U.S. 405, 9 EPD#10, 230, 10 FEP 1181 (1975).

[3]See Division of Industrial-Organizational Psychology, *Principles for the Validation and Use of Personnel Selection Procedures* 2nd ed. (Berkeley, Cal.: American Psychological Association, 1980) for a more detailed discussion.

[4]R.D. Arvey, *Fairness in Selecting Employees* (Reading, Mass.: Addison-Wesley, 1979).

[5]B. Schneider, *Staffing Organizations* (Glenview, Ill.: Scott, Foresman, 1976).

[6]American Psychological Association, *op. cit.*

[7]American Psychological Association, *op. cit.*

[8]Schneider, *op. cit.*

[9]American Psychological Association, *op. cit.*

[10]R.M. Guion, Open a new window: Validities and values in psychological measurement, *American Psychologist* 29 (1974): 287–296.

[11]See R.M. Stogdill, *Handbook of Leadership* (New York: Free Press, 1974); C. Behn, Can intelligence tests predict executive competence?, *Personnel* 56 (July-August, 1979): 52–58.

[12]M.D. Hakel, Employment interviewing, in K.M. Rowland and G.R. Ferris, *Personnel Management* (Boston: Allyn and Bacon, 1980).

[13]American Psychological Association, *op. cit.*

[14]American Psychological Association, *op. cit.;* F.L. Schmidt and J.E. Hunter, The future of criterion-related validity, *Personnel Psychology* 33 (Spring 1980): 41–60.

[15]American Psychological Association, Inc., *Technical Recommendations for Psychological Tests and Diagnostic Techniques* (Washington, D.C.: APA, 1954).

[16]D. Magnusson, *Test Theory* (Reading, Mass.: Addison-Wesley, 1967).

[17]*Ibid.*

[18]See administration manuals for the Thematic Apperception Test and the Rorschach Inkblot Test.

[19]T.A. Jeswald, Issues in establishing an assessment center, in J.L. Moses and W.C. Byham, eds., *Applying the Assessment Center Method* (New York: Pergamon, 1977).

[20]J.E. Hunter and R.F. Hunter, Validity and utility of alternative predictors of job performance, *Psychological Bulletin* 96 (1984): 72–98; W.A. Owns, Background data, in M.D. Dunnette, ed., *Handbook of Industrial and Organizational Psychology* (Chicago: Rand McNally, 1976).

[21]Evaluating employment applications, *Personnel Journal* 63 (January 1984): 22–24.

[22]*Ibid.*

[23]B.D. Wonder and R.S. Keleman, Increasing the value of reference information, *Personnel Administrator* 29 (March 1984): 98–103; R. Deland, Reference checking methods, *Personnel Journal* 62 (June 1983): 458–463.

[24]E.L. Levine and S.M. Rudolph, Reference checking for personnel selection: The state of the art (Alexandria, Va.: American Society for Personnel Administration, 1978).

[25]M. Zippo and K. Greenberg, Reference checks—myth or facts, *Personnel* (November-December 1982): 52.

[26]*Ibid.*

[27]R.S. Lowell and J.A. DeLoach, Equal employment opportunity: Are you overlooking the application form?, *Personnel* 59 (July-August 1982): 49–55.

[28]See the administration manuals for these instruments and the catalogues from the test development companies.

[29]Hunter and Hunter, *op. cit.*

[30]*Ibid.*

[31]J.P. Campbell et al., *Managerial Behavior, Performance and Effectiveness* (New York: McGraw-Hill, 1970).

[32]Schneider, *op. cit.*

[33]*Ibid.*

[34]E.E. Ghiselli, *The Validity of Occupational Aptitude Tests* (New York: Wiley, 1966).

[35]J.J. Asher and J.A. Sciarrino, Realistic work sample tests: A review, *Personnel Psychology* 27 (1974): 519–533.

[36]Schneider, *op. cit.*

[37]W.C. Byham, Assessment centers for spotting future managers, *Harvard Business Review* 48 (July-August 1970); J.L. Moses, The assessment center method, in Moses and Byham, *op. cit.;* W.C. Byham, Application of the assessment center method, in Moses and Byham, *op. cit.*

[38]See V.R. Boehm, Assessment centers and management development, in Rowland and Ferris, *op. cit.,* for a detailed discussion of assessment centers; see also Jeswald, *op. cit.*

[39]W.E. Souder and A.M. Keksich, Assessment centers are evolving toward a bright future, *Personnel Administrator* 28 (November 1983): 80–87.

[40]Jeswald, *op. cit.*

[41]Task Force on Assessment Center Standards, Standards and ethical considerations for assessment center operations. Paper presented at the International Congress of the Assessment Center Method, New Orleans, La., June 1979.

[42]Boehm, *op. cit.*

[43]B.M. Cohen, J.L. Moses, and W.C. Byham, *The Validity of Assessment Centers: A Literature Review* (Pittsburgh, Pa.: Development Dimensions, 1974); A. Howard, An assessment of assessment centers, *Academy of Management Journal* 17 (1974): 115–134; A. Boche, Management concerns about assessment centers, in Moses and Byham, *op. cit.;* Byham, *op. cit.*

[44]R.J. Klimoski and W.J. Strickland, Assessment centers—valid or merely prescient?, *Personnel Psychology* 30 (1977): 353–361.

[45]*Ibid.*

[46]*Ibid.*

[47]Boche, *op. cit.;* Byham, *op. cit.*

[48]W.T. Woltz, How to interview supervisory candidates from the ranks, *Personnel* 57 (September-October 1980): 31–48.

[49]*Ibid.*

[50]S.G. Ginsburg, Preparing for executive position interviews—questions the interviewer might ask or be asked, *Personnel* 57 (July-August 1980): 31–44.

[51]B. Felton and S.R. Lamb, A model for systematic selection interviewing, *Personnel* 59 (1982): 40–48.

[52]F.M. Lopez, *Personnel Interviewing: Theory and Practice* 2nd ed. (New York: McGraw-Hill, 1975).

[53]*Ibid.*

[54]Jain and Murray, *op. cit.*

FURTHER READINGS

American Psychological Association, Division of Industrial-Organizational Psychology. *Principles for the Validation and Use of Personnel Selection Procedures* 2nd ed. Berkeley, Cal.: American Psychological Association, 1980.

.merican Psychological Association. *Standards for Educational and Psychological Tests and Manuals.* Washington, D.C.: American Psychological Association, 1973.

Arvey, R.D. *Fairness in Selecting Employees.* Reading, Mass.: Addison-Wesley, 1979.

Ledvinka, J. *Federal Regulation of Personnel and Human Resource Management.* Boston: Kent, 1982.

Lopez, F.M. *Personnel Interviewing: Theory and Practice* 2nd ed. New York: McGraw-Hill, 1975.

Moses, J.L., and Byham, W.C., eds. *Applying the Assessment Center Method.* New York: Pergamon, 1977.

Schneider, B. *Staffing Organizations.* Glenview, Ill.: Scott, Foresman, 1976.

CHAPTER 5

Addressing the Need for Decruitment

CHAPTER OUTLINE

LEARNING CHECKPOINTS

After completing the reading and activities in this chapter, students will be able to

- diagnose the situation that calls for decruitment;
- show how decruitment decisions relate to human resources planning;
- specify alternative approaches to reducing the supply of human resources;
- evaluate the completeness and responsiveness of decruitment in an organization;
- discuss the significance of obsolescence for human resources management;
- offer strategies for combatting obsolescence;
- describe the causes of plateauing in organizations;
- offer strategies for dealing with the plateaued performer;
- identify and offer a plan for dealing with an employee experiencing burnout;
- show how a manager or human resources professional can help a troubled employee;
- conduct an interview to fire an employee;
- design a decruitment system.

INTRODUCTION

> Pittsburgh—U.S. Steel Corp. said yesterday it will close all or part of about 30 steel mills, coal mines and other facilities, at a permanent cost of 15,400 jobs, in a bid to boost its sagging bottom line.
>
> The top steelmaker said it will write off $1.2 billion in assets—one of the largest write-offs in U.S. history—by slicing 16 percent of its steelmaking capacity. Most cutbacks are scheduled to take effect next April.
>
> The company also said it broke off talks on a controversial import deal with British Steel Corp. for "financial and economic reasons," said chairman David M. Roderick.
>
> Speaking after the company board held its year-end meeting, Roderick said that "while the decisions to suspend operations at the affected units are difficult for the employees and communities involved, they were unavoidable in light of global economic and market conditions in steel.
>
> "We intend to serve only those markets that we can supply with quality product at profits necessary to maintain viable operations," he said.
>
> . . . Steelworkers said they were stunned by the massive round of cutbacks.
>
> "I don't think I can do anything about it. It just tears you up," said Don Thomas, president of United Steelworkers Local 1219 at the Edgar Thomson works near Pittsburgh.
>
> . . . The closing would eliminate the jobs of 4590 active and 10,896 already laid-off employees in all U.S. Steel operations. In steelmaking, 3607 active and 7477 inactive workers will be affected.
>
> . . . At the Fairfield Works, however, some operations will be revived, creating 1600 jobs, the company said. And at the Gary Works, a continuous caster will be installed, increasing production capacity for strip steel.[1]

This article describes another in a series of decruitment activities at the United States Steel Company; to cope with increasing competition and inflation, U.S. Steel reduced its work force, through layoffs, to reduce costs. *Decruitment* refers to those activities designed to reduce the labor supply within an organization or any part of it. But are layoffs the only alternative available when an organization has a surplus of employees?

Altogether, there are several decruitment options open to organizations. *Layoff,* such as that announced by U.S. Steel, refers to an organization removing individuals or groups from their positions for the short, medium, or long term. *Attrition* refers to allowing the work force to diminish naturally, over time, as a result of employees' resignations and retirements. *Lateral transfer* refers to the movement of individuals from one job to another one with different responsibilities, but at the same level in the organizational hierarchy. *Downward transfers* resemble lateral transfers except the new position is lower in the organizational hierarchy. *Firing* refers to an involuntary termination of an employee, generally in response to performance or attitudinal problems.

The choice of a decruitment option depends in part on the amount of time available to reduce the oversupply of workers. Good human resources planning always takes into account which jobs are likely to experience an oversupply of workers in the short run and the long run. Most human resources planners should increase the time frame available for implementing successful decruitment programs; that is, plan ahead more than they currently do. Not all organizations face the necessity of decruiting but it has become an increasingly frequent problem. Too often, reducing the labor force is difficult because no systematic procedure for decruitment exists.

In this chapter we develop a framework for evaluating the quality of a decruitment program. First, the chapter examines the reasons for decruitment. Next, it traces the steps in a comprehensive decruitment program. Then it investigates individual performance dilemmas that decruitment may address. Finally, the chapter concludes with questions that can help evaluate decruitment programs and reviews the appropriate roles played by managers and human resources professionals.

REASONS FOR DECRUITMENT

What conditions have made decruitment a major issue for organizations? Declining economic conditions or shifts in demand for a product or service may mandate decruitment. For example, U.S. Steel thought that decruitment (layoff) was necessary to reduce costs so as to compete more effectively in the steel industry nationally and internationally.[2]

The introduction of new technology may also require decruitment. Automation can call for less-skilled workers or reduce the total number of employees necessary to do the same jobs as previously.[3] Product or market changes might require personnel changes as well. Layoffs or lateral transfers may be necessary to deal with shifting skill requirements. The increasing computerization of all industrial functions reduces the demand for employees who lack computer skills.[4] The demographic characteristics of the organization's work force, too, such as a large number of workers with seniority, or an overabundance of management-level employees, can call for decruitment. Economic constraints may demand a reduction in salary costs. Or concern for the development of key talent in the organization may call for unblocking management positions. Human resources professionals need to identify where staff changes are needed. Organizations may respond to these dilemmas by laterally moving employees to different jobs or demoting them from managerial to nonmanagerial positions; but in any case the design and implementation of a decruitment program should follow a systematic plan.

STEPS IN DECRUITMENT

Decruitment involves four steps: (1) a situational audit to determine the nature of the oversupply; (2) identification of decruitment options; (3) selection of the best option or options; and (4) implementation of the program. Both human resources professionals and managers should be involved in performing all steps.

Identifying the Nature of the Oversupply

The implementation of any decruitment system begins with the human resources forecasts described in Chapter 2. These forecasts should indicate far enough in advance whether a surplus will exist so that the organization has flexibility in determining the most appropriate decruitment programs. Shifts in demand for a product or service can arise for different reasons and influence the extent and nature of the oversupply. So environmental, organizational, and job analyses should all influence program decisions.

Environmental Analysis. The environmental analysis should allow a human resources professional to answer two questions about an oversupply. (1) How long will it last? (2) Is the oversupply organizational, industry-wide, or geographical? U.S. Steel had to address these questions to determine feasible options. As a result, U.S. Steel may have decided that the oversupply would last three to five years and was industry-wide. (Top management may also have determined that the workers' skills could not be used elsewhere in the organization as a result of an organizational analysis.) In general, unpredicted changes in the environment, or predicted changes that occur earlier than expected, can force organizations to adjust their staffing more rapidly than their original human resources plans would suggest.

Organizational Analyses. Probably the most significant determinants of decruitment activities are the financial resources available to the organization. Organizations with extra resources can maintain an oversupply of employees longer than can organizations with limited resources. The availability of resources in the short and long run not only determines the necessity for decruitment but the most appropriate type of decruitment programs. Organizations also vary in the ways they are willing to expend resources. Some organizations provide job-hunting support and counseling for laid-off employees. Others offer financial incentives for early retirement.

The organizational analysis must consider the climate of the organization in determining appropriate decruitment activities. For example, those activities that involve movement within the firm, such as lateral or downward transfers, are often voluntary and negotiated and therefore require the cooperation and support of several individuals and groups within the organization. If organizational members feel that their organizations strongly support individual prerogatives then they are more likely to support decruitment programs that shift employees to other jobs inside the organization than if they view top managers as autocratic despots. And of course the ability of individual managers to negotiate creative means of reducing the work force depends on the support these activities receive from top management.

Job Analyses. These form the cornerstone of the decruitment analysis. First of all, human resources professionals use job analyses in employment planning, which also determines where there is a surplus of employees. Using the detailed job descriptions, specifications, skills inventories, and other data, a manager can then assess the skills and knowledge required to perform a variety of jobs to determine the feasibility of moving job holders to other positions within the organization, rather than shifting them out altogether.

The specific staffing needs for each job, department, and division in the organization must be assessed before a manager can select a decruitment option. To assess these needs, the manager should ask four questions:

1. What other jobs exist that require the same skills as those with the surplus of employees?
2. Where are these jobs located?
3. Do these jobs have a demand for more employees?
4. How can employees be moved into these jobs?

Identifying Decruitment Options

As increasing numbers of organizations have faced an oversupply of staff, they have used a variety of decruitment programs to reduce the number of employees. In this section we examine the following basic approaches to decruitment: (1) attrition, (2) transfers, (3) layoffs, (4) involuntary termination, (5) early retirement, and (6) phased retirement.

Attrition. Attrition allows an organization to reduce its work force with a minimum of secondary consequences. It is the reduction of the number of staff through resignations and retirements only; employees who leave the organization simply are not replaced. This process reduces the labor pool in a relatively slow and tension-free fashion. Because it does not threaten the job security of other organizational members, they generally view it positively. The major drawback is often an uneven distribution of work in the short and medium run until the system reaches equilibrium.

To implement this approach, however, human resources plans must accurately project the number of employees needed three to five years hence; attrition only effectively responds to relatively slow environmental changes. But when predictions of a changing technology or economic situation call for different types of labor over a three- to five-year period, the use of attrition can often address the needs without the dysfunctions of other decruitment methods.

Transfers. This approach can solve two types of staffing problems: (1) an oversupply in some departments or jobs while there is a demand for employees in others and (2) deficiencies in an individual's performance.

In the first case, the organization has an oversupply of one type of employee but not of another. To alleviate this situation, the organization can attempt to shift employees into jobs where demand still exists. For example, bookkeepers can be moved from the accounts receivable to the accounts payable departments; middle managers can be moved from operations to sales; and other staff can be moved from financial analyst positions to market research positions.

Such lateral transfer programs can be legitimized by including job rotation programs in normal training and development activities. In such programs organizational members are regularly moved from job to job, so lateral transfers for decruitment purposes have no stigma attached to them. Such programs also encourage organizational members to regularly seek new job opportunities, thus creating a climate that supports job mobility in general.

In the second case, where individuals have performance problems in a particular position, lateral transfers can result in a better fit between the individual and the job. For example, someone who performs poorly in the quality control group for the production department may do better in the engineering group. Or a clerk-typist in the finance department may perform better in a department that deals more with words and less with numbers.

Downward transfers; that is, transfers to lower positions in the hierarchy, can address these same two situations. They typically occur when individuals experience performance problems in their current jobs. But decruitment by downward transfer can also reduce an oversupply of individuals in certain jobs. It may unblock advancement opportunities for some highly qualified individuals as well.

One Canadian manufacturing firm, for example, initiated a downward transfer program to reduce a surplus of managers.[5] Executives moved some employees to lower positions, guaranteeing them their current compensation level for approximately one year. After that, compensation was adjusted to a level appropriate to the new position. This compensation arrangement was designed to reduce employee resistance to this type of staffing program.

Layoffs. This decruitment approach is most commonly used to reduce the number of job holders in more than one job category. Layoffs mean that management removes individuals from their positions but would be willing to rehire them if conditions in the organization improve or change. For example, both the automobile and steel industries used layoffs extensively as a way of reducing their work force and responding to economic pressures in the early 1980s, as described in the introduction to this chapter.[6]

Although large-scale layoffs can send ripples—or even waves—through a community, they offer organizations flexibility in dealing with an oversupply of labor: some of those laid off may be rehired at a later time. Particularly in unionized organizations, where financial benefits may continue during the first year of a layoff, individuals can and do delay seeking other employment.[7] They expect, sometimes correctly so, that they will be reemployed at some time in the future. Because of these expectations, organizations have a responsibility to inform employees as accurately as possible about the likelihood of their reemployment. Of course, layoffs can become permanent: many of the steelworkers described in the introduction to this chapter were not rehired.

Layoffs can have significant emotional consequences for the remaining organizational employees. Typically they begin to question their own job security. They may also feel that they are performing twice the work that they did before the layoffs.

Many organizations have conducted *outplacement* activities to help laid-off or terminated employees find new positions and adjust to their new status. Outplacement counseling is "a process of helping terminated employees face the crisis of job loss with renewed self-esteem and to conduct a positive job placement or retraining campaign."[8] In 1981 one estimate indicated that approximately 15,000 executives and managers in the United States received outplacement counseling.[9] Outplacement typically offers (1) career counseling, (2) psychological counseling, and (3) job hunting assistance.[10] Companies hire professionals to teach leaving employees to assess the value of their experiences, talents, personality, and accomplishments for other jobs; establish a job and career strategy; prepare a strong resume; use diverse sources for job information and contacts; succeed in employment interviews; and choose the best job offers."[11]

Organizations have offered laid-off employees the use of offices and telephones for a month after their last work day, free reproduction of resumes, and career counseling in job hunting skills. In one hospital, the human resources department conducted the entire outplacement program. They hung posters that described and located the outplacement office; posted lists of available jobs in three places; organized orientation meetings and a meeting between the president and those workers being separated to share information; gained union support and cooperation; sent mailings to other personnel directors to alert them to the advantages of employing the laid-off workers; invited other personnel directors to lunch to further promote hiring; assembled a benefits entitlement package; provided individual career counseling; and maintained the records for all the new hirings and other contacts between employees and potential employers.[12] Likewise, Pfizer Pharmaceuticals established an outplacement center that served as a command post for 250 ex-executives. The center offered a suite of offices where they could work, extensive reference materials, access to a staff of counselors, trainers, and psychologists, resources for phoning and photocopying, and workshops on job campaigns.[13]

In general, outplacement activities follow four phases: (1) orientation—planning and negotiating for services with the organization, providing counseling, and introducing life/career planning; (2) evaluation—testing and self-assessment; (3) job targeting—choosing job objectives, developing job targets and resumes, selecting possible job employment arenas; and (4) job campaign—obtaining interviews, making the job decision, following up and reporting progress.[14]

A number of organizations have absorbed the costs of such activities to facilitate the exit of employees and because they believed they had a moral obligation to do so. But maintaining the organization's positive image in the marketplace in this way can pay off with consumers' good will in the future; it can also pay off when hiring in the future, since the organization is viewed in the labor market as compassionate.

Few managers have the skills to act as outplacement counselors themselves, so they should lobby for outplacement services in their organizations if they do not already exist. Human resources professionals, on the other hand, often have the knowledge and skills to act as outplacement counselors. But if it is not feasible for them to perform in this capacity they may choose to hire outside outplacement consultants.

Involuntary Termination. Most managers find firing employees distasteful and avoid it. Still, employee termination is necessary in response to five types of problems: (1) defective job performance due to incompetence, negligence, changed job requirements, or lack of attention to the job; (2) violation of plant rules, including absenteeism, chronic alcoholism, or drug abuse, (3) violence or fighting at work, (4) insubordination, and (5) objectionable or illegal personal behavior such as sexual harassment or dishonesty.[15] Firing should occur only if these situations are well documented and if training or counseling fails to correct the problems. Firing must also meet legal requirements, as discussed in Chapter 13. Managers must learn to identify situations where there is a misfit between the worker and the job that cannot be corrected through future training. Human resources professionals can assist managers in spotting these situations.

Consider for example, the employee who is absent at least two days per month and frequently comes to work late. Attempts to introduce attitudinal and behavioral changes through training programs have failed. The manager seems to have no other option but to fire the employee. Or consider the small organization that hires an employee and discovers that he or she lacks the skills claimed; after six months of training no improvement occurs. Both cases illustrate situations where firing the employee is most appropriate.

All organizations should have a written termination policy.[16] It should clearly state that managers must document the case for termination with concrete business reasons. An example of such a policy could be termination for three consecutive below-average performance appraisals or missing at least three performance objectives. In addition, the policy should identify, in writing, the payment arrangements for the terminated employee, if any. For example, an employee receiving less than $30,000 in salary might receive one month's severance pay; an individual with a salary greater than $30,000 might receive four months' severance pay. The policy should also specify who will give references for the terminated employee, and those involved should agree among themselves about what they will say. Finally, the policy should specify whether the terminated employee will receive outplacement services.

In firing an employee, the manager should do the following:

- clearly list the performance deficiencies that exist;
- clearly specify the conditions for the firing;
- be sensitive to the personal situation of the employee;
- offer early retirement instead, if possible;
- limit the amount of time the worker can remain employed in the organization.[17]

When an employee is dismissed for cause, the manager should neither encourage nor discourage inquiries about him or her.[18] The manager who fires an employee must inform other employees about the reasons for the firing, while at the same time maintaining confidentiality for the terminated employee. Managers often face a dilemma, therefore, about what information to convey to other employees, since the firing of an employee who coworkers perceive to perform well can create dysfunctions throughout the organization. The manager should point out obvious job failures and mention that these were discussed in frequent conversations with the individual. Management's position should be the following: the decision to terminate was not made abruptly; it occurred after many discussions with the individual; management thought the change was necessary; not all of the facts are known to others; management does not think it appropriate to go into detail; and the manager is willing to discuss with any employee his or her own job situation.[19] Of course clarity and consistency in dealing with poor performers should also reduce perceptions of unfair or arbitrary firing. Reading 5–1, "When the News Is Bad: Leveling with Employees" by Gary G. Whitney, provides additional guidelines for terminating an employee.

Early Retirement. Another approach to decruitment involves speeding up the attrition process through encouraging early retirement. This means that for a specified period of time, ranging from a few months to a year, older and more senior employees are offered incentives if they retire voluntarily.[20] Common incentives include early receipt of pension monies, a cash bonus, the continuation of full or partial salary for a period of time, and other financial supplements.

Organizations can use early retirement to reduce a high seniority level so as to reduce salary and benefit costs, or to open promotional opportunities by decreasing the number of high-level managerial employees. Early retirement can also be an alternative to employee layoffs. Those who elect early retirement have the opportunity to retire with dignity rather than being laid off, receive extra monetary benefits, begin a new career, or initiate a major job change.

Polaroid Corporation introduced an early retirement incentive program in the early 1980s that had dramatic results.[21] Employees were offered as much as one year's salary to leave the organization. A much larger number of employees accepted the offer than Polaroid had expected. Employees at all levels of the organization used the salary bonus as an opportunity to pursue further education, start their own businesses, or retire early. From the organization's perspective, the cost associated with the program was worthwhile; it maintained positive attitudes of employees toward the company while at the same time reducing the labor force.

Phased Retirement. Many organizations believe their employees can contribute to the organization regardless of their life stage. Thus, in addition to early retirement incentives, organizations increasingly offer special programs to prepare individuals for retirement. They attempt to identify the diverse preferences of different segments of their work force to create opportunities for the organization and advantages for the individual employees.[22]

One survey indicated that 15–20 percent of organizations allow gradual retirement or extended leaves, vacations, and sabbaticals prior to retirement; 20 percent provide tuition assistance; and 50 percent allow employees to continue work beyond normal retirement age, while deferring or receiving pension benefits.[23] Human resources professionals can assist employees with retirement by conducting programs that prepare them early in their careers for the middle-to-later years by providing educational assistance and making alternative work options available.[24] In addition to counseling and financial planning, organizations can provide ways of reducing an individual's work load prior to retirement.

When designing a preretirement program, human resources professionals must carefully define the nature of the target population, use a variety of resources in planning, carefully choose appropriate materials to present, and focus on life planning rather than retirement planning.[25] These programs can facilitate exit from the rigors of organizational life while still ensuring that retiring employees do not feel stranded or isolated.

Choosing among Decruitment Options

The human resources professional should counsel managers at all levels about the most appropriate decruitment programs for a given set of circumstances. Some questions that help determine the appropriate options include:

1. Is the decruitment permanent or temporary?
2. How fast must the reduction occur?
3. For what purpose is the decruitment necessary (e.g., to reduce costs, unblock positions, deal with performance problems)?

Table 5–1 summarizes the various decruitment options on these dimensions.

Implementing a Decruitment Program

Once the decruitment needs have been identified and the appropriate staffing options selected, implementation can begin. Implementation should involve systematic, thoughtful, and consistent use of the options selected and should consider the ramifications of the program throughout the organization. Managers in all involved departments must be prepared for the program's operation: they must be trained in its procedures and psychologically ready to implement it.

So far, we have discussed decruitment, for the most part, as a way to reduce the overall number of employees in an organization, or the number of employees in certain departments or types of positions. But a decruitment program should also address individual performance problems.

Option	Permanency	Speed	Uses		
			Reduce Costs	Deal with Performance Problems	Open Promotion Opportunities
Attrition	Permanent	Slow	Yes	No	Yes
Lateral Transfer	Either	Fast	No	Yes	Yes
Downward Transfer	Either	Fast	No	Yes	Yes
Layoffs	Either	Fast	Yes	No	Yes
Involuntary Termination	Permanent	Fast	No	Yes	No
Early Retirement	Permanent	Slow-Fast	Yes	Yes	Yes
Retirement	Permanent	Slow	Yes	No	Yes

Table 5–1 COMPARISON OF DECRUITMENT OPTIONS

INDIVIDUAL PERFORMANCE DILEMMAS

What types of difficulties in individual performance call for decruitment strategies? In this section we examine (1) employee obsolescence, (2) the plateaued performer, (3) the burned-out employee, and (4) the difficult employee.

Employee Obsolescence

Obsolescence refers to "the degree to which organizational professionals lack the up-to-date knowledge or skills necessary to maintain effective performance in either their current or future work roles."[26] As the rate of technical advancement increases, the number of employees who become obsolete at the earlier stages in their careers also increases. Without constant upgrading technical employees, in particular, find that their educational training becomes outdated within a five- to ten-year period.[27]

Managers can also experience obsolescence. In this case, it results from the creation of new production methods due to technological changes; mergers, acquisitions, new products, and new markets that cause organizational changes; increased computerization; greater numbers of white-collar workers; and increased quantification of managerial activities such as operations research and systems analysis techniques.[28]

Managerial obsolescence has been positively associated with a manager's age and work experience. It is also associated with the functional area in which the manager works, the level in the organization's hierarchy, the manager's decision-making responsibility, and the challenge of the job.[29] On the other hand, obsolescence is negatively associated with mobility, a manager's perceptions of his or her own learning ability, attitudes about the importance of updated knowledge, and membership in professional associations. It has not been significantly related to educational and professional/technical qualifications or type of updating activities in which the manager has engaged.[30]

Supervision has been shown to contribute to a subordinate's growth and development.[31] In light of this, managers must play a major role in reducing obsolescence among their employees. In addition, managers and human resources professionals can and should alter any organizational characteristics that encourage obsolescence.[32] To do this managers must facilitate communication among employees, managers, planners, and those initiating technological change; defuse any defensive attitudes about new knowledge and skills; and focus on both current performance and long-term development. Top managers must recognize that technological change occurs and support practices and programs that encourage individuals to grow, develop, and learn for the future. Simultaneously, human resources professionals must provide adequate training programs and as much knowledge as possible about future human resources management requirements.

How can organizations deal with obsolescence? The most common strategies include training/development and career management activities. However, certain types of decruitment activities can also act as incentives for employees to deal with obsolescence. For example, the regular use of lateral transfers forces individuals to learn new areas and remain effective. Downward transfers can be used as a disincentive for employees who do not remain technically current. And of course the threat of involuntary termination can prod individuals to remain current.

The Plateaued Performer

Related to obsolescence is the problem of the performer who has moved as high in the organizational hierarchy as he or she ever will.[33] In this case, although the plateaued performer does well in his or her present position, organizational constraints prevent further advancement. "What happens to the individual and how does the organization react when the glowing prospects of steady advancement are replaced by a five-, ten-, or 20-year horizon offering the same job, the same challenges, the same colleagues?"[34] "For management, the basic challenge is not to weed out deadwood but to maintain the motivation and performance of managers who no longer see the carrot of vertical mobility."[35]

How does a manager recognize that a subordinate (or even himself or herself) is a plateaued performer? Answers to the following questions can provide early warning signals: Have you been in the same job longer than others in similar jobs? Do you have as much or more managerial and technical ability than others? Have you made some, but not a very large number of, job changes in your career? Do you have outstanding accomplishments? Have you received positive performance ratings in your jobs? Has your personal growth progressed at the same or faster rate than that of your peers? Do you have a mentor (see Chapter 8)?[36]

In dealing with a plateaued performer the manager must try to keep him or her from being bored through job rotation or assignment to special projects. In addition, the manager must determine the worker's perceptions of his or her own skills and abilities, and provide frequent feedback (see Chapter 6 for discussion of performance evaluation). The manager should also help the worker develop realistic expectations about advancement and encourage steady performance through the use of both feedback and various kinds of incentives, such as merit pay raises or bonuses.

When a plateaued employee loses motivation and stops performing adequately, the manager must also engage in frequent counseling directed at instruction, evaluation, discipline, problem-solving, and development of the subordinate.[37] Sometimes the manager can institute lateral or downward transfers to motivate such employees, which will then free the positions for other employees.

Helping the Burned-out Employee

Rather than the organization causing a worker to plateau, the worker himself or herself may become so tired of the work that advancement—or even adequate performance—stops. Employee *burnout* has been used to describe the worker who is "fed up with his or her job."[38] The term was originally used to describe "a syndrome of emotional exhaustion, depersonalization, and reduced personal accomplishment that can occur among individuals who do 'people work' of some kind."[39] But the definition has since been extended to include all types of work; the data processing workers, for example, who frequently experience burnout because they feel trapped in an assignment that goes on year after year.[40]

Working harder and accomplishing less, getting cynical and disenchanted, becoming more irritable and short-tempered, and tiring easily signal the occurrence of burnout.[41] Other symptoms are (1) feelings of emotional exhaustion about a once-pleasurable job; (2) negative, cynical attitudes toward the job, organization, and its customers; (3) unhappiness with oneself; (4) dissatisfaction with job accomplishments; (5) boredom, depression, hopelessness, and feelings of being trapped in the job; (6) frequent illness; (7) frequent job turnover, often not for career reasons; (8) overdedication and overcommitment to the job, which leads to cynicism when the job does not meet expectations; and (9) low morale, high absenteeism, drug or alcohol reliance, and family problems.[42]

The organizational setting, the job, or personal characteristics can all cause burnout. Organizations contribute to it if work conditions are unpleasant or stressful, treatment of employees is dehumanizing, and rewards given are inadequate or inappropriate.[43] Jobs that are repetitive provide few opportunities for creativity, require intensive and prolonged interpersonal interactions, or are overly complex can also contribute to burnout. And the individual's tolerance for stress and ambiguity influence whether he or she will experience burnout.

Treating burnout requires diagnosing and understanding its causes, determining the changes necessary for the individual to return to normal work function, developing individuals' sensitivity to the signs of burnout, and developing skills for discussing feelings and emotions so that burnout will be less likely.[44] The organization must develop programs that help individuals cope with the causes of burnout. These include, for example, good selection practices that ensure the person-job-organization fit (see Chapter 4), job enrichment (see Chapter 14), and stress management training programs. Reading 5–2, "Preventing Employee Burnout," by Susan Jackson and Randall Schuler, offers additional remedies for burnout.

Dealing with the Difficult Performer

Like burned out performers, recalcitrant employees may display negative attitudes or show signs of alcoholism, drug abuse, or other personal problems. Managers must deal with the declining productivity of such workers. How should the manager react to such a situation?

The manager must first diagnose the causes of the difficulty. The human resources professional can act as a valuable resource in the diagnostic phase. Those trained in psychological evaluation can apply their expertise; others can hire consultants to assist managers in diagnosis.

Next the manager must determine whether he or she can change the conditions causing the poor performance. Does the employee need to address alcoholism or drug dependence? Does the employee need more flexibility to deal with family problems?

Having identified the nature of the problem, the manager should implement remedial action. Such action can incorporate permanent or temporary transfers, layoffs, or even firing of the employees. Or the action may require disciplinary measures of some kind. When individuals do not perform adequately, organizations should rely on *progressive discipline procedures.* Such procedures typically involve four steps:

1. The manager meets with the employee to counsel him or her about ways to improve unsatisfactory behavior.
2. The manager issues a written reprimand that describes the deficiencies, reports discussions held about the subject, establishes expected levels of performance, and specifies a timetable for correcting the behavior.
3. The manager issues a final warning.
4. The manager dismisses the employee.[45]

Remedial action can emphasize the use of an organization's special employee assistance programs instead. Employee assistance programs provide counseling and rehabilitation activities for workers experiencing personal problems that hinder effective job performance.[46] They frequently combine actions directed at the troubled employee and his or her manager. One company offers 24-hour telephone counseling as well as a corporate counseling program to deal with both personal problems and work problems, including compensation and benefits, performance disputes, transfers and promotions, policies and procedures, interpersonal relationships, and career development.[47]

As part of these programs, the manager, worker, and counselor agree on acceptable job performance for the difficult employee. They emphasize early identification of problem employees and the development of diverse strategies for meeting each worker's unique needs.[48]

AN INTEGRATED DECRUITMENT SYSTEM

Effective human resources management requires a decruitment system that can be called on as needed and that is integrated with other human resources management functions, particularly performance appraisal, training and development, and career management. The decruitment system must motivate managers to regularly initiate activities to help them diagnose the existence of an oversupply of employees or individual performance problems.

After identifying the decruitment needs, the manager selects an option from those in place in the organization. The organization should have detailed procedures that facilitate implementation of the various options, and should include provisions for outplacement activities, retirement support, and exit interviews.

The Exit Interview

Some organizations always interview employees when they resign voluntarily. In these enterprises management believes the exit interview can reduce turnover by gathering information about the problems employees have encountered in the workplace. But modified exit interviews can also be conducted when an employee leaves any position for any reason—early retirement, transfer, or even layoffs. Human resources professionals can conduct such interviews without threatening the terminated employee.

A recent survey of eighteen major organizations indicated that two-thirds of them conduct exit interviews.[49] In most of these organizations, the personnel department conducts the interview to determine the reasons for employee turnover. Topics covered include the reason for departure; the nature of the new job and salary; a rating of job, supervision, working conditions, advancement opportunities, training, and pay; whether the departure could have been prevented; the most-liked and least-liked aspects of the jobs; and any suggestions for the organization.

Figure 5–1 shows a sample exit interview questionnaire. Although this questionnaire is directed primarily toward employees leaving voluntarily, an adapted version can be used in conjunction with other decruitment activities. Human resources professionals and managers can use the information gathered in such an interview to investigate and correct problems identified by employees.

Employee's Name	☐ Exempt Salaried ☐ Hourly ☐ Salaried Non-Exempt	Date of Birth	EEO Code
Job Title	Grade	Date Hired	
Group or Corp. Function	Ending Base Salary	Eff. Date of Term.	
Department	Time in Present Job yrs. mos.	Total GAF Service yrs. mos.	
Location	Other GAF Positions		

Type of Termination: ☐ Resignation ☐ w/notice ☐ w/o notice ☐ Layoff ☐ Discharge ☐ Early Ret. ☐ Normal Ret. ☐ Release ☐ Other (explain)

☐ Voluntary Term.
☐ Involuntary Term.
Reason(s) for (excl. Normal Ret.)

Was it Preventable ☐ Yes ☐ No (explain)

Name and Address of New Firm | Job Title | New Rate of Pay

Employee's Opinion About:

Salary

Benefits

Working Conditions

Work Load

Progress with Company

Employee's Morale (feelings toward work and the company)

Department, Plant, etc. Morale (his/her opinion of **others'** feelings toward work and the company)

Relationship with Co-Workers (and comments regarding working relationship)

Immediate Supervisor's Name and Title (and comments regarding working relationship)

Figure 5–1 SAMPLE OF AN EXIT INTERVIEW FORM

Continued

Any Needed Changes in Dept., Plant, etc. to Improve Operations and Conditions

____

Comments on Other Company Policies and Procedures

____

*Not to be completed by immediate supervisor unless completely unavoidable.

Termination Checklist
(Use "X" where applicable, "O" where not applicable)

Benefits Discussed

- ☐ Group Insurance Conversion
- ☐ State Disability Insurance
- ☐ Retirement Plan
- ☐ Vacation Eligibility
- ☐ Severance Pay (if eligible)
- ☐ Unemployment Insurance

Notification

- ☐ Credit Union
- ☐ In-Plant Bank Facility
- ☐ Employee Associations
- ☐ Plant Security Force
- ☐ Union Representative
- ☐ Facility Security Officer*

*Any employee who has a security clearance must complete a security termination statement.

Return of Property

Company Accounts (explain)

- ☐ Travel Advance ______________________________
- ☐ Misc. Unpaid Balances (for safety equipment, etc.) ______________________________

Credit Cards

- ☐ Air Travel
- ☐ Telephone
- ☐ Rail Travel
- ☐ Car Rental
- ☐ Other (specify) ____________

Disposition of Above: ______________________________

Keys

- ☐ Plant
- ☐ Desk
- ☐ Auto
- ☐ Other
- ☐ Office
- ☐ Files
- ☐ Lockers ____________

Disposition of Above: ______________________________

Equipment, Samples, Tools

- ☐ Automobile
- ☐ Sample Equipment
- ☐ Office Equipment (dictation equipt., calculators, etc.)
- ☐ Tools
- ☐ Memo Account Items
- ☐ Audio-Visual Equipment

Disposition of Above: ______________________________

Manuals, Books, Documents, etc.

- ☐ Security
- ☐ Organization Charts/Tables
- ☐ Notebooks
- ☐ Classified Documents (DOD)
- ☐ Designs
- ☐ Sales Figures
- ☐ Books
- ☐ Company Policies
- ☐ Papers
- ☐ Memoranda
- ☐ Formulae
- ☐ Customer List
- ☐ Price Lists
- ☐ Profit Figures, etc.

Disposition of Above: ______________________________

Miscellaneous

- ☐ Identification Card/Badge
- ☐ Safety Equipment (indicate) ______________________________
- ☐ Other (indicate) ______________________________

Disposition of Above: ______________________________

Figure 5–1 Continued

Continued

All employees are to be reminded of their obligations under the Invention and Secrecy Agreement signed at time of employment. ☐ Accomplished

Interviewer's Comments and Evaluation of Reasons for Termination:
Include references to terminee's mood. (If additional comments and/or rebuttals by members of management should be made, attach them on a separate sheet).

Interviewer's Signature	Interviewer's Name and Location	Date

(please print)

From "Exit Interviews: Don't Just Say Good-Bye," by Andrew Sherwood, copyright September 1983. Reprinted with the permission of *Personnel Journal,* Costa Mesa, California; all rights reserved.

Figure 5–1 Continued

Implications for Human Resources Professionals

Human resources professionals have a major responsibility in the design and implementation of decruitment activities. Effective programs include

1. monitoring the environment for any changes that might necessitate decruitment activities (conscientious human resources planning facilitates this)
2. evaluating organizational resources that limit employment and constrain various decruitment activities;
3. knowing the types of activities conducted in other organizations and continually thinking of creative alternatives for dealing with employee surpluses and individual performance problems;
4. systematically weighing the pros and cons of all decruitment options, considering the speed, permanency, and type of problem to be handled;
5. initiating and overseeing outplacement activities when appropriate; and ensuring the existence of employee assistance programs for difficult employees and career development programs for plateaued performers; and
6. conducting exit interviews with all terminated or laid-off employees and communicating the information gathered in this way to managers for corrective action.

Implications for Managers

Managers have primary responsibility for conveying information about decruitment to employees in cases of an oversupply, and in dealing directly with performance problems. To do this effectively, managers must

1. be well informed about existing decruitment policies and be trained in the implementation of newly introduced procedures;

2. monitor individual performance and deal with deficiencies directly, using progressive discipline procedures; and terminate employees expediently but with compassion and sensitivity when performance cannot be improved;
3. diagnose and respond to obsolescence, plateaued performers, and employee burnout; and attempt to prevent these problems by the use of job rotation, training and development programs, referring employees for counseling, providing diverse career paths, and offering educational opportunities.

READINGS

Reading 5–1

WHEN THE NEWS IS BAD: LEVELING WITH EMPLOYEES

Gary G. Whitney

How much can it cost a company when a manager fails to communicate bad news to a subordinate? A large hotel chain recently found out when it was required to pay a $2,000 discrimination claim because one of its supervisors couldn't level with an employee about his inadequate performance. In this case, the supervisor had become increasingly dissatisfied with the performance of the employee, who had been on the job for a month. Unable to bring himself to confront the employee with charges of unacceptable performance (a subjective judgment), he fired the employee for "excessive absenteeism" (a less subjective judgment).

The employee filed a claim because, in fact, he had missed only one day in his month of employment. Having no defense, the hotel chain paid the claim; to have argued poor performance at that point would not have been an acceptable defense. The claim could have been avoided, however, if the supervisor had been prepared to deliver bad news. And, with a little help from his personnel department, he might *literally* have been prepared to deliver it!

Occasionally managers must deliver such bad news as: "Your request for transfer has been denied," "Your project has been cancelled," or, in an extreme situation, "You're fired." Neither formal management training nor informal training currently offer any help for coping with these stressful situations. Personnel textbooks typically have several chapters instructing managers on how to interview, select, and socialize new employees, but they rarely devote even a paragraph to instructing managers on how to tell subordinates that their employment is terminated. A search of the psychiatric and social work literature on separation anxiety (dying) discloses that there is no agreement in theory or practice on how to deliver bad news to patients or to their families. In both business and medical literature, the advice on this issue generally makes the assumption that the bad news has already been delivered; consequently, only advice on how to cope with the resultant stress is offered.

NEGATIVE SPIRAL

Managers need to develop this confrontation skill because the way in which bad news is delivered has a major impact on the amount of stress created. When a message will cause stress, a poor delivery unnecessarily increases that stress; a skillful delivery helps the receiver successfully adapt to new circumstances.

A manager delivering bad news ought to anticipate the recipient's stress and resulting negative reaction—a reaction that may well be against the manager. This anticipation, coupled with a lack of knowledge about managing stress, is likely to create anxiety for the manager, thus decreasing his or her ability to effectively control the situation. The result is a vicious negative spiral—the greater the stress for the deliverer, the less effective he or she will be at delivering the bad news and the greater will be the recipient's stress and the probability of an overtly negative response. Anticipating this reaction further escalates the manager's own stress.

The manager may react to this anxiety by avoiding the confrontation entirely. When referring to a manager's inability to fire an employee, Lawrence Steinmetz calls this avoidance "dehiring." Dehiring is the act of indirectly driving the undesirable employee to resign. Steinmetz argues that this approach is not effective, for three reasons: The manager loses control of the situation; it is least effective with the poorest performers; and it is unethical because it sabotages the employee. This is similar to physicians' practices as reported in one study, which stated that 70 to 90 per cent of the responding doctors reported that they do not tell their terminal patients straightforwardly that they are going to die. Such indirect methods of communication fail to allow recipients of bad news to work through their grief and, further, they prevent other resources (family, colleagues, friends, and institutions) from helping recipients adapt to the new situation.

Forewarned Is Forearmed

Knowing the recipient's probable responses can help the deliverer plan and control the situation for the benefit of both parties. Thus the deliverer with advance knowledge has the opportunity and, I believe, the responsibility to prepare a minimally stressful confrontation. This will attenuate the negative spiral of anxiety.

With this end in mind, this article presents a general model of stress reaction that is derived from Richard S. Lazarus's book *Psychological Stress and the Coping Process* (McGraw-Hill Book Co., 1966) and that is based on various psychiatrists' and sociologists' observations. The model is then used to derive some guidelines for managers who want to deliver bad news in an effective, but least stressful way. The organizational form of "capital punishment," termination for cause, is used as an example of the bad news that must be delivered.

THE STRESS-REACTION MODEL

The stress-reaction model is divided into a primary and a secondary appraisal process. In the primary process, the reality and severity of the threat are assessed. If the primary appraisal leads to the conclusion that a significant threat to one's situation exists, then the individual begins the secondary appraisal in which implicit decisions are made about the type of responses, both behavioral and emotional, that are possible and appropriate.

Primary Appraisal

The primary appraisal has three phases: (1) A threat to the person's need fulfillment or motives exists. (2) The person becomes aware of the threat. (3) The threat is appraised to decide whether any response is needed.

Here, a stress-causing threat is created by the anticipation of future harm, rather than from the threat of immediate harm for which there is no time for appraisal. Appraisal is a cognitive process that requires the receiver to call upon past memories of similar situations and past ways of coping with threat.

The reality and severity of the threat are appraised in the light of several factors. Each of these (spelled out below) should be considered by the manager preparing to deliver bad news.

1. The more intensely the threatened need fulfillment is felt, the greater the threat. When, for example, an employee whose most salient need is social acceptance is transferred to a job that requires working alone, he or she may evaluate the situation as very threatening. Another worker, whose most salient need is security, might not feel threatened at all by the same transfer.
2. If the individual has other resources that allow him or her to satisfy the threatened need, the threat is reduced. For example, financial needs may be met through investment income, and esteem needs through hobbies or sports.
3. The more imminent the potential harm is, the higher the level of threat is. Thus, the further in the future that the harm will actually occur, the less threatening it seems. Termination on two days' notice, for example, is far more threatening than termination on two months' notice.
4. Ambiguity of information increases the perceived level of threat. When the nature of the potential harm is not clear, the individual is less able to marshal forces to neutralize the threat. This increases the feeling of helplessness. Ambiguity of information may also cause the individual to perceive a greater threat than really exists. Ambiguity tends to intensify idiosyncratic reactions to threat. An individual lacking reality-based information, but feeling that his or her needs are frustrated, is more likely to use personal coping responses such as aggression against the deliverer, than if he or she had clear information and could thus use appropriate coping responses.

If the primary appraisal indicates that important motives will be frustrated, the individual begins the secondary appraisal. In reality, of course, the primary and secondary appraisal are interdependent and may overlap in time, or the sequence of events may be different from that outlined here.

Secondary Appraisal

The secondary appraisal involves the cognitive process of evaluating and selecting methods of coping with the threat. Lazarus distinguishes between primary and secondary appraisals as follows: ". . . with primary appraisal, the issue is *how much am I in danger from a situation;* with secondary appraisal, the issue concerns *how much am I in danger from anything I do about the threat* or *to what extent will any particular action relieve the danger.*"

Overall, a perceived high degree of threat increases the likelihood of primitive or regressive coping mechanisms. A threat that is perceived as mild is more likely to result in reality-based coping, whereas an extreme threat is more likely to evoke a pathological response. A response to mild threat may be merely an increased alertness to alternatives as they occur. Severe regressive responses include displacement, defensive dissociation, apathy, denial of reality, or aggressive violence.

The secondary appraisal includes three decision steps that are taken on the basis of the answers to these questions.

1. *What is the source of the threat?* If the source is clearly identified, then the individual can search for alternative coping responses—but if the source cannot be identified or is ambiguous, anxiety is heightened and a defensive reappraisal is likely. This reappraisal may include projecting responsibility to the wrong source. For example, a person who is being fired for inability to cooperate with fellow employees, but is given a vague rationale about economic cutbacks, is more likely to find scapegoats or to project his or her deficiencies onto others (especially the person who delivers the bad news).
2. *Do I have some alternatives?* If viable alternatives are available, then problem solving can begin, and the adaptive coping process is under way. If no alternatives are identified, then question 3 is asked.
3. *Do I have enough power to attack?* The response to this results in a classic "fight or flight" tactic. If the answer is "yes," then some form of attack may occur. In the organizational context this may involve filing a lawsuit or engaging in slander, sabotage, or even aggressive violence. More often in organizations, however, the answer is "no," and the response is to feel anger but flee by withdrawing from the situation or refusing to face the reality. While such actions might not harm the organization, they are destructive for the individual because they prevent him or her from beginning the process of adaptive coping with the new situation.

THE ORGANIZATIONAL CONTEXT

Guidelines for delivering bad news depend on the goals of the manager delivering it and on the organizational context in which the situation arises. To begin with, the manager is assumed to have such objectives as:

1. Minimizing personal stress.
2. Ensuring that the message is understood and accepted with a minimum of distortion, defensiveness, and dysfunction; for example, getting the employee to realize that the job is unequivocably terminated and that he or she must leave the organization at the stipulated time.
3. Ensuring that the recipient will use an effective coping behavior—for example, that he or she will begin a job search.

The manager must be careful not to try to reduce his or her own stress by failing to communicate the full impact of the bad news. For example, in a skill-building roleplay a "supervisor" was supposed to tell a hotel desk clerk that body odor was causing guests to complain; in an attempt to soften the blow, however, the supervisor spent so much time praising the "clerk" that the clerk asked for a raise before the supervisor got around to mentioning body odor!

Other assumptions that are relevant to bad-news delivery in the organizational context include these:

1. The deliverer of the bad news has more authority than the recipient.

2. The deliverer of the bad news has access to organizational resources.

3. There is no need to fear overt violence by the recipient, because there are strong social constraints against it.

GENERAL GUIDELINES

In this final section, I spell out general guidelines for delivering bad news in organizations. In specific terms, as applied to the example of firing an employee, these guidelines are as follows:

1. *Deliver the bad news as soon as it becomes a certainty.* A sufficiently long lead time between the delivery of the bad news and the manifestation of its threat increases the receiver's chances of doing something constructive about it.

2. *Emphasize the authority you have over the recipient.* The greater the power differential between the source of the threat and the recipient, the more likely it is that the recipient will give credence to the threat.

3. *Be clear and unambiguous when delivering the bad news.* The receiver must understand that some of his or her needs will be frustrated before effective problem solving begins. The receiver must recognize that some aspect of her or his life will not continue as it has in the past; some important change will occur because of forces beyond his or her control. Vital to this understanding is clear information. Clarity provides a realistic basis for decision making and makes self-deception more difficult, thus leading to more effective problem solving.

4. *Accurately identify the person responsible for the decision.* Closely related to the matter of clarity is the matter of accurately identifying the source of the threat so the recipient does not waste time and energy fruitlessly trying to find the source(s) of his or her bad fortune.

5. *Provide alternate ways to meet the needs that will be frustrated.* Be prepared with information on severance pay, retirement income, and so forth, for example.

6. *Identify resources that may be useful to the recipient in adapting to the new situation.* Both step 5 and step 6 are methods of directing the recipient toward realistic problem solving. At no other time will the recipient be as open to suggestions for methods of coping as when the news is first received and understood.

DELIVERY OF DISMISSAL NOTICE

How can a manager who must dismiss an employee for poor performance use these guidelines to manage this stressful situation more competently? In general, he or she should do so clearly and unambiguously and then suggest alternate ways in which the recipient might fulfill the needs that will be frustrated.

A careful diagnosis of the situation is the first step. Such a diagnosis is best accomplished by referring to the stress-reaction model and answering the following questions:

1. Is the employee anticipating dismissal?

2. What is the power relationship between us?

3. What needs will be frustrated, and how intensely are they felt?

4. What is the probable response to hearing this news: apathy, denial, hostility, understanding, and so forth?

5. How well can I (the manager) handle the stress of delivering this dismissal notice and the recipient's probable response?

6. What alternatives does the employee have? Many needs will necessarily be frustrated when an employee is dismissed—but pointing toward alternate means of satisfying them will reduce the stress involved. Obviously, another job can meet most of the needs, but there may be other ways to meet specific needs. For instance, economic needs may be met by severance pay, retirement funds, or personal wealth. Social needs may be met by clubs, advisory relationships, and so forth. The most difficult needs to meet elsewhere are those esteem needs that many people satisfy through their jobs—but these, too, may be met in other ways.

7. What resources and constraints face the employee in the search for a new job or for other ways to meet frustrated needs (retirement, for example)?

8. How long will it take the employee to find a new job?

Each of these questions should be answered, and appropriate actions planned, to meet personal objectives of minimizing your own and the employee's stress.

The timing of the dismissal news should be planned so that there is enough lead time before the final day of employment to allow the employee to go through a period of (1) denial and (2) "mourning"—and then to make realistic adjustments. At least two weeks may be necessary for a dismissed employee to begin to assess his or her strengths and weaknesses and to start an effective job search. The length of time needed to complete a job search varies—depending, of course, on the job involved and the job market for the employee's skills.

The manager should set the stage so that the delivery emphasizes his or her power in relation to that of the employee. This is not simply personal ego building; it is to help ensure that the message comes through clearly and unambiguously; the employee is more likely to accept the message as final if it is delivered by a legitimate authority.

Power differential can be emphasized by place (use your office, not the employee's), position (have him or her sit while you stand), clothing (wear your three-piece suit that day), and association (make sure that you have legitimate organizational power behind you. For example, you have the authority to say, "I have decided and the personnel committee concurs . . ."). The emotional control and mutual support you need to maintain power can be achieved by careful mental preparation for the confrontation and by the presence of a colleague during the confrontation.

Making sure that the employee to be dismissed fully understands the reality of the situation requires three things: anticipation by the employee, bluntness by the manager, and a written document to add credibility to the message. The time for compassion comes later.

The employee who can anticipate his or her dismissal gains the time necessary to mentally prepare for the grief to follow. Such anticipation also serves to catch his or her attention during the delivery of the news. Of course, an effective personnel appraisal system that resulted in negative ratings, warnings, or notices of failure to meet established objectives will have prepared the employee for the ultimate decision. During the actual delivery of the news, the manager can alert the employee with such a simple statement as, "Your performance has not measured up to our standards and, as a result, I have some bad news for you."

Bluntness can be achieved by using short sentences and common words. "Your employment at our firm is terminated." If a careful diagnosis of the needs that will be threatened has been made, this is the appropriate time to bring them out.

Take personal responsibility for making the decision to dismiss the employee, and give specific reasons. Avoid succumbing to the temptation to be indirect or vague, or to pass the final responsibility to another person. If the dismissed employee cannot identify who or what is the source of the frustration, he or she is more likely to make baseless assumptions and/or accusations. Either course interferes with the ability to adapt to the new situation.

A person who has been dismissed in an ambiguous cloud of innuendo and vagaries is robbed of an opportunity to learn and grow from the experience. Ambiguity makes scapegoating and denial of reality easier, thus interfering with the internal personal confrontation that is necessary to change. This is especially important when the reason for dismissal is poor technical or interpersonal skills. A written document summarizing all of the essential information should be handed to the dismissed employee at the end of the confrontation to reinforce the verbal message.

The last two guidelines (provide alternate ways of meeting needs and identify resources) are directed at getting the recipient to begin coping immediately with the new situation. A manager dismissing an employee may be able to soften the blow with information such as, "Your pay will continue for another two months while you search for a new job."

These two guidelines (5 and 6) are helping functions and can best be executed by someone other than the person responsible for the dismissal. This, of course, is a variation of the good guy-bad guy routine. The deliverer of the news is the bad guy and will be the object of some hostility; therefore, it is useful to have a "good guy" waiting in the wings to be a compassionate helper. Someone from the personnel department is the most appropriate compassionate helper.

The compassionate helper should be prepared to help the dismissed employee realize he or she truly has been fired—a perception that is not always clear after the first confrontation. The letter prepared by the deliverer and given to the dismissed employee will help clarify this perception too.

Making sure that the dismissed employee can manage his or her feelings immediately after hearing the news is important. The compassionate helper can serve this function by being a good listener, by encouraging the dismissed employee to discuss her or his feelings and to accept them as a normal reaction to an unpleasant situation. Expressing and working through negative feelings is the first step on the road to coping with the new situation.

Finally, the compassionate helper should encourage the dismissed employee to begin looking at personal and institutional resources that will help him or her to find a new job or take whatever action is appropriate. At this point, some firms call in "outplacement consultants" to help dismissed employees focus quickly on problem solving. Other firms provide similar services with their own staffs, but many have no policy at all. At this time, the dismissed employee is particularly vulnerable to feelings of hopelessness and helplessness, and the slightest effort to help can have a strong positive impact. If the organization has no one assigned to perform outplacement services, the bearer of the bad tidings should make arrangements before the event with a colleague or staff person to be the good-guy helper immediately after the news is delivered.

SUMMARY

It is apparent that managers or others who must deliver bad news must perform two functions: First, he or she must deliver the news and make certain that the message is received and understood by the recipient. To accomplish this the deliverer must be blunt and provide specific details. If this part of the job is done well, the recipient will realize that there is a real threat and will move on to decide how to cope with the threat. At this point the second function comes into play, and another person's help may be effective.

The second function involves providing the recipient of the bad news with information that will help him or her cope with the event. Because the deliverer of the bad news may be tainted in the recipient's mind with the onus of being the cause of that event, another person may be more successful in filling the role of compassionate helper—that is, someone who can help the recipient deal with the psychological issues and rationally evaluate the alternatives available.

DISCUSSION QUESTIONS

1. What options are available to organizations when financial and employment conditions are deteriorating?
2. What communication skills are significant for leveling with employees?
3. What role should managers and human resources professionals play in leveling with employees?
4. Offer a plan for firing employees.

Reading 5–2

PREVENTING EMPLOYEE BURNOUT

Susan E. Jackson and Randall S. Schuler

Can you remember an employee who, just after being passed over for promotion, died (figuratively, of course) on the job? Or do you recall a new employee who joined the company full of enthusiasm and energy but became a real disappointment when the smoke settled? Or, closer to home, can you recall feelings of being emotionally wasted, of becoming more callous toward others, or of feeling personally ineffective on the job? If you can answer yes to any of these questions, you've probably had personal experience with employee burnout.

Unfortunately, if you've had such an experience, you are not alone. Increasing numbers of once qualified, energetic, and productive employees are becoming victims of burnout. And unless organizations act now, it is likely that these numbers will continue to increase. Because burnout is so detrimental to organizations as well as individuals, it is critical for employers to move now to prevent employee burnout. In this article we describe strategies that human resources managers can use to help prevent employee burnout in their organizations. First, however, it would be useful to examine employee burnout more closely.

WHAT IS EMPLOYEE BURNOUT?

Employee burnout can be thought of as a psychological process—a series of attitudinal and emotional reactions—that an employee goes through as a result of job-related and personal experiences. Often the first sign of burnout is a feeling of being *emotionally exhausted* from one's work. When asked to describe how she or he feels, such an employee might mention feeling drained or used up, at the end of the rope, and physically fatigued. Waking up in the morning may be accompanied by a feeling of dread at the thought of having to put in another day on the job. For someone who was once enthusiastic about a job and idealistic about what could be accomplished, feelings of emotional exhaustion may come somewhat unexpectedly, but the boss or co-workers may see the person's emotional exhaustion as a natural response to working too hard. In turn, their natural response is to tell the victim to "Take it easy," or to say "You need a vacation."

Instead of doing either of these things (neither of which would provide permanent relief anyway), the victim does what many employees in similar situations have done—she or he copes by *depersonalizing* relationships with the boss and co-workers. She or he develops a detached air, becomes cynical of relationships with others, and feels callous toward others and the organization. Managers who become burnout victims are especially harmful to organizations because such managers create a ripple effect, spreading burnout to their subordinates. Unfortunately for the friends and family of an employee who has reached this stage, the cynical and uncaring attitudes that develop toward co-workers, boss, or subordinates may also be directed at nonwork contacts, having a negative effect on all of the person's social interactions.

In addition to emotional exhaustion and depersonalization, a third and final aspect of burnout is a feeling of *low personal accomplishment.* Many individuals begin their careers with expectations that they will be able to make great contributions to their employer and society. After a year or two on the job, they begin to realize they are not living up to these expectations. Many systemic reasons may contribute to the gap that exists between a new employee's goals and the veteran's accomplishments, including (1) unrealistically high expectations because of a lack of exposure to the job during training, (2) constraints placed on the worker by organizational policies and procedures, (3) inadequate resources to perform one's job, (4) co-workers who are frequently uncooperative and occasionally rebellious, and (5) a lack of feedback about one's successes.

These and other characteristics almost guarantee that employees will be frustrated in their attempts to reach their goals, yet these employees may not recognize the organization's role in causing their frustration. Instead they may feel personally responsible and think of themselves as failures. When combined with emotional exhaustion, feelings of low personal accomplishment may reduce motivation to a point where performance is in fact impaired and that, in turn, leads to further failure.

CONDITIONS THAT CAUSE EMPLOYEE BURNOUT

Although we have already alluded to a few conditions that cause employee burnout, it would be useful to spell them out more specifically. As shown in Table 5–2, two types of conditions—organizational and personal—may trigger employee burnout.

Organizational conditions that can potentially cause burnout include these: (1) a lack of rewards;

Causes	Psychological Reactions	Consequences
Organizational Conditions:		
Lack of rewards.	Emotional exhaustion.	Withdrawal.
Lack of control.	Depersonalization.	Interpersonal friction.
Lack of clarity.		Declining performance.
Lack of support.		
Personal Conditions:		
Idealistic expectations.	Low personal accomplishment.	Family problems.
Personal responsibility.		Health suffers.

Table 5–2 CAUSES AND CONSEQUENCES OF EMPLOYEE BURNOUT

(2) excessive and outdated policies and procedures, work-paced jobs, and close supervision—all of which undermine an employee's "feeling of control"; (3) a lack of clear-cut expectations and job responsibilities, combined with conflict—both of which prevent an employee from being productive; and (4) the lack of support groups or cohesive work groups, which, in turn, prevent an employee from acquiring information needed to cope with the other three conditions. Note that these four organizational conditions *may* be behind employee burnout, but several personal characteristics usually interact with these organizational conditions to actually cause employee burnout.

Such personal characteristics include the following:

1. *Idealistic expectations.* The employee has unrealistic expectations about how the organization will work, and these, when combined with actual organizational experience, produce "reality shock." For example, the employee might expect rewards for good work, the chance to influence decisions affecting the job, friendly and understanding co-workers and supervisors, a clear understanding about what's expected, and adequate resources (including time and money) to get the job done.

2. *Idealistic job and career goals.* Organizational conditions that interfere with performance are bothersome only to employees who want to attain high levels of performance. An employee who thinks it is possible to do everything becomes a natural target of burnout. Employees in mid-career crisis reflect burnout reactions, especially feelings of low personal accomplishment. Although many of these employees may have been doing well by others' standards, by their own standards (for example, a goal of becoming president of the company by age 50) they may regard themselves as failures.

3. *Personal responsibility for low personal accomplishment.* Employees with feelings of low personal accomplishment, those who feel most personally responsible for their own failure, experience the most burnout. Essentially, the employees who care the most can get burned (out) the most.

CONSEQUENCES OF EMPLOYEE BURNOUT—TO THE ORGANIZATION, TO THE INDIVIDUAL

A legitimate question at this point may be, "Okay, so some people experience burnout. Organizations aren't perfect and never will be. And even if they could do something, what's the big deal about burnout?" The big deal is that the organization as well as the individual suffers many severe consequences as a result of employee burnout. The first paragraph of this article suggested a few. Others include the following:

1. *Withdrawal behaviors develop.* Employees want to avoid what discomforts them, and those organizational conditions that can cause burnout are certainly discomforting. Under these circumstances a logical reaction is to withdraw—leave work early, arrive at work late, take long breaks, and stay away from the workplace as much as possible.

2. *Interpersonal friction results.* As employees begin feeling cynical and callous toward others, small differences lead to monumental arguments, work

assignments begin to seem like insurmountable challenges, and friends begin to look like foes.

3. *Performance declines.* As a subtle result of burnout, the quantity of an employee's performance may not diminish but the quality may. Consider the job of an intake interviewer in a legal aid office as an example.

For the organization, the intake interview serves as a screening device through which all potential clients must pass. During the interview, specific information about the nature and details of a case must be assessed and an evaluation of the "appropriateness" of the case for the office must be made. Because as many as 40 intake interviews may be conducted each day, it is important that the interviewer work as efficiently as possible. Here the major index of efficiency is the number of forms accurately filled out for further processing. Thus the interviewer's attention must be focused on gathering information needed by the organization for its evaluation. To the extent that time is spent in talking about problems that are not relevant for these forms or this procedure, efficiency decreases.

Now consider the client's perspective. Upon arriving for an interview, the client is likely to be fuming inside at injustices that have been suffered and the retaliations hoped for. The client does not think in terms of the precise statutes that pertain to the problem nor of the essential details that make her or his case worthy of attention. Rather, the client is concerned with family problems arising from the situation. The primary concern is that emotional and physical life return to normal and that the law seems to offer a solution. For the client, the intake interview may be the first chance to explain the problems. From the client's perspective, an interviewer who lends a sympathetic ear is doing a good job.

How will the interviewer handle this situation? Typically, the person conducting the interview is a relatively recent graduate of law school with little or no clinical experience. The only guidance that he or she has received are generalities about the professional approach to analyzing cases. Professional training has emphasized the supremacy of objectivity. But clearly, an objective, analytic attitude combined with the pressure to efficiently fill out forms does not lead to the sympathetic ear the client is looking for. Because of these differing expectations about the interview the client and the interviewer perceive each other as obstacles. The objective interviewer appears unconcerned, and the client becomes frustrated. The emotionally involved client becomes an obstacle to detached efficiency, frustrating the interviewer. Whether or not open hostility erupts, the participants are aware of their antagonistic relationship.

One way for the interviewer to cope with this situation is to develop a limited set of case types and then focus on determining which type a client fits into. Once a case has been "typed," the unique nuances of the case can be ignored. Processing of the case then proceeds as it does for all other cases of that type. This method of coping can lead an interviewer to adopt a rigid line of questioning governed by the papers to be filled out rather than by the clients and their concerns. Although the interviewer will probably recognize that this strategy is less than optimal, it may be the only feasible way to deal with the myriad complexities and details of each case. Under these circumstances, the client perceives the interviewer as just another petty bureaucrat who is more concerned with paper than with people.

4. *Family life suffers.* Just as burnout leads to behaviors that have a negative impact on the quality of one's work life, it can also lead to behaviors that cause a deterioration of the quality of home life. In a recent study by Susan Jackson and Christina Maslach, burnout was assessed in 142 married, male police officers. Their wives were asked, independently, to describe how these officers behaved when interacting with their families at home. Emotionally exhausted officers were described by their wives as coming home tense, anxious, upset, and angry, and as complaining about the problems they faced at work. These officers were also more withdrawn at home—preferring to be left alone, instead of sharing time with their families. The wives' reports also revealed that officers who had developed negative attitudes toward the people they dealt with also had fewer close friends.

5. *Finally, burnout may eventually lead to health-related problems.* In the study of police families described above, burnout victims were more likely to suffer from insomnia and to use medications of various kinds. The officers also reported using alcohol as a way of coping with their burnout as did female nurses in an unpublished study, suggesting that using alcohol to cope with burnout is not unique to police officers or to males.

PREVENTING EMPLOYEE BURNOUT

Organizations can do many things to prevent employee burnout. On the basis of our employee burnout model in Table 5–2, organizations can change any one or all of the organizational conditions causing burnout. For example, supervisors could be trained to provide more contingent (based on performance) rewards to employees, thus eliminating the comment, "If you don't hear anything, you must be doing okay." Organizations could redesign jobs to enable employees to have more control over their work. Compensation could be more closely related to the level of employee performance. Although such programs could be successfully implemented by human resources managers, the cost and time required by them may be greater than that for the three programs described below—that is, anticipatory socialization programs, participative management programs, and/or feedback programs. The first of these is appropriate for new employees and the other two for current employees. Because of the relatively low cost of these programs, many organizations are already moving to adopting them. Thus the discussion here will provide arguments to persuade others to adopt them.

Anticipatory Socialization Programs

In *Reality Shock: Why Nurses Leave Nursing,* Marlene Kramer argues that a major source of burnout in the nursing profession is the gap between the expectations that nurses have when they begin their first job and the realities that they actually find. Nurses and others who enter human services professions are often strongly motivated by a concern for humanity and a desire to help people. When they start their first job, they anticipate being able to make visible improvements in other people's lives, and although they may not realize it, they also expect their contributions to be recognized as valuable. As any seasoned human services worker has discovered, the lofty expectations and goals they had as a novice were unrealistic. From the beginning they were doomed to failure if success meant achieving those naïve goals. Similar findings were reported by Edgar Schein in his study of employees across many different organizations.

What can be done to prevent the devastating shock that occurs as a result of the discrepancy between naïve ideals and reality? Kramer presents convincing evidence that anticipatory socialization programs can help decrease the magnitude of reality shock and its consequences. The philosophy underlying anticipatory socialization programs is that reality shock should be experienced before an individual begins his or her first full-time job. Furthermore, the reality shock should be experienced in a context that permits and encourages the development of constructive strategies for coping with the unexpected reality one faces. Throughout such a program, ideals are purposely challenged, and conflicts—such as the difference between the way things should be done based on personal or professional standards and the way things actually are done—get exposed. Individuals are then taught how to survive within the existing system without compromising their standards.

Kramer has demonstrated that anticipatory socialization can be an effective method for decreasing the severity of the reality shock experience on the job. This, in turn, decreases turnover rates and absenteeism. Because Kramer's anticipatory socialization program can serve as a model for any occupational group in any type of organization, it is outlined briefly below.

- *Phase 1.* The purpose of the program's first phase is to produce a mild form of the reality shock that an uninitiated worker might experience on the job. This is accomplished by presenting examples of real, on-the-job incidents that have been experienced by others.
- *Phase 2.* New employees are exposed to the negative aspects of policies and practices that characterize most organizations. During phase 2, new employees are encouraged to actively think about possible solutions for improving the situation. By thinking about the problems and trying to devise solutions, the new employees come to appreciate and better understand the reasons why certain imperfect conditions exist.
- *Phase 3.* Phases 1 and 2 focus on the employee's own expectations of how he or she should behave, but phase 3 of Kramer's program aims to teach the employees what others expect. For example, the nature of the nurse-physician relationship is presented by a panel of physicians and nurses. Similarly, a panel of head nurses,

supervisors, and administrators expose the novice to the expectations held by their immediate superiors. Another important aspect of phase 3 is a panel discussion by recent nursing graduates who describe what they are, and are not, able to accomplish on their jobs—thereby providing a realistic baseline against which the program participants can evaluate their own future success and failure.

- *Phase 4.* The final phase of Kramer's program is to teach theories and techniques of conflict resolution and negotiation. The intention of this phase is to teach skills that can aid the nurse in her or his role as an agent for change. These skills give the novice the option, in the future, of working toward changing those parts of a system that present conflict to something that is acceptable.

In summary, these are the pertinent features of anticipatory socialization. First of all, its major goals are to give new employees a realistic picture of the jobs they are about to enter and to provide skills for coping effectively with the difficulties they will face. Because the jobs are not ideal, negative aspects are exposed. While this exposure is not intended to dissuade people from starting a job, it may, of course, do so. Therefore, employers may be reluctant to conduct such programs for fear of losing potential future employees. On the other hand, the employer may conduct anticipatory socialization programs but downplay the negative aspects of the organization, thereby defeating the purpose of narrowing the gap between expectations and reality. Anticipatory socialization programs, however, are most beneficial when they convey the negative as well as the positive aspects of the job. A second important feature of anticipatory socialization programs: While they are aimed at burnout prevention, they are most appropriate for new employees. Exposing a 5-year veteran to such a program would probably do little to prevent burnout.

A third important feature of anticipatory socialization programs: They are not designed to change reality, but merely to expose it in hopes that forewarning will lead to better preparation. As such, anticipatory socialization programs are likely to be useful for decreasing the frustrations that occur during the first two or three years. However, simply being prepared for the negative aspects of one's job does not guarantee that long-term exposure to that job will not lead to burnout. Changes in the job itself or other organizational conditions may also be needed.

Increasing Participation in Decision Making

The importance of being able to control, or at least to predict future outcomes, is well-recognized by organizational researchers. Having opportunities to make one's own choices and the freedom and ability to influence events in one's surroundings can be intrinsically motivating and highly rewarding. When opportunities for control are absent and people feel trapped in an environment that is neither controllable nor predictable, both their psychological and physical health are likely to suffer.

In most organizations, employees are and feel controlled by organizational rules, policies, and procedures. Often these rules and procedures have their roots in an earlier era of the organization and are no longer as appropriate as they once were. Nevertheless, they are enforced until new rules are developed. Then, too, frequently new rules are created by people in the highest levels of the organization and then imposed upon those at the lower levels. Sometimes the new rules are an improvement over the old rules; other times they are not. Regardless of whether the new rules or procedures are an improvement, lower-level employees are likely to perceive them as another organizational event over which they have had no control.

Fortunately, recent studies of burnout suggest that increasing employees' participation in the decision-making process and thus increasing their control can be an effective way to prevent burnout. In addition to increasing employees' feelings of control, participation in decision making may help prevent burnout by clarifying role expectations and giving employees an opportunity to reduce some of the role conflicts they experience. The level of role ambiguity (lack of clarity) and role conflict that people experience are strongly related to burnout. In particular, a high level of role ambiguity leads to emotional exhaustion and feelings of low accomplishment. Role conflict causes emotional exhaustion also, as well as the development of cynical attitudes towards other employees.

Besides giving workers a feeling of control, participation in decision making gives them the power to remove obstacles to effective performance, thereby reducing frustration and strain. One way in which employees can use their increased power is to persuade others to change expectations for the employees' behavior that conflict with the employees' own views. Through the repeated interchanges required by participative decision making, organization members can also gain a better understanding of the demands and constraints faced by others. When the conflicts other people face become clear—perhaps for the first time—negotiation over which expectations should be changed to reduce inherent conflicts is likely to occur. Another important consequence of the increased communication that results from participative decision making is that people become less isolated from their co-workers and supervisors. Through their discussions, employees learn more about others' formal and informal expectations. They also learn about the organization's formal and informal policies and procedures. This information can help reduce feelings of role ambiguity. It also makes it easier for the person to perform his or her job effectively.

In addition to preventing burnout by reducing role conflict and ambiguity, participation in decision making helps prevent burnout by encouraging the development of a social support network among co-workers. Recent studies have found that social support networks help people cope effectively with the burnout they experience on the job. Among employees, one of the most important functions of a social support network is that it can assure the worker that he or she is not the only one who is experiencing difficulties on the job.

Making Increased Participation Work

While participative decision making appears to be a very promising strategy for keeping burnout to a minimum, organizations that plan to use it should be aware of a number of factors that can determine whether increasing participation is likely to be effective or to backfire. Among the most difficult issues in setting up a participative procedure is specifying the types of decisions in which employees will be allowed to participate. These two guidelines should be followed when making this decision: (1) An employee's input is most valuable when the decisions involved will have a direct impact on his or her day-to-day activities; (2) Asking employees to provide input into a decision and then ignoring their advice is worse than never having asked their opinions.

Most employees recognize that there are some decisions for which they are unprepared to provide meaningful input because they do not have all of the relevant information. However, most employees do consider themselves to be experts at their own particular jobs and in the workings of their own particular units. By necessity, people in other jobs and in other departments in the organization are less in tune with the factors that affect how well one is able to perform his or her job. Therefore, to have such people making decisions about procedures and policies that will affect one's own job creates frustration and a sense of lack of control. By giving employees the opportunity to provide input into decisions that affect them directly, supervisors and managers will find that better quality decisions are made because the unintended, negative side effects of a particular decision are more likely to have been foreseen by the workers. In addition, employees will have more positive attitudes toward implementing decisions that they helped make.

Increasing Feedback about Performance

A final job-related change that organizations concerned about burnout should consider is increasing the amount of feedback that workers receive about their job performance. In many organizations jobs are structured so that the employee seldom hears when things go right, but always hears when things go wrong. This is especially true in jobs where the main service the employee provides is advising people about how to solve their problems. For example, in human services organizations, there is a built-in bias that prevents employees from receiving positive feedback for a job well done. However, this is true for almost any organization. Therefore, organizations need to make a conscious effort to devise ways of obtaining such feedback for employees.

One such method in a human services organization is to ask clients to indicate how satisfied they are with the service they received using a *Client Feedback Survey.* When client feedback surveys are conducted on a regular basis, they not only provide feedback about how well the service provider is currently performing, they also give the employee information about whether his or her performance has improved or declined.

Co-workers are also a potential source of feedback about how well employees are doing on their jobs. Just as an organization might ask clients to complete a feedback survey, co-workers can be asked to make evaluations of each other, assuming they are able to observe each other's performance on the job. Co-worker evaluations have an advantage in that they are being made by a person who is fully aware of the constraints placed on employees by the organization. Whereas clients will tend to evaluate the service they received against an ideal standard, the evaluations of co-workers will be based on an understanding of professional ethics and practices and organizational realities.

Finally, subordinate feedback is a great way for supervisors and managers to find out how well they are doing. Because we all tend to gradually adapt to and get comfortable in the conditions in which we find ourselves, we forget to ascertain how others feel we're doing. Because managers are responsible for others, it is imperative for them to find out what their subordinates think of them. The employees are first to know if the boss is becoming callous. Because employees are usually reluctant to give the boss bad news, the personnel department can play a critical organizational role by conducting surveys and feeding the results back to the managers. These survey results can also be used to help spot areas of conflict or ambiguity or particularly irksome rules and procedures. The personnel department can also be effective in helping to detect employee burnout levels by surveying employees with a survey specifically designed to measure burnout.

CONCLUSIONS

Employee burnout has some extremely serious consequences for employees and employers. Fortunately there are a number of things that the personnel department can do—such as implementing participatory management programs like quality circles or conducting organizational surveys—to help prevent employee burnout. However, rather than assume that one cure exists for all situations, we should assume that each organization is somewhat unique, and this uniqueness must be taken into account when potential burnout prevention programs are being considered. For example, if employee opinions are already actively solicited before most major decisions are made, increasing participation in decision making is unlikely to affect future burnout levels.

Not only is it prudent for organizations to recognize the need to be cautious in selecting an intervention strategy, it is prudent for them to accept the possibility that the particular intervention they choose may not be effective. Therefore, organizations should evaluate the effects of any intervention they implement.

DISCUSSION QUESTIONS

1. What is employee burnout?
2. Give two examples of employee burnout.
3. What causes employee burnout?
4. What are the consequences of employee burnout to an organization?
5. Offer three strategies for preventing employee burnout.

ACTIVITIES

Activity 5–1

LOIS JONES

Step 1: Read the Lois Jones case.

Step 2: Prepare the case for class discussion.

John sat staring in disbelief at the summons to an unemployment benefits appeals hearing. It was incredible that an employee quitting her job could cause this much of a hassle. But here it was, a second hearing to attend and he had not even fired the person.

Lois, one of John's maids, had been hospitalized four months before and John had tried to hold the job open for her. She might have a lot of personal problems but John liked Lois. After three months her co-workers demanded that John find someone else to replace Lois. He first talked to Lois and then her doctor but neither could say when she would be able to return to work. Only then did he file a pink slip (Notice of Separation) with the state's Department of Employment Security and start looking for a replacement. No sooner had he engaged Bertha than Lois came looking for her job back. One month later after having filled out some twenty odd State and Federal forms, John received this summons which he angrily reread. He wondered what he should do next. Was it worth fighting Lois, a very sympathetic person, for the unemployment benefits? Could he win this step in the appeals process and how about the next appeal which was her due process? Maybe Lois deserved unemployment, and if he denied it to her, which was within his legal rights, what would she do for money? Was he pushing yet another person into the ranks of the permanently unemployed who gave up all hope of ever working again and lived on public assistance?

John was the manager of his family's funeral business which employed twenty-five people in a large southern city. The staff was small but the nature of the business called for five different groups of employees.

There was the professional staff which included the licensed personnel and the assistant managers; the apprentice-trainees who were finishing up the formal college curriculum for licensure and doing the required apprenticeship; the secretarial and clerical staff; the unskilled maintenance staff made up of mechanics, painters and carpenters; the unskilled labor which included chauffeurs, grounds maintenance, porters and maids. All the employees were a close knit group; for they had to work side by side under pressure. Most of the professional staff and apprentices lived in company housing on the premises. This facilitated their on-call duty shifts.

A further complication was the twenty-four hours per day, seven days per week nature of the business. Since it was an emergency service business, there was little routine. All of this made supervision difficult; for there were some employees John was lucky to see once a week due to the shifts they worked.

The unskilled laborers were the largest group and they gave John the most problems. The nature of their jobs was such that they were little better than household servants, except they had to deal with demanding strangers at odd hours. This group consisted of people who at most had a high school education. Some could not write. Job enrichment was impossible and increasing the pay had not attracted higher calibre people. A good employer/employee relationship and job enlargement were the only possible remedies. This consisted of remembering birthdays and anniversaries and giving maids and yard people errands to run so they might get off the premises. Another help was having them set up their own work schedules. Yet, there continued to be high turnover.

The apprentice/trainees were the next most troublesome. They were young, just getting out of school, and, in general, immature and suffering from their first disillusions in the work-a-day world. The professional schools filled their heads with ideals of what the students thought to be a glamour filled profession. Instead, they found hard, dirty work and long hours. Lack of responsibility, failure to come to work when they did not feel like it, and no sense of morals, a lack of basic honesty, were common problems. Most lasted no more than six months with 85% leaving the profession for good. In spite of this, John felt his apprenticeship program had merit if he got one good employee every so often. While this was the benefit, he wondered what was the effect of the high turnover on the morale of the long-term, steady employee who was so important to the firm. The professional staff looked down on the trainees because of these problems. They even went so far as to threaten to walk out 'en masse' if John hired another female apprentice. Since there were a limited number of staff positions, there was tension between the apprentices and the professional staff. Both were competing for the same positions.

The professional licensed staff was subdivided into two groups: the embalming technicians and the funeral directors who met with the public. In a large firm the former were a traditional source of problems (discontent, high turnover, alcoholism, unions) because they "never saw the light of day," their job being embalming. John tackled this problem through job enrichment by having the embalmers also direct funerals and perform clerical duties during slack periods. This helped break their work routine and prevent boredom. But it meant finding and retaining versatile and at times over-qualified personnel.

The only part of the skilled labor force which presented problems was the painters. They were usually drunks and John could not tolerate any drinking on the job since alcoholism was a major problem with the embalming profession. There was the traditional problem of lack of skills with the secretarial staff but added to this was the fact that the funeral business was a 98% male profession. It took a very strong woman to work in an all male office. A good secretary made all the difference to John's job so he just kept replacing them, hoping to hit on a good one sooner or later.

Thinking back over his career John recalled that he first got involved in the family business due to firing someone over ten years ago. At that time John was not employed by the firm but had his own contracting business. Yet, as with all family businesses, he was involved in an advisory capacity. He also had an emotional attachment to the business for while growing up his family lived next door to the funeral home. Dick, the manager at that time, had been with the company over twenty years . . . longer than John could remember. Dick had come to work for the firm when John was a small child and was like the uncle he never had, taking him fishing on weekends and buying him firecrackers when his parents forbade them to him. Dick was in a car accident and hospitalized for an extended period of time. Because of his absence Dick's duties fell to other employees, including his collection work on past due accounts. It was discovered that some "unpaid" accounts had actually been paid for in cash and the clients had signed receipts from Dick. It came out that Dick would pocket the cash, leave the account on the books and do no follow-up collection work. After a period of time he would recommend it be written off as uncollectible. A similar scheme was discovered with the prepaid funeral arrangements. Over a period of six years, Dick had embezzled in a systematic manner over $45,000.00. The current management was unable to confront Dick because he was in the hospital and because he was like a family member due to his long tenure. Yet, Dick had to be fired because the other employees had become aware of the situation. Employee morale was plummeting and management appeared to be very weak due to their inaction. John knew that the sooner this situation was dealt with the better it would be for all. Because of this John had to do the firing.

What John had thought was going to be very difficult, confronting Dick in the hospital, was relatively easy: a presentation of the facts and no denial from Dick and it was over. The difficulty came not from the confrontation, but from living with it afterward. Here was a person whom John felt close to and whom he had to fire. Here was a middle aged person whose future in the funeral industry was non-existent, for John could never give Dick a recommendation for any job where he would come in contact with money. While John could rationalize that Dick had got himself in trouble, he always wondered what had become of him. Whenever he would drive through skidrow John would keep an eye out for Dick.

It was another incident of employee theft that

convinced John that the firm needed some direct family management. Shortly after Dick was fired, Bob Hill was caught stealing money. Bob was a young man who was well educated and aspired to Dick's position with the company. It was discovered that the bank deposit was $1,000.00 short after Bob had taken it to the bank. When confronted he confessed and wept, saying he was being blackmailed for a sexual indiscretion. He had taken the money to pay off the blackmailer. Because of his story, the current management kept him on and employee morale dropped to an all time low. At that point John decided that he had better join the firm or else recommend that the family divest the business. Things were getting out-of-hand and rapidly falling apart. Once on board, John was unable to fire Bob for management had already forgiven him. He blamed Bob for the poor employee morale and made it clear to him that there was no chance of advancement in the firm. In four months, John had succeeded in driving Bob away. But this victory was short lived for Bob took an expensive parting shot by instituting a federal Wage-and-Hour examination. This meant that the investigators examined all hourly employee time cards for the past three years and if anyone had worked over 40 hours during a 168 hour period they were due time and one half. The firm's pay period had been Friday through Thursday and the only employees not considered hourly workers were management. A manager was defined as someone who had the power to hire and fire. Because it was a seven-day-a-week business and because management wanted to give every employee at least every other weekend off, they worked a "heavy" week and "light" week which averaged to 38 hours per week. During the "heavy" week they worked in excess of 40 hours. In aggregate, John had to pay $10,000.00 in back overtime assessed. He was able to remedy the overtime problem for the future by simply redefining the work week as beginning on Thursday morning instead of Friday. This balanced the two weeks without having to change any work schedules.

Employee theft did not end with Bob. A few years later John hired an excellent porter named Jay Treemont who had been in Angola Penitentiary but did not mind hard work. Jay was most happy when he had a shovel in hand and was very good natured. It was company practice that when there were only checks to be deposited in the bank, Jay would take the deposit, for everyone knew that all you could do with a corporate check was deposit it into the company account. Jay figured out a way to negotiate one of the company's checks and spent the money before the theft was discovered. The bank made good on the money but John lost a good worker. He hated firing someone he liked as much as Jay. Jay said he was sorry. A long time afterwards, John realized that he put temptation before Jay which was too great for him to resist ($1,800.00). Maybe he was as much to blame for losing Jay as Jay himself was.

John tried to clear his head and think back over his entire relationship with Lois. Lois had been working for the company for two years and from the very beginning had presented some unique problems. She was a very simple but intelligent person, heavily involved in her revivalist church. Related to her strong religious belief, Lois had illusions of persecution which she freely talked about in her more lucid moments. At one point she went so far as to threaten another employee with a knife. John did not make anything of it, for before he learned of the incident the employee had forgiven Lois. Lois told John that sometimes she felt spells coming over her and that she could not help herself. John told her that if it ever happened again at work she should just leave and no explanation would be necessary. Most of the time Lois did her work, maintained her distance and gave John few problems.

Everything appeared to be all right with Lois until four months before. One day she told John's secretary that she had to go to the hospital because she had radiation poisoning from the caskets. A few days later the Admitting Office of the neighborhood hospital called to verify her health insurance. Lois was in the psychiatric ward. Three months later she was released and filed for unemployment.

John first learned of Lois's unemployment claim when he received a "Notice of Claims for Benefits." At first glance it appeared that John's company's unemployment account would be liable for $2,016.00 in benefits. He then realized that this amount only covered 28 weeks and extended benefits could add on an additional 56 weeks. John checked his employment records and found that he had paid Lois approximately $12,000.00 over the past two years. The unemployment benefits could effectively double the annual cost of this employee to the firm.

Each firm maintained with the state's Department of Employment Security an account into which it paid contributions on a cumulative basis. The rate of contribution was determined by the firm's annual payroll and its experience rating. The experience rating was the amount of unemployment benefits awarded to past employees and charged against the firm's account. John quickly calculated that if Lois received only 28 weeks of benefits the firm's contribution rate would double. His failure to pursue this matter could cost the company thousands of dollars.

Since Lois had been ill and thus unavailable for work and since her illness was not job related, John got her disqualified. Lois filed an appeal. John wondered what Lois would do for money to exist on. She had no family to turn to and he doubted she had any savings.

Lois's social worker told John that she had applied for disability benefits from the Social Security Administration but she would have to wait five months before receiving any benefits if she were found to be eligible. She was receiving Food Stamps but the Welfare Department was disputing her inability to return to work.

Shortly after John determined that Lois had no means of support, he went to the first appeals hearing and related the facts. Thereafter, John received the Appeals Referee's decision, and Lois was again disqualified. Only at this point did the unemployment office begin in earnest to try to find Lois a job. Until then they had concerned themselves only with her rights to benefits. This presented a new dilemma for John . . . a reference for Lois. All she was capable of doing was household work and everyone demanded references. The first prospective employer to call John was an acquaintance who was looking for someone to care for her two small children. As much as he would have liked to see Lois employed he could not take the responsibility of recommending Lois for such a job. John wished one of his current employees would quit so he could rehire Lois. He could not rationalize firing anyone to create an opening for her.

It was at this point that he received the second appeal's notice summons. If he dropped his opposition Lois would be awarded unemployment benefits. If he would give her a reference she would probably get a job. If he had an opening he could rehire her. Here was a case of human subsistence and John did not know what to do.

Step 3: Individually or in small groups, orally or in writing as directed by your instructor, answer the following questions:

1. Was Lois Jones a problem employee?
2. What environmental or organizational contingencies contributed to the situation?
3. What action should be taken?

Step 4: Discussion. In small groups, with the entire class, or in written form, share your answers to the questions above.

Activity 5–2

SPECTOR INDUSTRIES

Spector Industries is a Fortune 100 conglomerate that includes subsidiaries in the defense, home appliances, book publishing, aircraft manufacturing, energy, and health services industries, among others. All subsidiaries have performed exceedingly well over the past five years, with the exception of their data services division. Originally a group that provided computer support for other subsidiaries, in the early 1970s the data services group was spun off into a separate subsidiary. The Data Services Division continued to provide computer assistance to other divisions through the development of computer-related hardware and software products. The DSD also sold their products to outside organizations.

While the 1970s saw DSD place their major effort into product development, initial sales remained significantly below projections. In 1980 they introduced an aggressive marketing campaign to increase sales. Still sales remained significantly below projections. Shortly thereafter, the market was flooded with comparable products, all at lower prices, and many from companies that already had major lines of computer products. DSD continued to lose millions of dollars each year. In 1984 Spector Industries decided to liquidate DSD.

Step 1: You are a member of the human resources department involved in planning for the liquidation. Your job is to specify a plan for dealing with the 700 employees of DSD. Individually or in small groups, outline an approach for dealing with these 700 employees; they include 100 hardware and software engineers; 100 professional staff in marketing, finance, and human resources departments; 200 programmers; 100 secretaries; 100 clerical and janitorial staff; and 100 managers in all departments. Be as concrete as possible. Be sure to indicate the roles that human resources professionals and managers should play in the program you outline.

Step 2: Discussion. In small groups or with the entire class, share your plans. Then answer the following questions:

1. What are the advantages and disadvantages of each plan?
2. What are the important components of an effective decruitment program at DSD?
3. What other supports must be included in this program?
4. What role should human resources professionals play?
5. What role should managers play?
6. How should the rest of Spector Industries be involved in the program?

Activity 5–3

DEVON MOTORS

Devon Motors is a large distributor of automobile parts. They have both wholesale and retail outlets. As part of their wholesale operation they sell parts to automobile dealerships, auto-body and repair shops, other retail distributors, and the federal government. Their retail operation includes 400 stores nation-wide that sell directly to the automobile owner; each store is staffed by several managers, a clerical staff of five to ten people, and between twenty to forty sales people. Because of declining economic conditions, Devon has decided to reduce its in-house sales force.

Step 1: You are the manager of the group that sells parts to auto-body shops. You have been directed by your boss to reduce the number of salespeople in your group by four. Which four of the following subordinates will you lay off?

Gerald Irons is a 42-year-old white male who has been with Devon for ten years. Originally a high performer, Irons's recent sales record has declined significantly. You know that Irons has been experiencing significant personal problems: his wife recently underwent serious surgery and he spent every free moment with her and his twelve children.

Marjorie Forbes is a 35-year-old white woman who was hired two and one-half years ago from a competitor as part of an affirmative action quota Devon was required to meet. Her performance has exceeded your expectations. Last year she was runner-up for salesperson of the year.

Robert Champion is a 30-year-old black male who was hired as part of the same affirmative action plan as Marjorie Forbes. Devon spent a great deal of money recruiting him because the industry had few black workers with sales experience. His performance has been satisfactory, although you feel that he could perform even better if he spent more time on the job and took fewer sick days.

Wanda Sipe is a 40-year-old black woman who has been with Devon Motors for 10 years, but has only been in sales for the past year and a half. Before that she held a clerical job in which she was viewed as a good, solid performer. Her performance as a salesperson has been only fair. You know that she works hard because she needs the extra income the sales position provides; she has six children, three of whom require special tutoring.

Michael Hill is a 55-year-old white male who has been employed at Devon Motors for 15 years, the longest of any in his work group. When you first hired him, he showed great potential. For the last five years his performance has been at the bottom of his group. Once a recovered alcoholic, he seems to be hitting the bottle again.

Thomas Hickman is a 31-year-old white male who has been with Devon Motors since his graduation from college ten years ago. His performance has always been high; he has frequently set new sales records.

John Bova is the eldest son of the owner's banker. Since joining the company three years ago, his performance has been average. He was one of the few white males hired during the period when the affirmative action program was in place.

Matthew Bowen is a 48-year-old white male who has been with the company for five years. His performance varies considerably, ranging from extremely good to extremely poor. Some feel that he has been struck particularly hard by a midcareer crisis and is trying to decide whether he wants to remain in sales for the rest of his career.

Lydia Jeffers is a 25-year-old white female who has been employed by Devon Motors for four years. Her performance has always been poor. She was hired originally because she was the only child of the boss's sister and could not find employment elsewhere.

Anthony Mentas is a 23-year-old white male who has been employed as a salesperson at Devon for one year. You had grave doubts about hiring him because as the son of very wealthy parents he has a trust fund of $1 million that becomes his when he is 25. He has surprised you because his performance has been extremely high; his sales have always been among the top three in the department.

Step 2: Indicate the four people whom you would lay off from the auto-body sales department. Explain your choices.

Step 3: Discussion. In small groups or with the entire class, answer the following questions:

1. Who should be included in the layoff? Why?
2. What are legitimate criteria for laying off employees?
3. What problems are created by laying off those with the least seniority? The most seniority?
4. Is performance a legitimate criterion to use in laying off employees?

Activity 5–4

THE CASE OF THE DISGRUNTLED EMPLOYEE

Step 1: Read the Case of the Disgruntled Employee and the Sequel.

Step 2: Prepare the case for class discussion.

In May, 1978, during a period of widespread concern over how effectively federal agencies audited their own expenditures, the Director of the Federal Home Financing Administration (FHFA), McDonald Graham, created an Internal Review Office (IRO) within his agency to conduct independent audits of agency operations and expenditures. To head the new office, Graham named Robert Morgenstern, a CPA with experience in both the private and the public sectors.

Since the agency had not had an official internal audit office before, Morgenstern faced an initial mistrust reflected in what he called "the two biggest lies when an auditor comes into an office: when the auditee says, 'We're glad to have you,' and the auditor says, 'We're here to help you.' " To counteract the skepticism, Morgenstern knew that he would have to set up a crack operation, efficient in its audits and responsible in its reporting. His first challenge was to assemble a staff. The IRO budget called for fourteen employees, some of whom would be transferred from other parts of the agency and some of whom would be recruited from outside. In regard to

This case was prepared by David H. Jernigan under the supervision of Stephanie Gould, Case Program Director, for use at the John F. Kennedy School of Government, Harvard University.

the former, Morgenstern was free to decide which of the existing audit positions scattered about the agency should be centralized in the new office, subject to Graham's approval. As Morgenstern began to do this and to negotiate the transfers with some of the affected department heads, he discovered that "anybody who was going to transfer an employee voluntarily into my office was not going to give up one of the better performers;" in fact, transferring was "one of the ways to get rid of people without firing them." Since Morgenstern had to take the actual people along with their functions, he had to accept the risk of lacklustre performance in exchange for managerial control over certain auditing operations. In two cases, Morgenstern determined this risk to be very real, but he wanted control of the job functions enough to take the risk in the hope that the transferred employees would either leave of their own accord or function better under his tutelage than they had in their previous posts. One of these men did in fact leave the agency soon after he was transferred to the IRO. The other, however, remained: a man named Neil Cooper.

Cooper was a youthful looking man in his mid-forties. A certified public accountant with a master's degree in business administration, he had transferred into the IRO from the Bureau of Financial Research, where he had been a senior accountant with substantial auditing experience. Previous supervisors in his seven years in the agency had all rated his performance "above satisfactory," but since over 90% of the employees in the FHFA receive this rating, it told Morgenstern little about Cooper's actual work. Although Cooper's resume and performance ratings were impressive, Morgenstern knew that the transfer would not have gone through had Cooper really been as top-notch a performer as the paper records indicated. So he checked with the personnel office and sought out Cooper's former supervisors, in an effort to uncover any information that might help him to encourage a better performance from his new employee. Morgenstern soon discovered that Cooper had a remarkable capacity for keeping a low profile: "The assistant personnel director, who knew everybody under every stone, didn't know this guy"—a fact made more remarkable by Cooper's high civil service grade (GS–13) in a Washington office with only five hundred-odd employees. Morgenstern further learned that by talking with former co-workers that, performance appraisals notwithstanding, his new employee had "a lousy reputation"—a reputation as a non-producer—and that, although his most recent job had been as an auditor, in fact in that post he had accomplished little in the way of auditing.

Since Morgenstern felt that his small office could not afford to carry a nonperforming employee, he felt constrained to make an effort to use whatever abilities the man might have, without seriously hindering the major work of the office or endangering its fledgling credibility with the agency. Also, he hoped that Cooper's performance would improve with a little good supervision. Accordingly, in September he assigned Cooper to the fairly simple task of auditing the FHFA's contract with Ramco, Inc., a construction engineering firm retained to oversee the interior finishing of the agency's new headquarters. Cooper initially estimated that the job would require five hundred person-hours, divided between him and an assistant, with an audit report to be completed by the end of October. After setting up a schedule of weekly meetings, Morgenstern pursued his own busy schedule and left Cooper on his own to complete the audit.

In addition to setting Cooper and the rest of his staff to work on various projects, in the early months of his tenure Morgenstern tried to find qualified outsiders to fill the remaining slots in his office. Several of these slots were below the GS–13 level, and were filled by bright young CPA's in their early twenties, but one of the jobs Morgenstern advertised for was at the GS–14 level, and Cooper wanted it very badly:

> I advertised for a GS–14, and I swear to God that guy got down on one knee and begged me for it. He wanted that job so bad there were tears that welled up in his eyes. He would sit there and talk to me for fifteen, twenty minutes, two or three times a week, about why he deserved that job.

Morgenstern, however, told Cooper that he wanted to see the results of Cooper's work on the Ramco audit before considering any promotions.

In their weekly supervisory meetings, Morgenstern discussed the progress of the audit with Cooper, including significant findings or problems and any anticipated changes in the schedule. Through these meetings, it soon became clear to Morgenstern that Cooper had "lost control" of the assignment. The audit failed to meet interim benchmarks, such as the timely completion of the audit survey and audit field work, and when the original five hundred hours had been used up, Cooper had "not even begun to draft a report outline." Morgenstern communicated his displeasure with Cooper's pace at their weekly meetings; but he continued to hope that Cooper would shape up "because he had had a lot of experience with the agency and he has a great resume." During this time the two men had only one substantive disagreement about the audit:

> At one point he came to me very excited, claiming that the agency had paid certain bills twice. And I said, "Fine, but I want to make sure that we have it documented." The whole figure was not that big—he claimed to have found $24,000 in overpayments on a $2 million contract. And it turned out that all but $1,000 had been caught and repaid long before we entered the picture. So he did not have the evidence, but he was ready to go with it. I told him, "You have to do these six steps before you can come out with a finding like that." He went back and did them, and found out that things weren't so bad after all.

Throughout the process of preparing the audit report, however, Morgenstern made many suggestions—further questions to ask, auditing procedures to follow, etc.—that Cooper didn't follow. The problem was not, apparently, one of open belligerence or even lack of conscientiousness: throughout this period, Cooper gave every appearance of diligence and willingness to cooperate. But he just didn't seem to be able to hear. As Morgenstern put it:

> Everyone has the ability to siphon off things that they don't want to hear—for every person there is a certain amount of distortion. He had gotten to the point of unbelievable distortion, where he was able to hear what he wanted to hear, and what he did not want to hear he did not hear. I tried to explain on several occasions why he should have been doing things differently, why it didn't need to take that long. It got to the point where I was beating a dead horse—things weren't changing. It was like a horse that was headed straight across a field and there was just no way to stop him. I didn't have the time. I should have taken over then and there and started spending twenty hours a week with him, but I didn't have the time to do it, and there was no one else in the organization who did.

Scuttlebutt around the office supported Morgenstern's suspicions that his message was not getting through:

> Sometimes he would confide in people that he was having problems and then two weeks later he would go back to the person and after nothing had changed, indicate that things were getting better.

As time wore on, Morgenstern repeatedly pressed for a final report:

> I started giving him deadlines and negotiating extensions with him. He would promise to give me the report in two weeks, then next week, then in a few days. It was driving me crazy. I didn't know what to do anymore. I had never encountered a situation like this before, and I'd been in the business several years.

Meanwhile, complaints began to filter in from the office he was auditing. "He would have the tendency to ask the same questions over and over again, and he became a pest," Morgenstern recalled. Knowing that Cooper never used foul language, an exasperated Morgenstern finally went to him and said, "Neil, when the **** are you going to give me that report?" "I said it to him just like that," Morgenstern recalled, "and he just fell apart. He very much resented that. But it was the first time he had listened."

Cooper finally turned in a summary of the report in January of 1979. Morgenstern rejected it as unsatisfactory, requesting a full report as soon as possible and offering a number of suggestions for revision. By this time, however, Morgenstern had begun to despair of turning Cooper into a productive employee:

> I went into it positively. I recognized that he was going to have some problems, and so I

> started him out on something that I thought would be relatively easy. Then when I realized the trouble he was having with the assignment, I made the decision that he was way over his head. He was making $40,000 but he was earning $20,000. I didn't have the time or the inclination to try to get him up to that point.

Knowing the complexity and infrequency of termination proceedings at the FHFA, Morgenstern was reluctant to begin proceedings at that point for two reasons: first, because he wanted a second opinion from someone fresh to the situation, namely that of his new deputy, before taking such a drastic step; and second because at that point in time he lacked an extra staffer to do the extensive documentation required for an adverse action such as termination. "It was a question of my biding my time until I could get some people on board [to take over Cooper's work], and in the meantime to keep him busy and out of trouble."

(Under FHFA regulations, a supervisor wishing to terminate an employee first had to inform the employee that his or her work was considered below satisfactory; then had to develop a corrective action work plan, identifying areas in which the employee's performance would have to improve; and finally had to allow a minimum of ninety days for implementation of this plan, with the employee's progress in the designated areas documented fully, before notice of termination could be given. The employee then had thirty days to respond to the charges contained in the notice of termination, and had the right to a subsequent appeal to the Merit System Protection Board (MSPB), the successor to the old Civil Service Commission.)

Between January and May, Cooper submitted four more unacceptable drafts, to Morgenstern's increasing dismay. By mid-May, Morgenstern finally had enough staff on hand to relieve Cooper of control of the audit, which he did, in effect (although not formally) demoting Cooper to assistant auditor. Cooper showed signs of dejection when Morgenstern told him of his demotion but he continued to work cooperatively:

> Very often in those situations I can envision someone refusing to cooperate and explain, because everything had to be explained. He explained everything, he didn't try to hold back—he was fully cooperative.

Since the new supervisor of the Ramco audit was only a GS–12, the disparity between Cooper's grade and performance and the new supervisor's grade and performance produced considerable tension in the ranks of all the junior employees. Some of these were only in their twenties—Cooper "had more work experience than they had life experience," Morgenstern recalled—but were clearly working more effectively than Cooper, knew it, and resented his higher grade and salary. Added to Morgenstern's other difficulties with Cooper, this pointed to a strong case for termination under the civil service stipulation that terminations must be shown to contribute to the efficiency of the office. In the presence of rising office tensions, and in light of the fact that his office by now was approaching its staffing capacity, Morgenstern reluctantly began to move towards terminating Cooper.

Initially, he hoped to convince Cooper to leave voluntarily by giving him a "below satisfactory" rating on his performance appraisal. (Annual performance appraisals are given each June at the FHFA, in accordance with civil service regulations, and a "below satisfactory" rating usually indicates that a civil service termination procedure will follow.) Morgenstern recalled Cooper's reaction at their June 3, 1979, meeting on the subject:

> He was shocked. He looked at me with his big eyes, and then looked at the floor, shook his head and said, "I don't agree with this."

The two men discussed the appraisal at some length, with Cooper claiming that his work had been affected by the difficulties of transferring into a new office and adjusting to new standards and procedures, and threatening to protest the rating to higher authorities. Cooper also threatened to look for a new job, and Morgenstern concurred that this would be a wise idea.

From that point on, all communications with Cooper had to be put in writing, to show that job instructions were clear and allowed for only one interpretation. Although Morgenstern had been aware from the start that he might eventually have to terminate Cooper, he had not begun to collect the kind of written documentation that would eventually be needed to justify such an action. In Cooper's first four months with the agency, Morgenstern did not want to jeopardize their relationship. Instructions at the FHFA are generally communicated orally. Shifting to written instructions which could later be used in termination proceedings would in Morgenstern's opinion have been a clear signal to Cooper that, rather than trying to help him, Morgenstern was trying to get rid of him:

> As far as employees are concerned, at least in our agency when you start putting everything in writing, you're trying to get rid of them—you're not trying to help them . . . it can have a really negative effect [on the employee].

Morgenstern also felt that, with his office and staff still in an embryonic state, and with his own life complicated by the fact that Chairman Graham asked him to serve as the agency's acting budget officer between December 1978 and March 1979, he simply did not have the time before the summer of 1979 to document all of his communications with Cooper: "I didn't have the time to sit down and write all those memos."

A week after giving Cooper his performance appraisal, Morgenstern received a call from Chairman Graham's assistant informing him that Cooper had filed allegations with the FBI that Morgenstern was suppressing the audit report of the Ramco, Inc. contract. It was Morgenstern's turn to be shocked: "You could never have told by looking at him that this was the kind of guy who would go to the FBI."

SEQUEL

By the time of the performance appraisal, Morgenstern had already delegated supervision of Cooper to his deputy. Advised by FHFA's General Counsel that there was no need for him to alter his behavior towards Cooper in any way, Morgenstern began to work with his deputy to develop a corrective action work plan for Cooper. Before they could complete a plan, however, Morgenstern became ill and was hospitalized for six weeks, during which no progress was made on the work plan. On his return, Morgenstern worked closely with the personnel office and the General Counsel's office to develop an airtight corrective action work plan. He knew the personnel office's reluctance to approve adverse actions, and since he had taken the leap towards termination with the negative performance appraisal, he wanted to ensure that the case against Cooper would not fail because of a technical error on Morgenstern's part. Morgenstern emphasized to the personnel office that he viewed his role as merely a documentor, leaving judgment in their hands:

> I got the General Counsel and the personnel office involved, and I told them, "All I'm doing is documenting in writing the performance of this individual. You tell me if you think he is not operating at the level he is supposed to be operating." Exactly what constituted grounds for removal I don't know—if we had written all those memos documenting his inefficiencies and they had come back to me saying it was not good enough, that it's not grounds for removal, I don't know what I would have done but I would have had to think of something else.

The work plan had to be tailored to Cooper's civil service grade and job description, so that the documentation collected would show whether Cooper's performance had indeed been well below what would normally be expected of a person in his job category, and would demonstrate that he actually had been given the opportunity to perform at a normal GS–13 level.

Upon gaining approval from the personnel office for the work plan in mid-August, Morgenstern presented it to Cooper for his approval (required by FHFA regulations), and Cooper balked. He submitted a several-page memo protesting the work plan in general terms, but giving no specific criticisms. Morgenstern nonetheless tried to revise the plan to bring it into a form that Cooper would agree to. Cooper, however, protested the revision in similarly general terms. After two weeks of dickering, Cooper finally agreed to the plan in its original form "without one word changed," according to Morgenstern.

The ninety-day corrective action work plan period finally began in September, and at this time, Morgenstern recalled,

> I got some more staff, and one person was assigned to be his supervisor in a hand-holding type of operation. He would be given an assignment, and be let go for two, three days, or maybe even one day. It was a very tight supervision, the type you would give someone with a GS–9 or GS–11. It took someone twenty hours a week for several months, just to get the memos back and forth—Neil agreed that everything would be in writing—and it was very difficult for us during this time, because we didn't want to send him out to do audits that we knew were not going to be of any use to the office. We also had a problem with our image to the rest of the agency if we sent someone like that out.

Informed at the start of the ninety days that he had the right to seek counsel, Cooper did so. After a cursory examination of the case, Cooper's lawyer advised him to "get the hell out of there," according to Morgenstern, and Cooper finally began to look in earnest for another job. He had little success at first, since every time he applied for a job his prospective employers would call Morgenstern for a recommendation. Morgenstern could not in good conscience give anything less than an honest appraisal of Cooper's work, nor could he leave himself open to a court suit claiming that he had written positively of Cooper's talents on a recommendation but negatively in the performance appraisal. Morgenstern began to despair of Cooper's ever finding a new job.

Effectively deprived of one and a half staff members during much of the summer and fall of 1979, Morgenstern attempted to maintain an atmosphere of business-as-usual. He continued to communicate with Cooper, and to encourage his efforts to find another job. During one of their conversations, Cooper indirectly referred to the allegations he had made to the FBI—which turned out to be more insinuation than actual accusation—and offered to apologize to the entire office. Morgenstern rejected this offer, thinking that it would render him liable to charges that he had initiated the termination process in order to extract an apology from Cooper. The atmosphere in the office remained calm but not cheerful—the strain on Cooper was visible, but while everyone was aware of the termination proceedings, the topic was avoided in day-to-day conversation.

As the ninety-day period neared a close, the legal and personnel departments began to prepare the written materials which had been collected during the documentation period—and which had been turned over to them with Cooper's knowledge—for the expected appeal hearing before the Merit System Protection Board. In the opinion of the agency's legal staff, the case was a shoo-in. Shortly before the end of the ninety-day period, however, a prospective employer from another agency called while Morgenstern was out of town and asked Morgenstern's deputy for an estimation of how Cooper would fit into his agency. Since the position Cooper was applying for had little to do with auditing, the deputy replied that she couldn't predict what Cooper's performance would be in a non-auditing function. Apparently satisfied, the caller hung up. When Morgenstern returned several days later, he was told of the incident but thought nothing of it, assuming that the hiring agency would make more than a cursory examination of Cooper's record. Soon afterward, the other agency offered Cooper a job, and in January 1980, before his case ever came before the Merit System Protection Board, Neil Cooper left the FHFA.

Step 3: Individually, in small groups, or with the entire class, as directed by your instructor, answer the following questions:

1. What contingencies influence Cooper's performance?
2. What skills, knowledge, and attitudes does the job require? Which behaviors does Cooper demonstrate?
3. What performance problems exist?
4. What explanations exist for the performance problems?
5. What systems exist for dealing with the performance problems?
6. What options are available to Morgenstern?
7. How should Morgenstern deal with Cooper's performance problems?

Step 4: Discussion. In small groups or with the class as a whole, orally or in written form, share your answers to the questions above.

Activity 5–5

SARAH JENSON—THE PLATEAUED PERFORMER

Step 1: Read the following scenario.

Sarah Jenson is the principal of the Hiram Gleason Elementary School in Evansville, Wisconsin. Her career began 25 years ago with her first job as a fourth grade teacher at the Gleason School. During her first ten years, she received several commendations for outstanding teaching. She was promoted to head teacher in the school after five years. During her first ten years she also earned a master's degree in education and completed the course requirements for her doctorate in education. When the principal at Gleason retired in her tenth year at the school, Sarah was promoted to principal.

Her first five years as principal saw Sarah institute major changes in the organization of Gleason Elementary. She encouraged team teaching and emphasized staff development. When asked, she remarked how invigorated she felt at the end of a day and how sad she was to see each school year end. She also earned her doctorate.

During the next five years, she repeatedly applied for positions as school superintendent. Each time she was among the finalists, but never chosen to be the new superintendent. Other positions opened in central administration in Evansville, but Sarah was not selected for any of these either.

During those years her energy seemed to wane. She seemed to be resting on her laurels. While the school still operated efficiently, and students received among the highest scores in the city on regional and national examinations, Sarah did not initiate any major changes or innovations. She arrived each day promptly at eight o'clock, completed the required activities for that day, and then left the building promptly at four o'clock. When asked, she expressed concern about the rest of her career. It seemed to her as if she were stuck in her job as principal.

Step 2: You are Sarah's boss, the assistant superintendent of elementary education in Evansville. Diagnose the situation described above and offer an action plan for dealing with Sarah. Base your plan on answers to the following questions:

1. How would you describe Sarah's situation?
2. How do you deal with plateaued performers?
3. Who is responsible for dealing with Sarah?
4. What role should human resources professionals play?
5. What role should Sarah's boss play?

Step 3: Discussion. In small groups or with the entire class, share your action plan.

Activity 5–6

CASE OF THE POOR PERFORMER

Step 1: Read the following scenario.

Rodney Harkness was hired by Sheldon Finch, the President of Interprogram, Inc., in October 1985 to fill a programmer position in Finch's four-person computer programming firm. Interprogram wrote programs under contract to clients. Finch did much of the C-language programming himself, but had decided to hire an additional programmer to help with the C-language programming so that he could spend more time managing the company.

Harkness had just received his undergraduate degree in Computer Science from Falcon State College. During his employment interview he showed Finch several programs that he had written, as part of his undergraduate requirements, in Fortran and C, the two languages that Finch required of his new staff member. After speaking with his references and reviewing his programs, Finch felt that Harkness had the basic skills to perform satisfactorily as a programmer. He expected Harkness to initially require some on-the-job training; however, he also expected Rodney to be working on his own by the end of the month, with Finch providing minimal direction.

During his first two weeks at Interprogram, Rodney spent most of his time studying a program that had been written by another programmer. Rodney's job was to make some modifications to the program. By the end of his first month in the company, Rodney was no closer to working independently than when he had joined Interprogram. By the end of November, Rodney still had not made the required modifications in the program. Throughout this time, Finch had to spend extensive time with Rodney, providing him with very specific directions about the way to modify the program. In December Finch was spending 50–75 percent of his time giving direction to Rodney in C-language programming. It seemed to Finch that he was spending more time training Rodney than he would have spent writing the modifications himself. In addition, Rodney did not seem to be making any progress toward becoming more independent.

Step 2: Assume you are Sheldon Finch. It is now January first and you must make a decision about Rodney Harkness. Should you spend more time with him? Provide additional training for him? Fire him? Individually or in small groups, develop a plan for dealing with Rodney.

Step 3: In small groups or with the entire class, share the plan you developed.

Step 4: Assume that Sheldon Finch has decided to fire Rodney Harkness. Your instructor will select one person to play the role of Rodney and another to play the role of Sheldon Finch. The remainder of the class will act as observers. When everyone is ready, Rodney enters Sheldon's office.

Step 5: Discussion. In small groups, with the entire class, or in writing, answer the following questions:

1. What is the appropriate action in this situation?
2. What determines whether an employee should be fired?
3. What are the elements of an effective termination interview?
4. What role should human resources professionals play in dealing with poor performers?
5. What role should managers play in dealing with poor performers?

SUMMARY

Decruitment, or the reduction of the number of workers, typically occurs in two situations: (1) when there is an oversupply of employees for a particular job or a particular set of skills, and (2) when an individual performs unsatisfactorily in his or her position. We have examined a variety of strategies for dealing with these situations. In the case of an oversupply, management can reduce the labor force by attrition, transfers, layoffs, early retirements, or phased retirements. In the case of poor performance the manager must deal with each situation individually by diagnosing and then correcting the problem. In either case, managers and human resources professionals should analyze the situation, determine the precise nature of the required change in the work force, specify decruitment options, choose among them, and then implement the chosen options.

We have proposed ways of reducing the number of employees at Spector Industries and Devon Motor Works. We have also offered solutions to performance problems experienced by Lois Jones, the Disgruntled Employee, Sarah Jenson, and the Poor Performer.

Human resources professionals have the major responsibility for the design and implementation of decruitment activities for dealing with surpluses of employees. They must monitor the environment and develop programs that respond to the changing needs for workers. They should design and oversee layoff, transfer, and early retirement programs. They should conduct preretirement workshops and inaugurate outplacement programs when appropriate. And they should act as sources of information for managers about available counseling, career development, and educational opportunities.

Managers have the responsibility for informing employees about these programs. They deal more directly with poor performers than do human resources professionals. Here they must prevent and correct situations encountered by plateaued, difficult, burned-out, or obsolete employees.

ENDNOTES

[1]From U.S. Steel closings affect 30 plants, *Boston Globe*, 28 December 1983. Reprinted courtesy of *The Boston Globe*.

[2]See Court says US Steel can close 2 plants, *New York Times*, 26 July 1980; US Steel warns of plant closings, *New York Times*, 9 December 1983; US Steel loses $983 million, *New York Times*, 1 February 1984; US Steel net fell 13% in third period; cost-cutting effort trimmed steel losses, *Wall Street Journal*, 19 October 1980.

[3]H.M. Levin and R.W. Rumberger, High-tech requires few brains: The jobs being created will demand less skill not more, *Washington Post*, 30 January 1983; L. Silk, Technology and jobless, *New York Times*, 1 April 1983.

[4]E.M. Fowler, Computer personnel in demand, *New York Times*, 15 October 1980.

[5]The white collar pay freeze: Companies risk loss of top personnel, *New York Times*, 23 June 1982; Alcan reduces spending plans, freezes wages: Capital outlays for year cut by $100 million, weak net seen for 2nd period, *Wall Street Journal*, 21 June 1982.

[6]US Steel layoffs, *New York Times*, 4 September 1980; Auto layoffs reach 251,490, *New York Times*, 6 November 1982.

[7]J.S. Lublin, On idle, the unemployed shun much mundane work, *Wall Street Journal*, 5 December 1980.

[8]L.M. Brammer and F.E. Humberger, *Outplacement and Inplacement Counseling* (Englewood Cliffs, N.J.: Prentice-Hall, 1984).

[9]Labor Letter, *Wall Street Journal*, 27 April 1982.

[10]T.M. Camden, Outplacement as a career development tool, *Personnel Administrator* 27 (1982): 35.

[11]*Ibid.*

[12]N. Shahzad, Outplacement services at Interfaith Medical Center, *Personnel Administrator* 29 (June 1984): 59–66.

[13]E. Silverman and S. Sass, Applying the outplacement concept, *Training and Development Journal* (February 1982): 70–85.

[14]Brammer and Humberger, *op. cit.*

[15]R. Coulson, *The Termination Handbook* (New York: Free Press, 1981).

[16]W.J. Morin and L. Yorks, *A Positive Approach to Terminating Employees* (New York: AMACOM, 1982).

[17]Coulson, *op. cit.*

[18]Morin and Yorks, *op. cit.*

[19]*Ibid.*

[20]D.H. Gravitz and F.W. Rumack, Opening the early retirement "window," *Personnel* 60 (1983): 53–57.

[21]Corrections and amplifications, *Wall Street Journal*, 31 March 1982; Polaroid's job cuts took key workers, *New York Times*, 19 July 1982.

[22]M.H. Morrison, Retirement and human resources planning for the aging workforce, *Personnel Administrator* 29 (June 1984): 151–159.

[23]*Ibid.*

[24]*Ibid.*

[25]D.F. Roth, Why sponsor a preretirement program?, *Personnel Journal* 62 (September 1983): 720–732.

[26]H.G. Kaufman, *Obsolescence and Professional Career Development* (New York: AMACOM, 1974).

[27]*Ibid.*

[28]A.N. Jones and C.L. Cooper, *Combating Managerial Obsolescence* (Oxford: Philip Allan, 1980).

[29]*Ibid.*

[30]*Ibid.*

[31]S.S. Dubin, *Professional Obsolescence* (New York: English University Press, 1972).

[32]E.H. Burack and G.C. Pati, Technology and managerial obsolescence, *MSU Business Topics* 18 (1970): 49–56; E.H. Burack and G.C. Pati, Every company's problem—managerial obsolescence, *Personnel* 2 (1970).

[33]See T.P. Ference, The career plateau: Facing up to life at the middle, *1978 MBA* (July/August, 1978); and E.K. Warren, T.P. Ference, and J.A.F. Stoner, The case of the plateaued performer, *Harvard Business Review* (January-February, 1975).

[34]*Ibid.*

[35]*Ibid.*

[36]E. Roseman, *Confronting Nonpromotability: How to Manage a Stalled Career* (New York: AMACOM, 1977).

[37]*Ibid.*

[38]M. Cherlin, Burnout: Victims and avoidances, *Datamayion* 27 (1981): 92–99.

[39]C. Maslach, *Burnout: The Cost of Caring* (Englewood Cliffs, N.J.: Prentice-Hall, 1982).

[40]Cherlin, *op. cit.*

[41]H.J. Freudenberger, *Burn-out: The High Cost of High Achievement* (Garden City, N.J.: Anchor Press, 1980).

[42]M.D. Glicken, A counseling approach to employee burnout, *Personnel Journal* 62 (March 1983): 222–229.

[43]*Ibid.*

[44]*Ibid.*

[45]Coulson, *op. cit.*

[46]M. Shain and J. Groeneveld, *Employee-Assistance Programs* (Lexington, Mass.: Lexington Books, 1980).

[47]D.J. Reed, One approach to employee assistance, *Personnel Journal* 62 (February 1983): 648–652.

[48]Shain and Groeneveld, *op. cit.*

[49]P. Garretson and K.S. Teel, The exit interview: Effective tool or meaningless gesture?, *Personnel* 59 (1982): 70–77.

FURTHER READINGS

Carone, P.A., ed. *The Emotionally Troubled Employee.* Albany: State University of New York, 1976.

Coulson, R. *The Termination Handbook.* New York: Free Press, 1981.

Freudenberger, H.J. *Burn-out: The High Cost of High Achievement.* Garden City, N.Y.: Anchor Press, 1980.

Jones, A.N. and Cooper, C.L. *Combating Managerial Obsolescence.* Oxford: Philip Allan, 1980.

Roseman, E. *Confronting Nonpromotability: How to Manage a Stalled Career.* New York: AMACOM, 1977.

Shain, M., and Groeneveld, J. *Employee-Assistance Programs.* Lexington, Mass.: Lexington Books, 1980.

Walker, J.W., and Lazer, H.L. *The End of Mandatory Retirement: Implications for Management.* New York: John Wiley, 1978.

PART 3

Personnel Systems for Evaluation and Development

CHAPTER 6

Implementing Effective Performance Evaluation

CHAPTER OUTLINE

LEARNING CHECKPOINTS

After completing the reading and activities in this chapter, students will be able to

- identify factors that influence performance appraisals;
- show the role of job analysis in performance evaluation;
- differentiate between performance appraisals for development and evaluation purposes;
- assess their own attitudes toward performance appraisal and the significance of these attitudes for effective evaluations;
- identify individuals who can perform appraisals most effectively in given circumstances;
- discuss the advantages, disadvantages, and uses of various types of appraisal instruments;
- design selected performance appraisal instruments;
- conduct an effective appraisal interview;
- discuss ways of improving communication about performance;
- develop a comprehensive evaluation system.

INTRODUCTION

John Elwing looked at his most recent paycheck. He was seriously considering quitting his job at Pittsburgh Plastics. Although he really enjoyed his work in market analysis and felt he was doing an excellent job, his paycheck told him otherwise. His most recent check reflected his annual performance increase. He had inferred from his boss's comments that he would be receiving a very high raise. Inflation had been approaching 10 percent, so he expected at least 12–15 percent. He felt his 5 percent increase did not reflect the time, effort, or skill he put into his job or the outputs he produced. Hadn't he almost singlehandedly suggested a new market for the company's most recent product? The introduction of the product into that market had netted the company several million dollars. John felt confused and hurt when he approached his boss for an explanation of the pay increase.

John's boss, Jennifer Fulton, expressed surprise when John complained about his increase. She thought that she had explained very clearly to him that his performance had not been up to par and that his raise would reflect that. In both the written appraisal and performance evaluation interview, she had tried to show his strengths and weaknesses, but wondered now if he had heard anything she'd said.

Pittsburgh Plastics had just introduced a new evaluation system. Managers were directed to sit down once a year with employees as part of the salary review process; they were to assess employee performance and talk about ways of improving it during the following year. Individual managers could choose their own specific approach to use. John's complaints made Jennifer wonder whether there was a better approach to evaluation and development of employees.

How could the process be improved? What approach should managers take in evaluating employee performance? What pitfalls are they likely to encounter?

In this chapter we examine ways of evaluating and improving individual performance. We first discuss the steps in preparing for performance evaluation. Next, we consider the implementation of formal evaluation approaches: Who should conduct appraisals? What formats are available? When should they be done? How can they be made more objective? Then we discuss appraisal interviews: how to communicate more effectively and set performance goals. Finally, we examine specific performance problems, as well as the elements of a comprehensive performance appraisal system.

PREPARING FOR A COMPREHENSIVE EVALUATION SYSTEM

How do human resources professionals and managers develop and implement a comprehensive evaluation system? What components comprise the system? How can a manager make an existing system more effective? As for other human resources management systems, the manager and human resources professionals must diagnose the problems in the existing situation. Together they should determine the purpose of the performance appraisal and investigate employees' attitudes toward it. In this section we examine these influences on performance appraisal: (1) characteristics of the situation; (2) the job description, specifications, and performance standards; (3) the purposes of performance appraisal; and (4) workers' and managers' attitudes toward evaluation.

Analyzing the Situation

How do the environment and the organization influence the conduct of performance appraisals in an organization?

The Environment. The environment places certain demands on organizations and its employees for productivity. As the environment becomes more competitive or as technological changes occur, assuring excellent performance becomes paramount. Thus managers must assess performance regularly and accurately. In addition, the legislative environment creates numerous legal constraints on the appraisal process. (See Chapter 13 for the equal opportunity laws that affect performance appraisals.)

Human resources professionals can support personnel evaluations by developing procedures and formats that facilitate assessment by managers. Identifying individuals' strengths and weaknesses allows managers to conduct activities that will correct performance deficiencies and augment strengths.

The Organization. Characteristics of the organization also influence the evaluation of performance. To begin, the organizational structure determines who has the responsibility for assessment. In structures that value the chain of command, an individual's boss alone performs the evaluation; neither peers nor subordinates contribute to the appraisal. In structures that value lateral communication, individuals in a variety of positions may conduct the evaluations.

The organizational climate—the internal environment of the organization that encompasses its communication, reward, leadership, and goal-setting processes, among others—also influences the type of assessment that occurs. The extent of decentralized decision-making, the existence of collaboration, and the nature of supervision in the organization may identify not only who will perform the performance appraisal, but the emphasis placed on development versus evaluation, and the general attitude of organizational members toward appraisal. For example, organizations that emphasize decentralized decision-making and collaboration tend to spread evaluation responsibility throughout the organization, as well as encourage evaluation *and* development. Organizations that encourage feedback are likely to involve employees in goal-setting and sharing the responsibility for their own evaluations.

The organization's resources influence the appraisal process by affecting its frequency, comprehensiveness, and sophistication. Generally, the more time managers spend in business-related activities, the less time they can devote to effective appraisal. The number of human resources professionals who can support performance appraisal also varies among organizations, in part as a function of the funds budgeted to human resources activities. Finally, some companies pay consultants high fees to develop sophisticated appraisal systems.

Using the Job Analysis

Job analysis should accompany the situational analysis and act as the cornerstone of the performance appraisal by establishing the criteria upon which an individual should be evaluated. Consider the job description for the position held by John Elwing, which is shown in Figure 6–1. John Elwing's appraisal must directly relate to his performance of each of these activities. Since different jobs have different job descriptions, the program for performance evaluation must provide a systematic way for considering these differences and ensuring consistent evaluations across jobs and the employees who hold them.

Human resources professionals or managers can use job descriptions, job specifications, and performance standards to design performance appraisal formats. For example, certain formats measure traits more effectively than behaviors, as discussed later in this chapter. Others identify general performance level rather than specific measures of performance. Managers must tie their assessment of a subordinate's performance to the particular performance required by the job description, specifications, and performance standards established for the job.

Specifying the Purpose of Performance Appraisals

Why do organizations conduct performance appraisals? Basically they serve two purposes (as summarized in Table 6–1): (1) evaluation and (2) development.[1]

In the *evaluation* approach a manager *assesses* an employee's past performance. The evaluator uses descriptive ratings to judge performance, and then uses the data in promotion, demotion, termination, and compensation decisions.[2] Jennifer Fulton, for example, used the data to help her determine pay raises. Evaluation helps answer such questions as: Does the individual deserve a relatively large or

1. Coordinates space advertising between the division's business areas and the advertising agency.
2. Meets with advertising representatives.
3. Evaluates advertising appearance and content.
4. Works with agency representatives in preparation of the bimonthly bulletin.
5. Composes and evaluates copy and layout.
6. Participates in the design, layout, and construction of displays for trade shows.
7. Reports on the effectiveness of each display.
8. Assists in the development of the advertising budget.
9. Establishes and maintains files about advertising activities.
10. Ensures accuracy and currency of mailing lists.

Figure 6–1 JOHN ELWING'S JOB DESCRIPTION

	Evaluation Approach	*Development Approach*
Purpose	provide data for administrative decisions	provide data for training and development decisions
Content	evaluative ratings or descriptions	counseling, goal-setting, and performance review
Role of manager	appraiser	joint goal-setter with employee
Focus	assess past performance	motivate and direct future performance
Uses	work planning, promotion and termination decisions, salary administration	internal placement, career planning, training, management succession

Table 6–1 **TWO APPROACHES TO PERFORMANCE APPRAISAL**

small pay raise? Should this person receive a promotion? What jobs will this person likely perform well? Does this person perform well enough to remain in the organization?

As their contribution to the evaluation system, human resources professionals can assist managers such as Jennifer Fulton by designing or selecting evaluation formats, training managers in their use, and monitoring the appraisals organization-wide to ensure their consistency for different jobs and raters.

In the *development* approach, in contrast, a manager tries to *improve* an individual's performance in the future. The manager counsels the employee about his or her career development and helps the subordinate to set performance goals.[3] He or she identifies the employee's training and development needs. In the scenario opening this chapter, Jennifer Fulton was not very effective at using the performance appraisal for developmental purposes.

The development aspect of appraisal encourages employee growth. It addresses the developmental needs of organizational members including the skills, experiences, or knowledge a person needs to perform the current job better; the skills or knowledge a person must acquire to perform future jobs; and the types of responsibilities a person should be given to prepare him or her for future assignments.

As for evaluation, human resources professionals can oversee the developmental phase of performance appraisals organization-wide; they can select appropriate formats and train managers in providing feedback effectively.

Appraisal for both purposes should be done in a context of an ongoing program of counseling, career planning, goal-setting, and performance monitoring.[4]

Individual performance appraisals can provide collective data for use in an integrated human resources system. For example, by aggregating performance deficiencies across jobs, top executives or human resources professionals can identify training needs throughout the organization. Aggregate data can also detect jobs where inappropriate selection criteria are used. By combining both evaluation and development aspects, performance appraisal should (1) provide a basis for personnel actions, including promotions, transfers, demotions, or layoffs; and (2) improve the utilization of staff resources through better job placement and specification of training needs. Figure 6–2 elaborates on these general uses of performance appraisals.

Checking Attitudes toward Appraisal

For maximum effectiveness, the appraisal system must have the support of all organizational members. All employees must understand its purpose and implement its procedures correctly and consistently. Too often, lack of commitment by top management limits the amount of resources, particularly staff time, available for appraisal activities.[5] Similarly, if middle management does not perceive that they are accountable for performing accurate evaluations, they will ignore appraisal activities and limit the appraisal's usefulness.[6] What do you think are Jennifer Fulton's and John Elwing's attitudes toward appraisal?

Managers and employees must also be committed to providing *accurate* feedback as part of the appraisal process. Too often managers feel uncomfortable in giving negative feedback.[7] They feel that it will affect the employees' attitudes in the short run and performance in the long run. Many also recognize that a negative appraisal will adversely influence a person's salary, even creating economic hardship for the employee. Managers must establish an organizational context that supports accurate and timely feedback.

Take a few moments to complete the questionnaire in Figure 6–3 about an organization in which you have worked. The questions help identify your attitude and the organization's attitudes toward performance appraisal. Now review your responses. How would you describe management's attitude? Your own attitude? How could these attitudes be changed? Managers and human resources profes-

1. Fosters improvements in work performance
2. Assigns work more efficiently according to workers' skills, abilities, and knowledge
3. Encourages promotion or decruitment based on merit or lack of merit
4. Warns of unacceptable performance
5. Reviews performance at completion of a probationary period
6. Recognizes and rewards past performance
7. Advises of the organization's expectations
8. Validates selection procedures
9. Improves job placement
10. Identifies training needs
11. Evaluates the impact of training programs
12. Addresses needs for growth
13. Recognizes potential for development to managerial positions
14. Assists in setting career goals

Figure 6–2 USES OF PERFORMANCE APPRAISAL

The following items ask your opinions about performance appraisal in general and as it is carried out within your organization as a whole. For these items, please indicate the extent to which you agree or disagree with each by circling the number which most closely corresponds to your opinion.

	Strongly Disagree	*Disagree*	*Slightly Disagree*	*Neither Disagree nor Agree*	*Slightly Agree*	*Agree*	*Strongly Agree*
1. Performance appraisal cannot be objectively and unemotionally carried out by managers.	[1]	[2]	[3]	[4]	[5]	[6]	[7]
2. Few people really understand what the objectives of performance appraisal are.	1	2	3	4	5	6	7
3. Most people have a real understanding of how performance appraisal results are used in my organization.	1	2	3	4	5	6	7
4. In my organization, *salary* decisions *are* based on performance appraisal results.	1	2	3	4	5	6	7
5. In my organization, *promotion* decisions *are* based on performance appraisal results.	1	2	3	4	5	6	7
6. Supervisors and subordinates pretty much agree on what constitutes good or poor performance.	1	2	3	4	5	6	7
7. Current performance appraisal practices provide accurate feedback to the subordinate.	1	2	3	4	5	6	7
8. Most supervisors are not rewarded for doing performance appraisal well.	1	2	3	4	5	6	7
9. Most managers would not carry out performance appraisal of their subordinates unless the organization required them to.	1	2	3	4	5	6	7
10. Most subordinates would not participate in performance appraisal unless the organization required them to.	1	2	3	4	5	6	7
11. Performance appraisals are fairly and honestly done in this organization.	1	2	3	4	5	6	7
12. Performance appraisal motivates individuals to improve their performances.	1	2	3	4	5	6	7
13. It wouldn't make much difference to our business if performance appraisals were not done.	1	2	3	4	5	6	7
14. Performance appraisal typically leads to productive changes in the subordinate's behavior.	1	2	3	4	5	6	7

Figure 6–3 ASSESSING ATTITUDES TOWARD PERFORMANCE APPRAISAL *Continued*

	Strongly Disagree	Disagree	Slightly Disagree	Neither Disagree nor Agree	Slightly Agree	Agree	Strongly Agree
15. Overall, subordinates (i.e., appraisees) are satisfied with our performance appraisal system.	1	2	3	4	5	6	7
16. Overall, supervisors (i.e., appraisers) are satisfied with our performance appraisal system.	1	2	3	4	5	6	7
17. Performance appraisals lead to better supervisor and subordinate understanding of what the subordinate's role should be.	1	2	3	4	5	6	7
18. Salary decisions *should* be based on performance appraisal results.	1	2	3	4	5	6	7
19. Promotion decisions *should* be based on performance appraisal results.	1	2	3	4	5	6	7
20. A subordinate's self-appraisal *should* be an important part of the performance appraisal process.	1	2	3	4	5	6	7
21. Performance appraisals *should* be based on goals previously agreed to by the supervisor and subordinate.	1	2	3	4	5	6	7
22. Performance appraisal *should* be done *only* for the subordinate's personal development.	1	2	3	4	5	6	7

Developed by Edward E. Lawler III, Steve Kerr, Chuck Maxey, Monty Mohrman, Bruce Prince, Janet Schriesheim, Department of Organizational Behavior, Graduate School of Business Administration, University of Southern California, Los Angeles, California 90007.

Figure 6–3 Continued

sionals can use these data to determine whether additional effort should be devoted to educating employees about the value and uses of performance appraisals.

Organizations can indeed institute formal evaluation procedures that encourage positive attitudes toward appraisal. To do so, the manager must view evaluation as useful, objective, and fair; be rewarded for performing job evaluations effectively; view other human resources management decisions as based on evaluation; understand the objectives of performance evaluation; and communicate standards of good performance to employees.[8] Employees too must view evaluation as useful, objective, and fair; be rewarded for accomplishing the performance being assessed; view other human resources management decisions as based on evaluation; understand its objectives; and understand the standards of quality performance.[9]

The formal performance appraisal system, then, must meet four criteria. First, it must legitimize evaluation in the organization. Second, it should always encourage an active dialogue between superiors and subordinates. Third, it must support self-improvement of employees by developing, not punishing, deficiencies. Fourth, it must identify and coordinate development activities within the organization that help accomplish the goals set in appraisal conferences. The next section discusses the formal approaches that meet these criteria.

INITIATING FORMAL EVALUATION APPROACHES

Organizations institute formal appraisal systems to ensure that managers regularly provide feedback to their subordinates. To develop and implement these systems, managers and human resources professionals must perform five steps. First, the manager or human resources professional must secure or perform a *job analysis* for each position being assessed. Second, based on this analysis the manager, with the assistance of a human resources professional, should identify the *appraisal criteria*—the standards on which an individual will be assessed—and communicate these to both raters and ratees. Third, the human resources professional should develop or secure an *appraisal format* and train managers in its use. Fourth, the manager must *implement the appraisal* by observing and documenting the employee's performance and communicating it orally or in writing. Fifth and finally, top executives, human resources professionals, and other managers must *review the performance data* obtained for various jobs, departments, or the organization as a whole; they can then use these data to revise human resources practices as necessary.

Analyzing the Job and Determining Evaluation Criteria

As described in Chapter 2, a job analysis determines required work outputs, tasks performed, individual competencies, supervisory activities, and budgetary responsibilities of a job holder. Based on this description, the manager must determine the four key facets—traits, behaviors, tasks, and outcomes—of job performance.

Traits refer to the personal characteristics of an individual, such as poise, motivation, or enthusiasm, that contribute to effective performance. Behaviors describe the actions required to perform job tasks; behavioral criteria might include making a specified number of sales calls, holding product development meetings, or placing advertisements. (The job analysis can also state the tasks required for job performance, as shown in Figure 6–1.) Work outcomes refer to the final performance or other result desired from a job holder. Outcomes may include levels of sales, profits, or costs; turnover or absenteeism; or quality of working life experienced by subordinates. In some situations, workers might have the traits required for successful job performance but fail to perform the required tasks or behaviors. Alternatively, they may behave appropriately, but environmental conditions, such as a poor economic situation or keen competition, may prevent them from attaining desired work outcomes. Both behaviors and traits can be drawn from job descriptions or job specifications, but work outcomes are derived from performance standards delineated by job analyses. Comprehensive analyses, then, should include all four components.

Traits, behaviors, tasks, and outcomes form the basic appraisal criteria. For example, the chief executive officer of an electronics company may evaluate his marketing vice president according to the extent he or she meets the departmental budget or according to the number of new product ideas generated by the department. Appraisal criteria for a customer service representative might include the number of customer complaints handled or the rep's attendance record. Figure 6–4 lists ten guidelines managers should follow in selecting these criteria. Identifying evaluation criteria for very complex jobs or poorly defined jobs can be extremely difficult. Appraisal of high-level managers, for example, is often based on such criteria as profit or sales levels because these are measurable, regardless of how well such criteria reflect successful job performance.

Appraisal Format

Design and implementation of the formal appraisal involves three decisions about format. (1) Who will conduct the appraisal? (2) When will the appraisal be conducted? And (3) what instruments will be used?

Assigning Responsibility. The organization should consider the following questions in choosing raters:

- What is the purpose of the appraisal?
- Who has the relevant knowledge of job performance?
- Who has relevant knowledge of job requirements and relationships?
- How frequently do potential raters observe ratee performance?

1. Define the criteria before selecting an appraisal instrument or format.
2. Do not assume performance cannot be defined or measured.
3. Look at personal knowledge and skills as well as performance criteria.
4. Look at behavior and outcome criteria.
5. Consider every aspect of the job.
6. Combine related, less-important criteria into a single criterion (combine sales levels for each product into one criterion—total sales level—for instance).
7. Keep data on the reliability and validity of criteria.
8. Review and develop criteria on a continual basis.
9. Use the criteria in other human resources programs.
10. Select criteria that are observable and measurable.

Based on S.J. Carroll, Jr. and C.E. Schneier, *Performance Appraisal and Review Systems: The Identification, Measurement, and Development of Performance in Organizations* (Glenview, Ill.: Scott, Foresman, 1982), pp. 57–58.

Figure 6–4 GUIDELINES FOR DEVELOPING APPRAISAL CRITERIA

- What must be done to corroborate ratings and assess their reliability?
- What are the costs associated with appraisal performed by each potential rater?
- Which raters are perceived as having legitimacy in the organization?
- Which raters support the appraisal process?
- Which raters are supported by the organizational structure and climate?
- Which raters have adequate skills for implementing the steps of the appraisal?
- Which raters have adequate work time to appraise performance?[10]

The person who best understands the organization's expectations of the job holder and observes or knows an individual's job performance typically performs the evaluation. This individual (or individuals) should have authority for gathering data for administrative decisions and be perceived as having legitimacy in giving feedback. For performance appraisals to be effective, the rater must support the appraisal process and have analytical, communication, counseling, and assessment skills. When there is a need to corroborate ratings, more than one rater should be used.

At Pittsburgh Plastics, for example, the supervisors performed the appraisals, although the responsibility can also be assigned to peers, subordinates, outsiders, or the employee. As shown in Table 6–2, there are advantages and disadvantages to using different types of raters. The use of multiple raters, where feasible, increases the accuracy of evaluations.

Timing Appraisals. How often and when should appraisals be performed? The manager must balance the time involved in completing an appraisal with the value of frequent feedback. The manager must assess an employee's performance at least once a year. Traditionally, appraisals have only accompanied yearly compensation decisions. Recent research suggests, however, that more frequent feedback correlates positively with improved performance.[11] Research has also indicated that appraisals for developmental purposes should be separated from those for salary administration[12]; thus, human resources professionals or managers should schedule evaluations at least twice a year.

One scenario that increases appraisal frequency and separates it from salary administration is as follows. Six months after the employee's hiring, the supervisor conducts an appraisal that focuses on development and goal-setting. On the employee's hiring anniversary the supervisor conducts an appraisal that emphasizes evaluation and provides data that can be used in pay decisions. The manager repeats these two appraisal activities each year.

In addition to regularly scheduled formal appraisals, the appraisal system should call for more frequent informal appraisals. The "one-minute manager" provides one minute of feedback as appropriate during the regular work day.[13] The manager can also schedule breakfast, lunch, or coffee break meetings with an employee to share or gather data about the employee's performance. When done on a more informal basis, appraisals have more power and result in less anxiety for the employee.

Raters	*Advantages*	*Disadvantages*
Superior	has legitimate authority to evaluate subordinates' performance controls rewards for performance has knowledge of ratee job performance	may hamper needed communication if assessment is low may be costly in time lost from other management functions
Peer	can facilitate inter-unit communication makes predictively valid ratings	may make inaccurate ratings due to competition for rewards may be influenced by acquaintance or friendship seldom used in industry
Subordinate	can foster participative and ownership feelings can uniquely evaluate leadership ability and potential	may fear reprisals may feel uneasy and experience superiors as defensive may have inadequate knowledge of or sensitivity to all crucial job dimensions
Self	has knowledge of job performance frequently and continuously observes job performance fosters development and less defensive appraisals	tends to inflate ratings may attribute problems to environment or others but not to self
External Specialist	possesses an unbiased view may have excellent knowledge of technical job requirements	may not have relevant job knowledge may not have adequate performance observation frequency may not be seen as legitimate by ratees may be costly

Based on L.L. Cummings and D.P. Schwab, *Performance in Organizations: Determinants and Appraisals.* Glenview, Ill.: Scott, Foresman, 1973.

Table 6–2 ADVANTAGES AND DISADVANTAGES OF VARIOUS RATERS

Choosing, Designing, and Using Instruments

Evaluation instruments have a variety of formats: (1) graphic rating scales, (2) behaviorally anchored rating scales, (3) essays or narrative formats, (4) critical incidents, (5) forced-choice scales, (6) rankings, (7) objective-based formats, (8) objective indices, and (9) combined formats. To assess the appropriateness of each type of instrument, the following factors should be used (see Chapter 4 for further discussion of these factors):

Validity—does the instrument accurately measure the appraisal criteria and correctly identify effective performance?

Reliability—does the instrument yield consistent and accurate ratings? For example, are the same ratings obtained by different raters, by the same rater at different times, on two halves of the same instrument, on reuses of the instrument, or on alternative versions of the same instrument?

Discriminability—does the instrument differentiate good from poor performers?

Freedom from bias—is there a tendency to assign extreme ratings or scores, or a trend to assign a certain type of ratings or scores? Does the instrument discourage the rater from making very high and very low ratings? Does the instrument encourage objective assessment of performance? Does the instrument discourage stereotyping; that is, assessing an individual and his or her performance based on a category (e.g., women, blondes, young professionals) to which the person belongs?

Relevance—does the instrument provide useful data to the rater and ratee?

Cost—does the instrument cost a reasonable amount to develop and use?

Ease of administration—does a rater require extensive training to use the instrument? Does the instrument require a reasonable amount of time to complete?

In the following sections we examine the nine formats in greater detail and comment about each format's value on the dimensions listed above.

Graphic rating scales compare individual performance to an absolute standard. The rater assesses performance on numerous dimensions, such as quality of work, acceptance of criticism, willingness to assume responsibility, and the like. The rater uses four-, five-, seven-, or even ten-point rating scales, ranging from low to high, poor to excellent, or unsatisfactory to very satisfactory performance. Figure 6–5 is an example of such a scale.

The human resources professional, manager, or outside consultant who designs a graphic rating scale should use the job analyses as the basis for deriving the dimensions to be rated. Frequently, however, those constructing the scale include traits, skills, or knowledge, such as "acceptance of criticism," that they feel distinguish good from poor performers in any job. In these cases, the appraisal form itself often becomes an operational job description.

Such scales have relatively low design cost and high ease of administration. They can readily pinpoint significant dimensions of the job. Because of these advantages, graphic rating scales are frequently used. The major drawback to these scales is their subjectivity and low reliability. Because the evaluative dimensions may not be traits, tasks, behaviors, or outcomes derived from job analysis, the rater may become confused about the "real requirements" of the job. And because the points on the rating continuum tend to be defined in relatively global, nonbehavioral terms, interpretation by different raters can vary significantly. Does "excellent ability to express self orally" mean the same thing to you and another person? How frequently is "always" or "sometimes"? These labels should be unambiguous and relevant to the dimensions being rated, while at the same time as specific and observable as possible.[14]

To design a graphic rating scale, a manager, human resources professional, or consultant first reviews the job analysis to determine the key dimensions of the job (typically traits) he or she desires to measure. After listing these dimensions, the designer determines what scale to use to assess them. For example, the scale might assess their frequency of occurrence (from never to always), the degree of their occurrence (from very low to very high), or how satisfied the rater is with

Considering the staff member's training and experience, evaluate him/her on each of the areas below based on performance for *this* assignment. 1) Outstanding 2) Above average 3) Average—what would normally be expected of a staff member at his/her level of experience 4) Requires improvement 5) Unsatisfactory 6) Not applicable. *Circle number representing your rating.*

		OVERALL
Auditing:		
Aptitude	1 2 3 4 5 6	
Imagination	1 2 3 4 5 6	1 2 3 4 5 6
Analytical ability	1 2 3 4 5 6	
Knowledge of accounting:		
Theory	1 2 3 4 5 6	
Current developments	1 2 3 4 5 6	1 2 3 4 5 6
Practical application	1 2 3 4 5 6	
Working characteristics:		
Judgment	1 2 3 4 5 6	
Acceptance of responsibility	1 2 3 4 5 6	
Ability to follow instructions	1 2 3 4 5 6	
Ability to plan, organize and complete work	1 2 3 4 5 6	1 2 3 4 5 6
Proficiency in preparing working papers	1 2 3 4 5 6	
Accuracy	1 2 3 4 5 6	
Productivity	1 2 3 4 5 6	
Supervision:		
Ability to train and develop staff	1 2 3 4 5 6	
Ability to direct staff	1 2 3 4 5 6	1 2 3 4 5 6
Ability to review work of staff	1 2 3 4 5 6	
Communication:		
Ability to express self in writing	1 2 3 4 5 6	1 2 3 4 5 6
Ability to express self orally	1 2 3 4 5 6	
Personal characteristics:		
Attitude	1 2 3 4 5 6	
Ability to maintain and/or develop goodwill of clients	1 2 3 4 5 6	
Ability to get along with other staff members	1 2 3 4 5 6	
Leadership	1 2 3 4 5 6	1 2 3 4 5 6
Independence and impartiality of mind	1 2 3 4 5 6	
Professional appearance and manner	1 2 3 4 5 6	
Business consciousness (such as ability to develop management reports, interest in service to clients)		1 2 3 4 5 6
Desirability on another of your assignments: Would this staff member be 1) Preferable 2) Acceptable or 3) Would you prefer another staff member		1 2 3

Reprinted with permission of Price Waterhouse.

Figure 6–5 SAMPLE OF A GRAPHIC RATING SCALE

their occurrence (from very dissatisfied to very satisfied). The designer then determines the number of points on the rating scale. Four, five, or six points are most common because distinguishing among more categories is difficult, and using fewer categories is not informative. The designer generally chooses an odd number of categories to allow the rater a middle ground. The designer then edits the items and scale. Next, he or she pilot-tests the rating scale with a small sample of evaluators in order to refine the scale to remove ambiguous or nondiscriminating items. Repeated pilot administrations of the scale should occur until the items are clear and discriminate among different levels of performance.

Behaviorally anchored rating scales (also known as BARS) attempt to reduce the subjectivity of absolute ratings such as graphic rating scales.[15] They use observable behaviors, rather than traits, knowledge, or skills, as the evaluative dimensions. As shown in Figure 6–6, behaviorally anchored rating scales resemble both graphic rating scales and critical incidents (described later in this chapter). Raters compare the performance of an individual on each dimension to a standard. Rather than using subjective standards, such as excellent, always, fair, or unsatisfactory, BARS use more objective, behavioral standards. The standard is a detailed description of observable behavior, such as "submits reports on time with no spelling, typing, or grammatical errors; writes clearly and succinctly."

Managers, human resources professionals, or outside consultants should derive the observable behaviors from the job description and performance standards. These behaviors often comprise a *process* whereby an employee accomplishes the desired work outcomes.

BARS have a greater reliability than graphic rating scales. But BARS also have high development costs because each job requires different behavioral standards; each job requires a different form.

Development of BARS resembles the development of graphic rating scales. The designer first identifies the key dimensions of the job, such as "verbal skills," "use of equipment," or "organizational ability." For each dimension, the designer writes six or seven narrative descriptions that reflect varying degrees of effective behavior, from the "best" to the "worst." The designer then refines these general descriptions into succinct behavioral anchors, often involving a panel of managers, human resources professionals, or experts in this step. As for graphic rating scales, the designer then repeatedly administers, tests, and refines the scales until they meet the characteristics of effective instruments discussed earlier in this chapter.

Essays or narrative formats ask the rater to assess an employee in fairly general areas. The rater might describe the strengths and weaknesses of an individual's performance. The effectiveness of these formats depends, more than other formats, on the rater's skill and effort in writing detailed comments. This format emphasizes evaluation of overall performance, rather than specific job dimensions; as such, it provides limited data for use in employee development and limits the ability of managers to make concrete comparisons to expected behavior for use in administrative decisions. Further, the relatively high cost and low ease of administration of essays and narratives create barriers to their use.[16]

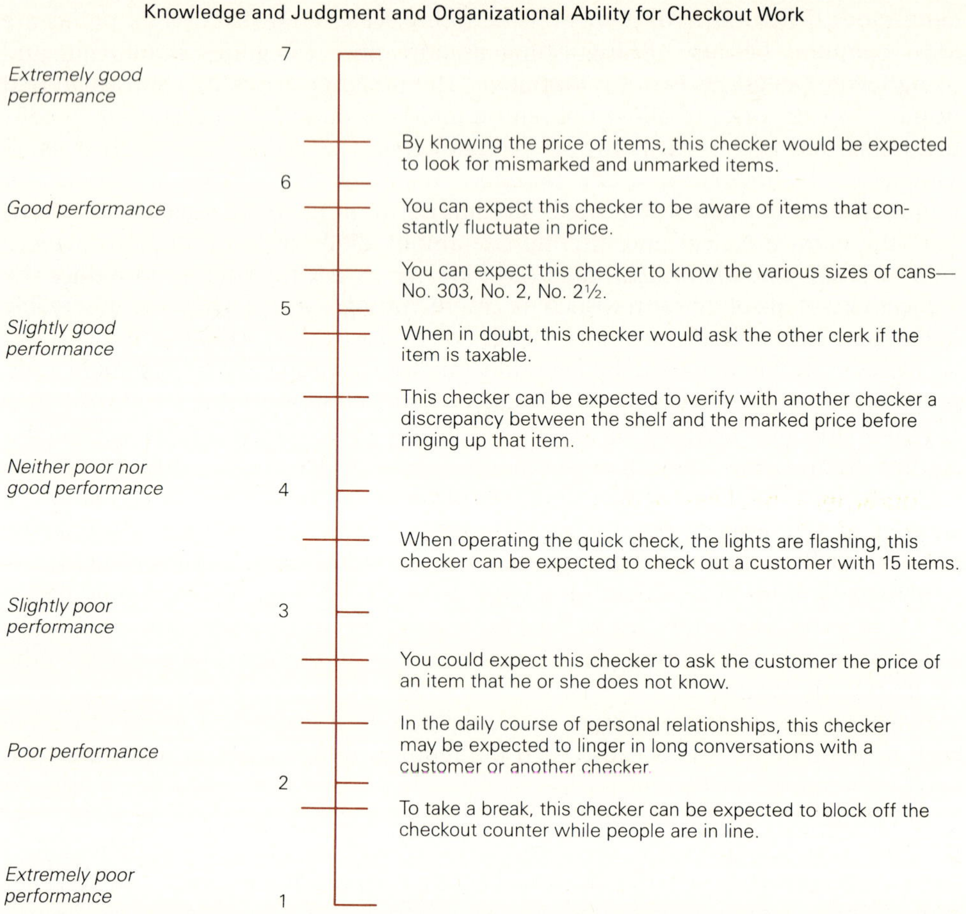

Source: From "Behavioral Job Criteria" by Lawrence Fogli, Charles L. Hulin, and Milton R. Blood (*Journal of Applied Psychology*, February 1971), © by the American Psychological Association. Reprinted by permission of the author.

Figure 6–6 SAMPLE OF A BEHAVIORALLY ANCHORED RATING SCALE

Managers, human resources professionals, or consultants tend to spend little time developing essay or narrative formats. To develop this instrument the designer thinks of general questions that would prompt a manager to describe and evaluate an individual's performance both globally and more specifically. For example, an essay appraisal might ask the evaluator to describe the areas in which the individual needs to improve, or the person's most outstanding characteristics. Developing a strong and discriminating essay format requires the designer to be clever in writing probing questions.

Critical incidents require the manager to record significant events that characterize the employee's performance.[17] The rater should choose events that reflect positive, negative, and typical behaviors. Originally, the critical incident technique used individual or group interviews , questionnaires, or recording forms to obtain data.[18] In interviews, for example, it asked questions such as the following: Think of the last time you saw one of your subordinates do something that was very helpful to your group in meeting its objectives; what were the general circumstances leading up to this incident? What did the person do that was so helpful in getting your group's job done?[19]

Today, managers using the critical incident format rely mainly on recording forms to obtain data. Figure 6–7 illustrates a form to help managers identify critical incidents in the performance of employees.

Because of the time required to write complete profiles of critical situations, managers can be asked instead to record sketchy notes of their observations noting the date and some other reminder of the event.[20] Later, they can either transform these brief notes into more detailed descriptions of the incidents, evaluate the anecdotes themselves, or use the notes as data for completing a rating scale of some kind.

Critical incidents, like behaviorally anchored rating scales, focus evaluation on an individual's *behavior*. But because critical incidents only sample behaviors, they may not accurately reflect an employee's overall performance. Also, the rater is likely to remember recent events most clearly; these may not represent overall

Employee's Name ______________________ Rater's Name ______________________

Think of the last time you saw one of your subordinates do something that was very helpful to your group in meeting its objectives. In the space below, please describe the incident. Include the general circumstances leading up to the incident, exactly what the person did, and why the incident was helpful to your group.

Think of the last time you saw one of your subordinates do something that was detrimental to your group in meeting its objectives. In the space below, please describe the incident; include the general circumstances leading up to the incident, exactly what the person did, and why the incident was dysfunctional for the group.

Figure 6–7 **SAMPLE OF A CRITICAL INCIDENT RATING FORMAT**

performance either. Finally, ensuring the comparability of incidents recorded for many employees can be difficult.

Forced-choice scales require raters to choose between pairs or trios of behaviors, or statements that describe individual performance. The responses are then scored using special statistical techniques. The items are designed to discriminate effective from ineffective workers as well as reflect valuable personal qualities.[21] They are meant to reduce the bias in ratings; specifically, the tendency to assign all high or all low ratings.

Although forced-choice scales are easy to use, unless very carefully developed and tested, they may suffer from low validity and reliability and a high development cost. Development of this type of scale is tricky and generally calls for designers with special training and experience in psychometric measurement.

Rankings compare one individual's performance to another's. The manager assigns to each employee a rank that reflects overall job performance. Or rankings on a series of job dimensions are summed to provide an overall evaluation of the individual. Although designing a ranking scale is straightforward, analysis of the data can require relatively sophisticated statistical techniques. Typically, managers and human resources professionals do more simplistic, and perhaps less informative, analyses.

Such an approach to appraisal can be relatively easy and inexpensive, but its reliability and validity may be questionable. In addition, managers and human resources professionals have trouble translating the data into recommendations for training or development.

Management-by-objectives, or similar formats based on setting objectives, combines development with evaluation. Management-by-objectives is a formalized approach that requires the development of detailed goal plans at all levels of the organization. Supervisors and subordinates jointly develop goals that serve as appraisal criteria, the focus of an employee's activities, and the basis for assessing training and development needs. Design of the format itself is relatively straightforward. The form should include a place to list the objectives, write the time frame for their accomplishment, specify any methods or activities that help to accomplish them, and describe the measurable outcomes that indicate the objective's accomplishment. Determining the goals themselves, however, is more difficult and time-consuming; this process is described in more detail later in this chapter.

When used for evaluation, goals should (1) identify specific results desired and actions to be taken, as a way of focusing activities; (2) set time limits that specify when goals should be accomplished; (3) specify costs for accomplishing objectives in terms of money, people, time, raw materials, and opportunity; (4) be measurable so that a reliable determination of their accomplishment can be made; (5) be realistic, challenging, yet attainable; and (6) be consistent with organizational plans, policies, and procedures.[22] When used for developing employees, goals must identify skills, knowledge, abilities, and experiences the job holder must acquire to perform well in the future.

In spite of its relative popularity and effectiveness, management-by-objectives has significant limitations. For example, the manager must acknowledge his or her responsibility in helping the subordinate accomplish the goals. The manager and subordinate must also discuss the process and resources required to accomplish the goals. Also, evaluations may encourage workers to accomplish their goals, regardless of the methods required to attain them. The manager must carefully monitor goal-setting, goal accomplishment, and goal evaluation.[23]

Objective indices, such as profits, sales dollars, and number of days absent or tardy, can serve as the basis of performance evaluation. These indices help assess work outcomes, rather than traits, behaviors, or tasks. Although such indices provide one of the most reliable estimates of performance, their usefulness is limited since they ignore the quality of the processes used to accomplish the outcomes. For example, a salesperson may not close any sales even though he or she behaves in an appropriate fashion; this lack of success may be due to a poor economic climate or a defective product, and not to poor performance. Or an employee may have no absences but do poor quality work. Such indices are excellent *supplements* to other measures of performance.

Combined formats reduce the shortcomings of using any single format. The advantages of one format can counterbalance the disadvantages of another. However, increasing the number of formats used almost always increases the cost of development and implementation, and decreases the ease of administration.

Maintaining Performance Records

The quality and usefulness of performance appraisals depend on the completeness and objectivity of the data on which they are based. Research suggests that raters frequently demonstrate bias in their evaluations. For example, they rate an employee's performance at a given time more positively if the performance is better than before than if it is worse than it was earlier.[24] Raters also tend to remember recent events better than remote ones.[25] Individuals remember particularly negative events longer than particularly positive or neutral ones.[26] Even the content of participative goal-setting interviews between a supervisor and an employee can play a role in subsequent performance appraisal ratings: a worker who sets high goals may receive inflated ratings from his or her supervisor later.[27]

Various training programs have attempted to reduce bias in observers' ratings.[28] Figure 6–8 provides some guidelines for doing this. In general, raters can reduce rating bias, and thereby improve performance appraisal, by gathering performance-related data on all employees on a regular basis, carefully and correctly attributing the causes of subordinate behavior, analyzing their assessments of subordinates for trends or biases, and noting all types of behavior, not just extremely positive or negative ones.

A manager who maintains performance records is likely to display less bias. Figure 6–9 shows an example of a useful performance log. In recording performance the manager should observe the following guidelines:

- Record objective facts concerning actual performance as they occur, rather than from memory.

1. Do not assume raters are aware of the bases of their judgments.
2. Encourage raters to gather performance-related information over time.
3. Encourage raters to identify their own stereotypes and expectations.
4. Recognize that unusually high or low performance may be given too much weight.
5. Recognize that ratings of traits may not measure performance.
6. Use performance-related data to help raters overcome their stereotypes.
7. Raters may thwart policies that specify the weights to be assigned to various criteria.
8. Raters may regularly misattribute causes of behavior; they may attribute their own failures to the environment and others' failures to their personal characteristics; and attribute successes in the reverse way.
9. The sex of the ratee may affect attributions; raters have historically attributed a woman's success to luck rather than ability.

Based on S.J. Carroll and C.E. Schneier, *Performance Appraisal and Review Systems: The Identification, Measurement, and Development of Performance in Organizations.* Glenview, Ill.: Scott, Foresman, 1982, pp. 80–81.

Figure 6–8 **WAYS TO INCREASE THE ACCURACY OF EMPLOYEE EVALUATION**

- Record only job-related behavior.
- Record direct observations rather than relying on hearsay reports from others.
- Describe specific behavior rather than making evaluative statements or describing an individual's personality.
- Record both positive and negative behaviors.
- Keep the same basic format and level of descriptive detail for each subordinate.
- Maintain documentation on all employees in a given work group.
- Periodically review the collective documentation to ensure that similar quantity, quality, and consistency are maintained.[29]

Documentation of behavior is particularly important when an employee has

Employee's Name ______________________ Supervisor's Name ______________________

For the employee named above, describe all significant or unusual behaviors that have contributed positively or negatively to the performance of his or her job. Also think of behaviors that are typical of the person.

Date	*Positive Behaviors*	*Negative Behaviors*	*Typical Behaviors*

Figure 6–9 **EXAMPLE OF A PERFORMANCE LOG**

performance problems. To guarantee the accuracy and legality of decruitment decisions, supervisors should maintain complete records of employee performance.

CONDUCTING APPRAISAL INTERVIEWS

Effective performance appraisal must include feedback to the employee about his or her performance. Most commonly this feedback includes oral communication during planned interviews as well as written feedback in detailed appraisal forms. Effective interviews depend on three factors: (1) the superior's knowledge of the subordinate's job and job performance; (2) the superior's encouragement and support of the subordinate; and (3) the superior's encouragement of the subordinate's participation in the appraisal process.[30]

The key to effective appraisal interviews is careful planning and communication. The manager should use the interview time to verify the data he or she has collected, convey evaluative information to the employee, and set future development goals. The employee should use the interview time to verify the data gathered by the manager, provide additional relevant data, and jointly set development goals for the next year. Recognizing the limits of the appraisal, one researcher notes that "management must . . . admit to employees that the appraisal process is a negative aspect of the supervisor/subordinate relationship and that it has some significant disadvantages and weaknesses."[31]

When an employee is unskilled in receiving feedback or a manager is unskilled in delivering it, the interview is less useful than it could be. The next sections present some general guidelines for communicating and setting goals effectively.

Guidelines for Effective Communication

Figure 6–10 shows the basic communication model. The manager must encode, or express, the message in language understood by the subordinate. The message passes through direct or indirect channels, using oral or written media, to the receiver. The receiver, in this case the subordinate, must decode the message accurately, determining as precisely as possible the superior's intent. Thus the interview format must provide an opportunity for feedback so that both parties can check that messages are encoded and decoded accurately. In the scenario at

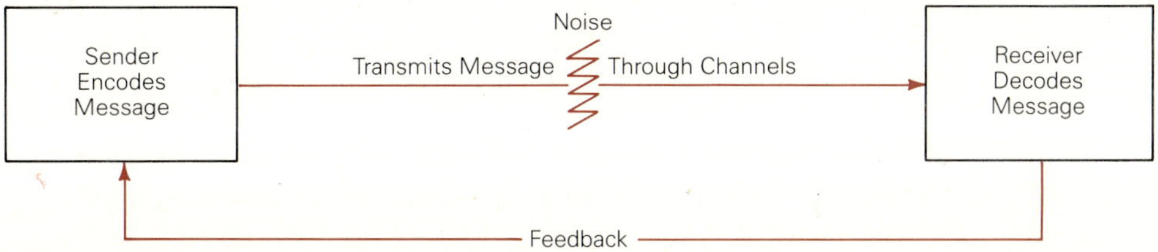

Figure 6–10 COMMUNICATION MODEL

the beginning of the chapter, it is clear that the communication between Jennifer Fulton and John Elwing during the appraisal interview was not effective.

To facilitate communication both interviewer and interviewee should create a supportive climate.[32] The manager should describe—not evaluate—events. For example, if a manager observes an employee acting in a way the manager thinks is inappropriate, the manager should describe the situation to the employee, not merely say, "You acted ineffectively." The manager should show that he or she has empathy not ambivalence toward the subordinate. The manager should never demonstrate superiority to a subordinate through using language such as "I know better because I've been doing it for so long," or "People with your background don't have the experience to understand this situation." The manager should take a collaborative approach toward problems experienced by the subordinate, viewing them as mutual problems that both of them must address jointly. The manager should not attempt to manipulate the subordinate into viewing the situation or acting in a certain way. Finally, the manager should show a willingness to experiment or change his or her own behavior.

There are three basic approaches to conducting an interview: (1) tell and sell, (2) tell and listen, and (3) problem-solving.[33] A manager who uses the *tell and sell* approach acts as a judge and tries to communicate an evaluation of subordinate performance as accurately as possible. The manager must persuade the subordinate to change in the prescribed fashion.

The manager who uses the *tell and listen* approach also acts as a judge, but communicates the evaluation and then waits for the subordinate's response. During the interview the manager both conveys assessments about the strengths and weaknesses of the worker's performance and explores the subordinate's feelings about the evaluation. The manager must demonstrate a willingness to accept the subordinate's reactions as a way of allowing the subordinate to retain dignity in the face of negative comments.

The *problem-solving* approach differs significantly from the other two approaches. The manager acts as a helper and works jointly with the subordinate to develop the employee's performance. The interviewer should use a problem-solving strategy where appropriate. In using this strategy the interviewer must

- define conflict as a mutual problem;
- pursue goals held in common;
- find mutually satisfying creative agreements;
- understand his or her own needs and show them honestly;
- try to equalize power;
- avoid threats;
- work at understanding and developing empathy of the other's position;
- communicate flexibility of position;
- behave predictably and consistently;
- emphasize exploring both differences and similarities in positions; and
- seek third parties to help.[34]

Table 6–3 compares these three approaches in greater detail.

Method	Tell and Sell	Tell and Listen	Problem-Solving
Objectives	To communicate evaluation To persuade employee to improve	To communicate evaluation To release defensive feelings	To stimulate growth and development in employee
Psychological Assumptions	Employee desires to correct weaknesses if he knows them Any person can improve if he so chooses A superior is qualified to evaluate a subordinate	People will change if defensive feelings are removed	Growth can occur without correcting faults Discussing job problems leads to improved performance
Role of Interviewer	Judge	Judge	Helper
Attitude of Interviewer	People profit from criticism and appreciate help	One can respect the feelings of others if one understands them	Discussion develops new ideas and mutual interests
Skills of Interviewer	Salesmanship Patience	Listening and reflecting feelings Summarizing	Listening and reflecting feelings Reflecting ideas Using exploratory questions Summarizing
Reactions of Employee	Suppresses defensive behavior Attempts to cover hostility	Expresses defensive behavior Feels accepted	Problem-solving behavior
Employee's Motivation for Change	Use of positive or negative incentives or both Extrinsic motivation is added to the job itself	Resistance to change reduced Positive incentive Extrinsic and some intrinsic motivation	Increased freedom Increased responsibility Intrinsic motivation—interest is inherent in the task
Possible Gains	Success most probable when employee respects interviewer	Employee develops favorable attitude toward superior, which increases probability of success	Almost assured of improvement in some respect
Risks of Interviewer	Loss of loyalty Inhibition of independent judgment Face-saving problems created	Need for change may not be developed	Employee may lack ideas Change may be other than what superior had in mind
Probable Results	Perpetuates existing practices and values	Permits interviewer to change his views in light of employee's responses Some upward communication	Both learn, because experience and views are pooled Change is facilitated

Table 6–3 COMPARISON OF THREE APPROACHES TO FEEDBACK

In addition, the manager must treat his or her subordinate as an adult, rather than a parent or a child. In this regard, transactional analysis can provide a useful framework for examining the interactions between individuals.[35] According to this model, individuals operate from one of three states: adult (rational), parent (judgmental), or child (dependent). Effective communication requires that both individuals in an appraisal interview (or elsewhere) act from and to adult states. They avoid communicating from two states simultaneously (one manifest and one latent) and they communicate openly and honestly.

In sum, the interviewer should observe the following steps in the appraisal interview: (1) get to the point of the interview; (2) outline observations in specific and descriptive terms; (3) invite self-evaluation; (4) listen; (5) set new goals and develop an action plan with the subordinate; (6) have the subordinate sum up the discussion; and (7) set a follow-up schedule.[36] The managers at two newspapers owned by Gannett Company were given the following pragmatic advice about conducting performance interviews, which is worth repeating here:

- Start with negatives and end with the positives.
- Define the problem.
- Criticize the work, not the person.
- When criticizing, soften the tone, not the message.
- Don't make assumptions.
- Don't criticize when you are angry. You will say something you'll regret.
- Don't exaggerate.
- Avoid absolutes. Words like "always" and "never" are easy to refute.
- Beware of your own biases (predispositions).
- Share responsibility. The burden for the staffer's failure falls, in part, on the manager.
- Ask questions to get information, not to confirm your beliefs or "test" the staffer.
- Expect disagreements, but don't get drawn into an argument.
- Draw on the staffer's strengths to overcome weaknesses.
- Listen. Listen. Listen.[37]

Reading 6–1: "An Active Feedback Program Can Spark Performance," by Fay Walther and Susan Taylor, summarizes key issues related to communicating about performance.

Conducting effective appraisal interviews is a two-way street. Employees must also be trained in their role in the appraisal. Such training should increase their investment in the organization and cause any frustration with their evaluation to be directed against themselves rather than the organization.[38] Training should also help employees

1. anticipate the appraisal interview by thinking about their performance before the interview (having a blank copy of the appraisal form so they can evaluate their own performance before the interview);

2. clarify the expectations their managers have of them;
3. know and document their personal strengths and weaknesses;
4. recognize expected behaviors (not voicing disagreements, never admitting mistakes, keeping a low profile, and the like) that adversely affect job performance;
5. accept help;
6. probe for information; and
7. avoid overly defensive behavior.[39]

Setting Development and Performance Goals

Joint goal-setting addresses both functions of performance appraisal: assessment of past performance and development of future performance. Managers and their subordinates can set goals for level of work output, improvements in work output, changes in personal behavior, and organizational improvements such as increased efficiency or cost reductions.[40] Research has shown that goal-setting involving the subordinate during the interview can produce positive outcomes such as work satisfaction, perceived fairness, and a desire to improve performance.[41] Subordinate participation is more effective if subordinates tend to be independent personalities and have information about the issues to be discussed.[42] In addition, the superior's support, encouragement of participation, and knowledge of the subordinate's job and performance contribute to the interview's effectiveness.[43]

"The purpose of a goal-setting session is to establish goals which are useful not only for performance evaluation at the end of the review period but for managing the work process during that period as well."[44] Goals should (1) identify specific results desired and actions to be taken; (2) set time limits for accomplishing objectives or completing activities; (3) specify costs in terms of financial, human, time, and materials resources; (4) be measurable; (5) be realistic, challenging, and attainable; and (6) fit with the organization's policies and procedures and with top management's goals.[45]

Figure 6–11 lists the steps involved in the effective setting of objectives. One scenario for an effective interview follows:

Step 1: The subordinate explains any problems that have arisen to the supervisor, who listens carefully.
Step 2: The subordinate leads and the supervisor more actively participates in a problem-solving discussion.
Step 3: The subordinate and supervisor reach agreement about performance problems and a plan for improvement.
Step 4: The supervisor concludes the interview by giving his or her own views about the issues raised, and by raising any issues the subordinate has neglected to raise.[46]

Figure 6–12 lists the steps in employee development as part of performance appraisal in more detail.

1. Review sources of objectives:
   a. Organization/unit plans, objectives, strategies
   b. Objectives of next higher level
   c. Key results areas
   d. Job or position descriptions
   e. Discussion with supervisor, subordinates, clients, etc.
   f. Organizational problems and opportunities
   g. Previous performance plan and objectives.
2. List major types of objectives which could be established within each of the key results areas.
3. Review the list with supervisor (and subordinates) to clarify their meaning and priority and preliminary thoughts on specific objectives.
4. Develop one or more draft objectives, including those of a continuing and project nature for each key results area.
5. Identify criteria and a rough action plan for each objective.
6. Omit/revise any objective for which no criteria exist, no practical action plan is possible, or which does not comply with the "Objectives Checklist."
7. Break objectives into subobjectives or components if required.
8. Note any conditions outside your control which would influence the attainment of the objectives.
9. Determine which objectives are critical.
10. Review the objectives, criteria, action plan, etc. with your supervisor.
11. Make any modifications necessary after supervisor's review.
12. Develop detailed action plan for each objective.
13. Begin to carry out action plans.
14. Periodically review sources listed in step 1, revising objectives, criteria, conditions, action plans, etc. as necessary and reviewing changes with supervisor and subordinates.

Figure 6–11 SETTING OBJECTIVES

TROUBLESHOOTING PERFORMANCE PROBLEMS

Managers experience difficulties in improving employee performance for three reasons. First, they react to their own assumptions about individual behaviors and attitudes. Second, managers fail to recognize that the organizational or environmental situation may contribute to performance problems; individuals may have the motivation to perform but not the opportunity, for example, due to a poor economic situation or lack of financial resources.[47] Third, no clear prescription for effective performance exists.[48]

Performance appraisal, more than any other human resources management system, addresses problems of poor performance (see Chapter 5). There are two major types of performance problems: (1) the performer lacks skills and knowledge to do the job effectively, and (2) the performer has the necessary skills and knowledge but lacks the motivation to do the job. Dealing with performance

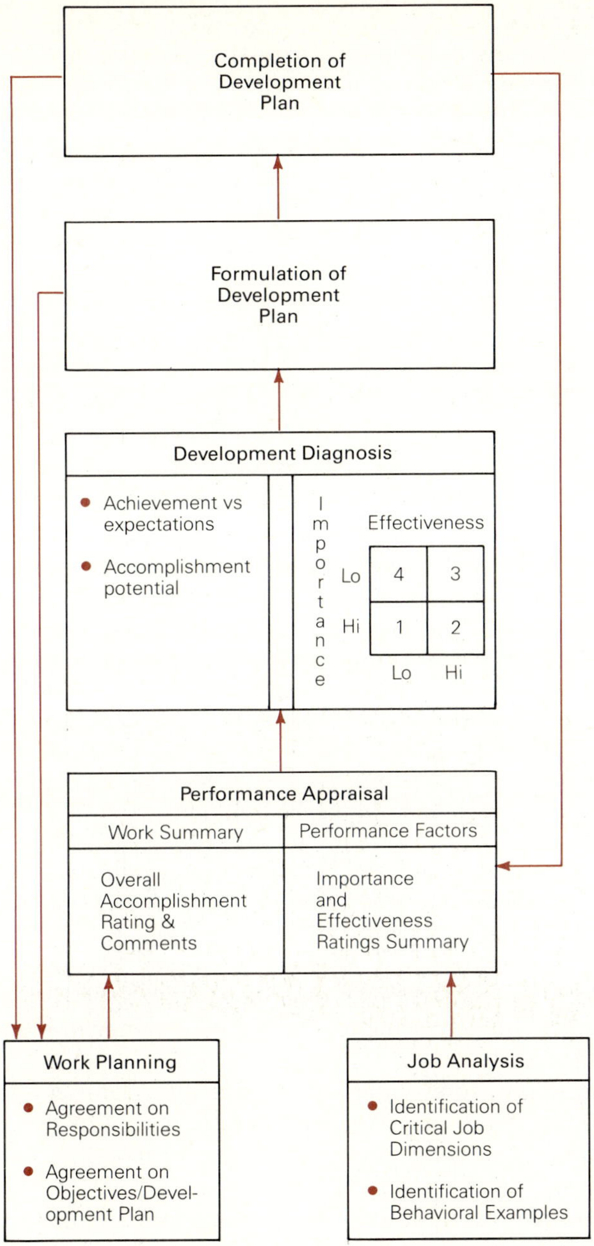

From L.R. Gomez-Mejia and R.C. Page, Integrating Employee Development and Performance Appraisal. Copyright 1983, *Training and Development Journal,* American Society for Training and Development. Reprinted with permission. All rights reserved.

Figure 6–12 A MODEL FOR INTEGRATING EMPLOYEE DEVELOPMENT AND PERFORMANCE APPRAISAL problems begins with diagnosis and continues with the development of strategies for modifying behavior.

Improving productivity should be a three-step process. Step 1 is to identify the area of poor performance. Step 2 is to determine its cause. And step 3 is to do something about the poor performance.[49] More specifically, a manager should (1) define expected or desired performance concretely, in observable behavioral terms; (2) reduce errors in the rating of performance; (3) set specific goals; and (4) establish positive consequences for employees who attain the goals.[50] Jennifer Fulton might need to follow these steps more carefully in conducting the appraisals of her subordinates.

DESIGNING A COMPREHENSIVE EVALUATION SYSTEM

The results of performance appraisals provide input for staffing, training and development, and compensation decisions. For example, the results of performance appraisals should complement needs assessments to determine training and development deficiencies and help determine pay increases. But managers and human resources professionals must also maintain the integrity of evaluation and feedback apart from these uses. Appraisal feedback should be separated from compensation decisions; evaluations should be separated from developmental counseling.[51] Computers can facilitate the coordination of data throughout the organization to ensure that appraisal programs are used systematically and with regularity and reliability.

Implications for Human Resources Professionals

Human resources professionals should design organization-wide appraisal systems, train managers in their use, and monitor their implementation. To do this effectively, they must act as follows:

1. Human resources professionals must assure that the program is rationally designed. They must find ways of encouraging consistency in ratings and feedback across the organization.
2. Human resources professionals must train the appraisers. Ongoing training in evaluation should focus on managers' understanding of the intricacies of the performance appraisal system, documenting performance accurately, and communicating information to employees effectively.
3. Human resources professionals can participate in an analysis of the environment and organization to ensure that the performance evaluation systems respond to their significant aspects.
4. Human resources professionals can maintain current job descriptions, specifications, and performance standards for all jobs for use in appraisals.

5. Human resources professionals should periodically check managers' and employees' attitudes toward appraisal; and conduct activities to decrease negative attitudes if necessary.

6. Human resources professionals can design or supply appraisal formats to managers. They should alert managers to the potential drawbacks of any forms used.

7. Human resources professionals should know the laws affecting performance appraisal (see Chapter 13) and be certain that all evaluation actions meet legal standards.

8. Human resources professionals should ensure that data from the evaluative component of performance appraisals fit with other human resources management systems; that compensation and promotion decisions are consistent with appraisal data, for example. They should use data from the developmental component to identify training needs and guide career development activities.

Implications for Managers

Managers should implement performance appraisal systems by completing evaluation forms and providing feedback to employees about their performance, as described below.

1. Managers can contribute to situational analyses by providing updated job information for all employees and should receive the results of any analyses performed by human resources professionals.

2. Managers must develop positive attitudes toward performance appraisals. They should clearly understand the purposes of evaluations, as well as their assets and liabilities.

3. Managers should be involved in the selection of appropriate appraisal instruments. They should be involved in determining appropriate assessment times and responsibility for performing the evaluation. Because the commitment of managers is crucial, they must fully accept the value of the performance appraisal formats used in the organization.

4. Managers must inform employees before the appraisal period about what will be appraised. They should make sure that evaluations of performance do not come as a surprise to the employee.

5. Managers must document subordinate performance regularly, completely, and accurately. In evaluating employee performance, they should apply specific standards which are objective and known to the employee.

6. Managers must practice effective communication during performance appraisal interviews. They should create an open, supportive climate; treat subordinates as adults, not children; and take a problem-solving approach to performance issues. Managers should focus discussions on identifying problems or obstacles that prevent optimal job performance.

7. Managers must set performance goals jointly with employees. Together they should develop and implement a plan for monitoring the accomplishment of these goals.

8. Managers should know the impact of performance evaluations on other human resources practices. They should use performance data in making staffing, training and development, and compensation decisions.

READING

Reading 6–1

AN ACTIVE FEEDBACK PROGRAM CAN SPARK PERFORMANCE

Fay Walther and Susan Taylor

Providing feedback to employees may be one of the most important and most overlooked processes in the practitioner's world of personnel management.

The concept is given lip service, but many managers fail to give their employees information about specific aspects of their job performance. Both research and practice suggest this sin of omission may have serious repercussions in terms of job satisfaction, performance and turnover.

One area of particular interest is the adequacy of feedback given to technical employees such as computer analysts, engineers and research scientists. Even in a tight job market, some skilled technical employees can virtually walk across the street to obtain better jobs. These training and turnover costs represent a loss of real dollars to management. Alternatively, one must consider the potential negative effects on the employee. Assuming employees change jobs for definite reasons besides compensation, one can question the role of appropriate communication between employees and management.

Utilizing a model proposed by Ilgen, Fisher and Taylor (1979), it is possible to constructively address the issue of feedback in employee communications. The term feedback means information relating to both positive and negative aspects of job performance. The model offers managers a method to more effectively organize feedback to their subordinates in an effort to increase its positive effects on attitudes and behaviors. Specifically, the model predicts that employees will respond with positive motivation to feedback that is consistent and timely, and includes some positive information. How many managers amidst the demands of their daily activities apply this basic principle?

Another area of new research interest is the effect of feedback on professional women employees in non-traditional occupations. The old stereotype of these women becoming emotionally upset about negative feedback from their supervisors is inadequate, but are we left in a theoretical void in predicting their responses? Taylor and Walther (1981) found evidence that these women do not have adverse reactions such as anger and decreased motivation to negative feedback as long as the information is perceived as accurate. Indeed, the acceptance of both positive and negative feedback was related to the employee's perception of the credibility of the supervisor.

Today, management is faced with the challenge of providing feedback to a diversity of well-educated employees whose specializations are essential to the performance of the corporation. By integrating research and common sense into a practical plan, managers can provide more effective feedback to their employees.

FEEDBACK MODEL

Ilgen, Fisher, and Taylor (1977) conducted an extensive review of the performance feedback literature and formulated a model that emphasizes the "effective use of feedback to members of on-going, task-oriented organizations." This model predicts that feedback on performance can influence the job-related behaviors of subordinates through a complex motivational process. In this process, several key ingredients are the power and credibility of the supervisor and the job experience of the subordinate.

The feedback process involves how the supervisor delivers the feedback and how the feedback is perceived by the subordinate. For a desirable response to feedback, such as more-effective pursuit of organizational goals, the employee must feel that the feedback is reasonable and must have the ability to respond to the information. If the employees accept feedback from trusted supervisors, they may have

Reprinted from the June, 1983 issue of *Personnel Administrator*, copyright, 1983, The American Society for Personnel Administration, 606 North Washington Street, Alexandria, VA 22314, $30 per year.

both the information and the motivation to improve their job performance.

How can managers integrate and apply good communication techniques in the real world of daily demands and crises? There appear to be several axioms to providing feedback to employees:

- Specificity: The employee needs feedback on specific aspects of his job performance. This information will help subordinates to maintain desired levels of performance and to correct deficiencies.
- Consistency: Information on specific aspects of job performance should not vary unpredictably between overwhelming praise and harsh criticism. For example, the employee should not be praised for good performance at periodic reviews and then given a poor annual performance rating. This behavior will be perceived by the employee as inconsistent, and the employee will be surprised or shocked by the outcome of the annual review. Instead, a consistent pattern of feedback about performance levels should begin to emerge over time in the communications between supervisor and subordinates.
- Timing: Feedback should be given as soon as possible after a specific event. While the event is still fresh in the employees' mind, this information encourages them to improve on performance or to maintain the desired response. If feedback is delayed or simply not provided to employees, they may not be able to gauge the success or failure of their job performance.
- Sign: Feedback should encompass a mixture of positive and negative information so that the employee is able to correct problem behaviors, but is not overwhelmed by the impact of the negative information. This combination of information can motivate the employee toward greater accomplishment of organizational goals.
- Credibility (expertise and trust): The manager must be perceived by the employee as a fair and accurate source of information. The implication of this statement is that the manager must be knowledgeable of the employee's job performance and be willing to systematically evaluate it.
- Accuracy: The communications from the supervisor to the subordinate must be perceived as accurate by the employee. If the supervisor introduces personal bias or demonstrates a lack of knowledge, the communication will not be accepted by the employee. Indeed, inaccurate communication may lower the employee's work motivation and organizational commitment.

THE OBSTACLES

While managers may appreciate these concepts in theory, what are some obstacles to their practical application?

- Time: Systematic feedback to subordinates must compete with productivity demands. If giving feedback takes time that is urgently needed to meet production schedules, which task will assume priority? The subordinate may be neglected unless his marginal performance is creating productivity problems.
- Unpleasantness: For many practitioners, it probably is not easy to initiate discussions of substandard job performance. The manager feels like the bearer of bad news, although the employee's behavior actually determines the level of job performance.
- Lack of skills: Some managers may have the best of intentions but simply lack the skills to communicate effectively. They may feel inept at providing useful information to employees and thus ignore both employee and organizational requests for such information.

COSTS OF FAILURE

The manager must weigh the benefits and costs of systematic feedback to subordinates. Both common sense and theory can be integrated to illustrate the real cost of failure to provide adequate feedback:

- Employees' overall job satisfaction is linked to their commitment to the organization.
- Low organizational commitment is related to the intention to leave the organization and with actual withdrawal behaviors such as absenteeism.
- Chronic poor performance: employees who do not recognize problems or deficiencies in their

job performance may feel justified in continuing that level of performance.

The cost of failure can be the loss of professional employees whose productive job performance is necessary to the organization. The myth that employees know how they're doing without adequate feedback from management can be an expensive fantasy.

The literature on the effects of feedback on the job performance and turnover of professional women is limited, so the manager must apply judgment and common sense in this area of employee communication. However, some recent research indicates feedback on performance is essential to maintaining the job satisfaction of women in technical occupations. Managers ignore the costs of poor or nonexistent feedback to employees at their peril.

One reason systematic feedback is probably essential to women in non-traditional jobs is that little information may be received from co-workers or from the job itself. Professional women may feel they are operating in a vacuum in which performance is not well defined and feedback on success or failure is minimal. This vacuum creates the profound questions: How am I doing? Can I advance? What is my potential with this organization?

Again managers must overcome the myth that women can't handle criticism. If the manager is perceived as fair and knowledgeable of their job performance, women can use negative criticism to improve aspects of their job performance. Since many of the real-world qualities of work are learned on the job, it is essential that women receive feedback on both the positive and negative aspects of their job performance.

FEEDBACK BENEFITS

Effective feedback can serve three important purposes: (1) relieving productive employees from worrying needlessly about their job performance and the security of their job; (2) helping marginal employees to improve their job performance; (3) providing systematic documentation in case of dismissal. In effect the supervisor can create a working environment that is more conducive to good job performance through the use of effective feedback. The payoffs for the supervisor are real and predictable; the time invested in effective feedback should have a positive effect on the employee's job satisfaction, performance, and organizational commitment. Instead of getting caught in the revolving door of training and losing valued technical employees, the manager can concentrate more time and effort on developing the talents of employees to meet organizational goals.

The manager can endeavor to correct performance problems before they reach a crisis stage, or until there is too much bitterness between the supervisor and employee to objectively evaluate the situation. The feedback on specific aspects of job performance should be timely, accurate, and incorporate both positive and negative aspects of the employee's performance. While constant negative criticism is probably not conducive to motivation or performance, the employees should know where they stand with management. Employees should not be left with the impression that their performance is meeting the supervisor's work standards if it is marginal. Again, the issues of credibility and fairness apply.

Finally, communication can serve as systematic documentation if an employee must be fired due to poor job performance. If over a specific period of time an employee's performance does not meet standards, the manager has the necessary data to defend his decision. More importantly, this information can help the manager to overcome any of her own guilt in terminating an employee. The manager's feedback to the employee serves as the basis for a systematic, rational decision.

TRAINING GROUNDS

Project management assignments can serve as a training ground for the development of effective communication skills. On project management assignments, which are frequently used in technical and scientific fields, managers can experiment with different feedback techniques. Since project management can entail a less-centralized hierarchy of authority, good feedback skills may become central to meeting scheduling and productivity goals. The manager must merge individual goals and abilities into a team effort to accomplish a specific mission. Frequent, systematic feedback on job performance could enhance the individual's contribution to the team effort.

Indeed project management assignments may be an ideal setting to develop a new or prospective manager's skills.

The project manager needs to provide timely feedback to colleagues on their job performance in reference to specific project goals. The feedback should entail some positive reinforcement and, if necessary, some structured negative information which will be perceived as accurate and fair by peers. Timing is critical, correcting mistakes in a tactful manner and praising successful goal efforts.

Using project assignments, prospective managers can develop effective skills which will serve them well in the daily demands of a management position. These assignments also encompass the potential for providing systematic feedback on leadership skills to professional women in non-traditional jobs. The practice of constructive feedback techniques can overcome one of the obstacles to effective communication. Because of competing priorities for a manager's time, the support of top management may be essential for the provision of systematic feedback to employees. Managers must develop effective skills and be supported by their supervisors in practicing these feedback techniques. When managers are able to use effective feedback to reach organizational goals such as reduced turnover and increased productivity, they should be systematically rewarded for their contributions. Top management can recognize, encourage, and reward managers who practice effective feedback with their subordinates.

Top management also can establish an organizational climate and direction which are conducive to providing effective feedback to employees. A climate of openness can be encouraged in which information is shared between managers and subordinates. This exchange of information in a non-punitive manner may reduce the defensiveness of employees' reactions to some negative feedback and enable them to improve their job performance. Organizational climate may have a major impact on the willingness of managers to provide both positive and negative feedback and on the employees' acceptance of this feedback.

REFERENCES

Huse, Edgar F., *"The Modern Manager,"* St. Paul, MN: West Publishing Company, 1979.

Ilgen, D.R., Fisher, C.D., and Taylor, M.S., *Performance feedback: A review of its psychological and behavioral effects.* Technical Report #1, Purdue University, February 1977.

Ilgen, D.R., Fisher, C.D., and Taylor, M.S., "Consequences of individual feedback on behavior in organizations," *Journal of Applied Psychology,* 1979, Vol. 64, pp. 349–371.

Kanter, R.M., *"Men and Women of the Corporation."* New York: Basic Books, 1977.

Mobley, W.H., Griffith, R.W., Hand, H.H., and Meglino, B.M., "Review and conceptual analysis of the employee turnover process," *Psychological Bulletin,* 1979, Vol. 56, pp. 493–522.

Muchinsky, P.M., "Employee absenteeism: A review of the literature," *Journal of Vocational Behavior,* 1977, Vol. 10, pp. 316–340.

Taylor, M.S., and Walther, F.T., *The relationship of feedback dimensions to work attitudes and behavior: Process and practical implications.* Paper presented at the Midwestern Academy of Management, Chicago, April 1981.

DISCUSSION QUESTIONS

1. State six techniques for improving feedback about performance.
2. What obstacles are there to effective feedback?
3. What are the costs of failing to provide effective feedback?
4. What are the benefits of providing effective feedback?
5. What roles should manager and human resources professionals play in providing feedback?

ACTIVITIES

Activity 6–1

DEVELOPING A BEHAVIORALLY ANCHORED RATING SCALE

Step 1: Review the job described in Figure 2–4.

Step 2: With a partner, identify the job-related behaviors composing that job. First, group them by dimension. Second, name the dimension. Third, list all the job-related behaviors that compose each dimension.

Dimension I:
Behaviors:

Dimension II:
Behaviors:

Continue as necessary.

Step 3: For each dimension, list below one to three anchors that describe excellent, very good, good, fair, poor, very poor, and unacceptable performance.

Dimension:
Excellent performance:

Very good performance:

Good performance:

Fair performance:

Poor performance:

Very poor performance:

Unacceptable performance:

Step 4: List these anchors in random order on a form such as the following:

Anchor	Dimension	Scale Value (1–7)

Step 5: Exchange your list of anchors with another partnership. For each anchor listed, you and your partner should record which dimension the anchor measures and what quality behavior the anchor represents (from 1 = unacceptable to 7 = excellent). Check each rating statement to ensure that it (1) describes a behavior, (2) does not evaluate the behavior or draw a conclusion about its effectiveness, (3) avoids quantitative values in describing behavior, (4) avoids using adjective quantifiers, and (5) describes behaviors, not knowledge of the job. Mark any anchors you feel lack clarity or about which you cannot reach agreement in assigning a dimension or rank.

Step 6: When both partnerships have finished step 5, review the assignment of dimensions and ranks to the anchors. Delete or change any anchors that the other partnership could not reach agreement on.

Step 7: Convert these anchors into a seven-step rating scale. Complete a scale such as the following for each job dimension:

Job Dimension ______________________________

7—
6—
5—
4—
3—
2—
1—

Continue on additional forms as necessary.

Step 8: In small groups share your rating scales. Critique each scale by assessing its objectivity, clarity, and comprehensiveness.

Step 9: Discussion. In small groups, with the entire class, or in writing, as directed by your instructor, answer the following questions:

1. What are the advantages and disadvantages of behaviorally anchored rating scales?
2. What difficulties did you encounter in developing such a scale?
3. What are the limitations in using such a scale?
4. Are BARS the best alternative available to organizations?
5. In what situations should they be used and developed?
6. What roles should managers play in the development and use of BARS?
7. What role should human resources professionals play in their development and use?

Activity 6–2

USING A MANAGEMENT-BY-OBJECTIVES APPRAISAL FORMAT

Step 1: Write a job description for a job you hold or have held in the past. (If you have not been employed, use your job as a student.)

Step 2: From this job description, develop a list of objectives you wish to accomplish during the next month, semester, year, and before graduation. For each objective, indicate (1) how the attainment of objectives will be measured, (2) in what time frame the objective will be accomplished, and (3) what must be done to accomplish the objective.

Step 3: Share your objectives with a partner. Together you should agree about the objectives for each individual.

Step 4: In a small group share your revised objectives. Check that each person's objectives include a specific outcome, the way the outcome will be measured, the time frame in which it must be accomplished, and the way it will be accomplished.

Step 5: Discussion. In small groups, with the entire class, or in written form, as directed by your instructor, answer the following questions:

1. What are the advantages and disadvantages of an MBO approach?
2. What role should a manager play in the development and implementation of MBO?
3. What role should a human resources professional play in its development and implementation?
4. What problems may be encountered in implementing the MBO system for your job as student?
5. In what situations will MBO be helpful?

Activity 6–3

ESSO A.G. (A–1)

Step 1: Read the case Esso A.G. (A–1).

Step 2: Prepare the case for class discussion.

As Manager of Employee Relations of the large German petroleum firm, Esso A.G., Mr. Otto Daniel was always interested in new personnel management approaches and techniques which might be useful additions to his company's existing practices. Thus, in 1974 Mr. Daniel had introduced an "upward appraisal system" under which employees could provide feedback to their superiors concerning their managerial behavior.

The upward appraisal system employed a 32-item questionnaire (shown in Figure 6–13) which was completed on a voluntary basis by a manager's subordinates. The managers themselves were under no obligation to use this system, nor were users required to reveal the results to anyone. Mr. Daniel explained to the casewriter that the system was intended "not so much as a means of control, but as a tool by which managers could increase their self-knowledge."

Recalling the introduction and development of the system, Mr. Daniel stated, "I first came across the idea in a German textile firm, where it appeared to be quite successful." It had taken nearly three years to perfect a questionnaire suitable for Esso A.G. and to achieve necessary support from line managers. In 1973 Mr. Daniel had invited his subordinates to use a pilot version of the questionnaire to evaluate him. As a second step Mr. Daniel had written to 120 senior managerial employees outlining the approach and asking for reactions. All of these managers had responded, 118 of them positively. Mr. Daniel smiled as he recounted the two negative replies. One manager had written, "I know exactly what my employees think of me. They need not write it down." The other wrote, "I'm the boss—that's enough."

Based on this positive response, the Employee Relations Department sent a draft questionnaire to the same senior managers for comment. Some forty managers replied with suggestions on phraseology and wording, many of which were incorporated in the final version of the questionnaire. Copies of the final questionnaire were then mailed to all senior managers along with a covering letter emphasizing that the exercise was strictly voluntary for both employees and supervisors.

If a manager elected to use the upward evaluation system, he would distribute questionnaires to his subordinates along with a letter explaining the process.* Those employees who chose to participate

This case was prepared by Miss Deborah Henderson under the supervision of Professors Stephen A. Allen and Alvar O. Elbing as a basis for class discussion rather than to illustrate either effective or ineffective handling of an administrative situation.

* Questionnaires were not sent to managers with less than three subordinates.

Employees rate their superiors on 32 statements related to various management attributes. The employee puts a cross against one of five possible responses to each statement: almost never, rarely, occasionally, frequently or almost always.
The statements, loosely translated from the German, are as follows:

1. He [the superior] analyzes and plans carefully.
2. He utilizes his employees and his means rationally.
3. Even under extreme conditions, he works safely and thoughtfully.
4. Employees have to do work which they think is unnecessary.
5. Employees have enough opportunity to use their capabilities.
6. He is always trying to develop efficient teamwork.
7. He gives enough scope to others in the team to express themselves.
8. He is prepared to listen to suggestions.
9. He likes to make decisions.
10. If employees, within their area of competence, make a decision, the superior feels he is not being consulted and does not like it.
11. He offers his employees the opportunity to make their own judgement, if that is in the interests of the work, and encourages them to co-operate in decisions.
12. He stands up for his employees against third parties.
13. He uses his employees as far as possible in accordance with their abilities and their will to work.
14. The employees have the impression that they have to work under unnecessary stress.
15. He gives his employees all available information which is necessary to fulfill their task.
16. He enables his employees to gather the necessary information for their work.
17. He has defined a clear line of responsibility.
18. He acts in conformity with his responsibilities and powers.
19. The employees get enough feedback of information to judge the results of their work.
20. The employees have to fulfill tasks without the necessary guidelines.
21. He understands the need to activate his employees not by hectic behavior but by well-directed activity.
22. The employees feel that they and their work are fairly judged.
23. He promotes his employees and looks after their development.
24. If employees have a work problem they can ask him for support.
25. If an employee makes a mistake, he criticizes him on a factual and unbiased basis.
26. In his conversations with his employees, he creates an easy-going atmosphere.
27. When he points out mistakes and shortcomings he helps by suggesting corrections.
28. If an employee has done a very good job, he tells him so.
29. He puts forward propositions by other people as if they were his own.
30. He deals with his employees as equals without losing their respect.
31. If he has personal problems, or problems with management, he doesn't vent them against his employees.
32. If one of his employees has made a mistake he does not continually hold it against him.

Figure 6–13 UPWARD APPRAISAL QUESTIONNAIRE

completed the questionnaires and delivered them to a colleague who had been designated to collect them. The completed questionnaires were then sent to the Computer Division for tabulation of mean scores and to become part of an anonymous company-wide data bank.** The manager received a confidential printout showing his mean scores and company-wide averages for each question.

Each manager was free to choose whether he wished to discuss results of the evaluation with his superior and/or subordinates. In cases where managers elected to discuss results with subordinates the Employee Relations Department recommended that the subordinates meet by themselves to discuss their opinions and then select a spokesperson to present the group's views in a separate meeting with the

** Company-wide results were used as one input in planning future management training seminars offered by the Employee Relations Department.

manager. Mr. Daniel explained the rationale for this approach as follows: "If a group meeting were held between the manager and his subordinates, it might become apparent how individuals had rated the manager. This would clearly harm the quality of the feedback." The Employee Relations Department further recommended that managers repeat the evaluation at intervals of between two and three years in order to allow for adequate time to achieve improvements in weaker areas of leadership.

Mr. Daniel estimated that 140 senior managers had administered questionnaires to over 800 subordinates between 1974 and 1977. In light of this level of acceptance at senior levels, the Employee Relations Department decided to introduce a similar voluntary system at middle management levels. Responses by these managers, however, proved less positive. As of July, 1976, only 25% of middle managers had volunteered to use the upward appraisal exercise. Mr. Daniel stated, "I suspect part of this is because they are still at the learning stage of management. A voluntary appraisal system such as this requires a certain degree of experience and maturity."

Step 3: Individually or in small groups, orally or in writing, as directed by your instructor, answer the following questions:

1. What is an upward appraisal system?
2. Where does the upward appraisal system fit in the overall performance appraisal program?
3. What were the roles of managers and human resources professionals in the upward appraisal system at Esso A.G.?
4. What are the advantages and disadvantages of this system?
5. Why was the response by the managers less than positive?
6. How could the upward appraisal system be improved?

Step 4: Discussion. In small groups, with the entire class, or in written form, share your answers to the questions above.

Activity 6–4

JASPER WRIGHT, INC.

Advance Preparation: Gather the following materials: (1) general instructions, (2) role sheets for Robin Smith and Lyn Jackson, and (3) instructions for observers. Set up a table in front of the room to represent the interviewer's desk, and two chairs arranged by the desk in such a way that the participants can talk comfortably and have their faces visible to the observers.

Step 1: The instructor will select two members from the class, one to role-play Robin Smith, the supervisor who conducts the appraisal interview, and one to role-play Lyn Jackson, the employee being interviewed. All other class members act as observers. All participants read the description of the situation below. The participants who play the roles of Smith and Jackson should study their roles. The instructor will distribute the roles of Smith and Jackson to these two players. Both should play their role parts without referring to their role sheets. The observers read the instructions for observers.

DESCRIPTION OF THE SITUATION

Jasper Wright, Inc., is a small brokerage firm in a large northwestern city. Each year on the anniversary date of hiring an employee, his or her supervisor must conduct a performance appraisal interview. Robin Smith is the head of the firm's analysts. Lyn Jackson has been with the firm for two years. This is the first appraisal Smith has conducted of Jackson since Smith assumed the supervisory position only four months ago.

INSTRUCTIONS FOR OBSERVERS

1. Observe the manner in which the meeting begins.
2. Observe how the interview is conducted.
3. Evaluate the outcome of the interview.

Step 2: When everyone is ready, Robin Smith calls Lyn Jackson into the office. They both take seats and begin the interview. The interview should last about thirty minutes and should proceed to completion unless stopped by the instructor.

Step 3: Discussion. In small groups or with the entire class, answer the following questions:

1. Was the interview effective?
2. How could the interview have been improved?
3. What assistance could a human resources professional provide in this situation?

VARIATIONS

1. One or two new pairs of participants role-play in order to permit comparison of different interview styles and their outcomes.
2. Smith and Jackson exchange roles and role-play the case again. Observers read the role instructions for both players.
3. The class is divided into small groups, each preparing the role of either Jackson or Smith, and then representatives are chosen to role-play in front of the class.

Activity 6–5

MANAGEMENT APPRAISAL AND HUMAN RESOURCE PLANNING

Step 1: Read the case Management Appraisal and Human Resource Planning.

Step 2: Prepare the case for class discussion.

Jim Nease had 17 years of experience at American Parcel, 14 at the managerial level. Presently, he was a center manager, with three well-salaried line supervisors reporting to him. These three supervisors had responsibilities for a total of 38 delivery personnel, and this number was increasing weekly.

Managers in the company were evaluated quarterly, the main criteria being the output of drivers according to standards developed by the Industrial Engineering department. The managers were also judged by the number of customer complaints against his or her drivers. In the ten months since he took over the center, Nease had fared well in the three evaluations.

Nease was well pleased with his progress until recently, when his drivers' outputs had declined considerably. This decline came at an inopportune time for the company, since the personnel department could not hire and train drivers fast enough to keep up with the increasing volume of packages caused by the recent postal rate hike.

At this same time, complaints had also risen rapidly, with no logical explanation. Nease was not only perplexed, he was downright angry that performance had slipped so badly. He called in the three supervisors to find out what the problem was.

Reprinted with permission of Dr. Kenneth A. Kovach, George Mason University.

Step 3: Individually or in small groups, orally or in writing, as directed by your instructor, answer the following questions:

1. Could anything be done to make the managerial evaluation criteria more accurate during periods of rapid hiring?
2. What could be done to make the standards themselves more realistic?
3. Would human resource planning help this company to avoid problems such as this one in the future?
4. What deficiencies exist in the performance appraisal system?
5. What roles do managers and human resources professionals play in this system?
6. What role should they play?
7. How could the evaluation system be improved?

Step 4: Discussion. In small groups, with the entire class, or in written form, share your answers to the questions above.

Activity 6–6

SLEEK-LINE, INC.

Step 1: Read the following description of Sleek-line, Inc.

Sleek-line is a large cosmetics firm that relies on "Sleek-line Ladies" who sell the products door-to-door rather than through retail outlets. Each Sleek-line Lady has a supervisor who oversees her performance. Regional managers supervise from five to ten supervisors each.

To date, the only feedback about a supervisor's performance has been the percentage of goods sold by the salespeople the supervisor oversees; supervisors receive 5 percent of the worth of the goods their Sleek-line Ladies sell. Recently, however, many sales supervisors have complained that they are operating in a vacuum. In particular, some feel that they could use some assistance in improving their management skills since most were promoted because they had been outstanding Sleek-line Ladies.

Top management has agreed to institute a feedback-evaluation system to respond to these needs. Although they want to provide additional information to the sales supervisors, they do not want the system to be cumbersome. At the same time, they want some consistency across the 100 sales regions of the country.

Step 2: In groups of four to six design an appraisal and feedback system for Sleek-line sales supervisors. Be sure to provide for written assessment and oral feedback. Where appropriate, develop the forms for managers to use.

Step 3: Discussion. In small groups or with the entire class, share your systems. Then answer the following questions:

1. What do these systems have in common?
2. How do they differ?
3. What are the strengths and weaknesses of each system?
4. What changes would you recommend?
5. What role do the managers play in the evaluation?
6. What role do human resources professionals play?

SUMMARY

Performance evaluation systems must provide for evaluation of past performance and development of future performance. But these components must be separated to serve such evaluation's separate functions—salary administration, determination of bonuses and other incentive awards, and assessment of an individual's promotability.[52]

We have examined the steps in preparing for performance evaluations, initiating formal appraisal systems, and conducting appraisal interviews. In the cases of Esso A.G. and Management Appraisal and Human Resource Planning, we have examined and critiqued existing performance appraisal systems. We have also designed appraisal formats and practiced conducting appraisal interviews. In this way we have examined and experienced some potential pitfalls in performance appraisal.

Recent research has suggested that the selection of an appraisal format depends on the organization's structure, the employee's need for independence, and the job itself.[53] For example, procedures emphasizing assessment of behaviors are most appropriate for individuals in highly routine jobs or those who have a low need for independence; goal-based formats are most appropriate for employees with moderate need for independence and moderately routine jobs; and formats that encourage multiple subjective judgments are most appropriate for employees with high independence and those who work on nonroutine tasks.

Both human resources professionals and managers can improve the design and implementation of performance appraisal programs by

1. separating the evaluation and development segments;
2. choosing appropriate performance data for both evaluation and development;
3. separating evaluations of performance and potential;
4. recognizing individual differences when designing the system;
5. using upward appraisal, where subordinates evaluate their superior's behavior;
6. improving the supervisor-subordinate relationship;
7. improving the appraisal interview by using both directive and participative problem-solving interviews; and
8. recognizing individual differences in the appraisal interview.[54]

But managers must be willing to admit that there are real problems in conducting performance appraisals: (1) appraisals are at least partly negative; (2) evaluations are always subjective; and (3) the supervisor acts as a judge.[55]

Managers and human resources professionals can increase management's credibility and improve the appraisal process by putting the evaluation in perspective, making it brief, admitting that management is fallible, and clearly stating the categories used in rating systems.[56] This can be accomplished by taking a win/win approach to performance appraisal, one that encourages the full participation of managers, supervisors, and employees.[57] We can evaluate the general effectiveness of a performance appraisal program by asking the following questions: Does the program fit the organization? Do all participants understand the program? Do all participants believe the program is worthwhile? Have appraisers been trained? Do controls to ensure its reliability and validity exist?[58]

Performance appraisal systems must serve both evaluation and development. The nature of the preparation for a comprehensive evaluation, the initiation of formal procedures, the conduct of appraisal interviews, and the response to performance problems all determine the overall effectiveness of the system. Performance appraisal provides basic data for use in other human resources management practices, such as training and development, career management, and employee compensation, topics we examine in the remainder of Part 3.

ENDNOTES

[1]See S.J. Carroll and C.E. Schneier, *Performance Appraisal and Review Systems: The Identification, Measurement, and Development of Performance in Organizations* (Glenview, Ill.: Scott, Foresman, 1982) for further discussion of these two approaches.

[2]C.E. Schneier and R.W. Beatty, Integrating behaviorally-

based and effectiveness-based methods, *Personnel Administrator* 24 (July 1979).

[3]*Ibid.*

[4]C.M. Kelly, Reasonable performance appraisals, *Training and Development Journal* 38 (1984): 79–82.

[5]See R. Henderson, *Performance Appraisal* (Reston, Va.: Reston, 1980) for a discussion of performance appraisals vis-à-vis the organization's mission; see also D.T. Hall, The effect of the individual on an organization's structure, style, and process, in F. Landy, S. Zedeck, and J. Cleveland, *Performance Measurement and Theory* (Hillsdale, N.J.: Lawrence Erlbaum Associates, 1983).

[6]C.M. Kelly, *op. cit.*; D.T. Hall, *op. cit.*

[7]See G.P. Latham and K. N. Wexley, *Increasing Productivity Through Performance Appraisal* (Reading, Mass.: Addison-Wesley, 1981); F. Walther and S. Taylor, An active feedback program can spark performance, *Personnel Administrator* 28 (1983): 107, for further discussion of attitudes toward performance appraisals.

[8]L.L. Cummings, Performance-evaluation systems in the context of individual trust and commitment, in Landy, Zedeck, and Cleveland, *op. cit.*

[9]*Ibid.*

[10]Based on L.L. Cummings and D.P. Schwab, *Performance in Organization: Determinants and Appraisals* (Glenview, Ill.: Scott, Foresman, 1973).

[11]C.A. O'Reilly, III and J.C. Anderson, Trust and the communication of performance appraisal information: The effect of feedback on performance and job satisfaction, *Human Communication Research* 6 (1980): 290–298.

[12]H. Levinson, Appraisal of what performance?, *Harvard Business Review* 54 (1976): 30–32.

[13]K. Blanchard and S. Johnson, *One-Minute Manager* (New York: Berkeley Books, 1982).

[14]R.S. Barrett, *Performance Rating* (Chicago: Science Research Associates, 1966); A.L. Edwards, *Techniques of Attitude Scale Construction* (New York: Appleton-Century-Crofts, 1957); J.P. Guilford, *Psychometric Methods* 2nd ed. (New York: McGraw-Hill, 1954).

[15]C.E. Schneier and R.W. Beatty, Developing behaviorally-anchored rating scales (BARS), *Personnel Administrator* 24 (1979).

[16]W. Cascio, *Applied Psychology in Personnel Management* (Reston, Va.: Reston, 1978).

[17]J.C. Flanagan, The critical incident technique, *Psychological Bulletin* 51 (1954): 327–358; W.K. Kirchner and M.D. Dunnette, Aptitudes, abilities, and skills, in M.D. Dunnette, ed., *Handbook of Industrial and Organizational Psychology* (Chicago: Rand McNally, 1976), pp. 473–520.

[18]*Ibid.*

[19]*Ibid.*

[20]See R.M. Guion, Recruiting, selection, and job replacement, in M.D. Dunnette, *op. cit.*; P.C. Smith and L.M. Kendall, Retranslation of expectations: An approach to the construction of unambiguous anchors for rating scales, *Journal of Applied Psychology* 47 (1963): 149–155.

[21]J.P. Guilford, *op. cit.*

[22]G. Labovitz and L.S. Baird, MBO as an approach to performance appraisal, in L.S. Baird, R.W. Beatty, and C.E. Schneier, *The Performance Appraisal Sourcebook* (Amherst, Mass.: Human Resource Development Press, 1982).

[23]C.D. Pringle and J.G. Longenecker, The ethics of MBO, *Academy of Management Review* 7 (1982): 305–312.

[24]A.S. De Nisi, W.A. Randolph, and A.G. Blencoe, Potential problems with peer ratings, *Academy of Management Journal* 26 (1983): 457–464.

[25]F.J. Landy and J.L. Farr, Performance rating, *Psychological Bulletin* 87 (1980): 72–107.

[26]*Ibid.*

[27]D.L. Dossett and C.I. Greenberg, Goal setting and performance evaluation: An attributional analysis, *Academy of Management Journal* 24 (1981): 767–779.

[28]G.P. Latham, K.M. Wexley, and E.D. Purcell, Training managers to minimize ratings errors in observation of behavior, *Journal of Applied Psychology* 60 (1975): 550–555.

[29]M. Smith, Documenting employee performance, *Supervisory Management* 24 (September 1979).

[30]D. Cederblom, The performance appraisal interview: A review, implications, and suggestions, *Academy of Management Review* 7 (1982): 219–227.

[31]C.M. Kelly, *op. cit.*

[32]J.R. Gibb, Defensive communication, *ETC: A Review of General Semantics* 22 (1965).

[33] N.R.F. Maier, *The Appraisal Interview: Three Basic Approaches* (LaJolla, Cal.: University Associates, 1976).

[34]D.W. Johnson and F.P. Johnson, *Joining Together: Group Theory and Group Skills* (Englewood Cliffs, N.J.: Prentice-Hall, 1975).

[35]E. Berne, *Games People Play* (New York: Grove Press, 1964).

[36]R. Brett and A.J. Fredran, Performance appraisal: The system is not the solution, *Personnel Administrator* 26 (1981): 62.

[37]R. Giles and C. Landauer, Setting specific standards for appraising creative staffs, *Personnel Administrator* 29 (1984): 40.

[38]B.L. Kaye and S. Krantz, Preparing employees: The missing link in performance appraisal, *Personnel* 59 (1982): 23–29.

[39]*Ibid.*

[40]G. Labovitz and L.S. Baird, MBO as an approach to performance appraisal, in L.S. Baird et al., *op.cit.*

[41]See R.J. Burke, W. Weitzel, and T. Weir, Characteristics of effective employee performance review and development interviews: Replication and extension, *Personnel Psychology* 31 (1978): 903–909; F.J. Landy, J.L. Barnes, and K.R. Murphy, Correlates of perceived fairness and accuracy of

performance evaluation, *Journal of Applied Psychology* 63 (1978): 751–754; M.M. Greller, The nature of subordinate participation in the appraisal interview, *Academy of Management Journal* 21 (1978): 646–658, for example.

[42]See E.A. Locke and D.M. Schweiger, Participation in decision-making: One more look, in B.M. Staw, ed., *Research in Organizational Behavior* 1 (1979): 425–478.

[43]Cederblom, *op. cit.*

[44]*Ibid.*, p. 52.

[45]*Ibid.*

[46]M. Beer, Performance appraisal: Dilemmas and possibilities, *Organizational Dynamics* 10 (Winter 1981): 24–36.

[47]Maier, *op. cit.*

[48]G.A. Rummler, Human performance problems and their solutions, *Human Resource Management* 19 (1972): 2–10.

[49]G.P. Latham, L.L. Cummings, and T.R. Mitchell, Behavioral strategies to improve productivity, *Organizational Dynamics* 10 (Winter 1981): 5–23.

[50]*Ibid.*

[51]D.B. Gehrman, Beyond today's compensation and performance appraisal systems, *Personnel Administrator* 29 (1984): 21–33.

[52]J.D. McMillan and H.W. Doyal, Performance appraisal: Match the tool to the task, *Personnel* 57 (1980): 12–20.

[53]M. Keeley, A contingency framework for performance evaluation, *Academy of Management Review* 3 (1978): 428–438.

[54]M. Beer, *op. cit.*

[55]C.M. Kelly, *op. cit.*

[56]*Ibid.*

[57]B. Kaye and S. Krantz, Performance appraisal: A win/win approach, *Training and Development Journal* 37 (1983): 32–35.

[58]D.L. Kirkpatrick, The ways to evaluate your performance appraisal system, *Training and Development Journal* 38 (1984): 38–40.

FURTHER READINGS

Baird, L.S., Beatty, R.W., and Schneier, C.E. *The Performance Appraisal Sourcebook.* Amherst, Mass.: Human Resource Development Press, 1982.

Carroll, S.J., and Schneier, C.E. *Performance Appraisal and Review Systems.* Glenview, Ill.: Scott, Foresman, 1982.

Landy, F., Zedeck, S., and Cleveland, J., eds. *Performance Measurement and Theory.* Hillsdale, N.J.: Lawrence Erlbaum Associates, 1983.

Latham, G.P., and Wexley, K.N. *Increasing Productivity Through Performance Appraisal.* Reading, Mass.: Addison-Wesley, 1981.

Morrisey, G.L. *Performance Appraisals for Business and Industry.* Reading, Mass.: Addison-Wesley, 1983.

CHAPTER 7

Designing a Training and Development System

CHAPTER OUTLINE

LEARNING CHECKPOINTS

After completing the reading and activities in this chapter, students will be able to

- diagnose the environment and organization and their influence on training;
- show the role job analysis plays in the training process;
- describe the steps in the training process;
- assess an individual's training needs;
- describe ten types of training programs and discuss their advantages and disadvantages in diverse situations;
- show the significance of organizational socialization strategies for training;
- differentiate among and illustrate the four levels of evaluation;
- plan an evaluation program for assessing training and development effectiveness; and
- design a comprehensive training and development program.

INTRODUCTION

Janice Lyons's assistant showed her a brochure that the training department had distributed to all administrative personnel in the organization. The training department was publicizing a course titled "Building Supervisory Skills." Janice's assistant wanted to participate in the course.

Although Janice generally encouraged her staff to receive training, she wondered if this course was worth her assistant's time. A well-known training and consulting group would conduct the seminar. One colleague had told her that this group "offered a flashy program with little substance, and that the trainers did not tailor their programs to the unique needs of the individual organizations for which they conducted the training."

Janice pondered the consequences of sending her assistant. Her assistant had shown her four programs already this year, and she had refused her assistant's request to participate in most of them. What should she do?

Why is Janice having difficulty making this decision? What are Janice's responsibilities regarding the training and development of her employees? What can Janice do to facilitate decisions such as the one she must currently make?

In this chapter we examine the elements of an effective training and development system. The chapter first provides an overview of the training process and the context in which it operates. Next, it offers an approach for assessing training needs. Third, the chapter describes diverse training and development options. It concludes by offering approaches to assessing the effectiveness of training and development.

THE TRAINING AND DEVELOPMENT PROCESS

Training is a set of activities designed to increase an individual's skills, knowledge, or experiences, or change an individual's attitudes. For example, when an organization computerizes its order-entry procedures, employees might be required to develop the skills required to use a computer, acquire knowledge of the new order-entry procedures, or develop a more positive (or less fearful) attitude toward computerization. *Development* refers to preparing individuals to assume higher-level or different responsibilities in the organization. Both training and development can occur in two situations: (1) when a job requires an individual to have skills, knowledge, or attitudes different from, or in addition to, those he or she currently has; and (2) when advancement in the organization requires an individual to have different or new skills, knowledge, or attitudes. Performance appraisals frequently identify whether either situation exists.

Training should increase employee effectiveness, increase employee satisfaction, satisfy equal employment opportunity and human rights programs, and prevent worker obsolescence.[1] Diagnosis of the environmental and organizational aspects of the situation, as well as job analysis, comprise the first step in developing training and development programs.

Diagnosing the Training and Development Context

How can the environment, organization, or job influence the nature of the training and development system?

Environmental Analysis. Technical and regulatory changes in the environment can require an organization's employees to have new and different skills from those they currently have. Consider, for example, the way the microcomputer revolution has affected organizations, particularly the skills required by employees. Or note the effect of environmental protection regulations on the design and operations of production lines and tasks.

Economic conditions also influence the need for training and development. In a strong economy, an open labor market may reduce employees' needs for training and development. An organization can hire an individual with the requisite skills, and employees without the required skills can find a better fitting job relatively easily. Where qualified individuals do not exist, organizations often choose to train current workers.

Organizational Analysis. An organization's goals, climate, structure, and resources frequently influence the extent and nature of training and development opportunities provided within an organization. Organizations that desire to grow and expand their operations tend to encourage training and development as a way of ensuring their ability to compete in the marketplace. Organizations that emphasize personal goals in addition to corporate goals generally view training and development activities favorably as well.[2]

Concurrently, the organization's climate may facilitate or hinder training and development. For example, an organization that pushes decision-making responsibility down into the ranks may also assign managers and other employees more responsibility for initiating training and development activities. Or an organization with a climate that emphasizes autonomy or creativity might encourage different training and development activities than an organization that encourages dependence or conformity. The content of training programs and responsibility for training and development may differ in organizations with different climates as well. To plan an extensive development program in an organization that discourages promotion from within the ranks or that has relatively blocked advancement opportunities may be dysfunctional. Alternatively, an organization that chooses to minimize obsolete and plateaued performers (see Chapter 5) most likely provides frequent training and development opportunities.

The structure of an organization also influences training and development activities. An organization with a separate human resources management and training function is most likely to encourage training and development. Where managers must orchestrate all development programs, training activities are less common. The extent to which an organization develops specialists versus generalists influences the type of training required. For example, job rotation programs help individuals learn numerous jobs and develop diverse skills; technical courses or workshops build more specific skills, such as knowledge of a new computer language, a respiratory therapy procedure, or curriculum changes.

Finally, the financial and human resources available within the organization influence the extent and type of training and development activities. During the recession of the early 1980s, for example, many organizations experienced significant cutbacks in their training programs.[3] They relied on on-the-job training rather than more expensive workshops. They also relied on line managers to conduct training rather than on a separate training staff whose salaries increased corporate overhead.

Job Analysis. Employees who lack skills or attitudes for a particular job may need training. Consider a production worker in a publishing company. Will a new hire have the skills needed to perform the job? Probably not. The typical worker brings basic skills and abilities to the job; however, every job has aspects unique to the specific organization in which it is performed, and the individual frequently requires training in these specific skills. The production manager should provide orientation to the job, as well as on-the-job training for the unique requirements of the job. Later, as the employee gains more skills and becomes promotable, the manager might provide supervisory training. Detailed job analysis should precede development of training and development programs.

Steps in Training and Development

Following analysis of the situation, managers or human resources professionals must perform three additional steps in designing the training and development programs. First they must assess the training and development needs of their employees. Are they deficient in specific technical skills? Could their supervisory skills be better? Do they need to develop a more corporate-wide or even industry-wide perspective? Do they need to develop greater commitment to developing their subordinates? Human resources professionals generally collect data about the employee needs across the organization so that they can contribute to diverse and appropriate program options.

Next, the manager learns about program options and selects those that best meet employee needs. Human resources professionals can advise on this choice.

Finally, managers or human resources professionals evaluate the impact of training and development on the needs originally identified. We examine each of these steps—needs assessment, program selection, and evaluation—in turn in the next sections.

ASSESSING TRAINING AND DEVELOPMENT NEEDS

How should Janice Lyons decide whether to send her assistant to the training session? First, she must determine her assistant's needs. What job responsibilities does she perform well? Poorly? Does her assistant have supervisory responsibilities? If so, does her performance of them show any deficiencies? Does her attitude toward other employees create difficulties? Does she have responsibility for communicating information to other employees? Will she have supervisory or communication responsibilities in the future? Does she have the skills to perform these responsibilities now or in the future? Managers can assess needs by observing performance or asking employees where they feel deficient. They can use specially designed questionnaires or commercially available instruments to compile data about training needs.[4] Table 7–1 shows other methods of assessing training needs. Needs assessment is conducted at three levels—(1) organizational, (2) job or operations, and (3) personal[5]—as shown in Figure 7–1 and described in the next sections.

Organizational Needs

Changes in the organization's strategy, market, and technology may call for employees to have new or different skills, knowledge, or attitudes. For example, the organization might introduce a new product to respond to a new market demand. Introduction of this product may call for new skills from a large number

Data Collection Techniques	Primary Strength	Primary Weakness
Business data review	Provides objective data	May take a long time
Interviews	Obtain in-depth information	Usually labor intensive
Focus groups	Provides qualitative focus	Direction of discussion may be swayed by informal leader
Questionnaires	Narrows direction of further investigation	Doesn't give in-depth information
Critical incident	Gathers observable investigation	Usually labor intensive
Observation	Provides a reality check	Usually labor intensive
Performance data reviews (e.g., performance appraisals)	Establishes criteria	May be confounded by other variables
Informal discussions	Provides input for other techniques	May be biased due to unsystematic approach
Job requirements review (e.g., job descriptions)	Provides objective data (if accurate)	Usually takes a long time

Table 7–1 **METHODS FOR ASSESSING TRAINING NEEDS**

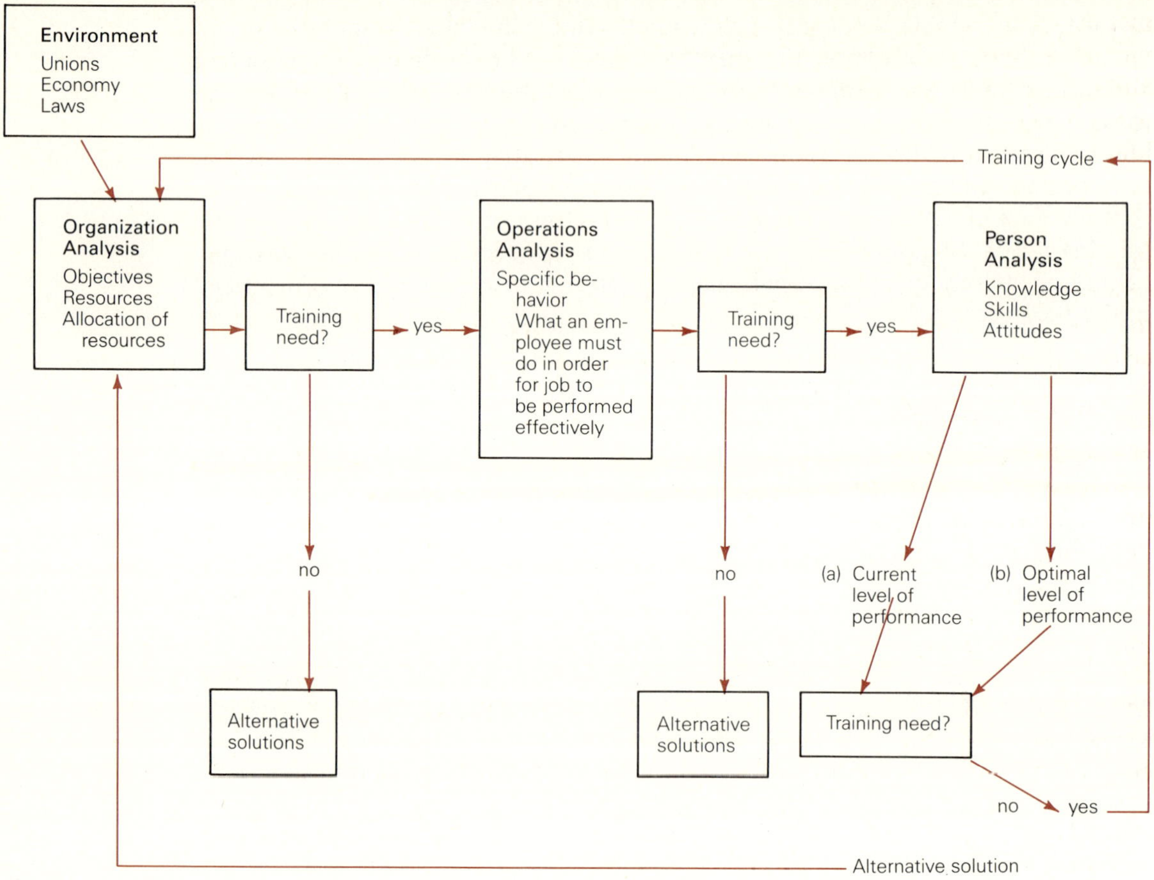

Reprinted from the November, 1983 issue of *Personnel Administrator*, copyright, 1983, The American Society for Personnel Administration, 606 North Washington Street, Alexandria, VA 22314, $30 per year.

Figure 7–1 SUPERVISORY TRAINING NEEDS ASSESSMENT MODEL

of employees in the marketing, engineering, or production departments. Or this change may require members of the marketing department to be more committed to the value of market research. Alternatively, the organization may move from a growth to a nongrowth strategy. In this case, some training may be instituted to allow current employees to change jobs as a way of avoiding layoffs.

Job Needs

When the requirements of a specific job change, some employees may lack the skills required for the changed job. Managers can respond to such a deficiency by initiating training and development activities. For example, increased automation of the assembly line may change the tasks of production workers. Or movement among levels of management may call for new skills or positive attitudes toward mobility or even job rotation. Table 7–2 lists the most frequent development needs of three levels of management, based on a survey of eighty-four typical organizations.

Personal Needs

Finally, an individual may lack the skills or attitudes required for job performance or career advancement. Individuals who enter with general skills and experience may need training in specific skills required for the job. Or an individual's advancement may require supervisory training or development in analytical and decision-making skills. Or the individual may lack a positive attitude toward particular job activities or responsibilities; he or she may require training directed at altering values or attitudes.

Performance appraisals can assist in identifying personal needs. A manager or human resources professional can use completed evaluation forms to identify individuals with unsatisfactory ratings. They can then determine if additional training might improve the performance represented by the ratings.[6]

Which type of needs does Janice's assistant have? Since there is no indication that the organizational requirements have changed or that the job has changed, the assistant may have personal needs for improved job performance and career development. Once a manager has identified a subordinate's needs or a human resources professional has identified organization-wide needs, they must select or design training programs to best meet these needs. In the next section we consider some factors that influence this choice.

TRAINING AND DEVELOPMENT OPTIONS

Training and development programs focus on three areas: (1) orientation, (2) training, and (3) management development. Programs in these areas meet different needs, but the formats used are similar.

Depending on the option selected, a trainer from the human resources management department, an external consultant, a manager, or another organizational member may design and implement the program. Outside consultants offer the following advantages: (1) they have expertise due to advanced degrees and experience with diverse organizations; (2) they most likely know state-of-the-art techniques and current information in their field; and (3) they can more objectively analyze a situation.[7] But they may lack knowledge of the organization—its informal structure and culture—and have difficulty keeping current in organizational problems because of irregular visits to the organization.[8] Some

Executive Level	Middle Level	Supervisory Level
1. Managing time	1. Evaluating and appraising employees	1. Motivating others
Team building	2. Motivating others	2. Evaluating and appraising others
3. Organizing and planning	3. Setting objectives and priorities	3. Leadership
Evaluating and appraising employees	4. Oral communication	4. Oral communication
5. Coping with stress	5. Organizing and planning	5. Understanding human behavior
Understanding human behavior	6. Understanding human behavior	6. Developing and training subordinates
7. Self-analysis	7. Written communication	7. Role of the manager
Motivating others	Managing time	Setting objectives and priorities
		Written communication
9. Financial management	9. Team building	10. Discipline
Budgeting	10. Leadership	11. Organizing and planning
11. Setting objectives and priorities	Decision making	Managing time
Holding effective meetings	Holding effective meetings	Counseling and coaching
13. Oral communication	Delegation	14. Selecting employees
14. Labor/management relations	Developing and training subordinates	15. Decision making
15. Decision making	15. Selecting employees	
Developing strategies and policies		

Reprinted, by permission of the publisher, from Management development: Needs and practices, by L.A. Digman, *Personnel*, April 1980, p. 56.

Table 7–2 MOST FREQUENT DEVELOPMENT NEEDS AT EACH LEVEL OF MANAGEMENT outside training consultants rely on training packages; Figure 7–2 provides an approach for assessing this type of training.

Inside consultants offer the opposite advantages and disadvantages. The solution may be to use an outside consultant and encourage him or her to become a partner with inside human resources professionals.[9] Table 7–3 compares the use of various types of trainers.

Any training program chosen then must meet organizational, job, or personal needs. It must also facilitate learning by participants. In addition, it most likely socializes workers to behave in certain ways on the job. In this section, we first examine principles of learning, then consider on-the-job training options, next

I. Determine Relevant Organizational Factors	Look at: • Objectives • Authority structure and style • Climate • Training history
II. Examine Your Training Objectives	Are your objectives congruent with organization's objectives? Look at: • Nature of training problem • Trainee characteristics • Potential benefits to organization
III. Examine Vendor Program Objectives	Are they clear and defined in behavioral terms? Are they measurable? Do they match closely your training objectives?
IV. Contact Other Vendor Program Users	Look at evaluations from organizations comparable to your own.
V. Research Vendor Program	Contact local business schools. Examine any written reviews.
VI. Examine Methodology	Look at: • Methodology of program • Methodology successful in your organization
VII. Decide on Vendor Program	Choose from alternatives. Have decision reviewed by colleagues. Sample the program, if possible.
VIII. Do Post-program Evaluation and Share the Results	Write review or document evaluation results for others.

Figure 7–2 ASSESSING VENDOR TRAINING

Type of Trainer	Advantages	Disadvantages
Human resources professional	Knows organization and its unique problems Knows participants and can use existing relationships with them Often has state-of-the-art knowledge Committed to solving the organization's problems Requires low out-of-pocket costs	May be too close to the organization and its members May have more pressing responsibilities May not be objective about problems
Manager	Committed to solving the organization's problems Requires low out-of-pocket costs Has good knowledge of the organization and its employees	May be ineffective as trainer May lack state-of-the-art knowledge May have more pressing responsibilities May not be objective about problems
Nonmanagerial employee	Has good knowledge of the organization May have good relationship with trainees	May lack detailed knowledge of problems May lack experience as a trainer May have more pressing responsibilities
Outside consultant	Has specialized knowledge Knows state-of-the-art techniques and information May be more objective about organizational situation	Lacks knowledge of organization May rely on packaged programs rather than tailoring them to organizational needs Call for higher out-of-pocket costs

Table 7–3 **COMPARISON OF DIFFERENT TYPES OF TRAINERS**

review off-the-job options, comment about fitting the options to assessed needs, and assess the consequences of these programs for organizational socialization.

Training, Development, and Learning

Learning is defined as the acquisition of new information, skills, or attitudes by an individual.[10] Learning occurs most effectively when

1. the learning situation *actively* involves the learner;
2. the learning situation recognizes and responds to *individual differences* in learners;

3. the learning situation provides *feedback* to participants about the acquisition of information presented by training materials; and

4. the learning situation encourages *transfer* of knowledge, skills, or attitudes to the work situation.[11]

The manager must determine the extent to which each training alternative fits these four criteria.

Figure 7–3 expands these general criteria into design principles to ensure that training programs result in learning. Managers and human resources professionals must evaluate each training option in terms of these learning principles, as well as the way each option meets training and development needs. Table 7–4 lists on-the-job and off-the-job training options, how well each meets various learning criteria and organizational factors. In the next two sections we examine each option in more detail.

On-the-Job Programs

Apprenticeships, internships, job rotation, and job training, among others, teach people skills and attitudes that directly relate to their job performance. Conducted as part of the employee's job activities and primarily performed by supervisors or coworkers, on-the-job training offers some clear benefits. It is highly relevant to the job, requires relatively low out-of-pocket costs, and helps motivate strong performance.

Its disadvantages include the expenditure of time by the supervisor who does the training and the possibility that the supervisor lacks the ability to train a subordinate well. In addition, an untrained worker may have a negative impact

1. The design should help people feel comfortable and capable and respond to participants' needs in the early stages of the program.
2. The design should help participants convert their personal experiences into learning.
3. The design should provide a comfortable setting and include rest breaks.
4. The design should allow for different learning and teaching styles.
5. The design should hold group or organizational activities until participants are willing to share their knowledge and feelings.
6. The design should be sufficiently flexible to allow the trainer to seize "teachable moments."
7. The design should recognize that participants vary in their involvement at different times during the session and that stress may be a prerequisite for learning.
8. The design should deal with behaviors that occur during the training session as well as behaviors that happen on the job.
9. The design should provide opportunities for participants to discover that others may face similar problems or situations.
10. The design should allow the trainer to share control of the session with the participants.

Adapted from J.J. Scherer, How people learn: Assumptions for design, *Training and Development Journal* 38 (January 1984): 64–65.

Figure 7–3 **PRINCIPLES FOR DESIGNING LEARNING ACTIVITIES**

Option	Learning Criteria				Organizational Factors			
	Active Involvement	Response to Individual Differences	Provide Feedback	Transfer of Learning to Work	Extra $ Cost	Interference with Normal Production	Involvement of Training Experts	Time Required from Supervisor
On-the-job Training								
Apprenticeship	High	High	High	High	Low	Moderate	Low	High
Internship	High	High	High	High	Low	Moderate	Low	High
Job rotation	High	High	High	High	Low	Moderate	Low	High
Job training	High	High	High	High	Low	High	Low	High
Off-the-job Training								
Lecture	Low	Low	Low	Moderate	Moderate	Low	High	Low
Role-play	High	Moderate	High	Moderate	Moderate	Low	High	Low
Case analysis	Moderate	Moderate	Moderate	Moderate	Moderate	Low	High	Low
Vestibule training	High	High	High	High	High	Low	Moderate	Low
Computer simulation	High	Moderate	High	Moderate	High	Low	High	Low
Computer-aided instruction	High	High	High	Moderate	High	Low	High	Low

Table 7–4 COMPARISON OF PROGRAMS ON LEARNING CRITERIA AND ORGANIZATIONAL FACTORS

on job and organizational performance; for example, an airline ticket agent receiving on-the-job training might grant too large a refund, not ticket a customer appropriately, or take too long to process a reservation, resulting in loss of revenue to the airline or a disgruntled customer.

In addition, on-the-job training may not be cost-effective when compared to a structured training program because the highest skilled employee is used as a trainer and the training is generally one-to-one.[12] Further, on-the-job training can result in more time devoted to performing the job—correctly or incorrectly—than in learning how to perform the job better.[13]

Apprenticeship. A new employee is assigned to a current employee for a prescribed amount of time. During that period the new employee works under the direction of the regular organizational member and is expected to gradually acquire job-related skills. Apprenticeship is used most often in manual labor or craft jobs.

Internship. Internships resemble apprenticeships except that they are more temporary. They provide individuals with experience in a particular job or an introduction to a job, organization, or industry. Used primarily for students, internships can be paid or unpaid opportunities that provide individuals with experience at relatively little cost to the organization.

Job Rotation. Individuals move through a series of jobs over a period of six months to two years. As they perform each job, they acquire new skills, experiences, and knowledge associated with that job. Frequently used for preparing individuals for management positions, job rotation provides an orientation to many job functions at a reasonably low cost.

Job Training. On-the-job training, in its simplest form, involves an employee being led through all the job functions as he or she performs the job's tasks. "Trial by fire" can promote the most rapid learning. However, the potential damage to employee morale or organizational performance caused by an individual who cannot learn on the job may be significant.

Off-the-Job Training

In contrast to on-the-job training, off-the-job training is performed at a separate location. It provides individuals with the skills or knowledge they need to perform the job at a time apart from their regular job activities. Courses, workshops, and seminars, using lectures, role-plays, videotaping, computer-aided instruction, and computerized simulations are typical examples of off-the-job training.

Management development programs frequently combine diverse types of off-the-job training but bring them "in-house" to respond to unique organizational needs. Organizations retain control of the programs' participants and content. Figure 7–4 shows a sample of in-house advanced management programs. To be successful, such programs must involve all levels of management, demonstrate

	Emphasis/Purpose	Position of Attendees	Length & Frequency
Oil Companies			
—Shell Oil U.S. (32,000 employees)	3 purposes — Time 1. In-depth look at Shell Oil Co. (50%) 2. How to be an effective manager (behavioral subjects) (30%) 3. Greater awareness of external forces (20%)	Upper middle managers • Those having capability of advancing to general management or higher • Also junior/senior staff personnel who need corporate overview	3 Wks. (One/Yr. at 24)
—Marathon (12,000 employees)	To develop business and managerial skills similar to an MBA degree with ⅓ of the time devoted to behavioral subjects	Upper middle managers and high potential employees	2 Wks.
Other Companies			
—General Electric Management Development Institute (350,000+ employees)	1. Management Development Course Provide department managers with business and managerial skills	High potential department managers	4 Wks. (5/Yr.)
	2. Business Management Course Business skills for a general manager position	Top functional managers; high potential section level managers whose next step is general manager	4 Wks. (4/Yr.)
—IBM (280,000 employees)	1. Advanced Management School 5 areas of concentration: • Process of decision making • Personnel management • Internal IBM environment • External social, political, legal environment • Personal development/career planning (45% external, 55% internal IBM issues)	High potential management personnel identified as executive replacements (typically out of district manager position)	3 Wks.
	2. Executive Seminar—intensive overview of current issues facing IBM executives (80% subjects external to IBM)	High potential executives	1 Wk. (2/Yr.)
	3. International Executive Program Greater understanding of internal IBM strategies and external international environment	Vice presidents, regional managers, directors, world trade executives	2 Wks.

Figure 7–4 SUMMARY OF IN-HOUSE ADVANCED MANAGEMENT PROGRAMS

Instructional Mix	Replacement For Univ. Ex. Programs	Location/Facility	Unique Characteristics (Comments)
50% provided by outside speakers 50% interaction with Shell top management	Very limited participation	Columbia Lakes Tennaco Facility, Houston, TX	—Effort has a 20-yr. history in Shell. —The effective manager topics do not stress business skill but interpersonal behavior and management style through developing information on subordinate perceptions of working environment and group behavior.
All teaching on Indiana University campus by I.U. faculty—(90%) At end of 2 wks. participants spend 3 days at home office for an overview of company operations	No—10 people per year still attend university programs	Indiana University and Corporate Headquarters	To maintain the benefits of campus they have contracted with Indiana to develop and administer a program fit to Marathon's needs. Marathon inputs into program design, instructional mix, controls and continually evaluates performance against their needs.
90% university faculty	Operations can spend budgets where they want to; a very few still attend Harvard AMP and Stanford	GE Management Inst. General Electric Campus Croton-on-Hudson, NY	These 3 programs are complemented by a host of short courses on specific subjects.
90% university faculty			
50% IBM executives 50% university faculty	No—40–50 high level vice presidents or presidents of divisions per year attend university executive development programs	IBM Country Club and Management Institute Sands Point, Long Island	This effort is preceded by 3 separate one-week "Middle Management Schools" Phase I –Role of the middle manager Phase II –Developing the entrepreneurial manager Phase III–The professional
50% IBM executives 50% university faculty			Cannot attend sooner than 4 yrs. after advanced management school.
1 wk. at Brookings 1 wk. by IBM executives			Attendee mix kept at ½ nationals, ½ internationals

Continued

Other Companies	Emphasis/Purpose	Position of Attendees	Length & Frequency
—Motorola Executive Institute* (51,000 employees)	Graduate level management education to technically oriented executives—closely related to MBA curriculum	Senior executives	4 Wks.
—St. Regis Paper Co. (30,000 employees)	Overview some concepts and principles of management	Upper middle management	2 Wks.
—Federal Executive Institute (2.8 million Civil Service employees)	1. Heighten responsiveness to national needs and goals. 2. Increase appreciation of the totality of the government system. 3. Improve knowledge of the managerial process.	GS-16 and above for a potential of 12,000 candidates	7 Wks. (5/Yr.)

*Motorola Executive Institute not currently functioning according to latest information.

Figure 7–4 Continued *Continued*

diversity and relevance, strive for excellence in presentation, and include evaluation and follow-up.[14]

What advantages does off-the-job training offer? Removing training from the job allows the employee to concentrate on learning the new skills or attitudes without having to simultaneously worry about job performance. It also reduces the risk to the organization of using a job holder who performs without sufficient knowledge.

What disadvantages are there? Often the fit between these types of training and the assessed needs is low. Too often managers are attracted by interesting-sounding training and development experiences and fail to check the fit with assessed needs. In addition, these types of training frequently require greater out-of-pocket costs.

Lectures. Probably the most common form of training, lectures present a wide range and amount of material in a short amount of time. Their cost tends to be relatively low. However, the lack of active learning and of limited opportunities for feedback reduces the effectiveness of this approach. In addition, retention of material from this method is relatively low; thus lectures should be supplemented by opportunities to practice or repeatedly recall the information acquired.

A trainer can overcome these limitations by using visual aids, encouraging and using questions, guiding note-taking, encouraging discussion, involving learners through written participation, using values-clarification exercises, using role-play or simulations, structuring a lecture to solve a problem, using brainstorming, preparing supplementary handouts, illustrating with a case study or critical incident, giving informal tests, conducting interviews, encouraging directed listening, making a concept diagram, asking for "I learned . . ." and "I wonder . . ." statements, lecturing as a team, and guiding follow-up.[15]

Instructional Mix	Replacement For Univ. Ex. Programs	Location/Facility	Unique Characteristics (Comments)
90% university faculty		Motorola Executive Inst. Scottsdale, AZ	Assessment by a trained psychologist takes place during the 4-wk. period.
90% university faculty		Harrison House, Glen Cove, NJ	Five months time between week one and week two.
95% FEI residential faculty 5% guest speaker		Own campus, Charlottesville, VA 95 Room Inn, 8 Acre Estate	Great deal of flexibility and option in the curriculum with emphasis on an individual's responsibility for learning and choice of courses.
			Emphasis on self-assessment and personal goal setting.

By M.M. Starcevich and J.A. Sykes. Reprinted by permission of the publisher from *Human Resource Planning*, Vol. 3, No. 3, 1980. Copyright 1980 by the Human Resource Planning Society.

Role-plays. These simulations of organizational situations allow an individual to approximate the experience of organizational life without influencing organizational performance. A participant is directed to act out a specific role, such as that of a supervisor giving an appraisal interview or a worker receiving unexpected negative feedback about his or her performance. The trainer or other participants in the training session then discuss the role-plays and offer suggestions for more effective behavior.

Particularly useful in developing management skills, role-plays combined with videotaping provide a powerful vehicle for feeding back information about individuals' listening skills, leadership style, conflict-handling style, and other communication, leadership, and interpersonal skills.

Case Studies. Popularized by the Harvard Business School, this method of study allows students to practice analytical and decision-making skills by reviewing a written description of a real-life situation. Participants analyze the problems faced by the individuals and organizations in the cases and offer recommendations for action. Cases allow students to (1) apply specific procedures, (2) analyze information, (3) offer approaches for solving a problem, (4) prescribe actions for dealing with a series of documents, (5) predict a sequence of events, or (6) assume roles in a case.[16]

Although opinions about the value of case studies vary, proponents have argued that they provide the experience of management, allow individuals to grapple with multiple issues, hold interest, encourage participation, and challenge students. Opponents contend that they are not realistic, encourage "the blind to lead the blind," can frustrate students with a lack of correct data, and are inefficient for transmitting data.[17]

Vestibule Training. This training technique simulates an organizational situation, such as the job of a supermarket cashier, bank teller, or airline ticket agent. It allows the individual to practice the job's tasks apart from the organization's regular operations. Vestibule training allows the worker to interact with the actual equipment and procedures he or she will use in the real-life job under conditions that resemble the job setting.

Computer Simulations. This technique allows an individual to experience the interactions between functional areas in an organization, between the organization and its competitors, or between the organization and its environment as part of a training experience. Individuals make marketing, production, or financial decisions which then act as inputs into the computer simulation; the program shows the impact of these decisions on the simulated organization's performance. Particularly useful for management development, computer simulations allow individuals to experiment with various responses to organizational situations and to see their impact, without actually affecting organizational functioning. The power of this approach is obtained at a relatively high cost, however.

Computer-aided Instruction. Companies such as Zenith, RCA, and other electrical companies have taught unskilled and semiskilled workers basic skills through the use of programmed instruction. Programmed instruction originally involved the sequential presentation of tasks in a workbook; an individual's answer to one question determined his or her next problem, question, or area of study, and so forth. More recently, trainers have computerized this approach and used it for teaching computer languages and other computer-related tools, such as spreadsheets or word processing. It incorporates significant amounts of feedback and is relatively active; thus this type of approach meets two criteria of effective training.[18]

Matching Training Programs to Training Needs

As described so far, the manager faces numerous training and development program options. Table 7–5 summarizes the advantages and disadvantages of each type. While no *best* program exists, a program's ability to respond to training needs and expedite learning is critical. Reading 7–1, "Training with a Focus on the Individual," by John D. Dickey, describes one of Corning Glass Works plant's attempts to respond to individual training needs.

Consider again the case of Janice Lyons's assistant. Should she send her assistant to the training program if it emphasizes budgeting skills and she has no budgeting responsibilities? Should she send her assistant to the program if it emphasizes decision-making skills and her assistant already has strong decision-making skills? Should she send her assistant if the program is directed toward Fortune 500 companies and Janice Lyons's company has only 200 employees? Should she send her assistant if the program includes only lectures and no hands-on training experiences?

Option	Advantages	Disadvantages
On-the-job	closely related to job high transfer of skills and knowledge acquired active involvement of participants relatively low out-of-pocket costs	takes supervisor from other job duties cost may be high may result in poor products supervisor may lack ability as a trainer
Off-the-job	greater variety of programs available often conducted by experts individuals can concentrate on learning skills or knowledge low risk of job holder performing without required skills or knowledge	may not meet learning criteria may be costly may not fit employees' needs

Table 7–5 ADVANTAGES AND DISADVANTAGES OF TRAINING OPTIONS

One type of training, called competency-based training or criterion-referenced training, focuses on meeting desired training outcomes as a way of ensuring that training meets assessed needs. Competency-based training "refers to the idea that if you want to teach someone to do something (like a job), you start by figuring out exactly what things successful performers do (what it looks like when it's done right), then train the learner until he or she is able to do all those things."[19] An instructional effort can be called competency-based if (1) it focuses on achieving clearly specified performance outcomes; (2) time is used flexibly; (3) learners can choose from a variety of learning experiences; (4) pre- and post-tests determine mastery of the subject; (5) demonstrated competencies are certified; and (6) decisions about program conduct are based on student performance.[20]

Determining the fit requires the manager to clearly specify the employee's and the organization's needs and then to research the content of the program extensively and carefully. Some misfits are obvious, but only a careful analysis reveals others.

Organizational Socialization

What does training and development do besides improve an individual's skills and knowledge or change the person's attitudes? Training and development can help people learn the ropes as well as the nature of acceptable behavior and attitudes in the organization.[21] That is, training and development can *socialize* employees to organizational expectations.

When does organizational socialization occur? We most commonly think of socialization occurring when an individual first enters an organization. Typically, orientation programs teach individuals the basics of acceptable behavior. New employees meet other organizational members, learn about policies regarding attendance and tardiness, and hear about the organization's philosophy and goals.

Socialization also occurs, though, when an individual moves up the hierarchy or becomes more central in the organization as a result of increased seniority or experience.[22] While formal training and development activities may accompany each movement and have socialization consequences, informal daily interactions between managers and subordinates often socialize employees to behave in certain ways as well.

Consider the introduction and orientation you received to your present job. What did you learn from that experience? How did the orientation contribute to your knowledge of organizational expectations? What outcomes resulted? In addition to teaching the ropes, orientation programs can also prepare new employees for subsequent training by accustoming them to the basics of learning—pay attention and concentrate, ask, don't guess, find out where to get help, check your understanding, when possible, take notes, find out how you're doing, and learn from mistakes.[23]

Now consider the most recent training or development experience in which you participated. The nature of these orientation, training, and development activities influences the way an individual will be socialized, and the extent to which a job holder will act in innovative or conforming ways on the job.

Table 7–6 lists seven pairs of socialization strategies and their anticipated consequences. How would you describe the socialization strategies incorporated into a morning-long orientation session for all new clerical employees at which members of the personnel department explain the requirements of employment and the benefits offered for job holders? This orientation uses formal, collective, fixed, investiture, and sequential socialization strategies. Is such a program likely to lead to innovation or role conformity? Consider, in contrast, a new receptionist whose only training is a half-day of watching the previous job holder. This approach uses informal, individual, variable, investiture, and sequential strategies. Are the same outcomes likely?

Managers must consider how the specific training and development activities socialize their employees. They must determine whether they desire innovative or conforming behavior, and what socialization strategies result in the desired outcome. Then the manager can design training and development activities that incorporate these strategies.

EVALUATION OF TRAINING PROGRAMS

Many managers focus their training and development efforts on program selection. They ignore the situational analysis, needs assessment, and evaluation steps of the training process. These steps are critical to the ultimate effectiveness of training and development. Human resources professionals can contribute to training effectiveness by establishing comprehensive and ongoing evaluation programs. Such evaluation can address four types of outcomes, as described in the next section.

Strategy	Definition	Predicted Outcomes
Collective	puts newcomer through a common set of experiences as part of a group	low stress, high conformity
Individual	processes recruits singly and in isolation from each other	high stress, high innovation
Formal	segregates newcomers from regular organizational members	low stress, high conformity
Informal	treats newcomers as not differentiated from other members	high stress, high innovation
Sequential steps	requires entrant to move through a series of discrete and identifiable steps to achieve a defined role	low stress, high conformity
Nonsequential	accomplishes achievement of a defined role in one transitional stage	high stress, high innovation
Tournament	separates clusters of recruits into different programs on the basis of presumed differences	high stress, high conformity
Contest	avoids sharp distinctions between clusters of recruits	low stress, high innovation
Fixed	gives the recruit complete knowledge of time required to complete passage	low stress, high innovation
Variable	offers a timetable which does not fix the length of socialization	high stress, high conformity
Serial	provides experienced members as role models for newcomers about to assume similar positions to follow	low stress, high conformity
Disjunctive	has no role models available since newcomers do not follow in footsteps of recent predecessors	high stress, high innovation
Investiture	ratifies and documents the usefulness of personal characteristics of new recruits	low stress, high innovation
Divestiture	seeks to deny and strip away recruits' personal characteristics	high stress, high conformity

Based on J. Van Maanen, People processing: Strategies of organizational socialization, *Organizational Dynamics* 6 (1978): 19–36.

Table 7–6 NAMES AND DEFINITIONS OF SOCIALIZATION STRATEGIES

Training Outcomes

Evaluation requires an assessment of the program's impact on short- and long-term behaviors and attitudes. Measuring training effectiveness involves assessing

1. *reactions*—how participants feel about the program;
2. *learning*—knowledge, skills, and attitudes acquired as a result of the training;
3. *behavior*—changes that occur on the job as a result of the training; and
4. *results*—impacts of training on the overall effectiveness of the organization or its accomplishment of organizational goals.[24]

Reactions. Participants' feelings about the training are frequently and easily measured. Did they like the program? Was it worthwhile? What were its strengths? Its weaknesses? What skills did the participants feel improved as a result of their participation? Did the program meet employees' goals?

Questions to evaluate reactions are typically answered through the administration of interviews or questionnaires. In preparing these questionnaires, human resources professionals or managers must first determine what information they want. They should use a written comment sheet that covers these items, design the form so that the reactions can be tabulated and quantified, make the forms anonymous to encourage honest reactions, and encourage the trainees to write in additional comments not covered by the questions.[25] Figure 7–5 is a sample of a questionnaire for assessing reactions.

This type of assessment is important because it provides the initial estimate of the training program's effectiveness. In addition, participants' feelings about a training experience later influence their application of the skills or attitudes acquired during the training. But assessment of reactions is not sufficient for a full evaluation of program effectiveness since reactions do not measure whether learning has really occurred or whether job performance has changed as a result of the training.

Learning. The knowledge and skills acquired or the attitudes changed as a result of the training program should be evaluated, using written tests or observations. For instance, a human resources professional can administer a test that measures knowledge of bank services before and after the training program. Pre-tests alone can increase trainees' readiness to learn, begin to educate the trainees, pull them into the context and content of the training program, sensitize them to important concepts, focus the trainer on key concepts, and establish a rigorous learning climate.[26] And end-of-class examinations can measure the mastery of particular skills.

The use of control groups and sophisticated statistical analysis, although not necessary to obtain some measurement of learning, increases the reliability of results but adds to the cost of evaluation. One option is for human resources professionals to assess the impact of training through the use of a *quasi-experimental research design.* This type of design divides participants into two groups: one that

PROGRAM EVALUATION

Seminar Title: ______________________ Name: ______________________

Date: ______________________ Title: ______________________

	Very Satisfied 10	9	8	7	6	5	4	3	2	Very Dis-Satisfied 1
1. Overall Rating of Meeting	☐	☐	☐	☐	☐	☐	☐	☐	☐	☐
2. How well were your objectives satisfied?	☐	☐	☐	☐	☐	☐	☐	☐	☐	☐
3. Speakers										
DAY 1 a) ______________ (Name of Speaker) — overall RATING	☐	☐	☐	☐	☐	☐	☐	☐	☐	☐
1) Level at Which Material was Presented	☐	☐	☐	☐	☐	☐	☐	☐	☐	☐
2) Ability to Communicate	☐	☐	☐	☐	☐	☐	☐	☐	☐	☐
3) Degree of Preparedness/Organization	☐	☐	☐	☐	☐	☐	☐	☐	☐	☐
4) Ability to Relate Material to your Needs	☐	☐	☐	☐	☐	☐	☐	☐	☐	☐

5) List constructive comments and/or criticisms and suggestions for improvement, if any: ______________________

____

____

____

	10	9	8	7	6	5	4	3	2	1
DAY 2 b) ______________ (Name of Speaker) — overall RATING	☐	☐	☐	☐	☐	☐	☐	☐	☐	☐
1) Level at Which Material was Presented	☐	☐	☐	☐	☐	☐	☐	☐	☐	☐
2) Ability to Communicate	☐	☐	☐	☐	☐	☐	☐	☐	☐	☐
3) Degree of Preparedness/Organization	☐	☐	☐	☐	☐	☐	☐	☐	☐	☐
4) Ability to Relate Material to your Needs	☐	☐	☐	☐	☐	☐	☐	☐	☐	☐

5) List constructive comments and/or criticisms and suggestions for improvement, if any: ______________________

____

____

____

	10	9	8	7	6	5	4	3	2	1
4. Administration and Facilities										
a) Registration Procedure	☐	☐	☐	☐	☐	☐	☐	☐	☐	☐
b) Room Seating/Atmosphere	☐	☐	☐	☐	☐	☐	☐	☐	☐	☐
c) Meals	☐	☐	☐	☐	☐	☐	☐	☐	☐	☐
d) Workbook Materials/Handouts	☐	☐	☐	☐	☐	☐	☐	☐	☐	☐

____

____

5. Please make any additional comments — or any suggestions — for improving this program and our overall offering:

____

____

____

____

____

6. May we refer future participants to you for comments? ☐ Yes ☐ No

7. May we quote your reaction to this program? ☐ Yes ☐ No

Figure 7–5 SAMPLE OF A REACTIONS QUESTIONNAIRE

receives training and the other that does not. The groups are either selected at random from a larger population or matched on key characteristics so they are as similar as possible. Their knowledge before and after the training is measured and compared. If the training has an effect on learning, we would predict that the group receiving the training would score better on post-training measures (after adjustments for differences in pre-test scores) than would the group that did not receive the training (the control group). The more alike the two groups are, and the more tightly controlled their training and nontraining experiences, the more valid are the results of the study.

Behavior. Assessment of on-the-job changes in behavior as a result of training most frequently occurs through supervisors' evaluation of subordinate performance. Analysis of performance appraisals before and after training can tell the rater which employees need training or retraining, what types of training they need, and whether a completed training program has been successful as well.[27] Changing behavior often requires extensive training and development activities, however; and participants must want to change, have the necessary knowledge and skills to try the new behavior, have a supervisor who encourages different behaviors, receive help during implementation of change, and receive rewards for changing.[28]

Frequently the use of repeated performance appraisals can provide documentation of the behavioral effects of the training. Thus if a performance appraisal is completed before training and then another one two to three months after it, we can often attribute the new behavior to training.

Results. The most difficult outcome to attribute to a training and development program is improved organizational effectiveness. Too often, there are several alternative explanations for the new results. Because of the difficulty in identifying the causes of these results, some organizational members justify training by simply assuming that training and development has an effect on organizational effectiveness. A few others conduct controlled experiments to show its impact. And others attempt to assess cost-benefits of training. The Deficiency Analysis Review Technique shows the value of a formal training program, for example, by quantifying the costs of deficient operations and unnecessary expenses. Then, by showing that training reduces these deficiencies, the dollar benefit value of the training can be approximated[29] (see Chapter 15 for further discussion of cost-benefit analysis). Table 7–7 illustrates such cost assessment and reduction.

Human resources professionals must continually attempt to show the relationship between training and development and organizational effectiveness. To do this, human resources professionals can track the pre- and post-training sales records of trainees, say, by comparing the records of trained and untrained employees during the same period, using statistical, graphical, or qualitative analysis.[30] Similarly, human resources professionals or managers can evaluate the impact of supervisory training by tracking changes in their subordinates' tardiness, absenteeism, turnover, and work quality or quantity.[31]

The assessment of reactions, learning, behavior, and results must be compre-

SET REALISTIC GOALS → Goal | ESTABLISH METHOD → Method | PERFORM COST/BENEFIT ANALYSIS → Annual Goal Value, Total Value (5 yrs.), Training Course Cost | CALCULATE NET SAVINGS → Net Savings

Sample Productivity Improvement/Cost Reduction Plan

Problem	Goal	Method	Annual Goal Value	Total Value (5 yrs.)	Training Course Cost	Net Savings	Means of Verifying
Sick Leave	Reduce by 20%	Training course	$ 72,000	$ 360,000	$15,000	$ 345,000	Sick leave data
Employee Accident	Reduce by 25%	Safety course	$ 30,000	$ 150,000	$15,000	$ 135,000	Accident data
Employee Turnover	Reduce by 15%	Benefits training course	$ 18,750	$ 93,750	$15,000	$ 78,750	Personnel records
Product Delivery Production	Increase by 15%	Work methods training	$240,000	$1,200,000	$15,000	$1,185,000	Work reports
Vehicle Damage	Reduce by 15%	Driving course	$ 38,250	$ 191,250	$15,000	$ 176,250	Accident data

Reprinted by permission of John M. McCullough, Director of Training Services Division, Roy Jorgenson Associates, Inc., International Management Consultants, Gaithersburg, Maryland; and *American City and Country*.

Table 7–7 AN ACTION PLAN FOR EVALUATING COST-EFFECTIVENESS OF TRAINING

hensive. Reading 7–2, "Putting the Evaluation Puzzle Together," by Gail Trapnell, discusses appropriate multidimensional approaches to evaluation.

STRATEGIES FOR INCREASING EFFECTIVENESS OF TRAINING AND DEVELOPMENT

How can human resources professionals and managers increase the effectiveness of training and development? They can follow a three-step process for controlling the quality of training programs. First, human resources professionals must prioritize training requests organization-wide and encourage managers to participate in the decision-making process. Second, human resources professionals can assist managers in determining whether there is a good fit between the proposed program and employee needs. Third, human resources professionals and managers should monitor the process of adjusting the program to ensure it is on target.[32] The next sections describe the implications for human resources professionals and managers in greater detail.

Implications for Human Resources Professionals

Human resources professionals should oversee or perform the design and implementation of training and development programs in the following ways.

1. They must perform or supervise the performance of regular environmental, organizational, and job analyses.
2. They must review various orientation, training, and development activities and consider the socialization strategies they use. They should inform managers or other trainers about the likely consequences of the activities for conforming and innovative behavior.
3. Human resources professionals must assist managers in analyzing the needs of their employees. They can then summarize the needs across the organization in preparation for identifying the types of training they should offer organization-wide.
4. They can organize or conduct off-the-job training and oversee on-the-job training. They should encourage the use of a diversity of training options, selecting those that best meet identified needs and ensure learning. Human resources professionals should keep themselves informed about new training techniques such as the use of audiovisual equipment and computers. They should maintain a data bank of the training programs available, as well as use and effectiveness of each in various organizational settings.
5. Human resources professionals must check the fit between available training options and the employee needs identified by managers.
6. They must make sure that all training activities are evaluated. Where possible, evaluation should focus on reactions, learning, behavior, and results.

Implications for Managers

Managers should assess training needs, help select training programs that meet these needs, and assist with the evaluation of the programs. More specifically,

1. Managers must provide for their subordinates to participate in training and development programs on a regular basis; and develop a climate that supports and rewards these efforts. If necessary, they should lobby for support from top management.
2. Managers should contribute to the situational analysis; in particular, they should provide up-to-date job analyses on a regular basis.
3. Managers must regularly assess their subordinates' needs. They can use data from performance appraisals, examinations, or other instruments to evaluate deficiencies in individual performance and areas of potential development.
4. Managers must match training programs to identified needs. They must actively ensure that the training programs in which their subordinates participate respond to the employees' needs. Likewise, they must be certain that employees do not participate in training programs that do not fit their needs.
5. Managers should investigate a wide range of training options using human resources professionals as resources in the identification or conduct of appropriate training programs.
6. Managers, again with the assistance of human resources professionals, should initiate a system for evaluating training and development programs. And managers themselves should be prepared to justify the value of training programs for their subordinates by analyzing the cost-effectiveness of each program.

READINGS

Reading 7–1

TRAINING WITH A FOCUS ON THE INDIVIDUAL

John D. Dickey

As we move forward, we must ensure the concept of "training with a focus on the individual" is foremost in our minds. With increased emphasis on productivity, we need to ensure that performance oriented training plays a key role in attaining the output we expect from our people. This output will be contingent upon how we manage our human resources. If as companies we manage our people with the same management skills and talent applied to planning, marketing, production and general business, we will be a long way toward attaining the desired productivity.

Many people responsible for establishing training programs, either for management or hourly employees, have had little direction as to which approach to take. For those in this situation, this article may be of practical value.

In some companies the corporate training and development staff spend hours writing their training philosophies. Corporate training philosophies may be of some value; however, for those who have the responsibility at a plant location the real need is guidance in the development of courses, and ultimately, assistance in the development of a plant-wide training program.

PHASES OF TRAINING AND DEVELOPMENT

At the Corning Glass Works plant in Harrodsburg, KY, we adopted a systematic approach in the development of a plant-wide training program. Our concept of training focuses on the individual.

Many plants have taken a different view by focusing their training on a department or operation. We at the Harrodsburg plant believe all employees, regardless of salary grade, position or department assignment, can benefit from quality training.

Individual training must come first. This includes an extensive orientation program for new employees. Formalized on-the-job training is administered for those who have transferred to a new job. Our process of on-the-job training will be addressed later in the article.

The second phase is classified as *departmental training*. The employees, regardless of whether they are hourly or management, are exposed to a myriad of specialized courses designed to increase department productivity. Within the framework of Corning Glass, a system has been established to document various operations. These documents, known as standard operating procedures (SOP), provide the instructor with a reference to develop a training program covering a particular operation. However, since we are in an age of rapid technology advances, additional departmental training is accomplished without the use of SOPs. These courses are technical and often deal with maintenance or troubleshooting aspects of equipment. Occasionally, resources outside Corning Glass Works are used, such as video tapes and other packaged courses for rent or sale. It should be the responsibility of the training coordinator to exhaust all possible sources for quality instruction.

The third phase of training is *plant/facilities training*. This includes safety training and courses offered at the local plant for personal and professional development. Priority is given to courses legally required by OSHA. For example, our plant gives high priority to a course covering the use of respirators. Those courses for personal and professional development might include a video tape on how to write an appropriation request for capital expenditures or a course on exceptional administrative skills.

Corporate and outside training and development account for the last phase. These include courses conducted at the corporate offices and courses offered by universities or management organizations.

Reprinted from the June, 1982 issue of *Personnel Administrator*, copyright, 1982, The American Society for Personnel Administration, 606 North Washington Street, Alexandria, VA 22314, $30 per year. By John D. Dickey, Education and Development Specialist, North American Operations, SunarHauserman, Cleveland, Ohio.

THE PROCESS OF DEVELOPMENT

A training program as comprehensive as ours does not evolve without detailed planning. The training professional would call it a "needs diagnosis." To the coordinator at a plant it is called "getting your act together."

The first step is to meet with department heads on an individual basis to determine their requirements for the upcoming year. To assist the department head in their selection of courses, the coordinator provides a list of all SOPs pertaining to that department's operation. At this point, a worksheet is given to the department head to complete. The department heads should be asked what problem areas their operations incurred over the last year and what future problem areas are anticipated. The department head then is given a list of required courses based on OSHA requirements and courses that top management feel would benefit the operation. Employees also need to feel they have input into the development of the courses. To accomplish this the department head and the training coordinator present the list of course offerings to several plant employees, allowing them to suggest further course context.

In some cases, the department head may not be the ideal person to provide the instruction for certain technical courses. To eliminate this obstacle, "engineering training consultants" have been established for each department to provide individual expertise and experience in the planning and presentation of various courses.

Once the training program for each department is established, the coordinator should publish a master training schedule. This schedule should be published on a monthly basis. Since the training plan for each department is established at the beginning of every year, circumstances may require a change in the plan several months after the initial writing. The training coordinator should therefore be advised by the department head prior to the presentation of a new course.

Once the training coordinator completes the process of establishing each department's training program, a catalog or training directory should be established. Listings are made according to whether the subject is operational, safety, plant-sponsored or departmental training. Each course has a corresponding number. The first three numbers identify the plant. This allows for other plants to use your courses (*i.e.,* video tapes or related material). The second three numbers identify the type of department receiving the training. If it is plant-sponsored, these numbers will be identical to the first three. The next number indicates the type of participants (exempt, non-exempt, hourly). The last two numbers indicate the sequence of the course. For example, 935-241-1-07, indicates: 935, plant; 241, inspection department; 1, hourly; 07, the seventh course made for this department. If there are a number of plants within the corporation that have this system, the ability to transfer educational material is made easier since each plant will have a master directory established by the corporate office.

WHAT IS THE COORDINATOR'S ROLE?

The responsibilities of the coordinator are to oversee the planning, development, implementation and monitoring of a comprehensive plant training program. In addition to the assistance he or she provides to the department head in preparing a training program for the year, the coordinator provides resources to facilitate professional instruction via training consultants or in-house video or slide presentations.

Video equipment professionalizes the training program. Our plant has produced video tapes for maintenance training, safety training, orientation, management training and as a means of supplementing the formalized on-the-job training.

PERFORMANCE ORIENTED TRAINING

The focal point of a plant-wide training program should be its on-the-job training. Many organizations waste man-hours on inefficient on-the-job training. The approach to on-the-job training is not to simply put the individual in the position to go it alone. This could result in the formulation of bad habits because the employee has no knowledge of the department's standards. Since the employee requires constant correction by the supervisor, time is wasted. On the other hand, giving the training requirements to a veteran may result in the trainee accepting methods and standards that are not the departmental standards.

On-the-job training is the responsibility of the

supervisor. The supervisor is evaluated on a set of standards. Those same standards may be applied to the employee during "formalized" on-the-job training (OJT). Our methods of formalizing the OJT process is quite simple. First, the employee is presented with classroom instruction. This may be supplemented by a video presentation. Then the employee is given an OJT training manual.

The training manual contains a check list. The list is comprised of all the tasks that the employee must perform in a satisfactory manner in order to meet the daily requirements of that position. All training manuals begin with the objective of the training. The objective should contain all the basic requirements of that job as outlined by the job description.

Following the objective are the instructions to both the employee and the supervisor. It is stressed in the instructions that to achieve credit for a particular task on the check list, it must be performed to the standard of the department. In some cases the check list contains time requirements for the completion of the program. Additionally, the check list will include questions to test the employee's overall knowledge of the operation, although the practical exercises are the most critical aspect. Effective on-the-job training must be performance oriented and to be performance oriented it must have practical application.

RESULTS ARE FAVORABLE

So, where have over two hundred various courses for our employees taken us? First, we have increased productivity. In one of our departments, we have seen record production runs following the introduction of employees who have completed formalized on-the-job training. Secondly, we have seen a standardization of concepts and applications. Employees are working to the standard of the supervisor and, most importantly, the standards are given meaning in a productive environment. Lastly, we have provided an in-house means of self-improvement. In our plant, the support is obvious from the management level. In addition, some of the greatest support has come from the production employees themselves. Finally, many favorable comments in this method of training have come from the union representatives.

As we move ahead in the 1980s, the demographics of our society are changing. Unfortunately, many do not favor business. For instance, there will be fewer qualified people we can bring into entry level positions in our hourly work force. Additionally, with rapid technological advances managers will, out of necessity, become experts in dealing with the topic of "managing change". Therefore, we must apply our talent to ensure that training programs reflect the importance we place on the individual employee; in short, we must focus our training on the individual.

DISCUSSION QUESTIONS

1. What does "training with a focus on the individual" mean?
2. What alternatives exist to focusing on the individual?
3. What are the advantages and disadvantages of each focus?
4. What were the key elements of the Corning training program?
5. What roles do human resources professionals and managers play in the training?
6. Was the training program effective?
7. What changes might make it more effective?

Reading 7–2

PUTTING THE EVALUATION PUZZLE TOGETHER

Gail Trapnell

The evaluation of training and development programs should be a multi-dimensional process for improving what we teach and how we teach. Evaluation helps trainers design and replicate successful training programs and determine the reasons for the failure of unsuccessful ones.

But piecemeal evaluation is not enough. We need

to assess the training and development program as a whole. In what environmental and political contexts does it exist? What fiscal, physical and human resources does the program use? What happens during the training process? What happens to a trainee's performance immediately after training, and six months later? What impact does the training program have on the organization? Each of these questions should be answered because each contributes bits of information toward the construction of a comprehensive picture of training.

CONTEXT EVALUATION

Context evaluation attempts to assess the environment, including managers', supervisors' and line workers' attitudes about the role of training and development. Broad identified 24 actions that management can take to support the transfer of training to the job. These actions also are indicators of the importance the management attaches to training. Are those who have completed training programs given preference for promotions? Does management guarantee salary increases to trainees who complete programs and improve on-the-job performance? Does management allow trainees time to prepare before training sessions? Top management must lend credence to training through such actions if training programs are to be successful and effective.

Middle management and supervisory personnel must display the same degree of support for training. If management and training and development cooperate in this way to make the work setting an extension of the training classroom, job proficiency will increase dramatically because trainees will put new skills to work immediately.

Context evaluation also deals with the purposes of specific training programs. Is a program to orient new employees? To instruct new employees in performing a task the company way? To develop new skills or enhance current skills? Is a program directed primarily toward the achievement of organizational goals and objectives? Is it to help eliminate causes of a company problem or address the consequences of the problem?

Finally, context evaluation focuses on the appropriateness of objectives. In many cases, the failure of a specific training program or training's general ineffectiveness may be caused by the lack of fit between individual programs and the organizational environment.

INPUT EVALUATION

Input evaluation assesses the appropriateness and adequacy of all resources that go into (or that should go into) a training program. It focuses on elements of the design, including performance objectives, instructional design and sequencing plans, as well as the training materials to be used by instructors and trainees. It also considers questions about facilities such as: Is the equipment to be used in training compatible with that used on the job? Is there enough equipment to allow each trainee hands-on practice? Are the facilities, equipment, materials and other physical resources congruent with the performance objectives outlined in the training guide?

Two of the most important elements of input evaluation are assessment of the instructor's competencies and evaluation of the behaviors trainees bring to the training program. If the program focuses on problem solving and uses case studies that require analytical ability, the trainee who has advanced no further than the knowledge or comprehension level of learning is doomed to fail. The instructor must be competent in the skills he or she will have to use in a particular training program. It is better to find out before the program whether the trainer is capable of using simulation and case study techniques.

PROCESS EVALUATION

What takes place during the training process? What elements can make or break a training program? In this assessment, trainers should be interested first in how effectively the instructor uses the resources and materials provided for the program. Is the instructor aware of the trainees' learning styles? Are training activities compatible with these styles? Are instructional strategies appropriate to objectives? Assessing these factors periodically during the course of training allows for interim adjustments that can enhance the probability of success.

Equally important is the assessment of trainees' interim performance gains. Correctly designed and sequenced training materials contain measurable achievement milestones. It is much better to know at the time that a trainee has not mastered the initial milestone than to wait for the final performance exam. Modifications can then be made while there is still time to succeed.

In general, process evaluation deals with the implementation of a program's design. For example, if the design calls for computer-assisted instruction, the evaluation would detail how such instruction is to be provided—whether it is to be offered in large or small groups or to individual students and whether time lines can be modified to meet individual needs and abilities.

PRODUCT EVALUATION

Product evaluation is the component with which trainers are most familiar. It assesses the competencies of trainees who complete programs and changes in on-the-job performance.

If pre-tests have been administered, post-tests can be used to determine trainees' gains in knowledge, skills and on-the-job performance. The design and selection of evaluation measures are of critical importance to this process. Choose measures that are congruent with training objectives and that truly measure what they purport to measure. Both criterion-referenced measures, which compare trainees' performances to job standards, and norm-referenced measures, which compare trainees' performances to group norms, can be useful.

For product evaluation, trainers must decide when and where to conduct the evaluation. It might occur in the training classroom or on the job site immediately after the program or three to six months later. Employees' supervisors also might be involved in the assessment, which might use a single test or a combination of tests.

IMPACT EVALUATION

Impact evaluation focuses on many factors that affect the bottom line. It assesses the cumulative difference training efforts have made in the organization's productivity, efficiency and profitability and offers training and development staff an opportunity to demonstrate to top management training's importance to the financial health of the company.

Impact evaluation is not a science. Many persons argue that other variables greatly affect long-term results and make training's effects difficult to assess. But the assessments can still be useful, especially if the training and development department is able to secure the help of other departments in the assessment effort. Top management, fiscal control officers and personnel and records staff could provide access to the necessary data—e.g., savings resulting from reductions in downtime, accident rates, absenteeism, customer returns, assembly line rejects, staff turnovers and employee grievances. This kind of information enhances the role of training and development professionals within the organization.

PUTTING THE PIECES TOGETHER

Yet it is not enough to conduct separate context, input, process, product and impact evaluations. The training and development staff must design and maintain a system that puts each piece of data in proper perspective. Only then can management understand the whole training picture and what each element of training contributes to the company's effort.

The first step in designing such a system is stating a rationale. If the evaluation is to be used solely for appraising instructors' or trainees' performances, the evaluation plan can be quite simple. On the other hand, if the evaluation seeks causes for success and failure, the plan must be much more comprehensive.

Although evaluation schemes differ in purpose and scope, all should contain the same six basic elements: objectives, identification of the data to be collected, standards, procedures, time frames and staff assignments.

Objectives are the specific purposes of an evaluation effort. They are usually stated in one of three ways:

- *As a question*—Does the trainee's individual use of filmstrips, cassette recordings and workbooks result in higher performance levels than the use of these same materials in large group instruction?

- *As a statement*—Top management perceives that training and development is critically important to the growth and prosperity of the organization. Data would either support or refute this statement.
- *As a traditional objective*—To determine the skill level of trainees in performing a certain operation after training.

Like performance objectives, evaluation objectives give specificity and precision to the process by forcing evaluators to focus on defined aspects of the training and development effort.

Data to be collected are the descriptors or types of information that will provide documentation of the achievement of objectives. The objectives statement should point to the types of data trainers need to collect. The definitions can be refined further through brainstorming sessions within the training and development group and in cooperation with supervisory groups, managers and former trainees.

Standards are predetermined measures of success or acceptability. Standards may be arbitrary—in fact, they almost always are—but they are useful if set collaboratively by training and development staff and management and supervisory personnel *before* the assessment. If the training and development staff does not involve management in setting standards before the assessment, the department might be subjected to disputes about the reliability of data and the effectiveness of programs. Also, standards should be modified as programs are repeated so that they become more realistic. A typical standard for product evaluation would read, "that 90 percent of the trainees perform 90 percent of the terminal objectives at the proficiency level called for in the objectives."

Procedures must be identified and appropriate to objectives. Zenger and Hargis have identified and assessed several evaluation procedures, including reaction sheets, anecdotes, incidents and testimonials, knowledge-gain measurements, observation checklists, questionnaires, pre- and post-tests, and multiple test administrations. Their article might help trainers decide which evaluation measures are appropriate for their purposes. Evaluators also might consider using longitudinal studies, interviews, third party evaluators and analyses of records.

Time frames add a sense of importance and priority to the evaluation plan. They set parameters for long-range and short-range evaluation efforts by identifying how frequently an evaluation will take place and when it will be conducted, with dates for beginning and completing the evaluation.

Staff assignments are the final critical element. By assigning specific responsibilities for evaluation to members of the training and development staff and to appropriate supervisory and management personnel, the training manager can make the organization's members aware that successful implementation of an evaluation plan must be a joint effort. Assigning these tasks ahead of time ensures that participants will take them seriously.

REFERENCES

Broad, M.L. (May 1982). Management actions to support transfer of training. *Training & Development Journal,* 124–130.

Zenger, J.H., & Hargis, K. (January 1982). Assessing training results: It's time to take the plunge. *Training & Development Journal,* 11–16.

DISCUSSION QUESTIONS

1. What are the components of the multidimensional evaluation process?
2. How does this process fit with the four aspects of evaluation described earlier in the chapter (measuring reactions, learning, behavior, and results)?
3. What roles should human resources professionals and managers play in a comprehensive evaluation program?

ACTIVITIES

Activity 7–1

IS THIS A TRAINING PROBLEM?

Step 1: Read each scenario below. For each situation, decide whether training could improve the situation.

Scenario I: Ronald McTavish has been working in your organization for almost five years since he graduated from State University with a degree in electrical engineering. During the first three years, his performance as a quality-control engineer was satisfactory. Since then his performance has gone consistently down hill. He doesn't seem to have any creative ways of dealing with the problems he now encounters. His coworkers feel that he is already over-the-hill, even though he is only twenty-seven years old. You are Ron's boss. Would training help?

Scenario II: Leslie Jacobs is a fashion designer in a ready-to-wear sportswear house. Les has lots of good ideas when you can get her to work. But she is frequently late, often spends much of the day roaming the office. She claims that she needs freedom and time to think of new ideas. Leslie's coworkers have told you that she has admitted to them that she spends most of the day dreaming. She seems to have lost her momentum. You are her boss. Would training help Leslie?

Scenario III: Marie Bowman has worked for Speedy Sneakers for four years as a cutting-machine operator. During her first two years she was the top performer in her group. Last year she was only average. This year, with the introduction of a new machine that was designed to increase production, her output has dropped way down. She just doesn't seem able to master the intricacies of the new machine. You are her boss. Would training help?

Step 2: For those situations in which training would help the situation, (1) identify the training needs, (2) describe a training program for meeting these needs, (3) offer a way of evaluating whether the program meets these needs.

Step 3: Discussion. What elements do the scenarios described in step 2 have in common?

1. What are the signs that training might be needed?
2. What needs can training programs meet?
3. What types of training programs meet various needs?
4. What kinds of evaluation procedures did you propose?

Activity 7–2

THE RESNICK COMPANY

Step 1: Read the Resnick Company case.

Step 2: Prepare the case for class discussion.

The Resnick Company is a large real estate and land development corporation with offices in major cities across the country. The Company had grown rapidly after World War II as the suburban housing market boomed. In the early 1950's, Jacob Resnick, the president and founder, had foreseen the emergence of suburban shopping centers as retail trade centers and had invested heavily in land parcels along major

 Material provided for this case was developed as a result of support from the Samuel Bronfman Chair in Democratic Enterprise, Graduate School of Business, Columbia University.

highways, particularly in the Southwest. This proved to be an extremely profitable venture, and Resnick soon became a leading force in the land development industry. The Company packaged and constructed the first industrial parks in the Chicago and Houston areas, and, in the late 1960's, added an urban division which specialized in major office complexes in downtown areas.

In 1962, with Mr. Resnick nearing retirement, the Company went public and used the resulting new equity to pursue a diversification strategy. This strategy led to the acquisition of an automobile rental company and a chain of fast-food stores, among others. Shortly after Mr. Resnick's retirement, the firm moved its corporate headquarters from New York City to its original industrial park outside Chicago.

The management of the firm also was transferred from architects and engineers who saw management as a diversion from their principal concerns to a team of professionals in such areas as finance, planning and systems analysis. Increasingly, management trainees were recruited from the graduate schools of business rather than from the construction engineers, land planners and others who worked on the field projects.

A number of the older construction managers who had "grown up" in the business with Mr. Resnick were unhappy with this shift in influence, and many left not long after the new "professional" management had taken over.

Mike Dorner was one of the "old guard" who had made the transition successfully. A civil engineer by training, he had worked his way up from site construction—where he had "driven nails on a roof and ridden an I-beam to the top of the Garber Building"— to his present position as Vice-President of Project Planning Services. Mike's department was responsible for providing management support to the four operating divisions of the development group—residential, commercial, industrial, and recreational. One of his major trades was to coordinate the efforts of the four divisions in developing multi-purpose, multi-use projects. His staff included land use planners, financial and capital markets specialists, engineering analysts and other professionals in environmental law, demography, transportation and so on. Despite this roster of specialists, Mike often said that "our principal function is general management. We are the operating arm of corporate strategy. It is our job to implement overall strategies to ensure that sound management practices are applied in all projects, and to develop and monitor the management of the divisions. It's clearly the best management job in the firm; we are central to the success of the firm, and the top managers of the future are going to come from this department."

Dorner had joined the company in 1945 after his discharge from the Navy and had completed his college degree at night. He frequently spoke fondly of the firm's early days and of Mr. Resnick's leadership:

> The old man had real vision and a firm opinion about almost everything. He took us into the suburbs and then into industrial parks when everyone said we were crazy. Somebody without his guts and self-confidence might still be building ranch houses one at a time in Long Island. He had learned the business from the ground up and believed everyone else should do the same. He had no patience for the lawyers and accountants and others he had to hire. He expected all of us to earn our way up to management through sweat and hard work; he said that good management came from knowing construction and that the other skills would take care of themselves.
>
> I agree with him—at least up to a point. There's no substitute for broad field experience if you want to be a top executive in this business. But the management skills don't take care of themselves. I had to learn them the hard way, and it was painful to me—and costly to the company! These young people coming out of the business schools have things we didn't—theories, models, perspective. We can't just turn the company over to them the day they arrive; they need experience in the business. But a person with a good education and several years' exposure to the operating divisions—driving nails, buying land, scheduling work—is an invaluable resource.
>
> A lot of youngsters who come to us are good sound people who can fill slots in the divisions. We can move them along fast for a few years until they reach their level. When we find those few who have real potential, I feel we have to move them along more carefully, expose them to a range of locations and operating problems. Then when they come to our department in five or ten years, they've got the

> background to move into positions of real responsibility. A person who stays in one area, perhaps becomes a project manager after three or four years, becomes too narrow and can't make that jump. The exposure, the broad perspective just isn't there.

Leroy Jamison was one of the young people identified by Dorner as having potential for top management. When Jamison joined the Company eight years ago after completing his master's in business administration, Dorner was impressed with his training and his personality and decided to lay out a program which would give Jamison exposure to each of the major divisions and to the particular problems of different sections of the country. Over the next eight years, Jamison had had six different assignments in five cities. After a short orientation program at headquarters in Chicago, he had spent a year in Portland, Oregon as a budget analyst in the commercial division. He next spent eighteen months in Houston in residential sales, two years in Atlanta as a field coordinator on a shopping center project, and eighteen months in Boston working with the financial staff in an industrial park development.

Throughout this period, Dorner had received appraisals at six month intervals from Jamison's supervisors and had had a personal appraisal interview with Jamison at the end of each year. The reports had been uniformly positive, praising Jamison for his initiative and enthusiasm and his ability to master quickly the intricacies of each location. Each of his supervisors had protested strongly when Dorner had transferred Jamison to his next assignment. Dorner had spoken with Jamison several times over the years when he had visited sites or when Jamison was called to Chicago. He continued to be impressed with Jamison's intelligence and ambition and was pleased with his professional development.

After the Boston assignment, Dorner was prepared to move Jamison back to Chicago as a senior program manager, a major promotion which would carry considerable responsibility and sizable salary increase. Unfortunately, a slight decline in business and the delayed retirement of two senior managers forced Resnick to put a freeze on promotions, and Dorner could not enlarge his staff. He decided to send Jamison to New Orleans to work as a budget analyst under Phil Jessup in the residential division.

At the end of his first six months in New Orleans, Jamison received his first unfavorable appraisal. Jessup reported to Dorner that Jamison was difficult to get along with and showed little interest in the division's work; he said that "Jamison completes his assignments more or less on time, but with no particular imagination and certainly no desire to go beyond the assignment."

Dorner was surprised; Jessup was respected throughout the Company as a high performing manager and as a developer of younger subordinates. His judgment could not be taken lightly so Dorner spoke with Jessup and Jamison individually on a trip to New Orleans. Jessup had indicated that he liked Jamison personally but was unimpressed with his work and his ability to work with the others in the office; he showed Dorner several of Jamison's reports which were not of the quality that Dorner had seen in earlier work.

Jamison was a bit defensive in his meeting with Dorner. He was critical of Jessup's methods and said that he did not feel comfortable in the office. "I don't feel like I'm accepted here; I've been a budget analyst before, but they treat me as if I just got out of school." Jamison also said that his oldest daughter had had to go into a new school in the middle of the first grade when he was transferred and had had some problems. Dorner left somewhat puzzled and more than a little concerned. He still felt confident in his original assessment of Jamison's potential but was disturbed by Jessup's criticisms.

When a position came open in the recreation division in Portland six months later, Dorner transferred Jamison again even though there was a headquarters position also available. After Jamison had been back in Portland for a year, Dorner brought him to Chicago for his annual appraisal interview. Dorner was approaching the interview with some discomfort. He had hoped by now to be able to move Jamison to Chicago as a program manager; after eight years, Jamison had completed the development program that Dorner had planned. Dorner had developed some doubts about his earlier enthusiasm, however; as he told his friend, Martin Stein, the Company's Controller:

> I thought I had a real winner in Leroy—engineering degree, MBA, family man—and his work in his first several assignments

> seemed to bear me out. He got along well with his supervisors and was full of excitement and ambition whenever he came back for his annual interviews. That's why I couldn't understand the problems he had in New Orleans. You know Phil Jessup—he's one of our top field managers and has a good record with young people—well, he and Leroy got along like oil and water. Phil claimed Leroy was indifferent about his work and surly and argumentative with him and his staff. Leroy knew Phil was displeased but really didn't seem too upset. He said he thought it was a personal thing—they just rubbed each other wrong. But Leroy was also critical of Phil's methods and said Phil wouldn't listen to his ideas. I tried to talk with them, but things didn't get any better.
>
> I wanted to get Leroy out of there, and I wanted to check out my judgment before I moved him into a big job here, so I sent him back out to Portland. He had done well there before, and I thought the change might help. I was half right. He hasn't had any personal problems with his supervisor or any of his coworkers, but his performance has been satisfactory but not really outstanding. It looks as if I was wrong about his potential. I'm really disappointed; I invested a lot in him, coached him, gave him an exposure to the whole Company that few young people get.

Stein felt that the New Orleans assignment might have been a particularly difficult one for Jamison and his family; "You know, Mike, five assignments in six years is a lot of moving. Phil Jessup's a good man, but he's from the old school. A bright young guy with a grad school background might have trouble communicating with him."

"I hear what you're saying, Marty, and I've thought up a lot of excuses for Leroy," said Dorner. "When I look at it carefully, however, the only conclusion is that his ambition and drive aren't as strong as I thought. If it were only the trouble with Phil, there would be no problem, but his work has fallen off in Portland too. I'm afraid that the senior program manager's job here at headquarters is out; there's a spot as a field manager open in Atlanta that I'm going to offer him. It looks like his career is in one of the field divisions."

Leroy Jamison was concerned about his interview with Dorner. He had always looked forward to his annual review. He liked Dorner, and Dorner had always been keenly interested in his work. Their yearly meetings had been lively discussions about Jamison's ideas and about new projects and developments in the company. This year was different, however; the troubles with Jessup in New Orleans had apparently disturbed Dorner, and Jamison had not been happy about the move to Portland. Jamison was concerned about where his career was going and felt that this year's interview would be critical. As he told his wife, Ruth, before leaving Portland,

> We've been bouncing around the country for the Company for eight years now, and I'd like to know where it's going to end. Mike Dorner has always been in my corner—or at least I thought he was—but last year, after he came down to New Orleans, things seemed to change. He seemed distant at the annual review meeting—it was the first time I ever felt I was on trial. In other years, there was nothing threatening about the review. Mike praised me a lot, but mainly he talked about the Company. It was a real education, but last year I really felt on the spot. When he said he wanted me to go back to Portland, I didn't want to go, but I didn't feel I could refuse.
>
> I've done some thinking this past year. Maybe I read too much into Dorner's interest in me. Other guys who joined the Company when I did aren't still on a shuttle, and most of them are a couple of levels above me making more money. Look at Fred Wilcox; he came a year after me, and he's a field manager in Houston. I knew him at school—he's a nice guy, but I always thought I was more capable. Either I'm wrong about myself, or someone's blocking me in the Company. I thought I had earned a promotion after Boston, and when they sent me to New Orleans, I was really down.

Ruth Jamison shared her husband's concerns and urged him to push Dorner for some clear signals:

> The only man you've ever had any trouble with is Jessup. If that's holding you up, you really should find out and try to clear it up. It's not good for us to keep moving around. I just don't want to move again. You've done what-

ever the Company asked. Now you have to ask them where we're going. If we aren't going anywhere—you have good contacts here in Portland and you could find another job.

Step 3: Individually, in small groups, or with the entire class, as directed by your instructor, answer the following questions:

1. What training needs does Mike Dorner have?
2. What training needs does Leroy Jamison have?
3. What training programs would you propose to meet these needs?
4. To what extent should Mike Dorner be involved in training Leroy Jamison?
5. To what extent are human resources professionals required?
6. What types of evaluation should be conducted?

Step 4: Discussion. In small groups, with the class as a whole, or in written form, share your answers to the questions above.

Activity 7–3

TRAINING AND DEVELOPMENT AT STATE BANK

Step 1: Review the following outline of a week-long training program for employees of State Bank. The State Bank is the third largest bank in a moderate-sized southeastern state. Top management at State Bank has regularly sent their high performing auditors and potential management talent to the training program described below. In fact, no one has been promoted to the position of Audit Manager until they have completed this program.

Day I	Overview of the Audit Function
Day II	Increasing Your Effectiveness as an Audit Supervisor—Motivating subordinates, Building audit teams, Fitting the leadership style to the situation
Day III	Increasing Communication Effectiveness—Improving oral presentations, Writing a good audit report, Conducting quality performance appraisals
Day IV	Strategic Planning and the Audit Function—Differentiating between operational and strategic plans, Designing long-term goals and plans
Day V	Implementation of Operational and Strategic Plans

Step 2: Read the descriptions of the following six candidates.

1. John Gibb has been a senior auditor with State Bank for four years since his graduation from a small liberal arts college. He has performed particularly well in the technical aspects of audits, but has received low ratings from his peers in his interpersonal skills. He has been rated very high in analysis and knowledge of bank procedures, but very low in organization, planning, and delegation. Employment tests have indicated that he lacks flexibility and adaptability.

2. Jennifer Ball has been a highly regarded customer service representative with State Bank for two years; she had worked as an auditor previously at a competitor. Jennifer received a B.S. in management from the state university and worked outside of banking for ten years before taking the position in auditing. She has performed well on diverse assignments. She is particularly strong in organizing work teams to accomplish tasks rapidly and effectively. Her knowledge of the technical aspects of audits is somewhat out of date, but she has been evaluated as being a fast learner. On her employment tests Jennifer received high ratings in budgeting, flexibility, and creativity, but average ratings in interpersonal skills and organizational ability.

3. Jane McDonald is the highest rated staff auditor currently employed at State Bank. Her supervisor has discussed the possibility of her being promoted directly into management, without her holding a senior auditor position. She has been employed at State Bank for two years since she graduated from a well-known eastern university. During that time she has worked on the most difficult projects, frequently heading teams of her peers. On employment tests, she scores high on management skills such as orga-

nization, flexibility, coordination. On the job she has high ratings in interpersonal skills, delegation, and knowledge of audit tasks. Her one negative performance rating is impatience she frequently shows with team members who do not perform as well or as quickly as she expects.

4. Hal Hennessey has worked at State Bank for ten years, five as a staff auditor and five as a senior auditor. Recently he was moved out of audit into loan review as a temporary replacement for an employee on personal leave. Hal's tenure at State Bank followed ten years of employment in a large insurance company. In spite of his extensive experience in senior positions, Hal has had limited experience in supervising other employees. He is technically strong and often serves as a technical advisor to most department projects, rather than as a team member on a small number of them. Because of his lack of management experience, limited data have been gathered about Hennessey's management skills.

5. Stan Andrews has been a senior auditor at State Bank for seven years; before that he was a staff auditor for two years at another bank following his graduation from the Institute of Technology. Andrews' performance ratings have been going consistently down hill since he became a staff auditor. Once rated as a very high performer, he currently receives average to below-average ratings. In his written response to these evaluations Stan claims that lack of cooperation from his supervisor has contributed to his declining performance. His interpersonal skills have received particularly low ratings, as has his ability to remain current in bank procedures. His organization, planning, budgeting, and technical skills have been rated acceptable. Employment tests indicate a lack of flexibility and creativity.

6. Sarah Dashiel has worked as a teller, customer service representative, bank manager, loan analyst, senior auditor and most recently as an operations manager for a total employment history of ten years at State Bank. Although Sarah's performance in each position has been considered outstanding, she has been unwilling to remain in a single department for more than two years, saying that she wants a variety of work experiences. Her performance evaluation shows strength in leadership, delegation, coordination, and organization; no weaknesses have been identified. Employment tests indicate that Sarah has high intelligence, maturity, and flexibility.

Step 3: Individually or in small groups, indicate the training needs of each candidate. Then nominate two candidates to send to the training program. Be prepared to justify your nominations.

Step 4: Discussion. In small groups or with the entire class, identify your candidates. Then answer the following questions:

1. What training needs does each person have?
2. What needs does the training program meet?
3. Which candidates will have their needs best met by the training program?
4. Which candidates will not have their needs met by the training program?
5. What type of training program would be appropriate for these candidates?

Activity 7–4

CREATIVE TRAINING DESIGN

Step 1: Read "The Unhappy Guest."

Jerry Smith is in charge of handling complaints for the Grand Hotel in St. Louis. His office is part of the Public Relations unit of the organization. Guests of the Hotel leave their complaints on forms which the Hotel leaves in every room. Mr. Smith and his two subordinates are supposed to compile the complaints, and take appropriate action.

Recently the President of the Grand Hotel received a letter from an angry guest who had asked, on his complaint form, that a letter be sent back explaining why room service had been slow. The guest also

By George H. Labovitz, Ph.D., President, Organizational Dynamics, Inc. From "The Applied Management Series," Performance Review, pp. 53–55 by Organizational Dynamics, Inc., Burlington, Mass., copyright 1985. Reprinted with permission.

wanted to know what steps would be taken to correct the situation. But the guest claimed to have received no letter at all. Hence his new complaint—this time to the President's Office.

Since the Hotel is divided functionally into two wings, Mr. Smith knew from the guest's room number that the subordinate who hadn't responded to the complaint was Kathy Bleer, in charge of the East Wing. Jerry approached Kathy at lunch one day in the Cafeteria.

SCENE I

Smith: Say, Kathy, I want to talk to you about something.
Kathy: Yes?
Smith: There's a real problem here. The President's Office has gotten a letter from an angry guest saying that you hadn't written back as he'd requested.
Kathy: What?
Smith: This guest was quite upset, and you know that doesn't make us look good in the President's eyes.
Kathy: I really don't know what you're talking about.
Smith: Come on, Kathy, this is really serious. Now let's talk about it.
Kathy: Let's not! (Walks out of the room.)

SCENE II

(Mr. Smith approaches the Director of Public Relations, Ms. Scott.)

Scott: What is it, Jerry.
Smith: I'm having a problem with Kathy Bleer. The President got a letter from a guest saying that Kathy hadn't written to him as he'd requested on his complaint form. Now the President is all upset. And when I approached Kathy to talk to her, she wouldn't say anything to me. She just walked right out of the room.
Scott: What in the world did you say to her?
Smith: Nothing, really. I just raised the issue, and she got all huffy and walked out on me. It was humiliating. There were other people around. I can't deal with her when she's put me in that kind of position.
Scott: Well what do you think I can do about it?
Smith: Maybe you could just talk to her. I don't seem to have any clout.
Scott: If that's what you want, Jerry, I'll see what I can do.
Smith: Yes, I wish you'd try it. Thanks.

SCENE III

(In Ms. Scott's Office.)

Kathy: Did you want to see me, Ms. Scott?
Scott: Yes, Kathy. I understand there's been some trouble between you and Mr. Smith . . . something about an unanswered request from a guest. Would you like to tell me your side of the story?
Kathy: There's nothing to tell. I don't know what this is all about. He just came over to me in the lunch room, and started getting all hot under the collar about a guest. What was I supposed to say? He could have waited until regular worktime to do that.
Scott: Perhaps so, Kathy, but this really could be a serious problem. I think it might look like Mr. Smith was being too strong in his criticism, but he really has the best interests of all of us in mind.
Kathy: Best interests? He just lit into me out there—and he didn't even explain himself.
Scott: Well, let me try to explain for him. You see, Kathy, it may not seem serious that some guest writes to the President. I know we have some pretty nutty people stay here, and they want the moon. But the President's Office is very sensitive to complaints like this, and it looks bad for all of us when he gets one.
Kathy: I do a good job, Ms. Scott. I handle complaints as well as anybody would. I don't even know who this guest is. He's probably one of those people who scribble something at the last minute, and you can't even read it.

Scott: You mean you wouldn't respond if something were hard to read?

Kathy: No, Ms. Scott, I don't mean that. I mean that some of them are just impossible to answer. You can't read them.

Scott: Well, Kathy, that's not a good attitude. It just won't do. Kathy, I can't stress enough to you that we are in a very sensitive position. We have to take the flack for everybody else's mistakes, and it's very hard sometimes. But a few oversights like the one you made, and we could be in serious trouble.

Kathy: Ms. Scott, it's not fair to ask 100% perfection. That's impossible on this job. I do the best I can. It's not fair.

Scott: Don't get upset, Kathy. I know you work hard. But look at Mr. Smith's position. He puts his head on the block when you make a mistake. We just have to be an *extra* bit more careful to do everything—including processing those illegible complaints—because what looks like a minor complaint here looks like a major problem at the top. That's just how it is, Kathy.

Kathy: I don't know what you want me to do.

Scott: Just try a little harder to realize that your actions are very important, and have consequences for all of us. I know you're a good worker, and I'm sure you'll be able to do better.

Kathy: O.K.—I understand, Ms. Scott.

Scott: Good, Kathy. Thanks for coming in.

Step 2: Identify Kathy's training needs.

Step 3: Assume that twenty people across the organization share Kathy's needs. Design a training program that meets these needs. In designing the program be as specific and detailed as possible. Include topical outlines, methods of presentation, and the qualifications of the trainers.

Step 4: Discussion. Individually, in small groups, or with the entire class, answer the following questions:

1. What training needs does Kathy have?
2. What types of training programs could meet these needs effectively?
3. What types of training programs would not meet these needs?
4. What are the characteristics of effective training programs? Of ineffective ones?

Activity 7–5

EVALUATING TRAINING

Step 1: The Wicket Paint Company has 200 managers who participate in various training programs. In the past year, Wicket has sent one-fourth of its managers to a program titled "Building Executive Skills." This program costs Wicket $500 per participant. The seminar includes the following topics:

I. The Roles of the Modern Manager
   - **A.** Examining interpersonal roles
   - **B.** Defining informational roles
   - **C.** Considering decision-making roles
   - **D.** The process of management: planning, organizing, implementing and controlling

II. The Manager as Motivator: Increasing Your Staff's Productivity and Satisfaction
   - **A.** Testing your assumptions about individuals
   - **B.** Assessing and meeting employees' needs
   - **C.** Understanding what motivates employees
   - **D.** Determining how motivating is your job and those of your employees
   - **E.** Rewarding employees: issues of compensation

III. The Manager as Leader: Improving Your Leadership and Power Skills
   - **A.** Assessing your leadership style
   - **B.** Considering whether your leadership style works
   - **C.** Increasing the fit between personal style and work situations
   - **D.** Evaluating how much and what kind of power you have
   - **E.** Improving your power relations

IV. The Manager as Monitor, Disseminator, and Spokesperson: Refining Your Communication Skills

A. Reducing perceptual distortions
B. Building a supportive climate
C. Improving interpersonal communication techniques
  1. Active listening
  2. Checking and clarifying
D. Using transactional analysis
E. Improving written and oral presentations
  1. Judging the audience
  2. Organizing your comments
  3. Running a meeting

V. The Manager as Decision-Maker: Developing Problem-Solving Skills and the Process of Decision-Making
A. Analyzing the situation
B. Setting objectives
C. Generating alternatives
D. Evaluating alternatives
E. Selecting an alternative
F. Implementing the decision

VI. The Manager as Resource Allocator: Delegating Responsibilities and Managing Time
A. Determining when to delegate
B. Improving how and to whom you delegate
C. Using your time wisely
D. Eliminating time wasters

VII. The Manager as Planner and Negotiator: Improving the Planning Process and the Implementation of Plans
A. Comparing planning and decision-making
B. Implementing plans
C. Negotiating: win-lose versus problem-solving orientation
D. Making competition constructive

VIII. The Manager as Change Agent: The Fundamentals of Organizational Structure and Organizational Development
A. Diagnosing and improving the structure of your organization
B. Redesigning jobs and work
C. Adapting and adopting organization development programs: MBO and others

IX. Developing Managerial Careers: Strategies for Career Development and Advancement
A. Assessing your own skills
B. Knowing available job and advancement opportunities
C. Setting personal goals and career objectives
D. Developing a career plan
E. Building career competencies
F. Interfacing work and family
G. Assessing yourself: dealing with reality
H. Negotiating promotions and salary increases

X. The Effective Manager

Step 2: Individually or in small groups, offer a plan for evaluating the effectiveness of this seminar for the Wicket Paint Company.

Step 3: Discussion. In small groups, with the entire class, or in writing, as directed by your instructor, share your evaluation plans. Then answer the following questions:

1. How does each plan measure reactions, learning, behavior, and results?
2. Which plan measures each type of outcome most effectively?
3. Which plan measures each type of outcome least effectively?
4. What are the characteristics of a comprehensive evaluation plan?

Activity 7–6

THE POOR PERFORMER

Step 1: Read The Poor Performer.

Step 2: Prepare the case for class discussion.

By George H. Labovitz, Ph.D., President, Organizational Dynamics, Inc. From "Motivational Dynamics II," pp. 295–296, by Organizational Dynamics, Inc., Burlington, Mass., copyright 1985. Reprinted with permission.

"It's not fair!" said Dave to his supervisor at his third bi-monthly performance review. "I'm working harder than anyone else. I've been in here every weekend for the past three weeks doing work my people don't seem to be able to do, and yet, here I get another lousy performance rating from you. I don't know what to do!"

Recent college graduates are selected each year by the large Metro Hospital to participate in their 12-month administrative training program. The program, created two years ago as a device to provide a continuous flow of administrative talent to the rapidly growing needs of the hospital, is widely known as being rigorous and competitive, providing ground for future hospital management personnel. The program is marked by bi-monthly performance reviews and a final retention review; not everyone who enters the program is retained by the hospital. While the other hospitals in the region are often willing to accept those who fail to make it at Metro, the pressure to remain in the program is intense.

"Unfortunately, Dave, the hospital cannot reward effort alone," said the supervisor solemnly. "We have to face up to the reality of poor performance when it happens. It's simply a matter of results, I'm afraid." The supervisor was holding the computer-generated "score card," which listed the late rates and error rates for the four administrative processing teams.

The rating given Dave during his last review was not good, and Dave knew that subsequent negative reports would pretty much eliminate his chances to get a position at Metro. As a result of his last review, Dave had redoubled his efforts and made great demands on his staff of four to reduce their error rate and to decrease their processing times. This increased pressure drove one person to transfer to another department, and another person had developed into a chronic absentee case. A week prior to this third review, Dave had received a replacement for the transferred clerk.

Dave's supervisor referred to the performance rating sheets in front of him. "Although your initiative remains high, Dave, and I've given you another 8 on that, I simply cannot in all fairness give you more than a 5 on 'quantity of work accomplished' and 'quality of work accomplished.' Your error rates and processing times are still both higher and longer respectively than any of the four processing teams. I'm sure with your abilities you will find a way to do better during this coming rating period. I have to say that if things don't improve, it doesn't look good for you here at Metro."

Step 3: Individually, in small groups, or with the entire class, as directed by your instructor, answer the following questions:

1. What needs is the Metro training program designed to meet?
2. How well does it meet these needs?
3. What changes would you propose?
4. How could human resources professionals improve the effectiveness of the training program?
5. What role is best for the managers at Metro to assume?

Step 4: Discussion. In small groups or with the class as a whole, or in written form, share your answers to the questions above.

SUMMARY

The design and implementation of training and development programs are a four-step process. Managers or human resources professionals should first analyze the environment, organization, job, and individuals as a prerequisite for needs assessment. Second, they should assess needs at three levels—individual, job, and organizational. Third, managers and their subordinates should select the appropriate training program. They must fit it to identified needs and ensure that it will promote learning. Table 7–8 shows the perceived effectiveness of nine training methods for six objectives, according to fifty-four of the training directors at the 200 U.S. firms with the largest number of employees.[33] Finally, human resources professionals or managers must evaluate the outcomes of training programs, assessing reactions, learning, behavior, and results. Figure 7–6 provides a set of questions that can be useful in assessing training.

	Training Objectives											
	Knowledge Acquisition		Changing Attitudes		Problem-Solving Skills		Inter-personal Skills		Participant Acceptance		Knowledge Retention	
Method	*Mean*	*Rank*	*Mean*	*Rank*	*Mean*	*Rank*	*Mean*	*Rank*	*Mean*	*Rank*	*Mean*	*Rank*
Case Study	3.35	4*	2.63	5*	3.89	1*	2.69	5	4.40	1*	3.04	4*
Conference (Discussion) Method	3.72	1*	2.93	3*	2.91	5	2.89	4	3.45	5*	3.26	2*
Lecture (with Questions)	2.57	8*	2.35	7*	2.47	7	1.72	8	2.79	8*	3.15	3*
Business Games	3.27	5	2.75	4*	3.68	2*	2.93	3	3.57	2*	2.98	7*
Movie Films	2.98	6*	2.41	6	2.06	9	2.00	6	3.50	4*	3.00	5*
Programmed Instruction	3.49	3*	2.21	8	2.85	6	1.81	7	2.69	9*	3.87	1*
Role Playing	3.59	2	3.63	2*	3.33	3*	4.06	1*	3.55	3*	3.00	5*
Sensitivity Training (T-Group)	2.74	7	3.65	1*	3.00	4*	3.80	2*	2.86	6*	2.57	9*
Television Lecture	2.43	9*	2.20	9	2.15	8	1.67	9	2.81	7*	2.76	8*

Rating Scale 5 = Highly effective 4 = Quite effective 3 = Moderately effective 2 = Limited effectiveness 1 = Not effective
*Items with asterisk were deemed acceptable for that objective, as judged in a literature review by Watson, (Reference No. 7).
From Evaluating effectiveness of training methods, by J. W. Newstrom. Reprinted from the January, 1980 issue of *Personnel Administrator*, copyright, 1980, The American Society for Personnel Administration, 606 North Washington Street, Alexandria, VA 22314, $30 per year.

Table 7–8 **PERCEIVED EFFECTIVENESS OF NINE TRAINING METHODS FOR SIX OBJECTIVES**

	Are we achieving our expectations? Verification	Are we prescribing the right things? Relevance	How can we do it better or cheaper? Diagnosis
Entry Capability	Do students who undergo the specified pre-training activities and experiences satisfy the prerequisites of the program?	Are the prescribed entry requirements for the program associated with success on the training outcomes?	What pre-training activities or experiences will enable students to quickly attain the requirements for attending the program?
End-of-Course Performance	Do students who satisfy the entry requirements and undergo the prescribed training activities attain the desired training outcomes?	Are the knowledge and skills taught in the program consistent with and supportive of prescribed mastery job performance?	What training activities or entry requirements will enable students to attain the desired training outcomes at the lowest possible cost?
Mastery Job Performance	Do graduates of the program exhibit mastery performance under normal job conditions after a practical period of on-job experience?	Are the behaviors prescribed by mastery job performance associated with success on organizational targets?	What training outcomes or operational actions can improve or expedite the occurrence of mastery job performance?
Organization Performance	Do graduates of the program meet or exceed organizational targets after a practical period of on-job experience?	Are the prescribed organizational targets consistent with and supportive of the mission of the organization?	What job behaviors or controllable environmental conditions can improve or expedite the attainment of organizational targets?

Figure 7–6 EVALUATION QUESTIONS

In this chapter we examined each of these steps. In Resnick Company and Metro Hospital we analyzed training needs and proposed ways of meeting those needs. In the remaining activities we determined whether training was the appropriate solution to organizational problems, determined the training needs of a group of supervisors, designed creative ways of meeting training needs, and evaluated an existing training program. Figure 7–7 summarizes the steps of a results-oriented human resources development model in more detail.

Human resources professionals must recognize that the organization should foster a climate of change and experimentation for a training program to have a long-term impact. They should encourage a multidimensional approach, not a single type of training or a single trainer. They should provide a procedure for

1. Conduct a needs analysis.
2. Identify purposes of evaluation.
3. Establish baseline data.
4. Select evaluation method/design.
5. Determine evaluation strategy.
6. Develop program objectives.
7. Estimate program costs.
8. Prepare and present proposal.
9. Design evaluation instruments.
10. Determine and develop program content.
11. Design or select development methods.
12. Test program and make revisions.
13. Implement or conduct program.
14. Collect data at proper stages.
15. Analyze and interpret data.
16. Make program adjustments.
17. Calculate return on investment.
18. Communicate program results.

Reprinted, by permission of the publisher, from "Training Programs: A Results-Oriented Model for Managing the Development of Human Resources", by J.J. Phillips, PERSONNEL, May-June 1983, p. 13.

Figure 7–7 STEPS IN A RESULTS-ORIENTED HUMAN RESOURCES DEVELOPMENT MODEL

regularly reassessing the training process. To develop their staff, managers should orient new employees, assess their needs and goals, plan developmental strategies, conduct on-the-job training, ensure transfer of learning, provide opportunities to practice new tasks, and offer performance feedback.[34]

ENDNOTES

[1]B.J. Middlebrook and F.M. Rachel, A survey of middle management training and development programs, *Personnel Administrator* 28 (November 1983): 27–31.

[2]T. Peters and R. Waterman, *In Search of Excellence* (New York: Harper & Row, 1982); W. Ouchi, *Theory Z* (Reading, Mass.: Addison-Wesley, 1980).

[3]More cuts in job training, *Washington Post,* 27 September 1983.

[4]'Fortune 500' firm coordinates training, *Training* 21 (February 1984): 56.

[5]W. McGehee and P.W. Thayer, *Training in Business and Industry* (New York: Wiley, 1961).

[6]R.B. McAfee, Using performance appraisals to enhance training programs, *Personnel Administrator* 27 (November 1982): 31–36.

[7]S.B. Wehrenberg, Inside or outside resources: Which are best for training?, *Personnel Journal* 63 (July 1984): 23–24.

[8]*Ibid.*

[9]*Ibid.*

[10]See W.J. Rothwell, Curriculum design in training: An overview, *Personnel Administrator* 28 (November 1983): 53–57, for a discussion of leading theories of learning.

[11]J.J. Scherer, How people learn: Assumptions for design, *Training and Development Journal* 38 (January 1984): 64–65.

[12]Use learner-controlled instruction to strengthen on-the-job training, *Training* 20 (April 1983): 13.

[13]T.L. Kainen, T.M. Begley, and M.J. Maggard, On-the-job training and work unit performance, *Training and Development Journal* 37 (April 1983): 84–87.

[14]P.B. Guild, How to involve the learner in your lectures, *Training* 20 (April 1983): 43–45.

[15]D.D. Simmons, *Notes on the Case Study* (Cranfield, England: Case Clearing House, 1974).

[16]*Ibid.*

[17]J.R. Eldridge and W.A. Boyd, Jr., Something old, something new: Trainers and computer-based learning, *Training and Development Journal* 37 (December 1983): 57–61.

[18]S.D. Truskie, Guidelines for conducting in-house management development, *Personnel Administrator* 38 (August 1984): 32–37.

[19]Competency-based training vs. criterion-referenced instruction: What's the difference?, *Training* 21 (March 1984): 81.

[20]*Ibid.*

[21]See E.H. Schein, Organizational socialization and the profession of management, *Sloan Management Review* 9 (1968): 1–16; J. Van Maanen, People processing: Strategies of organizational socialization, *Organizational Dynamics* 7 (1978): 57–77.

[22]See Schein, *op. cit.*

[23]Make training new employees a joint responsibility, *Training* 20 (February 1983): 69–70.

[24]D.L. Kirkpatrick, Four steps to measuring training effectiveness, *Personnel Administrator* 28 (November 1983): 19–25.

[25]*Ibid.*, p. 19.

[26]B. Mezoff, Six more benefits of pre-testing trainees, *Training* 20 (August 1983): 45–47.

[27]McAfee, *op. cit.*, p. 33.

[28]J.M. McCullough, To measure a vacuum, *Training and Development Journal* 38 (June 1984): 68–70.

[29]Kirkpatrick, *op. cit.*

[30]A.I. Kelley, R.F. Orgel, and D.M. Baer, Evaluation: The bottom line is closer than you think, *Training and Development Journal* 38 (August 1984): 32–37.

[31]*Ibid.*

[32]M.T. Garen and J. Daniel, Construct a training quality control system, *Personnel Administrator* 28 (November 1983): 33–38, 79.

[33]J.W. Newstrom, Evaluating the effectiveness of training methods, *Personnel Administrator* 25 (January 1980): 58.

[34]T.E. Zorn, Jr., A roadmap for managers as developers, *Training and Development Journal* 38 (July 1984): 71–73.

FURTHER READINGS

Connor, J.J. *On-the-job Training*. Boston: International Human Resources Development Corp., 1983.

Craig, R.L., ed. *Training and Development Handbook*. New York: McGraw-Hill, 1976.

Donaldson, L., and Scannell, E.E. *Human Resource Development—The New Trainer's Guide*. Reading, Mass.: Addison-Wesley, 1978.

Goldstein, I.L. Training in work organizations. *Annual Review of Psychology* 31 (1980): 229–272.

Moore, M.L., and Dutton, P. Training needs analysis: Review and critiqie. *Academy of Management Review 3* (1978): 532–545.

Phillips, J. *Handbook of Training Evaluation and Measurement Methods*. Houston, Tex.: Gulf Publishing, 1983.

Stockard, J.G. *Career Development and Job Training*. New York: AMACOM, 1977.

Varney, G.H. *An Organization Development Approach to Management Development*. Reading, Mass.: Addison-Wesley, 1976.

CHAPTER 8

Improving Career Management

CHAPTER OUTLINE

LEARNING CHECKPOINTS

After completing the reading and activities in this chapter, students will be able to

- identify the components of a career management system;
- specify the ways of preparing for career management;
- discuss individual and organizational contributions to individual career management;
- offer ways of gathering data for individual self-assessment;
- specify the stages of career development and the issues associated with each stage;
- describe at least one organizational career development program;
- show the significance of mentoring to individual and organizational career development and performance;
- describe the interaction of biological, career, and family life cycles;
- discuss the issues faced by dual career families and their implications for organizations;
- design a comprehensive career management system.

INTRODUCTION

Sam Conklin had just completed his second year as an employee at the Columbus Reserve Bank; he had worked there as a computer analyst since receiving his degree in electrical engineering from the Cleveland Technical Institute. Sam had significant responsibility for the development of state-of-the-art computer systems for the bank. When asked about his job, Sam said, "What I like best is becoming immersed in a computer system—its complexities and its beauties." Nothing seemed to please him more than working forty-eight hours without a break to perfect part of the system.

His supervisor, Warren Wyatt, gave Sam extremely positive performance ratings. During the previous two years Conklin had received three pay increases and had moved up three job grades. As much as he liked his job, Sam found his most recent conversation with Wyatt extremely disappointing. Wyatt had informed him that he could not continue giving Sam pay raises unless he assumed significant supervisory responsibilities. Sam threatened to quit if he were required to become a supervisor. Two months later Wyatt changed Sam's job description to include less time for technical system development and more time for overseeing other analysts' work on the system. Two weeks later Sam resigned.

What caused Sam's resignation? Although ineffective selection, training and development, compensation, or performance appraisal may have contributed to this situation, we can trace the problem more directly to deficiencies in career management by both Sam and the bank. Sam did not adequately assess the job opportunities in the bank. And the bank's management failed to provide career paths for talented, technically-oriented employees like Sam.

A *career* has alternatively been defined as a set of attitudes and behaviors associated with work and accumulated role-related experiences over time[1]; a sequence of work-related positions occupied throughout a person's life[2]; or a sequence of positions defined by an organization.[3] Career management refers to the orchestration of these experiences to result in a meaningful set of jobs that meet individuals' and organizations' needs. Organizations have increasingly moved from a top-down, traditional model of career control by organizations to one in which individuals participate equally in their own career development.[4] In this chapter we examine this more contemporary view of career management, from both individual and organizational perspectives.

We begin with the first step in career management—performing a situational analysis. Second, we trace the stages of a career. Third, we look at individual career management. Here an employee must assess his or her own goals and needs, evaluate how well existing and potential opportunities meet these needs, and make career decisions. Fourth, we view career management from the organization's perspective, examining career planning programs and activities, discussing mentoring for employees, and looking at the development of diverse and effective career paths. Fifth, we address the interaction between work, family, and leisure. We conclude the chapter by summarizing the components of an effective career management system.

ANALYZING THE CONTEXT OF CAREER MANAGEMENT

Effective career management does not occur spontaneously or in a vacuum. Rather, it begins with a careful assessment of the situation in which the career occurs as well as a recognition that employees, managers, and human resources professionals must take deliberate planning steps.

Environmental, organizational, and job characteristics all affect diverse aspects of career management, including the extent to which organizations support and fund individual career planning, the range of job opportunities inside and outside an organization, the types of career paths available, and the way work and family obligations interact.

The Environment

A changing, complex, and unpredictable environment creates unique dilemmas for individual and organizational career management. Individuals must continually prepare themselves for job and career changes; they must find ways to refine their present skills and develop new knowledge and skills to ensure their marketability. Organizations must constantly reevaluate the typical job sequences that they offer different kinds of employees. Individuals and organizations must monitor the environment to recognize changing work roles. Then they must seek ways to adapt to these changes. Career management must be proactive rather than reactive. Human resources professionals, managers, and other workers must actively seek ways to prepare for future work roles so they can adapt to the new requirements of our dynamic environment.

The Organization

An organization's resources, climate, goals, and structure influence its career management system. Financial resources are needed, for example, to conduct career workshops; time resources are required to involve employees and managers in career planning activities; and human resources are needed for counseling, mentoring, or pathing activities.

Some organizations create a climate that encourages comprehensive career management. An example would be an organization that introduces a performance appraisal system emphasizing development, as described in Chapter 6. In such a one, top management might reward managers for how well they develop their subordinates. The human resources management department might support further education by offering tuition reimbursement or other training and development programs. The extent to which organizations are employee-centered—that is, their primary emphasis is employee satisfaction and development—or product-centered—that is, their focus is on maximizing profitability or revenues, developing products, or encouraging worker productivity—contributes to the emphasis on career planning and development.

An organization with goals of flexibility and adaptability requires more career management than one that expects to remain stable. Thus many high technology organizations emphasize career management. As organizations shift their goals to respond to a dynamic, unpredictable environment, they frequently introduce programs for employee self-assessment, development of alternative career paths, and cross-training of workers. Unions in the automobile industry, for example, have required manufacturers to institute cross-training and career management programs.[5]

The allocation of responsibility for career management to different levels or departments in the organization's hierarchy influences managers' and employees' perceptions of its importance. The extent and formality of career management in the organization is often greater when human resources professionals are responsible for its introduction and implementation. Making middle and lower management accountable for their subordinates' career management often extends the value attached to career management programs throughout the organization.

The Job

The environment and the organization provide the context for career management, but the job is the ultimate focus of many career management activities. Managers and human resources professionals can institute career management programs that help individual career planning by informing employees about the number and nature of existing or future jobs. Regular analysis of jobs is a prerequisite for updating organizational components of career management systems, such as the development of career paths or use of career tracking systems. The situational audit and knowledge of available jobs by employees, managers, and human resources professionals is the first step in determining career strategies.

Career management must consider the stages through which careers pass, as well as characteristics of the situation, to ensure that planning by individuals and organizations is effective. In the next section we examine these stages in detail.

CAREER DEVELOPMENT

Recent research has indicated that careers pass through a series of relatively predictable stages, beginning with early exploration and investigation of career opportunities and ending with post-retirement.[6] Career planning must take into account the different issues and tasks individuals face at each of these stages.

Table 8–1 illustrates three career stage schemas. The early stages focus on investigating and choosing a career, followed by career entry and becoming a

Age	Super	Schein	Miller and Form
0			
5		Growth, Fantasy	Preparatory
10	Growth	Exploration	Pre-work
15			
20	Exploration	Entry into work	Initial work period
25		world/training	
30		Full membership:	Trial work period
		early career	
35	Establishment	Midcareer	
40		Midcareer crisis	
45			Stable work period
50		Late career/	
55	Maintenance	decline and	
60		disengagement	
65			
70	Decline	Retirement	Retirement

SOURCES: See D. Super, *The Psychology of Careers* (New York: Harper and Row, 1957); D.C. Miller and W.H. Form, *Industrial Sociology* (New York: Harper, 1951); E.H. Schein, *Career Dynamics* (Reading, Mass.: Addison-Wesley, 1978).

Table 8–1 EXAMPLES OF CAREER STAGES

bona fide member of an organization. In the middle career stage individuals stabilize their work experience by performing well or becoming a mentor; here many also experience midcareer insecurity. Late career includes stardom, renewal, and pre-retirement concerns. Table 8–2 lists these stages and the issues or tasks associated with each. Consider again Sam Conklin; what career stage is he experiencing? In this section we examine the early, middle, and late career stages in turn.

Early Career

While organizations provide internships or summer employment opportunities so that individuals can experiment with different career options, and individuals may test different occupational options through courses in college or even high school, the key human resources management concerns begin when an individual enters the organization. Managers and human resources professionals, as well as the employees themselves, must ensure that individuals effectively move through the organization. The challenge of a first job, and the nature of supervision on that job, contribute significantly to individuals' later career development.[7]

Employees go through three stages when they enter an organization.[8] During the *getting-in* phase the employee tries to get a realistic picture of the organization and find the job that best fits his or her skills, experiences, preferences, and interests. During the *breaking-in* phase the employee tries to become an accepted participant in a work group; he or she establishes relationships with peers and supervisors, demonstrates competence, and defines his or her role. Finally, as

Stages	Issues	Specific Tasks
Growth, fantasy, exploration	Developing a basis for making realistic vocational choices Obtaining education or training	Developing and discovering one's own needs and interests Getting maximum career information
Entry into world of work	Becoming a member of an organization or occupation	Learning how to look for and secure a job
Basic training	Becoming an effective member quickly	Overcoming the insecurity of inexperience Learning to get along with boss and coworkers
Full membership in early career	Accepting the responsibility and discharging duties Developing and displaying special skills	Performing effectively Accepting subordinate status Developing initiative and realistic expectations
Full membership, midcareer	Choosing a specialty Remaining technically competent Establishing a clear identity	Gaining a measure of independence Assessing own motives, talents Assessing organizational and occupational opportunities
Midcareer crisis	Reassessing own progress relative to ambitions Deciding relative importance of work and family	Becoming aware of career anchor Making specific choices about the present and future
Late career in nonleadership role	Becoming a mentor Broadening interests Deepening skills	Remaining technically competent Developing interpersonal skills Dealing with younger persons
Late career in leadership role	Using skills and talents for organization's welfare Selecting and developing subordinates	Becoming more responsible for organization Handling power Balancing career and family
Decline and disengagement	Learning to accept reduced power and responsibility	Finding new sources of satisfaction
Retirement	Adjusting to more drastic life style changes	Maintaining a sense of identity and self-worth without job

Table 8–2 STAGES, ISSUES, AND TASKS OF THE CAREER CYCLE

part of the *settling-in* phase the employee resolves conflicts outside work life as well as conflicting demands within the job. Here the job holder clarifies the interaction of work demands with family demands and prioritizes job responsibilities and activities.

The early career does not always proceed smoothly. Individuals commonly experience the following problems:

1. Early frustration and dissatisfaction due to expectations that are not met by reality

2. An incompetent first supervisor
3. Insensitivity to the political aspects of the organization
4. Passivity and failure to monitor the internal and external environments
5. Ignorance of the real criteria for evaluating performance of new hires or those in early career
6. Tension between younger and older professionals and managers due to different experiences, needs, or interests
7. Uncertainty about the type and limits of loyalty required by the organization
8. Anxiety about integrity, commitment, and dependence
9. Ethical dilemmas[9]

Figure 8–1 offers advice for avoiding these problems.

Middle Career

Having resolved the problems of early career, individuals next move into a period of stabilization where they are viewed as productive, become increasingly visible, accept higher levels of responsibility, and implement a more long-range career plan.[10] Establishment and advancement characterize this stage. It "often involves new experiences such as special assignments, further transfers and promotions, offers from other organizations, chances for visibility at higher organizational levels, and establishing one's value to the organization. . . . This is also a period of establishing oneself as a professional and developing a level of expertise that is valuable to the organization and contributes to self-worth."[11]

Halfway through this stage many individuals experience a midcareer transition or change, which becomes a midcareer crisis for some.[12] In this stage the individual

1. Be a good performer—know the criteria by which good performance is judged and meet those criteria.
2. Take responsibility for managing your own career.
3. Find a superior who is advancing in the organization; encourage him or her to act as your mentor.
4. Try to complement your superior; develop significant skills that he or she lacks.
5. Learn your job; and develop your own subordinates so that you have a replacement when advancement opportunities occur.
6. Be visible in the organization.
7. Ask for available positions you feel would enhance your career; do not wait for others to nominate you.
8. Frequently assess your own strengths and weaknesses; be sure you have the competence to fill any position you are asked to hold.
9. Test the boundaries of your job description; try to act creatively in accomplishing your tasks.
10. Find ways of coping with any ethical dilemmas you face; periodically reexamine your personal values and their influence on your job performance.

R.A. Webber, Career problems of young managers. © 1976 by the Regents of the University of California. Adapted from *California Management Review*, Volume XVIII, no. 4, pp. 19 to 33 by permission of the Regents and the author.

Figure 8–1 ADVICE ON CAREER MANAGEMENT

reassesses his or her accomplishments to date, and the likelihood of attaining personal career and life goals in the future. Positive factors, such as rethinking of career decisions, search for financial security, continued education, or early retirement; or negative factors, such as boredom, restlessness, depression, conflict between work and life stage, deterioration of the organizational climate, unused knowledge, skills, or ideas, and changing work-force requirements, can prompt changes at midcareer.[13] The plateaued and obsolete performers (described in Chapter 5) frequently experience difficulties at midcareer. Situational analysis and self-assessment, examination of alternatives, goal-setting, and planning can help individuals cope with this career stage.[14]

Late Career

A return to productivity, or decline and early retirement, may follow a midcareer crisis. Productive individuals may assume senior staff or top management roles, or they may continue as contributors in nonleadership roles. In this stage individuals must clarify for themselves and other organizational members the precise role they want to play in the organization.

Ultimately, they begin to disengage from work and prepare for retirement. Training successors, reducing their work load, or shifting responsibilities to less senior employees may precede retirement.

In one career development schema for professionals, these three stages have been elaborated into four, as shown in Table 8–3. Employees evaluated as effective and productive move through their career from helping and learning at the beginning, through contributing independently in the next part of their career, to training and interfacing at midcareer, to shaping the organization's direction at the end of their career.[15] Individual career management focuses on different concerns depending on the employee's stage of development, as described in the next section.

INDIVIDUAL CAREER MANAGEMENT

Individuals plan their careers to increase their status and salary, ensure job security, and maintain their marketability in a changing employment market. Organizations encourage individual career management because they want to (1) develop and promote employees from within, (2) reduce a shortage of promotable talent, (3) express interest in their employees, (4) improve productivity, (5) meet affirmative action program commitments, (6) reduce turnover, (7) allow managers to express personal interest in subordinates, and (8) create a positive recruiting image.[16]

Career planning by individuals includes

1. self-assessment to determine strengths, weaknesses, goals, aspirations, preferences, needs, or anchors;

	Stage I	Stage II	Stage III	Stage IV
central activity	helping learning following directions	independent contributor	training interfacing	shaping the direction of the organization
primary relationship	apprentice	colleague	mentor	sponsor
major psychological issues	dependence	independence	assuming responsibility for others	exercising power

SOURCE: Reprinted, by permission of the publisher, from "The Four Stages of Professional Careers: A New Look at Performance by Professionals," by G.W. Dalton, P.H. Thompson and R.L. Price, ORGANIZATIONAL DYNAMICS, Summer, 1977, p. 23.

Table 8–3 STAGES OF PROFESSIONAL CAREERS

2. assessment of the job market to determine the types of opportunities available both within the organization and external to it;
3. formulation of career goals based on these evaluations;
4. matching of opportunities to needs and goals and development of a career strategy; and
5. planning for career transitions.

Self-Assessment

A regular evaluation of personal strengths and weaknesses provides a foundation for career planning. Self-assessment means taking an inventory of skills, interests, experiences, personality traits, and other personal characteristics.

Self-assessment helps identify job options, training and development needs, and career goals. It provides information for determining (1) the jobs and positions to seek or avoid, (2) the strategy to use in securing a certain job, (3) which job to select from among alternative offers, (4) which assignments and transfers to accept, and (5) the sequence of job changes that help attain a preferred job.

Determining Career Anchors. Self-assessment can first focus on identifying career anchors, which are "a syndrome of motives, values, and self-perceived competencies which function to guide and constrain an individual's career."[17] (See Figure 8–2 for a list of possible career anchors.) Individuals function best when their jobs fit with their career anchors. For example, the individual with technical-functional competence as a career anchor organizes his or her career around the actual work; thus this person should seek positions that emphasize work in a technical or functional area, such as marketing researcher, financial analyst, or systems programmer.

The career anchor model is designed to guide people in contemplating career changes and to assist organizations in helping individuals plan their careers.[18] An individual with a technical-functional competence anchor would typically fit

1. Managerial Competence. Individuals with this anchor wish to demonstrate (a) interpersonal competence or the ability to influence, supervise, lead, manipulate, and control people toward the most effective achievement of organizational goals; (b) analytical competence or the ability to identify, analyze, and solve complex conceptual problems under conditions of uncertainty and incomplete information; and (c) emotional stability or the capacity to be stimulated by emotional and interpersonal crises rather than becoming exhausted or debilitated by them.

2. Technical-Functional Competence. Individuals with this anchor organize their career around the challenge of the actual work they are doing; it is the technical or functional area and the analytical work that "turns on" this individual.

3. Security. Individuals with this anchor tie their careers to a particular organization as a way of stabilizing and ensuring career security.

4. Creativity. Individuals with this anchor express a strong need to create something of their own.

5. Autonomy and Independence. Individuals with this anchor are concerned about their sense of freedom and autonomy.

6. Service. Individuals with this anchor are concerned with helping others or working on an important cause.

7. Identity. Individuals with this anchor emphasize status and title in their careers; they value the prestige that accrues to a particular job or career.

8. Variety. Individuals with this anchor want an endless variety of challenges; they are motivated by being able to use their talents in a number of different ways.

Based on E.H. Schein, *Career Dynamics* (Reading, Mass.: Addison-Wesley, 1978) and T.J. DeLong, Reexamining the career anchor model, *Personnel* 59 (May–June 1982): 50.

Figure 8–2 POSSIBLE CAREER ANCHORS

better with a series of technically-focused jobs than would an individual with a managerial competence career anchor. Lack of fit between anchor and job can cause people to leave an organization or "turn off" to work altogether. Thus individuals and organizations should both identify employees' career anchors; and organizations should provide a range of opportunities for individuals with different anchors.

Steps in Self-Assessment. More generally, self-assessment should involve the following three steps. First, the individual should collect extensive information about himself or herself from multiple sources. Figure 8–3 provides an example of self-assessment exercises. The individual can write an autobiography, complete one of the interest profiles listed in Figure 8–4, list skills and significant experiences, or interview peers about their perceptions of him or her. In a program titled "Self-Motivated Career Planning" individuals complete a series of exercises requiring a reconstruction of their personal history as a way of assessing and understanding their career progress.[19] There are many approaches and aids to self-assessment, but they all have one thing in common: participants must collect and analyze extensive data about themselves.[20]

Next the individual should analyze these data, looking for common themes. Through analysis the data may suggest a personal preference for and skill in

1. Take ten sheets of paper. Write on the top of each one the words: Who am I?
2. Then write, on each sheet, one answer to that question. At the end of the ten sheets, you'll have the same question written, but ten different answers.
3. Now go back over the ten again, and looking at each answer, write below it on the sheet what turns you on about that particular answer.
4. Now go back over the ten sheets, and arrange them in order of priority. Your most important identity goes on top. Then, in order, on down to the identity that is to you of least importance among the ten.
5. Finally, go back over the ten sheets, looking particularly at the answer you wrote (on each page) to What turns you on? and see if there are some common denominators.
6. If so, you have begun to put your finger on some things that your career (calling, vocation, job or whatever) must use if you are to be truly happy, fulfilled, used and effective—to the height of your powers.

From R.N. Bolles, *What Color Is Your Parachute? A Practical Manual for Job-Hunters and Career Changers*, 1985 Revised Edition, by Richard N. Bolles. Used with permission of the author and Ten Speed Press, Box 7123, Berkeley, CA 94707.

Figure 8–3 SAMPLE OF SELF-ASSESSMENT EXERCISES

dealing with people; or they may reflect a strong technical orientation. Analysis "starts by focusing on specifics (information generated by various devices) and from that slowly develops generalizations (themes). It involves sifting through large amounts of information looking for clues, drawing tentative conclusions, and then testing these conclusions against still more data."[21]

Finally, after verifying the analysis, the individual should draw implications for career decision-making from the themes. For example, an individual with strong interpersonal skills and interests would be a more appropriate candidate for a

Allport Vernon Lindzey Study of Values
Houghton Mifflin
Boston, MA

California Psychological Inventory
Consulting Psychologists Press
Palo Alto, CA

Career Development Inventory
Consulting Psychologists Press
Palo Alto, CA

Edwards Personal Preference Scale
The Psychological Corporation
New York, NY

Personal Career Development Profile
The Institute for Personality and Ability Testing
Savoy, IL

Self-Directed Search
Consulting Psychologists Press
Palo Alto, CA

Self-Motivated Career Planning
The Institute for Personality and Ability Testing
Savoy, IL

Strong Vocational Interest Blank
Stanford University Press
Stanford, CA

Vocational Preference Inventory
Psychological Assessment Resources
Odessa, FL

Wide Range Interest Opinion Test
Psychological Assessment Resources
Odessa, FL

Figure 8–4 STANDARDIZED INSTRUMENTS FOR SELF-ASSESSMENT

sales or managerial career than would a person lacking these skills. Repeated self-assessment should help the individual monitor any changes in personal characteristics.

Self-assessment offers four major benefits: "(1) It allows identifying strengths and weaknesses which help establish realistic career objectives. (2) It provides an information base from which to present oneself on a resume and in job interviews. (3) It provides a framework for generating questions to be answered in the career exploration process. (4) It suggests compatible and incompatible work roles."[22]

The Career Assessment Program developed at the Naval Underwater Systems Center is an example of a comprehensive approach to self-assessment for lower level employees.[23] This program includes inventories of abilities and interests, bibliographies, occupational information that employees use independently and at their own pace, and four hours of a career counselor's time for assistance. Employees use the program to test out career plans and goals. As a result of participating in the program individuals either make tentative career plans or have confidence that they should implement their existing plans.

Assessment of the Job Market

As part of individual career management employees must continually monitor the job market. Company bulletins, recruiting literature, annual reports, listings from the Department of Labor, placement bulletins, professional newsletters, trade publications, newspaper articles, and other publications describe available jobs.

Individuals can also conduct informational interviews to learn about job opportunities. In these interviews individuals meet with current job holders to learn about the job and related career paths.[24] These interviews might include questions such as "What is a typical day on the job like?"; "What has been your career path?"; "What do I have to do to get a job like yours?" Additional sources of information include friends and family; people in industry and professions (members of alumni groups, trade associations, and professional societies); social, religious, and political organizations (Kiwanis, Rotary, or church groups); and people with contacts (bankers, physicians, lawyers, or accountants).[25]

Formulating Career Goals

Based on self-assessment and analysis of available jobs and careers, an individual should then formulate specific career goals. These should focus subsequent career activities. Establishing career objectives means knowing "(1) the work related activities one is seeking, (2) the social and political aspects of the position, (3) the demands the position will place on one's personal time and family, and (4) the series of possible positions which would prepare one to perform effectively."[26]

An individual who aspires to be a plant foreman, for example, should know the job's content, the organizational constraints on that particular position, the amount of overtime required, and jobs that should be held before reaching the foreman position. He or she can then establish goals about the nature and timing of specific job steps, the development of informal contacts, and the acquisition of interpersonal, technical, and other skills required for the position.

Matching Individuals to Jobs

In the short term, individuals must check that a specific job opportunity fits with the individual's needs and goals. In the longer run a person should ensure that his or her career is on track by planning career moves and then assessing whether personal objectives have been met at each step. Such objectives might include specific jobs, salaries, supervisory responsibilities, or job tasks; or might be more general goals such as increased responsibility, more diverse job content, or greater power and centrality in the organization. How effectively has Sam Conklin matched his own needs to job opportunities at the bank? To what career planning activities should he devote more time? How could the Columbus Reserve Bank have helped Sam's career management?

For years, individuals and organizations operated in a relatively ad hoc manner with regard to career development. Adages such as "All good things come to those who work long hours"; "All good things come to those who perform well"; and "it's important to keep your home life and work life separated" guided career development. But managers and other employees now view these and other principles as myths.[27] According to many human resources professionals, consultants, and researchers, only active career management leads to individual success.[28]

An effective career strategy from an individual's perspective generally has

1. flexibility—the individual can adjust career direction in response to shifting goals or changing resources;
2. purposeful orientation—the individual feels he or she is developing along a long-term career path;
3. activity orientation—the individual translates his or her goal or purpose into a plan of action;
4. role orientation—the individual focuses on holding a particular role, independent of the activities or purpose involved;
5. future orientation—the individual takes a long-range perspective;
6. willingness to take risks—the individual is willing to commit personal resources for a long enough time to reach an objective;
7. ability to resolve conflict—the individual can reconcile multiple dimensions of a career that conflict;
8. reality orientation—the individual develops plans based on reality; he or she is involved with people in positions of responsibility, learns different ways of fulfilling needs, and uses experiences as the basis of self-assessment;
9. broad perspective of work—the individual recognizes that career does not take place in isolation from the organization, family, and self;

10. tolerance for ambiguity—the individual can accept some uncertainty in his or her career development;

11. clarity and specificity—the individual establishes clear and specific activities and objectives, particularly in the short-run.[29]

Planning for Career Transitions

"Transitions may result in a change of job or profession, or a change in one's orientation to work while continuing the same job."[30] A career transition is "the period during which an individual is either changing roles . . . or changing orientation to the role already held."[31] Both individuals and organizations must plan for such transitions. Individuals, for example, must find ways to regularly test their expectations about the nature of future roles they might hold. They must also learn the organization's expectations of their performance in roles other than their current ones. In addition, they must perform the following transition tasks effectively: (1) learning the basics of the job, (2) building a clear role identity, (3) building relationships with relevant others for the position held, (4) constructing new frames of reference that fit with the new role, (5) identifying relevant individuals and their interactions with the new role, (6) locating oneself in task or social networks, (7) learning the special language of the new role, and (8) assessing how well the job is being done and the general performance of the new unit.[32]

As organizational representatives, human resources professionals can conduct workshops that help support such transitions. They can also help individuals analyze the transition situation by sharing with them the characteristics of typical transitions, and by helping individuals to identify their preferences for and attitudes toward transitions.[33] Executives can create a climate that eases movement among roles, by encouraging job rotation programs or funding sufficient orientation and training for new job holders. They can also provide supports for the ambiguities and dilemmas of the transition period by clarifying their expectations of new job holders and providing them with enough information to understand the job, organization, and players in the new situation.

ORGANIZATIONAL CAREER MANAGEMENT

Career management programs include counseling employees; tracking jobs, skills, and other relevant experiences of workers; offering workshops in career and life planning; emphasizing developmental performance appraisal (as described in Chapter 6); and conducting assessment centers (as described in Chapter 4). Table 8–4 summarizes various career planning activities and their likely contribution to meeting organizational career management objectives. These activities focus on (1) assisting individual career planning; (2) providing mentors to help individuals effectively move through the organization; and (3) developing diverse job

Activity	Potential Advantages	Potential Shortcomings	Probable Impact on Psychological Success and Identity Integration
Individual Activities			
1. Personal planning with possible aid of self-help materials.	a. For persons with strong motivation and adequate sources of information, may be adequate for goal setting. b. Cost is minimal.	a. Most people need interpersonal feedback to develop a complete and accurate self-evaluation. b. No built-in mechanism for checking completeness of information on occupational opportunities or for correcting distorted views of self. c. No opportunity to explore new occupational possibilities.	Considerable potential contribution because individual sets own goals. Actual contribution likely to be minimized, however, because the activity lacks mechanisms for exploration of new potentials, interpersonal feedback, and social support to maintain motivation.
Counselor-Client Activities			
2. Testing Approach: Guidance counselor administers vocational interest and aptitude tests and feeds data back to client—may also provide information on occupations, job market, and job-hunting techniques.	Test results and information supplied may be of considerable value for client.	a. Usually expensive. b. Client has no way of testing validity of counselor's views or test results. c. Interpersonal feedback likely to be minimal.	Since people do not readily accept disconfirming data in situations where there is no opportunity to validate the information, contribution may be relatively limited.
3. Counselor Approach: Emphasis on interpersonal exploration of client's needs with counselor.	Skillful counselor may provide valuable input for self-assessment.	a. No mechanism for checking validity of counselor's perceptions. b. Most helpful in exploring personal needs; minimal stress on occupational information. c. Usually expensive.	Potentially helpful, subject to the limitations that client must experience insights produced as valid and must check validity with other persons outside of the counseling situation.
4. Combination Testing and Clinical Approach.	a. Combines benefits of both Testing and Counseling Approaches. b. Checking test results against perceptions of counselor provides some mechanism for "validating" information.	a. Potentially very expensive. b. Most counselors are not equally proficient in both approaches. c. Counselor may experience a need to see client in a manner consistent with test results.	Essentially the same as for #3.
Boss as Counselor or Coach			
5. Superior regularly or periodically assesses	a. Superior may have an excellent opportunity to	a. The superior's power can be highly threatening, causing	a. If done as a part of performance appraisal, depends on format.

Table 8–4 CHARACTERISTICS OF VARIOUS CAREER PLANNING ACTIVITIES AND PROBABLE CONTRIBUTION TO CAREER SUCCESS

Continued

Activity	Potential Advantages	Potential Shortcomings	Probable Impact on Psychological Success and Identity Integration
subordinate's performance and provides feedback and suggestions for improving performance and/or career opportunities.	observe subordinate's behavior in a number of work activities. b. Superior knows career opportunities within the organization. c. Superior can provide assignments to expand subordinate's capabilities.	subordinate to be defensive, cautious, and closed to feedback. b. Superior's first loyalty is likely to be seen as to the interests of the organization, not subordinate. c. Not likely to integrate nonwork aspects of subordinate's life with career issues.	Traditional performance appraisal unlikely to be productive. MBO with substantial self-evaluation by subordinate may be helpful, since subordinate sets own goals, etc., and takes lead in assessment. b. If done as informal coaching, can be very effective to the extent that superior provides relatively nondirective assistance which maximizes subordinate's freedom to choose.
Group Activities			
6. Assessment Center: Usually conducted by or sponsored by employer. Employee is tested by a number of pencil and paper tests and is presented with situational tests and interviews where performance is observed and evaluated. Evaluators are often other managers trained in the technique. Psychologists design Center and interpret test results.	a. Substantial amounts of data can be developed quickly. b. Multiple judges on panel and results of several tests provide variety of perspectives for candidate. c. Moderate cost—usually borne by employer. d. Some evidence for more valid predictions than available through counselor-client approaches.	a. High threat situation: 1. Employee likely to feel "on the spot" and anxious about results—not an optimal situation for feedback. 2. Center serves interests of employer first, which may be incompatible with interests of employee. b. Primary emphasis is not on setting personal goals. c. Data generated primarily applicable to career with employing organization only. d. Interpersonal feedback frequently not a prime or major objective. e. Does not provide information on other job possibilities especially outside of employing organization.	a. Likely to be minimized to the extent that employee: • Cannot really choose not to attend. • Is not involved in design of activities. • Is threatened by long-term career implications of evaluation. • Receives minimal or threatening feedback. b. No explicit provision for goal-setting. c. No support group for planning or dealing with career crises.

Table 8–4 Continued

sequences, or career paths, for employees. We discuss programs in these three areas in the next sections.

Programs and Activities to Assist Individual Career Planning

Organizations use a variety of approaches to help individuals plan their careers. A major organizational effort in individual career management has been the design and implementation of individual career planning programs. These programs help individuals assess their own skills, learn about job opportunities inside and outside the organization, and fit the individual to the available job. Many provide counseling, workshops, and other self-assessment programs.

The First National Bank of Kansas City introduced a career development program designed to help employees define their career goals and better understand the options at the bank.[34] The program includes four phases, each with one to four seminars. Phase I—Awareness—is an orientation to career development, as well as presentations about the stages of adult development. Phase II—Understanding—includes self-assessment activities such as completion of personality inventories and values clarification exercises, testing for career interests, and skill mapping, and introduction to careers at the bank. Phase III—Information—tells participants how to find and use career information. Phase IV—Action—concludes the program by integrating all materials into an action plan.

Other companies have introduced activities that respond to varying issues individuals face at different career stages. At the early career stage the organization must provide the employee with opportunities to work with a supervisor who can act as a role model and give the new employee chances to learn. Careful monitoring of the supervisor-supervisee relationship, regular scheduling of appraisal conferences, and provision of unique opportunities through job rotation, apprenticeships, or careful job placement, can aid in movement through this first stage. Periodic career planning and career counseling should help employees crystalize their career direction. To help new hires, for example, organizations must match them to effective supervisors, provide strong orientation and on-the-job training, assign them to organizational sponsors, and provide clear career paths.

Figure 8–5 summarizes the activities an organization can implement at this career stage. A project designed to enhance the work experience of entry-level professionals at General Electric encouraged the provision of challenging work, described and supported effective coaching, and identified the organizational barriers to providing challenging first assignments.[35] For example, managers and human resources professionals audited job content, utilization of skills, worker involvement, outcomes, and the interfaces among organizational positions and members to ensure that the first assignment was stimulating. In addition, managers structured formal discussions about orientation, initial assignments, work plans, career planning, and performance; they instituted informal contacts for new workers and provided broadening experiences for them through temporary

Stage 1: Getting In

Give prospective employees information not only on particular job duties, but also on the work group, and promotion and transfer opportunities.

Design selection and placement programs that make realistic assumptions about the relationships between personal characteristics and job performance, consider needs of job applicants, and allow for flexible career paths.

Stage 2: Breaking In

Design orientation programs that allow new recruits to meet the rest of the staff, involve them with both social and technical skills, provide time for informal task learning, and keep them out of interpersonal or intergroup conflicts.

Structure a program that provides training for job-relevant skills, provides frequent feedback, and integrates formal and informal training.

Provide a performance evaluation system that allows face-to-face meetings between supervisor and subordinates, has objective performance criteria, and trains supervisors to give feedback effectively.

Use the addition of new work group members as an opportunity to reallocate tasks more effectively and redesign work projects.

Stage 3: Settling In

Provide counseling for employees to help them deal with work and home conflicts.

Be as flexible as possible in scheduling work for employees with particularly difficult conflicts outside of work and particularly bad conflicts at work.

Recognize and deal with structural or interpersonal problems that generate conflicts at work.

Adapted, by permission of the publisher, from "Reexamining the Career Anchor Model", by T.J. DeLong, PERSONNEL, May-June 1982, pp. 56–7

Figure 8–5 WAYS OF INCREASING THE EFFECTIVENESS OF SOCIALIZATION

assignments or job rotation. Finally, they noted that for the career development process to work effectively organizational members had to confront the risk associated with assigning important work to a new employee, the time pressures on managers, business factors such as competition or new technology, the length and timing of training assignments, the reactions of experienced employees, the shortcomings of program administration, and the unrealistic expectations of new workers.

In the middle career stage, the organization should provide opportunities for independent contributions by their employees. To do this, human resources professionals and managers can identify the expertise of each person and match it to organizational requirements and activities. The organization should have a system for periodically evaluating the individual's strengths and weaknesses and his or her placement in the organization. For example, at Southern Railway, one career development program prepared managers for key vacancies by having department heads select candidates early, identify their developmental needs for a two year period, and become personally involved in helping candidates meet these needs.[36] Organizations should also provide periodic workshops to upgrade skills and offer counseling to check the employee's fit with the job and organization.

Organizations must also recognize that due to the post-war baby boom a larger percentage of individuals than ever before will reach career plateaus in the late 1980s and '90s (see Chapter 5); and that they will plateau at a younger age.[37] Thus individuals may experience content plateaus, where their job's content remains the same for too long; or they may experience structural plateaus, where there is no room for advancement because there are fewer positions above them in the hierarchy. Organizations can reduce content plateauing by introducing job rotation, sabbaticals, or similar programs. They can decrease structural plateauing by introducing alternative career paths, reducing hiring from outside, and slowing the pace of career advancement.[38]

Midcareer crises are fairly common and organizations can deal with them in several ways. Initially they can provide counseling to help individuals confront their problems and find personal strategies for dealing with them. Second, they can offer job rotation programs that reduce obsolescence and plateauing and revitalize stalled careers. Third, they can provide midcareer individuals with educational opportunities to help them shift to a career path that is valued by the organization.

In late career the individual's ability to assume a broad organizational perspective and exercise personal influence on the organization's direction should be assessed. The organization can increase the individual's supervisory or technical responsibility, encourage him or her to act as a mentor for younger or less senior employees, or provide more autonomy than earlier. The organization must assure that active career management does not stop after midcareer. It must provide new job opportunities for individuals in this phase and continue to support their movement through the organization.

An effective career strategy from an organization's perspective (1) provides flexible career options for employees, (2) ensures that hard work pays off, (3) translates objectives into an action plan, (4) provides diverse roles for organizational members, (5) balances both long-term and short-term plans, (6) offers approaches for resolving conflicts among multiple career dimensions, (7) makes sure the experiences of senior employees are passed on to junior ones, (8) helps individuals reduce or tolerate ambiguity, and (9) provides specific and clear career directions and paths for organizational members. Both individuals and organizations can implement such strategies by identifying basic competencies and motives (career anchors) to guide careers, identifying appropriate job sequences, and planning for career transitions.[39]

Lawrence Livermore National Laboratory encourages such career development by providing a career center that includes 3000 resources. It offers information about educational opportunities, career planning, the world of work, personal growth, and management and supervision. It also includes computerized information banks, periodicals, self-study vehicles, and lists of off-site training.[40]

Productive career planning has three results: "(1) broad conclusions about one's own capabilities, interests, aspirations, and objectives—life planning;

(2) targets for future job assignments, developmental activities to make that progress happen, and plans for other future career decisions—development planning; and (3) specific goals and plans, work priorities, and reward expectations on the current job assignment—performance planning."[41]

Mentoring and Career Management

A mentor is a person who acts as teacher, role model, and promoter of one or more subordinates.[42] They help their proteges learn the ropes quickly, make significant contacts in the organization, and advance with greater ease. Indeed, employees who have mentors seem to move through their organizations more effectively than others all around. However, the mentor-protege relationship has been described as intense, emotionally charged, exclusionary, and elitist.[43]

Mentoring a junior employee serves two purposes: (1) career functions, by providing challenging work assignments and introducing the junior person to senior managers, to enhance career advancement, and (2) psychosocial functions, by counseling and role modeling, to enhance feelings of self-competence and effectiveness.[44] For maximum benefit, both parties must contribute to and work at the relationship. In selecting a mentor or a protege a person should choose someone whom they admire, respect, and trust.[45]

Over time, the relationship between mentor and protege changes. Although mentors and proteges may remain connected for a long time, the intensity of the relationship varies. It passes through four stages: (1) initiation, (2) cultivation, (3) break-up, and (4) redefinition or lasting friendship.[46]

Mentoring occurs spontaneously in many organizations. But the Internal Revenue Service, Presidential Management Internship Program, A.T.&T., and Merrill Lynch have provided formal vehicles for managers and other employees to link up with mentors.[47] Such programs encourage more widespread mentoring than would occur naturally and more equitable treatment of all employees. Junior employees are directly assigned to a more senior person for a prescribed length of time. If effective as a mentor, the senior manager provides advice in establishing career goals and formulating strategies for advancement; offers technical and social-managerial instruction; increases the protege's visibility and exposure; and counsels the junior employee about problems.[48]

Not all of the outcomes of mentoring are positive. The relationship can limit a protege's advancement if the mentor fails to advance. Mentoring can also make an employee overly dependent on another worker. In some cases, when the mentor overprotects his or her protege, it can limit the protege's visibility to other organizational members.

Role modeling has extended beyond the workplace. Increasingly, individuals look for a mentor who represents success in many aspects of life, including family, leisure, *and* career.[49] This type of search may influence whether people seek mentors of the same or opposite sex. Alternatively, they may seek sponsors, who interact more intensely than role models or mentors in developing an individual's career.[50] Or they may seek peer relationships instead of mentor-protege ones.[51]

These generally involve more reciprocity and mutuality than do mentor relationships, which tend to be more unidirectional, from mentor to protege.

For maximum success, any mentoring, sponsoring, role modeling, or peer program should (1) get top management support; (2) integrate the program into career development and training and development programs; (3) make participation voluntary; (4) keep each part of the program short; (5) select partners carefully; (6) provide orientation to the program; (7) allow mentors "structured flexibility" where they are provided a range of ideas for beginning the relationship; (8) prepare participants for potential challenges, such as releasing the proteges for special activities; and (9) build in a monitoring system.[52]

Career Pathing

Career paths are "objective descriptions of sequential work experiences"[53] by an individual through an organization. Career management should include the provision of diverse avenues for career advancement. A job progression program might include among its objectives identification of the following: (1) rational paths to target jobs; (2) fast tracks to a target job; (3) lateral moves (that is, slower career growth); (4) rational downward moves; (5) career path clusters; (6) good development moves from any given job; (7) training needs for future jobs; and (8) "people pools" for open staff jobs.[54] Sam Conklin's case at the beginning of this chapter is an example of a progression program that is too limited since only one avenue of advancement existed, as shown in Figure 8–6.

To develop realistic career paths, managers and human resources professionals must carefully define work activities by specifying the jobs' content, identifying the personal skills and knowledge required for the job, and grouping jobs into natural clusters or families.[55] They can also conduct realistic job previews (see Chapter 3) as part of their determination of appropriate paths. "Formalized career paths communicate to employees specific step-by-step objectives, and identify the positions of possible role models for them to follow."[56]

Job holders can watch the performance of their supervisors or of others holding jobs ahead in their career path and learn both acceptable behaviors and pitfalls to the job. The career path program instituted by Sears, Roebuck and Company in the 1970s, for example, assumed that when a person has a rational sequence of job assignments, he or she will be able to target the skills necessary for future jobs and learn them more quickly.[57]

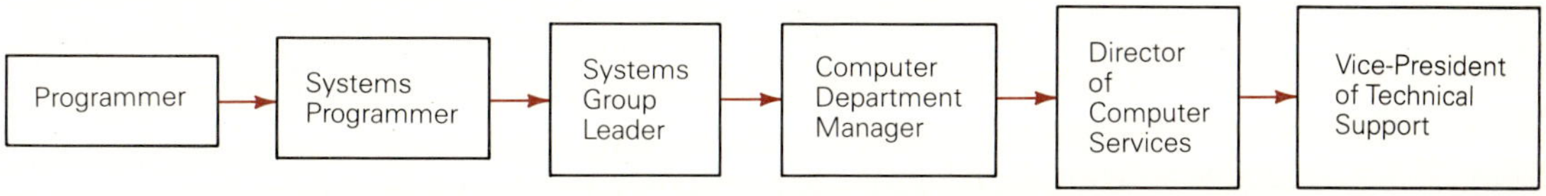

Figure 8–6 THE ONE CURRENT CAREER PATH POSSIBLE FOR SAM CONKLIN

Career paths should have four characteristics.[58] First, they should represent real progression possibilities, whether laterally or upward. Second, they should respond to changes in job content, work priorities, organizational structure, and management needs. Third, career paths should be flexible; they should consider the qualities of the particular individuals, managers, subordinates, or others influencing the way work is performed. Finally, they should specify acquirable skills, knowledge, and other specific attributes required to perform the work on each position along the paths. They should not merely use educational credentials, age, or work experience, which could preclude career opportunities from some capable performers.

What are some alternatives for Sam Conklin or others in his position? Figure 8–7 shows some possibilities. Notice that these paths include advancement along technical as well as managerial dimensions.[59]

Managers have traditionally advanced along functional lines, from the bottom to the top of the hierarchy in marketing, finance, or production. But five variations on the traditional functional career path are possible:

1. Lateral cross-unit advance—the manager retains the same title but is put in charge of ever larger work units.
2. Generalist tracks—the manager retains the same title, but is put in charge of ever larger products and programs.

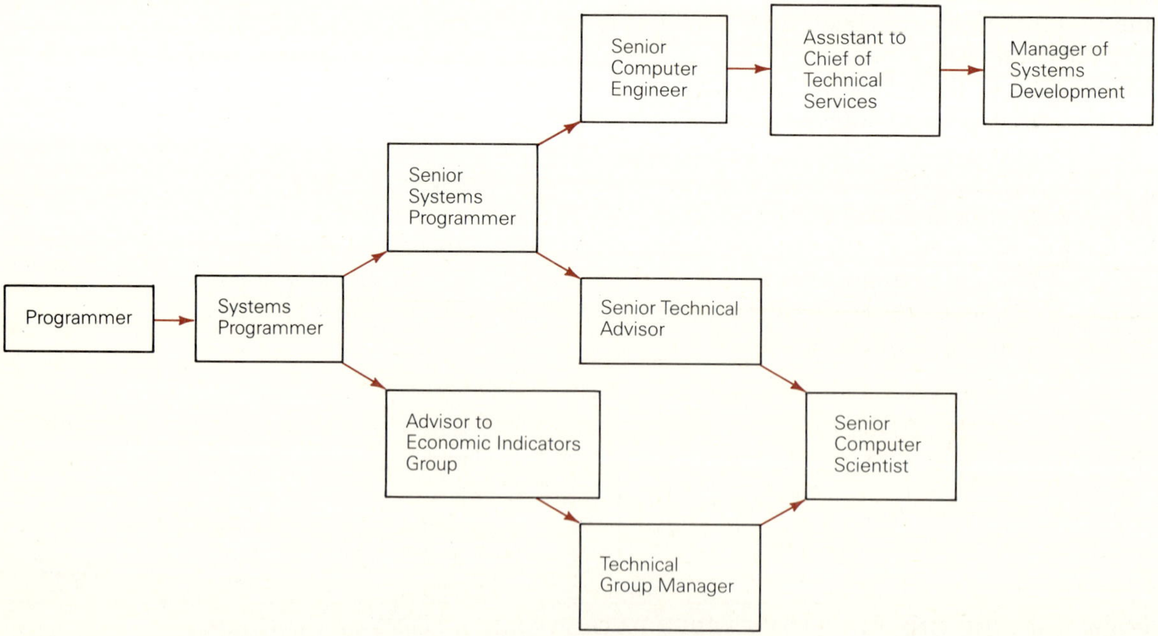

Figure 8–7 ALTERNATIVE CAREER PATHS FOR SAM CONKLIN

3. Extra-hierarchical leap—the manager makes unusual career moves that are unpredictable from looking at either the job chain or the organizational chart.
4. Dual or professional ladder—the professional or technical employee advances along a technical track that parallels, and receives rewards equal to, advancement along the managerial track.
5. High-level analyst pattern—the organization brings in a few analysts close to the top of the hierarchy to solve particular problems or to advise on major aspects of strategy.[60]

To implement career paths such as these, human resources professionals can assist by fleshing out the job descriptions that fit into each path and working with managers to integrate the diverse paths.

INTERFACING WORK, FAMILY, AND LEISURE

Career advancement does not occur independently of other, nonwork activities. A change in an individual's family status such as marriage, or the development of nonwork interests such as involvement in religious, political, or community organizations can alter a person's commitment to his or her work and career. Individuals use diverse strategies for resolving the dilemmas created by the interactions of work and nonwork concerns, but increasing numbers use an accommodative strategy—they orient toward *both* work and family.[61] In the next sections we discuss (1) the interaction of career and life cycles and (2) the interaction of work and family in dual career families.

Career and Life Cycles

"Most of the critical conflicts between work and family come at career path junctures, where major changes in life style are likely to occur."[62] An individual may enter the uncertainty of a first job at the same time he or she marries; or a more senior worker may plateau in his or her job and receive lower compensation at the same time that the employee has college-age children who require extra financial support. Just as individuals experience different stages of careers, they also experience different stages of biological and family development.

After childhood, the first life stage typically occurs between ages sixteen and twenty-two; here individuals leave the family and build strong peer relationships.[63] Following this, in the early twenties, individuals first reach out to significant others. Upon marrying, they focus more on spouse than on peers.

In the early thirties individuals often question their identity. At the same time they focus their attention even more intensely on the family. During the next decade individuals may experience a severe questioning of their progress to date. Recognizing their own mortality, individuals between ages 35 and 50 may uproot themselves, leave their families, or resolve the dilemmas of midlife. Resolution of this crisis results in settling down, and stabilizing family and other, nonwork relationships.

The dilemmas faced at each family stage can have a significant impact on an individual's career development. Attention that is devoted to build a marriage, rear children, or deal with the empty-nest syndrome, detracts from the time, effort, and energy an individual can devote to his or her career.

Consider Sam Conklin. A recent college graduate, Sam is twenty-three years old and single. What biological stage is Sam experiencing? What family issues must he deal with?

Table 8–5 shows the family stages, issues, and tasks individuals normally face over the course of their lives. Now look at Table 8–2 again. Where are the

State or Stage	Issues	Specific Tasks
Dependent child	Learning to adapt to the environment	Getting own needs met
Transition to adulthood	Managing the delicate balance between total and partial independence to allow for some trial and error in an environment of safety and support	
Single adult	Managing relations with other sex	
Married adult	Learning to live with a mate Making a long-term commitment to a family style and financial requirements	Balancing one's own needs and styles with those of another
Parent of young child	Adjusting to parenthood emotionally	Setting up workable schedule of child care
Parent of adolescents	Dealing with the independence needs and rebellion of own children Coming to terms with changing values	Setting reasonable standards and limits Enforcing limits
Parent of grown children	Adjusting to the departure of children Building new relationship with spouse	Developing new work role, hobbies, etc.
Grandparent	Establishing a relationship with a small child Dealing with own children in parent role Assessing own role as a mentor	

Edgar Schein, CAREER DYNAMICS, © 1978, Addison-Wesley, Reading, Massachusetts. Pgs. 50, 51, & 52, Table 5.1. Reprinted with permission.

Table 8–5 STAGES, ISSUES, AND TASKS OF THE FAMILY CYCLE

potential conflicts? We can identify the following times: (1) early twenties, where individuals are trying to establish their careers, as well as making family decisions; (2) midcareer, where individuals are confronting significant changes in family life, a decline in biosocial status, and questions about career choice; and (3) preretirement, where a decline in biosocial status accompanies a decline in career. Organizations must seek ways of managing these stages.

Individuals and organizations must learn to balance work and nonwork activities. Because of the interrelationship of the two, career planning must consider the impact of nonwork activities on work. Different people exhibit different work-nonwork patterns. And there is no single pattern that consistently correlates with job success[64]; different patterns influence the performance and satisfaction of individuals differently. Thus career management programs must include provisions for monitoring these relationships and encouraging patterns that lead to the most effective behaviors and attitudes for each person.

Dual Career Families

Organizations have recently been forced to expand career planning into life planning. This is partly a result of the dramatic increase in the number of women in the work force over the last ten years. Many of today's working women are married and have children; thus organizations have increasingly had to deal with the implications of two-worker families. Whereas the man's career was paramount in the past, now it must fit with a spouse's (or important other's) career. Organizations cannot assume that an employee is willing to transfer to another location or will even accept a more demanding job.

Dual career couples face a series of problems and concerns, depending on their career stage.[65] In the early career phase, they must choose where to locate for their first jobs. When opportunities are unequal in different locations, they must frequently decide which career is to be more important than the other. If both individuals have equal career commitment, similar needs, but little experience in resolving conflicts, they struggle somewhat but eventually find mutually acceptable solutions. Couples at midcareer have more experience in coping, are committed to their families, and generally have clearer priorities. But the overload created by family and career conflicts can create significant problems for dual career couples at this stage as well.

To manage two careers the people involved must be committed to both careers, show personal and job flexibility, and develop coping mechanisms. Common coping mechanisms are planning, scheduling, and organizing better; establishing clear priorities; overlooking less important tasks such as housecleaning; or eliminating social contacts outside of work and family. And they increasingly demand that their organizations respond to their special needs.

Organizations have responded to the demands of dual career families in numerous ways. They have revised nepotism policies so that spouses can work in the same organization. They have allowed transfers not essential for upward mobility. They have provided more flexible work environments through the introduction of flexible work schedules, maternity and paternity leaves, or additional personal days. They have offered counseling and training for dual career couples.[66]

A COMPREHENSIVE CAREER DEVELOPMENT SYSTEM

A career development system must provide opportunities for both employees and the organization to identify the most appropriate jobs for individuals in the short and long term. A good career development system can also contribute to the organization's effectiveness, as discussed in Reading 8–1, "A Cost-Effective Career Planning Program Requires a Strategy," by Milan Moravec. Both human resources professionals and managers must provide employees with information about job opportunities, provide counseling for the best job fit, and facilitate movement through the organization.

An effective career development system identifies and resolves any of the following potential career development problems:

- Employees who feel stuck or lack career mobility
- Unclear career paths
- Little information on career opportunities
- Managers who feel inadequate in coaching employees about their careers
- Plateaued performers
- Little planning for succession
- Rapid turnover of nonexempt employees
- A slow-growth or shrinking organization
- Loss of high-potential employees
- Employees who are unaware of how to manage their careers
- A shortage of promotable employees
- Inadequate communication of organizational mission and goals to employees
- Rapid expansion or decentralization of the organization
- Need to adapt to a rapidly changing technology
- New employees who leave soon after starting their jobs [67]

Implications for Human Resources Professionals

Human resources professionals can participate in the design and implementation of a career planning system. In particular, they can be involved in career counseling, conducting career workshops, and ensuring that career paths exist in the organization. Effective career management activities by human resources professionals include those described below.

1. Human resources professionals should help organizations and their members prepare for career management by diagnosing the environment, the organization, and their effects on career development.

2. Human resources professionals must train organizational members in the development and implementation of appropriate career strategies.

3. Human resources professionals should help organizations and individuals plan for career transitions by outlining the characteristics of typical transitions, diagnosing individuals' preferences, and analyzing the situation for its fit with the employees' needs.

4. Human resources professionals must offer diverse career planning programs that respond to different employee needs at various career stages.

5. Human resources professionals must help map various career paths; they should track job sequences and their utility for the individual and the organization.

6. Human resources professionals should introduce policies that facilitate the effective interaction between work and family; they should help support dual career families by offering workshops and counseling addressing the dilemmas these couples face.

Implications for Managers

Managers must oversee the ongoing career development of their subordinates. They should assist in self-assessment, identify appropriate career paths, and act as mentors for junior employees. In effective human resources management, managers act in the following ways:

1. Managers must facilitate career transitions for their subordinates; they should clarify their expectations to subordinates, build relationships among them, and help them master the basics of their jobs.

2. Managers should ensure that individuals have the necessary resources for self-assessment, evaluation of job opportunities, goal formulation, and matching individuals to jobs.

3. Managers must recognize that not all of their subordinates are in the same career stage; thus they must create a number of performance and advancement opportunities to fit with the needs of each phase.

4. Managers should track the job progressions of their subordinates; they should provide resources for helping them to identify and prepare for appropriate goals and directions for the future.

5. Managers must encourage their organizations to introduce diverse career planning programs.

6. Managers should act as mentors for their subordinates.

7. Managers should recognize the nonwork interests and responsibilities of their subordinates and minimize whenever possible their conflict with work.

READING

Reading 8–1

A COST-EFFECTIVE CAREER PLANNING PROGRAM REQUIRES A STRATEGY

Milan Moravec

Corporate management has taken a hard look at career planning in the last few years. In most cases, this is a new phenomenon. Career planning programs used to be relegated to staff departments, with line management hoping the fallout from this form of "philanthropy" would benefit the organization in the long run. That is, career planning was something that the organization (prompted by EEO requirements) did "for" the employees, and it was supposed to increase their motivation, sense of direction and loyalty to the company.

Recent experiences of some organizations indicate career planning is not just something to be done for the employees, but something that should be done for the organization. If a career planning program is properly planned and managed, it can be a cost-effective human resource management tool. For example, one bank's career counseling program saved $1.95 million in a year. This estimate, based on tabulations by an industrial engineer, reflected a 65 percent reduced turnover, 85 percent improvement in performance, 25 percent increased productivity and 75 percent increased promotability.

ESTABLISH A STRONG TOP-DOWN SYSTEM

All too often career planning programs are neither properly planned nor carefully managed. Too little thought is given to the ways they can be used to meet specific organizational needs. Although many companies claim they have adopted a career planning system to "improve the use of managerial talent," "increase ability to develop and promote from within," "improve productivity" and so forth, few have even been able to measure whether their programs have furthered these goals. Nevertheless, fearful of the spectre of Revised Order 4, they continue to invest in the programs. With no way to ensure the outcome, the result is usually a waste of both employee and management time and money.

Failure to establish a strong, top-down system for career planning can not only fail to produce positive fallout; it can result in negative results, such as:

- Cynicism on the part of subordinates who participate in career planning programs and then perceive no change in their career progress.
- Annoyance on the part of supervisors who grumble, "This takes too much time away from my real responsibilities." They don't see the company using the information they collect and they are not rewarded for their job in career development.
- Confusion on the part of middle managers. One department head confided, "I'm supposed to be responsible for career planning in those areas of the organization under my purview, but I don't see how that, in practice, ties into our three-year operating plan."

How, then, should an organization proceed in order to avoid these pitfalls? The following is a suggested approach, based on a review of a variety of corporate career planning strategies and an application of management theory.

ARRIVING AT STRATEGIC DECISIONS

Like any other type of corporate strategic planning, career planning should be directed from the top. It is essential that senior line management be involved in—if not the moving force behind—strategic decisions regarding the program. The reason for this is a career planning program must fit the nature of the business, its competitive employment practices, the organizational structure and management's person-

Reprinted from the January, 1982 issue of *Personnel Administrator,* copyright, 1982, The American Society for Personnel Administration, 606 North Washington Street, Alexandria, VA 22314, $30 per year.

ality. Ideally, senior line and personnel department management should work together to design and implement a career planning system.

To build an effective strategy, executives should examine 15 key questions.

1. *Why do we want a career planning program and what do we want it to do for us?*

The answer will indicate the basic goal toward which the management strategy will lead. Career planning programs at most organizations are expected to provide one or more of the following:

- More effective development of available talent to aid when promoting from within.
- Self-appraisal opportunities for employees considering new or nontraditional career paths.
- More efficient deployment of human resources within and between divisions and/or geographic locations.
- A demonstration of a tangible commitment to EEO, affirmative action and the corporate image.
- Satisfaction of employees' personal development needs.
- Improvement of performance through on-the-job training experiences provided by horizontal and vertical career moves.
- Increased employee loyalty and motivation, leading to decreased turnover.
- A method of determining training and development needs.

These options should all be considered in light of the organization's key business goals. The answer or answers will indicate the desired scope of the plan and make the next question easier to answer.

2. *For which specific groups of employees do we want to provide career planning?*

Selected groups might include: management trainees; fast-track management candidates; protected classes of employees; pre-retirees; professional trainees; technical trainees; mid-career employees; people going on international assignments; individuals being transferred from one locale or division to another; people who have requested career planning assistance; non-exempt and exempt employees as well as others.

3. *Should a career planning program be mandatory or voluntary for any of these groups?*

Some organizations found a completely voluntary career planning program does not provide management with data on all its human resources; only on those who chose to participate. On the other hand, mandatory participation of numerous people can be time-consuming and expensive.

4. *How do we identify members of groups for which the program might be mandatory? Voluntary?*

Some questions that could be asked here are: who should be considered "fast-track"? What skills and knowledge are at a particularly low level in the organization? Where will the organization be growing the fastest in the near term? Long term? What skills and experience will be necessary to fill future openings? What groups of employees need to upgrade their skills, knowledge and experience to achieve special goals? Given the organization's three-year operating plan, does any group of technical, administrative, supervisory, managerial or staff employees need to be specially monitored?

5. *Should our program be generic or custom-tailored to each selected group?*

Generic is certainly the most economical and may be perceived as the most fair. Yet, such an approach may not be consistently useful for certain groups of employees.

6. *How much responsibility for career planning should be given to the employee? How much to the organization? If primary responsibility rests with the employee, how can the organization benefit?*

The question of who assumes the responsibility for career planning can result in a wide spectrum of answers with the employee at one end and the organization at the other. In the latter case, a personnel specialist or an appropriate member of management is responsible for examining the employee's job path, performance record, other work-related background, skills and goals, and making recommendations based on a knowledge of how these fit current and future needs of the organization. In other cases, generally in smaller or more simply structured organizations, the burden of career planning is on the employee with the specialist doing no more than providing materials.

When the responsibility rests almost entirely with the employee, management may not get the data it needs to plan for future staffing, job rotation, replacement and so on. Also, unless the supervisor clearly informs the employee of the needs of the organization, the employee has no opportunity to tailor his or her career plan to fit in with the organization's requirements.

7. *What should the components of the program be?*

There are so many possible approaches to career planning that selecting the most effective combination can be difficult. Some components to consider are: informal counseling by the personnel staff; reference assistance by the personnel staff; career discussions led by supervisors with training of supervisors in career discussion; career counseling by specialized staff counselors; life/career planning workshops; annual career planning conferences; supervisory and management development workshops; workshops on retirement preparation; individual self-analysis and planning; referrals to external counselors and resources.

GEAR ELEMENTS TO THE EMPLOYEES

The element selected will depend on the groups of employees for whom career planning is provided, resources available to the company, the company philosophy and attitude toward its employees (paternal, laissez-faire, etc.) and previous company experience with any of these components.

Many companies are already implementing various combinations of these elements. For example, a large research institute has a career/life planning program for all its employees. It is staffed by in-house counselors who have psychological and technical backgrounds and it involves individual counseling, a career information center and a workshop series. An insurance company's package includes a career planning workshop, catalogs on career and training and development opportunities, a career resource center and a retirement planning workshop. The employee and his or her supervisor select the appropriate options.

A West Coast utility has instituted a career development center that is much like an assessment center for detecting managerial potential. After the employee spends one day participating in a series of exercises designed to reveal his or her ability to solve company-related problems, the results are evaluated by a panel of three specially-trained managers who prepare a skills profile and feedback report. This "diagnostic" center helps the employee plan for more effective future training and helps company management select appropriate training and work opportunities. It is not used for selection, promotion or disciplinary purposes.

8. *How much of our resources (people, time, money) are we willing to commit?*

This depends on the company's financial status and competitive employment practices, the attitude of senior management toward career planning and the seriousness of any problems (*i.e.*, shortage of available managerial candidates, high turnover, low productivity) the program might be able to ameliorate. These programs all require out-of-pocket expenditures and a commitment of supervisory time.

Before making a significant financial investment in career planning, budgets must be allocated for developing the scope of a program tailored to fit the firm.

9. *Who should have the primary organizational responsibility for a career planning system?*

Among the options are: a personnel staff (part- or full-time); line managers and supervisors; a separate consulting unit (in-house or external).

Primary responsibility does not mean sole responsibility. A cooperative line/staff effort is required if individual, unit and company-wide goals are to be met. People who have the responsibility for the overall integrity of the system may not be the best at helping the employee. The group responsible for the integrity of the system should be clearly identified, as should the people who do the counseling.

10. *What career planning aids are needed?*

Depending on the components of the program, these might include: workbooks; career path manuals; self-study (audio/video) cassettes; other visual aids (films, slides, etc.); manuals explaining career planning responsibilities; periodic corporate communications; announcements of training and development programs; career planning forms, self-analysis materials, etc.; training materials for career counselors/discussion leaders.

11. *How can training be provided for line managers and how can line management support of staff specialists be assured?*

It is generally agreed among companies with career planning programs that training is essential for the people who do the counseling. Some companies hire career counselors who are already trained or whose training was part of their development as staff specialists. When career counseling is assigned to staff specialists, it is important that they constantly communicate with line management so they will be aware of organizational practices and needs regarding current open positions, long-range staffing requirements, etc.

Some companies, on the other hand, train (to a greater or lesser extent) supervisors and managers to be career counselors. Line managers who do career counseling usually do well when properly instructed. They are often trained by a counselor from a staff area or by an outside consultant.

12. *How can we link career planning to supporting personnel systems?*

Results-oriented career planning must be linked to other personnel activities such as: performance evaluation policies; promotion and transfer policies; educational assistance plans; training and development programs; management succession and replacement plans; affirmative action plans; recruitment practices; job rotation plans; management assessment centers or systems.

FRAGMENTED SYSTEMS

The greatest failing of many systems is they are fragmented so there is no way of utilizing data obtained through career planning in any other personnel system. Linkage between systems must be carefully thought through. Although it is not accurate, for example, to say that "career counseling is a part of our performance evaluation system" because they are two distinct processes (one looking backward at past performance and the other looking forward to future opportunity), information gained from performance appraisal sessions and forms can be effectively used in career discussions.

Information gleaned in career discussions should never remain locked in the minds of mentors and managers nor in personal confidential files. If the organization is to make full use of data gathered in career discussions, some mechanism must be found to coordinate this information with that of the other personnel systems. For instance, when a career discussion reveals training needs related to both individual and organizational priorities, the training department should be informed so it can provide the appropriate courses and programs.

13. *How can we take advantage of new techniques in human resources management?*

When an organization already has advanced personnel systems such as a computer-based personnel information system or a systematic projection of future staffing requirements, career discussion information can be added to them. The information contained on career planning forms should be structured in a way that can be entered into and retrieved from the systems where it will be used. It is not, however, recommended that advanced information systems be tied into the career planning program until the program has been proven effective.

14. *Can we respond adequately to employees whose expectations are raised?*

If the career planning system produces no results visible to the employee (for example, a rewarding assignment), dissatisfaction will far outweigh its benefits. A common mistake occurs when the career counselor promises, directly or indirectly, more than can be delivered. The career counselor, whether a personnel specialist or line manager, should make a commitment only when he or she has the authority for the final outcome; otherwise, he or she should do no more than promise to consult with those who have the decision-making authority.

15. *How can we ensure accountability?*

It is not enough for a division manager to direct the personnel department to set up a career planning program or for the personnel department to produce forms and workbooks and send memoranda to line managers on the need for career discussions. Some method of follow-up is necessary. It should include a method of measurement and a reward system. Some accountability procedures are:

- Setting goals regarding the numbers of employees who are to participate; requiring supervisors to report these numbers to the personnel department and senior management.
- Setting timetables for career planning discussions.
- Scheduling periodic meetings between line and staff management to review program priorities and share ideas.
- Assigning the responsibility to a specific person or group to help employees follow through with their plans.
- Developing a system for circulating information among managers concerning participating employees.
- Evaluating and rewarding managers and career counselors according to their ability to meet targets and goals.

WORKING TOGETHER

In a major West Coast bank, career counseling forms are completed by the employee and development plans are completed jointly by the supervisor and the employee. A procedure has been set up to make sure all employees who want to participate do so. The manager (supervisor) informs the staff planning and development department about all plans made so they can be used by the departments and regions and as a tool when making personnel decisions.

The plans are used to monitor the supervisor's efforts, identify needs for new development programs and assist in decisions about promotions, transfers, special assignments and replacement planning. Even here there is no method for determining whether the employee has actually taken action to implement his or her plans.

An East Coast manufacturing organization has instituted an annual development review for employees and an annual organization audit. The results are taken to corporate headquarters by the manager of each division. This audit tells top management (of the parent company) how well each division is developing employees/future managers. It also identifies people who are capable of replacing others and those whom the organization might lose because of a lack of appropriate promotional opportunities within a projected five-year period. Thus, accountability reaches to the top of the organization.

If success cannot be clearly demonstrated, career planning will be one of the first programs to fall victim to an economic cutback.

TAILOR THE SYSTEM

A career planning system should include methods for meeting specific organizational as well as employee needs. Because there is no one "right" system for all companies, senior management must choose the best combination of counseling and training components, linking mechanisms, accountability systems and decision-making processes for the organization.

First, the system should meet the organization's minimum requirements. We can learn from early experiences with computer systems. When such systems attained credibility in the business environment, some companies acquired complicated, expensive hardware that far exceeded their needs—and thus caused more problems than they solved. Similarly, bigger is not necessarily better in the area of career planning. The cost effectiveness of each component should be carefully considered. It is easier and less expensive to add to a program than to subtract from it.

Second, the system should fit the personality of the company and its management. Overly formal programs with complex procedures do not fit simply structured, informal organizations. An informal, strictly voluntary employee-centered program will not be responsive to the management requirements of complex organizations with turbulent growth patterns.

Finally, the competition should be considered. Because one of the primary motives for installing a career planning program is to attract, develop and retain the best people, its results should match the results of similar programs of organizations sharing the marketplace (marketplace, not just the business or the industry).

GETTING STARTED

When initiating a career planning system, the first thing to do is to identify elements already in the organization. Most companies have performance appraisal systems; these can be adapted to include career planning. Similarly, parts of the affirmative action program, the training and development package and management assessment center might be adapted to career planning. It is possible that appropriate coordination of systems already in the organization could serve as the foundation of a pragmatic and responsive career planning program. Avoid redundant activities.

Line management input is vital during the system design period, not only to identify organizational needs in relation to the development and utilization of personnel, but also to identify any areas of weakness in the systems already in use.

DISCUSSION QUESTIONS

1. What is the value of a strong top-down career management system?
2. What questions should be asked in an audit of an effective career planning strategy?
3. How can the career planning system be tailored to the needs of the organization, individuals, and managers?

ACTIVITIES

Activity 8–1

CAREER ANCHORS

Step 1: Complete the following questionnaire by circling the answer that best describes your feelings about each statement. For each item, circle your response according to the following:

SA = Strongly Agree, A = Agree, D = Disagree, SD = Strongly Disagree.

1. I would leave my company rather than be promoted out of my area of expertise.	SA	A	D	SD
2. Becoming highly specialized and highly competent in some specific functional or technical area is important to me.	SA	A	D	SD
3. A career that is free from organization restriction is important to me.	SA	A	D	SD
4. I have always sought a career in which I could be of service to others.	SA	A	D	SD
5. A career that provides a maximum variety of types of assignments and work projects is important to me.	SA	A	D	SD
6. To rise to a position in general management is important to me.	SA	A	D	SD
7. I like to be identified with a particular organization and the prestige that accompanies that organization.	SA	A	D	SD
8. Remaining in my present geographical location rather than moving because of a promotion is important to me.	SA	A	D	SD
9. The use of my skills in building a new business enterprise is important to me.	SA	A	D	SD
10. I would like to reach a level of responsibility in an organization where my decisions really make a difference.	SA	A	D	SD
11. I see myself more as a generalist as opposed to being committed to one specific area of expertise.	SA	A	D	SD
12. An endless variety of challenges in my career is important to me.	SA	A	D	SD
13. Being identified with a powerful or prestigious employer is important to me.	SA	A	D	SD
14. The excitement of participating in many areas of work has been the underlying motivation behind my career.	SA	A	D	SD

Adapted, by permission of the publisher, from "Reexamining the Career Anchor Model", by T.J. Delong, PERSONNEL, May-June 1982, pp. 56–7.

15. The process of supervising, influencing, leading, and controlling people at all levels is important to me.	SA	A	D	SD
16. I am willing to sacrifice some of my autonomy to stabilize my total life situation.	SA	A	D	SD
17. An organization that will provide security through guaranteed work, benefits, a good retirement, and so forth, is important to me.	SA	A	D	SD
18. During my career I will be mainly concerned with my own sense of freedom and autonomy.	SA	A	D	SD
19. I will be motivated throughout my career by the number of products that I have been directly involved in creating.	SA	A	D	SD
20. I want others to identify me by my organization and job.	SA	A	D	SD
21. Being able to use my skills and talents in the service of an important cause is important to me.	SA	A	D	SD
22. To be recognized by my title and status is important to me.	SA	A	D	SD
23. A career that permits a maximum of freedom and autonomy to choose my own work, hours, and so forth, is important to me.	SA	A	D	SD
24. A career that gives me a great deal of flexibility is important to me.	SA	A	D	SD
25. To be in a position in general management is important to me.	SA	A	D	SD
26. It is important for me to be identified by my occupation.	SA	A	D	SD
27. I will accept a management position only if it is in my area of expertise.	SA	A	D	SD
28. It is important for me to remain in my present geographical location rather than move because of a promotion or new job assignment.	SA	A	D	SD
29. I would like to accumulate a personal fortune to prove to myself and others that I am competent.	SA	A	D	SD
30. I want to achieve a position that gives me the opportunity to combine analytical competence with supervision of people.	SA	A	D	SD
31. I have been motivated throughout my career by using my talents in a variety of different areas of work.	SA	A	D	SD
32. An endless variety of challenges is what I really want from my career.	SA	A	D	SD
33. An organization that will give me long-run stability is important to me.	SA	A	D	SD
34. To be able to create or build something that is entirely my own product or idea is important to me.	SA	A	D	SD
35. Remaining in my specialized area, as opposed to being promoted out of my area of expertise, is important to me.	SA	A	D	SD
36. I do not want to be constrained by either an organization or the business world.	SA	A	D	SD

37. Seeing others change because of my efforts is important to me.	SA	A	D	SD
38. My main concern in life is to be competent in my area of expertise.	SA	A	D	SD
39. The chance to pursue my own life-style and not be constrained by the rules of an organization is important to me.	SA	A	D	SD
40. I find most organizations to be restrictive and intrusive.	SA	A	D	SD
41. Remaining in my area of expertise, rather than being promoted into general management, is important to me.	SA	A	D	SD
42. I want a career that allows me to meet my basic needs through helping others.	SA	A	D	SD
43. The use of my interpersonal and helping skills in the service of others is important to me.	SA	A	D	SD
44. I like to see others change because of my efforts.	SA	A	D	SD

Step 2: Score your responses by writing the number that corresponds to your response (SA = 4, A = 3, D = 2, SD = 1) to each question in the space below next to the item number.

1 _____	2 _____	3 _____	4 _____	5 _____	6 _____	7 _____	8 _____	9 _____
10 _____	11 _____	12 _____	13 _____	14 _____	15 _____	16 _____	17 _____	18 _____
19 _____	20 _____	21 _____	22 _____	23 _____	24 _____	25 _____	26 _____	27 _____
28 _____	29 _____	30 _____	31 _____	32 _____	33 _____	34 _____	35 _____	36 _____
37 _____	38 _____	39 _____	40 _____	41 _____	42 _____	43 _____	44 _____	

Now obtain subscale scores by adding your scores on the items indicated and then divide by the number of items in the scale, as shown:

Technical Competence	_______________ #1, 2, 27, 35, 38, 41	÷ 6 = _______
Autonomy	_______________ #3, 18, 23, 36, 39, 40	÷ 6 = _______
Service	_______________ #4, 21, 37, 42, 43, 44	÷ 6 = _______
Identity	_______________ #7, 13, 20, 22, 26	÷ 5 = _______

Variety	____________ #5, 12, 14, 24, 31, 32	÷ 6 = ______
Managerial Competence	____________ #6, 10, 11, 15, 25, 30	÷ 6 = ______
Security	____________ #8, 16, 17, 28, 33	÷ 5 = ______
Creativity	____________ #9, 19, 29, 34	÷ 4 = ______

Step 3: Discussion. Form into groups with four to six others who have the same predominant anchor as you. In these small groups answer the following questions:

1. On which anchor did you receive the highest score?
2. What jobs fit best with your highest-scoring anchor?
3. What jobs fit poorly with your highest-scoring anchor?
4. What would an ideal career look like for you? For others in your group?

Step 4: With the entire class, compare the responses of different anchor groups to these questions:

1. Do the responses for the groups differ significantly? In what way?
2. Are the differences predictable from your knowledge of career anchors?
3. Are individuals with different anchors likely to have different career paths?

Activity 8–2

CAREER PLANNING FOR INDIVIDUALS

Step 1: Complete the following charts.

WORKSHEET 1

Career Development Issues

1. What do we mean by a *career?*

2. Do you have a career? Explain.

3. What are the advantages and disadvantages of simply "holding a job"?

4. What are the advantages and disadvantages of "building a career"?

WORKSHEET 2

Job Experiences and Skills

Think about the positions you currently hold and have held previously. First, list the tasks or activities which are/were part of these jobs. Then, beside the activity, list the skills or special knowledge you needed to do that task. You should begin each different position on a new sheet.

Job Title: ______________________

Tasks/Activities	Skills/Knowledge
(1)	(1)
	(2)
	(3)
(2)	(1)
	(2)
	(3)
(3)	(1)
	(2)
	(3)
(4)	(1)
	(2)
	(3)
(5)	(1)
	(2)
	(3)

WORKSHEET 3

Career Paths

1. What job would you like to hold 3–5 years from now?

2. What job would you like to hold 10 years from now?

3. Are there any other possibilities?

WORKSHEET 4 PART I

Career Path Analyses—Skills

Skills Needed	Rating of Competence low (1) to high (5)	How Important Is Skill for: Job 3–5 Years Hence	Job 10 Years Hence	Other Possible Jobs
		Unimportant (1) to Very Important (5)		

WORKSHEET 4 PART II

Career Path Analyses—Other Factors

Other Factors/Constraints	How Important Is Skill for: Job 3–5 Years Hence	Job 10 Years Hence	Other Possible Jobs
	Unimportant (1) to Very Important (5)		

WORKSHEET 5

Career/Life Plan

Given the ratings on Worksheet 4, you should be able to begin to formulate a plan. List below:

	Strategy	Priority
I. The *skills* you need to develop		
1.		
2.		
3.		
4.		
5.		
6.		
7.		
II. The *other factors* you need to address		
1.		
2.		
3.		
4.		
5.		
6.		
7.		
III. *Additional information* you require about yourself and/or job possibilities		
1.		
2.		
3.		
4.		
5.		
6.		
7.		

Now, go back and think of a way of strengthening your position on each, that is, develop a strategy for accomplishing each. Finally, assign a priority to each activity or strategy.

Step 2: With a partner, review the data you have collected. Then answer the following questions:

1. What are your major strengths and weaknesses?
2. What skills and experiences are most important in planning your career?
3. What types of jobs are you interested in holding?
4. Do you have the skills and experiences required for those jobs?
5. What skills must you obtain before securing those jobs?
6. Offer a plan for obtaining the required skills.

Step 3: Discussion. In small groups or with the entire class, discuss the key factors that influence your career plan. Share your plans for securing future jobs. What role does self-assessment and knowledge of job opportunities play in your career development?

Activity 8–3

SANFORD JARVIS

Step 1: Read the Sanford Jarvis case.

Step 2: Prepare the case for class discussion.

On Thanksgiving weekend of 1975, Sanford Jarvis yielded to an uncharacteristic impulse and wallowed ever so briefly in a micro-orgy of introspection. For the past couple of months he had experienced a muted but gnawing premonition that he was about to come to some sort of crossroads in his professional and personal life. Ever since Labor Day he'd been putting the capital budget for Buchanan Industries in shape for the November meeting of the Board of Directors. Visiting plant managers all over the country to assess their needs and supervising budget preparation back at headquarters had kept him pretty well stretched out. He hadn't been able to take the time to think his own thoughts for months. But the Board meeting before Thanksgiving had gone well, the capital budget was approved, and he was at home—unencumbered at least until Monday. Even the weather had conspired to set the mood. A grey, drizzly Friday almost compelled a few logs on the fireplace and a bottle of Scotch to be sampled sparingly. And so he let his mind play.

When Sanford (Sandy) was engaged in the job-hunting ritual in the second year of his MBA training, he had concentrated on large, multi-functional organizations that would give him immediate hands-on exposure to problems and opportunities in financial management. He received four job offers in the Spring of 1971, and he eventually accepted Buchanan Industries' offer because it seemed to give him the best shot at early responsibility. (See Figure 8–8 for a view of general organizational relationships.)

His first job assignment was in Augusta, Georgia, and his subsequent moves are described in the resume reproduced in Figure 8–9. Sandy's exposure to opportunity and his progress in the company are described in Table 8–6.

As Sandy sat by the fire and sipped on his Scotch, he asked himself,

> "What's gotten into me to make me think about doing something else? Aren't I doing what I'd wanted to do ever since I started planning for a career in management? What's eating at me?"

Taking a reflective look at those parts of his four-year career with Buchanan that seemed least satisfying, Sandy could identify a few trouble spots. They weren't really trouble spots, Sandy said; they were just clouds on the horizon that kept him from feeling 100% self-actualized. Take salary, for example. He knew that the mean salary for Virginia MBA's in 1971 was around $14,000, but he took the Buchanan job on the basis of potential for advancement. Besides, $13,000 in Augusta, Georgia, was certainly a living wage and he and his family had lived quite comfortably in the more than two years they were there. However, living in Wilmette (in a modest house that they had got "for a song" because it was 45 years old and needed some fixing up) was eating up more of his take-home pay than he had experienced in Augusta.

"Augusta—that was a neat operation. Why did I ever want to leave there? There was a job that had everything!" Sandy remembered back in the summer of 1973 when his boss, Frank Morrow, had died suddenly and the Plant Manager, J.G. Ross, asked him to take the job of Controller. "Yes, I know you're young, that you've been here only two years, and that this is a big responsibility to saddle you with. But you've done a good job here of learning what goes on at Augusta, you've handled yourself well in your contacts with management, and there's no one else we can break in with such short notice."

And so Sandy took the job. It was a hassle sometimes. He worked his share of 12-hour days, but life at business school had prepared him for that. The best part of it was that he was pretty much his own boss. He knew more about financial management than anyone else at the Augusta plant, and he was sufficiently removed from Headquarters in Chicago so that he was not conscious of top management looking over his shoulder. Given the requirements of corporate life, he was pretty well able to work at his

This material was prepared by Professor John L. Snook.

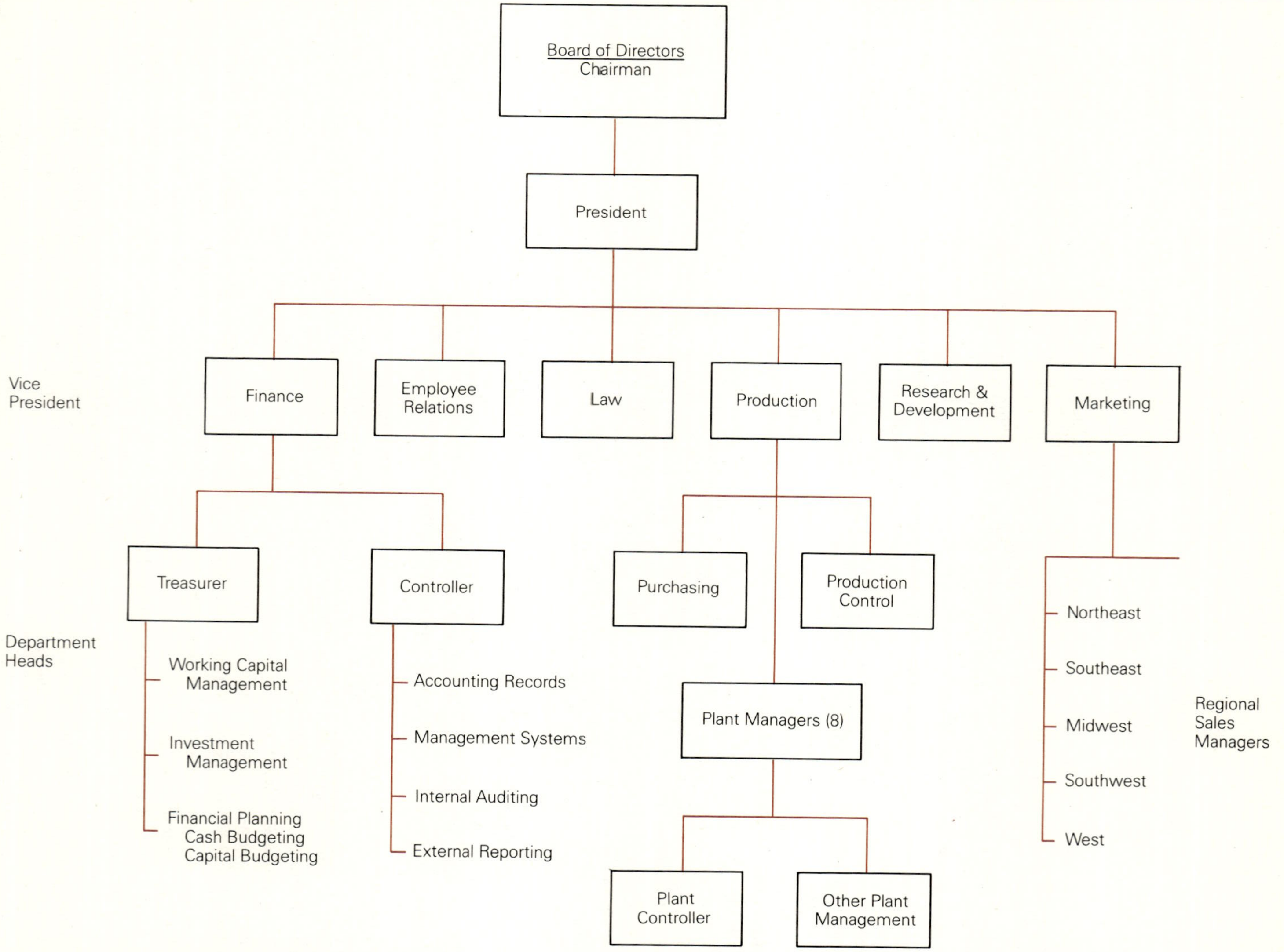

Figure 8–8 BUCHANAN INDUSTRIES

Sanford Jarvis
210 Chestnut Avenue
Wilmette, Illinois 60091

Telephone: Home (312) 635-4768
Office (312) 721-3900

EMPLOYMENT OBJECTIVE

Responsible position in financial management, in either the treasurer's or controller's role, which will lead to diversified responsibilities in top management.

EDUCATION

Sept. 1969–June 1971	MBA, The Colgate Darden Graduate School of Business Administration, University of Virginia, Charlottesville, Virginia.
Sept. 1963–June 1967	B.A., Economics, Lafayette College (President, Freshman Counseling System; Secretary, Student Council; Varsity Golf Team)

EMPLOYMENT EXPERIENCE

April 1974–Present	Senior Financial Analyst, Buchanan Industries, Chicago, Illinois. As a member of the Financial Planning Group of the Treasurer's Department of a multi-plant manufacturer of textiles and packaging products with sales in 1975 estimated at $1.2 billion, I am responsible for preparing capital budgets for the approval of the Board of Directors. In the most recent fiscal year, responding to the needs of plant managers, regional sales managers, and other performance centers, I was involved in the analysis of 43 capital projects totalling $94 million. Working with these diverse projects I have had close contact with many other departments and levels of management in Buchanan Industries. These associations have given me valuable first-hand experience in participating in top-level company decisions.
Aug. 1973–April 1974	Controller, Augusta Division of Buchanan Industries. Reporting directly to the plant manager of a major division producing paper and packaging products, I was responsible for maintaining accounting records, performed internal audits, and developed and perfected management control systems in a facility which employed 1,600 persons and produced products valued at $87 million. The controller's department employed a staff of three professional and seven non-professional personnel. As Plant Controller I maintained frequent relationships with the Controller's Department in Chicago, and was subject to the accounting methods and reporting systems of Buchanan Industries. At the same time I worked closely with department heads throughout the Augusta division in maintaining appropriate financial and managerial controls for the Division. I left the Augusta division in order to take a position in corporate headquarters' Financial Planning staff.
May 1972–Aug. 1973	Assistant Controller, Augusta Division of Buchanan Industries. Assisted the controller in the activities described above.
July 1971–May 1972	Financial Analyst, Augusta Division of Buchanan Industries. In an entry-level job in the Controller's Department, I engaged in analysis of capital projects, cost accounting procedures, and of the adequacy of computer facilities to process financial information.
June 1970–Sept. 1970	Summer Intern, Morgan Guaranty Trust Company. Worked on the Bank's quarterly review and prepared a detailed analysis of selected account profitability statements for presentation to the Services Policy Committee.

MILITARY EXPERIENCE

Sept. 1967–Aug. 1969	U.S. Army Lieutenant. As Signal Officer in a Signal Battalion stationed in Germany, served as Platoon Leader for a 95-man platoon before moving to the job of Company Operations Officer. As Operations Officer was responsible for organizing and coordinating signal maneuvers for a 320-man company.

PERSONAL

Date of Birth May 13, 1945; Weight 160; Height 5′10″; Health good.

Interests include music (as performer and audiophile), golf (middle 80's), bridge (especially duplicate). Participation in community fund drives (usually heading our election district), and church activities (teacher of adult class).

Figure 8–9 SANDY JARVIS'S RESUMÉ

own pace according to his own standards of performance.

He had been assured by Mr. Ross that he was performing to his and the company's satisfaction, and he fully expected to remain in Augusta for a number of years consolidating his understanding of financial management and his knowledge of Buchanan Industries' policies and procedures. It came as a genuine surprise to him, then, to be called into the office of Mr. Ross, who delivered to him an offer that he didn't know quite how to assess. "Headquarters in Chicago has suddenly developed a need for another person in the Financial Planning Group of the Controller's Department. They say they've looked around throughout the company and couldn't find anyone who has the right combination of training and experience to help them jack up a part of the organization that has been less effective than top management would like. They've looked at your record and at my assessment of your performance, and they want to offer you a position on the Headquarters Financial Planning Staff. I told them I'd hate like hell to have to give you up, but I certainly wouldn't stand in your way if you want to accept the offer."

Sandy was ecstatic at the offer. This would provide him with more exposure to top management financial circles than he could ever hope to get in Augusta. If he really wanted a top position in a major organization, this move might short-cut the process by four or five years. He called the controller in Chicago whom he had met a couple of times before, ascertained that the offer was genuine, and arranged to visit the Headquarters office in the following week to see whether this opportunity was truly as good as it seemed.

After engaging in a few of the amenities in the Chicago office, Sandy spent most of the day with Henry Craig, head of the Financial Planning Group. Mr. Craig was a brisk, alert, and personally charming man who seemed to be in his mid-50's. He had worked as a C.P.A. in a small regional accounting firm in the Chicago area, but when the firm dissolved in 1960, he took a job as financial analyst in the Treasurer's Department. In 1965, when the company developed a need to engage in some formal financial planning, Craig was put in charge of the operation. Under his leadership it had developed into two primary functions—capital budgeting and cash budgeting. He was in particular need of a person who could lend greater sophistication to the analysis of capital needs throughout the company so that the budgetary procedure could be used more to solve problems than merely to deny proposals. As Craig described his needs and objectives for the Group, Sandy warmed to the challenge. He was assured of a salary increase to reflect the higher cost of living in an urban center, his relocation costs would, of course, be paid, and he would be working in Chicago in close proximity to the Vice President of Finance, the Controller and the Treasurer.

Sandy's wife, Helen, had been brought up in Ohio,

	Name Sanford Jarvis Department Treasurer's			Birth Date 5/13/45 Employment Date 7/1/71	
Date	Job Title	Location	Salary Group	Salary	Increase
7/1/71	Jr. Financial Analyst	Augusta	5	13,000	
1/1/72	Financial Analyst	Augusta	4	14,300	1300 Promotion
5/13/72	Asst. Controller	Augusta	3	15,000	700 Promotion
3/1/73	Asst. Controller	Augusta	3	16,500	1500 Merit
8/1/73	Controller	Augusta	2	18,000	1500 Promotion
4/15/74	Sr. Financial Analyst	Chicago	3	20,000	2000 C-O-L
2/1/75	Sr. Financial Analyst	Chicago	3	22,000	2000 Merit

Table 8–6 COMPENSATION RECORD

and she rather missed the mid-West. She had not resisted Augusta, but when Sandy mentioned this new opportunity Helen was totally supportive of his interest in moving to headquarters. And so, after a careful assessment of the pros and cons, Sandy accepted the job in Chicago.

By and large, it was a good job. Sandy was given a good deal of latitude in visiting plants, gathering data, interrogating local managers about their needs and expectations, and suggesting new approaches to the formulation of capital budgets. Mr. Craig seemed strangely ambivalent at times about Sandy's performance. When Sandy would leave for Augusta or other field visits Craig would say, "Go get 'em, Sandy. Keep the troops happy, as long as it doesn't cost any money." He would deal with field personnel on a most affable basis, but if Sandy were to suggest a capital expenditure that had the slightest risk associated with it, Craig might remove it from the budget proposal.

Sandy had always taken pride in his ability to present complex data in a way that would make sense to unsophisticated listeners. He spoke well, he could organize data logically, and he could add just a little passion at the right moment to make people believe that what he said really mattered. He had done well in Analysis and Communication at business school, and his presentations to management at Augusta were uniformly well received. It came as a surprise to him when, after preparing the capital budget for presentation by him to the Board, Mr. Craig said, "It's been customary for the Group Head to appear before the Board, so it'll be necessary for you to brief me thoroughly before I go up next week." Unfortunately, the briefing didn't take into account all of the possible questions, and a couple of proposals made by Mr. Craig were shot down. Sandy caught hell from a plant manager who thought Sandy was on his side.

"What am I going to do with Craig?", Sandy asked himself. "Right now he's a real roadblock. He doesn't really understand what I'm trying to do with capital budgeting or with financial planning. There's a whole new world of analytical techniques out there, and he's still wearing his green eyeshade and sleeve garters. Should I try to get back in plant management, should I try to sneak around Craig, or do I have to sweat out his retirement?"

Sandy hadn't given much conscious thought to "Am I happy?" or "Is my career proceeding on schedule?" or "In the competition for fame and fortune, how am I doing?" If anyone had asked him, the response would certainly have been positive. And yet as he reflected on events of the past few months, he wondered. . . .

- A gossipy letter from an MBA classmate who had gone to work with General Foods told of his promotion to Product Manager and of buying a new home in Putnam County, New York.
- Helen, who went to a twice-a-week exercise class with several other Buchanan Industries wives, reported that the wife of the head of the Management Systems Group had told her that the Vice President of Finance had told the Controller that his department was the key to the continued success of the company. The Systems guy, two years older than Sandy, had just bought a Volvo station wagon and his wife was talking about investing in commodity futures.
- When Sandy was Controller at Augusta he knew about the ranges for the classified salary groups and that he was one of the youngest Group 2 employees in the plant and probably in the whole company. Back in 1973 the range for Group 3 was $15,000–22,500, and the range for Group 2 was $18,000–27,000. He didn't have ready access to that information in his current job, and he didn't know whether the ranges had gone up to reflect the inflation of the past two years. If they hadn't changed, he'd have to get reclassified (and promoted) within the next few months. On the other hand . . .

And so Sandy let his mind play, and the tune it played had a persistent theme: "How am I doing? Shall I polish up my resume and send it to Steve Bredin (Placement Director) at the business school? Where do I go from here?"

Step 3: Discussion. Individually in writing, in small groups, or with the entire class, as directed by your instructor, answer the following questions:

1. What career stage is Sanford Jarvis at?
2. Through what career stages has he passed?
3. What key issues and dilemmas does he face now? Has he faced in the past?
4. What types of assistance could his company provide? What should they provide?
5. How does his work interact with the nonwork parts of his life? What problems do you predict will occur?
6. What should Sandy do now?
7. What should the company do now for Sandy?

Activity 8–4

HOW CAN THIS CAREER BE HELPED?

Step 1: Read each of the vignettes below.

I. THE CASE OF JACK WEBSTER

Jack Webster is employed as a compensation analyst by a high technology firm that manufactures state-of-the-art biomedical equipment. He joined Biomed, Inc., upon graduation from college as a clerk in the human resources department. During his first two years of employment, he advanced quickly up the organizational hierarchy in the human resources department, moving into positions of personnel assistant, personnel professional, and then compensation analyst. He had moved into the highly specialized position in compensation because the director of human resources had advised him that this sequence of jobs was good preparation for higher-level managerial responsibilities.

Jack has held his current position for two years. During the past year he has complained frequently about the lack of challenge on the job. He also feels that he is ready to assume significant managerial responsibilities. Jack's performance appraisals have always been positive. He has been promised a promotion for over a year. He assumes he has not yet received one because no position has become available. Jack has informed his supervisor that he is willing to transfer out of compensation, or even out of human resources management, to secure a managerial position. Recently, however, his supervisor has implied that Jack's lack of a graduate degree is hindering his advancement.

II. THE CASE OF FRANK ROBERTSON

Frank Robertson has been employed by the Stateline Door Company as a salesperson for the last fifteen years. When he originally joined the company after graduating from college, Frank's father owned Stateline. After Frank had worked there for ten years, a large home-products conglomerate offered Frank's father an extremely generous offer for the firm and ultimately bought Stateline. The new owners gave Frank's father a five-year management contract and retained most other employees, including Frank. Before the sale of Stateline, Frank's father had implied that when he retired Stateline would become Frank's. Even though he concentrated on sales and marketing, Frank tried to learn all aspects of the business. Not surprisingly, Frank was disappointed when his father sold Stateline instead of turning the company over to him.

Since the sale of the company, Frank's unease with his job has increased. Although Frank has always felt that he has pulled his weight, he has not received any real performance appraisals because of his relationship with the former owner of the company. He has become increasingly uncertain about his future at Stateline, even though the new president has assured him that there will always be a position for him. In addition, in many ways he feels more qualified to run Stateline than any manager they might bring in.

III. THE CASE OF SARAH CALDMAN

Sarah Caldman joined Smith Associates, a firm of ten consultants and five staff assistants, as a senior consultant after she received her doctorate in educational psychology. Sarah worked previously as a counselor in several social service agencies. At Smith Associates she was expected to develop her own base of clients, bill sufficient hours to make a profit, and market the other services Smith Associates offered. Her major business is educational and psychological testing.

Sarah enjoyed her first two years at Smith Associates. She felt that she had mastered the basics of being an entrepreneur within a consulting organization. She had built a large client base that generated sufficient revenues for her "division" to contribute a significant profit to Smith Associates. Yet now she is considering leaving the firm because she feels she has learned all she can from the other consultants employed there. She is the only person with expertise in educational and psychological testing; the remaining consultants are involved in areas in which she has no real expertise and little interest. She is seriously considering seeking a position as an internal consultant in an industrial or educational organization.

Step 2: Individually or in small groups, answer the following questions for each vignette:

1. What is the problem with this career?
2. What can the organization do to correct this problem?

Step 3: In small groups or with the entire class, share your answers. Then consider the following:

1. What types of career problems exist in organizations?
2. What strategies can individuals use to correct them?
3. What strategies can managers use to correct them?
4. What strategies can human resources professionals use to correct them?
5. What roles should human resources professionals, managers, and other employees play in career management?

Activity 8–5

ALLWOOD AND MASTERS, INC.

Step 1: Read the following scenario.

Allwood and Masters employs 200 professionals in the development and sale of software for diverse industrial, educational, and personal uses. The company is divided into three major divisions, as shown in Figure 8–10. Each division is headed by one of four senior partners in the firm; the fourth partner acts as the managing director of the entire firm.

The managing partner has responsibility for overseeing the staffing of the organization, as well as the development of current employees. The firm encourages promotion from within; therefore, most hiring occurs for entry-level positions. These are filled primarily from college recruiting and referrals by current employees. Because Allwood and Masters, Inc., has an excellent reputation, employees tend to be high-quality professionals with excellent educational backgrounds.

In its five years of existence, Allwood and Masters has quickly obtained a reputation as a creative and innovative organization. The company has at least doubled its number of employees each year. So far, it has not been plagued by the high turnover many similar organizations have experienced.

Now the managing partner feels that it is important to extend the firm's creativity to career development issues. She wishes to develop a comprehensive career development program for Allwood and Masters, Inc.

Step 2: Individually or in small groups, design a comprehensive career management program for Allwood and Masters. Describe the types of programs and career development activities you will implement; list who will be responsible for and involved in each activity; and indicate a schedule for implementation. Be as concrete in your description as possible.

Step 3: Discussion. In small groups or with the entire class, share your plans. What elements do they have in common? How do they differ? What are the ingredients of a comprehensive, effective career management system?

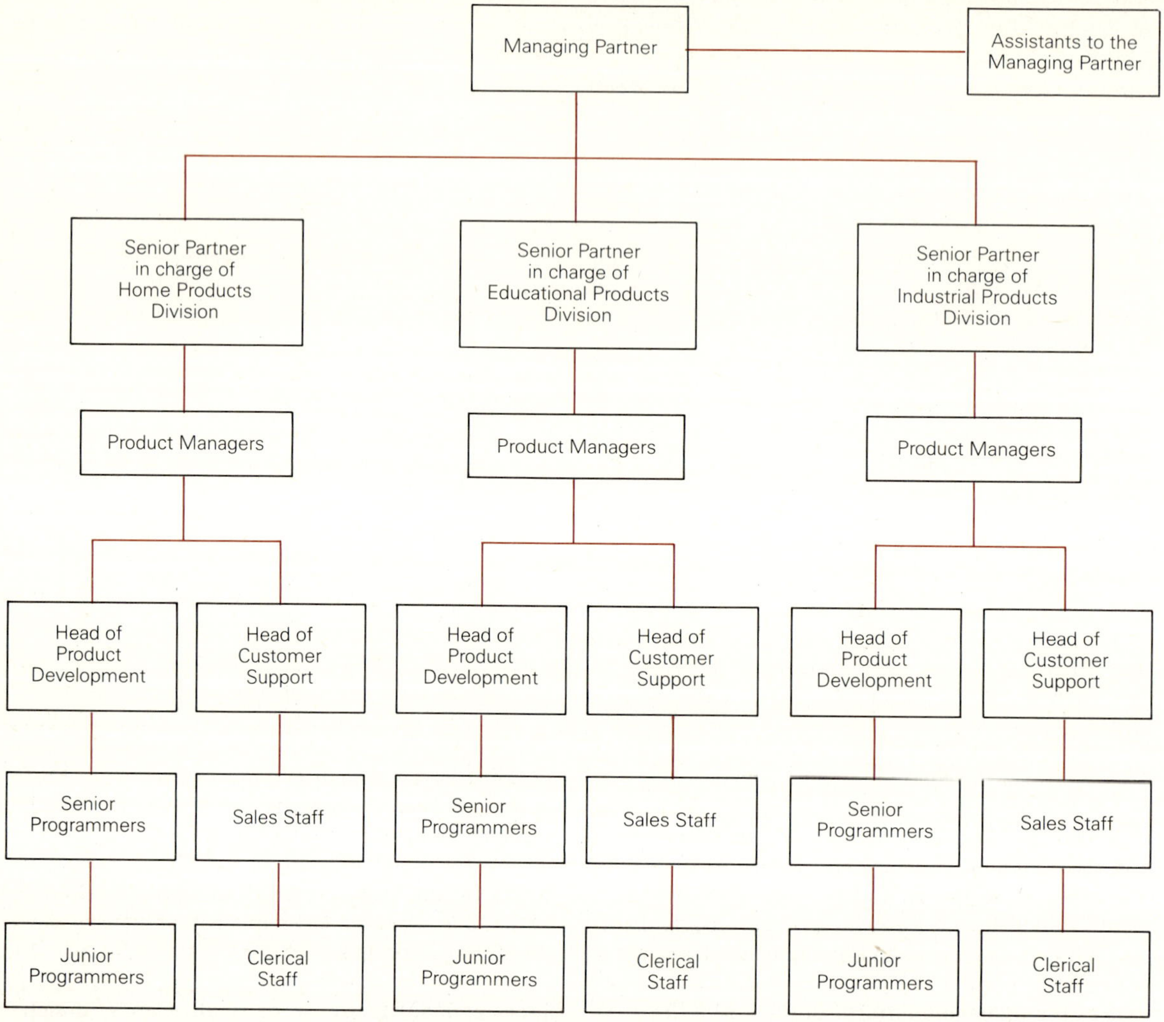

Figure 8–10 ORGANIZATIONAL CHART FOR ALLWOOD AND MASTERS, INC.

SUMMARY

Career management should be addressed from two perspectives: (1) the individual view and (2) the organizational or institutional view. In either case, it should begin with a situational audit, followed by the development of overall career strategies. Such strategies might include planning for transitions or identifying resources available for career management. Programs must also respond to the stages through which individual careers pass; the concerns of individuals entering their careers in their early twenties differ considerably from those at midcareer, and the concerns of those at late career or preretirement are different still. Thus individuals and organizations must conduct a range of activities to respond to the needs at each career stage.

Individuals are primarily concerned with planning and tracking their own careers. Planning should include regular self-assessment and evaluation of career and job opportunities. Based on these analyses individuals can formulate career goals and select the job or career that best fits with their skills, interests, abilities, and preferences. In the activities in this chapter you had the opportunity to participate in such career planning activities and to analyze the career planning performed by Sanford Jarvis.

Organizations can assist with career development activities. Human resources professionals can conduct career planning workshops, act as sources of information, and provide career counseling; managers can help subordinates to identify appropriate jobs and monitor their performance. Top management and human resources professionals can also identify various career paths for organizational members and assist individuals in the pursuit of appropriate options. Here you had the opportunity to propose a career management program for Jack Webster, Frank Robertson, and Sarah Caldman, as well as for Allwood and Masters, Inc.

The sophistication of career management varies from one organization to another. Activities range from simple, informal, and traditional ones to more complete and complex, formal, and innovative ones.[68] Leading-edge organizations may vary in size, age, and industry, but all have a commitment to effective career development for their employees.

Finally, organizations and individuals must be conscious of the interaction between work and family. With the increase in the numbers of dual-career families, as well as changing attitudes toward work, organizations are required to become more flexible than ever before in response to employees' needs in nonwork domains. The introduction of in-house day care programs, increased use of flexible work schedules, and elimination of nepotism rules are some of the ways organizations have responded.

ENDNOTES

[1]D.T. Hall, *Careers in Organizations* (Santa Monica, Cal.: Goodyear, 1976).

[2]M. London and S.A. Stumpf, *Managing Careers* (Reading, Mass.: Addison-Wesley, 1982).

[3]G.T. Milkovich and J.C. Anderson, Career planning and development systems, in K.M. Rowland and G.R. Ferris, *Personnel Management* (Boston: Allyn and Bacon, 1982).

[4]B.M. Glitzer and B. Maher, Six steps to contemporary career development, *Training* 19 (December 1982): 48.

[5]Ford-UAW Contract, February 13, 1982, Ford Motor Co., The American Rd., Dearborn, Mich.

[6]See E.H. Schein, *Career Dynamics: Matching Individual and Organizational Needs* (Reading, Mass.: Addison-Wesley, 1978); Hall, *op. cit.;* and others for discussions of the stages of careers.

[7]R.A. Webber, Career problems of young managers, *California Management Review* 18 (1976): 19–33.

[8]D.C. Feldman, A practical program for employee socialization, *Organizational Dynamics* 4 (1976): 64–80.

[9]Webber, *op. cit.*

[10]Schein, *op. cit.*

[11]London and Stumpf, *op. cit.*, p. 77.

[12]D.J. Levinson, *The Seasons of a Man's Life* (New York: Knopf, 1978).

[13]C.D. Orth, How to survive the mid-career crisis, *Business Horizons* 17 (October 1974): 12–18.

[14]*Ibid.*

[15]G.W. Dalton, P.H. Thompson, and R.L. Price, The four stages of professional careers: A new look at performance by professionals, *Organizational Dynamics* 5 (Summer 1977).

[16]J.W. Walker and T.G. Gutteridge, *Career Planning Practices: An AMA Survey Report* (New York: AMACOM, 1979).

[17]E.H. Schein, Career anchors and career paths: A panel study of management school graduates, in J. Van Maanen, ed., *Organizational Careers: Some New Perspectives* (New York: John Wiley, 1977).

[18]T.J. Delong, Reexamining the career anchor model, *Personnel* 59 (May-June 1982): 50.

[19]V. Walter, Self-motivated career planning: For productive human resource management, *The Career Development Bulletin* 3 (1983).

[20]See J.P. Kotter, V.A. Faux, and C.C. McArthur, *Self-assessment and Career Development* (Englewood Cliffs, N.J.: Prentice-Hall, 1978) for a comprehensive approach to self-assessment and career planning.

[21]*Ibid.*, p. 8.

[22]London and Stumpf, *op. cit.*, p. 43.

[23]L. Kapurch, Career assessment program at the Naval Underwater Systems Center: A study in self-paced career planning, *The Career Development Bulletin* 3 (1983).

[24]See, for example, E. Bronstein and R.D. Hisrich, *The MBA Career: Moving on the Fast Track to Success* (New York: Barrons, 1983); Kotter et al., *op. cit.;* R.N. Bolles, *What Color Is Your Parachute?* (Berkeley, Cal.: Ten Speed Press, 1980).

[25]London and Stumpf, *op. cit.*

[26]London and Stumpf, *op. cit.*, p. 44.

[27]A.H. Souerwine, *Career Strategies: Planning for Personal Achievement* (New York: AMACOM, 1978).

[28]Bolles, *op. cit.*; Bronstein and Hisrich, *op. cit.*; Souerwine, *op. cit.*, among others, call for active career planning.

[29]Souerwine, *op. cit.*

[30]M.R. Louis, Career transitions: Varieties and commonalities, *Academy of Management Review* 5 (1980): 330.

[31]*Ibid.*

[32]M. Louis, Managing career transition: A missing link in career development, *Organizational Dynamics* 10 (Spring 1982): 68.

[33]*Ibid.*

[34]Career development at First National Bank of Kansas City, *The Career Development Bulletin* 3 (1982): 5.

[35]Enhancing the early work experience of entry level professionals at General Electric, *The Career Development Bulletin* 2 (1981): 3.

[36]C. Allen, Development of middle level operating managers at Southern Railway, *The Career Development Bulletin* 3 (1984): 1.

[37]C.M. Dawson, Will career plateauing become a bigger problem? *Personnel Journal* (January 1983): 78.

[38]*Ibid.*

[39]E. Moir, Career resource centers in business and industry, *Training and Development Journal* 35 (February 1981): 54.

[40]This list is modeled after the one offered by Souerwine, *op. cit.*

[41]J. Walker, *Human Resources Planning* (New York: McGraw-Hill, 1980).

[42]See Levinson, *op. cit.*, for further discussion of these stages.

[43]D.M. Hunt and C. Michael, Mentorship: A career training and development tool, *Academy of Management Review* 8 (1983): 474–485.

[44]K.E. Kram, *Mentoring Processes at Work: Developmental Relationships in Managerial Careers,* unpublished doctoral dissertation (New Haven, Conn.: Yale University, 1980).

[45]N.W. Collins, *Professional Women and Their Mentors* (Englewood Cliffs, N.J.: Prentice-Hall, 1983).

[46]K.E. Kram, Phases of the mentor relationship, *Academy of Management Journal* (1983): 608–625.

[47]L. Phillips-Jones, Establishing a formalized mentoring program, *Training and Development Journal* 37 (February 1983): 38.

[48]*Ibid.*

[49]See E.C. Shapiro, F.P. Haseltine, and M.P. Rowe, Moving up: Role models, mentors, and the "patron system," *Sloan Management Review* 19 (1978): 51–58; and N.A. Roeske and K. Lake, Much Ado about mentors, *Harvard Business Review* 57 (January-February 1977): 14–31.

[50]Walker, *op. cit.*

[51]K. Kram and L. Isabella, Much ado about mentors, not enough about peers, *The Career Development Bulletin* 3 (1983).

[52]Phillips-Jones, *op. cit.*

[53]Shapiro et al., *op. cit.*

[54]H.L. Wellbank et al., Planning job progression for effective career development and human resources management, *Personnel* 55 (1978): 54–64.

[55]J.W. Walker, Let's get realistic about career paths, *Human Resources Management* 55 (Fall 1976): 2–7.

[56]London and Stumpf, *op. cit.*, p. 139.

[57]H.L. Wellbank et al., *op. cit.*

[58]Walker, 1980, *op. cit.*, p. 313.

[59]See J. Raelin, *Professional Careers* (New York: Praeger, 1983) for discussion of technical careers.

[60]R.M. Kantar, Variations in managerial career structures in high technology, *The Career Development Bulletin* 3 (1983): 13.

[61]L. Bailyn, Involvement and accommodation in technical

careers: An inquiry into the relation to work at mid-career, in Van Maanen, ed., *Organizational Careers: Some New Perspectives* (New York: Wiley, 1977).

[62]J.A. Hunsaker, Work and family life must be integrated, *Personnel Administrator* 28 (August 1983): 87.

[63]See Levinson, *op. cit.*; and G.E. Vaillant, *Adaptation to Life* (Boston: Little, Brown, 1977) for further discussion.

[64]B. Kabanoff, Work and nonwork: A review of models, methods, and findings, *Psychological Bulletin* 88 (1980): 60–77.

[65]F.S. Hall and D.T. Hall, Dual career couples—How do couples and companies cope with the problems?, *Organizational Dynamics* (Spring 1978): 57–77.

[66]*Ibid.*

[67]Z.B. Leibowitz, C. Farren, and B. Kaye, Will your organization be doing career development in the year 2000?, *Training and Development Journal* 37 (February 1983): 15.

[68]E.H. Burack and N.J. Mathys, *Career Management in Organizations: A Practical Human Resource Planning Approach* (Lake Forest, Ill.: Brace-Park, 1980).

FURTHER READINGS

Bolles, R.N. *What Color Is Your Parachute?* Berkeley, Cal.: Ten Speed Press, 1980.

Bronstein, E. and Hisrich, R.D. *The MBA Career: Moving on the Fast Track to Success.* New York: Barrons, 1983.

Burack, E.H. and Mathys, N.J., *Career Management in Organizations: A Practical Human Resource Planning Approach.* Lake Forest, Ill.: Brace-Park, 1980.

Collins, N.W. *Professional Women and Their Mentors.* Englewood Cliffs, N.J.: Prentice-Hall, 1983.

Hall, D.T. *Careers in Organizations.* Santa Monica, Cal.: Goodyear, 1976.

Hall, F.S. and Hall, D.T. *The Two-Career Couple.* Reading, Mass.: Addison-Wesley, 1979.

London, M. and Stumpf, S.A. *Managing Careers.* Reading, Mass.: Addison-Wesley, 1982.

Raelin, J. *The Professional Career.* New York: Praeger, 1983.

Schein, E.H. *Career Dynamics: Matching Individual and Organizational Needs.* Reading, Mass.: Addison-Wesley, 1978.

CHAPTER 9

Building a Compensation System

CHAPTER OUTLINE

LEARNING CHECKPOINTS

After completing the reading and activities in this chapter, students will be able to

- specify the characteristics of an effective reward system;
- show the relationship of various forms of compensation to motivation theories;
- describe the process of establishing a wage structure and wage levels;
- compare and contrast four methods of job evaluation;
- discuss the types of benefits available;
- describe the advantages and disadvantages of a flexible benefits program;
- construct an incentive system for increasing sales;
- evaluate an existing compensation program; and
- design a comprehensive compensation program.

INTRODUCTION

Tim Carmichael, manager of the midwest district office for Connected Network Telephone, reviewed his list of appointments that day in preparation for submitting his weekly report to central headquarters. He had met with five of the fifty employees in his office. Each had requested the meeting to discuss his or her compensation.

Connected Network had experienced rapid growth during the past five years, increasing its work force from fifty to 2000 nationwide. All personnel matters were handled in corporate headquarters in New York. Top management had recently centralized human resources management because the executives felt that each office was becoming too independent. Although there was no comprehensive pay system, the central office had recently handed down general guidelines regarding pay increases for the first time.

Tim summarized the complaints he had heard from his workers:

1. Roger Dey, an accounts receivable clerk—he had received an outstanding performance evaluation but only a cost-of-living pay increase.
2. Carol Hovey, a night supervisor who had been with the company since its founding—a recently-hired night supervisor was receiving a higher salary than Carol.
3. Ray Francis, one of five marketing representatives—he was the best performer in his group and had the most difficult product to sell, but he had received the same pay increase as his four coworkers.
4. Helen Reid, assistant manager—she had been promised yearly bonuses when she was hired; she had received none to date although profits had increased dramatically.
5. Robert Maloney, accounts supervisor—he felt that he was losing benefits because his wife was employed and their medical coverage overlapped.

In thinking about the comments he wanted to include in the report, Tim pondered why these compensation problems had arisen. He wondered whether the complaints were justified. Perhaps Connected Network really had an effective compensation system.

Does Connected have an effective system? What problems do these complaints reflect? Compensation in an organization has two major objectives: first, to obtain and keep the best employees for the organization, and second, to motivate employees to work at their highest possible productivity. To meet these objectives compensation should (1) reward employees' past performance, (2) remain competitive in the labor market, (3) maintain salary equity among employees, (4) motivate employees' future performance, (5) maintain the budget, (6) attract new employees, (7) reduce unnecessary turnover, (8) maintain company profits, (9) increase employees' job satisfaction, (10) avoid conflict in the work unit, (11) weed out poor performers (by encouraging their turnover due to dissatisfaction with wages), and (12) meet employees' personal needs.[1]

In this chapter we discuss the characteristics of a compensation system that serves these purposes. We begin by looking at the role of individual motivation and other situational influences in an effective reward system. Second, we examine the development of a wage structure that brings equity to the compensation system. Third, we look at various benefit options. Fourth, we examine incentive programs. Finally, we offer strategies for ensuring effective compensation policies and practices.

THE BACKBONE OF AN EFFECTIVE COMPENSATION SYSTEM

Does Connected Network have the underpinnings for an effective compensation system? In this section we examine two key considerations. First, the compensation system should respond to the situation. It should fit with the environment and consider the organization's goals, resources, and structure. Second, the compensation system should motivate employees. It should meet their needs, ensure equitable treatment of employees, and reward performance.

Situational Influences

The nature of the environment and the organization influence the types of compensation expected and desired by employees, the amount of money available for compensation, and the diversity of rewards offered.

Environmental Influences. Competition for workers, local, regional, and national economic conditions, the demographic composition of the work force, and federal and state legislation influence the extent and type of compensation available to workers. Where worker shortages exist, managers may use compensation to attract scarce types of employees. Wages for engineers, for example, skyrocketed in the late 1970s and early 1980s for this reason.[2] In contrast, universities employing faculty in the humanities could hold the line on salaries because of a surplus of human resources in those areas.[3]

The rate of inflation and general economic situation may influence pay increases. When inflation ran between 15 and 20 percent in the early 1980s in the United States, many workers lost money when formerly good pay increases failed to keep pace. As the supply of money tightens, fewer funds are typically available for pay increases, additional benefits, or bonuses.

The entry of more women into the work force has increased the number of dual career family members and workers with preschool or school-age children. Managers in some organizations have recognized that these employees prefer different types of compensation than in years past. To respond to new worker needs, some organizations provide day care centers, job search assistance for spouses, and more flexible sick leave policies.[4] In addition, organizations have introduced flexible benefit plans, as described later in this chapter, to better meet the diverse needs of a heterogeneous work force.

Legislation introduced in the 1960s and 1970s, such as the Equal Pay Act of 1963 and the Age Discrimination in Employment Act of 1972, revised in 1978 (see Chapters 2 and 13 for elaboration), calls for equity in compensating employees. In response, many organizations introduced wage systems (also described later in this chapter) to systematize the level and range of wages offered and ensure equity in compensation.

In evaluating the influence of the environment, managers or human resources professionals should answer questions such as the following:

1. What aspects of the environment influence compensation?
2. Have any changes occurred in the environment that should be accompanied by changes in compensation policy?
3. What compensation policies do other organizations—in the same or different industries—have?
4. How should compensation be changed in response to environmental contingencies?

Organizational Influences. The organization's resources, goals, and composition also affect the amount and type of compensation given. An organization facing a strong financial future may offer more generous pay increases to employees than an organization with an uncertain financial situation. If top management feels that the economic situation is likely to remain strong, they may increase the compensation offered. Some organizations increase the level of benefits received by employees. Others introduce profit-sharing plans. Still others increase the money available for bonuses. Similarly, organizations with limited financial resources may be forced to cut back in many aspects of compensation.

Organizations consider their goals in determining the type of job performance that is rewarded. Organizations that wish to emphasize their revenues, for example, may offer performance incentives different from those that wish to reduce costs. Organizations that wish to diversify into new markets may encourage product development by offering bonuses for patentable inventions. Similarly, organizations that emphasize individual over team performance may introduce individual incentive systems or individual bonuses rather than group or departmental rewards.

The presence of labor unions in an organization significantly influences compensation practices. Unions affect the compensation level, the freedom of organizations to offer pay increases, the types of benefits allowed, and the willingness of organizational members to participate in incentive programs.[5] Chapters 10, 11, and 12 discuss these influences in more detail.

The Job Analysis

The results of job analysis (described in Chapter 2) contribute to an effective pay system. Data collection must focus on establishing the similarities and differences between jobs and assessing the jobs' relative value or contribution.[6] The job analysis should emphasize the most important aspects of the job. These may become significant components or compensable factors in subsequent job evaluations, as described later in this chapter.

MOTIVATION AND COMPENSATION

Why should Tim Carmichael be concerned about his employees' dissatisfaction with their wages and benefits? Organizations use compensation to motivate their employees. For example, organizations give employees who come to work daily and complete their required activities their regular paycheck. Executives may encourage individuals to work extra hours by giving them compensation for that additional effort. Or managers may give bonuses to individuals who sell more than other workers or innovate new projects.

1. *Individuals are motivated to perform when they perceive that rewards are equitably distributed.* The design and administration of the compensation system must ensure that external equity, internal equity, and individual equity exist through design and implementation of an effective wage structure and appropriate wage levels.[7] *External equity* refers to wage rates that correspond to those prevailing for similar jobs in external labor markets (those from which an employer hires). External compensation levels are influenced by (1) labor market factors, such as the nature of the demand and supply of workers; (2) product market factors, such as the degree of competition, the level of product demand, industry characteristics, and other factors affecting the health of the industry and its ability to pay; and (3) the price of capital and the degree to which it can be substituted for labor in productive processes.[8] A wage system ensures external equity through setting appropriate wage levels, as described later in this chapter.

External equity, in the broadest sense, is always preserved in the long run because employees leave the organization if it does not exist. In the short term, external inequity can cause great stress in the organization as employees decide whether to leave the organization or whether the situation will pass. And since different organizations are desirable, or not, for reasons other than compensation, workers always measure the external equity in their compensation; for example, the more they are rewarded in proportion to workers holding similar jobs in competitive organizations, the more they value employment in their particular organization.

Internal equity refers to wage rates that conform to the job's internal worth to the employer.[9] Internal equity is a function of the relative status of an occupation in the organization, the economic value of job outcomes, or the social status of a job, such as its power, influence, and status in the hierarchy.[10]

There is little theory or research to guide the selection of criteria for determining internal equity.[11] Some propose job evaluation as the solution. As described later in this chapter, the development of a systematic wage structure helps ensure internal equity. In addition, the issue of comparable worth (discussed in Chapter 13) relates to internal equity. When comparable worth problems exist, the employer pays at the market rate for a job, but jobs typically held by women receive lower wages than jobs typically held by men, even though the jobs are of equal worth to the employer.

Individual equity means that individuals perceive that they are treated equitably compared to their coworkers.[12] Equity theory states that individuals make social comparisons in assessing their own rewards and status. An individual, *A*, determines the ratio of his or her inputs (effort, education, experience, skills, responsibilities, work conditions, or expected results) to outcomes or rewards O_A/I_A. Person *A* compares this ratio to his or her perception of person *B*'s ratio O_B/I_B. Depending on the individual's perception of the relative size of these ratios (is O_A/I_A greater than O_B/I_b? less than? equal to?), he or she is motivated to act in certain ways. It predicts, for example, that if worker *A* feels he or she devotes more effort to a job than coworker *B* but is paid less or receives smaller rewards (e.g., O_A/I_A is less than O_B/I_B) worker *A* will be less motivated to perform than if the ratios were the same. As one of the most visible indicators of status and perceived responsibility, compensation must be administered equitably within the organization. The wage structure and wage levels must encourage individual equity in compensation.

It looks as if there are equity problems among Tim Carmichael's work group. Some workers complained that they are not being paid in proportion to their effort relative to other workers—lack of individual equity. One worker complained that he only received a cost-of-living pay increase for outstanding performance, implying that his compensation is not comparable to that of the general labor force—lack of external equity. (Figure 9–1 shows the relationships between equity and satisfaction with pay.) Thus Tim questioned whether Connected Network had considered equity in its compensation program, and felt they had not considered the implications of lack of equity on worker motivation and productivity.

2. *Individuals are motivated to behave so that they receive rewards in proportion to their performance.*[13] This principle is based primarily on expectancy theory. Expectancy theory states that motivation is a function of three characteristics: (1) the worker's perception that his or her effort leads to performance; (2) the worker's perception that performance is rewarded (e.g., with pay, time off, or praise); and (3) the value the worker attaches to the rewards given. Oversimplifying the theory for purposes of clarity, if a person (1) works hard and produces at a high level, (2) is rewarded for that production with pay, and (3) values pay, he or she will be motivated to perform. On the other hand, if the person values pay but does not receive pay for performing, motivation will be lower; or if the person does not value pay but receives it for performing, motivation will be less. Like equity theory, expectancy theory offers implications for designing a wage structure and wage levels.

3. *Individuals are motivated to satisfy needs.*[14] Needs vary from person to person, and for the same individual at different times. Thus different forms of compensation

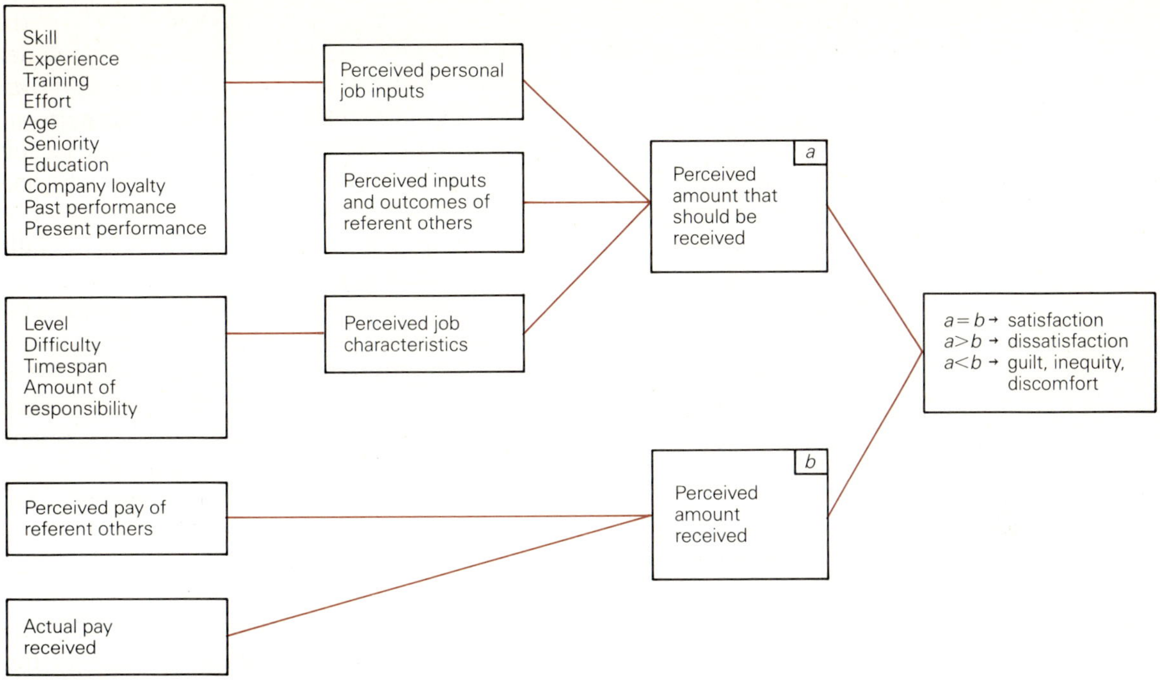

Edward Lawler, PAY AND ORGANIZATION DEVELOPMENT, © 1981, Addison-Wesley, Reading, Massachusetts. Pg. 13, Fig. 2.1. Reprinted with permission.

Figure 9–1 DETERMINANTS OF PAY SATISFACTION

may be appropriate for individuals with different needs. Benefits, in particular, should respond to individual needs. A migrant worker, for example, may have physiological needs for food and shelter but a plant foreman might have social or esteem needs instead. Organizations can satisfy these needs through the compensation system, by offering various benefits, bonuses, or wages that meet specific needs. A worker with a need for self-esteem, for example, may be more motivated to perform well if managers recognize performance with bonuses or announced merit rewards. A worker with safety and security needs may perform better if the organization rewards good performance with pensions or tenure. Since one of Tim's subordinates was given benefits he did not need, receiving these benefits most likely would not motivate him to perform.

4. *Individuals are motivated to behave in a way that receives reinforcement from their managers or other organizational members.*[15] Reinforcement theory suggests that a person can be encouraged to behave in a specific, desired way if a reinforcer (reward or punishment) is at first attached to the behavior each time it occurs, and later randomly attached to the behavior. For example, if employees receive a bonus for each month of perfect attendance, this association of a reward (bonus) with a behavior (perfect attendance) should motivate the individual to be present

at work. This principle has implications for the design of incentive systems described later in this chapter.

5. *Individuals are motivated to accomplish goals they personally set and accept as both specific and difficult.*[16] Thus a clerk-typist who agrees to increase the number of pages he or she types per day by 25 percent should be motivated to perform more than a person who is simply told to work harder. The first person has set an accepted goal that is specific and probably difficult; the second person has been given a goal that may not be accepted, is general, and may not be difficult. Managers and human resources professionals can integrate goal-setting into an incentive system, as described later in this chapter.

To use compensation (including wages, benefits, and incentives) to motivate individuals, organizations must analyze the characteristics of organizational members and the work situation. The compensation system should have five characteristics.[17] First, it should tie rewards to performance. Second, rewards should be sufficiently plentiful. Third, the criteria for the allocation of rewards should be clear and complete. Fourth, individuals should be treated differently when appropriate and similarly when appropriate. Fifth, organizational rewards should compare favorably with rewards in similar organizations.

Overall job satisfaction is influenced by how satisfied employees are with the rewards they receive from their jobs.[18] Thus the compensation system should also encourage worker satisfaction with pay since dissatisfaction may result in decreased performance, more strikes and grievances, a search for a higher paying job, high absenteeism, turnover, and other symptoms of job dissatisfaction. Instituting a systematic and comprehensive wage structure and determining appropriate wage levels, as described in the next sections, should encourage worker satisfaction with compensation.

WAGE STRUCTURE AND WAGE LEVELS

Many organizations have developed wage structures that increase the objectivity of pay decisions. These structures can apply to both hourly and salaried workers as well as to those exempt and nonexempt from overtime laws.

Classifications of Pay

Pay can be classified along a variety of dimensions, as described below.

1. Hourly pay versus salaries. Hourly employees are paid for each hour they work; salaried employees receive a specified amount regardless of the number of hours they spend on the job. Some organizations have no hourly employees. They reason that by salarying all employees a more professional work force is created; and that the organization can more easily require overtime without paying for it.[19]

2. Nonexempt versus exempt. Nonexempt workers are subject to overtime laws. These typically call for additional pay, such as time and a half or double time for overtime or Sunday work. Exempt employees are not guaranteed pay for overtime work.

Regardless of the type of pay, effective compensation calls for organizations to have a systematic way of determining pay level and pay increases. Although there are many consulting firms who specialize in developing these systems,[20] human resources professionals can also develop them for their organizations. Development of the wage structure includes the following steps: (1) performing job evaluations, (2) conducting compensation surveys, (3) collecting data to rank jobs, and (4) organizing jobs into an ordered sequence.

Methods of Job Evaluation

Job evaluation provides the basis of a fair pay system by systematically determining the relative worth of jobs to the organization. Should a newly hired janitor be paid more or less than a newly hired clerk typist? When should two different individuals holding the job of plant foreman receive different wages? Job evaluation compares jobs and determines their level within an occupational group and then compares jobs in different occupational groups in the same organization.[21] Job evaluation analyzes jobs and offers a preliminary assessment and ranking of their relative worth to the organization. Job evaluation helps specify the relative value of the jobs of accounts receivable clerk, marketing analyst, or field services manager to the organization, and helps determine which job should have higher typical or average wages.

At Connected Network, job evaluation should answer questions such as the following:

- Do the jobs of marketing representative and night supervisor differ substantively? Which holds greater value to the organization?
- Across departments, which jobs are comparable?
- Which jobs should receive the same pay?

Job evaluations can be conducted in four major ways, as summarized in Table 9–1, or in variations on these approaches. *Subjective ranking methods* evaluate the whole job in comparison to other jobs. *Grade description* or *classification methods* compare the whole job to a set of standards. *Factor comparison methods* rank specific job factors in comparison to similar factors in other jobs. *Point methods* evaluate job factors and compare them to an absolute standard. Typically a human resources professional or outside consultant oversees the job evaluation activity. Managers may assist in the collection of data and may even serve on panels empowered to rank or compare the jobs. Other employees often play a prominent role in job evaluation by offering their perceptions of the relative value of various jobs.

	Evaluation of Whole Job	Evaluation of Job Factors
Comparison of Job to Other Jobs	Ranking Method	Factor Comparison Method
Comparison of Job to Absolute Standards	Grade Description/ Classification Method	Point Method

Table 9–1 THE FOUR MAJOR JOB EVALUATION METHODS

Subjective Ranking Methods. Using this type of method, managers or human resources professionals judge the relative value of a job based on their general impression of its overall worth. They may consider the skills, experience, responsibility, or other characteristics required to perform the job in determining its absolute value. But jobs can be evaluated on different bases; for example, one may be ranked higher than another because of skills required; a second may receive a higher ranking because of education required. Job analysts may rank the job of accounts receivable clerk lower than the job of marketing representative primarily because the first requires little education and the second calls for analytical skills.

To rank jobs, evaluators can place a deck of index cards, one for each job, in order.[22] Or rankers can use the more sophisticated paired-comparison method, where they compare each job with every other job and then indicate which job of the pair ranks higher. Either way, using relatively simple mathematical techniques, a score for each job is obtained; which are then ordered to rank-order the jobs.

Grade Description or Classification Method. This method begins with a specification of a series of levels. The levels are determined based on a general consideration of the skills, experience, or responsibility required for the job. Jobs are then fitted into the most appropriate level or category. Figure 9–2 shows such a category system.

The U.S. Civil Service Job Classification Scheme uses this method of job evaluation. Job levels range from GS1 to GS18. Detailed descriptions exist for each level; for example, GS2 includes positions with the duties "to perform, under immediate supervision, with limited latitude for the exercise of independent judgment, routine work in office, business, or fiscal operations, or comparable

Class II

Ability to perform unskilled routine jobs which are almost entirely manual, requiring the use of simple tools or equipment.

Jobs usually do not require a knowledge of company methods or the exercise of judgment and decision.

Versatility may be the prime characteristic and assignments will coincide with ability to assume tasks dependent on training and skill. Work performed under direct or limited supervision.

Benchmarks

Casual plant and field labor	Guard
Car and truck loaders	Janitor
Apprentice factory mechanic	Apprentice machine operator

Class III

Ability to perform tasks of a semiskilled nature, either manual or nonmanual. Mechanically must have ability to operate or to examine machines for defects, dismantle, reassemble and adjust for efficient operation without direct or constant supervision.

May have ability to perform work of nonmechanical status, but work which requires the making of some general decisions as to quality, quantity, operations, and the exercising of independent judgment.

Benchmarks

Stockroom clerk	General truck operator
Semiskilled mechanic	Research technician
Semiskilled machine operator	

Class IV

Ability to perform work of a skilled or specialized nature. Mechanically must have the ability to set up, repair, overhaul, and maintain machinery and mechanical equipment without being subject to further check. Must have ability to read blueprints, material specifications and the use of basic shop mathematics or comparable experience with the company layout to offset these requirements.

Work may be specialized of a nonmechanical nature requiring the ability to plan and perform work where only general operations methods are available and requires the making of decisions involving the use of considerable ingenuity, initiative, and judgment. Work under limited supervision.

Benchmarks

Skilled machinist	Packaging supervisor
Skilled electrician	
Skilled mechanic	Shipping supervisor

Class V

Ability to perform work of the highest level in a trade or craft. This skill may be recognized with a license or other certification after formal apprenticeship training; or, after a considerable period of formal on-the-job training by demonstrated competence to perform equivalent level of skill.

Other employees to be considered for classification into grade V must regularly supervise others in the technical and other aspects of their work, perform other supervisory functions and may, in addition, perform work of a nonsupervisory nature.

Benchmarks

Master electrician	Factory supervisor
Master (chief) mechanic	Maintenance planner
Power plant—chief engineer	

From G.T. Milkovich and J.M. Newman, *Compensation* (Plano, Tex.: Business Publications, Inc., 1984). Reprinted with permission.

Figure 9–2 CLASSIFICATION SCHEME FOR EVALUATING JOBS

subordinate technical work of limited scope in a professional, scientific, or technical field, requiring some training or experience; or to perform other work of equal importance, difficulty, and responsibility, and requiring comparable qualifications."[23] Jobs such as secretary, mechanic, budget analyst, and director must be fitted into the appropriate category.

The grade description/classification technique is most effective in a moderate-sized organization with relatively stable jobs. It can be introduced fairly quickly and inexpensively. However, like the ranking approach, the job classification approach may lack clearly defined criteria for comparing jobs, as well as a detailed procedure for determining job levels. Further, the job performance of current job holders may influence the rankers. Quantitative methods such as factor comparison and point methods overcome some of these deficiencies.

Factor Comparison Method. The factor comparison method focuses on the evaluation of specific job factors. Job evaluation begins by identifying the key factors of each job that relate to or deserve compensation; traditionally these factors include mental requirements, physical requirements, experience requirements, skill requirements, supervisory and other responsibility, accountability, and working conditions, among others (see Figure 9–3). After obtaining job descriptions for all positions in the organization, the human resources professional or outside consultant selects ten to fifteen key jobs[24] (see Table 9–2 for evaluations of ten key jobs). Each key job is ranked on each key factor, as listed across the top of Table 9–2; these rankings are the numbers shown in parentheses. Next, the evaluators take the market rate for each key job and apportion that rate across the factors; these rates are the italicized numbers in Table 9–2. Then the pay within each column is ranked; these rankings are the starred numbers. The two sets of rankings, those in parentheses and those starred, should show little difference if jobs selected were really key jobs. If the ranks are discrepant, as for Job H, then the job should be discarded as a key job and replaced with a better selection.

Hay System

1. Know-how: practical procedures, managerial, human relations
2. Problem-solving: thinking environment, thinking challenge
3. Accountability: freedom to act, job impact on end results, magnitude

Bass System

1. Skill: intelligence or mental requirements; knowledge required; motor or manual requirements; learning time
2. Working conditions: physical application, nervous application, occupational working conditions
3. Responsibility

National Metal Trades Association System (currently known as AAIM Plan)

1. Skill: education, experience, initiative, and ingenuity
2. Effort: physical demands, mental or visual demands
3. Responsibility: equipment or process, material or product, safety of others, work of others
4. Job Conditions: working conditions, unavoidable hazards

Based on E.N. Hay and D. Purves, The profile method of high-level job evaluation, *Personnel* (September 1951): 162; E.N. Hay and D. Purves, A new method of job evaluation: The guide chart-profile method, *Personnel* (July 1954): 72; A.W. Bass Jr., Evaluating shop jobs by the point system, *The Iron Age* (September 1936): 42; American Association of Industrial Management, *Job Rating Manual (Shop)* (Melrose Park, Pa.: AAIM, 1969).

Figure 9–3 FACTORS IN SAMPLE PAY SYSTEMS

Job	Experience	Supervision	Mental Responsibilities	Physical Demands	Other Responsibilities	Market Rate
A	(1) *3.75* 1*	(1) *3.80* 1*	(1) *3.90* 1*	(4) *2.40* 4*	(7) *1.85* 6*	15.70
B	(2) *3.70* 2*	(4) *2.35* 4*	(2) *3.85* 2*	(5) *2.20* 5*	(2) *2.45* 2*	14.55
C	(3) *3.40* 3*	(2) *3.75* 2*	(6) *2.40* 5*	(8) *1.75* 8*	(8) *1.70* 8*	13.00
D	(4) *2.80* 4*	(3) *3.60* 3*	(5) *3.10* 4*	(9) *1.60* 9*	(6) *1.90* 5*	13.00
E	(5) *1.65* 5*	(6) *2.25* 6*	(3) *3.80* 3*	(6) *2.00* 6*	(1) *2.50* 1*	12.20
F	(6) *1.60* 6*	(5) *2.30* 5*	(7) *2.35* 6*	(7) *1.90* 7*	(5) *2.00* 4*	10.15
G	(7) *1.45* 7*	(7) *2.00* 7*	(8) *2.25* 8*	(1) *2.90* 1*	(9) *1.50* 9*	10.10
H	(8) *1.30* 8*	(8) *1.30* 10*	(4) *2.30* 7*	(2) *2.85* 2*	(3) *1.75* 7*	9.50
I	(9) *1.20* 9*	(9) *1.70* 8*	(9) *1.90* 9*	(10) *1.55* 10*	(4) *2.20* 3*	8.55
J	(10) *1.15* 10*	(10) *1.50* 9*	(10) *.60* 10*	(3) *2.65* 3*	(10) *1.45* 10*	7.35

Table 9–2 **JOB RANKING FOR KEY JOBS**

Once the key jobs have been completely identified, a job comparison table for another set of jobs is prepared as shown in Table 9–3. The left-hand column of this table is a list of monetary amounts; the remaining columns refer to the job factors. One (or more) key job is placed on the chart; in Table 9–3 only the key job of inventory manager, which corresponds to Job D in Table 9–2, is included. Then each job in the second set is placed higher or lower in a column than the key job, depending on a comparison of each factor.[25] Thus a managerial job would be placed higher in the accountability column than would the job of assistant to the manager. Likewise, the worth of the job of packer is determined by comparing each factor to that of the key job of file clerk. The job of packer has relatively more physical demands and relatively less mental requirements, experience, skills, supervision, and other responsibilities than the key job of inventory manager. The monetary value assigned for each factor is recorded—experience (.80), supervision (1.20), mental demands (1.00), physical demands (2.40), and other responsibilities (.60)—to yield a total rate, in this case an hourly rate—6.00. Managers or human resources professionals must then compare this rate to industry data to further check the accuracy of the job evaluation.

Next, the raters compare additional jobs to key jobs on each factor and place them in the appropriate places on the job comparison table. Finally, they record the monetary value associated with the job's position on each characteristic and add these values for all factors to yield total pay for each job. This total should correlate positively with the compensation paid for comparable jobs in other organizations, collected through the compensation survey. Where major deviations occur, reformulation of the factor comparison table may be necessary. This type of job evaluation system identifies wage levels in addition to the wage system.

Because this method requires significant agreement by a committee of professionals, it is time consuming. Further, the identification of appropriate key jobs is essential to its effective implementation. In general, the point method has replaced the factor comparison method.

Point Method. This method begins, as does the factor comparison method, by identifying the *compensable factors* (see Figure 9–3 again for examples). Each factor is described in detail. For example, the effort factor might include physical and mental effort; responsibility might include responsibility for equipment or for the safety of others. Each factor or subfactor is then weighted. Figure 9–4 presents a simplified list of factors and weightings; typically the description of factors and subfactors is more detailed. For example, a possible total of 200 points is assigned to experience; these points are awarded as shown. Similarly, 60 possible points are assigned to job complexity and 200 to supervisory responsibility.

To evaluate a job, its content on each factor or subfactor is assigned points and then the points for all factors or subfactors are totalled. In some point schemes, the points received on a factor may be multiplied by a weight that reflects the importance of that factor and summed. Jobs can then be ordered or grouped according to the number of points. Later, wage levels are assigned to various groups.

$ Value	Experience	Supervision	Mental Responsibilities	Physical Demands	Other Responsibilities
4.00		dock foreman	financial analyst		
3.80					
3.60		inventory manager			
3.40			dock foreman		
3.20	secretary				
3.00	dock foreman		inventory manager		
2.80	inventory manager		secretary		
2.60	file clerk			dock foreman	janitor
2.40				packer	
2.20	janitor				
2.00	financial analyst		janitor		
1.80				janitor	inventory manager
1.60		financial analyst		inventory manager	
1.40		file clerk	file clerk		
1.20		packer		financial analyst	
1.00			packer	file clerk	financial analyst
0.80	packer	secretary		secretary	file clerk
0.60		janitor			dock foreman
0.40					packer
0.20					
0.00					

Table 9–3 JOB COMPARISON TABLE

Factor: Experience **200 points**		
Level 1	0–2 years	30 points
Level 2	3–5 years	60 points
Level 3	6–10 years	90 points
Level 4	11–15 years	120 points
Level 5	16–20 years	150 points
Level 6	21 or more years	200 points

Factor: Complexity **60 points**		
Level 1	a few clear-cut tasks	20 points
Level 2	various related tasks or steps	40 points
Level 3	different and unrelated tasks	60 points

Factor: Supervisory Responsibility **200 points**		
Level 1	no subordinates	50 points
Level 2	1–3 subordinates	100 points
Level 3	5–10 subordinates	150 points
Level 4	11 or more subordinates	200 points

Figure 9–4 ASSIGNMENT OF POINTS TO JOB CHARACTERISTICS

Table 9–4 offers a simple application of the point method of job evaluation. Each job is evaluated on the factors listed in the left-hand column and assigned points that reflect the degree of that factor in the job. Job 1, for example, receives more points on knowledge of equipment than does Job 3. Overall, Job 2 receives the most points, followed by Jobs 1 and 3; thus Job 2 should receive more compensation than Jobs 1 and 3.

The assignment of points to a job on each characteristic is frequently done by a committee that includes human resources professionals, managers, and employees (or their representatives in unionized organizations). This method allows easy comparison of jobs in different occupational groups, considers a range of characteristics, and favors analytical comparison. The point method resembles the factor comparison method in its assessment of jobs by factors; it also emphasizes the quantification of job dimensions before, rather than after, the rank-ordering of jobs.

Although both methods are analytical, neither technique is necessarily statistically valid. Points or dollar values can easily be manipulated to create shifts in the positioning of jobs in the wage schedule. These methods lack clear principles for selecting the key characteristics, selecting the key jobs, determining the differential weights, and using mathematical manipulations to ensure statistical justification.[26] Still, research has suggested that traditional and hybrid systems, such as factor comparison or point methods, that use standardized instruments are at least as accurate, reliable, and objective in accurately determining grade levels as are statistical methods.[27]

Compensable Factors	Number of Points		
	Job 1	Job 2	Job 3
Education	40	120	55
Experience	120	100	75
Knowledge of equipment	60	20	40
Knowledge of procedures	45	75	45
General knowledge	110	150	100
Judgment	90	230	175
Mental Skill	75	150	120
Physical Effort	100	30	30
Mental Effort	300	350	200
Responsibility for others' work	175	180	90
Responsibility for others' safety	60	40	25
Responsibility for equipment	40	20	20
Job conditions	30	40	20
Total	1245	1505	995

Table 9–4 **APPLICATION OF THE POINT METHOD OF EVALUATION**

Table 9–5 reports the results of a survey of job evaluation policies and practices in 117 companies.[28] The results suggest that the point factor method is most commonly used. Job evaluation is most commonly conducted by a job analyst from the human resources department and frequently reviewed by a personnel officer for needed revisions. Evaluation of specific jobs can often be appealed through formal procedures. Because job evaluations are not inexpensive—one survey reported a median cost of $10,000[29]—organizations must ensure that they are as reliable, valid, and useful as is possible.

Compensation Surveys

Once the wage structure has been designed, organizations use compensation surveys to get information about the going rate for each job in order to determine wage levels. Figure 9–5 shows an excerpt from a compensation survey. Such surveys usually collect the following information:

1. General information—identification data, location of the organization, industry, size indicators, organization chart, work-week characteristics, and union representation
2. Wage and salary policies—the job evaluation system in use, the overall salary structure, merit adjustments, across-the-board increases, performance-related payments, and pay differentials
3. Benefits policies—pension policy, insurance, pay for time not worked, and miscellaneous benefits
4. Individual job data—job incumbent data, wage and salary data, and miscellaneous data[30]

	Exempt Only or All Employees (N = 84)	Nonexempt or Office Only (N = 63)	Plant Only (N = 25)	All Plans (N = 172)
A. Evaluation methods used:				
Point system	46	56	68	53
Factor comparison	31	35	36	33
Job classification	24	22	32	24
Hay Associates plan	23	2	0	12
Simple ranking	17	13	4	9
B. Evaluation is conducted by:				
Job analyst from personnel department	63	60	60	62
Job evaluation committee	40	38	36	39
Job analyst from department other than personnel	7	6	24	9
Outside consultant	1	1	0	1
C. Evaluations are reviewed by:				
Personnel officer	33	29	32	32
First level supervisor	18	21	20	19
Evaluation or salary committee	15	16	16	16
Top line officer/manager	17	14	16	16
Department head	7	6	0	6
Union	0	0	20	3
D. Evaluations are reviewed for possible revision:				
As needed	24	21	16	22
Annually	17	16	20	17
Every two years	7	11	8	9
Upon request	11	8	8	9
Periodically/no set time	10	10	0	8
When job changes	6	5	16	7
Other	11	11	12	12
(No response)	(14)	(18)	(20)	(16)
E. Evaluations can be appealed:				
Through formal procedure	65	60	72	65
Informal procedure only	12	11	4	10
No appeals procedure	22	20	12	20
(No response)	(1)	(8)	(12)	(5)

*Figures are percentages of plans covering employee groups indicated. For example, 46% of the 84 plans that covered exempt-only or all employees were point plans. (The five categories of evaluation methods used are not mutually exclusive.)

From Mary G. Miner, *Job Evaluation Policies and Procedures*, Survey No. 113. Reprinted by permission from *Personnel Policies Forum*, copyright 1976 by The Bureau of National Affairs, Inc., Washington, D.C.

Table 9–5 JOB EVALUATION POLICIES AND PROCEDURES SURVEY RESULTS*

Human resources professionals or executives can purchase these surveys, use a consultant to gather information, or conduct their own surveys. Sources of data include the AMA Executive Compensation Service, the United States Department of Labor, and surveys conducted by consulting firms for their own clients or

Staff and Hours

Number of employees? ______

How many hours per week do your employees normally work? ______
How much time allotted for lunch? ______
How many breaks? ______ How much time allotted for them? ______

Do you have a 4-day workweek? YES ____ NO ____

Do any of your employees work on shifts? YES ____ NO ____
If YES, answer below:

Shift	*Shift Hours*	*% Premium Pay*
Evening (2nd)	______	______
Late Night (3rd)	______	______
Other	______	______

Do you have any form of Flexitime (allowing employees to choose working hours)?
YES ____ NO ____

Salary Payment Policies

If your standard number of hours worked per week is less than 40, do you pay overtime for hours in excess of the normal workweek but less than 40? YES ____ NO ____

If certain groups within the organization have less than a 40-hour workweek, please list them.

Group	*Hours*
______	______
______	______
______	______

What is overtime rate for individuals required to work on regularly scheduled holidays?
1½ times normal pay ____ 2 times normal pay ____ Other ____

Have you paid a bonus or made a supplemental salary payment at any time within the past 12 months?
YES ____ NO ____ If YES: Date of last one ______
Approximate % of Salary ______

Have you granted any general across-the-board adjustments in salary within the past 24 months?
YES ____ NO ____ If YES:

	Date	*Approximate % Adjustment*
1.	______	______
2.	______	______

Are they linked to the Bureau of Labor Statistics Consumer Price Index?
YES ____ NO ____ If linked to any other price index, please indicate. ______

Starting Salaries—High School Graduates

What is your average starting salary for a high school graduate with *no* work experience who cannot type or take shorthand?
$ ______

What is your average starting salary for a high school graduate with *no* work experience who can type 50–60 words per minute accurately? $ ______

Figure 9–5 SAMPLE OF A COMPENSATION SURVEY *Continued*

What is your average starting salary for a high school graduate with *no* work experience who can type 50–60 words per minute and take shorthand 80–90 wpm? $ ________

Starting Salaries—Community College-Technical School Graduates

What is your average starting salary for a technical school graduate who has a usable technical skill? $ ________

What is your average starting salary for a community college graduate with an Associate Degree pursuing a *non-technical* occupation in your firm? $ ________

Starting Salaries—College Graduates

What is your average starting salary for a college graduate with a Bachelor's degree in Business Administration, Accounting, Finance, Economics, Management, etc., pursuing a *non-technical* occupation in your firm? $ ________

What is your average starting salary for a college graduate with a Bachelor's degree in Engineering, Mathematics, Statistics, etc., pursuing a *technical* occupation in your firm? $ ________

Employment Policies

Do you pay employment agency fees for non-college graduates? YES ____ NO ____
If YES: Do you pay fee at time of employment? YES ____ NO ____
If NO: When? ________

Do you require that aptitude tests be passed prior to employment? YES ____ NO ____

Employee Benefits

Paid Vacations

What paid vacations are allowed?

Years Service	*Weeks of Vacations Allowed*		
(inclusive)	Nonexempt	Exempt	Executive
0–1	____	____	____
1–4	____	____	____
5–9	____	____	____
10–15	____	____	____
Others	____	____	____

Can unused vacation be carried over the following year? YES ____ NO ____
If YES, how many days? ____

Paid Holidays

How many paid holidays do you grant? ____

Christmas Day	____	Memorial Day	____	Veteran's Day	____
New Year's Day	____	Independence Day	____	Thanksgiving Day	____
Washington's Birthday	____	Labor Day	____	Employee's Birthday	____
Good Friday	____				

Sick Leave

Do you have an official sick leave plan? YES ____ NO ____

How many days of sick leave do you grant per year? ____

Do you have a waiting period before an employee is eligible for sick leave? YES ____ NO ____

Figure 9–5 Continued

Do you have a lifetime maximum number of sick leave days an employee can take? YES ____ NO ____

Do you have a plan that permits the employee to convert sick leave to other uses? YES ____ NO ____

If YES, check the applicable conversion:

Cash ____ Vacation ____ Carryover to future years ____ Credit at retirement ____

Other Leaves

Do you grant leave with pay for any of the following reasons?

Reason	*Number of Days*	*Reason*	*Number of Days*	*Reason*	*Number of Days*
Jury Duty	____	Family Illness	____	Dental Appointment	____
Marriage	____	Death in Family	____	Other	____
Graduation Exercises	____				

Job Data

Our Job Title ________ Job Code ________ Other Possible Titles ________

Thumb-Nail Job Description:

Special Notes: This section of the form must be completed by the surveying organization prior to the printing of the form.

PLEASE COMPLETE THIS FORM FOR YOUR COMPARABLE JOB:

Job Title: ________ Minimum Pay: ________ (or entry-level hiring rate)
Job Code: ________ Maximum Pay: ________ (or maximum longevity rate)

Please indicate on each line the number of employees receiving the particular rate of pay and indicate the rate under the applicable column.

Number of Employees	Dollars				Average Years on This Job
	Per Hour	Per Week	Per Month	Per Year	

Richard I. Henderson, COMPENSATION MANAGEMENT, 4th Edition, 1985. Reprinted by permission of Reston Publishing Company, 11480 Sunset Hills Road, Reston, VA 22090.

Figure 9–5 Continued

general publication, such as Project 777, the Philip Weber Survey, and the SIRS survey.[31]

A compensation survey typically asks a representative of the organization surveyed to provide wage information for selected *key* or benchmark jobs; these are jobs for which analysts can determine what comparable employers pay for comparable jobs.[32] Obviously, the selection of key jobs is important:

1. Key jobs should be readily definable and describable.
2. Many organizations should employ people in each of the key jobs.
3. Key jobs should vary in terms of job requirements such as education and experience, and in terms of other compensable factors.
4. Key jobs should represent all salary levels within the organization.
5. Key jobs should not be in the process of changing.
6. The twenty-five to thirty key jobs should account for a sizable part of the employee population.
7. Key jobs for an organization will probably include any jobs with which the organization is having problems such as an inability to hire or excessive turnover.
8. Key jobs should probably include those jobs traditionally used on wage and salary surveys.[33]

Not only can human resources professionals conduct surveys but they should be prepared to provide data to other organizations conducting surveys as well. Consequently, there is a dilemma in obtaining accurate information. The survey is typically restricted to a specific geographical area. The organizations surveyed should include those who hire similar kinds of employees, that use a comparable job evaluation system, that are in the same industry, and that vary in size.[34] Although many organizations want salary information, they are at the same time reluctant to reduce their competitive advantage by providing other organizations with salary information. Using industry-wide surveys conducted by neutral parties helps solve this problem.

Finalizing Pay Levels, Grades, and Ranges

Once the organization has obtained both internal and external information about pay for the key or benchmark jobs, human resources professionals or the job evaluation committee can finalize the ranking of jobs within the organization. Jobs then must be grouped into between ten to twenty levels. Within each level, jobs are further ordered. Next, pay ranges are assigned to each level. In comparing levels, there will be some overlap, but the midpoints of each level should differ from between five to fifteen percent. The width of a range can be linked to market-rate data. Or a percentage band above and below the midpoint of the range can be identified. In many pay structures, the difference between midpoints remains a constant percentage. In an expanding pay structure, in contrast, the distance between midpoints may increase as the jobs move up the hierarchy, as shown in Figure 9–6. Here the difference between midpoints for entry-level jobs

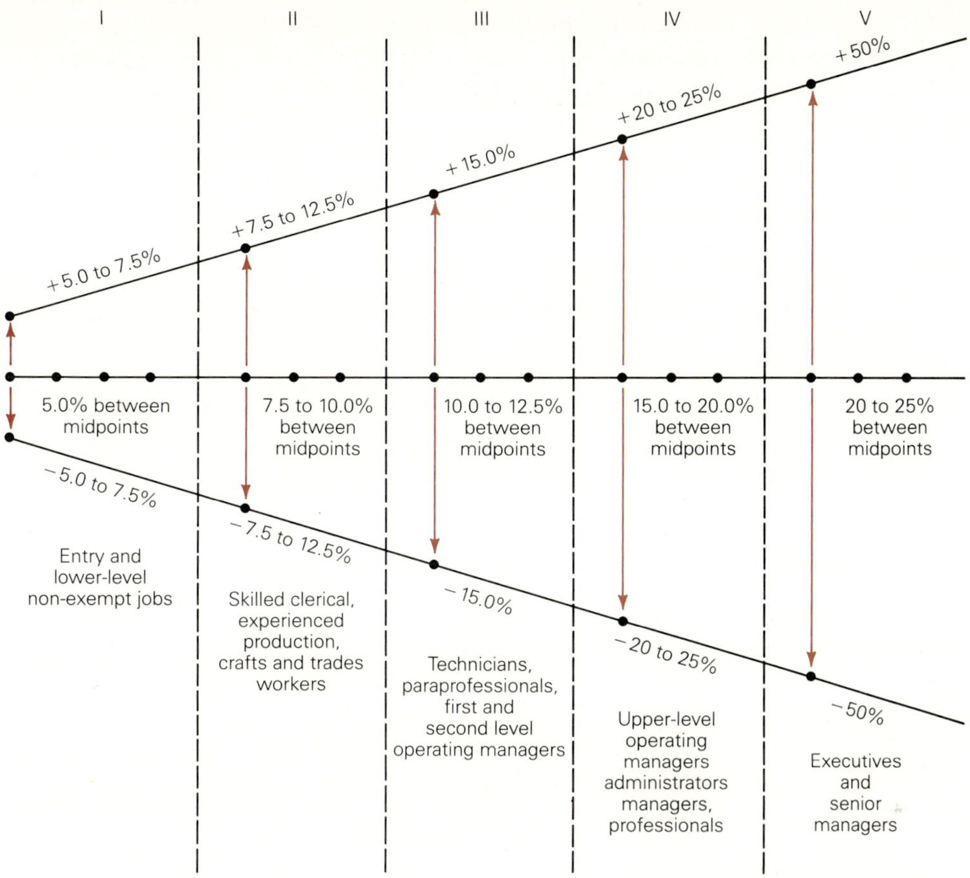

Richard I. Henderson, COMPENSATION MANAGEMENT, 4th Edition, 1985. Reprinted by permission of Reston Publishing Company, 11480 Sunset Hills Road, Reston, VA 22090.

Figure 9–6 THE EXPANDING OR FAN TYPE PAY STRUCTURE

is five percent, whereas the difference between midpoints for executives and senior managers is 20–25 percent. Fanning the structure, as it is called, and using different rates for exempts and nonexempts allows managers additional flexibility while still ensuring consistency between and among levels.[35] Some overlap in ranges cannot be avoided, but of course care must be taken to ensure that promoted employees do not receive a cut in pay, or that subordinates do not make more money than their superiors.

Within each level, there are usually between five and fifteen steps. Their size may increase absolutely, by a constant percentage, or randomly. Seniority and sometimes education exert a major influence on the step position of an individual within a level. A person new to the job is usually at step one. For each year of experience in the job or for each advanced educational credential, such as a master's degree or even credits toward the degree, individuals move up one or more steps. Significant changes in a person's current job activities and responsibilities or promotion to a new job most likely result in movement to a new pay level. Figure 9–7 illustrates the setting of pay levels and pay steps.

I. Setting pay ranges; the following illustrates overlapping hourly pay rates.

	Minimum	Midpoint	Maximum
Grade Level 1	3.50	4.25	5.00

II. Setting steps within pay level; the following illustrates pay rates within grade level 1 above.

Step 7	5.00
Step 6	4.75
Step 5	4.50
Step 4	4.25
Step 3	4.00
Step 2	3.75
Step 1	3.50

III. Determining overlaps between pay levels; the following illustrates the overlap for three levels.

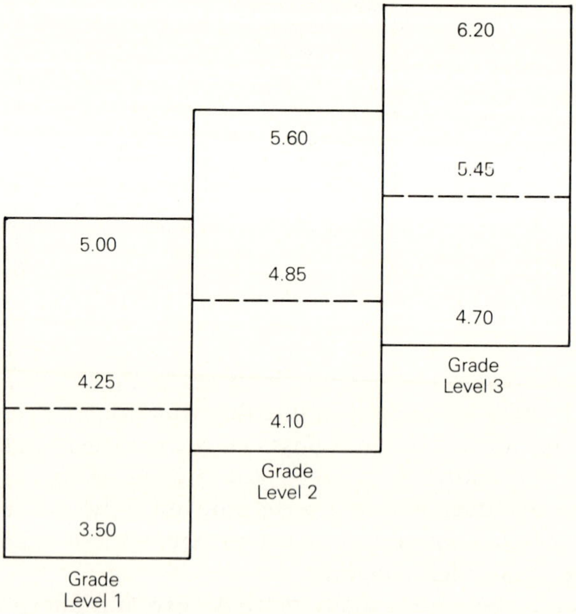

Overlap between levels 1 and 2: $.90. Overlap between levels 2 and 3: $.90.
Range of levels 1, 2, and 3: $1.50.

Figure 9–7 **SETTING PAY GRADES AND PAY STEPS**

Implementation of Results

Many well-designed pay programs fall short in implementation because of a failure to communicate the program effectively. Organizational members must be informed about and involved in the program's development and operation. It is also beneficial that they know the outcomes resulting from implementation of a thoroughly systematic program.

Organizations often question the extent to which individual pay information should be made public. Many managers favor secrecy because it gives them more freedom in administering pay, but employees counter that managers may abuse this freedom. Research suggests that making pay public can lead to a higher quality of work life and improved work climate, and prevent the dissatisfaction resulting from overestimation or underestimation of others' pay that accompanies secrecy.[36]

Merit Pay Plans

Some organizations emphasize merit pay over cost-of-living increases. The wage structure we have just reviewed can incorporate either or both emphases. Proponents of merit pay argue that it rewards those who contribute most to the organization's performance. And one research study suggests that merit pay systems closely tying performance to rewards are likely to generate higher levels of performance.[37] Opponents question the objectivity of merit pay and the amount of time supervisors must spend documenting performance. Others argue that merit pay leads to an overemphasis on individual performance at the expense of teamwork and group productivity.

For merit increases to be effective, the following conditions must be satisfied:

- Workers must trust and believe in management so they feel that merit judgments are accurate;
- a valid job analysis must exist;
- supervisors and job holders must agree about the job's tasks and criteria;
- criteria for evaluation must be job-specific and results-oriented;
- performance appraisals must be conducted regularly and accurately;
- the merit pay system must be accompanied by appropriate administrative practices;
- managers must provide regular and quality feedback to their subordinates about performance;
- managers must be trained in implementing merit systems;
- human resources professionals should implement information systems to track the administration of merit pay; and
- follow-up research about the effectiveness of merit pay must be conducted.[38]

The difficulties in implementing a merit pay system must be acknowledged. If workers, managers, and human resources professionals are committed to and competent in accurately evaluating and reporting performance, then implementation of a merit pay system is possible.

Pay Compression

Inflation has caused the salaries of entry-level employees to rise dramatically in many industries. This has resulted in new employees having comparable or even higher salaries than long-term employees. Pay compression results when new employees have high pay rates; when there are limits on pay raises, preventing the pay of current more senior employees from keeping pace with new hires; and when new employees work extensive overtime and their overtime pay is translated into higher salaries than those of longer-term employees.[39]

Pay compression can occur for the following reasons: (1) newer employees are considered more valuable because their education is more current (engineers) or because they work harder or have less security (professors); or (2) older employees lack mobility because of specialization or dearth of similar work in the geographic area where they have established roots. Pay compression typically demotivates current employees, who feel that they have worked very hard and are not rewarded at the same level as someone with no experience.

Although many organizations have dealt with this problem by automatically increasing the salaries of current employees, it is the wage structure that should reduce pay compression. Great care must be taken, however, to ensure that all relevant variables are considered in determining pay.

Other solutions include the following:

1. Organizations must view overtime with an eye toward employees' and supervisors' year-to-date earnings to ensure they are equitable. Supervisors do not necessarily have to be paid more than their subordinates, however. For example, it is not unreasonable to pay supervisors less than those they supervise if the subordinates' function is more important—as often happens with high technology expertise—or is in greater demand, as with sports players, who earn more than their managers.
2. Starting pay rates should be viewed not only in terms of external competitiveness but also internal equity.
3. Application of general increases must be preceded by study of the effects on any positions not receiving the increase.
4. Promotional increases must be legitimate and not of excessive amounts; the effects on other employees within the new classification should be examined before reaching any decisions on the amount of the increase.
5. Salary grade assignments should be developed so that each job within a promotional hierarchy is at least two pay grades above the next lower job.
6. The percentage spread between grade midpoints must be large enough to allow promotion without compression.
7. The compensation policy must allow employees to move upward within their ranges in a reasonable span of time.
8. Relocation of employees to different plants, divisions, or areas of the country must be administered with potential compression in mind.[40]

One solution to pay compression problems is to compensate for lower salary with higher benefits. In the next section we examine the types of benefits organizations offer to their employees.

BENEFIT PROGRAMS

In addition to pay, compensation also includes a wide range of benefits. Employee benefits are payments and services that protect and supplement base pay; and the employer pays for all or part of these. Estimates suggest that organizations spend on benefits an amount equal to 36 percent of the total cost of compensation.[41]

Benefits are used to help organizations meet one or more of the following objectives: (1) improve employee morale, (2) motivate employees, (3) increase job satisfaction, (4) attract good employees, (5) reduce turnover, (6) keep unions out, (7) use compensation dollars better, (8) enhance employee security, (9) maintain a favorable competitive position, and (10) enhance the organization's image among employees.[42] Too often, employees take benefits for granted, and the organization does not derive any clear value from the dollars spent.

Each benefit must be assessed in terms of how well it accomplishes the benefit program objectives. Does a flexible benefits program improve the use of compensation dollars? Does a new sabbatical program attract better employees? Benefits frequently have more favorable tax consequences for workers than does increased compensation. Benefits should, in general, be considered part of the total compensation package, and as such, linked to worker performance; for example, high performers could get larger contributions to their retirement plans than low performers.[43]

In addition to helping accomplish specific objectives, benefits programs must respond to legal or statutory requirements. The Employee Retirement Income Security Act of 1974 (ERISA), for example, imposed significant constraints on the use of pension funds and their disbursement to employees by organizations (see Chapter 13 for further discussion). Similarly, the HMO Act of 1973 required that all organizations offering medical benefits provide workers with the option of a health maintenance organization plan.[44] And the Pregnancy Discrimination Act of 1978 mandated that pregnancy be treated the same as any other disability in the benefits plan.[45]

Benefits should be chosen to respond to the needs of workers. With the increasing number of two-worker families, for example, as in the case of Robert Maloney at the beginning of this chapter, some workers may have multiple medical insurance policies with overlapping coverage. This overlap prevents the worker from receiving the full value of the benefit. Other organizations may offer educational benefits that pay for degree-related education; if most employees already have advanced degrees this benefit is useless to certain workers.

Finally, benefits must be selected to have value in proportion to their costs. Dental benefits have only recently become common because their cost is now affordable for more organizations. Likewise, some universities have eliminated the payment of tuition for faculty children to go to other universities because they found that the expense outweighed its value to the organization.

Organizations must also determine who is to be covered by particular benefits. To make this determination, executives or human resources professionals can ask the following questions:

1. What probationary periods (for eligibility for benefits) should be used for various types of benefits? Does the employer want to cover employees and their dependents more or less immediately upon employment, or provide such coverage for employees who have established more or less permanent employment with the employer? Is there a rationale for different probationary periods for different benefits?
2. Which dependents of employees should be covered?
3. Should retirees (as well as their spouses and perhaps other dependents) be covered, and for which benefits?
4. Should survivors of deceased active employees (and/or retirees) be covered? And if so, for which benefits? Are benefits for surviving spouses appropriate?
5. What coverage, if any, should be extended to employees who are suffering from disabilities?
6. What coverage, if any, should be extended to employees during layoffs, leaves of absence, strikes, and so forth?
7. Should coverage be limited to full-time employees?[46]

Reading 9–1, "Develop a Proactive Approach to Employee Benefits Planning," by Michael Carter and Kenneth Shapiro, offers an approach for answering these and other questions involved in benefits planning. In the next sections we examine four types of benefits available: (1) income and health protectors, (2) time off with pay, (3) income supplements, and (4) miscellaneous.[47] Figure 9–8 lists the benefits included in each category.

Income and Health Protectors

Five situations can prevent individuals from earning their regular wages: (1) loss of earnings because of sickness or accident, (2) inability to work because of permanent disability, (3) inability to work because of old age, (4) unexpected death, and (5) layoff or involuntary job termination. Most organizations have benefits that maintain some flow of income to individuals experiencing these situations. Benefits that respond to these circumstances include disability pay, life and accident insurance, workers' compensation (in most states), pension plans, social security, unemployment compensation, supplementary employment benefits, health insurance, and sick leave. By law, employers must pay unemployment compensation, workers' compensation (in most states), and social security benefits.

Income and Health Protectors	*Income Supplements*
Accidental death insurance	Bonuses
Disability insurance	Commissions
Life insurance	Gain-sharing plans
Medical insurance	Profit-sharing plans
Supplementary unemployment benefits	Stock bonus plans
Workers' compensation	Stock options
Time Off with Pay	*Other Benefits*
Holidays	Business and professional memberships
Personal days	Club memberships
Sick leave	Company automobile
Vacations	Credit union
	Day care
	Dental insurance
	Education costs
	Flexible work hours
	Parking facilities
	Recreation Facilities

Figure 9–8 LIST OF BENEFITS

Disability income guards against the first and second of these situations. *Life and accident insurance* can be used to provide benefits for families of workers. Workers' compensation, sick pay, long-term disability payments, and pension plans also provide this type of protection.

Workers' compensation provides money for medical care and support to workers injured on the job. Private insurance carriers, the state, or the organization, through self-insurance, provides workers' compensation coverage.[48] In states where insurance coverage is not compulsory, employers may elect not to obtain coverage but are then liable to lawsuits by employees. Premiums are a function of the types of jobs covered and the wages of job holders. Payment to injured employees depends on the workers' wages and varies according to the type of injury.

Retirement income provides a basic income for older employees. This income can come from payments to either *social security* or *pension plan* programs. Organizations typically contribute a certain percentage of an individual's salary to the pension plan.[49] The individual becomes vested in the plan after he or she has worked for the organization for a specific amount of time; initial vesting is for a percentage of the fund, increasing to 100 percent vesting after a certain number of years. Three typical approaches to vesting are derived from the Employee Retirement Income Security Act of 1974: (1) the ten-year service rule—the employee receives 100 percent of the accrued pension rights after ten years of employment; (2) the graded five-to-fifteen year service rule—here the employee is vested 25 percent after five years, then gains five percent additional vesting in each of years six through ten, and ten additional percent for each year of employment in years eleven through fifteen; (3) the rule of forty-five—50 percent vesting when the sum of the employee's age and number of years' service equals 45, then 10 percent vesting for each year of service thereafter; the person begins vesting after five years of service, must be 50 percent vested after ten years, and 100 percent vested after fifteen years.[50] Vested employees who leave the organization before retirement age may withdraw from the pension plan to the extent of their vesting.

Pay for unemployment protects income for those fired or laid off. Automobile workers, for example, receive Supplemental Employment Benefits that replace salaries for laid-off workers for three to twelve months.

Health benefits include health coverage provided by Blue Cross/Blue Shield, health maintenance organizations, and self-funding plans. Self-funding plans have become more popular as health costs have risen dramatically; organizations pay claims directly rather than providing insurance coverage for employees. Because of the increasing costs of health coverage, organizations must actively manage the financing of medical benefits and attempt to eliminate excess services, claims, and costs.[51] Some organizations are looking for ways to transfer the costs to employees, encourage second opinions and more outpatient medical care, and coordinate payments with coinsurers.

Time Off with Pay

Vacations, holidays, personal days, and sabbaticals have become so common in most organizations that workers frequently forget that they are not automatically owed these benefits.

Policy with regard to time off with pay varies considerably. Some organizations grant new employees two weeks vacation; more senior employees receive three or four weeks. Some organizations require individuals to use their vacation time each year; others allow employees to accrue it indefinitely. Organizations are increasingly introducing sabbaticals as ways of rejuvenating employees. Personal leave for military duty, jury duty, funerals, weddings, or elections may also be given. Organizations must decide which holidays to observe, who is eligible, and at what rate individuals who work on holidays are to be paid.

Sick leave policy can also vary significantly. Organizations must determine who receives sick leave, how much they receive, whether it accrues indefinitely or just for a year, and whether employees receive part or all of it upon leaving the organization. Because of the significant cost associated with sick leave, organizations are looking for ways to reduce its abuse. To do this, some organizations have even instituted a well-pay policy, where bonuses are paid to employees with no absences during given time periods.[52]

Income Supplements

These plans typically reward employees for exceptional performance or longevity in the organization. They include profit sharing plans, stock bonus plans, suggestion award plans, and productivity gain-sharing plans. These benefits share the following characteristics:

- They are usually available to all or a large segment of employees in the company.
- Rewards can be related to an individual's or a group's contribution to increased profitability, reduced costs, and improved operations.
- These plans can create additional income or capital for employees.
- There is no requirement to work extra hours to receive extra compensation.
- These plans frequently offer employees distinct tax advantages over cash bonus plans.[53]

Profit sharing plans redistribute a percentage of the organization's profits to the employees.[54] This type of plan provides employees with long-term benefits in proportion to the company's performance. Thus the better their personal performance, the better should be the organization's performance. Profit sharing plans may pay workers shares of the profit shortly after profits have been determined, or reinvest these shares for payout when the individual leaves the organization or retires. Some plans combine cash and deferred payments. Executives of organizations that have experienced takeovers have received special profit sharing bonuses called *golden parachutes,* which are designed to protect them financially after the change in organizational control.[55] Care must be taken in establishing such plans to ensure that executives have both long-term and short-term views of corporate performance.[56]

Productivity gain-sharing plans became popular with the introduction of the Scanlon Plan in the 1930s. Scanlon believed that a company that would use employee ideas and reward employees for their efforts would increase its profitability and thus increase workers' job security and pay; workers received bonuses for increasing profits by certain amounts.[57]

In gain-sharing plans employees offer suggestions for improving productivity and then share in the gains.[58] Gain-sharing plans are based on a formula that yields a monetary pool for organizational members. The plans establish a standard based on past performance.[59] The most common base ratio equals labor costs divided by the sales value of production. Thus, if labor costs are reduced, the ratio decreases, and a contribution is made to the bonus pool. If labor costs increase, the ratio increases, and no bonus, or in some cases a deduction from the pool, is made. The costs included in the bonus calculation vary; they may include labor, materials, or utility costs. Organizations must decide how much to share, who will share, how the money is to be divided, and how frequently the bonus is to be calculated.

A successful plan results in the following:

1. The plan enhances coordination, teamwork, and sharing of knowledge at lower levels.
2. Social needs are recognized via participation and mutually reinforcing group behavior.
3. Attention is focused on cost savings, not just quantity of production.
4. Acceptance of change due to technology, market, and new methods is greater because higher efficiency leads to bonuses.

5. Attitudinal change occurs among workers, and they demand more efficient management and better planning.
6. Workers try to reduce overtime—to work smarter, not harder or faster.
7. Workers produce ideas as well as effort.
8. More flexible administration of union-management relations occurs.
9. Unions are strengthened because they are responsible for a better work situation and higher pay.[60]

Programs fail when the formula for determining workers' financial shares is not accurate or fair, bonuses are not paid regularly, managers do not support the program, the plan focuses on labor costs to the exclusion of other controllable costs, workers do not understand the plan, unions do not cooperate, or supervisors feel threatened by the plan.[61]

To some extent these resemble profit sharing plans, except the amount paid to workers is not tied to profits, but rather to reduced costs and increased productivity, which are generally more under workers' control. Table 9–6 lists the conditions favoring a gain-sharing plan.

Stock bonus plans resemble profit sharing plans in that they distribute a share of the company to employees as a way of encouraging their performance. However, these distributions are in the form of company stock. A recent survey of twenty-one high technology firms indicated that 67 percent use stock purchases to encourage a team approach among top executives.[62] In firms where a family or only a few people own stock, stock bonus plans can experience problems because of subjectivity involved in determining the worth of stock; owners can adjust the value upward or downward in light of their own objectives. The valuation of stock may not then be the most favorable one for employees.

Recently *employee stock ownership plans* (E.S.O.P.) have been used to raise capital for organizations. Employee stock ownership plans come in three forms: (1) a stock bonus plan—the organization gives stock to a trust to benefit employees; (2) a leveraged ESOP, in which the trust can borrow money to buy stock in the organization; and (3) a TRASOP, in which both employer and employees contribute equally to the trust fund but stock cannot be distributed for seven years.[63] ESOPs have the following advantages: (1) working capital remains constant because payment is in stock; (2) employees who "own" the organization are assumed to be more motivated; (3) takeovers can be more easily avoided; (4) contributions are not based on profit; and (5) employers do not owe employees pension money for the time before the ESOP was established.[64]

Suggestion award plans are the final way for employees to earn additional income. Employees are rewarded for demonstrating innovation in solving difficult problems, offering ways of cutting costs, or suggesting new products. Management either divides a pool award among all individuals whose suggestions were used by the organization, or management assigns a value to certain types of suggestions. In either case, these programs should encourage employees to be more creative, help employees gain recognition, help organizations target more innovative employees, and assist in communication between management and employees.[65]

Organizational Characteristic	Favorable Condition
Size	Small unit, usually less than 500 employees
Age	Old enough so that learning curve has flattened and standards can be set based on performance history
Financial measures	Simple, with a good history
Market for output	Good, can absorb additional production
Product costs	Controllable by employees
Organizational climate	Open, high level of trust
Style of management	Participative
Union status	No union, or one that is favorable to a cooperative effort
Overtime history	Limited to no use of overtime in past
Seasonal nature of business	Relatively stable across time
Work floor interdependence	High to moderate interdependence
Capital investment plans	Little investment planned
Product stability	Few product changes
Comptroller/Chief financial officer	Trusted, able to explain financial measures
Communication policy	Open, willing to share financial results
Plant manager	Trusted, committed to plan, able to articulate goals and ideals of plan
Management	Technically competent, supportive of participative management style, good communications skills, able to deal with suggestions and new ideas
Corporate position (if part of larger organization)	Favorable to plan
Work force	Technically knowledgeable, interested in participation and higher pay, financially knowledgeable and/or interested
Plant support services	Maintenance and engineering groups competent, willing, and able to respond to increased demands

Table 9–6 CONDITIONS FAVORING GAIN-SHARING PLANS

In selecting a pension program, the employer must answer the following questions:

1. What mix of pension, profit-sharing, ESOP, and option benefits are to be offered?

2. How much are employees to get?
3. How are differences in benefits to be determined? Seniority, profits, salary level, age, or a mix?
4. How much should employees contribute to the plan?
5. Should benefits be subject to cost-of-living adjustments?
6. Should other employee income (such as Social Security) affect benefit levels?
7. When are benefits to start? Can employees retire early for reduced benefit levels?
8. What happens to benefits if employment terminates for reasons other than retirement?
9. How are payouts to be made (lump sum, income flow, or a combination)?
10. How is vesting to be handled?
11. Can the employee draw on benefit funds (e.g., borrow against them) while still working for the organization?
12. How is the fund to be administered?
13. To what extent should employees participate in fund administration?
14. How is the fund to be insured against economic adversity?[66]

Answers to these questions then determine the type of pension program introduced, its funding, the determination and distribution of benefits, and the administration of the fund by the organization.

Other Benefits

Organizations have created a range of benefits to respond to the unique needs of their members. These include education benefits, matching charitable contributions, moving expenses, product discounts, credit unions, subsidized food services, employee assistance programs, and others.

Flexible work schedules have come into much greater use over the last decade.[67] Here, individuals are given a choice in the specific hours they work, so long as they include a set of core hours. For example, one worker may work from 7 A.M. to 3 P.M. with an hour for lunch, while another worker may work from 9 A.M. to 5 P.M. with an hour for lunch. The worker negotiates the precise hours with his or her supervisor and coworkers. Other forms of flexible schedules include compressed work weeks where individuals work their entire work week in four instead of five days, or part-time employment where employees work between one-half to three-quarters of the normal work week.

Some organizations offer special services to their employees. They may include savings plans, credit unions, charter flights, food services, legal services, child care, company care, parking, or uniforms.

Flexible Benefit Plans

In response to the duplication of benefits or the failure of some benefits to respond to individual needs, organizations have begun to introduce programs where employees can choose from a smorgasbord of benefits.[68] Also known as *cafeteria fringe benefit plans,* these programs provide employees with some choice of benefits. First introduced in the mid-1970s at TRW Systems, Educational Testing Service, American Can Company, Northern States Power, and Pepsico, these plans address the new needs created by a changing work force that includes many more women than before.[69] Workers with spouses who have sufficient medical insurance can choose additional vacation time rather than health insurance as part of their benefits package. Likewise, workers who do not want educational benefits might choose additional life insurance instead.

Individuals are given a certain dollar value or number of points they can allocate to benefits, depending on their seniority, job type, or other factors. Each benefit also has a dollar value or number of points associated with it. For the most part, employees may spend their points the way they want to, though selection of benefits may be subject to certain constraints since organizations typically require some core benefits as a way of protecting employees and themselves against disastrous choices. For example, employees are generally required to have a certain level of medical insurance.

While the cost and difficulty of administering these plans initially limited their use, the availability of computer programs for administering them, and changes in the costing of group benefits, have made them more accessible to organizations. In one study at TRW, workers in flexible divisions felt that their benefits were better than those in nonflexible divisions.[70] Robert Maloney, the employee of Connected Network Telephone, would most likely be enthusiastic about a flexible benefit plan.

Communication of Benefits Plans

Too often workers take benefits for granted. Organizations must communicate to their workers the dollar value of benefits plans. To do this, some organizations provide individual employees with a yearly or bi-annual report of the value of their benefits; Figure 9–9 shows an excerpt of such a report. In a unique communications effort, one hospital conducted a benefits fair that drew individuals' attention to the nature and value of available options.[71]

INCENTIVE PROGRAMS

Incentive programs pay an individual or group of individuals for precisely what is produced. For example, if the worker assembles toy tea sets, then he or she receives a certain amount of money for each tea set assembled. Similarly, a sales team would be paid a specific amount for each tea set it sold. Piecework, commission plans, and bonuses are the most common incentive systems, although some compensation specialists classify the profit-sharing and gain-sharing plans

About Your Booklet

This booklet briefly summarizes the major Benefit Plans and provides you with a personal statement of the value of your insured benefits. With this booklet, you can review your total benefit package at the University and see how much it's worth to you.

Certain benefit amounts and information shown in this booklet are based on your personal data, such as age, salary, length of service, and plan membership, as of December 31, 1980.

Before you read about each benefit separately, please look at the following figures. They show the University's cost for your Life and Disability Insurance, Medical Insurance, Retirement Plan and Social Security coverage. (This does not include costs for benefits such as vacations, tuition remission, and Worker's Compensation insurance.)

Annual Value—in addition to your salary

$5,503 This is the approximate total cost to provide your insured benefits.
$1,943 This is your share of the cost including $1,494 for Social Security.
$3,560 The difference, therefore, is the **Annual Value** of your insured benefits, a sum paid for you entirely by your employer.

Note: Your Social Security number appears in the lower right-hand corner of this page, as well as pages 3, 5 and 10 to assure that all financial information is yours.

Employer provides the following Sick Leave and Disability Benefits:

Sick Leave. In the event of a long-term illness or disability, you would be eligible to receive: full base pay for up to 6 months as long as you have completed 1 year of service.

TIAA Total Disability Insurance Plan. Plan members who remain totally disabled for longer than 6 months are eligible for an **Income Benefit** until recovery or age 65.

$1,123 per month is your benefit.

In addition, for TIAA Retirement Plan members, under the **Annuity Premium Benefit** the Disability Insurance will contribute to a member's TIAA-CREF Retirement Fund at the same level as before disability (subject to 13% maximum).

The plan will contribute 10% of your salary as the premium benefit.

For employees receiving Disability Benefits, Employer will also continue to provide **Group Life Insurance** and **Medical Insurance** coverage at no cost to the employee.

Employer offers the following program for your survivors:

Lump Sum Benefits

$45,000	Group Life Insurance
$437	TIAA-CREF Death Benefit
$255	Social Security Lump Sum
$45,692	Lump Sum Total

If accidental death occurs while traveling on university business, an additional $50,000 would also be paid to your beneficiary.

Monthly Family Income Benefits

Your surviving spouse and/or dependent children together may qualify for Social Security Survivors Benefits currently estimated at:

$418 monthly if your surviving spouse has no dependent children and is at least age 60 (the minimum age requirement);

or

$877 monthly if your surviving spouse has one dependent child;

or

$438 monthly for each surviving dependent child up to a $1,024 family maximum

Additional employee death benefit paid by your employer: 3 months salary after 5 years of service, or 6 months salary after 10 years service.

Reprinted with permission of Leo Sullivan, Director of Personnel, Boston College, Chestnut Hill, Mass.

Figure 9–9 EXCERPT FROM A BENEFIT REPORT

described earlier as incentive programs. Incentive plans can be tied to individual, group, plant, or organizational productivity.

Piecework systems tie compensation to individual performance; individuals are paid for each item produced. That is, the employee is paid for each circuit board assembled, each application processed, or each new client recruited. In establishing their pay an analyst would consider a market rate in determining fair pay associated with a certain level or *standard* of performance. If, for example, welders earn fifteen dollars per hour and job analysis shows they should be able to weld thirty pipe joints per hour, then the piece rate should be 50 cents, or the market rate ($15) divided by the output standard (30 pipe joints). Piece rates generally guarantee a minimum wage, with high producers exceeding it.

In a *straight piece rate plan*, the worker receives a certain amount of pay for anything he or she produces above the standard. In a *differential piece rate plan*, there are two pay rates. Under the latter system, when a worker completes the work in a set time and in an acceptable condition, he or she receives a higher pay rate per unit produced; but when the worker takes longer than the established time to complete the work, he or she receives a lower rate per unit.[72]

The major advantage of this pay approach is that individuals see that performance is rewarded. Implementing an incentive program for production jobs is relatively straightforward, but implementation of such a program for more complex jobs is more problematic. Either way, dissatisfaction can occur if inappropriate standards are set; workers may resent managers or discourage high producers by isolating them.

Lincoln Electric Company is an example of an enterprise that has a company-wide incentive program.[73] Workers are guaranteed thirty hours of work fifty weeks a year, but are not guaranteed a specific level of pay. Most workers are on a piecework incentive program, with a merit-rating program supplementing the piecework program. Workers receive ratings on dependability, quality, output, ideas, and cooperation. In addition, they can purchase twenty-five shares of stock each year. Profits are divided among the corporation, the shareholders, and the employees. Employees also receive an annual cash bonus, which is a function of the total labor cost, the individual's merit rating, and total profit.

Commissions link pay to sales rather than to production. Individuals may receive a certain percentage of sales, a certain percentage of new sales, or pay for reaching sales quotas. Some salespeople receive a base amount and then earn a commission above the base.

Bonuses are lump-sum payments that are tied to exceptional performance. A baseball pitcher, for example, may receive a bonus for a certain number of wins. An advertising account executive may receive a bonus for signing a new client.

Figure 9–10 offers a list of steps that should be followed in designing a short-term incentive program. Should Tim Carmichael consider introducing such a program at Connected Network? What effect would it be likely to have on his subordinates' attitudes about their compensation?

Incentive systems offer the following advantages: (1) they can contribute to

1. Who should be eligible to participate? Why should these executives be included and not others? Will this definition be accepted by those not eligible? Is such acceptance important?

2. How important is performance of the individual, the unit, and the corporation? What should be the relative weighting of each?

3. What measurable factors will quantify performance? How should they be weighted?

4. What factors can alter the attainability of the target? What is the probability and severity of each? To what extent will these factors be reflected in revised targets?

5. How much should the participants receive for meeting pessimistic, most likely, and optimistic performance targets? Should there be a maximum payment? If yes, why, and at what performance level? If no, why not?

6. Is the reward in balance with the responsibilities and degree of risk? How much downside risk in total pay is reflected in the incentive program?

7. How will the long-term incentive plan integrate with the short-term program?

8. How will SEC requirements impact the plan design? What shareholder action is required? How will the plan and its payments be disclosed in the proxy statement?

9. If this is a unit of the company and the incentive opportunity is significantly greater than for comparable positions in other units within the company, how is this reconciled? How will transfers of executives be accommodated?

10. When will payments be made and in what form? Will deferred amounts be contingent upon continued employment? Will such amounts be credited with some type of interest?

11. Will earned, vested, or actual payments be the basis for determining competitiveness of the executive's total pay package?

12. How will payments be considered for employee benefit programs (for example, will such amounts be treated as earnings for life insurance and pension plans)?

13. How will disability, death, and retirement be treated when it occurs during the plan period?

14. How will the plan be communicated? What data will be provided to participants before and during the plan period to enable them to estimate potential payout?

15. Having considered all of the above, what five factors are basic to the design of an effective short-term incentive plan for the unit considered, and what is the relative importance of each of these factors?

Figure 9–10 SHORT-TERM INCENTIVE PLAN DESIGN CONSIDERATIONS

increased productivity, lowered production costs, and increased earnings; (2) they can require less direct supervision to maintain specific output levels; (3) they encourage workers to reduce lost time and make more effective use of time and equipment; and (4) they can result in a more accurate determination of labor costs.[74]

The disadvantages include the following: (1) the quality of the product may deteriorate; (2) if the results are unreasonable, employee efficiency and morale may decline; (3) the risk of accidents may increase; (4) inaccurate rate-setting may lead to inequitable earnings; (5) the administration of the system requires some additional costs; and (6) workers may be resistant to changing the conditions of production.[75] Incentive programs may fail because they do not meet employees' needs, the likelihood of success is too low, or the plan is not equitable.[76]

STRATEGIES FOR EFFECTIVE COMPENSATION

Employee compensation is the biggest overhead expense for organizations. Careful determination of the costs and making compensation cost-effective are important. A comprehensive compensation program assigns pay according to a prescribed, systematic structure, includes a range of benefits to fit individual needs, and involves incentive programs for directly rewarding performance. Pay must be tailored to organizational strategies, organizational culture and values, employee needs, and union requirements. Compensation policy influences individuals' decisions to accept a job offer, leave or remain with an employer, or perform at a certain level.

Organizations should develop a comprehensive statement of their compensation philosophy. This statement should address the following questions:

1. What are the goals of the compensation system?
2. What aspects of compensation should be communicated to organizational members and how should communication occur?
3. Who is to be involved in making compensation decisions?
4. Does the organization want to be a high, average, or low payer in its industry?
5. How centralized or decentralized is the formation and administration of compensation policy to be?
6. What is the desired mix between benefits and cash?
7. What is the role of performance-based pay?
8. How do performance appraisal and compensation practices interface?
9. Does the compensation policy reinforce or contradict the management philosophy of the organization?
10. How are changes in compensation policy and practices to be managed?[77]

Both human resources professionals and managers should be involved in the design and implementation of these systems. They must recognize that different aspects of compensation have different values. For example, salary has high value for attracting and retaining employees and moderate value for motivating them; benefits have low value for attracting and motivating employees and moderate value for retaining them; short-term incentives have high value for attracting and motivating employees and moderate value for retaining them; long-term incentives have moderate value for attracting and motivating employees and high value for retaining them.[78]

Implications for Human Resources Professionals

Human resources professionals should oversee the design and implementation of compensation systems. Effective compensation management includes the following practices:

1. Human resources professionals can perform a comprehensive situational audit to determine the environmental and organizational factors that are to lead to the amount, type, and apportionment of compensation given to employees. They must be certain that there are current job descriptions, specifications, and performance standards for all jobs.

2. Human resources professionals must ensure that the organization has a systematic and equitable wage structure which motivates individual organizational members to perform in desired ways. They can act as compensation analysts and design the system themselves, or hire compensation experts to develop an appropriate wage structure.

3. Human resources professionals should conduct periodic salary surveys to determine market conditions for various positions in their organizations; they should also subscribe to the most appropriate salary reports for their industry.

4. Human resources professionals must monitor the wages of new workers and institute programs directed at preventing pay compression.

5. Human resources professionals should recommend and introduce flexible benefits programs so that benefits respond to workers' needs and meet organizational objectives; they should regularly audit the benefits program to ensure its cost-effectiveness and motivational characteristics.

6. Human resources professionals should design individual and group incentive programs that emphasize the accomplishment of such organizational goals as profitability, cost reduction, and productivity; and they should monitor the environment for innovative incentive programs that could work in their own organizations.

Implications for Managers

Managers must understand the existing compensation system so that they can implement it effectively. Effective human resources management in compensation includes the following:

1. Managers should be involved in the collection of accurate data about jobs to ensure that job analyses are current.

2. Managers should communicate the details of pay plans to their subordinates; they must understand the design and implementation of the wage structure.

3. Managers should encourage the use of merit pay for performance; they must keep accurate performance records and communicate their assessment of employees' performance to their workers.

4. Managers must assist human resources professionals in reducing pay compression; they must consider ways of moving current employees to higher paying positions where appropriate.

5. Managers must diagnose their subordinates' needs so they can recommend appropriate benefits to the human resources professionals or top executives involved in the design of benefits plans.

6. Managers should implement incentive programs, such as suggestion awards, bonuses for outstanding performance, or cost-reduction rewards where possible; and lobby top management for the financial support for such programs, if necessary.

READING

Reading 9–1

DEVELOP A PROACTIVE APPROACH TO EMPLOYEE BENEFITS PLANNING

Michael F. Carter and Kenneth P. Shapiro

In the first half of this century, employee compensation consisted primarily of "cash"—wages, salary, and bonuses—modestly supplemented by "fringe" benefits. Since World War II, however, employee benefits have increased significantly, moving from the "fringe" to the "fabric" of employee compensation.

Today, the average U.S. employer spends an additional 30% of payroll on benefits such as pension; health, disability, and life insurance; thrift, profit sharing, and stock plans; and mandated benefits (Social Security and worker's and unemployment compensation). Moreover, paid time off (vacations, holidays, and sick leave)—representing 10% of payroll costs—brings the total benefit expenditure of the average employer to 40% of payroll.

Despite the size of this expenditure, management has generally not actively planned or managed benefits programs, but instead has reacted to current trends and practices.

However, due to the growing size of benefits in the total remuneration package, differing employee needs, benefits program complexity, and legal, tax and competitiveness issues, it is now clear that benefits planning must be not only thoughtful, but proactive.

THE PLANNING CYCLE

Benefits planning, like most planning, should not be a one-time exercise, but rather an ongoing process. The steps in this process are illustrated in Figure 9–11. Because of the cost of benefits, and the importance of business strategy and management style in the total remuneration planning process, remuneration planning should be conducted by senior management as a group, rather than by compensation and benefits specialists alone.

Such a committee approach should ensure that the organization's goals and strategies are supported by an effective remuneration program, and that the program will be attractive to, and suitable for, the kinds of employees that are best for the organization. The right program will reinforce the objectives of the organization.

To be most effective, benefits planning should be conducted as a part of a total remuneration program: base salary, incentives, benefits, executive perquisites, and intangible rewards. The ultimate goal of a total remuneration program is to attract, retain, and motivate employees to fulfill the organization's goals

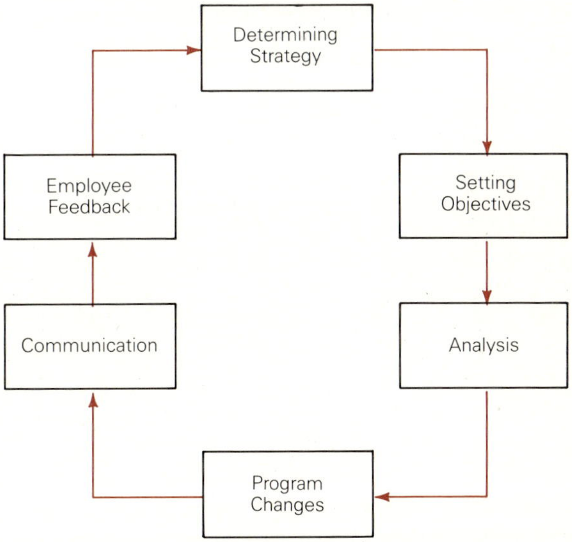

Figure 9–11 THE BENEFITS PLANNING CYCLE

"Develop a Proactive Approach to Employee Benefits Planning," by Michael F. Carter and Kenneth P. Shapiro, copyright July 1983. Reprinted with the permission of *Personnel Journal*, Costa Mesa, California; all rights reserved. Excerpted from M.F. Carter and K.P. Shapiro, HANDBOOK OF WAGE AND SALARY ADMINISTRATION (New York: McGraw-Hill, 1983).

and objectives. Attracting and retaining the right kind of people is aided by developing a total remuneration program with a mix of compensation elements that best fits the organization.

Determining that best mix is a step-by-step process that starts with an analysis of the organization's business cycle and business type and includes primary consideration of management style (as demonstrated in Figure 9–12).

MATCHING STYLES AND CHARACTERISTICS

Examples of how to best match the total remuneration mix with the organization's style and characteristics are shown in Table 9–7. For instance, an industrial company with a competitive product in a growing market would be in a developing business cycle and therefore would probably have a strategy of investment and growth. An appropriate management style could be entrepreneurial, which requires dynamic risk-taking individuals.

An appropriate total remuneration mix under these circumstances would be a lower level of benefits, and a higher level of cash compensation—particularly incentive compensation. The benefits provided could be short-term, stressing medical and dental coverage and time off.

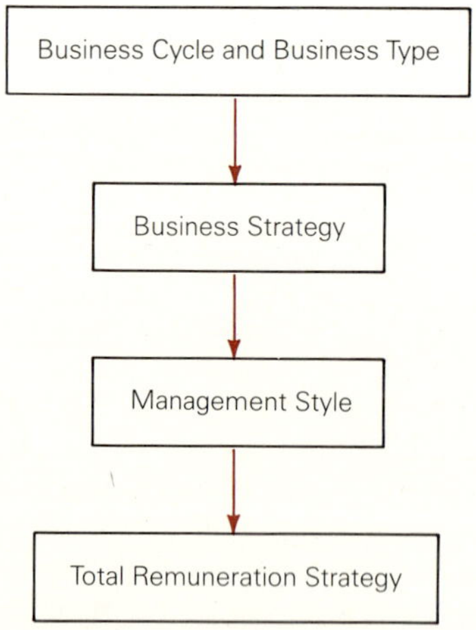

Figure 9–12 **THE PROCESS OF DETERMINING TOTAL REMUNERATION STRATEGY**

In contrast, a conservative financial organization would have very different business characteristics and would thus be best served by a different total remuneration mix. Business strategy here, which might be controlled growth coupled with protection of assets, would generate a conservative management style and require security-oriented individuals.

The total remuneration package in this kind of organization might stress benefits rather than cash compensation. In particular, it would probably be appropriate to have limited or no cash incentives. The benefits provided could be long-term and security-oriented, emphasizing retirement income and protection coverages such as life and disability insurance.

Finally, in determining the total remuneration strategy, management must consider developing different programs for different employee types within the total organization. For example, the total remuneration mix is often different for sales positions than for other jobs in the company.

SETTING OBJECTIVES

Once strategies are set, specific objectives should be developed. A checklist of major benefit objective issues is shown in Figure 9–13. One primary objective concerns competitive position. The organization's desired competitive compensation position is a result of its total remuneration mix (as determined in the previous step).

Related to competitiveness is benefits adequacy. Decisions are made here regarding the desired level of disposable income replacement after retirement, disability or death; appropriate levels of health insurance; and the level of employees' responsibility in protecting themselves through their own personal savings, individual insurance, premium cost sharing, and deductibles and coinsurance.

Flexible benefits programs can be considered in the objective setting phase. Most companies already offer some modest degree of flexibility by allowing a choice of an insured medical plan or health maintenance organization, a supplemental life insurance or other plan, and other options.

Type of Organization	Working Climate	Reward Management Components: Cash — Base Salary	Cash — Short Term Incentives	Noncash — Level	Noncash — Characteristics
Developing Industrial	Growth, Creativity	Medium	High	Low	Short Term-Oriented
Mature Industrial	Balanced	Medium	Medium	Medium	Balanced
Conservative Financial	Security	Low	Low	High	Long Term, Security-Oriented
Nonprofit	Societal Impact, Personal Fulfillment	Low	None	Low-Medium	Long Term, Security-Oriented
Sales	Growth, Freedom to Act	Low	High	Low	Short Term-Oriented

SOURCE: Hay Huggins Bulletin, December 1980.

Table 9–7 ORIENTING COMPENSATION MIX TO ORGANIZATIONAL STYLE

There is a growing awareness that most firms are composed of a divergent employee population of various ages and different marital and dependents status. These employees, therefore, have very different benefit needs. To better address these needs, and thereby achieve greater employee satisfaction and awareness, additional forms of flexible benefits should be considered. One caveat: Although the advantages of flexible benefits programs can be great, setting up related administrative and communications procedures can be expensive and very time consuming.

☐ Competitive Position
☐ Adequacy
☐ Flexible Benefits
☐ Funding
☐ Cost Containment
☐ General Plan Design
______ Early/Late retirement
______ Benefit comparability for different employee groups
______ Benefits taxation

Figure 9–13 CHECKLIST OF BENEFIT OBJECTIVE ISSUES

MANAGEMENT CONSIDERATIONS

When setting objectives, management may want to bring employees into the planning process by surveying their benefits preferences and perceptions. Such employee involvement can be very valuable in determining the range of employees' needs and desires. Employee opinions can be used to ensure that the company makes changes that provide employees with benefits they most want and need.

If employee input is desired in the planning process, the most reliable approach is to use a written questionnaire. Wording must ensure that the right questions are asked in the right way. In addition, management must be prepared to respond to issues that employees raise. If employee expectations are raised and then not fulfilled, the project will be self-defeating.

Management must also develop objectives about funding issues. Certainly all employers want their programs to be effectively funded. There may, however, be a trade-off between lowest cost and administrative convenience. Where cost savings are absolutely critical, the organization should seek the lowest possible cost regardless of administrative difficulties.

Where cost savings are not as critical, the organization may want to choose one carrier—or perhaps two—for all coverages, even though the overall cost of this approach may be slightly higher than using separate carriers and trustees for each coverage.

The use of self-insurance should be reviewed during the funding analysis. If used, the appropriate balance of insurance and self-insurance can then be determined.

COST CONTAINMENT MEASURES

A related matter concerns cost containment. Deductibles and coinsurance are commonly used to control benefits costs—particularly for health care. Requiring employees to pay part of the premium cost is another way to control benefits costs. An objective that aims to maximize such cost savings may, however, cause a conflict with the desire to provide a competitive plan.

Other cost containment approaches include using effective plan design to avoid overuse or abuse of the plan, or encouraging employees to use a less expensive form of medical treatment—such as outpatient services, home care, preventive medicine, and generic drugs. Finally, several general plan design objectives should be addressed. Management must develop an appropriate approach to encouraging or discouraging early, normal, and late retirement. Provisions in the pension and other plans can then reinforce the company's retirement orientation.

Another example of a plan design issue is whether to give different benefits to different employee groups. For instance: Should you differentiate between exempt and nonexempt groups; among employees in different locations or different divisions; among employees in different job groupings; or among employees who are in a union and those who are not?

Also important is the degree of tax effectiveness desired. If an organization believes that a goal of total remuneration should be a high degree of tax-effectiveness (primarily for higher-paid employees), then more benefits and nontaxable perquisites—rather than incremental cash compensation—could be emphasized.

PROGRAM ANALYSIS

After specific objectives have been set, the organization's current benefits program should be reviewed to find out if the plans are consistent with those objectives.

A major step here is to analyze if the competitive position of an organization's benefits program is consistent with the organization's objectives. A benefits program includes several major plans (pension, medical, etc.) which in turn consist of dozens of major provisions. Attempting to compare a benefit plan by comparing the individual provisions can be very difficult, while comparing overall benefit programs this way is virtually impossible. In order to make an overall program comparison, a bottom line approach is necessary.

This is accomplished by comparing an organization's program using an actuarial model that develops average costs of providing benefits. Using this approach, all of a plan's provisions can be valued in common terms. For example, a pension plan that has a below-average benefit formula could have a favorable overall competitive position because of above-average vesting, cost-of-living adjustments, annuity forms, early retirement, subsidies, and other plan provisions.

A COMPARISON OF OVERALL VALUES

In addition to helping compare whole benefit programs, this approach also has the advantage of allowing a comparison of total remuneration. Because benefits and perquisites are stated in dollar value terms, they can be added to cash compensation to derive a total cash and noncash compensation position.

For example, an organization may want to stress security and provide slightly below-average pay, which will be offset by above average benefits. The total remuneration valuing approach would enable this organization to see if its benefits were high enough to offset a less competitive pay position.

The adequacy of benefits can be assessed by determining the amount of income needed to replace disposable preretirement, death, or disability income. This replacement ratio can then be compared with the ratio amounts that the organization's pension, death, and disability plans provide. For example, a pension plan that provides 35% of final pay, with Social Security providing 20%, would result in a combined replacement ratio of 55%. This can then be compared to the preretirement disposable income target at that specific age, service, and income level.

DETERMINING FUNDING EFFECTIVENESS

When considering a flexible benefit program, a company should conduct an employee benefits preference study to determine if there is a need for the program, and, if so, where the major variations in need and interest occur. Such a study could compare the perceived value of the program to the actual cost of benefits to determine the return on benefit investment.

Funding effectiveness can be determined by analyzing the financial characteristics—rates, reserves, retention, and cash flow features—of the existing funding arrangement, and then comparing these financial characteristics with the alternatives. Alternative approaches include: changing carriers, consolidating coverages, splitting out coverage to separate carriers, incorporating cash flow features, and changing to a different degree of self-insurance. Such an analysis is best done by an experienced and objective third party.

The remaining objective areas of cost containment and general plan design can be reviewed through a general benefits study. In such an analysis, the organization's program plan design could be reviewed for consistency with objectives in all areas. Any problem areas can then be reconciled. When the analysis has been completed, needed plan changes can be developed so the program will be consistent with the organization's objectives.

Once plan changes are implemented, they should be communicated to employees. However, communications should not be limited to these changes only; communications should be an ongoing activity.

COMMUNICATION

To reinforce the idea that benefits are part of a total remuneration package—benefits and pay—communication should present a total remuneration concept. Such an approach would explain total remuneration, possibly by presenting pay and benefits issues alternately to emphasize their interrelationship. Effective communication of benefits enhances employee understanding and appreciation; failure to communicate effectively deprives the employer of receiving fuller value for the substantial cost of those benefits.

THE COMPLETED CYCLE

As the final step in benefits planning, employee feedback can be either a formal or informal process. However, like communications, employee feedback must be ongoing and use informal channels, exit interviews, perhaps a question and answer column in an in-house publication, and formal questionnaires every few years.

Feedback is the link that completes the planning cycle shown in Figure 9–11. The planning cycle, however, also must be an ongoing process—one that considers continual changes in the work force, competitive practices, government regulations, tax treatments, the general nature of the individual organization, management style, and the content of employee feedback itself.

DISCUSSION QUESTIONS

1. What are the major steps in the benefits planning cycle?
2. What issues should managers and human resources professionals consider in setting objectives?
3. What are the key management considerations in benefits planning?
4. How does compensation mix interact with an organization's style?
5. How can managers and human resources professionals determine the cost-effectiveness of various benefits?

ACTIVITIES

Activity 9–1

COMPENSATION RATINGS

Step 1: You are the director of marketing at a rapidly growing high technology organization. Many of your professionals move into other divisions in your firm after several years. Others, after two or three years, move into better positions in your competitors' companies. You want to be sure to keep those who work hard and make significant contributions. You must determine pay increases for the marketing professionals described below. Beside each name, write the percentage increase you would give that person. Each currently earns between $25,000 and $35,000.

________ *Hal Hartwood.* Hal has been with your company for four years. At the end of his first year he was one of your best workers. But since then his work has gotten poorer. His coworkers have repeatedly said that he doesn't do his share, even though he seems to you to be working quite hard. Others say that he just doesn't need the money because of a huge trust fund he inherited from his grandparents.

________ *Elsa Diamond.* Elsa's rich father complains that he never sees her because she is always working. She regularly works ten to twelve-hour days. During her two years with your company she has become one of the most respected of her peers because of her excellent work. She is creative and productive.

________ *Samson Glynn.* Sam is viewed by all his coworkers as the company clown. He is always making jokes and leads the group's social excursions after hours. But he has always seemed to be a very hard worker to you. He is one of the best performers in the department. You are constantly surprised at the quality of his work because Sam never seems to work very hard. You only hired him because he was your wife's brother.

________ *Harvey Howard.* Harvey always looks as if he will collapse from exhaustion—he always seems to be the hardest working person in the department. But the quantity of work he produces seems to be below that of his coworkers. Still, his coworkers always want him to work with them, saying that he is one of the best workers in the department. You wonder if his lack of an MBA is still a problem. You thought he would learn on the job and make up any deficiencies he had. You know he has been under great pressure at home because his son requires special education that is very costly.

________ *Carol Capwell.* Carol has worked for you for six years. She has the most seniority of any of your subordinates. Although she has been an average worker overall, her work has declined in quality and quantity recently. She comes to work late and leaves early and doesn't seem to be working very hard. Her coworkers have repeatedly complained that she doesn't do her share of the department's work. Carol has said she may take several months off to travel around the world.

________ *Hilary Mouton.* Hilary always works extra hours, takes work home with her, but still has difficulty finishing it. You know that as a widow she has to spend a great deal of energy taking care of her five children. Maybe she is just too tired to concentrate on her work. Or she may still be suffering from her lack of recent technical education. Although she received a good recommendation from her last boss, the job was much less technically demanding. Some of her coworkers have recommended that you provide her with additional training.

________ *Matthew Watchford.* Matthew received his MBA from one of the most prestigious programs in the country two years ago. He graduated with honors and has been doing top-notch work since then. His work is always finished promptly; he even takes work home if it is required. His coworkers agree that his work is excellent. You know that Matthew has done some moonlighting because he needs extra money to meet family obligations.

______ *Jesse Long.* Jesse's family has significant medical and financial problems. In spite of this, she continually produces high-quality work. You are not sure how she manages to do this since she frequently comes to work late and leaves early. Her coworkers complain, however, that she doesn't have the skills needed to do the job. You had some questions about her academic background when you hired her, but are now quite satisfied that any deficiencies have been corrected.

Step 2: Now, in groups of four to six, reach consensus about the percentage increase each person should receive. Be prepared to justify them.

Step 3: Discussion. In small groups or with the entire class, answer the following:

1. What increases did you propose?
2. Explain the reasons for each increase.
3. Use any relevant theory of motivation to justify the increases.

Activity 9–2

MIDLAND CHEMICAL COMPANY

Step 1: Read the Midland Chemical Company case.

Step 2: Prepare the case for class discussion.

Dr. Philip M. Hart, Director of the Basic Research Division of the Midland Chemical Company, regarded himself as a scientist and not a philosopher. He did not care for idle ruminations about truth, justice, and the meaning of life. His training in organic chemistry had not equipped him to think in philosophical abstractions. And he was a busy man.

Most of his colleagues recognized Phil Hart as a "comer", energetic and with a flair for selling his Division's research ideas to top management. He had been promoted to Director of Basic Research at age 37, after only 10 years with Midland Chemical. Senior executives valued him for his sound science, his quick and relentlessly logical mind, and his practical ability to transform colleagues' wild ideas into commercially plausible proposals. Colleagues valued his willingness to extend full credit to those who originated such ideas.

But although Hart tried to avoid philosophic issues, notions of "justice" and "fairness" began to crowd in upon his thinking as he read the latest policy memorandum endorsed by the Board of Directors—"Midland's Employee Relations Objectives". He didn't usually spend much time on formal employee relations plans, but he had taken an interest in the compensation program, which he considered a means to stimulate and reward creative people. He wondered how these new objectives would affect his own compensation practices.

MIDLAND'S ORGANIZATION

Midland Chemical Company was one of the nation's leading producers of complex organic chemicals, medicinal chemicals, antibiotics, vitamin products, and radio isotopes. It manufactured nearly 500 different products in 1980, and its sales amounted to nearly $750 million. Some of its products were produced under license or assignment agreements with other companies.

The Company's executive offices, main plant, and research laboratories were located in upstate New York, but it had eight manufacturing facilities elsewhere in the United States and three foreign countries—Argentina, Italy, and Turkey. Branches for sales and service were maintained in principal cities of the United States and 18 foreign countries.

Midland Chemical's senior executives had recognized the vital importance of research and development to the Company's future by making this activity a separate functional area with its own Vice-President, Dr. R.F. Vance, who also sat on the Board of Directors. (See Figure 9–14 for the corporation's organization chart.) R & D was organized into five divisions:

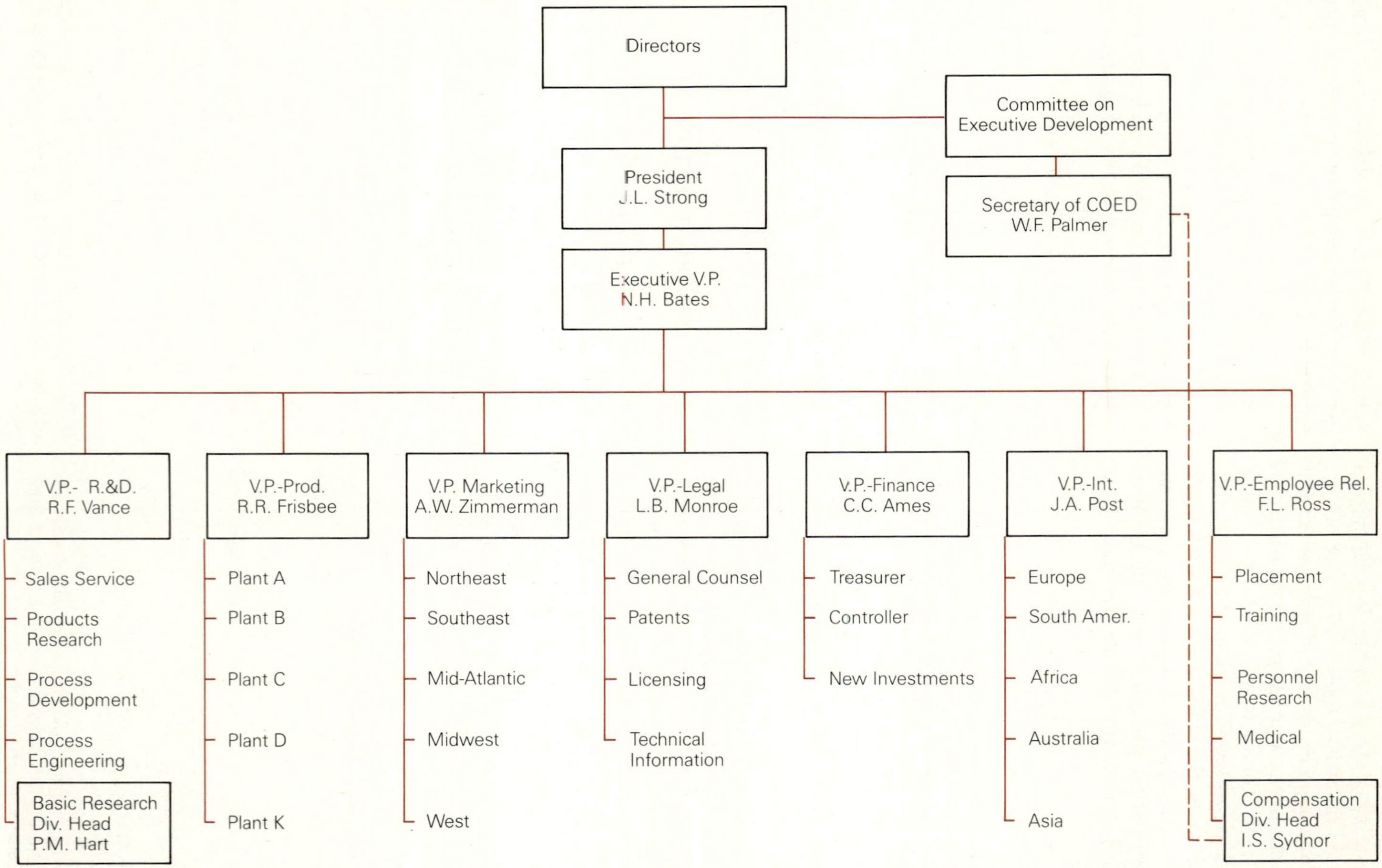

Figure 9–14 CORPORATE ORGANIZATION CHART

1. Basic Research, which explored the fringes of scientific knowledge with no certain expectation that discoveries could be exploited commercially.
2. Products Research, which investigated ways of refining existing products.
3. Process Development, which evaluated the economics of production against preferred product characteristics.
4. Process Engineering, which fixed production techniques and established specifications for the design and construction of plants and equipment.
5. Sales Service, a technical liaison between customer, sales organization, and manufacturing.

Research and Development was autonomous. Dr. Vance submitted expense, capital, and manpower budgets each year to the Board of Directors. So long as he operated within these budgets, observed a few company-wide policies (including those governing salary administration), and fulfilled the Board's expectations for R & D, he was free to run the unit without interference.

RESEARCH AND DEVELOPMENT EMPLOYEES

In 1980 the Board authorized a $45 million operating budget for R & D and approved Dr. Vance's manpower budget of 480 employees. The Division's needs varied. Basic Research employed 97 people. Of these, 51 were Ph.D. chemists; other employees included several M.S. chemists, chemical engineers, pharmacologists, physicists, and 30 laboratory assistants, "a bunch of long-hairs" whom the professionals grudgingly respected. Products Research involved less rarified research; its 105 employees included a number of Ph.D. chemists, but M.S. and B.S. degrees were more common, and 40 laboratory assistants conducted more routine investigations. Process Development primarily employed chemical engineers, several with Ph.D. degrees, many with the M.S., and a few with M.B.A.'s. Engineers of this department were generally regarded as the elite among the Company's engineering personnel. Process Engineering employed nearly 60 M.S. or B.S. engineers from several disciplines, along with 25 semi-professional designers and draftsmen and about 25 pilot plant operators. Employees of the Sales Service Division had more diversified backgrounds than others in R & D. They were B.S. or M.S. chemists or chemical engineers who came from research, marketing, or manufacturing. They were valued more for interpersonal skill than for technical ability—a stereotyped evaluation which often irritated the Sales Service personnel.

All of these Divisions occupied a common building next to the Company's executive offices. Despite occasional invidious comments which reflected long standing prejudices, the scientists worked well together.

Phil Hart was conscious of similar feelings among the diverse backgrounds of the people in his Basic Research Division. (See Figure 9–15 for the Division's organization chart.) The Division could not hope to span all the uncharted areas of chemistry, so Dr. Vance and the Board of Directors had agreed to limit research to a few fields, using contracted research with universities and private research groups to meet other needs. Basic Research concentrated on four fields. The Polymer Section, composed primarily of Ph.D. organic chemists and bio-chemists, synthesized new chemical substances for technological developments. This section was divided into three groups, and while each group was somewhat self-contained, the 43 people collaborated well. The Medical Chemicals Section was divided into two groups, one working on enzymes, the other on steroids, particularly hormones. Their technical personnel were biochemists, organic chemists, and pharmacologists, almost all of them with Ph.D.'s. The Radio Isotopes Section was comprised mainly of physical and organic chemists who investigated the consequences of irradiation from various sources of nuclear energy. These scientists worked in the "nuclear cave" and were regarded by others in the Company (although not necessarily by members of the Basic Research Division) as having glamorous and exciting jobs. The Cryogenics Group, established for only a year, explored the possibility of low temperature processing and storage for several of Midland Chemical's products. This group included mechanical and chemical engineers as well as chemists. Some members of the other groups who regarded themselves as pure scientists felt that the Cryogenics people were only one step above refrigeration and air conditioning mechanics.

Hart was aware of the diverse interests and conflicting attitudes toward basic research among mem-

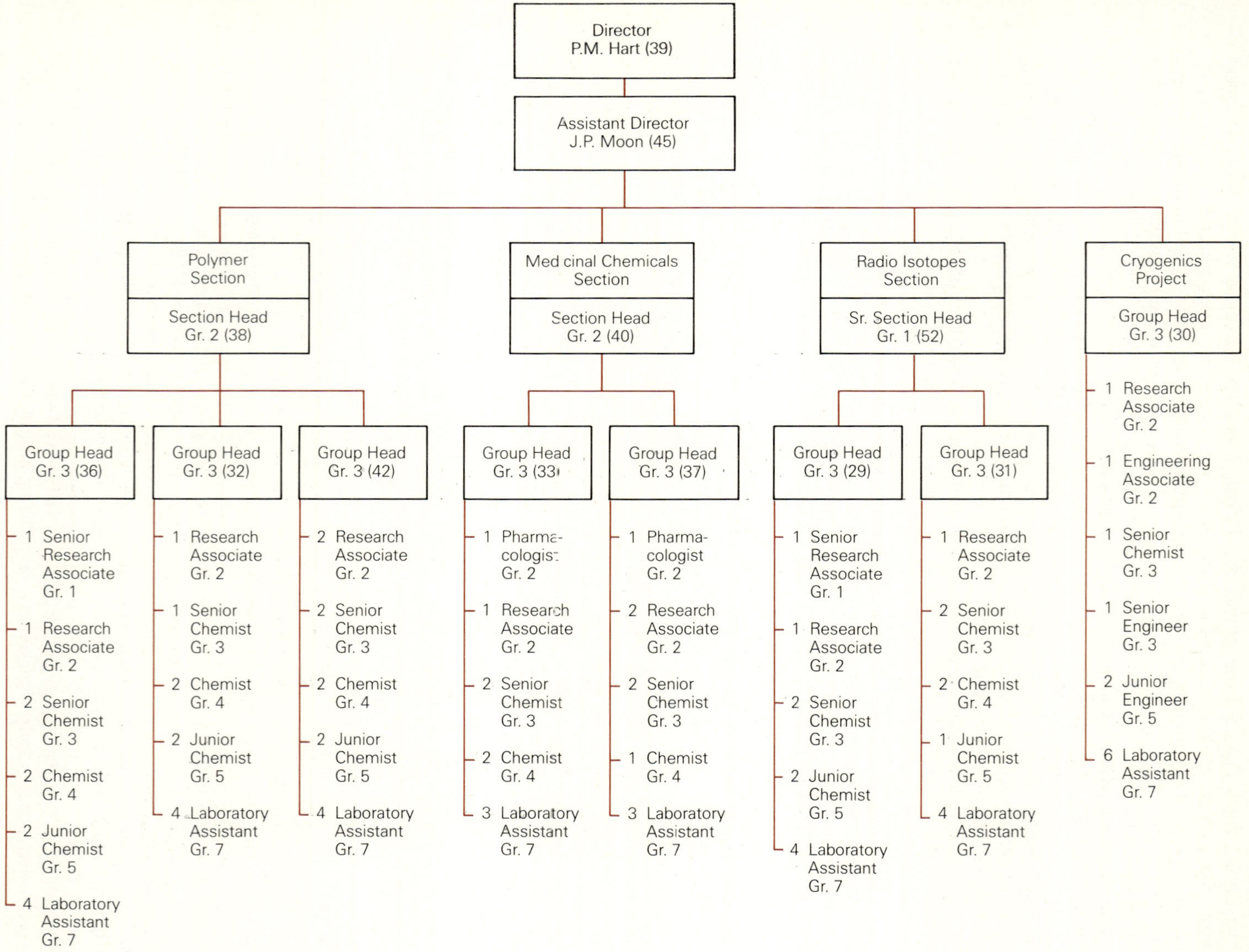

Numbers in parentheses show age of incumbent

Figure 9–15 ORGANIZATION CHART, BASIC RESEARCH LABORATORIES

bers of his Division. He was pleased (and slightly surprised) that professional differences seldom got in the way of this work. Whether they were pushing back the frontiers of knowledge or doing cookbook chemistry, they got along well with one another.

PRE-1980 SALARY ADMINISTRATION

As he stared at the new policy memorandum, Phil Hart thought about the system that Midland Chemical had used for the past twenty years. It was a pretty complex salary administration program, to be sure, and not everyone understood it, but its logic appealed to him. Phil dipped into his CONFIDENTIAL file to look again at the well-thumbed "Salary Administration Guide for Supervisors." He re-read the following excerpts:

"The career payment plan is based on the premise that salary increases should be provided to employees throughout their careers as incentives and rewards for their contributions. Midland's career payment plan considers both current performance and future potential to determine the degree and frequency of these increases.

"The plan is tailored to meet the problems specific to evaluations of technical and research personnel. Unlike research positions, production, marketing, and managerial positions entail duties that can be defined fairly accurately. Hence these employees' performances can be evaluated and priced in the competitive market with relative ease. A job hierarchy controls and limits the contributions that these employees can make, as well as the corresponding compensation that they can receive, without moving up to a higher level in the hierarchy.

"In contrast to such positions, professional research positions cannot be accurately defined. Specific projects can be assigned to a scientist or engineer, and his or her performance can be evaluated after the task is completed. But the value of most research assignments is determined less by the specific project than by the technical competence, initiative, and creativity with which the scientist approaches the assignment. These qualities cannot be defined rigidly. Thus job classifications and personnel evaluation is difficult and perhaps even meaningless in research work.

"However, there remain differences in the levels of creative work that people can be expected to accomplish. We believe that these differences should be recognized through appropriate job titles and compensation. Although we cannot predict in advance the specific tasks that a research scientist will perform, we can anticipate the level of intellectual activity that he or she is likely to engage in throughout his or her career.

"We have identified these levels of intellectual activity by job titles (see Table 9–8), using competitive data to set the salary ranges for these positions. To determine compensation, an employee's first and second level supervisors evaluate current perfor-

		Salary per Month		Job Title	
	Group	Minimum	Maximum	Technical	Administrative
Professional	1	3750	5625	Senior Research Associate	Senior Section Head
	2	3250	4875	Research Associate	Section Head
	3	2750	4125	Senior Chemist	Group Head
	4	2250	3375	Chemist	Project Leader
	5	1750	2625	Junior Chemist	
*Non-professional	7	1000	2000	Laboratory Assistant	

*Laboratory assistants were members of the United Chemical Workers, AFL-CIO; they were covered by the wage-hour provisions of the Fair Labor Standards Act; their salaries were fixed by contract for the first several years in grade, but they were eligible to be considered for merit salary increases.

Table 9–8 1980 CLASSIFIED SALARY RANGES

mance and simultaneously assess the employee's long range value to the company. The performance rating is then expressed in terms of the highest job level that the employee can reach during his or her career, in the supervisor's estimation. For example, a rating of "2" means that the employee's past and current performance demonstrates that he or she has the potential to become a Section Head or Research Associate.

"Allied to each job level is a salary guide line, expressed graphically by a curve, that terminates at the maximum salary for each position (see Figure 9–16). This guide line determines the employee's salary progress while he or she is still classified at a lower level position. The periodic rating may be altered to reflect any change in performance. If the rating changes, subsequent salary increases will correspond to the revised rating. Because career development and compensation are presumed to follow the slope of the appropriate salary guide line during the employee's career, we do not grant promotional increases.

"Midland Chemical follows three main principles in using these professional guide lines to administer salaries.

1. Current performance and contribution is the basis for granting raises, regardless of whether the guide line says a raise is possible.
2. The guide line is the salary ceiling. A merit

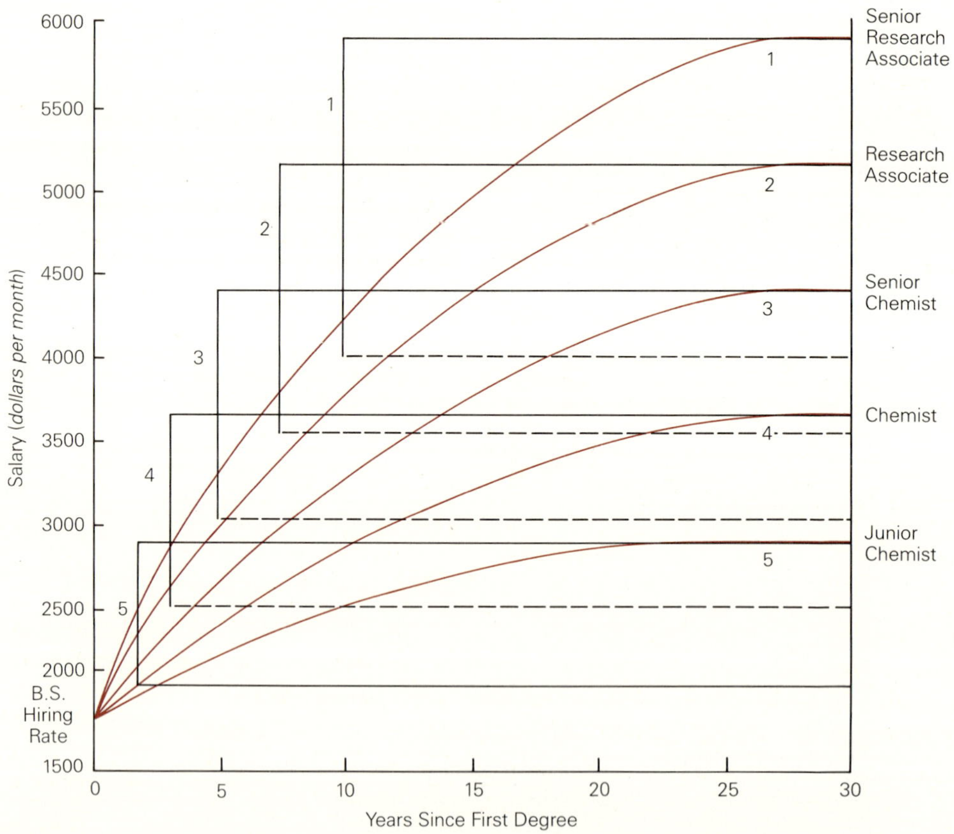

Figure 9–16 SALARY RATE RANGES AND CAREER SALARY CURVES

increase may raise salary up to but never above the guide lines.

3. Anniversary dates and similar increase patterns should be avoided. Usually, because of the decreasing slope of the guide line, intervals between salary increases gradually get longer."

Phil Hart remembered well enough how he had slaved over salary budgets in previous years. Early in September he would compile the ratings on each employee made by section heads. After receiving an appraisal of an employee's current performance, Hart would discuss with the appropriate supervisors the employee's career prospects. Then Hart would rank all of the 65 classified technical personnel in the Basic Research Division according to his judgment of who was most useful in the Division, who was least useful, who was second most useful, who was second least useful, and so forth until all 65 were listed *seriatim.* In order that his bias for his own men might not contaminate the impartiality of salary administration for the nearly 300 technical personnel in the Research and Development function, Hart and other Division Heads met for a stormy day with Dr. Vance to prepare a master ranking for all 300. At this session, for example, the Head of the Sales Service Division would be required to justify the contribution of Mr. Jones, B.S. Chemist and effective liaison with the pharmaceutical industry, in relation to that of Dr. Smith, a Ph.D. Physical Chemist whose imaginative research design for the Radio Isotopes Section of the Basic Research Division had not produced the anticipated results. And Phil Hart would have to justify his assessment of Dr. Smith in relation to that made of Ms. Parks, an M.S. Chemical Engineer in Process Engineering. At these meetings the usually repressed feelings of inferiority and discrimination that some of the division heads had harbored for the prior year sometimes broke out. But Dr. Vance was usually able to smooth ruffled sensibilities, and division heads regarded this annual session as a useful cathartic as well as an important managerial gathering.

When the division heads reached a consensus regarding the relative value of each classified technical employee in Research and Development, the *seriatim* ranking was divided into segments. The top 10% were presumed capable of rising to the highest managerial or technical positions in the unclassified realms beyond Group 1; the next 15% were regarded as having potential to rise to Group 1 positions; the second quartile were felt to have Group 2 potential; the third quartile, Group 3; the next 15%, Group 4; and the bottom 10% were believed not capable of advancing beyond the Group 5 Junior Chemist position. Many of this low potential group would be "counselled out" sooner or later. Hart then compared the designations of potential suggested by the consensus for all Research and Development Divisions with the assessments of potential that he had already made in his own Division. He was expected to resolve any discrepancies by consultation with the other Division Heads.

In October, when questions of overall value and potential had been mediated, Hart would then compute the position on the salary chart of every technical man in the Basic Research Division. For example, Tom Jacobs, head of the Cryogenics Research Group, received his B.S. degree eight years ago. Hart believed that he had Group 1 potential. His current salary was $3120 a month, $350 below the Group 1 guideline. His last salary increase of $240 a month had been given in July, 1979. Next year the guideline would move up to $3600. On the basis of this data, Hart felt justified in recommending a $300 increase to take place in October, 1980.

"But that was last year's approach," Hart reflected, as he looked again at the new policy memorandum. "What's it going to be this year?"

1980 EMPLOYEE RELATIONS OBJECTIVES

In 1979 the Board of Directors had asked Mr. F.L. Ross, Vice-President of Employee Relations, to take a fresh look at the Company's employee relations objectives. His new recommendations were summarized in a policy memorandum endorsed by the Board and distributed to all supervisory personnel in the Company. Pertinent excerpts follow:

"Midland's investment in professional, technical, and managerial personnel has grown steadily in proportion to total personnel. These people, representing the vital, creative force of Midland's future, must be given maximum incentive. A cradle-to-grave concept of compensation is no longer appropriate. New, dynamic stimuli must be developed if we are to use our highly talented personnel to the greatest advantage.

Management of Creative Professionals

"The need for highly educated professionals has expanded more than 50% in the past decade. Current estimates point to a rise in professional and technical workers of about 6% per year, despite America's chronic unemployment. The managerial, professional, and technical sector of the workforce now represents 40% of Midland's domestic employment, and is compensated by 70% of that payroll.

"High-talent personnel are scarce and promise to become even scarcer. We must use more effectively those educated minds that we secure and seek to retain. We must substitute professional for less skilled employees and develop each professional to his or her full capacity. We must determine what motivates professionally trained people, and we must provide them with innovative leadership.

Recasting Career Management

"These changing personnel requirements mean that Midland can no longer consider lifetime career employment as the primary objective of employee relations policies. We can no longer sustain the assumption that we do not expect Midland career people to compete with the best talent in the labor market. Today's rapidly changing technology can make Midland's home-grown talent obsolete. High personal security, long tenure, and lifetime careers are valuable to the individual and to the organization. Yet while the organization seeks to build stability, it may inadvertently create sinecures for half-hearted people who have lost their sense of striving. Employees may become more dependent, less agile, and too tolerant of their own limitations. The aging employee population remains in the company. We must develop a new balance that recognizes the importance of stability but avoids the penalty of mediocrity.

Strengthening Economic Incentives

"Money, advancement, and status are important goals for ambitious, able people. They are therefore important factors in employee relations. We are not modernizing Midland's salary administration to recognize promotion as the most important incentive that we can provide. Promotions can no longer be considered merely opportunities and rewards for individual employees. Promotions should instill maximum competition and participation among employees. Frozen job classifications, narrow ladders of advancement, and supervisors who hoard talent or block promotions by idiosyncratic evaluations constrict the growth of highly talented people and of Midland Chemical.

Recognizing Personnel As An Investment

"Plant and equipment are investments of capital. Employees are regarded as a cost. A chemical plant has an asset value. An employee has none. And yet we know that every employee represents an investment—an investment of $10,000 to hire a technical employee, an investment of a million dollars to pay his or her salary on a career basis, a further investment for training and development, a still further investment in his or her annuitant status. How do we determine the company's return on that investment? Some have claimed that every technical employee generates $7 million of new business in the course of his or her career. How valid is such a guess? What criteria can we use to evaluate the contribution of professional personnel, who cannot be measured by output-per-manhour data? Can we identify marginal personnel investments as reliably as we can screen out marginal investments? As senior executives devote more attention to investment policy, those responsible for employee relations must be prepared themselves to answer these questions."

Phil Hart's Reactions

Hart found these objectives hard-nosed. While he liked to consider himself business-like, he was alarmed at the effect these policies might have on his people if they became aware of it. He called Ivan Sydnor, the Head of the Compensation Division, who had moved into Employee Relations several years ago after a productive ten years in Process Development.

"Ivan, let's talk."

"O.K., Phil, come on over."

Hart launched into a monologue. "Look, Ivan, this thing that Ross put out on employee relations objectives—this is lousy. If this is the new look, you can shove it. What's it going to do to my research people? You can't take these guys and explain that they're competing with one another. Science is unselfish in working toward company objectives. But now we've got to compete for promotions. It's going to be dog-eat-dog in the laboratory.

"And how can you put a 'return on investment' label on a man who's playing with steroids and may work for two years on a synthesis that doesn't pan out? If he gets zero return, does he get zero raises? None of us wants a bunch of mediocrities populating the Company. But the fact is that not all of our people are going to turn out as well as we'd thought when we hired them. Are we supposed to fire everybody in the bottom half of the class?

"I agree that salary is a great motivator, but if you administer it unfairly you'll knock the props right out from under these guys, and you'll wind up worse than you were before. How do you in Compensation plan to put these objectives into operation without wrecking what we've got?"

"Well, Phil, that's a pretty blanket indictment of objectives that we thought nobody could object to, sort of like Home and Mother. You can't knock competition. And if old J.L. Strong keeps saying 'people are our most important asset', I don't see why we can't think at least metaphorically in terms of getting a return on investment. Of course, I know what you're saying, and I can imagine that some of the long-hairs in your shop who don't understand management's point of view could get pretty upset at drastic changes in our salary administration.

"The truth is, Phil, we're not sure we're getting value received for our compensation dollars. Bearing in mind our employee relations objectives—even if you don't like the way they're phrased—and your own feelings about how professional people should be compensated, what sort of a salary administration program would you suggest for us? Don't just gripe; give me some constructive suggestions."

Step 3: Individually, in small groups, or with the entire class, as directed by your instructor, answer the following questions:

1. What aspects of the environment and organization are important for an effective compensation system at Midland?
2. What would a job analysis of the professional positions at Midland reveal?
3. What are the characteristics of the existing wage structure at Midland?
4. What are the assets and liabilities of this structure?
5. What problems does the structure create?
6. What would you recommend that Phil Hart do about the new structure?

Activity 9–3

JOHNSON SHOE COMPANY

Step 1: Read the following description of the Johnson Shoe Company.

Johnson Shoe Company was founded in 1940 in a small New England manufacturing town. It grew from a small job shop of ten employees to a highly automated factory employing 750 workers. In 1970 the company moved into retail sales of moderately priced, highly styled shoes. Beginning with two outlets, they expanded to twenty outlets throughout New England.

Between the two types of businesses, Johnson employs a diverse group of individuals. The factory organization includes hourly workers, supervisors and foremen, a small staff in the marketing, finance, and human resources departments, and executives in each functional area. The sales outlets include full- and part-time salespeople, assistant managers, and store managers.

Johnson has always been known for its generous compensation; the wages received by the manufacturing workers are among the highest of its local competitors. But recently employees in the retail outlets have been complaining that their benefits are much too limited. The company offers full individual medical coverage or its equivalent, seven paid holidays, and ten paid sick days, and contributes to an employee pension plan after an employee works for ten years.

The work force at Johnson has also changed in

the last ten years. For example, it now includes more women of all ages, more MBA graduates, more members of dual career families, more workers with preschool and school-age children, and more workers over the age of sixty.

Step 2: Propose a benefits program for Johnson Shoe Company. Consider the different types of employees at Johnson as well as their different needs. List the different benefits you want to offer. Specify who is to receive each benefit as well as the conditions that are required to receive it, such as length of employment or holding a managerial job. To the extent possible estimate the costs of various benefit combinations.

Step 3: Discussion. In small groups or with the entire class, share your benefits plans. Then answer the following questions:

1. Which benefits are mandatory?
2. Which benefits are voluntary?
3. Which benefits are more costly? Less costly?
4. To what needs does each benefit respond?
5. Should all employees receive the same benefits?

Activity 9–4

MADISON ELECTRONICS COMPANY

Step 1: Read the Madison Electronics Company case.

Step 2: Prepare the case for class discussion.

The Madison Electronics Company manufactures electrical components for a variety of major U.S. firms. The standards for the components vary with the customer but usually must conform to rather close tolerances. Despite receiving some large orders for components in recent years, MEC is currently being forced to lay-off employees.

Part of this lay-off can be attributed to an efficiency team brought into the organization one year ago to redesign jobs and work flow to increase productivity and reduce per unit costs. One of the recommendations of this group of consultants was the implementation of a bonus system. MTM was used to establish rates for the various jobs throughout the facility. While there was initial resistance to using such a system, most employees have discovered that they can exceed the rate and so earn more than their base pay.

One of the jobs which has been unable to meet the rate is that of the employees which trim the various parts prior to their being assembled and sold to the customers. The parts are sent directly to the trimmer from the casting department. The trimmers insert the part into a shearing machine which trims away burrs and other irregular formations on the parts. After trimming, the parts are sent to milling where they are smoothed and prepared for assembly and shipped to the intended customer as shown in Figure 9–17. If the part does not fit into the shearing equipment, it is rejected and returned to the casting department for possible reworking.

The standard rate set for the trimmer is 500 units per hour or 40,000 units per day. When the casting machines are properly adjusted this rate can be attained by a diligent worker. However, if the trimmer rejects a part because it does not fit the shearing machine, it is not counted as a unit completed and does not count toward the rate set for the operator. Since the dies in the casting department are allowed to become quite worn before replacement, it becomes increasingly difficult for the trimmer to achieve the established rates of production. This creates special problems, since once the parts are trimmed, other workers in assembly and shipping are able to achieve their rates and earn their bonus. Trimmers are quite dissatisfied with the existing system, and turnover for the department is excessive.

The manager of the trimming department has asked the casting manager numerous times to replace the dies before they become so worn. The casting manager is reluctant to replace the dies sooner than is

This case was prepared by Professor Joe Thomas of Middle Tennessee State University as a basis for class discussion rather than to illustrate either effective or ineffective handling of an administrative situation.

Figure 9–17 WORK FLOW OF CAST COMPONENTS

absolutely necessary because this increases the down time for his workers and keeps them from achieving their established rates. Doing maintenance also causes increased operating costs for the department.

The personnel manager has been very reluctant to change the established bonus system. The standard reply has been that the system was developed by specially trained time and motion experts and that they knew what they were doing.

Step 3: Individually, in small groups, or with the entire class, as directed by your instructor, answer the following questions:

1. Is an incentive system appropriate for Madison Electronics?
2. What are the characteristics of the existing system?
3. What are the problems associated with the existing system?
4. What are the major concerns facing the manager of the trimming department?
5. What are the major concerns facing the personnel manager?
6. How would you advise the managers in this case to resolve the problems?

Activity 9–5

DESIGNING AN INCENTIVE PROGRAM

Step 1: Read the following scenario.

Feelwell Pharmaceuticals distributes 150 drugs that are sold over the counter in pharmacies, supermarkets, discount stores, and other miscellaneous retail outlets. They have a national sales force of 300 men and women who are assigned to various geographical areas across the United States.

Basically, the country is divided into 300 equal geographical areas, and each salesperson is assigned to one area. Some areas include one or more metropolitan areas; others include only small, suburban towns; still others are primarily rural in nature. Some salespeople service many large stores; others have primarily small grocery stores in their territory. Salespeople receive a flat 2 percent of all sales. Occasionally they receive a special prize for selling a specified amount of a new product.

When a vacancy arises in a sales territory, the most senior individual has the first choice of moving into that territory. New employees are hired for vacant territories into which no existing employee wants to move.

Turnover at Feelwell Pharmaceuticals ranges from 5 to 30 percent a year, depending on the general economic conditions. The top executives feel that this turnover is becoming very costly for them because of the costs associated with recruiting and training new employees. They also feel that their sales force is not as productive as it could be.

Step 2: Individually or in small groups, design an incentive program for the sales force at Feelwell Pharmaceuticals.

Step 3: Discussion. In small groups or with the entire class, share the plans you developed. Then answer the following questions:

1. What elements do these plans have in common?
2. Will the employees be motivated to perform better? To remain in the organization? Why?
3. What options are available at a reasonable cost to organizations that want to pay for performance?
4. What problems are there with the use of incentive plans at Feelwell Pharmaceuticals?

Activity 9–6

JOSLIN FAMILY SERVICES CENTER

Step 1: Read the following scenario.

Joslin Family Services Center is a privately owned social services agency. It provides counseling services for individuals and families; special recreational programs for area children, adolescents, and adults; and acts as an interface between its clients and other federal, state, and local agencies. Joslin employs fifty full-time workers: fifteen social workers, seven administrative assistants, one recreation director, ten recreation aides, two bookkeepers, four financial aid officers, three program administrators, two assistant directors, one executive director, and five secretaries. They also employ about thirty college students on a part-time basis.

As the executive director of the agency, you have a $3 million budget. From those funds must come all program expenses, including all salaries and benefits. Any money that you do not spend for employee compensation can be devoted to providing additional services.

Step 2: Individually, in small groups, or in writing, as directed by your instructor, design a compensation system for the Joslin Family Services Center. Include provisions for the determination and distribution of wages and benefits. Also include any incentive programs you feel are appropriate. In designing the compensation system, include the approximate costs of all components. Be sure to state any assumptions you make in designing the system.

Step 3: Discussion. In small groups or with the entire class, share your compensation systems.

1. What assumptions did you make in designing the compensation system?
2. What are the key elements of the plans?
3. What components are most costly? Least costly?
4. Do all employees receive the same wages and benefits?
5. How do you prioritize the various parts of a compensation system?

SUMMARY

Compensation serves diverse functions, including attracting, retaining, motivating, and rewarding employees. To design an effective compensation system, human resources professionals and managers must begin with environmental, organizational, and job analyses. Such analyses provide data for determining the amount, type, and distribution of compensation that will encourage effective performance. In addition to ensuring equity, the compensation system should motivate individuals by meeting their needs and reinforcing desired behaviors. Workers must value the rewards as well. In the Compensation Ratings activity you had the opportunity to consider the implications of various pay raises for individual motivation.

Development and implementation of a systematic wage structure encourages equity in the distribution of wages. Analysis of jobs, identification of compensable factors, evaluation of jobs, conduct of compensation surveys to determine wages in related organizations, specification of pay levels and steps, and association of pay with the levels and steps comprise the process for developing the wage structure. In the Midland Chemical Company you had the opportunity to identify the problems associated with an imperfect wage structure.

Compensation also includes benefits. Flexible benefit plans have become increasingly popular in response to a changing work force. Organizations have also become more conscious of the costs of benefits and are seeking ways of increasing the benefits while reducing their costs. You considered some of these issues at the Johnson Shoe Company.

Incentive plans often complement the more traditional wages and benefits. Individuals, groups, or organizations as a whole can receive monetary or other rewards when they perform at certain prespecified levels. In the Madison Electronics case you examined some of the difficulties associated with such a plan, and in the Designing an Incentive Program activity you had the opportunity to design your own incentive plan.

The key to effective compensation is a comprehensive, diverse set of wages, benefits, and incentives that respond to individual needs and fit with organizational goals. You developed such a system for the Joslin Family Services Center. Careful diagnosis of the situation, as well as creative design and integration of the components of a compensation system, should contribute to its effectiveness.

ENDNOTES

[1]See S.M. Freedman, J.R. Montanari, and R.T. Keller, The compensation program: Balancing organizational and employee needs, *Compensation Review* (Second Quarter 1982): 47–53, for a complete description of the survey in which 277 compensation managers ranked these goals for their organizations.

[2]Oil companies, to keep the best people, treat engineers like top executives, *Wall Street Journal,* 9 February 1982, pp. 8, 16; Engineering graduates again top most-wanted list in college hiring study, *New York Times,* 20 April 1981, p. 8; Engineers, scientists to find bright career future: Salaries, opportunities booming, *Los Angeles Times,* 22 February 1983, p. 56.

[3]Colleges paying more to teachers in demand, *New York Times,* 13 December 1982, p. 10, A–16.

[4]F.S. Hall and D.T. Hall, Dual career couples—how do individuals and companies cope? *Organizational Dynamics* 6 (Spring 1978): 57–77.

[5]See Bureau of National Affairs, *Basic Patterns in Union Contracts* (Washington, D.C.: Bureau of National Affairs, 1979) for discussion of some constraints.

[6]See G.T. Milkovich and J.M. Newman, *Compensation* (Plano, Tex.: Business Publications, 1984).

[7]The discussion of equity follows the organization of M.J. Wallace Jr. and C.H. Fay, *Compensation Theory and Practice* (Boston: Kent, 1983).

[8]See Milkovich and Newman, *op. cit.;* Wallace and Fay, *op. cit.*

[9]See Wallace and Fay, *op. cit.*

[10]See Wallace and Fay, *op. cit.*

[11]See Wallace and Fay, *op. cit.*

[12]See J.S. Adams, Inequity in social exchange, in *Advances in Experimental and Social Psychology,* ed. L. Berkowitz, 2 (1965): 267–300. See also E. Walster, W. Walster, and E. Berscheid, *Equity: Theory and Research* (Boston: Allyn and Bacon, 1978).

[13]See V.H. Vroom, *Work and Motivation* (New York: Wiley, 1964); E.E. Lawler III, *Motivation in Work Organizations* (Belmont, Cal.: Brooks/Cole, 1973).

[14]See A.H. Maslow, *Motivation and Personality* (New York: Harper & Row, 1954); D. McClelland, *The Achieving Society* (Princeton, N.J.: Van Nostrand, 1961); C.P. Alderfer, *Existence, Relatedness, and Growth: Human Needs in Organizational Settings* (New York: Free Press, 1972) for further discussion of needs theories.

[15]See B.F. Skinner, *The Behavior of Organisms: An Experimental Approach* (New York: Appleton-Century, 1938); W.C. Hamner and E.P. Hamner, Behavior modification on the bottom line, *Organizational Dynamics* 4 (1976): 8–21; S. Kerr, On the folly of rewarding A, while hoping for B, *Academy of Management Journal* 18 (1975): 773.

[16]See E.A. Locke. The ubiquity of the technique of goal-setting in theories of and approaches to employee motivation, *Academy of Management Review* 3 (1978): 599; see also research conducted on lumber workers such as G.P. Latham and S.B. Kinne III, Improving job performance through training in goal-setting, *Journal of Applied Psychology* 59 (1974): 187–191; G.P. Latham and J.J. Baldes, The 'prac-

tical significance' of Locke's theory of goalsetting, *Journal of Applied Psychology* 60 (1975): 122–124.

[17]E.E. Lawler III, New approaches to pay: Innovations that work, *Personnel* (September-October 1976).

[18]See E.E. Lawler, *Pay and Organization Development* (Reading, Mass.: Addison-Wesley, 1981).

[19]See R.D. Hulme and R.V. Bevan, The blue collar worker goes on salary, *Harvard Business Review* 53 (1975): 104–112.

[20]Hay Associates and Cole Associates are well known for their compensation systems.

[21]D. Elizur, *Job Evaluation: A Systematic Approach* (Hants, Eng.: Gower, 1980).

[22]*Ibid.*

[23]H. Suskin, ed., *Job Evaluation and Pay Administration in the Public Sector* (Chicago: International Personnel Management Association, 1977).

[24]This description is based on R. Beatty et al., *How to Administer Wage-Salary Programs and Perform Job Evaluations* (New York: Penton Learning Systems, 1980).

[25]E.J. Benge, *Job Evaluation and Merit Rating* (New York: National Foreman's Institute, 1946) was an early description of factor comparison methods.

[26]Elizur, *op. cit.*

[27]L.R. Gomez-Mejia, R.C. Page, and W.W. Tornow, A comparison of the practical utility of traditional, statistical, and hybrid job evaluation approaches, *Academy of Management Journal* 25 (1982): 790–809.

[28]Milkovich and Newman, *op. cit.*

[29]M.G. Miner, *Job Evaluation Policies and Procedures, Survey no. 113* (Washington, D.C.: Bureau of National Affairs, June 1976).

[30]See Wallace and Fay, *op. cit.*

[31]J.G. Berg, *Managing Compensation* (New York: AMACOM, 1976); R.I. Henderson, *Compensation Management* (Reston, Va.: Reston, 1985).

[32]Henderson, *op. cit.*

[33]Wallace and Fay, *op. cit.*, p. 113.

[34]Wallace and Fay, *op. cit.*

[35]R.J. Greene, Issues in salary structure design, *Compensation Review* 14 (1982): 28–33.

[36]See E.E. Lawler III, Secrecy and the need to know, in *Readings in Managerial Motivation and Compensation*, M. Dunnette, R. House, and H. Tosi, eds. (East Lansing: Michigan State University Press, 1972) for further discussion of the secrecy and pay issue.

[37]R.E. Kopelman and L. Reinharth, Research results: The effect of merit-pay practices on white collar performance, *Compensation Review* 14 (1982): 30–40.

[38]N.B. Winstanley, Are merit increases really effective?, *Personnel Administrator* (April 1982): 37.

[39]*Ibid.*

[40]D.R. Marshall, *Successful Techniques for Solving Employee Compensation Problems* (New York: Wiley, 1978).

[41]R.B. Dunham and R.A. Formisano, Designing and evaluating employee benefit systems, *Personnel Administrator* (April 1982): 29.

[42]R.C. Huseman et al., Getting your benefit program understood and appreciated, *Personnel Journal* (October 1978).

[43]G.P. Brunker, The potential for performance-based benefit plans, *Compensation Review* 14 (1982): 23–32.

[44]HMO Act of 1973, U.S. Code 1976 Title 42, §§280d, 300e *et seq.*, Re. 29, 1973, P.L. 93–222: 87 Stat. 914.

[45]Pregnancy Discrimination Act of 1978, D.C. Code 1973, §§46–310, 46–327; EEOC Guidelines of 1979, *Equal Opportunity Handbook* (Washington, D.C.: Dept. of Health, Education and Welfare, 1979).

[46]J. Rosenbloom and G.V. Hallman, *Employee Benefit Planning* (Englewood Cliffs, N.J.: Prentice-Hall, 1981).

[47]This classification resembles that offered by R.M. McCaffery, *Managing the Employee Benefits Program* (New York: AMACOM, 1983); other classifications are equally valid and useful. See, for example, Milkovich and Newman, *op. cit.*; Wallace and Fay, *op. cit.*; Henderson, *op. cit.*

[48]See M.W. Elson and J.F. Burton Jr., Workers' compensation insurance: Recent trends in employee costs, *Monthly Labor Review* (March 1981): 45–50.

[49]These plans are governed by ERISA (see Chapters 2 and 13).

[50]Wallace and Fay, *op. cit.*

[51]See G.T. McIlroy, Health care cost containment in the 1980s, *Compensation Review* 15 (1983): 15–31, for further discussion.

[52]F.C. Jordan, A fair system of time off the job: Combine sick days, vacation days, and holidays into paid days, *Modern Business Practice* (1974).

[53]McCaffery, *op. cit.*, p. 110.

[54]See B.L. Metzger, *Profit Sharing in 38 Large Companies, vol. I* (Evanston, Ill.: Profit Sharing Research Foundation, 1975); B.L. Metzger, *Profit Sharing in 38 Large Companies, vol. II* (Evanston, Ill.: Profit Sharing Research Foundation, 1978).

[55]J.D. McMillan and G.S. Reisinger, Takeover protection for executives: The 'golden parachute,' *Compensation Review* 15 (1983): 34–43.

[56]P. Meyer, Executive compensation must promote long-term commitment, *Personnel Administrator* 28 (May 1983): 37.

[57]F.G. Lesieur, ed., *The Scanlon Plan . . . A Frontier in Labor Management Cooperations* (Cambridge, Mass.: MIT Press, 1958).

[58]See B.E. Moore and T.L. Rose, *The Scanlon Way to Improved Productivity: A Practical Guide* (New York: Wiley, 1978); Lesieur, *op. cit.*; F.G. Lesieur and E.S. Puckett, The Scanlon Plan has proved itself, *Harvard Business Review* 47 (1969): 109–118; C.F. Frost, J.H. Wakeley, and R.A. Ruh, *The Scanlon Plan for Organization Development: Identity, Par-*

ticipation, and Equity (East Lansing: Michigan State University Press, 1974).

[59]The Scanlon Plan, Rucker Plan, and Improshare Plan are examples of gain-sharing programs; see M. Schuster and G. Florkowski, Wage incentive plans and the Fair Labor Standards Act, *Compensation Review* 14 (1982): 34–46.

[60]B.E. Moore and P.S. Goodman, *Factors Affecting the Impact of a Company-wide Incentive Program on Productivity* (Washington, D.C.: National Commission on Productivity, 1973).

[61]Lawler, *Pay and Organization Development, op. cit.*

[62]Compensation currents, *Compensation Review* 15 (1983): 2.

[63]R.G. Swad, Stock ownership plans: A new employee benefit, *Personnel Journal* 60 (June 1981): 453–455.

[64]*Ibid.*

[65]McCaffery, *op. cit.*

[66]Wallace and Fay, *op. cit.*, pp. 209–210.

[67]B. Stein, A. Cohen, and H. Gadon, Flextime: Work when you want to, *Psychology Today* 10 (1976): 40–43; J.W. Newstrom and J.L. Pierce, Alternative work schedules: The state of the art, *Personnel Administrator* 24 (1979): 19–23; A.O. Elbing, H. Gadon, and J.R.M. Gordon, Flexible working hours: The missing link, *California Management Review* 7 (1975): 50–57.

[68]Flexible benefits combined with salary reduction: A new trend, *Employee Benefit Plan Review* (May 1983).

[69]D. Gifford, The status of flexible compensation, *Personnel Administrator* 29 (May 1982): 19.

[70]*Ibid.*

[71]S.N. Gerberding, Communicate your benefits program through an employee fair, *Personnel Administrator* 28 (May 1983): 51.

[72]F.W. Taylor, A piece rate system, *Transactions of the American Society of Mechanical Engineers* 16 (1895): 856–905, cited in Henderson, *op. cit.*

[73]*Lincoln's Incentive System and Approach to Manufacturing* (Cleveland, Ohio: Lincoln Electric Co., 1972).

[74]Milkovich and Newman, *op. cit*, p. 303.

[75]*Ibid.*

[76] S.R. Collins, Incentive programs: Pros and cons, *Personnel Journal* 60 (1981): 571.

[77]Lawler, *Pay and Organization Development, op. cit.*

[78]B.R. Ellig, Total compensation design: Elements and issues, *Personnel* 61 (January-February 1984): 22.

FURTHER READINGS

Berg, J.G. *Managing Compensation.* New York: AMACOM, 1976.

Elizur, D. *Job Evaluation: A Systematic Approach.* Hants, Eng.: Gower, 1980.

Henderson, R.I. *Compensation Management.* Reston, Va.: Reston, 1984.

Lawler, E.E. III. *Pay and Organization Development.* Reading, Mass.: Addison-Wesley, 1981.

McCaffery, R.M. *Managing the Employee Benefits Program.* New York: AMACOM, 1983.

Milkovich, G.T. and Newman, J.M. *Compensation.* Plano, Tex.: Business Publications, 1984.

Rock, M.L., ed. *Handbook of Wage and Salary Administration.* New York: McGraw-Hill, 1984.

Wallace, M.J. Jr. and Fay, C.H. *Compensation Theory and Practice.* Boston: Kent, 1983.

PART 4

Labor Relations Systems

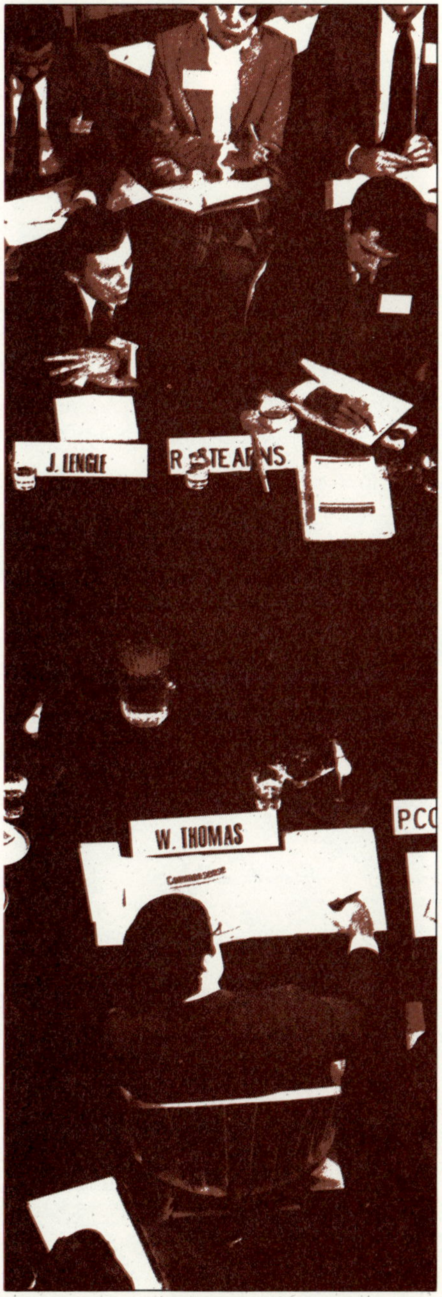

CHAPTER 10

Dealing with Unionized and Nonunionized Organizations

CHAPTER OUTLINE

LEARNING CHECKPOINTS

After completing the reading and activities in this chapter, the student will be able to

- offer five reasons why individuals would want to join a union;
- present the advantages and disadvantages of unionization to individuals and organizations;
- describe the major legislation that influences unionization;
- trace the history of the labor movement and its significance for workers, managers, and human resources professionals;
- specify the procedures for organizing a union;
- specify the procedures for decertifying a union;
- offer a strategy for organizing a union in union and nonunion organizations;
- offer a strategy for remaining or becoming nonunion.

INTRODUCTION

American Wood Products was an owner-operated manufacturer of fences, frames for water beds, and other wooden products in a large midwestern city. It employed fourteen workers in a single location. Jobs included running the cutting and nailing machines, overseeing the storage of products manufactured, loading products onto trucks and flatcars, driving trucks to deliver the products, and unloading them at the customer's location. For the first ten years of its existence the plant was nonunion. One-half of the workers had been employed by American Wood Products since its founding.

Workers were paid an hourly rate according to the difficulty of their jobs and their length of employment. In general, wages were competitive with those in comparable organizations, whether or not those organizations were unionized. Workers received ten paid holidays and five sick days yearly, and one day of vacation for each two months they worked at American.

Some of the workers felt that they were underpaid in comparison to their friends with similar jobs. When they approached the owner of American Wood Products—who prided himself on being accessible to his employees—he told them that the company could not afford increases in pay or benefits.

In 1982, one of the workers met a representative of the local union at a social gathering. The worker shared his dissatisfaction with the union representative. The representative suggested that the worker schedule a meeting to discuss bringing a union into American Wood Products. Scheduling the meeting upset the owner and general manager at American. They expressed outrage that their workers, whom they had treated more than fairly, would consider joining a union. If the workers at American Wood Products choose to unionize, they would join the more than twenty-two million workers—close to one-fourth of the nonagricultural labor force—who belong to unions.[1] In fields such as transportation and construction, more than 75 percent of the workers belong to unions; in mining, petroleum, manufacturing, telephone and telegraph, and the federal government, more than 50 percent of the workers are union members.[2]

Should the workers at American join a union? Should the owner and general manager be angry or insulted if the workers decide to unionize? What advantages and disadvantages does union membership offer? If the workers feel that unionization is appropriate, which union should they join? How do they become unionized? How can American's executives guard against unionization? Would these employers want to guard against unionization?

In this chapter we address questions such as these. We begin by answering why members of an organization would choose to unionize. Next we look at the historical context of unionization. We continue by examining the structure of unions. Then we look at the steps in organizing a union. We also examine the alternative of remaining or becoming nonunion. We conclude the chapter with a discussion of the role of human resources professionals and managers in the unionization process.

THE EMPLOYEE PERSPECTIVE: WHY UNIONIZE?

Why would the employees at American consider joining a union? Workers join unions for a variety of reasons. First, they expect that union membership would result in increased compensation; most union leaders argue that they have succeeded in obtaining improved wages, benefits, and hours for their members. Second, some workers, particularly those in blue-collar jobs, may feel that union membership would provide them with greater status—in some communities, membership in a union has significant prestige. Third, union membership may satisfy their social needs. Union members frequently socialize at the union hall outside the workplace. Fourth, union membership may satisfy self-esteem needs. Some workers feel more confident and competent when they are part of a highly visible and powerful organization. Fifth, individuals may join unions because their coworkers or other peers exert pressure on them to join. Would you be able to resist joining a union if the majority of your coworkers belonged to a union? Finally, in some organizations, employees automatically belong to a union. The *union shop* describes an organization where all employees in certain jobs must join the established union.

If the workers at American Wood Products were to unionize, their interaction with management would probably change. Management would have to deal with employees as a group, not as individuals. They would be dealing with a separate organization—the union—with its own goals, financial status, and officers. Unions act as intermediaries between management and workers; in this role they can facilitate or hinder communication between these groups. Because unions act as watchdogs on management, the management of unionized organizations must be particularly consistent in formulating and implementing policies that affect employees.

HISTORICAL CONTEXT OF UNIONIZATION

What protection would the workers be provided if they were to join the union? During the twentieth century, laws have been passed to regulate union-management relations. Figure 10–1 summarizes the key legislation that regulates and monitors management/union activities. Figure 10–2 lists the agencies designated with responsibility for administering the provisions of the legislation.

Prior to 1925

Labor law prior to 1925 provided significant protection for management. From an early nineteenth-century Supreme Court case that dealt with shoemakers in Philadelphia (1806), a doctrine evolved that identified employee union activities

Railway Labor Act, 1927. Designed to protect rights of railroad and airline employees; created the National Mediation Board, National Railway Adjustment Board, and Public Law Board to resolve disputes between workers and management.

Norris-LaGuardia Act, 1932. Reduced the use of injunctions in repressing union activity; forbade yellow-dog contracts.

National Labor Relations Act (Wagner Act), 1935. Stated mandatory subjects of bargaining; specified unfair labor practices by management; created the National Labor Relations Board.

Labor-Management Relations Act (Taft-Hartley Act), 1947. Prohibited the closed shop; stated unfair labor practices by unions; provided for the handling of national emergency strikes; created the Federal Mediation and Conciliation Service.

Labor-Management Reporting and Disclosure Act (Landrum-Griffin Act), 1959. Regulated internal union affairs.

Figure 10–1 **SUMMARY OF LABOR LEGISLATION**

as a "conspiracy against free trade."[3] At that time—prior to the Industrial Revolution—this doctrine was viable to the economy since workers could negotiate one-on-one with their employers in the cottage industry environment that existed. Unionization would have been a conspiracy or an unfair advantage to the employee.

After the Industrial Revolution the pendulum swung to the employer's advantage. For example, the average steelworker in the nineteenth century could

National Labor Relations Board (NLRB). Administers the National Labor Relations Act as amended by the Taft-Hartley and Landrum-Griffin acts, conducts union representation elections, and adjudicates unfair labor practice complaints.

Federal Mediation and Conciliation Service (FMCS). Provides mediation services to unions and management in collective bargaining and assists these parties in selecting arbitrators in grievance administration.

U.S. Department of Labor. Performs many labor-related services: conducts research, administers wage laws, and enforces federal contract compliance under OSHA and EEO.

National Mediation Board. Handles union representation issues under the Railway Labor Act, provides mediation services to parties in negotiations, assists in disputes over contract interpretation, and in cases involving emergency disputes proposes arbitration and certifies the dispute to the President as an emergency.

National Railroad Adjustment Board. Hears and attempts to resolve railroad labor disputes growing out of grievances and interpretation or application of the labor agreements.

State and Local Administrative Agencies. Enforce and administer state laws and local ordinances involving labor relations issues.

Figure 10–2 **MAJOR ADMINISTRATIVE AGENCIES**

not negotiate one-on-one with Andrew Carnegie about wages and conditions of employment. Thus a Supreme Court decision in the 1840s *(Commonwealth* v. *Hunt,* 1842) modified this conspiracy doctrine.[4] It allowed employees to gather collectively to engage in union activities so long as the activities did not interfere with the employer's commerce. If there was interference, however, the employer could seek an *injunction* from the courts; this decree barred the union from continuing the activities. Although workers had the right to strike, management could file a request with the federal courts to halt the strike, and this right of injunction was granted freely.[5] It provided management with significant power in curbing union activity. Subsequently, during the twentieth century, legislation was passed to maintain a balance of power and prerogative between employees and employers.

Railway Labor Act

An early act designed to protect workers' rights was passed in 1926. The Railway Labor Act encouraged the fair treatment of railroad employees. It attempted to reduce work stoppages by providing avenues of appeal for worker complaints.

The National Mediation Board, composed of three presidential appointees, provided mediators who acted as go-betweens in helping management and union members reach agreements about problems. The Act also established the National Railway Adjustment Board (NRAB) in Chicago, which handled grievances under existing agreements between labor and management. While the National Railway Adjustment Board acted effectively in those cases it heard, its backlog of cases quickly increased, resulting at one point in an eight-year backlog. The creation of the Public Law Board in 1966, which also handled cases, reduced the time-to-hearing to two years.

Under this law, *mediation* played a significant role in resolving disputes between workers and management. A third party (the mediator) attempted to help the two parties reach an agreement (see Chapter 12). Yet this approach was not fail-proof. In the case of failures, binding arbitration (where the two parties agreed to abide by a third-person's [arbitrator's] judgment regardless of the nature of that decision) could be used (see Chapter 12). If the parties refused arbitration, the President of the United States could call an emergency board of investigation. This Board investigated the situation, submitted a report within thirty days, and then allowed thirty additional days for the parties to reach resolution. If no resolution were reached at the end of sixty days, workers could call a strike.

The Railway Labor Act was designed to

1. avoid interruptions of commerce;
2. forbid any limitation on employees' rights to organize and join labor unions;
3. provide complete independence for both parties in carrying out the purposes of the act;
4. provide prompt and orderly settlement of disputes over pay, rules, and working conditions; and

5. provide prompt and orderly settlement of disputes over grievances and contract interpretation.[6]

While the general provisions of this act set the stage for subsequent legislation, the Railway Labor Act itself did not cover the categories of workers at American Wood Products.

Norris-LaGuardia Act

This act, also called the Federal Anti-Injunction Act, moved public policy from repression to strong encouragement of union activity; it freed collective activity from the court interference that had restricted it. It further strengthened the power of workers in their interactions with management in an attempt to reduce the advantage still held by employers.

Passed in 1932, the Norris-LaGuardia Act, named after the Senator and Congressman (later Mayor of New York), respectively, who sponsored the legislation, increased the protection of workers by restricting the use of injunctions. Federal courts could still issue injunctions under conditions such as the following:

1. Unlawful acts had been threatened or committed
2. Substantial and irreparable injury to the employer's property would follow
3. Greater injury would be inflicted upon the employer by denial of an injunction than upon the union by granting injunction
4. The employer had no adequate remedy under the law
5. Public officers were unable or unwilling to furnish adequate protection
6. The employer had made every effort to settle the dispute through collective bargaining (including mediation, voluntary arbitration, and so on) before going to court[7]

This act also extended the protections of the Railway Labor Act to any interstate business. Thus workers at companies such as American Wood Products, which bought, sold, and transported products between states, are entitled to appeals and mediation as a result of provisions of the Norris-LaGuardia Act.

The Norris-LaGuardia Act also forbade *yellow dog contracts.* Such a contract required an employee to agree *not* to join a union as a condition of employment. The passage of this act ensured that workers at American Wood Products can join a union and may not receive retaliatory actions from management if they do so. The individual employee is guaranteed "full freedom of association, self-organization, and designation of representatives of his own choosing, to negotiate the terms and conditions of his employment . . . free from interference, restraint, or coercion of employers."[8] Thus the owner and general manager at American Wood have little power to prevent unionization as a result of the provisions of the Norris-LaGuardia Act and subsequently passed legislation.

National Labor Relations Act (Wagner Act)

The National Labor Relations Act (NLRA), also known as the Wagner Act, was passed in 1935 and extended the rights of workers beyond those specified in the Norris-LaGuardia Act. This passage of this act reflected the active role the federal government planned to play in national economics. Passed while the United States was experiencing its most severe depression, the Act "acknowledged that inequality of bargaining power between employees and employers affected the flow of commerce and aggravated recurring economic depressions by depressing wages and purchasing power and thereby prevented the stability of wages and working conditions . . . and recognized that protection by the law of the right of employees to organize and bargain collectively would promote the flow of commerce, restore equality of bargaining power, and encourage friendly adjustment of industrial disputes."[9]

This act, more than any other, provides for and ensures that management does not abridge the rights of workers. It guarantees the rights of employees to organize; bargain collectively; and strike, boycott, or picket in certain situations. Figure 10–3 is an excerpt from the Wagner Act; you should review the language used and the specificity of these illustrative provisions that guide labor-management relations.

COMPARISON OF THE NATIONAL LABOR RELATIONS ACT OF 1935 WITH TITLE I OF THE LABOR MANAGEMENT RELATIONS ACT OF 1947

Key to Comparison

Portions of the National Labor Relations Act which have been eliminated by the Labor Management Relations Act are enclosed in black brackets; provisions which have been added to the National Labor Relations Act are in italics; and unchanged portions of the National Labor Relations Act are shown in roman.

NATIONAL LABOR RELATIONS ACT

[AN ACT]

[To diminish the causes of labor disputes burdening or obstructing interstate and foreign commerce, to create a National Labor Relations Board, and for other purposes.]

FINDINGS AND POLICIES

Section 1. The denial by *some* employers of the right of employees to organize and the refusal by *some* employers to accept the procedure of collective bargaining lead to strikes and other forms of industrial strife or unrest, which have the intent or the necessary effect of burdening or obstructing commerce by (a) impairing the efficiency, safety, or operation of the instrumentalities of commerce; (b) occurring in the current of commerce; (c) materially affecting, restraining, or controlling the flow of raw materials or manufactured or processed goods from or into the channels of commerce, or the prices of such materials or goods in commerce; or (d) causing diminution of employment and wages in such volume as substantially to impair or disrupt the market for goods flowing from or into the channels of commerce.

Figure 10–3 EXCERPT FROM THE WAGNER ACT *Continued*

The inequality of bargaining power between employees who do not possess full freedom of association or actual liberty of contract, and employers who are organized in the corporate or other forms of ownership association substantially burdens and affects the flow of commerce, and tends to aggravate recurrent business depressions, by depressing wage rates and the purchasing power of wage earners in industry and by preventing the stabilization of competitive wage rates and working conditions within and between industries.

Experience has proved that protection by law of the right of employees to organize and bargain collectively safeguards commerce from injury, impairment, or interruption, and promotes the flow of commerce by removing certain recognized sources of industrial strife and unrest, by encouraging practices fundamental to the friendly adjustment of industrial disputes arising out of differences as to wages, hours, or other working conditions, and by restoring equality of bargaining power between employers and employees.

Experience has further demonstrated that certain practices by some labor organizations, their officers and members have the intent or the necessary effect of burdening or obstructing commerce by preventing the free flow of goods in such commerce through strikes and other forms of industrial unrest or through concerted activities which impair the interest of the public in the free flow of such commerce. The elimination of such practices is a necessary condition to the assurance of the rights herein guaranteed.

It is hereby declared to be the policy of the United States to eliminate the causes of certain substantial obstructions to the free flow of commerce and to mitigate and eliminate these obstructions when they have occurred by encouraging the practice and procedure of collective bargaining and by protecting the exercise by workers of full freedom of association, self-organization, and designation of representatives of their own choosing, for the purpose of negotiating the terms and conditions of their employment or other mutual aid or protection.

Sec. 3. (a) [There is hereby created a board, to be known as the "National Labor Relations Board" (hereinafter referred to as the "Board"), which shall be composed of three members, who shall be appointed by the President, by and with the advice and consent of the Senate. One of the original members shall be appointed for a term of one year, one for a term of three years, and one for a term of five years, but their successors shall be appointed for terms of five years each, except] *The National Labor Relations Board (hereinafter called the "Board") created by this Act prior to its amendment by the Labor Management Relations Act, 1947, is hereby continued as an agency of the United States, except that the Board shall consist of five instead of three members, appointed by the President, by and with the advice and consent of the Senate. Of the two additional members so provided for, one shall be appointed for a term of five years and the other for a term of two years. Their successors, and the successors of the other members, shall be appointed for terms of five years each, excepting* that any individual chosen to fill a vacancy shall be appointed only for the unexpired term of the member whom he shall succeed. The President shall designate one member to serve as Chairman of the Board. Any member of the Board may be removed by the President, upon notice and hearing, for neglect of duty or malfeasance in office, but for no other cause.

(b) *The Board is authorized to delegate to any group of three or more members any or all of the powers which it may itself exercise.* A vacancy in the Board shall not impair the right of the remaining members to exercise all of the powers of the Board, and [two] *three* members of the Board shall, at all times, constitute a quorum [.] *of the Board, except that two members shall constitute a quorum of any group designated pursuant to the first sentence hereof.* The Board shall have an official seal which shall be judicially noticed.

(c) The Board shall at the close of each fiscal year make a report in writing to Congress and to the President stating in detail the cases it has heard, the decisions it has rendered, the names, salaries, and duties of all employees and officers in the employ or under the supervision of the Board, and an account of all moneys it has disbursed.

(d) *There shall be a General Counsel of the Board who shall be appointed by the President, by and with the advice and consent of the Senate, for a term of four years. The General Counsel of the Board shall exercise general supervision over all attorneys employed by the Board (other than trial examiners and legal assistants to Board members) and over the officers and employees in the regional offices. He shall have final authority, on behalf of the Board, in respect of the investigation of charges and issuance of complaints under section 10, and in respect of the prosecution of such complaints before the Board, and shall have such other duties as the Board may prescribe or as may be provided by law.*

Sec. 4. (a) Each member of the Board *and the General Counsel of the Board* shall receive a salary of [$10,000] *$12,000* a year, shall be eligible for reappointment, and shall not engage in any other business, vocation, or employment. The Board shall appoint [without regard for the provisions of the civil-service laws but subject to the Classification Act of 1923, as amended,] an executive secretary, and such attorneys, examiners, and regional directors, and [shall appoint] such other employees [with regard to existing laws applicable to the employment and compensation of officers and employees of the United States,] as it may from time to time find necessary for the proper performance of its duties. [and as may be from time to time appropriated for by Congress.] *The Board may not employ any attorneys for the purpose of reviewing transcripts of hearings or preparing drafts of opinions except that any attorney employed for assignment as a legal assistant to any Board member may for such Board member review such transcripts and prepare such drafts. No trial examiner's report shall be reviewed, either*

Figure 10–3 **Continued** *Continued*

before or after its publication, by any person other than a member of the Board or his legal assistant, and no trial examiner shall advise or consult with the Board with respect to exceptions taken to his findings, rulings, or recommendations. The Board may establish or utilize such regional, local, or other agencies, and utilize such voluntary and uncompensated services, as may from time to time be needed. Attorneys appointed under this section may, at the direction of the Board, appear for and represent the Board in any case in court. Nothing in this Act shall be construed to authorize the Board to appoint individuals for the purpose of conciliation or mediation, [(or for statistical work), where such service may be obtained from the Department of Labor.] *or for economic analysis.*

(b) [Upon the appointment of the three original members of the Board and the designation of its chairman, the old Board shall cease to exist. All employees of the old Board shall be transferred to and become employees of the Board with salaries under the Classification Act of 1923, as amended, without acquiring by such transfer a permanent or civil service status. All records, papers, and property of the old Board shall become records, papers, and property of the Board and all unexpended funds and appropriations for the use and maintenance of the old Board shall become funds and appropriations available to be expended by the Board in the exercise of the powers, authority, and duties conferred on it by this Act.]

[(c)] All of the expenses of the Board, including all necessary traveling and subsistence expenses outside the District of Columbia incurred by the members or employees of the Board under its orders, shall be allowed and paid on the presentation of itemized vouchers therefor approved by the Board or by any individual it designates for that purpose.

Sec. 5. The principal office of the Board shall be in the District of Columbia, but it may meet and exercise any or all of its powers at any other place. The Board may, by one or more of its members or by such agents or agencies as it may designate, prosecute any inquiry necessary to its functions in any part of the United States. A member who participates in such an inquiry shall not be disqualified from subsequently participating in a decision of the Board in the same case.

Sec. 6 [(a)] The Board shall have authority from time to time to make, amend, and rescind, *in the manner prescribed by the Administrative Procedure Act,* such rules and regulations as may be necessary to carry out the provisions of this Act. [Such rules and regulations shall be effective upon publication in the manner which the Board shall prescribe.]

RIGHTS OF EMPLOYEES

Sec. 7. Employees shall have the right to self-organization, to form, join, or assist labor organizations, to bargain collectively through representatives of their own choosing, and to engage in *other* concerted activities for the purpose of collective bargaining or other mutual aid or protection, *and shall also have the right to refrain from any or all of such activities except to the extent that such right may be affected by an agreement requiring membership in a labor organization as a condition of employment as authorized in section 8 (a) (3).*

UNFAIR LABOR PRACTICES

Sec. 8. (*a*) It shall be an unfair labor practice for an employer—(1) to interfere with, restrain, or coerce employees in the exercise of the rights guaranteed in section 7;

(2) to dominate or interfere with the formation or administration of any labor organization or contribute financial or other support to it: *Provided,* That subject to rules and regulations made and published by the Board pursuant to section 6, [(a)] an employer shall not be prohibited from permitting employees to confer with him during working hours without loss of time or pay;

(3) by discrimination in regard to hire or tenure of employment or any term or condition of employment to encourage or discourage membership in any labor organization: *Provided,* That nothing in this Act, or in [the National Industrial Recovery Act (U. S. C., Supp. VII, title 15, secs. 701–712), as amended from time to time, or in any code or agreement approved or prescribed thereunder,] any other statute of the United States, shall preclude an employer from making an agreement with a labor organization (not established, maintained, or assisted by any action defined in *section 8 (a) of* this Act as an unfair labor practice) to require as a condition of employment membership therein *on or after the thirtieth day following the beginning of such employment or the effective date of such agreement, whichever is the later,* (*i*) if such labor organization is the representative of the employees as provided in section 9 (a), in the appropriate collective-bargaining unit covered by such agreement when made; *and* (*ii*) *if, following the most recent election held as provided in section 9 (e) the Board shall have certified that at least a majority of the employees eligible to vote in such election have voted to authorize such labor organization to make such an agreement: Provided further, That no employer shall justify any discrimination against an employee for nonmembership in a labor organization (A) if he has reasonable grounds for believing that such membership was not available*

Figure 10–3 **Continued** *Continued*

to the employee on the same terms and conditions generally applicable to other members, or (B) if he has reasonable grounds for believing that membership was denied or terminated for reasons other than the failure of the employee to tender the periodic dues and the initiation fees uniformly required as a condition of acquiring or retaining membership;

(4) to discharge or otherwise discriminate against an employee because he has filed charges or given testimony under this Act;

(5) to refuse to bargain collectively with the representatives of his employees, subject to the provisions of section 9 (a).

(b) It shall be an unfair labor practice for a labor organization or its agents—

(1) to restrain or coerce (A) employees in the exercise of the rights guaranteed in section 7: Provided, That this paragraph shall not impair the right of a labor organization to prescribe its own rules with respect to the acquisition or retention of membership therein; or (B) an employer in the selection of his representatives for the purposes of collective bargaining or the adjustment of grievances;

(2) to cause or attempt to cause an employer to discriminate against an employee in violation of subsection (a) (3) or to discriminate against an employee with respect to whom membership in such organization has been denied or terminated on some ground other than his failure to tender the periodic dues and the initiation fees uniformly required as a condition of acquiring or retaining membership;

(3) to refuse to bargain collectively with an employer, provided it is the representative of his employes subject to the provisions of section 9 (a);

(4) to engage in, or to induce or encourage the employees of any employer to engage in, a strike or a concerted refusal in the course of their employment to use, manufacture, process, transport, or otherwise handle or work on any goods, articles, materials, or commodities or to perform any services, where an object thereof is:

(A) forcing or requiring any employer or self-employed person to join any labor or employer organization or any employer or other person to cease using, selling, handling, transporting, or otherwise dealing in the products of any other producer, processor, or manufacturer, or to cease doing business with any other person;

(B) forcing or requiring any other employer to recognize or bargain with a labor organization as the representative of his employees unless such labor organization has been certified as the representative of such employees under the provisions of section 9;

(C) forcing or requiring any employer to recognize or bargain with a particular labor organization as the representative of his employees if another labor organization has been certified as the representative of such employees under the provisions of section 9;

SOURCE: U.S. Code 1976 Title 29, § 151 *et seq.*, July 5, 1935, C. 372, 49 Stat. 449.

Figure 10–3 Continued

The Wagner Act mandated that union and management must bargain about three subjects: (1) wages, (2) hours of employment, and (3) terms and conditions of work. These subjects may seem fairly restricted, but they have since been extended to include a wide range of issues, as shown in Figure 10–4. Wages, for example, include hourly compensation, overtime, time off with pay, and benefits, among others. Hours of employment refers to the length of the normal work day, the number of hours worked per week, staffing of overtime hours, and introduction of flexible or alternative work schedules (see Chapter 14). Conditions of work include issues as diverse as safety in the workplace, such as wearing hard hats or required maintenance of equipment, and the presence of vending machines on the shop floor. The Act states that bargaining regarding the labor contract must include these three subjects; management may not take unilateral action in these three areas.

The National Labor Relations Act has three major provisions: (1) it banned five management actions as unfair labor practices; (2) it required secret ballot union elections, as well as a majority rule for electing representatives to bargain for employees; and (3) it created the National Labor Relations Board (NLRB).

Hours

Wages

actual rates of pay	shift differentials
overtime rates	incentive plans
pension plans	merit pay
profit-sharing plans	bonuses (in some situations)

Terms and Conditions of Employment

sick leave	grievance procedure
vacations	safety
holidays	pensions
job classifications	child-care facilities
work rules	management rights
scheduling	union security
layoffs	payment of union dues

Figure 10–4 EXAMPLES OF MANDATORY BARGAINING ISSUES

Unfair Labor Practices by Management. Should the workers at American Wood choose to unionize, what protections do the five unfair labor practices grant them?

1. Management must allow employees to organize if they wish. They cannot bribe, blacklist, or transfer employees for the purpose of preventing self-organization.

2. Company representatives cannot interfere with the formation or administration of unions. For example, supervisors cannot organize a company-sponsored union that has dues lower than union dues.

3. A company cannot discriminate in hiring or granting tenure to employees as a way of influencing their membership in a union. For example, a manager cannot promise a subordinate job security if he or she does not join the union.

4. A company cannot discriminate against an employee who files an unfair labor practice or gives testimony in an unfair labor practice case. For example, the company cannot suspend, demote, or reduce the salary of such a worker.

5. Employers cannot refuse to bargain collectively. They must participate in contract negotiations and must *bargain in good faith.* This means that management or its representatives must attempt to reach an agreement. For example, the employer must supply information requested by the union, such as wage rates and increases, that is relevant and necessary to allow union representatives to bargain intelligently and effectively (see Chapter 11 for further discussion of good-faith bargaining).

Secret Ballot Election. To further protect workers' rights to choose union membership, the Wagner Act requires secret balloting in all elections regarding unionization or election of union representatives. Either employees or management can petition for an election. In such an election workers can vote for any of several union choices or can choose not to have a union. The provisions of this act would guide the election process at American Wood Products.

An NLRB representation election is prohibited for twelve months after a union wins the right to represent employees.[10] An NLRB rule called the *contract bar doctrine* can extend this time limitation for up to three years, or the duration of a valid contract between union and management.[11] The election procedures are described later in this chapter.

National Labor Relations Board. Empowered with the responsibility for overseeing union and management activities, the National Labor Relations Board (NLRB) is a quasijudicial body.[12] It includes a five-member Board (nominated by the President and confirmed by the Senate), general counsel, and fifty regional and field offices. The Board establishes policy and judges final appeals; the general counsel investigates and issues complaints and oversees the regional and field offices, which interact directly with organizations under their jurisdiction.

The National Labor Relations Board supervises union elections, oversees collective bargaining activities, and provides assistance in some cases of contract violations. In 1980 the agency handled 55,587 cases; 42,047 were cases of unfair labor practices and 13,540 were cases of union representation.[13] Although administratively the agency has been successful, it lacks the power to impose severe penalties, award damages, or recoup for individuals the wages lost during periods of improperly deprived employment. The federal or state courts retain this power.

National Labor-Management Relations Act (Taft-Hartley Act)

After the passage of the Wagner Act, strikes, boycotts, and walkouts increased, and unions incurred public disfavor. The Taft-Hartley Act was viewed as a fine-tuning of the system to ensure a balance of power between the two parties involved in labor negotiations. The role of the federal government in this has been perceived as providing a structure in which neither employer nor employee has an inappropriate amount of leverage over the other. The Labor-Management Relations Act was passed in 1947 to reduce the perceived imbalance in favor of unions created by the provisions of the Wagner Act. The Taft-Hartley specified unfair labor practices by unions, the rights of employees as individuals, the rights of employers, and provisions for handling national emergency strikes. It also prohibited the closed shop and created the Federal Mediation and Conciliation Service.

The *closed* shop prohibited a worker from being employed unless he or she was already a member of a union. Clearly this restricted the work force significantly. The Taft-Hartley allowed instead the *union* shop. In this case individuals could be required to join a union *once they were hired by an organization.* Thus union membership could no longer be used as a selection criterion. Approximately twenty-five states, primarily in the south and west, subsequently passed *right-to-work* legislation which prohibited a requirement of union membership at any time.[14]

Unfair Labor Practices by Unions. Just as the Wagner Act prohibited certain behaviors by management, the Taft-Hartley Act instituted a parallel set of controls for union leaders. These controls provide protection for the owner and general manager at American Wood Products. The unfair union practices defined in this act included the following:

1. Union leaders cannot prevent employees from exercising their collective bargaining rights, such as the right to negotiate wages, hours, and conditions of employment;
2. union leaders cannot ask an employer to discriminate against an employee as a way of influencing union membership;
3. unions cannot refuse to bargain in good faith;
4. unions cannot conduct certain types of strikes or boycotts, such as actions against another employer who is neutral (secondary boycott), to get recognition for an uncertified union;
5. unions cannot charge excessive dues; and
6. unions cannot engage in *featherbedding;* that is, they cannot require an organization to pay for services not performed. For example, the union cannot insist that extra, unnecessary workers be assigned to a packing area and receive pay for not working.

Rights of Employees As Individuals. Not only are unions prohibited from engaging in specific unfair labor practices, but they, as well as management, must ensure that certain rights of individual employees are not abridged.

The Taft-Hartley Act guaranteed individuals the right to present grievances, or complaints about their treatment at work, *directly* to the employer without intervention of the union. In most cases, the union represents the workers in presenting complaints to management. Where unions decide that such complaints are not justified, they must still allow workers to present their complaints.

The final protection for an individual offered under this act was the prevention of the automatic deduction of union dues from that person's paycheck unless he or she authorizes direct payment; unions could not insist on the automatic deduction of dues.

Rights of Employers. Employers can advertise and speak against the union; they can develop and distribute attractive, eye-catching brochures, leaflets, or booklets that promote the advantages of remaining nonunion, often by describing the disadvantages of unionization. They can also conduct formal or informal informational meetings to discuss the disadvantages of unionization. But employers cannot meet with employees within twenty-four hours of an election since this does not allow the union sufficient time to rebut any unsubstantiated charges.

Nor can they lobby employees individually to vote against the union; this pressuring of individuals is contrary to fair practice. Thus the owner and general manager of American Wood Products can actively campaign against unionization. They cannot, however, promise to change wages, hours, or conditions of employment for the purpose of avoiding unionization.

National Emergency Strikes. When a strike affects national health and safety, the government can intervene. The President of the United States can appoint a board of inquiry to make recommendations, seek a court injunction, and restrain the strike for sixty days. If no agreement is reached, this provision allows the President to extend the restriction for twenty more days. Employees are then polled in a secret ballot about their willingness to accept the employer's offer. The board of inquiry submits a final report to the President. If no resolution has been reached, the President submits a recommendation to Congress. By 1980, this provision had been invoked thirty-five times, most recently when President Jimmy Carter ordered the National Guard to operate the coal mines in 1977–1978. It is unlikely that this provision would apply to the situation at American Wood Products.

The *Federal Mediation and Conciliation Service* provides individuals to act as mediators (see Chapter 12). These neutral third parties facilitate union's and management's attainment of collective bargaining agreements by suggesting procedures and encouraging communication between the parties.

Labor-Management Reporting and Disclosure Act (Landrum-Griffin Act)

The Taft-Hartley regulated internal union affairs to some degree, by requiring unions to file certain financial and constitutional information yearly with the National Labor Relations Board, for example, and the Labor-Management Reporting and Disclosure Act (Landrum-Griffin Act), passed in 1959, extended these responsibilities.[15] While the Wagner Act can be viewed as a document that defines the rights of labor by limiting the actions of management, and the Taft-Hartley as defining the rights of management by limiting the actions of labor, the Landrum-Griffin Act can be viewed as the document that defines the rights of union members by limiting the actions of union leadership. The Act may have been motivated by the federal government's pursuit of criminal charges against Jimmy Hoffa, president of the Teamsters Union, for inappropriate use of union monies.[16]

The Landrum-Griffin Act provided for detailed regulation of internal union affairs. For example, union officers must file a yearly report about union spending. Increases in dues and fees must respond to members' needs and desires. Each union member must receive a copy of the negotiated agreement. This act also laid ground rules for union elections, calling for election of national and international officers at least every five years and local elections at least every three years.

Labor Law Reform Since 1960

Although the Taft-Hartley Act was meant to equalize the balance between union and management prerogatives, union advocates felt that the law created significant barriers to unionization. In 1977 labor lobbied for the passage of the Labor Law Reform Act. It was designed to expedite the union election process by imposing stiff penalties on employers who violated labor policy. Fines would be assessed if management did not bargain in good faith.

The proposed Act also placed deadlines on action by the National Labor Relations Board, which had become overwhelmed by the number of cases it had to handle. Management that wanted to avoid unionization often committed an unfair labor practice, knowing that the union would appeal to the NLRB. Because of the backlog of cases faced by the NLRB, this appeal became a useful way of delaying unionization. The J.P. Stevens Textile Company, for example, avoided unionization for approximately ten years by utilizing a variety of appeals to the NLRB to delay elections.[17]

The Labor Law Reform Act passed the House of Representatives by a vote of 257 to 163, but in 1978 the Senate blocked its passage with a filibuster. Thus the balance between union and management remains that established by the Landrum-Griffin Act. Together with the Wagner Act and Taft-Hartley Act, these laws represent the three identifiable parties in labor relations activity. The specific players, as well as the organizational and environmental context in which these laws operate, are described in the next section.

THE SITUATIONAL AUDIT

Factors in the environment and characteristics of the organization both influence whether individuals join a union.

The Environment

The nature of the political, social, and geographical environments all affect unionization. The nature of labor law, for example, is linked to the political party in power. Traditionally the Democratic party has supported union prerogatives more than has the Republican party.

Similarly, blue-collar organizations typically provide a fairly conducive social environment for unions. In general, blue-collar workers have joined unions in numbers disproportionate to white-collar workers.[18] Union membership is most common in transportation, construction, paper, and machinery industries, with more than 50 percent of the workers in these industries unionized; it is less common in nonmanufacturing, service, and agricultural industries, where less than 25 percent of the workers belong to unions.[19] Some argue that if union membership is to increase in the future, it must attract more white-collar workers.

Why have they chosen not to join unions? Would the decision of the workers at American be the same if they were white-collar rather than blue-collar workers?

White-collar workers have not been receptive to unionization for a variety of reasons. Historically unions have had a poor image, and the involvement of some union officials in corruption has contributed to this negative image.[20] Further, because white-collar workers have felt superior to and different from blue-collar workers, they do not feel that union membership gives them increased status. Rather, they have been unwilling to join unions because they perceive that it *reduces* their status in organizations. White-collar workers typically aspire to managerial positions; thus they feel that union membership would jeopardize their advancement. Also, white-collar workers have included a relatively large percentage of women, to whom union membership has not been attractive; for years job security was less important to women than to men and few union leadership positions were held by women. Some white-collar workers have felt that the labor movement has been led by uninspired, bureaucratic leadership, which has not motivated white-collar workers to join.

Finally, certain parts of the United States are more receptive to unionization than are others. The highly industrialized midwest expects and accepts union activity more readily than the south, southwest, or west. As the midwest becomes less reliant on heavy manufacturing and becomes more service-oriented, unionization efforts face greater cultural, social, and political opposition. As the south becomes more unionized, anti-union sentiment may decrease.[21]

The Organization

The way an organization structures and manages its internal environment also influences whether employees perceive that they need representation. If the organization meets employee needs, employees do not feel that they must find another organization—a union—to meet their needs. In these cases, unions tend not to be found in an organization. If an organization has not adequately managed its human resources by designing, developing, and implementing appropriate systems, however, employees often seek the services of a union to ensure that appropriate human resources management occurs. Thus organizations tend to face union activity if they are inadequately managed.

The goals of an organization, too, influence the support or resistance to unionization. If an organization perceives that unionization would hinder accomplishment of its goals, resistance would be high. Where unions already exist, the addition of another union may face less opposition than would the first union in a currently nonunionized organization.

Union advocates and opponents must analyze the organization to determine top management's likely receptivity or resistance to unionization. At American Wood Products, for example, it is clear that management would resist unionization, stressing the excellent treatment received by workers and the possibility that unionization would have negative consequences for the organization's financial stability. Management's attitudes toward and experience with particular unions and their leaders might also influence their receptivity to unionization.

TYPES OF UNIONS

In considering unionization, which union should the workers at American Wood Products join? In this section we consider options that have historically existed as well as current organizations.

Historical Options

Prior to the industrial revolution labor unions as we know them today did not exist. Employees belonged to guilds—joint associations of employers and craftspeople—that attempted to improve conditions for both groups. Only a few strikes occurred, primarily regarding wages.

1869 to World War I. The period between the rise of large manufacturing concerns and World War I heralded the formation of three national labor organizations: (1) Knights of Labor, (2) American Federation of Labor, and (3) Industrial Workers of the World. Founded in 1869, the *Knights of Labor* encouraged the use of producer and consumer cooperatives, the increase of workers' rights, and the improvement of work conditions through political action. They wanted to reduce the depersonalization of industrial mass production and create a morally improved society. The Knights actively avoided the use of strikes, preferring education as a way of instituting change. In addition, they promoted an eight-hour work day.[22] Membership reached 700,000 at its peak.

The Knights of Labor felt that all workers could belong to one big union since they would all have the same interests. This parochial view contributed to their downfall, as did their (incorrect) assumption that technical progress could be halted and their perceived association with the Haymarket Riot and other strikes in 1886.[23]

Samuel Gompers attempted to improve the material conditions of members of craft unions by using, rather than rejecting, the existing capitalistic system. In 1886, he organized craft unions into the *American Federation of Labor* (AFL). Unlike the single union approach taken by the Knights, the AFL was a collection of unions whose goal was pure and simple unionism. Membership in unions that comprised the AFL was restricted to crafts workers, who were viewed as the industrial elite; it did not include less skilled workers.

The AFL attempted to secure increased status for organized labor and to institute collective bargaining (contract negotiations) between labor and management. It used strikes as a weapon, was involved in the political arena through extensive lobbying of and support for selected political leaders, and relied on exclusive jurisdiction—each union had complete control over a particular group of workers—and decentralized authority to increase the local power of unions. These principles reinforced the uniqueness of each trade group. The AFL's emphasis on building union size and strength rather than instituting societal change contributed to its success because workers could easily relate to the AFL's goals.

The final union alternative, *Industrial Workers of the World* (IWW) was organized by Big Bill Haywood as an alternative to the AFL. He wanted to destroy capitalism and overthrow the existing political system. The IWW failed, however, because it did not appeal to its members' interests, lacked a permanent membership and financial base, encouraged sabotage and violence, and alienated the news media and government officials.[24]

Between the World Wars. The 1920s saw a decline in union membership due in part to an increasing number of strikes. These resulted from the rising cost of living after World War I and the greater power accrued by unions during the war.[25] At the same time, employers aggressively opposed union growth and tried to devise acceptable alternatives to unions. Some employers blacklisted employees who had a pro-union sentiment; others used violence against individuals trying to unionize; still others took a paternalistic approach and tried to convince employees that they knew what was best for them.[26]

The 1930s saw an increasing empowerment of industrial unions who represented semiskilled and unskilled workers in many occupational groups. They increasingly competed with craft unions for members. In large part because the AFL refused to represent unskilled industrial workers, John L. Lewis, president of the United Mine Workers, organized the industrial unions into the *Congress of Industrial Organizations* in 1935.

Originally formed within the AFL as the Committee for Industrial Organizations with an espoused educational and advisory purpose, it encouraged the organizing of unskilled workers. When the Committee refused the AFL's demand to disband, seven unions with one million members broke from the AFL and formed the competitive Congress of Industrial Organizations (CIO). This resulted in a significant increase in union membership, with the steel, automobile, rubber, marine, and textile industries being organized.

The growth of both the AFL and CIO continued until World War II, occurring because of

1. strong and aggressive leadership by John L. Lewis, Sidney Hillman, and other CIO leaders;
2. realistic goals of short-term gains and pure unionism by both the AFL and CIO;
3. effective use of *sitdown strikes*—where employees stayed inside the plant rather than picketing outside—to get management to accede to union demands;
4. the passage of the Wagner Act; and
5. changes in employees' attitudes toward the potential of using unions to obtain job security, wage increases, and improved work conditions.

Post–World War II. Worker strikes during World War II spurred negative attitudes by the public toward unions.[27] These strikes intensified after the war, and unions repeatedly attempted to extend their collective bargaining agreements to include new areas such as job security in the face of technological advancement, wages to meet increases in the cost of living, and employee benefits.

This period saw the merger of the AFL and CIO, in 1955. The new leaders of these organizations did not feel the antagonism toward each other that earlier leaders (such as Gompers and Lewis) had felt. Also, the slow growth of unions overall suggested a need for more collaborative rather than competitive efforts in securing new members. National unions became more powerful during this period. Declines in union raiding also resulted.

Unions increased their efforts in organizing white-collar workers and public workers, with some success. From 1960 to the present, many states granted public employees the right to organize and bargain collectively.[28] During this period white-collar unions have grown faster than blue-collar ones.[29]

Still, unionization efforts among engineers typify some of the problems encountered in unionizing white-collar workers.[30] Organization of these professionals has usually failed as a result of (1) the opposition of employers, who conduct active anti-union campaigns and promise a tough negotiation posture if unionization occurs; (2) the employees' view of unionization as a challenge to their professionalism and status; (3) a lack of bargaining power, since engineers often cannot easily paralyze the organization's operations (except perhaps in high technology organizations); and (4) the unions' historical projection of a blue-collar image.

Table 10–1 shows the changes in union membership from 1960 to 1980. Declines have been explained by

1. decreases in the number of employees in heavily unionized industries, such as manufacturing and railroads, due to automation and financial decline;
2. shifts in product and labor markets that have resulted in plant closings or relocations, causing unions to fail in maintaining promised employment;
3. shifts to new, high-technology industries;
4. movement toward more professional, technical, and service employees;
5. management's increased success in resisting unionization;
6. changing demographics of the work force (e.g., more women and minorities);
7. rapid expansion of legal rights that protect employers;
8. deficiencies in labor relations laws, such as time delays and lengthy appeals; and
9. union commitment of resources to servicing member needs rather than organizing new members.[31]

The results of a 1983 survey of union presidents and research and education directors suggests that there is some difficulty ahead for unions due to major environmental changes.[32] The survey sees barriers to union growth stemming from factors outside the labor movement, such as the economy, managerial attitudes, government policies, and technological change.[33] To increase membership unions must rely on increasing the number of (1) women, as they become dissatisfied with low-level jobs, (2) southern workers, as the south becomes more

Year		Total Labor Force		Nonagricultural Employees	
Unions and Associations	Union Membership (in Thousands)	Number (in Thousands)	Percent Members	Number (in Thousands)	Percent Members
1968	20,721	82,272	25.2	67,951	30.5
1970	21,248	85,903	24.7	70,880	30.0
1972	21,657	88,991	24.3	73,675	29.4
1974	22,809	93,240	24.5	78,265	29.1
1976	22,662	96,917	23.4	79,382	28.3
1978	22,757	102,537	22.2	86,697	26.3
1980	22,366	106,821	20.9	90,657	24.7
Unions					
1960	17,049	72,142	23.6	54,234	31.4
1962	16,586	73,442	22.6	55,596	29.8
1964	16,841	75,830	22.2	58,331	28.9
1966	17,940	78,893	22.7	63,955	28.1
1968	18,916	82,272	23.0	67,951	27.8
1970	19,381	85,903	22.6	70,920	27.3
1972	19,435	88,991	21.8	73,714	26.4
1974	20,199	93,240	21.7	78,413	25.8
1976	19,634	96,917	20.3	79,382	24.7
1978	20,238	102,537	19.7	85,762	23.6

SOURCE: U.S. Department of Labor, Bureau of Labor Statistics, *News* (Washington, D.C.: Government Printing Office, September 18, 1981).

Table 10–1 NATIONAL UNION MEMBERSHIP, 1960–1980

industrialized and racial tensions and anti-union attitudes are reduced, and (3) college-trained workers, as they fail to attain managerial or professional jobs.[34] In addition, they must find ways to increase union membership in organizations, such as textiles and other heavy manufacturing, that are declining due to a poor economy and competition from abroad (resulting from a lack of trade barriers).

Current Union Alternatives

In selecting the union to represent them, workers typically have several choices. They must select a union that can serve their occupational group and represent them effectively. Most unions have fairly broad mandates. The Teamsters, for example, originally founded as a union for truck drivers, now includes workers in diverse manufacturing and service areas.

The vote of workers, an agreement between management and workers, or the vote of the National Labor Relations Board determines which bargaining unit represents employees. The National Labor Relations Act includes the following rules for determining the bargaining unit:

1. The unit cannot include both professional and nonprofessional employees unless a majority of professionals concurs;

2. the unit cannot include craft members who have previously been included in a larger unit;
3. the unit cannot include both guards hired to enforce rules and other employees; and
4. the unit cannot include supervisors and managers.[35]

The specific number and type of employees represented by the bargaining unit is decided by the NLRB or negotiated between union and management. For example, a bargaining unit in a hospital might include all nonsupervisory nurses but no laboratory technicians.

Workers typically are most active in the union at the local, rather than regional or national, level. Union members have most contact with local officials, particularly the negotiating committee and union steward. The committee bargains contracts and decides whether to pursue grievances. The union steward represents the workers in interactions with management and files grievances for union members. The national union gives the local union its constitution, bylaws, and rules. Craft unions have considerable independence from their national union, though members may work under the same agreement at different sites. Craft unions have typically tried to limit their members, acting almost as a closed shop; they have insisted on certain apprenticeship requirements or priority hiring from among union members.

Industrial union members are frequently covered by agreements negotiated between the company and the national union. The United Auto Workers, United Mine Workers, or Teamsters are examples of this type of union. The president of the local union assists in the day-to-day administration of the contract.[36] He or she participates in local negotiations, maintains the union headquarters, and assists in the administration of grievances. The business agent is the full-time chief administrator of the local. The shop steward is the first union person to handle employee grievances and contact the business agent if needed. Figure 10–5 shows the organization chart of a typical union and its relationship to management. Note the separate hierarchies of union and management[37]; these can exert conflicting pressures on the workers.

Union members frequently do not devote much attention to union governance. Attendance at union meetings rarely exceeds ten percent of membership, although a relatively large percentage of union members votes when electing officers, supporting or refusing strikes, or ratifying contracts.[38] The union meeting allows members and leaders to communicate about problems, current negotiations, and other concerns.

Some unions have regional or district offices that coordinate the activities of the locals in a particular area. Others participate in joint councils of local unions for sharing information and gaining increased leverage in bargaining. Some intermediate organizations sponsor trade conferences for industrial union groups or convene conference boards that represent locals within a particular industry.

More common than regional or district unions are national unions, sometimes called international unions when they include a significant number of Canadians.

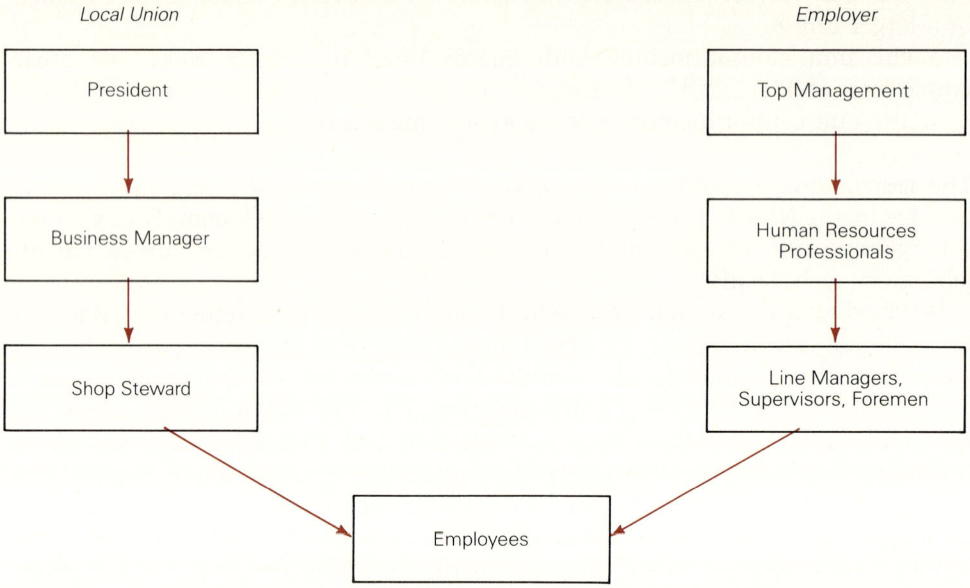

Figure 10–5 ORGANIZATION CHART FOR UNION AND MANAGEMENT

Table 10–2 lists the largest national unions in 1980. Unions such as the United Automobile Workers and the United Mine Workers frequently bargain at the national level for all their members. National unions charter and exert considerable influence over local unions. Because of their larger size, they bring extensive resources and expertise to negotiations. Then locals must ratify the contracts.

To increase their size and clout many labor unions merged between 1979 and 1984, more than in any similar period since the AFL-CIO merger in 1955. For example, in 1981 the United Food and Commercial Workers with 1.3 million members merged with the 22,000-member United Retail Workers.[39] These mergers were a function of the union leaders' goal of unity, the need to reduce disputes over the jurisdiction of competing unions, the need to gain a strong and united voice in collective bargaining, dwindling membership, and the resulting loss of dues.[40] These mergers increased membership, extended the financial resources of the merged unions, and expanded the jurisdiction of the unions to encompass more individuals—unions' ways of increasing their control over a changing environment.

These mergers generally did not succeed immediately because of members' desires to retain their geographical or craft identity, union traditions, and autonomy.[41] In some cases past rivalries created ill-will. However, the resulting larger unions had more power and resources, allowing them to negotiate as equals with large companies, hire better trained and qualified leaders, and ensure their longevity in the face of a dynamic economic and technological environment.[42]

Union	Membership
Teamsters	1,891,000
National Education Association	1,684,000
Automobile Workers	1,357,000
United Food and Commercial Workers	1,300,000
Steelworkers	1,238,000
Electricians	1,041,000
Carpenters	769,000
Machinists	754,000

Preliminary data from U.S. Department of Labor, Bureau of Labor Statistics, *News* September 1981, p. 2. Reprinted with permission.

Table 10–2 LARGEST INTERNATIONAL UNIONS

As another way of increasing their influence, many unions belong to the AFL-CIO. This group speaks for organized labor before Congress and in other political affairs. It coordinates community services and lobbying. It also helps organize nonunion employees. Annual or biennial conventions act as the governing body for the national union. The convention can revise the union's constitution, pass new union rules, act as a judge in union decisions, and elect union officers. Each local union sends a certain number of delegates. Each year these delegates discuss

1. internal government—dues, financial matters, authority of the president, executive board, and locals;
2. collective bargaining—problems with current agreements, membership requests for future negotiations, bargaining priorities, and determination of strategy for the next negotiations; and
3. resolutions in support of or against domestic and international public policies—labor law reform, inflation, interest rates, unemployment, international balance of payments, or loss of jobs to foreign countries.[43]

Figure 10–6 illustrates the structure of the AFL-CIO.

THE ORGANIZING CAMPAIGN

What are the steps the workers at American Wood Products must follow if they choose to become unionized? Because employers can lose extensive control and not all workers have the same attitude toward unionization, there are a great number of rules to ensure fairness in union organizing attempts.[44]

Union Certification

Union certification can occur in several ways, but if workers at American Wood Products were to unionize they would probably proceed as follows. Generally a

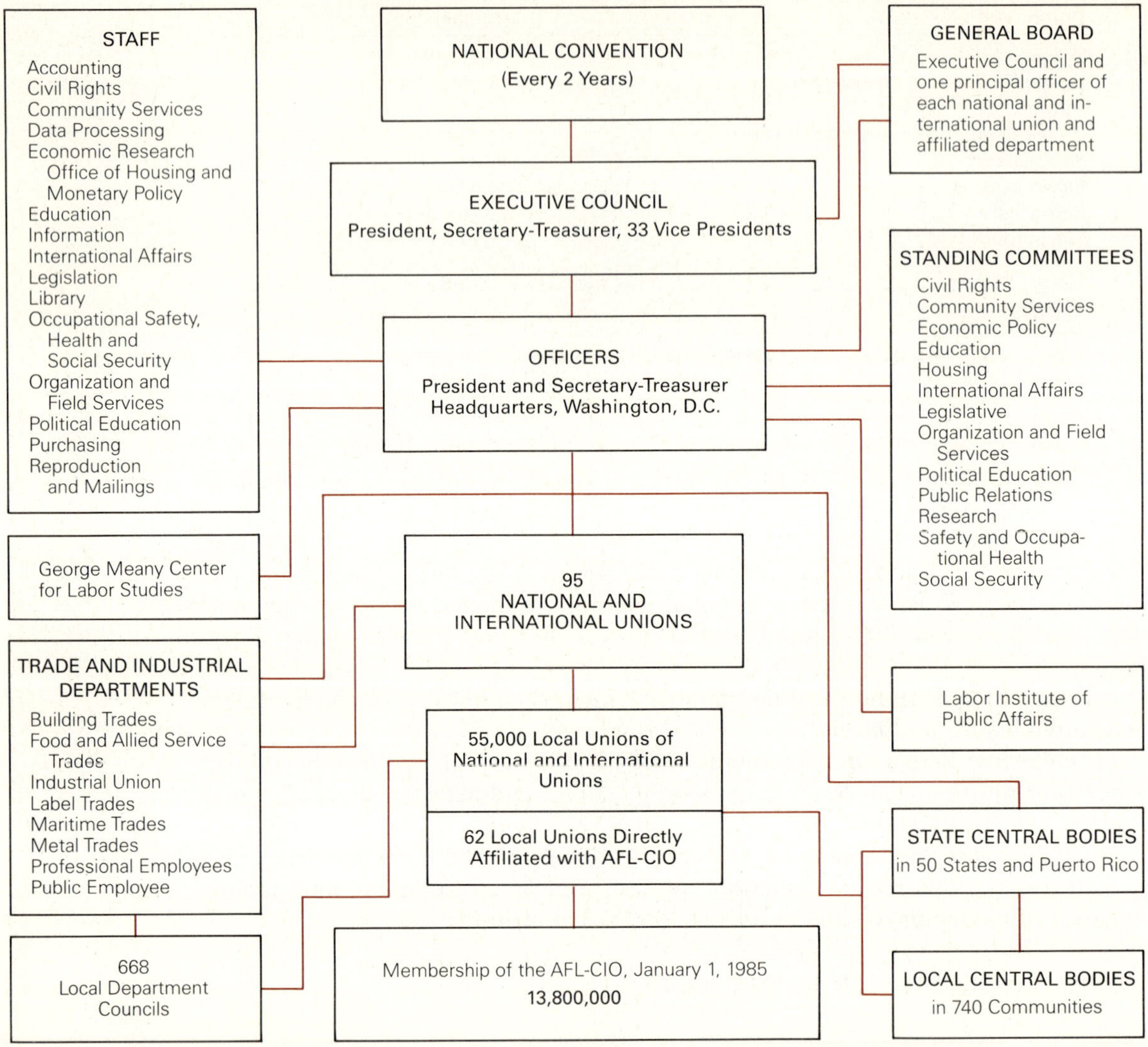

Reprinted by permission of the AFL-CIO.

Figure 10–6 STRUCTURAL ORGANIZATION OF THE AMERICAN FEDERATION OF LABOR AND CONGRESS OF INDUSTRIAL ORGANIZATIONS

unionization campaign begins with either a worker or a union initiating contact with other workers to discuss the possibility of unionization. At American Wood Products, for example, a representative of the local union approached the employees. The early discussions conducted by union advocates such as this representative tend to focus on the benefits of union membership by workers.

For example, when workers desire more fringe benefits, unions argue that they can negotiate better benefits for their workers. Or when workers complain about difficulty in altering their work days or hours, unions argue that they can negotiate improved rules and policies about work schedules and ensure their fair implementation.

Frequently union representatives from one or more unions conduct informational sessions at off-site locations, since they can be barred from the organization's property.[45] The employees of American Wood Products would probably attend such sessions, which are designed to convince the workers of the value of joining their union. Sometimes the pro-union forces try to hide their activity so management cannot mount an effort to remain nonunion.[46]

The union organizers can ask management to conduct a representation election. If management does not consent to this request, the union organizers next request the workers to sign authorization cards. These cards say that employees who sign want an election to take place; signing the cards does not necessarily mean that the workers want the union to represent them. To call a union election, 30 percent of the bona fide workers of the potential bargaining unit must sign the cards. In practice, most unions do not call for an election unless 60–65 percent of the workers sign cards. Since the union infers that a signed card reflects a worker's support for unionization, and the union does not want to call an election unless it can win, the union needs a large enough positive response—at least 60 percent—to ensure an ultimate election victory.

If the union decides to proceed, the signed cards are then submitted to the National Labor Relations Board for authentication. If the board determines that at least 30 percent have indeed signed, it can then call an election, assuming that the union has committed no unfair labor practices. If more than 50 percent sign cards, the union can ask for recognition from the organization. An organization, such as American Wood Products, rarely accedes to such a request for union recognition without a challenge or an election. Generally, the organization challenges numerous cards, which then require the NLRB to authenticate them.

If the NLRB determines that management has committed unfair labor practices, such as coercing workers not to sign cards or meeting with them at times prohibited by law, the NLRB can call an election without the required percentage of signatures. An employee, group of employees, labor organization, or employer can petition for an election.

When the NLRB issues an order for an election, management must supply the names and addresses of employees who would be in the proposed bargaining unit. If the NLRB issues such an order to executives of American Wood Products, they must provide this information. Representatives of the NLRB may request a consent election, where both parties agree to the proposed bargaining unit, voter eligibility, and election procedures. If they do not agree to a consent election, the NLRB holds a hearing to determine if an election should be held. This allows the union to contact potential members and campaign more actively. At this point, unions emphasize their ability to present worker grievances, improve wage levels, and increase worker participation in decision-making.[47]

For its part, the management of organizations such as American Wood Products can hold anti-union meetings on company time. These meetings emphasize the lack of value in unionization, the cost of union dues, the fairness with which the employer has treated workers in the past, and the increased likelihood of costly strikes.[48] They may hire an outside consultant to direct the campaign. Employers' threats, actions taken against union supporters, written communications, and captive-audience speeches affect voting, generally in support of management's position.[49] But neither unions nor management can campaign within twenty-four hours of the election since the other side does not have sufficient time to rebut inflammatory statements.

Management (supervisors) sometimes make mistakes that contribute to successful union organization attempts. For example, they may (1) prevent pro-union workers from distributing information to employees in public areas; (2) excessively limit access by pro-union individuals to areas surrounding a plant, such as outside plant gates; (3) prevent employees from soliciting support and distributing union material in a lunchroom; or (4) forbid employees from wearing union insignia.[50]

For a union to be organized, the majority of those workers voting must vote *for* unionization. If 100 workers vote, then 51 must vote for the union; if 3 workers vote, then 2 must vote for the union. At American Wood Products, 8 of the 14 workers must vote positively for unionization to occur. Thus to ensure a decision that represents the wishes of the workers, a large voter turnout is important.[51]

In certain cases of unfair management practices, the NLRB can certify a union without a majority vote. Similarly, in certain cases of unfair union practices, the NLRB can overthrow a majority vote and not certify a union. Recent election outcomes have favored unionization less than 50 percent of the time.[52] Union success has occurred more often when bargaining units are small, are agreed to by both unions and management, and represent only some of the workers.[53]

If the election supports unionization, the NLRB must then certify the union. This involves negotiations about the precise composition of the bargaining unit. Either the organization or union may file unfair labor practice charges with the NLRB at this point. Final certification is delayed until these charges are resolved. Figure 10–7 summarizes the steps in certification. Reading 10–1, "Employee Relations and Union Organizing Campaigns," by James Hopkins and Robert Binderup, discusses issues related to union organizing further.

Decertification

Once a union has been authorized, no attempts to decertify it can occur for at least one year and possibly as many as three years (the duration of the first contract). If employees believe that the union is not representing the interest of the majority after one year they can file for decertification. This request is made when the employees feel that their employer treated them more fairly before unionization, when unions do a poor job of providing services, when unions fail

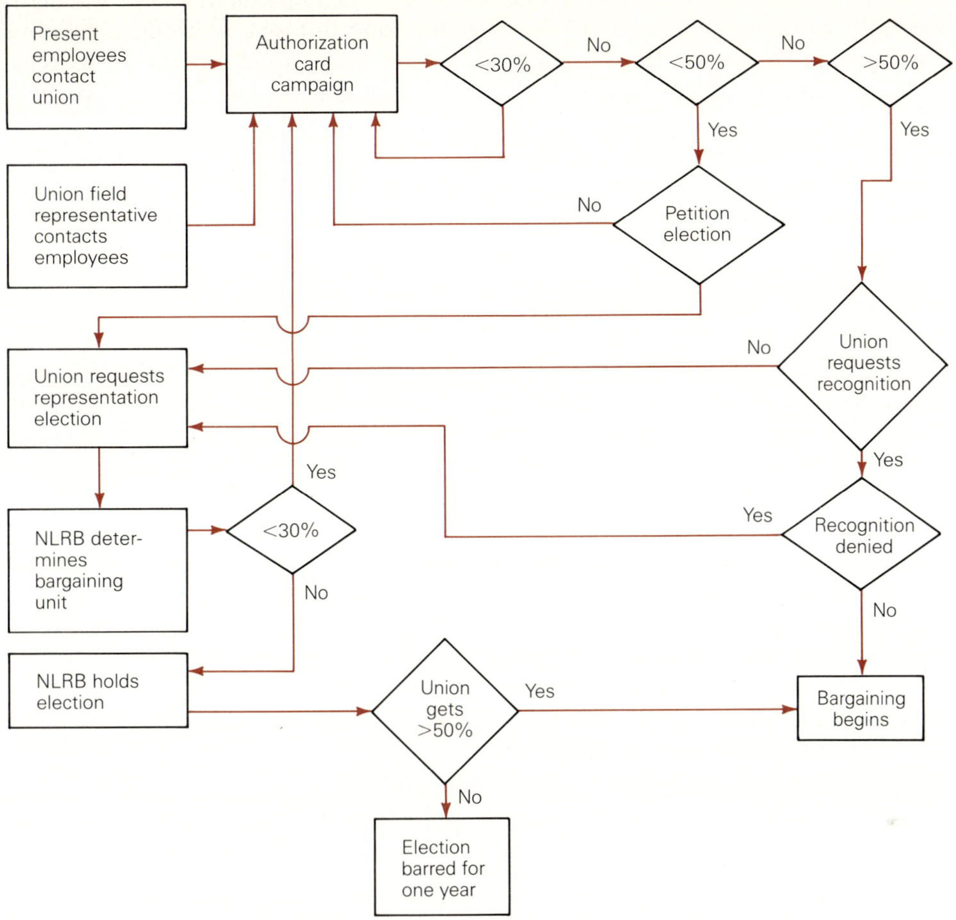

SOURCE: J.A. Fossum, *Labor Relations: Development, Structure, Process* (Dallas, Tex.: Business Publications, 1979), p. 130. Reprinted with permission.

Figure 10–7 SEQUENCE OF UNION ORGANIZING EVENTS

to effectively negotiate a first contract, when unions have established precedents in a contract and workers feel these benefits will continue without union membership and paying the required dues, or when an employer hires replacements for striking employees.[54] Decertification, or removing a certified union, is more likely in locals that are small, lack member involvement, fail to develop positive relations with management, change their composition, and fail to act during a decertification campaign.[55]

Although management cannot file to decertify a union, it can encourage a decertification request by workers. Managers often conduct meetings with employees to describe the disadvantages of the unions, implement letter campaigns to remind workers about costs of unionization, and improve working conditions to discourage continued unionization. But employers can*not* obtain forms from the NLRB for employees interested in decertification, provide services such as typing to help employees launch a decertification campaign, initiate discussions about such a campaign, or allow supervisors or management to promote such a campaign.[56] Figure 10–8 summarizes the steps in decertifying a union.

THE NONUNION ALTERNATIVE

Most employers prefer their organizations to remain nonunion. Among the best-known nonunion firms are International Business Machines, Kodak, and Delta Airlines. Reading 10–2, "How Top Nonunion Companies Manage Employees," by Fred K. Foulkes, cites the characteristics that companies such as these tend to have. These include

1. the absence of symbols of rank and status;
2. locations in quality neighborhoods and near universities;
3. overall corporate strength;
4. programs that emphasize employee security;
5. promotion policies that emphasize advancement from within;
6. influential human resources management department and professionals;
7. competitive pay and benefits;
8. management that listens to employees; and
9. grooming of managers that emphasizes long-term results and competence.[57]

Employees or a rival union can file a petition for decertification of a union. In very limited circumstances employers can also file.

The following actions generally result in a decertification:

1. At least 30 percent of the employees in a bargaining unit sign a request stating that they want a decertification election; or no longer want the union to represent them.

2. They file the petition for the election with the NLRB at least one year after the union was originally certified.

3. They file the petition when
   a. there is no contract in effect, OR
   b. it is between ninety and sixty days to the end of the current contract if the contract is in its third year, OR
   c. it is after the end of the three-year contract, before a new contract has been signed, OR
   d. the contract in effect is not valid.

4. At least 50 percent of those who vote in the decertification election vote against the union.

Based on J.W. Hunt, *Employer's Guide to Labor Relations* rev. ed. (Washington, D.C.: Bureau of National Affairs, 1979).

Figure 10–8 **STEPS IN DECERTIFICATION OF A UNION**

Why would the management of American Wood Products want to remain nonunion? Unionization removes some of the flexibility management has in making job assignments, determining compensation and benefits, and generally managing the organization. Once employees have designated a bargaining unit, management can no longer act unilaterally in areas specified in the labor contract. Another reason is cost: one estimate of the cost of unionization alone is from $580 to $1568 (1980 dollars) per person.[58]

Union avoidance practices include the following: (1) lessening the need for unionization by introducing equitable labor practices; (2) making union organizing difficult; (3) detecting and addressing union organizing at an early stage; (4) responding with a campaign to win employee votes if organizing occurs; (5) reviewing employee complaints and personnel records to identify dissatisfaction; (6) training supervisors and security personnel to be alert for covert union activity; (7) developing employee sources of information; and (8) establishing outside sources of information, such as employers' associations.[59]

Other widely recommended devices for discouraging unionization include locating plants and offices in nonunion areas; designing plant layout to restrict contact between nonunion employees and potential outside union organizers; selecting new hires on the basis of their anticipated attitudes toward unionization; restricting employee solicitation on employee property before, during, and after working hours; controlling access to employee names, addresses, and job classification data; and informing all employees that the employer intends to remain nonunion.[60]

Some companies use more drastic tactics to avoid unionization. These include developing a spy network (tattletales) to identify possible union supporters; refusing to hire former employees of unionized companies (but giving the applicant a reason other than prior union affiliation for employment denial); establishing a case for discharge (including documentation) of known union advocates; seeking to determine prospective employees' attitudes toward unions from interviews, references, and so on, then refusing to hire them (again giving another reason) if they are pro-union; giving psychological tests (job interest questionnaires) to determine the likelihood that an applicant will be interested in a union; locating new plants in areas where union membership is low and expanding the company's nonunion plants; or using an application form which asks applicants whether they have been a member of a union.[61]

Some companies go to great lengths to avoid becoming unionized. They may commit unfair labor practices to delay unionization.[62] J.P. Stevens Textile Corporation fought unionization in its southern plants for over a decade.[63] Similarly, Darlington Manufacturing spent from 1956 to 1968 trying to overthrow a vote of 256 to 248 for unionization; in 1968 they were ordered to negotiate on final appeal, but as late as 1974 the union was attempting to reinstate back pay.[64]

The use of consultants to keep unions out of companies has increased dramatically. Labor's success in representation elections dropped significantly from 1969 to 1979, from 55 to 45 percent.[65] Union organizers attributed many defeats to the so-called union busters. Firms such as Modern Management, Inc., of Illinois boasts a 93 percent success rate at keeping firms nonunionized.[66] There is some question about the legitimacy of the tactics used by some of these firms. The best strategy for organizations that want to remain nonunion is to eliminate the need for a union's services. Management can accomplish this by using the good human resources management practices described throughout this book.

STRATEGIES FOR DEALING WITH UNIONS

Unionization is an organizational reality for many manufacturing and governmental agencies. To date, the unionization of white-collar workers has been less successful than that of blue-collar workers but seems to be increasing. How should human resources professionals deal with attempts to unionize organizations? How should managers respond? Should human resources professionals and managers attempt to keep their organizations nonunion?

Implications for Human Resources Professionals

Human resources professionals must be aware of potential union organizing attempts so they can help organizations respond effectively. Effective practice in this regard is as follows:

1. Human resources professionals must understand the reasons employees unionize so they can consider meeting employees' needs in ways that fit with organizational goals. They must propose ways to meet these needs within organizational and environmental constraints.
2. Human resources professionals must know the legislation that influences union activity. They can then develop legal strategies for dealing with unions.
3. Human resources professionals must help top management determine the implications of unionization for their organization. They can forecast and plan for changes that would be likely to accompany unionization.
4. Human resources professionals should know and advise management about unfair labor practices. Union certification should proceed if workers wish it.

Implications for Managers

Managers should reflect the organization's goals, strategies, and philosophy in encouraging or discouraging unionization. To do this effectively managers should act in the following ways:

1. Managers must know the legislation that has an impact on their actions in dealing with potential unionization, to avoid unfair labor practices. They must assure that they act within the constraints imposed by the legislation.
2. Managers should know the rights of management and workers in dealing with labor issues. If top management wants to avoid unionization, managers must actively promote the value of nonunionization to employees.

3. Managers should thoroughly apprise any subordinates who are supervisors of the boundaries of legitimate union organizing practices; and they should monitor supervisors' behavior to ensure that they act legally.

4. Managers should develop positive relations with union leaders to facilitate resolution of labor-management problems. They should understand the union hierarchy and division of responsibility so that they and their subordinates can deal with the appropriate union representatives.

READINGS

Reading 10–1

EMPLOYEE RELATIONS AND UNION ORGANIZING CAMPAIGNS

James H. Hopkins and Robert D. Binderup

The threat of a union organizing drive is a continuing concern that each personnel professional and line manager, operating in a non-union environment, must face. Union elections are seldom won or lost during the campaign prior to election—the outcome is determined by a firm's overall employee relations climate.

This article reviews why labor unions desire to organize and represent employees, why employees may feel a need to support a union and what practices can be followed to create a positive employee relations climate which should minimize those needs. Also outlined is the organizational drive including preliminary signs, National Labor Relations Board (NLRB)[1] procedures for a determination election and what the company can and cannot do during the campaign prior to election.

Many employers feel secure that their employees would never approach a union to request assistance in organizing fellow workers. Those employers are usually shocked to find that generally union organizing efforts are indeed "inside jobs". Most often the union becomes a willing and enthusiastic participant which coordinates and finances the organizational attempt for several reasons.

First, union memberships, while holding stable at about 19.4 million since 1970, are declining as a proportion of the workforce represented from about 25 percent to 20 percent.[2] Unions are businesses and any business which has suffered a marketshare loss of such proportion would jump to regain lost revenue. Increased memberships mean increased dues (revenue).

Second, recent union election statistics reflect a poor showing on a percentage basis. In the fiscal year ended September 30, 1977, the NLRB conducted 9,626 conclusive representation and related elections. Unions won 4,424 of these, or 46 percent. In elections dealing specifically with collective bargaining representation, unions lost 52 percent; they lost 76 percent of decertification elections.[3] Unions need a high volume of elections to gain membership since their winning percentage is low.

Third, unions sometimes target a company or an industry for organization. A non-union company in a heavily unionized area is a likely objective. Certain industries with low wage structures such as retailing, health care and other service industries are attracting increased organizational activity.

Finally, union leadership truly believes that the rank and file worker needs the protection of collective bargaining. Employers who ignore the needs of the modern employee will undoubtedly find that unions can and do provide a countervailing power structure for disenchanted workers.

VULNERABILITY

The needs of the modern employee cannot be conveniently categorized and satisfied. Some employees enjoy hard work, accept reasonable pay and expect a tyrannical boss. Some employees want little or no work, high pay and reject any type of supervision. Fortunately, in most organizations employees are reasonably satisfied with their jobs, pay and supervision. If this reasonably satisfactory condition deteriorates, workers can withdraw and quit or they can stay and fight, often by turning to a union. It is important to remember that what seems fair and reasonable to management often seems arbitrary and even ridiculous to the worker. To explore some areas of dissatisfaction we present a fairly typical scene:

Time: 9:30 a.m.
Place: Cafeteria
Event: Coffee Break

Reprinted from the March, 1980 issue of *Personnel Administrator*,

Participants: Alice, Shipping Department Secretary; Henry, Fork Lift Operator

Henry: Can you believe I paid 25¢ for this dry roll . . . and I hear they're jacking up the coffee prices again!

Alice: Inflation . . . we just can't win.

Henry: Yeah, and our company's jumped on Carter's seven percent bandwagon . . . you didn't see the UAW settle for seven percent. I'm sick of making $6 an hour.

Alice: You're sick? I went to college for two years and graduated from secretarial school and I make $2 an hour less than you do.

Henry: We both should be plumbers . . . they make $14 an hour—but they're in a union.

Alice: You see that Shipping Clerk job posting?

Henry: You mean Mary's job—she's the only one qualified the way they customized the specifications to match hers.

Alice: That really burns me up! But I expected it since the boss is so chummy with her. I should file a grievance—that would end my career here (laughing).

Henry: (Laughing) You're right there! You ever worked for a boss like him?—What a mess. He treats us like kids and he has no idea what's going on.

Alice: Yeah, but he's only following the example upper management sets. If they really cared for us, they'd hire better supervisors. I'd sure like to get a chance at management, but it's not what you know—it's who you know around here.

Henry: Why don't they listen to us anyway? We could show them how to save money and get more profits so they could pay us more!

Alice: Pay us more? I heard there's a big layoff coming. Now that Mary's getting promoted around me, I'd be the first to go.

Henry: I heard that too—I guess we better keep our mouths shut. Let's get back to work—I don't want to get chewed out.

Alice: Yeah, managers are the only ones that get away with long breaks around this place.

This conversation dramatizes some main areas of dissatisfaction that cause employees to sign union cards: inequitable pay, favoritism, poor supervision, lack of appreciation, no outlet for gripes or suggestions, job insecurity, unfulfilled leadership aspirations and "we" (the workers) versus "they" (management). Firms failing to address these employee concerns are vulnerable to union organization.

POSITIVE CLIMATE

Employers who feel that remaining non-union is in the best interests of management and the employees eligible for union membership can create an employee relations climate that will prevent unionization. Book after book is written and seminar after seminar is taught concerning methods available to management in its effort to remain non-union. This article does not attempt to provide a detailed analysis of those methods. Rather, we suggest a common-sense approach to positive employee relations, capsulizing those practices essential to running a non-union business. The main areas covered are compensation, policies and practices, supervisory awareness and employee participation.

Companies that hold down wages and benefits to increase profitability will soon share reduced profits with a union bureaucracy. Rates of pay and the total benefit package must fairly and competitively reflect the marketplace for employees. This external equity is not difficult to maintain. Surveys of local, regional, or national wage rates are used depending on the recruiting pattern. Key or "benchmark" jobs provide adequate comparison. Traditional methods of delivery are the automatic progression to job rate in "blue-collar" jobs and merit pay for "white-collar" jobs. Progression systems are much safer to administer than are merit programs due to a reduced perception of favoritism. Keeping updated on benefit improvements is a matter of knowing what your competitors offer and what your employees want. A younger, mobile workforce is probably not as interested in a retirement program as is the typical general manager who often decides new benefits on his/her inaccurate perception of what the "troops" really need (whether they know it or not). Recent inflationary times have created more demand for monetary reward rather than for increased benefit levels.

Once a firm is confident that it is externally competitive, that information should be communicated to the employees. The company need not match every wage in the community, but the overall wage and benefit package must be defendable.

Perceived internal equity problems are nearly impossible to eliminate. Virtually every employee can name at least one other employee who contributes less and makes more. But each company should strive to maintain internal equity among the various job classifications. Whether by ranking, by point/factor, or by other more sophisticated systems, employers should be able to explain why certain jobs pay more than other jobs. Job titles can also cause perceived inequity. In one company, a technician signed some correspondence as "administrator", causing other employees to feel that an under-the-table promotion to an exempt category had transpired. Promotion practices in general are covered in the next section. To summarize, employers must be aware of the external environment by providing competitive wages and benefits and should strive to minimize internal problems realizing that total elimination of perceived internal inequity is nearly impossible.

POLICIES AND PRACTICES

Once an adequate compensation program and method of updating (usually annual) is established and communicated, the employer should address its policies and practices concerning method of promotion, outlet for grievances and procedure for layoff.

Contrary to most managers' aspirations, many employees most susceptible to unionization have no lofty ambition for promotion. But when an employee does desire promotional opportunity, he/she expects to be treated fairly. The safest method of promotion is to use seniority as the basis. Charges of favoritism are negated, but employees who stay with the firm move up regardless of qualifications or performance. No formal system leads to the "who you know" syndrome. A method that provides for notification of available openings, for seniority as the first criterion, for defined minimum qualifications and performance levels will provide equitable promotion paths.

Being passed over for promotion hurts enough, but having no outlet for complaint without fear of reprisal pours salt in the wound. Employers must encourage employees to bring grievances to the attention of someone who has the authority to respond. Formal grievance systems, open-door policies, ombudsmen—all these methods can be effective if employees can use them, get results and fear no adverse effects.

The final area of concern for employees that many managers neglect is the issue of job security. When times are good and overtime is common, no one thinks about layoffs. But let inventories rise and news accounts of impending recession strike—then workers fear the loss of their jobs. Companies should establish a plan to follow when reductions in workforce are necessary. Most plans follow seniority for non-exempt employees and performance for exempt employees. The plan should be referred to when questions surface concerning layoffs.

Formal policies and practices help to alleviate certain employee concerns; however, many needs of the employee can be dealt with only by good common sense supervisory practices. First-line supervisors undoubtedly get tired of hearing that they are "on the firing line" or the "first line of defense" in an organization's attempt to remain non-union. So we will refrain from saying that (even if it's true). Some brief examples will highlight the key role played by the supervisor:

Employee Question No. 1: Why did Mary get to leave early today when you didn't let me leave early last week?

Supervisor's Answer: Because she had a good reason.

Result: Employee feels that favoritism is present. The supervisor should set parameters so employees will know rationale for decision-making.

Employee Question No. 2: Why don't you discuss my performance when I make standard?

Supervisor's Answer: That's because you're expected to make standard.

Result: Employee feels unappreciated since the only time the supervisor discusses performance is to "chew".

Employee Question No. 3: Why don't we buy this chemical in bulk instead of in individual containers?

Supervisor's Answer: Engineers decide processes; they must have a good reason. Just follow the process. When I get time, maybe I can look into it.

Result: Employee perceives his/her role as being insignificant. The supervisor's lack of concern breeds employee apathy.

Employee Question No. 4: How do you get promoted to supervisor?

Supervisor's Answer: Why would you want a job like this? You've got it made.

Result: Supervisor has created a double put-down of the employee's leadership aspiration and of the role of management.

The supervisor must make time to learn what "turns on" each employee—all are not motivated by the same needs and desires. This supervisory awareness is a critical factor in creating a healthy work climate.

Finally, unions promise employees the opportunity to *participate.* A company that pays little or no attention to the ideas, suggestions and general concerns of their workers will have a difficult job in refuting the union's argument that its employees need a union to be heard. Some traditional methods of participation are the question box, suggestion systems, attitude surveys and general communication meetings. Many companies are setting up systems that allow for employees (often randomly selected) to meet with upper management for more extended communication sessions. Of course, workers must see some results from the input if they are to feel that it is effective.

This listing of positive management practices is surely not exhaustive, but it should provide basic ideas that will assist in strategic planning to provide the type of climate that will prevent a successful unionization drive.

ON THE ALERT

Even if a company follows sound management practices, it may be faced with a union attempting to organize the employees of the company. The best and hopefully the first way management will become aware of any union activity is through the first-line supervisor. A union election is not, for the most part, won or lost at the ballot box, but requires constant vigilance, 365 days a year. First-line supervisors of any company must develop credibility with their employees so every employee will feel comfortable in coming to the supervisor with any concern. In this way, any union activity should be brought to the supervisor's attention. The company's responsibility is to see that all management employees are trained in and develop good human relations skills.

Other ways that management may be alerted to possible union activities are: individuals handing out handbills or leaflets to employees as they enter company premises (these same handbills/leaflets may appear mysteriously on company bulletin boards or cafeteria tables). Generally these are one or two page papers outlining issues that may concern the people and how the union can help rectify them. An obvious way is when authorization cards are being passed out among employees to sign and return to the union. An authorization card is generally a 3″ × 5″ card that may request an election for a particular union or it may be a membership card in a union. With the former, if the union wins the election, it must still obtain members; with the latter, if the union wins the election, the employees who signed are automatically members of the union. Still another way is if employees are acting out of the ordinary; this will best be detected by the first-line supervisor who is sensitive to his/her employees. Some signs to watch for are employees meeting in unusual groupings and employees discontinuing a conversation when a supervisor approaches. These actions are ambiguous at best and should not be taken automatically as a sign of union activity. Finally, union officials may contact a company directly, by telephone, letter, or personal visit.

It is best to combat any feeling of need by employees for representation by a third party before the NLRB becomes involved and orders an election. This is done, as has been outlined above, with a sound employee relations program followed continuously.

The majority of a company's employees in any appropriate bargaining unit may choose a union to represent it in its dealings with the company. To determine an appropriate bargaining unit, the NLRB reviews the similarity of duties, skills, wages and working conditions of the employees; the collective bargaining history of the industry involved; the request of the employees (union); and, the appropriateness of the unit in relation to the organization.[4] If a union gathers what it feels is a sufficient number of authorization cards, it will petition the company. Company officials then have two choices of action: 1) If the company is convinced the union represents a majority of its employees, it may voluntarily recognize the union, or 2) if the company officials have a good faith basis for doubting the union's claim of majority status, they may petition the NLRB for a representation election. A caveat is appropriate at this point: if a company has determined that the union has the support of the majority of the employees, but still refuses to bargain, the NLRB may issue a bargaining order without an election.[5] With this in mind, company officials should not take a private poll of their employees or review any authorization cards presented by the union. Before the NLRB will order an election, they will determine if there is enough interest in the appropriate bargaining unit. This has been defined by the NLRB as 30 percent or more.[6] The biggest issue at this stage will be identifying the appropriate unit. The company and the union are obviously in a numbers game and it will be in the best interest of the company to have a larger unit with any pro-management employees being part of the unit. This will make the required 30 percent more difficult to obtain; remember, the company is better off if an election is never ordered.

If the NLRB directs an election, a simple majority of those employees voting[7] is all that is required to have the union certified as the bargaining agent for the employees. To put this in perspective, if the appropriate unit consists of 10 employees, four may petition for an election. If four vote in the election, three voting for the union can bring about recognition. It is in the company's best interest to have all employees vote. This can be accomplished by the company scheduling section by section the employees' time to vote.

During the organizing campaign, the company may not restrain, coerce or interfere[8] with an employee's right[9] to join or refrain from joining or voting for a union. This does not mean that an employer must keep its opposition to a union quiet. An employer has the right to let its employees know it is opposed to unions.[10] But there can be no direct or indirect promise of benefits if an employee doesn't support the union or threats of retaliation if they do.

RESTRICTIONS DURING A CAMPAIGN

Some specific items to keep in mind during the campaign are: first, employees may solicit their fellow employees for union support during non-working "free time". This has been defined as lunch time, scheduled coffee breaks, time before or after the start of a regularly scheduled shift and even time standing in line to punch a time clock.[11]

Second, the company can prevent solicitation during work time which is obviously time other than that outlined above. There seems to be a danger here if an employer attempts to keep employees from verbalizing their union feelings during work time when they do not otherwise restrict visiting among employees. This would appear to be a form of prohibited discrimination against union activity.

Third, employees may distribute union handbills or leaflets to other employees in non-working areas, but not in work areas.[12] Examples of non-work areas are an employee lunchroom, lounge, restroom, etc. A company should have a solicitation policy that prohibits the solicitation of employees by non-employees on company premises. The United States Supreme Court has taken the position that a company may withhold permission from a non-employee union organizer to come on company premises to distribute literature.[13] However, this can happen only if the company has refused permission uniformly against all non-employees and is not simply discriminating against the union organizer. Having a no-solicitation rule is part of the 365-days-a-year program. A company cannot institute such a rule at the outset of a union organizing campaign and expect to be upheld.

Fourth, generally, a company cannot forbid the wearing of union buttons or insignias by its employees.[14] There are exceptions to this, such as when employees have customer contact, etc., but if a company wants to enforce such a ban, it must review circumstances carefully.

Fifth, once a union campaign gets under way, a

company cannot unilaterally change wages or benefits.[15] Although there seems to be no clear rule as to when the campaign begins, it would seem to be when the company becomes aware of the union's intent to organize the company's employees. This does not mean that the union can notify the company in an attempt to keep them from making changes with no actual organizing intended. The facts of each situation will be determinative. Once again, there are exceptions to this—the main example being if the change was planned before the campaign began. Before any changes are made, the company should evaluate the circumstances carefully.

Sixth, a company may make predictions as to the possible consequences that may result if they are unionized, provided the results are beyond the company's control.[16] This means a company cannot threaten to close down a plant or move a plant because it is unionized. The company can state that the added financial burden could put the company out of business. The company may indicate whether it prefers one of two competing unions, provided no threats or promises are made.[17]

Seventh, the company can and should discuss the benefits that its employees have enjoyed in the past while being non-union. After all, an employee may not realize the extent of their company's total benefit package. This "selling" of a company's benefits to its employees is another part of the 365-days-a-year program.

Eighth, the company may bring to the attention of its employees the union's policies and practices in dealing with members. This can be done by obtaining copies of the union's constitution and highlighting areas like special assessments, discipline procedures, etc. and ensuring that each employee is provided a copy.

Finally, neither the company nor the union can make speeches to the employees during the 24 hour period just prior to the election.[18]

This article is in no way a comprehensive study of the subject and any personnel professional should continually educate himself and his company on the subject of good employee relations. A thought that should be kept in mind: an outside union organizer is like any other vendor—you are not obligated to buy his product, but you owe him the courtesy of treating him professionally.

REFERENCES

[1]National Labor Relations Board, established by Congress with the National Labor Relations Act of 1935.

[2]Labor Relations Yearbook—1978, The Bureau of National Affairs, Inc., Washington, D.C. (1979), 264.

[3]Ibid, From the Forty-Second Annual Report of the NLRB; Fiscal Year 1977, 271.

[4]Primer of Labor Relations-Twentieth Edition—BNA Publications (1975), 29.

[5]Sullivan Electric Co., 199 NLRB 97.

[6]"LABOR- RELATIONS, BNA Policy and Procedure Series", 83:2.

[7]Ibid, 83:581.

[8]Labor-Management Relations Act of 1947, Section 8(a).

[9]Ibid—Section 7.

[10]*NLRB* v. *Scott & Fetzer Co.*, 97 LRRM 2881 (8th Cir. 1978).

[11]"LABOR RELATIONS, BNA Policy and Procedure Series", 36:201.

[12]Ibid, 36:201.

[13]*NLRB* v. *Babcock & Wilcox Co.*, U.S. Sp. Court (1956), 38LRRM2001.

[14]*Republic Aviation Corp.* v. *NLRB* (1945) 16LLRM620.

[15]"LABOR RELATIONS, BNA Policy and Procedure Series," 46:421.

[16]Ibid, 40:101.

[17]Ibid, 40:101.

[18]Ibid, 83:633.

DISCUSSION QUESTIONS

1. Why do unions participate in union organizing campaigns?

2. What areas of dissatisfaction does the scene in the cafeteria illustrate?

3. How can organizations address these areas of dissatisfaction?

4. How can a supervisor influence the outcome of union organizing efforts?

5. What warning signals foreshadow a unionization attempt?

6. What restrictions are there on a union, management, and employees during a unionization campaign?

Reading 10–2

HOW TOP NONUNION COMPANIES MANAGE EMPLOYEES

Fred K. Foulkes

What is the primary advantage large corporations gain from operating without unions? Many might answer that the biggest advantage is lower costs for pay and benefits.

I would strenuously dispute that answer, however, on the basis of a study I recently carried out of 26 large corporations that are either predominantly or entirely nonunion. My study suggests that such companies benefit most from the flexibility they have to improve productivity in both the short and the long run.

I should add right away that these 26 companies were not chosen randomly. Rather, they were picked because they are respected leaders in their fields and, in many cases, are recognized for their innovative personnel policies. The corporations studied include Black & Decker, Eli Lilly, Gillette, Grumman, IBM, and Polaroid. (For details on the study, see the ruled insert on page 470.)

The experiences of these companies are especially instructive for companies without unions, because these experiences suggest that companies willing to take creative approaches to employee relations can improve productivity. The experiences are also potentially useful for unionized companies, since innovative approaches to employee relations are possible for them too.

Executives of the 26 companies studied believe they achieve higher productivity than they would if they were organized. Their companies, they say, have achieved a high degree of employee loyalty, a low rate of turnover and absenteeism, and a low degree of worker resistance to technological change. One of the companies studied, for example, enjoys a turnover rate of .5% monthly, considerably below the average for its industry. The annual turnover rate of another of the companies studied is 3%. A third company employs fewer people per dollar of sales than any other company in its industry. And a fourth has achieved such a reputation as an attractive place to work that it has its pick of job applicants—it receives an average of 8,000 to 10,000 applications annually for its 500 nonexempt job openings.

In the view of many of those interviewed, such benefits accrue from their freedom to experiment with employee relations plans, their opportunity to deal directly with workers, and the absence of an adversary relationship between employees and management.

Not surprisingly, the accomplishments of many of these companies cannot easily be copied or duplicated. My study revealed that strong top management concern for employees becomes institutionalized through implementation of various policies. Also important are the intangibles of leadership, personal example, and use of symbols. These companies' rich legacies and traditions affect their managers and employees profoundly.

My study disclosed a set of nine common attributes, policies, and attitudes among large nonunion companies against which the managers of nonunion as well as unionized corporations can measure the effectiveness of their own personnel practices.

1 A SENSE OF CARING

First and perhaps foremost, many of the founders of the nonunion companies in my sample held fiercely egalitarian views about treatment of employees. Today, many of the customary symbols of corporate rank and status are absent. In many of the companies, everyone from vice president to sweeper has access to the same parking spaces, receives identical medical benefits, and eats in the same cafeteria. Frequently, executive offices are Spartan or even nonexistent. Employees at all levels call each other by their first names.

Moreover, the salaries of some of the top-level executives are modest by *Fortune* "500" standards. Many of these companies eschew such perquisites as company cars and club memberships that symbolize a visible ruling class of management.

Top management's commitment to employees is demonstrated not only symbolically but also through certain policies and practices. Hewlett-Packard, for example, is committed to job security, innovative training programs, promotion from within through job posting, cash profit sharing, an attractive stock purchase plan, widely granted stock options, and flexible working hours.

In most cases, the founders articulated and put in writing top management's commitment to effective personnel practices when the companies were quite small:

- At IBM, Thomas Watson stated almost half a century ago the personnel principles that still govern the company; respect for the individual was and is one of those principles.
- Edwin Land, founder of Polaroid, spoke early in the corporation's life of Polaroid's objectives: "We have two basic aims. One is to make products that are genuinely new and useful to the public, products of the highest quality and at reasonable cost. . . . The other is to give everyone working for the company a personal opportunity . . . to make his work here a fully rewarding and important part of his life."
- At the Eli Lilly Co., J. K. Lilly wrote in 1916 a *Report on the Subject of Employment* that still guides the company. He noted in part, "The employment function is so important to good organizations as well as right relations that the 'Hiring Office' should be looked upon as one of the most important departments of the Company."
- Some of Hewlett-Packard's corporate objectives with respect to employees are as follows: "To help HP people share in the company's success, which they make possible; to provide job security based on their performance; to recognize their individual achievements; and to help people gain a sense of personal satisfaction and accomplishment from their work."

What is important, of course, is the way Hewlett-Packard or any other similarly committed company achieves its objectives. While philosophy is important, it is action that counts.

2 CAREFULLY CONSIDERED SURROUNDINGS

Several situational factors are also important both in fostering an effective personnel program and in encouraging a climate of trust and confidence. These factors include, among others, plant location and size and the handling of "sensitive work" and particular employee groups.

Determining Location & Size. The companies I studied consider carefully effects on employees and the chances of remaining nonunion when they select sites for new plants. Among the criteria used by one company are the quality of the public schools and the proximity to a university—as well as the area's attitude toward unions.

A personnel vice president at another company reported why a certain city would not be a good place to construct a blue-collar, production-type plant: "That city is sixth among the top 50 cities in the United States in downtime due to strikes, jurisdictional disputes, and other, related union conflicts. Moreover, there are more EEO charges in that city than in all but two other major cities. It is third in the number of fair employment practice cases and unfair labor practice charges. The city has several militant and aggressive unions."

Not only do many of the companies carefully choose rural or suburban plant sites, but they frequently limit the size of their facilities—between 200 and 1,200 employees—to promote personal and responsive employee relations. In the words of one personnel director, "We like to keep our plants small. We don't want them to grow larger than 200 employees. Beyond that size, both management and personnel lose personal contact with the employee."

Taking Care with Traditionally Union Work. Many of the companies studied are also careful about how they handle sensitive work—work that unionized employees often do. Some companies subcontract sensitive or strategic jobs. One company, for example, subcontracts its printing work, while many of its unionized competitors do their own printing. Sometimes sensitive jobs are done in-house but by the unionized employees of a subcontractor.

The idea is to make an organizing drive less likely. If a company's own nonunion employees do sensitive work, management usually pays close attention to their working conditions and wages, attempting to ensure that their treatment is equal to or better than that of comparable unionized personnel.

3 HIGH PROFITS, FAST GROWTH, & FAMILY TIES

Certain financial and ownership characteristics seem to have an important bearing on personnel policies. Most of the companies studied are profitable—some, extremely so. Many are high technology growth businesses, have dominant market positions, and are leaders in their industries. Growth enables them to offer many promotion opportunities, provide full employment, and make profit sharing pay off.

Another important company characteristic is close ties between ownership and management. Two of the companies in my sample are privately owned, and members of the founding family are still active in management. In several of the public companies, a significant percentage of the stock is owned by one or more families, whose members remain active in top management. Thus, management is pushed to endorse the ideals of the founders and owners.

I should emphasize that no company studied displays all these attributes. Nor are these factors a sine qua non for achieving the desired organizational climate. They can even get in the way. For instance, while rapid growth provides many promotion opportunities, it also sometimes leads to such problems as communication difficulties and cramped quarters.

4 EMPLOYMENT SECURITY

Many of these companies attempt to minimize workers' usual nagging uncertainty regarding future employment. Several of the companies use various techniques to ensure full or nearly full employment.

During its early years, for example, Hewlett-Packard rejected large government contracts that would have created huge fluctuations in work load, forcing the company often to lay off and then rehire people. Moreover, during the 1970 recession, Hewlett-Packard cut everyone's pay and work time 10% for a six-month period rather than lay anybody off. The pay cut applied to everyone, from chairman of the board to assembly-line worker, as did the practice of not working every other Friday.

Other methods of weathering peaks and troughs in the work load include hiring freezes and the use of temporary or retired workers. This latter method, of course, simply transfers unemployment from the permanent labor force to part-time and temporary workers. Some companies prefer to devote periods of overstaffing to building up their inventories. Others encourage employees to take voluntary leaves of absence—thus guaranteeing continued employment.

Permitting employees to bank their vacation time can also ensure some flexibility in lean times. Work sharing is another way in which some companies avoid or minimize layoffs. Some companies that experience seasonal work loads hire their own retired or former workers during the peaks.

To some extent, one company's full-employment practice becomes its subcontractors' unemployment problem. At one company studied, part of the full-employment strategy is to use subcontractors to help absorb necessary production cutbacks. During tight periods, such subcontracting is curtailed or eliminated.[1]

Costs of Full Employment

Although companies that provide employment security boast of the flexibility gained from their nonunion status, they of course lose the option to lay workers off in response to changed business conditions.

Table 10–3 catalogs the costs and benefits of avoiding layoffs. As it indicates, the costs can be significant. Yet the benefits of employment security cannot be overestimated. Eliminating workers' fears about layoffs can be a cornerstone of effective employee relations.

If layoffs become necessary nonetheless, management must implement a system that is perceived as equitable. The companies in my sample that do not practice full employment rely nearly exclusively on the principle of seniority. They also attempt, through a variety of means, to delay layoffs and cushion their

1. See Warren M. Lowry, "Two-Way Contracting," HBR May-June 1967, p. 131.

Costs	Benefits
Extra payroll and payroll-related expenses: • training costs • extra overtime because of reluctance to hire • possible temporary red circle rates • extra costs of any special early retirement plans	Flexibility to reassign workers
Extra employment costs associated with extreme selectivity in hiring	Productivity advantages because of high employee morale
Productivity losses associated with people assigned to different jobs	Greater acceptance of changes in methods and technology
Moving expenses	Lower unemployment insurance costs
Extra financial charges because of larger-than-necessary inventories	Savings of training costs due to layoffs
Possible slower delivery schedule	Favorable image in the community and recruiting advantages
Possible slower rate of change in methods or technology due to need to avoid displacing permanent employees	

Table 10–3 COSTS AND BENEFITS OF A FULL-EMPLOYMENT POLICY

impact. Curiously, none of these companies uses a supplemental unemployment plan.

A point to remember about full-employment practices: they always require effectively coordinating manpower planning and business planning. If a company has a policy of no layoffs, personnel people and line managers must cooperate when formulating strategies.

5 PROMOTION FROM WITHIN

A policy of promoting from within—accompanied by training, education, career counseling, and (frequently) job posting—is most attractive when a company's growth rate opens up many advancement opportunities. When computerized operations were expanded at one company, it chose to train current employees to be programmers instead of hiring qualified applicants. The training opportunities were simply posted, and interested employees who bid and passed the aptitude tests were trained to be computer programmers on company time and at company expense.

Like employment security, such efforts go a long way in building employee loyalty. Indeed, two-thirds of the companies in my sample have institutionalized the principle of promotion from within by routinely posting job openings. Some companies even provide plant workers extensive training and education so they can move into white-collar positions.

Promotion of insiders to good jobs gets attention from company employees. Up-from-the-ranks supervisors who have benefited from such a policy have reason to be loyal and enthusiastic. Indeed, their attitude may contribute to the higher rates of productivity that many of these companies claim.

Promotion from within also helps a company maintain a consistent philosophy as the organization grows larger. Homegrown managers know and respect the company's values and traditions. Unlike newcomers, veteran managers know many employees personally and are familiar with several different jobs and operations. They also serve as excellent role models for employees wishing to follow in their tracks. But remember: extensive reliance on promotion from within requires reliable initial hiring practices and good career development programs.

6 INFLUENTIAL PERSONNEL DEPARTMENTS

Not only are the personnel departments of the companies studied usually extremely centralized, they also have access to and in many cases are part of top management. More than half of the personnel vice presidents I interviewed report directly to the presidents of their companies. At a few of these companies, the head of personnel is a member of the board of directors.

The personnel departments of the companies studied are well staffed. Many have at least one professional person per 100 employees. Many also devote much attention to training and encouraging personnel people. At one predominantly nonunion company, trainees in employee relations get experience in a union plant, a nonunion plant, and finally in a corporate staff assignment. One company employs a staff person whose sole function is to help plan the career paths of the company's personnel people.

One reason for the influence of the personnel departments at the companies I studied is that line managers' competence is measured partly in terms of employee relations. When a department manager is accountable for the results of an employee attitude survey or the number of complaints filed by his or her subordinates, the expert advice of the personnel department suddenly takes on relevance.

7 COMPETITIVE PAY & BENEFITS

As might be expected, the 26 companies in my sample work hard to ensure that employees perceive their pay and benefits policies as equitable. All of them, therefore, compensate their employees at least as well as their unionized competitors do. The companies studied thus pay well by both industry and community standards. The nonunion companies watch carefully the union settlements of competitors.

Also, the nonunion businesses make careful and thorough attempts to communicate with workers about their pay increases and benefit improvements. Few of the companies studied will likely ever be vulnerable to a union drive on the basis of either benefits or pay.

These companies also give particular attention to making their benefits visible. One company, for example, presents an annual slide show at each local office comparing its benefits with those of its organized competitors. Black & Decker personnel and benefits professionals present all major benefit changes in group meetings. They not only tell managers and supervisors about the changes beforehand, but personnel staffers also provide them with answers to possible questions from employees.

Some nonunion companies argue that what might appear to be very generous provisions are highly cost effective. For instance, the medical facilities for employees at some companies seem lavish. Polaroid, for one, has on call its own orthopedists, dermatologists, and other specialists—in company facilities. Polaroid managers argue that this is much less expensive than medical insurance payments. Furthermore, employees spend less time away from work when medical professionals come to them.

Many nonunion companies also place heavy emphasis on merit increases, which either substitute for or supplement across-the-board pay increases. According to its proponents, such pay systems can serve

---

The 26 companies in the study were defined as nonunion based on the fact that all or nearly all of their production and maintenance employees located in the United States were not members of any union. Twenty of the companies in the sample appear on the *Fortune* "500" list of industrials; and five other either privately owned or service companies had sales figures that would have qualified. Half of the companies studied had sales of $1 billion or more at the time of the study.

The companies each employ between 2,200 and 150,000 people in the United States; 60% employ more than 10,000 in this country. All but three of the companies are engaged in manufacturing, in a range of industries. The three remaining companies are service organizations. No banks or insurance companies were included in the study. Many of the companies studied enjoy leadership positions in their respective fields. The names of most of them are household words. But the names of most are anonymous as a condition for their cooperation in the original study.

This field study used the case-study interview approach. More than 500 key line managers—including chairmen, presidents, operating executives, lower-level management people, and personnel executives—were interviewed.

HOW THE STUDY WAS DESIGNED

as an incentive and will encourage greater work effort.

In the same spirit, many of the companies studied pay blue-collar workers salaries instead of hourly wages. About half of the companies have no hourly employees at all. The practice of bestowing the status of a salary on blue-collar workers represents another attempt to eliminate the "we-they" distinction between management and labor or between office and plant personnel.

The allowances for illness or personal business included in salaries impart respect and responsibility to the worker that are absent when labor is rewarded strictly by the time clock. Besides being consistent with the principle of equal treatment, salary plans differentiate the employee in status from his or her friends at other companies in the same industry or community.

Other common forms of supplementary compensation include profit sharing, company-matched savings and investment plans, and employee stock purchase plans. Profit sharing and stock ownership can also help employees to identify with the company, motivate them to work for its success, and further their understanding of the economics of the business.

Such programs often distinguish large nonunion companies from comparable organized corporations in the eyes of employees. For example, unionized employees at AT&T and General Motors were allowed to participate in their companies' savings and investment plans only two years ago, long after workers in many of the 26 companies I studied were offered that perquisite.

8 MANAGEMENTS THAT LISTEN

The companies studied use a variety of mechanisms to learn employees' views on various matters. Attitude surveys "take the temperature" of the organization and expose developing employee concerns. Some companies regularly conduct "sensing sessions," or random interviews to understand employees' sentiments.

A number of these companies exclude supervisors from the upward communication process, so employees feel freer to speak out. For example, one company keeps its local managers out of its annual benefits presentations, which include a suggestion, complaint, and discussion session.

These managers now conduct their own regular meetings with employees, in turn excluding the foremen and supervisors. In this way, management believes, it can forestall serious labor problems on the local level. Supervisors are also encouraged by this system to resolve employee problems quickly, because they may fear higher-level investigations or complaints to higher management that reflect negatively on them.

Speak-out programs, which allow employees' anonymously written inquiries to be answered by management, are another common communication device. According to executives of companies that use speak-out programs, 5% to 10% of their employees submit a question at least once a year.

Like other communication programs, speak-outs can backfire if handled gracelessly. At one company, a hardworking technician wrote to inquire why parking at the plant was not on a first-come, first-served basis. This man arrived early every morning, parked his car, and then walked one-quarter of a mile across an empty management parking lot. His letter was answered by a low-level official, who suggested that managers have a divine right to convenient parking. The president of the company later learned of this gaffe, so now a top officer at each location reviews and signs the answers.

The dominant grievance procedure in the companies studied is the open-door policy. However, two companies have (and pay for) formal arbitration programs for certain grievances that can't be otherwise resolved. Two other corporations have appeals boards to which employees can take their grievances. One of the boards includes hourly employees and makes recommendations to the president. The other, which consists of managers, is a decision-making body.

Discussions with representatives of several nonunion companies have convinced me that open-door policies whose reviews and investigations are formal and rigorous can be effective. The office of the chairman of one company usually receives several hundred open-door complaints a year. Investigators working out of the chairman's office follow up on these complaints under an exacting timetable. Because managers usually settle in advance those cases in which the employee is obviously right, the cases that reach the chairman's office tend to be those in which management is right; thus, about three-fourths of the decisions support managers and about one-fourth back employees.

Top management's reactions to complaints demonstrate to lower-level management and employees alike whether the higher echelons care about the way employees are treated. When top management wants the decisions to be fair and is willing to investigate and review lower-level decisions, its credibility is enhanced.

The principal value of the formal complaint procedure seems to be the encouragement it gives to managers and supervisors to resolve employee problems before they become formal complaints. Management in a nonunion environment should not expect a formal grievance procedure to be used frequently; nor should such a procedure be relied on as a primary feedback device.

However, in my view, a nonunion company today should not be without some kind of formal complaint procedure. This is especially so in today's environment because employees who feel discriminated against because of race, sex, or age or who think their work area is unsafe can take complaints to an outside agency for investigation. Wise executives prefer to respond to complaints through their own mechanisms rather than deal with requirements set by a government agency.

9 CAREFUL GROOMING OF MANAGERS

Managers in these companies know that effective management of people is an important part of their jobs. Many of the companies studied avoid bonuses that reward short-term performance. Instead, they emphasize long-term results, including successful employee relations. They use stock options or other incentives associated with longer-term company success.

Thus, the selection of managers is a carefully considered procedure. Some nonunion companies use a series of panel interviews to evaluate potential managers instead of the traditional process whereby the boss picks his or her favorite for a promotion. Other companies send managerial candidates to "assessment centers" for a series of rigorous and imaginative tests that assess their ability to identify priorities and subdue crises in the managerial ranks.

At the lower levels of the organization, considerable resources are devoted to supervisory training. The supervisors, after all, deal with employees on a day-to-day basis, while top management has only occasional contact with them.

As a consequence of such training and reward systems, managers at all levels are keenly aware of the importance of good employee relations. Results of surveys are viewed as indicators of managerial competence. In many companies, managers believed that a stigma would be attached to their careers if their units had union-organizing drives or major personnel problems.

"People who demonstrate that they can manage well within the ethic of the organization are promoted," said a general manager of one company. At another company, performance is evaluated in terms of both "competence" and "relationships."

Because top management's personnel concerns often focus on the lowest-level employees, the supervisor may have the most difficult role of all in these nonunion companies. In some cases, the preoccupation of the founder with the welfare and security of the hourly workers appears to have depreciated the role of the supervisors, who may feel less secure than those they supervise. If supervisors come to feel insecure and experience too much anxiety, of course, the long-run health of the organization can suffer. Some of the nonunion companies have therefore begun tracking the feelings of supervisors through attitude surveys and other means.

PRIDE & PROFITS

The 26 companies studied clearly try to create a climate of cooperation between employees and management. However, skeptics may still wonder if the rewards of positive employee relations are financially significant. I noted at the beginning of this article that the top managers of many large nonunion companies have expressed the belief that they can justify their personnel policies as providing great economic incentive. However, it may be impossible to determine precisely by what amounts the personnel practices previously outlined actually alter the bottom line. It certainly is costly to hire your own doctors, conduct attitude surveys, train your own employees for promotion, and offer profit sharing.

But in the view of many of those interviewed, the freedom to experiment with employee relations plans, the opportunity to deal directly with employees, and the absence of adversary relationships between employees and management result in a more profitable enterprise in the long run. Many of the managers take obvious pride in their personnel philosophies and accomplishments and are convinced that their efforts contribute directly and positively to productivity and profits.

Thus, I would argue that, for a large company to remain nonunion, top management needs to be personally involved in personnel management and to constantly demonstrate to non-exempt workers and managers alike its interest and concern for employees.

DISCUSSION QUESTIONS

1. What advantages do organizations gain from operating without unions?
2. What disadvantages result from an organization's operating without unions?
3. How would you characterize nonunion companies?
4. What strategies can organizations implement to remain nonunion?
5. What human resources management policies contribute to an organization's remaining nonunion?
6. Are there any drawbacks to human resources management policies designed to help an organization remain nonunion?
7. What role should human resources professionals and managers play in keeping their organizations nonunion?

ACTIVITIES

Activity 10–1

INTERVIEW OF A UNION MEMBER

Step 1: Identify a member of a union who is willing to talk with you about his or her perceptions of being a union member.

Step 2: Individually or in small groups, formulate a series of questions to ask the union member you are interviewing. You might ask questions such as the following:

1. Why did you join a union?
2. How long have you been a member?
3. What roles does the union play in the organization?
4. Does the union help or hinder the organization?
5. What are the advantages of belonging to a union?
6. What are the disadvantages of belonging to a union?

Step 3: Interview the union member.

Step 4: Prepare a written or oral report, as directed by your instructor, that indicates the reasons the person joined the union, the benefits he or she derives from union membership, any drawbacks membership creates for that person or the employing organization, and the relationship between the union and the organization.

Step 5: Discussion. In small groups or with the entire class, share your observations.

Activity 10–2

UNION MEETING VISITATION

Step 1: First, attend a regular union meeting. During the meeting, observe the agenda used by the union leaders. Also note the types of concerns expressed by the members. If possible, speak with several members afterward about their reactions to the meeting.

Step 2: Individually, in small groups, or in writing, as directed by your instructor, answer the following questions:

1. What is the purpose of the organization?
2. What typically occurs at its meetings?
3. What occurred at the meeting you attended?
4. Was the meeting valuable to the members? Why?
5. What were your overall reactions to the meeting?

Activity 10–3:

SECRETARIAL SERVICES

Step 1: Read the following scenario.

Fairview University employs 200 secretaries who work in various university offices. These secretaries receive pay that is typically 25 to 30 percent below the average for secretaries in the metropolitan area in which they work. The executives of the university justify this lower wage rate in terms of the secretaries' ability to take courses at the university free of charge. In addition, the secretaries get one-half of their individual medical insurance paid, receive five sick days, ten holidays, and two weeks vacation per year.

Most secretaries work for between two and ten faculty members or administrators. Recently, with the addition of a word processing capability, the number of secretaries has been declining since the top administrators feel that technological advancements allow the secretaries to service more faculty. To best take advantage of the equipment available at the university, many secretaries have been moved from private offices to larger secretarial pools, where four to six secretaries may work in the same "bullpen."

During the past ten years, several limited attempts have been made to unionize the secretaries. Each time, there has been little interest among the secretaries, who view themselves as professionals. However, recent comments by a number of secretaries suggest that they may be ready for unionization. They have been complaining about their low wages, poor working conditions, and heavy work loads.

Step 2: Assume you are a member of the Secretarial Workers Union. Individually or in small groups, design a campaign to unionize the workers in the secretarial pool. Provide as much detail as possible about the campaign, including copies of any publications and posters, schedules of meetings and other events, as well as the arguments you would use to convince the workers of the value of unionization.

Step 3: Discussion. In small groups or with the entire class, share your proposed campaigns. Critique each campaign in terms of its legality and likely effectiveness. Summarize the key issues involved in ensuring a legal and effective unionization campaign.

Activity 10–4

THE CHALLENGED ELECTION RESULTS DUE TO ALLEGED EMPLOYER MISCONDUCT

Step 1: Read the Challenged Election Results case.

Step 2: Prepare the case for class discussion.

Company: The Singer Company, Albuquerque, New Mexico
Union: International Association of Machinists and Aerospace Workers (IAM), AFL-CIO

BACKGROUND

The Singer Company had operated a calculating machine production plant at San Leandro, California, where the International Association of Machinists and Aerospace Workers (IAM) had represented the employees of the plant for the preceding 25 years. In an effort to attain lower labor costs and thereby to compete more favorably with foreign-produced calculating machines which Singer believed had caused a drastic decline in its share of the domestic market, Singer in 1969 established a new manufacturing facility at a temporary location in Albuquerque, New Mexico. The new plant was moved to its permanent facility in August 1970.

In June 1970 the IAM union began a campaign to organize and represent the employees of the new plant. The campaign was characterized by the distribution of extensive literature and numerous general meetings with the employees by both Singer and IAM. On September 11, 1970, the union notified Singer of its campaign activities, and on October 22, 1970, the union requested recognition on the basis of a card check. Singer refused and insisted on an NLRB election, which was held on December 10, 1970. The election resulted in the union's being rejected by a 63–44 margin. The union filed objections with the NLRB to certain preelection conduct by Singer and requested that the election results be set aside because of alleged violations by the company of Sections 8(a) (1) and 8(a) (3) of the LMRA.

Adapted from the National Labor Relations Board case. Reprinted from Schoen and Hilgert, *Cases in Collective Bargaining and Industrial Relations* 4th ed. (Homewood, Ill.: Richard D. Irwin, 1982).

POSITION OF THE UNION

The IAM union's objections were based primarily upon three charges of preelection misconduct on the part of the company.

The first alleged misconduct involved an incident on September 17, 1970, when seven employees reported to work wearing shirts colored in a manner and with insignia displayed to identify them as union shirts. The men were told by an officer of Singer that they would not be permitted to work in the plant while wearing the shirts. Under protest, the men removed the shirts. According to the union, the right to wear union insignia on an employer's premises during working hours is guaranteed by Section 7 of the Act, as long as such wearing of union insignia does not interfere with the normal duties of employees and their efficient and safe work performance. In this case, the shirts in no way interfered with the employees' plant duties, or anything else. The company's prohibition of the employees' rights to wear union insignia was primarily designed to interfere with the union election campaign in the plant.

The second allegation of misconduct was that George Vasquez,[1] a plant supervisor, held "coercive interrogations" of employees concerning the union sympathies of employees under him. This took place in a series of interviews held by Vasquez during September 1970, in which Vasquez tried to get employees to indicate their feelings and their estimates of the union's supporters in the plant.

Closely related was a third allegation that Singer had "exerted coercive pressure" on its employees through statements made by it during its preelection campaign. These statements were made verbally by company representatives and also in company literature distributed to employees. According to the union, the dominant theme of Singer's antiunion campaign was that the IAM union would bring strikes, a loss of jobs, and possible closure of the plant itself. The company's literature attributed the loss of 14,000 jobs to unionization at various plants, and it was illustrated by specific examples of other plants which had, after voting for union representation, been closed with an attendant loss of jobs to the work force. In the union's view, these types of statements were clearly threats aimed at the possible consequences of unionization at the Albuquerque facility.

Because of these alleged violations of Sections 8(a) (1) and 8(a) (3) of the Act, the union argued that the results of the election should be set aside by the NLRB. The union argued that the Board should order the union to be certified to represent the plant employees; or at the very least, that another representational election should be held under Section 9(c) of the Act; and that the company should be required to cease and desist in its unfair labor practices accordingly.

[1]The names of all individuals have been disguised.

POSITION OF THE COMPANY

The company argued that all the union's allegations of unfair labor practices committed by the company were unfounded and should be dismissed for the following reasons:

1. The company's prohibition against the employees' wearing union insignia in the plant was necessary in view of interfactional hostilities between union supporters and nonunion advocates at the plant, and the possibility of further disruption if the shirts were permitted in the plant. As proof, Singer pointed to a drop in production on the particular day (September 17, 1970) in question. The company had the right to maintain discipline in the plant, which it sought to do in this matter.

2. The interviews which supervisor George Vasquez had with various employees were "nothing more than casual conversations." Vasquez did not make any coercive statements. He was simply "curious" about the union's strength among plant employees. Regardless, these interviews had no influence on the outcome of the representational election.

3. The company contended that various statements made by company representatives and included in its literature during the election campaign were merely "an attempt to disclose the economic facts as they existed and to indicate possible eventualities if the economic situation changed unfavorably for Singer." An employer's statements which are not coercive are protected under Section 8(c) of the Act,

and cannot form the basis for a Section 8(a) (1) violation.

The company emphasized that it made no statements to the effect that the Albuquerque plant would be closed as a consequence of unionization.

In summary, the company claimed that its activities and statements during the union representational campaign were both permissible and legal under LMRA. The union's unfair labor practice charges should be dismissed, and the results of the election should be certified by the NLRB.

Step 3: Individually, in small groups, or with the entire class, address the following:

1. Trace the steps in the organizing campaign.
2. Why did the union file objections?
3. What were the union's objections?
4. Were these examples of unfair labor practices?
5. How should the Singer Company have acted during the election?
6. Did management violate any provisions of the Wagner or Taft-Hartley Acts? Did the union?

Activity 10–5

DELI-LITE FOOD PRODUCTS

Step 1: Read the following scenario.

Deli-lite is a catering service that employs 100 people. The company prepares and serves foods at weddings, graduations, and other social events. Of its 100 employees, 10 hold managerial positions, 10 hold clerical positions, and the remainder are cooks, food preparation assistants, bartenders, waiters, waitresses, or van drivers.

With the exception of management, all workers receive hourly pay which to date has been slightly above average for the industry. Employees are credited with a paid day for each 200 hours they work. They also have medical, disability, and unemployment compensation in proportion to amount of time worked with the company.

The Food Workers Union has made two attempts to unionize the company. So far management has successfully prevented unionization.

Step 2: You are a member of the management team of Deli-lite Food Products. You have been asked to plan a strategy for keeping the company nonunion. Individually or in small groups, offer a detailed strategy.

Step 3: Discussion. In small groups or with the entire class, share your strategies. What elements do they have in common? Are they likely to be effective or ineffective? What are the components of an effective strategy?

SUMMARY

In this chapter we have examined the reasons for and the process of unionization. Workers unionize to meet personal needs, in response to peer pressure, and for social purposes. Most importantly, they unionize to improve the wages, benefits, hours, and working conditions on the job. You interviewed a union member about his or her reasons for joining; you attended a union meeting and observed some of the concerns of union members.

A series of legislative acts has guided the unionization of workers since the beginning of this decade. Beginning with the Railway Labor Act, continuing with the Norris-LaGuardia Act, and concluding with the Wagner Act as amended by the Taft-Hartley Act and the Landrum-Griffin Act, the process for unionization has been prescribed and controlled. The National Labor Relations Board and the Federal Mediation and Conciliation Service were initiated to oversee the implementation of these laws.

During the first half of the century, union organizing focused on blue-collar workers. Today the emphasis has shifted to the organization of white-collar workers. This has occurred in response to declining percentages of unionized workers—from 35 percent in 1950 to about 20 percent in the 1980s.[67]

Both employers and employees should know and understand the mechanics of union certification and decertification. Accordingly, you planned an organizing campaign for Secretarial Services, Inc.; evaluated the actions by the management of the Singer Company during a union election; and planned a campaign for keeping Deli-lite Food Products nonunion. Workers should also carefully assess whether unionization meets their needs before becoming involved in a campaign. Management, for its part, typically chooses to avoid unionization at all costs; thus the nonunion alternative is a primary goal of management.

ENDNOTES

[1]U.S. Department of Labor, Bureau of Labor Statistics, *News*, 18 September 1981.

[2]Bureau of Labor Statistics, *Directory of National Unions and Employee Associations* (Washington, D.C.: Government Printing Office, 1980).

[3]J.R. Commons and E.A. Gilmore, *A Documentary History of American Industrial Society* (Cleveland, Ohio: A.H. Clark, 1910).

[4]Commonwealth v. Hunt, 45 Mass. 4 (1842).

[5]See F.R. Dulles, *Labor in America: A History* 3rd ed. (New York: Crowell, 1966); J.G. Rayback, *A History of American Labor* (New York: Free Press, 1966); and P. Taft, *Organized Labor in American History* (New York: Harper & Row, 1964).

[6]44 Stat. 577 (1926) as amended 1934, 1936, 1940, 1951, 1964, 1966, and 1970.

[7]W.H. Holley Jr. and K.M. Jennings, *The Labor Relations Process* 2nd ed. (Chicago: Dryden, 1984), p. 74.

[8]47 Stat. 70 (1932).

[9]*Ibid.*, p. 77.

[10]National Labor Relations Board, *A Guide to Basic Law and Procedures Under the National Labor Relations Act* (Washington, D.C.: Government Printing Office, 1976).

[11]*Ibid.*

[12]See F.W. McCulloch and T. Bornstein, *The National Labor Relations Board* (New York: Praeger, 1974); and J.A. Gross, *The Making of the National Labor Relations Board* (Albany, N.Y.: State University of New York Press, 1974).

[13]National Labor Relations Board, *45th Annual Report of the NLRB* (Washington, D.C.: Government Printing Office, 1981).

[14]The Wagner and Taft-Hartley Acts, as amended, provide states with the opportunity to pass right-to-work laws; see M. Estey, *The Unions* 3rd ed. (New York: Harcourt Brace Jovanovich, 1982) for further details.

[15]See J.R. Bellace and A.D. Berkowitz, *The Landrum-Griffin Act: Twenty Years of Federal Protection of Union Members' Rights* (Philadelphia: University of Pennsylvania Press, 1979).

[16]A.L. Goldman, *The Supreme Court and Labor-Management Relations Law* Lexington, Mass.: Heath, 1976).

[17]W.B. Gould, *A Primer on American Labor Law* (Cambridge, Mass.: M.I.T. Press, 1982).

[18]See G.W. Latta, Union organizing among engineers: A current assessment, *Industrial and Labor Relations Review* 35 (1981): 29–42; and T.A. Kochan, How American workers view labor unions, *Monthly Labor Review* 102 (1979): 23–31, for discussion of the image of unions.

[19]U.S. Department of Labor, Bureau of Labor Statistics, *Directory of National Unions and Employee Associations 1975* (Washington, D.C.: Government Printing Office, 1976).

[20]Kochan, *op. cit.*

[21]G. Strauss, Industrial relations: Time of change, *Industrial Relations* 23 (Winter 1984): 1–15.

[22]D.L. Bemmerer and E.D. Wickersham, Knights of Labor in 1885–1886, *Industrial and Labor Relations Review* 3 (1950): 213–220.

[23]See S. Lens, *The Labor Wars, From Molly McGuires to the Sitdowns* (Garden City, N.Y.: Doubleday, 1973).

[24]Holley and Jennings, *op. cit.*

[25]*Ibid.*

[26]See S. Alinsky, *John L. Lewis: An Unauthorized Biography* (New York: Vintage Books, 1970).

[27]See R. Dulles, *Labor in America: A History* 3rd ed. (New York: Thomas Y. Crowell, 1966); and A. F. McClure, *The Truman Administration and the Problems of Post-War Labor, 1945–1948* (Cranburry, N.J.: Associated University Presses, 1969).

[28]L.T. Adams, Labor organization mergers 1979–1984: Adapting to change, *Monthly Labor Review* 107 (September 1984): 21–27; C.N. Chaison, A note on union merger trends, *Industrial and Labor Relations Review* 34 (1980): 114–120.

[29]G. Strauss, Industrial relations: Time of change, *Industrial Relations* 33 (Winter 1984): 1–15.

[30]Latta, *op. cit.*

[31]Holley and Jennings, *op. cit.*

[32]B. Hershizer and H. Graham, Are unions facing a crisis? Labor officials divided, *Monthly Labor Review* 107 (August 1984): 23–25.

[33]T.A. Kochan, R.B. McKersie, and P. Cappelli, Strategic choice and industrial relations theory, *Industrial Relations* 23 (Winter 1984): 16–39.

[34]Strauss, *op. cit.*

[35]J.E. Abodeely, *The NLRB and the Appropriate Bargaining Unit (Labor and Public Policy Series Report No. 3)* (Philadelphia: Industrial Research Unit, Wharton School of Finance and Commerce, University of Pennsylvania, 1971).

[36]K.S. Koziara, M.I. Bradley, and D.A. Pierson, Becoming a union leader: The path to local office, *Monthly Labor Review* 105 (February 1982): 44–46, discusses the process of becoming president of a local labor union.

[37]L.S. Gray, Unions implementing managerial techniques, *Monthly Labor Review* 104 (June 1981): 3–13, discusses the selection and training of professional union staff.

[38]J.C. Anderson, Local union participation: A re-examination, *Industrial Relations* 18 (1979): 18–31.

[39]Adams, *op. cit.;* G.N. Chaison, Union mergers and integration of union governing structures, *Journal of Labor Research* 3 (Spring 1982): 139.

[40]Adams, *op. cit.*

[41]Chaison, *op. cit.*

[42]C.J. Janus, Union mergers in the 1970s: A look at the reasons and results, *Monthly Labor Review* 101 (October 1978): 13.

[43]J. Barbash, *American Unions* (New York: Random House, 1967).

[44]W.E. Fulmer, Step by step through a union campaign, *Harvard Business Review* 59 (July-August 1981): 94–102, elaborates on the organizing concerns faced by union and management.

[45]NLRB vs. Babcock & Wilcox, Inc. 351 U.S. 105 (1956).

[46]J.A. Fossum, Union-management relations, in K.M. Rowland and G.R. Ferris, *Personnel Management* (Boston: Allyn and Bacon: 1982).

[47]J.G. Getman, S.B. Goldberg, and J.B. Herman, *Union Representation Elections: Law and Reality* (New York: Russell Sage, 1976).

[48]*Ibid.*

[49]W.T. Dickens, The effect of company campaigns on certification election: Law and reality once again, *Industrial and Labor Relations Review* 36 (1983): 560–575.

[50]F.L. Sullivan, Limiting union organizing activity through supervisors, *Personnel* 55 (July-August 1978): 55–65.

[51]H.G. Heneman and M.H. Sandvers, Predicting the outcome of union certification elections: A review of the literature, *Industrial and Labor Relations Review* 36 (1983): 537–559, summarizes twenty-nine studies of certification outcomes.

[52]National Labor Relations Board, *45th Annual Report, op. cit.*

[53]M.H. Sandver, Regional differentials in outcomes in NLRB certification elections. Paper presented at the annual meeting of the Academy of Management, Detroit, Mich., August 1980.

[54]See I. Chafetz and C.R.P. Fraser, Union decertification: An exploratory analysis, *Industrial Relations* 18 (Winter 1979): 68; J.B. Dworkin and M. Extejt, Why workers decertify their unions: A preliminary investigation. Paper presented at the Annual Meeting of the Academy of Management, Atlanta, Ga., August 1979.

[55]See J.C. Anderson, G. Busman, and C.A. O'Reilly III, What factors influence the outcome of union decertification elections? *Monthly Labor Review* 102 (1979): 32–40; J.C. Anderson, C.A. O'Reilly, and G. Busman, Union decertification in the U.S.: 1947–1977, *Industrial Relations* 19 (1980): 100–107; W.A. Fulmer and T.A. Gilman, Why do workers vote for union decertification?, *Personnel* 58 (March-April 1981): 28–35; J.J. Lawler and G. Handley, Determinants of certification and decertification activity, *Industrial Relations* 22 (Fall 1983): 335–348.

[56]W.A. Krupman and G.I. Rasin, Decertification: Removing the shroud, *Labor Law Journal* 39 (April 1979): 234.

[57]P. Voos, Does it pay to organize? Estimating the cost to unions, *Monthly Labor Review* 107 (June 1984): 43–44.

[58]F.K. Foulkes, How top nonunion companies manage employees, *Harvard Business Review* 59 (September-October 1981).

[59]A.A. Porter and K.F. Newman, A survey of employer union avoidance practices, *Personnel Administrator* 28 (November 1983): 66.

[60]Holley and Jennings, *op. cit.; ibid.*

[61]Porter and Newman, *op. cit.*

[62]C.R. Greer and S.A. Martin, Calculative strategy during union organizing campaigns, *Sloan Management Review* 19 (1978): 61–74.

[63]K.A. Kovach, J.P. Stevens and the struggle for union organization, *Labor Law Journal* 29 (May 1979): 300–308.

[64]D.P. Twomey, *Labor Law and Legislation* 6th ed. (Cincinnati, Ohio: Southwestern: 1980).

[65]J.S. Lublin, Labor strikes back at consultants that help firms keep unions out, *Wall Street Journal,* 15 May 1982.

[66]*Ibid.*

[67]Strauss, *op. cit.*

FURTHER READINGS

De Maria, A.T. *The Process of Deunionization.* New York: Executive Enterprises Publications, 1982.

Estey, M. *The Unions* 3rd ed. New York: Harcourt Brace Jovanovich, 1982.

Fossum, J.A. *Labor Relations: Development, Structure, Process.* Dallas: Business Publications, 1982.

Herman, E.E. and Kuhn, A. *Collective Bargaining and Labor Relations.* Englewood Cliffs, N.J.: Prentice-Hall, 1981.

Holley, W.H. Jr. and Jennings, J.M. *The Labor Relations Process* 2nd ed. Chicago: Dryden, 1984,

Lewis, R. and Krupman, W.A. *Winning NLRB Elections: Management Strategy and Preventive Programs.* New York: Practicing Law Institute, 1979.

Nash, P.G. and Blake, G.P., eds. *Appropriate Units for Collective Bargaining.* New York: Practicing Law Institute, 1979.

Schlossberg, S.I. and Scott, J.A. *Organizing and the Law.* Washington, D.C.: Bureau of National Affairs, 1983.

Twomey, D. *Labor Law & Legislation* 6th ed. Cincinnati, Ohio: Southwestern, 1980.

CHAPTER 11

Smoothing the Collective Bargaining Process

CHAPTER OUTLINE

LEARNING CHECKPOINTS

After completing the reading and activities in this chapter, students will be able to

- describe the steps in the collective bargaining process;
- offer guidelines for management and unions in preparing for negotiations;
- specify the legal and quasilegal constraints on collective bargaining;
- compare and contrast four types of bargaining;
- discuss the tactics often used in negotiations;
- list the primary bargaining issues;
- explain the conditions under which successful and unsuccessful negotiations take place;
- discuss the differences between public and private sector labor relations;
- discuss the causes of strikes;
- discuss strategies for avoiding strikes;
- compare the labor relations systems in Canada, Western Europe, Eastern Europe, and Japan to that in the United States;
- offer an approach for increasing the effectiveness of collective bargaining.

INTRODUCTION

> The nurses employed by the Visiting Nurses Association of Bay City recently certified the State Nurses Union to act as their bargaining unit. Most nurses voted for unionization because the Union promised significant improvements in wages, benefits, and working hours in their first contract.
>
> The United Food Workers' contract is due to expire in thirty days. Negotiations between their representatives and Center City Hospital have been conducted for the past sixty days. Many members feel that Center City has not bargained in good faith. A preliminary poll indicates that union members may be willing to strike if agreement is not reached.
>
> The Textile Workers of America negotiated a new collective bargaining agreement for all workers in New England six months ago. The contract allowed negotiations to reopen if inflation exceeded 8 percent. Recent indicators showed that inflation has reached 8.2 percent.

What steps should union and management take in each of these situations? How is the collective bargaining agreement reached? What influences its content? When should negotiations be started? Stopped? When should or do workers strike?

In this chapter we answer these and other questions. We begin by examining the collective bargaining process in which the State Nurses Union, United Food Workers, and Textile Workers of America; and representatives of the Visiting Nurses Association, Center City Hospital, or organizations employing textile workers in New England would be engaged. Next, we discuss the steps in negotiating the collective bargaining agreement. Third, we examine the issues on which union and management focus during negotiations. Then we consider work stoppages, including strikes, lockouts, and walkouts. Finally, we offer ways of improving the collective bargaining process.

THE COLLECTIVE BARGAINING PROCESS

Collective bargaining is a process by which union and management establish, revise, and administer the rules of the workplace, determine amounts of compensation, and specify methods for the settlement of disputes during the life of an agreement between labor and management. As a result of collective bargaining, union and management might agree, for example, to pay higher hourly wages to nurses who work the third (night) shift, or to pay all rather than a fraction of health insurance for employees with more than five years in the organization. The union might agree to allow management more flexibility in promoting food workers; they might agree to let managers use criteria other than seniority alone. Or the union might agree to reduce wages of textile workers in exchange for guarantees of job security for workers.

Under collective bargaining the rules that govern behavior in the workplace are written down in explicit terms and incorporated into the labor-management agreement. "Collective bargaining therefore consists of interaction between unions and managers. It takes place within limits set by formal rules, accepted practices, laws, and conventions. It has the purpose and result of regulating relations between an organization under management, and its workers."[1]

The collective bargaining process has been described as (1) a poker game that combines deception, bluff, luck, and ability; (2) a debating society with long-winded rhetoric and name-calling; (3) power politics where the party with greatest brute strength forces its terms on the weaker party; and (4) a rational process in which each side relies on facts and logic to be persuaded and is willing to reconcile conflicting interests in light of common interests.[2] Most likely the process includes all four elements at different times.

Union and management must try to reach an agreement acceptable to both sides. Each party typically has a set of positions that it would accept. The union, such as the Textile Workers of America or United Food Workers, might accept at least a 6 percent wage increase; management might accept at most a 7 percent increase. Collective bargaining attempts to find where these sets overlap. Overly simplistically, both sides would accept a 6 to 7 percent increase. Or, the union might be willing to accept a wage increase slightly less than 6 percent if management increases its contribution to employee pension plans. Although each side can hold out for extremes—management could insist on a 4 percent increase and the union a 10 percent increase—by doing so they risk being unable to reach an acceptable agreement. A key task of negotiations is for each party to determine its opponent's bargaining range without revealing its own. Unionized organizations must bargain about hours, wages, and conditions of employment.

NEGOTIATING THE AGREEMENT

Most negotiations today involve the revision and renewal of existing contracts; these expire at intervals ranging from one to three years.[3] Or, as for the Textile Workers mentioned in the introduction, the contract may be subject to renegotiation unexpectedly. The *contract* specifies the rules that govern employees' work. Figures 11–1 and 11–2 show excerpts from a national and a local labor contract. These documents can range from a few to hundreds of pages. Typically, with each additional negotiation, the contract becomes more extensive and the work rules more detailed. For an automobile assembler, for example, the contract would specify at least his or her wages, benefits, length of shift, rights due to seniority or lack of it, and the right to present grievances (complaints), among others. For a bus driver, the contract would specify length of shifts, right to select routes, duration and timing of rest periods, as well as wages, benefits, and other conditions of employment. The contracts negotiated by the State Nurses Union, United Food Workers Union, and Textile Workers of America likely would vary

(b) Employes On Layoff From Unit Other Than Basic Unit

Any employe who has basic seniority in one unit and who, as of May 25, 1959, is on the active employment rolls of another unit or who subsequently is placed in or transferred to another unit under circumstances where he does not carry his seniority with him, shall, at his first layoff thereafter in a reduction in force, have his seniority determined by whichever of the following he then elects:

(i) Such employe may irrevocably waive his seniority in his basic unit and retain at the other unit his latest date-of-entry seniority, which will then become his basic seniority (it being understood that such waiver will not break the employe's "Company seniority" for purposes of such plans as the vacation, holiday pay, jury duty pay, SUB or retirement plans where Company, rather than plant, seniority is taken into account); or

(ii) Such employe may elect to return to his basic unit, in which event he shall be placed in, or on the recall list of, his basic seniority unit with full credit for seniority accumulated while working in the other unit to be included in determining his seniority in such basic unit, and he shall retain no seniority rights in any other unit, except as otherwise provided in Article VIII, Section 23(c) with respect to skilled trades seniority.

Any employe who does not elect (i), above, in writing at the place designated by the Company within five calendar days after his layoff shall be deemed to have elected (ii).

This Subsection (b) shall not supersede or preclude local or area agreements pertaining to the seniority date of an employe on layoff from a plant other than his basic unit approved by the National Ford Department and Labor Relations Staff.

Section 2. Employes on Rolls June 20, 1941—Seniority Break Period

For those Local Unions which have not locally negotiated a "seniority break period" for use in computing the seniority status of employes who were on the payroll on June 20, 1941, a four-year break period shall be considered established.

Employes who were receiving Workmen's Compensation on June 20, 1941, will be considered as having been on the payroll and shall have cumulative seniority, provided that they do not have a seniority break as provided for by local agreement between the Company and the Union.

Section 3. Local Seniority Agreements

Seniority agreements, which have been negotiated locally and which are still in effect, shall remain in full force and effect unless changed by local agreement approved by the National Ford Department of the UAW and the Labor Relations Staff of the Company.

Section 4. Acquiring Seniority; Probationary Employes

(a) Acquiring Seniority

New employes and rehired employes shall be regarded as probationary employes and shall establish seniority after the first three (3) months of continuous employment with the Company, and if retained thereafter shall be placed upon the seniority list in the seniority group in the Unit or plant where they are then working with seniority as of the date of hiring.

In order to become a seniority employe, a probationary employe must have been employed for a total of three (3) months within the year following the date he was hired or last rehired, whichever is the later. For the purposes of this Section, periods during which the employe was laid off, or on leave of absence for any reason, or employed on an excluded classification, shall not be considered as periods of employment.*

Following completion of his probationary period, the employe shall be given seniority as of the date he was hired or last rehired, whichever is the later, as set forth in the first paragraph of this Subsection.

(b) Rights to Transfer and Discharge Probationary Employes

The Company may discharge or transfer employes at any time during the probationary period. However, any claim by a probationary employe that his layoff or discharge after 30 days of employment is not for cause, or any claim of discrimination in connection with his transfer or discharge may be taken up as a grievance.

(c) Probationary Employes—Layoff and Recall

When possible, the Company shall adhere to a policy of laying off and rehiring probationary employes, within an occupational group, or within the Labor Pool, in accordance with their date of hire, provided that the Company shall retain the sole discretion as to the laying off, transferring and rehiring of probationary employes, except in cases of claimed discrimination.

When a probationary employe is laid off, his employment shall be terminated unless it is anticipated that the layoff will be temporary. If the employe is recalled within a period not exceeding the period he was employed continuously by the Company immediately preceding the date of layoff, the Company shall reinstate rather than rehire him.

Figure 11–1 EXCERPT FROM A NATIONAL LABOR CONTRACT *Continued*

(d) Probationary Employes—Medical Leave

If a probationary employe is absent on medical leave for a period not exceeding the period he was employed continuously by the Company immediately preceding the date such absence commenced, he will be reinstated and returned to work if there is work available in his Unit which he can perform.

If his period of absence exceeds his preceding period of employment, the Company shall be under no obligation to reinstate him.

(e) Rights of Probationary Employes

With respect to matters where provision otherwise has not been made, probationary employes are covered by the terms of this Agreement and shall have access to the Grievance Procedure for the enforcement of their rights thereunder.

Section 5. Loss of Seniority

Seniority shall be broken for the following reasons:†

1. (Quit)
If the employe quits.

2. (Discharge)
If the employe is discharged and the discharge is not reversed through Grievance Procedure.

3. (Absent from Work)
If a seniority employe with less than six months' seniority is absent for three (3) working days without properly notifying the Company and giving a satisfactory reason for his absence, unless it is not possible for him to do so.

4. (Failure to Report)
If the employe does not, within five (5) working days (excluding Saturdays, Sundays and Holidays) after notice to report has been sent to him, either report for work or give a satisfactory reason for his absence, unless it is not possible for him to comply with either

*For crediting of periods of military service, see Article VIII, Section 33(b) of this Agreement.

†For expiration of sick leave, see Article VIII, Section 30 of this Agreement.

"Agreements between Ford Motor Company and the UAW," Agreements dated February 13, 1982, Vol. I, Article VIII, Section 1(b)–5, pp. 68–71. Reprinted with permission, International Union, UAW.

Figure 11–1 Continued

OVERTIME EQUALIZATION AGREEMENT

It is mutually agreed between Ford Motor Company, Plastics Paint and Vinyl Division, Saline Plant, and the International Union, UAW, Local 892, on May 24, 1982 at Saline, Michigan, that the following provisions, within the constraints and guidelines allowed under Article IV, Section 6 of the Master Agreement, shall govern the procedure for overtime equalization at the Saline Plant.

1. Weekend overtime will be posted no later than noon Thursday prior to the overtime. The department overtime schedule will be posted by name, date, and classification unless scheduled 100 percent. The overtime posting will be placed at one established location each week in each department. Department employees will be responsible for checking their schedule. The department supervisor will be responsible to notify affected employees of changes to the posted weekend schedule.

2. Overtime shall be equalized by classification within a department by shift.

3. Overtime records will be maintained on the basis of hours paid, not hours worked.

4. Employees not available to work overtime for any reason, except on the day of Personal Holidays, will be charged for such missed opportunity when properly notified.

5. Hires, rehires, reinstates, transfers, and reclassifications shall be charged hours equal to the highest employee on the classification on the shifts in the department who is within spread. Employees assigned to another shift for a period of not to exceed two weeks for the purpose of breaking in new hires or to launch a new product or to start a new shift production or employees on temporary layoff, shall not be charged with high hours upon his return to his original classification and shift. However, he will be charged with any overtime worked or refused while off his regular shift.

6. A temporary reclassified employee will be charged hours equal to the highest employee who is in spread on

Figure 11–2 EXCERPTS FROM A LOCAL LABOR CONTRACT *Continued* such classification on the shift in the department and will equalize his hours in that classification. Upon return to his original classification, shift, and department, he will be charged hours equal to the highest employee in that classification, who is within spread.

7. Employees who have been granted overtime as a result of a grievance settlement shall be charged with the number of hours paid.

8. Employees loaned to and working overtime in another department shall be charged the overtime on their regular classification and department.

9. Saline Plant overtime records will revert to zero the second Monday after ratification. On January 1, 1983, and on January 1, 1984, overtime hours will be adjusted so as to reflect the overtime spread condition only.

10. The overtime spread on a shift, within a department and classification, will be 36 hours or less.

11. When an employee is out-of-spread the Union may request in writing that the Industrial Relations Manager confer with the appropriate superintendent and provide a written explanation as to why the employee is out-of-spread and the planned remedial action.

12. When distribution of overtime between shifts becomes unbalanced, at the Union's request, the Union and Management will meet to discuss remedies to correct the situation.

13. It is the policy of the Saline Plant that an employee may be bypassed, at his request, in scheduling overtime when less than all of the employees on his classification and shift within the departments are scheduled, providing another qualified employee within his classification, shift and department is available to work such overtime. Such overtime not worked will be charged.

14. Voluntary overtime worked outside their home department by Supplemental Overtime Pool Employees will not be charged back to the home department, but will be reflected in a separate overtime group for pool employees. Overtime worked in the home department by pool employees will be charged in both home and pool overtime lists.

15. Weekly overtime lists will be posted at an established location in each department. They shall be posted by the department supervisor, with any corrections to be noted on the overtime sheet and to appear on the following week's printout.

16. The employee initiating a shift preference bump shall assume the highest hours within spread on the overtime sheet on his new shift. The employee being bumped shall assume the hours of the employee that bumped, if within spread, otherwise of the highest employee within spread.

17. Once the original overtime list has been posted for scheduled overtime, any addition to or correction of the list will be the responsibility of the employee's supervisor to notify the employee.

18. Any employee other than Supplemental Pool Employees refusing to accept overtime out of his department and shift shall not be charged.

19. When an employee accepts available overtime and is AWOL for the overtime assignment, he shall be charged double the amount of the accepted overtime.

20. All skilled trades and Appendix F employees shall rotate overtime by classification, by shift, plantwide.

21. When a skilled trades or Appendix F employee refuses overtime and is then forced to work because the supervisor has gone through the entire list, he shall be charged double the offered hours so that the overtime list will continue to be rotated.

22. a. If an employee has been scheduled and accepts an overtime opportunity for overtime assignment and he is absent on the day prior to the assignment, he must advise the Company no later than one hour prior to the end of his regular shift on the day prior to the premium time assignment that he will or will not report to work.

b. If the employee does not call, he will be charged double the hours he would have been paid had he worked the premium assignment and a low houred employee within the equalization group may be scheduled to work in his place. If the employee, when calling in, advises the Company that he will not report for work, he will be charged in the normal manner.

c. In the event the employee reports for work on the premium assignment and he did not notify the Company, he may be sent home without liability of call-in-pay.

23. Overtime for apprentices shall be equalized with journeymen of their respective trade after completion of 2000 hours of their indenture apprenticeship program.

VOLUNTARY OVERTIME SUPPLEMENTATION POOL EXCLUDING CHROME PLATER

1. Any employee working in the unit who desires to be included in the pool may apply during business hours at the Labor Relations and Hourly Personnel Office. Accepted applicants will be included on the list of pool employees no later than the second Monday following such application.

2. Selections for the pool will be based on a review of medical restrictions, attendance and workmanship records

Figure 11–2 Continued

Continued

for six months immediately preceding the date application is made.

3. An employee cannot refuse overtime in his own department to work voluntary overtime in another area.

4. Except for compelling reasons, an employee selected for the pool will be expected to work offered overtime. Scheduled employees who must be absent are required to call in to notify the Company of such absence as soon as possible.

5. An up-to-date list of pool employees will be maintained by the Labor Relations Office, who will furnish the list to the Superintendent's Clerks. This pool list will be in hours order (low to high). It is expected that all members of the pool will receive a fair share of the overtime assigned to the pool.

6. A sign-up sheet will be posted for each shift in a central location by Monday noon each week. Pool employees desirous of working weekend overtime must sign the sheet in order to be scheduled for the following weekend. Pool employees may sign only one sheet. The sign-up sheets will be taken down Tuesday at noon. Voluntary overtime will be scheduled and the list of scheduled pool employees posted by noon Thursday. Pool employees will be required to check the posted schedule to determine their job assignment if scheduled.

7. Each production area, by Superintendent, will attempt to schedule employees who work in their own production area and are familiar with the operations prior to scheduling pool employees who work in other production areas.

8. If a pool employee should be scheduled for overtime in his home department after being scheduled for voluntary overtime, he must notify the Superintendent's Clerk in the assigned area, so that a replacement can be obtained.

9. Supplemental pool employees voluntary overtime hours outside the regular equalization group will be maintained in a separate overtime group. Voluntary overtime hours outside this equalization group will not be charged to the home department, however, overtime hours charged in the home department will be added to the supplemental pool overtime list.

10. Unsatisfactory job performance by pool members on voluntary overtime will be reviewed by the parties for possible reassignment.

"Local Agreement between Ford Motor Company and UAW Local 892 Saline," Agreement dated May 24, 1982, pp. 6–11. Reprinted with permission.

Figure 11–2 Continued

in length and detail because of differences in the age, membership, and experience of the union. Figure 11–3 lists the components of a typical contract.

Negotiating the agreement involves three steps: (1) preparing for the negotiations, (2) conducting the negotiations, and (3) concluding the negotiations.

Preparing for Negotiations

At this stage, both management and union attempt to gain information that can help them to accomplish their bargaining objectives.

Preparation by Management. Management picks its negotiating team, formulates a series of proposals, and plans its course of action. The negotiating team can be composed of the top management of the organization, such as the president, senior vice president, or chief executive officer, a labor relations manager, or legal counsel to the firm. At Center City Hospital, for example, management's negotiating team might include the hospital administrator, director of human resources, and legal counsel. The negotiating team should include people with patience, perseverance, and expertise in both organizational and negotiation issues.

Union Security and Management Rights

The bargaining unit—people for whom union speaks
Form of recognition—extent of bargaining rights
Duration and renewal—length of bargaining rights
Management rights—nature of management's rights

The Wage and Bargaining Effort

Pay for time worked—wage or incentive rate
The effort bargain—established standards for task performance
Premium pay—pay for overtime
Pay for time not worked—pay for holidays, bonuses
Contingent benefits—pensions, unemployment benefits, health plans

Individual Security

Job rights—seniority
Due process—grievance procedure

Administration

Internal (on-the-job representation)—who represents union members
External (arbitration)—powers and appointment of arbitrator

Based on E.F. Beal and J.P. Begin, *The Practice of Collective Bargaining* 6th ed. (Homewood, Ill.: Irwin, 1982).

Figure 11–3 COMPONENTS OF A CONTRACT

Once the team has been selected, it formulates and costs a series of proposals. The proposals specify the components of the agreement acceptable to management. They include a description of acceptable levels of compensation, benefit changes, hours of employment, including overtime and payment for it, and other conditions of employment. Each proposal lists wages, hours, and conditions of employment, as well as the costs associated with them. As much as possible, management should calculate the cost of various alternatives in advance so that they can respond to union demands with concrete counterproposals. Table 11–1 shows an approach for costing out changes in contract terms.[4]

Finally, the team must plan its action. Should it begin with a generous or conservative offer? Which areas should it address first? In which areas should it be willing to yield? To plan an effective course of action, management's negotiating team must understand the union's position and psychology, specify and rank its own objectives, and think about the procedures that will help accomplish these objectives.

As part of its preparation, management frequently gathers the following information:

1. A summary of previous negotiations—commentary about the issues raised and settled or vetoed by each side during previous negotiations, including

Changes in Costs	Increased Cost
1. Direct payroll—annual	
Straight-time earnings—36¢ per hour general increase	
100 employees × 2,080 hours × 36¢	$74,800
Premium earnings—second shift established differential—10¢ per hour	
30 employees × 2,080 hours × 10¢	6,240
Overtime—overtime cost increased by increased straight-time rate—average straight-time rate increases 39¢	
39¢ × 12,000 overtime hours × .5 overtime rate	2,340
Bonus	None
Other direct payroll cost increases	None
Total increase in direct payroll costs	$83,460
2. Added costs directly resulting from higher payroll costs—annual	
F.I.C.A.—5.85 percent times increase in average straight-time earnings below $9,000 annual	
100 employees × 36¢ × 5.85% × 2,080 hours	$4,380.48
Federal and state unemployment insurance tax	
number of employees × 4,200 × 2.5% tax rate	No change
Workmen's compensation (total cost or estimate)	No change
Other	No change
Total additional direct payroll costs	$4,380.48
3. Nonpayroll costs—annual	
Insurance—company portion	
Health insurance	No change
Dental insurance	None
Eye care	None
Life insurance—added employer contribution $100 per year	
$100 × 100 employees	$10,000
Pension costs—fully vested pension reduced from 25 years and age 65 to 20 years and age 62	
Estimated additional cost	52,000
Miscellaneous	
Tuition reimbursements (addition)	600
Service rewards	No change
Suggestion awards (addition)	350
Loss on employee cafeteria	No change
Overtime meals	No change
Cost of parking lots	No change
Company parties	No change
Personal tools	No change
Personal safety equipment (addition)	1,200
Personal wearing apparel	No change
Profit sharing	No change
Other	No change
Total additional nonpayroll costs—annual	$64,150
4a. Changes in nonwork paid time	
Holidays—2 new holidays added to 6 already in contract	
100 employees × 8 hours × 2 holidays × $3.96 average new wage	$6,336
Vacation—new category added—4 weeks	
(160 hours annual vacation) with 20 or more years service—former top was 3 weeks after 15 years	

Table 11–1 **COSTING CONTRACT TERMS** *Continued*

Changes in Costs	Increased Cost
Average number of employees affected annually	
15 employees × 40 hours $3.96 average new wage	2,376
Paid lunch time—paid ½ lunch time added to contract	
100 employees × ½ hour × 236 days worked yearly × $3.96	
average new wage	46,728
Paid wash-up time	None
Coffee breaks	No change
Paid time off for union activity—new 1 hour per week per shop steward	
10 shop stewards × $4.20 shop steward average new wage	
× 1 hour × 52 weeks	2,184
Paid sick leave	None
Paid time off over and above workmen's compensation	
paid time	None
Jury service time off—no change	None
Funeral leave time off—no change	None
Paid time off for safety or training—no change	None
Other	None
Total change in hours paid for but not worked—annual	$57,624
4b. Financial data derived from costing out (Items 1–4, above)	
Total increase in contract costs	
Item 1 + item 2 + item 3	$151,990
Average total increase in contract costs per employee payroll hour	
Item 1 + item 2 + item 3 ÷ 2,080 hours	.73
Average total increase in direct payroll costs per man-hour	
Item 1 + item 2 ÷ 2,080 hours ÷ 100 employees	.422
Average total increase in nonpayroll costs per payroll hour per employee	
Item 3 ÷ 2,080 hours ÷ 100 employees	.308
Average total increase in nonwork paid time expense per payroll hour per employee	
Item 4 ÷ 100 employees	.277
Average total increase in direct payroll costs per productive (worked) hour per employee	
Item 1 + item 2 ÷ 1,888 hours ÷ 100 employees	.49
Average total increase in nonpayroll costs per productive (worked) hour per employee	
Item 3 ÷ 1,888 hours ÷ 100 employees	.34

Reprinted by permission from "Positive Collective Bargaining" by Reed C. Richardson, p. 7-127–7-129 in *ASPA Handbook of Personnel and Industrial Relations*, Dale Yoder and Herbert G. Heneman, Jr., eds., copyright © 1979 by The Bureau of National Affairs, Inc., Washington, D.C.

Table 11–1 Continued

specification of those issues that received most and least attention from union and management

2. A copy of the current agreement

3. Data about the firm's labor costs—specification of the wage rates and productivity of workers covered by the contract

4. Data about labor costs of competitors—results of compensation surveys

5. Information about the union's leadership, history, and finances—reporting

of the concerns, experiences, style, and vulnerabilities of the union negotiating team, history of dues assessed and their use during the past five years, and existence of strike funds

6. A list of likely union demands and their impact on the organization
7. A list of people in the company who can provide additional information as required—names and telephone numbers of relevant managers, supervisors, and human resources professionals
8. Analysis of previous grievances—listing of areas in which grievances occurred, as a way of identifying ambiguous provisions and significant areas of the contract
9. Costs of various management proposals—specification of the costs of each provision as well as the total costs of likely combinations
10. Financial forecasts listing costs associated with different agreements (showing, for example, that a high-cost agreement may result in decreased profits, and thus hardship and potential loss of job security for employees)

Preparations for negotiations can begin from three months to two years before the expiration of the existing agreement.[5] Table 11–2 illustrates a typical planning timetable for management.

Union's Preparations. The extent and sophistication of the union's preparations can vary significantly, depending on its size and visibility. Large international unions, such as the United Automobile Workers or United Mine Workers, whose contracts can affect the national economy, engage in extensive, ongoing preparations. The three unions mentioned in the introduction to this chapter would probably devote less time and fewer resources to preparation.

The union begins its preparations by selecting a negotiating team. The team can include key members of the local union, members of the national union, or legal representatives of the union. Team members should have expertise in negotiations and legal matters. They must also be able to represent the range of interests of the union's members. The major function of the union team is to work out an agreement by presenting the union's demands, reaching agreement, and then selling the agreement to the members.

A major component of preparation is the formulation of *demands.* These are the specific wages, hours, and conditions of employment the union wants to include in the contract. Data collected during a meeting of union members, a poll of union leaders, and analysis of contracts held by the organization's competitors from the basis of demand formulation. The State Nurses Union, for example, would poll its members and analyze contracts of similar nursing associations in the region to determine the demands they should present to the hospital's negotiating team.

Once the union formulates a *wish list*—a list of those demands wished by each union member—it next reduces the list to a set of "reasonable" demands. The union leaders must reduce the list carefully to ensure that all members' wishes are represented, since it is the members who will ultimately accept or reject the

	8 to 12 Months Before Contract Expires	4 to 8 Months	1 to 4 Months Prior Commencement of Negotiations	During Negotiations	Postnegotiations
Local Unit Management	1. Assigns responsibilities for community surveys estimating union demands and employee attitude. 2. Assesses the total corporate community and union compensation/benefit plans. 3. Assesses union/employee motivation and goals for impending negotiations.	1. Develops with division management, corporate E.R. and corporate insurance project alternate benefit proposals that are to be designed and costed. 2. Continues all steps in the planning process.	1. Secures division approval of strategy negotiating plans and cost estimates.	1. Continues negotiations clears significant cost variances from plan with division management. 2. Integrates benefit negotiations with all other items. 3. Secures agreement in accord with plan. 4. Agrees with union on method and expense to inform employees of new contract terms.	1. Evaluates previous negotiations against plan within 30 days. 2. Assigns responsibilities for the planning process so as to integrate with the division's plans. 3. Identifies tentative objectives for next contract. 4. Completes wage/benefit adjustment form.
Division Headquarters Management	1. Assures local unit is preparing for negotiations. 2. Plans through annual financial plan project impact of inventory build-up. Possible settlement costs, etc. 3. Identifies internal responsibilities and relationships (corporate, law, E.R. insurance, benefits, etc.).	1. Coordinates the development of strategy and negotiating plan, consulting with corporate employee relations and benefits. 2. Develops with local management, corporate E.R. and insurance project alternative benefit proposals that are to be designed and costed.	1. Approves negotiating plan strategy. 2. Clears benefit and corporate policy variances from plan with corporate employee relations. 3. Communicates progress to senior management and corporate employee relations. 4. Approves cost variances from plan.	1. Provides in addition to those points in "1 to 4 months" column, identification of "end" position and supports local negotiators in maintaining such position.	1. Evaluates all aspects of the previous negotiations within 45 days. 2. Identifies and communicates all long-range needs to executive management and corporate employee relations. 3. Integrates planning process in the division growth plan.

Table 11–2 SUMMARY OF MANAGEMENT'S PLANNING TIMETABLE

	4. Keeps corporate employee relations informed.	3. Makes broad judgment on impact of company and expected proposals in relation to division and corporate goals, strategy and plans. 4. Evaluates plans to control costs and deviations from plan/strategy.	5. Identifies strike issues.		
Corporate Employee Relations	1. Advises division and local management of union's national position on economics. Benefits and other issues. 2. Counsels on any anticipated conflict with corporate policy other divisions, etc. 3. Provides available historical information pertinent to planning.	1. Assists division, local management, and corporate insurance in projecting and preparing alternate benefit proposals that are to be designed and costed. 2. Keeps division and local unit informed of any external developments having impact on its planning.	1. Consults with division on strategy and plans; available for on the scene assistance or to consult with international union officers; recommends corporate point of view on issues. 2. Approves all variances from corporate personnel policy and benefit plan proposals. 3. Assures that all issues are resolved at the required levels.	1. Provides same as "1 to 4 months" column. 2. Identifies to division management potential problems having corporate impact; if necessary advises corporate management of unresolved major issues.	1. Counsels with union and/or unit management on negotiating experiences and/or evaluation of new contract. 2. Informs other units of results. 3. Initiates needed objectives for study policy change or corporate decision.
Corporate Law Department	1. Counsels on request.	1. Counsels on request and reviews current contract as required. 2. Approves benefit plan drafts to assure legal compliance.	1. Counsels and drafts contract language on request. 2. Makes counsel available to review contract language before signing.	1. Provides same as "1 to 4 months" column.	1. Reviews new contracts for possible problems; advises division and corporate employee relations.

SOURCE: Audrey Freedman, *Managing Labor Relations* (New York: Conference Board, 1979), p. 24. © The Conference Board, 1979, reprinted by permission.

contract. They also must gather extensive documentation to support the validity of the demands.

The union also tries to collect information that helps it assess the organization's strength, intentions and competitive position (profitability, costs, sales); it tries to learn about the state of the industry as well. And the union tries to assess the organization's ability to withstand a strike and willingness to make *concessions*—to yield to the union's demands.[6]

In deciding whether to push to reopen their contract, the Textile Workers must assess their organization's current financial situation. If the organization is in a state of financial health, management may be more responsive to demands for increased wages in response to the increased cost of living than if it is in financial difficulty. However, the union often does not tally the cost of its demands because it lacks complete information about costs, may not be overly concerned with the costs of the demands, or views cost control as a managerial function.[7]

Finally, the union must publicize and explain the demands to its members and garner their support. The union uses meetings, newsletters, and informal discussions to keep members informed about the intended direction of the negotiations. Those who draft the proposals at the local level meet with the membership to present the demands and solicit their agreement to the proposed contract. Representatives of the State Nurses Union, United Food Workers, or Textile Workers of America must maintain open and ongoing communication with their workers during the preparations and negotiations.

Conducting the Negotiations

Collective bargaining can be conducted at the local or national level, in collaboration with or isolation from other unions.

Bargaining Patterns. The *national union* can conduct the bargaining, as is typical in the steel industry. Each local union must then approve the agreement reached by the national union. National bargaining provides more power to the union's position because of the large number of members represented; if an agreement is not reached, there is the potential for a major work stoppage. Since most national unions include a relatively diverse membership, they may experience difficulty in adequately representing the desires of all members.

A variation of this is that elected representatives of local unions form a *conference board* that negotiates the contract. Ford Motor Company and General Motors take this approach with the United Automobile Workers, as does the Westinghouse Conference Board of the International Brotherhood of Electrical Workers.[8] The Textile Workers of America, described earlier, might take this approach. In this approach, the bargaining settles certain issues at the national level, such as across-the-board wage incentives or job security provisions. Other issues are left for local settlement, such as manning, seniority, and other work rules.

Alternatively, the *local union* can conduct the bargaining, with the national union coordinating the actions of several locals. The United Food Workers might negotiate this way. This type of collective bargaining attempts to take advantage of the power of the national union while still carefully responding to the demands of local union members.

Several independent local unions can also band together to conduct the bargaining, without coordination at a national level. Representatives of these unions comprise a *trade council* that acts on behalf of all unions during the negotiations. In this situation the unions gain strength through their numbers but can respond better to local conditions than when a national union negotiates the contract.

In some cases each local union conducts the bargaining independently. The local of the State Nurses Union might negotiate this way. Here the negotiations best respond to the needs of union members but the union may have limited power if it represents only a small number of members.

Who should conduct the bargaining for the unions described in the introduction to this chapter? Table 11–3 summarizes the advantages of each approach discussed above.

Employers, too, can form associations to bargain with local unions. Industrial associations in the trucking, garment, mining, and construction industries typically operate in this fashion.[9] In the trucking and garment industries, a number of employers hire workers who belong to the same union. In these industries, where labor costs are a significant component of total costs, bargaining by an association attempts to reduce competition between companies in the wage area.

In the construction industry, different employers hire workers who belong to diverse local and national unions. Here the association bargains for numerous employers with many unions. This approach reduces the necessity of an organization negotiating multiple contracts on a regular and time-consuming basis.

Pattern	Advantages	Disadvantages
National union conducts bargaining	Increases union's power Union has more resources to use in bargaining	High potential for major work stoppage May not represent membership well
Conference board of representatives bargains	Settles issues at appropriate level (national or local)	May be unable to resolve different preferences of locals
Trade council negotiates on behalf of independent locals	Increases unions' strength through greater numbers Responds better to local conditions	May experience difficulty in resolving differences among locals
Local union conducts negotiations	Represents workers' interests best	May lack power to attain demands May lack financial clout

Table 11–3 ADVANTAGES AND DISADVANTAGES OF EACH PATTERN OF BARGAINING

Should employer associations conduct the bargaining for the organizations described in the introduction to this chapter? Problems with association bargaining relate to the voluntary nature of the employer associations and the necessity of ensuring that all competitors belong to the association.[10] Nonmembers can significantly reduce the association's power by granting concessions that association members have agreed not to accept.

The Bargaining Process. Once a bargaining pattern has been determined, the team has three general negotiating strategies to choose from.[11] In the *piecemeal approach,* negotiators try to settle issues one by one from the easiest to the most difficult, or from the beginning to the end of the draft demands. Thus they might reach agreement about wages first and then negotiate the number of paid sick days. In the *total approach,* negotiators settle nothing until everything is settled. They discuss *bargaining points* but do not resolve them until they complete the whole agreement. They might discuss the wages acceptable to both sides, but do not finalize the wages until other issues are also discussed and decided. By *combining strategies* negotiators agree to minor issues, leaving the opportunity for compromise on major ones. They combine aspects of unsettled issues until an appropriate mix is reached. For example, they might agree to small adjustments in health benefits or the number of sick days, but wait to reach agreement on wages and job security provisions.

Recent literature suggests that both management and unions can benefit by combining any of these general strategies with a problem-solving approach to negotiations. Often known as *integrative bargaining,* this approach assumes that both parties can "win" in the distribution of benefits. This means that they acknowledge a common ground where both parties can agree; negotiations then focus on identifying this common ground and emphasizing common goals.[12]

Accomplishing win-win bargaining outcomes is not easy. The different requirements of the four parties involved—management, labor, management representatives, and labor representatives—makes it quite complex. Interacting in a political arena, representatives of both sides must reach an agreement that is viable and workable to the other side; they must also reach an agreement that satisfies the multiple individuals they represent.

The necessity of combining numerous, often conflicting, issues into an acceptable bargaining package also limits the feasibility of win-win negotiating. Negotiators must consider *all* the issues simultaneously; win-win bargaining on specific issues is impossible. For example, management's gain on wages is labor's loss and vice versa. Win-win bargaining succeeds only when the parties can adjust their positions on several issues in ways that, overall, are acceptable to all. The following conditions facilitate the accomplishment of mutually satisfactory goals: the issues are stated clearly and specifically; commitment and positions are withheld while both parties consider solutions; negotiations are free from preimposed constraints; the issues are broad and far-reaching rather than shortsighted; and both parties have necessary economic, social, and attitudinal information.[13]

To be successful, the win-win approach must also be a major goal of both the union and management bargaining teams. Often the various parts of the team represent different constituencies and have varying needs. For example, on management's side, the attorney may represent the chief executive officer, who wants a fast settlement; the human resources manager may want to ensure that the new contract is fair to all employee groups; and the managers of the bargaining unit in question may want particular contract provisions relating to work performance. The negotiation process must strive to balance these wishes and satisfy each party as much as possible.

Reading 11–1, "Guidelines for Productive Negotiating Relationships," by Johanna Hunsaker, Phillip Hunsaker, and Nancy Chase, offers directives for conducting win-win bargaining. The contract negotiated between the United Automobile Workers and the Ford Motor Company in 1982 is the result of such integrative bargaining, the proposed provisions of which are summarized in Figure 11–4.

FRAMEWORK FOR A NEW FORD-UAW AGREEMENT

Ford Motor Company is proposing to the UAW a **MUTUAL GROWTH PROGRAM** that is reasonable, realistic, and responsive to the concerns and needs of employes and the Company.

The Company has carefully assessed the major concerns the Union has introduced and has fashioned a program that will enable us to work together to achieve mutual objectives that are crucial to all of us.

We believe this **MUTUAL GROWTH PROGRAM** to be responsive to the special interests and needs of Ford employes and to the unique circumstances of the Company. We believe we have responded to all of the major issues that the Union has said are deeply troubling its members and that must be addressed. Our responses—many of which involve innovative approaches that would break important new ground in labor-management relations—are embodied in the elements of the Program as listed on the following pages.

This is a *growth* Program in the true sense of the word. There will be no wage reductions, and during the terms of the proposed Agreement Ford employes will experience an *increase* in their compensation.

The Company believes it is vital that Ford and its employes look to the future when shaping this Agreement. By recognizing our responsibility to each other, we can grow together.

MUTUAL GROWTH PROGRAM

1. A principal focus of the new Agreement would be on providing **JOB PROTECTION** for Ford employes.

   - Plant closings are sometimes unavoidable for clearly volume-related reasons including those attributable to market conditions and product changes such as instances where certain components are no longer required. Barring such developments, there would be a moratorium during the first 12 months of the new Agreement on plant closings except for those concluded or announced.

   - Mechanisms would be negotiated to reserve future job opportunities for laid-off Ford employes through various forms of seniority protection and preferential placement consideration arrangements.

Figure 11–4 SUMMARY OF THE FRAMEWORK FOR THE 1982 FORD–UAW AGREEMENT *Continued*

- Additionally, there would be arrangements for employe counseling, placement and moving assistance.

2. Substantially **IMPROVED INCOME SECURITY** would be provided by two new programs:

- A **REDUNDANCY PROGRAM** would include greatly improved income protection through SUB Plan revisions.
- A **GUARANTEED INCOME STREAM,** an entirely new program, would provide income protection beyond the SUB Plan for higher seniority employes.

(In order to provide these programs, inverse seniority provisions would be eliminated.)

3. A **COOPERATIVE PRODUCTIVITY ENHANCING ARRANGEMENT** would be developed to ensure operating competitiveness to the extent possible in order to contribute to employe job security and Company growth and success. Among other things, the Union will continue to assist positively during the Contract term to:

- Eliminate local inefficiencies and improve local competitiveness.
- Consolidate job classifications and expand duties.

4. A **PROFIT SHARING PLAN** would be developed which would allow all employes to share in the success of the Company as well as serving to provide a new source of income beginning January 1, 1984.

5. A jointly administered comprehensive **EMPLOYE DEVELOPMENT AND TRAINING PROGRAM** would be instituted to serve the parties' mutual interests relative to enhancing employe job skills and educational levels and energizing and sustaining the Employe Involvement process.

6. Establish a **NEW ONGOING FORUM** for joint discussion of certain business developments and for joint constructive, cooperative problem resolution as a highly visible new adjunct to the collective bargaining process.

7. The Company would pledge that **ECONOMIC ADJUSTMENTS** by hourly employes would be *applied comparably to salaried employes,* recognizing salaried adjustments already made.

8. A new **COMPREHENSIVE MAJOR MEDICAL PLAN** would be implemented, *Retirement Benefits* would be increased and **CERTAIN FIXED AMOUNTS WOULD BE UPDATED** in dental and vision plans.

9. **ECONOMIC ADJUSTMENTS** would be negotiated to moderate the growth of wage and benefit costs; however, there would be *no reduction in current wage rates* or the current COLA level for time worked by present employes. Profit sharing over time will provide the prospect for future additional income. For new employes, provisions for grow-in for full wage and benefits would be included.

10. The proposed new Agreement would *be effective* February 1, 1982, and would terminate September 14, 1984.

11. All local agreements would continue in effect for the life of the new Agreement.

This framework should be viewed in its entirety, and specific items are not available in respect to any other framework. Obviously, this program involves new concepts which will be costly to the Company and can be impacted by competitive factors. Therefore, it is subject to withdrawal, depending upon actions taken by our primary domestic competitor. (January 15, 1982)

"Framework for a New Ford–UAW Agreement," a company proposal to the UAW dated January 15, 1982. Reprinted with permission.

Figure 11–4 Continued

Previous to the 1982 negotiations at Ford, and more typically in most negotiating situations, *distributive bargaining* occurs. Financial and noneconomic privileges are thought to exist in a fixed total amount; thus one party's gain is the other's loss. Accordingly, each party tries to increase its power relative to the other to secure more of the "pot." Each side attempts to do this by making it costly for the other side to disagree (for example, by emphasizing the high costs of a threatened strike); or relatively inexpensive for the other side to agree (by emphasizing the advantages of rapid settlement). Since the assumption is that there can only be distribution of a fixed amount of privileges between the two parties, this type of bargaining typically involves conflict. Nevertheless, distributive bargaining can be successful when individuals commit to a firm (clear and specific) position early in the negotiations.[14]

Many negotiations of this type still include rituals and tactics designed to outfox the other party, rather than to identify common areas of agreement. Both management representatives and labor representatives often have to strike certain postures to keep those not involved in the negotiations happy. Labor negotiators are aware, for example, that the management team must take a hard line on wages to satisfy top management. Likewise, management negotiators know that the labor team cannot reach agreement too quickly or the workers will think they have sold out.

Management's first offer is usually low, while the first demands of the union are high.[15] This ritual allows each side to determine the other's position and still leave room for bargaining. A second ritual is that no agreement is reached before the expiration date of the existing agreement.[16] This ritual allows some last-minute bargaining and protects negotiators from appearing to concede to the other side's demands too easily. At the last minute, concessions then appear necessary to avoid the costs of a strike or lockout. This ritual, however, does create the threat of unwarranted work stoppages if the parties cannot finally and quickly reach agreement. A third ritual is that most negotiations involve some name-calling. If any of the negotiators are unfamiliar with the underlying causes of the various rituals or tactics, false assumptions can lead to severe and long-term impasses. This most frequently occurs when one side (or both) is new to negotiation.

Tactics used to gain advantage, by either side, include holding something back, bluffing, lying, using decoys, making contrived emotional outbursts or deliberate errors, or assigning "good guy–bad guy" roles to members of the negotiating team (i.e., one person offers an unreasonable proposal while another person offers a proposal that seems reasonable by contrast).

In addition to integrative and distributive bargaining, which focus on allocating wages and benefits between the two parties, there are two other types of bargaining. *Attitudinal structuring* focuses on developing relations between union and management. The attitudes of the two parties determine whether the relationship is characterized as one of conflict, containment-aggression, accommodation, cooperation, or collusion.[17] These attitudes include (1) the parties' motivational orientation and action tendencies toward the other party, (2) the parties' beliefs about the legitimacy of the demands of the other, (3) the level of trust in the other party, and (4) the degree of friendliness between parties. Table 11–4 shows the attitudinal components of various relationships between union and management. The tactics used by each party, described above, can also influence their bargaining attitudes.

Intraorganizational bargaining attempts to achieve consensus within either the union or the management organization. Often intraorganizational bargaining is necessary before union members will agree to the contract negotiated by their representatives. When intraorganizational bargaining fails to consider certain groups—older or younger workers, skilled or unskilled employees, for example—contract ratification may be in jeopardy.[18]

Figure 11–5 summarizes the conditions that lead to integrative, distributive, attitudinal, or intraorganizational bargaining. These influences include the bargaining power of each side, the nature of relationships, trust, and contact between the parties, the size of the teams, the time allowed for bargaining, and the estimated cost and likelihood of a work stoppage. Note that the different types of bargaining can occur singly or in combination. For example, intraorganizational bargaining or attitudinal structuring often accompanies integrative bargaining or distributive bargaining.

Legal Influences. Collective bargaining is monitored by the provisions of the Wagner Act as amended by the Taft-Hartley Act (see Chapter 10). One provision is that both union and management must negotiate in *good faith.*[19] To bargain in good faith means that management must meet with the union to negotiate, may not announce wage increases or other changes in compensation policies without consulting the union, must supply data about group issues, and cannot insist on its proposals to the point of impasse. It is not good-faith bargaining to begin negotiations with a final offer. Boulwarism—named after the vice president of General Electric, who used a bargaining approach where management made a fair and firm take-it-or-leave-it offer after carefully examining the facts and polling employees about their needs—is an approach the NLRB determined is in violation of the good-faith bargaining provisions.[20]

Other provisions of the Acts are that unions must negotiate about mandatory subjects (wages, hours, and terms and conditions of employment), must meet with representatives of management to negotiate, and cannot insist on discriminatory hiring or closed shops. An impasse can occur, however, even when bargaining is conducted in good faith.

Good-faith bargaining at General Electric and elsewhere is judged by *totality of conduct.* The following behaviors, when considered together, provide tentative evidence of a lack of good-faith bargaining:

- Going through the motions of bargaining without progressing toward an agreement
- Demonstrating an unwillingness to compromise

	Pattern of Relationship				
Attitudinal Dimensions	Conflict	Containment-Aggression	Accommodation	Cooperation	Collusion
Motivational orientation and action tendencies toward other	Competitive tendencies to destroy or weaken		Individualistic policy of hands off	Cooperative tendencies to assist or preserve	
Beliefs about legitimacy of other	Denial of legitimacy	Grudging acknowledgment	Acceptance of *status quo*	Complete legitimacy	Not applicable
Level of trust in conducting affairs	Extreme distrust	Distrust	Limited trust	Extended trust	Trust based on mutual blackmail potential
Degree of friendliness	Hate	Antagonism	Neutralism—Courteousness	Friendliness	Intimacy—"Sweetheart relationship"

SOURCE: Richard E. Walton and Robert B. McKersie, *A Behavioral Theory of Labor Negotiations* (New York: McGraw-Hill, 1965), p. 189. Reprinted with permission of the author.

Table 11–4 ATTITUDINAL COMPONENTS OF RELATIONS BETWEEN UNION AND MANAGEMENT

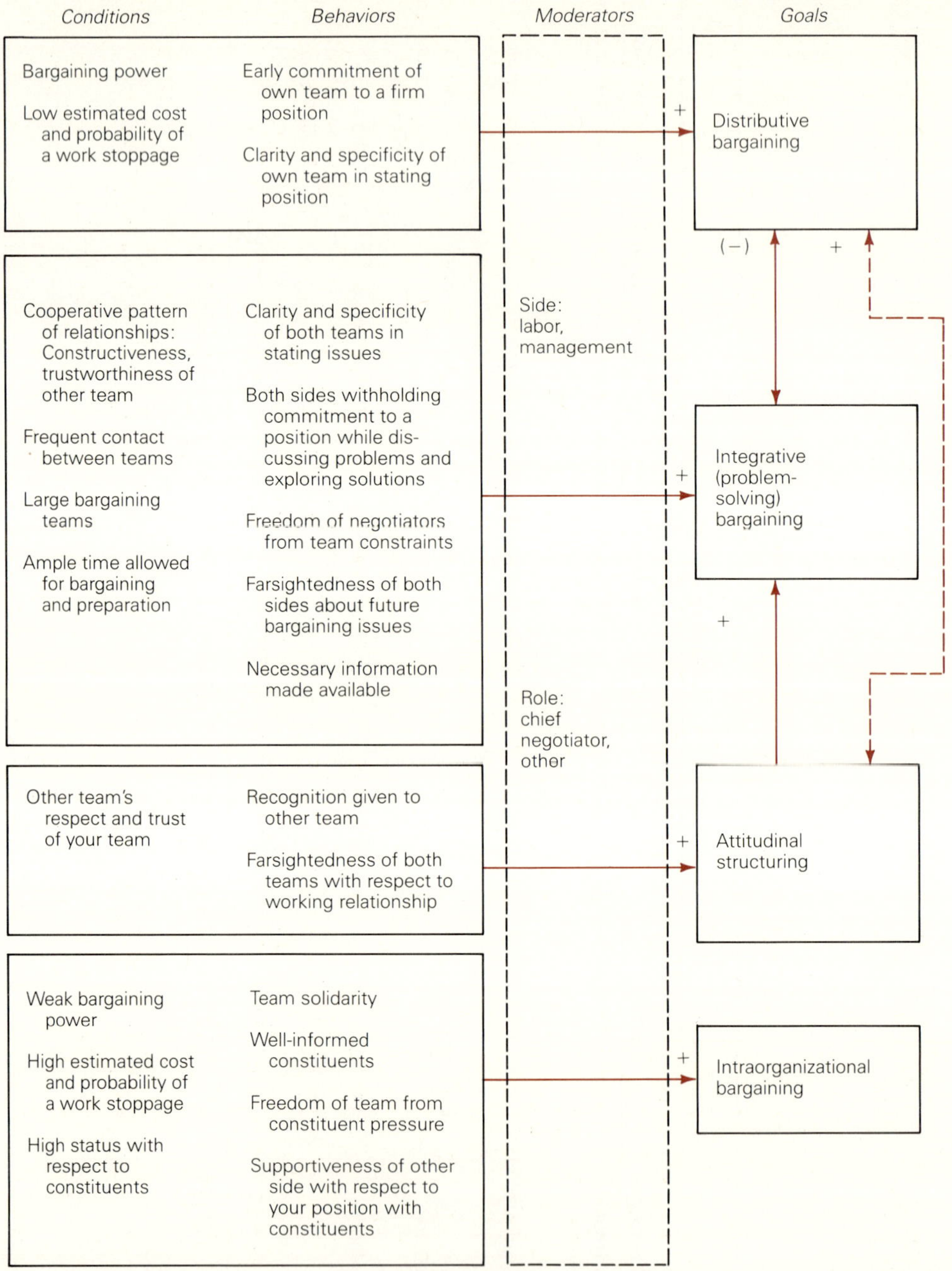

SOURCE: Richard B. Peterson and Lane Tracy, "Testing a Behavioral Theory Model of Labor Negotiations," *Industrial Relations*, February 1977, p. 37. Reprinted with permission.

Figure 11–5 FOUR TYPES OF BARGAINING

- Offering proposals that foreclose future negotiations, such as stating "This is our final, nonnegotiable offer"
- Imposing unreasonable conditions on bargaining, such as stating that it must be completed within the next two hours or it will cease
- Unilaterally changing conditions of employment, such as eliminating certain fringe benefits or performance of certain work, without consultation
- Procrastinating unreasonably in scheduling meetings or refusing to meet at all
- Bypassing the union representative and trying to negotiate directly with the union's members
- Committing unfair labor practices, such as threatening to close the plant if the union does not accept management's proposal

Figure 11–6 is a list of questions to assess whether good-faith bargaining is occurring.

In addition to bargaining in good faith, effective bargaining procedures include

- exchanging contract proposals well in advance of contract expiration;
- avoiding eleventh-hour bargaining (delaying bargaining until just before the contract is due to expire);
- using mediators when stalemates occur or seem likely;
- negotiating at the table, not in the press;
- fully understanding the implications of a strike before it occurs;
- considering possible alternatives before a strike occurs; and
- building respect, honesty, and credibility.[21]

Concluding the Negotiations

Concluding the negotiations involves finding the overlap between management's and union's demands. In the later stages of bargaining, each side knows clearly

Do the parties meet frequently enough?
Do the parties engage in "real" bargaining, as opposed to inflexibly adhering to their own demands?
Do the parties show a willingness to compromise?
Do the parties show a willingness to make proposals, demands, and counterproposals?
Do the parties avoid delays in scheduling meetings?
Do the parties avoid stipulating preconditions for reaching agreement?
Do the parties avoid Boulwarism?
Do the parties communicate offers to their members?
Do the parties avoid unilateral changes in bargaining areas that would prevent bargaining?
Do the parties offer proposals that encourage future discussions?
Do the parties deal with the representatives of the other side?
Do the parties avoid unfair labor practices?

Figure 11–6 **TESTS OF GOOD-FAITH BARGAINING**

what it is fundamentally seeking and how much it is willing to concede. Skilled negotiators who want to avoid a strike will remain flexible. They will attempt to create a pattern of agreement by trying to reach concord on each of a series of issues. Negotiators may formulate a series of packages and then work to select the most appropriate one. Management may establish alternative packages by *trading points;* that is, agreeing to one demand in return for a concession on another demand, or by making *counterproposals* that focus on compromise on several demands at once.

Recently unions have been asked to make concessions in the face of difficult economic times.[22] In return for concessions in wages, such as acceptance of a lower wage rate, union workers might obtain the following:

1. Symbolic improvements—management receives the same cuts as the union and pledges to consider union interests in the future.
2. Job security—no-layoff clauses are offered in exchange for wage reductions or work rule changes.
3. Implicit job security—management promises to limit *outsourcing,* that is, subcontracting certain parts of the manufacturing process to other companies.
4. Contingent compensation—improvements in future compensation are promised through stock ownership, profit sharing, or tying future pay to performance.
5. Participation in company decisions—union leaders join boards of directors and participate in organizational decision-making.
6. Union bargaining gains—management improves the bargaining relationship by providing the union with more information.[23]

Reading 11–2, "Concession Bargaining: The Time Is Now!," by John Falahee, examines the process of concession bargaining in greater detail.

The bargaining concludes with formal *ratification* of the agreement. Ratification votes show that the membership supports the action of the bargaining committee and indicate that the union has fairly represented its members. It typically involves members casting secret ballots regarding their acceptance or rejection of the agreement. A majority of the members of the State Nurses Union, United Food Workers, and Textile Workers of America described in the beginning of this chapter must vote in favor of the agreement. Most proposals are ratified on the first vote; about 10 percent are rejected by members. Rejection frequently leads to strikes.

BARGAINING ISSUES

What issues are the focus of negotiations in collective bargaining? They can be divided into three legal categories[24]:

1. *Mandatory issues*—wages, hours, and terms and conditions of employment; practices that have direct and immediate effects on union members' jobs
2. *Permissive issues*—issues that may be raised but do not require a response

because they lack a direct impact on the job, such as the placement of vending machines on shop floors

3. *Prohibited issues*—issues that are statutorily outlawed, such as the closed shop[25]

The issues can also be classified into five content categories: (1) wage issues, (2) economic supplements, (3) institutional issues, (4) administrative issues, and (5) production standards and staffing. Figure 11–7 provides examples of these five types of issues.

Ability, Definition of
Absence
Reporting of
With Leave
Without Leave
Arbitration
Bargaining Unit,
Definition of
Benefits, Employee
Funeral Pay
Glove, Hat, and Shoe Allowance
Jury Duty
Layoff Allowance
Nonoccupational Disability Pay
Occupational Disability Pay
Pension and Insurance
Vacation
Bidding
Bulletin Boards
Call-out
Definition of
Holiday
Regular
Seventh Consecutive Day, in P/R
Sixth Day Worked in Holiday Week
Change of Rate
Permanent
Temporary
Company Service Credit Rules
Contract
Duration
Purpose of
Termination
Differentials, Shift
Disability Pay Plans
Nonoccupational
Occupational
Discipline
Discharge
Unsatisfactory Attendance
Dues Deduction
Authorization Form
Duration
Withdrawal, Method and/or Date of
Funeral Pay
Glove Allowance
Grievances
General Committee
Procedure—General
Other
Discharge
and
Suspension
Job Rate
Establishment
Handicapped Employees
Hat Allowance
Health and Safety
Holidays and Holiday Pay
Hospitalization Agreement
Hours of Work
Insurance Plan
Interchange of Work
Job Classifications and Rate Schedule
Job Rate Establishment
Job Sequence Charts
Jury Duty Allowance
Layoff
Allowance Plan
Procedure
Recall after
Seniority Rights during
Temporary
Leave-of-Absence
General
Military
Seniority, Accumulation of
Service Credit, Accumulation of
Union Business
Lunch, Overtime
Maintenance of Union Membership
Management Rights
Master Overtime Agreement
Military Service
Nonoccupational Disability Pay
Occupational Disability Pay
Overtime
Daily
Distribution of
Lunch
Pyramiding of
Weekly
Pay
Call-out
For Grievance Meetings
Hiring
Holiday
Overtime
Progression
Rate Schedule
Report-in
Seventh Consecutive Day in Workweek
Shift Differential
Sixth Consecutive Day in Workweek
Sunday Premium

Figure 11–7 EXAMPLES OF BARGAINING ISSUES *Continued*

Pension Plan
Probationary Period
Progression
Rate Schedule
Recall
Recognition, Union
Rehire and Reinstatement
Company Service Credit
Rate of Pay
Seniority Rights
Vacation Eligibility
Safety and Health
Safety Shoes
Seniority
Application of
Bidding in
Curtailment in
Definition of
Departmental
Equality of
Handicapped Employees
Layoff during
Loss of
Plant
Recall after
Rehire after
Reinstatement after
Strike Notice during
Supervisors
Ties of
Veterans
Seventh Day, Overtime Pay for
Shift Differential
Shoe Allowance
Sixth Day, Overtime Pay for
Stewards
Strikes and Lockouts
General Provisions
Suspension
Temporary Change of Rate
Termination of Contract
Time and One-Half Pay
Transfers (Vacancies)
Out of Bargaining Unit
Pay Changes Because of
Temporary
Within Bargaining Unit
Transportation
Union
Bulletin Boards
Officials, Leave-of-Absence
Plant Visit of Business Representative
Recognition
Security
Vacancies
Permanent
Temporary
Vacation Plan
Voting Time
Wages (Pay)
Hiring Rate
Progression
Rate Schedule
Work
Conditions
Day, Basic
Hours of
Supervisors
Week, Basic

Figure 11–7 Continued

Wage Issues

The major issue addressed is wages. Both the State Nurses Union and the Textile Workers of America would likely focus negotiations on wage issues. The agreement should answer questions such as the following:

- What wages should each type of employee receive?
- Which employees should be hourly or salaried? Exempt or nonexempt?
- Will cost-of-living increases be granted automatically? How large will they be?
- Under what conditions can wage negotiations be reopened?
- Will workers receive additional pay for working night shifts, or doing hazardous or dirty work?
- What additional wages will workers receive if they work overtime? When does overtime start? At what rate is overtime paid?

Unions use three criteria in formulating pay demands (see Chapter 9 for discussion of pay and motivation): (1) equity for union members with regard to peers in comparable situations; (2) ability of the organization to pay; and (3) maintenance of workers' standard of living through increases that keep pace with inflation or other cost-of-living indicators.

Management may be particularly sensitive to the secondary consequences of *roll-up,* so-called—"the automatic increase in the cost of certain existing wage-related benefits that results from an increase in wages."[26] When wages increase 5 percent, proportional increases occur in overtime pay, shift pay, disability insurance when the benefit is a percentage of base pay, and the company's payment of social security tax. Both union and management must recognize the implications of wage increases when trying to reach an acceptable agreement.

With regard to wages, the contract might specify, for example, that the members of the Textile Workers of America receive a wage keyed to inflation. The visiting nurses can expect their contract negotiations to make very clear the amount and nature of pay they would receive for various types of nursing services. Figure 11–8 illustrates the components of the wage demand issue. Equity, the ability to pay, and standard of living are key determinants of the total wage demand.

Economic Supplements

In addition to wages, most collective bargaining agreements specify the benefits that workers receive (see Chapter 9). For example, the number of vacation days, holidays, personal days, and sick days with pay are subject to negotiation. Some unions may negotiate Lincoln's birthday as a holiday with pay; others may negotiate the Friday after Thanksgiving as a paid holiday.

Details about employer contributions to health insurance plans and pension plans are included in the contract. Some employers pay for comprehensive health insurance for the workers and their families; others pay a portion of individual health coverage. Details about pension plans include the extent to which the employer can and must contribute, the extent of employee contributions, and the length of time required before an individual becomes vested. Again, these areas are subject to negotiations and can be changed in subsequent contracts.

Some contracts also specify that a certain amount of pay will be received by workers who are dismissed or laid off. In the case of layoffs, many industries have introduced *supplemental employment benefits.* These provide wages and health benefits for workers for a specified amount of time after a layoff occurs.

Some union contracts include provisions that workers will earn *reporting pay*—money received if the company tells them not to report to work on a day they were normally scheduled to work. Again, all economic supplements are subject to collective bargaining.

Institutional Issues

These issues relate to union formation and membership, as well as the workers' responsibilities to the union. The agreement may specify the bargaining unit and the types of employees it represents. The contract typically grants the bargaining unit exclusive bargaining rights for all employees in the unit, regardless of whether they belong to the union.

Where there is a *union shop* the employer must make union membership a condition of employment. In right-to-work states (see Chapter 10) *agency shops* may exist; here union membership is not required. Employees who do not wish

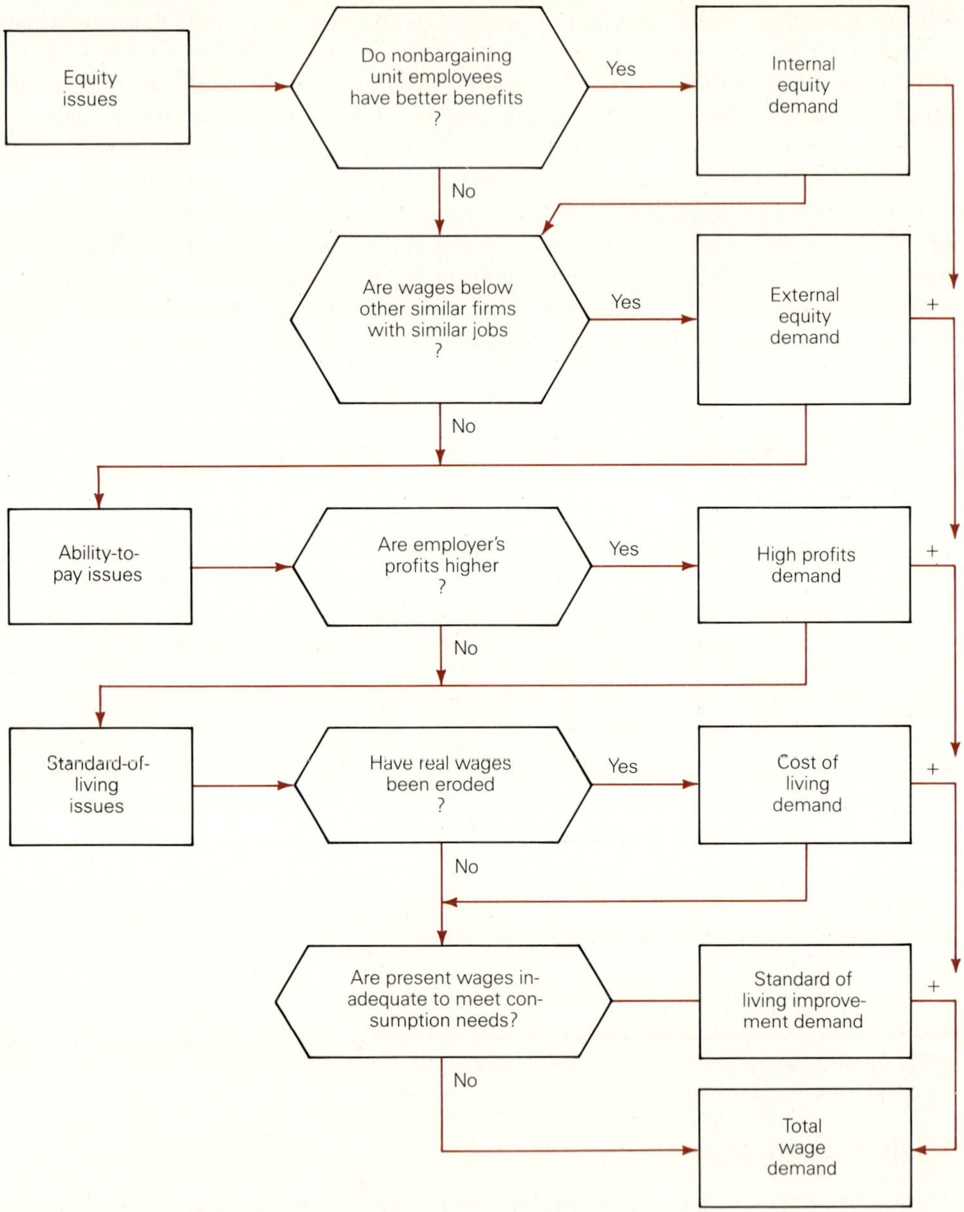

Reprinted with permission from *Labor Relations* Revised Edition (1982) by John A. Fossum. Homewood, Ill.: Richard D. Irwin, copyright 1982.

Figure 11–8 **WAGE DEMAND COMPONENTS**

to join or participate in union activities may instead pay the equivalent of the initiation fee and dues to the union.

In addition to specifying whether an individual has an obligation to join a union, some contracts also state whether union *checkoff* exists; that is, whether union dues will automatically be deducted from workers' paychecks. Unions want this provision to ensure that their members pay dues, and management can use it as a bargaining chip to obtain other provisions from the union.

Some unions also agree to a no-strike provision. In these cases, disagreements are resolved through arbitration or other grievance procedures (see Chapter 12). A few contracts also include provisions for workers to play a major role in organizational decision-making. Contracts negotiated at Chrysler Motor Company in the early 1980s provide that the president of the United Automobile Workers has a seat on the Board of Directors of the firm.[27]

Administrative Issues

These issues include policies regarding seniority, affirmative action, discharge and discipline, and safety and health in the workplace. To avoid favoritism in promotion, firing, or rehiring, seniority provisions call for decisions to be made on the basis of seniority, departmentally, occupationally, plant-wide, or organization-wide. In such provisions, employees are generally bumped from jobs according to least seniority and rehired in reverse order, most senior first. Lately, however, organizations have been asked to lay off more senior employees to maintain sufficient percentages of minorities in the work force. Recent court decisions have supported neutral seniority systems—those that do not intentionally discriminate—over affirmative action plans (see Chapter 13).[28]

Production Standards and Staffing

Contracts also focus on issues relating to staffing of work activities. These provisions are often used to resist the reduction in work force that accompanies automation. Some contracts state that employers must notify the union and its members of layoffs or shutdowns in advance, provide for the retraining of employees, and limit subcontracting. Increasingly, employers have agreed to shorter work weeks. The award of production incentives must also be specified in the labor contract.

PUBLIC SECTOR LABOR RELATIONS

Since the issuance of Executive Order 10988 by President John Kennedy in 1962, which allowed federal employees to unionize and specified the scope of bargaining, state and local governments have passed significant amounts of legislation directed at unionization and collective bargaining by public employees. Labor relations in the public sector differs somewhat from what has been described so far for the private sector.

Collective bargaining in the public sector, as in the private sector, involves the negotiation of a contract between workers and management for a specified period of time. But problems have arisen in identifying which individual has responsibility and accountability for representing the employer. Does a city's mayor, school committee, or superintendent of schools represent the taxpayers in negotiating with teachers? Is the governor or state legislature the employer of state workers?

Unions or employee associations also represent workers in the public sector. Originally, employee associations professed greater concern for the professional aspects of public employment, whereas unions expressed greater interest in wages, benefits, and working conditions; today the distinctions have blurred.[29] Larger unions include the American Federation of State, County, and Municipal Employees (AFSCME), which represents workers in diverse occupations; the American Federation of Government Employees (AFGE), which represents federal employees, and the American Federation of Teachers (AFT). The largest public employee association is the National Education Association (NEA).

Constituting a bargaining unit in the public sector can be complex. Should supervisors join a union? Should they join the same union as nonsupervisory workers? Many collective bargaining systems in the public sector must operate side by side with existing civil service systems. These regulate, to varying degrees, hiring, promotions, terminations, and compensation—traditional topics of collective bargaining. The Civil Service Reform Act of 1978, for example, forbids the negotiation of wages and position classifications of federal employees.[30]

Differences between the Public and Private Sectors

The major differences between public and private sector collective bargaining include the following:

1. The sovereignty doctrine calls for only unilateral action by an employer (the government) since a governmental source of law is final.
2. Vital public interest is often present in public sector bargaining.
3. Regulation and protection is greater for public sector employees.
4. Market constraints and employer mobility are less significant factors in the public sector.
5. Public employees can often influence the composition of the management side through elections since the political party in power fills many positions.[31]

Perhaps the most striking difference between the public and private sectors is that public employees frequently lack the right to strike. This denial has occurred because many public employees—police, firefighters, teachers, and garbage collectors—provide essential services, which are described in greater detail in the next section. Chapter 12 describes the use of mediation, fact-finding, and arbitration as ways of resolving impasses during collective bargaining in the public sector.

Enforcement Agencies

Title VII, Federal Service Labor-Management Relations Act, passed as part of the Civil Service Reform Act of 1978, established the Federal Labor Relations Authority (FLRA). Like its counterpart in the private sector, the NLRB, the FLRA oversees labor-management relations in the federal government. Responsibilities of the FLRA include filing and prosecuting unfair labor practice cases, conducting representation elections, and seeking enforcement of its decisions in the U.S. Circuit Court of Appeals. The FLRA protects the bargaining rights of federal employees while ensuring their fulfillment of their obligations to the public.

At the state and local levels, responsibility for overseeing labor relations varies. Some states establish penalties by legislation and rely on the executive and judicial branches to enforce them. Other states establish labor relations policies that call for mediation, fact-finding, or arbitration in given situations.

STRIKES, LOCKOUTS, WALKOUTS, AND SLOWDOWNS

What options are available to union and management when they cannot reach agreement? Unions can stop work by calling a strike or walkout. The visiting nurses might stop working if their union does not reach an agreement with the management of the Visiting Nurses Association. Likewise, management can stop their employees from working by locking them out.

A *strike* occurs when employees refuse to come to work until changes are made in compensation, hours, or conditions of work, or until a new collective bargaining agreement is reached.

A *walkout* occurs when workers leave the job while a workday is in progress to show dissatisfaction with existing conditions under a bona fide collective bargaining agreement. Walkouts can be short in duration (several hours) or turn into strikes.

Closely related to walkouts are two types of work actions designed to *slow down* the performance of work by union members who lack the legal right to strike. Police officers and firefighters have contracted the *blue flu,* named for the color of their uniforms and the type of illness they claimed to have. In this type of slowdown workers call in sick in large numbers on a prespecified day or days. Their absence is intended to paralyze the organization and thus obtain support from the public for their demands.

Teachers and other public-union members have used *work-to-rule* actions to support their demands. In these actions employees follow the rules of their contracts to the letter. Teachers, for example, may refuse to write recommendations, perform voluntary bus duty, or hold parent conferences outside the school hours designated in the contract. Their intent is to alert the community to all the "extras" they perform and obtain support for their contract demands. Unions in the public sector frequently lack the legal right to strike, reflecting the feeling that public safety must be guaranteed. These unions must resort to interest arbitration or mediation (see Chapter 12) to resolve a contract impasse.

A *lockout* occurs when an employer closes the plant or facility in which there is a labor dispute. Lockouts have become relatively uncommon due to the success of other approaches in reaching labor accords. Of the stoppages described in this chapter, strikes are the most common.

Reasons to Strike

Although workers do not have a constitutional right to collective action, the Wagner Act provides employees "the right . . . to engage in . . . concerted activities for the purpose of collective bargaining or other mutual aid or protection."[33] There is "nothing in this act . . . to interfere with or diminish in any way the right to strike."[34]

Workers undertake a strike when they feel that a work stoppage will cause the organization to concede to a bargaining demand. Often strikes occur when workers believe prolonged negotiations will never result in an agreement.

Why do workers strike? Workers strike when they feel that management is ignoring their needs or wants. Strikes do not always have to do with benefits or pay.[35] Table 11–5 lists the top reasons for striking in 1980 and 1981. Although

	Stoppages			
	1980		*1981*[a]	
Major Issue	Number	Percent	Number	Percent
General Wage Changes	2,601	66.9	1,442	65.8
Supplementary Benefits	79	2.0	43	2.0
Wage Adjustments	52	1.3	27	1.2
Hours of Work	9	0.0	6	0.3
Other Contractual Matters	204	5.3	101	4.6
Union Organization and Security	205	5.3	139	6.3
Job Security	202	5.2	117	5.3
Plant Administration	383	9.9	259	11.8
Other Working Conditions	55	1.4	25	1.1
Interunion or Intraunion Matters	65	1.7	27	1.2
Not Reported	30	0.8	5	0.2
Total	3,885		2,191	

SOURCE: Bureau of Labor Statistics, *News*, 29 January 1982. (Washington, D.C.: U.S. Department of Labor), p. 6. Reprinted by permission.

Table 11–5 TOP REASONS FOR STRIKING IN 1980 AND 1981

dissatisfaction with wages and benefits was the primary motivator, in the past decade increases in automation have shifted workers' concern to job security. In craft unions, workers may also be concerned with jurisdictional issues; for example, they may strike if employment of nonunion workers is encouraged.

The decision to strike is affected by the perceived costs of a strike to each side, the ability of union members to withstand the strike financially, the attitude of the community toward the strike, and the ability of the organization to operate without union members.[36] If workers' friends, relatives, and neighbors complain that a strike would disrupt their lives, workers are less likely to strike. If the workers can easily be replaced, a threat to strike would hold less bargaining weight than if workers were irreplaceable.[37] Management may decide to "take a strike" if it reasons that the costs of demands or the decline in management's flexibility associated with the demands exceeds the cost of the strike.

Both unions and employers prepare for strikes. The union must make sure that most or all members of the bargaining unit participate in the strike. It organizes picket lines to keep the strike effective and provides financial support for the strikers. The employer must prepare for operations during the strike by training supervisors or new hires to perform the strikers' jobs. Or management may hire new, nonunion workers to replace strikers. Known as *scabs,* these individuals frequently must cross picket lines designed to discourage their entry into the plant or work site. If the community supports the union cause, the use of scabs is a less viable option than if the community does not condone the union's stance. Management must also consider the impact of picket lines on distribution of goods and services. Some unions have agreed, for example, not to cross picket lines of sister unions, thus preventing deliveries of supplies.

The Strike Vote and the Strike

During the early stages of negotiation union leaders frequently take a strike vote. This action is designed to strengthen the union's hand. Management usually treats this threat as a bluff and may challenge the union by assuring it that the company can withstand a strike.

Strike votes taken at later times during negotiation may be used to indicate union members' sentiments about the progress of bargaining. These votes strengthen the union's position until the union presents an ultimatum to management.

The last vote to strike typically occurs near or after the expiration of a contract (in the case of an initial agreement the vote may hinge around a deadline promised or stated by the union or management). If progress toward agreement continues, even in the face of a deadline, the union will most likely postpone the final strike vote.

Different unions react differently during strikes. Where the striking laborers are irreplaceable, the workers' best strategy is to wait for management to concede. Occasionally management will lock out employees of a union that has struck another member of an employer association.

Industrial unions typically cannot wait for management to concede; rather, they use *political* methods, such as gathering community support for their cause and against the use of nonunion replacement, to increase the impact of a strike.[38] In manufacturing organizations, for example, the union attempts to control physical access to the plant as a way of halting production by preventing materials from entering, and finished goods from leaving, the plant.

Beginning a strike involves the following steps:

1. Union leaders call the workers off the job.
2. The union shuts down the plant by ensuring that shift workers do not report.
3. The union tries to keep workers and possible replacements from going to work.[39]

The union uses a *picket line*—a group of union members who walk back and forth in front of the plant—to remind people about the strike and discourage them from entering the facility. Mass picketing effectively blocks the entrance to the facility, but it is illegal[40]; so-called peaceful picketing, which is less intense and more orderly, may in fact lead to greater violence because strikebreakers can cross the picket line and intensify the negative attitudes of the strikers.

Consequences of Strikes

Although a strike can encourage union and management to rapidly solve areas of disagreement about a contract or its implementation, more often it has less functional economic and psychological consequences for both union and management. Studies of the cost of strikes indicate that lost profits "represent only the tip of an iceberg."[41] Prestrike costs include productivity loss during contract negotiations and lost purchases when customers discover a strike might occur. Costs during the strike include lost profits and executive time. Longer term costs include loss of trained employees, overtime expense, loss of customers, and lowered sales effort.[42] Additional costs may include sabotage, arbitration, plant closing, and duplication of equipment and staff in a second plant.[43] Some estimates placed the total costs at $200 to $300 per worker-day in 1979 dollars; today they would be significantly higher.[44]

Because of the cost of strikes to organizations, some industries have formulated mutual aid pacts as a way of providing insurance against them. In the airline, railroad, and newspaper industries, mutual aid pacts have succeeded in reducing the cost of strikes.[45] These pacts are private, formal agreements between cooperating employers to help them withstand a strike through the payment of benefits by nonstruck employers to struck employers. When some airlines were struck in the 1970s, they received revenue from other operating airlines that approximated their lost receipts. Because of the cost of these plans, however, many of them have been discontinued.[46]

Costs of the strike to workers include more than wages lost during the duration of the strike. Employees run the risk of losing their jobs in the short and long term. Even if workers are reinstated after the strike, management may have learned that the organization can function with fewer employees and ultimately reduce the size of the work force.

Strategies for Avoiding and Settling Strikes

The major way of avoiding strikes is for both parties to begin negotiations early enough to allow time to reach agreement, bargain in good faith, and compromise.

The 1970s saw a decline in the number of strikes because of the declining economy: unions faced a choice between accepting a less-desirable agreement or losing their jobs, replacement labor was easy to find, and the prospect of unemployment was threatening. The increased ability of companies to operate during strikes; unfavorable consumer response; increasingly complex issues that prevented eleventh-hour settlements, and threats of long-term retaliation of management (such as through mutual aid pacts) also contributed to the reduction.[47] A major strategy for resolving strikes already begun is the use of arbitration, described in Chapter 12.

LABOR RELATIONS ABROAD

Unionization and collective bargaining is not limited to the United States. Canada, Western Europe, Eastern Europe, and Japan, for example, have equally strong labor relations systems. But these systems differ from the United States' in labor's ties to political parties, trade unions' representation of political, philosophical, or economic ideologies, relationships between union and management, the existence of formal collective bargaining agreements, and the nature of the laws that govern labor relations.

In Canada, for example, three major factors influence labor relations.[48] First, the large number of United States corporations with divisions in Canada results in labor decisions frequently being made in the U.S.; such decisions may be less representative of Canadian workers' needs, resulting in worker discontent. Second, the bilingualism and biculturalism (French and English) of Canada have exacerbated the often-adversarial relationship between labor (often French-speaking) and management (often English-speaking). Third, labor regulations and control of union activities have been placed under the authority of the provinces, rather than centralized under the national government.[49] This has resulted in a lack of coordinated control and large numbers of local disruptions, since agreements tend to be between one union and one organization only.

Labor relations in Western Europe and Great Britain differ from those in both the United States and Canada.[50] Unions lack the exclusive representation of workers; as a consequence, employers bargain with a number of unions, not just the legally certified one. Representatives of employer associations, rather than a single employer, frequently conduct negotiations with representatives of an association of unions. Also, labor has closer ties to political parties than in the United States.

In Great Britain, almost one-half of the workers are unionized. However, collective bargaining is voluntary and strikes, either official or unofficial, are more frequent.[51] No system of laws regulates union-management interactions.

In other Western European countries, such as Sweden and Germany, worker participation in decision-making through work councils or representation on company boards of directors is more common than here (discussed in Chapter 14). Legislation in these countries governs the participation.

Eastern European labor relations are closely linked to the dominant political party—the Communist party. Trade unions represent all employees—approximately 90 percent of the population.[52] Union members have extensive duties, few rights, and cannot meet without the permission of union officials.[53] The trade unions encourage worker productivity and disciplining workers; they also politically indoctrinate them through education and raising their political consciousness.[54] Poland's Solidarity Union has recently received extensive publicity because of its leaders' attempts to reduce the Communist party's control of trade unions and increase the workers' freedom to strike and their freedom of speech.[55] Relationships between the union and the government remain stormy.

Japanese industrial relations, in contrast to all the systems discussed so far, emphasizes the life-time employment of workers and the formation of company-sponsored unions. These characteristics typically result in less antagonism between labor and management than elsewhere. In addition, wage policies that link pay to seniority rather than to skill, and offer pay in the form of salaries reduce the distinctions between workers and management. Unions in Japan use pattern bargaining: during the Spring Shunto, workers publicly demonstrate their contract demands,[56] and then one union takes the lead and negotiates a new contract that acts as the pattern for subsequent negotiations. Recent challenges to the traditional system, such as increased automation, a decline of worker loyalty to the organization, higher unemployment, and the elimination of automatic pay increases, may ultimately inspire changes in the Japanese labor relations system.[57]

IMPROVING THE COLLECTIVE BARGAINING PROCESS

The goal of collective bargaining is to reach a contract acceptable to both union and management. Human resources professionals can contribute to effective negotiations by regularly implementing effective human resources practices and gathering information about likely bargaining issues. Managers can contribute by scouting their subordinates' needs and preferences, as well as establishing a positive working environment.

Implications for Human Resources Professionals

Human resources professionals often represent the organization in collective bargaining. They are responsible for monitoring the existing agreement and gathering data for use in revising it. More specifically,

1. Human resources professionals must know the provisions of the current contract and the laws that affect the collective bargaining practice. They can act as resources to other managers about the legality of managerial or employee actions.
2. Human resources professionals can advise management on the process of local negotiations and the content of resulting agreements. They must be experts on local unions—they should know the leaders, their way of operating, and their concerns.
3. Human resources professionals can organize training for foremen or managers of unionized employees about ways to build support for the collective bargaining agreement. They can then implement the training and evaluate its outcomes.
4. Human resources professionals can negotiate for the organization at the local or even national level. They must prepare for negotiations aggressively and completely.
5. Human resources professionals should research present concerns and predict future issues. They can advise management about ways to deal with these concerns in advance of the negotiations.

Implications for Managers

Managers must inform the organization's negotiators of their perceptions of employees' needs and monitor the implementation of the present contract. To do so effectively they should act as follows:

1. Managers must know contract provisions so that they can conform to them; they must try to maintain good (or at least nonadversarial) relations with the union, its leaders, and members.
2. Managers should measure productivity and assess which contract provisions contribute to or hinder performance. They should feed back this information regularly to those who represent management in negotiations.
3. Managers should regularly provide management with data about workers' needs and any changes in these needs. In so doing, they might help management's negotiators anticipate demands the union will make.
4. Managers should monitor the ability of individual workers to withstand a strike so that they can provide data to management about the possibility of strike and its likely duration. They should develop strategies for withstanding strikes in their own group, department, or division.

READINGS

Reading 11–1

GUIDELINES FOR PRODUCTIVE NEGOTIATING RELATIONSHIPS

Johanna Hunsaker, Phillip Hunsaker, and Nancy Chase

The Any Occasion Card Company is preparing to print its latest line of Christmas greeting cards. In the past, the sale of Christmas cards has accounted for half of the company's annual gross revenues.

This year Any Occasion Card Company's three-year contract with the Printer's Union is up for renewal. Negotiations are currently underway but progress has halted because agreement cannot be reached regarding three new requests that the printers are asking for:

1. $1.50, 1.00, .50 per hour, respectively, wage rate increases over the next three years, on top of their present $5.00/hour wage rate;
2. a reduction in working hours from five eight-hour days to five seven-hour days;
3. a change in vacation policy from: two weeks for up to 10 years employment, three weeks for up to 20 years, four weeks after 20 years to: two weeks for up to five years employment, three weeks for up to 15 years, four weeks after 15 years.

Any Occasion Card Company currently offers 10 company paid holidays: Memorial Day, Independence Day, Labor Day, Thanksgiving Day, three days at Christmas and two at New Years and employees have birthdays off.

Any Occasion Card Company's chief competitor, the across-town firm of Every Occasion Cards, Ltd., has just settled its three-year contract with the printer's union, but only after company management threatened to hire non-union printers if a strike occurred. The printers at Every Occasion Cards finally agreed to the present $5.00/hour wage rate being increased by $1.00, .75, .50/hour, respectively, over the next three years. Their work week was reduced from five eight-hour days to four nine-hour days. Their earned vacation rate remains the same: two weeks for up to 10 years employment, three weeks for up to 20 years, and four weeks after 20 years. However, Every Occasion has increased its paid company holidays from 10 to 15: Memorial Day, Independence Day, Labor Day, Thanksgiving Day and the Friday following, plus two weeks off during the Christmas/New Year period.

Any Occasion Card Company management and the printer's union have not yet reached a contract settlement. The contract expires at midnight tonight, and the union has threatened to strike if a contract is not agreed on before expiration of the old one. It is now 10:55 p.m. and final negotiations are scheduled to begin in 15 minutes.

Reprinted from the March, 1981 issue of *Personnel Administrator*, copyright, 1981, The American Society for Personnel Administration, 606 North Washington Street, Alexandria, VA 22314, $30 per year.

WHY WAIT FOR A CRISIS?

The Any Occasion Card Company's situation is not unusual. A relatively straightforward contract negotiation has reached a crisis predicament, probably because of skill deficiencies on the parts of the negotiating parties. With increasing needs for autonomy and the surfacing of more complex human needs considerations by workers, managers and personnel administrators need updated skills in handling negotiations. This is especially true when negotiation is defined broadly to include any transaction between two parties where the intent is to resolve a conflict.

Negotiations occur at all levels of human interactions among friends to events of worldwide importance. The individuals involved in negotiation may be representing themselves, a group, or an entire organization. This article describes the characteristics of negotiations, strategies for facilitating productive outcomes and a case, role-play exercise for use as a negotiations training vehicle.

KEY CHARACTERISTICS OF NEGOTIATION

As can be derived from the Any Occasion Card case every negotiation involves at least *two parties* who have met to resolve a *conflict* between them. The parties have come together voluntarily because they are partially dependent on one another and each stands to gain more by participating in the sequential, give-and-take negotiation process than abdicating their rights or attempting power tactics *(Rubin & Brown, 1975)*.

Ignorance is another critical factor in the negotiating relationship. If a fair and equal settlement for all parties were known prior to the negotiation, there would be no call to hold it. The complete knowledge of all involved would preclude anyone from asking for more than a fair share *(Swingle, 1970, p. 47)*. Since some degree of ignorance is most often the case, the opening demands of negotiators are usually quite high and decline to more modest levels as more complete information is obtained. An unawareness of this strategy to offset ignorance, quite often found in a negotiation with lower expectations, almost guarantees a less-than-equitable solution.

This partial or total ignorance of the true interests of the negotiators requires an *information exchange*. The mistrust implicit in this exchange makes the skilled negotiator a master in "the handling of other people's mistrust" *(Nierenberg, 1968, p. 4)*.

Although there are many strategies employed in negotiations, some are better than others. Flexibility in strategy is important so that participants take advantage of opportunities not anticipated originally. Keep in mind that a negotiation that deteriorates to the game stage will most likely fail. A successful negotiation means everyone wins.

GUIDELINES FOR PRODUCTIVE NEGOTIATING

Integrity, trust and openness are necessary for the creation of win-win situations. These conditions are impossible when a competitive atmosphere exists and high degrees of skepticism exist. Recognition of the opponent's competence and point of view can help establish the cooperative atmosphere needed for a productive negotiating relationship. Following are guidelines for establishing a productive and satisfying negotiating relationship.

1. *Recognize assumptions* made by both negotiators concerning each other. Some of the information gathered about the other party is bound to lead to assumptions. They should be treated as such and separated from what is known to be fact. Of course, some assumptions are necessary as a starting point for negotiations, but disasters can occur when all assumptions are taken as being true. Assumptions can be valuable tools but any action based on them has a certain risk factor. The hardest assumptions to recognize are those that are hidden or caused by misinterpreting given information. They interfere with listening and the consequential loss of otherwise valuable information *(Nierenberg, 1968)*.

2. The negotiator should always enter a negotiation with an *open mind*. Preconceived ideas tend to block the creativity essential in negotiating. All individuals to be dealt with in negotiating are different and the negotiator must make appropriate adjustments. It helps to keep in mind that rational behavior is relative to the situation at hand.

3. Negotiation should aim toward the *satisfaction of the needs of all the parties* involved. Dealing with an individual representing an organization in a negotiation means confronting his or her individual needs as well as the organization's. Appreciation of the individual's needs leads to their satisfaction and ease in handling the organization's own needs. All parties stand a better chance of maximizing their gains and reaching an agreement if they are able to anticipate and satisfy the needs of others. A win/lose situation is not a true negotiation.

4. The sequential *give and take* of negotiation should be emphasized to underline the importance of compromise. The other party should not be cornered and pressed into agreement. Being overly cooperative, however, could find all parties losing if they concentrate on satisfying the other's needs and not properly presenting and clarifying their own *(Rubin and Brown, 1975)*.

5. The agenda is the guiding force behind the information exchange involved in any negotiation. It determines what will be discussed and in what order. No one party in a negotiation should be allowed to have complete control of the agenda and its content should have mutual agreement prior to its implementation *(Karrass, 1974)*.

6. Two dilemmas are encountered in the information flow of negotiation: the dilemma of trust and the dilemma of honesty and openness *(Rubin and Brown, 1975)*. Trust is needed among negotiating parties to bring about an information flow through effective communication, but the question remains about how open one should be. It does not pay to show the other party all of your cards when he or she is not responding likewise. An information exchange should be a two-way street making negotiation a sequential activity. The initial discussions reveal much regarding each party's tendency to cooperate. The degree of openness manifest in later exchanges will demonstrate each party's perception of the other and whether the needed trust is present.

7. By remaining emotionally detached, danger signals from the other can be more easily detected, allowing the negotiation to be redirected to the facts. Keeping the pace slow can help. Rushing increases the chances of over-involvement and may head the process in a negative direction with little chance of recovery.

8. Paying attention by listening and observing for clues to changes in attitudes can provide valuable information. Interruptions should also be avoided so that important information won't be lost. Finally, be aware of gestures, tone of voice, facial expressions and other key non-verbal forms of communication. They are the media of many key communications *(Hunsaker & Alessandra, 1980)*. Paying attention is a must for understanding the other and behaving effectively when you are on the receiving end of a question that requires a correct response.

9. When other strategies are failing in a negotiation, a much better tactic than threats would be *promises*. A promise can have a positive impact similar to that of a concession. The amount of conviction perceptible in the promise governs the opponent's reactions and could lead to concessions on his or her part and further progress towards mutual agreement.

10. Properly phrased questions can be a powerful negotiating tool. Their primary use is to lend clarity to the negotiating session. They should be sincere and not a device to lead the other party into a corner. As in other forms of communication used in negotiation, the intent of a question is to learn of the opponent's true needs and interests. Good judgment in questioning means knowing how, what and when to ask. A straightforward question can aid all parties by possibly revealing new information and insight.

11. Affirmative statements can have a calming influence during the negotiating session. Phrasing, tone of voice and choice of words are special considerations. By maintaining an unemotional tone throughout the discussion of a difficult negotiating point, it may be possible to continue the information flow through affirmative statements and avoid an impasse situation. Making the other aware of his or her gains can also help shift an apparently rigid position.

12. Time is a very important consideration in the negotiating process. "If it did not matter when the parties agreed, it would not matter whether or not they agreed at all" *(Cross, 1969, p. 13)*. When the negotiation is between organizations, a lengthy negotiation could prove to be very costly.

In addition, a steadily dwindling relationship may call for a change of direction and the timing of such a change would be crucial. Any change presented by a negotiator to an opponent also needs time to be accepted.

13. The essence of successful negotiations is cooperation. Any succession of moves toward agreement can only be made through cooperation. In striving to reach mutually acceptable solutions, everyone must win. A win/lose finale rarely brings an end to the negotiating issue. Only a cooperative win/win solution is the long-lasting type.

14. As a negotiator, you must know yourself. Ignorance of your personal needs and behaviors is a crucial factor contributing to stalemates and hard feelings in negotiations. For example, negotiators with low self-esteem may be overly competitive in order to prove themselves, or negotiators with a high need for power may use exploitative moves. Because of the "self-ignorance" factor, negotiators should seek feedback on their own behavior in order to gain self-insight and develop strategies for increased interpersonal effectiveness.

15. Finally, the negotiator should be prepared. This factor includes much more than gathering factual information and understanding rules and regulations. It means investigating the other party's needs, styles and incentives. Investigation of past negotiations may reveal comparable situations and provide an understanding of these factors. The information gathered may also give clues to predicting the other party's reactions to situations which may occur during the negotiation.

In better knowing yourself in preparation for negotiation, you should act out the negotiation in advance. With the help of others, you should play both roles. Traits that interfere with negotiating ability, such as not listening carefully, may be uncovered. The insights that are gained to the opponent's side would allow thought to be given to what solutions may be acceptable and what possible compromises could be made.

NEGOTIATION ROLE PLAY

The following role play has been developed to provide negotiators with an opportunity to assess and improve their negotiation skills. It is based on the Any Occasion Card Company presented at the first of this article. The role play scenario follows.

This exercise may be effectively conducted with from three to 15 participants. All participants should be thoroughly familiar with the Any Occasion Card Company case. A mediator for the negotiation should be chosen from the participants. The remainder of the participants should divide into two groups: 1) Any Occasion Card Company management group; and 2) a union group. Each group should select a negotiator to represent it in the upcoming session. The remaining group members will act as observers during the negotiating session.

The mediator will utilize the 15-minute preparation time to become familiar with the negotiating items and develop an agenda for the negotiating session. There will be a 10-minute break during the negotiating session to allow the negotiators to hold a caucus with their respective group. The mediator's role in the session will be to direct the negotiation to the agenda items and keep notes on any agreements.

The two groups participating in the session will use their preparation time to decide on positions to take on the negotiating items, including acceptable limits for agreement, alternative solutions and possible compromises. They should also spend some time making assumptions about the other group's possible stances on the negotiating issues.

NEGOTIATING SESSION

The mediator should present the negotiating session agenda he or she has prepared and proceed to conduct the session accordingly. This negotiation continues for 20 minutes. Then there is a 10-minute break, followed by a final 20-minute time period to conclude negotiations. The observers should take notes during the session of such things as:

1. How clear are the goals of each negotiator to the other?
2. How effective is the communication?
3. Is there a spirit of cooperation or competition?
4. Are concessions being made equally by both sides?
5. Do the negotiators seem trustful of each other?

At the end of negotiations, a discussion should be conducted by the entire training group. Observers should report their observations including the suggested questions and other relevant observations. Other points of discussion for the entire group are:

1. How accurate were the assumptions made by both sides about each other?
2. Did the negotiators reevaluate assumptions which were proved incorrect?
3. How much empathy was shown between the negotiators as to the other side's needs?
4. Was the agenda easy to follow?
5. Which agenda items were/were not agreed upon and why?
6. What transpired during the caucus?
7. Was the negotiation a win/lose or a win/win exercise?

EXERCISE SUMMARY

The negotiation exercise began with both sides on an equal footing—management needed the printers at this critical time of their business year, but could consider going outside the union if necessary and the union could go on strike and hurt the company, but they could be risking losing their jobs and hence income during the holidays. Each group was partially dependent on the other to gain their objectives, but this dependency also had an element of ignorance in that it was not known how far each group would go in obtaining their objectives. The comparison of the settlement at Every Occasion Cards, Ltd., with the demands of the Any Occasion Card Company printer's union suggested possible negotiating agreements and at the same time forced management and union officials to make assumptions as to the true interests of each other.

REFERENCES

Cross, John G., *The Economics of Bargaining.* New York: Basic Books, Inc., 1969.

Hunsaker, Phillip L., and Alessandra, Anthony J., *The Art of Managing People,* Englewood Cliffs, NJ: Spectrum Books, 1980.

Karrass, Chester L., *Give and Take.* New York: Thomas Y. Crowell Co., 1974.

Nierenberg, Gerald I., *The Art of Negotiating.* New York: Hawthorne Books, Inc., 1968.

Rubin, Jeffrey Z., and Brown, Bert R. *The Social Psychology of Bargaining and Negotiation.* New York: Academic Press, 1975.

Swingle, Paul G. (Editor), *The Structure of Conflict.* New York: Academic Press, 1970.

DISCUSSION QUESTIONS

1. What are the key characteristics of negotiation?
2. Offer guidelines for productive negotiating.
3. Think of a recent negotiation in which you were a participant. Did you follow the guidelines for productive negotiations in that situation? How could your performance as a negotiator have been improved?

Reading 11–2

CONCESSION BARGAINING: THE TIME IS NOW!

John Falahee

The wage-price spiral that has plagued the American economy for decades is coming to an end. Unions and their membership are listening and yielding to economic realities. Everybody is responding—automotive original equipment manufacturers, suppliers, trucking companies, airlines, the retail food industry, etc. In light of the happenings in industry today, all employers should ask themselves these hard questions: Why not my business? Am I passing a golden opportunity?

This article examines the process of concession bargaining and its likely outcomes. This type of negotiating, though not essentially different from normal collective bargaining, has some special considerations and techniques. The process includes establishing the rationale for reopening the current agreement, timing, special proposals, union concerns and areas for mutual agreement.

WHY BARGAIN?

The essence of successful concession bargaining is the development of mutual trust and respect by the parties involved. The company has to be the moving party in the negotiations and this role reversal must be understood and appreciated to begin the process. In this instance the company makes demands and the union counterproposes. The union has to be convinced of the need to give up what it's gained through years of difficult contract negotiations. The current agreement is a living document and can be changed.

The first step in bringing about concessions is to examine carefully and realistically why the company must have concessions. The most basic reason is the survival of the business. If this is demonstrated convincingly, the bargaining task is made more simple, but it still must be done correctly to maximize gains. Proving the need for concessions takes many forms: lay-offs, personnel reductions and temporary shutdowns; documented customer pressure asking for price concessions; and/or documented loss of contracts or business because of price.

Obviously, losing money is the ultimate proof. If this is your tactic, be prepared to open your books. Fear, distrust, exposure of pricing policy and family secrets and simple reluctance always well up in any manager's mind when faced with this union demand. In reality, these concerns aren't pertinent. The usual method is to agree on an objective third-party profes-

Reprinted from the January, 1983 issue of *Personnel Administrator,* copyright, 1983, the American Society for Personnel Administration, 606 North Washington Street, Alexandria, VA 22314, $30 per year.

sional accountant to verify the economic condition of the company since the union committee isn't qualified for this task and shouldn't be allowed to see the details.

FINANCIAL OBJECTIVES SHOULD BE KEPT IN MIND

Preparation of a complete proposal is important. The first requisite is to determine, through the financial analysis of lost bid proposals, the amount of economic relief needed to obtain profitable business and stabilize employment. Always keep this overall financial objective in mind and make it an integral part of your initial proposal. How the company and the union finally agree to arrive at the full number can vary. The company must remain flexible and open to union suggestions. The total objective must be realized and the pieces or way to get there shouldn't be controlling.

Analyze the present agreement clause by clause to generate cost saving proposals. Generally, elimination of pay for time not worked is more palatable to employees rather than outright wage reductions. Contract provisions to be especially studied for this type of relief are:

1. **Vacation pay.** Lengthening service or work time requirements and shortening length of time off are usually acceptable.
2. **Holiday pay.** Elimination of paid personal holidays or lowering the number of general days granted generates savings and more production time with fewer employees.
3. **Break periods.** Eliminate or shorten rest periods and wash-up time to produce relief but not in direct ratio to minutes saved. Productive output is more often merely spread over the extra time. Breaks are very necessary in some operations, so approach proposals in this area cautiously.
4. **Non-productive down time and classification inflexibility.** Propose work be done for all time paid so a productive effort is given even when the standard job is not operating because of irregularities. This can eliminate indirect labor costs in custodial or quality control areas.
5. **Pension benefits.** This is a complex area. There are real cash flow benefits to be realized from changing assumptions and delaying or postponing contributions. Changing from a defined benefit plan to defined contributions or, even better, a profit sharing plan, will shift the costs to more profitable times and not hold corporate assets hostage.
6. **Insurance program.** Benefit amount, timing and deductibles can be changed to save considerable costs in this area. Pay particular attention to health, medical, sickness and accident coverages, which are most costly. Pay for extended coverage on layoff, leave of absence and retirement can be eliminated or paid by employees. Preserve flexibility to change carriers to obtain premium reductions.
7. **Seniority provisions.** Streamline bidding and bumping procedures to eliminate excessive turmoil and retraining. Ensure assignment of qualified, experienced personnel to jobs to maintain peak efficiency.
8. **Overtime assignment.** Provide for only qualified people to work and eliminate unnecessary make-work assignments.
9. **Bonus payments.** Eliminate or reduce extra payments.
10. **Wages.** Consider eliminating or suspending future increases and cost-of-living allowances. If this doesn't achieve your economic objective, propose a wage reduction. Reductions of over $1 per hour have been approved in many companies.

NEGOTIATIONS

The timing and length of the actual negotiations vary with the local situation; however, concession negotiations are rarely as long or arduous as normal negotiations. Usually an intense period of a week to 10 days is all that is required. Request a meeting with the union to discuss the overall economic condition of the company. During this meeting demand a reopening of the contract and present your total proposal. Give the union time to thoroughly study the proposal and your reasons for it. Emphasize the urgency of need and welcome their ideas and approaches to solving the problems. Problem-solving, not prerogative or confrontational bargaining must be initiated. Joint respect and cooperation are key. Both parties must keep the rank and file members informed so ratification of the new pact is assured.

The union must respond even if it declines renegotiation of the contract. It must then accept the responsibility for jobs lost or operation shut down. Most likely, the negotiations will commence tentatively to reach an agreement. The union will look for job guarantees, equality of sacrifice by the officers and non-union employees (a reasonable request if the entire organization is to survive). Profit-sharing will be high on the union's list so the good is shared with the bad. The company negotiators must remain flexible and open to other solutions. The total economic objective is important, not the details or specific elements of the package.

Many creative and extraordinary solutions to economic recovery have been negotiated. Besides profit-sharing and specific job guarantees, new and innovative savings plans are now in place. Concessions in all areas of wages and benefits, as well as elimination of restrictive contract clauses have been won. Guard against reopeners and try to provide profit level triggers to improve or restore benefits when economically feasible.

There is no risk to concession bargaining when properly conducted. The result of failure is that your current agreement continues. Any improvement from that is a gain. The least gain is to learn the real concerns of the work force and whether there is any solution to the economic problem other than liquidation of the company. That, in itself, might be a real plus. Prepare carefully and be rewarded with a cooperative, resourceful work force building a stronger, more stable business.

DISCUSSION QUESTIONS

1. What is an effective procedure for concession bargaining?
2. What issues could be included in concession bargaining?
3. What are the likely outcomes of concession bargaining?

ACTIVITIES

Activity 11–1

ELECTRICAL WORKERS AND THE HIGH TECHNOLOGY COMPANY

Step 1: Read the Electrical Workers and the High Technology Company case.

Step 2: Prepare the case for class discussion.

The Electrical Workers Union and the High Technology Corporation have been negotiating their first contract on and off for three months. The negotiations have been difficult and strained. During this period, the parties have agreed to many aspects of the contract, including medical benefits and union representation. Negotiations about the following issues remain:

Issues	*Present Positions*	
	Management	*Union*
Wages	5% increase first year 4% increase second year 4% increase third year	10% increase first year 8% increase second year 8% increase third year
Cost of Living Allowance	8% cap	No cap
Layoff	Job seniority	Plant-wide seniority
Contract Reopener	No reopener	Inflation above 6%
Third Shift	No premium pay	25% premium pay

One hour remains before the strike deadline. The Electrical Workers Union has stated that the deadline is firm.

Step 3: Discussion. Individually, in small groups, or with the entire class, as directed by your instructor, answer the following questions:

1. What areas of disagreement are there between union and management?
2. How should union and management prepare for the bargaining?
3. What approach should they take to the bargaining?
4. What will be the key bargaining issues?
5. What other packages might union propose? Management?
6. What factors will determine whether a strike will occur?

Activity 11–2

OAKLAND MANUFACTURING CORPORATION

Step 1: Read the Oakland Manufacturing Corporation case.

From T. Kennedy and J.H. Stamm, *Cases in Labor Relations*. Copyright Sherborn-Exeter Company.

Step 2: Prepare the case for class discussion.

In February of 1981 Local 421 of the United Auto Workers (UAW) notified Oakland Manufacturing Corporation (OMC) that the local wished to renegotiate the parties' collective bargaining agreement which was due to expire on Friday, April 24, 1981. The company's Personnel Manager, Mr. Robert Hills, was hired in late 1978, a few months after that agreement had been negotiated. Although he had dealt with the union President, J.J. Shaver, during the last two years over grievances and other labor-management problems, the renegotiation of the agreement would constitute their first encounter across the bargaining table. They each set about preparing with their respective bargaining committees for these important negotiations.

I. COMPANY HISTORY

Oakland Manufacturing Corporation was founded in 1915 in Battle Creek, Michigan to machine parts for various industries including the young automotive industry. OMC was acquired by Precision Motor Parts in 1927 after which it began to specialize in machining camshafts. A midwestern company purchased OMC in 1931 and continued ownership until 1952 when the firm was bought by an individual investor, Mr. R.J. Phillips, who took over as President of the firm.

During the early 1960s Oakland purchased some other, unrelated businesses in an attempt to emulate the successful conglomerates of the day. These moves soon proved financially disastrous. Bankruptcy proceedings began in 1965 and continued until a plan for reorganization was approved four years later. Hayworth-Clarke, a Connecticut-based corporation which had been OMC's principal supplier, accepted its bankruptcy settlement in the form of OMC stock. It acquired, through the settlement, a one-third interest in Oakland. The remaining two-thirds was purchased by a syndicate comprised of local businessmen headed by Mr. Phillips. In 1973 local interests decided to liquidate their holdings and Hayworth-Clarke made a tender offer for the available shares. The tender offer was accepted and Hayworth-Clarke assumed full ownership.

After Hayworth-Clarke took over the management of Oakland in 1973, Mr. Paul Richardson was appointed Vice-President and General Manager. R.J. Phillips continued to hold the position of President but he did not participate in the day-to-day management of the firm. He retired fully in 1980. That same year Paul Richardson was promoted to head up Hayworth-Clarke's entire midwest operations. This new position required Paul to spend more and more time at other locations and Jerry Sadat, Plant Manager, assumed responsibility for many of the daily operations at OMC. However, all major decisions continued to be made by Hayworth-Clarke through Mr. Richardson.

Oakland Manufacturing Corporation was one of the larger employers in the Battle Creek area, where many of the major companies were controlled by outside organizations. OMC's production facilities and product lines have been subject to some changes over the years. In 1971 OMC opened its second plant three miles away from its original Battle Creek location. At the time the original plant was over sixty years old and in poor condition. The second plant, Plant #2, was expanded in 1978 and in 1979 all operations were consolidated in Plant #2. In November 1980 Oakland introduced a new, numerically-controlled machine tool to its production facilities and announced its intention to introduce additional machines beginning in the summer of 1981.

Prior to World War II, OMC had specialized in machining camshafts for the automobile industry. Automobile production ceased during the war and OMC shifted to the machining of parts for military engines and industrial diesel engines. Following the war, Oakland returned to the machining of camshafts, primarily for diesel engine manufacturers in the automotive and heavy-duty vehicle industries. Sales of OMC products were made to approximately six major customers with giant Turbo-Diesel by far its largest customer. Management was quick to point out that, in addition to foreign competition, their customers were potentially their biggest competitors. If Oakland's price became prohibitive, delivery poor, or quality unacceptable, the firm's customers could embark upon camshaft machining themselves.

II. LABOR-MANAGEMENT RELATIONS

Oakland Manufacturing had been engaged in collective bargaining for many years. Local 421 of the United Auto Workers was certified by the National Labor Relations Board in the early 1940s. Although the only contract negotiation strike against Oakland occurred over twenty years ago and lasted only four days, it would be remiss to assume that relationships have been overly cozy. Mr. Phillips used to characterize the parties' relationship as one of "mutual respect and competition with a degree of cordiality."

Initially the union's leadership was composed of older employees. However, over the years younger workers have moved into leadership positions. Local 421's President, J.J. Shaver, at 350 pounds, has carried much weight within the company. Shaver, 41 years old and the son of an OMC retiree, was initially hired as an employee in 1960. He has been the union President since 1971, and was a member of the union's bargaining team for the last three negotiations.

J.J. Shaver has been a great soapbox orator, embellishing his speeches with earthy analogies. He also has been an astute politician. His political savvy has been demonstrated by his scheduling of union elections to coincide with contract negotiations. He has pointed out to the membership, on more than one occasion, that it would be unwise to change the union's helmsman in the midst of a negotiating storm. JJ has fought hard for members of his local, including those who have already retired. Almost all grievances have been processed vigorously. He has spent a good deal of time cultivating rank and file support, devoting much of his workday to union business. Oakland management has acknowledged, if reluctantly, that no member of management understands the contract as well as JJ.

During the late 1960s Battle Creek, like many American cities with a black population, experienced some racial unrest. OMC was not immune to the racial tension of the city. One racial incident actually resulted in the closing of the plant to allow a cooling off period of a few days. The last decade has benefited from an improvement in race relations within the city and Oakland's has established an affirmative action program. This has resulted in a slight decrease in the number of family relationships among bargaining unit members. However, close to fifty percent of the unit remain related, by either blood or marriage, to at least one other member of the workforce. Three years ago union members elected, for the first time, a black member to serve as Vice President.

Wages at OMC had been quite low prior to Hayworth-Clarke assuming control. This had contributed to the "country club" atmosphere which prevailed prior to the 1975 negotiations. Management's lack of control over the operation was due to a number of factors. The company was not able to attract and retain the best workers due to the low wages. Union members often refused to follow orders, with no disciplinary action taken by management. Management had developed a defeatest attitude which contributed to the problem. They felt overwhelmed by the strength of the union and did not know how to respond. A past practices clause in the contract helped to perpetuate the "country club" environment.

Faced with this situation when it took control of OMC in 1973, Hayworth-Clarke established three management objectives:

To regain managerial control of the plants.
To tie increased wages to increased productivity.
To establish a solid no-strike clause.

III. 1975—A CHANGE IN DIRECTION

Two years after taking control of OMC, Hayworth-Clarke was at the bargaining table negotiating a contract with Local 421. In an effort to attain the goals it had established, Hayworth-Clarke brought in a team of industrial engineers from one of their other operations to negotiate their first agreement with the UAW. The company traded higher wages for increased management rights in an attempt to end the lax working conditions. Oakland gave the employees a substantial wage increase, although some employees may have disagreed as to the amount of the increase. In return, OMC instituted an incentive plan, the Engineered Work Standards Plan; obtained a clause prohibiting strikes on almost all issues; eliminated the past practices clause; and acquired generally stronger management rights. Negotiation of the 1975 contract had not been an easy matter, there had been many, many negotiating sessions and the agreement was rejected on the first vote of the union membership.

Increased productivity and the end of a temporary peak in production resulted in the layoff of over two hundred hourly employees in 1975 and early 1976. Anticipation of these layoffs may have accounted for the initial rejection of the parties' tentative agreement. As a result of the layoffs the work force had dropped from about 650 to 420 employees.

Approximately half of the hourly-rated employees were covered by Engineered Work Standards. The standards had been developed for individual jobs, for a group of jobs or for part of an entire production line. Industrial engineering methods, as set out in the Engineered Work Standards Manual, were used to determine the time it took a qualified operator to perform a specific operation or operations. While the incentive system resulted in higher earnings, employees did not realize the substantial earnings expected in the first year or so due to certain changes in the diesel industry. By 1977 OMC had started to get a handle on the problems resulting from these changes and many incentive employees began to earn large pay checks for their increased efforts.

IV. THE 1978 NEGOTIATIONS

The 1978 OMC-Local 421 negotiations proved less than satisfactory to both sides for a number of reasons. The company did not have the benefit of the experience and skill of those who had played a major role in the 1975 negotiations. The company's entire negotiating team had been killed in the unfortunate crash of the Hayworth-Clarke company plane shortly after conclusion of the 1975 negotiations. OMC's new Personnel Manager, Mr. James Smithe, headed the 1978 negotiating team. Although a qualified individual, this was Jim's first experience in contract negotiations. He and JJ had many heated exchanges during the course of negotiations, some because of their strong personalities, others because of the firm positions taken by each side on certain issues.

Throughout negotiations Local 421 took the position that any multi-year contract had to contain annual wage increases and an unlimited cost of living allowance (COLA). Management was equally adamant in its opposition to including an increase each year together with an expensive, unlimited COLA. Smithe insisted that any COLA clause had to include a cap. The union did not even wish to discuss the possibility of a cap on their COLA. While the parties differed on many other issues, including more flexible use of skilled workers, extent of incentive coverage, pension improvements and a past practices clause, wage protection and the length of the contract remained at the center of their dispute.

The company was steadfast in its refusal to discuss pension improvements. In 1975 the parties had agreed to a six-year pension agreement which was to span two contract negotiations, 1975 through 1981. The union attempted to obtain some improvements in 1978 but management would not discuss the matter because of the six-year pension agreement. The union finally dropped their demand for improvements in 1978.

The wage issue was finally resolved when, realizing that JJ and the other union representatives would not agree to a multi-year contract which included a cap on COLA, management agreed to drop its insistence on a cap. In exchange management obtained the union's agreement to update the consumer price index used in the calculation of the quarterly COLA adjustments. This breakthrough, together with some other improvements in wages and benefits, resulted in the union representatives agreeing to take management's offer to the rank and file for a vote. The union recommended neither acceptance nor rejection. The company also announced at this time the expansion of the more modern Plant #2. The union membership accepted management's offer by a slim margin on the afternoon of April 21, 1978, thereby averting a strike.

V. THE 1981 NEGOTIATIONS

In the fall of 1979 management closed the old plant, Plant #1, and consolidated all production and office operations in the expanded Plant #2. This resulted in some layoffs of junior, low skilled employees. Additional layoffs were caused during the term of the 1978 agreement due to a slight downturn in business. Management was somewhat concerned with foreign competition. Imported camshafts of a quality superior to OMC's products were being purchased by some of OMC's customers. Management was convinced quality had to be improved.

In order to improve quality and become more competitive, Oakland embarked upon a Capital Equipment Program. The first new, numerically controlled milling machine was introduced into the plant in November 1980. The company had a number of meetings, not only with union officials but with the employees as well, and explained their plan to modernize production machines and equipment. The program would have its major impact during the term of the next agreement.

In early 1980 OMC instituted a Point System to control absenteeism. The system involved the accumulation of points for unexcused absences or tardiness in reporting for work. The accumulation of nine (9) points by an employee resulted in an automatic suspension, whereas twelve (12) points resulted in discharge. Without doubt the Point System has been as effective in reducing absenteeism as it has been in generating the animosity of employees. When it installed the program management contended that the Point System was a management policy and not subject to negotiation under the National Labor Relations Act. Management was also aware that the union had received numerous demands for the elimination of what the members viewed as a draconic, oppressive system.

Jim Smithe had resigned from OMC in 1979 in order to join his family's business. Robert Hills had been hired to replace Jim and it was Hills who would head the company's negotiating team for the 1981 negotiations. Bob Hills was 34 years old, had been trained as an engineer but had moved into labor relations with his former employer. Bob had participated in two rounds of negotiations as a member of the negotiating committee of a Fortune 500 company. The UAW had also represented those employees. The 1981 negotiations would be Bob's first negotiations as Oakland's chief spokesman.

Bob was a bit concerned with the recent increase in grievances. Traditionally the grievance rate had been fairly low but constant. However, in recent weeks he sensed a spurt in the number filed and it seemed that the union was more reluctant than ever to settle pending disputes. On Tuesday, March 17th, he was faced with a more pressing problem. The entire second shift walked off the job in a wildcat strike in order to press a demand for a full-time nurse on the second shift. While each employee who participated in the walkout received a one day suspension (paper penalty) the company did hire a nurse for the second shift.

Bob reviewed the union's sixty day notice which indicated that it wished to renegotiate the 1978 agreement. He was aware that the union membership had passed a resolution of No Contract—No Work. Bob also knew JJ was under pressure from certain groups within the local. He also wondered what effect the elimination of the government's wage-price program would have on this round of negotiations.

In starting to prepare for the 1981 contract negotiations, each side attempted to evaluate those they would soon face across the bargaining table. They also began to get to know their own team members and to research the demands they intended to put on the bargaining agenda.

Step 3: Discussion. Individually, in small groups, or with the entire class, as directed by your instructor, answer the following questions:

1. How did labor/management relations change through the case?
2. How will the history of relations between union and management likely influence the bargaining?
3. What were the union's and management's attitude toward the negotiations?
4. What are the major issues of the 1981 negotiations? How do they differ from the issues during the previous negotiations?
5. How likely is a strike?
6. How should union and management act to ensure effective negotiations?

Activity 11–3

PRISONERS' DILEMMA EXERCISE

Step 1: The facilitator explains that the group is going to experience a "risk-taking" situation similar to that experienced by guilty prisoners being interrogated by the police. Before interrogating prisoners suspected of working together, the questioner separates them and tells each one that the other has confessed and that, if they both confess, they will get off easier. The prisoners' dilemma or risk is that they may confess when they should not or they may fail to confess when they really should. (The facilitator carefully avoids discussing goals.)

Step 2: Two teams are formed and named Red and Blue. The teams are seated apart from each other. They are instructed not to communicate with the other team in any way, verbally or nonverbally, except when told to do so by the facilitator.

Step 3: Prisoners' Dilemma Tally Sheets are distributed to all participants. They are given time to study the directions. The facilitator then asks if there are any questions concerning the scoring.

Step 4: Round 1 is begun. The facilitator tells the teams that they will have three minutes to make a team decision. He instructs them not to write their decisions until he signals them that time is up, so that they will not make hasty decisions.

Step 5: The choices of the two teams are announced for Round 1. The scoring for that round is agreed upon and is entered on the scorecards.

Step 6: Rounds 2 and 3 are conducted in the same way as Round 1.

Step 7: Round 4 is announced as a special round, for which the payoff points are doubled. Each team is instructed to send one representative to the chairs in the center of the room. After representatives have conferred for three minutes, they return to their teams. Teams then have three minutes, as before, in which to make their decisions. When recording their scores, they should be reminded that points indicated by the payoff schedule are doubled for this round only.

Step 8: Rounds 5 through 8 are conducted in the same manner as the first three rounds.

Step 9: Round 9 is announced as a special round, in which the payoff points are "squared" (multiplied by themselves: *e.g.*, a score of 4 would be $4^2 = 16$). A minus sign should be retained: *e.g.*, $(-3)^2 = -9$. Team representatives meet for three minutes; then the teams meet for *five* minutes. At the facilitator's signal, the teams write their choices; then the two choices are announced.

Step 10: Round 10 is handled exactly as Round 9 was. Payoff points are squared.

Step 11: The entire group meets to process the experience. The point total for each team is announced, and the sum of the two team totals is calculated and compared to the maximum positive or negative outcomes (+126 or −126 points). The facilitator may wish to lead a discussion about win-lose situations, zero-sum games, the relative merits of collaboration and competition, and the effects of high and low trust on interpersonal relations.

VARIATIONS

I. The competition can be carried out using money instead of points.
II. Process observers can be assigned to each team.
III. Teams can be placed in separate rooms, to minimize rule-breaking.
IV. The number of persons in each team can be varied.
V. In Round 10, each team can be directed to predict the choice of the other. These predictions can be posted before announcing the actual choices, as in the following diagram. (Actual choices are recorded in the circles after the predictions are announced.)

Predicting Team	Predicted Choice	
	Red Team	Blue Team
Red	○	
Blue		○

PRISONERS' DILEMMA TALLY SHEET

Instructions: For ten successive rounds, the Red Team will choose either an A or a B and the Blue Team will choose either an X or a Y. The score each team receives in a round is determined by the pattern made by the choices of both teams, according to the schedule below.

Payoff Schedule

AX—Both teams win 3 points.
AY—Red Team loses 6 points; Blue Team wins 6 points.
BX—Red Team wins 6 points; Blue Team loses 6 points.
BY—Both teams lose 3 points.

SCORECARD

Round	Minutes	Choice		Cumulative Points	
		Red Team	Blue Team	Red Team	Blue Team
1	3				
2	3				
3	3				
4*	3 (reps.) 3 (teams)				
5	3				
6	3				
7	3				
8	3				
9**	3 (reps.) 5 (teams)				
10**	3 (reps.) 5 (teams)				

*Payoff points are doubled for this round.
**Payoff points are squared for this round. (Retain the minus sign.)

Step 12: Discussion. Individually, in small groups, or with the entire class, answer the following questions:

1. How does this simulation relate to labor/management negotiations?
2. What did you learn that would help you be more effective as a party to labor/management negotiations?
3. How can you encourage win-win situations in such negotiations?

Activity 11–4

RELIANCE TEXTILES, INC.

Step 1: The instructor divides the class into management and union teams. Each team receives a role.

Step 2: Read the following description of the situation at Reliance Textiles, Inc.

Reliance Textiles manufactures and sells a line of sportswear for men and women. Located in a small town in Michigan, Reliance employs approximately 750 workers, including sales and manufacturing personnel as well as corporate support staff. The International Clothing Workers Union organized Reliance approximately twenty-five years ago when the company grew from a small, cottage-industry form of organization to one that emphasized mass production. Reliance Textiles has grown significantly, benefiting from the emphasis on leisure activities and the trend to more informal attire in the United States. For the most part, workers have experienced increases in wages and benefits and improvements in working conditions since the company was unionized.

Reliance has combined an emphasis on high-quality clothing with the ability to mass produce garments at a low cost for sale in middle-level discount stores and certain specialty stores. Recently Reliance has encountered significant national and international competition. Management has stated that it may be forced to reduce the work force if the union is unwilling to make concessions in wages, overtime, and benefits. The general economic situation has fluctuated significantly in the past five years, from great prosperity to recession to moderate stability. Management has expressed concern about the economic situation the company will face in the next three to five years.

The most recent three-year union contract expires in one hour. Management and union have been negotiating about the terms of a new contract for about two months and have made little progress. The following bargaining issues seem to prevent the parties from reaching a new agreement:

1. *Wages*
   Current situation: wage increases are tied to the cost of living; the average wage increase is 1 percent above the rate of inflation for the previous six months
   Management: 5 percent increase first year, 6 percent increase second year, 6.5 percent increase third year
   Union: 7 percent increase each year
   Competitors: average of 5.5 percent increase over three years
2. *Overtime*
   Current contract: all overtime, Sundays, and holidays paid at time and one-half
   Management: all overtime, Sundays, and holidays paid at time and one-half
   Union: all overtime paid at time and one-half; Sundays and holidays paid at double time
   Competitors: all overtime, Sundays, and holidays paid at time and one-half
3. *Shift Differential*
   Current contract: no shift differential
   Management: $.20 per hour extra for third shift
   Union: $.40 per hour extra for third shift
   Competitors: $.35 per hour extra for third shift
4. *Paid Sick Leave*
   Current contract: five (5) days of paid sick leave
   Management: five (5) days of paid sick leave
   Union: ten (10) days of paid sick leave
   Competitors: eight (8) days of paid sick leave; after five years of employment, ten (10) days
5. *Medical Insurance*
   Current contract: company pays 75 percent of individual medical insurance
   Management: company pays 75 percent of individual medical insurance until an employee has been employed for ten years, then company pays all individual medical insurance
   Union: company pays all individual medical insurance and adds dental insurance
   Competitors: company pays 50 percent of individual medical insurance and no dental benefits
6. *Cost of Living Increases*
   Current contract: wages are tied to one estimate of cost of living
   Management: remove cost of living clause from contract
   Union: provide for contract reopening if cost of living exceeds 8 percent for any three-month period
   Competitors: contract provides for no wage reopeners
7. *Profit Sharing*
   Current contract: no provision for profit sharing

Management: no provision for profit sharing
Union: institute a profit-sharing plan whereby workers share in 10 percent of the profits as determined by a joint union-management committee
Competitors: profit-sharing clauses are very unusual

8. *Job Security*
Current contract: specifies that every attempt will be made to retrain and transfer employees rather than lay them off
Management: agrees that every attempt will be made to retrain and transfer employees rather than lay them off
Union: layoffs restricted to 5 percent of the work force during any year period; all other employees will receive cross-training; employees with twenty-five or more years of employment will be guaranteed life-time employment
Competitors: the provisions range from those offered by union to those offered by management

9. *Vacations*
Current contract: two paid weeks per year
Management: two paid weeks per year
Union: two paid weeks per year; after five years three paid weeks per year
Competitors: two paid weeks per year

10. *Automation*
Current contract: no provision for dealing with employees displaced because of technological advancements
Management: cross-training of employees displaced because of new technology
Union: guarantees of job security and cross-training of employees displaced because of new technology
Competition: cross-training of employees displaced with every attempt made to guarantee the job of those employed more than ten years

Step 3: Each negotiating team should meet to discuss its approach to the negotiations. They should consider the acceptable bargaining range for each issue described above. They should consider under which circumstances they would or would not be willing to accept an agreement.

Step 4: Representatives of union and management teams have 60 minutes to reach agreement about these issues. (Failure to reach an agreement means that the union will strike.)

Step 5: Discussion. With the entire class, share the agreements reached by each management-union negotiating team. Compare and contrast the agreements. What types of concessions were offered by union? By management? Which issues showed the greatest variation in the agreements? Which issues were most difficult to resolve? What techniques helped and hindered the reaching of an agreement? Did any groups fail to reach an agreement? What explains their failure?

Activity 11–5

THE STRIKE FUND

Step 1: You are faced with the following problem:

You are the union steward for a local of truck drivers. Your national union bargaining team recently agreed to a new contract. The members of your local have refused to ratify the contract and have voted to strike. You know that there is $100,000 in the local strike fund. The fifty members' wages average $30,000 per year.

Step 2: Individually, in small groups, or with the entire class, develop a plan for proceeding at this time.

Step 3: In small groups or with the entire class, share the plans you developed. Consider their similarities and differences. What are the goals of the plans? What are the elements of an effective plan? What role does the strike fund play in the plan?

Activity 11–6

THE PLANT CLOSING ROLE PLAY

Step 1: Your instructor will divide you into groups.

Step 2: Read the following scenario:

Acme Parts is located in Cedar Bend, Michigan, in the western part of the State. It is a wholly-owned subsidiary of Great Western Manufacturing, Incorporated, a shareholder-owned corporation headquartered in Chicago. Great Western's Parts Division owns 5 plants which make sub-assemblies for the major domestic automakers. Due to the recent recession, declining auto sales and efforts on the part of the automakers to reduce the number of suppliers with whom they do business, Great Western has cut back production in all 5 of the plants. Moreover, there are indications that some of the automakers are considering purchasing parts from Japanese competitors; such a move would be a significant loss to Great Western. In an effort to increase their cost competitiveness, Great Western has announced its decision to close 3 of the 5 plants and to substantially upgrade/update the technology and machinery of the remaining two. At this point, the plants have roughly equivalent machinery; thus, none would seem to be an obvious choice for renovation on the basis of recent capital investments in equipment.

Acme Parts has been an employer in Cedar Bend since 1938. Until 1973 it was a privately-owned company but it was bought out by Great Western as part of the latter's expansion in auto parts production. The plant is covered by a contract with the Parts Makers International Union (PMI) and Local 1090 of PMI has represented Acme workers since 1946. PMI has approximately 350,000 members nationally in the auto parts supplier industry; but the union has suffered organizationally and financially as a result of the recession and the increasing incidence of out-sourcing (domestic automakers contracting with foreign suppliers for parts). In the last round of contract negotiations (in 1981), Great Western bargained for and won a 10% decrease in hourly wages from PMI for its parts division. However, Acme workers remain the highest paid production workers in the county, earning on average $10/hour.

Shown below are some statistics describing the labor force at Acme:

Production Employees (300 total)		*Non-Production Employees (40 total)*	
Unionized:	100%	Management:	10 White males
Male:	70%	Supervisors:	20 White males
Female:	30%	Clerical:	10 White females
Black:	10%		
White:	85%		
Hispanic:	5%		
Skilled: (millwrights, tool and die, electricians, machine repair)	10%		
Unskilled: (assemblers, machine operators, cleaners)	90%		
Avg. Age:	46		
Avg. # Dependents: 3			

Of all employees, 2/3 are homeowners in Cedar Bend. Since 1979, around 50% of the unionized employees have been laid off.

Acme Parts has long been viewed in the county as the last bastion of relatively stable employment, in spite of the high lay-offs in recent years. There have already been four major plant closings in the county since 1979 and those amounted to a loss of nearly 5000 jobs. Due to the ripple effect of industrial plant closings, it has been estimated that Cedar Bend would lose an additional 75–100 (e.g., in retail sales, services and city employment) jobs should Acme Parts close down. Total employment for the county in early 1979 was approximately 74,000; as of January 1984, total employment has dipped to less than 60,000.

Cedar Bend is the county seat. It has a population of around 30,000. The county has a population of 110,000. However, figures from the 1980 Census indicate that both the city and the county have decreased in size nearly 10% since 1970. The city is about 20% Black, 10% Hispanic and Asian and 70% White. It is ringed by an agricultural sector (mostly made up of financially strapped small vegetable and orchard farms) which employs seasonal workers in the summer and fall. Aside from the dwindling industrial base and seasonal agriculture, major employers in the city and the county are: government (schools, social services, city and county), tourism (which is somewhat seasonal) and service sectors. In recent years, there has been a 5% default rate on mortgages in Cedar Bend, an indication that the area is pretty depressed economically.

Since 1981 the City Economic Development Committee (CEDC), appointed by city council, has been working hard to attract new business to the area. To date, the CEDC has not been successful in finding new tenants for the two small plants that closed in Cedar Bend. Most people agree that the loss of Acme would have multiple negative effects, including: a setback to CEDC's efforts to attract new business to Cedar Bend; a psychological loss to the community owing to the long-standing role Acme has played in civic affairs; and an increase in demands for social services which are already suffering under the strain of high unemployment and dwindling state and federal financial aid. There is a feeling in some quarters that the high wage rates paid to workers at Acme Parts are a strike against keeping the plant open—even in the face of the last concession contract.

Rumor has it that Great Western's decision to renovate only two of its five plants will set off a competition between all five to see which pair keeps its plants.

THE PARTICIPANTS

Great Western Manufacturing, Incorporated. Most of what is known generally is described above. However, for the Public Forum and subsequent discussions, Great Western has sent a representative from its Corporate Strategic Planning office.

Parts Makers International Union (PMI) and PMI Local 1090. Described above. PMI is represented at the Public Forum by the President of Local 1090. However, Local 1090 is a relatively heterogeneous group: included in its membership are a strong contingent of retired Acme workers, a vocal (but numerically small) caucus opposed to the present local leadership, and a majority of members who only occasionally participate in union affairs.

Cedar Bend City Government. Cedar Bend city government consists largely of the city council and the mayor. The mayor is elected directly in Cedar Bend and in this instance the mayor is a Democrat with a slim majority of Democrats on the city council. The mayor, who will be representing city government in the Public Forum, was recently elected to the top slot in city government on a platform of continued commitment to human and community services despite declining state aid to the cities.

Small Business. Small businesses in Cedar Bend have been hard hit by the recession and by the economic troubles of companies like Acme Parts. Local banks have been suffering from mortgage defaults and high interest rates on consumer and business loans. Local retailers have seen their sales droop and have been forced to cut back, where possible, on the number of people they employ—adding to the unemployment figures in the city. Many fear that they will be unfairly taxed to help the city continue financing social services. Representing the small businesspeople of Cedar Bend will be a grocery store owner who is president of the local Chamber of Commerce and a member of the City Economic Development Committee.

Low-Income Activists. The low-income community of the city of Cedar Bend has been growing as a result of the recession and it is disproportionately Black and Hispanic. In the late 1960s and early 1970s, the low-income community was actively involved in organizing and administering a complex array of federally-financed social welfare programs. Though those funds have diminished significantly in the past decade, a core of organizers remains in the community. They have been concentrated in local churches, especially a Black Baptist church and a predominantly Hispanic Roman Catholic church. Among other things, these allied groups have organized two local day-care centers, a neighborhood food co-op, and a chapter of Alcoholics Anonymous. In recent years, they have focused attention on voter registration and in the last local election were a significant factor in the election of the present mayor. It is believed that the Mayor's promise of an additional $150,000 in city funds—a significant chunk of the city's budget for the fiscal year—for local social services has been a reward to the low-income groups for their support. In the Public Forum, the low-income group is represented by one of the most vigorous activists.

Step 3: Your instructor will give each group a role, which is described in detail on the role sheet. Each group must select one person to act as the representative for the group. Read the role sheet carefully. It will give you information about both the group of which you are a part and the person who is serving as the representative for that group (e.g., what the group does or is, where it fits into the local community, who the representative is, and where he or she fits in the larger context).

Step 4: In your role group, you will have 30 minutes to complete the following:

1. Define your interests in this plant closing situation.
2. Based on your interests, decide what course of action (or inaction) you want to pursue in this situation.
3. Plan a strategy that includes both a *public statement* (no longer than 4 minutes in duration) for the Public Forum and a *private plan* for the meeting which follows the Public Forum. There will be a 10 minute break between the two meetings so that you can bargain with other groups privately, should you so choose.
4. Choose one person from your group to speak at the Public Forum at the City Auditorium. You may divide other speaking and/or discussion tasks as your strategy requires. All role group members are permitted to sit in on the discussion after the Forum.

Step 5: The rest of the participants will join the Public Forum at City Auditorium. This forum is very well attended, with a significant number of people from each of the groups in the audience. The audience includes members of the press. The moderator will introduce each speaker. Speakers have 4 minutes to make their statements. After the statements, the meeting will adjourn.

Step 6: As the auditorium clears out, you have 10 minutes to talk privately with any other group or group members.

Step 7: People remaining go to the coffee shop across the street for further discussions. During this time try to advance your strategy as much as you can within the context of the meeting that is taking place. Everyone at the meeting is aware that its purpose is to come to some understanding about the possible plant closing. You have 20 minutes to reach a solution.

Step 8: The instructor will reconvene the entire class. The class will then discuss the solutions reached.

1. What alternatives were considered?
2. How well were they examined?
3. How would you evaluate the quality of negotiations?
4. What factors helped or hindered the negotiations?
5. How could the situation have been handled more effectively?
6. What impact does a plant closing have on labor/management relations?

SUMMARY

> Framingham (Massachusetts)—There has been a drastic change in labor relations at the General Motors Plant here. It showed yesterday. By a vote of 2009 to 94, Local 422 of the United Auto Workers became the first General Motors assembly plant in the nation to approve a local conditions contract.
>
> This is the same local that struck twice since 1970. In 1974 the strike lasted 10 weeks, causing the local union to be called "the most troublesome" by a General Motors official.[58]

Do situations such as this one signal a change in the collective bargaining process in the United States? Observers of the labor relations system increasingly feel that management can improve relations with unions through communicating more effectively and treating labor more equitably.[59]

In this chapter we have examined the components of collective bargaining and offered ways of increasing the effectiveness of this process. The text first described the preparations for negotiations made by union and management. Next it presented the negotiating process, including the patterns used to bargain, general negotiating strategies, and the legal influences on bargaining. Then the text commented about ways of effectively concluding negotiations. It also examined the issues on which negotiations typically focus. In the activities, you had the opportunity to examine and participate in several negotiations.

In this chapter we also considered the factors that influence strikes and the consequences of work stoppages. In the strike fund activity you investigated the economic realities of striking, which illustrated their dysfunctional consequences and have contributed to their decreased frequency since 1970.[60]

Unions and management are working toward a new partnership. Bargaining concerns are increasingly focusing on job security in the face of technological advancements. Both workers and management are seeing that the benefits of stable employment outweigh the gains from layoffs, even during a recession.[61] The Scanlon Plan (see Chapter 9) and Quality of Work Life Programs (see Chapter 14) offer other alternatives for improving the effectiveness of labor-management relations.[62]

ENDNOTES

[1]E.F. Beal and J.P. Begin, *The Practice of Collective Bargaining* 6th ed. (Homewood, Ill.: Irwin, 1982).

[2]J.T. Dunlop and J.J. Healy, *Collective Bargaining* (Homewood, Ill.: Irwin, 1953).

[3]Editors of *Collective Bargaining Negotiations & Contracts, Basic Patterns in Union Contracts* 9th ed. (Washington, D.C.: Bureau of National Affairs, 1979).

[4]See E.E. Herman and A. Kuhn, *Collective Bargaining and Labor Relations* (Englewood Cliffs, N.J.: Prentice-Hall, 1981) for detailed discussion of issues related to costing the contract.

[5]I. Rothenberg and S.B. Silverman, *Labor Unions, How to: Avoid Them, Beat Them, Out-Negotiate Them, Live with Them, Unload Them* (Elkins Park, Pa.: Management Relations, Inc., 1973) talk about the "extravagance of over preparation."

[6]R.E. Walton and R.B. McKersie, *A Behavioral Theory of Labor Negotiations* (New York: McGraw-Hill, 1965).

[7]D.Q. Mills, *Labor-Management Relations* (New York: McGraw-Hill, 1978).

[8]Beal and Begin, *op. cit.*

[9]*Ibid.*

[10]*Ibid.*

[11]*Ibid.*

[12]R. Fisher and W. Uri, *Getting to Yes: Negotiating Agreement without Giving In* (Boston: Houghton Mifflin, 1981).

[13]R.B. Peterson and L. Tracy, Testing a behavioral model of labor negotiations, *Industrial Relations* 16 (1977): 35–50.

[14]*Ibid.*

[15]See C. Karass, *Give and Take: The Complete Guide to Negotiating Strategies and Tactics* (New York: Crowell, 1974); F.L. Acuff and M.F. Villere, Games negotiators play, *Business Horizons* 19 (February 1976): 76.

[16]*Ibid.*

[17]Walton and McKersie, *op. cit.*

[18]D.R. Burke and I. Rubin, Is contract rejection a major bargaining problem?, *Industrial and Labor Relations Review* 26 (1972): 820–833.

[19]B.W. Justice, *Unions, Workers, and the Law* (Washington, D.C.: Bureau of National Affairs, 1983).

[20]See L.R. Boulware, *The Truth about Boulwarism* (Washington, D.C.: Bureau of National Affairs, 1969); NLRB v. General Electric, 72 LRRM 2530 (1969); T.P. Brown, Hard bargaining: The board says no, the courts say yes, *Employee Relations Law Journal* 8 (Summer 1982): 37–51.

[21]D.Q. Mills, *Labor-Management Relations* (New York: McGraw-Hill, 1978).

[22]J.H. Falahee, Concession bargaining: The time is now!, *Personnel Administrator* 28 (January 1983): 27.

[23]P. Cappelli, What do unions get in return for concessions?, *Monthly Labor Review* 107 (May 1984): 40–41.

[24]Editors of *Collective Bargaining Negotiations and Contracts, op. cit.*

[25]J.A. Fossum, *Labor Relations: Development, Structure, Process* rev. ed. (Dallas: Business Publications, 1982).

[26]R.G. Steckel, The misuse of roll-up in costing contract settlements, *Personnel Administrator* 25 (March 1980): 33.

[27]Labor voice on the board (Chrysler board labor representation), *Newsweek,* 26 May 1980, p. 13.

[28]A right turn on race? In placing seniority rights over affirmative action goals, the Supreme Court may be signalling a new era, *Newsweek,* 25 June 1984, p. 63.

[29]Mills, *op. cit.*

[30]See I.B. Helburn, The scope of bargaining in public sector negotiations: Sovereignty reviewed, *Journal of Collective Negotiations in the Public Sector* 3 (Spring 1974): 147–166.

[31]J.M. Weisberger, The appropriate scope of bargaining in the public sector: The continuing controversy and the Wisconsin experience, *Wisconsin Law Review* 3 (1977): 688–689.

[32]*Federal Labor Relations Authority Fact Sheet*, mimeo, 1979, cited in Herman and Kuhn, *op. cit.*

[33]Wagner Act as amended by the Taft-Hartley Act.

[34]*Ibid.*

[35]W. Imberman, Who strikes—and why? *Harvard Business Review* (November-December 1983): 18–28.

[36]*Ibid.*

[37]J.P. Goodman and W.R. Sandhey, A contingency approach to labor relations strategies, *Academy of Management Review* 6 (1981): 145–154, offers a contingency theory that describes strike proneness and likelihood of settlement according to a company's resources and type of industry.

[38]Beal and Begin, *op. cit.*

[39]*Ibid.*

[40]*Ibid.*

[41]W. Imberman, Strikes cost more than you think, *Harvard Business Review* (May-June 1979): 133–138.

[42]*Ibid.*

[43]*Ibid.*

[44]*Ibid.*

[45]M.J. Levine and L.W. Helly, The airlines mutual aid pact: A deterrent to collective bargaining, *Labor Law Journal* 28 (January 1977): 44–55.

[46]S. Marshall, Curbing mutual aid pacts, *AFL-CIO American Federationist* (February 1979): 10.

[47]U.S. Department of Labor, Bureau of Labor Statistics, *Work Stoppages, 1980* (Washington, D.C.: Government Printing Office, 1981), p. 3.

[48]W.H. Holley, Jr. and K.M. Jennings, *The Labor Relations Process* 2nd ed. (Chicago: Dryden, 1984).

[49]J. Crispo, Multinational corporations and international unions: Their impact on Canadian industrial relations, in R.J. Flanagan and A.R. Weer, eds., *Bargaining without Boundaries* (Chicago: University of Chicago Press, 1974).

[50]O. Farweather, Western European labor movements and collective bargaining: An industrial framework, in A. Kanan, ed., *Western European Labor and the American Corporation* (Washington, D.C.: Bureau of National Affairs, 1970).

[51]Mills, *op. cit.*

[52]Holley and Jennings, *op. cit.*

[53]J.L. Porket, Industrial relations and participation in management in the Soviet-type Communist system, *British Journal of Industrial Relations* 16 (March 1973): 70–71.

[54]Holley and Jennings, *op. cit.*

[55]See T. Lowit, The working class and union structures in Eastern Europe, *British Journal of Industrial Relations* 20 (March 1982): 67–69; H. Brand, Solidarity's proposals for reforming Poland's economy, *Monthly Labor Review* 105 (May 1982): 43.

[56]An aging work force strains Japan's traditions, *Business Week*, 20 April 1981, pp. 72–85.

[57]R.C. Simpson, The significance of legal status of trade unions in Britain and Australia, *Journal of Industrial Relations* 18 (September 1976): 229–242.

[58]New attitude at GM-Framingham, *Boston Globe*, 2 August 1984.

[59]See S.A. Levitan and C.M. Johnson, Labor and management: The illusion of cooperation, *Harvard Business Review* (September-October 1983): 8–16; D.N. Scobel, Business and labor: From adversaries to allies, *Harvard Business Review* (November-December 1982): 129–136.

[60]U.S. Department of Labor, *op. cit.*

[61]See J.F. Bolt, Job security. Its time has come, *Harvard Business Review* (November-December 1983): 115–123; M. Mooney, Let's use job security as a productivity builder, *Personnel Administrator* (January 1984): 38–44, for discussion of the job security issue.

[62]J.W. Driscoll, Working creatively with a union: Lessons from the Scanlon plan, *Organizational Dynamics* (Summer 1979).

FURTHER READINGS

Editors of *Collective Bargaining Negotiations & Contracts, Basic Patterns in Union Contracts.* Washington, D.C.: Bureau of National Affairs, 1979.

Herman, E.E. and Kuhn, A. *Collective Bargaining and Labor Relations.* Englewood Cliffs, N.J.: Prentice-Hall, 1981.

Justice, B.W. *Unions, Workers, and the Law.* Washington, D.C.: Bureau of National Affairs, 1983.

Kochan, T.A. *Collective Bargaining and Industrial Relations.* Homewood, Ill.: Irwin, 1980.

Walton, R.E. and McKersie, R.B. *A Behavioral Theory of Labor Negotiations.* New York: McGraw-Hill, 1965.

CHAPTER 12

Using Third Parties in Negotiations and Grievance Resolution

CHAPTER OUTLINE

LEARNING CHECKPOINTS

After completing the reading and activities in this chapter, students will be able to

- compare and contrast three types of third-party interventions that can facilitate collective bargaining;
- discuss the issues involved in administering the collective bargaining contract;
- differentiate among the ways of resolving grievances (arbitration, mediation, and fact-finding);
- compare and contrast various types of arbitration;
- list the various agencies that can help in grievance resolution;
- offer a judgment in an arbitration case;
- describe the bases on which arbitrators make awards;
- offer a plan for resolving grievances in a union organization;
- offer a plan for resolving grievances in a nonunion organization;
- define the roles of managers and human resources professionals in arbitration and mediation.

INTRODUCTION

> When an employee with a record of overstaying his work breaks was late returning from a break, he was called into his supervisor's office and informed that he was being suspended for three days. The worker challenged the action, however, pointing out that under the organization's progressive discipline policy, he should receive only a warning, not a suspension. Leaving the meeting, the supervisor went to an adjacent office to check the personnel records and found that the worker was correct. According to the supervisor, he then returned to the meeting, and advised the employee that the discipline was being reduced to a warning. However, at that point, the supervisor contended, the employee turned to a coworker and said, "I've got my three days off—let's go."
>
> The supervisor instructed the coworker to follow the employee to the parking lot and tell him to be at work the next morning. Later the supervisor also tried to locate the worker at home and at his mother's house, and left word with the mother that the employee was subject to termination if he failed to report to work the next morning. Nevertheless, the employee did not return to the job until three days later. Management then informed him that he was fired for being absent without notice.
>
> Protesting the discharge, the employee maintained that he was unaware that the suspension had been changed to a warning since he had left while the supervisor was away checking the records. The employee also insisted that he had not received the message from his mother in time to return to work.[1]

What recourse did the employee have? Could management rightfully discharge the employee? How can the dilemma be resolved? How should a contract be administered to ensure that such situations are handled correctly?

In this chapter we begin by examining the process for settling and administering a contract. We examine the role of *grievances*—disputes that arise from the interpretation or application of the collective bargaining agreement[2]—in the administration of the contract. We also look at arbitration, mediation, and fact-finding as alternative means of resolving contract disputes. We examine strategies for resolving grievances in nonunion organizations as well. Finally, we propose ways for improving contract administration.

THE PROCESS OF CONTRACT RESOLUTION AND ADMINISTRATION

Third-party intervention occurs under two circumstances: when two parties cannot reach a collective bargaining agreement acceptable to both of them, and when a worker files a grievance. In either case, a third party can facilitate resolution.

Third Parties in Collective Bargaining

Union and management sometimes reach an impasse during the collective bargaining process. In the last chapter we discussed the use of a *strike* as a response to the parties' inability to reach an agreement acceptable to both sides. In this chapter we consider several other mechanisms for reaching an agreement. Interest arbitration, mediation, and fact-finding are third-party interventions designed to help union and management resolve their differences. Because unions in the public sector frequently are forbidden from striking, they often turn to these types of conflict resolution, as described later in this chapter.

Use of Grievances

Grievances arise for a number of reasons.[3] Ambiguous contract language may encourage the filing of grievances that are designed to increase the contract's precision. Interpersonal conflict between an employee and his or her supervisor may lead to the employee's filing a grievance. Often supervisors lack a detailed knowledge of contract provisions and may inadvertently violate them by acting inconsistently or inappropriately, causing a worker to file a grievance, as in the introductory scenario. A negative attitude toward the contract or the union can foster intentional contract violations that lead to grievances. And the union can challenge the contract and management's rights by filing an onslaught of grievances.

Grievances generally charge that a violation of contract language occurred, that inappropriate application of the contract occurred, or that past practice was ignored. For past practice to become established as a required condition of work in an organization, four conditions must exist: (1) the practice must be an employee benefit or favorable condition, (2) the contract must say nothing about that condition, (3) the practice must be of significant frequency or duration, and (4) the practice must extend beyond a simple gratuity.[4] For example, the contract may not specify that workers receive two ten-minute rest periods during the day. If the employer has regularly given such breaks, then the employer has established a practice and condition of employment. Thus an employee may grieve if management unilaterally ceases to provide these rest breaks.

Workers file grievances about a variety of situations that range from meal allowances to layoffs and terminations.[5] Figure 12–1 categorizes the most common ones. A study of grievances filed by one West Coast union representing 4000 workers indicated that the most common grievances relate to suspension and seniority issues; the least common focus on training or performance of work outside the worker's job description.[6] In that study, whose results seem typical of grievance-resolution behaviors, outcomes went in favor of the union more often than management in the following categories: safety, grievance process, seniority, excused and complementary time, pay, scheduling, union representation, and management doing union members' work. In addition, unions tend to benefit in grievance resolution in areas where the contract language is explicit rather than ambiguous. Resolution favored the company more often than the union in the

Suspension: Employee charges he or she was unfairly ordered not to work.
Seniority: Employee charges he or she has been bypassed for overtime, transfer, promotion, training, or scheduling.
Transfer: Employee complains that a transfer for which he or she applied has been refused.
Termination: Employee complains he or she has been unjustly fired.
Disciplinary Memoranda: Employee receives a warning that more serious consequences are to follow if the specified unacceptable behavior continues.
Vacation: Employees complain that they do not receive the vacation dates they prefer or deserve.
Grievance Process: Union charges company has not met in good faith on a grievance.
Management Performing Productive Work: Union charges that management is doing work that should be restricted to union members.
Safety: Union complains that a procedure or a condition involving employees is unsafe.
Discrimination: Employee charges that he or she is not being treated the same as other workers.
Performance Evaluations: Employee charges that his or her annual performance evaluation does not fairly represent performance.
Union Representation: Union complains that an employee has been denied union representation in a discipline hearing.
Sick Benefits Denial: Employee complains that the company has unfairly refused to pay for sick leave.
Pay: Employee complains about nonpayment of special pay provisions, such as meal allowances or night shift differentials.

Based on D.R. Dalton and W.D. Todor, Win, lose, draw: The grievance process in practice, *Personnel Administrator* (March 1981): 25–29.

Figure 12–1 CATEGORIES OF GRIEVANCES

following categories: denial of sick benefits, termination, transfer, suspension, training, work outside of job classification, discrimination, disciplinary memoranda, and vacation.[7]

The next sections describe three types of resolution: (1) arbitration, (2) mediation, and (3) fact-finding.

ARBITRATION

Arbitration is the process of dispute resolution by a third party. It is a quasilegal proceeding: the process resembles a formal judicial procedure (and is described later in this chapter) but does not take place in a court of law. Arbitration focuses on clarifying the provisions of an agreement or the disposition of an employee complaint. The third party, who is selected by the parties involved, generally acts as an arbitrator and offers a judgment about the case.

In arbitration each party presents its position on disputed matters to the arbitrator. The arbitrator then judges the situation and decides on the disposition of each issue. For example, if no resolution can be reached regarding the extent of medical coverage or wage increases to include in a new contract, an arbitrator may be called in to make the decision. Or if a worker files a grievance against an employer that says he or she was unfairly discharged, as in the introduction to this chapter, an arbitrator may resolve the dispute.

Types of Arbitration

Arbitration can be categorized in a variety of ways. The first contrasts interest arbitration to rights arbitration. *Interest arbitration* is the resolution of disputes about the terms of a collective bargaining agreement. If union and management (or any two parties) cannot reach agreement about a contract, they may call in an arbitrator to judge which are the best or most appropriate terms. The arbitrator examines the positions of both parties and makes a judgment about the appropriate content of the agreement. Although this type of arbitration is relatively rare in the United States, it has been used to resolve impasses in the public sector; public unions have endorsed compulsory, binding, interest arbitration to avoid work stoppages.[8] States where strikes are illegal for public sector employees have also agreed to this type of arbitration, as discussed in Chapter 11. But interest arbitration removes the incentive for either party to withdraw or concede on any important issue; the prospect of arbitration colors the bargaining.[9]

Rights arbitration refers to a third party's resolution of grievances filed by individuals. We discuss rights arbitration in the next section.

The second categorization terms arbitration as either binding or nonbinding. In *binding arbitration* the parties are committed to accepting the arbitrator's decision. In *nonbinding arbitration* the parties can choose whether to accept the decision or not.

The third categorization describes arbitration as either *voluntary* or *compulsory*. In most cases, the two parties can voluntarily decide whether to call in an arbitrator to resolve a dispute. In some few others, contracts require arbitration in certain situations.

The final categorization defines arbitration as either final-offer or not final-offer. In *final-offer arbitration* the arbitrator asks each party to make a final offer. He or she then selects the "better" offer. This approach is sometimes chosen because an arbitrator's award is perceived to be more attractive. It is frequently used for public employees where expedient resolution of grievances is essential. In practice, most often the arbitrator does not make a decision about a final offer; he or she tries to mold a decision that is acceptable to all parties.

Rights Arbitration

Grievance or rights arbitration occurs when workers perceive that their rights have been violated, complain to management, and do not receive a satisfactory resolution to their complaints. The worker described in the introductory scenario might submit his claim to arbitration. A formal grievance procedure has the following purposes:

1. It provides a mechanism to adjust employees' complaints or to clarify disputes over the rights and obligations of the employer.
2. It brings the matter in a formal, prearranged way to the attention of union officials and management.
3. It defines and narrows the nature of the complaint.

4. It provides a structure of meetings between union and management at various levels that may result in settlement of the grievance.[10]

The grievance procedure has been linked to employee discipline as well:

> Employee discipline is the real drama of labor relations. It is a panorama of industrial conflicts. It is the nerve center of the network of interrelationships between management and employee. Here are no small issues. . . . On a broader canvas employee discipline is a process of control. It is a method for the maintenance of authority by management. . . . A reprimand or layoff or a discharge are the prerogatives which management uses as a control to keep these objectives in focus.[11]

But management can abuse workers by misusing discipline or misapplying the collective bargaining agreement. As noted earlier, grievances can be filed in response to perceived violations of the collective bargaining agreement, federal or state law, past practice, or company rules. Workers typically file grievances to protest unfair treatment or contractual violations, draw attention to a problem in the plant, such as a safety hazard, or exercise power as a test of union-management prerogatives. Only workers, not management, may file grievances: management acts, workers grieve.

Steps in the Grievance Procedure

Grievance procedure includes a series of complaints, responses, and appeals, which are summarized in Table 12–1. In the early stages, the aggrieved employee presents his or her complaint orally to the union steward. The union steward interviews the grievant and any witnesses to the situation being grieved, views relevant records, and consults with union officials. The steward for the employee in the introductory scenario should gather data in these ways. At this stage, the union steward who is processing a grievance should answer the following questions:

Action	Approximate Timetable
1. The aggrieved employee presents the complaint orally to the first-line supervisor and union steward.	3 days
2. The supervisor and steward forward the grievance in writing to the plant manager and union grievance committee or business agent.	3–5 days
3. The plant manager and union representative refer the grievance higher in their respective hierarchies, to the company's president, vice president of labor relations, or legal counsel, and the president of the local union.	5–10 days
4. Management and union submit the grievance to arbitration.	5–10 days
5. The arbitrator hears the case and renders a decision.	1–10 months

Table 12–1 STEPS IN THE GRIEVANCE PROCESS

1. Who was involved?
2. What happened that led to the grievance?
3. When did the incident or action occur?
4. Where did the events take place?
5. Why did the actions occur?
6. How were the actions taken?
7. Have there been any other grievances filed on the same subject?
8. If so, how did each side respond?
9. Did the case go to arbitration?
10. What was the arbitrator's ruling?[12]

The union steward should act empathetically toward the grievant and promise a full investigation of the complaint, but not guarantee the union's support in case the grievance lacks merit.

Either the grievant or the union steward can present the grievance to the line supervisor. Figure 12–2 illustrates a form used to file a grievance. Once the

Date:

Name of Grievant:

Position:

Description of Grievance:

Description of Contract or Past Practice Violation:

Response by Supervisor:

Subsequent Actions:

Figure 12–2 SAMPLE OF A GRIEVANCE FORM

grievance has been filed in this way, management interviews the supervisors and witnesses involved, reviews documentation of the incident, and checks with higher management to determine its position on the grievance. Figure 12–3 illustrates the interaction of the individual grievant, the union steward, and management at the early stages of grievance-handling. Union and management try to informally resolve grievances filed by individuals with a positive propensity to grieve; they more likely proceed to formal grievance procedures if an individual with a negative propensity to grieve files the complaint.

Next, union and management meet to try to resolve the grievance. The steward represents the grievant and tries to present a persuasive case. The internal organizational structure and management, the history of union-management relations, and any precedence in grievance-filing and -handling will influence whether and how the grievance is settled. For example, where union-management relations are cordial and management wants to maintain a cooperative work environment, the parties are likely to make every attempt to resolve the grievance at this early stage.[13] Most likely the company referred to in the introductory scenario would try to resolve the grievance without submitting it to arbitration.

The line supervisor submits his or her decision about the grievance in writing. At this time, the union (represented by the steward) or grievant can choose to proceed to the next step if either is dissatisfied with the decision. These steps of investigation, meeting, response, and appeal can be repeated until the grievance reaches arbitration.

Assuming no settlement occurs, the supervisor and steward then forward the grievance in writing to the plant manager and union grievance committee or business agent. They may also investigate the situation, analyze existing records, meet with the relevant parties, and reach a decision. Again, assuming no

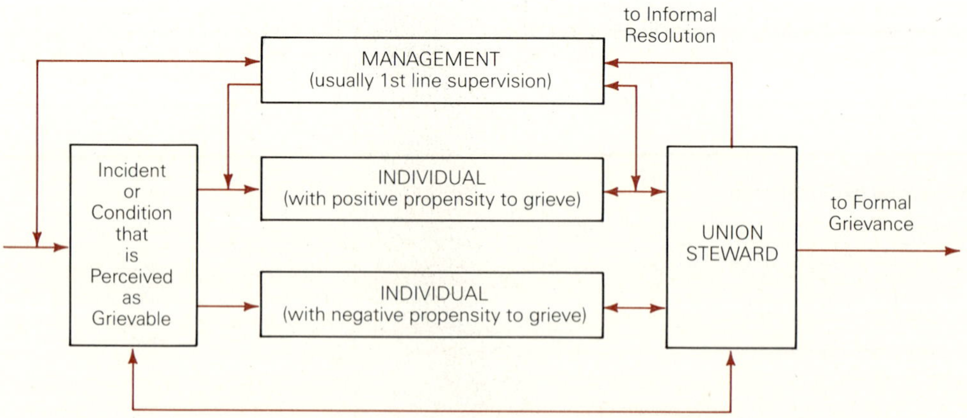

Reprinted with permission from D.R. Dalton and W.D. Todor, Antecedents of grievance filing behavior: Attitude/behavioral consistency and the union steward, *Academy of Management Journal* 25 (1982): 158.

Figure 12–3 EARLY STAGES OF THE GRIEVANCE PROCESS

resolution occurs, the union representative and plant manager refer the grievance higher in their respective hierarchies, to the president of the local union and to the company's president, vice president of labor relations, or legal counsel. Failure to resolve the grievance at this level most often results in its presentation to an arbitrator.

Most contracts specify the procedures and time required at each step in the grievance process. Figure 12–4 is an example of such contract language.

In grievance arbitration the union decides whether to go through the grievance process. It may not press for a third-party action if it views the process as too

ARTICLE VIII—ADJUSTMENTS OF GRIEVANCES

Section 1. The procedure under this Section is available to either the Company or the Union for the presentation and settlement of grievances arising hereunder.

Section 2. Any employee who believes that he has a justifiable request or complaint shall discuss same with his foreman with or without his Union committeeman being present, as he may elect, in an attempt to settle his request or complaint. Any such request or complaint which involves a question of the interpretation or application of, or compliance with the terms of this Agreement, shall constitute a grievance within the meaning of this Article. A grievance shall be processed in the manner set forth below and the specified time limitations, which shall be exclusive of Saturdays, Sundays and holidays, shall be strictly observed. When the grievance is not processed to the next step of the grievance procedure within the time limitations specified herein, it shall be considered settled on the basis of the answer given in the step of the grievance procedure in which it was last discussed.

Step 1. If, in the discussion with the foreman, the grievance is not satisfactorily disposed of, the employee may have his grievance presented to his department superintendent by his grievance committeeman, with or without the employee being present, as the employee may elect. Any such grievance must be submitted in writing to the department superintendent within thirty (30) days from the date the cause of the grievance occurs, except as specified in Article XI. The department superintendent shall answer the grievance in writing, within three (3) days of the presentation to him of such written grievance. If such written answer is unsatisfactory, the grievance may be presented to the Union Committee.

Step 2. The Union Committee, if it determines to carry the grievance further, shall, within five (5) days of the department superintendent's written answer in Step 1, present the written grievance to the Plant Manager for discussion at the next regularly scheduled monthly committee meeting. If the grievance is not satisfactorily disposed of in such a meeting, the Plant Manager shall, within ten (10) days answer the grievance in writing, unless a longer period for such answer is mutually agreed upon.

Step 3. The grievance, if not satisfactorily disposed of in Step 2, shall, within ten (10) days of the Plant Manager's written answer, be referred by letter, jointly addressed, to an official of the International Union and the Director—Personnel Services of the Company. They, or their designees, shall meet in the Hannibal area, preferably at the Hannibal Plant of the Company, as promptly as possible after they have been officially notified that the grievance is to be carried to Step 3. The Local Union shall be represented by the Chairman of the Local Grievance Committee, or his designee, and the local Plant Management by the Plant Manager or his designee. At such meeting no others shall be present except those deemed necessary by the parties for the purpose of giving information relevant to the grievance.

Figure 12–4 SAMPLE OF CONTRACT LANGUAGE REGARDING THE GRIEVANCE PROCESS

Continued

Step 4. If no agreement is reached in Step 3, either party may request in writing that an impartial umpire be appointed to determine the issue. Such request shall be made within fifteen (15) days of the Step 3 meeting. The designation of an impartial umpire shall be by mutual agreement between the parties. The fees and incidental expenses incurred by the impartial umpire in the determination of the controversy shall be shared equally by the Company and the Union. The decision of the umpire shall be final and binding upon both parties. Grievances involving the provisions of the collective bargaining Agreement and occurring so as to be processed to arbitration at the same time will be at the request of either party arbitrated before the same arbitrator. However, it is agreed that not more than four (4) cases will be heard at one series of hearings.

Section 3. An umpire to whom any grievance is submitted in accordance with the above procedure, shall only have jurisdiction and authority to interpret and apply the provisions of this Agreement insofar as it shall be necessary to the determination of such grievance, but he shall not have jurisdiction or authority to add to, or detract from or alter in any way the provisions of this Agreement.

[3]1975 Agreement between Universal Atlas Cement Division of United States Steel Corporation, Hannibal, Missouri plant, and Local 205, United Cement, Lime, and Gypsum Workers International Union, AFL-CIO, pp. 38–41.

Figure 12–4 Continued

costly or time-consuming, or if it believes the worker's case lacks strength or appropriateness. If the union does not support the grievance, the aggrieved worker still has the right to appeal the grievance through to arbitration and the union must represent the worker in these cases.

Research suggests that the more committed stewards are to their unions, the more they discuss grievances with members and resolve them before filing.[14] Stewards act in this way because they recognize that filing costs both union and management money and time, and it may not produce guaranteed (positive or negative) results. Research also indicates that company commitment to the resolution of grievances decreases as the number of grievances filed increases; as the union encourages members to file grievances; or as the union files grievances without the support of its members. The number of grievances actually filed tends to be a function of differences in union stewards' behaviors and attitudes, not differences among rank and file members.

A union must provide both *fair* and *adequate* representation of its members. If the complainant in the chapter opening scenario wishes to press his claim, the union must represent him through all steps. The union's duty to fairly represent employees has increasingly resulted in charges by members of the bargaining unit that (1) the union does not file grievances on their behalf and (2) the union mishandles grievances that are filed.[15] Workers can litigate against a union in these situations, claiming that the union breached the collective bargaining agreement. In one case, where the union represented senior workers after jobs were given to the most qualified rather than the most senior, the courts concluded that the union must advocate for *both* groups.[16] To protect themselves from failure-to-represent charges, some unions process all grievances—a time-consuming and costly process. Recently the NLRB has faced more than three times the number of these failure-to-represent cases than it did ten years ago.[17]

The Process of Arbitration

Arbitrators are generally chosen from the American Arbitration Association (AAA) or the Federal Mediation and Conciliation Service (FMCS). The American Arbitration Association had 16,669 cases filed with it in the twelve-month period ending October 31, 1979, as compared to 4007 in 1966.[18]

Arbitrators are typically trained as lawyers, professors of industrial relations, or economists. Internships with practicing arbitrators serve as the basic training ground.[19] Some private services provide a computer listing of arbitrators who have heard cases about specific issues; union or management can use this information to try to select arbitrators who have experience with their issues and have made favorable decisions.

To select an arbitrator, one or both parties requests that the AAA or FMCS furnish the names of three arbitrators. Union and management each eliminate one name from the list, with the remaining person being appointed the arbitrator. They can instead rotate cases among four or five mutually acceptable arbitrators. Or they can agree to a permanent arbitrator who handles all their cases. A study of thirty arbitrators and thirty-six representatives from labor and management agreed that name recognition was the most significant factor in choosing an arbitrator[20]; sex and ethnic characteristics were viewed as relatively unimportant.

Once an arbitrator is selected, the arbitration process lasts from one-half to one and a half days. Before the hearing each party typically

1. studies the original statement of the grievance and reviews its history through every step of the grievance process;
2. reviews the collective bargaining agreement from beginning to end;
3. assembles all documents and papers needed at the hearing;
4. interviews all witnesses to make sure they understand the basis of the case and role-plays a possible cross-examination;
5. writes a summary of the testimony of each witness;
6. studies the case from the other side's point of view and prepares to deal with opposing evidence and arguments;
7. discusses the outline of the case with others in the organization; and
8. reads published awards on the issues that seem pertinent to the case.[21]

The arbitrator acts as a judge in this proceeding. The parties may file prehearing briefs that present the basics of their arguments and supporting data. The arbitrator may request an opening statement from each side. Each side then presents its case by calling witnesses, with the union generally presenting first. The parties may file formal briefs that outline and support their cases. Each party next presents a summary. The parties may also file posthearing briefs offering any additional information not presented at the hearing. The arbitrator reviews the materials, then gives the decision, known as the *award,* and the analysis of the case to each party in writing. The analysis states the issues, facts, union and management contentions, and the relative weight he or she has assigned to the facts and contentions. Arbitrators have different styles, and thus proceedings can range from very formal to very informal.

In general, arbitrators base their decisions on the weight of the evidence. Would the evidence (interviews with relevant parties) indicate that the employee in the chapter introduction was unaware that the suspension had become a warning, and that he had not received the message from his mother in time to return to work? Arbitrators would answer this question by using the provisions of the labor agreement, the intent of the parties, past practice, the significance of the violation, and the nature of previous arbitration awards to determine the content of the award. A study of 400 Arbitration Case Report Forms indicated that the arbitrator upheld the grievance in 25 percent of the cases, denied it in 54 percent, and had a mixed response in 21 percent of the cases.[22]

Ten common errors in presenting an arbitration case include the following:

1. Using it as a harassment technique by arbitrating grievances that can't be won
2. Overemphasizing the grievance (by the union) or exaggerating an employee's fault (by management)
3. Preparing insufficiently and relying on a minimum of facts and a maximum of arguments
4. Introducing witnesses who have not been properly prepared as to demeanor or the importance of their testimony in the case
5. Unsuccessfully attempting to conceal essential facts or to distort the truth
6. Refusing to show books, records, and other documents until required to do so by subpoena
7. Clogging the procedure with legal technicalities
8. Withholding full cooperation from the arbitrator
9. Disregarding the ordinary rules of courtesy and decorum
10. Engaging in a debate with the other side (The time to try to convince the other party is before arbitration, during grievance discussions; at the arbitration hearing, efforts should be concentrated on convincing the arbitrator)[23]

Although a trilogy of court decisions in 1960 established the integrity of the arbitration process and the validity of the arbitrator's judgment, court decisions in 1974 and 1976 threw the finality of the arbitrator's award into question.[24] Parties who initially agree to arbitration are increasingly filing suit later to have the decision overturned. The increasing number of court challenges to arbitration awards threatens to undermine the finality of the process.[25] The courts are most likely to review appeals that concern procedural matters, such as claims that the arbitrator acted arbitrarily, exceeded his or her authority, or violated a federal statute.[26]

Problems with the arbitration process include the capability and ethics of the arbitrator, as well as procedural difficulties. Often management is dissatisfied with the decisions of the arbitrator, particularly when he or she reinstates employees who were dismissed. Yet one study showed that reinstated employees tend to be satisfactory workers, make normal progress, have a positive attitude, and tend not to commit problems requiring further discipline.[27] Arbitration is expensive—recent estimates have placed the cost of arbitration at $621 (1976 dollars) to $5000 (1984 dollars) per case. And a limited number of arbitrators is available so there are time lags in the process. Estimates indicate that the lapse between filing and resolution of the grievance averages 223 days.[28]

To reduce the cost and time lag, some organizations have introduced an expedited arbitration procedure.[29] In the steel industry, for example, with mutual agreement between union and management, the grievant can bypass the review by top management and union officials and proceed to arbitration. In addition, the arbitrator must conduct an informal hearing, allow no briefs or transcripts, suspend formal rules of evidence for the testimony, and render a decision within forty-eight hours.[30] A previously designated local representative presents each party's case. The arbitrator must ensure that the representatives present all necessary facts and considerations. Table 12–2 summarizes five expedited arbitration procedures.

MEDIATION AND FACT-FINDING

Two other approaches to resolution of contract disputes and grievances—mediation and fact-finding—can be used independently or in conjunction with arbitration. These procedures are most commonly used by organizations in the public sector. They often occur in the following sequence (if resolution does not occur at the preceding step): mediation, then fact-finding, and then arbitration.

Mediation

Grievance mediation can be used as an alternative to arbitration to facilitate labor and management reaching acceptable collective bargaining agreements or handling grievances.[31] In *mediation* a neutral party tries to help disputing parties reach a settlement of the issues that divide them. The neutral party does not act as a judge and therefore does not resolve the case. Rather, the mediator focuses on bringing the parties to agreement. Mediation can range from conciliation, where the mediator persuades the parties to meet and discuss their problems, to proposals of potential solutions.

Mediation can also be used as a final step before arbitration. It "helps identify and solve the underlying problem that caused the dispute; teaches 'settlement skills' to the parties involved so they can solve future problems in the workplace without recourse to either mediation or arbitration; and expedites the grievance-settlement process while leaving open the possibility of arbitration."[32] In one study of thirty-seven grievances, mediation resolved them more quickly, less expensively, and with greater management and worker satisfaction than arbitration.[33] Grievance mediation assists parties in resolving differences in a mutually

	Steelworkers— Basic Steel Industry	American Arbitration Association Service	AIW Local 562 Rusco, Inc.	American Postal Workers— U.S. Postal Service	Mini-Arbitration Columbus, Ohio
Source of arbitrators	Recent law school graduates and other sources	Special panel from AAA roster	FMCS roster	AAA, FMCS rosters	Its own "Joint Selection and Orientation Committee" from FMCS roster
Method of selecting	Preselected regional panels Administrator notifies in rotation	Appointed by AAA regional administrators	Preselected panel by rotating FMCS contacts	Appointed by AAA regional administrators	FMCS regional representative by rotation
Lawyers	No limitation, but understanding that lawyers will not be used	No limitation	No lawyers	No limitation but normally not used	No limitation
Transcript	No	No	No	No	May be used
Briefs	No	Permitted	No	No	May be used
Written description of issue	Last step grievance report	Joint submission permitted	No	Position paper	Grievance record expected
Time from request to hearing date	10 days	Approximately 3 days depending on arbitrator availability	10 days	Approximately 7 days depending on arbitrator availability	Not specified
Time of hearing to award	Bench decision or 48 hours	5 days	48 hours	Bench decision written award 48 hours	48 hours
Fees (plus expenses)	$100/½ day $150/day	$100 filing fee Arbitrator's normal fee	$100/½ day $150/day	$100 filing fee $100 per case	$100/½ day, 1 or 2 cases; $150/full day, 1 or 2 cases; $200/day, 3 or 4 cases

SOURCE: J. Zalusky. "Arbitration: Updating a Vital Process," November 1976 *AFL-CIO Federationist,* the official monthly magazine of the AFL-CIO. Reprinted with permission.

Table 12–2 **EXPEDITED ARBITRATION PROCEDURES**

satisfactory fashion. This type of resolution assumes, however, that both parties consider grievances a solvable problem.

Mediation involves three components:

1. Procedural suggestions—the mediator schedules and conducts meetings, establishes or extends deadlines, and keeps records.
2. Communication functions—the mediator keeps channels of communication open, presents one party's plan to the other to test reactions, or offers opportunities for the parties to exchange demands.
3. Affirmative actions—the mediator establishes priorities, softens extreme stands, and offers creative solutions.[34]

The effective mediator has good communication skills, knows how to manage crisis situations, and has good timing. One researcher suggests that to qualify as a mediator an individual must have "the patience of Job; the physical endurance of the marathon runner; the broken-field dodging abilities of a halfback; the guile of Machiavelli; the personality-probing skills of a good psychiatrist; the confidence-retaining characteristic of a mute; the hide of a rhinoceros; and the wisdom of Solomon."[35] In addition, the mediator must know

- when to intervene,
- with whom to intervene,
- how to conduct, control, and schedule meetings,
- how to listen,
- how to evaluate the importance of each issue to the parties,
- how to get commitment to a solution by the parties,
- the importance of remaining neutral,
- when to make a substantive suggestion,
- how to paraphrase,
- how to manage crisis situations,
- how to establish and maintain open, relevant, and accurate communication, and
- the significance of the context in which the negotiations occur.[36]

A good mediator can improve an unhealthy labor-management relationship. He or she tries to determine the true intentions of each party and communicates them to the other, often proposing alternate solutions. The mediator attributes the alternative solutions to himself or herself so that both sides can save face. In this way, the mediator can determine the intentions of both sides and test the other side's reactions to them. In one study of the nature and function of mediation in disputes between public school teachers and their school board, teachers rated the mediator's ability to quickly comprehend aspects of the case and general knowledge of labor relations as the most important factors in resolving disputes; mediators rated persuasiveness and energetic persistence as most important; and school board members evaluated the mediator's knowledge of labor relations and persistence as most essential.[37]

Mediators use a variety of strategies and tactics to facilitate reaching an agreement. Some mediators try to make deals, while others try to orchestrate agreements; some emphasize the importance of content knowledge about similar agreements and the circumstances at hand, while others focus on encouraging a process likely to result in fair and appropriate outcomes.[38] In Reading 12–1, "Strategy and the Tactics of Mediation," Deborah Kolb discusses the differences between FMCS and state mediators.

Mediation can be broken down into three stages. In the early stages the mediator achieves acceptability, identifies the issues in dispute, specifies obstacles, and tries to develop an attitudinal climate of collaboration. He or she takes a passive, listening role. In other words, the mediator establishes his or her role as well as credibility with the two parties. In the second stage, the mediator helps the two parties exchange proposals and counterproposals. He or she holds probing conversations with the parties to identify their priorities and outstanding issues. In later stages, pressure for settlement builds. The mediator becomes more aggressive, trying to get the parties to face reality and adjust their expectations so that they can find common areas of acceptance. The mediator may formulate proposals for the parties to discuss or, in rare cases, offer proposals from which to choose (assuming a more judgmental role).

Fact-finding

Fact-finding is a process somewhere between mediation and arbitration. Fact-finders may trace the history of the parties and the dispute, specify the issues, state each party's position on the issues, and summarize the arguments supporting the positions.[39] Fact-finding can take place with or without recommendations. If recommendations are given, they can focus on procedures or on the bargaining issues themselves. Fact-finders gather and assess the facts relating to the situation and display them publicly in hopes that the parties will feel obligated to accept the validity of their analyses and conclusions. In fact-finding, management and union define the issues. Each then proposes its own resolution with a supporting argument.[40] The fact-finder then attempts to structure the presentation and discussion of opinions to allow an agreement to occur.

Fact-finding attempts to avoid strikes by postponing them. By revealing the facts it tries to build public sentiment against unreasonable demands and to encourage their withdrawal. It may identify new considerations for the parties to evaluate. Finally, when recommendations are offered, fact-finding may shift the burden of proof to the party that rejects them.[41] No legal proof is required in fact-finding; rather, the burden of proof is left to the public's judgment.

Fact-finding shares the following advantages with arbitration:

1. It helps conclude the negotiations process.
2. The neutral third party provides a fresh perspective and approach to unresolved issues.

3. It offers political advantages in resolving an impasse by allowing the parties to "pass the buck" to a third party.
4. It can help structure public opinion and prepare the public for the settlements.
5. It can encourage parties to resolve disputes on their own.

However, fact-finding also has some disadvantages in common with arbitration:

1. It may leave the two parties in disharmony.
2. It may not resolve the basic causes of their differences.
3. It may not give access to complete information and thus prevent the true interests and priorities of the parties from being considered.
4. It may cement positions.
5. It may discourage the parties from giving any power to a third party who is not viewed as accountable.[42]

The effectiveness of fact-finding is not clear. Research in Wisconsin and New York indicated a relatively high rejection rate of fact-finders' recommendations.[43]

APPROACHES TO RESOLVING GRIEVANCES IN NONUNION ORGANIZATIONS

Nonunion organizations, as well as unionized ones must have procedures for resolving employee grievances. A recent study of nonunion companies indicates that approximately two-thirds have an employee complaint system.[44] Such systems can provide mechanisms to (1) identify and resolve employee dissatisfactions, (2) identify the practices, procedures, and policies that cause dissatisfaction, (3) gauge temperaments, (4) settle complaints, (5) improve worker morale and productivity, (6) communicate upward, (7) provide justice in the workplace, and (8) at least potentially reduce the threat of unionization.[45]

There are five general types of nonunion grievance systems: (1) open-door policy, (2) ombudsperson, (3) juries of peers, (4) hearing officers, and (5) binding outside arbitration.[46] In an *open-door program,* employees can go to any manager with a complaint. In this case justice may not be served because the manager who handles the grievance is frequently a party to it. If so, he or she lacks credibility and is unlikely to act fairly.

Use of an *ombudsperson* adds objectivity to the grievance process. The ombudsperson listens to complaints and designs corrective action. The ombudsperson acts as a mediator who can fairly settle the grievance. He or she must have strong interpersonal and communication skills, good knowledge of organizational goals and policies, and the trust and respect of workers. Human resources professionals can act as ombudspersons, bringing their objectivity and knowledge of organizational behavior to the solution of the problems presented to them.

Peer decision is a review procedure where a panel of coworkers and managers acts as a quasijudicial body. It reaches an advisory decision about complaints presented to it. In one experiment, nonunionized hourly workers have convened and led a grievance review panel to handle complaints. This mechanism has ended disputes and helped the company to avoid unionization.[47] Too often, however, management fails to act on the board's recommendations, and the system loses credibility. Because the decisions are not made by people with human resources management expertise, they are often poor ones.

Hearing officers are professionals, often in human resources management, employed by the organization to make judgments about grievances. Their effectiveness depends on workers and management perceiving them as expert and fair. Because the position of hearing officer is traditionally a full-time one, most frequently it is large organizations that have this type of grievance system.

Finally, nonunion organizations can also use an outside arbitrator, as described earlier in this chapter for union organizations. Because of the cost and its association with union situations, however, this system is relatively rare in nonunion organizations.

Regardless of the type of grievance system used, employees should receive a detailed description of the procedures. Such a description should specify the purpose of the procedure, the groups covered, the steps of the process, an assurance of management's objectivity, and encouragement of employees to use it.[48] If the organization described in the opening scenario of this chapter were nonunion, any of these grievance systems would be appropriate for handling the dispute.

IMPROVING CONTRACT ADMINISTRATION

Both human resources professionals and managers can assure that effective procedures exist and are implemented for hearing and resolving employee grievances. Grievance procedures have frequently been used as adversary proceedings.[49] Too often, the phrasing of the grievance calls for a win-lose outcome, rather than one both parties can accept. To facilitate effective grievance resolution, contract language should include the following requisites:

1. The parties must identify the problem, its dimensions, and the priorities assigned to its resolution.
2. The parties must offer the possible causes and explanations of the grievance as a focus of discussion and exploration.
3. Each party should specify an acceptable outcome of the grievance.
4. Both parties should examine diverse alternatives (e.g., different resolution procedures or possible awards) to reach a desired outcome.
5. The parties must assign responsibility for reaching and implementing the solution.
6. The parties should establish follow-up procedures to reduce the likelihood of similar grievances in the future.[50]

A sample of contract language emphasizing these principles is shown in Figure 12–5.

One estimate of the cost of resolving grievances stated that, on the average, resolution required 9.1 work hours per grievance for formal meetings alone; disruptions of regular work increase its cost.[51] Both human resources professionals and managers can improve the contract resolution and administration process.

Implications for Human Resources Professionals

Human resources professionals should establish and monitor grievance procedures. They should facilitate the prompt settlement of disputes inside the organization by acting as follows:

1. Human resources professionals should participate in the design and specification of a clear grievance system, in both union and nonunion organizations. They should ensure that the system expediently and fairly responds to the workers' and organization's needs.
2. Human resources professionals should conduct training for supervisors and managers about the provisions of the grievance system. They should monitor its implementation to ensure that it is applied appropriately.
3. Human resources professionals should track all grievances, recording the type of grievance, the nature of resolution, the level of resolution, and the time required by all personnel to resolve the complaint. Where possible, they should encourage changes in organizational practices or in subsequent labor contracts to help reduce the number of grievances.
4. Human resources professionals should oversee any cases that reach arbitration; they should contribute to the selection of an arbitrator, assist in the

---

Third Step: The matter shall be referred to the next meeting of the labor management relations committee. At this meeting, members of the union and management will each specifically define the problem that is to be resolved, establish a joint objective in resolution of the problem and identify at least three alternatives to the resolution of the grievance. If no settlement is reached upon conclusion of this labor relations meeting, then—

Fourth Step: The matter shall be referred to a conference between the company's corporate director of industrial relations and a duly authorized representative of the international union. The parties will have the responsibility to review the stated problem, the objectives to be accomplished and the alternatives. At this step, both parties should refine, if necessary, and add alternative solutions. If a settlement does not result from such conference within a 30-day period, the grievance may, at the discretion of the union, be referred to arbitration in accordance with the arbitration provisions of this agreement.

SOURCE: J.F. Rand, Creative problem-solving applied to grievance/arbitration procedures. Reprinted from the March, 1980 issue of *Personnel Administrator*, copyright, 1980, The American Society for Personnel Administration, 606 North Washington Street, Alexandria, VA 22314, $30 per year.

Figure 12–5 EXCERPT OF CONTRACT LANGUAGE THAT FACILITATES EFFECTIVE GRIEVANCE RESOLUTION

preparation of the case, attend the arbitration proceedings, and record the decision. They should also analyze the outcomes of all cases that reach arbitration to determine trends and possible corrective actions.

Implications for Managers

Managers should understand grievance procedures within the organization and implement them correctly. Effective practice involves the following:

1. Managers in a unionized organization should know the provisions of the union contract so that they can implement them correctly or recognize when they deviate from specified procedures.
2. Managers should train any subordinate managers in the provisions of the contract and insist on their careful implementation of them. They should monitor managers' conduct with regard to union workers.
3. Managers in nonunionized organizations should implement a grievance procedure that encourages the rapid and fair resolution of grievances. They should act as prescribed by the system and as objectively as possible.

READING

Reading 12–1

STRATEGY AND THE TACTICS OF MEDIATION[1]

Deborah M. Kolb[2]

Labor mediators see the achievement of a settlement as their objective. From this point of convergence, mediators will differ on the strategy to be used to achieve this end. Tactics refer to the specific actions mediators take in the service of these strategic ends. Based on a participant observation of 10 mediators on 16 cases, the strategies and tactics of mediators from a state agency are contrasted with those used by mediators from a federal agency. The state mediators use a building strategy and emphasize directive tactics to gather information, assess priorities, and encourage parties to move the parties on discrete issues. In contrast, the federal mediators favor a narrowing strategy and emphasize tactics to encourage the parties to continue to meet and progressively refine their proposals in order for an acceptable package to emerge. Mediators from both agencies see their strategic approach as responsive to the parties they serve.

INTRODUCTION

Mediation is often described as an art. The basis for this claim is thought to rest with the highly individualistic means by which the mediator brings parties to a settlement (Rehmus, 1965; Kochan & Jick, 1978). These "means" are indeed the essence of mediation—how does the mediator, faced with a situation where the parties cannot agree on the provisions of a contract, ultimately enable them to reach agreement? The term "strategy" is used in the literature to describe these means (Stevens, 1963; Kressel, 1972; Kochan & Jick, 1978). Although the term is widely used and accepted, there appears to be some confusion about its precise meaning.

From the perspective of practicing mediators, the actions they take to bring the parties to settlement are inseparable from the intent of the action, which is in turn based on the interpretation they make of the parties' needs at a particular point in time.[3] When mediators describe what they do, therefore, they emphasize both the concrete action taken as well as the purpose for taking the action:

> You see, I asked them (the union) for the work schedule at other broadcasting stations. I want them to think of management's proposal in terms of practice in other stations. They are upset, but the proposal may not be that different from others. (Comment from a mediator)

In the empirical research on mediation, strategies have been conceptualized and measured in ways that tend to differ from, and in some situations actually misrepresent, the ways mediators understand their activities. This misrepresentation occurs because the differences between strategies—what mediators say they do—and tactics—what they actually do—have not been fully appreciated. In most of the recent research on mediator strategies, presentational strategies (see Van Maanen, 1979), which refer to the abstract and general statements mediators make about what they do to get a settlement, have been the primary focus of interest. Kressel's (1972) interview study of 12 practitioners presents an inventory of such strategies. The problem is that these abstract generalizations do not neatly map to the actions the mediator actually takes in a particular situation. For

Reprinted with permission from *Human Relations*, 36 (1983) pp. 247–268.

[1]To the mediators who gave generously of their time and wisdom, I give my special thanks. To John Van Maanen, Lotte Bailyn, and Thomas Kochan, I am indebted for their analytic insights and the special contributions they made to the production of this paper and the larger study of which it is a part.

[2]Requests for reprints should be sent to Deborah M. Kolb, Associate Professor, Simmons Graduate School of Management, 409 Commonwealth Avenue, Boston, Massachusetts, 02215.

[3]The term strategy puts a particular connotation on the mediator's activities. It makes them appear more scientific, planned, and methodical than they may be. It is interesting to note that the term strategy is not one used by practitioners themselves, for they frequently emphasize the unpredictable over the planned in accounting for what they do.

example, an often reported presentational strategy is that mediators "get the parties to face reality" (Kressel, 1972; Kochan & Jick, 1978). Mediators would probably agree that such an objective is indeed an important element of a mediator's strategy. Where they might disagree is on how operationally or tactically they can accomplish such an objective. In recent cross-sectional studies, presentational strategies and operational tactics are lumped together. As a result, it becomes difficult to separate what the mediator is trying to accomplish, e.g., "educate the parties to the bargaining process," from the tactics he uses to accomplish this end, e.g., "by pressing the parties hard to make compromises" (Kochan & Jick, 1978, p. 240).

This paper presents an alternative approach to the conception and study of mediator strategies and tactics. It starts with the assumption that the goal of the mediator is to get a settlement. Starting from this point of convergence, however, mediators will often differ on what strategy should be used to achieve this end. Similar to its military and planning usage (Anthony, Dearden, & Vancil, 1965; Manning, 1979), strategy, as used here, refers to an overall plan, approach, or method a mediator has for resolving a dispute. All things being equal, it is the way the mediator intends to manage the case, the parties, and the issues. Strategy is presentational in that it describes what the mediator believes he is trying to accomplish and how he intends to do it.

What the mediator actually does (and may be observed doing) to bring the parties to settlement, to learn the issues and priorities, and to encourage movement I have labelled mediation tactics. There are several characteristics that are important to note about tactics.

1. Tactics are operational. They are concrete behaviors that may be observed.
2. As behaviors, tactics have no meaning in and of themselves (Manning, 1979). They can only be understood in the context of strategy, i.e., what the mediator plans to do. Indeed, tactics are the behavioral specifics of strategy.
3. Although one observes much variability in the use of tactics, i.e., no two mediators are likely to use the same tactic in precisely the same way, there are patterns that can be observed. Consistent with his strategy, a mediator will tend to emphasize certain types of tactics and time their use in particular ways. Indeed, by observing these patterns, one can infer the strategy that underlies them.

To study mediation tactics, therefore, requires that they be analyzed and interpreted within the context of the particular strategy of which they are a part. In this paper, the contrasting strategies used by mediators from two government agencies and the tactical patterns associated with them are presented. The findings are inductively based on an observational study of 16 mediation cases. Ten of the cases were conducted by practitioners from a state agency whose jurisdiction is primarily in the public sector. The remaining six cases were conducted by mediators from a field office of the Federal Mediation and Conciliation Service, in a variety of private sector settings. By observing the mediators at work on their cases and discussing the observed activities with them, I was able to begin to decode how strategies and tactics are understood and used by mediators over the course of a case.[4,5]

Observation of the mediators' effort to settle disputes between the parties suggests that mediators from these agencies start with a similar objective—to bring the parties to settlement. Their strategies for accomplishing this end differ. The contrasts can be seen in the ways the mediators handle the basic activities of the process—how they learn the issues in dispute, decipher the parties' priorities, assess and interpret these priorities, and encourage them to

[4]A more complete account of the methods used in this study is contained in Kolb (1981a) and in the Methods Appendix of my dissertation (Kolb, 1981b). To analyze the mediator's strategy and tactics, I arrayed every action I had observed according to the chronology of the cases and collapsed these tactics into sets of categories that appeared generalizable across the sample.

[5]My presence on the cases affects this discussion of strategy in interesting ways. Mediators take many actions in the context of a case, only some of which may be considered strategic. As they work on a case, they may be observed acting in ways that one would be hard pressed to call strategic—e.g., getting angry, laughing. These are merely reactions. However, when mediators talked to me about why they were angry or why they laughed, they couched their descriptions in deliberate, strategic terms. Thus, when analyzing a mediator's strategy, it is important to bear in mind that much of what passes for strategy are figments of retrospective constructions and not of preplanned method (see Weick, 1979). Basically, mediators act and then account for their actions in language that signifies intentionality. What I have tried to do in this paper, because I was present at the cases, is describe and analyze what the mediators actually did and not rely solely on retrospective constructions.

make moves toward settlement. The differences in strategy were consistent over the two caseloads. Tactics, however, do not fall as neatly into consistent patterns. Rarely were particular tactics unique to one group of mediators or the other. Rather, the tactics observed were similar for both the state and federal mediators. What differed were the frequencies and timing of the tactics used, differences which may be traced to contrasting underlying strategies.

STRATEGY AND CONTEXT: STATE AND FEDERAL MEDIATORS

The state and federal mediators in this study have contrasting strategies rooted in the definitions they hold of the mediator's role (Kolb, 1981a). State mediators define their role as one of "deal-making." Based on their perception that the parties in the public sector are inexperienced in the ways of collective bargaining and have reached an impasse in their efforts to resolve their own dispute, the state mediators believe that responsibility for creating an acceptable deal rests with the mediator. To this end, they rely on a strategy of *building an acceptable package* from priority issues. To accomplish this, the state mediators plan to gather a great deal of information about the *facts* surrounding the dispute and the *priorities* of the parties. They assess this information primarily within the context of comparable geographical *patterns* and attempt to move the parties on an *issue-by-issue* basis. To implement their strategy, the state mediators make use of directive information-gathering and movement tactics and initiate these efforts early in the case.

In contrast, the federal mediators see themselves as "orchestrators" of the process. Based on their perception that settlement is ultimately inevitable and that the parties must "live under" the contract they set, the federal mediators manage the mediatory process in such a way that responsibility for the substantive elements of the settlement rests with the parties. To achieve this end, the federal mediators favor a "narrowing"[6] type of strategy that relies heavily on the slow, but consistent exchange of increasingly refined proposals and counteroffers. What remains after the narrowing process is an acceptable package. To accomplish this narrowing process, federal mediators try to clarify the *issues* in dispute, give the parties *time and space* to establish their own priorities, which the mediators continually assess according to *situational* categories of relevance. Finally, movement is accomplished in terms of the *total package*. Tactically, the federal mediators use indirect techniques to gather the minimal information they need, and use movement tactics that assist the parties in proposal preparation. More directive movement tactics, if used at all, are observed late in the case, once considerable narrowing has been accomplished.

Learning the Issues in Dispute: Facts Versus Issues

According to all mediators, the first step in the case is to learn the issues in dispute. This may be accomplished in many ways. For example, it may occur in a joint meeting where one side presents its demands and the other party signals its agreement that the presented issues are indeed the ones in dispute. Or the mediator may learn the issues through extensive private meetings with the parties, where each side presents its understandings of the outstanding issues. There are, however, several observed differences in the way the state and federal mediators go about this basic task.

State mediators try to "learn the facts." These facts cover not only the parties' demands, but also include information about the constraints and opportunities inherent in the situation. Depending upon the case, these facts may include the economic climate of the community, the personalities on the bargaining committee, the political posture of the town managers, settlements in comparable jurisdictions, as well as the history of negotiations prior to impasse. These facts start to frame the state mediator's thinking about the range of an acceptable package. (See Table 12–3 for the types of initial information sought in a state and federal case.)

The federal mediators use their first session with the parties to "learn the issues in dispute." If the parties are to narrow the differences between them successively for a package to result, federal mediators believe that there must be initial consensus on the

[6]The term narrowing is somewhat ambiguous. The federal mediators do not actually do the narrowing themselves. Rather they use tactics that allow the parties to narrow the differences between them. However, getting the parties to narrow is the strategy. In shorthand and in the interests of comparability, I have shortened this to "narrowing."

	State mediation	Federal mediation
Purpose	Learn the facts	Learn the issues
Forum for starting the case	Separate meetings	Joint meeting
Tactics: Information sought about:	(1) Basics of proposal	(1) Last proposal from each side
	(2) Mechanics of some provisions	(2) Mechanics of some provisions
	(3) Negotiating history	(3) Status of provisions under existing contract
	(4) Political climate of town	
	(5) Tax status	
	(6) Budgetary process	
	(7) Composition, personality, and authority of bargaining committees	

Table 12–3 COMPARISON OF STRATEGY AND TACTICS OBSERVED IN THE FIRST MEETING OF A STATE AND FEDERAL CASE

areas of disagreement. When the parties attempt to introduce "facts" into the discussion, the mediators typically request that such information be held until the parties adjourn to separate meetings. In practice, when learning the issues is uncoupled from learning the facts, it means that the parties can work from the same, agreed-upon areas of disagreement. In the building strategy, learning the issues, learning the facts, learning priorities, and encouraging movement may occur in the same initial form. As a result, the parties may make moves before they have agreed upon the issues in dispute. (See Kolb, 1981b.)

Gathering Information About Priorities

Ascertaining the likelihood of a settlement and the probable contents of an agreement are facets of a case that continually preoccupy all mediators. In particular, the mediator is interested in priorities. Priorities mean several things to the mediator. In terms of the demands that comprise a party's proposal, priorities mean those issues which are crucial or "musts" as opposed to those which may be "nice, but not necessary." Wages are usually considered priority issues. Work rules such as shift preference and manning levels and fringe benefits such as medical plans, vacations, and maternity leaves may or may not be priorities depending upon the particular situation. But priorities do not refer solely to the issues themselves, they also refer to the level of benefit as well—i.e., how many vacation days, duration of maternity leave, etc. What interests the mediator, then, are those issues that the parties consider of top priority and compensated at what level. It is quite obvious that if the mediator were privy to all this information, he would know the parties' "bottom lines." The need to have this information on priorities and bottom lines and the tactics used to secure such data differed between the state and federal mediators.

Since state mediators are attempting to build a package, they need to identify the priority issues that such a package must at a minimum contain. One state mediator described what he needed to know to fashion a package:

> You need to get to the core of the matter. You try to get the bottom line. You may have to sweat it out of them. You keep asking directly and keep hammering it down. Often the parties don't know what it is. So priority issues are not just what they [the parties] say they are, but your experience about what's important and your determination of what's attainable.

To get to the core of the matter, state mediators work through the parties' respective proposals on an issue-by-issue basis. Early in the case, through the use of directive tactics, the state mediators attempt to discover what moves it will take for the parties to settle.

1. They may *ask* directly, as one mediator did in the first meeting he had with the union:

> Joe [union attorney], you know the way I work. I know all 26 of these [demands] are important, but which are more important than the others? Which ones would really make a difference? Why don't I go through them and you whisper in my ear what can go?

Another state mediator asked the union committee for its bottom line on wages in an early meeting in the case:

> You have to tell me what it will take. I can't do anything until you give me the percentage. How about 16% for two years? Will that do it?

2. The state mediators also made suggestions and used their own arguments as a way to test the firmness of a negative response on a particular issue. For example, when a management negotiator in the first meeting refused to discuss the union's sick leave bank proposal, the mediator countered with suggested alternatives that were responsive to the negotiator's objections to the demand:

> You see, I showed him how we could "condition" it to take care of his problems. When he still said no, I knew it was off the table.

Certainly, the state mediators developed a sense of priorities from the proposals they were given and from confidences uttered by chief negotiators off the record. But on balance, the state mediators were more likely to seek information on priorities directly and early in the case, then wait for such information to be divulged.

The federal mediators were also concerned about priorities. However, they believe that priorities are difficult to decipher. The parties may not know them until they have been forced to make trade-offs in the course of bargaining. Or, if the parties know their priorities, they are likely, in the interests of maximal bargaining leverage, to keep such information to themselves. Finally, the federal mediators believe that priorities will often change as a result of narrowing, so that information gathered early in the case may later prove to be unreliable. One federal mediator described how he viewed the process of learning priorities:

> I know from experience what the key issues are, but it's their priorities that are important. They have to get a fix on what they want, and they can't do it until they bring their proposal into focus. . . . As for management, I know them. They'll tell me when the time is right.

Early in the case, the federal mediators are more concerned about the parties' intentions to continue to meet and make incremental moves than they are about identifying substantive priorities. As a result, the federal mediators do not make much of an effort to learn priorities directly. They seem content to wait for information to be given them through (1) the formal exchange of refined and narrowed proposals that start to suggest which issues are priority ones and (2) confidences given them by the spokesmen. However, the substance of these confidences differs between the early and later stages of the case. Early in the case, discussions between the spokesmen and mediators mostly touch on the process of the mediation and not the issues themselves. For example, the spokesman might brief the mediator on his plans for the upcoming joint meeting, or they might discuss whether to separate economic from noneconomic issues for consideration, or they may use such off-the-record meetings to set a date for the next mediation session. Later in the case, if the mediator is to play a more active role—e.g., convey a final offer—these off-the-record meetings then become the forum to discuss substance.

Like the tactics used by the state mediators, those of the federal mediators are intimately tied to their strategy. Since they want a package to result from a narrowing process, they are more concerned that the parties demonstrate progress toward that end, than they are to ascertain the precise nature of the priorities, particularly during the early stages of the case. Their indirect and rather passive approach gives the parties the time and space to refine their own priorities, and allows the mediator to monitor that, at a minimum, progress is continually made.

"Reading" Priorities: Categories of Interpretation

As mediators learn of the parties' intentions and develop a sense of the priorities each side has for settlement, they begin to make predictions about whether the parties are likely to settle, and if so, what form the agreement will take. To make such predictions, mediators rely on interpretative categories that allow them to make sense of what they hear[7] (see Spradley, 1970). Three categories are of general concern and appear to underlie the actions of both the state and federal mediators.

First, the relative bargaining power of the parties must be assessed. Relative bargaining power refers to the mediator's assessment of which side is more likely to realize its demands, and complementarily, which party will have to "move the furthest" for a settlement to be reached. The mediators' estimation of bargaining power seems to be based on two intertwined criteria: (1) how critical the employees are to the functioning of the organization, and relatedly, (2) how capable the union is to strike and management to withstand the action.

Second, the relationship between the demands and "patterns and standards of practice" must be assessed. Whereas estimations of bargaining power help the mediator predict the shape of the final agreement, mediators tend to assume that the form of the agreement, that is, the contract provisions, will conform to certain patterns and standards of practice. As mediators use the term patterns, they refer to historical settlement ranges, wage scales, and practice with regard to fringe benefits and work rules in comparable industries and/or contiguous communities. Thus, as demands are introduced and modified, they are assessed by the mediator according to their conformance or deviation from what are thought to be patterns.[8]

Third, mediators develop an assessment of the chief negotiators based on first-hand knowledge and reputation. A subset of chief negotiators, described by the mediators as "pros," are distinguished by their experience and familiarity with collective bargaining and mediation and their immediate and previous behavior in mediation. Statements from the pros have the power to modify the mediator's assessments about settlement and contract provisions that were based on relative bargaining power and patterns. For example, if a pro indicates that a certain provision is a "must," or that a demand from the other side that appears logical or rational will not be conceded, or that a bottom line has been reached, the mediator will tend to believe the pro.

The state and federal mediators made use of all these categories (power, patterns, and pros) in their assessments of the likely settlement range, but they differed in terms of when, how, and to what use they put these assessments.

Relative Bargaining Power. Because their caseload is primarily in the public sector where unions are denied the legal right to strike, the state mediators see the balance of power always tipped in favor of management. Thus, they enter a case with the assumptions that (1) the mediator will have to devote more effort to moving the union, for they will have relatively more concessions to make, and (2) the union, as the weaker party, will need the mediator to press its positions with management, for without such efforts, the union would realize few of its demands. One mediator described this belief system:

> There is no replacement for the strike. The bottom line in the public sector is what management wants to do, given a few percentage points either way. What you try to do as a mediator is get management to do the fair thing, because you know the union will eventually have to go along.

For the federal mediator, assessment of bargaining power is more situational. Since the unions in the

[7]Categories of relevance are the means by which raw information about issues, people, and bargaining environments are made meaningful. Categories allow the mediator to identify the people and their behavior as recognizable features of the situation and to gauge his own behavior accordingly (see McHugh, 1968; Spradley, 1970).

[8]Although economic patterns seem to exist in certain industrial sectors (Dunlop, 1957; Ross, 1948; Bourdon, 1979) and occupational groups (Anderson, 1979; Kochan, 1980), what the mediator refers to as a pattern is neither as systematic nor as empirically demonstrable. A mediator may make reference to a pattern if he encounters regularities in his caseload, or if he has read about industry averages recently, or even if he had a case the previous day that settled in a particular way. Patterns, however, as loosely constructed as they are, seem to have an existence in the mind of the mediator apart from the particular context of a case and appear to him as an "objective" standard to apply in any dispute. Often when mediators say a demand is reasonable or rational, they mean that it conforms to a pattern with which they are familiar.

private sector have the legal right to strike,[9] determination of relative bargaining power is an ongoing preoccupation of the federal mediator. The federal mediator is often not sure until late in the case whether the union plans a strike or not. Indeed, a major rationale for a narrowing strategy is that it makes it increasingly more costly for the union to go on strike:

> This is why the process of narrowing down is so important. The final wage offer is the union's. The complete health and welfare package is theirs. They got the COLA (cost of living escalator) they asked for. When you get them to narrow down, many of the issues are theirs (based on their counterproposals), and it becomes harder for them to take a walk (strike).

Patterns. During the early phases of the case, most of the state and federal mediators' assessments of the issues are described in terms of patterns and standards of practice. However, there are several differences in the emphasis placed on patterns, and on how these assessments are used. The caseload of the state mediators exposes them to bargaining relationships that affect similar occupational groups—teachers, firefighters, police—in contiguous cities and towns. As a result, it is quite natural that comparisons between the demands in a current case and settlements in other similar communities with the same occupations are made. Further, since the state mediators start to build a package early in the case, and these are the kinds of assessments that tend to predominate at that time, this criterion of patterns and standard practice tends to be overriding. In this first session with the union committee, a state mediator described the importance of patterns:

> In the public sector, we are very primitive, but we do have a first measurement—to compare your proposal with other towns. And of course you realize that what happened with other units here in Unionville will also affect what happens to you.

[9]The federal mediators' caseload comprises the private industrial sector and private, nonprofit hospitals jurisdiction given them under the National Labor Relations Act. Under Executive Order, they have jurisdiction for workers in the federal government who do not have the right to strike.

The federal mediators also assessed the issues in terms of patterns and standards of practice. Early in the case, they use patterns as a way to assess how realistic the opening positions are:

> The wages they want are 10% and the 1% from COLA. That's 11%. The average we've been getting is 7%. 11%, no way. They have as much chance of getting that as flying.

In addition to cross-sectional comparisons, the federal mediators used the previous contract in making assessments about the form of the one currently in dispute. They believe that it is difficult for the parties to depart from past practice:

> Bill's smart [management attorney]. He knows he has to put the bonus in, because they had it in the last contract. But he's going to save it until the union makes substantial moves.

Although the federal mediators consider patterns in "reading" the issues, and take these readings early in the case, they do not make direct use of their assessments and in fact, rarely mention them to the parties at all. Later in the case, these assessments may be used as movement tactics, but only after considerable narrowing has already been accomplished.

Pros. The state and federal mediators see pros in a different light and view their contribution to the mediator's strategy differently (Kolb, 1981a, 1981b). In brief, the state mediators believe that pros are resources to the mediator who provide him with information about priorities and support him in his effort to build and sell a package. Thus, the state mediators expect that pros will share their conviction about patterns and will support the mediator's efforts to convince the rest of the bargaining committee to act accordingly. At the end of the first session of a three session case, one state mediator described how he intended to build a package and how he expected that the pro, in this case on the management side, would accept his assessment:

> This deal can be put together. I thought the sick pool made sense, but the school committee attorney convinced me it was not war-

> ranted given the leave policy. On the maternity provision, I think the attorney will go along. He knows that other towns do it—it makes sense comparability wise. I understand the school committee on money and longevity: you can't depart from the pattern (settlements made with other units). . . . My goal always up front is to make a contract and I think maternity will do it.

The federal mediators see the pros as knowledgeable and experienced practitioners who are as well acquainted with settlement patterns and standard practice as the mediator, but who are better informed about the local character of the issues in dispute. Therefore, federal mediators temper their assessments of the issues in light of information proffered by the pro. Further, since the mediators believe that the pros have their own timetables for when events should occur in mediation, the federal practitioners do not expect to be given such information until the time is right. But when it is given, it exerts a strong effect on the mediator's thinking:

> I know they'll settle. You see he [union pro] didn't tell me last time, but he told me today that it was settleable as long as they get the 8¢ on the pensions. He needs it because of ERISA. Now Dick [management pro] knows he needs it. So I can be pretty sure it will be in.

As the comments from the mediators make clear, these categories of relevance are not mutually exclusive, and indeed, overlap to a considerable degree. For the state mediators, the union's lack of bargaining power makes patterns an attractive way to think about what management can be expected to concede. Further, since building starts early in the case, these are the first assessments to be made and tend, unless pros fail to support the mediator, to shape the development of the package. The federal mediators spend the early stages of the case monitoring the process by which the parties narrow their differences. They tend, therefore, to make the assessments according to pattern, but not make use of them directly until later in the case at which point more information about relative bargaining power and the positions of the pros have been assessed. In one manufacturing case, the federal mediator never discussed the fact that he deemed the union's vacation demand to be above average until the very end of the case. By that time he knew from the union pro that three of the five bargaining committee members were personally affected and from the management pro that the president of the company refused to grant additional vacation time. Thus, when vacation time was the only outstanding issue separating the parties, he could marshall all these arguments to convince the union committee to concede this issue.

Movement Tactics: By Issue or Total Package

Movement tactics cover a wide range of mediator activities. Using Simkin's (1971) taxonomy, it is possible to categorize these tactics into three broad types.

1. Communication tactics refer to the actions taken by the mediator that allow the parties to communicate more effectively with each other even when they are not physically in the same room. The major way this is accomplished is when the mediator carries or conveys a position from one side to the other. The tactics the mediator may use are: (1) to be a "conduit" and merely report the position as prepared by one bargaining committee to the other, (2) to present in addition to the position, the committee's arguments or rationale for its position, and (3) to knowingly alter or distort the position as a means to inject his own perspective. In addition, the mediator may (4) raise points of clarification or carry questions and responses back and forth from one committee to the other.

2. Substantive tactics refer to specific, usually mediator-initiated input concerning the issues in dispute. These tactics are: (5) calculating the cost of particular demands, (6) identifying how demands deviate from patterns or standard practice, (7) proffering an opinion or "reading" on whether a demand is reasonable or attainable, (8) making suggestions and/or recommendations for how a bargaining committee might reformulate its demands.

3. Procedural tactics refer generally to actions the mediator takes to facilitate the mediation process. Structuring the format and sequencing of meetings which I have discussed elsewhere are tactics of this sort (see Kolb 1981a, 1981b). Other tactics include (9) offering strategic suggestions, e.g., on concession strategy, on timing and preparation of proposal

presentations and extramediation activities such as additional meetings or lobbying activities. (10) A mediator may make threats, e.g., to withdraw his services, convene excessive meetings or, in the public sector, threaten to certify the dispute to fact-finding.

These 10 types of tactics constitute the major ways both the state and federal mediators attempt to convince, pressure, or persuade the parties to move over the course of the strategic cycle. Drawing from the same tactical pool, however, there are significant contrasts in the way these tactics are used by the state and federal mediators in terms of purpose, frequency, and timing.

1. *Purpose.* The state mediators attempt to move the parties on an issue-by-issue basis, whereas the federal mediators want the parties to make compromises and trade-offs in the context of the full proposals. Thus, tactics that may appear similar on their face are directed toward different ends. For example, the state mediators will often calculate the costs of a particular demand as part of an argument to convince a bargaining committee to change its position on the issue. One mediator made such a calculation on the cost of a stipend for emergency medical treatment (EMT) work and presented it along with the rationale of pattern, his "reading," and a threat, to convince management to concede on that issue:

> In a single 24 hour period, you have two men. Work it from two men who work 7 days. At 365 days, you get 712 tours, times \$5. So you have \$3560 as a cost factor. It's nothing. I think if you don't do something fair on EMT, I'll have to certify you to fact-finding. . . . The way I read it, they won't settle without the EMT stipend and I don't blame them. Other towns do it and so should you.

As the state mediators try to build a package on an issue-by-issue basis, they apply their movement tactics to one issue at a time. If agreement cannot be reached on certain priority issues, these may be deleted and new ones, called "sweeteners," are brought in to compensate for the loss of the priority. In the case cited above, management refused, despite the mediators' tactics, to concede on EMT, and increased payment on the firefighters uniform allowance was used as a sweetener.

The federal mediators may use the identical tactic, but with a different purpose in mind. When a federal mediator calculated the costs of provisions for the parties, he did so to aid them in their consideration of possible demand trade-offs within the context of the full package:

> Let me think for a minute. You say the standard average hourly rate is \$5.22. So if you want an extra holiday, the employee's birthday, that's about 2.5¢. The dental plan is going to cost 7.5¢. Extended coverage on the Sickness and Accident will be 1¢. You have to decide whether you want to take it off the wages. I know they are all nice, but are they necessary? As you prepare your counter, you have to keep these things in mind.

Whereas the state mediators work on proposals issue by issue, the federal mediators encourage the parties to think in terms of full proposals and counters. Their movement tactics, at least in the early stages, are geared to proposal preparation and not to movement on particular issues.

2. *Timing.* The timing of tactical usage also differs between the state and federal mediators. Table 12–4 contrasts both the purpose and timing of movement tactics in a particular state and federal case both of which settled after three full 8-hour sessions. As Table 12–4 indicates, the state mediator used movement tactics to pressure for particular concessions right from the start of the case. In contrast, the federal mediator emphasized tactics to keep the narrowing process moving and facilitate proposal preparation for most of the first, second, and indeed the third session of the case. Only in the last meeting did he explicitly attempt to persuade the parties to make a move on a particular issue. At that point, he marshalled all the "bullets" he had husbanded by not taking a position during the early phases, and argued that the union needed to consider seriously dropping its vacation demand to get a settlement:

> On the vacations, how many people does it affect? At 23, that's 2.5–3¢ per hour. So you're talking .5% to get it. You have to decide whether .5% off the wages is worth it for 23 people. My reading at this point is that the package you have is the best you can get.

	Federal case			State case		
Tactic	Observed	Purpose	Timing	Observed	Purpose	Timing
(1) Convey position	+	Pressure for concession	Session 3	+	(a) Represent position	Throughout
					(b) Pressure for concession	Throughout
(2) Alter position	0			+	Pressure for concession	Throughout
(3) Obtain clarification	+	Explain confusing issues	Throughout	+	Start negotiations	Session 1
(4) Calculate costs	+	(a) Facilitate proposal preparation	Sessions 1 & 2	+	Pressure for concession	Session 2
		(b) Pressure for concession	Session 3			
(5) Highlight pattern	+	Facilitate proposal preparation	Throughout	+	Pressure for concession	Sessions 1 & 2
(6) Make substantive suggestion	0			+	(a) Learn priorities	Sessions 1 & 2
					(b) Pressure for concession	Throughout
(7) Make strategic suggestion	+	Keep process moving	Throughout	+	Bring pressure on management	Sessions 1 & 2
(8) Make a threat	0			+	Pressure for concession	Session 2

Table 12–4 **CONTRASTING TACTICS TO ENCOURAGE MOVEMENT: INCIDENCE, PURPOSE, TIMING**

3. *Frequency*. Finally, the state and federal mediators differ in the frequency with which they use certain kinds of tactics.[10] (See Table 12–5.) Since the federal mediators favor the joint exchange of proposals across the table (see Kolb, 1981a), they do not often (unless pressed) convey proposals from one committee to another. But when they do convey proposals, federal mediators tend to transcribe them and report them verbatim. In separate meetings with the parties, they tend to emphasize the reasoning and rationale behind proposals and to clarify areas of confusion or misunderstanding. The substantive tactics they use are tailored primarily to proposal preparation, i.e., making cost calculations and identifying pattern deviations. Strategic suggestions relate primarily to proposal preparation and how best to run the process. For example,

> It's getting late today. When they come back with their counter, why don't you caucus for a few minutes and tell them that you want more time to consider it. If you rush through and present a counter, you'll waste a move.

In contrast, the state mediators use more tactics and a greater variety of them. Since they prefer to keep the bargaining committees separate from each other, they are usually carrying positions themselves (see Kolb, 1981a). As a result, they typically provide the supporting rationale behind the positions as well, and they frequently alter the information they carry in ways that suit their strategic ends. Substantively, they make extensive reference to geographical patterns and quite liberally offer their own opinions and suggestions for compromise. When they make strategic suggestions, this advice often relates to lobbying activities the union might undertake to sway the town bargaining committee:

> You said you have some friends in the town. Now is the time to contact them and publicize your position. They won't move on the salary schedule without some pressure. Maybe you need to light some fires.

[10]During the case observations, handwritten semicomplete transcripts were used to capture the mediators' verbal and nonverbal actions. The number of times a mediator transmitted a proposal, offered an opinion, noted a standard practice or pattern was tabulated. From these crude frequencies emerged the data presented in Table 12–5. They are not meant to stand on their own, but rather to supplement the selected examples presented in the paper.

These differences in timing, frequency, and purpose may be traced to the contrasting strategies of the state and federal mediators in this study. These strategies are in turn rooted in differing perceptions the mediators have about how they help the parties reach a settlement. The state mediator's strategy, to build a package through the use of directive and aggressive tactics early in the case, is based on the view that the parties, by dint of their inexperience and the union's lack of bargaining power, need the active assistance of the mediator to structure an agreement. Further, given the strategic position of the mediator, he is uniquely placed to meet the parties' needs. As one state mediator commented:

> Parties camouflage their positions with each other, but with the mediator, they are more open to discussing things directly. You cut right to the heart of the matter and are in a unique position to guide the direction a package takes.

In contrast, the federal mediators look more to the parties themselves, particularly the chief negotiators, to structure a package agreeable to them:

> These guys know as much as I do about where this thing should settle. I don't have to draw pictures for them. They'll move their committees when the time is right.

Thus the strategies of building a package or of narrowing proposals until a package is left is seen by each group of mediators as the appropriate strategic response to the contingencies they face.

COMMENT

In this paper, I have tried to show how strategies and tactics are used by two groups of mediators in the service of a settlement. Observation of a set of state and federal cases suggests that the mediators have different strategies for accomplishing these ends. Tactics are the observed behavioral practice and are given meaning (and indeed can only be understood) in the context of particular strategies. Although there were similarities in the tactics observed, there were notable contrasts in the meaning, frequency, and timing of their use. That these differences exist seems clear, but uncovering the source of the differing

	Federal cases ($N = 6$)			State cases ($N = 10$)		
	No. of federal[a] cases in which tactic observed ($N = 6$)	Average use of tactic across all federal cases[b]	Range of use across all federal cases[c]	No. of state[a] cases in which tactic observed ($N = 10$)	Average use of tactic across all state cases[b]	Range of use across all state cases[c]
Communication tactics						
(1) Present proposal as given	6	4.0	(1–9)	5	1.3	(0–3)
(2) Provide rationale behind position	6	7.8	(4–12)	10	8.2	(2–13)
(3) Knowingly alter position	1	.2	(0–1)	10	7.0	(3–13)
(4) Obtain clarifications and response to questions	6	9.0	(3–16)	10	1.4	(1–8)
Substantive tactics						
(5) Calculate costs	6	5.8	(1–12)	10	5.9	(1–14)
(6) Identify pattern deviations	5	3.8	(0–5)	10	8.9	(2–15)
(7) Give opinions	6	4.8	(1–8)	10	12.9	(4–18)
(8) Make substantive suggestions	6	2.6	(1–7)	10	9.7	(5–17)
Procedural tactics						
(9) Strategic suggestions	6	12.6	(9–17)	10	3.9	(1–9)
(10) Threats	0	0	(0)	6	2.2	(0–7)

[a]Multiple tactics observed in the case.

[b]Sum across the cases of the total number of times tactic observed in each case divided by number of cases.

[c]The range in the number of times tactic was observed in each case across the caseload.

Table 12–5 TACTICS USED TO ENCOURAGE MOVEMENT: OBSERVATIONS BY CASE, AVERAGE USE, RANGE ACROSS CASES

strategic approaches is more complex and confounded.

Recent studies of mediation in the public sector suggest that when mediators use "aggressive" or "intensive" strategies, more concessions are made by the parties (Kochan & Jick, 1978), and settlement seems to result at an earlier stage in the dispute-resolution process (Gerhart & Drotning, 1980), than if the mediator is more passive in his approach. Noted practitioners have also argued that mediation in the public sector somehow compels mediators to use more active and aggressive strategies and tactics (Robins, 1972; Liebowitz, 1972).

The state mediators observed in this study, who work primarily in the public sector, use a building strategy, emphasize tactics that might be characterized as aggressive, and can point to a settlement rate of 70% as support for their strategy. The strategy of the federal mediators is less directive and aggressive, yet they have a settlement rate that is close to 100%, a fact that is in part attributable to the caseload they serve.[11] These observations raise the question of whether the environment (sector) or social milieu (organizational practices) account for the strategic differences.

Lack of bargaining experience, legal bars to the strike, and the political character of bargaining are often singled out as the major distinguishing characteristics of the public sector that call for more aggressive mediation strategies (Robins, 1972; Liebowitz, 1972; Kochan & Jick, 1978). Indeed, these factors figure prominently in the state mediators' "readings" of their cases, as do the contrasting factors in the federal mediators' interpretations. There are other facets of sector noted in this study which may contribute as well. In the private sector, the federal mediators tended to have more pros on their cases. The state mediators had pros on their cases, but not with the same degree of regularity. It may be that, since state mediators cannot expect to be as regularly surrounded by pros, they develop a strategy that is effective, regardless of the spokesmen's experience and expertise.

The fact that state mediation practice is composed of similar occupational groups in contiguous geographical communities means that comparisons to patterns are quite easily made. The federal mediator's private sector caseload is apt to be more diverse, and therefore the opportunity to apply such criteria is more limited. Findings from another study are interesting in this regard. In his study of federal mediators, Lovell (1950) found that when a mediator considered himself a "specialist" in a particular industry, he was more likely to become involved in the substance of the dispute. This observation suggests that specialization, not necessarily sector, is important in understanding the use of certain tactics.

The histories and organizational practices of the two agencies also differ (see Kolb, 1981a). Procedures for recruiting, training, and assigning cases, opportunities for collegial interaction, and setting and impression management differ between the two agencies, and create contrasting organizational cultures from which strategies emerge. But the process is even more complex. Features of sector may interact with those of the social setting to reaffirm a particular strategy. Since state mediators are assigned cases only after the parties have declared an impasse, they are always supported on their assumption that the parties are inexpert and inexperienced, a rationale for an active mediation strategy. Familiarity with patterns and practices that cover the full complement of issues from wages to EMT to maternity to layoff may tempt the state mediator to apply this knowledge to each discrete issue. Considering a dispute on an issue-by-issue basis puts the state mediator continually into a series of "single-issue" situations. A single-issue case conducted by a federal mediator is noteworthy in this regard.

After the union rejected an earlier package, the parties came to mediation to consider and resolve only one issue—the formula for the cost of living clause. In this federal case, the mediator was observed using and timing his tactics in ways that were more characteristic of the state mediators. The federal mediator attempted to learn the facts about the rejected package, asked each party directly for the bottom line on the issue and used this information to offer, right from the start of the case, suggestions and alternatives to resolve the one issue. He commented afterward,

> With a one issue case like this, you are working from suggestions, not proposals, and nei-

[11]For most of the parties served by the federal mediators, there is no further dispute-resolution machinery if mediation fails to yield a settlement. Thus at some point in time, however distant, all federal mediation cases are settled. In the state caseload, fact-finding is available to all parties and arbitration to the uniformed services.

> ther side wants to get committed. So you carry the suggestions back and forth and present them as your own. They also looked to me to come up with some ideas and I did.

Thus, to consider a proposal as a set of single issues seems to lead rather directly to the use of what might be called "aggressive" tactics. Our knowledge about the other ways such aggressive strategies are born—whether from sectoral needs or organizational cultures—is still quite rudimentary.

These observations have implications for mediation practice. If a mediator wants to be aggressive, then specialized knowledge can be brought to bear early in the case on the discrete issues in dispute. If the mediator wants to be more passive, then a slow strategy of narrowing will place responsibility for determining the substance of the package with the parties. Under what conditions is one or the other strategy or some variant to be preferred? From the mediator's perspective, it appears that the major factor to be considered is the competence of the parties, particularly the chief negotiators. To the degree that the negotiators are "pros," and have the credibility, authority, and willingness to move their committees, a narrowing type of strategy might be deemed a good fit. If there are no pros present, or if present, they lack such "movement" abilities, then the mediator may adopt more of a building strategy. Although such flexible approaches are desirable for mediators, it may be that the ways sector, organizational practices, and the process itself act to subtly reaffirm a particular strategy preclude such situational tailoring. For like the patterns they are so willing to quote, a mediator's strategy—the artistic rhetoric notwithstanding—seems to be guided by standard practice as well.

REFERENCES

Anderson, J. Determinants of bargaining outcomes in the federal government of Canada. *Industrial and Labor Relations Review,* January, 1979, *XXXII,* 224–241.

Anthony, R., Dearden, J., & Vancil, R. *Management control systems.* Homewood, Ill.: Richard D. Irwin, 1965.

Bourdon, C. Pattern bargaining, wage determination and inflation: Some preliminary observations on the 1976–78 wage round. In M. Piore (Ed.), *Unemployment and inflation.* White Plains, N.Y.: M.E. Sharpe, Inc., 1979.

Dunlop, J. Wage contours. In G.W. Taylor & F.C. Pierson (Eds.), *New concepts of wage determination.* New York: McGraw-Hill, 1957.

Gerhart, P., & Drotning, J. Dispute settlement and the intensity of mediation, *Industrial Relations,* Fall 1980, *XIX* 352–359.

Kochan, T. *Collective bargaining and industrial relations.* Homewood, Ill.: Richard D. Irwin, Inc., 1980.

Kochan, T., & Jick, T. The public sector mediation process. *Journal of Conflict Resolution,* June 1978, *XXII,* 209–241.

Kolb, D. Roles mediators play: State and federal practice. *Industrial Relations,* Winter 1981, *XX,* 1–7. (a)

Kolb, D. *The mediators: Practice in a state and federal agency.* Cambridge, Mass.: MIT Press, 1981. (b)

Kressel, K. *Labor mediation: An exploratory survey.* New York: Association of Labor Mediation Agencies, 1972.

Liebowitz, J. Public sector mediation: Some observations on techniques. *Journal of Collective Negotiations in the Public Sector,* February 1972, *I,* 91–95.

Lovell, H. *The mediation process.* Unpublished doctoral Dissertation, MIT, 1950.

Manning, P. *Police work: The social organization of policing.* Cambridge, Mass.: MIT Press, 1979.

McHugh, P. *Defining the situation: The organization of meaning in social interaction.* New York: Bobbs-Merrill, 1968.

Rehmus, C. The mediation of industrial conflict: A note on the literature. *Journal of Conflict Resolution,* March 1965, *IX,* 118–123.

Robins, E. Some comparisons of mediation in the public and private sector. In J.J. Lowenberg & M. Moskow (Eds.) *Collective bargaining in the public sector.* Englewood Cliffs, N.J.: Prentice-Hall, 1972.

Ross, A. *Trade union wage policy.* Berkeley: University of California Press, 1948.

Simkin, W. *Mediation and the dynamics of collective bargaining.* Washington, D.C.: Bureau of National Affairs, 1971.

Spradley, P. *You owe yourself a drink.* Boston: Little, Brown, 1970.

Stevens, C. *Strategy and collective bargaining negotiations.* New York: McGraw-Hill, 1963.

Van Maanen, J. The fact of fiction in organizational ethnography. *Administrative Science Quarterly,* Winter 1979, *XXIV,* 539–551.

Weick, K. *The social psychology of organizing.* Reading, Mass.: Addison-Wesley, 1979.

DISCUSSION QUESTIONS

1. What are the major characteristics of mediation tactics?
2. What are the major sources of mediators?
3. How do federal and state mediators differ?
4. How do the strategies and tactics used by the two groups differ?
5. Which are more effective?

ACTIVITIES

Activity 12–1

THE SELLERS MACHINE COMPANY

Step 1: Read the Sellers Machine Company case.

Step 2: Prepare the case for class discussion.

The Sellers Machine Company produces electrical machinery in a rural plant in eastern Pennsylvania. Its primary customer is the paper industry. Employing about 150 workers, it is much smaller than its major competitors and relies upon its long-established reputation for quality work and upon its flexibility in operations which frequently permits it to quote earlier delivery dates than its competitors.

The day-to-day direction of the company is vested in a general manager, sales manager, plant superintendent, and personnel manager. No formal delineation of duties or authority exists. Where decisions may impinge on several areas of the business, they are arrived at by informal consensus among the managers. All of the managers and a majority of the employees are of native Pennsylvania-Dutch stock and have known each other most of their lives.

The employees were organized by the International Union of Electrical Radio and Machine Workers in 1946, and relations between the company and the union have been described as excellent by company and union. Both parties take pride in the fact that they have never experienced a strike. As an indication of its cooperative attitude with the union, the company each month holds information meetings with the five union officers who composed the local union leadership to discuss various subjects, such as order backlogs, new products, and recruitment needs, many of which transcend the usual matters of collective bargaining.

Late in the year 1964, the Sellers Company was merged into a large nationally known machinery manufacturer. The parent company retained the local management to operate the company as an independent division with relatively broad autonomy. One change introduced in the labor relations function was the parent company's insistence upon having its representative present at third-step grievance meetings.[1]

During the spring of 1965, the company experienced a substantial increase in orders, and sales forecasts indicated that the increase in orders would continue at least through 1967. A general management meeting was called to determine means of accommodating the increase without major additions to plant or equipment, for a general modernization program had been budgeted for the plant by the parent company for the year 1967. Moreover, it was recognized that additional machinery could not be placed in operation quickly enough to accommodate to the sudden surge in orders.

The plant superintendent pointed to two particular problems in adding new employees. Recruitment of skilled hands would be difficult in the rural area surrounding the plant. He pointed out that existing employees were working a six-day week, and in some cases a seven-day week. Secondly, the two shifts currently operating were scheduled over a 17-hour period (7 A.M. to 3:30 P.M., 3:30 P.M. to 12 A.M.), since each shift was entitled under the labor agreement to a half-hour unpaid lunch break. Were the company to add a third shift, it could only effectively operate six and one-half hours, since in all likelihood employees would demand a lunch break. The sales manager suggested the idea of overlapping shifts but was convinced by the other managers that neither parking facilities nor plant facilities could support doubling up of shifts and that

Case written by Wayne E. Howard, Wharton School of Finance and Commerce. Reprinted with permission.

[1]The contract-established grievance procedure provides for three steps: first, discussion between the employee and/or the shop steward and the departmental foreman; second, discussion between the chief steward and the personnel manager; third, discussion between the international representative of the union and the general manager. If satisfactory settlement of grievances cannot be reached after the above procedure has been exhausted, either party may appeal the dispute to arbitration.

only chaos would result, should that alternative be tried.

It was decided that the plant superintendent would attempt to work out plans for a third shift for the machining department on a trial basis, since operations within that department were currently the most critical from a scheduling standpoint. The personnel manager brought up the advisability of notifying the union, but the consensus of the management group was that notification should be delayed until the feasibility of adding a third shift could be determined and the details of the manning schedule could be worked out.

On May 27, 1965, the plant superintendent and personnel manager held a regular information meeting with local union officers, at which time they discussed certain quality problems in production and the substantial increase in forecasted business. According to company minutes of the meeting, the company discussed the latter problem as follows:

> To meet the forecast we will add 10 or 12 people as soon as possible. Unfortunately, there is a shortage of skilled help in the valley and we have to depend to a great extent on green hands. As you know, we have a class for upgrading our skilled classifications which fits into this program.

At the conclusion of this meeting, Mr. Jacob Bruder, chief steward of the union asked, "Is there any truth to the rumor that the company intends to establish a third shift?"

Mr. L. G. Harker, the plant superintendent, replied, "We should keep this an information meeting." Mr. Bruder said, "But the guys in the shop have been asking about this rumor all week." Mr. Harker stated, "All I'm interested in is getting enough machinery to have a full complement of personnel on the second shift."

On Tuesday, June 1, at 9 A.M., Personnel Manager Robert Kraus called the union Grievance Committee into the personnel office and handed them seven job postings.[2] Six of these postings were for a newly created third shift in the machinery department to be established on Monday, June 7, with the shift hours running from midnight Monday until 7 A.M. Tuesday morning.[3]

Chief Steward Bruder raised his voice and said, "You can't do this to us; you got to sit down and bargain the wages, hours, and conditions first. There can't be any third shift without us agreeing to it." Personnel Manager Kraus replied, "Look, Jake, we're going to do it. Why can't we discuss it sensibly?"

"What about a lunch period?"

"We'll give them a paid lunch period."

"What about a shift differential?"

"They'll get the same shift differential as those on the second shift, 10 per cent."

After about a 30-second pause and without any inflection, Jake Bruder said, "We'll think it over." The committee then left the personnel office, but later in the day filed the following grievance:

> The Union is grieving the unilateral action of the Company in establishing a 3rd shift in violation of the present working Agreement (Art. I, Sec. 1 and Art. III, Sec. 1).[4]

Recognizing the policy nature of the grievance, Bob Kraus immediately contacted Plant Superintendent Harker and General Manager Koch. All agreed that the corporate manager of industrial relations should be notified, and Kraus placed a conference call to the parent company.

The corporate manager of industrial relations, Warren Wilson, after hearing the background of the dispute suggested the position the company should take in denying the grievance and suggested that the company attempt to set up a third-step grievance meeting for June 9, at which time he would personally attend. From notes taken during the telephone

[2]Article VII, Section 1 of the Agreement provides: "Whenever a vacancy occurs in the plant, it shall be posted for a period of three (3) working days and filled on the basis of seniority for those applicants who are qualified to perform the posted job."

[3]Because the third shift would be likely to be composed of less experienced employees, the company believed that greater efficiency could be achieved by having this shift follow the existing shifts and merely carry forward work initiated on the existing shifts. Therefore, they scheduled the workweek for this shift to begin at midnight Monday, rather than the more common workweek schedule starting at midnight Sunday.

[4]See Figure 12–6 for the relevant provisions in the collective bargaining agreement.

Article I—Union Recognition

Section 1. The Company recognizes the Union as the sole and exclusive bargaining agent for all production and maintenance employees with regard to rates of pay, hours of employment, and other conditions of employment.

Article II—Management Rights

Section I. It is the responsibility of the Management of the Company to maintain discipline and efficiency in the plant. The Management has the sole right to hire and to lay off employees, in accordance with the terms of this Agreement. The right of the Management to discipline and discharge employees for just cause and relieve employees from duty because of inefficiency is expressly recognized subject to the right of appeal through the Grievance Procedure provided in Article XV. In addition, the products to be manufactured, the schedule of production, the methods, processes, and means of manufacturing are solely and exclusively the responsibility of the Company. Previous rights of the Management in the past history of labor relations between the Company and the Union shall be continued.

Article III—Hours and Overtime

Section I.

(a) The regular workweek shall consist of forty (40) hours, five (5) days from Monday to Friday inclusive, consisting of eight (8) hours each day.

(b) Any changes in the regular workday and/or week as referred to in Section 1 (a) of this Article shall not be made effective until mutually agreed to by both parties.

Section 2. All work performed in excess of eight (8) hours in any single day, or in excess of forty (40) hours in any week and all work performed on Saturdays shall be paid at the rate of time and one half.

Article VIII—Wages

Section 7. All employees working on shifts other than the regular day shift shall receive a rate of pay which will be ten per cent (10%) above the day hourly rates.

Article XIV—Grievance Procedure

Section 1. There shall be no suspension of work by the Union or lockout by the Company on account of any differences, grievances, or disputes that may arise between the Company and the Union, its members, or any employees covered by the bargaining unit.

Figure 12–6 APPLICABLE CONTRACT PROVISIONS

conversation, Bob Kraus framed the following answer to the union's grievance:

> This letter is in reply to your Grievance #792 relative to the establishment of a third shift in our plant.
>
> The establishment of a third shift to meet the production needs of our plant is clearly within the rights of Management in accordance with our working agreement.
>
> We specifically recognize the Union as the sole and exclusive bargaining agent for the production and maintenance employees whom we would employ on the third shift, and we are willing to bargain with you in accordance with Article I, Section 1 of our Contract. Meeting our production needs is solely and exclusively the responsibility of the Company as covered under Article II of our Labor Agreement.
>
> With respect to your reference to Article III, Section 1, we believe that our proposal is consistent with the provisions contained therein.
>
> Therefore your grievance is denied.

After reading the company response, Bruder agreed with Kraus that a third-step grievance meeting should be scheduled for June 9. Since this date was only two days after the planned establishment of the third shift, Kraus convinced Koch and Harker that the establishment of the third shift should be deferred pending the results of the grievance meeting.

At the meeting of June 9, Warren Wilson acted as spokesman for the company group and presented the following points to the union committee and to International Union Representative John Barker:

1. Under the labor agreement, the company has the right to unilaterally establish a third shift.
2. The establishment is necessary because of the sudden upsurge in business.
3. The use of a seven-hour shift is necessary to avoid the chaos of overlapping shifts.
4. The company is willing to discuss any details of the third shift, its hours, conditions, and pay, but will not entertain any discussion of changes in the existing shifts, their hours, conditions, or rates of pay.
5. Regardless of the outcome of the meeting, the third shift will be placed in operation at midnight on June 10.

John Barker who had apparently expected the meeting to be one of general negotiation was enraged. "Of all the double-dealing tricks," he shouted. "Let's get the hell out of here and take the men with us!"

"You do and you'll be saddled with a nice fat damage suit," Wilson retorted. "Our agreement has an ironclad no-strike clause in it."[5]

Barker and Wilson shouted at one another for the next few minutes. Barker accused the company of bad faith, and Wilson accused the union of attempting to pressure the company into renegotiation of the contract in the middle of its term. The union committee, however, made no move to leave the meeting.

Bob Kraus caught the eye of Jake Bruder, and they left the meeting for a conversation in the corridor outside the conference room. "Look, Jake," Bob pointed out, "we're not getting anywhere here today, and we're not likely to with both sides in this frame of mind. Why not get your side to recess, and I'll work on my guys, and we'll try to thrash this thing out tomorrow. Nothing's going to be done before then anyway."

Jake Bruder agreed, and the two men returned to the conference room to find Barker and Wilson still shouting. A short time later, however, Bob Kraus requested a short recess and broached his idea to Warren Wilson, who agreed to stay over for another day in an effort to settle the dispute. Jake Bruder was equally successful with his committee, and the parties arranged to meet the following morning.

After leaving the meeting, John Barker felt that the local union should have the benefit of legal counsel on the points raised by the company. Jake Bruder at first felt that it was a waste of local union funds, but was won over when John Barker pointed out that Wilson had taken an adamant and legalistic position and that if the union did not make a strong showing on this issue, the parent company would, in all likelihood, "force other decisions down the local's throat." Accordingly, International Representative Barker contacted a nearby attorney who frequently represented the international union on labor matters. The committee met with him that evening. After hearing the facts as presented by the local committee, he agreed to represent them at the meeting the following morning, but cautioned the committee not to take precipitate action, regardless of the outcome of the meeting.

Thursday morning, June 10, the union committee again met with company representatives, and the union counsel, Louis Somerson, acted as spokesman. Somerson immediately took the initiative. "Gentlemen," he stated, "I've examined the position you took at yesterday's meeting, and there's no question in my mind, and there should be none in your own minds, that you have committed a deliberate violation of the agreement." He spelled out the union's present position with the following arguments:

1. The right of the company to establish a third shift does not encompass an establishment on some basis other than it is applied to the first and second shifts, nor in a manner contrary to the plain language of the agreement.
2. Establishment on a basis different from what the current agreement provides must be

[5]See Figure 12–6 for the relevant provisions of the collective bargaining agreement.

negotiated with the union. Failure to negotiate infringes on the union's rights as the collective bargaining representative of the employees and violates Article I, Section 1 of the agreement.[6]

3. Third-shift employees under the company's plan will receive numerous benefits not available to first- and second-shift employees: a paid lunch period; eight hours of pay for six and one-half hours of work; premium overtime pay after six and one-half hours of work. Thus, the company has discriminated in favor of certain employees and against other employees.

4. Moreover, if the company establishes the shift on a regular Monday midnight through Saturday 7 A.M. basis, without specific negotiation with the union, it will be liable for premium overtime payments for all time worked by the third shift after midnight Friday under Article III, Section 2 of the agreement.[7]

5. Since the union was taken by surprise by the job posting for the third shift and immediately filed a grievance, employees who otherwise might have availed themselves of this opportunity did not do so because of uncertainty over how the grievance would be resolved. Therefore, the union demands that once the issue is finally resolved, the company repost the jobs.

6. Finally, if the issue is not resolved at this meeting the union will seek immediate arbitration of the grievance.

[6]See Figure 12–6.

[7]See Figure 12–6.

The company management team pleaded surprise over items 4 and 5, above, and asked for a recess to consider them. During the recess, Warren Wilson was contacted by the parent company and was asked to return to the home office. He requested that he be kept informed of all developments. The company team again convened with the union committee, pointed out that the team needed further time to consider the union position, and requested that the group convene again on Tuesday, June 15. The union agreed to meet again on that date.

On the evening of June 10, General Manager Koch called a meeting of company management to determine the course of action the company should pursue.

Step 3: Individually, in small groups, or with the entire class, answer the following questions:

1. Describe the history of relations between the union and management at Sellers.
2. What impact did the merger have on union-management relations?
3. Did the personnel manager Kraus act appropriately and effectively?
4. Was the grievance legitimate?
5. Could the grievance have been avoided by actions of management or human resources professionals?
6. Did the company act in good faith?
7. How would you resolve this situation?

Activity 12–2

POST-NEWSWEEK STATIONS

Step 1: Read the Post-Newsweek Stations case.

Step 2: Prepare the case for class discussion.

Decision of Arbitrator

In re POST-NEWSWEEK STATIONS MICHIGAN, INC. and NATIONAL ASSOCIATION OF BROADCAST EMPLOYEES AND TECHNICIANS, AAA Case No. 54 30 0511 83, January 18, 1984

Arbitrator: William P. Daniel

DISCIPLINE

—Failure to prepare properly edited tape ▶ 118.651 ▶ 118.301

Broadcast station had right to impose discipline on video tape editor who failed properly to prepare edited tape for use on air because of his failure to review whole tape that he thought was all right, but one-day suspension is reduced to written reprimand, in light of evidence that grievant's misconduct was of lower level than originally charged and he had not received benefit of progressive discipline.

Appearances: For the company—Walter O. Lambeth, Jr. and Thomas A. Pogue, attorneys. For the union—Judith A. Sale, attorney.

MISCONDUCT

Facts

DANIEL, Arbitrator:—The grievant had previous experience when he was hired April 4, 1981, as a video tape editor in the News Department. The television news stories which he works on are originated by a reporter in the field who, along with the crew, makes a basic video tape and conducts interviews. When the reporter returns to the station he writes out the story or script, records whatever comments he wishes to be added as additional audio and then works with the film editor to combine the video and audio tape into a finished product. This finished product is then to be in proper form to run as a scheduled news story.

On July 5, 1982, a reporter was sent into the field to film various scenes on the Detroit River to be included in a short presentation entitled "Busy River". Frazier, the reporter, returned to the studios with the tape and audio and wrote a script to put the various pieces into an order. He recorded his voice portion of the story but was unable to remain any longer to work with the grievant as editor because he was to anchor the 5:30 p.m. news and had to have time to prepare for that. He left the editing room at approximately 5:00 p.m. Bergson, the Assignment Manager, told the grievant he would take over in the place of the reporter to work on putting the pieces in proper and suitable order. Bergson was having problems of his own and from time to time had to leave. By 5:30 p.m. Bergson had finished putting together the audio portions of the story and left the grievant to match the video to that track. As he left, Bergson told the grievant that if he had any problems or questions to contact him since he would be in the immediate area.

According to the grievant, there was no script for him to use as was common when he started the job and it was when the job was almost completed that Bergson finally provided one. Furthermore, the grievant notes there was no log of the video on the field tape to help him find the various shots that he needed to match with audio and this further complicated the job. According to the grievant and another witness presented by the union, this particular spot was to run approximately two minutes and normally such a segment with the number of elements that were involved—three different speakers and six different interviews—would take approximately two hours to complete.

From approximately 5:35 to 5:55 Bergson was working on his own problem regarding the signal from the helicopter. He heard nothing from the grievant and the grievant acknowledges that he did not interrupt his work to contact Bergson. The story was originally scheduled to go on no later than 6:03 or 6:05 but was moved up at the very last minute by Bergson because they were unable to make the contact with the helicopter. He informed the grievant of this at 5:58 with the intention of showing the story at 6:01. When a minute later, he learned that the grievant had not yet brought the story in for broadcast, Bergson returned to the booth, finding the grievant reviewing the story. At this point, the grievant advised Bergson that he had not seen the completed tape, that he thought it was ready but he could not be sure. Bergson said the story had to run as is and told him to rewind the tape and give it to him. The story ran at 6:01.

There is no dispute that the tape was seriously deficient. There were three different types of mistakes—improper match of audio with the video, black screen with no video at all and extraneous video in the middle and at the end of the tape. Bergson immediately confronted the grievant who admitted that there were errors on the tape and that it should never have aired. News Director Warfield saw the segment and asked for an explanation from Bergson. According to Warfield when he learned all of the facts, he considered the matter along with the past problems that the grievant had had and decided that a one day suspension would be necessary to emphasize to the grievant the necessity to improve his job performance.

The company detailed a number of past incidents

which had been made known to the grievant where his performance was unacceptable. These included taking long periods of time to edit stories and substituting personal preferences or artistic view for getting a job done on time or the way that the supervisor wished. A number of meetings were held with the grievant for such counseling or critiques. Warfield testified to having met with the grievant three or four times to make sure he understood what was expected of him. He indicated that the grievant understood he was being criticized and that his job performance was expected to improve. In mid-November 1981 there was an occasion when a film edited by the grievant was not done on time and missed the broadcast. A similar problem arose on November 30, 1981; it was finished only at the last minute. December 1, 1981, brought another problem of editing relating to certain shots which the station, as a matter of policy, did not wish on the air. The grievant failed to remove certain sequences and it went on the air; he was again called to task for his failure. Warfield's testimony emphasized that there was very specific discussion on these occasions to assure that the grievant understood.

Apparently other incidents arose during the interim, because in May 1982 Warfield again counselled the grievant regarding his attitude in general. At this time he emphasized to the grievant that he had to work within the station's severe time constraints so that the quality of broadcasts could be maintained. It was at this time that Warfield informed the grievant "The very next time that you do something that directly and adversely affects our air product, I will impose disciplinary action." The next event which took place was the instant matter of July 5, 1982. The penalty selected by the company was a one day suspension which was immediately assessed.

Positions of the Parties

EMPLOYER: The grievant had over a considerable period of time demonstrated an inability to meet the fair standards of performance. He had been repeatedly warned and counselled and, in fact, on the last occasion prior to this he had been notified that disciplinary action could result for the next offense. He was guilty of negligent and careless performance on July 5, 1982, and this subjected him to disciplinary action. The employer properly considered his entire record to determine at what level it would be necessary to discipline him to bring about a realization of the need to comply with the directions of management.

Since there was a basis for disciplinary action, the penalty selected should not be disturbed and the grievance should be denied.

UNION: The grievant's past problems certainly have no relevance here because he was disciplined only for the single incident of July 5, 1982. In that respect, it must be noted that he was given an insufficient amount of time to accomplish the work and lacked basic and necessary aids such as the log and the script. Furthermore, the reporter was unavailable throughout the period to help. All of these matters complicated the grievant's work and of necessity brought the time constraints into play. If he had an opportunity to review the work, he would not have released it to go on air.

The facts clearly indicate that it was not his fault and therefore he should be given no penalty at all. If there is any fault found on his part, it is not sufficient to justify the penalty in this case and it should be modified.

Contract Provisions

The contract is silent on disciplinary matters except for discharge but in that respect speaks in terms of "just and sufficient cause". In presenting this matter to arbitration the parties have conceded that disciplinary action short of discharge may be subject to grievance and to the arbitration procedure. It is the intent, then, of the arbitrator to apply to this incident, the same standard which the parties have adopted for discharge cases—just and sufficient cause.

Issue

Was there just and sufficient cause for disciplinary action against the grievant and, if so, was a one day suspension appropriate?

Discussion

It is very clear that had the events of July 5, 1982, not taken place the grievant would not have been disciplined. To that extent then it was the trigger or the proverbial "straw that broke the camel's back."

It was in that regard that substantial time was spent at the hearing considering the implication and relevance of past problems and incidents. It was the ruling of the arbitrator that the basis for disciplinary action would have to be found in the events of July 5, 1982, since the employer had not on the previous occasions taken disciplinary action. Nevertheless, as it was pointed out, previous incidents certainly were proper evidence of warning to the grievant and knowledge on his part of what was expected and what was deficient in his job performance.

To weigh the disciplinary action taken in this case, it is necessary to be cognizant of the particular industry involved. This is not an industrial operation—scrap can not be neatly piled in a corner some place to be reworked. There are, as the company has pointed out, time constraints and enormous pressures applying right up to the very last minute before some story or program goes on the air. This is to emphasize that people involved in preparing films to be shown must be able to competently and fully perform their work the first time. The station has well explained the extreme detriment that can result from incompetent, incomplete and careless work by a film editor.

There can be no doubt, then, that in this industry the employer has the right to expect a high level of performance and competence with a full realization on the part of the employee of the necessity for quality and timeliness. There simply can be no doubt that the grievant was aware of this. His past history at this station reflects numerous incidents of similar problems which were called to his attention and in great detail defined and explained in terms of what was expected in the future.

It is contended that there was some explanation for the grievant's failure; but there is no doubt whatsoever that he did fail to prepare a properly edited tape for use on the air. The explanation or excuse centers around the claim that he was not given enough time to do the work. Of course, he has had this problem in the past and should be well aware of it. Some testimony asserts that the time was less than that normal for such assignment. No doubt his task would have been easier and, perhaps, better performed if the reporter had been available. Bergson simply was not an adequate substitute in this instance because of his own responsibilities and duties. Perhaps, as the grievant contends, the lack of a script from the very beginning and absence of a log also slowed up the process. However, the fact that Bergson decided to run the story two or three minutes earlier than originally scheduled is no basis for complaint. If the story was ready to go at 5:58 then it would not have made any difference whether it aired a couple of minutes early.

What this case comes down to is the question of whether or not the grievant was subject to disciplinary action for the events of July 5, 1982. The arbitrator has real doubts that the grievant is entirely to blame for the condition of the tape that he turned over for broadcast. There is enough fault to be shared here. However, it is incomprehensible how the grievant could have been unaware of the types of errors that were in the tape. His caution to Bergson that he had not reviewed the whole tape but thought that it was all right is inadequate and irresponsible under the circumstances. It was in this respect that he failed to perform his duties. He should never have turned the tape in when he must have known it was not appropriate for airing. If he did not realize this, he is to blame for a competent workman would have.

It must be concluded, then, that though the grievant may not be to blame altogether for the condition of the tape, he was wrong in failing to reveal that it was inappropriate for broadcast. In this respect he is at fault and subject to some disciplinary action.

The issue is not only whether there was just and sufficient cause for discipline but also whether the penalty meets that standard. The purpose of disciplinary action is not simply to punish an employee but rather to cause a realization that certain actions are improper and that there must be an improvement and change. It is expected that discipline will bring about a change and it is for this reason that concepts of progressive discipline commencing at the lowest level are universally recommended and observed. Progressive discipline means exactly that—application of discipline at such a level as will likely bring about improvement in behavior or performance—but no greater than that. If, when first applied, such does not bring about the necessary change then a more severe penalty should be assessed and upheld.

Here we have an employee who has never received any discipline before. Perhaps the company should have done something before this but it is not to be criticized for restraint in dealing with the grievant—attempting by counselling to get him on the right track. In a system of progressive discipline oral warnings are generally followed by written warnings so as to establish a clear-cut record and notice as to what is expected and future penalty for failure. There have been no written warnings here and the last oral "reprimand" was vague as to what might occur the next time the grievant did something wrong. Merely mentioning discipline leaves an employee uncertain of his status; if he is in jeopardy of a substantial penalty, he should be told. The loss of wages is severe discipline and a step to be undertaken only where other solutions have failed. To place on the grievant's record a one day suspension would jump a rung on his disciplinary ladder and expose him to very severe discipline in the event of some subsequent misconduct. This simply is inappropriate under the circumstances here.

Considering his lesser degree of fault for the incident of July 5, 1982, and the lack of progressive disciplinary procedures here, it is found that just and sufficient standards would require no more than a written reprimand for the offense involved.

AWARD

The grievance is denied but the penalty is modified because the grievant's misconduct was of a lower level than originally charged and he has not received the benefit of progressive discipline. There is no reason to believe a lesser penalty would not have achieved the same intended result without exposing the grievant to financial detriment. The penalty is reduced to a written reprimand and he is to be made whole for the one day's wages which he lost.

Step 3: Individually, in small groups, or with the entire class, answer the following questions:

1. What was the basis of the grievance?
2. What evidence supported the grievance?
3. What evidence negated the grievance?
4. On what evidence did the arbitrator base his decision?
5. Do you agree with the arbitrator's decision?

Activity 12–3

ARBITRATION CASES

Step 1: Presented below are four cases. Read each case, then answer the following questions:

1. What are the key issues in the case?
2. If you were the arbitrator, would you uphold the employer's decision? Justify your decision.

CASE 1: PREPLANNING PREVENTS PAY

"How can you say that this was no emergency?" protested George Mullins. "My child had a serious problem and this was the earliest that we could get her into the hospital."

"We're following the same standard with you that we have with everyone else," responded personnel manager Joe Hollis. "Her hospitalization was scheduled ahead of time—it didn't just suddenly crop up. We're sorry, but we have to stick with our rules."

Was the employer's decision proper?

Facts: When an employee's daughter was hospitalized for one day after suffering an attack of asthma, management granted the employee's request for a day of paid emergency leave. The daughter continued to have asthma attacks, and two months later, on her physician's recommendation, was taken by automobile to a distant hospital for treatment where she remained for several days. During the auto trip she was on a life support oxygen system. Urging that the employee's "time off should be covered as if it were an emergency situation," the child's physician advised the employer that "referral to the University Hospital was of utmost urgency and accomplished at the only time available." Nonetheless, management denied the worker's request for paid emergency leave, explaining that the automobile trip did not qualify as an "emergency situation" since it had been "scheduled, not unforeseen."

Pointing out that the dictionary definition of an emergency includes "a trying or dangerous time or state of affairs," the employee insisted that "without question, the situation was dangerous and of a life or death nature." According to the employee, "emergencies can be created by man in quest of corrective treatment."

CASE 2: UNSAFE EXIT

"OK, so I squealed my car tires leaving the parking lot," John Hardy said. "What's so awful about that? I didn't endanger myself or anyone else, and lots of people put a little rubber down on their way out of here."

"Hot-rodding in the parking lot is not only immature, it's dangerous," responded supervisor Terry Hall. "Several people told us you revved up and tore out of the lot. In view of your poor safety record, that just convinces us you're not a safe employee. The discharge stands."

Was the discharge for just cause?

Facts: Late one afternoon, a worker got into his car in the employer's parking lot, revved up the motor, and left the area very fast with the car tires squealing. One of the people who observed the incident was a manager, who notified the employee's supervisor that the worker had been behaving in an unsafe manner. The supervisor then called a meeting with the employee and suspended him for five days, pending a decision on whether or not he should be discharged for committing an unsafe act. At that time, the worker refused to acknowledge that he had done anything unsafe, claiming that his tires had squealed only because there was loose sand and gravel on the parking lot. After reviewing the worker's safety record and discovering that he had been cited for two previous safety violations, management decided to terminate the employee.

The employee protested the discharge, arguing that the discipline was discriminatory and too harsh for the offense. Management had never notified its employees that such conduct would be grounds for discipline, the worker maintained, pointing out that no one had ever before been disciplined for such an offense, despite the fact that many employees customarily squealed their tires and drove through the parking lot at high speed. Management, on the other hand, insisted that reckless driving in its parking lot was a dangerous and dischargeable offense. Moreover, management pointed out, the employee had compounded his error by failing to acknowledge the danger of such conduct and admit his guilt.

CASE 3: PERFORMANCE PROCRASTINATION

"Look, the important thing is I got the job done, even if it was a few minutes late," protested Charlie Jackson. "Even if we don't see eye to eye about that little delay, there's no way you can justify suspending me for seven days."

"You were told to do that job at 9:00 o'clock, not 10:00 o'clock," replied supervisor Hank Higgins. "You've got to learn that we're not kidding around when we hand out job assignments, and maybe this suspension will get that point across."

Facts: At 8 a.m., an employee was given a work assignment that required him to be at another location by 9 a.m. The worker expressed concern to his supervisor about the availability of transportation, but a co-worker offered the use of his vehicle. Nevertheless, after the supervisor left the area, the employee telephoned a manager at his assigned workstation and said that he was unable to get to the location since he lacked transportation. The manager agreed to postpone the job, made arrangements with other affected employees for a new date, and then asked the worker to check with his supervisor to make sure that he would have transportation on the new date. When the supervisor learned of the change, he objected to the employee's failure to carry out the original instruction. The assignment was rescheduled for the same day, and was performed by the employee within an hour of its original scheduled time. Subsequently, management imposed a seven-day suspension on the worker for failing to carry out a work order.

The employee protested, emphasizing that he had, in fact, complied with the supervisor's order and carried out the assignment. Maintaining that workers in the past often had rescheduled assigned tasks, the employee argued that he was being unfairly punished because a recent change in management ranks had resulted in a reduction in the former operating flexibility.

CASE 4: BOTCHED BATCH

"All right, I admit I made an error in preparing those data processing cards, but I told the operations manager about it right away, and he could have stopped the computer run," protested Bonnie Flint. "Seeing as how I've always been one of your best workers, how can you justify suspending me and rescinding my promotion, and not doing anything to him?"

"The simple fact is that if you hadn't been negligent, we wouldn't have had to deal with a whole string of problems that cost us several thousand dollars to correct," replied personnel manager Judy Martin. "Since you were primarily responsible for the foul-up, you deserve the discipline."

Was the disciplinary decision proper?

Facts: A computer department employee made an entry error on a program control card that botched up an entire run of computer cards. Efforts to rectify the situation produced a second set of improperly run cards. As a result of the series of errors, the employer incurred extra costs of $2,400, plus a weekend of overtime work by other computer department staffers. Management suspended the employee for three days for negligence, and also revoked a promotion for which she previously had been approved.

Protesting the discipline, the employee stressed that she had attempted to correct her error in the early stages of the run by notifying the manager of computer operations of her mistake. Maintaining that the resulting string of errors could have been avoided if the manager had followed up on her report and stopped the initial run, the employee argued that she had been treated unfairly because the manager had not been disciplined even though he compounded the problem, while she was severely punished. Moreover, citing her "impeccable" work record and management's acknowledgment that she had always been a "model employee," the worker insisted that the denial of her previously-approved promotion was "unconscionable."

Activity 12–4

A PENALTY FOR NOT PILING ON

Viking Machine Company manufactures finished engine blocks from basic parts. Barry Faith has just filed a grievance regarding the stacking of engine blocks.

Step 1: Your instructor will assign you to a group of four to six members. Each group will receive one of the following roles:

1. Barry Faith, grievant
2. Harry Thiel, foreman
3. Charles Gilroy, general supervisor

Step 2: The groups should spend approximately fifteen minutes discussing their character's perception of the situation, and thinking about how the role should be played. At the end of that time each group should appoint members to play the roles of Faith, Thiel, and Gilroy at a meeting.

Step 3: The instructor will choose one of the groups to play the roles. The role-play should last approximately twenty minutes or until there is some resolution of the grievance.

Step 4: The instructor may choose a second group to play the roles again.

Step 5: Discussion. In small groups or with the entire class, answer the following questions:

1. What were the strengths and weaknesses of each position?
2. How well did the role-players represent their positions?
3. What decision was reached?
4. Was the decision effective?
5. How could the resolution process have been improved?

Activity 12–5

SCRUBBING JOBS

Atozed Lubrication Products Company has recently decided to contract out janitorial service at the plant, effective May 15. The union has filed a grievance since work has never been contracted before.

Step 1: Your instructor will assign you to a group of four to six members. Each group will receive one of the following roles:

1. Sam Snyder, Chief Steward
2. Edgar Harpster, Union President
3. Glenn Callahan, Maintenance Supervisor
4. Donald Taylor, General Manager

Step 2: The groups should spend approximately fifteen minutes discussing their character's perception of the situation, and thinking about how the role should be played. At the end of that time each group should appoint members to play the roles of Snyder, Harpster, Callahan, and Taylor at a meeting.

Step 3: The instructor will choose one of the groups to play the roles. The role-play should last approximately twenty minutes or until some resolution of the grievance occurs.

Step 4: The instructor may choose a second group to play the roles again.

Step 5: Discussion. In small groups or with the entire class, answer the following questions:

1. What were the strengths and weaknesses of each position?
2. How well did the role-players represent their positions?
3. What decision was reached?
4. Was the decision effective?
5. How could the resolution process have been improved?

Step 6: Assume that this case has progressed to outside arbitration. What are the pros and cons of each position? If you were the arbitrator, how would you decide this case?

SUMMARY

Third party interventions in labor-management relations focus on eliminating barriers to contract agreement and handling grievances. Particularly in public sector organizations that lack a legal right to strike, mediation, and less frequently fact-finding and interest arbitration, are used to help resolve contract impasses. Arbitration is most commonly used to resolve grievances. In this chapter we have examined the use of these interventions in contract resolution and administration.

In the activities you have had the opportunity to act as a third party in a variety of organizational situations. You may have noticed that the outcomes of decisions actually made by arbitrators vary considerably. One study of five steel companies suggested that the following factors, summarized in Figure 12–7, influence the grievance and resolution process: (1) the task organization and work environment; (2) technological changes experienced by the organization; (3) socioeconomic conditions that influence workers and management; (4) union leadership, organization, and policies; and (5) management leadership, organization, and policies.[52]

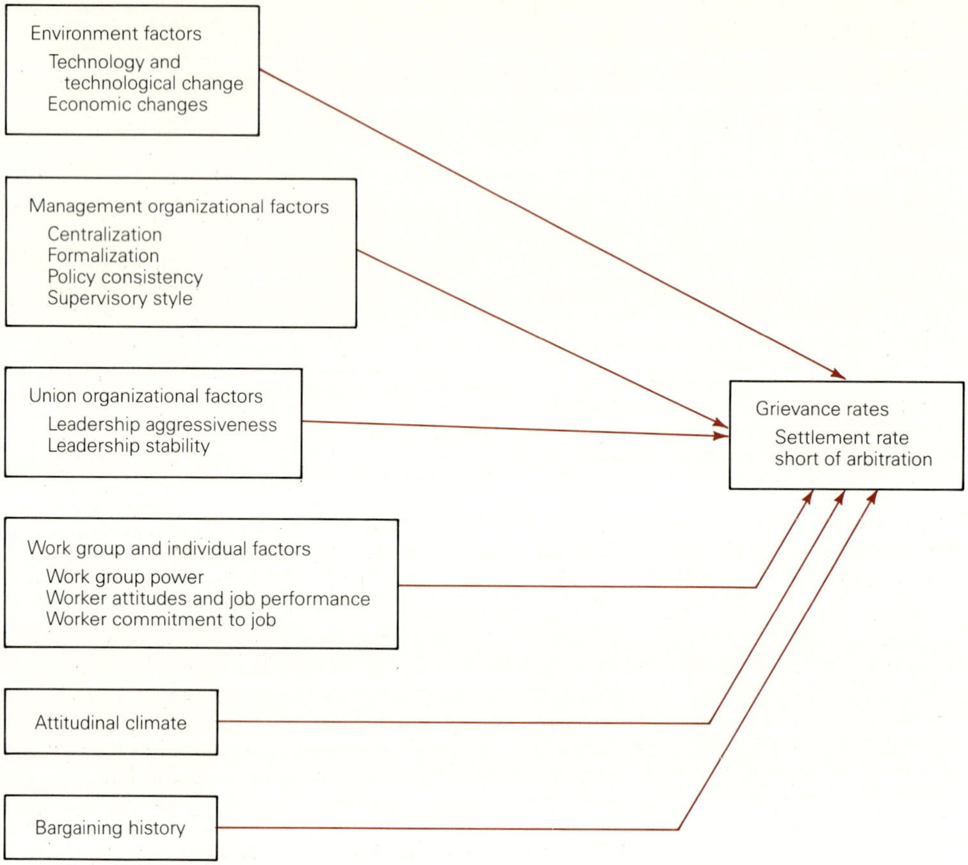

SOURCE: Thomas H. Kochan, Professor of Industrial Relations, Sloan School of Management, MIT. From Determinants of grievance activity, *Collective Bargaining and Industrial Relations* (Homewood, Ill.: Richard D. Irwin, 1980). © 1980 by Richard D. Irwin, Inc.

Figure 12–7 DETERMINANTS OF GRIEVANCE ACTIVITY

The grievance procedures should promote an orderly process for reducing anxiety experienced by employees, act as a mechanism for equitable and just interpretation of the contract, and prevent capricious, unreasonable actions against employees.[53] An audit of the resolution process should indicate the types of disputes handled, the process for collecting facts and information, the training of supervisors, the time limits on each step, the consistency of agreements with the contract, the encouragement of early settlement, the existence and composition of a grievance committee, and the results of the grievances.[54] Both human resources professionals and managers should understand and be involved in the contract and grievance resolution processes.

ENDNOTES

[1]Reprinted by permission from *Bulletin to Management,* copyright 1984 by The Bureau of National Affairs, Inc., Washington, D.C.

[2]Sam Kane Publishing Company vs. Meat Cutters, Local 17, 477, F.2d 1128, 83 LRRM, 2294, 5th Circuit, 1972.

[3]D.S. McPherson, *Resolving Grievances: A Practical Approach* (Reston, Va.: Reston, 1983).

[4]*Ibid.*

[5]D.R. Dalton and W.D. Todor, Win, lose, draw: The grievance process in practice, *Personnel Administrator* 26 (March 1981): 25–29.

[6]*Ibid.*

[7]*Ibid.*

[8]R. Johnson, Interest arbitration reexamined. *Personnel Administrator* 28 (January 1983): 53–57.

[9]*Ibid.*

[10]D.Q. Mills, *Labor-Management Relations* (New York: McGraw-Hill, 1978), p. 205.

[11]L. Stessin, *Employee Discipline.* Washington, D.C.: Bureau of National Affairs, 1960), p. vii.

[12]McPherson, *op. cit.*

[13]See J.T. Turner and J.W. Robinson, A pilot study of the validity of grievance settlement rates as a predictor of union-management relationships, *Journal of Industrial Relations* 14 (1972): 314–322, for empirical study of the impact of cooperative attitudes between union and management.

[14]D.R. Dalton and W.D. Todor, Antecedents of grievance-filing behavior: Attitude/behavioral consistency and the union steward, *Academy of Management Journal* 25 (1982): 158–169.

[15]See G.W. Bohlander, Fair representation: Not just a union problem, *Personnel Administrator* 25 (March 1980): 36; and J.W. Kuhn, *Bargaining in Grievance Settlement* (New York: Columbia University Press, 1961).

[16]Smith v. Hussman Refrigerator Co. & Local 13889, United Steelworkers of America 619 F.2d 1229 (1980).

[17]Bohlander, *op. cit.*

[18]*The Wall Street Journal,* 25 March 1980, p. 1; American Arbitration Association, *News and Views* 1 (January-February 1976).

[19]See J.V.N. Dorr III, Labor arbitrator training: The internship, *Arbitration Journal* 36 (June 1981): 4–10; A.M. Zack, Who is responsible for the development of arbitrators—the parties or the arbitrators?, *Arbitration Journal* 36 (June 1981): 11–14, for discussion of one type of training.

[20]E.W. Lawson, Jr., Arbitrator acceptability: Factors affecting selection, *Arbitration Journal* 36 (December 1981): 22–29.

[21]R. Coulson, *Labor Arbitration—What You Need to Know* (New York: American Arbitration Association, 1973), pp. 43–44.

[22]P.A. Zirkel, A profile of grievance arbitration cases, *Arbitration Journal* 38 (March 1983): 35–38.

[23]Coulson, *op. cit.*

[24]United Steelworkers of America v. Warrior & Gulf Navigation Co., 363 U.S. 574 (1960); United Steelworkers of America v. American Manufacturing Co., 363 U.S. 564 (1960); United Steelworkers of America v. Enterprise Wheel & Car Corp., 363 U.S. 593 (1960); U.S. Supreme Court Case No. 72–5847 (February 19, 1974); Hines v. Anchor Motor Freight, 96 U.S. Sup. Ct. 1048 (1976).

[25]F. Ashe, Arbitration finality: Myth or reality, *Arbitration Journal* 38 (December 1983): 42–51.

[26]W.E. Baer, *Strikes* (New York: AMACOM, 1975).

[27]A.A. Malinowski, An empirical analysis of discharge cases and the work history of employees reinstated by labor arbitrators, *Arbitration Journal* 36 (March 1981): 31–46.

[28]See J. Zalusky, Arbitration: Updating a vital process, *American Federationist* 83 (November 1976): 2; and *BNA Bulletin to Management,* 5 July 1984.

[29]M.H. Sandver, H.R. Blaine, and M.N. Woyar, Time and cost savings through expedited arbitration procedures, *Arbitration Journal* 36 (December 1981): 1–21.

[30]*Ibid.*

[31]See *BNA Bulletin to Management,* 5 July 1984.

[32]*Ibid.*

[33]S.B. Goldberg and J.M. Brett, An experiment in the mediation of grievances, *Monthly Labor Review* 106 (March 1983): 23–30.

[34]W.E. Simkin, *Mediation and the Dynamics of Collective Bargaining* (Washington, D.C.: Bureau of National Affairs, 1971).

[35]*Ibid.*

[36]R. Walton, *Interpersonal Peacemaking: Confrontations and Third Party Consultation* (Reading, Mass.: Addison-Wesley, 1969).

[37]P.A. Zirkel and J.G. Lutz, Characteristics and functions of mediators: A pilot study, *Arbitration Journal* 36 (June 1981): 15–20.

[38]D.M. Kolb, Roles mediators play: State and federal practice, *Industrial Relations* 20 (Winter 1981): 1–17.

[39]E.E. Herman and A. Kuhn, *Collective Bargaining and Labor Relations* (Englewood Cliffs, N.J.: Prentice-Hall, 1981).

[40]R.E. Doherty, Fact-finding: A one-eyed man lost among the eagles, *Public Personnel Management* 5 (September-October 1977):18–20; A. Zack, *Fact-finding and Arbitration in the Public Sector* (Washington, D.C.: U.S. Government Printing Office, 1974).

[41]Herman and Kuhn, *op. cit.*

[42]See A. Zack, *Fact-finding and Arbitration in the Public Sector* (Washington, D.C.: U.S. Government Printing Office, 1974); J.R. Grodin, Political aspects of public sector interest arbitration, *California Law Review* 64 (May 1976): 678–701.

[43]See W.R. Word, Fact-finding in public employee negotiations, *Monthly Labor Review* 95 (February 1972): 60–64; J.L. Stern, The Wisconsin Public Employee fact-finding procedure, *Industrial and Labor Relations Review* 19 (July 1966): 8; L.B. Gatewood, Fact-finding in teacher disputes: The Wisconsin experience, *Monthly Labor Review* 97 (October 1974): 47–51.

[44]R. Berenheim, *Non-union Complaint Systems: A Corporate Appraisal,* Report No. 765 (New York: The Conference Board, 1979).

[45]S.L. Yenney, In defense of the grievance procedure in a non-union setting, *Employee Relations Law Journal* 2 (Spring 1977): 437; J.F. Wandschneider, Nip the grievance in the gripe, *Supervisory Management* 8 (September 1973): 34; A. Balfour, Five types of non-union grievance systems, *Personnel* 61 (March-April 1984): 67–76.

[46]Balfour, *op. cit.*

[47]R.T. Boisseau and H. Caras, A radical experiment cuts deep into the attractiveness of unions, *Personnel Administrator* 28 (October 1983): 76–79.

[48]W.L. Beavers, Employee relations without a union, *ASPA Handbook of Personnel and Industrial Relations* (Washington, D.C.: Bureau of National Affairs, 1974); S. Briggs, The grievance procedure and organizational health, *Personnel Journal* 60 (June 1981): 471–474.

[49]J.F. Rand, Creative problem-solving applied to grievance/arbitration procedures, *Personnel Administrator* 25 (March 1980): 50–52.

[50]*Ibid.;* see also adaptation of principles specified in C.H. Kepner and B.B. Tregoe, *The Rational Manager* (New York: McGraw-Hill, 1977).

[51]Dalton and Todor, Win, lose, draw, *op. cit.*

[52]E.R. Livernash and D.A. Peach, *Grievance and Resolution: A Study in Basic Steel* (Cambridge, Mass.: Harvard University Press, 1974).

[53]D. Yoder and P.D. Staudohar, Auditing the labor relations function, *Personnel* 60 (May-June 1983): 36–56.

[54]*Ibid.*

FURTHER READINGS

Elkouri, F. and Elkouri E.A. *How Arbitration Works* 3rd ed. Washington, D.C.: Bureau of National Affairs, 1973.

Evarts, W.R., Greenstone, J.L., Kirkpatrick, G.J., and Leviton, S.C. *Winning through Accommodation: The Mediator's Handbook.* Dubuque, Iowa: Kendall/Hunt, 1983.

Grossman, M.M. *The Question of Arbitrability.* Ithaca, N.Y.: ILR Press, 1984.

Kolb, D.M. *The Mediators.* Cambridge, Mass.: MIT Press, 1983.

Prasow, P. and Peters, E. *Arbitration and Collective Bargaining: Conflict Resolution in Labor Relations.* New York: McGraw-Hill, 1983.

Teple, E.R. and Moberly, R.B. *Arbitration and Conflict Resolution.* Washington, D.C.: Bureau of National Affairs, 1979.

PART 5

Organizational Effectiveness

CHAPTER 13

Responding to Legal Constraints

CHAPTER OUTLINE

LEARNING CHECKPOINTS

After completing the reading and activities in this chapter, students will be able to

- describe the major legislation that has influenced human resources management in the last twenty-five years;
- discuss the major provisions of equal employment opportunity legislation;
- cite the components of an affirmative action plan;
- illustrate three ways of determining adverse impact;
- cite ways of preventing and dealing with sexual harassment in the workplace;
- describe the regulations affecting occupational safety and health;
- list the major issues affecting employee pensions and benefits;
- offer a general strategy for responding to legal constraints.

INTRODUCTION

Consider the following scenarios:

Scenario I: Several women in an electronics assembly and distribution facility complained that the company discriminated on the basis of sex in selecting participants for its supervisory development program. Most of the supervisors were men, and 90 percent of the participants in the development program were men. Employees were chosen for the program based on the performance appraisal given by their supervisors. Supervisors were asked to rate the following characteristics from outstanding to unsatisfactory: knowledge of work, dependability, productivity, safety, quality of output, cooperation, relationships with others, initiative, organizing ability, and judgment.

Scenario II: Supervisors in the Central City Bank were told that their pension fund no longer existed. The executors had invested it in a 'sure-fire' real estate deal that had gonc bankrupt.

Scenario III: An airline refused to promote a black applicant into its management training program because he did not have a college degree and had poor performance evaluations. The applicant charged the airline with racial discrimination.

Scenario IV: Joan Smith was not selected as a police recruit in Centerville City. Since there were no women on the police force she was not surprised until she discovered that she missed the cutoff on the selection test by one point.

Scenario V: Jacqueline Eliot was recently diagnosed as having lung cancer. She did not smoke, but had worked in a plant that had large quantities of asbestos in the workplace. She asked her employer to pay her medical bills, but the president of the company refused to pay anything.

Were the individuals in these scenarios treated fairly? What protection does federal and state law provide them? What recourse do they have to the decisions made in their cases? How can organizations ensure fair treatment of employees without incurring prohibitive costs?

In this chapter we examine the legal and regulatory influences on human resources management in three primary areas: (1) equal employment opportunity, (2) safety and health in the workplace, and (3) employee benefits. For each area, we examine the pertinent legislation and consider its impact on organizational life. Then we look at selected areas in personnel and labor relations and discuss the impact of legislation on them. We conclude the chapter with some general strategies for organizations to improve the quality of working life through appropriate responses to legal and regulatory requirements.

EQUAL EMPLOYMENT OPPORTUNITY

The Equal Pay Act of 1963 and Title VII of the Civil Rights Act of 1964 form the basis of antidiscrimination law in the United States. Together, these laws provide women, blacks, and ethnic minorities the ammunition in their struggle for equal employment opportunities in the workplace.

Legislation

The *Equal Pay Act* prohibits discrimination in compensation for jobs requiring the same skills, effort, responsibility, and working conditions on the basis of sex.[1] Figure 13–1 is an excerpt from this act. It allows pay differences that are due to differences in skill, effort, responsibility, working conditions, seniority, merit, and quantity and quality of production. The failures of organizations to comply with provisions of the Equal Pay Act can be tried and appealed through the U.S. judicial system.

Since the act was passed, disputes about the definition of equal worth have arisen. Differences in pay between men and women have been allowed if their job titles differed, even if the jobs involved substantially equal worth. The Equal Employment Opportunity Commission—the federal agency charged with enforcement of this and other laws directed against discrimination—has recently advocated the extension of equal pay for jobs of equal worth to equal pay for jobs of *comparable worth,* which is discussed later in this chapter.

Title VII of the Civil Rights Act extended the Equal Pay Act to prohibit discrimination in more areas of employment: hiring, promotion, and discharge as well as compensation. This act governs the treatment of the women in the electronics facility, the black applicant in the airline industry, and Joan Smith, the police recruit applicant described at the beginning of this chapter. It mandates that no employment decisions can be made on the basis of race, color, religion,

Section 3(d)(1): No employer having employees subject to any provisions of this section shall discriminate, within any establishment in which such employees are employed, between employees on the basis of sex by paying wages to employees in such establishment at a rate less than the rate at which he pays wages to employees of the opposite sex in such establishment for equal work on jobs the performance of which requires equal skill, effort, and responsibility, and which are performed under similar working conditions except where such payment is made pursuant to (i) a seniority system; (ii) a merit system; (iii) a system which measures earnings by quantity or quality of production; or (iv) a differential based on any other factors other than sex: Provided, that an employer who is paying a wage rate differential in violation of this subsection shall not, in order to comply with the provisions of this subsection, reduce the wage rate of any employee.

SOURCE: U.S. Code 1976 Title 29 §206, June 10, 1963, P. L. 88.38, 77 Stat. 56.

Figure 13–1 EXCERPT FROM THE EQUAL PAY ACT OF 1963

sex, or national origin in industry, state government, local government, labor organizations, and educational institutions. It also provides guidelines for the use of professionally designed tests for selection purposes, which are also described later in this chapter. Figure 13–2 shows excerpts from this act.

The Bennett Amendment to Title VII precludes any provisions of the 1966 Civil Rights Act from countermanding contradictory provisions of the 1963 Equal Pay Act. Recent judicial interpretations of the Bennett Amendment have supported the comparable worth doctrine.[2]

(a) It shall be an unlawful employment practice for an employer

(1) to fail or refuse to hire or discharge any individual, or otherwise to discriminate against any individual with respect to his compensation, terms, conditions, or privileges of employment, because of such individual's race, color, religion, sex, or national origin; or

(2) to limit, segregate, or classify his employees or applicants for employment in any way which would deprive or tend to deprive any individual of employment opportunities or otherwise adversely affect his status as an employee because of such an individual's race, color, religion, sex, or national origin.

(b) It shall be an unlawful employment practice for an employment agency to fail or refuse to refer to employment, or otherwise to discriminate against any individual because of his race, color, religion, sex, or national origin, or to classify or refer for employment any individual on the basis of his race, color, religion, sex, or national origin.

(c) It shall be an unlawful employment practice for a labor organization

(1) to exclude or to expel from its membership, or otherwise to discriminate against, any individual because of his race, color, religion, sex, or national origin;

(2) to limit, segregate, or classify its membership or applicants for membership or to classify or fail or refuse to refer for employment any individual in any way which would deprive or tend to deprive any individual of employment opportunities, or would limit such employment opportunities or otherwise adversely affect his status as an employee or as an applicant for employment, because of such individual's race, color, religion, sex, or national origin; or

(3) to cause or attempt to cause an employer to discriminate against an individual in violation of this section.

(d) It shall be an unlawful employment practice for any employer, labor organization, or joint labor-management committee controlling apprenticeship or other training or retraining, including on-the-job training programs, to discriminate against any individual because of his race, color, religion, sex, or national origin in admission to, or employment in, any program established to provide apprenticeship or training.

(e) Notwithstanding any other provision of this title, (1) it shall not be an unlawful employment practice for an employer to hire and employ employees . . . on the basis of his religion, sex, or national origin in those certain instances where religion, sex, or national origin is a bona fide occupational qualification reasonably necessary to the normal operation of that particular business or enterprise.

SOURCE: U.S. Code 1976 Title 28, §1447, U.S. Code 1976 §§1971, 1975a et seq., 2000a et seq., July 2, 1964, P. L. 88.352, 98 Stat. 241.

Figure 13–2 EXCERPT FROM TITLE VII OF THE CIVIL RIGHTS ACT OF 1964: SECTION 703

The *Equal Employment Opportunity Act of 1972* amended the 1964 Civil Rights Act. It provides additional mechanisms for enforcement and extends its coverage to many sectors of the economy not covered by the original act.

The *Civil Service Reform Act of 1978* extended this law to federal agencies. Only where religion, sex, or national origin can be shown to be *bona fide occupational qualifications* (known as BOQ or BFOQ) can they be used as criteria in employment decisions. There are few situations where bona fide occupational characteristics are legitimate—selection of actors or washroom attendants, to name two. Flight attendants can no longer be selected on the basis of sex[3]; and the traditionally male roles of airline pilots and telephone switchers also have been shown to be appropriate for women.[4]

Title VII agrees with the Equal Pay Act that different standards of compensation or employment can be provided because of a bona fide seniority system, merit system, system measuring earnings by quantity and quality of production, or system treating employees who work in different locations differently, provided the intention of these practices is not to discriminate.[5]

Recent interest has focused on protecting workers against national origin discrimination occurring because of an individual's dress, accent, or name.[6] For example, height and weight, fluency in English, and education and training have been shown to be discriminatory because of their correlation with national origin.[7] More specifically, the decision in a recent court case concluded that speaking English as a qualification for a job must be shown to be job-related.[8]

National origin harassment, which can be verbal or physical and conducted by supervisors, coworkers, or non-employees, is also illegal. To avoid harassment, management should

1. inform all managers and supervisors about the guidelines and the organization's intent to comply;
2. never withhold an application form from an individual;
3. make sure recruitment has equal impact on all parts of the labor pool;
4. make sure recruiters can interview in all relevant languages (depending on the labor pool);
5. specify only job-related characteristics for recruiting by employment agencies;
6. select enough sources of recruitment to represent the labor pool;
7. establish a committee to review all written employment materials for compliance;
8. let employees know where English-only rules apply; and
9. make sure management is aware of and sensitive to harassment.

Additional legislation extends equal employment opportunity to groups disenfranchised because of age or physical ability. The *Age Discrimination in Employment Act of 1967* (ADEA), as amended in 1978, prohibits organizations from discriminating in employment against individuals over forty years old but less than seventy years old. According to ADEA, organizations cannot mandate retirement for individuals less than seventy years old. Recent legislation in some states, Massachusetts for one, has extended the protections to virtually eliminate a mandatory retirement age for any employee.[9]

Public awareness of the provisions and implications of the law has increased significantly: the number of age discrimination complaints increased in the early 1980s.[10] Since most ADEA cases deal with discriminatory termination, management should

1. make all personnel decisions on the basis of carefully collected data and systematically documented analysis of worker competence;
2. sensitize managers to the importance of avoiding any reference to age in termination interviews;
3. encourage the human resources department to disseminate information concerning their antidiscrimination policies and to maintain records of the information they distribute;
4. keep current about ADEA provisions;
5. choose a replacement for a protected employee with great care;
6. document an offer of transfer or demotion to a fired or laid-off protected employee;
7. have the employee sign a waiver that relinquishes his or her rights to sue the employer under ADEA if he or she chooses an option such as early retirement;
8. avoid any defense of discriminatory actions based on the costs of employing older workers;
9. create and regularly update an age chart of the entire organization to identify workers subject to ADEA provisions; and
10. view older workers as an asset, not a liability.[11]

Equal employment legislation protects two additional groups. The *Vocational Rehabilitation Act of 1973* prohibits discrimination against physically handicapped individuals by federal contractors or the federal government. It also calls for affirmative action in the recruiting and hiring of handicapped individuals, as described later in this chapter. The *Vietnam Era Veterans Readjustment Assistance Act of 1974* requires the government to take affirmative action (see below) in hiring and promoting Vietnam era and all disabled veterans. Figure 13–3 summarizes the equal employment opportunity legislation.

Types and Causes of Discrimination

Equal employment opportunity is directed at the prevention of both disparate treatment and disparate impact.[12] *Disparate treatment* involves direct discrimination, where different standards are applied to different groups. It includes using illegitimate reasons for rejecting or selecting different employees or treating a minority applicant unfairly by hiring someone with equal or fewer qualifications. For example, if an employer rejects a woman who lacks certain work experience but hires a man with the same deficiency, it is a case of disparate treatment.

Equal Pay Act of 1963 prohibits discrimination on the basis of sex in compensation for jobs that require the same skills, effort, responsibility, and working conditions.

Title VII of the Civil Rights Act of 1964 prohibits discrimination in employment (e.g., hiring, promotion, or discharge) on the basis of race, color, religion, sex, or national origin, in industry, state government, local government, labor organizations, and educational institutions unless race, color, religion, sex, or national origin can be shown to be a bona fide occupational qualification.

Equal Employment Opportunity Act of 1972 amended the Civil Rights Act of 1964; created the Equal Employment Opportunity Commission, which is empowered with the authority to investigate and file suits on behalf of individuals experiencing discrimination.

Age Discrimination in Employment Act of 1967, as amended in 1978, prohibits discrimination in employment (e.g., hiring, promotion, retention, and compensation) for individuals over forty years old but less than seventy years old, and forbids mandatory retirement for individuals less than seventy years old.

Executive Order 11246 prohibits discrimination by federal contractors and subcontractors, and calls for affirmative action plans by employers.

Executive Order 11478 requires affirmative action plans in federal agencies.

Vocational Rehabilitation Act of 1973 prohibits discrimination against physically handicapped people by the federal government or federal contractors and requires affirmative action to employ qualified handicapped individuals.

The Vietnam Era Veterans Readjustment Assistance Act of 1974 requires the government to take affirmative action in hiring and promoting Vietnam era and all disabled veterans.

Figure 13–3 SUMMARY OF LEGISLATION INFLUENCING EMPLOYMENT DECISIONS

Discrimination results from unequal treatment or prejudiced actions. It also results from employers making decisions based on a racial or sexual premise, such as automatically excluding blacks or women from the hiring pool.

Disparate impact is less direct discrimination, where the same standards are applied, but with different consequences for different groups. In these situations, some groups are not adequately represented in the organization's work force. For example, it is a case of disparate impact if middle management includes a significant percentage of women, but top management includes few or none. Thus the concept applies to any employment practice that has unequal impact on the groups in question—men versus women, whites versus blacks, and so forth. Many tests with cutoff scores that result in the exclusion of women or minorities have been shown to create disparate impact.

The following screening devices have been rejected under some circumstances because of disparate impact: educational requirements, prespecified test scores, experience requirements, height and weight requirements, physical agility test scores, credit record requirements, arrest-conviction records, and requirements to designate marital status, nature of discharge from the military, and the names of relatives employed by the company. In addition, the use of walk-in or word-of-mouth recruiting, reference checks, promotion from within, and promotion based on supervisory recommendations have led to disproportionate representation of minorities and women, which can then lead to disparate impact in subsequent selection procedures.[13]

Equal Employment Opportunity Commission

Created by the Equal Employment Opportunity Act of 1972, the Equal Employment Opportunity Commission (EEOC) is a federal agency that processes complaints of discrimination and issues written regulations governing employment practices. In addition to its regulations prohibiting discrimination based on sex, religion, age, and national origin, EEOC has issued guidelines about pregnancy disability, employee selection, sexual harassment, record keeping and reports, affirmative action for state and local governments, and equal employment opportunity in the federal government.[14]

In processing complaints, EEOC follows three steps.[15] First, it investigates the complaint. Second, it terminates its involvement if the investigation shows no probable cause for the complaint. If it finds a probable cause, EEOC attempts to settle the matter through conciliation with the relevant parties. Third, if conciliation is unsuccessful, EEOC litigates the complaint in court.

If the women in scenarios I and IV or the black applicant in scenario III earlier in this chapter felt they were victims of discrimination, they could file a complaint with EEOC. EEOC would then investigate the complaint, determine its accuracy, and recommend the appropriate action. Once it determines that a discrimination complaint is valid, the organization involved must rectify the complaint unless it wishes to go to court. If the organization elects to ignore EEOC and consequently ends up in court, a *prima facie* case must be established by the plaintiff. A plaintiff demonstrates *prima facie discrimination* if he or she can show either disparate treatment or disparate impact, as discussed earlier.[16] If so, then the burden of proof shifts to the organization, which attempts to prove that it has not been guilty of discrimination. If proven guilty, the court makes an award to the plaintiff or plaintiffs, such as reinstatement or promotion and back pay.

Affirmative Action

Executive Order 11246 in 1965 required that federal contractors receiving more than $15,000 per year "take affirmative action to ensure that applicants are employed, and that employees are treated during employment, without regard to their race, color, religion, sex, or national origin."[17] This order also requires organizations to take affirmative action to employ, promote, and equalize pay for groups that have experienced discrimination.

Under this order, federal contractors and subcontractors must submit an affirmative action plan to the government. Such a plan must include the grouping of jobs by similarity of tasks and responsibility; a *utilization analysis,* which compares the number of women, minorities, or other protected groups in the organization to the number of those available for employment; the identification of cases where women or minorities are not employed in numbers proportionate to their numbers in the labor supply; and goals and timetables to correct the situation.[18] Executive order 11478 extends these requirements to federal agencies and the Office of Federal Contract Compliance enforces affirmative action requirements. Violation of the order can result in the withdrawal of the federal contract, which can be a significant loss of revenue to many organizations.

In different situations affirmative action has meant (1) recruiting underrepresented groups, (2) changing management's prejudicial attitudes, (3) changing practices that work to the disadvantage of underrepresented groups, and (4) preferentially hiring and promoting underrepresented groups.[19]

To determine whether minorities are being underutilized in any job group the government contractor should consider at least the following factors:

1. The minority population of the labor area surrounding the facility (i.e., the relevant external labor market, which could be the local geographical area, the nation, or the world)
2. The number of unemployed minorities in the labor area surrounding the facility
3. The percentage of the minority work force compared to the total work force in the immediate labor area
4. The general availability of minorities having requisite skills in the immediate labor area
5. The availability of minorities having requisite skills in the immediate labor area
6. The availability of promotable and transferable minorities within the contractor's organization
7. The existence of institutions capable of training minorities in the requisite skills
8. The amount of training the contractor is reasonably able to undertake as a means of making all job classes available to minorities[20]

These data are collected in much the same way as data for determining the supply of human resources and the availability of various categories of employees, as described in Chapter 2. Basically, affirmative action officers count the number of women, minorities, and members of other protected groups inside and outside the organization; sometimes they use published data to determine the size of the relevant external labor market. They then compare the percentage employed to the percentage available and determine whether the numbers are sufficiently and significantly alike.

Affirmative action plans offer ways of correcting underutilization by setting goals and establishing timetables. Affirmative action planning should follow these steps:

1. Identify areas of underutilization in the organization by means of the utilization analysis
2. Determine how the organization's employment policies might be contributing to the underutilization
3. Plan for changes in those policies

4. Set affirmative action employment goals
5. Later, examine the organization's successes and failures in meeting affirmative action goals
6. Try to identify the reasons for the failures
7. Take the reasons into account in the next cycle of planning and goal setting[21]

Overreaction to equal employment opportunity laws and affirmative action requirements can be costly to organizations.[22] In some cases organizations hire unqualified workers to meet affirmative action quotas. In other cases *reverse discrimination* has occurred. In 1978 the U.S. Supreme Court agreed to review the constitutionality of the admissions program of the medical school of the University of California at Davis in response to such a complaint. Plaintiff Allan Bakke claimed that the school's Equal Opportunity Program discriminated against him by reserving admissions for less qualified applicants. Figure 13–4 summarizes the allegation. Later that year, the Supreme Court ordered that Bakke be admitted to medical school. Although the ruling alerted federal agencies and contractors that affirmative action programs would be under broader scrutiny than before, it did not affect earlier rulings requiring organizations to remedy the effects of past discrimination.[23]

The ruling did not eliminate the use of quota systems for affirmative action purposes. *Weber* v. *Kaiser Aluminum* supported the legality of a quota system for minorities applying to an on-the-job craft training program that was included in a collective bargaining agreement. In this case, the Supreme Court emphasized

The University of California established its medical school at Davis in 1968. Concerned with the need to boost minority enrollment, the faculty resolved in 1968 to set up a special Task Force to fill 16 seats. The regular admission committee continued to select 84 regular candidates. The Task Force Committee, composed mostly of minority faculty members and students, was empowered to select 16 "economically and educationally disadvantaged" applicants. In 1974, application forms were changed to add questions asking students to identify themselves by race and whether they wished to be considered as minority applicants.

Allan Bakke, a civil engineer of Norwegian ancestry applied under the regular admissions procedure in 1973 and again in 1974. He was rejected on both occasions, despite high undergraduate grades and high scores in the Medical School Admissions Test. Bakke also had received a favorable "benchmark" rating from the regular admissions committee, which included such factors as community involvement and character, as revealed by recommendations and a personal interview.

Bakke filed suit shortly after the second rejection. The Supreme Court of California sustained his claim, and ordered that Bakke be admitted after the school stipulated that he probably would have been admitted had the 16-seat admissions program not been in effect. The state court declared that Bakke's constitutional rights were violated by the grant of a "preference on the basis of race to persons who, by the university's own standards, are not as qualified to the study of medicine as nonminority applicants denied admission."

SOURCE: *United States Law Week*, 18 October 1977, p. 3249.

Figure 13–4 **SUMMARY OF THE ALLEGATION IN *BAKKE* V. *THE REGENTS OF THE UNIVERSITY OF CALIFORNIA***

the fact that the affirmative action plan resulted from negotiations between the company and the union and must be viewed within the historical context in which Title VII was passed—to deal with the plight of minorities in the United States economy. The Court upheld voluntary quotas and quota systems that do not produce reverse discrimination.[24]

Sexual Harassment

In a 1977 case, a woman alleged that she was reassigned and her job abolished because she refused to have sexual relations with a male supervisor. The Court of Appeals for the District of Columbia Circuit stated that "discrimination as portrayed was plainly based on (plaintiff's) gender." Plaintiff had alleged facts showing that "retention of her job was conditioned upon submission to sexual relations—an exaction which the supervisor would not have sought from any male."[25] Title VII is violated "when a supervisor, with actual or constructive knowledge of the employer, makes sexual advances or demands toward a subordinate employee and conditions that employee's job status—evaluation, continued employment, promotion, or other aspects of career development—on a favorable response to these advances or demands, and the employer does not take prompt and appropriate action after acquiring such knowledge."[26]

During the late 1970s, courts treated cases of sexual harassment inconsistently, particularly with regard to the responsibility of the employer in such cases. In 1980, however, EEOC amended its guidelines to state unequivocally that harassment on the basis of sex violates Title VII.[27] The guidelines now require employers to maintain a workplace free of sexual harassment and intimidation. Unwelcome sexual advances, requests for sexual favors, and other verbal or physical conduct of a sexual nature constitute sexual harassment when (1) submission to such conduct is made, either explicitly or implicitly, a term or condition of an individual's employment, (2) submission to or rejection of such conduct by an individual is used as the basis for employment decisions affecting such individual, or (3) such conduct has the purpose or effect of unreasonably interfering with an individual's work performance or creating an intimidating, hostile, or offensive working environment.[28]

If an employee guilty of sexual harassment is a supervisor or agent for the organization, the *employer* is liable for sexual harassment under Title VII, regardless of whether the act was authorized or forbidden by the employer or whether the employer knew of the act. To avoid liability, employers must have a clear company policy that opposes sexual harassment. They should formulate a grievance procedure, investigate complaints actively and responsively, and take disciplinary action immediately and strongly. Reading 13–1, "Effective Training and the Elimination of Sexual Harassment," by George Kronenberger and David Bourke, offers some guidelines for helping employers meet current EEOC guidelines. In summary, the employer should take the following actions:

1. Establish a procedure for handling complaints of harassment, or adapt the existing complaint procedure for this purpose.

2. Determine whether there might be a sexual harassment problem.

3. Seek legal counsel about what the organization should do.

4. Prepare a policy statement on harassment, signed by the highest possible members of the organization, and distribute it to all employees (possibly in their pay envelopes).

5. Be aware of, and train the personnel staff about, sexual harassment.

6. Include a discussion of sexual harassment and company responsibility at training sessions or staff meetings for executives, middle management, and supervisory personnel.

7. Assign responsibility for coordinating the overall effort to prevent harassment to an equal employment coordinator, a personnel officer, or other specially assigned personnel.[29]

EMPLOYMENT SAFETY AND HEALTH

Estimates have placed the cost of industrial accidents at $27.3 billion (1979 dollars), or $13,600 per accident. In 1979 alone, 13,200 people lost their lives and 2.3 million received disabling injuries in work-related accidents.[30] The Occupational Safety and Health Act (OSHA) mandates a range of safe and healthy working conditions, and workers' compensation laws in most states try to compensate individuals for disabilities they receive in the workplace.

Occupational Safety and Health Act

The Occupational Safety and Health Act was passed in 1970 to respond to the increasing number of job-related injuries, the increasing costs of work-related accidents, and inadequacies in states' workers' compensation laws. Its purpose is "to assure so far as possible every working man and woman in the Nation safe and healthful working conditions and to preserve our human resources."[31]

The Act states that the employer must provide employees with a safe place of employment and that each employee must follow all safety and health standards, rules, and regulations. "Each employer (1) shall furnish to each of his employees employment and a place of employment which are free from recognized hazards that are causing or are likely to cause death or serious physical harm; (2) shall comply with occupational safety and health standards promulgated under this Act. Each employee shall comply with occupational safety and health standards and all rules, regulations, and orders issued pursuant to this Act which are applicable to his own actions and conduct."[32]

If the costs to meet the legal requirements for providing a safe and healthful working environment are high, the costs associated with accidents, injuries, and occupational diseases are even higher. They include not only the direct, measurable costs for treating illness or injury and those associated with loss of work time, but the expense to repair damaged equipment, clean up the workplace, compensate an injured employee beyond funds provided by workers' compensation, investigate and process the accident report, complete work interrupted by the accident or illness, pay for legal services, and hire, train or promote a replacement, among others.[33]

OSHA Agencies

The Occupational Safety and Health Act created several agencies to monitor and enforce its provisions and conduct research regarding safe and healthful employment. The Occupational Safety and Health Administration (OSHA) establishes safety standards, rules on requests for variances, conducts inspections, and issues citations for violations. The Occupational Safety and Health Review Commission (OSHRC) acts as a quasijudicial body that hears appeals to citations issued by OSHA; appeals can also be made to the U.S. Court of Appeals. The National Institute for Occupational Safety and Health (NIOSH) conducts training of OSHA inspectors and conducts research into job safety and health standards.

OSHA Enforcement Procedures

The Act established procedures for both employers and employees to follow in identifying and dealing with safety and health hazards. Employees (or their representatives) have five rights:

1. They may request in writing that the Department of Labor make an inspection.
2. They may accompany the compliance officer on the inspection (known as the *walk-around right*).
3. They may participate in subsequent hearings if the employer protests a fine or inspector's decision.
4. They may examine their exposure record in the case of toxic materials or other harmful agents, and they may monitor the company's monitoring processes.
5. They may request that the government determine if there are potentially toxic substances in the workplace and require it to set standards for safe levels.[34]

In addition, employees can refuse to work in dangerous conditions if their fears are objectively reasonable, if they have sought correction of the dangerous conditions, or if resorting to normal enforcement procedures is inadequate or too slow to deal with the danger.[35]

The employer also has certain rights:

1. It may request and receive proper identification from OSHA compliance officers.
2. It must be advised of the reasons for the inspection.
3. It may participate in the walk-around inspection and in opening and closing conferences with the compliance officer.
4. It may contest a citation for violation of a safety or health standard.
5. It may apply for a temporary or permanent variance of a standard.[36]

OSHA inspections are conducted for the following reasons: (1) employees feel they are in imminent danger; (2) a catastrophe or fatal accident has occurred; (3) valid employee complaints have been made about working conditions; (4) special-emphasis programs, such as target industries and target health hazards, have been introduced; (5) the organization has been chosen for a random inspection; and (6) reinspections are made.[37] The inspection procedure typically begins with the OSHA compliance officer presenting his or her credentials, asking to see the appropriate person, citing the reasons for the inspection, and requesting to see any existing documentation related to the complaint. The compliance officer meets with the employees' representatives to discuss the complaint, then conducts the walk-around inspection. The officer then discusses any violations with the employer. If the officer finds a violation, he or she issues a written warning or citation as soon after the inspection as possible. Where violations are particularly dangerous, the officer may order the employer to cease operations. In any case, the employer is ordered to correct the violation within a specified time period; but the employer may appeal the penalty to the Occupational Safety and Health Review Commission, hoping the judge will rescind the order. Figure 13–5 lists possible compliance responses when violations of health and safety provisions are found.

To protect against safety and health violations, and the disruptions they cause, the employer should

- be aware that he or she has a general duty and responsibility to provide a place of employment free from recognized hazards and to comply with occupational safety and health standards promulgated under the Act;
- familiarize management with mandatory occupational safety and health standards;
- make sure employees know about OSHA;
- examine conditions in the workplace to make sure they conform to applicable safety and health standards;
- remove or guard hazards;
- make sure employees have and use safe tools and equipment, including required personal protective gear, and that they are properly maintained;
- use color codes, posters, labels, or signs to warn employees of potential hazards;
- establish or update operating procedures and communicate them so that employees follow safety and health requirements for their own protection;
- provide medical examinations when required by OSHA standards;
- seek advice and consultation as needed by writing, calling, or visiting the nearest OSHA office.[38]

One organization addressed the safety and health issues through establishment of an occupational health management-by-objectives program (see Chapter 6 for a discussion of management by objectives).[39] The basic objectives focused on early recognition of hazards, evaluation of the risks posed, and formulation and

Technical responses

Maintenance
- Monitoring the effect of engineering controls
- Routine maintenance checks

Equipment Change
- Retool a machine
- Add new engineering controls
- Install or adjust ventilation system
- Install noise control equipment
- Replace offensive materials with less dangerous one
- Eliminate a hazardous operation
- Install or purchase air monitoring equipment

Worker Protection
- Provide workers with new protective equipment
- Re-instruct in or increase use of existing protective equipment

Informational responses

Training
- Stepped up safety and health training (through booklets, films, job training institutes) for workforce
- Training of supervisors in safety and health management
- Motivation or incentive systems
- Policies and procedures manual developed or utilize trade association manual
- Training employees in the use of monitoring equipment

Planning
- Track costs of OSHA compliance
- Develop grievance system for workers' complaints
- Establish contingency fund for safety and health or OSHA compliance
- Develop own data collection system for lost-time accidents
- Computer analyze lost-time data
- Conduct safety and health research and development

Administrative responses

Structural
- Establish safety committee
- Modify safety committee structure
- Create new positions; loss control officer, government relations manager, industrial hygienists
- Upgrade position of safety engineer
- Move safety and health function from one functional area to another
- Increase plant security

Procedural
- Modify safety committee responsibility
- Pay workers for walkaround
- "OSHA administrative solutions," i.e., reducing eight hour day, rotate workers' exposure to hazard

Policy
- Add or amend safety and health clauses in union-management contract

External responses

Political
- Gather economic data, argue for deregulation
- PR efforts toward employees or the public, image advertising
- Solicit employee contributions to PAC
- Lobby for changes in standards
- Contact congressman or senator regarding safety and health concerns

Legal
- Require entry warrant of inspectors
- Contest a citation or penalty
- Hide an operation, spike a sample

From "How Does Your Company Respond to OSHA?" by Barbara Gray Gricar and H. Donald Hopkins. Reprinted from the April, 1983 issue of *Personnel Administrator*, copyright, 1983, The American Society for Personnel Administration, 606 North Washington Street, Alexandria, VA 22314, $30 per year.

Figure 13–5 OSHA COMPLIANCE RESPONSES

implementation of appropriate control measures. Other worksite health programs emphasize prevention of disease: employers have instituted programs to help workers stop smoking, detect and control high blood pressure, control cholesterol level, control weight, increase general fitness, and manage stress.[40]

Overall, the impact of the Act has been limited. The list of standards is so extensive that inspectors have had difficulty becoming fully versed in them. In addition, some standards are viewed as spurious; others are considered overly rigorous. Enforcement problems are rampant. Most important, the costs of OSHA are perceived to be too high relative to its benefits, particularly in light of recent political pressures to cut the cost of government. Figure 13–6 traces the dynamics of OSHA ineffectiveness. In the 1980s some dismantling and reduction of OSHA's activities has occurred.[41]

Still, OSHA has the potential to (1) raise the productivity of those who would otherwise have been injured or ill, (2) increase their enjoyment of life, (3) reduce the costs of treatment and rehabilitation, (4) reduce the costs of administering worker compensation, insurance, and training for replacements, (5) reduce the need for private-sector efforts to encourage job safety and health, (6) reduce damages to plants and equipment, and (7) decrease disruption of work.[42]

Workers' Compensation

Workers' compensation laws provide workers with income when they are disabled. In almost all states employers must provide their employees with insurance that provides benefits in a variety of situations. Occupational hazards that are typically covered include accidents, partial or total disabilities, death, occupational disease,

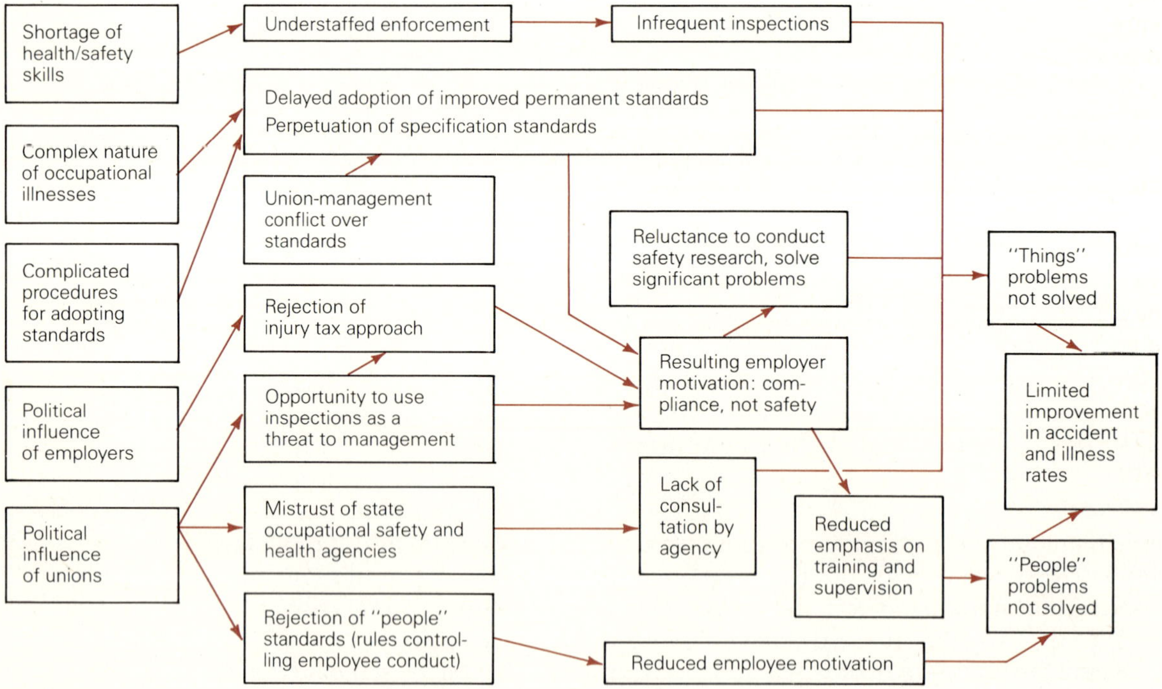

From James Ledvinka, FEDERAL REGULATION OF PERSONNEL AND HUMAN RESOURCE MANAGEMENT (Boston: Kent Publishing Company, 1982), p. 192. © 1982 by Wadsworth, Inc. Reprinted by permission of Kent Publishing Company, a division of Wadsworth, Inc.

Figure 13–6 DYNAMICS OF OSHA INEFFECTIVENESS

job-related or job-connected physical impairments, or injuries and disabilities attributable to an employer's gross negligence.[43] The amount of the payments in these situations are a function of state law as well as employee longevity with the company and the level of the employer's coverage. (See Chapter 9 for additional discussion of these laws.)

EMPLOYEE PENSIONS AND BENEFITS

The third major area of the government's regulation of organizations focuses on employee benefits. Because these regulations are extremely complex, technical, and dynamic, this section highlights some of the issues only briefly.

The major regulation underpinning benefits legislation is the *Employment Retirement Income Security Act* (ERISA). ERISA was passed in 1974 to safeguard against the misuse of pension monies. It details provisions related to participation, eligibility, vesting, termination, and funding of pension plans (see Chapter 9 for additional discussion of these plans). This Act protects the pension funds of supervisors in the Central City Bank from misuse, for example.

A pension or retirement plan is a program, established or maintained by an employer or an employee organization, that either provides retirement income to employees or results in a deferral of income by employees.[44] There are two types of plans:

1. *Defined benefit plans* provide a certain fixed income after retirement.
2. *Defined contribution plans* require an organization to make a regular deposit into a retirement account in the employee's name.

Employers most often contribute to these plans, but sometimes individuals may also add to them. In this case, the employee is allowed to contribute up to a maximum percentage of his or her compensation. Why would an employee want to make such a contribution? Typically, these plans defer income until retirement, a time when the individual will most likely pay taxes at a lower rate than when working.

The plans vary in the time required before an individual can become a participant and become vested; that is, acquire a nonforfeitable right to the retirement benefit. Under ERISA, the following are permissible minimum participation requirements: (1) not older than age 25 and completion of one year's service; (2) not older than age 25 and completion of three years' service, if the plan provides full and immediate vesting of accrued benefits; or (3) one year of service alone, generally defined as at least 1000 hours worked over a twelve-month period.[45] Part-time employees and workers hired five years or less before normal retirement age can be excluded. Exclusion of lower-paid employees is not allowed; and any plan must cover 70 percent of all employees, or 80 percent of those eligible if 70 percent of an organization's total work force is eligible.

Vesting can be full and immediate or can meet one of the following rules: (1) 100 percent after ten years of service; (2) 25 percent after the first five years of service, 5 percent for each of the next five years, and 10 percent for the next five years; (3) 50 percent when age plus service equals 45, and 10 percent per year thereafter (the rule of 45); (4) 40 percent after four years' service, increasing incrementally to 100 percent after eleven years' service, if the plan can demonstrate a rank-and-file turnover of less than 6 percent.[46] In any case, vesting at ten years of service must be at least 50 percent and increase 10 percent each year thereafter; and the employee must be 100 percent vested at his or her normal retirement date. In addition to issues of participation and vesting, recent legislation has facilitated the transferability of pension monies among funds should an individual change organizations.

ERISA requires employers to communicate information about the retirement plans to all participants. Such information must include a description of the plan, amendments to the plan, an annual report of the plan's financial status, a statement of benefits to those who terminate, and a written explanation of any denial of benefits. The organization must also provide a statement of the participant's accrued and vested benefits on request. "The summary plan description . . . shall be written in a manner calculated to be understood by the average plan participants, and shall be sufficiently accurate and comprehensive to reasonably apprise such participants and beneficiaries of their rights and obligations under the plan."[47]

Three agencies oversee the implementation of ERISA.[48] The Internal Revenue Service's Office of Employee Plans and Exempt Organizations reviews retirement and pensions plans, with emphasis on determining their tax-deferral status. The United States Department of Labor's Labor-Management Services Administration also reviews program structure and operation. The Pension Benefit Guaranty Corporation investigates the termination of plans, collects insurance premiums for individuals in terminated plans, and makes pension payments to participants in place of terminated plans.

LEGAL INFLUENCES ON PERSONNEL AND LABOR RELATIONS SYSTEMS

The legislation discussed so far influences human resources management in the areas of recruitment, selection, decruitment, performance evaluation, compensation, and collective bargaining.

Recruitment

The various acts influence recruitment (see Chapter 3) in two ways: (1) during recruitment interviewing, managers and human resources professionals must limit their questions to those that are legally acceptable; and (2) the selection of sources of recruits must not inherently eliminate any group of applicants on the basis of race, color, religion, sex, or national origin.

In other words, in their recruitment practices, managers and recruiting organizations may not discriminate on the basis of race, religion, sex, or ethnic origin. They may not discriminate on the basis of age. Managers must recruit only on the basis of job-related characteristics. They may not discriminate on the basis of physical handicaps. Thus, managers or human resources professionals cannot request an individual's age, sex, citizenship, religion, race, ethnic origins, or criminal record as part of recruiting data unless these data have been shown to be job-related. Finally, all advertisements must meet legal criteria. Figure 13–7 lists the areas often addressed illegally on application blanks or during employment interviews.

Selection

Employers can select among individuals only on job-related criteria. *Job relatedness* means that any selection criterion must be shown to be related to an individual's performance on the job (see Chapter 4 for discussion of selection). For example, sex was shown not to be a bona fide occupational qualification for flight attendants[49]; but professing a certain religion would be a bona fide occupational qualification for the clergy, and being male could be a bona fide qualification for an actor.

The *Uniform Guidelines for Employee Selection* issued by the Equal Employment Opportunity Commission specify that instruments used in selection may neither have adverse impact nor demonstrate differential validity for different population groups. *Adverse impact* in selection refers to a screening device's yielding a differential selection rate for applicants in different ethnic, racial, gender, or demographic groups. If an employer uses an aptitude test as a screening device and if a cutoff score is arbitrarily chosen, the cutoff could systematically eliminate women or minorities from the selection pool. The cutoff selected would then

Name used previously	National origin
Title (Mr., Mrs., Miss, Ms.)	Education
Sex	Military background
Age	Arrest records
Marital status	Relatives
Height and weight	Notification in case of emergency
Religion	Membership in organizations
Race/Color	Physical handicaps
Citizenship	

Based on R.S. Lowell and J.A. DeLoach, Equal employment opportunity: Are you overlooking the application form?, *Personnel* 59 (July-August 1982): 49–63.

Figure 13–7 DANGER AREAS IN RECRUITMENT APPLICATION BLANKS AND INTERVIEWS create adverse impact. In this situation employers use a nominally neutral employment practice, such as a test, to discriminate. To show that there is adverse impact, "one must demonstrate that a protected class is being treated in some fashion that places that class in an unfavorable position compared to the majority employment group, e.g., being denied employment at a more frequent rate."[50]

One criterion for adverse impact directs that the percentage of a minority group selected must be at least 80 percent of the percentage of a majority group selected. Table 13–1 illustrates the computation of adverse impact in this way. Alternatively, individuals have shown adverse impact by demonstrating that the percentage of a protected group employed by a given organization is significantly less than the percentage in the overall population.[51]

In a third approach, used for an individual filing suit or when too few minority job candidates exist, the Supreme Court offered the following procedure:

> The complainant in a Title VII trial must carry the initial burden under the statute of establishing a prima facie case of racial discrimination. This may be done by showing: (i) that he belongs to a racial minority; (ii) that he applied and was qualified for a job for which the employer was seeking applicants; (iii) that, despite his qualifications, he was rejected; and (iv) that, after his rejection, the position remained open and the employer continued to seek applicants from persons of complainant's qualifications.[52]

Applicant	Sex	Test Score
1	Female	99
2	Female	98
3	Male	90
4	Male	85
5	Male	84
6	Male	83
7	Female	79
8	Female	77
9	Male	75
10	Female	70
11	Male	70
12	Male	70
13	Female	67
14	Male	55
15	Male	50
16	Male	50

Using a cutoff score of 80:
2 of 6 (33%) of women earned scores above 80.
4 of 10 (40%) of men earned scores above 80.
Is 33% greater than 80% of 40%?
33% = 83% of 40%.
Since 83% is greater than 80%, there is no adverse impact on women according to this criterion.

Table 13–1 CALCULATION OF ADVERSE IMPACT USING THE 80 PERCENT RULE

In this case, once an individual has shown that adverse impact exists, the employer must show that the selection instrument produces job-related information.

To be legal, selection instruments cannot show differential validity.[53] When "technically feasible a test should be validated for each minority group with which it is used. . . . A test which is differentially valid may be used in groups for which it is valid but not for those in which it is not valid."[54] Questions exist, however, about the best way to measure such differences, or whether differential validity even exists.

The criterion used by the Uniform Guidelines for Employee Selection in determining discrimination is whether a test score has criterion validity (see Chapter 4). A regression equation of a predictor (e.g., a test score) and a criterion (e.g., work performance ratings) that yields significantly different regression coefficients for protected and nonprotected groups means that there is adverse impact.

Organizations do not have to select unqualified or poor performing minority workers, women, or protected workers for an open position simply because they are protected. Thus the airline described in Scenario III in the introduction to this chapter does not have to promote an unqualified black worker into a management training program.

Decruitment

The legislation outlined earlier also affects the discharge of workers. Employers can discharge workers with unsatisfactory work records, poor attendance, or attitude problems (see Chapter 5).[55] To protect themselves, however, employers must document the performance of employees, keep them informed about performance problems, show that a progressive discipline process was used, and equitably punish employees who violate rules.

Employers must also recognize that they can no longer practice termination-at-will.[56] *Termination-at-will* means that employers "may dismiss their employees at will . . . for good cause, for no cause or even for cause morally wrong without being guilty of legal wrong."[57] Current legislation prohibits termination-at-will, implying that once employed, workers have the right to hold their jobs unless they fail to live up to their part of the bargain or unless the employer has a just business cause, such as an economic slowdown.[58] To maintain their full right to terminate employees, employers should check their orientation and training material to see if a promise of steady employment is stated or implied, and try to eliminate any statements that allow termination only for just cause.[59]

Performance Evaluation

Two major principles underlie effective performance appraisal (see Chapter 6): (1) individuals must be evaluated on job-related behaviors that are observable and measurable; and (2) appraisal systems must be validated and may not discriminate against any group of employees. Figure 13–8 is a series of questions to test your knowledge of the legal principles affecting performance appraisal. Take a few minutes to complete the test.

Indicate whether each of the following statements is true or false.

_______ 1. An employer who employs fifteen or more people for at least twenty weeks must keep accurate records on the results of employment decisions.
_______ 2. An employer can integrate records on the results of employment decisions into selection and performance appraisal programs.
_______ 3. Most human resources decision-making processes are subject to scrutiny for adverse impact.
_______ 4. An employee who files an action under Title VII has the burden of establishing a prima facie case of employment discrimination.
_______ 5. To establish a violation of Title VII it is not necessary to prove that the defendant intentionally discriminated against one or more people.
_______ 6. A plaintiff can claim that a superficially neutral practice has an adverse impact on nonwhites, women, or other protected groups.
_______ 7. Statistical proof can be used as one indicator of discrimination in lawsuits.
_______ 8. The courts have developed extreme skepticism of appraisal techniques involving supervisory judgments that depend almost entirely on subjective evaluation.
_______ 9. The best defense against a charge of adverse impact in performance appraisal is a properly validated appraisal system.
_______ 10. Quotas cannot be used instead of validated personnel appraisal systems.
_______ 11. Employees should participate in the identification of critical elements of their jobs.
_______ 12. Employees may be legally evaluated on the extent to which they fulfill any job-related behaviors.
_______ 13. Rewards should be tied to performance.
_______ 14. An individual can receive less than thirty days' notice of a demotion or termination decision.
_______ 15. An individual should have the opportunity to respond to a termination or demotion decision orally or in writing.
_______ 16. Performance measures must be based on critical or important requirements of the job.

Figure 13–8 PERFORMANCE APPRAISAL AND THE LAW QUIZ

Managers and human resources professionals must know the characteristics of nondiscriminatory performance appraisals. All of the statements in Figure 13–8 are true and describe good practice. Additional principles of good practice include the following:

1. Appraisal of job performance must be based upon analysis of job requirements as reflected in performance standards.
2. Appraisal of job performance only becomes reasonable when performance standards have been communicated and understood by employees.
3. Employees should be evaluated on specific dimensions of job performance rather than on a single, global or overall measure.
4. Performance dimensions should be factorially pure; only homogeneous activities should be grouped together.
5. Performance dimensions should be behaviorally based so that all ratings can be supported by objective, observable evidence.

6. Abstract traits, such as loyalty or honesty, should be avoided unless they can be defined in terms of observable behaviors.

7. The adjectives associated with ratings, called anchors, should be kept brief and logically consistent.

8. Appraisal systems must be validated, as must the ratings given by individual raters.

9. When possible, more than one rater should be used, particularly when ratings are to be closely tied to important personnel decisions.

10. Documentation of extreme ratings should be required.

11. A mechanism for appeal should be provided in case an employee disagrees with a supervisor's appraisal.

12. The system should be formal and standardized.

13. If a supervisor's subjective evaluations are used, other measures should also be used.

14. The system should include well-publicized opportunities for transfer or promotion that can be initiated by either rater or ratee.

In one sample of discrimination suits, characteristics of the systems in organizations that successfully defended against the charges included the following: (1) the organization was nonindustrial; (2) the appraiser had specific written instructions about how to complete the appraisals; (3) job analysis was used to develop the content of the appraisals; (4) appraisals were behavior-oriented, not trait-oriented; (5) the results were reviewed by the appraised employees.[60]

Compensation

Compensation policy is increasingly addressing the issue of comparable pay for comparable worth. Recent interpretations of the Equal Pay Act and Title VII of the Civil Rights Act, as well as the legislatures of numerous states, have supported the concept.[61] *Comparable worth* means that to ensure internal equity (see Chapter 9) "jobs that are equal in their value to the organization ought to be equally compensated, whether or not the work content of those jobs is similar."[62] Of course, determining whether jobs have the same value is difficult.[63] But implementation of a valid job evaluation system should assist organizations in identifying comparable jobs and offering comparable pay for them.

The notion of comparable pay for comparable worth has pros and cons.[64] By ensuring internal equity—paying for the relative value of jobs within the organization—productivity and commitment should be encouraged. In addition, this practice should increase women's living standard since jobs held by women have typically received lower pay than those traditionally considered men's jobs. But comparable worth can be hard to implement since there are no accurate methods for computing a job's worth; it can create legal problems if inaccurate measurements are used; it can have an adverse impact on men; and it can increase the cost of labor to an organization. To date, there is no federal legislation specifically mandating comparable pay for comparable worth, and states are slow to pass such legislation as well. Reading 13–2, "The Employer's Liabilities Under Comparable Worth," by Judy Fulghum, examines the comparable-worth issue in more detail.

The laws regarding employee pensions and retirement plans described earlier must also play a significant role in effective compensation. In developing compensation policy, organizations should seek creative ways of offering employees diverse benefits that have strong economic power. In addition, these benefits should consider relevant tax laws and offer the greatest financial benefit to workers.

Collective Bargaining

Contract negotiations between union and management must consider the legal ramifications of any items they include. For example, promotion and layoff policies must not discriminate among groups of employees. Seniority and merit systems must be clearly defined. Any pension plans must be carefully monitored for their legality.

STRATEGIES FOR RESPONDING TO THE LAW

Both human resources professionals and managers at all levels of the organization must be knowledgeable about the laws and regulations that influence human resources management.

Implications for Human Resources Professionals

Human resources professionals can serve a useful role by providing all organizational members with frequent memoranda regarding current government regulations, and by auditing organizational practices to ensure that they conform to the law. Effective practice includes the following:

1. Human resources professionals should know the provisions of all legislation that relates to discrimination in the workplace. They should monitor human resources management practices to ensure they are legal, and correct any violations they find.
2. Human resources professionals should assist in the formulation of affirmative action plans should they be mandated for the organization.
3. Human resources professionals should convene an organizational safety board charged with the responsibility of ensuring safe working conditions. They should monitor the enforcement of safety provisions and train all managers in safe and healthy work practices.
4. Human resources professionals should remain current about the benefits that offer greatest tax advantages. They should ensure that pension plans and other retirement plans meet the criteria specified in ERISA and other legislation.

5. Human resources professionals should train managers in the legal provisions affecting supervision of their subordinates. They should periodically schedule training sessions to update managers' knowledge of allowable policies and procedures.

Implications for Managers

Managers must implement human resources management practices within the requirements specified by federal and state legislation, as follows:

1. Managers should remain current about regulations that apply to equal opportunity in recruitment, selection, and other aspects of personnel administration.
2. Managers should analyze recruitment procedures to ensure compliance with equal employment opportunity and related laws and regulations.
3. Managers should look for evidence of discrimination in staffing, identify the practice responsible for it, determine if the practice is job-related, and eliminate it if not job-related.
4. Managers should regularly audit their own practices for intentional or unintentional discrimination.
5. Managers should conduct regular safety and health audits of their work area to ensure that they comply with OSHA requirements.

READINGS

Reading 13–1

EFFECTIVE TRAINING AND THE ELIMINATION OF SEXUAL HARASSMENT

George Kronenberger and David Bourke

Since the EEOC's very inception, few of its dictates have raised as much dust as its November 1980 guidelines on sexual harassment. Though the dust has begun to settle and corporate personnel departments have had the opportunity to review the interpretive issues, a general confusion still exists as to which preventive and protective measures should be selected to assure compliance. The guidelines attempt to channel employers in the right direction by encouraging them "to take all steps necessary to prevent sexual harassment."[1] Plus, a plethora of articles has already been written recommending model programs which include policy statements, sanctions and inhouse grievance mechanisms.

The emphasis, however, has not been placed on a mechanism for disseminating information on this sensitive topic. The importance of an effective and comprehensive training program as the method for relaying pertinent information to employees has been neglected. Prominent communication of corporate policy opposing harassment in the workplace, and of the existence of inhouse complaint procedures, are mandatory since a number of judicial actions have placed strong reliance upon such measures.[2] Therefore, training modules should not only supplement other actions, but should also be the foundation for efforts to prevent sexual harassment and to educate employees on this new aspect of EEO law.

A static and perfunctory training program will not fulfill the two-pronged objectives of informing employees of the new EEOC guidelines and of ultimately eliminating sexual harassment from the workplace. An effective program will be dynamic without overwhelming an audience with technical jargon. To emphasize the serious nature of the issue, the program should illustrate how the courts have ruled on sexual harassment claims and should demonstrate the company's firm commitment towards a harassment-free environment. This can readily be accomplished with a detailed program that reviews relevant legal actions and sexual harassment grievances that have arisen within the company.

THE CREDIBILITY PROBLEM

A real credibility problem exists between employees and personnel departments over the issue of sexual harassment. When disseminating information and policies regarding the EEOC guidelines, many administrators may encounter a general disbelief among many male employees who cannot believe that their language, attitudes and jokes can now be construed as sexual harassment.

Also, sexual harassment as defined by the new guidelines is very nebulous. Since no parameters really exist on the terms "offensive, hostile and intimidating," employees may be confused when company officials cannot adequately answer the many questions that arise or explain the concept properly.

If a training program is designed to relay the new meaning of sexual harassment and to transmit information that will arm supervisors against potential claims, this credibility problem may be reduced. The following items should be considered when an EEOC training program is being planned:

Technical Level. The program should not be too technical. Some brief description of federal and state law is necessary, but the discussion need not go into such great detail so as to confuse and alienate the audience.

Corporate Policies. The issue of sexual harassment may present a timely opportunity for managers to renew and reaffirm existing corporate EEO policies and training. When fundamental concepts and terminology are reviewed, they will provide good background for further discussion on sexual harassment.

Judicial Examples. Actual judicial actions (as discussed later) should be reviewed to emphasize the seriousness of the issue and show how the courts will view acts of sexual harassment.

Corporate Examples. If there have been incidents in which company employees have been disciplined for sexual harassment, these cases should also be reviewed. Of course, such cases can be more readily used in larger organizations where confidentiality can be maintained.

Employee Participation. The presentations should be given to all employees if possible, but at least to first-line supervisors if space, time, manpower or costs are limiting factors. If only supervisors are trained, all employees should be made aware of important aspects of the training program. Informal staff meetings at which handouts reviewing EEOC guidelines and company policy are distributed are a good solution.

Competent Trainers. To assure credibility, the training program should be administered by persons with sufficient company experience and adequate background in EEO so that all questions can be answered properly and concisely.

Sexual harassment is a sensitive subject that is both complicated and ill-defined. Make every effort to know your audience and not be viewed as condescending or dogmatic. The wrong attitude may alienate the group and render the program ineffective. By establishing an open communications environment, members of both sexes may engage in a free exchange of ideas, and males may become more aware of behavior that women consider to be harassing.[3]

THE JUDICIAL VIEW OF TRAINING

To assuage the credibility problem on the harassment issue, several court actions that illustrate the serious nature of potential liability for all employees should be used in a training program. Cases that are concise but are not full of legal jargon, quickly and easily convey the concepts of supervisory liability, burden of proof, and intolerable working conditions.

The following cases best illustrate these points:

Miller vs. Bank of America.[4] Margaret Miller, female, alleged that she was discharged from the Bank of America after refusing her supervisor's demands for sexual favors. The Bank of America argued that it had an established policy prohibiting sexual harassment and an inhouse grievance mechanism, and that it was, therefore, not liable for its supervisors' actions. The Ninth Circuit Court of Appeals ruled that, regardless of administrative policies and mechanisms, Bank of America was still liable because supervisors were acting as its "agents."

Miller is a good case to use in a training program because it demonstrates that personnel officials and supervisors must take affirmative efforts to stop alleged acts of sexual harassment and that concerted action is necessary to limit liability for the company.

Kyriazi vs. Western Electric.[5] Kyriaki Kyriazi, female, was discharged from an industrial engineering position at Western Electric for refusing to seek psychiatric care. She linked her discharge to her complaints of sexual misconduct by her male co-workers in the form of tasteless behavior, joking and innuendos. In addition, Kyriazi expanded her complaint into a class action lawsuit on behalf of nearly 2,000 other women. The U.S. District Court of New Jersey ruled in 1979 that Kyriazi was entitled to reinstatement, back pay, promotions and benefits. (Because of the class nature of the lawsuit, thc total cost of the case has yet to be determined, but several million dollars have already been awarded in back pay settlements and attorneys' fees.) The key element, however, was that the co-workers who engaged in the harassment and the supervisors who were aware of the behavior were each fined $1,500 with the stipulation that Western Electric could not pay the penalty.

Kyriazi demonstrates that employees may be affected where it hurts most—in the pocketbook. Co-workers may be fined for sexual misconduct and supervisors may be fined for having knowledge of the misconduct without taking action. In addition, this case expands upon points made in *Miller:* that the company cannot defend employees who engage in sexual harassment or supervisors who are aware of such conduct but do nothing about it. Also, *Kyriazi* demonstrates clearly the potential financial liability in class action lawsuits.

Bundy vs. Jackson.[6] Sandra Bundy, female, charged that she had been subjected to numerous propositions, but she had not been denied "tangible employment benefits" as a result of her resistance to the advances of her supervisor. The U.S. Court of Appeals, District of Columbia Circuit, adopted the EEOC guidelines, holding that an employer is liable for creating "a substantially discriminating work environment" even though Ms. Bundy had not been denied any tangible employment benefit.

Bundy illustrates the EEOC's expanded definition of sexual harassment: the linking of sexual favors to promotions, salary increases, etc., is not the only definition of sexual misconduct. But conduct which ". . . has the purpose or effect of substantially interfering with an individual's work performance or creates an intimidating, hostile or offensive working environment" may also be construed as illegal behavior.

INHOUSE CASES

The EEOC guidelines explicitly state that a company can limit its liability in cases of sexual harassment by showing that it took "immediate and corrective action." Cases resulting in disciplinary action may have already occurred in medium and large organizations. By reviewing these cases in training sessions (without mentioning names), a company can: 1) Convey the organization's commitment to a harassment-free work environment; and 2) Show that swift and appropriate disciplinary action (discharge, demotion, etc.) will follow any substantiated acts of sexual harassment.

The use of inhouse cases makes the issue of sexual harassment relevant to an employee's work environment. From our experience, inhouse cases used for training purposes force employees to sit up and listen since their own co-workers have been affected.

In order to choose the most effective inhouse examples, a number of elements should be considered:

1) Use examples that illustrate the discipline of both top-level management and blue-collar employees.

2) Use examples that hit employees' pocketbooks. An audience's attentiveness will increase dramatically when their paycheck becomes an issue.

3) Include cases that describe "intolerable working environment," not simply ones that tie sexual favors to employment decisions.

Smaller companies may not have had the opportunity to act on a charge of sexual harassment and would not, therefore, be able to use inhouse examples. In this instance, information from other organizations could possibly be obtained to illustrate employer and employee liability.

Our discussions with various companies have uncovered cases similar to the hypothetical examples presented below, which illustrate varying degrees of sexual harassment and subsequent disciplinary actions.

Example One. A female sales representative came to the personnel department and complained about the conduct of the male sales department manager. On several occasions he had, in private, questioned the female employee about her sexual habits, method of birth control and social acquaintances. He had also asked her to his home in the evenings, but never in the presence of co-workers. The employee turned down his requests and asked for a transfer out of the department. The manager denied her a transfer and eventually retaliated against her and gave her a poor performance appraisal.

The personnel department confronted the manager with the employee's allegations. He unequivocably denied ever making any advances or remarks of a sexual nature. However, statements were taken from other females under the manager's purview. Though they never heard him make any remarks or advances to the employee making the complaint, most of the women were themselves recipients of sexual comments that were both inappropriate and unprofessional.

Though the manager denied the allegations, the personnel department had enough evidence to believe that the woman's complaint was valid. The company took immediate and corrective action against the manager in order to limit potential liability.

Example Two. A male supervisor believed he had a good rapport with a female subordinate. He had a habit of making tasteless jokes with sexual overtones to her in front of co-workers, though he made no sexual advances. She appeared at the time to take no offense and made no complaints to anyone. She had been given favorable salary increases and performance appraisals.

Approximately two years after she began working under this particular supervisor, she was denied a promotion given to a male employee. She believed that the denial of promotion was based upon her gender since she believed she was more qualified for the position so she complained to the corporate EEO office. In her complaint, she also stated that several months previous, the same supervisor who denied her a promotion made demeaning sexual jokes to her in the presence of co-workers.

The EEO office did an investigation and refuted the female's claim that she was more qualified than the male promoted into the position in question. However, through contacts with co-workers, the EEO office substantiated that the male supervisor had made sexual jokes, which were directed to the female subordinate and other employees.

To limit the company's liability, the EEO office recommended that the supervisor be suspended for a period of one week. The director of the department accepted the recommendation.

POLICY STATEMENT

A corporate policy statement on harassment should not only emphasize sexual harassment, but it should also address racial, ethnic and religious harassment since the same concepts of liability apply.

Below is a sample company policy on harassment:

> Since the founding of __________ Company, it has been our policy to provide all employees with a work environment free of any form of discrimination, including harassment.
>
> In addition, The (State) Fair Employment Practices Act and Title VII of the 1964 Civil Rights Act prohibits discrimination on the basis of race, color, sex, national origin, religion and pregnancy. Under both of these laws, it is illegal for an employee to engage in unwelcome sexual advances, requests for sexual favors, verbal or physical conduct of a sexual nature, or any other verbal conduct that might be construed as a racial, sexual, ethnic, or religious slur.
>
> Such behavior, regardless if committed by a supervisor or co-worker, will be considered employee misconduct and will be subject to employee disciplinary action, up to and including termination.
>
> Any questions regarding corporate policy, state or federal law or complaints regarding any form of harassment should be addressed to
>
> ____________________________.

CONCLUSION

Comprehensive training programs may actually increase the number of complaints filed against a company. However, by informing employees of their civil rights, the company is also informing them of their obligations under the law and telling them how to protect themselves from potential complaints. Problem areas in the company's workforce, such as latent employee dissatisfaction and performance discrepancies, may also be discovered when sexual harassment complaints are investigated. Personnel administrators and corporate managers may also find, if training programs are successful, that problems of absenteeism, negative attitudes, and social problems associated with harassment situations may be reduced if not eliminated.[7]

REFERENCES

[1]EEOC Guidelines on Sexual Harassment, November 1980, 29 CFR Part 1604.

[2]William C. Strock, "Address on Workplace Sexual Harassment," 27th Annual Institute on Labor Law, Dallas, Texas.

[3]Kathryn A. Thurston, "Sexual Harassment: An Organizational Perspective," *Personnel Administrator* (December 1980), Volume 25, No. 12, p. 62.

[4]*Miller vs. Bank of America,* 600 F.2d. 211. For an indepth discussion of this case, see Darrel L. Tillian, "Sexual Harassment, New Rules To The Game," *Forum* (July 1980).

[5]*Kyriazi vs. Western Electric,* 476 F.Supp. 335.

[6]*Bundy vs. Jackson,* 24 FEP 1155 (D.C.C.A. 1981).

[7]James C. Renick, "Sexual Harassment at Work: Why It Happens, What To Do About It," *Personnel Journal* (August 1980), Volume 59, No. 8, p. 660.

DISCUSSION QUESTIONS

1. What responsibilities do employers have in preventing sexual harassment?
2. What are the key issues that should be considered in designing a training program to combat sexual harassment?
3. What judicial cases best illustrate the concepts key to preventing sexual harassment?
4. Choose an organization in which you have worked and design a company policy on harassment for that organization.
5. What role should managers play in designing a training program to prevent sexual harassment?
6. What role should human resources professionals play in designing a training program to prevent sexual harassment?

Reading 13–2

THE EMPLOYER'S LIABILITIES UNDER COMPARABLE WORTH

Judy Fulghum

In recent months, testimony before three U.S. House of Representatives' subcommittees on the issue of comparable worth has led industry leaders to reconsider the importance of this topic as being one of the major issues to be faced in the 1980s. Under the banner of pay equity (semantically more easily understood than comparable worth), women's organizations and labor unions are clamoring for recognition of the issue and examination of the factors that cause pay disparity between the sexes.

The politicians, too, are pledging their support to the issue. Anita Gottlieb, organizer of last fall's congressional hearings, contends that every major Democratic hopeful for the 1984 nomination is a comparable worth supporter. She envisions that the 1984 Democratic Convention will include a majority of delegates committed to the pay equity movement.[1]

Just what is comparable worth? Although no true legal definition has arisen from the Congress or the courts, the concept broadens the scope of the Equal Pay Act's commitment of equal pay for equal work to include comparisons of separate jobs of equal value to an employer (based on that employer's system of internal job values). Thus, jobs historically held by females would be looked at for comparability with predominantly male jobs.

Seventeen states have passed legislation with comparable worth implications. Individual states, cities, and municipalities are studying the extent of comparable worth liability in their own job-structure systems. Results of these studies are expected to be alarming in terms of potential employer liabilities, as these studies will highlight problem areas of personnel systems previously unexamined by most companies.

It is imperative, therefore, that personnel professionals reacquaint themselves with the issue, particularly from the standpoint of examining the potential impact of comparable worth on their own human resource programs.

UNDERSTANDING THE STATUTES

The wage discrimination issue involving employees working in two separate job classifications, one predominantly male, the other female, was resolved in the landmark court case decision of County of Washington vs. Gunther, settled by the Supreme Court in 1981.[2] In essence, the court's ruling in favor of the plaintiffs opened the courts to examination of the wage setting process itself and the applicability of claims involving disparity in wages between the sexes for similar—but not identical—jobs.

In order to understand the significance of Gunther and its potential ramifications, it is important to briefly review the three legislative statutes that form the basis for comparable worth litigation.

The Equal Pay Act of 1963 sets forth the concept of equal pay for equal work. Determination of equal work rests on the establishment of four factors: skill level, effort, responsibility, and working conditions. The law permits four exceptions to equal pay requirements. (These are important to remember when considering the Bennett Amendment, which is discussed below.) Three exceptions extend circumstances whereby an employer can justify sex-based pay differences for reasons of seniority systems, merit systems, or when pay is measured by the quality or quantity of work produced.

The fourth exception is the most difficult to interpret. It is also the exception used most successfully by defendant companies. This exception permits a differential based on any factor other than sex. Comparable worth was not addressed in the act, nor has any subsequent litigation based upon alleged Equal Pay Act violations been interpreted to apply to dissimilar jobs.

Title VII of the Civil Rights Act of 1964 prohibits discrimination on the basis of race, color, religion, sex, or national origin and expressly prohibits discrimination in compensation practices based on these factors. The law does not appear to limit claims of sex-based compensation discrimination to cases involving "equal" jobs.

THE BENNETT AMENDMENT

The Bennett Amendment to Title VII of the Civil Rights Act allows employers to differentiate wages paid to employees on the basis of sex as long as this variance is authorized under the Equal Pay Act.

Prior to Gunther, two interpretations of this amendment prevailed. The first interpretation, upheld by some lower courts, would have limited Title VII wage discrimination claims specifically to equal work situations. Comparable worth advocates, on the other hand, argued that the amendment was intended only to incorporate the four Equal Pay Act exceptions to liability into Title VII, thus allowing discrimination claims based on dissimilar jobs.

Favorable interpretation of the Bennett Amendment, from a comparable worth standpoint, was first decided in the Gunther case of 1981. This case involved two separate job classifications—male jail guards and female jail matrons. The county's outside market study recommended that the matrons be paid 95% of the guard's wages; however, the county chose to pay the matrons only 70%. In finding for the plaintiffs, the court stressed that this was not a comparable worth claim, but rather one of intentional sex discrimination in the setting of wages. The Bennett Amendment was interpreted in this case not strictly in terms of equal work, but as an incorporation of the four exceptions outlined in the Equal Pay Act into Title VII. Most significantly, by addressing separate job classifications, it opened the door to future pay claims based on dissimilar jobs.

After Gunther, many subsequent suits were filed and decided regarding dissimilar jobs. These suits have focused primarily on four key elements of typical personnel programs that have been targeted by special interest groups for future claims in the comparable worth-pay equity cause. These elements, to be discussed in detail, are: job evaluation systems, market pricing, job classification systems, and performance appraisal systems.

JOB EVALUATION SYSTEMS

The various formal job evaluation systems, such as point-factor, ranking, Hay, guideline, etc., were originally scorned by comparable worth advocates as being a major cause behind pay disparity between the sexes. However, as the courts and the public have become exposed to the mechanics of formal evaluation systems, these very systems have offered a way of rectifying and overcoming pay disparities.

The job evaluation systems have yet to be proven discriminatory. Rather, the administration of these programs and the deviation from the results of these programs have been the focus of the litigations.

A prime example of this occurred in the case of Wilkins vs. University of Houston.[3] In this case, although the university had developed a formal evaluation system for its professional and administrative employees in 1978, it did not properly administrate it. Testimony given by a university EEO officer indicated that one of the motives behind the 1978 evaluation plan was to solve inequity problems between salaries paid to male and female employees. The plaintiffs successfully proved that females were subsequently paid below the range minimum disproportionately to the men, and that range maximums were never exceeded for females although they were for males. Reclassifications to lower job levels were also disproportionate.

The university had obviously not followed through in the use of its wage plan, so it learned an expensive lesson regarding the administration of established salary structures.

DOCUMENTATION IS ESSENTIAL

A well documented and communicated job evaluation system applied consistently is mandatory to employers wishing to build defensible compensation programs. These systems need to be reviewed, and updated if necessary, in line with legislative developments. Westinghouse Electric Corporation faced this dilemma in 1980 and 1981.

In the now famous case of IUE vs. Westinghouse Electric Corp., a job evaluation system put in place over 40 years ago was questioned.[4] Although the system was revised in 1965, the union argued that discrimination was carried over from the older system. The court ordered back pay for approximately 600 females who successfully proved that wage rates were discriminatory between male and female jobs that had been ranked equally in the initial evaluation, yet were paid at a lower rate.

All of the cases since Gunther in which the court decided for the plaintiff were argued based on documented evidence of intentional wage discrimination. In each case, it was apparent that the individuals with authority over final compensation decisions made a deliberate deviation from the recommendations of the job evaluation system.

If a manager or management group attempts such a deviation, personnel professionals should promptly point out the implications of this move. The question becomes: Does the company have legitimate grounds for the pay differential based on one of the four exceptions? If so, it is perhaps safe to proceed. If not, rethink the decision or proceed forewarned.

THE PERSONNEL GUARDIANS

Prudent compensation professionals should systematically examine their current job evaluation programs and test them throughout for factors that discriminate, in light of recent court decisions. For example, are dissimilar jobs evaluated on different criteria? Are production jobs evaluated on criteria differing from that used in the evaluation of clerical jobs? If so, potential liability exists.

In general, the following guidelines will help evaluate existing job evaluation programs:

1) Apply the mechanics of the evaluation system consistently, and don't deviate from initial evaluation results without legitimate reason.

2) Be sure any disparities are documented accurately and completely in terms of the four exceptions to equal pay.

3) Document the system's mechanics—it's hard to prove an evaluation system is nondiscriminatory if the mechanics can't be explained through formal written procedures and guidelines.

4) Monitor wage relationships between males and females in both equal jobs and similar jobs rated equally.

5) Ensure that employees actually involved in the evaluation process are properly trained and are up-to-date on legislative trends.

THE WASHINGTON STUDY GROUP

The threat and potential impact of pay equity liabilities has grown so significantly that personnel professionals from industry, educational institutions, and trade associations have founded the Washington Study Group. The group closely monitors and attempts to influence judicial, legislative, and regulatory developments on the comparable worth/pay equity issue.

The group is sponsored by the law firm of Chadbourne, Parke, Whiteside & Wolff. Daniel Leach, former vice chairman of the EEOC and now a member of the firm, recently testified before House subcommittees on the comparable worth issue. Quarterly meetings of the group are held to brief members on the latest related court rulings and to discuss relevant trends throughout the country. A quarterly newsletter, which recaps current legislative actions, is also distributed to members.[5]

Ronald Heddings of Tektronix, Inc., of Beaverton, Oregon, and co-chairman of the Washington Study Group encourages the awareness and participation of smaller organizations in the group. Many of these smaller firms do not have a formal job evaluation program at all. What is their expected liability? Heddings offers the following suggestions:

Understand that job evaluation is a process. Companies must establish the basis on which they are willing to pay for certain values and ensure that these values are nondiscriminatory. Examine the process you use for placing jobs in value relationships to each other within your company. Test these values against court rulings and ensure that your system could withstand legal scrutiny. If you have problems, begin researching a systematic approach to establishing proper values and place your employees accordingly.

MARKET PRICING

Most companies at some point in their job evaluation process "go to the market" to insure competitive wages. Many salary surveys are available for purchase or participation. In many cases, employer associations conduct their own.

These employer associations, however, have been accused of violating antitrust laws by allowing the identification of individual company data. A Boston coalition by the name of 9 to 5 recently was successful in its charges against a local survey group. The group alleged that such practices deliberately kept clerical wages low. The survey group denied any intentional wrongdoing, but as a result of the charges has reformatted survey results to generalize and summarize data rather than report individual company statistics.

Other employer associations are reviewing their own surveys in light of this action and have, in some cases, turned the survey effort over to third party consultants. Should this trend continue, employers can expect marked changes in the survey data available and in the effectiveness of survey results.

To date, each time a plaintiff has presented a case to the courts alleging that market pricing is discriminatory, the court has upheld the validity of the market pricing concept as a valid "differential based on a factor other than sex."

Two pre-Gunther decisions on this issue upheld the supply and demand theory behind the market pricing approach. In both Christensen vs. State of Iowa[6] and Lemons vs. City and County of Denver,[7] the plaintiffs charged that the use of local salary survey data perpetuated the historical underpayment of wages for females. Both employers, in defense, cited the local labor market as a valid tool, and the court agreed. In Lemons, the court refused to consider evaluation of skills across job description lines.

RELATED COURT CASES

Subsequent to the Gunther decision, two particular cases have been brought to the courts and again have been denied.

In Briggs vs. City of Madison,[8] the court staunchly upheld the market system by declaring that under Title VII such defense is valid where "different skills are required for the performance of the jobs."[9] (This obviously is not valid under equal pay cases in which the jobs are identical.) The court further upheld Gunther's interpretation of the Bennett Amendment by recognizing that such claims do not have to meet Equal Pay Act standards.

Another post-Gunther case has far reaching implications in several areas. Spaulding vs. University of Washington involves faculty member wages at a nursing school.[10] The female teachers charged discrimination under both Title VII and the Equal Pay Act, by stating that their pay was less than male teachers in other departments. They felt that the fact that different subject matter was taught by the male teachers was irrelevant, as the same basic skills were required. This is a new interpretation of equal work.

The university cited the use of market data for the setting of wages as a legitimate defense. The plaintiffs further alleged that the setting of salaries in this manner is discriminatory. The court dismissed the case; currently it is in the process of appeal.

A CONTROVERSIAL SOLUTION

It is likely that the whole market pricing system is going to continue to come under fire from women's organizations and will be used as a recruiting tool by the labor unions. In looking at the validity of market pricing, it is interesting to consider that the salaries of high-paying predominantly male production jobs (upon which comparisons might be made to "equivalent" high-level predominantly female administrative jobs) have been significantly clouded by the labor union movement. This in itself can be used favorably by the unions ("we helped the guys, now we can help the gals''). Conversely, it can give further credence to the employers' complaint that unions intensified the problem originally.

Many compensation professionals feel that the market truly does reflect the internal worth of jobs. When looked at in terms of technical skills required, responsibility, effort, working conditions, discretion (cost of error), etc., they feel that the market bears out the classification hierarchy correctly. However, these professionals widely agree that the problem lies in the job opportunity and placement system. (See Figure 13–9.)

If you use the market as a tool in your job evaluation process, recent court decisions suggest you keep several elements in mind. The most widespread error made by companies when analyzing survey results is the matching of survey jobs to actual company positions. Never make a comparison based purely on title alone—be sure the job description summary matches the job. This also applies to inputting data to a survey. Be suspicious of local surveys or even telephone surveys in which a title only is given. The results of such surveys have to be questioned.

Documentation is again important when using market data. On age-dated survey results, document the how and why. If surveys call out specific company codes, document how and why certain company data was excluded. So far, market pricing has been a legitimate defense, but only when all the documentation was in order.

- Understand the legal parameters, particularly the four exceptions to equal pay, and insure that job evaluations are kept abreast of legislative developments.
- Examine employment practices and work to eliminate job segregation in the selection process.
- Involve top management in the communication of personnel systems to employees.
- Take an active role in assuring the validity of market surveys in which you participate.
- Administer job posting systems fairly and communicate their value to employees.
- Ensure that line management is adequately trained in the performance appraisal process and that sufficient time is given to the accurate documentation of employee performance.
- Document and administer job evaluation system mechanics consistently—don't deviate from initial evaluation results without legitimate reason.
- Document thoroughly all system disparities in terms of the four exceptions of equal pay.
- Monitor wage relationships between males and females in both equal jobs and similar jobs rated equally.
- Consider current employee salaries and skills when making starting salary decisions.

Figure 13–9 GUIDELINES FOR A POSITIVE COMPARABLE WORTH PROGRAM

JOB CLASSIFICATION SYSTEMS

Although many facets of job classification systems and promotion and transfer policies are now open to courtroom scrutiny, none has received the attention recently given to the practice of setting starting salaries.

Two 1981 cases specifically addressed this issue. Neeley vs. MARTA was an Equal Pay Act claim.[11] The case centered on a guideline that set starting salaries no more than 10% above the preceding salary, without additional approval. The court found for the plaintiff on the basis that "the lower salary levels traditionally paid to females doing the identical work of males" placed a disparate impact on salaries paid to males and females.[12] The court felt such a practice would further affect the potential earning levels of females as the result of company policy granting increases based on the employee's current salary.

Fortunately, for employers, the court did stress that employers can differentiate starting salaries to employees in substantially equal jobs on the basis of superior background or experience, in much the same way that merit can distinguish the pay of employees performing the same job.[13]

A LEGITIMATE EXCEPTION?

Past training and experience was acknowledged in the appeal case of Kouba vs. Allstate as being legitimate factors under the "other than sex" exemption.[14] In the initial trial, brought in 1981 under the Equal Pay Act, the issue was raised concerning the starting wages for entry level sales agents. Allstate based starting wages in part on the prior salary level of the applicant. (An important point to remember here is that this case related specifically to an entry level job.) The employer's use of past salary history was found to be discriminatory. The lower court found for the plaintiff, asserting that past salary history is not a legitimate exception to equal pay on the grounds of a factor other than sex.

In the appeal, the initial decision was reversed and remanded. The appeal court felt that the district court misinterpreted the exception based on a factor other than sex, and cited the fact that the Equal Pay Act does not limit the exception to job evaluation systems only, but was meant to be applied in a much broader sense. The appeal court found in its conclusion that:

> The Equal Pay Act does not impose a strict prohibition against the use of prior salary. . . . The court must find that the business reasons given by Allstate do not reasonably explain its use of that factor before finding a violation of the Act.[15]

Prior unrelated salary history should be irrelevant in an entry level job. It would be alarming if, for example, a company based an entry-level college graduate engineer's salary on what he or she was earning in an unrelated job prior to graduation. Employers looking for guidelines on this subject should examine not only outside market rates but also internal incumbent relationships to those rates when determining starting salaries. Merely looking at a past salary when determining salary offers provides too limited a perspective to ensure equitable decisions.

PROMOTIONS AND TRANSFERS

Job promotion and transfer policy contains almost as many traps for the unwary as starting salary.

To alleviate potential discrimination liability, many companies have created job posting systems that advertise promotional opportunities. However, these systems have been bypassed in some cases when positions are filled either before posting occurs, or were never posted at all. To minimize liability, employers must understand the necessity of a valid process in meeting affirmative action goals and in eliminating possible discriminatory actions. All open jobs should be posted and posted with accurate statements of job requirements.

Another ticklish situation occurs when a company posts a job for a specific level position and subsequently decides to hire (or promote) a candidate with qualifications below the minimum stated in the job posting. Unless the job is reposted with new minimum qualifications, the employer can be accused of denying a promotional opportunity to an undetermined number of applicants who never had the chance to apply under the "actual" minimum qualifications. The job should be reposted, and the selection process should begin anew.

Readers interested in court case references on the transfer and promotion issues are referred to Taylor vs. Charley Brothers Co.[16] and Greenspan vs. Automobile Club of Michigan.[17]

One of the thorniest problems is misclassification of employees. What personnel professional cannot remember a situation in which employees were classified into higher positions for which they were not qualified, or subsequently could not perform at the level of job responsibility that was inferred at the time of job evaluation. Guidelines for exemption under the Fair Labor Standards Act have also been caught up in the misclassification melee.

Make no mistake; the courts are willing to examine every facet of employment practice. The comparable worth-pay equity doctrine allows the broadening of this exposure to include areas previously unavailable to courtroom scrutiny.

PERFORMANCE APPRAISAL SYSTEMS AND AGE DISCRIMINATION

One additional topic in which increasing liability is being seen is in the area of performance appraisal systems.

Recently a court case has arisen under the Age Discrimination in Employment Act, which has focused attention on this issue. The employer in EEOC vs. Sandia Corp. had a system of granting salary increases at established intervals that varied according to the employee's age.[18] The court found for the plaintiff, ruling that Sandia's subjective performance appraisal system discriminated against older workers.

Consistently applied and documented performance appraisal systems are becoming increasingly important as work force reductions result from current economic conditions. Predictably, more and more age discrimination charges and lawsuits are appearing in the courts. A recent newsletter from the Washington Study Group stated:

> The courts have ruled against companies that have terminated or forced early retirement of older, higher-salaried employees in order to achieve a budget reduction. Employers able to demonstrate objectively that younger employees were retained due to superior work performance or some other basis directly related to their ability to perform the job will have a greater chance of persuading a government agency or jury to view such criteria as a "reasonable factor other than age." A subjective performance rating system, however, will increase the plaintiff's chances of persuading the fact-finder that the employer's articulated reason was in reality a pretext to cover up age discrimination.[19]

Employers must reinforce with supervising managers the importance of documenting true work performance. It's hard to explain a voluntary layoff to an employee with "superior" performance reviews when employees with lower ratings were retained.

USE ACTUAL STANDARDS

Performance appraisal systems are subject to a number of problems, many of which could be solved by implementing actual performance standards against which employees can be measured. This is often ignored, though the benefits of such a system are immense. For example, employees would have an exact document outlining precisely what is expected for satisfactory performance, rather than a vague notion of what they're supposed to do. Supervisors would have a document against which performance can be measured, thus easing the task of dealing with superior or inferior performers or justifying average performance.

Having a system makes biting the bullet on slipping performance a less bitter pill to swallow for both the manager and the employee. Administering a merit pool system also becomes tied less to the whims of favoritism or the tendency to grant identical increases to everyone as a cop-out to truly rewarding performance. Employees respect such a performance appraisal system, when fairly and consistently applied, because performance expectations are never in question.

Too often, managers fail to give performance appraisal systems enough of their time and commitment. As a result, reviews are late or are performed improperly, and both the employee's morale and the manager's credibility with the employee suffer. A good corporate investment is to train managers to develop performance standards, and to prepare and conduct performance reviews. The company's commitment to fair treatment of employees will be enhanced, and its liability for discrimination charges will be lessened.

COMPARABLE WORTH LIABILITIES

At the heart of the comparable worth issue is the job selection process and the way it perpetuates job segregation practices. Example: A female enters an employment office and files an application for any entry level job. Is she funneled to the clerical pool and mail room, or is she counseled about employment opportunities in the plant? Too often, it's the former. Until women recognize that all jobs are open to them, initial hiring will remain the area in which the most blatant discrimination exists.

Marcia Carpeni, an attorney with Chadbourne, Parke, Whiteside & Wolff of New York, estimates that 90% of the working women in America are classified into eight of the 400 job classifications listed by the Department of Labor (basically clerical, service, and sales oriented). Women's wages approximate 60% of those earned by males. In order to correct this wage disparity, says Carpeni, two-thirds to three-fourths of working women would have to change jobs.[20]

Now that the courts are open to examination of all forms of employment discrimination practices, positive selection tactics are necessary to lessen an employer's vulnerability to such claims.

POSITIVE SUGGESTIONS

All unskilled entry-level jobs should pay the same rate to eliminate bias between traditionally sex segregated jobs. Employment interviewers must be skilled in discussing various career paths leading from entry level positions, in order that female applicants are aware of the nontraditional career paths open to them. If a woman elects to accept a female-dominated job, she should make that decision based on a knowledge of total job opportunities and potential advancement possibilities.

Carpeni offered an additional suggestion to members of the Washington Study Group during her 1982 speech:

> Employers should take care to have job applicants specify which jobs they are applying for. This specificity will do away with the employer's responsibility to make the initial assignment.

Many professionals feel that the whole comparable worth pay equity issue will be resolved in time as women become encouraged to enter nontraditional jobs. This is a long-term process with definite socioeconomic consequences.

Part of this solution rests with employers, in both selection philosophies and procedures and in changing management attitudes regarding traditional role relationships. Part of the burden falls on the women themselves to broaden their own outlooks on the types of jobs available and the skills they must acquire in order to qualify. But most importantly, society itself must be re-educated to overcome biases about women's role in the workplace, which have been in place for generations.

TOP MANAGEMENT SPONSORSHIP

As with any program, the commitment of top management to equity is essential. It is first the task of personnel and human resource professionals to counsel other executives on the scope and liabilities of the issue. Management must understand all aspects of the issue, from its statutory requirements to the way in which these affect company employment and compensation programs. The increasing employee awareness of rights, laws, and personnel management systems means that managers must become better educated.

Good management education, in turn, builds a solid foundation for the way in which formal business practices are established and applied. Without this understanding—the systematic review of all facets of human resource programs for potential discrimination, liabilities will continue to exist, litigation will continue to result, and the problem will not be resolved. Top management must assume its share of the burden in assuring all employees of their opportunities for equal employment.

Personnel professionals must emphasize the realities of this issue. This is not a problem that will go away by itself. The laws are there, and the time is ripe for ensuring that companies make the most of this awareness by implementing systems that are fair, consistent, and well documented. Practitioners must assume a leadership role by taking positive action to ensure that our companies are indeed an equitable place in which to work.

REFERENCES

[1]Gottlieb, Anita. "Comparable Worth—Legal Update, Congressional Perspective and Recent Union Activities," speech delivered to the Washington Study Group on February 3, 1983.

[2]452 U.S. 68 L.Ed.2d 751, 25 FEP Cases 1521 (No. 80-429 decided June 8, 1981).

[3]654 F.2d 388 (5th Cir. 1981).

[4]631 F.2d 1094, 23 FEP Cases 588 (3rd Cir. 1980), cert. denied, 449 U.S. 1009 (1981).

[5]For more information about the Washington Study Group, contact the author at 6685 S.W. Sagert St., Ste. 28, Tualatin, OR 97062, 505/692-0127. Upon request, a packet including the group's charter statement and copies of past newsletters will be mailed to prospective members.

[6]563 F.2d 353 (8th Cir. 1977).

[7]620 F.2d 288 (10th Cir.), cert. denied, 449 U.S. 888 (1980).

[8]28 FEP Cases 739 (W.D. Wisc. 1982).

[9]Id. as quoted in the *Washington Study Group Comparable Worth Report,* Vol. 1, No. 1, p. 1.

[10]No. 80-3528, 9th Cir. (currently in appeal)

[11]24 FEP Cases 1610 (N.D. Ga. 1908), aff'd without opinion, 641 F.2d 877 (5th Cir. 1981).

[12]24 FEP Cases at 1612.

[13]Id. at 1613.

[14]523 F. Supp. 148 (E.D. Cal. 1981), reversed on appeal (See *Daily Labor Report,* No. 214, Nov. 4, 1982, at page D-1, published by the Bureau of National Affairs.)

[15]Id. at Section V.

[16]25 FEP Cases 602 (W.D. Pa. 1981).

[17]495 F. Supp. 1021 (E.D. Mich. 1980).

[18]15 EPD ¶ 7902 (D.C.N.M. 1977), aff'd, 23 EPD ¶ 31,175 (10th Cir. 1980).

[19]*Washington Study Group Comparable Worth Report,* Vol. 1, No. 2, pages 2,3.

[20]Carpeni, Marcia. "Comparable Worth Presentation," speech delivered to the Washington Study Group on January 14, 1982. Copies of this speech will be sent, upon request, to prospective members (see reference above).

DISCUSSION QUESTIONS

1. What are the provisions of the statutes that define the wage discrimination issue?
2. How do job evaluation systems address the comparable worth issue?
3. What must be included in a job evaluation system for it to effectively deal with comparable worth?
4. Offer your own guidelines for a positive comparable worth program.
5. What other employment practices besides compensation must consider comparable worth? How should this issue be incorporated into those areas?
6. What role should top management play in addressing comparable worth effectively?
7. What role should human resources professionals play in addressing the comparable worth issue?

ACTIVITIES

Activity 13–1

RAY HAGEN (A), (B), (C), AND (D)

Step 1: Read Ray Hagen (A).

"From the loading dock in back of my company's warehouse, I watched George Perrilli, assisted by his wife, walk slowly across the street. George had suffered a heart attack six months earlier, and I knew that he was coming to my office to ask for his old job back. I wasn't sure what I should say." Ray Hagen leaned back in his chair as he described a difficult situation he had faced not long ago.

RAY HAGEN'S BACKGROUND

"But first, let me give you a little background to the story. When I graduated from the University of Notre Dame, I went to work for a family-owned company, a large company, in Louisville. We manufactured equipment for the chemical and food processing industry. I was hired by the man who was the sales manager—he had been sort of a family friend for a number of years—and went to work for them in the sales capacity. I guess you might say I got on the fast track and achieved some success in the company.

"We were a company of 275 employees doing approximately $6 million in sales. About 1970 the man who was the president of the company, one of the family owners, passed away. Now that the president was gone, other family members from the parent corporation—people who had never taken a strong interest in the company—suddenly started to become involved. The man I had worked for was sort of shoved off to the side, and they brought in a new man. He was from Westinghouse, and he'd been exposed to 1960 methods of running a business: managing and forecasting.

"So all of a sudden I was answering to a man who was asking me for reports and asking me to forecast what I was going to do, and I had never been asked to do these kinds of things. It had been a sort of—not a loose corporation, but not as tight a ship as the new situation, and I guess I wasn't totally comfortable with that, but I did respect that type of discipline and began to see its merits. My boss was not a warm person in his dealings with the salesmen. He split the company into three regions—three profit centers—and I was made the regional manager in Atlanta. While there I worked very hard, but I never could seem to get the total job done, all the reporting and the paper work of the business. Basically, that's because I'm a salesman.

"So I began to look around for opportunities either to go to another company or to have my own business. I had an opportunity in 1974 to go in with another man and buy an old company, the oldest distributorship of its kind in Louisville. I knew nothing about the business, absolutely nothing, except that I was a little bit familiar with the products that the company handled because they were used on some of the equipment that we built. During the negotiations, I learned that the lady (an older woman about 60) who was selling knew something about the man I was going in with that I didn't know, and she didn't want to have anything to do with him because of some almost illegal things he had done. I decided to make her an offer on my own.

"So, while living in Atlanta, and traveling to Louisville for meetings or conferences or something, I was also negotiating to purchase this company, and I did in October 1975. I moved back to Louisville, and although I knew nothing about the business, all of a sudden one day I'm the Chief Operating Officer and responsible for everything in the company. I looked at the situation and told myself that the most important thing I needed to do was learn about the products—who buys them, why they buy them, and what they are used for. Again, sort of a salesmen's mentality, not worrying about the other parts of the business.

"There were only 5 employees when I bought the company: the woman who had owned the business, three men, and an old maid bookkeeper upstairs who paid the bills. I was the sixth employee. I had no outside salesman, so I felt that in order to pay for this company as soon as possible, I had to work hard.

"We closed out 1975 with just a little under $500,000 in sales. It took me about ten to twelve months to get a grasp of the business—what the products were, who they were sold to, the companies that we were distributor for, the people who worked for them. And I learned that the only business this company had was the business that came in off the street or came in over the phone.

"The name of my company was Louisville Power Transmission, and I was a distributor for what was called power transmission equipment—things that make machinery go, big V-belts and motors and chains and gears and gear boxes. In my business, I was a buyer, a middle man, if you want to call it that. I bought from maybe twenty different companies, and I inventoried those products. I had about a half a million dollars of inventory. Then I turned around and sold them to basically two classes or two types of accounts: Industrial Users that had machinery in operation—a bakery, a concrete plant, or a plastic plant making plastic bottles. I also sold to what we called the OEM accounts, Original Equipment Manufacturers. My business was divided up about 70% to the first group and the balance to OEM accounts.

"My strategy was to keep that type of mix as close as I could because, needless to say, I got a lot of small orders with big margins on the one end, and big volume and low margins on the other end, so you needed a proper mix. Working with the OEM accounts enhanced my buying position. In other words, I could go to the manufacturer and instead of buying 100 widgets, I could buy 1,000 widgets because I knew that I could move volume to the OEMs, but when I sold it to the Industrial User I got a bigger margin because I bought it on volume.

RECRUITING

"I took one of the young men who was working in the back putting up stock, making deliveries, and I said, 'I don't know a great deal about this business, I'm not an engineer' (some of the products required some technical expertise in their sales), 'but if you teach me about the business and how these products are used, I'll teach you about selling.' He said 'okay,' so I sent him to a sales training program in Atlanta and then I worked with him, and we began to get some business.

"I called on some of the people that I'd known from years past—they became my customers, and the business started to grow. About the early part of 1977, I thought maybe I should get another salesman outside, particularly somebody who knows the business, has some technical expertise, and maybe is known around the city because he's sold these products. In other words, maybe I should go pirate somebody. So, I looked around. My competitors didn't really worry too much about me, because they had heard that I didn't know anything about the business. They knew something about the old business that I bought, and it was just a mom-and-pop grocery store sort of operation.

"I did meet one fellow who was with a competitor, and he impressed me, and I thought, maybe this is my man. In the Spring of 1977, I called him and said, 'if you are downtown, why don't you stop by some evening—I would like to talk to you about possibly going to work for me.'

"Now, one of the reasons I told you about my background was because I'm basically a salesman. I didn't know about good management practices, and I didn't recognize all the responsibilities of a Chief Operating Officer or of a General Manager of a company, so I was handling things with the same mentality as the guy who had come in from Westinghouse and became my boss. I placed most of my emphasis on getting to know a guy. I felt like I was a good judge of people and if this particular fellow was a good guy, I would worry later about what talents he had. He seemed like a nice enough fellow, so I offered him a job, and he accepted. It wasn't very long after that that I regretted my decision.

"He started raising hell with a lot of people. He was always bitching, 'You don't make my deliveries, you're not talking nice to my customers, you're not handling them like you handle the other customers, you charge them too much, you people really don't know the business—if you only knew half of what I knew, it would be easy for you.' Saying this to my inside people. And, he would say these things openly in the office. You know, he would be speaking to one fellow, but he'd say it loud enough so everybody could hear. So, I'm getting all of these vibrations. The other employees would say, 'Just get that guy away from me.'

"Then he would come in and raise hell and yell at one of the delivery boys: 'I told you you should always take that to the back of that guy's store!' or 'You give these items to me so I can deliver them, because that's how I get in the back door!' He used to do a lot of what they call 'back door selling.' In other words, this guy would take the delivery and when he did, he would go in to see the customer. There's not anything really wrong with that, but it makes some customers uncomfortable. They don't like people wandering around in their plants. I heard from a couple of customers that, if possible, they'd prefer the deliveries to be sent UPS or by truck because they didn't want this guy wandering around in their plants.

COACHING

"But, I said, maybe I could work with him. I will be kind to him because one of the things he was telling me was that every body had dumped on him every place he'd been. And you know, I have always been sort of dumped on, and I thought, well, maybe I could turn that around—maybe if I'm kind to him and if I'm nice to him, show some interest in him, just do a few nice little things for him, give him a few perks, maybe he'll turn around.

"About two months after he came to work for me, I received a call from a customer who said George had passed out and looked like he'd had a heart attack, and that he was being taken by the rescue squad to the hospital. I immediately went to the hospital. George was in intensive care, but the doctor said he didn't think it was a heart attack. They weren't sure what had happened. They kept him there for a couple of days.

"He came back about a week later. He said that his blood pressure had dropped down to a very low point. I guess the symptoms of very low blood pressure are like a heart attack. At least, that's what the doctor said.

"He had had a history of heart problems. In 1968 he had gone to work for a company out of Indianapolis and had started a branch in Louisville. He had worked very hard, but never was really productive. That is, he didn't manage his time properly, and he worried too much about things that he didn't need to worry about. As a result, he had a very serious heart attack and was out of work for about 6–7 months.

"I made a real conscientious effort to work with the guy and to put up with his idiosyncrasies. This went on for several years. I hired several other salesmen, and they saw how I was coddling this guy and trying to be nice to him, and they became a little upset with me. They told me, 'you shouldn't let that guy run you around like that.' One instance I remember very vividly. Every fall I would get the salesmen and the non-sales people together, and we'd talk about what had happened that year, and what we'd look for next year, and what things we wanted to do the coming year. Basic, simple planning—setting up some objectives. This one dinner in October turned into a shouting match—all of a sudden, things that had been boiling just under the surface came out. This fellow, George, called another guy an 'SOB,' who then called him an 'AH.' You know, right then and there. I just ended the meeting.

"I really didn't know what to do. I felt like I should terminate the man, but he was bringing me some business, and I was growing. I was getting a lot of pressure particularly from the general manager inside, a young guy in charge of sales and the warehouse. He kept saying, 'you have just got to get rid of this guy; he's causing too damn much trouble around here, raising hell.' And I was saying, 'well, he's bringing me some orders.' But it concerned me that we weren't a real profitable business, and George was not a good salesman. He tried to sell his technical expertise where in a lot of cases, people didn't want it. Then he would just cut the price. His approach to selling was that if he came in to see you, he would say, 'How much do you pay for these items?' And somehow he would get it out of you, and say, 'Well, I'll sell them to you for 10% less.' Arbitrarily, without consulting me, without saying whether we were even in the business—it could have been products that we didn't even handle as a distributor. It put us in a difficult position. But he WAS bringing us some business, and I was going through some very heavy growth years. I closed out in 1979 with about 2 1/2 million dollars in sales.

"George was 55 years old then, and he had a history of moving from company to company. That was another thing I learned—about my naivete. I didn't know that the man had had three jobs before he came to me. I also didn't know that at two of the places, he had been asked to leave. Sometime later, one of the managers of the company from whom I hired him told me that they were sure glad that I took him off their hands because they didn't know what the hell they were going to do with him. He said they'd been telling the people in headquarters that they needed to get rid of him because he was such a problem in the business.

GROWTH AND OTHER CRISES

"I was reaching a point where I couldn't do it all. There was just no way. I mean, I couldn't be the bookkeeper, I couldn't be the sales manager, I couldn't be the floor sweeper, I couldn't be it all. I began to recognize that I had to get some people in to help me.

"Meanwhile, George had had a heart attack at Christmas of 1979. A BAD heart attack. He was 58. In January of 1980 I began looking around for a man to help me manage some of the other salesmen, someone who had technical expertise and had good accounts of his own, but who could help me assume some of the responsibilities managing the men. So I hired Bob Dreyer in January. He was to come in as sort of a sales manager, but he was really to be more of a shepherd to take care of the salesmen and to help me.

"So I said to the staff, 'Mr. Dreyer isn't in here as a true sales manager; he's going to help us get organized. If I need to get a plan put through the sales area, I hope that he'll get that message to you so we can implement it. George is in the hospital in intensive care for about three weeks, so we really won't know what his condition is until the end of January. We spoke to his wife, and she indicated that he would probably be in the hospital for another month to six weeks and then there'll be a period of three or four months' recuperation. They still don't know how severe the heart damage is—his doctor wouldn't give us any indication about his future—whether he could ever go back to work again, whether he might require surgery. He might be out for another six or eight months.'

"As it turned out, while George was gone, the company suddenly started working smoothly. Everybody was getting along well, and people are happy. We were experiencing tremendous growth. I was getting some positive feedback from customers. I had to have the general manager and Dreyer take over George's accounts, and we were generating new sales from these companies. They liked Dreyer, and it looked like they would probably do more business with us.

"About the first of April, I had a conversation with George's doctor, who said George might be able to come back to work in June, but he wasn't sure. George was resting at home then. He couldn't drive a car; if he had to go somewhere his wife took him.

"This last time, the doctor told me that the earlier low-blood-pressure episode was in fact a heart attack, though a very slight one. I guess they can tell through tests, you know, how many times the heart has been injured or damaged. They found evidence of this first serious one and then of the tiny little one that happened in September.

RAY'S FATHER'S CASE

"Now, my father died when he was 52 years old. I don't know whether I've ever totally gotten over that. I remember my mother being so upset about it—upset with the men that he'd worked for. My father had several heart attacks and when he had the third one, I remember the men from the company coming to visit my father and asking him to help them with something or give them some advice, and asking, 'when are you coming back to work?'

"My father was a conscientious guy, and he went back to work. I can remember my mother in tears at the funeral, screaming at the President and the Executive Vice President of the company, 'You killed my husband! You made him come back to work, and you've killed him, and here I am with these seven young children. If you hadn't made him come back . . .' When I thought about my father, deep down, I guess I didn't want the responsibility of having George come back to work for me.

"I remember that when George had the slight heart attack, he was anxious to come back immediately. I didn't want the responsibility then, either. So now I wondered if I were using responsibility to cover up my real feelings—maybe I just didn't want him back. But after thinking about it seriously, I really believed that I didn't want the responsibility of his coming back to work.

GEORGE'S VISIT

"I had talked to George on the telephone occasionally. He'd been telling me that the doctor really doesn't want him to come back to work, but that if George says he's okay, then the doctor will agree. So, he's sort of telling the doctor, 'I'm okay, I want to go back to work.' The doctor isn't totally sure, but if he's the patient, and he's telling the doctor that he's okay, and he wants to go back to work, then I guess you sort of have to give him the benefit of the doubt.

"I knew I had to face this problem. I hadn't seen George in six months when I asked him to come down and talk to me. It was a warm June day—the doors were all open in the back on the dock, and I was talking with one of the warehousemen. I looked across the street. George and his wife—she was driving—pulled up in the parking lot. He had a tough time getting out of the car, and his wife helped him cross the intersection. She wasn't exactly holding him up, but she was just sort of guiding him as you would guide an older person. I told him to go upstairs. It took him five minutes to go up two flights because he had to stop and rest before he could go on. So, we went up to talk in the office.

"I asked how he was feeling, and what he wanted to do, and this was when he told me, 'I'll be ready to come back to work in three weeks. I'm getting stronger every day, and I know I can come back to work. My wife might have to drive me around a little bit, but I think I can start back on at least a three-day basis.'"

Step 2: Individually, in small groups, or with the entire class, answer the following questions:

1. What are the forces that are influencing Ray?
2. What are Ray's options?
3. Should George be reinstated?
4. What would you say to George?

Step 3: Read Ray Hagen (B).

"I said to myself, I just don't think that this fellow . . . there's no way. So I said, 'George, I will not let you come back to work. I do not want the responsibility.'

"Now remember, I was the younger man. I was only 39 years old, and I'm telling a man who's 18 or 19 years my senior how he should take care of his health, how he should take care of himself. But, I tried to do it in as kind a way as I possibly could. Again, I guess it's the salesman personality, if you will—not trying to approach it from the standpoint of the Chief Executive Officer, but maybe more as a friend.

"I said, 'if you want to, you know, maybe you could come back at the end of the year or maybe at the first of next year.' Now I was sort of postponing the problem. I didn't know what to do, but I sincerely believed that it was in his own best interest not to come back to work. So I finally said, 'You cannot come back to work.' I knew that he needed time to think about this, and so I said he could come back in three weeks. He told me that he was going to get a release from the doctor, and we could make a final decision later.

"I did say at that time, 'George, you know, we've had an opportunity here in the last six months to examine how you got along with your fellow employees, and I really don't like to say this to you, but a lot of people have not missed you. I don't want to be real harsh, but those are the facts. The people would prefer that you don't come back.'

"But, I did leave it open. I said, 'If you could take the next three weeks to think about what you want to do, then I would let you come back to work in a year. But I also want it understood that if you do come back, you're going to change. You just haven't been able to get along with your fellow employees. You have a responsibility to work with them, and you have the responsibility to the company to respect its structure. I will take you back, but I want you to consider that this will be your responsibility.

"So, he came back three weeks later and he said, 'Yeah, I'll do a good job, and I want to come back to work now.'"

Step 4: Individually, in small groups, or with the entire class, answer the following questions:

1. What forces are influencing George?
2. What would you say to George now?

Step 5: Read Ray Hagen (C).

"I said, 'Well, if you want to come back at the first of the year, that's okay. But if you want to come back to work right now, then the decision I would have to make is that I'll have to let you go, because I will not accept that responsibility for you to come back.'

"I said to him, 'I know that you are a conscientious guy, but I just would never forgive myself if your wife came in here in two months screaming at me that I made you go back to work and I killed you.'—I really believe that that was my overriding motive, if that's the right word, in the whole matter. I was thinking that if a man didn't do a good job, you would just say, 'Hey Joe, I'm sorry, you just aren't cutting it—you're just going to have to leave: hit the road, Jack. See the sign over the door: My way or the Highway.'

"So on July 1, I let him go. I said 'We'll pay you through the end of August, and if you wish, we'll give you your part in the profit-sharing plan. And I wouldn't be against it if you wanted to go to your doctor and get a disability claim—we'll give you disability.'

"Well, he didn't want that. He was a person with a tremendous amount of pride. He could've taken disability for a year and then gone back to work. Maybe not for me, but for someone else. And, I told him that.

"So that was it and he left. He didn't go back to work right away. He sort of floated around looking for a job. He found out that people really did not want him. He thought that he would be accepted immediately, you know, be able to go and get on board somewhere. Instead, he went to work part-time for a competitor so that he could get back out on the street, and he spread a lot of bad stuff about us. You know, that I was a terrible guy, that I fired him when he'd had a heart attack. That I didn't give him his benefits.

"About the middle of August, I received a certified letter from the state's Civil Rights Commission informing me that he had filed suit claiming age discrimination in letting him go. Shortly thereafter I received another certified letter indicating that he had filed suit against me for age discrimination with the Federal Civil Rights Commission. I also was contacted by the sheriff and told that he had filed a civil action against me for age discrimination.

"The guy wanted some money from me. He knew that it wouldn't cost him anything, except for the attorney in the Civil action, to get the money from me, and he was suing me for a year's wages. And so, you know, the attorney tells me, in these kinds of cases we can go to Court and fight it, but do you want all of this to come out in public? I said no. The attorney says he knows that, so we'll have to agree on some offering. He had asked for $21,000, and I said he wouldn't get $21,000 from me."

Step 6: Individually, in small groups, or with the entire class, answer the following questions:

1. What legal constraints confront Ray now?
2. What would you do in Ray's position?

Step 7: Read Ray Hagen (D).

"Here I was, a young entrepreneur, trying to run a good business. Incidentally, my sales in 1981 closed out at a little over 4 1/2 million dollars. About $4.6 million dollars to be exact. In 1982, I'll do about $6 million. So, here's a little company that has grown from a half a million seven years ago to over six million. Pretty good little company. I was saying to myself, maybe the salesman mentality can do it!

"But, when I got these actions against me, I went to the law office. They said, 'Well, where is your file on this guy?' And I said, 'Well, I don't have any.' And so we tried to reconstruct what happened in these meetings. One of the attorneys went and talked to the people at the state's Civil Rights Commission. He handled the civil suit and then handled the Federal suit after these other two.

"My attorney talked to his attorney and handled the Civil case first; we made a settlement with him. It cost me almost $10,000. He signed off on the Civil suit. He also worked through the action in the state's Civil Rights Court and the action in the Federal Civil Rights Commission.

"But, there are a couple of lessons to be learned here, I guess. You know, you reach a point when the size of your business forces you to have to run it in a more business-like manner. One of the reasons I am here is to learn to think in a business-like way and to think of some of the responsibility that a chief executive has. If my business continues to grow the way it has, I'm projecting by 1985, it will be a 10-million-dollar-a-year business. And, when a business reaches that size, you certainly can't run it like a mom-and-pop grocery store. Your problems begin to multiply.

"I didn't have a personnel officer. I was the personnel officer. I did it on my own, but since this has happened, one of the things I've done is make a file on everybody. I went around and asked everybody to fill out an application form like they were coming to work. I had to have some point to start. I said, 'I have to keep a file on all of you. And, if I have a problem with you or we have a misunderstanding or we talk about something, then I've got to keep a record of it. So, this is day #1. This is the first day you've come to work for me and so I'm going to ask all of you to fill out an application form and then I'm going to start the file.'

"Even today I guess I'm still the personnel manager, but in May of this year I brought on a young man, 26 years old, as my Comptroller/Chief Financial Officer. I did it because I was reaching the point where my accountants were asking for this kind of information or that kind of information and I had no idea what they were talking about. The accounting people and the law firm and the guys at the bank were saying, 'You've got to do something! Get somebody in there to run the business part of your business!' The only thing I'm interested in, like a salesman, is how much money am I going to make.

"Two years after the thing with George was settled, I have twenty employees. Until just recently, I had the old maid bookkeeper that I had when I bought the company. She was 57. And she'd brought on three other women to work for her. What I didn't know—because I had just totally left that department to her responsibility—was that she wasn't doing anything up there. She had these other three women doing lots of things she could be doing. She just sort of sat there and had them do it all.

"I didn't discover this until I hired the young financial guy. He began observing things and making notes. We got to saying we've got to do this and we've got to do that. And one day we had a conversation, the three of us, and she said the office wasn't big enough for the new financial guy and her both. He said to her, 'I think that it's obvious, then, that if it's not big enough for both of us, one of us has to leave—and, I believe it's time that you consider leaving.' And she said, 'Am I fired?' And he said, 'If that's the way you look at it, yeah.' And, she left the office."

Step 8: Individually, in small groups, or with the entire class, answer the following questions:

1. What advice would you give Ray at this point?
2. What responsibility does Ray have to the organization? To people like George?
3. What legal constraints must Ray consider?
4. What type of protection is George offered under the law?
5. What role should managers play in dealing with employees such as George? What skills do they require?
6. How can human resources professionals help managers such as Ray deal with employees such as George?
7. What repercussions might occur from the company's treatment of the bookkeeper?

Activity 13–2

SEXUAL HARASSMENT IN THE OFFICE AND SEQUEL

Step 1: Read Sexual Harassment in the Office.

Step 2: Prepare the case for class discussion.

This case was written by Esther Scott under the supervision of Stephanie Gould for use at the John F. Kennedy School of Government, Harvard University. Names of individuals and organizations in this case have been disguised.

On a Friday afternoon in early May 1981, Tina Wallinsky, secretary for the Technical Information Unit of the federal government's National Chemical Research Agency, requested an interview with the unit director, Dan Newcomb. Newcomb recalled, "She needed to talk. It was pretty apparent that something was very troubling to her"; but Wallinsky appeared extremely reluctant to say directly what was on her mind. Only after a great deal of hemming and hawing, and questioning from Newcomb, could she bring herself to tell her story.

The story really belonged to Terry Rizzo, a high school senior who, as part of her work/study program, had been employed as a part-time clerical worker in the Technical Information Unit.* Rizzo had come to the unit with poor office skills but hoped to improve enough to get a full-time job there after graduation. She had found the unit a warm and supportive environment; during a period of personal problems with her family, office personnel had responded with concern, advice, and even financial assistance. Two months before Newcomb's conversation with his secretary, however, Rizzo had suddenly announced her intention to leave the unit and work instead as a cocktail waitress. Her parting, as Newcomb recalled, was quite amicable:

> The issue was that she could make so much more money [as a cocktail waitress] and this would permit her to keep going to school, because she could work part-time late at night and on the weekends. . . . I didn't put in a lot of thought about [her quitting]. She had considered these options before. She didn't seem to me too well adjusted; I knew she was going through a lot of personal problems. I had given her my advice several times; I really felt it would be better for her not to try to [work as a cocktail waitress]. But nonetheless, it was her decision, and she made it, and that was fine.†

A month after her resignation, however, Rizzo had met Wallinsky and, over coffee, explained "the real reason" for her departure. Several weeks before resigning, Rizzo told Wallinsky, she had agreed (after "numerous requests") to pose for the unit's assistant director, Jack Hayes, who was known to be a "photography buff." During lunch hour, Hayes had driven Rizzo several miles from the office to a fairly remote outdoor location and, after she had posed for awhile, had begun pressing her to undress for the pictures. How much, if at all, Rizzo obliged was not clear to Newcomb, since Wallinsky did not want to relate the details of Rizzo's story. However, it appeared certain that Hayes had spent some time trying to persuade Rizzo to oblige and even showed her some of his earlier photographs, which Rizzo considered pornographic. Hayes did not resort to force and, when Rizzo refused to go further with the posing, took her back to the office. "It wasn't," related Newcomb, "a hostile, 'I want out of here' kind of thing. Apparently [Rizzo said] 'No, I don't want to do that' and [Hayes replied] 'Well, fine, we'll start again another day.' So apparently she wasn't too highly offended. I'm not sure."

Hayes didn't seem to think Rizzo was deeply offended, either, and asked her several more times to pose for pictures. It was this persistence, however amicable, that Wallinsky indicated may have decided Rizzo on leaving the Technical Information Unit. As Wallinsky related it to Newcomb, "[Rizzo] is afraid to come back, and afraid to have anything more to do with the office because of possible reprisals from this guy [Hayes]."

Newcomb felt that in relating this story, Wallinsky, a woman in her mid-twenties whom he regarded as a frank, down-to-earth person, was not inclined to exaggerate Rizzo's innocence. (Newcomb himself characterized Rizzo's manner as "rather flirtatious.") For instance, Rizzo had stated that she wouldn't "go out with [Hayes] any more after I found out what he wanted," but Wallinsky suspected that Rizzo had been out with Hayes on more than one occasion. Nevertheless, she clearly believed that the basic facts of the story were true, and she was upset. One reason, Newcomb felt, for the upset was the disillusionment with Hayes, who, as assistant director, had supervisory authority over about fifteen people in the Technical Information Unit, including Terry Rizzo. Wallinsky and Rizzo had greatly respected Hayes, especially as a model husband and father. (They had met Hayes' wife and children several times at office parties and outings.) Rizzo, in particular, had re-

*The Technical Information Unit employed approximately 25 people, largely clerical workers, chemical engineers, and computer programmers. Women comprised about 45% of the unit, with a few holding senior positions. The unit was headed by a director (Dan Newcomb) and his assistant director (Jack Hayes); because of the way Newcomb and Hayes divided up office duties, Hayes was given direct supervisory responsibility for over half of the unit staff. The Technical Information Unit was part of the agency's Biomedical Products Research Division; Newcomb's immediate supervisor was the division chief.

†Newcomb had also speculated at the time that Rizzo might have decided to leave because she had received several warnings that, unless her basic office skills improved significantly, she would not be offered full-time employment.

garded Hayes (who was in his mid-forties) as a "father figure" who had been a source of support during a time of personal difficulties. "He really went out of his way," recalled Newcomb, "to be of assistance, and to comfort her." More seriously, though, than her disillusionment, Tina Wallinsky expressed concern for the women still working in the unit. "She was afraid of what would happen," said Newcomb. "Might the guy do something like this with some other person in the office?"

At the same time, Wallinsky insisted on absolute secrecy. Terry Rizzo had asked her not to repeat the story to anyone, and had disavowed any intention of filing a complaint against Hayes, feeling, according to Wallinsky, that "it's over now, and it would disrupt the office."* In turn, Wallinsky asked Newcomb not to approach Hayes or anyone on the matter and wanted him to promise to take no action.

Newcomb refused to make that promise, but felt at a loss for what to do. He did not feel particularly close to Hayes, whom he had hired as assistant director, using routine civil service channels, only a few months before the alleged photography session. While Hayes had not exactly sparkled on the job, he had proved, in Newcomb's estimation, "reasonably competent." Newcomb thought that with some people in the office Hayes did "tend to contrive and connive," but that with him (Newcomb) he had always been very honest. Newcomb remarked:

> If you had told me that one of the two people [Rizzo or Hayes] were lying, [I would have said] it was the girl. . . . If she told me this and he told me that, I'd go with him nine times out of ten, based on my feelings about her integrity at the time.

Nevertheless, Newcomb was troubled by some circumstantial evidence that appeared to support Rizzo's story. He recalled that Hayes had recently gone through a period of apparent upset:

> He suddenly became very distraught, and it was seriously affecting his job, to the point where I finally had a long talk with him and asked him, "What the hell is happening? Your tail is dragging, you look run down, you just seem to be churning and not accomplishing anything. What is it? Can I help?" And he almost cried and [said] . . . "I just am physically not able to keep up with the work. I am not making the progress that I want to make, and I'm getting frustrated." [This period] happened to correspond very closely to the time right after [Rizzo] left.

Newcomb was also disturbed by Tina Wallinsky's report of a conversation she had had with Hayes not long after Rizzo had left (but before Rizzo had met with Wallinsky). Hayes had asked Wallinsky for her opinion of Rizzo "from the standpoint of, 'Do you think she would be the kind to file a sexual harassment complaint?' " And further, although nothing on Hayes' employment record indicated any questionable behavior, Wallinsky, who had worked with Hayes in another office, seemed to recall otherwise. "She implied that something had happened at one stage," said Newcomb. "She didn't want to go into it but [she indicated] something that she now recalled did fit, that there had been some kind of episode."

Finally, there was a nagging concern about Rizzo's sudden change in jobs. As far as Newcomb could tell, Rizzo was now working "under age and on false pretenses"* as a cocktail waitress "in a pretty rough bar." Newcomb remembered that, on the promise of full-time employment in the unit if she improved, Rizzo had worked on her own time to upgrade her skills:

> She was practicing her typing. . . . We actually had a series of exercises that she was doing during her lunch time and any other breaks between tasks. I got the impression that, by God, she might make it. And then—zing—she was gone. . . . So maybe in fact the episode did force her into a line that she wouldn't have taken otherwise.

Uncertain of what to do, Newcomb decided to give himself the weekend to mull over the problem.

*The Technical Information Unit was just beginning to settle down after a period of unpleasant turmoil. Shortly before Rizzo's departure, a black employee, whom Newcomb was about to fire for poor performance, had filed a series of grievances and discrimination complaints. Between the employee's efforts (unsuccessful, Newcomb reported) to win support from among office workers, and the presence of federal investigators inquiring into the complaints, the unit had, Newcomb felt, experienced considerable disruption of its normally tight-knit, supportive environment.

*Rizzo, who was only 18 years old, had a forged I.D. that enabled her to work as a cocktail waitress.

Step 3: Individually, in small groups, or with the entire class, answer the following question: What should Newcomb do?

Step 4: Read Sexual Harassment in the Office, Sequel.

Over the weekend, Dan Newcomb came up with only a few, less than satisfactory options for dealing with a possible case of sexual harassment in his Technical Information Unit. One line of action would be to talk to Terry Rizzo, to verify her story (which he had only heard secondhand) and to see if she wanted to file a formal complaint against the unit's assistant director, Jack Hayes. The drawback, however, was that Rizzo had asked Tina Wallinsky, the unit secretary, not to repeat her story and that Wallinsky, in turn, had requested complete secrecy. "So if I got in touch with anybody," remarked Newcomb, "I violated somebody's confidence."

A second option would be to confront Hayes directly, but Newcomb found that equally troubling:

> [I felt] I couldn't go after him and accuse him of something that was based on hearsay. And I was not positive that I had a right to base it on the testimony of a secretary who asked not to be identified. . . . I was not positive that I could [talk to Hayes about it] without an accusation of sorts creeping into the conversation. How do you ask somebody if they've done something like this? That in itself indicates a judgment. . . . Certainly people pose in the nude for artists, and there's nothing from that perspective that's pornographic or out of place. And, by my asking him about [the incident], I might seem to be making a judgment. "That thing I heard you might have done is wrong."

While Newcomb continued to doubt the veracity of Rizzo's story, he worried that he might be wrong: "If [the story] was true, the young lady was in a particularly vulnerable situation. She had an awful lot of confidence in [Hayes] and, if it happened, then he clearly took advantage of her." Further, if there were any grain of truth in what Rizzo had told Wallinsky, Newcomb felt he had ample grounds to be critical of Hayes. Even if Hayes had exerted no overt pressure on Rizzo, he had, Newcomb believed, shown

> poor judgment for a supervisor. If you need models, go out and find them somewhere else; but for God's sake, don't ask the people who report to you. Whatever happened, if he did in fact ask [her to model], I think he was wrong. Whether he asked her to go further and she didn't want to, or he wanted to force pornographic pictures on her, or whatever, is immaterial. The first error is that he was improper in asking.

Finally, Newcomb settled on a third option—to tell his boss, the head of the Biomedical Products Research Division. That Monday morning, he related Rizzo's story, in private:

> I simply told him the bare essentials of what I had heard, and that I had decided that I would not discuss it with [Hayes]. I felt that I ought to keep it to myself, because it was too fragmented and there was too much hearsay to actually speak to [Hayes] about it.

Later, Newcomb explained his decision to talk with his boss:

> I felt that I needed, in some way, to seek the advice of somebody. I don't [typically] ask my boss what to do. . . . I tell him what I've decided to do. That's more our way of conversing—I simply tell him, "Here's what happened and here's what I've decided to do." I don't ask his advice, although frankly that's what I wanted. The way I ask his advice is to tell him what I've done, and it gives him the opportunity to offer it if he wants. But [in this case] he didn't.

And so, Terry Rizzo's story, at least in theory, stopped there. Newcomb's main concern in mulling over the incident had been, "What if it happens again? What if it goes further with someone else? Should I do something on behalf of the young women in the office, or should I forget it?" While acknowledging Rizzo's vulnerability to Hayes, Newcomb concluded that, in general, the women in his unit "know how to handle" sexual harassment—"[they would] just tell the guy where to go." Still, he felt ambivalent. Newcomb explained, "I guess I concluded it wasn't all that serious after all, but I'm not sure. I have a funny sort of feeling about it."

Step 5: Individually, in small groups, or with the entire class, answer the following questions:

1. Evaluate the options that Newcomb considered.
2. How should a manager deal with a possible case of sexual harassment?
3. What should top management at the National Chemical Research Agency do?
4. What responsibility do managers in an organization such as National Chemical have in dealing with sexual harassment?
5. Did Newcomb act appropriately?

Activity 13–3

AFFIRMATIVE ACTION PLAN

Step 1: Read the following scenario.

The Acme Construction Company is bidding on a federal contract of $300,000 for the construction of low-income housing. One condition of the contract is that all finalists undergo a federal audit before the contract is awarded. This audit would evaluate both the financial status of the company and the effectiveness of its human resources management. In the latter area, great concern has arisen in Acme's regional EEOC office about the employment of minorities in the construction industry. Approximately 20 percent of the regional population are black or Spanish-American; 50 percent are men and 50 percent women; and 15 percent are over the age of sixty-five.

The following profiles Acme's 100 employees:

10 managerial, 90 nonmanagerial
90 members belong to the union
98 white men, 2 white women
75 under the age of 40, 25 between the ages of 40 and 65

Acme claims not to have a mandatory retirement age. In general, recruitment has occurred by word of mouth or by posting of job notices in the union hall. Because the region has experienced significant growth in the building industry, there has been a shortage of qualified workers.

Step 2: Individually, in small groups, or with the entire class, offer a plan for preparing for the federal audit from the perspective of the president of the company, the director of human resources, and the managers. The federal contract office has informed Acme that they can expect the audit to occur in one to two months.

Step 3: Discussion. In small groups or with the entire class, answer the following questions:

1. Is Acme in compliance with EEOC regulations?
2. If Acme is in compliance, how do you prove it to the federal auditors?
3. If Acme is not in compliance, what steps can be taken to bring the company into compliance?
4. What obligation does Acme have to hire minorities and more women?
5. Should Acme bid for the contract?
6. Should Acme expect to get the contract?
7. What role should human resources professionals play in ensuring compliance?
8. What role should managers play in ensuring compliance?

Activity 13–4

IMPROVING OCCUPATIONAL SAFETY AND HEALTH

Step 1: Read the following scenario.

The Welling Pipe Company supplies pipes for large office buildings, land development projects, and street repairs. Employing approximately thirty workers, the company buys large steel pipes, sorts them according to size, cuts them to customer requirements, loads them onto delivery trucks or railroad cars, and unloads them at the customer's site. The company has a large, unheated warehouse where the cutting and sorting occur and a smaller yard where the loading takes place.

The company is nonunion. However, recent attempts by several unions have almost succeeded. The major complaint by workers is the poor repair of machinery, the lack of safety procedures, and the general lackadaisical attitude of management toward safety issues.

Step 2: Assume that you are the general manager of the company. You think that something should be done to respond to the employees' complaints. You think the workers have a right to a safe environment. You also know that the company would never pass an OSHA inspection; an inspector would close you down immediately and everyone would lose their jobs. But the owner has told you that the costs required to improve health and safety conditions would bankrupt the company. Nevertheless, you think that something should be done.

Step 3: Individually, in small groups, or with the entire class, prepare a statement to present to the president of the company that describes the action you propose to take to improve the working conditions at Welling Pipe Company.

Step 4: Discussion. In small groups or with the entire class, answer the following questions:

1. What plans were offered? What were the advantages and disadvantages of each proposal?
2. Should the general manager threaten to file a complaint with OSHA?
3. What would an OSHA inspector likely do if he or she visited Welling Pipe Company?
4. What steps could the general manager take at little or no cost?
5. What steps could the workers take?
6. What types of costs cannot be avoided?
7. Do you support the president's statement regarding health and safety in the workplace?

Activity 13–5

ASSESSING ADVERSE IMPACT

Step 1: Examine the test scores for twenty-five job applicants shown below.

Applicant	*Sex*	*Race*	*Score*
1	Male	White	170
2	Male	White	169
3	Female	White	167
4	Female	Black	167
5	Male	Black	160
6	Male	Black	159
7	Male	White	158
8	Male	Black	155
9	Female	White	150
10	Male	Black	140
11	Male	White	137
12	Female	White	120
13	Female	White	120
14	Female	White	120
15	Male	Black	104
16	Male	White	93
17	Male	White	90
18	Male	Black	90

Applicant	*Sex*	*Race*	*Score*
19	Male	Black	80
20	Female	White	80
21	Male	White	80
22	Female	White	79
23	Male	White	79
24	Male	White	79
25	Male	White	78

Step 2: If a cutoff score of 154 is used, does this test demonstrate adverse impact on women applicants?

Step 3: If a cutoff score of 94 is used, does this test demonstrate adverse impact on black applicants?

Step 4: Discussion. In small groups, with the entire class, or in writing, as directed by your instructor, answer the following questions:

1. Are these data adequate to show adverse impact?
2. Would any additional information strengthen the case?
3. What action should the organization take based on this information?
4. What responsibility do human resources professionals have?
5. What actions should managers take?

Activity 13–6

IS THIS DISCRIMINATION?

Step 1: Read each situation below.

Case I. Jennifer Howe had worked for the Data Research Company for one year as a research associate when Hugh Hoyt was hired as a research associate. Both associates had received Master's degrees in education in the same year from state universities in different parts of the country. After Hoyt had worked at Data Research for approximately three months, Jennifer Howe was promoted to an assistant vice president and given the responsibility for supervising Hoyt and four other male employees on various research projects. Two months later Jennifer learned that Hugh Hoyt (who was married with one child) received a salary $2000 higher than hers.

Case II. James Mahoney had been employed by the Adrian Service Corporation for over thirty years. As he approached the age of sixty-five, he decided he really did not want to retire. None of his benefits precluded his continuing employment. But company policy specified that all employees had to retire at the age of sixty-five or their pensions would be systematically reduced for each year that they continued to work after that age.

Case III. Thomas Piper was the first black American faculty member in the School of Management at Central State University. Central State had been under an affirmative action decree for approximately three years, but had been unable to find any qualified minority employees. Piper had a Master's degree from a reputable university, and was hired at a salary slightly above the average for new hires at the university. Edward Grayson had also applied for the position that was ultimately awarded to Piper. Grayson had a Doctorate from an Ivy League university, as well as exceptional teaching and research experience for a new Ph.D. When Grayson learned that

Piper received the position, he claimed that reverse discrimination had occurred.

Step 2: Individually, in small groups, or with the entire class, answer the following questions:

1. Did discrimination occur?
2. What law was violated?
3. What complaint should the individual file and with whom?
4. What evidence should the organization present that discrimination did not occur?

Step 3: Discussion. In small groups or with the entire class, answer the following:

1. What conditions must exist for a charge of discrimination to be valid?
2. What laws specify these conditions?
3. What rights do employees have in cases of discrimination?
4. What evidence must employees provide to show that discrimination occurred?
5. What evidence must companies provide to show that discrimination did not occur?

SUMMARY

Legislation passed since 1960 has had a dramatic effect on the management of human resources in organizations. The Equal Pay Act, Title VII of the Civil Rights Act, and the Age Discrimination in Employment Act, among others, provide significant employment protection for workers. The Occupational Safety and Health Act directs organizations to improve the safety and health conditions in the workplace. The Employment Retirement Income Security Act offers safeguards for pension monies and other retirement funds for employees.

Human resources professionals and managers should be knowledgeable about the laws that influence their performance and that of subordinates. Most organizations have been required to review, and in many cases redesign, their staffing, promotion, compensation, and career development policies to ensure that they comply with recent federal and state legislation.

In this chapter you had the opportunity to learn the provisions of various laws as well as their implications for organizations. In the activities you had the opportunity to examine a variety of situations that call for changes in organizational policies and practices to ensure compliance with antidiscrimination, health and safety, and benefits legislation.

Organizations must develop approaches for ensuring that their employment practices meet current legislative requirements. First, top management must make certain that all managers are informed about relevant legal provisions. Second, they should assign to human resources professionals and managers the responsibility for monitoring the organization's compliance with various legislation. Finally, they should provide regular avenues of appeal for employees who think their legal rights have been violated.

Enforcement of federal and state legislation varies, depending on the political climate and the amount of resources devoted to the task, but all organizations must assess their ethical responsibility to comply with the statutes described in this chapter.

ENDNOTES

[1]P.J. Greenlaw and J.P. Kohl, The EEOC's new equal pay act guidelines, *Personnel Journal* 61 (July 1982): 517–521.

[2]J.B. Fulghum, The employer's liabilities under comparable worth, *Personnel Journal* 62 (1982): 400–412.

[3]Diaz v. Pan American Airways, 311 F.Supp. 559 (U.S. Dist. Ct. Fla. 1970); see also T.S. Neuberger, Sex as a bonafide occupation qualification under Title VII, *Labor Law Journal* 29 (1978): 425–429.

[4]See Bureau of National Affairs, *Labor Relations Reporter, State Laws,* 4 SLL 1 (November 1977):11–14; *Los Angeles Times,* November 1976, Part 1-A, pp. 6–7; *Seattle Times,* 21 February 1972, p. A-7 for discussion of new roles for women.

[5]Civil Rights Act of 1964, Title VII, provision h.

[6]P.S. Greenlaw and J.P. Kohl, National origin discrimination and the new EEOC guidelines, *Personnel Journal* 60 (August 1981):634–636.

[7]O.A. Ornati and M.J. Eisen, Are you complying with EEOC's new rules on national origin discrimination?, *Personnel* 58 (March-April 1981):12–20.

[8]See Espinoza v. Farah Manufacturing Co., Inc., 35 *Federal Register* 421, 414, U.S. 86, 92 (1973).

[9]Mass. legislature acts on mandatory retirement bill, *Boston Globe,* 5 October 1984; Mass. Gov. Dukakis signs bill banning mandatory retirement, *Boston Globe,* 17 October 1984.

[10]R.A. Snyder and B. Brandon, Riding the third wave: Staying on top of ADEA complaints, *Personnel Administrator* 28 (February 1983):41–47.

[11]*Ibid.*

[12]J. Ledvinka, *Federal Regulation of Personnel and Human Resource Management* (Boston: Kent, 1982).

[13]Bureau of National Affairs, *Fair Employment Practices Manual* (Washington, D.C.: Bureau of National Affairs, 1976); B.L. Schlei and P. Grossman, *Employment Discrimination Law* (Washington, D.C.: Bureau of National Affairs, 1976).

[14]Ledvinka, *op. cit.*

[15]J. Ledvinka and H.J. Watson, Processing of discrimination charges by EEOC, *Journal of Business Research* 3 (1976):149–156; Schlei and Grossman, *op. cit.*

[16]Ledvinka, *op. cit.,* bases these on McDonnell-Douglas v. Green, 411 U.S. 972 (1973), and Griggs v. Duke Power Co., 401 U.S. 424 (1971).

[17]Executive Order 11246 Sec. 202 (1).

[18]Revised Order No. 4, 41 Code of Federal Regulations, Part 60, At sec. 2.10 (1979).

[19]Ledvinka, *op. cit.*

[20]Revised Order No. 4, *op. cit.*

[21]Ledvinka, *op. cit.,* p. 129.

[22]J.A. Belohlav and E. Ayton, Equal opportunity laws: Some common problems, *Personnel Journal* 61 (April 1982):282–285.

[23]The dismantling of OSHA, *Nation* 233 (September 12, 1981):205.

[24]Weber v. Kaiser Aluminum and Chemical Corp., 564 F.2d 216 (5th Cir. 1976) reversed, 443 U.S. 193 (1979).

[25]Barnes v. Costle, 561 F.2d. 983 (DC Cir. 1977).

[26]Tomkins v. Public Service Electric and Gas Co., 568 F.2d. 1044, 1048—1049 (3d. Cir. 1977).

[27]M.L. Greenbaum and B. Fraser, Sexual harassment in the workplace, *Arbitration Journal* 7 (December 1981):30–41.

[28]EEOC, Guidelines on Sex Discrimination Because of Sex, 29 C.F.R. 1604.11 (a).

[29]Massachusetts Advisory Committee to the U.S. Commission on Civil Rights, *Sexual Harassment on the Job: A Guide for Employers* (Boston: Massachusetts Advisory Committee, 1983).

[30]See *Accident Facts, 1980 edition* (Chicago: National Safety Council, 1980); *Insurance Facts, 1980–1981 Edition* (New York: Insurance Information Institute, 1980).

[31]Public Law 91–956, 91st Congress, S. 2193, December 29, 1970.

[32]Occupational Safety and Health Act, Public Law 91–596, 91st Congress, S. 2193, Sec. 5 (a),(b).

[33]D. Petersen, *Safety Supervision* (New York: AMACOM, 1976).

[34]See F. K. Foulkes, Learning to live with OSHA, *Harvard Business Review* 51 (November-December 1973); U.S. Department of Labor, *OSHA: Your Workplace Rights in Action* (Washington, D.C.: Occupational Safety and Health Administration, 1979).

[35]J.J. Hoover, Workers have new rights to health and safety, *Personnel Administrator* 28 (April 1983):47–51.

[36]U.S. Department of Labor, *All About OSHA* (Washington, D.C.: Occupational Safety and Health Administration, OSHA 2056, 1974).

[37]U.S. Department of Labor, *OSHA Inspections,* Programs and Policy Series (Washington, D.C.: Occupational Safety and Health Administration, OSHA 2098, June 1975.

[38]U.S. Department of Labor, *All About OSHA, op. cit.*

[39]H.M. Taylor, Occupational health management by objectives, *Personnel* 57 (January-February 1980):5–70.

[40]J.J. Brennan, Worksite health promotion can be cost-effective, *Personnel Administrator* 28 (April 1983):39–42.

[41]V. Cahan, The overhaul that could give OSHA lite under Reagan, *Business Week,* 19 January 1981; A lighter schedule of OSHA inspections, *Business Week,* 14 September 1981.

[42]B.J. Whiting, Jr., Regulatory reform and OSHA: Fads and realities, *Labor Law Journal* (August 1979):514–527.

[43]R.L. Greenman and E.J. Schmertz, *Personnel Administration and the Law* 2nd ed. (Washington, D.C.: Bureau of National Affairs, 1979).

[44]ERISA, Sec. 3.2.

[45]Greenman and Schmertz, *op. cit.*, p. 148.

[46]Greenman and Schmertz, *op. cit.*

[47]ERISA, Sec. 102 (a) (1).

[48]Ledvinka, *op. cit.*

[49]Diaz v. Pan American Airways, *op. cit.*

[50]R.D. Arvey, *Fairness in Selecting Employees* (Reading, Mass.: Addison-Wesley, 1979).

[51]*Ibid.*

[52]*Ibid.*, p. 54.

[53]See J.E. Hunter, F.L. Schmidt, and R. Hunter, Differential validity of employment tests by race, *Psychological Bulletin* 86 (July 1979):721–735; C. Fincher, Differential validity and test bias, *Personnel Psychology* 28 (Winter 1975):481–500.

[54]Uniform Guidelines of Employee Selection, 29 Code of Federal Regulations, Part 1607.

[55]J. Klotchman and L.L. Neider, EEO alert: Watch out for discrimination in discharge decisions, *Personnel* 60 (January-February 1983):60–66.

[56]M. Leonard, Challenges to the termination-at-will doctrine, *Personnel Administrator* 28 (February 1983): 49–56.

[57]L.E. Blades, Employment at will vs. individual freedom: On limiting the abusive exercise of employer power, *Columbia Law Review* 67 (1967):1402.

[58]Leonard, *op. cit.*

[59]*Ibid.*

[60]W.H. Holley and H.S. Feild, Will your performance appraisal system hold up in court?, *Personnel* 59 (January-February 1982):59–64.

[61]Fulghum, *op. cit.*

[62]*Women, Work, and Wages: Equal Pay for Jobs of Equal Value* (Washington, D.C.: National Academy of Sciences Committee on Occupational Classification and Analysis, 1981).

[63]R.J. Schonberger and H.W. Hennessey, Jr., Is equal pay for comparable work fair?, *Personnel Journal* 60 (December 1981):964–968.

[64]S. DeForrest, How can comparable worth be achieved?, *Personnel* 61 (September-October 1984):4–11.

FURTHER READINGS

Greenman, R.L. and Schmertz, E.J. *Personnel Administration and the Law* 2nd ed. Washington, D.C.: Bureau of National Affairs, 1979.

Massachusetts Advisory Committee to the U.S. Commission on Civil Rights. *Sexual Harassment on the Job: A Guide for Employers.* Boston: Massachusetts Advisory Committee, 1983.

Ledvinka, J. *Federal Regulation of Personnel and Human Resource Management.* Boston: Kent, 1982.

U.S. Department of Labor, *All About OSHA.* Washington, D.C.: Occupational Safety and Health Administration, OSHA 2056, 1974.

CHAPTER 14

Implementing Change in Organizations

CHAPTER OUTLINE

LEARNING CHECKPOINTS

After completing the reading and activities of this chapter, students will be able to

- define quality of work life;
- describe ten organization development interventions and their uses;
- describe situations in which job redesign is appropriate;
- redesign a job using four different approaches;
- list five circumstances in which organization redesign will improve quality of working life;
- illustrate how six contingencies influence effective organizational structure;
- redesign an organization;
- list five types of resistance to change and offer ways to overcome each;
- describe the roles of managers, human resources professionals, and consultants in organizational change.

INTRODUCTION

The Lexington Travel Agency offers diverse travel services to customers in a large metropolitan area. The one hundred agents at Lexington's twenty branches book charter flights and trips, plan individual travel itineraries, book all required reservations, and ticket airline, railway, and bus passengers. Although a significant part of the business is conducted in the twenty offices, Lexington Travel also maintains a telephone sales office that serves customers twenty-four hours a day. Customers can call the telephone sales department instead of visiting an office in person.

The telephone sales group is located in a small corner of the main office building, next to the accounting department. The group has added two or three agents during each of the previous four years, but the space allocated for telephone sales has remained the same. The sales agents are in cramped quarters; clumsy dividers are used to provide privacy and soundproofing. Each member of the group has a small desk, a telephone, and the *Official Airline Guide.* Along one wall of the office is a small library of a dozen or so reference books and brochures used most often by the agents. If they require additional materials they must go to the first or second floor of the main office, where a larger supply of materials is available, or telephone other agents for assistance.

As a telephone call is received, it is automatically transferred to an agent. The sophisticated telephone system that has been installed in all Lexington's offices rings the first available agent highest on the telephone-sales random-access list. This agent is then expected to handle the customer's request. The agent may make follow-up calls at a later time if he or she needs additional information to answer the customer's question. If a customer calls a second time, the second call is not referred to the original agent; rather, the agent highest on the list must pick up where the other agent left off. The telephone system monitors the length of each call and the number of calls handled by each agent. It also monitors the number of callers put on hold and those who ultimately hang up before reaching a telephone sales agent.

Agents are evaluated according to the number of calls they handle in a day. On completing each call, the agent is expected to record the type of action that resulted from the conversation—purchase of an airline ticket, mailing of information about charter trips to Europe, and so on. These reports, together with the telephone records, are tabulated periodically by the telephone sales manager to obtain information about the group's performance.

Jessica Talley, Vice President of Sales at Lexington, has recently acquired supervisory responsibility for the telephone sales department. Previously the department operated fairly autonomously, with limited reporting to the company's president. Jessica's review of the department indicates a decline in the agents' performance. The number of calls handled by various agents has been very uneven; some handle three to five times as many calls in a period as others. Almost twenty percent of the calls placed on hold were never answered because the customer hung up while waiting to be helped. The vice president has recently received a number of complaints about the telephone sales office; customers complain that the agents lack knowledge, never follow up on their requests, or insist that a follow-up call is necessary to answer a simple question because the sales agent lacks required information. Comparison of the time spent on calls to the results in terms of sales are disappointing. Often very long calls have not resulted in any sales.

Jessica attributes the poor performance, in part, to ineffective management by the department manager. The manager spends most of the day monitoring the agents' telephone conversations. In conversations with the agents Jessica has learned that they think the manager's "spying" is unnecessary, and that the manager should be handling calls from the queue a larger portion of the time. The telephone sales agents also indicate that the manager is not helpful in solving their problems, lacks up-to-date information about travel services, lacks strong interpersonal skills, and continually tells the agents to "speak faster and handle more calls."

Absenteeism has risen significantly during the past year. Many agents have requested transfers to branch offices. The vice president detects low morale and lethargy when she visits the telephone sales area. Even some of the best agents are showing a decline in productivity.

Is human resources management at Lexington Travel effective? The quality of working life and productivity in the telephone sales department are low. These indicators suggest a need for some changes in the organization.

Quality of work life (QWL) is the employees' perceptions of various components of their jobs, as well as the organizational context in which they occur. "QWL is . . . a new system . . . in which management attitudes toward employees . . . move from the orthodox rigidity of scientific management to a clear recognition of the dignity of human beings."[1] It is concerned with the extent to which work "provides an opportunity for an individual to satisfy a wide variety of personal needs—from the need to survive with some security to the need to interact with others, to have a sense of personal usefulness, to be recognized for achievement, and to have an opportunity to improve one's skills and knowledge."[2] QWL encompasses an individual's perception of adequate and fair compensation; safe and healthy working conditions; immediate opportunity to use and develop human capacities; future opportunity for individual growth and security; social integration in the organization, including freedom from prejudice, egalitarianism, mobility, supportive work groups, a sense of community, and interpersonal openness; constitutionality in the workplace, including privacy, free speech, equity, and due process; compatibility of work and extra-work life, including family and leisure; and social relevance of work life.[3] Jessica Talley should consider implementing changes in the organization to improve the department's quality of work life and productivity.

In this chapter we examine various changes that a human resources professional or manager can use to improve the department's quality of work life. We consider organization development programs that emphasize behavioral interventions, the redesign of work, and the redesign of organizations. Then we look at lessons that can be learned from human resources management practices outside the United States. We also briefly consider the process of change; specifically, overcoming resistance to change and the selection of a change agent. We conclude the chapter with a discussion of strategies for effective organizational change.

ORGANIZATION DEVELOPMENT INTERVENTIONS

Organization development refers to a wide range of interventions that attempt to alter personal and interpersonal interactions. It has been defined as a long-range effort to improve an organization's problem-solving and renewal processes, particularly through a more effective and collaborative management of organizational culture—with special emphasis on the culture of formal work teams—with the assistance of a change agent or catalyst; and the use of the theory and technology of applied behavioral science, including action research.[4] (Note that *organizational culture* has been defined as "the pattern of basic assumptions that a given group has invented, discovered, or developed in learning to cope with its problems of external adaptation and internal integration."[5]) It has also been defined as an effort that is planned, organization-wide, and managed from the top, to increase organizational effectiveness and health through planned interventions in the organization's "processes," using behavioral-science knowledge.[6]

Organization development (OD) interventions attempt to change individuals' skills, knowledge, or attitudes.[7] Change must begin with a needs assessment—or in the terms of the practical approach described in this book, diagnosis. Experienced human resources professionals, outside consultants, or, in some cases, line managers must diagnose the organizational situation and determine where there are deficiencies. At Lexington Travel, for example, Jessica Talley might hire an outside consultant to assess conditions and recommend strategies for meeting identified needs.

The following sections describe strategies to address four frequently identified needs. They are the need to (1) increase personal or interpersonal effectiveness, (2) build collaborative teams, (3) reduce intergroup conflict, and (4) increase overall organizational effectiveness.[8] Table 14–1 lists the interventions discussed to meet each need. Although many of these strategies should only be implemented by trained professionals, line managers and human resources professionals should be aware of the options available when planning for organizational change.

Increasing Personal and Interpersonal Effectiveness

When individuals have difficulty functioning in the workplace, interventions addressing improvement of their personal effectiveness may be appropriate. Individual performance problems can occur because a person's style does not fit with the work situation or with the style of supervisors, coworkers, or subordinates, or because he or she lacks effective communication or leadership skills.

Problems experienced by the telephone sales department and similar groups may also result from the ineffective interaction of two or three coworkers. The first agent who handles a client might try to hide information from another agent to prevent the second from making a sale; competition between individuals can prevent effective communication.

Psychological counseling or long-term individual training are probably the best ways to alter personal style so that quality of work life is improved. *Structured*

Intervention	Primary Target
Behavior modification	Personal or interpersonal effectiveness
Collateral organizations	Organizational effectiveness
Confrontation meeting	Intergroup conflict
Grid Organization Development	Team skill-building
Job expectation technique	Team skill-building
Organizational mirror	Intergroup conflict
Process consultation	Personal or interpersonal effectiveness
Quality circles	Organizational effectiveness
Role analysis technique	Team skill-building
Role negotiation technique	Team skill-building
Sensitivity laboratory training	Personal or interpersonal effectiveness
Structured training programs	Personal or interpersonal effectiveness
Survey feedback	Organizational effectiveness
Team-building	Team skill-building
Third-party interventions	Intergroup conflict
Transactional analysis	Personal or interpersonal effectiveness

Table 14–1 TYPES OF INTERVENTIONS

training programs (see Chapter 7) offer individuals opportunities to diagnose their personal effectiveness, and completion of questionnaires that assess personal style can provide data for such diagnosis. Role plays or other activities where individuals can practice communication and leadership skills can ultimately influence performance favorably. These approaches require workers or managers to participate frequently in training sessions to ensure they have learned the new skills well enough to use them in the work situation. Structured training is fairly commonly used today, but more often for teaching specific skills or knowledge than for changing personal behavior. To do the latter effectively requires extensive time and resources for each individual. Still, the manager of the telephone sales department might benefit from this type of training.

Behavior modification can also be used to improve individual behaviors.[9] Here, managers or human resources professionals design and implement programs that reinforce desired behaviors. If a manager wants a problem worker to arrive at work promptly, then each time the employee comes to work on time the manager reinforces the behavior by, say, praising the employee. Or each time a supervisor implements a new, profitable idea without direction from top management, his or her manager might give the supervisor a bonus. Human resources professionals can help managers design these and other incentive programs such as those described in Chapter 9.

Behavior modification has received renewed attention in the past decade since these programs are relatively inexpensive to administer, have had significant impact on diverse types of behavior, and can be introduced by managers after relatively little training. The major drawback to this approach is the necessity for managers to precisely identify the behavior to be modified and to change only that behavior without accompanying, sometimes undesirable, side effects.

Sensitivity laboratory training has been used to improve interpersonal effectiveness.[10] Small groups of individuals meet together to share perceptions of each other's behavior and offer suggestions for improving interpersonal style. They participate in a series of unstructured activities designed to provide practice in communicating and diagnosing their performance in group situations. The objectives of sensitivity training include

1. increased understanding, insight, and awareness about one's own behavior and its impact on others, including the ways in which others interpret behavior;
2. increased understanding and sensitivity about the behavior, thoughts, and feelings of others, including better interpretation of both verbal and nonverbal clues;
3. better understanding and awareness of group and intergroup processes, both those that facilitate and those that inhibit group functioning;
4. better diagnostic skills in interpersonal and intergroup situations;
5. increased ability to transform learning into action, so that real-life interventions will be successful in increasing participants' satisfaction, output, or effectiveness;
6. improvement in individuals' ability to analyze their own interpersonal behavior, as well as to learn how to help themselves and others to achieve more satisfying, rewarding, and effective interpersonal relationships.[11]

The use of sensitivity training in organizations has declined over the past fifteen years. It is currently limited by the lack of individuals qualified to conduct this type of training. In addition, there are significant doubts about its long-term cost-effectiveness; research has questioned the transferability of learning from the workshop to the workplace.[12]

Transactional analysis focuses on improving communication by analyzing the nature of communication between two people.[13] In this model, the individual is considered to operate from one of three ego states: (1) the parent, who judges or tries to control others; (2) the adult, who acts rationally toward others; and (3) the child, who depends on others. Here, intervention calls for individuals to diagnose the basis of their communication and offer strategies for communicating between appropriate ego states—generally adult to adult. This approach reached a peak in popularity in the 1960s and early 1970s. Although transactional analysis can be useful, its view of communication and other interpersonal interactions as a highly structured "game" offers too limited an understanding of them.

Process consultation can also assist in evaluating and improving interpersonal interactions. It is "a set of activities on the part of the consultant which help the client to perceive, understand, and act upon process events which occur in the client's environment."[14] A process consultant gathers data about the effectiveness of individuals or groups, feeds back the data to the individuals involved, and then jointly develops strategies for improving communication, leadership, or decision-making. A manager or human resources professional can act as a process consultant after some training in its methodology. For example, Jessica Talley could ask a human resources professional at Lexington Travel to act as a process consultant if she perceives that interpersonal communications problems are the major cause of the sales group's ineffectiveness.

Building Collaborative Teams

Team-building activities can focus on the roles individuals play within a team, or on the integration of an entire group. Role analysis, job expectation, and role negotiation techniques attempt to clarify roles held by individuals within a team. Teamwork skill-building and Grid Organization Development aim to facilitate team integration and coordination.

In the *role analysis* technique, group members discuss the purpose of the pivotal role in the group, determine its prescribed and discretionary components, and examine its links to other roles.[15] For this last step, the role holder lists his or her expectations of others in the group, and the others list the role holder's obligations to them. Team members might analyze a project leader's role, such as that of the telephone sales manager at Lexington Travel, and then try to reach agreement about its major activities and their impact on the activities of other team members.

The *job expectation* technique follows a similar approach.[16] Individuals and management separately list their roles or job expectations. Discussion typically begins with the easiest role—for example, that of the most recently hired telephone sales agent—and ends with the leader's role. The group then negotiates until agreement is reached about the expectations held for each job.

The *role negotiation* technique focuses on role behavior, and includes four steps.[17] In the first—contract setting—individuals write down their expectations and demands of specific roles. The second step—diagnosis—calls for participants to analyze the performance of all the roles in the group and list what they would like others to do more, less, or the same; then they exchange lists for clarification. The third step—negotiation—requires pairs of individuals to negotiate behaviors to be changed. Each person agrees to change a behavior in return for a change in the other person's behavior. This continues until all parties are satisfied. The final step—follow-up—asks the group to live with its agreements and then meet again to review and renegotiate if necessary.

Teamwork skill-building brings work teams together to share information, set goals and priorities, examine the way the group is working, and analyze relationships among group members.[18] A range of activities, including management simulations, decision-making exercises, and diagnostic discussions, can be used at the meetings to develop the work groups into effectively functioning teams. Because of the wide variety of activities available in this type of intervention, it can be tailored to specific situations and currently has relatively high popularity.

Grid Organization Development is a more structured approach to team development.[19] This six-stage program moves individuals, work teams, and ultimately organizations to a high level of concern for both people's needs and production results. In the first phase, individuals assess their work styles and learn how to carry out the desired behaviors. In phase 2, focus shifts to the development of teamwork through identifying group norms and receiving feedback about interpersonal styles. Phase 3 emphasizes intergroup development by reducing win-lose behavior among groups. In phase 4 each group develops a strategic plan—a description of the ideal organization. Phase 5 involves implementation of the plan. In phase 6, participants critique the change to date and identify barriers that still exist to attaining a high concern for people and production. Because trained consultants must perform this intervention, its cost is relatively high and top management's commitment is essential.

To conduct the various types of team building interventions may require special expertise. Human resources professionals may be trained to implement them, or they may need to hire outside consultants to oversee the change process. Another possible drawback is that these interventions can lead to unexpected consequences: the role analysis, job expectation, and role negotiations techniques can sometimes result in scapegoating rather than improving teamwork. In addition, unless reinforced, teamwork skill-building often has only a short-term impact. And finally, Grid Organization Development requires a commitment to change throughout the organization; if only one group wants to improve its collaborative skills this approach is not effective.

Reducing Intergroup Conflict

Team-building interventions can be used to reduce conflict, but third-party interventions, confrontation meetings, and the organizational mirror are designed specifically to address intergroup conflict.

Third-party interventions can resolve interpersonal, intergroup, or interorganizational conflict. The third party synchronizes efforts to resolve confrontation, introduces incentives to improve intergroup interaction, builds support for openness in the organization, proposes new interaction styles that facilitate confrontation and collaboration, makes tension more productive, and helps to define issues clearly.[20] As discussed in Chapter 12, third parties frequently intervene in labor-management disputes. For the purpose of dealing with intergroup conflict, however, human resources professionals and managers as well as outside experts can act as third parties. Normally they must have appropriate training to fill this role.

A *confrontation meeting* resolves problems by generating and analyzing data about the interaction of two groups.[21] A top manager first introduces the issues and goals in dispute. Next, in randomly chosen small groups, participants collect information about organizational problems. Third, representatives from each small group report their list of problems to the rest of the groups. Fourth, participants convene with their usual work groups to set priorities for the problems and establish the first action steps. Fifth, a top management team meets to plan follow-up action. Finally, all the participants reconvene four to six weeks later to report progress. Like some interventions directed at improving teamwork, the confrontation meeting, if not properly conducted, can intensify rather than reduce the conflict.

The *organizational mirror* intervention also addresses intergroup ineffectiveness, through "a particular kind of meeting that allows an organizational unit to collect feedback from a number of key organizations to which it relates (e.g., customers, suppliers, users of services within the larger organization). The meeting closes with a list of specific tasks for improvement of operations, products, or services."[22] A consultant interviews members of all groups about the difficulty they have in interacting with the other groups. The consultant then reports the data from the interviews, after which the groups discuss the data openly. Finally, heterogeneous subgroups develop action plans for each problem.

Most typically, specially trained human resources professionals or outside consultants orchestrate the latter two types of intervention; managers can assist by recognizing situations that call for them.

Developing Organizational Effectiveness

Collateral organizations, survey feedback, and quality circles improve organizational effectiveness through encouraging worker participation in decision-making and innovative problem-solving.

Collateral organizations are supplementary organizations of employees from various departments and levels that coexist with the formal organization and focus specifically on solving difficult problems.[23] Typically, they emphasize innovation rather than output by using a relatively flat structure (few levels of authority) and low job specialization. The collateral organization provides people with new ways of working together. In a collateral organization, all information channels are open, allowing managers and nonmanagers to communicate directly. Members are encouraged to analyze and question assumptions, methods, alternatives, and goals, and any manager in the larger organization can request problem-solving assistance from the collateral organization.[24] Organizations facing a dynamic environment are increasingly using this intervention as an alternative to total redesign or restructuring. Human resources professionals at Lexington Travel might organize some telephone sales agents, managers, and other employees into a collateral organization to identify the department's problems and offer solutions to them.

Survey feedback polls employee attitudes and uses the responses to improve organizational effectiveness.[25] Survey feedback involves two steps. During the first stage—survey—a human resources professional or external consultant administers a questionnaire to determine employees' perceptions of the organization's management. During the second stage—feedback—the change agent (consultant) reports the results of the survey to those who completed the questionnaire. Feedback is provided in phases, beginning at the top of the organizational hierarchy and moving downward; each unit or team receives a summary of the results and discusses its significance with their group.[26] Unless managers act on the suggestions offered, however, surveys can do more harm than good because they create an expectation of change in the respondents. Still, this intervention remains popular because of the relative ease of its implementation and the large amounts of information it generates.

Quality circles also use group meetings to increase individual, group, and organizational productivity. Groups of five to twenty people meet weekly to offer suggestions for the improvement of the conduct of work. Often the group receives technical training that it uses for analysis and recommendations.[27] Quality circles recommend changes in procedures, interpersonal interactions, reporting relationships, or the jobs themselves. Though enthusiastically adopted by many organizations in the early 1980s, Japanese management techniques such as quality circles are no longer imported ''as is.'' Managers have found that they must modify such interventions to meet the unique needs of their situation.

REDESIGNING WORK

The nature of work itself can affect the quality of working life. That is, managers or human resources professionals can change the activities performed by a job holder to make the work more satisfying and productive. At Lexington Travel, for example, a needs assessment might suggest deficiencies that redesigning the telephone sales agents' jobs would address. If the agents find that they do not have the opportunity to complete a job the human resources professionals (or Jessica Talley) could restructure the tasks each agent performs by reducing the number of different activities. Or they might redesign the jobs to assign each agent more tasks to complete. In this section we examine four approaches to redesigning work: (1) work simplification, (2) job enrichment, (3) quality of work life programs, and (4) alternative work schedules.

Work Simplification

Work simplification breaks down a job into its component parts and then reassembles the parts into a more productive work process than before. Work simplification emphasizes (1) mechanical pacing of work, (2) repetitive work processes, such as those on an assembly line, (3) work on only one part of a product, (4) predetermining of tools and techniques, (5) restricted interaction among employees, and (6) few skill requirements.[28] Lexington Travel could institute work simplification for the telephone sales agents by having one agent make only plane reservations, another book only hotel reservations, and so on. Would this improve the situation at the agency? How does this type of job redesign influence quality of working life?

Work simplification influences productivity by giving individuals extensive experience in performing a small part of a larger task. Work simplification has the potential to help people feel more competent at their jobs, reduce feelings of work overload, and control the expenditure of effort. Often, however, work simplification leads to boredom and monotony. Any of these positive or negative consequences might result at Lexington Travel.

Job Enrichment

When jobs are overspecialized, workers experience boredom and there are no opportunities for personal growth. In this case, a more effective way to redesign a job is to *enrich* it. This means changing the job by giving individuals more responsibility and autonomy (vertical enrichment), more variety of tasks (horizontal enrichment), and more growth opportunities.[29] How might you enrich the job of the agents in Lexington Travel's telephone sales department? Proponents of job enrichment would suggest increasing the agents' responsibility, autonomy, and growth opportunities by giving them, for example, responsibility for booking all reservations needed for any tours in a given geographical area.

A more prescriptive form of job enrichment, the job characteristics model, focuses on changing core characteristics of a job to improve motivation, performance, satisfaction, absenteeism, and turnover.[30] The model specifies five core job dimensions (see Figure 14–1):

1. Skill variety—the degree to which a job requires performance of activities that challenge the worker's skills and abilities
2. Task identity—the degree to which a job requires completion of a whole and identifiable piece of work; that is, doing a job from beginning to end with a visible outcome

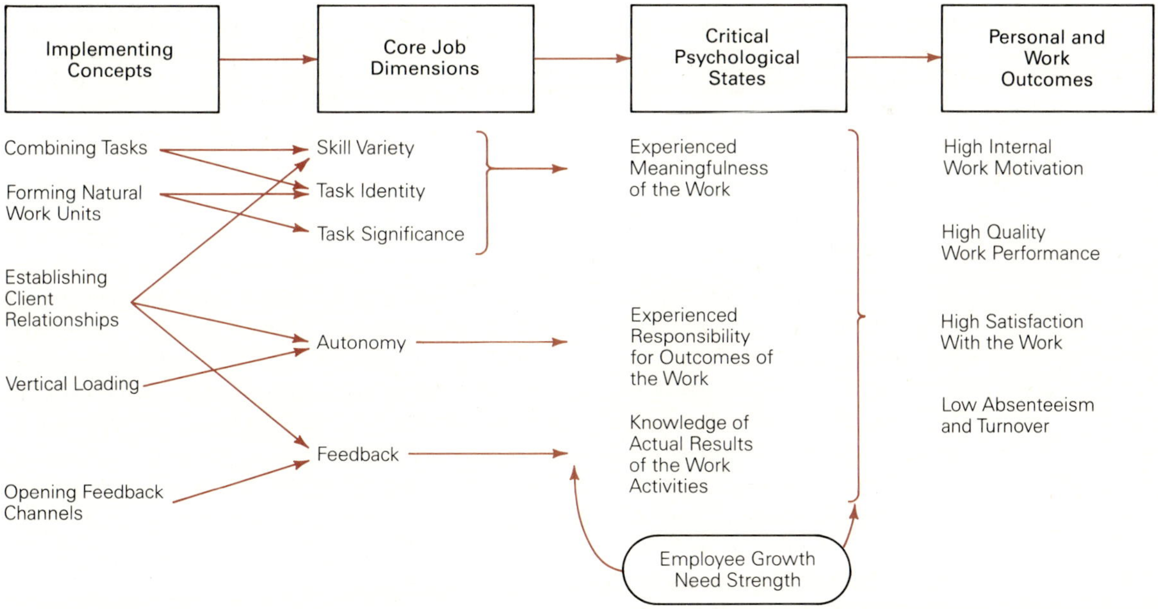

From J.R. Hackman et al., A new strategy for job enrichment. © 1975 by the Regents of the University of California. Reprinted from CALIFORNIA MANAGEMENT REVIEW, Volume XVII, no. 4, p. 58 by permission of the Regents.

Figure 14–1 JOB CHARACTERISTICS MODEL

3. Task significance—the degree to which a job has a substantial and perceivable impact on the lives of other people

4. Autonomy—the degree to which a job gives a worker freedom, independence, and discretion in scheduling work and determining how he or she will carry it out

5. Feedback—the degree to which a worker carrying out the activities required by a job gets information about the effectiveness of his or her efforts[31]

As shown in Figure 14–1, these core dimensions influence the degree to which an individual experiences a job as meaningful and responsible, and knows the results of his or her performance. To enrich a job means to improve it along one or more of the core dimensions. Combining tasks, forming natural work units, establishing client relationships, loading a job vertically to combine implementation and control, and opening feedback channels are all typically implemented. This approach to job enrichment has been tested in numerous work settings; and the results to date provide some, although inconsistent, support for the model. The problems seem to be in the methodology used to test the model and in its ability to accurately predict performance.[32]

How could a manager enrich the job of telephone sales agent? What would be the likely outcome of such enrichment? At Lexington Travel, Jessica Talley might consider organizing the agents into calling teams. One agent or team could handle all travel requests for a particular client group such as "swinging singles," young marrieds, or "young urban professionals." By having total responsibility for a particular type of client, task significance, task identity, and autonomy would increase. The agent would also receive feedback directly from the client and increase the skills used on the job.

Quality of Work Life Programs

Quality of work life programs focus on improving the internal work environment of an organization. They have become an important part of collective bargaining. Unions in the automobile industry, for example, have bargained for and won the introduction of such programs for their workers in many organizations and industries. This call for improved quality of work life (QWL) and programs that address it has occurred in spite of unions' suspicions that managers support it because they view it as a way to broaden their decision-making authority.[33] In many cases, however, workers and management have addressed QWL issues through the institution of joint labor-management committees.[34] These committees have focused on increasing workers' involvement in decision-making, improving working conditions, and establishing more autonomy and control over their work.

At General Motors approximately fifty QWL programs existed in 1980.[35] The success of these programs depended, first, on union and management developing a collective bargaining climate characterized by mutual respect; second, by conducting pilot programs that emphasized workers' involvement in problem-solving and decision-making, and finally, by joining together to solve problems in the workplace.[36] Reading 14-1, "The Quality-of-Worklife Project at Bolivar: An Assessment," by Barry Macy, describes one of the earliest QWL programs. Reading 14-2, "Helping Labor and Management Set Up a Quality-of-Worklife Program," by Michael Maccoby, describes a more recent effort.

Alternative Work Schedules

An employee's work schedule refers to the times during which work is performed. The most typical work schedule requires an employee to work thirty-five or forty hours a week, and divides the hours equally over Monday through Friday, generally between 8 A.M. and 6 P.M. Alternative work schedules are variations on this pattern. This type of job redesign addresses the context rather than the content of the work.

In a compressed work week, the number of days worked per week is reduced and the number of hours worked per day is increased. A worker might work four ten-hour days instead of five eight-hour days. The total number of hours worked per week remains the same, but the distribution of hours worked each day may vary.

A discretionary system, in contrast, allows a worker to decide which hours to work during the day. In a *flexitime system* (also called flextime), employees choose their own starting and stopping times within management's guidelines.[37] For example, a worker might work the required eight hours a day as follows: starting time, 7 A.M.; break, 11–11:30 A.M.; ending time, 3:30 P.M. Another worker might choose the following schedule for working the eight hours: starting time, 9 A.M.; break, 12–1:30; ending time, 6:30 P.M. Management often identifies a core time or times, such as 10 A.M. to 12:00 noon and 1 P.M. to 2 P.M., when workers are required to be present.

Four types of flexitime have been described:

1. Flexiform—workers pick a schedule and stick with it thereafter
2. Gliding time—workers' schedules vary from day to day but always equal eight hours
3. Variable day—workers' schedules vary daily, and the number of hours worked in a day may vary during the week, but hours must total a certain number by the end of a week or month
4. Maxiflex—employees vary their daily hours and have no required core time[38]

In part-time employment the number of hours worked per week is less than thirty-five or forty. One innovative type of part-time employment is job-sharing, where two workers hold a single job. Each works part-time and the two workers, not their supervisor, have the responsibility for coordinating activities so that all the work is accomplished.

Alternative schedules such as these provide workers with greater flexibility in their lives, which can ease family-work conflicts and even reduce traffic congestion. They also give individuals greater control over their work.[39] Flexitime seems to reduce unpaid absences and increase performance efficiency,[40] but some organizations still lack the ability or willingness to offer it. In some cases, either the organization's tasks or its employees do not have characteristics that respond well to this type of change.

Human resources professionals who design or monitor such programs must eliminate the typical causes of failure: lack of involvement of supervisors and workers in planning alternatives; supervisors' fear of loss of control over workers; introduction of schedules that are not appropriate to workers' needs; employees' failure to meet deadlines or record hours worked; and rigidity of managers.[41] Properly instituted, however, both the flexibility and autonomy encouraged by such programs can contribute to improved quality of working life. Should Lexington Travel introduce alternative work schedules? Would this change address the problems in the telephone sales group?

RESTRUCTURING ORGANIZATIONS

A third type of intervention changes the formal reporting relationships in an organization rather than redesigning the work or changing individual behavior. A needs assessment usually turns up the advisability of such a change. Organizational redesign can improve an enterprise that fails to innovate, produces at low levels, produces redundant work, communicates ineffectively, requires extensive red tape to accomplish goals, uses workers' skills ineffectively, or fails to respond to a changing environment. Rapid technological changes, the higher educational level of workers, and multi-nationalization of companies have all combined to call for structural change to allow for more rapid, appropriate, and flexible functioning. Changes in an organization's strategy (described in Chapters 2 and 15) can also necessitate changes in its structure.[42]

Structural Options

Although organization structure has been described in a variety of ways, in this section we classify it into one of three categories: (1) functional, (2) product/project, and (3) matrix.

Functional. The functional structure groups employees according to their specialty. Manufacturing firms that adopt a functional structure generally assign personnel to a manufacturing, research and development, marketing, finance, or personnel department or division. Within this type of structure finance staff members work only with other finance personnel, marketing with marketing, and so forth.

Reporting relationships are vertical, with clear lines of authority specified and

Product or project management appears to be effective at allowing organizations to focus on problems unique to a particular product or client, responding quickly to changes in the project, product, or client, and encouraging personnel with different expertise and professional loyalty to focus on a common goal. But some firms are reluctant to move to this more flexible structure. Project management can reduce economies of scale and thus increase costs. Often, there are duplicate positions (such as market researcher or systems analyst) on several project teams, and the job holders consequently perform the same tasks or generate the same information independently rather than consolidating activities and resources and sharing information. Furthermore, some managers fear the decreased control and authority that they perceive accompanies this structure.

Matrix. The matrix structure combines the benefits of functional and product/project structures. It consists of temporary, multidisciplinary teams composed of members from both project and functional units.[44] By adopting a matrix structure an organization opts for neither a functional nor project/product configuration; rather, it chooses both. Employees report to at least two superiors—one in the functional division and one in a project group. Thus they are evaluated by both members of the functional division and members of the project. Figure 14–4 shows a possible matrix structure for Lexington Travel.

A matrix structure responds to an organization's need for great flexibility. It is particularly effective for enterprises facing very dynamic, complex, uncertain environments. It reinforces professional identity and development, as in the functional structure, while simultaneously encouraging flexibility and lateral communication, as in the project structure. It facilitates the development and effective utilization of employees, encourages specialization, and can lead to innovation.[45] However, the matrix structure can lead to conflict between functional and project responsibilities, ambiguity in reporting relationships, and high overhead costs because of the additional management required as well.[46]

Contingencies Influencing Organizational Design

How should Lexington Travel go about choosing the best design? Effective structure depends on the environment, technology, work force, goals, age, and size of an organization. Some general precepts for designing responsive organizations are as follows:

1. A dynamic, unpredictable environment requires an organic structure, such as a product or matrix design; a stable, predictable environment requires a more bureaucratic (typically functional) structure; a complex environment calls for decentralized decision-making; a simple or hostile environment calls for centralized decision-making.[47]
2. An organization's technology using machines and equipment to control the employee's work calls for a bureaucratic (typically functional) structure, whereas a technology that relies on knowledge (such as in service organizations) fits best with a project or matrix structure.[48]

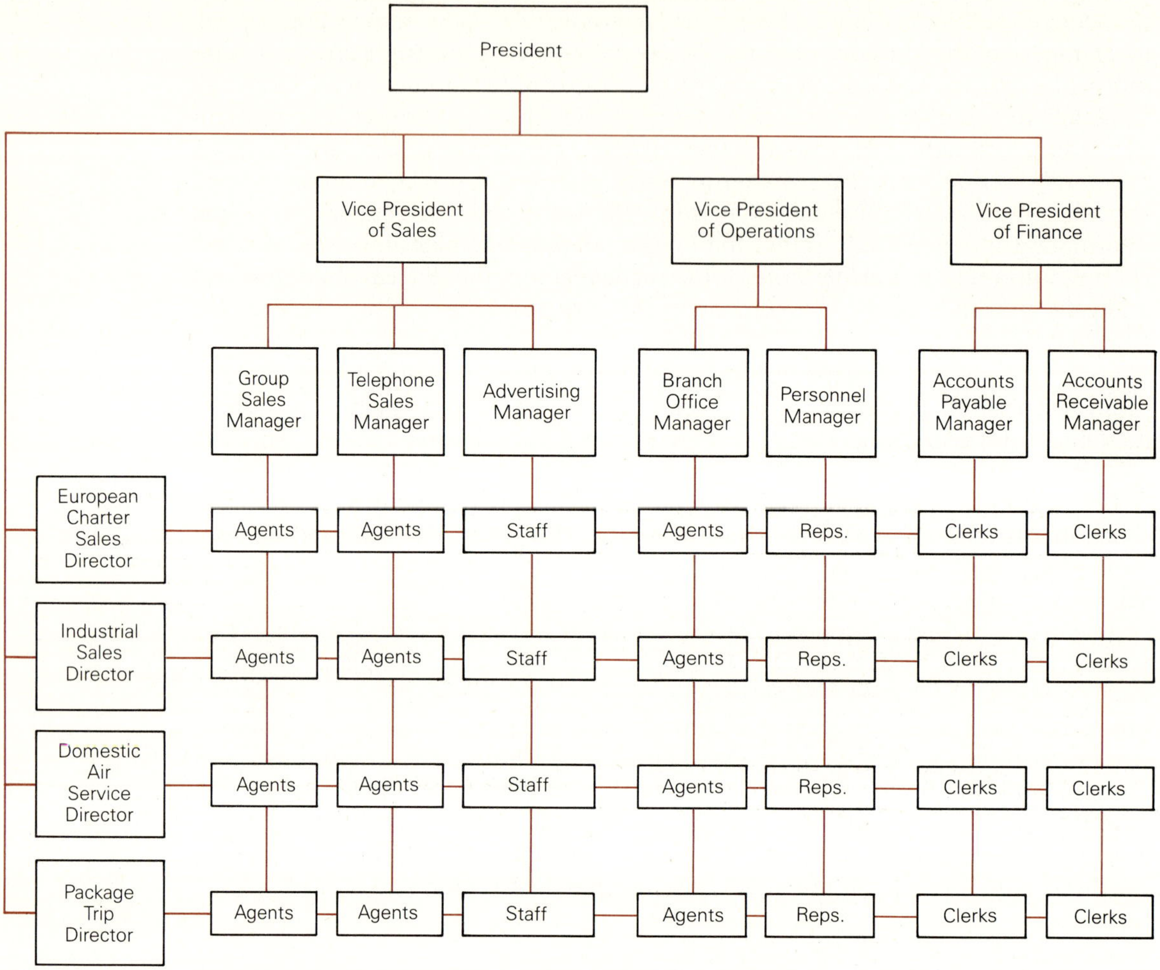

Figure 14–4 LEXINGTON TRAVEL WITH A MATRIX STRUCTURE

3. A sophisticated, complex, and intricate technology needs more support staff with special expertise and structures that emphasize lateral communication between groups.[49]

4. The more professional the work force, the more the organizational structure must build in opportunities for the professionals to interact.

5. As an organization increases in size or age, it typically becomes more specialized and bureaucratic[50]; thus human resources professionals and top management must ensure that these characteristics continue to fit the other contingencies.

6. Parts of an organization that have different goals should be separated and possibly have different structures.

Steps in Redesigning an Organization

In addition to determining the general structural configuration that fits best with the contingencies, redesign of an organization should follow these principles:

1. Group jobs together homogeneously, in a way that focuses on the organization's goals or specialized expertise.
2. When a group becomes too large, break it down into two or more groups.
3. Develop ways of integrating different groups through the hierarchy, task forces, linking roles, or project teams.
4. Make sure that groupings respond to the particular environment, technology, and work force.
5. Make sure that larger and older organizations are not too formal or rigid.
6. Expedite the collection and analysis of information for decision-making, where appropriate, through the creation of slack resources (extra people or financial resources), self-contained tasks (tasks performed from beginning to end by one person), and lateral relations (use of task forces, project teams, and the like); and investment in computers.[51]

LESSONS FROM HUMAN RESOURCES MANAGEMENT ABROAD

In addition to the organization development, work redesign, and organization redesign interventions described above, human resources professionals and managers have introduced two approaches to management from outside the United States: worker ownership and Japanese management.

Worker Ownership

In West Germany, the Scandinavian countries, and elsewhere managers have heavily involved workers in the operation and decision-making of their organizations. Worker cooperatives, such as the Mondragon Cooperatives in Spain, where workers own and manage the member organizations, have increasingly served as a model for employee ownership of steel, plywood, and meat-packing companies in the United States.[52] Cooperatives offer workers the opportunity to exert significant control over their organization's direction and operation. For example, at Mondragon, the board of directors consists only of members elected from among the workers—a secretary, bank teller, mechanic, plant foreman, and middle manager might sit on the board at any given time.[53] In Yugoslavia, such cooperatives are seen as the most appropriate and efficient way to use resources to achieve societal goals.

Instead of worker ownership, some countries have mandated worker representation on their organizations' boards of directors. Known as *codetermination,* this type of management gives worker representatives voting privileges on the board, but otherwise the precise nature of participation and number of representatives differ from country to country.[54] Germany, for example, extended in 1976 the earlier Works Constitution Act to require all companies with more than 2000 employees to elect an equal number of worker-directors and stockholder-directors. Here, stockholders select the chairperson of the board, who can cast a double vote in the event of a tie, and thus retain control of the company. Since 1976, Swedish companies with more than 25 employees have been required to include two worker-directors on their boards; likewise, in Austrian companies with more than 300 employees, workers elect one-third of the board. This type of representation clearly increases workers' participation in managing their organizations, but a recent trend toward including union representatives—often nonemployees—instead of worker representatives on the boards may dilute the impact of workers' participation in the future.[55]

The quality-of-worklife programs described in the text and readings in this chapter borrow from worker participation ideas instituted as part of job enrichment efforts at Saab and Volvo in the 1970s.[56] In both companies, groups of workers have responsibility for assembling a particular part of a car or truck. The specific activities of each assembler are determined through negotiations with the rest of the group and can vary daily. Should Lexington Travel consider worker ownership or codetermination? The former approach might increase worker commitment and productivity, but worker ownership is normally used only as a last-resort solution to very serious problems; the owners of Lexington Travel are unlikely to sell the company to the workers. Similarly, because Lexington Travel is a family-owned company, codetermination is unlikely to be acceptable.

Japanese Management

In the early 1980s, the philosophy of management typical throughout Japan exerted a major influence on human resources management in the United States. Most Japanese companies consider their employees to be the firm's most important and profitable assets in the long run.[57] Thus Japanese companies offer the following employment conditions to their workers:

1. Long-term and secure employment
2. Emphasis on a concern for employee needs and teamwork
3. Hiring workers who will fit into the company
4. Continuous development of employees' skills
5. Multiple criteria used for evaluation
6. Open communication about and worker participation in decision-making[58]

By contrast, approaches to management in the United States are typically characterized by (1) short-term employment, (2) individual decision-making, (3) individual responsibility, (4) rapid evaluation and promotion, (5) explicit, formalized control, (6) specialized career paths, and (7) segmented views of family and work life.[59]

Theory Z management represents an attempt to integrate the most effective of both the United States and Japanese practices. The following characteristics describe Theory Z management: (1) long-term employment, (2) consensual decision-making, (3) individual responsibility, (4) less frequent evaluation and promotion, (5) implicit, informal control with explicit, formalized standards and procedures, (6) moderately specialized career paths, and (7) holistic concern for employees' lives, including family relationships.[60] As shown by an early 1980s study of top-performing U.S. companies, management that incorporates most or all of these principles can indeed increase an organization's effectiveness.[61]

THE PROCESS OF CHANGE

Identifying and Overcoming Resistance to Change

The success of an intervention to improve organizational effectiveness depends first on its fit with needs identified during a diagnostic needs assessment. Success also relates to the willingness of the organization and its members to change. Resistance to change arises for numerous reasons. Individuals may distrust the managers, human resources professionals, or outside consultants who design and implement the change. They may fear the change itself, or want to maintain power that the change might reduce. Workers might show resistance to making adjustments because they lack the resources to support change, disagree with organizational goals, or are simply apathetic.

Resistance often arises when (1) the change ignores the needs, attitudes, and beliefs of organizational members; (2) individuals lack specific information about the change; (3) individuals do not perceive a need for change; (4) organizational members have a "we-they" attitude leading them to view the change agent as an enemy; (5) members view change as a threat to the prestige and security of their supervisor; (6) change is neither voluntary nor requested by organizational members; and (7) employees perceive threats to their expertise, status, or security.

How can human resources professionals or managers overcome resistance to change? Strategies include educating those affected, involving them in the change process, introducing change relatively slowly, and assuring employees that their jobs are secure. The change agent—manager or human resources professional—chosen to implement the change can also help overcome resistance.

Selecting a Change Agent

Managers, human resources professionals, and outside consultants can all act as change agents. When managers are the change agents they have the advantage of knowledge of and experience with a particular situation; but they may lack objectivity. Human resources professionals, in contrast, may be trained in intervention techniques or skills, and may bring greater objectivity to the situation, but workers may see them as surrogates for top management and resist or fear their change efforts. External consultants generally offer the greatest knowledge of and experience with intervention strategies, but may lack critical information

	Managers	Human Resources Professionals	External Consultants
Advantages	possess best knowledge of the situation are readily available require low out-of-pocket costs are a known quantity	possess best knowledge of both the situation and change strategies are readily available require low out-of-pocket costs	possess best knowledge of change strategies have more objective views of the situation have more experience dealing with diverse problems
Disadvantages	may be too close to the problem may hold biased views may better spend time in other ways may create resistance if viewed as part of the problem may lack expertise as change agents	may be perceived as representatives of top management may lack knowledge of the situation may hold biased views may lack expertise as change agents	may lack knowledge of the organization require higher out-of-pocket costs are an unknown quantity require longer start-up time

Table 14–2 ADVANTAGES AND DISADVANTAGES OF THE THREE TYPES OF CHANGE AGENTS

about the organization's operations. Table 14–2 summarizes the advantages and disadvantages of each of these change agents.

Managers should be involved in any changes they have the expertise to implement, any that directly influence their work group, and any that are tied to their objectives. Human resources professionals can act as resources for managers, but they can also implement interventions themselves, particularly those that are comprehensive, require expertise that they alone have, or that form the basis of human resources policy formulation. Consultants should be called upon when they have unique expertise and when there is enough money available to pay them.

In selecting a change agent, the organization must consider the purpose of the change, the type of help needed to effect it, the type of help available within the organization, who has the expertise, the constraints on the change, and the pluses and minuses of the various potential change agents.

STRATEGIES FOR ORGANIZATIONAL CHANGE

Human resources professionals and managers should be actively involved in diagnosing the need for change, selecting the appropriate option, and implementing the change. But effective change efforts should also include an evaluation of the benefits obtained. Such evaluation can parallel that described in Chapter 7 for assessing training outcomes. Human resources professionals, managers, or outside consultants can perform the necessary evaluations using a variety of assessment techniques.

Implications for Human Resources Professionals

Human resources professionals can design, implement, or oversee change efforts in the following ways:

1. Human resources professionals should act as resources in diagnosing the need for change and in selecting the intervention strategies.
2. They should monitor change programs in other organizations and recommend those that can be adapted for implementation in their own organizations.
3. Human resources professionals should identify appropriate organization development interventions for changing behaviors and attitudes in their organization. They should then select the appropriate change agent for implementing the intervention and assist in overcoming resistance to change.
4. Human resources professionals should regularly analyze the design of jobs in the organization. They should propose job enrichment, work simplification, QWL, or alternative work schedule programs wherever appropriate.
5. They should audit the organization's environment, technology, work force, and goals to track changes that call for consequent modification of the organization's structure. Together with top management, they can propose new structures that respond better to these contingencies.

Implications for Managers

Managers typically provide data for diagnosing the type of intervention needed or participate with other workers in implementing the change. Effective change efforts include the following actions:

1. Managers should regularly diagnose the quality of working life and organizational productivity of their subordinates. Where there are problems or deficiencies, they should collaborate with top management or human resources professionals to introduce or implement new human resources practices.
2. They should participate in behavioral interventions that will improve the quality of work life or employee performance.
3. Managers should regularly analyze the design of their subordinates' jobs. They should propose and implement job enrichment, work simplification, or alternative work schedule programs wherever appropriate.
4. They should alert top management or human resources professionals where structural problems limit their own or subordinates' performance. If they have enough knowledge of organizational redesign, they might also propose new structures.
5. Managers should help reduce resistance to change among their subordinates by rewarding innovative performance, educating them about the advantages of potential changes, and resolving power conflicts.

READINGS

Reading 14–1

THE QUALITY-OF-WORKLIFE PROJECT AT BOLIVAR: AN ASSESSMENT

Barry A. Macy

The quality-of-worklife project[1] at Harman International Industries, Inc., in Bolivar, Tennessee, is a cooperative change effort between the company and the United Automobile Workers of America (UAW). The project is structured so that both parties can jointly determine and implement organizational change according to mutually agreed-upon principles. The objectives of the project are to improve employees' quality of worklife and enhance organizational effectiveness.

The explicit internal goals were identified as job security, job equity, worker humanization, and worker democracy. These were ambitious undertakings in 1973—ahead of their times in many respects—particularly because they were shared and agreed to by both labor and management. However, some of the objectives of the project have been reached and surpassed, while others have yet to be reached. Other outcomes and critical process events are discussed in an assessment study by Macy and others.[2]

According to the five intervention phases of the Bolivar experiment, each composed of 11 months beginning with the baseline phase through plant-wide experimentation to coincide with the change program, the following changes were measured:

Job Security. More jobs were created, as the hourly employment level rose 55 percent to 839. Once the program was underway, the cooperative union-management climate stimulated an effort to develop a joint bid on a particular product, and the company and the UAW established joint efficiency rates with the goals of increasing employees' quality of worklife and improving job security. Ultimately, this venture saved 70 jobs. Voluntary turnover rates declined by 72 percent, while involuntary turnover (discharges, retirements, and so forth) rates decreased by 95 percent.

Health and Working Conditions. Accident rates, as defined by the Occupational Safety and Health Administration, declined 60 percent, while minor accidents decreased 20 percent even with the presence of many new and inexperienced employees. Rates of short-term absences due to sickness declined 16 percent. However, not all of the changes were favorable, as the rate of minor illnesses rose 71 percent and the rate of medical leaves increased 19 percent. (Perceptions of Bolivar employees' health appear later in this report.)

Financial Security. The average hourly rate remained constant and the wage rates relative to area standards did not change (during this time, the wage rates for the whole country did not increase relative to real wages). The fringe benefit package increased by a small amount. Proposals for the introduction of a gain-sharing compensation plan (a negotiable issue) were discussed but none was adopted.

Job Security Based on Organizational Performance. Daily output per hourly-paid employee, adjusted for inflation, rose 23 percent. Two other measures of productivity—efficiency and standard performance—verify this positive change in plant performance. On the product side of the financial ledger, net product reject cost rates declined 39 percent, while the rate of customer returns decreased by 47 percent. Once again, not all was positive as the rate of manufacturing supplies used rose 22 percent and the rate of machine downtime increased slightly. What is so striking about productivity and product quality at the Harman International plant is the fact that both of these performance measures increased. Moreover, these measures have held positive and significant

Reprinted from *Monthly Labor Review* 103 (July 1980), by Dr. Barry A. Macy, Director, Texas Center for Productivity and Quality of Work Life and Associate Professor, Management Area, College of Business Administration, Texas Tech University, P.O. Box 4230, Lubbock, Texas 79409.

trends for approximately 3 years. Some of the gains are attributable to technological and capital inputs; however, many can be attributed to the cooperative labor-management change.

Cost-benefit. The cost-benefit calculations for the project reflect the program costs and benefits per hourly-paid employee per phase, summed over 55 months. The results show a net discounted benefit per hourly-paid employee to the company of more than $3,000. There are multiple reasons for this net savings, but nevertheless, the plant improved its performance through a combination of forces, including the cooperative quality-of-worklife program.

In summary, the evidence shows that because of the quality-of-worklife program, jobs objectively became more secure; productivity and product quality rose; accidents decreased at a faster rate than their industry average; minor accidents declined while minor illnesses rose; short-term absences due to sickness declined; manufacturing supplies and machine downtime increased; and employee earnings held steady. Also, grievances decreased 51 percent and absences due to lack of work decreased 94 percent.

These positive behavioral and organizational performance gains seem to have had some practical implications for both the company and the union in their contractual process. The company's 1976 contract with the UAW was signed earlier than ever before and benefited both the company and the union membership by reducing the need for higher product inventories while maintaining the same employment level. These bargaining sessions, as contrasted to previous ones, were accomplished and concluded in a mutual atmosphere of cordiality, creativity, and trust. Absent was the win-lose philosophy and counterthreats that often accompany traditional labor-management bargaining. This is not to indicate that the adversary relationship between the UAW and Harman International Industries has vanished. It has not! The union still grieves contract issues; however, the spirit or climate in which grievances are handled has improved.

Generally, the behavioral and performance findings were positive, while the attitudinal indicators showed mixed results. Thirteen indicators of the quality of worklife and 24 measures of job and work environment characteristics known to be associated with higher quality of worklife are assessed in Table 14–3. (The data refer only to UAW members; however, these indicators represent fairly well the different types of employees surveyed at the Bolivar plant.) Some of the gains have been offset by losses or no change. It must be remembered, however, that over the extended period studied, there were some unmeasured changes in the employees' level of aspirations and expectations. These changes in expectations and aspirations were enhanced by the quality-of-worklife program and the later conditions were probably judged more critically than the earlier conditions. When asked a series of questions pertaining to the goals and outcomes of the quality-of-worklife program, the employees responded generally with positive opinions about the impact, the desirability of the program, the effectiveness of the union-management relationships, and the ability of the UAW to represent membership concerns. For example, 60 percent found the program to be desirable; a majority found the joint union-management committee responsible for designing and implementing the program to be effective without domination from either party; and 67 percent indicated that the program strengthened the local union. In addition, 90 percent of the UAW membership were satisfied with the local union in 1976, compared with 78 percent in 1973. This is substantially higher than the satisfaction level of a national sample of blue-collar union members with their union during this period.[3] Moreover, union membership at the Bolivar plant has increased from 65 percent to more than 90 percent, and 100 percent of the union membership responded affirmatively when asked: "If there were an election today on whether or not the union should be kept at Harman International Industries, how would you vote?"

These results and other outcomes not reported here[4] seem to indicate that the union members prefer to use joint union-management programs to deal with quality of worklife and other important domains of their life at work. Recently, many other reports and studies[5] have indicated similar trends and like results with other union members. One trend seems very clear. The time is ripe for the U.S. industrial relations system to seriously consider cooperative union-management programs along with their traditional contractual and collective bargaining structures and processes.

Gains	No change	Losses
	Quality of Worklife	
Less alienation	Job satisfaction	More reports of physical stress symptoms
Treated in a more personal way	Job offers opportunity for personal growth	More reports of psychological stress symptoms
Job involved more use of, or higher level, skills	Working conditions	Less satisfaction with pay level
	Work equity	
Job is more secure	Fringe benefits	Less satisfaction with pay equity
	Work Environment	
Supervisors more participative	Role conflict	Supervisors are less work-facilitating, supportive, and respectful
	Job variety	
More work-group participation	Supervisory closeness, favoritism, and feedback	
More employee influence over task-related decisions	Work-group feedback	Less satisfaction with work group
More adequate work resources	Employee influence over work-schedule decisions	Less association between work performance and reward received (3 indicators)
More work improvement ideas provided by employees	Association between job security and intrinsic motivation with work performance	Less job feedback
	General organizational climate	
	Work improvement suggestions	

Note: Assessment based on 85 matched UAW members.

Table 14–3 ASSESSMENT OF QUALITY-OF-WORKLIFE INDICATORS AND WORK ENVIRONMENT CHARACTERISTICS

FOOTNOTES

[1]The project was independently assessed during 1972–79. The behavioral and performance outcomes were evaluated for 55 consecutive months during 1972–76. Support for this article was provided by the Ford Foundation and the Economic Development Administration, U.S. Department of Commerce.

[2]B.A. Macy, G.E. Ledford, Jr., and E.E. Lawler III, *An Assessment of the Bolivar Quality of Work Life Experiment: 1972–1979* (New York, Wiley-Interscience, forthcoming).

[3]R.P. Quinn and G.L. Staines, *The 1977 Quality of Employment Survey* (Ann Arbor, University of Michigan, Survey Research Center, 1978). A general discussion of the survey results is described in an article by G.L. Staines and R.P. Quinn, "American workers evaluate the quality of their jobs," *Monthly Labor Review,* January 1979, pp. 3–12. For a more in-depth discussion of union attitudes, see T.A. Kochan, "How American workers view labor unions," *Monthly Labor Review,* April 1979, pp. 23–31.

[4]See Macy et al., *An Assessment.*

[5]For example, see T.A. Kochan, D. Lipsky, and L.

Dyer, "Collective Bargaining and the Quality of Work—the Views of Local Union Activists," *Proceedings of the Twenty-Seventh Annual Meeting* (Madison, Wis., Industrial Relations Research Association, 1975), pp. 150–62; A. Ponak and C. Fraser, "Union Activists' Support for Joint Programs," *Industrial Relations,* Spring 1979, pp. 197–209; B.A. Macy, "A Progress Report on the Bolivar Quality of Work Life Project," *Personnel,* August 1979, pp. 527–30 and 557–59; P.S. Goodman and E.E. Lawler III, *New Forms of Work Organization in the United States* (Geneva, Switzerland, International Labor Organization, 1977); J. Drexler and E.E. Lawler III, "A Union-Management Cooperative Project to Improve the Quality of Work Life," *The Journal of Applied Behavioral Science* (July-August-September, 1977), pp. 351–86; I. Bluestone, "The Quality of Work Life Project Between UAW and Harman International Industries," paper presented at the Thirty-Seventh Annual Meeting, The Academy of Management, Aug. 14–18, 1977; E.E. Lawler III and L. Ozley, "Winning Union-Management Cooperation," *Management Review* (March 1979), pp. 19–24; E.E. Lawler III, and J. Drexler, "The dynamics of establishing cooperative quality-of-worklife projects," *Monthly Labor Review,* March 1978, pp. 23–28; D. Nadler, "Hospitals, Organized Labor and Quality of Work: An Intervention Case Study," *The Journal of Applied Behavioral Science* (September 1978), pp. 366–81; J. Perry and others, *The Impact of Labor-Management Relations on Productivity and Efficiency in Urban Mass Transit* (Institute of Transportation Studies and Graduate School of Administration, University of California at Irvine, 1979); B.A. Macy and M. Peterson, "Evaluating Attitudinal Change in a Longitudinal Quality of Work Life Intervention," in S. Seashore, E. Lawler III, and others, eds., *Observing and Measuring Organizational Change: A Guide to Field Practice* (New York, Wiley-Interscience, forthcoming); P.S. Goodman, *Assessing Organizational Change: The Rushton Quality of Work Experiment* (New York, Wiley-Interscience, 1979); B.A. Macy and A. Nurick, *Assessing Organizational Change and Participation: The TVA Quality of Work Experiment* (New York, Wiley-Interscience, forthcoming); and M. Duckles, R. Duckles, and M. Maccoby, "The Process of Change at Bolivar," *The Journal of Applied Behavioral Science* (July-August-September, 1977), pp. 387–99.

DISCUSSION QUESTIONS

1. Describe the quality-of-worklife project at Harman International Industries.
2. What goals did the project have?
3. What impact did the project have?
4. How could the project be adapted to other organizations?
5. What role did managers and human resources professionals play in this QWL project? Were they effective?

Reading 14–2

HELPING LABOR AND MANAGEMENT SET UP A QUALITY-OF-WORKLIFE PROGRAM

Michael Maccoby

Editor's Note: During the past 3 years, the American Telephone and Telegraph Co. (AT&T) and the Communications Workers of America have cooperated in a quality-of-worklife program unique in scope and intensity. The program is based on a memorandum of agreement covering half a million workers in 21 Bell System companies, including operating telephone companies, Western Electric, and Bell Laboratories. About 40,000 Bell System employees have participated in the program, which survived a 1983 strike and in which the parties agreed to continue after divestiture of AT&T. A subsequent survey indicated that more than 80 percent of the employees would volunteer to participate in the program.

Reprinted from *Monthly Labor Review* 107 (1984):28–32.

My involvement in this project began in 1977 when the management of American Telephone and Telegraph Co. invited me to lecture on quality-of-worklife programs at a corporate policy seminar. I was asked to talk about the Bolivar project, a quality-of-worklife experiment in an auto parts factory in Tennessee, which was the first successful American union-management experiment to improve the quality of working life.[1]

However, most Bell System managers were not interested in the Bolivar experiment. They wanted to hear about my studies of managerial character.[2] As company men/craftsmen, they felt threatened by the gamesmen-marketeers newly recruited to the company, and wanted advice on how to deal with them. However, a few recognized that the traditional Bell System managerial character was too cautious and inflexible for a fast-arriving competitive market.

Among the latter was Rex Reed, Bell System's vice president of industrial relations. He saw the quality-of-worklife experiment at Bolivar and at the GM assembly plant in Tarrytown, N.Y., as promising models for the Bell System. He had surveyed Bell employees over a 5-year period and found disturbing trends. Although satisfied with pay and benefits and motivated to work productively, both workers and supervisors were dissatisfied with technology and perceived too much supervisory control. They believed they were mismanaged, pushed around, not listened to, and that the spirit of service was being eroded by the drive to increase profit.

PERSUADING MANAGERS

In January 1978, Reed met with Bell System regional presidents to present new approaches to raising morale and improving service. He cited examples from Ohio and Pacific Northwest Bell, and asked me to describe how employee involvement had increased both satisfaction and productivity in other companies.

I stressed to the Bell presidents the importance of cooperation with the union. Those present agreed they should moderate the rigid bureaucratic system, but there was no consensus about how to do so. Their concern at this point, before competition and divestiture had forced a new outlook on management, was as much humane as economic. They mentioned their own work history, how some had started as linesmen or clerks and had moved up with the help of friends. "Working for the Bell System has been more than making a buck," one said. "We have the obligation to make it a good place to work for others. Everyone should feel important, respected, needed."

This meeting, together with support from Charles L. Brown, the Bell System's new chief executive officer, reinforced experimentation in participative management in some of the Bell companies, but most of the experiments were without union involvement. In fact, some middle managers reacted with anger at the idea of cooperating with the union.

Relations between Communications Workers of America (CWA) and AT&T had been stormy in some companies and always complex. Strikes had caused violence and bitter feelings in certain areas. The processing of grievances had become a sizable business. Although relationships at the top, between AT&T vice president of industrial relations Rex Reed and CWA President Glenn Watts, were cordial and respectful, at lower levels there was considerable distrust.

As in many American companies, management tended to view the union as a symptom of failure to create a good workplace. Bell System managers were proud of their achievement—building a great company, providing effective universal service, and creating new technology. In the view of executives, management was identified with science and productivity, while the union represented unproductive politics. This sense of superiority seemed to divide union and management, obscure shared values, and impeded productive cooperation.

In the spring of 1978, Robert Gaynor, vice president of Long Lines in Kansas City, began a change project with his managers. Gaynor was a leader in shifting AT&T to a more market-oriented business. He believed this could not be achieved by decree, that managers had to analyze the new competitive demands together, combine knowledge, and agree on goals. Through interviews with their peers, a research team of managers defined problem areas, including the need for innovative leadership; the need to maintain a spirit of service; the need to make measurements and control systems more flexible; and the need to improve the planning process which, like most large companies at that time, was mainly a matter of extrapolation.

Most managers believed change was essential, but were concerned that AT&T's positive values—caring about people, the spirit of service, high standards and integrity, and technical excellence—be preserved. How to begin this process of change became the subject for task forces, and I was asked to help create more open and participative management, starting with Gaynor's team. By January 1980, we had improved management teamwork and addressed interdepartmental problems, but the process had not reached the worker level and did not include the union.

CWA BECOMES INTERESTED

In January 1980, Ronnie J. Straw, director of research at CWA, asked if I was interested in studying the various forms of union participation in management, with recommendation for the union on how it should approach AT&T. The CWA was interested in a range of possibilities, from membership on the board to shop floor participation. Was I interested?

Very much so. The CWA was an exceptionally forward-looking union. Its members were affected by changing technology and were asking the leadership to do something about job stress. The union had a good research department and creative leadership. I believed that a strong informed CWA would both further the interests of its members and put pressure on the Bell System to improve its management, and that both union and management would benefit from the project I was being asked to undertake.

But there was a problem: I had been an AT&T consultant. CWA President Watts would have to decide whether this made a difference. Also, I would not take the job unless it was approved by Rex Reed. There were two reasons for this: first, I would be bringing knowledge of Bell System management to the union; and second, I wanted to keep alive the chance to work with both.

Watts liked the idea that I was familiar with the Bell System; it would save time. Furthermore, John Carroll, CWA executive vice president, had attended the AT&T corporate policy seminar at which I urged management to cooperate with the union. Reed had no objections. In fact, he agreed that a stronger, more knowledgeable union would push management to improve, while a weaker, more reactive union would be less able to understand and support change.

To develop a strategy for CWA, I proposed that Straw and I together interview CWA leadership on its views of what changes were needed. Previous recommendations to the union had not been acted on, largely because those who had to make use of the findings were not involved in the study process. All proposals for change are a likely threat to those who are adapted to the status quo. I wanted CWA to own the study and the strategy, which meant that it had to participate from the start.

Straw and I, assisted by others, interviewed the union executive board and more than 100 local officers from all over the country. We asked AT&T for examples of participative management projects, and asked the local union leaders for comments.

A consensus emerged: the union leaders believed that in recent years, management had tightened to prepare for deregulated competition; workers believed they could give better service if there was less monitoring, both technological and supervisory.

The union noted a number of attempts to improve morale through increased participation, but they were often short-lived. A few of the attempts tried to involve the union, and some had become the cause of grievances, as "participation" resulted in actions considered in violation of the contract. (An example was one which encouraged employees to criticize those who were less productive.)

The local presidents we interviewed did not favor participation on the board and were skeptical of joint

---

DEFINING QUALITY OF WORKLIFE

Quality of worklife grew out of the collective bargaining process. It is a commitment of management and union to support localized activities and experiments to increase employee participation in determining how to improve work. This process is guided by union-management committees and facilitators, and requires education about the goals of work and training in group process.

In the Bell company and AT&T, I see quality of worklife as a means to move from the bureaucratic-industrial model of scientific management with its fragmentation of jobs and hierarchical control, to a flexible, broadly skilled, participative team. This is a more effective way of managing market-driven technoservice work while protecting the rights and dignity of employees.

The new automated workplace requires decentralization, responsiveness to customers, and ability of workers to solve problems where they occur without waiting for hierarchical approval. Quality of worklife develops the flexibility essential for effectiveness and at the same time strengthens the union.—MM

---

committees which in the past had done little. They liked the idea of a quality-of-worklife program in offices and garages, based on the Bolivar or Tarrytown models. In fact, the most enthusiastic union leaders were those currently taking part in joint initiatives of this sort.

JOINT COMMITTEE DEVELOPED

When I reported these findings to the union executive board in July 1980, Watts asked me to draft an article for the contracts he was then negotiating with Reed. I recommended joint sponsorship of participative experiments, including a National Committee on Joint Working Conditions and Service Quality Improvements with the following function:

1. Developing and recommending principles and objectives relative to working conditions and service quality improvement which will guide experiments or projects such as quality circles, problem-solving teams, and the like, in various work situations. These should be designed to encourage teamwork, to make work more satisfying, and to improve the work operation.
2. Reviewing and evaluating programs and projects which involve improving the quality of the work environment.
3. Arranging for any outside consultants which it feels are necessary or desirable to assist it, the expenses thereof to be shared equally by the company and the union.

The national committee first met in the fall of 1980. It agreed on a set of principles but had trouble developing a strategy. Some management members wanted to take a relatively passive role, basically supporting whatever local companies initiated. They viewed quality-of-worklife programs as a means toward healthy decentralization, and were sensitive to playing the traditional controlling role. The union distrusted this approach: it believed that Bell companies interpreted quality-of-worklife projects as participative management without union involvement, and union officials were getting messages from local leaders that such programs were causing problems. If the national committee was not to direct the quality-of-worklife programs, CWA members wanted it to at least control the quality of the programs and set minimum standards. The union proposed that I be retained as consultant to the committee. Management resisted the idea.

The debate was not so much about me as about the committee's role. When management agreed to hire me, it meant a decision had been made to experiment with a more active strategy. I organized a series of meetings with union leaders, district vice presidents and their assistants, and company counterparts, including personnel vice presidents and their labor relations assistants. I described the quality-of-worklife project to them, its potential benefits and risks, and the development in skills and relationships necessary for both management and union to make it work. I emphasized that management had to share power, to treat the union as a partner, and that the union had to learn more about the business, to learn to work cooperatively, and to agree that ongoing quality-of-worklife projects would not be held hostage during unrelated conflicts. Quality-of-worklife projects should not be a substitute for collective bargaining, but a development of bargaining into issues of mutual interest.

Union and management groups then met separately to discuss what they wanted from quality-of-worklife projects, and what they thought the other side wanted. Then they shared their deliberations. There were high levels of trust in some companies, especially in companies in which top management invited union leaders to discuss changes and ways of decreasing grievances. In other companies, there was little trust or communication. Even in instances where top leaders had created a good relationship, lower levels might view each other warily. The fault might be in either side or both. Managers might be insecure and inflexible, overcontrolling, or paternalistic; union leaders might want to make all the deals themselves, and fear giving more power to members who might criticize them or discover they do not need either managerial or union bosses.

We established quality-of-worklife committees in each company, with union and management coordinators who would communicate with the national committee. The strategy was to educate and train facilitators from both sides so there would be no need to hire outside consultants. This strategy avoided having to deal with approaches which might distort the shared goals and principles. It strengthened internal skills, gave a sense of ownership to both union and management, and created a group of dedicated proponents.

The national committee developed a quality-of-worklife training package, designed by CWA District 5 and Mountain Bell. It included four modules which described quality-of-worklife, its implementation, how a group would identify and solve problems, and how to deal with interpersonal relations within the group. This became the basic training required for all levels, from workers to the problem-solving team.

The strategy announced by the national committee was to start with voluntary leadership from both sides. The first stage was to create successful models which could be copied by others.

The committee planned a series of meetings to stimulate union and management to consider quality-of-worklife projects in relation to an organizational vision. The participants were chief operating and personnel vice presidents from each Bell company with the corresponding union vice presidents. Professor Richard Walton of the Harvard Business School and I conducted the seminars, using Harvard Business School cases to describe a range of visions, from Japanese paternalism to European work councils. We persuaded management that the union was not seeking control of their decisions, and persuaded the union that management respected their role as representing workers' needs for security, fair rewards, and a chance to develop skills. This was the first time some of the operating officers had ever met union leaders; they testified that these traditional adversaries were responsible and intelligent about business needs, and were potential allies in the task of making the Bell companies more competitive in a deregulated environment.

By the summer of 1982, the national committee had achieved its first goals—designing a cooperative structure and training for teams and facilitators—and were organizing a meeting to showcase its success.

For the next stage, we invited leaders from both sides for discussions. They concluded that good models existed, but required initiative and involvement from management, and only a few innovative leaders were willing to take the risk. Support from the top was needed, including rewards for risk-takers, and a roadmap showing how to manage the process. To encourage support, the national committee planned meetings with the top management of the new regional companies. To develop a roadmap, union and management staff interviewed exemplary leaders, representing levels from company president and regional vice president to district manager and local union presidents.

Both management and union leaders believe that quality-of-worklife projects are meant to strengthen their organizations, and that a quality-of-worklife project requires teamwork, trust, and coordinating committees that manage the process, but not the content (which must come from the workers). All the leaders interviewed had invested liberally in training and used internal consultants. They stayed with the process, holding frequent meetings, in contrast to some managers who give their blessing and then withdraw.

Union leaders reported the quality-of-worklife projects require them to gain new skills and knowledge. They also commented that intra-union struggles over turf impede the process. It is clear that quality-of-worklife projects deteriorate unless union leadership maintains an active, informed role.

The strike of August 1983 slowed down the momentum, but quality-of-worklife programs emerged intact. Watts is convinced the strike would have been longer and more violent without them. Local presidents I have interviewed agree. They say members recognized the difference between areas which demand cooperation, and those, such as wages and benefits, which are areas of disagreements. In one Bell company where such projects have widespread support, the company president talked to picketing workers and congratulated them for their loyalty to the union. Since the strike, that company has made rapid strides to extend quality-of-worklife programs.

WILL DIVESTITURE AFFECT COMMITMENT?

Both union and management leaders in the divested Bell companies have declared their commitment to quality-of-worklife projects. Internally, the union has used the process to improve its own management at headquarters and in the district teams. But further development depends on the willingness of management to work cooperatively with the union on all factors that influence the quality of working life, and the willingness of the union to understand the new problems of a competitive market. Quality-of-worklife projects must include the design of technology and the organization of work. As management builds more efficient systems, it must consider from the start whether such changes create good jobs. Will workers be "deskilled"? Will work be organized to allow broad learning, including problem-solving skills that are not made obsolete by change? In a monopoly that has been able to maintain high levels of job security, how will management deal with downturns and technological unemployment?

The growth of quality-of-worklife projects requires a developing relationship between management and union built on mutual respect for institutional interests and values. CWA leaders have seen that quality-of-worklife can strengthen the union's ability to serve all its members, not just those with grievances. Indeed, such projects make the union more attractive to educated service workers. But no union can operate if management threatens its existence. If the new Bell companies pursue a strategy of cutting costs by becoming nonunion, quality-of-worklife projects will wither. If management sees the union as a potential ally to be brought into strategy, quality-of-worklife projects can guarantee the new companies a highly motivated, flexible, and productive work force.

FOOTNOTES

[1]In 1972, Irving Bluestone, then vice president of the United Automobile Workers, and Sidney Harman, Bolivar chief executive officer, had asked me to help them design and direct that project which pioneered many of the practices subsequently used by GM, Ford, and AT&T. This included a union-management plant-level committee and department-level teams trained to analyze problems and to propose solutions. Bolivar went farther than most subsequent programs in supporting general education and arts and crafts, as well as technical training. The project was effective not only in terms of work satisfaction, but also in union-management cooperation to gain new business, cut costs, and achieve mutually beneficial early bargaining.

[2]See Michael Maccoby, *The Gamesman* (New York, Simon & Schuster, 1976).

DISCUSSION QUESTIONS

1. What constitutes high quality of work life?
2. What characteristics of the situation at AT&T prompted initiation of a QWL program?
3. What approach did AT&T use?
4. How effective has the QWL project been?
5. What role did managers and human resources professionals play in the QWL project?
6. Were they effective? If not, what role should they play?

ACTIVITIES

Activity 14–1

DATA-ENTRY CLERK JOB REDESIGN

Step 1: Read the following scenario.

Foxwood Appliances has forty data-entry clerks who report to one of two supervisors. They enter data into a video terminal for a variety of work that is supplied by a number of departments and groups at Foxwood. Some jobs are small, while others involve extensive data transfer. Most work comes with a due date, although some does not.

The work is supplied to the clerks by their supervisor. The supervisor attempts to see that each person gets exactly one-fortieth of the work. The supervisor looks at the work before giving it to the clerks to make sure the writing is legible. If not, the supervisor returns it to the originating department.

Usually each clerk is able to enter between 10,000 and 15,000 characters a day. Because of the exact nature of the work and the lack of skilled entry clerks, the output is then sent to proofreaders for review to minimize the number of errors. However, the departments still complain about large numbers of mistakes. Many due dates and schedules are not met. The department has high absenteeism and turnover.

Step 2: Diagnose the situation.

1. How effective is the human resources management?
2. What human resources management problems are there?

Step 3: Redesign the job using the following approaches:

1. work simplification
2. job enrichment
3. quality-of-worklife programs
4. alternative work schedules

Step 4: In small groups, share your job design. Decide which approach would be the most effective and which the least effective.

Step 5: Offer at least two other approaches for solving the problem at Foxwood Appliances.

Step 6: Discussion. With the entire class, share your group's conclusions. Then address the following:

1. Compare and contrast the three methods of work redesign.
2. What problems does each solve? Create?
3. What advantages and disadvantages does each offer?
4. What role should managers and human resources professionals play in redesigning the work?
5. What other approaches to change are appropriate for this situation?

Activity 14–2

SUBURBAN HOSPITAL REDESIGN

Step 1: Read the following scenario.

Suburban Hospital is a 300-bed neighborhood hospital that services several suburban communities in a large metropolitan area. It admits 25 to 100 patients each day. Figure 14–5 shows a partial organization chart of the hospital.

The admissions clerk greets the patient when he or she arrives for admittance, gives the patient a hospital identification bracelet, and takes the patient's possessions for storage.

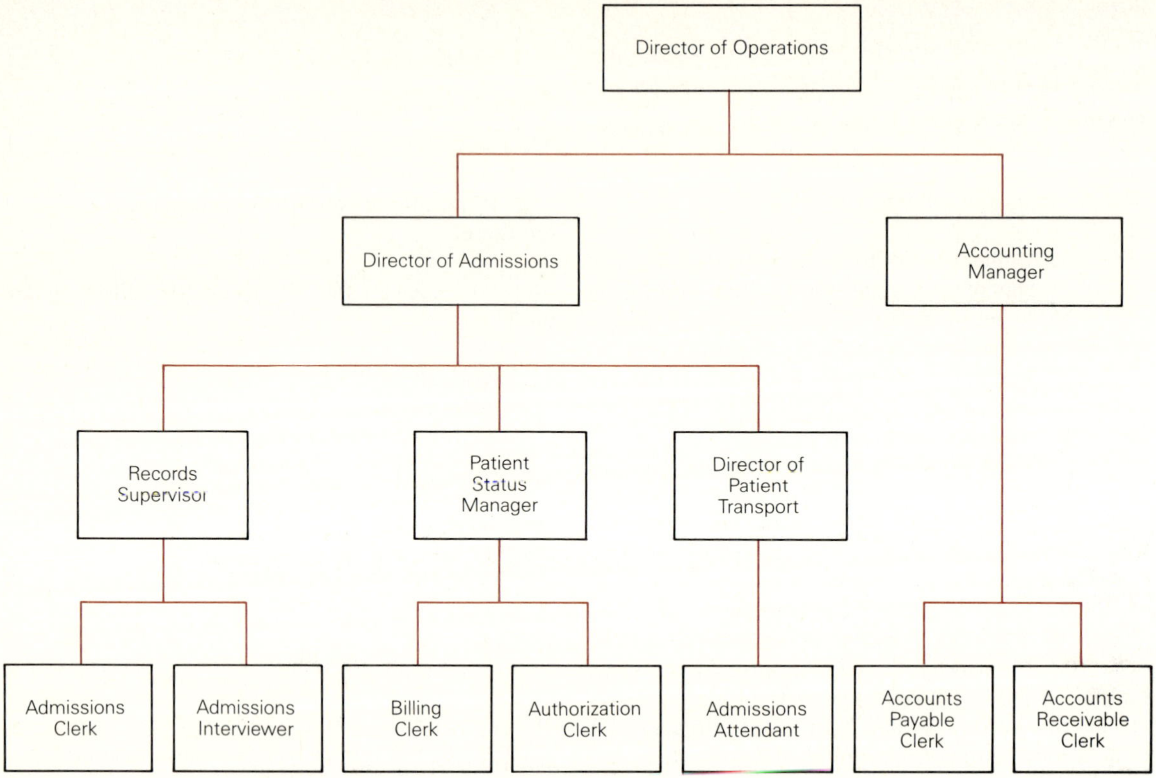

Figure 14–5 PARTIAL ORGANIZATION CHART OF SUBURBAN HOSPITAL

The admissions interviewer takes a preliminary medical history of the patient.

The billing clerk discusses the patient's plan for paying for the hospitalization. He or she enters the patient's name, personal data, and payment plan into the daily log. The clerk sends one copy of the log to the authorization clerk and one copy to the accounts receivable department.

The authorization clerk verifies the patient's ability to pay. He or she passes an authorization for admission to an admissions attendant.

The admissions attendant delivers the patient to his or her room. Delays in admitting a patient can occur at any step if the appropriate person is not available to process the patient. The patient carries no paperwork; each admissions employee must wait for the previously completed paperwork before performing his or her admissions task.

Step 2: Individually, in small groups, or with the entire class, answer the following questions:

1. What method of organizing is used?
2. What kinds of problems does this type of organization solve? Create?
3. Is this the most effective kind of organization?
4. How would you redesign this organization?
5. What role should managers and human resources professionals play in redesigning the organization?

Activity 14–3

ERICSSON DE ARGENTINA (A)–(F)

Step 1: Read Ericsson de Argentina (A)–(F).

Step 2: Prepare the case for class discussion.

ERICSSON DE ARGENTINA (A)

The Ericsson Group is a major international producer and distributor of telecommunications equipment and business information systems. Sales in 1981 were approximately U.S.$3 billion. Headquartered in Stockholm, Sweden, Ericsson was engaged in local manufacturing in over 30 different countries. In 1981, the company employed approximately 70,000 people world-wide. Major customers of switching and transmission equipment included public agencies such as national telecommunication nets (P.T.T.'s). Ericsson also enjoyed a private market for its business information systems, including small telephone switchboards, paging systems, intercoms and other intercommunication devices.

In the early 1980's, major competitors included ITT, Siemens, Philips, Plessey, Thomson, Nipon Electric and a number of other firms. Ericsson management believed that technological leadership, service, distribution and technical assistance, price and local production were important criteria for success in their industry. In the late 1970's, Ericsson had bolstered their reputation for technological excellence with their development of electronic switching equipment. Although not first to market with electronic telephone exchange equipment, their efforts represented one of the most successful early ventures into electronic switching.

While generally far more complex than the present technology, some elements of electronic production were less complex than electromechanical production. For example, electronic assembly required considerably less training than electromechanical assembly. While electromechanical assemblers required as much as one full year to reach a high level of proficiency, electronic assemblers could be expected to be producing at high levels within two months or less. However, Ericsson had learned that Computer-Controlled testing of electronic switching equipment was considerably more complex than testing of electromechanical switching equipment. Until 1978, all of Ericsson's electronic switching equipment was manufactured in plants located in Sweden. In late 1978, the Ericsson factory in Argentina received its first local order for electronic switching equipment.*

Top management of the Ericsson Group was quite interested in the success of its first overseas venture in the manufacture of electronic switching equipment. The company had already converted a number of Swedish factories to electronic switching and believed that they could provide valuable technical support for the Argentinian startup.** Detailed documentation was available on equipment needed for production, materials, plant layout and production processes. Video tapes had been produced in Swedish plants, demonstrating in great detail the various tasks, elements and processes involved in electronic assembly and testing.

Ericsson de Argentina (E.D.A.)

Ericsson de Argentina (E.D.A.), a wholly-owned subsidiary of the Ericsson group, had been involved in manufacturing electromechanical switching equipment for approximately 10 years. The factory in Buenos Aires was managed by Eric Martenson, a 30-year-old graduate in mechanical engineering from the Chalmers University of Technology in Göteborg, Sweden. Martenson had previously been involved in

This case was prepared by Professor Richard B. Higgins as a basis for class discussion rather than to illustrate either effective or ineffective handling of an administrative situation.

*Ericsson manufacturing in various countries throughout the world was in response to local, country orders.

**In contrast to Sweden, where electronic switching production had achieved a fairly high level of automation, the decision was made to begin production in Argentina using manual processes in the assembly operations.

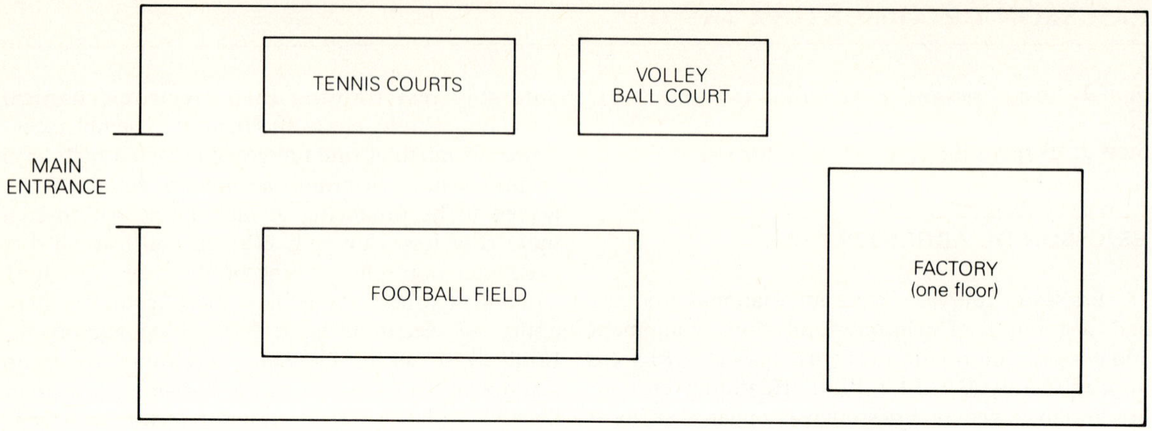

Figure 14–6 FACTORY LAYOUT PRIOR TO 1978

a production startup operation in another South American plant. When Martenson arrived in Argentina in late 1976 to take over the plant manager's position at E.D.A., he found the factory located in an old warehouse in the industrial area of Buenos Aires, while all other departments were located in the center of the city (see Figure 14–6 for an overall layout of the factory).

Organizationally, the factory manager reported to the managing director of Ericsson de Argentina (see Figure 14–7 for an organization chart of Ericsson de Argentina). Within the factory, Martenson had four department heads reporting to him: (1) Administration, responsible for accounting, personnel, purchasing and general services; (2) Planning; (3) Control; and (4) Production (see Figure 14–8 for an organization chart of the factory). Administration, planning and control were considered to be factory

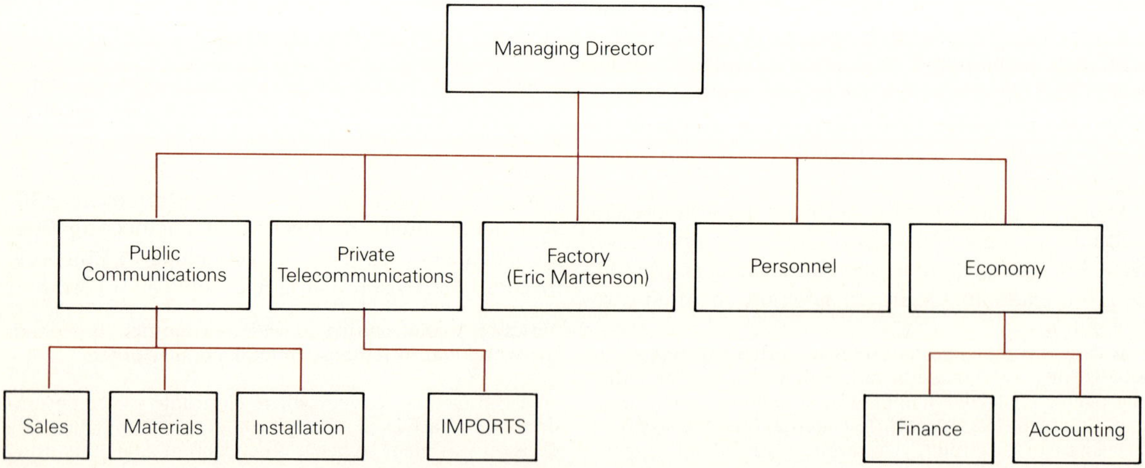

Figure 14–7 ORGANIZATION PRIOR TO 1980

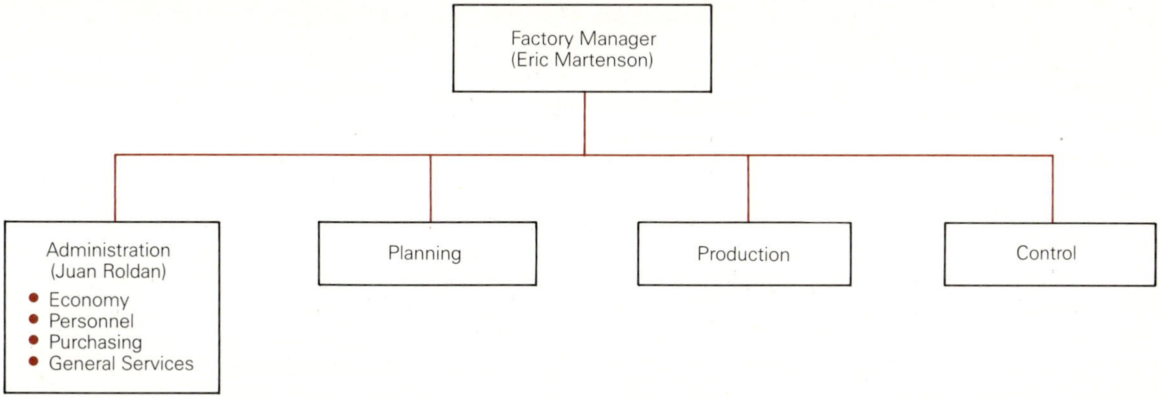

Figure 14–8 FACTORY ORGANIZATION PRIOR TO 1980

office positions. Production employed approximately 130 "direct" workers out of a total factory work force of 200.

Although factory management at E.D.A. had been engaged in preliminary planning for possible conversion to electronic production, it was not until late 1978, with a firm local order in hand, that Eric Martenson realized that his plant would be Ericsson's first overseas venture in manufacturing electronic switchgear. In preparation for the startup of electronic production in Argentina, Eric Martenson was recalled to Stockholm for an intensive briefing by engineers and headquarter's personnel who had considerable experience with a number of Swedish plant conversions.* In November of 1978, Martenson, with three suitcases filled with equipment specifications, plant layouts, blue prints, a tentative schedule for conversion and many videotapes, boarded flight no. 521 for his return trip to Buenos Aires, Argentina.

ERICSSON DE ARGENTINA (B)

Immediately upon his return from Stockholm, Sweden, Eric Martenson called a series of meetings, first with factory office employees and then with production workers. The purpose of these meetings was to brief employees on the company's plans to begin electronic production. To assist in his presentation, Martenson had brought along a number of printed boards made in Sweden. He used the boards as visual aids to describe the new technology and the impact that the new production process would have on employee staffing, training requirements and compensation policies and practices.

*In the next two years, Martenson was to make five additional trips to Stockholm.

ERICSSON DE ARGENTINA (C)

Plant management decided to proceed with a planned phase-in at its Buenos Aires factory. Phase no. 1, referred to by some as a "debugging" period, called for transferring 30 Argentinian production workers, formerly involved in electromechanical manufacturing, to electronic production.

Eric Martenson decided to select the 30 factory employees with the best production records for transfer. His reasoning was based on two major considerations: (1) He wanted to maximize the chances for success in the changeover; and (2) He wanted to establish the idea that electronics manufacturing was a very desirable job (more employees would be needed in later phases of the conversion). In the process of selecting the electronics work group, plant management was guided by another consideration. They did not want to remove all of their most productive employees from electromechanical manufacturing. As Eric Martenson said, "We couldn't do this, otherwise you would lose too much efficiency and, secondly, we would lose all of our 'models' of high performance."

Martenson believed that training the new electronics work group was an activity of highest priority. He was aware that training for electronic assembly tasks, aided by elaborate and detailed documentation and videotape demonstrators, would be considerably less difficult than electronics testing training. It was decided that training for testers would be conducted in two phases, (1) six months pre-training at the Buenos Aires plant, followed by (2) six months further training in Sweden. In order to provide an incentive, as well as provide backup support if needed, factory management decided to select two more testers than required during Phase 1 of the changeover. Hoping to foster competition among the testing trainees, Martenson "unofficially" informed the testers that only 4 out of the 6 would be chosen to go to Sweden for follow-on training.

Initially, a number of prospective electronic employees showed serious concerns regarding their compensation under the new manufacturing process.* They reasoned that, during the training and early production phase, their output would be at such a sufficiently low level that their paychecks would suffer. Plant management hoped eventually to establish a piece-rate compensation system for all electronics production tasks, but realized that it would take time to develop and install such a system.** In the meantime, plant management assured electronics production workers that their compensation would not be adversely affected during the training and initial production startup phases.

ERICSSON DE ARGENTINA (D)

"1979–1980 was a learning year for all of us," said Eric Martenson, factory manager at Ericsson de Argentina. "As planned, it took us a full year to begin to move into high levels of production. All of us were learning the new technology. Sweden was helpful in providing technical support wherever possible, but it was our job to make the thing work. Of course, if the transition were occurring in Sweden, the changeover probably would not have taken as long. For one thing, with all of the expensive, automated equipment in use in Sweden, management would have been under considerable pressure to reduce startup time. At the end of the year, however, we knew all about the new technology and we knew about a lot of the problems. When we brought in a new batch of employees to train, we were much more prepared."

In the meantime, in early 1978, the managing director of Ericsson de Argentina (see Figure 14–7) was reviewing final plans to relocate all offices and departments, currently situated in the Center of Buenos Aires (with the exception of private telecommunications), to the factory site located in the industrial area of Buenos Aires. Two reasons were cited by the managing director for this move: (1) to improve communications between office workers located in the center and factory office workers located at the manufacturing plant, (2) to allow for a consolidation of some functions formerly performed at the different locations. In addition, the managing director was well aware that:

(1) The working environment of the factory (located in an old warehouse) did not measure up to Ericsson standards.

(2) Production of electronic switching equipment at the factory would require plant expansion with new facilities designed to accommodate the new technology.

In order to respond to the diverse needs of the downtown office (Center of Buenos Aires) and the factory, a relocation plan was drawn up that would gradually consolidate offices and factory and provide for plant expansion. The following time schedule had been established:

Mid-1978	New canteen New factory offices for factory office workers
Mid-1979	New electronic production areas
Mid-1980	Move some downtown offices to factory site
Mid-1981	Move remainder of downtown offices to factory site

*Under the present compensation system, employees' total compensation included a base salary plus incentives.

**Industrial engineers with the Ericsson Group in Sweden had developed standard times for Swedish electronic manufacturing methods, but these were based on a highly automated manufacturing process.

At the completion of the relocation in 1981, management visualized the following layout at the factory site as shown in Figure 14–9.

The consolidation of downtown and factory offices would increase the size of the workforce at the plant from 200 to approximately 525 employees. Currently, factory employees, both in the office and in production, worked an 8 1/2 hour day, 42 1/2 hours per week. Factory office workers regarded themselves as a rather close-knit, cohesive group. Frequently, smaller groups within the factory office would get together for off-the-job social activities. Volley ball, tennis and table tennis were popular at the factory and organized competition among different departments and groups within the factory generated considerable interest and enthusiasm.

Office employees located downtown currently worked a 37 1/2 hour, flexitime, work week. A long standing tradition in the downtown offices extended the normal lunch hour to 1 1/2 hours, permitting office workers to go home for lunch.

ERICSSON DE ARGENTINA (E)

Factory employees were generally pleased with the first two phases of the relocation and modernization program. Everyone seemed to enjoy the new canteen and factory office workers welcomed their new facilities. While the old tennis court had been selected as the site of the new office building for downtown workers, this did not appear to cause a major problem. In mid-1979, the new electronic production area was completed on schedule.

By mid-1980, some of the downtown office workers were relocated to the factory. Almost immediately factory employees, particularly factory office workers, began to express a number of concerns to factory management. "Who are these people who are arriving in broad daylight, 1/2 to 1 hour late and going home 1/2–1 hour early?" "Are these downtown workers going to take our parking space, just like they took our tennis courts?" "Who are these people that go for lunch anytime they want to, causing us to wait in line in our own canteen?" By mid-1981, when the remainder of the downtown office personnel were transferred to the factory site, relations between office and factory employees were described by one observer as "less than cordial."

In the early 1980's, factory management decided that something must be done to remove some of the more visible differences in working conditions between the two groups. A long term goal of a standardized 40 hour work week for all employees was discussed but met considerable resistance from the "downtown" office workers. Used to a 37 1/2 hour week, they strenuously resisted an increase in their working hours to 40, although management had proposed an 8% wage increase to accompany the increased work week. Unable to convince the

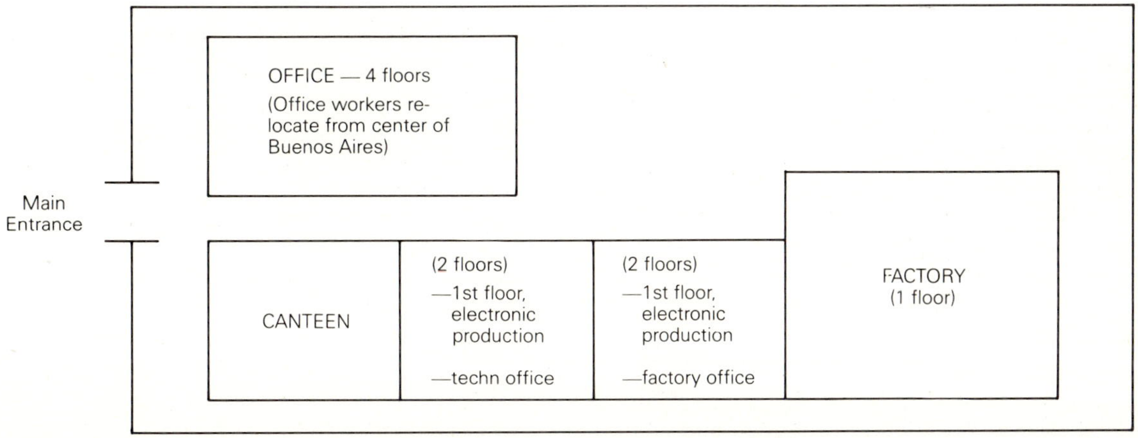

Figure 14–9 FINAL LAYOUT—CONSOLIDATED OFFICES & FACTORY 1981

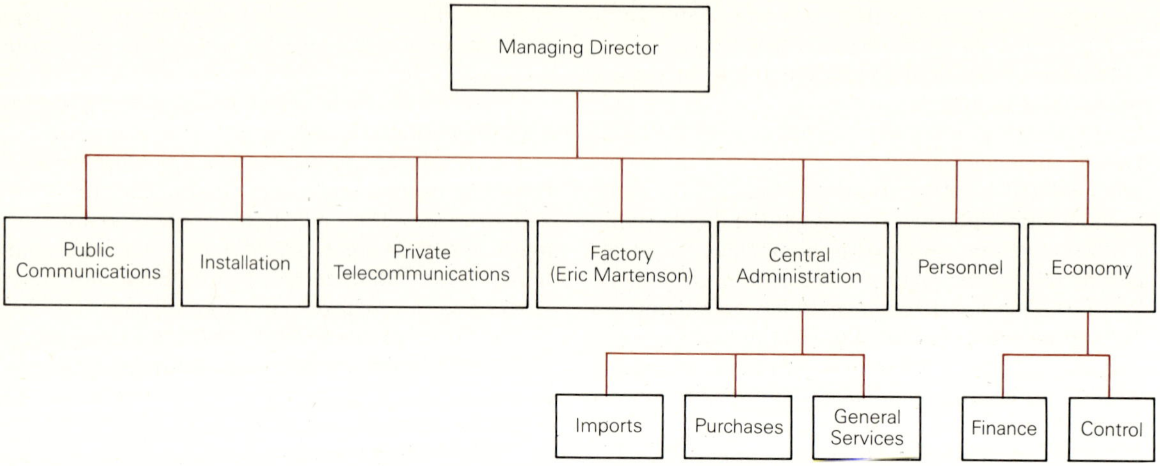

Figure 14–10 **ORGANIZATION AFTER 1980**

office workers to accept this package, factory management was reluctant to reduce the factory employee work week to 40 hours and factory employees continued to work a 42 1/2 hour work week.

In 1980, the relocation plan moved into its final phase. One of the initial reasons for relocation was to consolidate a number of office functions formerly performed at the factory and at the downtown location. Management had already decided to remove the purchasing and personnel functions, formerly performed by the Factory Administration department, under Juan Roldan. These activities were to be merged with the recently relocated downtown personnel department and the newly created central administration department (see Figures 14–10 and 14–11). This consolidation was fully accepted by factory management.

Juan Roldan was about 50 years old, had been an employee of Ericsson de Argentina for 30 years, and planned to retire in another five years. He held a Bachelor of Economics degree and, at the time, was continuing with his post graduate Economics studies

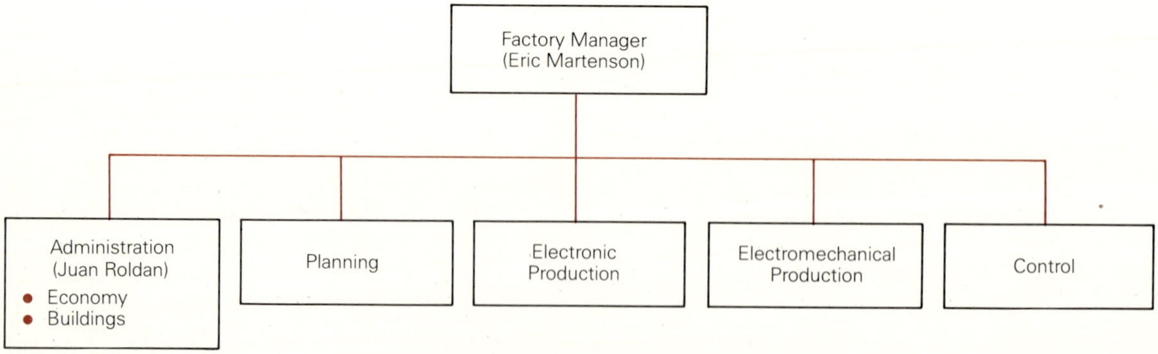

Figure 14–11 **FACTORY ORGANIZATION AFTER 1980**

in the evening. Plant management had been generally satisfied with Juan's performance. "The personnel administration activities under his section had worked out well and also the purchasing activities were well run."

ERICSSON DE ARGENTINA (F)

Although Juan Roldan did not openly complain about the consolidation of the Personnel and Purchasing functions, his behavior indicated that something was bothering him. He became more reserved and much less involved in project meetings and other factory discussions. The remaining function within the Administration dept. was economy.* Even here, Juan's boss, Eric Martenson, had expressed some concern over Juan's apparent lack of imagination in his cost analyses. Working very well with routine tasks, Martenson believed Juan to be a rather rigid, autocratic person, who found it difficult to tackle new and complex tasks.** Although Juan was very respectful in his relationships with Eric, Martenson had heard, through the grapevine, that he was a very difficult person to work for. Martenson knew, from first hand experience, that Juan had had some problems with his two sons. His eldest son had run away from home at 17 years old and continued to have little contact with the family. His younger son had also run away from home for a few days.

Eric Martenson was convinced that he had a serious motivational problem with one of his employees. One evening in mid-1980, Martenson was pondering the reasons for Juan's apparent frustration. Eric was not certain how significant each of the following factors were, but he thought that they might help to explain Juan's behavior in recent months:

> "Juan resented preparing a rather comprehensive, written report for me each month, showing progress achieved towards targeted activities. He had never had to do this before and he obviously did not like it, at first."

- "Roldan was no longer considered as my 'natural deputy,' as he had been in the past."
- "Juan was aware that his salary was considerably lower than (25% lower) the two other Bachelor of Economics within the factory."
- "He had functions and responsibilities taken away from him (personnel and purchasing)."
- "He thought that he had the capacity to do much more and he also thought that I did not give him the chance."
- "Juan had serious family problems."
- "He had difficulties in developing a new managerial style, the 'modern' way of treating subordinates."
- "He could have found it difficult to take orders from a younger man (me)."
- "He did not feel my support."

After reviewing his list, Eric Martenson concluded that there were more than enough reasons to account for Juan's rather dispirited behavior of recent months. However, Martenson kept returning to the same question: "What can I do about the current situation with Juan?"

Four hours later, Martenson was still staring at his notes scribbled on a single piece of paper. He was considering the following options:

1. *Try to get Roldan to understand and accept the current situation.* How can you tell someone that the goals that they have set up are not going to be reached and then tell them why not?
2. *Undertake an active program of personal development,* identifying weaknesses and providing support for improvement. This of course sounds very good and maybe if I had undertaken it sooner, it would have worked. But how do you teach a guy to be more creative?
3. *Clearly define his new job and my expectations for performance* in cost control and electronic production. This, I did not do.
4. *Transfer Roldan to another department.* This may be very difficult to do.
5. *Terminate his contract with the company.* This would be next to impossible, given Juan's 30 years' service.

*At the time of consolidation, Juan was also put in charge of buildings.

**This impression was reinforced, in Martenson's view, when Juan Roldan resisted Eric's urging to become more involved in the new electronics manufacturing process.

Step 3: Individually, in small groups, or with the entire class, address the following:

1. Evaluate the process of introducing the new technology.
2. Assess the role of Martenson in this process.
3. Was the management of human resources effective?
4. How effective was the relocation process?
5. How could the relocation problems have been avoided?
6. How could Martenson have been a more effective human resources manager?
7. What assistance could trained human resources professionals have provided?
8. How should Martenson handle Roldan?

Activity 14–4

LABOR/MANAGEMENT PARTICIPATION TEAMS

Step 1: Read Labor/Management Participation Teams.

Step 2: Prepare the case for class discussion.

Few American industries felt the impact of the recent recession more keenly—or welcomed the signs of recovery with greater relief—than the steel industry.

Today, as those signs grow stronger, a new sense of optimism and determination is growing at the Riverdale, Illinois, steelmaking plant of Interlake's Iron and Steel Division. But increased orders from automotive and consumer durable goods manufacturers are only part of the reason why.

Step into one of the plant's meeting rooms on a typical afternoon, and you'll see another aspect of this new vitality. It's a group of Interlake employees—a division superintendent, general foremen, a plant engineer and several hourly employees.

This is an advisory committee meeting of Interlake's Labor/Management Participation Team (LMPT) program.

LMPT is a system in which employees, both hourly and salaried, have the opportunity to work together. Not just in their traditional roles, but on problem-solving teams, in a joint effort to solve the serious problems which face all employees at the Riverdale plant.

In short, LMPT is a program based on the premise that every employee has a stake in the mill's success.

Since the program was initiated in late 1982, it has been expanded into all five divisions at the Riverdale steelmaking operation: hot mill, cold mill, primary rolling mill, maintenance and steel production, as well as the manufacturing and processing division of Acme Packaging, with 275 employees at the Riverdale plant.

Each of the six LMPT advisory committees—one for each operating division—reports to a central policy committee. And each reviews and coordinates the activities of two or more operating teams. Currently, 28 teams have completed training in problem-solving and are working to improve plant efficiency, product quality and cost control. By early March, 1984, although several teams had been organized for just a few months, 89 different projects were under consideration, underway or already completed.

Interlake's LMPT program, while not unique, is one of the fastest-growing and most successful in the industry. In little more than a year, it has attracted nationwide attention from industry management and labor leaders alike.

For a clearer view of how the program began and where it's heading, *InterViews* spoke with Brian Marsden, president of the Iron and Steel Division.

InterViews: Mr. Marsden, what led to the formation of Labor/Management Participation Teams at Riverdale?

Mr. Marsden: I think three ingredients must be present for successful LMPT. There has to be the need, the desire and the organization to make it work.

We certainly had the need. Starting in 1975, the Riverdale works had shown a declining profit picture. And while various efforts were made to explain this to union membership, we really hadn't been successful. There was always an element of doubt—mistrust, you might say—which prevented an exchange of ideas between the union leadership and the management of Riverdale.

In 1980, the plant lost a significant amount of money. And even in 1981, a relatively good year from a volume standpoint, Riverdale was headed for a significant loss. The union contract would not expire until '83. but we decided in the fall of 1981 that the situation was critical. Under the existing union contract, Riverdale was not a viable operation. The plant had to renegotiate or close. We needed a major program to make everyone at Riverdale clearly understand where the profit picture was taking us.

We started with a videotape message from Fred Langenberg, who was president and chief operating officer at the time, Al Ward, president of Acme Packaging Division, and myself. This was shown to all employees—management and union—with a question and answer period following each showing. In that videotape, we pulled no punches. We showed the profit picture. We showed the decline and the fact that we were losing money.

InterViews: How did the union respond?

Mr. Marsden: The union sent in their staff representatives from Pittsburgh, whom we invited to verify our numbers. They confirmed that the Riverdale plant was indeed losing money. That employment costs were higher than the industry average. That Riverdale had certain inherent penalty costs because of the nature of the product mix, small heat sizes, coil sizes, slab sizes and operations that require a lot of man hours. They finally determined that if union membership was concerned about their future job security, they should be prepared to discuss concessions that could help keep Riverdale a viable operation.

This all transpired in early 1982. From there, we entered serious negotiations with the union, and a new three-year contract was signed in September, 1982.

InterViews: What happened in those negotiations?

Mr. Marsden: It was mutually agreed that with Riverdale's future viability at stake, it made a lot of sense to have labor/management participation teams to try to improve plant efficiency.

InterViews: Was that happening at other steel mills at the same time?

Mr. Marsden: Not to the same degree. At that point, other steel companies had not been successful in reopening negotiations with the union. I don't think any other steel companies established the degree of confidence and trust that we had. There *had* been some attempts at labor/management teams. But I don't think the climate at other plants was as conducive to moving ahead. At Riverdale, the need was there, and the desire was there—from both the union and management. The third thing we had to put in place was the organization.

InterViews: How did you do that?

Mr. Marsden: We worked jointly to select a management consulting firm that would be the catalyst. After interviews and discussions, a New Jersey firm, Participative Systems, was selected. I guess that was the first case of cooperation: jointly we said yes, these are the people we want.

Participative Systems came in with a 3-tiered organization structure—a policy committee, the advisory committees and the actual team committees out in the plant. Each of these three levels is a working group that attacks problems.

InterViews: Has this structure been effective?

Mr. Marsden: I have to say that I had some reservations at first. But they've proven to me that the structure works. It really involves all employees. It ensures a good flow of information up and down the stream.

InterViews: What has impressed you most about the program at Riverdale?

Mr. Marsden: Two things. One is the speed with which the LMPT teams have expanded. We started with three divisions, and we've expanded probably about twice as fast as expected. In fact, we had to go back to our senior management and ask for more money—for training expense, our people's time and the consultants' time—because we were expanding faster than we had planned.

Secondly, I'm impressed by the projects that have been chosen. In the last six months, the teams have really addressed some long-standing problems in the plant. And we have gained the benefit of experienced people on the job, who often know the problems better than we do.

InterViews: Can you project the benefits of the program in terms of cost savings?

Mr. Marsden: We have a long-standing cost improvement program in this division which saves probably $3 million at Riverdale per year. I believe it would be reasonable for the labor/management participation teams eventually to save an equal amount.

We're not near that yet. It's an ongoing thing.

InterViews: Do you think you can maintain the level of enthusiasm for LMPT that exists now?

Mr. Marsden: It's going to have to be maintained. Bear in mind that we really didn't get the teams formed until about the end of the first quarter of '83. We made considerable progress last year. But there's a lot more to be done.

If we're going to remain viable, we've got to go on proving our quality and efficiency. I think everybody at the Riverdale plant realizes this. And the best way we know to utilize all the talents and all the experience we have in this good workforce is the LMPT teams.

It's like any organization you're in: you're going to get out of it what you put into it. It requires thinking and effort—sometimes effort over and above the normal call of duty. We have counted heavily on involvement . . . continued involvement, support and enthusiasm. We've got to keep it up.

InterViews: What do you foresee for the Riverdale plant over the next five years?

Mr. Marsden: When I addressed that subject at the LMPT Activity Review Meeting in early March, it was the first time in recent years I felt I could talk confidently about our position five years hence.

We think we can capture more of the market. But we've got to improve our quality, remain close to our customers and ship our products on time. We've got to be more cost-efficient. And I see labor/management participation teams as a very important mechanism for achieving these three objectives.

LMPT ROUND TABLE

Today at Interlake's Riverdale facility, hourly and salaried employees are facing problems and opportunities together—from a shared perspective. How do they view the LMPT approach to problem-solving now, 16 months after the original policy statement was drafted?

To find out, *InterViews* met with four of the Interlake employees most closely involved with the formation and activities of LMPT at Riverdale. All participated in the 1982 contract negotiations and are members of the LMPT central policy committee:

Mike Batka, plant manager, Riverdale Plant

George Chandler, president, Local 1053, United Steelworkers of America, BOF shop employee

Don Pearson, trustee, Local 1053, United Steelworkers of America, primary mill employee

Jerry Shope, manager of employee relations, Iron and Steel Division

InterViews: Was the LMPT system a part of the contract negotiated in 1982?

Mr. Shope: It was actually part of the 1980 labor agreement. When we negotiated in 1982, we reaffirmed the commitment to enter into the process.

Mr. Chandler: I guess we couldn't get together prior to that . . . for reasons both on the union side and the company side. The only way we in the union would go with the concession agreement in '82 was to make sure LMPT was instituted.

Mr. Shope: I think *survival* was something that really got us moving. There was an understanding that the concessions themselves weren't our salvation. We had to go way beyond concessions. LMPT looked like it had the potential.

InterViews: What was the next step?

Mr. Shope: To find out exactly what the labor/management participation process was. That involved talking to three different consulting firms. Participative Systems out of Princeton, New Jersey, seemed to have the best record of experience and expertise. We brought their personnel on site, and they talked to us for several months.

Mr. Batka: An interesting point—they looked us over as much as we looked *them* over. They wanted to have a reasonable chance of success, or they wouldn't have made the commitment to come with us.

Mr. Shope: They wanted to know that we were serious, that it wasn't just a negotiating ploy or something we agreed to because we had to.

InterViews: When did the program really get started?

Mr. Chandler: In early December of '82, we held a joint meeting—about 60 people—union officials plus company officials, superintendents and so on.

That was the planning meeting. Over a three-day period we were oriented on what LMPT is. Then we developed a policy statement covering our common objectives. We also went through some exercises in building trust relationships. At the conclusion of the meeting, we established a policy committee whose first task was to decide how to go from there.

Mr. Batka: That three-day conference was probably the first instance where union and management got together in a non-adversarial situation. Most of the time, my only contact with George had been to discuss a problem at the plant, usually in the form of a grievance. And now here we were, in a three-day conference together. Day two was a little better than day one. And by day three, we were standing next to each other drinking coffee.

Mr. Shope: We found out that we had a common objective: job security. We wanted to do the same thing.

Mr. Pearson: I had never worked with anybody from management before. I worked for Mike when he was a superintendent in the melt shop, but had never worked *with* management.

InterViews: How did you communicate this new spirit of cooperation to employees?

Mr. Pearson: We had plant-wide orientations, meeting department by department on the floor. It was very difficult. There were all kinds of questions.

Mr. Chandler: We passed out information and policy statements at the gate as people came in and went home.

Mr. Shope: We communicated however we could. And the communication is still going on. There are still skeptics.

Mr. Batka: From the management standpoint, from the line foreman on up the line, this process means relinquishing some authority. It means asking the worker, "What's your thought on this? How do you think we should proceed?" This sharing of authority and responsibility was new and different. And it caused some apprehension.

Mr. Pearson: It was a threat to the established union official, and it caused us some apprehension, too.

Mr. Shope: It really is a traumatic thing to go through, and it's slow. But we're further along than other companies might be because of the environment we're in. Job security motivated us to work harder than we might have otherwise—if we were all comfortable and complacent, and there was no threat of the plant closing.

InterViews: Could you explain briefly how the three-tiered LMPT structure works?

Mr. Chandler: The policy committee is made up of key union and management people whose basic responsibility is to create the proper environment for the process, help it grow and monitor the progress. We established divisional advisory committees which not only administer and support the teams but also solve problems themselves. That's one of the unique features of the structure: all of these groups are problem-solving groups—not just administrative bodies—and they consist of both hourly and salaried people. Participation is strictly voluntary. That was established from the start.

LMPT AT RIVERDALE

InterViews: What's involved in the training process?

Mr. Pearson: Each team gets 40 hours of problem-solving training. People talk about what's going on in their area and look for problems. Then the exercises are directed toward those problems.

Mr. Batka: The emphasis is on problem-solving, but the training encompasses other areas, too. There's a lot of orientation on LMPT, the objectives of people on the teams, group dynamics and interpersonal skills—solving problems as a group.

Mr. Chandler: We also have four coordinator-trainers who underwent a three-week course in New Jersey. They both train the teams and help them after the initial training period. Without the coordinator-trainers, I don't think we'd be where we're at now.

InterViews: How did you set priorities for selecting problems to address?

Mr. Batka: One of the key things that led to our current success in working together was the dissemination of information at the policy committee meeting. The employees asked, "What areas should we look at?" We had our chief industrial engineer come out to make a presentation, describing practically all the major cost items in the plant—labor, energy, material yields and so on. It was another indication that we were interested in the process for real. We opened our books to show actual cost information.

Mr. Shope: That information filtered down all the way to the shop floor teams. Since everybody had the same information, most people picked the same priorities. That really helped in our problem selection.

Mr. Batka: From my perspective, improving our product quality is the single most important task we have at Riverdale. It's not only a dollars-and-cents area but the key to the plant's survival. We could be the most efficient producer in the world . . . reduce our labor costs, energy costs and increase our productivity far beyond our competitors. But if the product we produce is not acceptable to the customer, all that's for naught.

Mr. Pearson: I don't think people ever thought about the millions of dollars involved in quality problems. I know I didn't. I just did my job. Now I hear people who have just finished their training say they never knew quality was so important.

One of our most successful projects to date concerns both quality and product yield in the primary rolling mill. The solution we implemented saved more than $8,500 the first month. When we expand that project, we expect to save about a quarter of a million dollars annually.

Mr. Shope: In another area, we have a joint activity on a quality problem, involving the hot mill, the cold mill and the manufacturing and processing division. They're trying to improve the quality of the product going from the steel division through manufacturing.

Mr. Chandler: That kind of joint effort is growing now. Before, a lot of people said, "I'll make it here the best I can and send it over there . . . and if they have trouble with it, that's their problem." Now we have joint teams between the divisions.

InterViews: Is the LMPT program helping to boost employee morale at Riverdale?

Mr. Batka: Once people get involved, they see the benefits to themselves—the excitement of being part of the decision-making process. Having something to say about their work activities.

Mr. Pearson: I think the shop floor teams get turned on when they ask for information from management people and get it. Teams have the right to ask any questions in any area they're working on. That really excites people.

Mr. Shope: The benefit is not just in the results; it's actually going through the process. When you can't do anything about your situation, you're frustrated . . . and that compounds the problem. But when you get involved in a productive, problem-solving process, you're contributing something. You just feel better about it.

InterViews: What are your opinions of the program's overall success at this point?

Mr. Batka: We're off to an excellent start. We're receiving recognition and credit from other people for our quick progress. But it really is just a start, and we're not out of the woods by a long shot. Without everyone's continuing support, it would collapse. Once people see the benefits of being involved, the program becomes self-perpetuating.

Mr. Shope: We started out with a meeting of 60 people and a policy committee of 11. Now I believe we have more than 200 people involved. We've deliberately avoided giving ourselves a lot of publicity and patting ourselves on the back because we have a long way to go. But we've seen some successes and encouraging response in the last 15 months. We're starting to get people interested in what's going on here, working on problems related to our survival.

Mr. Pearson: One indicator of the response is our low rate of drop-outs from the teams. We calculated it at about 5% since the LMPT process began here. From what I gather talking to people involved in programs at other plants, that's very low.

Mr. Chandler: From my eyes, the success of this program depends on keeping as many people employed as we can without losing benefits. We've lost a lot of active employees in the past few years.

Mr. Batka: The process is not a panacea. It won't solve all the problems at Riverdale. But it *is* a very substantial part of the progress made in the plant during the past year. I'd like to see us move faster, but some things can't be pushed. We're talking not only about structural changes but cultural changes, too. It's a different way of life for us, and will continue to be different.

Mr. Pearson: There's a relationship that's changed. People are working together. And the relationship comes out of solving problems.

Mr. Batka: Right. That relationship develops not because of altruistic statements but by getting together and doing some hard knocking. That's solid. That's fundamental. And that's what's going to make this thing last.

Step 3: Individually, in small groups, or with the entire class, answer the following questions:

1. What effect will LMPT likely have on the quality of work life?
2. What human resources management practices should accompany introduction of LMPT to increase the likelihood of the program's success?

3. What is management's reaction to LMPT? Workers'?

4. What is the role of managers in LMPT? What should the role of managers be?

5. What is the role of human resources management professionals in LMPT? What should their role be?

6. What is the role of workers in LMPT? What should their role be?

Activity 14–5

DIGITAL TRYING THE BOSSLESS SYSTEM

Step 1: Read the following description of the Bossless System at Digital Equipment Corporation.

Enfield, Conn.—The inside of the Digital Equipment Corp. plant here looks much less like a factory than a warehouse full of machines and office desks deposited haphazardly.

Equipment, people and the odd potted plant seem randomly scattered about the cavernous, 10,000-square-foot building. No neat aisles divide the space, no obvious paths cut through the maze.

In one particular touch of incongruity, a volleyball net stands ready at one end of the room.

This, it turns out, is new management. It's an experiment—or, as one Digital official calls it, "an investment"—in the team management approach.

And according to Digital officials, it works.

The plant's 180 employees produce printed circuit board modules for computer storage systems. At other Digital plants, similar modules are made in assembly lines, where one person does the same job, or operates the same machine, all day.

At Enfield, by contrast, each board is put together from start to finish by one of several teams. The 18 people on each team divide the work among themselves and assemble the modules from the moment the raw materials are delivered to the plant to the time the finished product is shipped out the door. Each person is expected to be able to do all the roughly 20 jobs involved in making a module.

Workers set their own hours, plan their own schedules, check their own work and take team responsibility for each board. There are no time clocks, no security guards, no quality control officers and every employee has a key to the building.

The system is not new—several thousand similar operations have emerged at other companies and plants across the country during the last 10 years. But it's new for Digital, and although it affects a very small portion of the company's 73,000 employees worldwide (including about 28,000 in Massachusetts), company officials are supportive and say they are willing to extend it to other parts of the company.

"We do a lot of experimenting as a company," says Greg Plakias, Digital's group manufacturing manager of storage systems. "We encourage it, we reward it. We believe that if the investment and the concept is successful, then other parts of the company will reach in and take segments that are most applicable to their organization."

Enfield plant manager Bruce Dillingham says the new system has decreased by 40 percent the time needed to produce one printed circuit board, reduced by half the amount of scrap that is common in the industry and has produced twice as many perfectly working modules than other production systems.

The theory behind such new forms of participatory management, says Homer Hagedorn, management consultant at Arthur D. Little in Cambridge, is basically that, "People will be more interested in what they're doing and do a faster and higher quality job."

Employees at the Digital plant say that's exactly how they feel.

"This gives me a little more experience in how to put the whole board together and how to check it," says Betty Stebbins, a grandmother from Springfield who's worked for Digital for five years and at the Enfield plant for one. "You're sort of proud because you see the end product."

"Digital Trying the Bossless System" by Wendy Fox, October 14, 1984. Reprinted courtesy of *The Boston Globe*.

Plakias won't give specific numbers on productivity and savings, but says the year-old experiment "is going very well."

"We have always felt that traditional hardware manufacturers invest enormously in robotics and automation and pay little attention to ways to improve the product through innovative work systems and people," Plakias says. Digital is trying to increase its productivity with fewer people, he says, while at the same time emphasizing individual involvement in the process and personal pride in the product.

As Plakias says, the company is trying to achieve a balance "between the social part of one's life and the work part of one's life."

The Enfield system was Dillingham's idea, and he, in turn, got the idea by talking with other plant managers across the country.

"It's just the stuff I believe in," he says now.

As the concept for the plant evolved and the Enfield building was built, employees were involved from the beginning. In addition to the usual architects, engineers and accountants, Digital also employed an anthropologist.

The simplicity and efficiency of the building alone, Dillingham says, saved Digital about $500,000 over the normal set-up costs of a new plant.

Digital elected to avoid tying up money in long-term supplies, and the plant was designed with very little stockroom space.

A four-walled modular conference room can be moved to any part of the vast plant floor for meetings. Some of the desks are arranged in clusters of four, radiating out from a floor-to-ceiling pillar that holds telephone and electrical lines. Others are in pairs, facing each other, to increase eye contact and communication between workers.

The volleyball net and exercise equipment at one end of the floor are for employees as well as their families. ("We're trying to balance work and family," Dillingham says.)

Team members interview and train new workers and give each other certification tests as they learn new parts of the manufacturing process. Pay increases are based on improved levels of skill, as opposed to seniority or authority. There are only three managers in addition to Dillingham.

"Everybody is a teacher here and everybody is a learner," Dillingham says. "People are responsible for themselves, that's the trick."

Hagedorn says that sometimes causes problems: "You have to get built into the system a willingness on the part of the peer group to reject very unsuitable people. Sometimes that's hard to do."

Dillingham says his goal is to have an atmosphere that is informal, relaxed and trusting, where people are self-motivated, creative, open and flexible.

"We don't want a lot of clones here," he says. "We want a lot of individuals. Everybody here knows everything I do. We're not paying you for a job here; we're trying to use the total person."

Plakias says Digital wants to produce at the Enfield plant in one day what is produced at other plants in 10. But the real goal, he says, is to emphasize each worker's achievement and involvement.

"Productivity is good, but it comes in many ways," he says. "Primarily, this is an investment in our most valued asset and that's people.

"The concept we have designed here is one of very few layers of supervision and management . . . We have an environment here that has no functional structure. It's a team concept."

The system is not without snags.

Because there are no large stocks of supplies, vendors who are late with their deliveries or deliver faulty raw materials for the modules "can shut us down immediately," says David LaBrecque, a team member. "But we've identified a small number of vendors with excellent track records," he says, and so far, small inventories haven't been a problem.

Although Dillingham believes his system "will work anywhere," he also acknowledges that "It's not for everyone.

"It's a threatening system. We don't need as many people. The role of professional people has changed to one of learning."

Many workers don't want to work in a place where all workers are equal in terms of authority and there is no opportunity to become a supervisor.

Plakias counters by saying, "Instead of getting better at what you're good at, you get better by adding to what you have. As you gain more knowledge about how to build a product and manage the administrative aspects of the product, you become more valuable."

And, in fact, some people, like Joseph Talbot who was a supervisor for nine years with Digital in Springfield before coming to Enfield, prefer being part of a team than wielding their authority over others.

"I had 17 people under me," he said recently at the plant, bending over a table, making miniscule adjustments to a circuit board. "After a while, it gets to be a drag. I have to learn the manufacturing end of it. This gives you the overall picture."

Hagedorn at Arthur D. Little says he expects to see management systems like the one here spread to other companies because, "Many people are a little more comfortable doing this kind of work."

But unions are not always comfortable when traditional job classifications are erased and positions are not defined. And, Hagedorn says, the Enfield system won't necessarily work everywhere for many reasons:

"The whole notion of job enrichment and job enlightenment has probably been somewhat oversold. As somebody said recently, it really isn't much of an enrichment of the job if what you do is wash the spoons on Monday and wash the glassware on Tuesday."

Step 2: Individually or in small groups answer the following questions:

1. What types of interventions were used at Digital?
2. Why were these interventions introduced?
3. What are the advantages and disadvantages of each intervention?
4. Will a bossless system work for Digital? What are its assets and liabilities?

Step 3: In small groups or with the entire class, offer top management a plan for ensuring that the bossless system will succeed.

Step 4: With the entire class, share these plans. Then answer the following questions:

1. What are the key elements of each plan?
2. What do the plans share? How are they different?
3. What considerations must be included in planning for change?
4. What roles should managers and human resources professionals play in the planning? In implementing the change?

Activity 14–6

CITIZENS SERVICE CENTER CONSULTING PROBLEM

Step 1: Your instructor will divide you into groups of four to six people; one group will represent management and the rest, competing consulting groups.

Step 2: Read the following description.

Citizens Service Center provides a wide range of social services to adults and children. Most employees have advanced degrees in human services, social work, or psychology. Whereas the Center originally provided one-to-one counseling for its clients, the high demand for services has forced the employees into primarily clerical roles—filling out food stamp vouchers, obtaining medical referrals for clients, and completing detailed information forms about every visit. Most case workers spend at least fifty hours on the job, even though they are paid for only forty. The supervisors assign incoming clients randomly to the first available employee. The supervisors keep what they consider to be the best cases for themselves.

Most employees complain that they are not using their skills. In addition, the pay is relatively low. The Center has operated as a nonprofit agency, obtaining most of its funding from state and federal sources. Top management recently decided to transform the agency into a profit-making organization.

Step 3: *The Management Group.* Assume that you are the top management of the Citizens Service Center. You are concerned with the high rate of turnover and the low productivity in your organization. You want to hire a group of consultants to diagnose your organization's problems and to recommend a plan for solving them. Shortly, several consulting teams will ask you for a preliminary meeting to gather information for use in formulating their consulting proposal. Be prepared to provide them with your timelines and other requirements, as well as with any constraints, financial or otherwise, that you see as relevant to their task. Then develop guidelines for judging the various proposals presented. (Expect that each will include, at a minimum, a diagnosis, change strategy, and plans for implementation, as well as the rationale on which these are based.)

The Consulting Groups. Your objective is to be hired as consultants to the organization described in the case. The organization's president is concerned with the high rate of turnover and low productivity of its employees. The president has asked you to diagnose the company's problems and to recommend a plan for solving them. Specifically, the president wants your answers to the following questions:

1. What do you think the real problems are and why?
2. What solution(s) would you propose and why?
3. How would you implement your plan?
4. What reasons would you give for doing it this way?

You will have the opportunity to meet briefly with the top management of the organization in a short while to get answers to preliminary questions you have about the organization. Then, on the date given by your instructor, you will be requested to present your plan.

Step 4: The management and consulting groups meet independently, and then together.

Step 5: The consulting teams present their proposals one at a time.

Step 6: The management team selects the consulting team they would like to hire and describes the criteria for selection.

Step 7: Discussion. With the entire class, address the following:

1. What group was hired? Why?
2. What intervention strategies were proposed? Would they be effective?
3. Describe the change processes proposed.
4. What makes an effective change effort?
5. What makes an effective consulting proposal?

SUMMARY

Ensuring high quality of working life and organizational performance are major concerns of organizational members. In this chapter we discussed organization development, work design, and structural interventions that can increase the quality of working life and productivity in organizations.

Organization development interventions attempt to alter personal or interpersonal effectiveness, build collaborative teams, reduce intergroup conflict, and increase overall organizational effectiveness. In the Ericsson de Argentina and Labor/Management Participation Teams cases you identified behavioral interventions that would facilitate change in these organizations.

Redesigning work focuses on the activities performed by a job holder. In the job redesign problem at Foxwood Appliances, you had the opportunity to apply work simplification, job enrichment, QWL programs, and alternative work schedules to redesigning a job.

Restructuring an organization itself may increase efficiency as well as improve the quality of working life. In examining the Suburban Hospital Admissions Department you considered the implications of various organization structures.

Managers and human resources professionals in the United States have imported the ideas of worker ownership and Japanese management from abroad as additional ways of improving the quality of working life in U.S. organizations.

Organizational change cannot occur, however, without first diagnosing the needs an intervention is meant to address, and evaluating the effectiveness of the change strategies afterward. In addition, during implementation change agents must overcome resistance to change. In analyzing the Bossless System at Digital and participating in the Consulting Problem you offered plans for overcoming resistance to change. You also examined the trade-offs involved in the selection of various change agents, as well as some of the characteristics of an effective change agent.

ENDNOTES

[1]Bluestone, Technology and the human factor, *Work Life Review* 3 (1984): 3–13.

[2]G. Lippitt and J. Rumley, Living with work—The search for quality in work life, *Optimum* 8 (January 1977): 38.

[3]R.E. Walton, Quality of working life: What is it?, *Sloan Management Review* 15 (1973): 11–21.

[4]W.L. French and C.H. Bell, Jr., *Organization Development: Behavioral Science Interventions for Organizational Improvement* 2nd ed. (Englewood Cliffs, N.J.: Prentice-Hall, 1978).

[5]E.H. Schein, The role of the founder in creating organizational culture, *Organizational Dynamics* (Summer 1983): 13–28.

[6]R. Beckhard, The confrontation meeting, *Harvard Business Review* 45 (1967): 149–155.

[7]L.E. Short, Planned organizational change, *MSU Business Topics* (Autumn 1973): 53–61.

[8]These strategies have also been characterized in other ways; see French and Bell, *op. cit.;* L. Spenser, Jr. and B. Cullen, *Taxonomies of Organizational Change—Literature Review and Analysis,* ARI Technical Report TR 78–A23 (Alexandria, Va.: U.S. Army Research Institute for the Behavioral and Social Sciences, 1978), cited in E.F. Huse, *Organization Development and Change* 2nd ed. (St. Paul, Minn.: West, 1980); M.B. Miles and R.A. Schmuck, The nature of organization development, in *Organization Development in Schools,* ed. R.A. Schmuck and M.B. Miles (La Jolla, Cal.: University Associates, 1976); R. Harrison, Choosing the depth of organizational intervention, *Journal of Applied Behavioral Science* 6 (1970): 181–202.

[9]See F. Luthans and R. Kreitner, *Organizational Behavior Modification and Beyond* (Glenview, Ill.: Scott, Foresman, 1985) for detailed discussion of behavior modification and operant learning.

[10]See J. Campbell and M. Dunnette, Effectiveness of t-group experiences in managerial training and development, *Psychological Bulletin* 70 (1968): 73–103; and E.H. Schein and W. Bennis, *Personal and Organizational Changes Through Group Methods: The Laboratory Approach* (New York: Wiley, 1965) for discussion of sensitivity training.

[11]Campbell and Dunnette, *op. cit.,* p. 75.

[12]Campbell and Dunnette, *op. cit.*

[13]E. Berne, *Games People Play* (New York: Grove Press, 1964).

[14]E.H. Schein, *Process Consultation* (Reading, Mass.: Addison-Wesley, 1969), p. 9.

[15]I. Dayal and J.M. Thomas, Operation KPE: Developing a new organization, *Journal of Applied Behavioral Science* 4 (1968): 473–506.

[16]E.F. Huse, *op. cit.*

[17]R. Harrison, Role negotiation: A tough-minded approach to team development, in *The Social Technology of Organization Development,* ed. W.W. Burke and H.A. Hornstein (La Jolla, Calif.: University Associates, 1972).

[18]R. Beckhard, Optimizing team building efforts, *Journal of Contemporary Business* (Summer 1972): 23–32.

[19]R.R. Blake and J.R. Mouton, *Building a Dynamic Corporation Through Grid Organization Development* (Reading, Mass.: Addison-Wesley, 1969); R.R. Blake and J.R. Mouton, *The New Managerial Grid* (Houston: Gulf, 1978).

[20]R.E. Walton, *Interpersonal Peacemaking: Confrontation and Third-Party Consultations* (Reading, Mass.: Addison-Wesley, 1969).

[21]Beckhard, Optimizing team building efforts, *op. cit.*

[22]J.K. Fordyce and R. Weil, *Managing with People* (Reading, Mass.: Addison-Wesley, 1971).

[23]D.E. Zand, Collateral organization: A new change strategy, *Journal of Applied Behavioral Science* 10 (1974): 63–89.

[24]Huse, *op. cit.*

[25]D.A. Nadler, *Feedback and Organization Development: Using Data-Based Methods* (Reading, Mass.: Addison-Wesley, 1977).

[26]W.W. Burke, *Organization Development: Principles and Practices* (Boston: Little, Brown, 1982).

[27]E. Yager, Examining the quality control circle, *Personnel Journal* (October 1979): 682–684, 708.

[28]F.W. Taylor, *The Principles of Scientific Management* (New York: Harper, 1911).

[29]F. Herzberg and A. Zautra, Orthodox job enrichment:

Measuring true quality in job satisfaction, *Personnel* 53 (September-October, 1976); F. Herzberg and E.A. Rafalko, Efficiency in the military: Cutting costs with orthodox job enrichment, *Personnel* 52 (November-December, 1975).

[30]J.R. Hackman et al., A new strategy for job enrichment, *California Management Review* 17 (1975): 59.

[31]*Ibid.*

[32]See K.H. Roberts and W. Glick, The job characteristics approach to task design: A critical review, *Journal of Applied Psychology* 66 (1981): 193–217.

[33]D. Lewin, Collective bargaining and the quality of work life, *Organizational Dynamics* 33 (Autumn 1981): 37–53.

[34]Hak-Chong Lee, *Lordstown Plant of General Motors Case* (Seoul, Korea: Yonsei University, n.d.).

[35]I. Bluestone, How quality-of-worklife projects work for the United Automobile Workers, *Monthly Labor Review* (July 1980): 39–41.

[36]*Ibid.*

[37]See A.O. Elbing, H. Gadon, and J.R.M. Gordon, Flexible working hours: The missing link, *California Management Review* 7 (1975): 50–57; and J.W. Newstrom and J.L. Pierce, Alternative work schedules: The state of the art, *Personnel Administrator* 24 (1979): 19–23, for discussion of flexitime.

[38]J.M. Rosow and R. Zager, Punch out the time clocks, *Harvard Business Review* (March-April 1983): 12–30.

[39]W.D. Hicks and R. Klimoski, The impact of flexitime on employee attitude, *Academy of Management Journal* 24 (1981): 333–334.

[40]J.S. Kim and A.F. Campagna, Effects of flexitime on employee attendance and performance: A field experiment, *Academy of Management Journal* 24 (1981): 729–741.

[41]Rosow, *op. cit.*

[42]A. Chandler, *Strategy and Structure* (Cambridge, Mass.: MIT Press, 1969) offers a classic discussion of this relationship.

[43]See A. Walker and J. Lorsch, Organizational choice: Product versus function, *Harvard Business Review* 46 (1968); J.R. Galbraith, Matrix organization design, *Business Horizons* 14 (1971): 29–40; and L.R. Sayles, Matrix organization: The structure with the future, *Organizational Dynamics* 4 (Autumn 1976): 2–17, for further discussion of project management.

[44]See L.C. Stuckenbruck, The matrix organization, *Project Management Quarterly* 2 (September 1979); S.M. Davis and P.R. Lawrence, *Matrix* (Reading, Mass.: Addison-Wesley, 1977); J.R. Galbraith, *Organization Design* (Reading, Mass.: Addison-Wesley, 1977); and H.F. Kolodny, The evolution to a matrix organization, *Academy of Management Review* 4 (1979): 543–553, for further discussion of matrix management.

[45]Davis and Lawrence, *op. cit.*

[46]H. Mintzberg, *Structure in Fives: Designing Effective Organizations* (Englewood Cliffs, N.J.: Prentice-Hall, 1983); H. Mintzberg, *Structuring Organizations* (Englewood Cliffs, N.J.: Prentice-Hall, 1978).

[47]*Ibid.*

[48]*Ibid.*

[49]*Ibid.*

[50]*Ibid.*

[51]See J.R. Gordon, *A Diagnostic Approach to Organizational Behavior* (Boston: Allyn and Bacon, 1983).

[52]H. Levin and B. Jackall, eds., *Worker Cooperatives in America* (Berkeley: University of California Press, 1984).

[53]"Mondragon Experiment," film (San Francisco: California Newsreel, n.d.).

[54]R.M. Mason, *Participatory and Workplace Democracy* (Carbondale: Southern Illinois University Press, 1982); and M. Poole, *Workers' Participation in Industry* (London: Routledge & Kegan Paul, 1978) elaborate on the examples of codetermination described here.

[55]Mason, *op. cit.*

[56]T.G. Cummings, Self-regulating work groups: A sociotechnical synthesis, *Academy of Management Review* 3 (1978): 625–634.

[57]N. Hatvany and V. Pucik, Japanese management practices and productivity, *Organizational Development* 10 (Spring 1981).

[58]*Ibid.*

[59]W. Ouchi and A.M. Jaeger, Type Z organization: Stability in the midst of mobility, *Academy of Management Review* 3 (1978): 305–314; W. Ouchi, *Theory Z: Meeting the Japanese Challenge* (Reading, Mass.: Addison-Wesley, 1980).

[60]*Ibid.*

[61]T. Peters and R.H. Waterman, Jr., *In Search of Excellence: Lessons from America's Best-Run Companies* (New York: Harper & Row, 1982).

FURTHER READINGS

Burke, W.W. *Organization Development: Principles and Practices.* Boston: Little, Brown, 1982.

Cummings, T.G. and Molloy, E.S. *Improving Productivity and the Quality of Work Life.* New York: Praeger, 1977.

French, W.L. and Bell, C.H., Jr. *Organization Development: Behavioral Science Interventions for Organizational Improvement* 2nd ed. Englewood Cliffs, N.J.: Prentice-Hall, 1978.

Hackman, J.R. and Oldham, G.R. *Work Redesign.* Reading, Mass.: Addison-Wesley, 1980.

Huse, E.F. *Organization Development and Change* 2nd ed. St. Paul, Minn.: West, 1980.

Mintzberg, H. *Structure in Fives: Designing Effective Organizations.* Englewood Cliffs, N.J.: Prentice-Hall, 1983.

Ouchi, W. *Theory Z: Meeting the Japanese Challenge.* Reading, Mass.: Addison-Wesley, 1980.

Pascale, R. and Athos, A. *The Art of Japanese Management.* New York: Warner Books, 1981.

U.S. Labor-Management Services Administration, *Resource Guide to Labor Management Cooperation.* Washington, D.C.: U.S. Government Printing Office, 1982.

The Work Life Review, published by the Michigan Quality of Work Life Council, Ann Arbor.

CHAPTER 15

Ensuring Effective Human Resources Management

CHAPTER OUTLINE

LEARNING CHECKPOINTS

After completing the reading and activities in this chapter, students will be able to

- discuss the indicators of effective human resources management;
- discuss the relationship of human resources management to organizational effectiveness;
- review the practical approach for each personnel and labor relations system;
- show three ways to assess the costs of human resources management practices;
- describe a way to quantify the benefits of human resources management practices;
- describe the components of a computerized human resources information system;
- discuss the value of a computerized human resources information system;
- discuss the key issues in strategic human resources management;
- offer three alternate scenarios for the future of human resources management;
- list the elements of comprehensive human resources management.

INTRODUCTION

Specialty Stores, Inc., is a major department store chain in the Southwest, owned by Enterprises, Inc. Specialty Stores includes fifteen branches, with the largest or main store in the downtown area of a large city. Specialty Stores employs approximately 4000 workers in its stores. Figure 15–1 provides a partial organizational chart.

During the early 1980s, Specialty experienced a significant decline in sales and profitability. Some analysts attributed this to the recession, but others felt that the chain's employees were not as productive as they once were. The new merchandising vice president, Joshua Fine, questioned the effectiveness of the merchandise buying groups. In particular, he was concerned about the quality of the jobs performed by the assistant buyers, the dissatisfaction expressed about the jobs by the buyers themselves and top management, and the high turnover rate of the assistant buyers.

Each buying group is composed of a buyer, a senior assistant buyer, and an assistant buyer. As a group they are responsible for the selection, purchase, and distribution of goods throughout the fifteen stores, and they are involved to some extent in displaying merchandise in each store.

Top management is becoming very concerned about the position of assistant buyer. Top managers have said that the assistant's job provides an opportunity to learn the buyer's job; however, most assistant buyers spend the majority of their time performing menial clerical tasks. No assistant buyer joins his or her buyer on buying trips to New York. Few assistant buyers leave the office in the downtown store to see the distribution and display of merchandise in the suburban stores.

In the past two years, turnover has been approximately 67 percent of the new hires. Management feels that significant time and expense are invested in recruiting and training the assistant buyers, and that this investment is lost every time an assistant leaves the organization. Recruitment emphasizes college recruiting and promotion from the store's sales clerks.

Individuals can enter the store's work force as assistant buyers, typically after receiving a degree from a junior college or college; no previous retailing experience is required. Approximately 50 percent of those hired have worked as salespeople in a retail store or have majored in retailing in college. Occasionally an assistant buyer is promoted from a sales position in the store or hired from a competitor. Assistant buyers receive relatively low wages for relatively long hours: a typical assistant buyer earns $11–14,000 and works sixty hours a week.

Assistant buyers attend a one-week orientation session conducted by one or two buyers, among whom the responsibility rotates. The personnel department recruits, hires, and pays employees, but assumes no other responsibilities for human resources management. After being hired, assistant buyers receive only on-the-job training, the quality of which is mainly a function of the quality of the supervision they receive from the buyer in their department. They are evaluated on their performance once a year, on the anniversary of their joining the store. The written form asks only for employee strengths and weaknesses, and is almost identical to that used when Joshua Fine was an assistant buyer

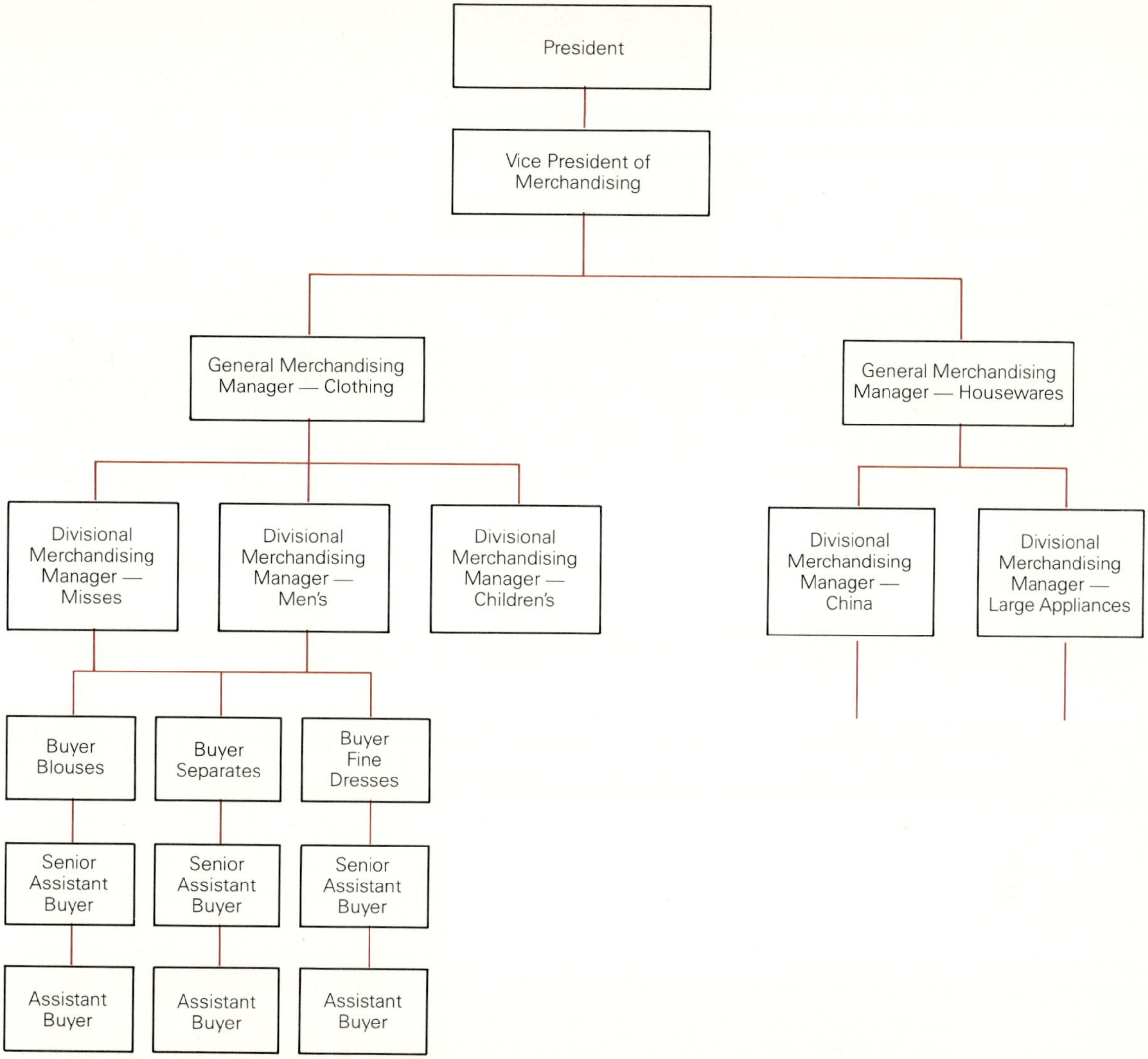

Figure 15–1 PARTIAL ORGANIZATIONAL CHART OF SPECIALTY STORES, INC.

almost twenty years ago. Some supervisors accompany the written report with an evaluation interview; others simply hand their assistant buyers the written review for their required signature.

Interviews with assistant buyers have indicated some dissatisfaction with their pay and hours. They seem more concerned, however, about the quality of their training, the lack of opportunities for advancement, and the absence of regular communication from their superiors about their performance. Several also have noted a cut-throat climate in the stores, where there seems to be little teamwork among buyers of related products, such as women's blouses and women's suits and dresses. They attribute this to the lack of promotional opportunities for buyers. Buyers never ask assistant buyers for their opinions, even in areas of style where some assistants have expertise.

Specialty Stores, Inc., clearly has problems in managing its human resources. How would you evaluate the effectiveness of human resources management practices for the assistant buyers?

In this chapter we conclude our discussion of human resources management by, first, summarizing the criteria for assessing its effectiveness. Second, we review the practical approach to human resources management, evaluating each area as it relates to the assistant buyers at Specialty Stores. Third, we examine ways of assessing the costs and benefits of various human resources management practices. Fourth, we look at the way computerized information systems can improve human resources management. We conclude with comments about the future of human resources management; we consider strategic human resources management, other future trends, and their implications for human resources professionals and managers.

CRITERIA OF EFFECTIVENESS

How do we determine whether human resources management is effective in Specialty Stores or another company? In this section we consider some general criteria.

Organizational Effectiveness

We can judge the effectiveness of human resources management practices in part by determining the organization's effectiveness. Organizational effectiveness depends on (1) employee characteristics, including job performance, (2) managerial policies and practices, (3) organizational characteristics such as structure and technology, and (4) characteristics of the internal and external environment.[1] Effective human resources management addresses each of these characteristics, and in turn influences organizational effectiveness. Diverse indicators, such as those listed in Figure 15–2, can be used to measure effectiveness. For example, if an organization has a high absenteeism rate, low worker morale, and inefficient production, it does not function at maximum effectiveness. Thus top executives and human resources professionals should identify the appropriate indicators for their situation and assess their organizations on each of them.

How effective is Specialty Stores according to these criteria? Certainly the declining sales, low profitability, and high turnover of assistant buyers suggest some areas of ineffectiveness. In addition, morale and quality of working life seem poor; productivity and efficiency seem low.

Overall Effectiveness	The degree to which the organization is accomplishing all its major tasks or achieving all its objectives. A general evaluation that takes in as many single criteria as possible and results in a general judgment about the effectiveness of the organization.
Quality	The quality of the primary service or product provided by the organization. This may take many operational forms, primarily determined by the *kind* of product or service provided by the organization.
Productivity	The quantity of or volume of the major product or service that the organization provides. Can be measured at three levels; individual, group, and total organization. This is not a measure of efficiency; no cost/output ratio is computed.
Readiness	An overall judgment concerning the probability that the organization could successfully perform some specified task if asked to do so.
Efficiency	A ratio that reflects a comparison of some aspect of unit performance to the costs incurred for that performance. Examples: dollars per single unit of production, amount of down time, degree to which schedules, standards of performance, or other milestones are met. On occasion, just the total amount of costs (money, material, etc.) a unit has incurred over some period can be used.
Profit or Return	The return on the investment used in running the organization from the owners' point of view. The amount of resources left after all costs and obligations are met, sometimes expressed as a percentage.
Growth	An increase in such things as manpower, plant facilities, assets, sales, profits, market share, and innovations. A comparison of an organization's present state with its own past state.
Utilization of Environment	The extent to which the organization successfully interacts with its environment, acquiring scarce, valued resources necessary to its effective operation. This is viewed in a long-term, optimizing framework and not in a short-term, maximizing framework. For example, the degree to which it acquires a steady supply of manpower and financial resources.
Stability	The maintenance of structure, function, and resources through time, and more particularly through periods of stress.
Turnover or Retention	Frequency or amount of voluntary terminations.
Absenteeism	The frequency of occasions of personnel being absent from the job.
Accidents	Frequency of on-the-job accidents resulting in down time or recovery time.
Morale	A predisposition in organization members to put forth extra effort in achieving organizational goals and objectives. Includes feelings of commitment. Morale is a group phenomenon involving extra effort, goals communality, and feelings of belonging. Groups have some degree of morale, while individuals have some degree of motivation (and satisfaction). By implication, morale is inferred from group phenomena.
Motivation	The strength of the predisposition of an *individual* to engage in goal-directed action or activity on the job. This is not a feeling of relative contentment with various job outcomes as is satisfaction, but more akin to a feeling of readiness or willingness to work at accomplishing the job's goals.
Satisfaction	The degree of feeling of contentment felt by a person toward his organizational role or job. The degree to which individuals perceive they are equitably rewarded by various aspects of their job situation and the organization to which they belong.
Internalization of Organizational Goals	The acceptance of organizational goals by individuals and units within the organization. Their belief that the organization's goals are right and proper.
Conflict-Cohesion	A bipolar dimension defined at the cohesion end by an organization in which the members like one another, work well together, communicate fully and openly, and coordinate their work efforts. At the other end lies the organization with verbal and physical clashes, poor coordination, and ineffective communication.
Flexibility-Adaptation	The ability of an organization to change its standard operating procedures in response to environmental changes, to resist becoming rigid in response to environmental stimuli.

Figure 15–2 INDICATORS OF ORGANIZATIONAL EFFECTIVENESS *Continued*

Evaluations by External Entities	Evaluations of the organization or organizational unit by those individuals and organizations in its environment with which it interacts. Loyalty to, confidence in, and support given the organization by such groups as suppliers, customers, stockholders, enforcement agencies, and the general public.
Climate*	The nature of the internal environment of the organization.
Quality of Working Life*	The quality of the employee's relationship to his or her working environment.

*These dimensions were added by the author of this book.

SOURCE: Adapted from J.P. Campbell, "Research into the Nature of Organizational Effectiveness: An Endangered Species?" Unpublished manuscript. Minneapolis: University of Minnesota, 1973; and J.R. Gordon, *A Diagnostic Approach to Organizational Behavior* (Boston: Allyn and Bacon, 1983).

Figure 15–2 Continued

Effective Human Resources Practices

Effective human resources practices should contribute to overall organizational effectiveness. Conversely, when organizational effectiveness is low, we might look to the quality of human resources management as one explanation. How do we characterize effective human resources management? On a general level we can assess the following:

1. Does human resources management respond to the needs of the individual organizational members?
2. Does human resources management contribute to organizational effectiveness?
3. Does it yield greater benefits than costs?
4. Does it use the expertise of managers and human resources professionals?
5. Do managers and human resources professionals interact in ways that encourage organizational effectiveness?
6. Does human resources management have the commitment of top management?
7. Does it have the unions' support?
8. Are the human resources management practices dynamic and responsive to changes in the environment, organization, job, and individuals?
9. Does human resources management use state-of-the-art knowledge about organizations and their members?
10. Does it use the practical approach described in this book?

Answering such questions involves interviewing organizational members, observing organizational behavior, and assessing organizational outcomes. The methods for collecting these data vary in sophistication from one organization to another, depending on the resources available, expertise of organizational members, and preferences of top management for accurate and detailed information. Preliminary answers to these and similar questions suggest that human resources management at Specialty Stores could be improved, however. For example, the lack of career development does not respond to the needs of the assistant buyers. Insufficient training, poor job design, or low compensation may be responsible for their declining productivity.

The high turnover increases the cost of recruiting and training assistant buyers; these costs may exceed the benefits derived if they never develop the skills required for effective performance. The training is conducted primarily by buyers who may lack the skills or knowledge for effective teaching. And there are questions about the cost-effectiveness of the training offered (see discussion of the costs and benefits of training later in this chapter).

In addition, the human resources professionals seem to be relatively uninvolved in human resources management; using their expertise would improve the situation in each of these areas. Finally, Specialty Stores has changed its human resources management little during the past twenty years. Consequently, practices do not respond to the increased education of new assistant buyers, the availability of new technology, or the shifts in consumer demands. Certainly the effectiveness of human resources management at Specialty Stores could be increased.

REVIEW OF THE PRACTICAL APPROACH

Throughout this book we have used a four-step approach for increasing the effectiveness of human resources management: (1) diagnosis of the situation, (2) evaluation of existing practices, (3) design of revised policies and practices, and (4) planning for and implementation of the recommended changes. How can Joshua Fine apply the practical approach to solving the problems at Specialty Stores?

Diagnosis

Joshua Fine must first determine the nature of the environment, organization, and jobs at Specialty Stores. The environment is dynamic, complex, and somewhat unpredictable. We can assume that competition is increasing, the work force is more educated than earlier, and individuals have higher expectations from their jobs. Because of the intense competition, Specialty Stores must ensure that all employees are productive, that turnover and absenteeism are low, and that the organization operates efficiently and effectively.

Organizational assessment suggests that limited resources may constrain the human resources management: a fixed and relatively small budget exists for the compensation and training of assistant buyers. Some resources devoted to recruitment could be shifted elsewhere, if turnover were reduced. The internal environment at Specialty Stores is described as cut-throat. It does not tolerate questions or mistakes, but a more supportive environment might change the nature of human resources management. Management could include workers in decision-making, provide opportunities for growth and advancement, and improve the quality of working life. Use of the hierarchy is strong, discouraging assistant buyers from acting creatively or autonomously. Their superiors neither encourage them to take risks nor pay much attention to their ideas.

The job itself has become highly clerical rather than professional. Its description, specifications, and performance standards seem to differ from the expectations of job holders. For individuals expecting professional opportunities, redesign of the job is essential.

Evaluation

Following the situational audit, we must evaluate human resources management practices in personnel and labor relations; specifically, the extent to which current practices in these areas meet the criteria of effective human resources management as described throughout this book. Figure 15–3 lists a series of questions that can

Planning

1. Does the organization regularly forecast the supply of and demand for employees in various categories?
2. Does the organization use a variety of techniques for forecasting?
3. Are human resources plans consistent with strategic plans?
4. Does the organization maintain replacement charts for all positions?
5. Does the organization maintain a data base for determining transitions among positions?

Work Analysis

6. Do job analyses—job descriptions, job specifications, and performance standards—exist for every position?
7. Does a regular review of job analyses take place?
8. Are the job analyses updated periodically?
9. Do skill inventories exist for all employees?
10. Are top management, human resources professionals, managers, and workers involved in the work analysis program?

Recruitment

11. Does recruitment include a detailed situational analysis and specification of criteria for each job?
12. Are all potential sources of recruits identified and evaluated?
13. Are both internal and external sources of recruits tapped?
14. Do recruiting methods selected reach those individuals who meet the recruitment criteria?
15. Are new sources tapped by innovative methods?
16. Is job posting used?
17. Does the organization maintain a data base of potential candidates?
18. Does the organization encourage use of realistic job previews?
19. Are managers trained in employment interviewing?

Selection

20. Are measurable selection criteria developed for each job to be filled?
21. Are the instruments used reliable, valid, and cost-effective measures of the selection criteria?
22. Are multiple instruments used in selection?
23. Do managers use interviews to measure selection criteria?
24. Is there a quantifiable screening process?
25. Does a data base maintain records of available employees inside and outside the organization?

Figure 15–3 QUESTIONS FOR EVALUATING HUMAN RESOURCES PRACTICES *Continued*

Decruitment

26. Do regular predictions of a possible oversupply of employees occur?
27. Do managers attempt to reduce an oversupply through attrition before using more drastic approaches?
28. Is there an outplacement program for employees experiencing a layoff?
29. Does the organization have a progressive discipline procedure?
30. Does top management look for innovative ways of reducing the work force when needed?
31. Are there programs to reduce employee obsolescence and plateauing?
32. Are there programs to deal with employee burnout?
33. What procedures dealing with difficult employees include a rehabilitation component?
34. Are exit interviews conducted regularly?
35. Are managers well informed about and trained in decruitment policies and practices?
36. Do managers level with employees when their performance is inadequate?

Performance Evaluation

37. Is there a performance evaluation system that includes both evaluation and development?
38. Do employees have a positive attitude toward performance evaluation?
39. Do appraisal criteria exist for every employee?
40. Do raters systematically observe each ratee's performance?
41. Do those with relevant knowledge of job performance perform the evaluation?
42. Are formal appraisals performed at least twice a year, and informal ones performed more often?
43. Are developmental appraisals separated from compensation decisions?
44. Do evaluation instruments have high validity, reliability, discriminability, freedom from bias, relevance, and cost-effectiveness?
45. Are multiple types of rating formats used?
46. Are managers trained in the conduct of evaluation interviews?
47. Are performance records maintained on all employees?
48. Do managers use effective communication techniques; i.e., create a supportive climate, operate on an adult-to-adult basis, and take a problem-solving strategy?
49. Does each employee and his or her supervisor regularly engage in joint goal-setting?

Training and Development

50. Do training and development programs exist?
51. Is the nature of organizational socialization understood and controlled?
52. Does regular assessment of training needs at the organizational, job, and personal levels occur?
53. Do managers and their subordinates participate in the needs assessment?
54. Is there a current inventory of training opportunities?
55. Is training designed to encourage learning?
56. Are diverse training programs offered to employees?
57. Are training programs selected to match training needs?
58. Are training programs evaluated for participant reactions, learning, behavior, and other results?

Career Management

59. Do managers determine a subordinate's career stage and meet the needs of that stage?
60. Do managers determine a subordinate's career anchor and fit job opportunities to that anchor?
61. Do self-assessment programs exist?
62. Do managers and human resources professionals act as career counselors?

Figure 15–3 Continued

Continued

63. Do managers and subordinates jointly formulate career goals?
64. Does the organization plan for career transitions?
65. Do diverse career paths exist?
66. Does the organization have a mentoring program?
67. Does succession planning exist?
68. Is extensive information available about career opportunities?
69. Are employees trained in career management?

Compensation

70. Is the compensation program designed to motivate employees?
71. Are rewards assigned equitably?
72. Do rewards meet individual needs?
73. Do rewards reinforce desired behaviors?
74. Is job evaluation performed regularly in order to update the wage structure?
75. Is the wage structure consistent and coherent?
76. Does the organization have access to data from current and relevant compensation surveys?
77. Do merit pay plans exist?
78. Are there provisions for preventing pay compression?
79. Are benefits comprehensive?
80. Do benefits respond to employee needs?
81. Does the organization have incentive programs that help accomplish organizational goals?

Unionization

82. Do managers and human resources professionals understand the implications of unionization?
83. Do managers and human resources professionals know employees' and their own rights regarding unionization?
84. Has top management determined their attitude toward unionization?
85. Have managers been trained in managing unionized employees?
86. If top management wishes to avoid unionization, have they taken positive steps to ensure effective human resources management?

Collective Bargaining

87. Do all organizational members know the provisions of union contracts?
88. Do human resources professionals or top management monitor contract negotiations at similar organizations?
89. Does management prepare thoroughly for union negotiations?
90. Do union and management take a problem-solving approach to negotiations?
91. Do union and management bargain in good faith?
92. Do union members use strikes infrequently and only as a last resort?

Grievance Resolution

93. Is there a grievance system?
94. Do all organizational members understand the provisions of the grievance process?
95. Does the grievance process encourage the rapid resolution of complaints?
96. Do union and management call in third parties to assist in negotiations when impasses occur?
97. Do workers file grievances only when their rights are violated?
98. Do workers avoid filing spurious grievances?
99. Are arbitrators, mediators, or fact-finders called in appropriately?

Figure 15–3 Continued

Continued

Legal Issues

100. Do all employees know the legal provisions that govern equal employment opportunity, safety and health, and benefits administration?

101. Does the organization have and disseminate information about antidiscrimination policies?

102. Does the organization have an affirmative action plan?

103. Is the organization meeting any affirmative action goals?

104. Is there a written policy prohibiting sexual harassment?

105. Does a safe and healthy work environment exist?

106. Does a safety committee monitor working conditions to ensure their compliance with good practice and OSHA requirements?

107. Do employee benefits meet legal reporting and distribution requirements?

108. Do recruitment, selection, decruitment, performance evaluation, compensation, and collective bargaining practices conform to legal requirements?

Organizational Change

109. Does the organization have a high quality of working life?

110. Have QWL programs been implemented?

111. Have behavioral, job redesign, or organizational redesign interventions been implemented?

112. Have some characteristics of Japanese management been introduced?

113. In introducing change, has the most appropriate change agent been selected?

114. Have attempts been made to overcome resistance to change?

115. Have interventions been matched to the problems diagnosed?

Figure 15–3 Continued

offer a preliminary evaluation of each area. In this section we discuss how well the company's treatment of assistant buyers satisfies these principles of good human resources management practice.

Planning. We have no indication that human resources planning is occurring. The organization should use a variety of techniques to forecast supply of and demand for workers. The high turnover rate underscores the importance of planning so that replacements can be made smoothly.

Work Analysis. No process currently exists for periodically analyzing the job of assistant buyer to ensure that it fits with the organization's needs. The clerical nature of the position compared to the relative skill level of the job holders suggests that the current job description may not be appropriate.

Recruitment. Specialty Stores successfully fills the open positions. We have little information about the recruitment process except that Specialty Stores relies on two types of recruitment. However, colleges and current employees may not be the most appropriate sources for the assistant buyer job as currently performed. Additional and diverse methods of recruiting should be considered.

Selection. The selection criteria may not be appropriate; the organization places college graduates in clerical positions. This selection of overqualified workers may contribute to the high turnover.

Decruitment. Decruitment is not necessary for the assistant buyer positions due to the high turnover. And the organization deals with a potential oversupply of workers for managerial positions by limited advancement opportunities within the organization. Top management seems to lack innovative ways of dealing with the number of potential managers versus the number of possible positions. Neither obsolescence nor plateauing seems to be a problem for the assistant buyers.

Performance Evaluation. No appraisal criteria exist. The performance evaluation system lacks a systematic approach to evaluation, and includes no development. The evaluation forms use only a single format, which seems to be out of date and shows unknown reliability and validity. Managers receive no training in completing the evaluation forms, nor do they maintain performance records. Performance interviews are conducted randomly and without clear objectives.

Training and Development. Training is limited to a brief orientation session and then on-the-job training. In neither situation do the trainers have sufficient expertise to conduct the training effectively. No assessment of the training needs of assistant buyers occurs. Specialty Stores does not maintain a current inventory of training opportunities, nor is there any evaluation of training.

Career Management. Little career management takes place at Specialty Stores. Buyers and other managers do little career counseling; nor do they assess workers' career stage, career anchor, or career goals. The organization does not plan for career transitions, offer diverse career paths, or offer a succession program. Most workers feel frustrated at the lack of career advice and advancement opportunities.

Compensation. Compensation seems inadequate for the assistant buyers; too low to motivate workers to remain with Specialty Stores. Further, no provisions have been made for merit increases. No discussion of benefits is included, but given the lack of assessment of employee needs in general, benefits may not be appropriate for the employees.

Unionization. The organization is not unionized. Given the low wages and poor working conditions, Specialty Stores could be subject to a unionization attempt.

Collective Bargaining. No collective bargaining occurs.

Grievance Resolution. The case provides no indication of whether there is a grievance system.

Legal Issues. We cannot assess whether Specialty Stores is an equal opportunity employer. Similarly, we cannot evaluate the quality of safety and health in the workplace. The legality of benefit pension plans also cannot be determined.

Organizational Change. The description of Specialty Stores provides no indication of attempts to change the organization. Behavioral interventions to improve the effectiveness of the buyers, job redesign for the assistant buyer position, and organizational redesign to respond to changes in the environment over the past two decades would be appropriate. The top management of Specialty Stores might also implement some quality-of-worklife programs to improve worker attitudes and productivity.

Design

Following assessment of existing human resources practices, managers and human resources professionals can specify any deficiencies in human resources management. For example, Specialty Stores lacks comprehensive career development and training systems. Top managers, human resources professionals, and managers should then *design* ways of improving these areas. Recommendations in these areas might include the following (among others):

1. Human resources professionals should assist managers in analyzing the assistant buyers' needs; then they should identify the types of training needed organization-wide.
2. Human resources professionals should organize or conduct the required off-the-job training and oversee on-the-job training conducted by the buyers.
3. Human resources professionals should institute a program to evaluate the training in which assistant buyers participate.
4. Managers should insist that human resources professionals provide the training needed by the assistant buyers.
5. Human resources professionals and managers should offer career counseling to assistant buyers; this counseling should emphasize an assessment of the assistants' strengths, weaknesses, and developmental needs.
6. Human resources professionals and executives should identify a set of career paths for assistant buyers.
7. Managers should receive training in career opportunities within Specialty Stores and related organizations; they should disseminate this information to their subordinates.
8. Managers should track the job progressions of their subordinates.

Alternatively, the human resources professionals or managers could do nothing; or they could redesign the job to be a clerical position. If they opt for the latter, design should address all current deficiencies. It must consider, to some extent, the cost of the proposed changes as well as their likely acceptance (the implementation stage later addresses these considerations more directly). Human resources professionals or managers should generate a wide range of design alternatives, and choices among these should then be subjected to cost-benefit analysis.

Implementation

Following the design of the relevant human resources systems, executives, human resources professionals, and other managers must develop a strategy for ensuring the success of the new systems. First, they must determine which individuals should implement and be affected by the change. Should managers or human resources professionals monitor a career development program, for example? Second, they must consider ways of overcoming resistance to change. Introduction of educational programs or changes in the reward system may facilitate the acceptance of new programs. Third, they must identify the resources available to implement new programs. Hiring a large staff of human resources professionals to implement training programs may be too costly; using a combination of on-the-job training by managers and workshops by external consultants may sufficiently address the training problems. Next, they must develop a schedule for introducing new programs. For example, selected buyers might pilot a career development program under the supervision of specially trained human resources professionals. Or, human resources professionals might redesign the compensation systems. Last, they must implement the prescribed changes in a systematic, step-by-step change effort.

INCREASING THE COST-BENEFITS OF HUMAN RESOURCES MANAGEMENT

Because human resources management cannot be tied directly to the "bottom line," there is some difficulty in determining both the financial costs and benefits of human resources management practices. This difficulty exists for four reasons: (1) human resources professionals do not know how to measure the costs of behavior; (2) top management believes that the effects of human resources activities cannot be quantified; (3) some human resources professionals do not want their functions to be measured; and (4) those human resources managers who want to measure their functions have lacked the knowledge to do so.[2] Recent efforts have offered ways of addressing three of these four reasons.

Analyzing Costs

While there is no generally accepted system for human resources accounting, several approaches have been used.[3] In the *historical* approach, costs under recruiting and acquisition, formal training, informal training, experience, and development are tabulated for each manager. Costs are then amortized over the expected working lives of the employees; any unamortized costs due to employee turnover are written off.[4] This and similar budgeting approaches treat workers as assets.[5] Although the historical approach emphasizes performance measurements, it includes significant subjectivity in evaluating and classifying expenditures and fails to measure the employees' value to the organization.[6]

The *replacement cost* approach measures the cost of replacing an employee: thus it tabulates the costs of recruiting and training a new employee.[7] Table 15–1 shows one way of measuring replacement costs. Although these calculations could provide some insight into the cost of ineffective human resources manage-

Cost Element	Formula			
Communicating job availability (R_1)	= [advertising and employment agency fees per termination	+ (time required for communicating job availability	× personnel department employee's pay rate)]	× number of turnovers replaced during period
Preemployment administrative functions (R_2)	= time required by personnel department for preemployment administrative functions	× average personnel department employee's pay rate	× number of turnovers replaced during period	
Entrance interview (R_3)	= time required for interview	× interviewer's rate	× number of interviews during period	
Staff meeting (R_4)	= time required for meeting	× (personnel department employees' pay rate	+ department representatives' pay rate)	× number of meetings during period
Postemployment acquisition and dissemination of information (R_5)	= time required for acquiring and disseminating information	× average personnel department employee's pay rate	× number of turnovers replaced during period	
In-house medical examinations (R_6) or	= [(time required for examination	× examiner's pay rate)	+ cost of supplies used]	× number of turnovers replaced during period
Contracted medical examinations (R_7)	= rate per examination	× number of turnovers replaced during period		

From Measuring manpower turnover costs, by Howard L. Smith and Larry E. Watkins. Reprinted from the April, 1978 issue of *Personnel administrator*, copyright, 1978, The American Society for Personnel Administration, 606 North Washington Street, Alexandria, VA 22314, $30 per year.

Table 15–1 **MEASURING REPLACEMENT COSTS**

ment at Specialty Stores, replacement costs account for only part of the cost of human resources management.

Valuation approaches to assessing costs include determining the present value of future earnings, or the value of a worker's services to the organization.[8] These calculations often lack precision because of the difficulty in calculating both present and future dollar values.

Beyond general human resources accounting, managers can determine the costs of various specific consequences of ineffective human resources management. Figure 15–4, for example, shows a way of estimating the cost of employee absenteeism. Or they can determine the costs of various different employment programs. Table 15–2 shows a way of estimating the costs of training programs, and Table 15–3 shows a way of estimating termination or separation costs.

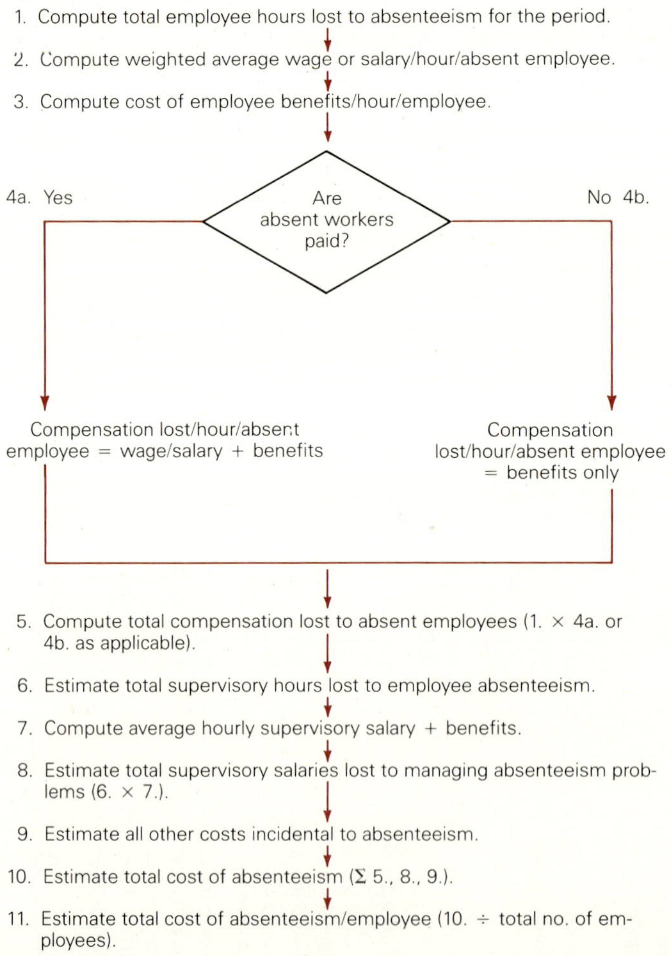

Figure 15–4 ESTIMATING THE COST OF EMPLOYEE ABSENTEEISM

Cost Element	Formula		
Informational literature (T_1)	= unit cost of informational package	× number of replacements during period	
Instruction in a formal training program (T_2)	= Length of training program	× [(average pay rate of trainer(s)	× number of programs conducted)
	+ (average pay rate per trainee	× total number of trainees during period)]	× proportion of training costs attributed to replacements
Instruction by employee assignment (T_3)	= number of hours required for instruction	× new employee's pay rate	× number of instructions during period

From Wayne F. Cascio, COSTING HUMAN RESOURCES: THE FINANCIAL IMPACT OF BEHAVIOR IN ORGANIZATIONS (Boston: Kent Publishing Company, 1982), p. 30. © 1982 by Wadsworth, Inc. Reprinted by permission of Kent Publishing Company, a division of Wadsworth, Inc.

Table 15–2 **MEASURING TRAINING COSTS**

Cost Element		Formula				
Exit interview (S_1)	=	cost of interviewer's time	= (time required prior to interview	+ time required for interview)	× interviewer's pay rate during period	× number of turnovers during period
		cost of terminating employee's time	= time required for the interview	× weighted average pay rate for terminated employees	× number of turnovers during period	
Administrative functions related to termination (S_2)	=	time required by personnel department for administrative functions related to termination	× average personnel department employee's pay rate	× number of turnovers during period		
Separation pay (S_3)	=	amount of separation pay per employee terminated	× number of turnovers during period			
Unemployment tax (S_4)	=	(unemployment tax rate—base rate)	× [($6,000 × number of employees earning at least $6,000) + (weighted average earnings if less than $6,000 × number of employees earning less than $6,000)]			

From Wayne F. Cascio, COSTING HUMAN RESOURCES: THE FINANCIAL IMPACT OF BEHAVIOR IN ORGANIZATIONS (Boston: Kent Publishing Company, 1982), p. 21.

Table 15–3 **MEASURING SEPARATION COSTS**

Executives, human resources professionals, and line managers are increasingly required to quantify human resources management practices. They should consider implementing one or a combination of these approaches to obtain estimates of the costs involved.

Determining Benefits

Human resources professionals and managers have even less experience in valuing the benefits of human resources management programs than in figuring costs. Typically such efforts have focused on determining the economic consequences of various programs. For example, one assessment of the benefits of training attempted to quantify the time required to reach job competency, performance of the job, and worker attitudes.[9] It measured the following: (1) time to reach competency, (2) production rate, (3) performance test results, (4) product quality, (5) raw material usage, (6) employee attitudes toward training and the jobs, (7) monetary value of performance, and (8) total return.[10]

Alternatively, human resources professionals and managers can assess the potential revenue impact of specific human resources management programs.[11] For example, they might determine the revenue obtained from reduced absenteeism or increased worker productivity as a result of training. At Specialty Stores, for example, top management might determine that a sales clerk generates, on the average, $50 of profit per day. Thus, reducing a worker's absenteeism by five days a year should increase the profits generated by that worker approximately $250 per year. Or, if training shows the sales clerk how to increase daily sales by $500, then the benefits of that training can be assessed as $500 per day for the worker; this revenue can later be compared to the cost of training.

Cost effectiveness of human resources practices, or anything else, means comparing the cost to the benefits derived. Clearly, this requires quantification of the benefits as well as the costs. Computers can assist managers or human resources professionals in developing an extensive data base and using statistical techniques to analyze the data. Such analysis should facilitate the computation of both costs and benefits. If cost-effectiveness is high, these data can help human resources professionals or managers to sell the value of human resources programs to top management. If cost-effectiveness is low, human resources professionals or managers can use the data to stimulate and refocus the design of human resources programs and systems.

IMPLEMENTING COMPUTERIZED HUMAN RESOURCES INFORMATION SYSTEMS

The availability of low-cost, high-speed computers can help managers and human resources professionals implement effective tracking and monitoring of human resources programs and systems. Human resources information systems (HRIS) should be structured to collect and analyze data in order to provide useful information to managers and human resources professionals.[12] An HRIS system must have a general data base management capability—facilities for data entry, data retrieval, and data manipulation. HRIS can assist with

1. tracking applicants;
2. developing employee rosters;
3. identifying new hires and reassignments;
4. tabulating total salary expenditures by employee category;
5. tracking employee turnover;
6. compiling training needs and matching programs to these needs;
7. maintaining replacement charts;
8. projecting attrition or future employment;
9. evaluating affirmative action effectiveness; and
10. monitoring benefits plans.[13]

An HRIS system should generally include modules for job evaluation, position control, skills inventory, payroll, benefits administration, attendance control, EEO and Affirmative Action, training, and health and safety.[14] Otherwise the precise configuration of an HRIS system depends on the organization's needs.

Designing and implementing an HRIS system typically requires that a human resources professional present a proposal to management; analyze the organization's needs; develop the system's specifications; design, develop, and install the system; convert the manual information system to a computerized one; and evaluate the new system.[15] Those installing such a system can select from existing software packages, or hire consultants to custom-tailor the system to the organization's needs.[16] Evaluation of software should include checking its documentation, warranty, flexibility, integration of diverse human resources functions, types of reports generated, and the nature of the audit trail for locating and correcting errors.[17] A computerized HRIS system can provide significantly greater amounts of information over manual systems at little extra cost. Nevertheless, organizations frequently expect too much of computerized HRIS. To guard against this, organizations must be careful in designing, developing, and introducing it. They should try to avoid the following common mistakes:

1. Trying to build a system that is all things to all people
2. Lacking individuals with knowledge of human resources management on the HRIS project team
3. Separating the HRIS system from related systems such as payroll
4. Creating superfluous complexity in the HRIS system
5. Lack of support from top management
6. Designing the system by committee
7. Introducing a system that is not user-friendly
8. Having loose project control
9. Promising savings due to a reduction in the work force, which does not then occur

10. Building a custom system when available noncustom systems would be adequate[18]

The integration of computer systems into human resources management should ultimately improve personnel and labor relations systems.

THE FUTURE OF HUMAN RESOURCES MANAGEMENT

In the early 1980s attention focused on the importance of human resources management for organizational effectiveness more than ever before. As noted earlier, an increasingly educated work force, greater competition from abroad, tight economic conditions, and new legal regulations are factors adding to its importance.

Strategic Human Resources Management

Effective human resources programs address strategic issues as well as managerial and operational ones (see Chapter 2 for additional discussion of the strategic backbone, particularly as it relates to human resources planning).[19] A study of how the most productive corporations are run suggested that the companies' strategic goals drive the efforts to improve productivity.[20] Thus plans and programs in human resources management and other areas must reflect both short- and long-term company goals. Strategic issues emphasize formulation of organizational policy, setting of organizational goals, and placement of the organization relative to its environment. In the area of performance appraisal, for example, strategic issues include the following:

Operational (short-term)—establishing an annual appraisal system and day-to-day control systems

Managerial (medium-term)—establishing validated systems that relate current conditions to future ones and introducing assessment centers for the development of employees

Strategic (long-term)—determining what should be valued in the long run, how to appraise these dimensions, and making an early identification of potential[21]

Effective human resources management in strategic terms emphasizes the fit between four components: (1) the environment; (2) the business mission, strategy, and objectives; (3) the human resources strategy; and (4) the human resources organization—its tasks, structure, people, informal organization, and processes.[22]

Human resources management of corporations that lead in productivity share five characteristics.[23] First, the human resources role includes substantial participation in business decisions and implementation of business strategies. For example, one company established a recruitment program anticipating the need for engineers five years hence, as the company moved to change product lines; this is in striking contrast to nonleading companies where the personnel staff merely hire, fire, maintain the department, and react to specific problems. Second, leading companies focus current resources on important problems and request additional resources only to respond to problems to be solved, such as funds for health care cost containment. Third, the human resources managers of leading organizations are more likely to initiate programs as a result of regular communication with line management, rather than wait for managers to make specific requests. Fourth, in leading companies line management shares responsibility for human resources management with the human resources professionals in the way described throughout this book. Fifth, responsibility for human resources policy formation and program administration is shared throughout the organization, not just at top corporate levels.

Implementing strategic human resources management involves the following principles:

1. Make sure the organization engages in strategic planning at the corporate or business level.
2. Identify the human resources tasks needed in order to support the organization's objectives at the strategic, managerial, and operational levels.
3. Identify any gaps in the current delivery of personnel service to managers and workers.
4. Use people trained as business generalists to carry out human resources functions so they can better respond to line management concerns.
5. Alter the reward and control systems to support strategic human resources functions.
6. Design systematic links between human resources functions and the line organization.[24]

Let us say that top management at Specialty Stores makes a strategic decision to focus their merchandising on young urban professionals. They must then hire human resources professionals who understand, and can help develop, the type of staff required to service this clientele. These human resources professionals may determine, for example, that the buying and selling staff require training in the styles preferred by young urban professionals, and the sales approach to which they respond best. The staff serving these professionals should probably have general management training (an M.B.A. or business degree) or line experience. And they should receive rewards for designing human resources programs that help the merchandising staff better serve the target customer.

Effective human resources management can be improved overall in organizations such as Specialty Stores by tightening the relationship between operational, managerial, and strategic practice. To accomplish this, the enterprise should

1. conduct an organization-wide human resources management audit;
2. make plans for the future based on market data;

3. make sure line management has input into the process;

4. make sure that managing strategic, managerial, and operational links is a joint responsibility of line management and staff; and

5. upgrade the human resources functions.[25]

Future Trends

Beyond significant participation in strategic planning, what else does the future hold for human resources management? The issues described below will probably receive the most attention during the next decade.

1. Increased emphasis on cross-training and retraining of workers to provide additional flexibility in job assignments. Since the management of unionized organizations has increasingly agreed to job security for workers, it must ensure that workers remain productive regardless of the jobs they hold.

2. Increasing numbers of two-career families, necessitating creative ways of providing men and women with compatible benefits, flexibility in scheduling work hours, and less need for geographical mobility as a prerequisite for advancement in the organization.

3. Changing tax laws encouraging individuals and organizations to look for new means of compensation to reduce the tax bite on earnings. Legal constraints on flexible benefit plans will motivate employees to look for new types of rewards and reward systems.

4. Continuation of the collaboration between union and management begun in the early 1980s. Increased employee involvement in decision-making and profit-sharing is likely.

5. Increasing sophistication of human resources planning. Even small organizations will track the supply of workers and analyze the demand for various categories of employees.

6. More implementation of computerized HRIS. The availability of sophisticated yet economical computers will increase the development of extensive data bases and complex analysis of the data.

7. Increased concern with the bottom-line consequences of human resources programs. Organizations will look for innovative ways to quantify the value of human resources programs and practices.

8. The shift in responsibility for human resources management from human resources professionals to managers. Human resources professionals will act as expert resources in the design and implementation of new human resources programs.

Implications for Human Resources Professionals

Human resources professionals must monitor the entire human resources management system for effectiveness. Specifically, they must act in the following ways:

1. Human resources professionals must regularly audit the human resources management in their organizations to determine the effectiveness of various programs.

2. They should apply the four-step practical approach described in this book to evaluating and improving human resources management. They must diagnose, evaluate, design, and implement quality human resources practices.

3. Human resources professionals must regularly evaluate the cost-effectiveness of human resources management systems in their organizations. They must develop and implement a convincing quantitative method of assessing costs and benefits.

4. Human resources professionals should encourage their organizations to install computerized HRIS systems as one way of managing information.

5. They should begin to instill in their organizations a strategic perspective toward human resources management.

Implications for Managers

Managers should provide data to top management and human resources professionals about the effectiveness of programs and practices in their organizations. Successful action includes the following:

1. Managers should regularly assess the effectiveness of human resources management in their unit, evaluating both processes and outcomes.

2. They should apply the practical approach where possible; they should diagnose, evaluate, design, and implement quality human resources management practices.

3. Managers should use computerized HRIS to obtain information for use in human resources management. They should maintain a readily accessible data base about current or potential employees.

4. They should assist human resources professionals in quantifying the costs and benefits of human resources management in the organization. They should gather data about the various programs they conduct and the outcomes that result.

5. Managers should be actively involved in the managerial and operational levels of human resources management. They should provide data for strategic decisions about human resources in the organization.

ACTIVITIES

Activity 15–1

ESSO A.G.

Step 1: Read ESSO A.G.

Step 2: Prepare the case for class discussion.

Mr. Otto Daniel, Director and Manager of Employee Relations at Esso A.G., discussed his company's management development and appraisal practices with pride. Since assuming his current position in 1971 much of Mr. Daniel's effort had been devoted to establishing and continually refining an integrated set of personnel systems and programs that would help Esso A.G. manage its human resources in as rational and objective a manner as possible. In discussing his department's activities with the casewriter Mr. Daniel stated, "We have tried to be innovative and have adopted several new and unique approaches."

This case describes the basic policies, programs, and techniques used by Esso A.G. in recruiting, training, appraising, paying and promoting its 1,400 managerial, professional and technical employees. Most of these practices had been introduced by 1973, and all were being applied in 1977, the time at which the case was completed.

BACKGROUND INFORMATION

Esso A.G. had been established in 1890 as a subsidiary of the U.S. based petroleum company, Exxon Corporation. The German subsidiary had grown substantially over the years, and in 1976 it represented the second largest component of Exxon's multinational operations in terms of sales. It employed 3,700 people approximately 1,500 of whom were located at the central offices in Hamburg. The remainder of employees worked in other parts of Germany in retail outlets, refineries, branch offices, and bulk plants. White collar employees constituted approximately two-thirds of the total. Seventy-five per cent of blue collar workers were members of unions (90% in refineries). Roughly 30% of white collar employees had signed union contracts (including 5% of those classified as managerial employees).*

Figure 15–5 shows the management organization of Esso A.G. Like all German A.G. companies, it was collectively managed by a *Vorstand* (Board of Management) consisting of a chairman and several directors which in turn reported to an *Aufsichtsrat* (Supervisory Board) made up of representatives elected by shareholders and by company employees. In addition to these reporting relationships, each *Vorstand* member also worked in close

*In addition to union membership most employees had legal rights to participation via a representative system of Works Councils which had been set up at various levels within all German enterprises.

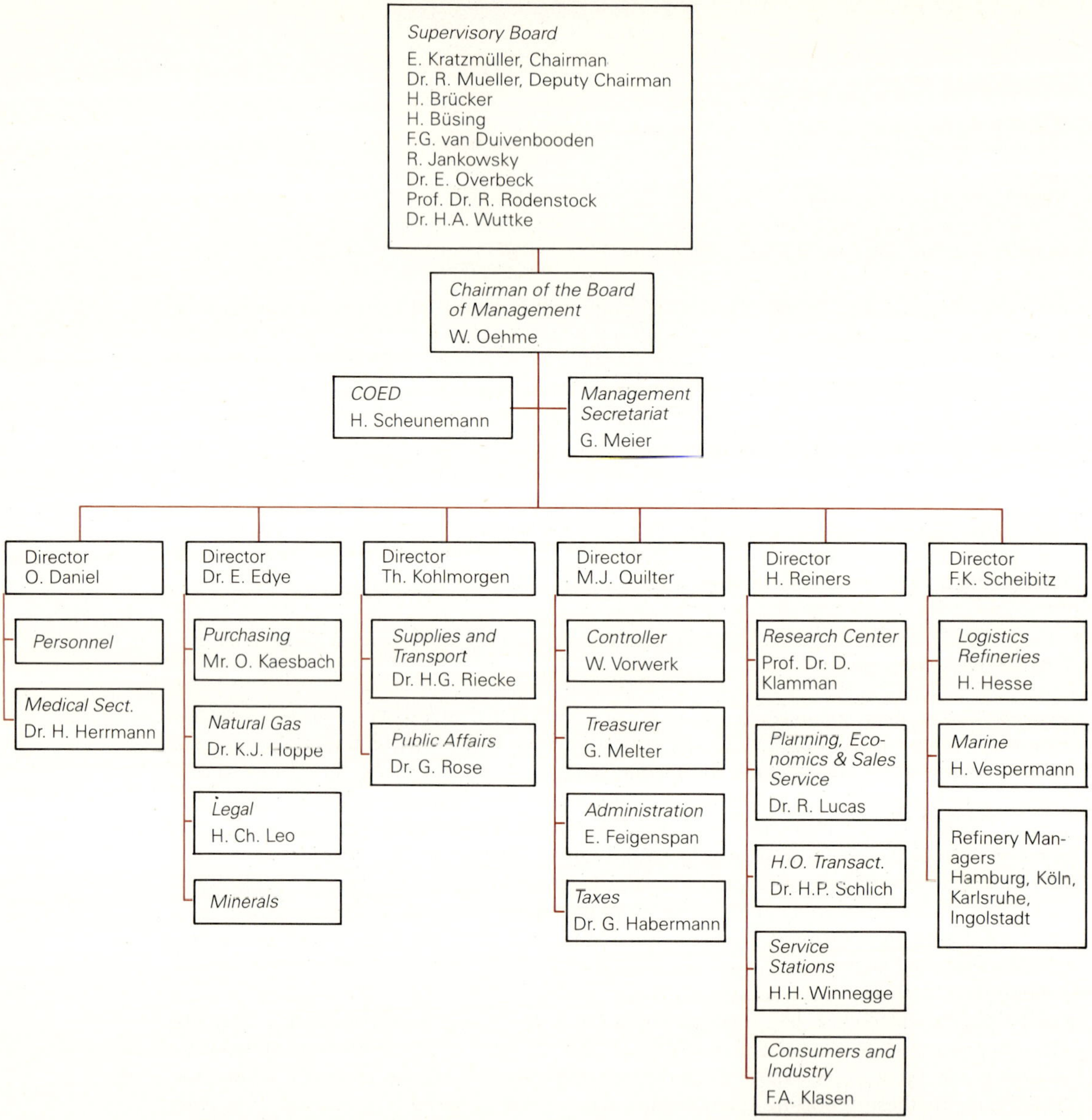

Figure 15–5 MANAGEMENT ORGANIZATION

contact with a corresponding functional manager at Esso European headquarters in London, England.

The Employee Relations Department at Esso A.G. consisted of 38 people working in eight functional areas (see Figure 15–6). Otto Daniel had been appointed as head of the department in 1971 after having spent more than twenty years in various executive

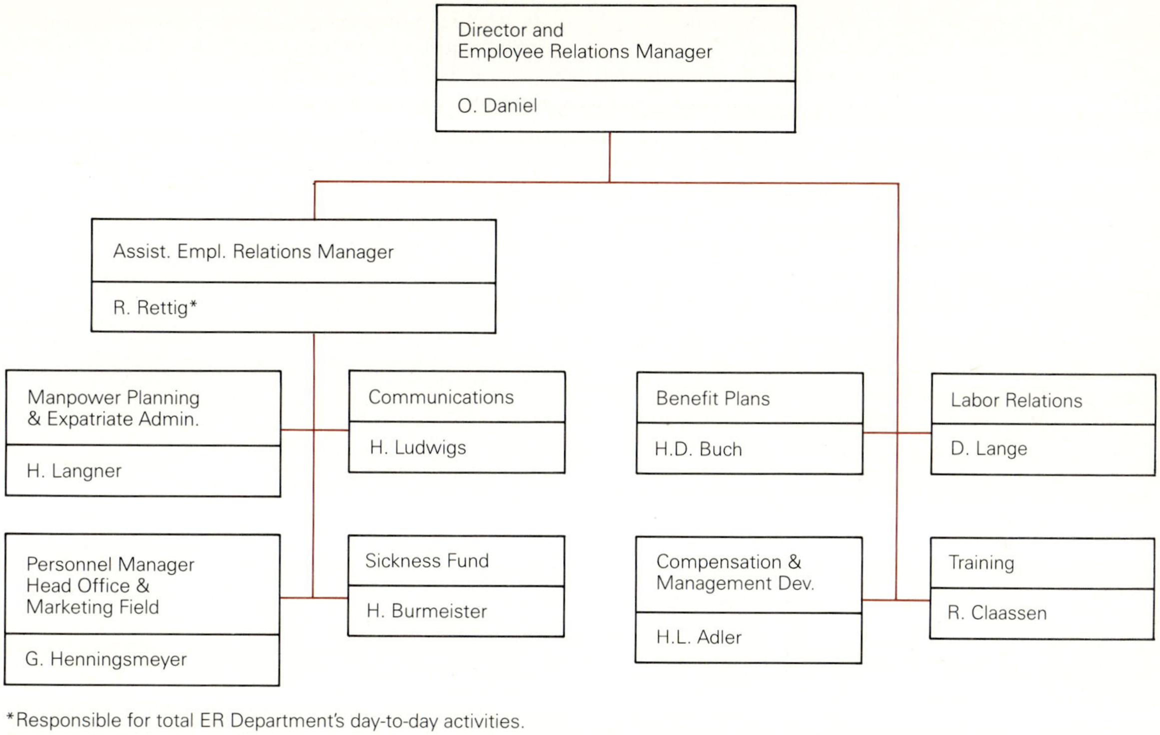

Figure 15–6 ORGANIZATION OF EMPLOYEE RELATIONS DEPARTMENT

positions in the marketing area. Shortly after his appointment Mr. Daniel had designated Dr. Rudolf Rettig as Assistant Manager and his "right-hand man." Figure 15–7 provides brief biographical sketches for these two managers.

MANAGEMENT DEVELOPMENT AND APPRAISAL PRACTICES

Esso A.G.'s management development and appraisal systems were designed to provide individual guidance and a central information base for all potential managerial employees throughout their careers with the company as well as maintaining a consistent and integrated framework for selection, training, performance evaluation, payment, and promotion decisions.

Recruiting

The company typically hired 30–40 young potential management employees annually, approximately 90% of whom held university degrees. Dr. Rettig explained, "It is our goal to increase the number of management employees with university degrees from 47% to 50% over the next few years." As of July, 1976, university graduates were divided among the various functions as follows:

Otto Daniel—age 59, joined Esso A.G. in 1950; worked in International Marine Sales department until 1959, then transferred to Hamburg central office as co-ordinator for all marine sales; later promoted to Marketing Manager for International Business, position held until 1971 when he became Manager of Employee Relations. Appointed Director in 1976.

Rudolf Rettig—age 53, doctorate in Modern History; joined Esso A.G. in 1955; worked in different Employee Relations functions in refineries, marine, marketing, and head office. Appointed Assistant Employee Relations Manager in 1970.

Figure 15–7 BIOGRAPHICAL SKETCHES OF MESSRS. DANIEL AND RETTIG

Function	*Percentage of University Graduates*
Refining	81%
Staff functions	65%
Marketing	43%
Controllers	33%

Although annual turnover of managerial, professional and technical staff was normally as low as 2.5%, the highest statistics occurred among business administration graduates of whom 10%, on average, left the company after the first or second year of service.

Training and Job Rotation

Two basic types of training programs were offered to all potential and current management employees: leadership seminars and seminars to improve job effectiveness. End of course appraisals by participants were used as one input in modifying and assessing the relevance of the company's training activities.

One-week leadership seminars were offered at three different stages in the manager's career:

Program	*Managerial Position*	*Average Number of Years with Company*
Supervisory Practice	First line supervisors, foremen	3–4
Leadership Awareness	Middle managers	5–6
Successful Leadership	Senior managers	7–10

Seminars to assist in improving job effectiveness focused on social policy on the one hand and business administration techniques on the other. In the social policy seminar managers were encouraged to develop an understanding of the political and social environment in which Esso A.G. operated. The fundamentals of Marxism, socialism, and free market economies were discussed; and the strategies of various political groups were analyzed. For managers who had not studied economics or business administration a four-week seminar was offered. This course, plus various follow-up seminars, focused on balance sheet analysis, profit contribution calculations, cost accounting, and capital expenditure analysis.

Job rotation was treated as another means of developing managerial abilities at Esso A.G. Under this program middle and senior managers were encouraged to get wider experience by accepting cross-functional assignments. Transfers of this sort were frequently arranged among the various plants and offices in Germany, and at management levels international exchanges were encouraged. Normally about 5% of managerial employees were working at various "developmental" assignments within Germany, while another 5% were participating in international exchanges. Internationally transferred managers officially remained Esso A.G. employees, although their salaries were paid by another subsidiary. In order to maintain employer/employee contacts, annual progress reports on these managers were sent to the headquarters in Hamburg.

Psychological Tests of Management Potential

In order to improve identification and development of employees with considerable management potential Esso A.G. had devised a battery of psychological tests, consisting of some 800 questions, which was administered to all recent recruits with university degrees at least two years after they had joined the company.* The results of these tests were intended to provide one input in evaluation of an employee's potential for advancement within the management ranks. Other factors considered were age, educational background, previous work experience, most recent position and salary, and performance appraisal records. Dr. Rettig explained the rationale behind the testing program as follows: "Although we devote considerable attention and resources to training and development, some aspects of good management and leadership are inherent in the person and cannot be taught."

The tests used by Esso A.G. were adaptations of a well known set of psychological measures used by its U.S. parent. In 1955 Exxon Corporation had begun a long-range research program aimed at developing and validating questionnaire measures which would predict future management potential. The initial testing program had involved some 500 executives in the New York area and was based on the following assumptions:

1. There are significant individual differences in the degree of success and effectiveness of present managers.
2. There are significant individual differences between the more successful and less successful managers.
3. A candidate for a management position will have a better chance of being successful if his individual characteristics are similar to those of the more successful rather than the less successful managers.
4. Some of these characteristics can be measured before the employee is assigned to a management position.

Pilot administrations in the U.S. between 1958 and 1963 produced relatively high correlations (the multiple correlation coefficient was as high as .70) between the test measures and two different criteria of managerial success within the Exxon organization. The first criterion, termed "overall success," was a composite measure which considered position level attained, salary history, superiors' ranking of managerial effectiveness, functional area and specialty, work patterns, and age.** The second criterion, termed "managerial effectiveness," was a score based on subjective rankings by three or more

*These tests were not used in arriving at initial hiring, or recruiting, decisions.

**The actual index measure was constructed by identifying highly interrelated component measures using factor analysis, a sophisticated multi-variate statistical technique.

superiors in terms of performance on most recent job and with particular emphasis on technical and professional achievement.* By the late 1960's these tests had been translated and were being used with comparable results by subsidiaries in Latin America, Japan, India, Australia, Holland, Norway, Denmark, and Finland.

Dr. Rettig recalled,

> When we saw that, in spite of differences in cultural settings, the tests still proved valid, we decided to adapt them for use in a German environment and try them out at Esso A.G. We had to change or delete some questions related to civic responsibilities, schooling, or American customs; but the basic tests are the same ones originally developed by Exxon in 1955.***

By early 1972 Dr. Rettig had completed a study of the validity of the adapted tests with a group of 160 Esso A.G. managers. The first step in this research had been to develop Esso A.G.'s own set of independent criterion measures of management potential, i.e., to establish valid measures of success against which test results could later be compared. The three criteria used were:

1. *Esso A.G. criterion:* Each manager was rated according to his position reached within Esso A.G. and his appraised potential for advancement, as compared with managers of the same age, educational background, and length of service with the firm.
2. *Success index:* Each manager was ranked, according to his relative degree of success, as determined by his age, salary, and the company's salary policy.
3. *Salary group:* Each manager was rated according to his actual salary received at the time of the test.

As shown in Table 15–4, the criteria were highly correlated with one another but not strongly related to two control variables, age and education. This relatively high level of "internal validity" supported the conclusion that the three criteria were suitable measures of managerial success.

The 800-item battery of tests consisted of two basic series which are outlined in Figure 15–8. Multiple correlations between the overall test battery and the various success criteria ranged from .63 to .70 (see Table 15–5 for patterns of correlations by test parts and overall).

Based on this study and comparable results reported by other Exxon units around the world, Esso A.G. decided to make the management potential tests a regular part of its personnel procedure. Subsequently tests have been administered at two different stages in a manager's career. Series I (consisting of the first four items in Figure 15–8) is administered to all university recruits after 1–3 years with the company. Series II (consisting of the last

*The managerial effectiveness criterion was one of the components of the overall success criterion. The researchers found that while ratings of managerial effectiveness were significantly correlated with overall success (as measured by level attained in the company and salary), they did not represent a totally reliable predictor of this latter criterion. For this reason both criteria were used in assessing management potential, and different scoring keys and weighting factors were developed for linking the psychological tests to each criterion.

**A question often raised by critics of Exxon's management potential test is whether there is a need to allow for change in standards and environmental requirements faced by managers. For example, would a successful executive of today also be successful 15 or 20 years from now? or 15 years ago? Appendix A presents a response to these questions by the Exxon researchers.

	Criterion Variables			Control Variables	
	Esso A.G. Criterion	Success Index	Salary Group	Age	Education
Esso A.G. Criterion	—	.72	.67	−.29	−.04
Success Index		—	.89	−.35	.13
Salary Group			—	.05	.19
Age				—	.15
Education					—

SOURCE: "Identifying Management Potential in Esso A.G.," report to *Vorstand*, January, 1972.

Table 15–4 VALIDITY OF MANAGEMENT POTENTIAL MEASURES: INTERCORRELATIONS AMONG THREE CRITERIA MEASURES AND TWO CONTROL VARIABLES

Series I

1. *Learning Ability Test.* This is a short, steeply scaled test of 54 items. Three types of items are included: block counting (non-verbal reasoning), vocabulary (verbal reasoning) and arithmetic (quantitative reasoning). Four alternatives, including the correct answer, are provided for each item.

2. *Non-Verbal Reasoning Test.* This test is a measure of abstract reasoning and was included because of the many problems in the company which require the mental manipulation of concepts other than words. The Non-Verbal Reasoning Test uses geometrical figures as a basis for problems to test the examinee's ability to reason without using words.

3. *Temperament Survey.* The Temperament Survey measures several different personality characteristics, some of which could be expected to be present in successful managers. Examples of these characteristics are emotional stability, objectivity and friendliness.

4. *Individual Background Survey—Early Items.* A series of questions concerning an individual's background has been one of the most useful tools in research studies for the selection of employees for a wide variety of jobs in Exxon and its affiliates. Areas covered include home and family background, education, vocational planning and experience, financial background, leisure time activities, health history, and social and community relations. In some ways the IBS resembles an interview on paper; everyone answers the same questions, and the responses are limited to the choices given. This procedure for recording information affords the researcher an opportunity to analyze differences in backgrounds and determine how these differences are related to managerial success. Enough has been learned about the IBS to recognize that it measures a number of personal characteristics such as independence, maturity, sociability, social responsibility, and certain kinds of vocational and avocational interests.

Series II

5. *Management Judgement Test.* This test describes problem situations and presents several possible choices of action or decisions. The examinee chooses the action he believes most appropriate. The purpose of this test is to determine the examinee's judgement insofar as managerial problems are concerned and to compare his judgement with that of other managers.

6. *Self-Performance Report.* Each participant in the study completes a report describing his own performance to determine whether differences in these self-ratings are related to differences in managerial success. For the most part, the items cover various aspects of supervisory and managerial job behavior. Scoring procedures yield six area scores plus an overall score: initiative, responsibility, leadership; specific job knowledge and skills; dependability, thoroughness, follow-through; ability to get along with others, cooperativeness; stability under pressure, self-control; and effectiveness of appearance, manner, work habits.

7. *Individual Background Survey—Later Items.* The items in this test cover the same general areas as those in the Background Survey—Early Items, but apply more to a person's early adult years.

SOURCE: "Identifying Management Potential in Esso A.G.," report to *Vorstand*, January, 1972.

Figure 15–8 COMPONENTS OF MANAGEMENT POTENTIAL TEST

Test Parts & Series	Criteria: Esso A.G. Criterion	Criteria: Success Index	Criteria: Salary Group
1. Learning Ability	.37	.21	.11
2. Non-Verbal Reasoning	.29	.32	.22
3. Temperament Survey—Success*	.36	.33	.28
—Effectiveness*	.42	.37	.28
4. Individual Background—Success	.49	.54	.45
(early items) —Effectiveness	.43	.49	.43
5. Individual Background—Success	.57	.61	.62
(later items) —Effectiveness	.57	.64	.60
6. Management Judgement—Success	.35	.40	.34
—Effectiveness	.39	.42	.34
7. Self-Performance	.20	.23	.20
8. Series I—Success	.55	.56	.46
—Effectiveness	.57	.55	.45
9. Series II—Success	.57	.62	.60
—Effectiveness	.59	.66	.60
10. Series I & II—Success	.61	.65	.60
—Effectiveness	.64	.70	.61
Total	.65	.70	.63

SOURCE: "Identifying Management Potential in Esso A.G.," report to *Vorstand*, January, 1972.

*Separate correlations on some tests for "overall success" and "managerial effectiveness" reflect the fact that different scoring and weighting procedures had been developed for linking these items to the original Exxon criteria. Esso A.G. had elected to use these same procedures.

Series I figures are multiple correlation coefficients for tests 1–4 and the criteria. Series II figures are multiple correlation coefficients for tests 5–7 and criteria. Total is the multiple correlation coefficient for both success and effectiveness scores and criteria.

Table 15–5 CORRELATIONS BETWEEN TEST PARTS AND SERIES AND CRITERION MEASURES*

three tests outlined in Figure 15–8) is administered after 5 years with the company. Non-university employees who have successfully advanced within the company also have been tested when it has been considered appropriate.

Direct access to individual test results has been limited to only the employee and the Management Development Advisor in the Employee Relations Department. When a departmental manager was considering promotion of an employee, the Employee Relations Department would, upon request only, submit either a positive or negative recommendation based on its interpretation of the individual's test results. This recommendation represented one potential input to help the supervisor in making the promotion decision. (For many years all promotions at Esso A.G. have been made from within the organization with the exception of a few in the medical department).

Performance Appraisal Practices

The performance appraisal system was intended to give a valid assessment of an employee's performance on the job, to provide an objective basis for wage and salary administration, and to provide information on the employee's suitability for present position as well as potential for further advancement. In addition, assessment of the employee's future training needs and his choice of job postings were influenced by his performance evaluation.

Each employee was evaluated at regular intervals determined by number of years with the company, as shown below:

Length of Service	*Frequency of Evaluations*
1–5 years	yearly
6–15 years	every 2 years
16 years of service and up to 55 years of age	every 3 years
over 55 years of age	no further assessments unless requested

Results of evaluations were recorded and computer tabulated to provide a basis for company salary rankings. Evaluation essentially consisted of an assessment of actual versus required performance as outlined in job descriptions, which accompanied all positions. Each position and title carried with it a standard remuneration range within which final pay decisions were required to fall.

One basic performance appraisal form was used for all employees—managerial and non-managerial (see Figure 15–9).* This form required the supervisor to establish a performance requirements profile for each employee from among 23 potential items by weighting each according to its importance for the job being evaluated. Each item was then rated in terms of a seven-point scale. Finally, the supervisor was required to arrive at a single, overall rating.

In assigning overall ratings supervisors were asked by the Employee Relations Department to remember that a "normal frequency distribution" was expected for the company's 3,700 employees:

Abbreviation	*Rating*	*Percentage of Employees to Receive Ratings*
h (hervorragend)	Outstanding	5%
s (sehr gut)	Very good	15%
g (gut)	Good	25%
v (voll zufriedenstellend)	Fully satisfactory	30%
z (zufriedenstellend)	Satisfactory	15%
n (noch genügend)	Poor	7%
u (ungenügend)	Unsatisfactory	3%
		100%

After completing the forms the supervisor would schedule individual discussions of the results with each employee. Results of all performance evaluation discussions were confirmed in writing by the employee using the form shown in Figure 15–10. If the employee indicated any objections or areas of dispute, a second meeting was scheduled, after which each party was required to confirm the results.

*Otto Daniel stated, "We believe it is important that the same form be used for all levels, so that everyone feels he is being treated equally. Of course, it also helps our administrative work considerably."

Surname:	First Name:	Personnel No.:	A member of my staff since:
______	______	______	______

Dept/Plant	Age:	Year's Service:	Wage/Salary Earner:	Place:	Date:
______	______	______	______	______	______

Position acc. to Job Description:	Present Activity/Position of the Employee:
______	______

Rating code:
h = outstanding
s = very good
g = good
v = fully satisfactory
z = satisfactory
n = poor
u = unsatisfactory

This code is to be applied to performance and analogously to knowledge, personality/conduct and leadership qualities.

Sections 1 to 4 serve the purpose of appraising the employee in relationship to the requirements laid down in the above mentioned job description. Sections 5 and 6 give the overall appraisal and related comments. The appraisal of the "boxed" criteria is essential; the respective requirements will determine which other criteria are to be appraised.

1. Performance	h	s	g	v	z	n	u	The appraisal item is of . . . . importance: little	medium	great
[10] Work Quality to be determined on the basis of the utilizability of the work produced, i.e. correctness (frequency of errors), completeness, time-keeping (work ready on schedule).										
[11] Work Volume to be determined on the basis of the work rate, utilization of working time (intensity and consistency).										
12 Constructive Ideas develops new ideas, makes realizable proposals, knows how to substantiate them.										
13 Initiative does not need stimulating to act soundly with good judgement.										
14 Cost-Mindedness pays attention to efficient working methods and working attitude.										
15 Success in Negotiations prudent and skilled negotiating tactician; supplies convincing arguments.										

Figure 15–9 PERFORMANCE APPRAISAL FORM

Continued

									The appraisal item is of . . . . importance		
2.	**Knowledge**	h	s	g	v	z	n	u	little	medium	great
20	Own Field of Work has full knowledge of his own specialist field; knows products, methods, technologies and new developments.										
21	Neighbouring Fields of Work is familiar with the objectives and procedures of those fields affecting his own field of work.										
22	Appreciation of Company Matters in General has knowledge of new organizational procedures, interrelationships and work of other functions.										
23	English Language reads, understands, speaks, writes.										
3.	**Personality/Conduct**										
30	Energy shown in the fulfillment of his work; has drive; dynamic and active.										
31	Authority shows perseverance, provides convincing arguments.										
32	Reliability takes his work and responsibilities seriously and justifies the faith put in him.										
33	Emotional Stability and Consistency is down to earth, calm and collected, is not nervous or moody.										
34	Judgement objective and critical observer.										
35	Workload Exposure also works effectively when subjected to stress, workload peaks and tight time schedules.										
36	Openness expresses his opinion frankly and critically.										
37	Cooperation supports others by way of information, advice; assistance; gives priority to practical aspects; willing to take up new ideas; is openminded and willing to discuss; is able to adapt himself to other personalities.										
38	Bearing and Manners confident, polite, pays attention to personal appearance.										

Figure 15–9 Continued

Continued

								The appraisal item is of . . . . importance	
4. Leadership Qualities	h	s	g	v	z	n	u	little	medium	great

(All items to be completed for supervisors: i.e. employees with leadership functions.)

40 Specification of Objectives, Planning and Organization
thoughtful and farsighted planning in accordance with the set objectives; rational employment of manpower, equipment and funds, i.e. practically and according to schedule.

41 Decision-Making and Responsibility
makes his own prudent decisions even in difficult situations, makes decisions promptly, realizes the importance of decisions and assumes responsibility.

42 Information and Delegation
gives his staff comprehensive information in good time, integrates them in the decision-making process, provides feedback on job results; delegates work responsibility and authorities in accordance with the aptitude and performance of the employees.

43 Leadership, Motivation, Promotion
passes on knowledge and techniques in a clear and precise manner; motivates others to independent thinking and action; develops and maintains the interest of his staff in their jobs. Good appraiser of performance and capability. Upholds the interests of his staff.

5. Overall Appraisal

under the appraisal codc h–u taking into consideration the importance of the individual items.

6. Comments on the Overall Appraisal

Mention of particular strong points and weaknesses. Reference to suitability for the present activity or mention of an activity for which the appraised employee would be better suited; required development of knowledge.

Date

Signature of Immediate Supervisor

Figure 15–9 Continued

Continued

Remarks of the next supervisor (to be given *prior* to the discussion of the appraisal):

____________________ ____________________

Date Signature

Note on the Result of the Appraisal Discussion. The discussion with the appraised employee took place on ________

____________________ ____________________

Date Signature of Immediate Supervisor

Figure 15–9 Continued

Salary Administration

Although performance appraisals were not conducted annually for all employees, wages and salaries were reviewed on a yearly basis. For managerial employees salary adjustments included an economic factor (cost of living/productivity) and a merit component. Size of merit increases were determined on the basis of overall performance ratings, potential, and promotability. Base wages or salaries for non-managerial employees were established annually by collective agreement with the unions. In addition, merit increases were granted on the basis of overall performance ratings. Depending on the employee's wage or salary group, merit increases ranged from 50 to 120 Deutschmarks per month.

APPENDIX A*

Researchers' Reply in Defense of Exxon Corporation's "Early Identification of Management Potential" Research Project and Test.

Would a successful executive of today also be successful 15 or 20 years from now? Will the application of the results of the research perpetuate the same kind of management that exists at the present time? If so, is this perpetuation desirable? How can one expect the company to grow and expand if it is always run by the same kind of people? Will the managers identified by these procedures be capable of keeping up with the many changes which are taking place in management philosophy and practices and the new theories of organizational effectiveness?

These questions, in one way or another, are challenging the criteria, or standards of management success, used in the study. Final answers to these questions will not be available for some time, but partial answers can be given to many of them.

In the first place, the standards of success against which the predictors were examined were not confined to one measure alone; several elements entered into the success criterion. Various combinations of these elements could give a manager a high rating on this criterion.

**Source:* "Summary Report of the Early Identification of Management Potential Research Project" prepared by Social Science Research Division, Employee Relations Department, Exxon Corporation, August, 1961.

Surname:	First name:	Personnel No.:	Rating Code:
______	______	______	
Department/Plant:	Age: Years of Service:		h = outstanding s = very good
______	______ ______		g = good
Wage/Salary Earner:	Position acc. to Job Descript.		v = fully satisfactory z = satisfactory
______	______		n = poor u = unsatisfactory

Present Activity/Position of the Employee:

______

My supervisor, Mr./Mrs./Miss
discussed with me today the ______
appraisal drawn up in respect of my performance in my present job.

The overall appraisal ______ in full ______
was made known to me and explained.

Space for any comments of the appraised employee: (if necessary continue on next page)

Place: ______ Date: ______ Signature: ______

Only to complete if renewed talks are to be held with the appraised employee on the grounds of the above comments:

1. Remarks of appraising supervisor:

   Date: ______ Signature: ______

2. Remarks of the next supervisor:

   Date: ______ Signature: ______

3. Acknowledgment of appraised employee:

   Date: ______ Signature: ______

Figure 15–10 APPRAISAL DISCUSSION FORM

In addition, there is evidence that the procedures developed will select effective managers in general and not simply managers who can be effective in a limited situation at a specific time. Those who scored high on the test battery were characterized by high intelligence, adaptability, willingness to experiment and innovate, and a degree of aggressiveness. These managers should be able to adapt to change; in fact, they should be capable of engineering changes as the needs arise.

One further point with respect to change is often overlooked: the successful managers today have not lived in a static situation. They have been called upon to adapt to many changes during their careers and they, perhaps, have been responsible for them. Change is not something for the future alone; it has also existed in the past to create the present.

Nevertheless, the importance of these questions should not be minimized. They should be kept clearly in mind as the results of this research are implemented and used, and those responsible for their use should be alert to changes which might influence their effectiveness. One phase of this effort might well be the development of clear-cut specifications in specific terms by the top executives of the corporation for the managers of the future. A comparison of these specifications with the qualifications of the individuals identified as high potential employees would reveal whether the predictors should be revised or augmented.

Step 3: Individually, in small groups, or with the entire class, as directed by your instructor, answer the following questions:

1. Is human resources management at Esso A.G. effective?
2. What role do managers play in human resources management? Are they effective?
3. What role do human resources professionals play at Esso? Are they effective?
4. Are the recruiting, training, appraisal, compensation, and development systems state-of-the-art?
5. What deficiencies are there in the recruiting, training, appraisal, compensation, and development systems at Esso?
6. What changes would you propose for human resources management at Esso A.G.?
7. Redesign the human resources systems at Esso.
8. What problems will probably arise in implementing these changes?
9. How can these problems be overcome?

Activity 15–2

STATE VOCATIONAL REHABILITATION AGENCY (A), (B), (C)

Step 1: Read the State Vocational Rehabilitation Agency case.

Step 2: Prepare the case for class discussion.

STATE VOCATIONAL REHABILITATION AGENCY (A)

As John Adams, Director of State Vocational Rehabilitation Agency, hung up the telephone, he felt apprehensive. He had taken a major step in an attempt to deal with the problems of his agency, but he did not know where it would lead.

Reprinted with permission of the author, Professor Roger Atherton, University of Oklahoma.

Several months ago he had hired a management consulting firm to study the Agency, to identify present and potential problems, and to give John recommendations on how to solve or prevent these problems. The phone call was from his secretary; the consultants had arrived and were ready to deliver their report to him.

The rehabilitation agency that John Adams directed was an independent state agency. John reported to a Commission of Rehabilitation composed of seven members appointed by the Governor for three-year terms. Further information and data on the agency's operations are given in subsequent paragraphs and exhibits.

The Development of Vocational Rehabilitation

During World War I, legislation was enacted by the U.S. Congress to provide vocational rehabilitation to discharged disabled veterans to assist them in obtaining civilian employment. In 1920, the Vocational Rehabilitation Act was passed to provide similar services to disabled civilians. The programs were to be organized by the states with fifty-fifty matching federal funds. Congress passed only temporary legislation to stimulate the development of such programs. The government intentionally limited its role to providing support funds and did not get involved in providing the states with program direction.

Funds were limited so that a priority of service was necessary, resulting in the highest priority being given to the indigent person with an obvious disability that could be corrected or minimized. The Social Security Act of 1935 provided for a permanent authorization, increased grants, and increased support for federal administration.

During World War II, new legislation was passed which resulted in the greatest period of expansion in the twenty-year history of vocational rehabilitation. The Selective Service Agency referred people who were rejected for the armed services because of disability and the Employment Security Commission and the War Manpower Office referred people who were needed as productive workers despite their disabilities. All administration, guidance, and placement costs, including salaries for professional and clerical staff, were paid by the federal government. This led to a rapid expansion of staff in the state programs. (Services to clients remained on a fifty-fifty matching basis.) Also, the mentally ill and the mentally retarded were made eligible for vocational rehabilitation services.

In 1954, a greatly enlarged program was passed which shifted the major emphasis from guidance and counselling of the most severely disabled to medical services for large numbers of less severely disabled who could more readily have their disabilities corrected or minimized so they could return to work.

In the late 1960's, the Vocational Rehabilitation Act was amended to extend services to socially handicapped people who were not specifically physically or mentally handicapped, but who could be helped by vocational counselling and training. Funding was changed to 80 percent federal and 20 percent state. Rehabilitation services were expanded to include follow-up services in maintaining an individual in employment as well as services to families of the handicapped individual, when the services could contribute substantially to the rehabilitation of a group of individuals.

In the early 1970's, political action groups of the physically disabled were formed and were able to get legislation passed which rescinded the inclusion of the socially handicapped. The new legislation also specified that the most severely disabled should receive priority. (Even with the historical and continuing expansion of funding, there were still fewer dollars available than required to serve the people needing rehabilitation.) The legislation also established that the states were responsible for assuring that the handicapped received equal rights with respect to others. Thus, the states had to provide technical assistance to employees and federally funded programs to assure accessibility to the handicapped.

In 1978, legislation was passed to authorize support services to improve the quality of life. These services were intended to provide help to those handicapped who would benefit from more independent living. The training provided would help those who are institutionalized for mental inadequacies to return to the community. It would also help the physically handicapped to be more independent, e.g., to do their own shopping and use transportation without help. The purpose of the amendment was to shift the emphasis away from vocational rehabilitation to more general rehabilitation. However, the exact meaning of the "quality of life" and the specific impact on vocational rehabilitation agencies were the subject of extensive debate. As of late 1979, the funding for these new programs had not yet been appropriated. The eventual impact on the state vocational rehabilitation agencies was unclear.

Each state agency was organized somewhat differently with varying levels of state support, and subject to different degrees of pressure from the Federal Government, state legislators, client groups, and vendor service groups (organizations outside the agency that provide subcontracted services). The Director was usually supported by a variety of staff and technical service groups. The direct contact with the handicapped person was the counselor who typically was highly educated and very client oriented. Since performance in the Agencies was typically measured by "closures", cases where the handicapped individual has been returned to employment (technically a "#26" closure), there was a kind of built-in conflict for the counselor, who had to choose between a large number of short-term cases and a smaller number of long-term cases.

As discussed above, the goals of these agencies shifted over time, future goals became less than clear, the environment was more and more turbulent, the political forces intensified, and inflation had reduced the real value of increased funding levels. Thus, there were increased pressures to use resources more efficiently coupled with greater managerial complexity. In addition, there were seemingly more and more constituents who wanted a voice in how the agencies were run.

John Adams' Agency

An organizational chart and budget information for the agency directed by John Adams are presented in Figure 15–11 and Table 15–6. A profile of agency employees, turnover data, and a brief demographic description of the state are provided in Tables 15–7, 15–8, and Figure 15–12.

Personnel Procedures

Recruitment and screening of personnel for all state agencies were handled by the State Civil Service Commission. When a position needed to be filled in the rehabilitation agency, the personnel manager requested a list of qualified applicants from the Civil Service Commission. The average length of time needed to obtain such a list was two months. Each list contained the names of the top seven applicants as scored by the Civil Service Commission. These applicants were interviewed by the Director, the Personnel Manager, and the immediate Supervisor. The Supervisor and the Personnel Manager made recommendations, but the Director made all of the hiring decisions.

Internal promotions did not go through the Civil Service Commission. The Personnel Manager circulated a notice of the promotional opportunity. Employees who were interested were interviewed by the Supervisor and the Director. The Director made the final decision.

Compensation

The legislature decided each year how much money to appropriate for employee pay raises. In 1979 every state employee was given an automatic 5% cost of living raise. In addition, agencies were authorized to use an amount not to exceed 2% of total salary budget for merit raises. The method of administration was left to the discretion of the individual agency. The rehabilitation agency decided to give the raises to all those who were recommended until the money ran out. The Director issued a memo to all supervisors asking them to be very careful about making recommendations for these raises.

Employee Attitudes

Almost half of the agency's employees had worked in the state system for ten years or more. Personnel practices had changed little if any in that time. Employees generally seemed satisfied and few expressed complaints.

An increasing number of the newer employees, however, expressed dissatisfaction with agency personnel procedures. Some even talked of unionization. Over the past two years a union which represented public employees had been trying to organize within the state. The formal employee grievance procedure had only recently been instituted to help alleviate some of the employee dissatisfaction.

Grievance Procedures

The State Civil Service Commission procedures provided few details on the handling of grievances. Emphasis was placed on the ability of supervisors to resolve complaints informally, often upon the basis only of an oral complaint. When a written complaint was submitted, the agency head had to respond within ten working days. If the complainant was still

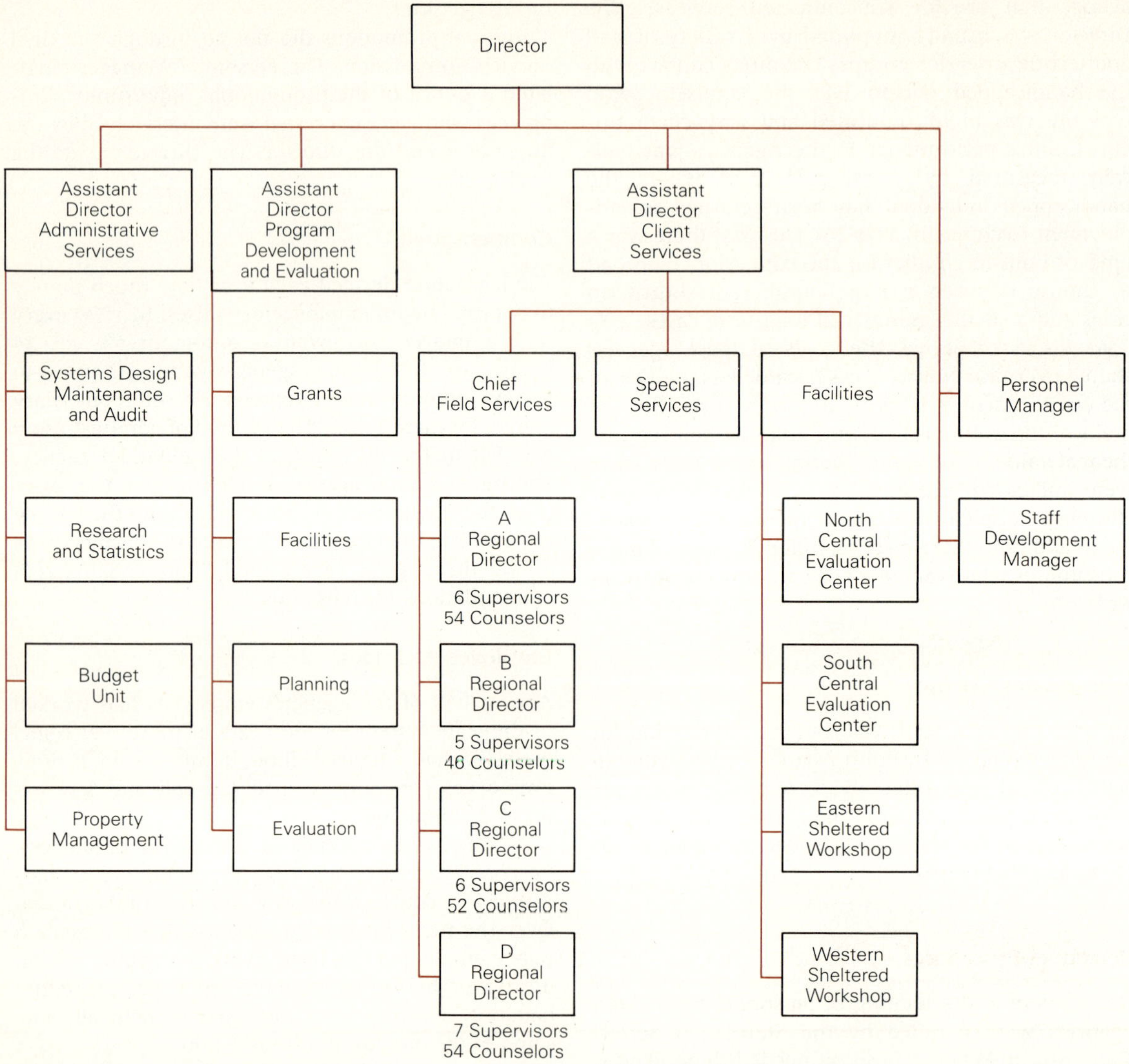

SOURCE: Adapted from agency charts.

Figure 15–11 ORGANIZATIONAL CHART

dissatisfied, an appeal could be made to the State Civil Service Commission for a hearing before an administrative law judge. A thirty day limit was set for completion of this step. The judge's decision could also be appealed to the full Civil Service Commission. It was also possible for a complainant to file a civil suit or to file a complaint, in cases of alleged discrimination, under Civil Rights legislation.

State Appropriation	$ 3,000,000
Federal Funds matched	12,000,000
	$15,000,000

	State		U.S.—All Agencies*		
	Amount (in 000's)	% of total	% of total expenditures		
			FY 78	*FY 77*	*FY 76*
Administration	$ 960	6.4%	9.1%	8.0%	8.2%
Counseling and Placement	4,725	31.5	34.7	35.7	34.9
Services for Individuals	8,265	55.1	51.3	50.6	52.1
Small Business	165	1.1	1.7	1.7	1.7
Establishment of Rehab. Facilities	630	4.2	1.7	3.3	2.4
Facilities and Services to Groups	60	0.4	1.0	0.5	0.7
Agency Operated Rehab. Facilities	60	0.4	0.1	0.1	0.0
Construction	135	0.9	0.4	0.1	0.1
Total	$15,000	100.0%	100.0%	100.0%	100.0%

*Figures may not add exactly due to rounding

SOURCE: Agency data.

Table 15–6 CURRENT FY BUDGET

	Professional		Clerical		Technical		Supervisory Administrative		Totals		
	M	F	M	F	M	F	M	F	M	F	Grand Total
Age 45+	61	32		20	1		21	11	83	63	146
Handicapped	9	7		11			1		10	18	28
Black	10	4		6			1		11	10	21
Native American				2						2	2
Spanish Surname	3	1		6	1				4	7	11
Oriental				1						1	1
Other											
Total of Above Classes	83	44		46	2		23	11	108	101	209
Total Agency Employees	107	139	3	226	6	6	30	23	146	394	540

SOURCE: Agency data.

Table 15–7 EMPLOYEE PROFILE

	Turnover by Type of Staff	# of Staff	% Total Staff Turnover
Clerical Staff	28%	65	60%
Professional Managerial Technical Staff	14%	43	40%
Overall	42%	108	100%

Source: Agency data.

Table 15–8 STAFF TURNOVER—ATTRITION RATE

Training and Development

The Agency had put increasing effort and money in recent years into Staff Development and Training. See Table 15–9 for specific details of the most recent year.

Background

For much of the past few months, John Adams had felt discouraged. He knew that he was no longer really enjoying the job he had held for over twelve years. Before becoming the Director, he had felt really in touch with what was going on in the Agency. Now he felt isolated. In addition, rapid growth of the agency and its programs, budget, and number of personnel had created an extremely complex organization over which he felt he had ever-decreasing influence and control. He suspected that changing conditions both within the Agency and outside it were creating problems. He was worried about the impact that these changes would have on his job and on his performance. He had given some thought to the problems, but was not certain whether any changes needed to be made, what the best approach to making changes might be, and whether it was really his responsibility to initiate changes.

As a counselor, many years ago, John had personally known everyone in the Agency. His caseload was self-determined, record keeping was at a minimum, he had close working relationships with vendor services, and he had always enjoyed good placement rates for his clients. Indeed, some of them still called on him as personal friends after all these years. His career with Vocational Rehabilitation had progressed nicely as he was promoted from counselor to supervisor, to regional manager, then to Chief of field services, all in 20 years. Throughout this time, he had been able to maintain close and satisfying working relationships with all of the Agency members. He had stayed particularly close to the counselors, giving them advice and counsel, supporting their decisions and protecting them when they were brought to account for mistakes. He strongly believed

1.	Total population:	4.24 million
2.	Racial distribution:	15% black (636,000); 5% Spanish (212,000); 1% Other Minorities (42,240); .04% American Indian (16,560).
3.	Population distribution:	11.1 average school years completed; 71% urban population; 29% rural population.
4.	Employment data:	27% manufacturing; 41% white collar; 32% agricultural.
5.	Income data:	$6,000 average yearly income; 15% over $12,000/year. 21% earn less than $3,000/year; 4% on public welfare.

Source: Agency data.

Figure 15–12 STATE STATISTICS

Staff Development and Training Agency Administered

# Programs	# Employees	Type Employee	Total Training Days	Man/Days	Percent Effort
2 (5 days)	20	All	10	200	8%
Orientation 6 (3 days)	95	Counselors Supervisors	12	1140	45%
Communication Skills 4 (3 days)	80	Counselors	12	960	38%
Medical Information 1 (5 days)	20	Counselors	5	100	4%
Counseling 1 (5 days)	15	Counselors	5	75	3%
Basic Supervision 1 (5 days)	10	Supervisors	5	50	2%
Management	0	Middle Management	0	0	0%
15	240		49	2525	100%

Staff Development and Training Non-Agency Administered

Programs	# Employees	Type Employee	Total Training Days	Man/Days
Counseling Skills	5	Counselors	5	25
Evaluation Skills	3	Evaluators	5	15
Assertiveness	10	Counselors Clerical	5	50
Case Management	3	Counselors	5	15
Placement	5	Counselors	5	25
	26		25	130

SOURCE: Agency data.

Table 15–9 MANPOWER DEVELOPMENT, TOTAL BUDGET $206,700

that the Agency counseling staff trusted him from the time he was a counselor through his tenure as Chief of field services. His subsequent promotion to Director, twelve years ago, had changed these relationships. He now felt isolated and alone.

In his years as a counselor and as a manager, he had no difficulty following orders which emanated from above. He consistently tried very hard to follow Agency rules and regulations, and to comply with the wishes of higher authority, which he felt almost always operated in the best interest of the Agency's mission. He was of the opinion that people should be content with performing their duties as prescribed by the Agency, without continually demanding that they be consulted before changes were implemented.

His top staff of five persons included three men who shared his values. They often discussed the deplorable state of affairs and wished for a return to the "good old days". The other two on his staff, however, frequently disagreed with his decisions and he suspected that they engaged in some covert actions against his policies through external consumer groups, legislative contacts, and even some internal meetings.

The Current Situation

One example of the problems of concern to John was his Staff Development Manager, Wilma Benson. Wilma would soon complete her doctorate in Education. She had been with the agency for three years.

She had never been a counselor but had worked for the State Personnel Division before being hired as a trainer in Staff Development. Wilma seemed to always disagree with his policies, and had indeed suggested that the Agency Executive Staff was incompetent to deal with managing their human resources. The current grievance on his desk supported his belief that Wilma was more concerned with individuals than with what was best for the Agency. She had attached a supportive letter to the grievance complaint which contended that the Agency had discriminated against a counselor, Mary Clark, in failing to select her for a recent promotion.

This grievance was the latest in a series of personnel grievances totaling eighteen in just the past year. The full impact of state-controlled hiring practices, civil-rights legislation, E.E.O., Affirmative Action, and most recently, the talk of unionization, were descending upon John. Additionally, Agency people were complaining more frequently about the ever-increasing control procedures. In recent years both federal and state-imposed report requirements had more than doubled; this took more and more time away from the professional role of counseling with clients. It seemed that a state or federal audit was continually in progress, so that his Agency spent an ever-increasing amount of time responding to audit exceptions. As a result of these and other changes, Agency people were becoming more and more vocal in their dissatisfactions with Agency work life, and they expected him to effect changes in these conditions, over which he felt he had little or no control. In addition, he felt it was his primary responsibility to direct the Agency according to the laws, rules, and regulations provided.

As John awaited the management consultants, he was wondering again how well his long and carefully developed views about his management of the Agency's human resources would fit with the consultant's report.

STATE VOCATIONAL REHABILITATION AGENCY (B)

Wilma Benson was proud of the fact that she was the highest ranking woman in the State Vocational Rehabilitation Agency. She had been appointed last year as the manager of staff development. In her view, she had achieved this position because of her hard work, outgoing personality, and academic credentials which would soon include an Ed.D. Wilma felt that she was developing a significant amount of influence within the agency as she had significantly increased staff development activities and had increased her subordinate staff from three to eleven.

She was upset, however, about a recent occurrence. Wilma had highly recommended a young woman who had an impressive education and training record for promotion to a supervisory position. The Director had instead chosen a black male with lesser qualifications for the position. Not only did Wilma think that this was highly inequitable for the counselor but also she considered it to be an undermining of her own position. The Director and most of his top staff were all middle-aged men who were former Vocational Rehabilitation Counselors. She frequently disagreed with their policies and told them so. In her view they often ignored her suggestions and opinions because she was not a member of the "old guard". Wilma recommended to the young counselor that she file a grievance; Wilma had written a strongly worded letter of support for her.

Background

As a young woman, some twenty years ago, Wilma had been a secretary in a private business firm. After three years on the job, she really knew more about the day-to-day operation than anyone else, including her boss. Recognizing this, he had allowed her to make many decisions and to commit the firm's money for certain routine things, in his absence. When the firm prospered and grew, a new position in management was created, for which she applied. She was shocked when her boss chose to hire a young college graduate, with no experience for the management position. He justified his decision on the basis of the young man's credentials. She felt betrayed that her hard work and commitment had not been recognized and rewarded. Vowing this would never happen to her again, she quit and enrolled in college. She was a very bright and energetic student, who finished at the top of her class, and then went on to graduate school. Prior to being employed by the State Vocational Rehabilitation Agency, she had worked for the State Personnel Division where she had learned the "system". The selection process with which she became familiar was strictly one of credentials. Promotions were mostly given to those with the longest list of degrees awarded, training courses completed, and documented educational efforts, regardless of whether or not the training was related to their work. Hard work and job accomplishments were only secondary considerations. This supported her earlier observations. She renewed her own career efforts by attending State training opportunities every time they were offered. Her strategy paid off when she applied and was selected for the position as Rehabilitation Staff Development Officer last year.

Staff Development

Since her appointment, Wilma had instituted project management in the staff development section. Her subordinate training specialists were allowed almost total freedom in the choice and design of the projects they wanted to work on. She did, however, reserve the right of final approval of those projects. She based her decisions in these matters on the anticipated contribution of the project to a participant's growth and career development. So far they had developed and instituted five new in-service training courses for agency staff. The courses in assertiveness and communication skills had been particularly well received. Wilma had established a close working relationship with the manager in charge of personnel. Wilma closely monitored new hires and promotions so that she could assess the training needs of the Agency.

Grievance

When the subject of filling the supervisory position came up at the Director's staff meeting, Wilma had strongly recommended Mary Clark as the best trained and most experienced person for the job. When the Director chose someone with less experience and training Mary Clark filed a grievance. Wilma provided complete support to Mary in this action because to her the Director's decision was so obviously wrong.

STATE VOCATIONAL REHABILITATION AGENCY (C)

Just three weeks ago, Bill Darrow, a 34 year old black man had been appointed unit supervisor. Bill had been a high school civics teacher until joining the Agency as a counselor three years ago. Those who knew him liked his easy going ways and friendly attitude. He had a reputation for following the rules, getting his closures, and for maintaining good relationships with his peers, his superiors, and his clients. A recently initiated case review had resulted in reports that documentation in his cases was weak, but everyone agreed that he was a nice guy who did a good job.

Mary Clark liked Bill, but thought that his appointment as supervisor was terribly unfair. She had been functioning as acting supervisor for the past five months. Mary also thought that her qualifications were obviously better than Bill's. She called the Staff Development Manager, and discussed the whole situation with her. Wilma immediately checked the files and found that in every aspect of training and experience Mary rated higher than Bill. In addition, Mary had taken an "Introduction to Supervision" course offered by the State. Wilma had encouraged Mary to take action in the matter. Mary promptly filed a grievance. The Regional Manager, Ken Evans, had replied that he could do nothing in the matter since the Director made all the hiring decisions. The grievance had now gone to step two and was on the Director's desk.

Background

Mary Clark had worked for the State Rehabilitation Agency for just over four years. She had first become interested in rehabilitation as a teen-ager when her older brother had become severely disabled after an automobile accident. The State Rehabilitation Agency had provided counseling and services that enabled him to finish school and lead a full life. She had talked to her brother's counselor at length and eventually decided to become a rehabilitation counselor. She had gone through the Rehabilitation Counselor program at State University. There her professors had strongly reinforced her belief that work with handicapped persons required a high degree of professional dedication to the clients and their needs.

Mary As A Counselor

With her M.R.C. degree, her record of involvement with the local client action group which her brother had helped to start, and high recommendations from her professors, Mary had no trouble getting a counselor position with the State Rehabilitation Agency. She was not prepared, however, for what she encountered. Mary found herself awash in a sea of rules, regulations, procedures, and reports which she saw as constraining her efforts as a counselor. Her supervisor was always sympathetic when she complained about the many bureaucratic blockages and the paper-work, contending that the organization itself was at fault. Mary reluctantly accepted these explanations, but continued searching for ways and means to circumvent the rules in order to better serve the needs of her clients. She seemed to always be in hot water with management due to her late reports and her low closure rates. She explained her actions by pointing out that she actively sought out and served those most severely disabled persons who needed her services the most. Her case-load had the highest percentage of severely disabled clients in the state. She did not close a case unless the person had a well-paying, meaningful job. She refused to "take a 26" (i.e., close a case) just to meet the numbers requirement of management. (Figure 15–13 is the performance appraisal form used by the agency and the State Civil Service Commission; the form is filled

Employee Name:______________________ Job Title: ______________________

	Above Average	Satisfactory	Below Average
1. Job Knowledge: Does employee know job requirements well?			
2. Quality of Work: Is quality of work good?			
3. Quantity of Work: Is quantity of work meeting standards?			
4. Safety: Does employee try to work safely and follow safety rules?			
5. Initiative: Is employee a "Self Starter"?			
6. Dependability: Can you count on this employee to follow instructions and do what you expect?			
7. Conduct: Does employee try to follow agency rules?			
8. Punctuality: Is employee at work on time regularly?			
9. Cooperation: Does employee try to work as a team member?			
10. Attitude Toward Job: Does employee seem to like present work?			
11. Attitude Toward Agency: Does employee seem to feel "at home" in present job?			
12. Has this employee been fully trained?			
13. Does he make production standards regularly?			
14. If he has not made production standards, is he making satisfactory progress in training and in meeting production standards?			
15. Do you think employee is satisfied with the job?			

16. How do you rate this employee on his job compared with other employees with equal experience?

Definitely Unsatisfactory	Substandard but Making Progress	Doing an Average Job	Definitely Above Average	Outstanding
______	______	______	______	______

17. Do you recommend this employee for salary increment? Yes ______ No ______

______________________ ______________________
Signature Date

Figure 15–13 EMPLOYEE PERFORMANCE APPRAISAL

out by the immediate supervisor for regular employees every twelve months.)

Mary As Acting Supervisor

Several months ago Mary's supervisor suddenly became very ill and had to take an extensive leave. Mary was appointed as acting supervisor. She energetically took on the added responsibilities while maintaining her own caseload. Whenever she or any counselor in her unit encountered obstacles to serving clients she actively challenged the system that caused these roadblocks. Her subordinates encouraged and supported her actions. The unit was developing into a cohesive and potent force in advocating for client services. Memos flew from the unit, to the district office, to the central office and back again with regularity. All of this time Mary gave a very liberal interpretation of all matters within the unit, yet never actually violated agency rules. The counselors in the unit responded very enthusiastically to this atmosphere and the office had become a more exciting place to work under her leadership.

Step 3: Individually, in small groups, or with the entire class, as directed by your instructor, answer the following questions:

1. Is human resources management at the State Vocational Rehabilitation Agency effective?
2. What role do managers play in human resources management? Are they effective?
3. What role do human resources professionals play at the Agency? Are they effective?
4. Are the personnel and labor relations systems at the Agency state-of-the-art?
5. Do the systems respond to the environment and organizational situations?
6. What deficiencies exist in human resources management practices?
7. What changes would you propose for human resources management at the Agency?
8. Redesign the human resources systems at the State Vocational Rehabilitation Agency.
9. What problems are likely to arise in implementing these changes?
10. How can these problems be overcome?

Activity 15–3

HUMAN RESOURCES PROGRAM ANALYSIS

Step 1: Choose a single human resources program (such as a training program, performance appraisal interview, or recruiting program) in which you have participated.

Step 2: Describe the program.

Step 3: Analyze the program's impact on you and the organization.

Step 4: Evaluate how well the program meets criteria of effective human resources management practice.

Step 5: Redesign the system if appropriate.

Step 6: Discussion. Share your analysis with the rest of the class in small groups, with the entire class, or in written form.

Activity 15–4

HUMAN RESOURCES PROBLEM ANALYSIS

Step 1: Choose a problematic situation you encountered in the management of human resources in an organization of which you were a member.

Step 2: Describe the situation.

Step 3: Diagnose the situation.

Step 4: Prescribe ways of improving the situation.

Step 5: Devise an action plan.

Step 6: Discussion. Share your analysis with the rest of the class in small groups, with the entire class, or in written form.

Activity 15–5

HUMAN RESOURCES MANAGEMENT ANALYSIS

Step 1: Choose an organization with which you have some familiarity.

Step 2: Evaluate the human resources management systems in that organization, considering the following systems:

human resources planning
recruitment
selection
training and development
decruitment
career development
performance appraisal
compensation
unionization
collective bargaining
grievance resolution
occupational safety and health
equal employment opportunity

Step 3: Describe each system.

Step 4: Evaluate each system.

Step 5: Redesign each system if appropriate.

Step 6: Devise an implementation plan.

Step 7: Discussion. Share your analysis with the rest of the class in small groups, with the entire class, or in written form.

SUMMARY

Effective human resources management is a prerequisite for organizational effectiveness. To assess the effectiveness of human resources management we can determine the cost-effectiveness, responsiveness to workers' needs, responsiveness to the environment, and state-of-the-art quality of personnel and labor relations systems.

Applying the practical approach to human resources management increases its effectiveness. Diagnosis of the situation in which human resources management occurs, evaluation of the quality of current programs and practices, design of state-of-the-art systems to respond to needs and deficiencies in human resources management, and implementation of the new systems comprise this approach. In the activities in this chapter you had the opportunity to apply each of these steps to the cases of Esso A.G. and the State Vocational Rehabilitation Agency, as well as to a human resources problem, a human resources program, and a human resources management system, using organizations of your choice.

Beyond the application of the practical approach, effective human resources management increasingly requires the use of computerized information systems. Computerized HRIS should assist in tracking and monitoring personnel and labor relations systems.

Finally, top management and human resources professionals should take a strategic approach to human resources management. This long-term orientation should complement the managerial and operational orientations of line managers.

ENDNOTES

[1]R.M. Steers, *Organizational Effectiveness; A Behavioral View* (Santa Monica, Cal.: Goodyear, 1976).

[2]J. Fitz-Enz, Quantifying the human resources function, *Personnel* 57 (March-April 1980): 41–52.

[3]W.F. Cascio, *Costing Human Resources: The Financial Impact of Behavior in Organizations* (Boston: Kent, 1982).

[4]R.C. Woodruff, Jr., Human resources accounting, *Canadian Chartered Accountant* 97 (1970): 156–161.

[5]B.G. Meyers and H.M. Shane, Human resource accounting for managerial decisions: A capital budgeting approach, *Personnel Administrator* (January 1984): 29–35.

[6]See J.J. Tsay, Human resource accounting: A need for relevance, *Management Accounting* 58 (1977): 68–78; and G.M.N. Baker, The feasibility and utility of human resource accounting, *California Management Review* 16 (Summer 1974): 17–23.

[7]See E.G. Flamholtz, A model for human resource valuation: A stochastic process with service rewards, *Accounting Review* 46 (April 1971): 253–267; and R. Likert, *The Human Organization, Its Management and Value* (New York: McGraw-Hill, 1967).

[8]Cascio, *op. cit.*

[9]J.G. Cullen et al., Cost-effectiveness: A model for assessing the training investment, *Training and Development Journal* 32 (January 1978): 24–29.

[10]*Ibid.*

[11]L.M. Cheek, Cost effectiveness comes to the personnel function, *Harvard Business Review* 51 (May-June 1973): 96–105.

[12]A.J. Walker, The analytical element is important to an HRIS, *Personnel Administrator* 28 (September 1983): 33.

[13]B.E. Graham-Moore and G.D. Jenkins, Jr., Computerized tracking of your relevant labor force, *Personnel Administrator* 28 (September 1983): 49.

[14]A.J. Walker, *HRIS Development* (New York: Van Nostrand, 1982).

[15]*Ibid.*

[16]See publications such as *Auerbach Computer Technology Reports* (Auerbach Publishers, Pennsauken, N.J. 08109); *DataPro Directory of Software* (DataPro Research Corporation, Delran, N.J. 08075); *ICP Software Directory* (International Computer Programs, Indianapolis, Ind. 46240); *Sourcebook I and II* (Information Sources, Glenview, Ill. 60025); *The Software Catalog: Business Software* (Elsevier Science Publishing, New York 10017).

[17]V.R. Ceriello, How do you pick the right software?, *Personnel Journal* 63 (November 1984): 53–58.

[18]Walker, *HRIS Development, op. cit.*

[19]See M.A. Devanna, C. Fombrun, and N. Tichy, Human resources management: A strategic perspective, *Organizational Dynamics* 10 (Winter 1981): 51–67; C. Fombrun, N.M. Tichy, and M.A. Devanna, eds., *Strategic Human Resource Management* (New York: Wiley, 1984).

[20]K.F. Mise and T. Stein, Strategic HRM and the bottom line, *Personnel Administrator* 28 (October 1983): 27–30.

[21]Devanna et al., *op. cit.*, p. 55.

[22]*Ibid.*

[23]Mise and Stein, *op. cit.*

[24]M.A. Devanna, C.J. Fombrun, and N.M. Tichy, A framework for strategic human resource management, in Fombrun et al., *op. cit.*

[25]Devanna et al., Human resources management, *op. cit.*

FURTHER READINGS

Cascio, W.F. *Costing Human Resources: The Financial Impact of Behavior in Organizations.* Boston: Kent, 1982.

Fombrun, C., Tichy, N.M., and Devanna, M.A., eds. *Strategic Human Resource Management.* New York: Wiley, 1984.

Walker, A.J. *HRIS Development.* New York: Van Nostrand, 1982.

Walker, J.W. *Human Resources Planning.* New York: McGraw-Hill, 1980.

Index

Continued

Continued